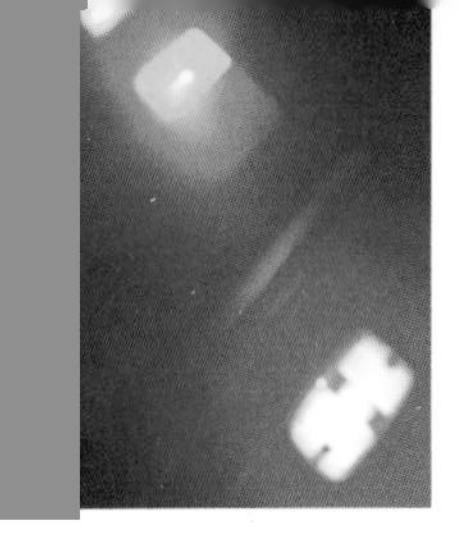

map page

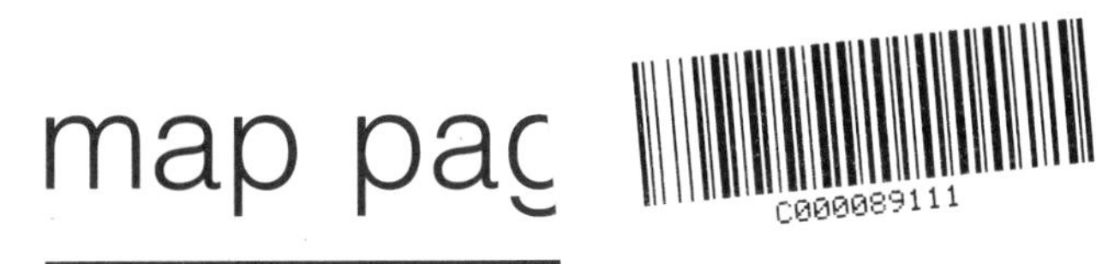

C000089111

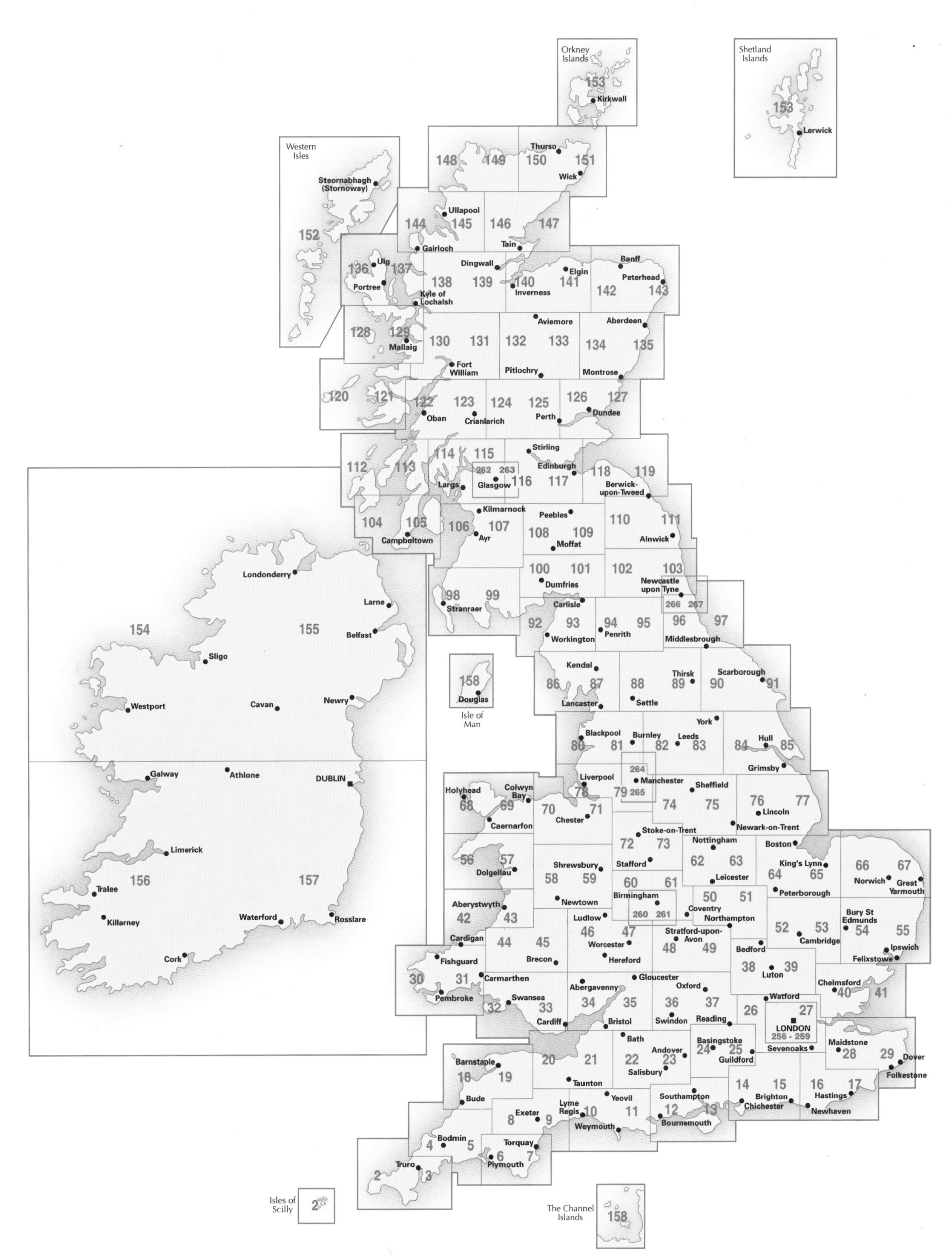

Orkney Islands
153
Kirkwall

Shetland Islands
153
Lerwick

Western Isles
Steornabhagh (Stornoway)
152

148 149 150 151 Thurso Wick

144 145 146 147 Ullapool Tain
Gairloch

136 137 138 139 140 141 142 143 Dingwall Elgin Banff Peterhead
Uig Portree Kyle of Lochalsh Inverness Aviemore Aberdeen

128 129 130 131 132 133 134 135 Mallaig Fort William Pitlochry Montrose

120 121 122 123 124 125 126 127 Oban Crianlarich Perth Dundee

112 113 114 115 116 117 118 119 Stirling Edinburgh Berwick-upon-Tweed
262 263 Largs Glasgow

104 105 106 107 108 109 110 111 Kilmarnock Peebles Moffat Alnwick
Campbeltown Ayr

100 101 102 103 Dumfries Newcastle upon Tyne
266 267

98 99 92 93 94 95 96 97 Stranraer Carlisle Workington Penrith Middlesbrough
Larne

154 155 Londonderry Belfast
Sligo Cavan Newry Westport

158 Douglas Isle of Man

86 87 88 89 90 91 Kendal Thirsk Scarborough
Lancaster Settle York

Galway Athlone DUBLIN

80 81 82 83 84 85 Blackpool Burnley Leeds Hull
Liverpool 264 Manchester Grimsby

156 157 Limerick Tralee Killarney Waterford Rosslare
Cork

68 69 70 71 72 73 74 75 76 77 Holyhead Colwyn Bay Chester Stoke-on-Trent Nottingham Lincoln Newark-on-Trent
Caernarfon 265 79 Sheffield Boston

56 57 58 59 60 61 62 63 64 65 66 67 Dolgellau Shrewsbury Stafford Birmingham Leicester King's Lynn Norwich Great Yarmouth
Newtown Peterborough

42 43 44 45 46 47 48 49 50 51 52 53 54 55 Aberystwyth Ludlow Worcester Stratford-upon-Avon Coventry Northampton Bedford Cambridge Bury St Edmunds Ipswich
260 261 Felixstowe

30 31 32 33 34 35 36 37 38 39 40 41 Cardigan Fishguard Brecon Hereford Gloucester Oxford Luton Chelmsford
Pembroke Carmarthen Swansea Abergavenny Cardiff Bristol Swindon Reading Watford
26 27 LONDON 256 - 259 Maidstone 28 29 Dover Folkestone

18 19 20 21 22 23 24 25 Barnstaple Taunton Salisbury Andover Basingstoke Guildford Sevenoaks
Bude Yeovil 14 15 16 17 Brighton Hastings Newhaven

8 9 10 11 12 13 Exeter Lyme Regis Weymouth Southampton Chichester
Bodmin 4 5 6 7 Torquay Plymouth Bournemouth

2 3 Truro

Isles of Scilly 2

The Channel Islands 158

AA
ROAD ATLAS
OF THE
BRITISH
ISLES
2001

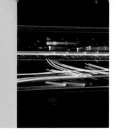

contents

Scale 1:200,000 or 3.15 miles to 1 inch

11th edition July 2000

Published by AA Publishing (a trading name of Automobile Association Developments Limited, whose registered office is Norfolk House, Priestley Road, Basingstoke, Hampshire RG24 9NY. Registered number 1878835).

Mapping produced by the Cartographic Department of The Automobile Association. This atlas has been compiled and produced from the Automaps database utilising electronic and computer technology.

ISBN 0 7495 2525 8

A CIP catalogue record for this book is available from The British Library.

Printed in Italy by Pizzi, Milan.

The contents of this atlas are believed to be correct at the time of the latest revision. However, the publishers cannot be held responsible for loss occasioned to any person acting or refraining from action as a result of any material in this atlas, nor for any errors, omissions or changes in such material. The publishers would welcome information to correct any errors or omissions and to keep this atlas up to date. Please write to the Cartographic Editor, Publishing Division, The Automobile Association, Fanum House, Basing View, Basingstoke, Hampshire RG21 4EA.

Information on National Parks provided by the Countryside Commission for England and the Countryside Council for Wales.

Information on National Scenic Areas in Scotland provided by Scottish Natural Heritage.

Information on Forest Parks provided by the Forestry Commission.

The RSPB sites shown are a selection chosen by the Royal Society for the Protection of Birds.

National Trust properties shown are a selection of those open to the public as indicated in the handbooks of the National Trust and the National Trust for Scotland.

Automobile Association Developments Limited would like to thank the following photographers, libraries and associations for their assistance in the preparation of this book.

British Waterways Board, Waterways Museum 22a, 23b
The Mansell Collection 6a, 6b, 7a, 7c
Museum of Rural Llife 26a
Nature Photographers Ltd 32a (P R Sterry), 41a (C Palmer), 41b (W S Paton), 41c (P R Sterry)
Pictures Colour Library Ltd 25c
Rex Features Ltd 18b (N Jorgensen)
Spectrum Colour Library 10, 11a, 11c, 25d

All remaining pictures are held in the Association's own library (AA Photo Library) with contributions from the following photographers:

M Alexander, A Baker, P Baker, V & S Bates, J Beazley, M Birkitt, I Burgum, D Corrance, S L Day, E Ellington, P Enticknap, A J Hopkins, C Jones, A Lawson, S & O Mathews, E Meacher, C Molyneux, J Morrison, R Mort, J Mottershaw, R Newton, A Perkins, M Short, R Strange, T Teegan, T D Timms, M Trelawny, A Tryner, R Victor, W Voysey, R Weir, L Whitwam, P Wilson, T Woodcock, T Wyles

Distances, journey times and map pages — inside front cover

The tourist's British Isles — 4–48

Information for motorists–air ambulance — IV–V

Route planner — VI–XI

Road signs — XII–XIII

Motorways
- Restricted junctions — XIV–XV
- M25 London orbital motorway — XVI
- M60 Manchester orbital motorway — XVII

Map symbols — XVIII–1

Road maps — **2–153**
- Scottish islands — 152–153
- Ireland — 154–157
- The Channel Islands & The Isle of Man — 158

Town plans — 159–232
- Key to town plans — 159
- Central London — 238–248
- Central London street index — 249–255

Ports and airports
- Major ports — 233
- Major airports — 234–236
- Channel Tunnel — 237

District maps
- London district — 256–259
- Birmingham district — 260–261
- Glasgow district — 262–263
- Manchester district — 264–265
- Tyne & Wear district — 266–267

Index to place names — 268–318
- County map — 268

Distances, journey times and map pages — inside back cover

CHURCH & HOME:
BUILDINGS IN THE LANDSCAPE

LOCAL STONE

In the border country of Somerset and Dorset some of the finest building stone is found. The exquisite golden stone of Somerset's Ham Hill was transported across the county border to give such splendid buildings as Sherborne Abbey their mellow hue. Hamstone has been lavished on great Somerset houses too, as much as on the charming vernacular buildings of so many of the county's villages. In the immediate hinterland of Ham Hill are the Tudor and Jacobean piles of Montacute House, Tintinhull and the restored Barrington Court, the latter enhanced even more by the 20th-century development of its gardens. All three are in the care of the National Trust and are open to the public.

In Devon and Cornwall the availability of durable granite has produced the solid four-square certainty of church tower and farmhouse alike, the roughness and earthy colour of the unadorned stone merging with the knuckly landscape of Dartmoor and the Atlantic coast of Cornwall. But in the non-granite country of Devon, cottages were often built of 'cob', unbaked mud that was remarkably durable. In Cornwall and Devon too, the use of less attractive slates and shales has resulted in darker, more sombre buildings that still merge satisfyingly with the landscape from which they emerged.

Granite is a rock that is often at its best when low to

Top: Egypt cottage at Chulmleigh is of Devon cob and thatch; right: Forde Abbey, a superb example of an ecclesiastical conversion into a home

For many people, the West Country means the picture-postcard thatched cottages of Dorset, Somerset and Devon, the cobbled streets of the famous coastal villages of Clovelly and St Ives, and the elaborate façades of seaside hotels in Torquay and Ilfracombe. But memorable images apart, it is the building materials that characterise the different parts of a region, as represented by cottages and castles, churches and cathedrals. Above all else the best buildings appear to have grown from the very landscape that they adorn.

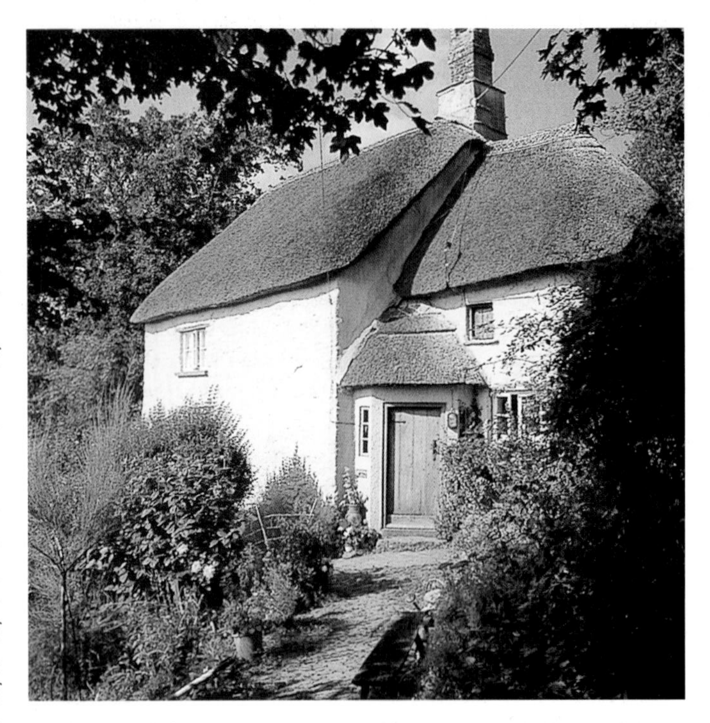

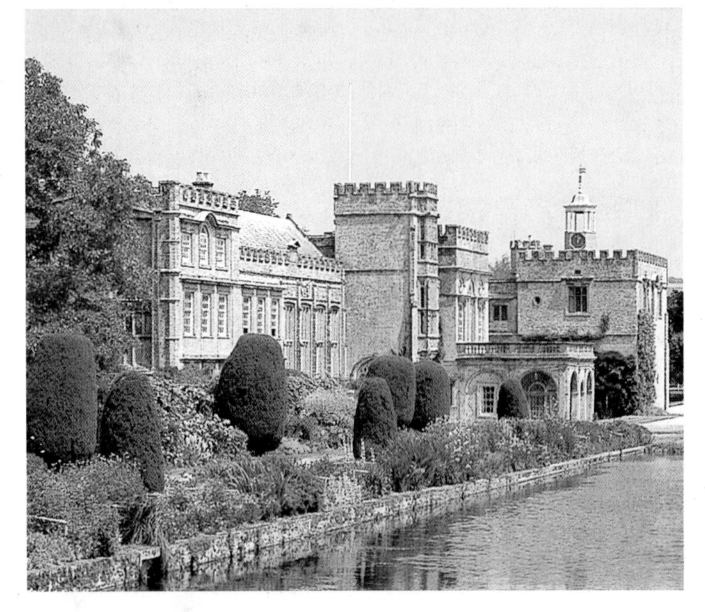

the ground, absorbed by the landscape rather than set monumentally upon it. Yet types of Cornish granite have produced such great buildings as Lanhydrock, near Bodmin, and the magnificent Antony House on the banks of the River Lynher opposite Plymouth.

CHURCH ARCHITECTURE

An enduring motif of West-Country architecture is the local church, with its stately tower rising fortress-like from surrounding woods, or dominating the lower roof-line of numerous towns and villages. Somerset is particularly noted for its elegant church towers. Spires were few in Somerset; instead the tall, square tower, with its characteristic Somerset tracery and its elegant lace-like pinnacles and statue niches, big windows and ornamental string courses, has been the glory of the West Country for centuries. There are especially fine church buildings at Glastonbury, Wells, Taunton, Shepton Mallet, Yeovil and Huish Episcopi.

There was less church building during the 17th and 18th centuries. That period saw the rise of non-conformist chapels and meeting places, and it was not until the 19th century that a new religious self-confidence produced such fine Regency churches as Teignmouth's St James's and the Norman-influenced St Paul's at Honiton.

Large numbers of non-conformist churches were built throughout the West Country during the 19th century. They were simple preaching places, although neo-classical and

Gothic themes emerged. Throughout Cornwall, stern-faced Methodist chapels still dominate the rural landscape, their main façades seemingly always to face the unsmiling north as if to deny even the sun its elevated place.

CHANGING STYLES

The Romans left few traces of their presence west of Exeter, the Anglo-Saxons likewise. But Norman influence was substantial in churches and castles, and there are numerous West-Country churches that have some element of Norman work that has survived the repeated restorations and extensions of the ensuing centuries.

It is the 15th and 16th centuries, however, that have bequeathed us fairly complete buildings. Rural buildings of the period were still vulnerable to structural erosion and decay from the impact of the heavy work that went on around them, but in Devon, good examples of larger farmhouses still exist. These include Sir Walter Raleigh's birthplace of Hayes Barton near Budleigh Salterton, constructed of cob and with a fine Devon thatch.

Good stone buildings of the period include the outstanding George Inn at Norton St Philip, between Bath and Frome. The George is pure medieval, its ground floor of stone with a fine entrance archway, the upper storeys timber-framed. In

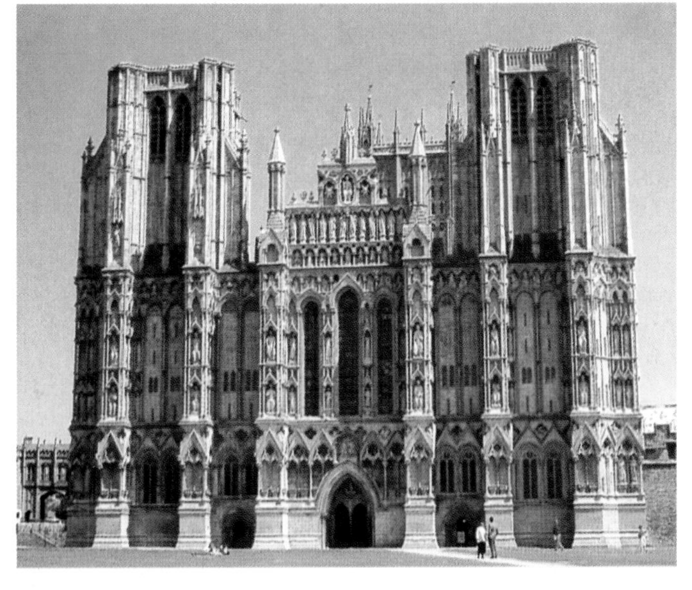

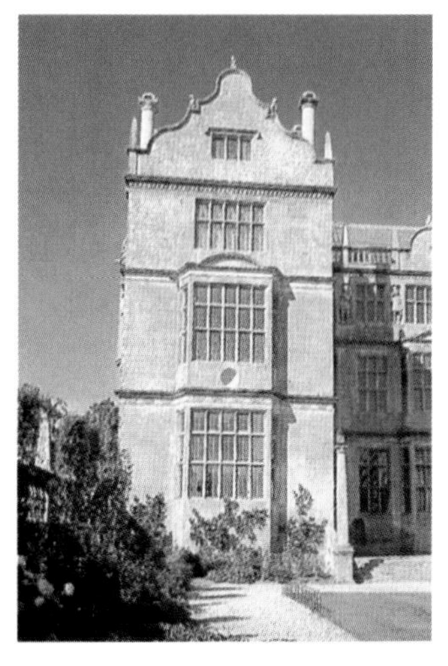

Glastonbury High Street is another famous Inn – The George and Pilgrim – this time in three storeys of ornamented stone. A few yards further along is the 15th-century Gothic building known as the Tribunal.

The great buildings of the late 16th century are well represented in the West Country by beautiful houses such as Montacute and by town buildings such as the Guildhall at Exeter. Later developments of the Stuart period produced Dorset's Forde Abbey, an example of how buildings evolve from earlier forms. Forde lies on the site of a 12th-century Cistercian Abbey and parts of the abbey are incorporated into the 17th-century house. Tintinhull, near Yeovil, is another example of incorporation, the mainly 17th-century building having absorbed parts of a 16th-century farmhouse.

*T*he George Inn at Norton St Philip is a fine medieval building

*A*bove: the wonderful West Front of Wells Cathedral; above right: Montacute House has the lovely golden glow of Hamstone

THE LAST 200 YEARS

By the 18th century urban architecture was becoming increasingly sophisticated, as the burgeoning merchant class expressed its aspirations. Great country houses also reflected this. Devon's Saltram House, the county's finest country mansion, is an outstanding early Georgian building with fine interiors, the whole maintained by the National Trust. But it was urban building that became the focus for fashionable architecture. The legacy of the Georgian and Regency periods, so evident in our great cities and in such places as Bath, can be seen in most West Country towns of any size. Even as far west as Truro the stylish neo-classicism of entire terraces, such as those of Lemon Street, matched the sophistication of those of Bath, and the red-brick elegance of Taunton's Hammet Street and The Crescent match the crescents and terraces of Exeter.

During the late 18th century and well into the Victorian period the 'seaside' architecture peculiar to holiday resorts produced some outstanding buildings in towns such as Sidmouth, Ilfracombe and Torquay.

Sidmouth still has some very fine Regency buildings, including the fascinating *cottage orné*, a mock-rustic style incorporating Gothic façades topped with lavish thatch. At Ilfracombe, the use of polychromatic brickwork resulted in some outstanding Victorian Gothic buildings.

It was a stylishness soon to be overtaken by the bland and brutal convenience architecture of the 20th century, as technology and commercial enterprise ensured the triumph of function over style. Yet good modern architecture is still given breathing space, even in the featureless world of supermarkets and tower blocks. Award-winning buildings include Truro's Crown Court, designed by the same architects who were responsible for the Tate Gallery at St Ives, and, as late as 1995, Sainsbury's superstore at Plymouth won an award for its bold design that features a white canopy made of overlapping sail-like armatures.

But it is in the surviving older buildings of Dorset, Somerset, Devon and Cornwall that the great legacy of good West-Country architecture is enshrined – the Hamstone villages, the thatched houses of quiet hamlets, and the lichened and mossy cottages of fishing villages. Above all, the marvellous churches and cathedrals and the great country houses of the west remain as priceless jewels within the landscape.

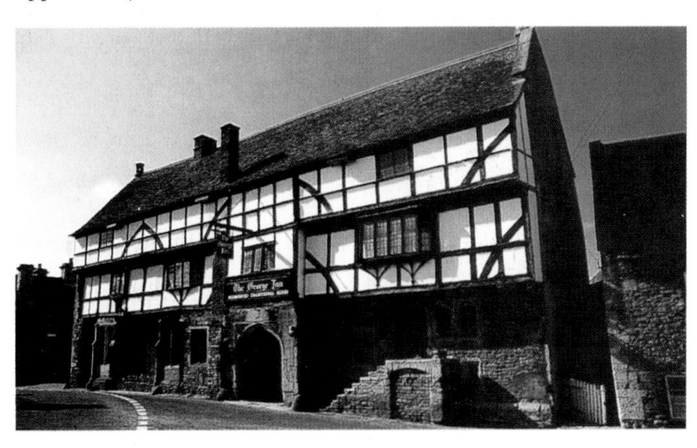

LITERARY SETTINGS: WRITERS IN THE WEST COUNTRY

The poet John Heath-Stubbs captured, grudgingly it seems, both the inspiration and the awe of the wildest parts of the west of England, when he spoke of '...a hideous and wicked country/Sloping to hateful sunsets and the end of time...' Most writers have been more happily captivated than that. For Heath-Stubbs, it seems, too much raw nature was unnerving. The poet's uneasy words were inspired by the powerful Atlantic coast of Gurnard's Head near Land's End, itself the *Belerium*, the 'Seat of Storms', of the Roman writer Tacitus, an early commentator within the literary setting.

From those Roman times until the present day, the West Country has continued to attract poets and writers. From the beautiful countryside of Dorset, Thomas Hardy created his own landscape of 'Wessex', at the gates of the West Country, yet he too was drawn further west, to the spectacular coastline of North Cornwall. Here he met his wife Emma at the exquisite little church of St Juliot, near Boscastle, and much bitter-sweet romance ensued. The pair strolled out at Beeny Cliff, just north of Boscastle, and above 'the opal and the sapphire of that wandering western sea' – lines in which Hardy captured the essence of the Cornish coast better, perhaps, than generations of writers since. But before Hardy, the north coast of Devon gave inspiration to Charles Kingsley, who grew up at the charming village of Clovelly, lived later at Bideford, and gave the breezy name of *Westward Ho!* to his most famous novel – and subsequently to a seaside village.

EVOCATIVE LANDSCAPES

The coast of North Cornwall more recently inspired John Betjeman, whose lifelong association with Padstow, further south from Hardy's Beeny Cliff, added a richer, more robust tone to the poetry of suburbia. South of Padstow, the rugged tin-mining coast of St Agnes and Perranporth inspired Winston Graham's marvellous *Poldark* saga, an epic narrative of life in 18th- and 19th-century Cornwall from the pen of a modern master.

The Atlantic coast of the west was ever inspirational, but so too were the high moors of Exmoor and the Quantocks. Amidst the wooded combes and soft rolling heaths of the Quantocks, the poet Samuel Taylor Coleridge and his friends, William and Dorothy Wordsworth, found the intensely pastoral inspiration for their great Romantic poems, even before the Lake District claimed them for its own.

Between Exmoor and the sea, Coleridge wrote his fevered, flawed masterpiece 'Kubla Khan', its opium-induced fantasies rudely interrupted by the unannounced visit of a 'a person from Porlock', who was thus immortalised as perhaps the most notorious full stop in literary history.

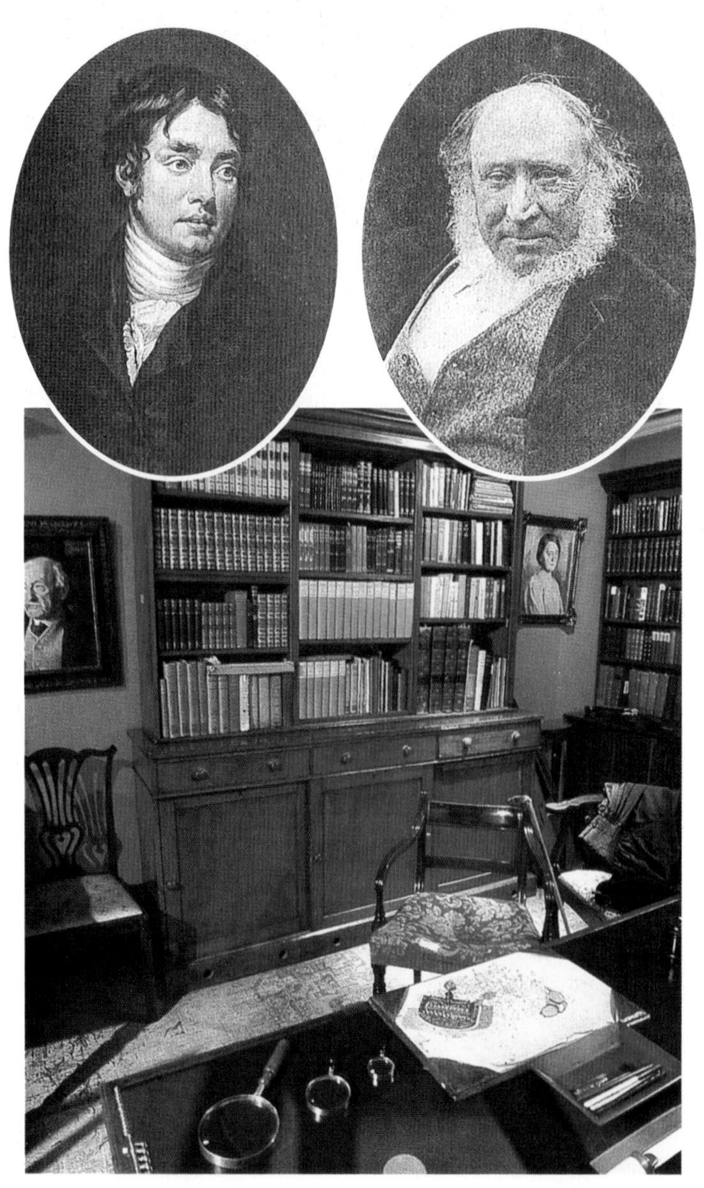

Directly inland from Porlock, around the heathy wastes of Badgworthy Water, is 'Doone Country', the inspiration for R D Blackmore's famously romantic novel *Lorna Doone*. The legends of the robber Doones of Badgworthy, said to originate from an exiled and disaffected Scottish noble family, were part of Exmoor lore long before Blackmore's masterly embellishment, but with all its lonely, compelling beauty, the moorland wilderness cried out for just such a rattling good tale. Blackmore's novel merged romance with reality, and turned into shrines of literary pilgrimage such places as the little church at Oare where Lorna was shot and wounded by Carver Doone during her wedding to John Ridd.

Main picture: Thomas Hardy's study, in Dorchester's County Museum; above left: Samuel Taylor Coleridge; right: R D Blackmore

ROMANCE AND MYSTERY

R D Blackmore's 20th-century counterpart was undoubtedly Daphne du Maurier, whose grasp of the romantic and the picturesque gave rise to such popular novels as *Jamaica Inn* and *Frenchman's Creek*. The former borrowed some of its imagery from the forlorn heights of Cornwall's Bodmin Moor; the latter focused on the tree-shrouded creeks of the Helford River on the county's south-west coast. But du Maurier's true literary setting was the lovely landscape of the River Fowey. Here, amidst the wooded parkland of Menabilly House were shaped the the novels *My Cousin Rachel*, and *Rebecca*, who woke and 'dreamt of Manderley'. It was here too that du Maurier was inspired to write a short story about predatory seabirds – subsequently filmed by Alfred Hitchcock as *The Birds* – after watching a cloud of screaming gulls foraging in the wake of a tractor as it drew its plough through the rich earth of the Cornish fields.

Similar inspiration for one of the greatest detective stories ever written, *The Hound of the Baskervilles*, was drawn from Dartmoor by Sir Arthur Conan Doyle. The novelist had stayed on the south-eastern edge of the moor, at Manaton, and had been gripped by the changing moods of its great waste, and by the Gothic atmosphere of the lonely granite tors that rise eerily like castles above the marshy low ground.

Following in the romantic spirit set by Blackmore in *Lorna Doone* and Hardy in *Tess of the D'Urbervilles*, 20th-century writer John Fowles established Lyme Regis as the setting for his powerful novel, *The French Lieutenant's Woman*, with its more complex literary romanticism. The novel is now

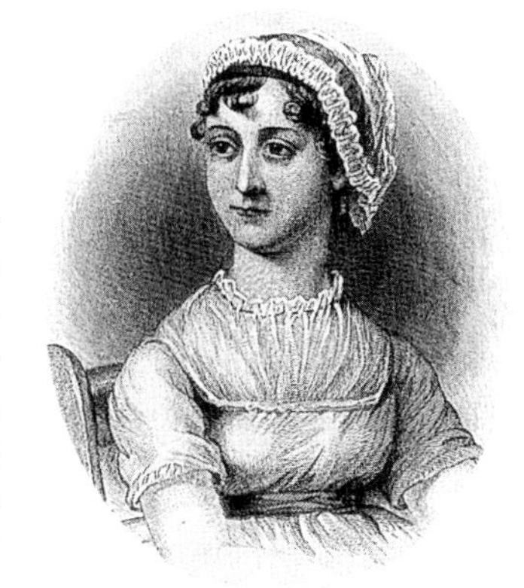

Jane Austen knew Lyme Regis well

immortalised on film, most dramatically by the image of the tragic heroine, the black-cloaked Sarah Woodruff, precarious in body and soul, on the storm-battered harbour wall of The Cobb at Lyme. Here also, the more formal romance of Jane Austen's *Persuasion* depicts the head-strong Louisa Musgrove falling from the Higher Cobb, intent on landing in Captain Went-worth's arms, but knocking herself unconscious instead; and so precipitating a crisis for all the characters in the novel.

CONTINUING INSPIRATION

The literary inspiration of the West Country continues today, its dramatic landscapes inspiring even those writers whose themes may not necessarily reflect a West-Country setting. Near Land's End lives the novelist John Le Carré, whose books range the cosmopolitan world of Europe and Asia, yet whose hard work of writing is often carried out against the background of the restless Atlantic. A near neighbour of Le Carré's is Derek Tangye, author of a gently sentimental series of autobiographical novels about his beloved west Cornwall. The novelist Mary Wesley lives in Totnes and writes more sophisticated novels than perhaps Daphne du Maurier would ever have dared. Wesley has based her

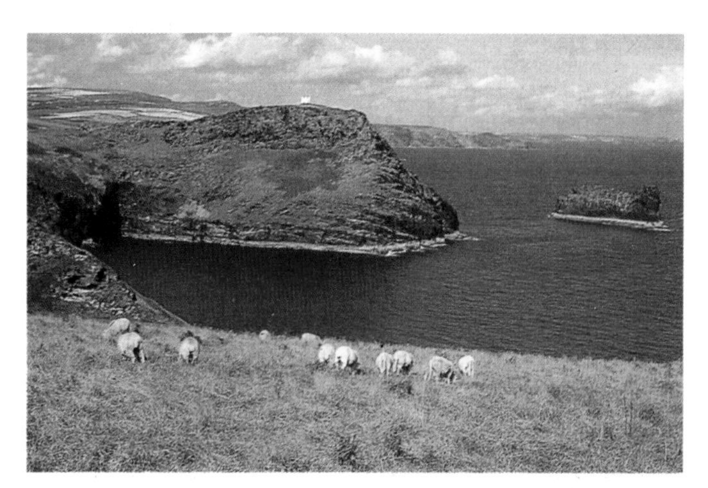

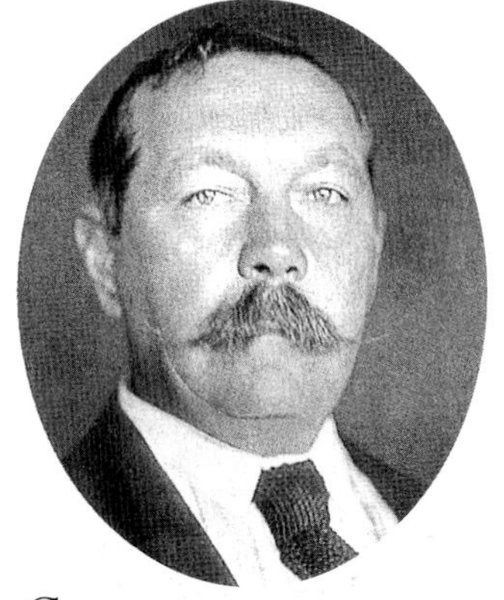

Sir Arthur Conan Doyle wrote of the mysteries of brooding Dartmoor

scintillating *Camomile Lawn* on Cornwall's Roseland Peninsula.

The popular novelist Rosamund Pilcher has strong connections with the north coast of west Cornwall near St Ives, and the film version of her novel *The Shell Seekers* was filmed in the town.

Earlier literary figures connected with the St Ives area were Virginia Woolf, who based her novel *To the Light-house* on the nearby Godrevy lighthouse. D H Lawrence lived at Zennor, along the coast from St Ives, for a period during World War I, hounded by the authorities because of his pacifist stance and because of his wife Frieda's German nationality. Lawrence described vividly his experiences during his time in Cornwall when he wrote the nightmare sequence in his novel *Kangaroo*.

Locations in the West Country have inspired some of the most seminal works of English poetry and prose. Near Yeovil is East Coker, ancestral

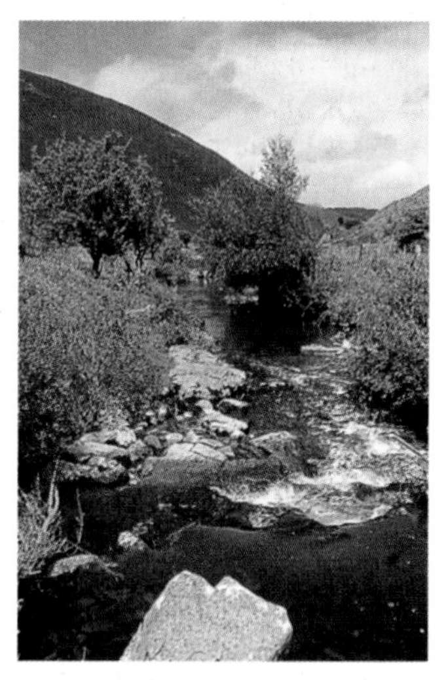

Top: the Boscastle coastline has romantic associations with Thomas Hardy; above: the Doone Valley

home of T S Eliot, whose ashes are buried here, and who attached the name of this archetypal English village to the second poem of his *Four Quartets*. Coleridge was born at Ottery St Mary. John Galsworthy lived for 18 years at Manaton in east Dartmoor, where he worked on *The Forsyte Saga*. At the unlikely setting of nearby Chagford, Evelyn Waugh wrote *Brideshead Revisited*, whose characters would have felt positively uneasy amidst Dartmoor's ruggedness. Torquay was the birthplace of Agatha Christie, who also lived on the inspiring Dart Estuary and wrote several of her famous crime novels on the nearby Burgh Island off Salcombe. And in the delightful valleys of the Rivers Taw and Torridge in North Devon Henry Williamson wrote *Tarka the Otter* and *Salar the Salmon*.

THE NEW FOREST

THE LIVING AND WORKING FOREST

Occupying a large part of south-west Hampshire, the New Forest is both a major tourist attraction and an area of wildlife and landscape conservation. A wide-ranging and detailed New Forest Heritage Area Management Strategy seeks to reconcile these conflicting functions, together with a third element – that of commercial timber production. Recent changes in the government's remit to the Forestry Commission mean that it is now, though not in name, very much closer to being a national park, and that the demands of commercial forestry are balanced against the conservation of ancient woodland and the growing of broad-leaved and ornamental species.

If the forest were a fully fledged national park, it would be in the English rather than the international sense, because it encompasses not just beautiful scenery and flora and fauna, but houses, villages and small towns too – and people, especially farmers and foresters, who earn their living from the land. The 1,500 deer, which are one of the Forest's great attractions, belong to the Crown and are managed by the Commission, while the 3,000 or so New Forest ponies belong to the Commoners. These are local people whose 11th-century predecessors secured grazing and other rights when the savage Forest Law deprived them of the right to hunt.

The traditional 'capital' of the New Forest – seat of the Commission's local administration, of the ancient but still important Court of Verderers, and these days also of New

The name, it has been observed, is doubly misleading. The New Forest was 'new' only in 1097, when William the Conqueror declared it a royal hunting preserve, and 'forest' then meant not a large area of woodland, as we think of today, but an area of land reserved for hunting. Then, as now, trees occupied less space than the heathland and the often rather marshy fields, but today, though 130sq miles (336sq km) of New Forest are still 'preserved', it is for public enjoyment and for conservation as an ecological and landscape asset, rather than for a monarch's days out in the saddle.

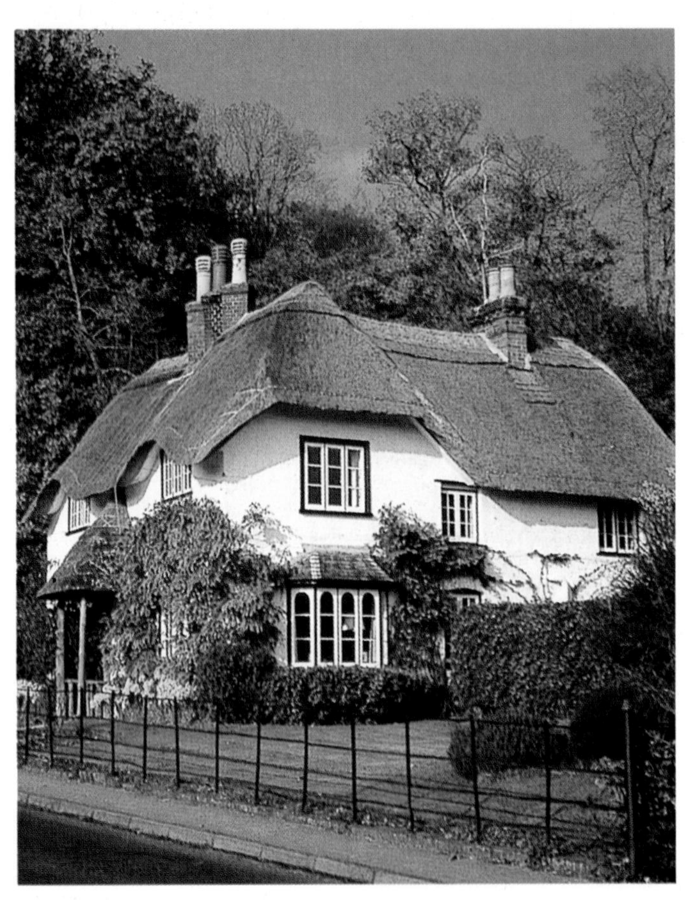

Above: thatch amidst the forest at Swan Green; right: the famous and sturdy little New Forest ponies can be seen grazing any clearings between the woodland

Forest District Council – is Lyndhurst. A town of a few thousand people, it is idyllically set with great forestry 'inclosures' to north and south, and open heathlands to east and west, its church spire a distinctive landmark. The New Forest Museum and Visitor Centre

adjoining the main car park at Lyndhurst provides both general tourist information and audio-visual and other displays on how the New Forest came into existence, its way of life and its customs and traditions.

FOREST ATTRACTIONS

As well as the obvious attractions of the landscape and wildlife, the Forest has a number of places of interest to visit. There is a Deer Sanctuary at Bolderwood (to the west of Lyndhurst), with the Reptiliary near by. A reminder of its days as a Norman hunting preserve exists in the Rufus Stone, which commemorates the allegedly accidental shooting of the unpopular, red-headed King William II (Rufus) while he was out hunting.

The Longdown Dairy Farm near Ashurst is a working farm which welcomes visitors, and near by is the New Forest Butterfly Farm, housed in tropical glasshouses. A good way to appreciate the best of the woodland is to venture along the magnificent Rhinefield and Bolderwood ornamental drives, and there are horse-drawn wagon rides as well as waymarked woodland walks, all with skilfully sited car parks.

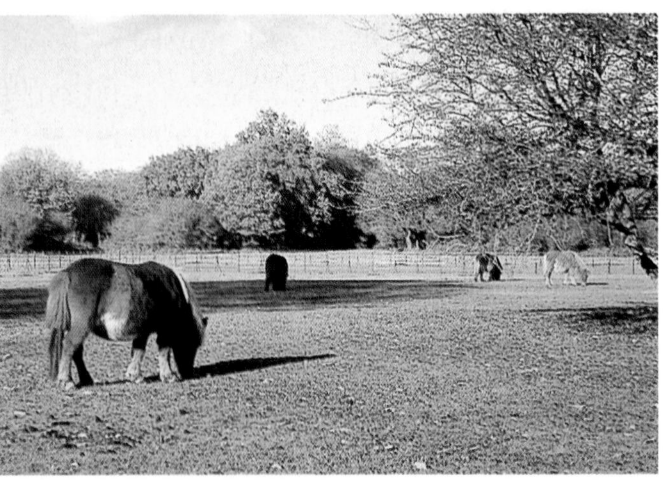

Of the Forest's half-dozen villages, Minstead is among the most visited, with its thatched cottages and well-preserved, largely 18th-century All Saints Church, notable for its three-decker pulpit, box pews and two galleries, one above the other. Furzey Gardens at Minstead consists of 8 acres (3ha) of flowering trees and shrubs. More famous are the Exbury Gardens, which are spectacularly colourful during the rhododendron season. Burley in the south-east of the Forest, set amidst bracing open heathland, is a good centre for walkers. Castle Hill, 1¼ miles (2km) north, is an Iron-Age camp and one of the best vantage points to view the Forest.

In the south-east of the Forest stands Beaulieu Abbey, founded by King John for the Cistercians, but home of the Montagu family since 1538. Its battlemented Palace House was once the abbey's gatehouse, though its present appearance owes much to an 1870s 'restoration' by Sir Arthur Blomfield for the 1st Lord Montagu. Understanding of the medieval remains is greatly helped by an exhibition about monastic life. Alongside the Abbey is the 3rd Lord Montagu's pride and joy, his splendid National Motor Museum, with 250 exhibits, including cars, commercial vehicles and motorcycles. There is also 'Wheels', described as 'a futuristic ride

on space-age pods through 100 years of motoring', as well as a monorail and veteran bus rides.

Buckler's Hard, 2½ miles (4km) down the Beaulieu River, is a remnant of an early 18th-century plan to build Montagu Town, a port to rival Southampton. Two rows of attractive brick cottages are all that was built, but the place was important for 80 years as a shipyard – Nelson's *Agamemnon* was built here, using 2,000 New Forest oaks. Buckler's Hard's Maritime Museum vividly evokes that era. On the next little river to the west stands Lymington, a lively yachting and ferry port and the New Forest's main market town. Its streetscape and roofscape, mixed with masts and culminating in the steeple of St Michael's Church, are as lively as the Saturday high-street market.

A CITY ON THE FOREST FRINGE

A large, modern city, port, and regional shopping and commercial centre, Southampton nonetheless has a long history. There was a Roman town on the east bank of the Itchen at Bitterne, and on the west bank a Saxon town called Hamwic. Despite World War II bombs and post-war development, a great deal of the past remains. South of the modern shopping centre Above Bar is a surviving

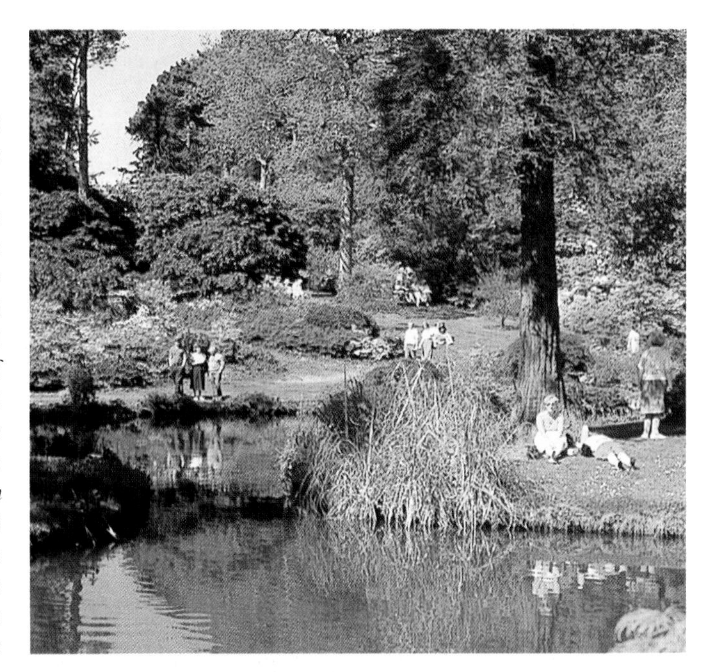

Exbury Gardens are a riot of colour during the rhododendron and azalea season in early summer

gateway of the medieval town, the fortified Bargate. Beyond stretches the high street, with the Red Lion, Dolphin and Star hotels reminding us that this was Southampton's 18th-century equivalent of a railway station or airport.

To right and left of Bargate run the impressive remains of the town walls with defensive towers, including the picturesquely named Catchcold Tower and Blue Anchor Postern. The Tudor House, a fine example of a rich merchant's town house of around 1500, is now a museum, and its finest exhibit is arguably its handsome banqueting hall. Other medieval and Tudor buildings have been converted to museum use, including the Museum of Archaeology in God's House Tower on the old Town Quay, and the Maritime Museum, housed in the early 15th-century Wool House.

More recent history is celebrated in the Hall of Aviation, which tells the story of aviation – particularly flying boats and seaplanes – in and around the

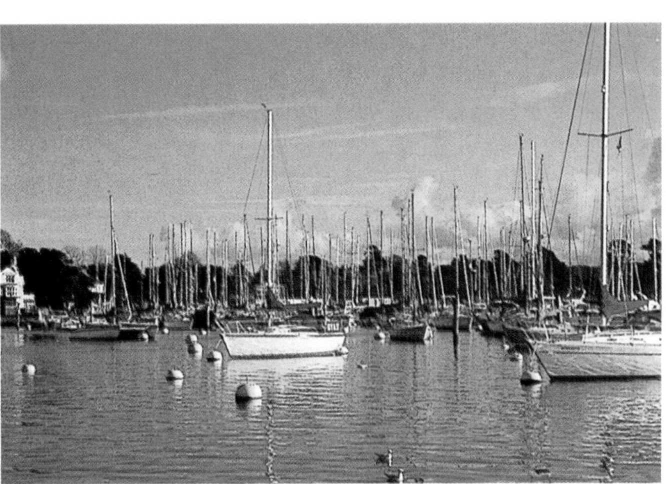

Lymington harbour is a delightful scene, popular with weekend sailors as well as with Isle of Wight ferry passengers

Solent. The name 'Supermarine' attaches not only to the Spitfire, first built in Southampton, but also to the racing seaplanes that took part in the Schneider Trophy races here in 1929 and 1931. The modern helicopter was also created in Southampton, and several are on show.

Southampton is very green, with a series of six parks right in the heart of the city, while to the north the 368 acres (149ha) of Southampton Common drive a generous green wedge between the adjacent suburbs. It is also turning its waterfront into a pleasant public amenity, with Mayflower Park looking out over the Test estuary between Town Quay and the Western Docks, and the more recent development of Ocean Village focusing on the 'festival market' concept, with speciality shops and restaurants by the waterside, alongside a marina and new waterside homes.

Tourist Information Centres

Lymington: St Barb Museum, New Street
(tel: 01590 689000).
Lyndhurst: New Forest Museum & Visitor Centre, Main Car Park
(tel: 01703 282269).
Southampton: Above Bar
(tel: 01703 221106).

CUSTOMS AND FESTIVALS

Traditional customs and festivals in south-east England are many and varied. Some, like 'first footing' on New Year's Eve, pancakes on Shrove Tuesday, and bonfires and fireworks on Guy Fawkes Day, are nationwide, but sometimes may have peculiar local variants. Many go back to pagan times, though the early Christian church took them over. The variety of traditional festivals celebrated is, moreover, being interestingly extended and enriched as schools and communities respond to an increasingly multicultural population.

Thus primary school children in Kent or Oxfordshire are quite likely to know about Holi (when Hindus celebrate the end of winter), Id-ul-Fitr (the end of the Ramadan fast for Muslims), Vesak (when Buddhists leave gifts on the doorsteps of the poor), Shavuot (when Jews celebrate the first fruits of the harvest), or the Chinese New Year marked with fire-crackers and (as in London's Chinatown) dragon dancers. But in these two pages we look at some of the more traditional customs and festivals of the south and south-east.

THE FIRST QUARTER

One curious New Year custom is Queen's College, Oxford's Needle and Thread Gaudy (feast), when the college bursar presents each guest at table with a needle threaded with silk, and says: 'Take this and be thrifty'. Sound advice, no doubt, but all a bit of a joke, in arcane Oxford style. Needle and thread in Norman French is *aiguille* and *fil* – a pun on the college's 14th-century founder, Robert de Eglesfield.

Solemnity and fun are mixed in a different way in London in February, with the annual Clowns' Service at Holy Trinity Church, Dalston. Clowns in full costume and make-up attending this service end with a prayer thanking God 'for causing me to share with others your precious gift of laughter'. It began relatively recently, in 1946, as a tribute to the great 19th-century clown Joseph Grimaldi.

In March people at Stockbridge in Hampshire elect jurors to the Courts Leet and Baron, which traditionally resolved disputes over the local commons. These now belong to the National Trust, but the revived ceremony is fun and provides a useful forum for discussion of local matters.

RITES OF SPRING

Easter and the period preceding it are rich in quaint and colourful customs, starting with Shrove Tuesday, which is traditionally associated with pancakes. This, it seems, is because pancake-making used up perishable foodstuffs before the 40 days of Lent.

A well-known variant is the pancake race at Olney, Buckinghamshire. Contrary to general belief, dropping the pancake does not disqualify the racer, though it may spoil the appetite.

On Maundy Thursday the sovereign distributes Maundy Money – specially minted silver coins – at Westminster Abbey and varying cathedrals. In London Easter Sunday sees the Easter Parade in Battersea Park, followed on Easter Monday by the Harness Horse Parade in Regents Park. On Dunstable Down in Bedfordshire they roll oranges down the hill to waiting children.

May Day ceremonies are perhaps most spectacular in Oxford, where at 6am choristers climb the 144ft (44m) tower of Magdalen College to sing a Latin hymn to the (surprisingly large) assembled crowd. The tower's bells ring out, and a day of celebrations begins with Morris dancing, punting parties and picnics. At Rye, Sussex, May Day is strangely celebrated by the throwing of hot pennies.

Towards the end of May the Vicar of Hastings blesses the sea, presumably to enhance local fisherman's catches (these days his pulpit is a lifeboat). Around the same time, the charter trustees of High Wycombe, Buckinghamshire, choose a mayor, who is weighed, then by the mayoress, out-going mayor and various

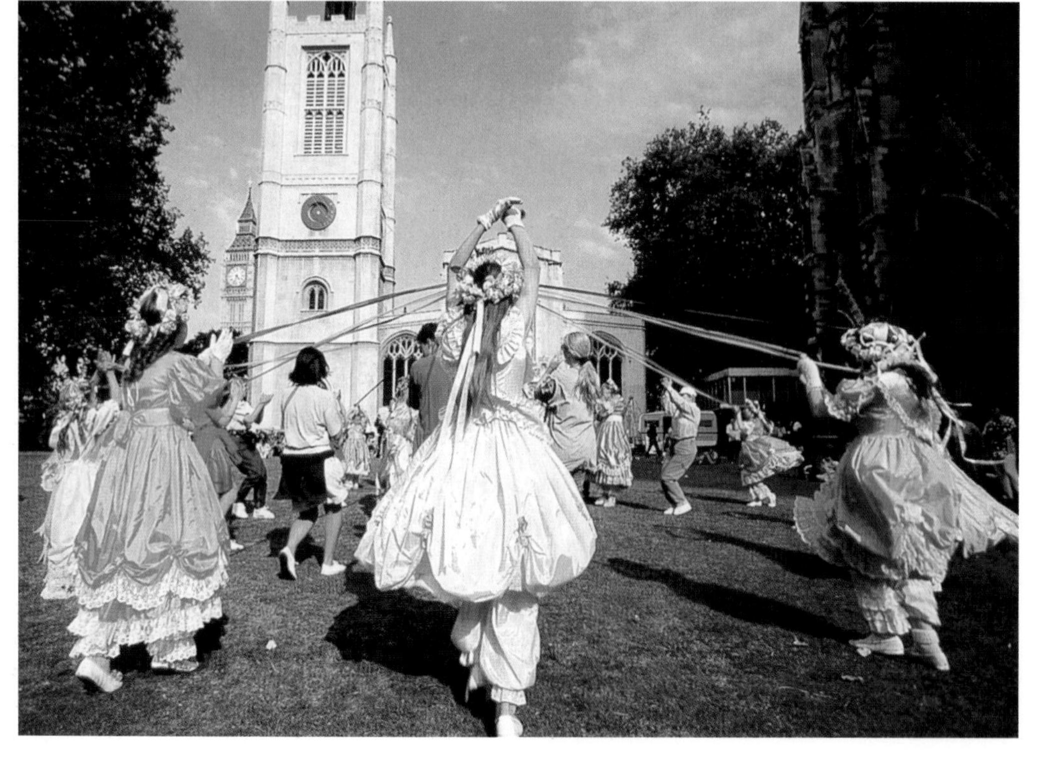

The country moves into the city with maypole dancers performing outside St Margaret's Church in London

others, the presiding weights-and-measures official pronouncing either 'Some more' (meaning 'You've put on weight since last year') or 'No more' (meaning 'You haven't').

SUMMER CELEBRATIONS

On a June Saturday in each leap year, Great Dunmow in Essex is the scene of the well-known Dunmow Flitch, a 900-year-old custom in which married couples seek to convince a local jury of 'six maids and six bachelors' that they have never been unfaithful nor had cross words. National celebrities dressed in wig and gown act as prosecuting and defending counsel; the prize for successful defendants is the flitch – a whole side of bacon.

On the second Wednesday in July the new Master of the Vintners' Company (a City of London livery company) processes from Vintners' Hall in Upper Thames Street to the Church of St James Garlickhithe, he and his entourage carrying nosegays against noxious fumes or infection, and preceded by their Wine Porter who sweeps a clean path with his broom. Later in the month the Vintners are concerned with Swan Upping on the Thames – the nicking of the beak of each swan to show whether it belongs to the Queen, the Vintners or the Dyers.

In August the Thames hosts the Doggett's Coat and Badge Race, when recently qualified Thames Watermen compete in a sculling race from London Bridge to Chelsea's Cadogan Pier. Thomas Doggett, an Irish actor-manager who died in 1721, inaugurated the race to show his patriotic support for George I and his new Hanoverian dynasty – the prizes being £5, a scarlet coat, breeches and shoes, and a huge silver badge.

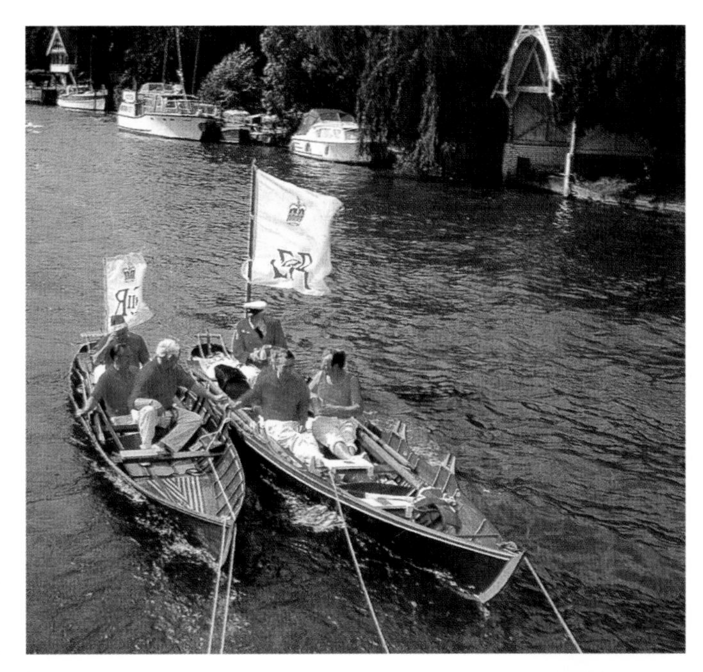

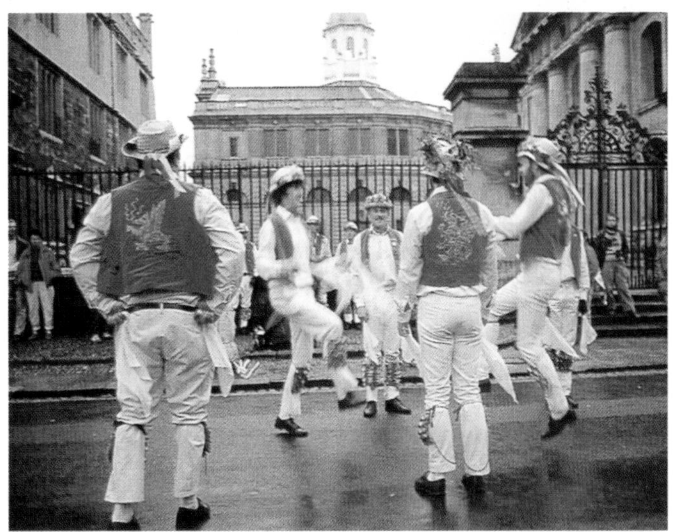

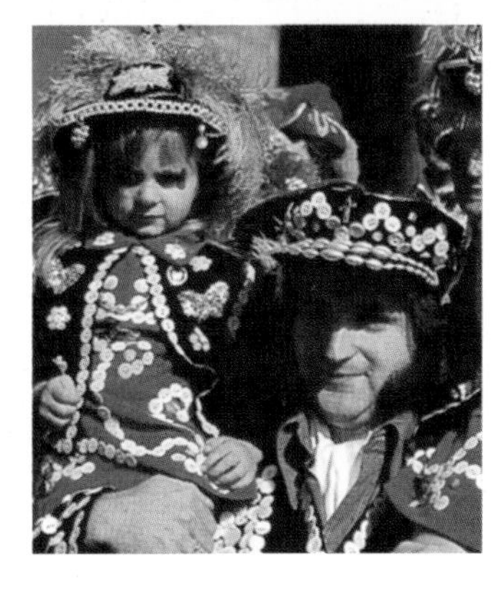

*T*op: swan upping on the River Thames; above: the best-known of all English traditions – morris dancing: right: Pearly Kings and Queens are a long-established London tradition

WINTER CUSTOMS

October 1 sees the Lord Chancellor processing from a service in Westminster Abbey to the House of Lords where he greets his guests and gives them 'Breakfast' (a reception for lawyers and others). On the first Sunday London's Coster-mongers congregate for their service in St Martin-in-the Fields, many of them kitted out in the dressy manner of 19th-century street traders, including 'Pearly Kings and Queens', their clothes studded with innumerable pearl buttons.

Following Guy Fawkes' unsuccessful attempt to blow up King and Parliament in 1605, bonfires and fireworks in England are mostly not at the New Year but on 5 November. Nowhere is this festival so thoroughly celebrated as in Lewes, Sussex, where the memory of 17 Protestant martyrs in the reign of Queen Mary led to a (these days not serious) anti-Papist tradition. Lewes has a number of bonfire societies in different parts of the town, who dress up, go in procession, and burn effigies of currently-hated politicians and others on giant bonfires. In London, the second Saturday in November sees the City's new Lord Mayor ride in his state coach to be sworn in at the Royal Courts of Justice. The procession accompanying him consist of mobile floats on various aspects of a theme chosen by the incoming Lord Mayor.

On Christmas Day the Serpentine in Hyde Park is the scene of an annual swimming race for the Peter Pan Cup, originally presented in 1864 by Peter Pan's creator Sir James Barrie. The swimmers, meeting at 9am, sometimes need to break ice first.

DAILY EVENTS

Finally, some customs and ceremonies take place every day of the year. At the ancient Hospital of St Cross in Winchester, the first 32 people to arrive can claim, with no questions asked, a slice of bread (presented on a wooden platter) and a drink of ale from a horn cup. And each evening at the Tower of London the Chief Yeoman Warder and his escort are challenged by a sentry, leading to the following exchange. 'Halt, who goes there?' 'The Keys'. 'Whose keys?' 'Queen Elizabeth's keys'. The sentry then presents arms, the Chief Warder removes his hat and proclaims, 'God preserve Queen Elizabeth', and the whole guard responds 'Amen!'

LONDON BUILDINGS, OLD AND NEW

Londons architectural riches range from great setpieces like the Palace of Westminster and Wren's two great waterside 'hospitals', or retirement homes (for old soldiers at Chelsea and old sailors at Greenwich) through to smaller, more hidden gems like the Blewcoat School in Caxton Street, Westminster, and the more out of the way City churches.

London has its grand sequences, like the Mall, with Nash's stuccoed, columned sweep of Carlton House Terrace, his great processional route from Regents Park along Portland Place and Regent Street, and Pall Mall with its succession of Italianate 19th-century gentlemen's clubs. But the capital generally eschews grand gestures; its townscape tends to be both more reticent and more anarchic.

THE HEART OF THE CAPITAL

Perhaps the place to start is at Charing Cross in the heart of London, and the hotel which fronts the station (Decimus Burton, 1834) is worth more than a glance. Trafalgar Square has two fine classical buildings. The first, St Martin-in-the-Fields Church (Gibbs, 1726), has a magnificent temple-like portico and steeple.

The other is the National Gallery (Wilkins, 1838), with its controversial but extremely likeable 1991 Sainsbury Wing, designed by American architect Robert Venturi after criticism by Prince Charles scotched the original plan.

Whitehall is full of architectural delights, outstandingly the Banqueting House (Inigo Jones), which, in the early 17th century, was shockingly modern. There is also the Horse Guards (1760), the ceremonial gateway to the parade ground and park beyond, and Richmond Terrace. A 1960s scheme for a new government precinct would have swept away this and the famous New Scotland Yard, but by 1970 the tide of conservation was running strongly enough to stop it. William Whitfield's attractive Department of Heath building, alongside Richmond Terrace, shows how modern infill can possess strength and character, and yet still exist in sympathy with its surroundings.

More MPs' offices on the Parliament Square corner await completion of a new station

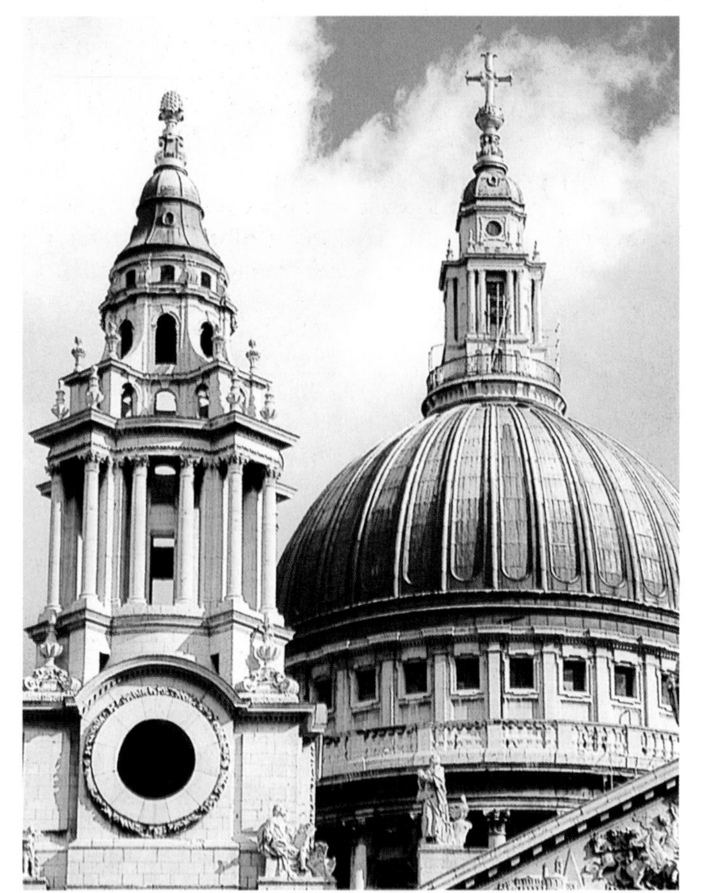

for the Jubilee Line. The architects of the 11 new stations on the line's extension have a brief to bring light and spaciousness into the underworld.

The Houses of Parliament and Westminster Abbey are, of course, the great architectural features of this square, but the Queen Elizabeth II Conference Centre (1986) demonstrates how large modern buildings can sit happily in a historic townscape.

Other notable buildings hereabouts include Westminster Cathedral (Bentley, 1903); and Channel 4's television studios and headquarters in Horseferry Road (Rogers, 1994).

THE CITY AND DOCKLANDS

The City of London has rather different planning policies from neighbouring Westminster, most of which is now a conservation area. The City has its historic jewels – Wren's St Paul's Cathedral, his 'wedding cake' St Bride's and a string of other churches, built after the Great Fire of 1666. The tranquil and beautiful Inns of Court are here, along with such monuments to commerce as the Bank of England, Royal Exchange, Custom House and the Mansion House and Guildhall. Just over the City boundary is that great riverside fortress, the Tower of London.

Because it is a money-making machine, the City has looked favourably on new developments designed to give

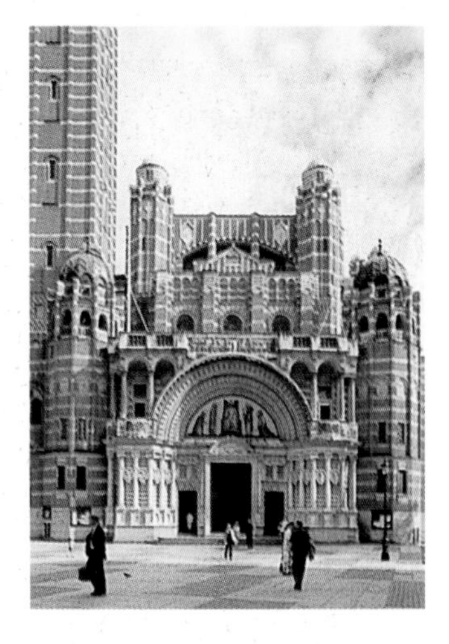

Top: St Paul's Cathedral is an impressive sight amidst the towering modern office blocks of the city

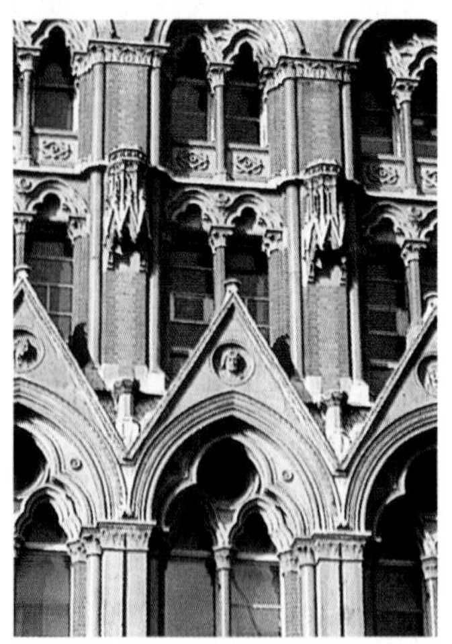

Above: Westminster Cathedral and St Pancras Station both reflect the flamboyance of the 19th century

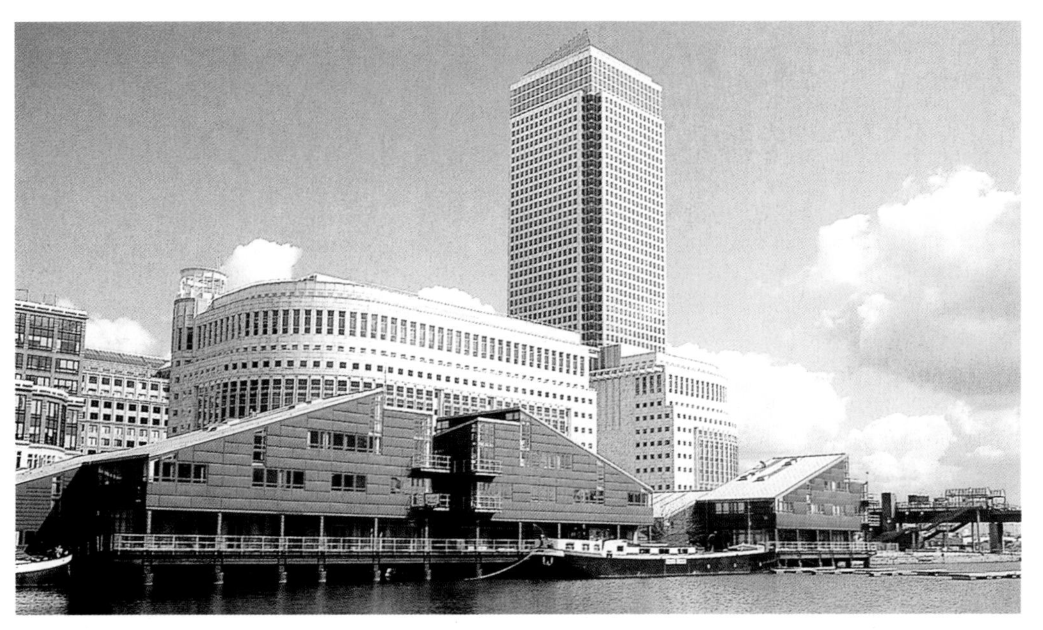

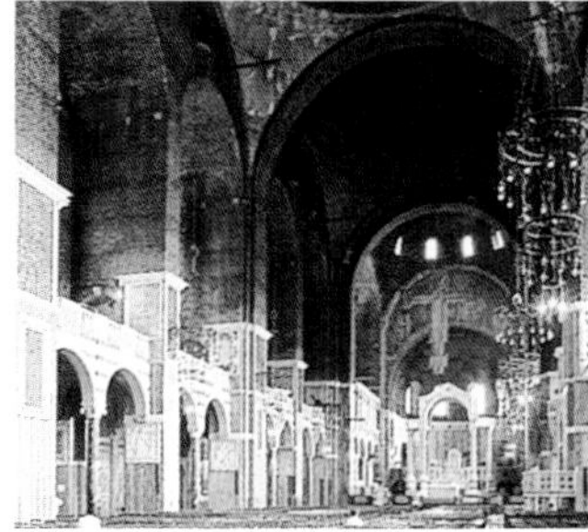

its money-makers the accommodation they want, resulting in many large, dull or ugly buildings, some bold and beautiful ones, and a striking new City skyline. Notable recent buildings include Rogers' 1986 Lloyds building in steel and glass, with a lofty atrium looking down on its underwriting room. Another is the stylishly upgraded Liverpool Street Station (British Rail architects) with the huge Broadgate office development (Arup Associates, Skidmore Owings Merrill). And there is the 1950s-1980s Barbican development, combining accommodation with entertainment venues and restaurants (Chamberlin Powell & Bon).

These days the Square Mile has a rival in its near neighbour to the east – London's renascent Docklands. Here is the capital's most spectacular and controversial group of buildings, Canary Wharf. Conceived as a sort of Wall Street-on-Thames, this £4 billion development extends more than half a mile (1km) across the Isle of Dogs, and includes London's tallest tower, by American architect Cesar Pelli. It has its own shopping centre and waterside restaurants, with a mixture of architectural styles that are often pastiche. Canary Wharf is best approached by the elevated Docklands Light Railway, but do get out and walk all round it!

AROUND THE CENTRE

On the north-central fringe of central London are four buildings of particular merit – the British Museum (1847, Smirke), University College's original Gower Street group (Wilkins, 1829), St Pancras Station and the new British Library. St Pancras's spectacular and recently restored High Victorian hotel front (1874, G G Scott) faces Barlow's great 1868 train shed, soon to be adapted for trains from the planned Channel Tunnel fast rail link; the Library, recently completed next door, and designed by Colin St John Wilson, is clad in red brick to match the station buildings.

The 'museums area' of South Kensington also merits a good, long look. Here is the expression of Queen Victoria's and (especially) Prince Albert's belief in the nation's intellectual and cultural advancement, and stylistically the site reflects that age. Impressively self-confident buildings in brick, terracotta and stone line spacious boulevards. They include the Victoria and Albert, Natural History and Science Museums; Imperial College tower and the Royal Albert Hall. There are plans to enhance the overall area ('Albertopolis') for the Millennium by submerging the road in front of the Royal Albert Hall and creating a piazza connecting it with the Albert Memorial.

On the South Bank the two most notable buildings are the Royal Festival Hall (Robert Matthew, Leslie Martin, 1951) and the Royal National Theatre (Denys Lasdun, 1975). A scheme currently being developed by Rogers aims to humanise and perhaps roof over the rather hostile area between them, demolishing the windswept upper walkways. This, and Millennium proposals for new cross-river footbridges, tramways and even cable cars, should do much to make the South Bank feel more like part of central London. A powerful magnet will be the conversion of the huge Bankside Power Station into an art gallery; the Tate Gallery have appointed the Swiss architects Herzog and de Meuron to design it.

Just downstream you see the thatched roof of the replica Globe Theatre, part of an international Shakespeare centre close to the site of the original Globe. Further on are Southwark Cathedral, London Bridge City, where lofty Hay's Galleria rises from a former dock basin, and (below Tower Bridge) Butler's Wharf, an area of 19th-century warehouses recycled into flats, restaurants and design studios – an ideal site for the Design Museum.

*T*he familiar Albert Memorial, restored to its full splendour after a recent extensive overhaul and cleaning-up operation

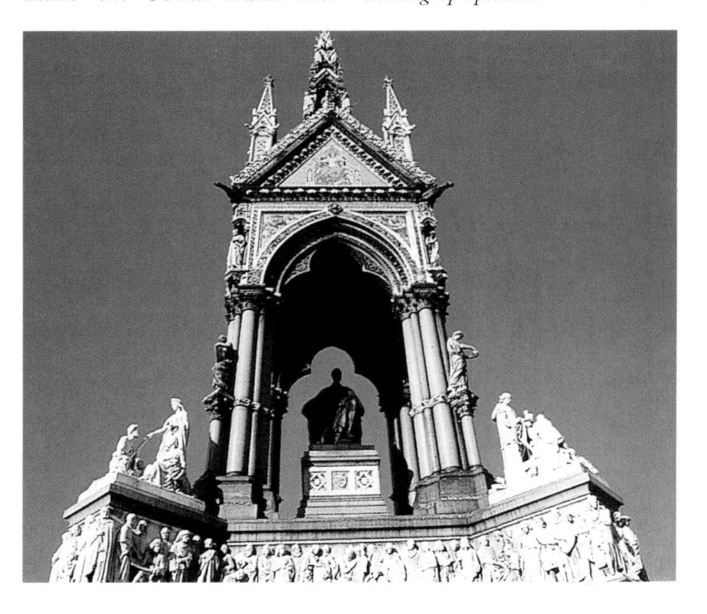

THE GREEN LUNGS OF LONDON

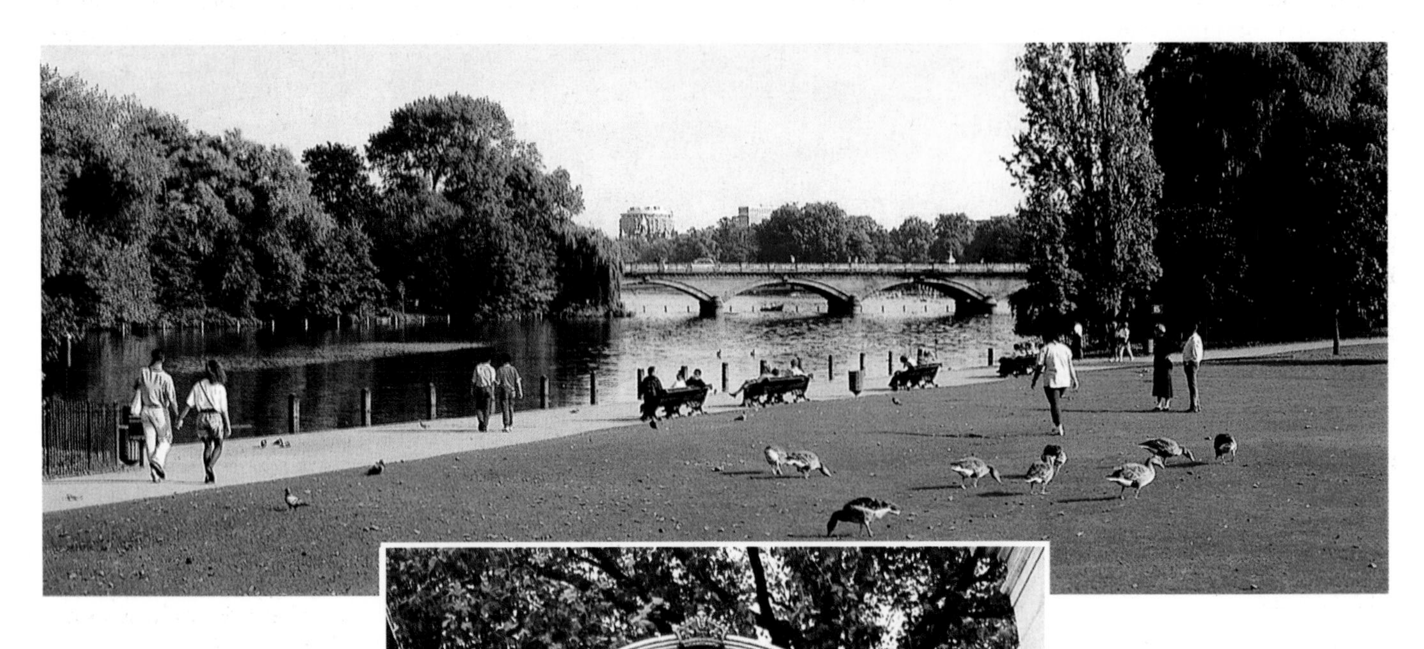

CENTRAL LONDON PARKS

Centuries ago these parks were mostly royal hunting forests outside the confines of a much smaller capital. Central London has now engulfed many of them, and the oldest is St James's Park, with its neat lawns, colourful flower beds and shrubberies around a lovely lake.

It is hard to imagine this as marshland, as it was until it was drained to provide Henry VIII with a bowling alley, tiltyard and deer nursery. Charles II redesigned it, and by the late 17th century it was already home to many species of wading birds, including two pelicans given to the king by the Russian ambassador. The variety and profusion of birdlife around the lake is one of its attractions; another is the splendid roofscape seen from the bridge.

St James's Park forms the first link in a great green chain, leading past Buckingham Palace into Green Park, then into the wide expanses of Hyde Park and Kensington Gardens. Lush and restful

Cities, and the people in them, need to breathe, and one feature of London that appeals to visitors and residents alike is the number and richness of green spaces. A recent survey carried out for the Royal Parks Agency showed that in that particular year its parks attracted some 30 million visitors, which put them collectively above such national tourist attractions as St Paul's Cathedral (2.6 million) and the Tower of London (2.4 million). Other research among visitors from abroad shows that they are drawn to London by the relaxed, civilised image created by its parks – particularly the Royal Parks.

Green Park is the smallest Royal Park, while Hyde Park is the largest of those in central London – quite exhilarating amidst this densely built-up area. Deer-hunting ceased here in the 1750s, and the deer have long gone, but people still ride horses along a sandy track called Rotten Row. The name is a corruption of *Route du Roi* (the king's road), because it is on the line of the road which led to Kensington Palace. Just north of Rotten Row is the Serpentine, which, with the Long Water, forms a long curving lake. In the park's north-east corner are Marble Arch and Speakers' Corner, where assorted soap-box orators, from anarchists to evangelists to flat-earthers, by tradition harangue passers-by.

Above: sweeping lawns beside the Serpentine in Hyde Park bring a taste of the countryside into central London; left: the ornate gates which lead into Green Park

Across the Broad Water lie Kensington Gardens, originally the gardens of Kensington Palace and now effectively a westward extension of Hyde Park, though it is more intimate and sedate. Features include the magnificently restored Albert Memorial, the Round Pond, Broad and Flower Walks, the Sunken Garden and the Orangery. Don't miss the intricately carved Elfin Oak, Frampton's statue of J M Barrie's eternally youthful hero, Peter Pan, and (near Lancaster Gate) the recently restored Italian Water Gardens with their fountains and statuary.

Regent's Park formed part of an inspired 19th-century property development scheme, a collaboration between architect John Nash and the Prince Regent. It was originally to be the grounds of a new palace, which was never built, and consists of landscaped, wooded parkland with a lake; villas lie hidden within it, and the park

is ringed by a sequence of grand stucco terraces. It is a magical combination of landscape and water, with a well-preserved architectural backdrop. Other features include the delightful Queen Mary's Rose Garden and the open-air theatre's summer season. On the northern boundary of the park are London Zoo and the Regent's Canal. The adjacent Primrose Hill, once part of the same hunting forest, retains a more rural atmosphere and where it rises to 207ft (63m) there are panoramic views over London.

FURTHER AFIELD

The outer Royal Parks include three huge open spaces near the Thames in west London, all associated with former royal palaces. Richmond Park still has ancient oak trees, a large herd of deer and lots of other wildlife. From Robin Hood Gate a pedestrian link connects with another huge belt of parkland – Wimbledon Common, with its lake and windmill, and adjoining Putney Heath. Bushy Park and Hampton Court Park lie west and north of Hampton Court Palace and are somewhat simi-

lar to Richmond's landscaped parkland, except that Hampton Court's gardens have a more urbane, cultivated character, with formal vistas, a canal lined with lime trees, statuary and the famous maze.

Greenwich Park, too, was a royal hunting park, walled in from adjoining Blackheath. Today it forms part of a unique sequence, which starts on the Thames waterside with Sir Christopher Wren's Royal Naval College. It then moves through the National Maritime Museum's grounds, along the twin colonnades flanking Inigo Jones's superb Queen's House and into the park, which contains Wren's charming hill-top Old Observatory, standing at zero degrees longitude. The sequence continues along a broad chestnut-lined avenue to the windswept, kite-flying Blackheath and terminates at the spire of All Saint's Church in Blackheath Village.

HEATHS, COMMONS AND SQUARES

London's unique inheritance of Royal Parks constitutes only the crème de la crème of

its green open spaces, but there are many other appealing tracts of land. Hampstead Heath, Kenwood and Parliament Hill to the north are famous for their wonderful views (Guy Fawkes' compatriots intended to watch the result of their conspiracy to blow up Parliament from here). Epping Forest, a huge green wedge stretching from Wanstead out into Essex, is real countryside on London's doorstep, and on the eastern edge are Lee Valley Park and Thames Chase, the latter a new forest, planted by the Countryside Commission.

Clapham, Tooting, Streatham, Wandsworth and Barnes all have their commons, and London also has a number of big municipal parks, providing relief from urban sprawl and a refuge for wildlife. The Grand Union and Regent Canals, forming an arc of waterways with towpaths round north inner London, offer tranquil walking and are an important part of a network of ecological corridors.

There remain many parts of London which are not so fortunate in having a green open space in their vicinity, and their saving grace is the London square. These railing-enclosed gardens with mature trees are sometimes open to the public, sometimes the private reserve of the residents, but are always a green lung among busy streets. There are over 600 squares in Greater London, with a huge diversity of character. They range from such fashionable and architecturally magnificent ensembles as Belgrave and Eaton Squares to unnumbered squares, crescents, and circuses with soft green centres all over London. These – like the parks – bring delight and refreshment to Londoners and visitors alike.

Below: colourful flower beds in St James's Park; below left: the Regents Canal is a peaceful backwater in North London; bottom: Richmond Hill looks down over the Thames

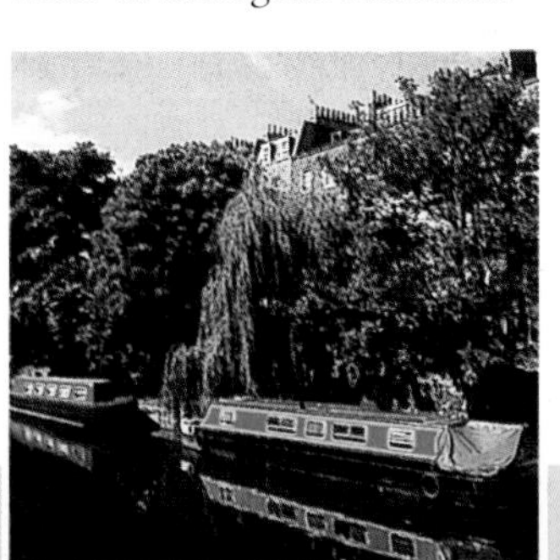

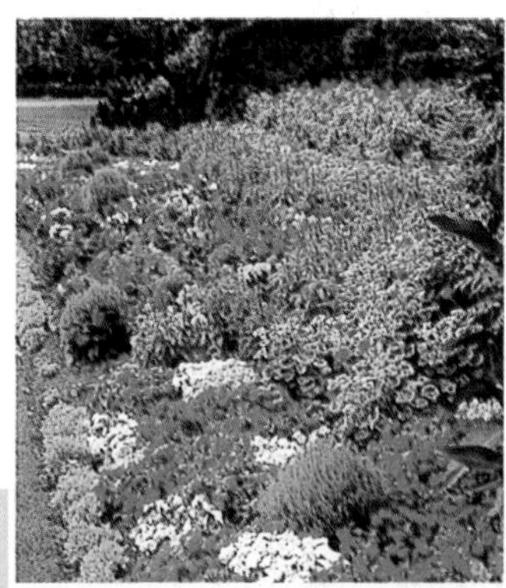

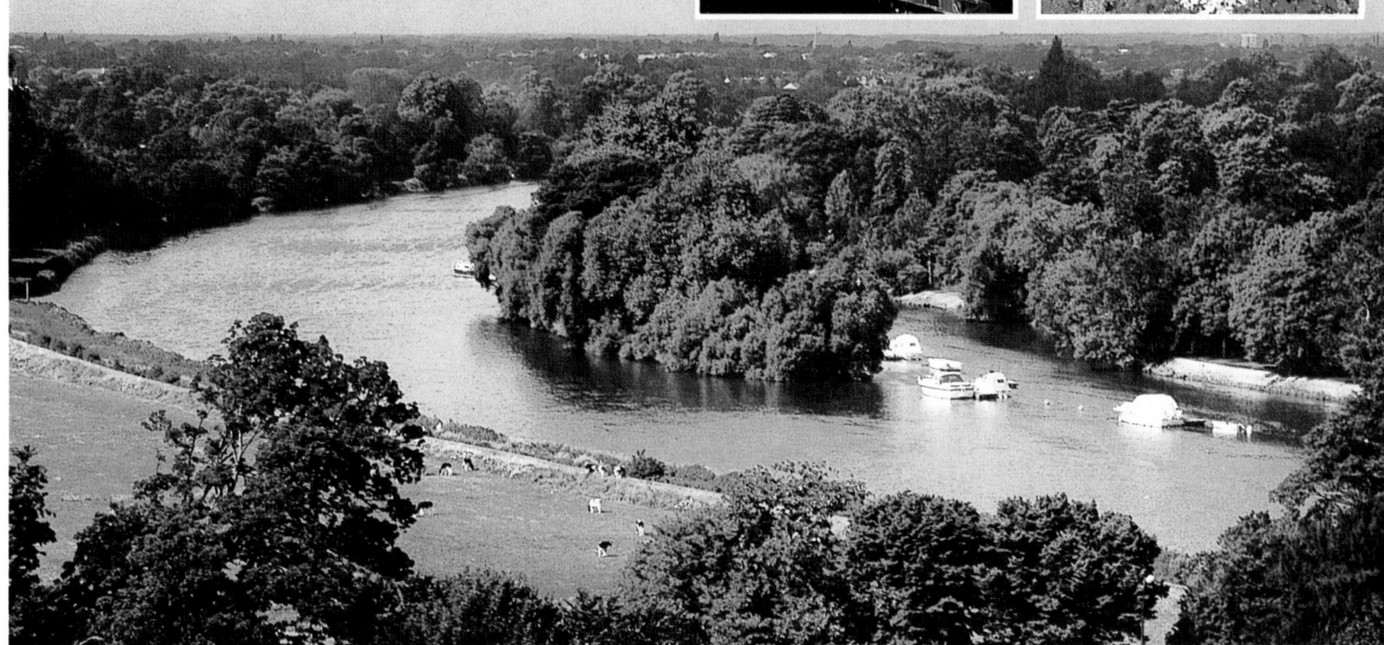

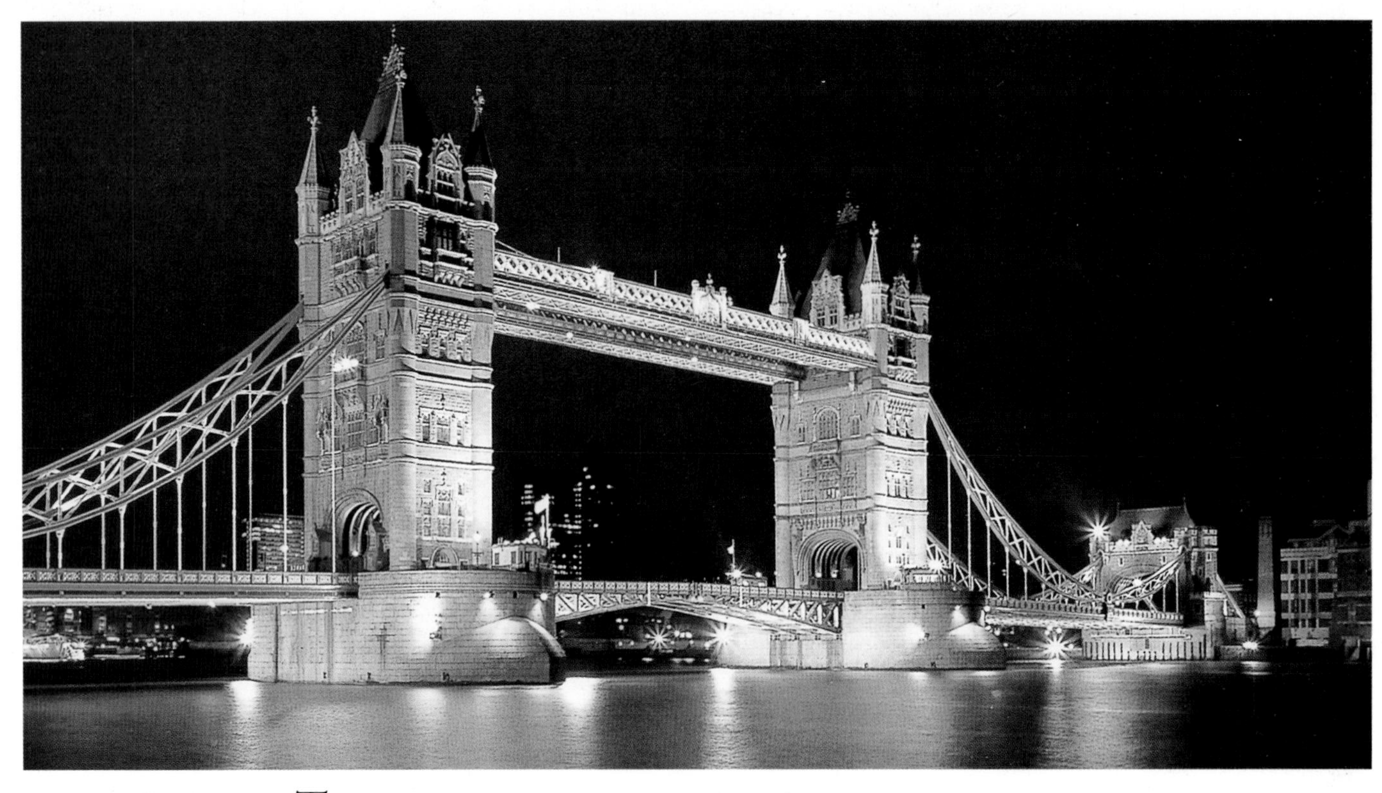

Tower Bridge is a spectacular and dramatic sight when floodlit against the night sky of the capital

CROSSING THE THAMES

CENTRAL LONDON BRIDGES

When it comes to bridges in London, most people tend to think first of Tower Bridge, London Bridge and Westminster Bridge. Tower Bridge – until 1991 the lowest bridge on the Thames – reflects the Victorian obsession with Gothic architecture. A glass-covered walkway, 142ft (43m) above the water, links the two towers and gives panoramic views along the river. The opening mechanism was electrified in 1976, but the original hydraulic machinery is now the centrepiece of a museum, which uses state-of-the-art effects to tell the story of the bridge in a dramatic and exciting way. Recent surveys suggest that the bridge is suffering from heavy traffic; its life may be prolonged by providing a replacement tunnel a little

The River Thames was once London's greatest thoroughfare – it was by far the easiest means of travelling in and out of the capital in the days of horses and carriages, rough, muddy tracks, footpads and highwaymen. But the great river always needed to be crossed, and there have been bridges over the Thames for about 1,000 years. Today there are some 30 of them within Greater London – for road, rail and pedestrians – not to mention the tunnels or the towering Queen Elizabeth II suspension bridge downstream, which doubles up with the twin Dartford Tunnels to carry the busy M25 across the river.

downstream and restricting Tower Bridge's use to pedestrians, cyclists and perhaps buses.

The next bridge upstream is London Bridge, the oldest and most famous, which has its origins in a wooden bridge built to connect Roman Londinium via the Kent section of Watling Street to the Roman ports of Dubris (Dover) and Rutupiae (Richborough). It was broken or burnt down several times until, in 1176, Peter de Colechurch erected the first stone bridge, with a chapel on

it dedicated to St Thomas à Becket. Soon after, houses were built alongside its roadway, and the gruesome custom developed of displaying the impaled heads of executed rebels and traitors on the bridge.

De Colechurch's bridge was not well designed. It had many narrow arches, and their piers obstructed the river's flow and made navigation hazardous. But it saw service until the 18th century, when the houses were removed and a wider central channel was created. In

1801 Thomas Telford designed a new and revolutionary single-span iron bridge, but it was too innovative for the powers-that-be. They built instead a five-arched stone bridge, by the Scottish engineer, John Rennie, and built by his more famous son who was knighted upon its completion in 1831. Rennie's bridge was bought and transported, stone by stone, to the USA, where it now stands incongruously in the Arizona desert.

The latest incarnation of London Bridge is a three-span construction, opened in 1972.

Next come Southwark Bridge and Blackfriars road and railway bridges before we reach Waterloo Bridge, which opened in 1942, replacing Rennie's much admired stone bridge of 1817. Hungerford (or Charing Cross) railway bridge, with a well-used pedestrian way, connects Charing Cross to the South Bank arts complex. Dating from 1864, the rail

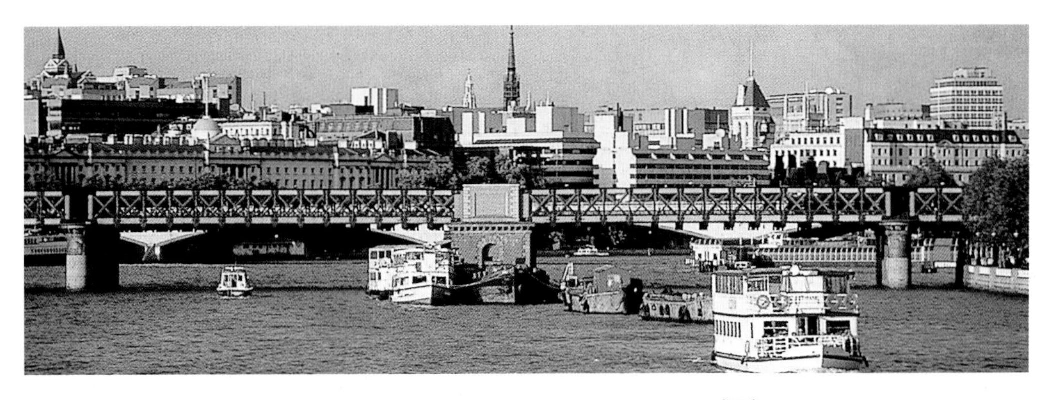

bridge replaced Brunel's suspension bridge, but used its brick piers; the chains were recycled into his Clifton Suspension Bridge in Bristol.

Westminster Bridge, alongside the Houses of Parliament, was the second bridge to be built in what is now central London. The present structure, was completed in 1862, but it replaced an earlier bridge, which opened in 1750. That was the bridge on which Wordsworth wrote his famous sonnet ('Earth has not anything to show more fair...'), but it later suffered - like others - from the notorious scouring action of strong Thames tides.

The idea of a second crossing at Westminster provoked strong opposition from vested interests – the Thames Watermen had to be bought off with £25,000 compensation; the Archbishop of Canterbury, owner of the horse ferry at Lambeth, collected £21,000 – considerable amounts in those days. Later, in 1862, Lambeth Bridge was completed, right where the Archbishop's ferry used to be – on its east side stands Lambeth Palace, the Archbishop's official residence; its western approach, Horse-ferry Road, is a lasting reminder of the ferry. The present bridge was built in 1932.

Upstream again are Vauxhall Bridge, Grosvenor railway bridge (carrying the lines out of Victoria) and Chelsea Bridge, a handsome suspension bridge. On the other side of Battersea Park is perhaps the most attractive of them all, Albert Bridge. Opened in 1873, it was designed by R M Ordish and may be described as a 'semi-suspension' bridge – the diagonal stays radiating so picturesquely from the towers to support the deck are rigid; the light suspension chains take only the weight of the stays.

Eighteen London bridges lie upstream of this, starting with Battersea (designed by Sir Joseph Bazalgette, who built

the Victoria Embankment). They include the monumental Hammersmith Bridge with its rather Empire-style towers and the suspension footbridge at Teddington Weir, ending with Hampton Court Bridge, of which only one side (Hampton Court) is in London; the other is in Surrey.

Tunnels under the river are numerous, and include several carrying Underground lines. Within London there are also three road tunnels: Rotherhithe, with bends definitely for horse-drawn rather than motor vehicles, and the two Blackwall Tunnels. Also downstream of Tower bridge are two pedestrian tunnels, the one at Woolwich providing an alternative to the free Woolwich Ferry, the other at Greenwich, connecting the Cutty Sark Gardens to Island Gardens on

*T*wo contrasting bridges across the Thames are the sturdy Lambeth Bridge, right, built in the 1930s, and the Albert bridge, below, looking like a metal cobweb across the water

the Isle of Dogs, the present terminus of the Docklands Light Railway (DLR). Another tunnel at this point will soon extend the line of the DLR to Greenwich, Deptford and Lewisham.

Just upstream of the Woolwich ferry and foot tunnel is something which is neither a bridge nor a tunnel, but is an important link between the north and south banks of the river. The Thames Barrier, completed in 1984, is a vital part of a £480 million flood defence scheme for London.

*T*he river near Westminster Bridge is busy with tourist boats, cruising the historic artery of the city

The Barrier has four enormous curving steel gates, each 200ft (61m) long, shaped like barrels sliced longways; each weighs 3,200 tonnes. These fit into concrete sills on the river bed and only rise if winds and the North Sea surge threaten to cause flooding in the capital. Immediately downstream is the south bank visitors' centre, with viewing esplanades, a café, and an exhibition.

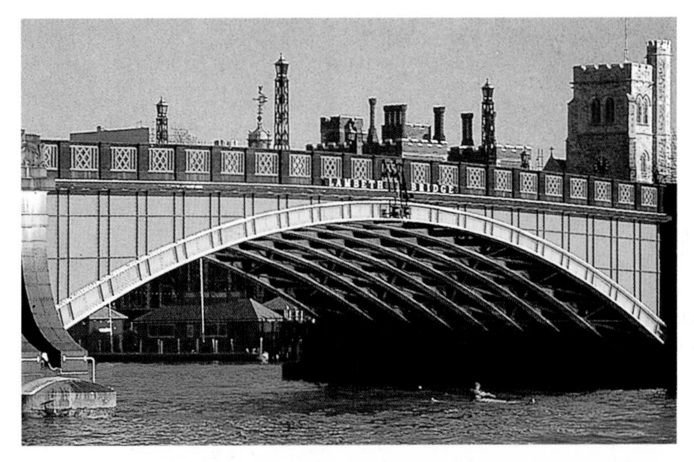

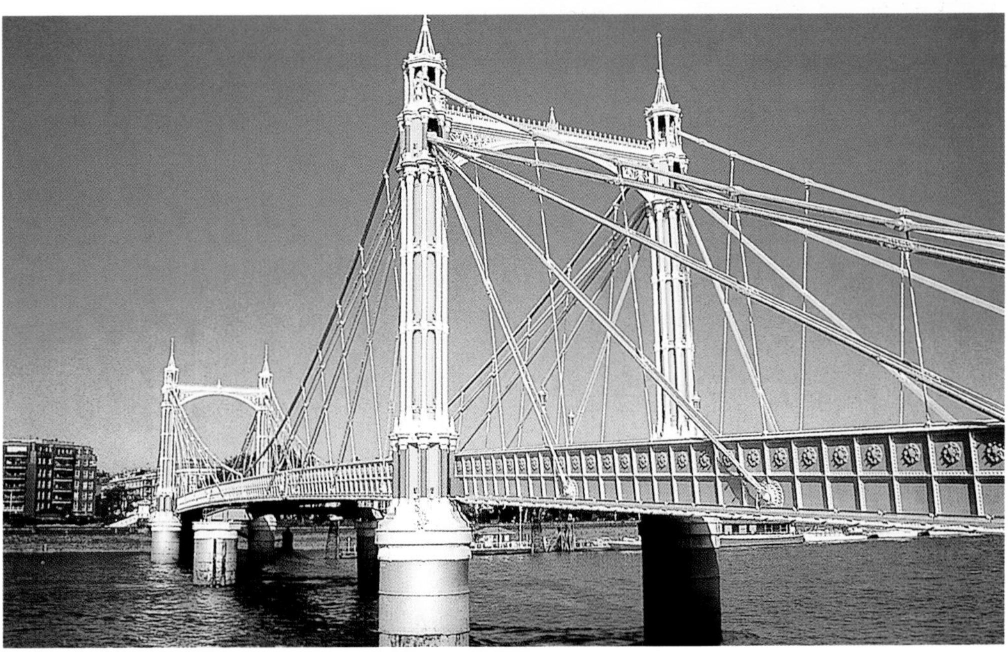

POMP AND CIRCUMSTANCE

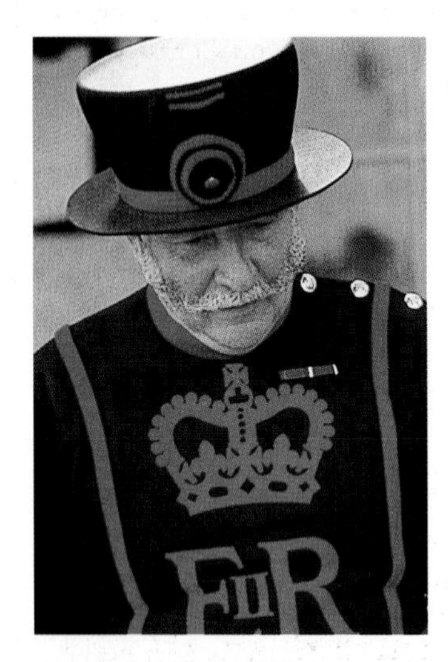

London has many odd and colourful ceremonies. Some are public, others private; some vouchsafe passers-by a glimpse of worthy-looking persons in bizarre old-fashioned costume, processing through the public street in the course of honouring some ancient tradition. Often the origins and purpose seem obscure; these are traditions kept alive when the reasons for them have long disappeared. But these quaint and colourful ceremonies can be savoured simply because they are quaint and colourful. Parliament, the monarchy, the armed forces, the law and the City of London are the main focuses of traditional ceremony.

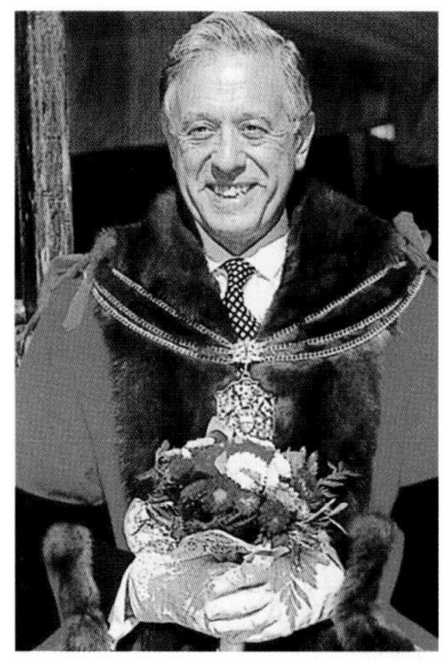

ROYAL TRADITIONS

Ceremonial relations between Crown and Parliament reflect the struggle of the elected House of Commons in the 17th century to assert its independence from the Stuart kings. Thus, when the Queen opens each new session of Parliament, it is not in the House of Commons – no sovereign has been admitted here since the Civil War and subsequent execution of Charles I – but in the House of Lords.

The State Opening of Parliament usually takes place in late October or early November and begins with a coach carrying the imperial state crown to Parliament, followed some 20 minutes later by the Queen in the splendid Irish state coach. From Buckingham Palace they drive down the Mall, through Horseguards Arch into Whitehall and thus to Parliament. As the Queen enters the Lords, guns in Hyde Park fire a salute; as she takes her seat on the throne, the Lord Great Chamberlain (a hereditary royal official) raises his wand to summon the Commons.

But when Black Rod, a House of Lords official, arrives at the Commons chamber,

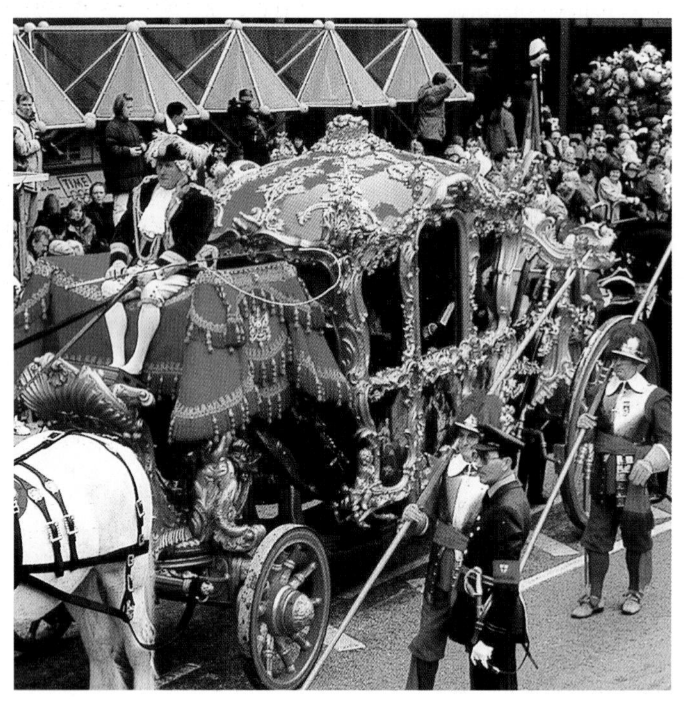

*F*ar left: the 'Beefeaters' of the tower are a daily attraction; above and left: the Lord Mayor's Show, led by his fairytale golden coach, takes place once a year in November

something odd happens. The Sergeant at Arms, a Commons official, slams the door in his face. This recalls Charles I's attempt to arrest five MPs in 1642, one of the events which led to the Civil War. However, eventually Black Rod gets to delivers his message, and MPs follow the Speaker of the House of Commons to the Lords to hear the Queen's Speech. In a curious way, this is proof of Parliament's triumph, because the speech is written not by the Queen, but by government ministers, and it sets out their policies and legislative programme for the new parliamentary session.

Earlier that day another historic ceremony is performed. The Queen's bodyguard of Yeomen of the Guard, in their picturesque red and black uniforms, search the cellars beneath of the Palace of Westminster for gunpowder – recalling the attempt on 5 November 1605 to blow up King James I and Parliament.

The most colourful of the public royal ceremonies is the annual Trooping the Colour which celebrates the sovereign's official birthday, usually on the second Saturday of June. The parade's original purpose was to show the men of a particular regiment their

'colour' or flag so that they would recognise it as a rallying point in battle. In today's ceremony, the Queen, dressed in the uniform of the Foot Guards she is reviewing, goes with an escort of Household Cavalry to Horseguards and inspects the parade; there is then a march past, and finally the Queen leads her Foot Guards back to Buckingham Palace. Until 1987, the Queen rode on horseback; now she rides in a carriage.

Beating the Retreat is another display of military precision involving the marching and drilling bands of the Household Division in their colourful uniforms. It takes place on Horseguards Parade in late May or early June and involves mounted bands, trumpeters, massed marching bands and pipes and drums. The name has nothing to do with defeat in battle – it goes back to the ancient custom of signalling or 'beating' the retreat of sunlight at nightfall.

For those who miss these annual parades, the Changing of the Guard is a colourful

daily ceremony which takes place at four royal palaces in London. Most impressive is that at Buckingham Palace, with one detachment of Foot Guards, in their scarlet tunics and tall bearskin helmets, taking over from another the duty of guarding the Queen's residence. Similar ceremonies also take place at the Horse Guards in Whitehall, St James's Palace, and the Tower of London.

CIVIC DIGNITARIES

Over the years London's local authorities have often been reorganised to suit new conditions, but the oldest, the City of London Corporation, which administers only the 'Square Mile' – the tiny area containing London's financial centre – has retained its independence. The authority combines an efficient (though arguably undemo-

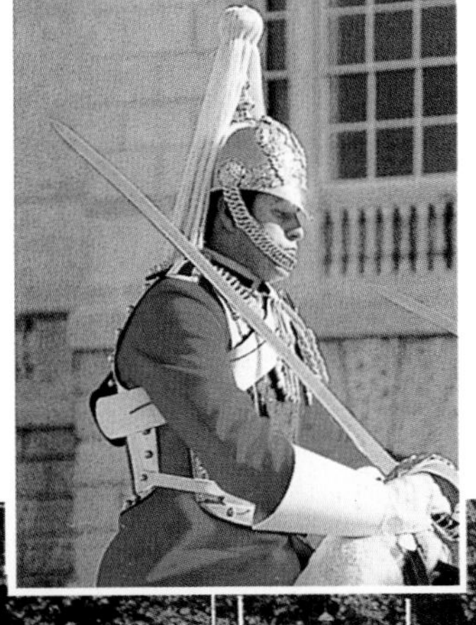

cratic) administration with the pomp and pageantry of 800 years of proud municipal independence.

Its figurehead is the Lord Mayor, elected each year in an unbroken 800-year tradition by the liverymen of the City livery companies, or guilds. When the reigning Lord Mayor and Sheriffs arrive at the Guildhall in their traditional robes of office, the Keeper of Guildhall presents them with nosegays of garden flowers. This tradition goes back to the days when they were believed to give protection not only against the evil smells of London streets, but against the diseases that were harboured there.

The election of the Lord Mayor takes place around Michaelmas Day (29 September), followed in November by the Lord Mayor's Procession (or Lord Mayor's Show). This dates back to Magna Carta in 1215 when King John, under pressure from his barons, sought support from the City in return for giving it a new charter allowing annual elections. His proviso was that

*T*rooping the Colour, with the Queen's guardsmen resplendent in their ceremonial uniforms, takes place in June to mark the official birthday of the sovereign

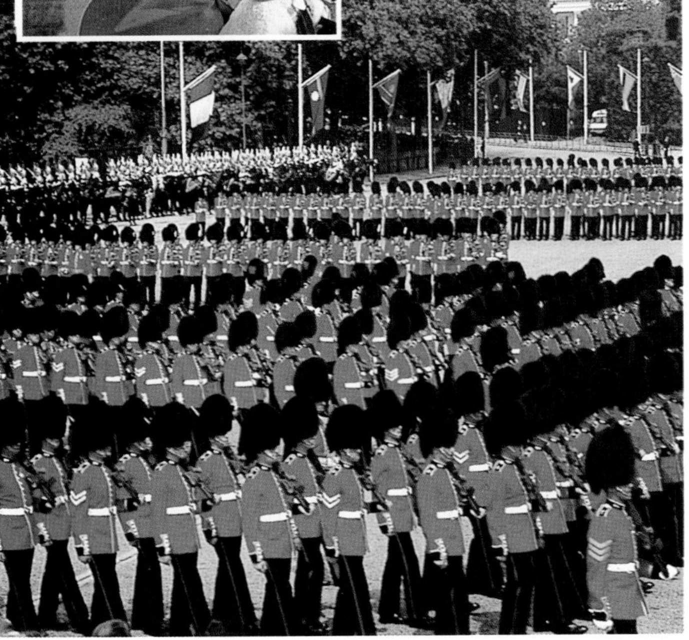

CEREMONY IN MUSIC

A different kind of Pomp and Circumstance is found in Elgar's five marches of that name, music redolent of the imperial pride of the Edwardian era.

At least one (Number 1) features each year at the festive Last Night of the Proms (the Henry Wood Promenade Concerts) at the Royal Albert Hall. Sung lustily by the audience of Promenaders to the words of 'Land of Hope and Glory', the enthusiastic chorus typifies the way in which Londoners enjoy celebrating the past without necessarily taking too seriously the attitudes lying behind the traditions.

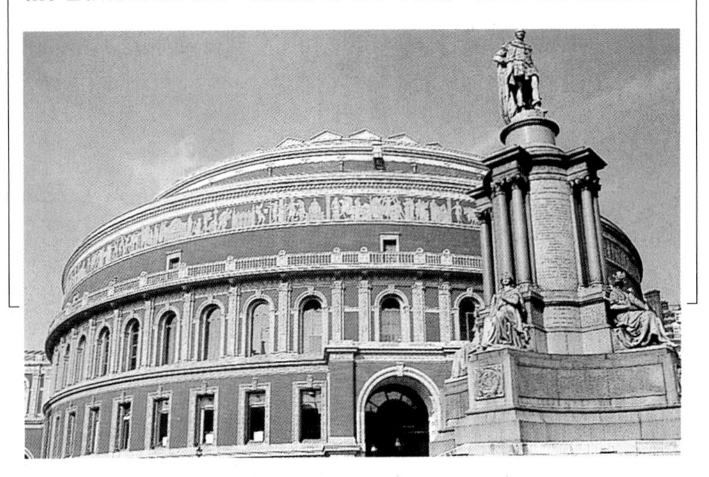

*T*he imposing Royal Albert Hall

each new Lord Mayor took an oath of allegiance before the king or his justices, and so, on a Saturday each November, the new Lord Mayor of London goes in procession to the Royal Courts of Justice in the Strand to swear loyalty to the Crown.

The processional route is along Cheapside, Ludgate Hill and Fleet Street to the Strand. The Lord Mayor's gilded coach, built in 1757 and looking for all the world as if it has come straight out of a fairy tale, has actually come straight out of the Museum of London, harnessed to six magnificent Shire horses; he is attended by a personal bodyguard of pikemen in armour

and musketeers from England's oldest regiment, the Honourable Artillery Company. A huge retinue of mobile floats or tableaux make up the procession, and illustrate various aspects of a theme chosen by the new Lord Mayor for his year of office.

Another highlight of the City calendar is the Lord Mayor's Banquet, held on the Monday following the Show, and the most important in a series of banquets and feasts which each Lord Mayor must enjoy or endure during his year of office. The new Lord Mayor and Sheriffs give this banquet in honour of the outgoing Lord Mayor, and invite some 700 VIPs, the most important of them welcomed with fanfares by splendidly costumed trumpeters. During the evening there is a major speech by the Prime Minister.

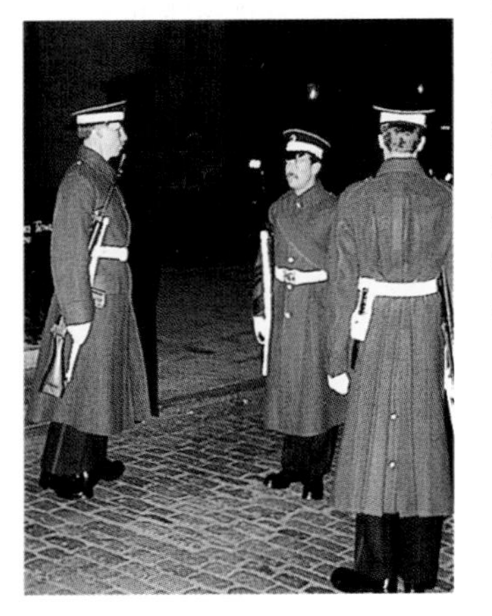

*T*he Ceremony of the Keys at the Tower of London has taken place at 10pm every night for centuries

OFF-CENTRE LONDON

GREENWICH AND THE SOUTH-EAST

On a nice day, you cannot beat the boat trip to Greenwich from the city, but travel to Greenwich by the Docklands Light Railway and you will alight at Island Gardens on the opposite side of the river. From here you can enjoy the finest view of the great architectural ensemble of the Royal Naval College and National Maritime Museum, before continuing on foot through a tunnel beneath the Thames. As well as the museum, there is a historic ship collection which includes the *Cutty Sark* clipper ship and *Gipsy Moth IV*, Sir Francis Chichester's round-the-world yacht. The restored Queen's House is also open, as is the Old Royal Observatory, standing at zero degrees longitude in Greenwich Park.

Woolwich, to the east, has the imposing Royal Artillery Barracks and Academy on the common, and the Museum of Artillery, housed in the Rotunda, by John Nash. Also at Woolwich is the Thames

Most visitors to London look at a few famous tourist attractions, perhaps take a bus tour round the centre, and think they have seen what the city has to offer. To do this is to miss out on some real treats, because 'off-centre London' has interesting and attractive places that are well worth visiting. Here we explore some of the more notable of them – moving clockwise, we start at about the four o'clock position at one of the best known of London's outer limits.

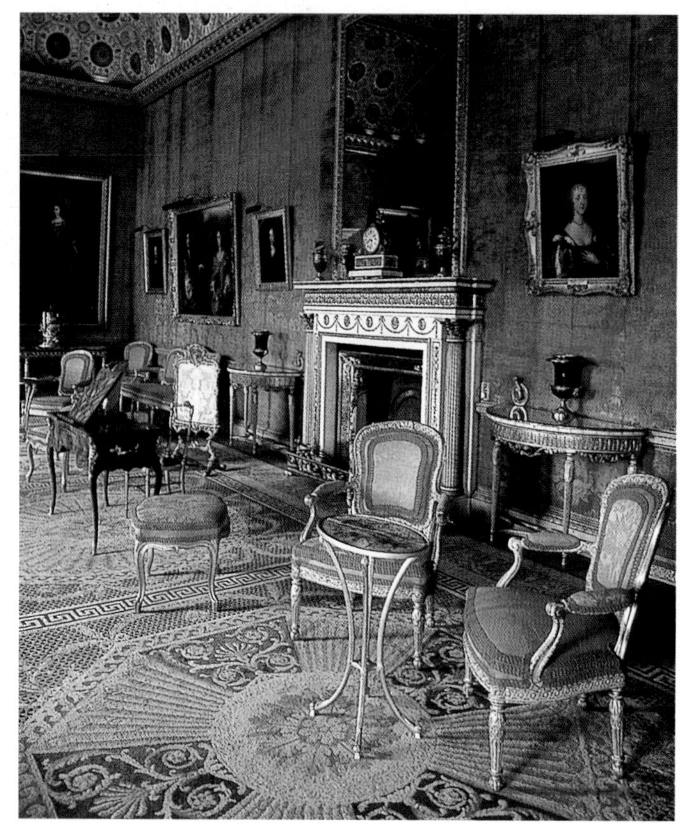

Barrier Visitor Centre, while at nearby Eltham are impressive ruins of a medieval royal palace.

To the south, near Bromley, are Chislehurst Caves, a mysterious labyrinth hewn out of the chalk over a period of 8,000 years. During World War II the caves became a huge air-raid shelter which even had its own church. North-west again, Dulwich has a historic 'village' centre, the impressive 19th-century Dulwich College and the Dulwich Picture Gallery, with many old masters.

ALONG THE THAMES

Richmond combines historic buildings and splendid Thames views with a bustling commercial centre and lively arts and restaurant scene. Architectural set-pieces include its two greens, with delightful old lanes, and Richmond Hill, with 18th-century houses and fine views.

Kew, downstream, is best known for the Royal Botanic

*S*yon House, left, and magnificent Hampton Court Palace, below

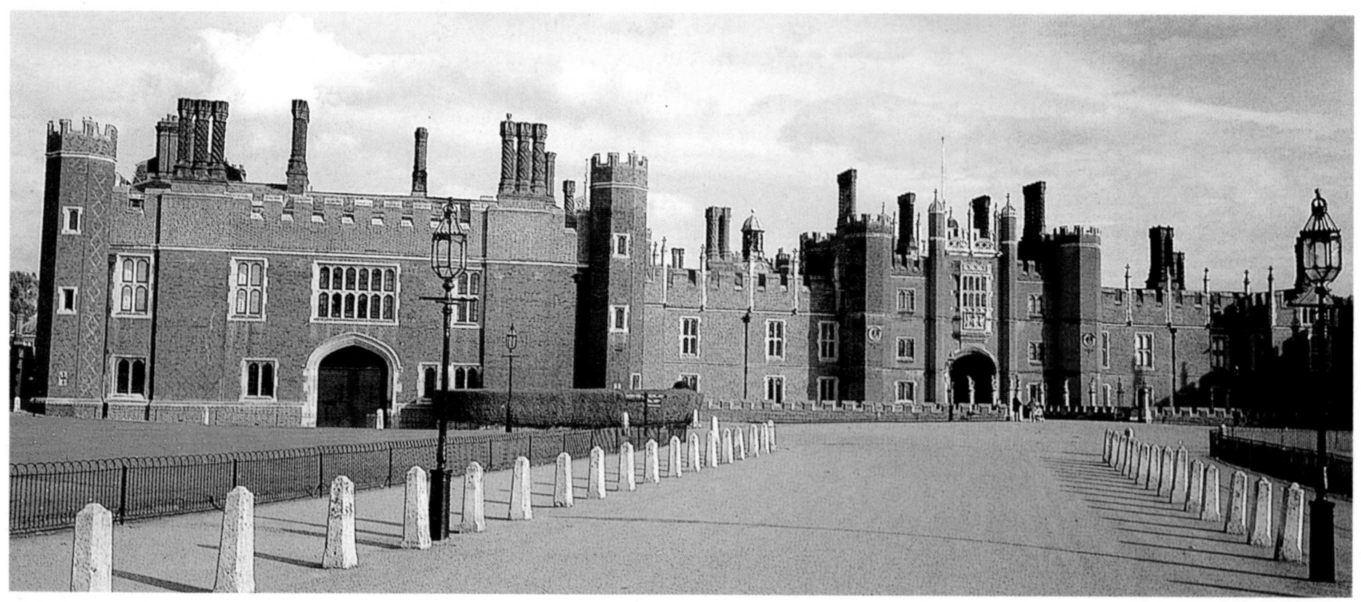

Gardens, 300 acres (122ha) of landscaped gardens, with some spectacular buildings. Seventeenth-century Kew Palace is the most modest but charming of royal residences, and Kew Village is charming too. In nearby Brentford is the Kew Bridge Steam Museum, a Victorian pumping station with enormous beam engines and London's only steam railway.

Upstream from Richmond are a string of splendid 18th-century buildings – Marble Hill House, a magnificent Palladian villa of the 1720s set in lovely parkland; Ham House, a large 17th-century house of exceptional interest; the early 18th-century Orleans House Octagon, its adjoining wing now an art gallery. A ferryman will row you from the Ham side to Marble Hill Park.

Further upstream is Hampton Court Palace, built by Cardinal Wolsey, Henry VIII's most powerful minister, who gave the palace to his monarch. His great gatehouse in Tudor brick dominates the main approach, and beyond the huge Base Court lies the Clock Court with its 16th-century astronomical clock and Great Hall. Later monarchs all left their mark here, notably the work carried out by Wren for William and Mary, with the arcaded Fountain Court and great East Front, looking out over the formal gardens and lovely parkland.

Downriver, the riverside is studded with attractions – Horace Walpole's 'Gothick castle' at Strawberry Hill, Syon House with its Adam interiors and spacious park, Old Chiswick with its 18th-century Chiswick Mall, and Fulham Palace in Bishop's Park. Chelsea, known for its King Road boutiques and cafés, also has Wren's Chelsea Hospital (home to the famous pensioners), a maze of streets

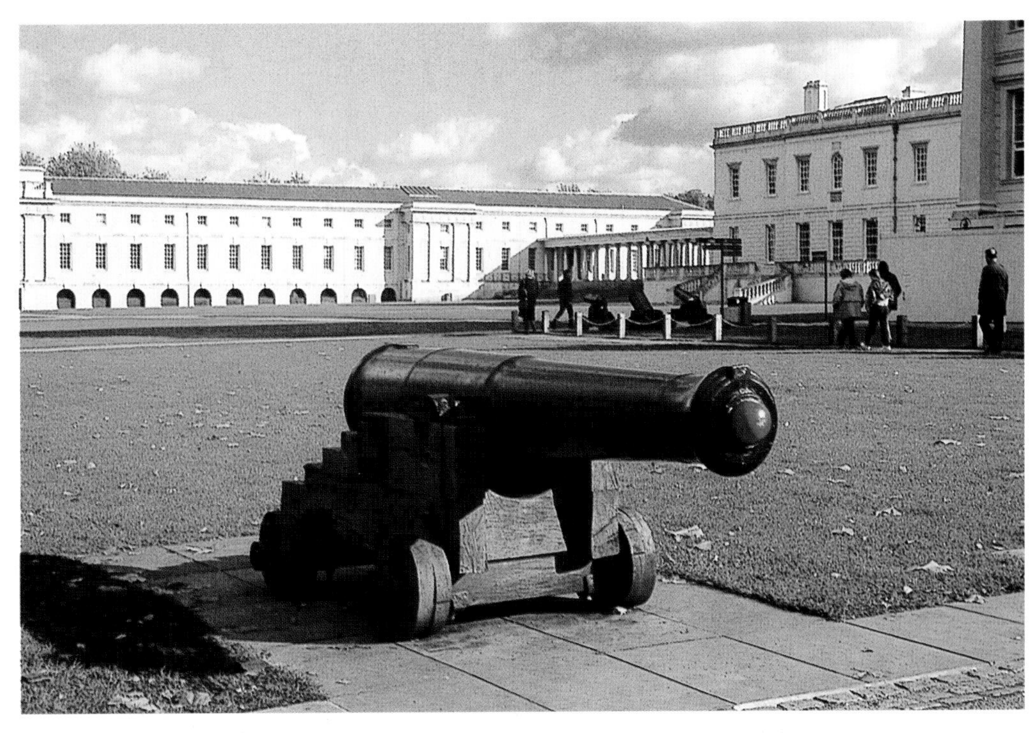

Ham House is a superb riverside mansion which was built in 1610

leading to the river and the 320-year-old Physic Garden, a pioneer botanical garden.

Further north are two notable historic houses – Lord Burlington's Chiswick House, an essay in Palladian style, and Osterley Park, built in the 16th century by Sir Thomas Gresham, merchant, Lord Mayor of London and founder of the Royal Exchange, and later splendidly remodelled in classical style.

AROUND NORTH LONDON

Harrow-on-the-Hill is noted for 400-year-old Harrow School. A little way to the east,

at Colindale, is the Royal Air Force Museum, with 70 aircraft and other exhibits, including flight simulators, cinema shows and the incredible 'Battle of Britain Experience'.

Hampstead's Fenton House was built in the late 17th century; it accommodates a collection of musical instruments, and often resounds to the sound of harpsichords or virginals. Keats House is now a museum devoted to the famous poet, and the house once occupied by Sigmund Freud contains his collection of antiquities and displays relating to his work, while Kenwood, in lovely wooded grounds, contains fine art collections. Highgate has the unusual

Greenwich is the centre of London's maritime heritage, with the superb Royal Naval College and museum and a collection of historic vessels down on the river

attraction of its impressive cemetery, housing the remains of many luminaries, such as George Eliot, Michael Faraday and Karl Marx.

The Georgian and Victorian Islington area has many delights, including the fascinating London Canal Museum. Walthamstow village is a conservation area which is well worth a visit. Here you will find the former home of William Morris, famous as a prime mover in the Arts and Crafts Movement.

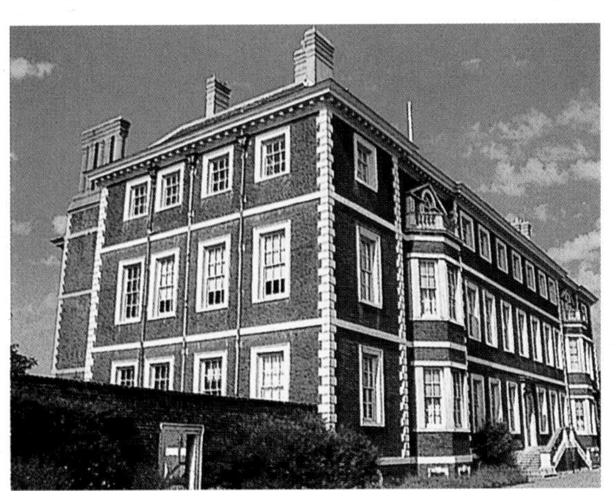

SPORTING MUSEUMS

Sports fans are spoilt for choice, with the MCC Museum at Lords Cricket Ground in St John's Wood, the Lawn Tennis Museum at the All England Club in Wimbledon, or the popular Wembley Stadium Tour.

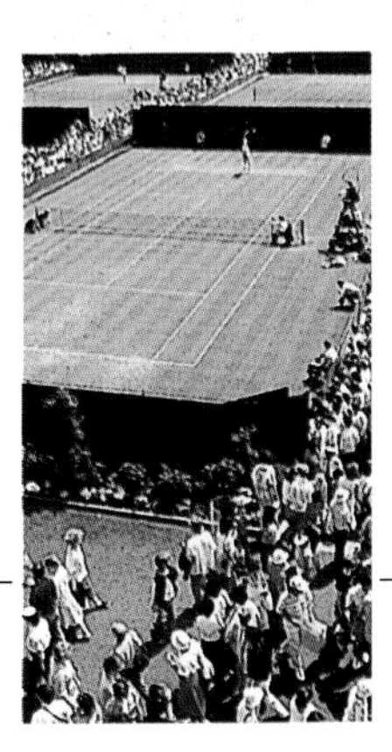

WATERWAYS OF CENTRAL ENGLAND

Before the proliferation of the canal system in the late 18th and 19th centuries, the movement of freight across large distances had been a practical impossibility, effectively limited to something like 12 miles (19.3km) by both the cost and the poor state of roads. The only exceptions were those areas lucky enough to be on one of the larger rivers like the Severn and, in the eastern part of the country, the Ouse.

Attempts to find a way of improving on river navigation date back at least to the days of the Romans, who constructed artificial waterways near Lincoln and Cambridge. From the 12th century onwards the idea was resurrected and small scale navigation allowed the passage of narrow barges here and there. The first pound locks in Britain were introduced in 1566 (having already been in existence in Holland for 200 years), after which the domestication of rivers, such as the Great Ouse, became much easier and their development and use increased throughout the 17th century. These projects were not generally government financed, but were instead in the form of investment by merchants, who were driven by the expectation of eventually being able to make a profit.

THE CANAL AGE

Large-scale construction was nonetheless surprisingly slow to get off the ground considering that most of the technical problems had already been overcome in the 17th century; the first long-distance canal was built only in the 1730s, in Ulster, running between Newry and the

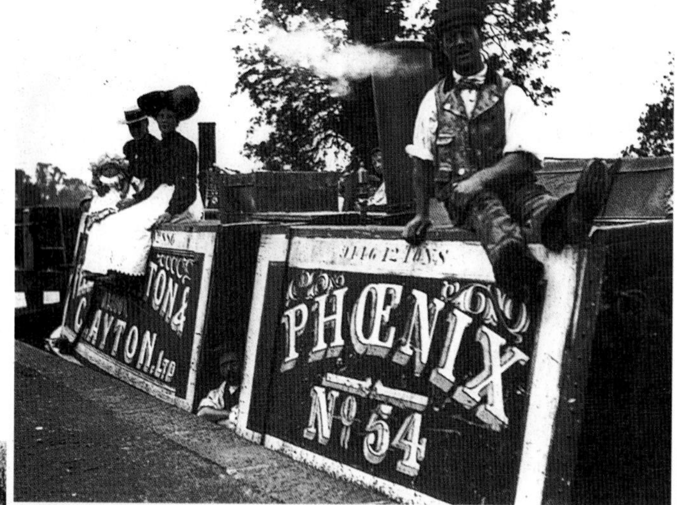

Upper Bann. However, it was really with the construction of the Bridgewater Canal, designed by James Brindley, that canals began to proliferate all over the country. Brindley gained his ideas through his experience as a millwright in Leek, Staffordshire – the

Whole families would once live and work on the narrowboats which are so popular today for holidays

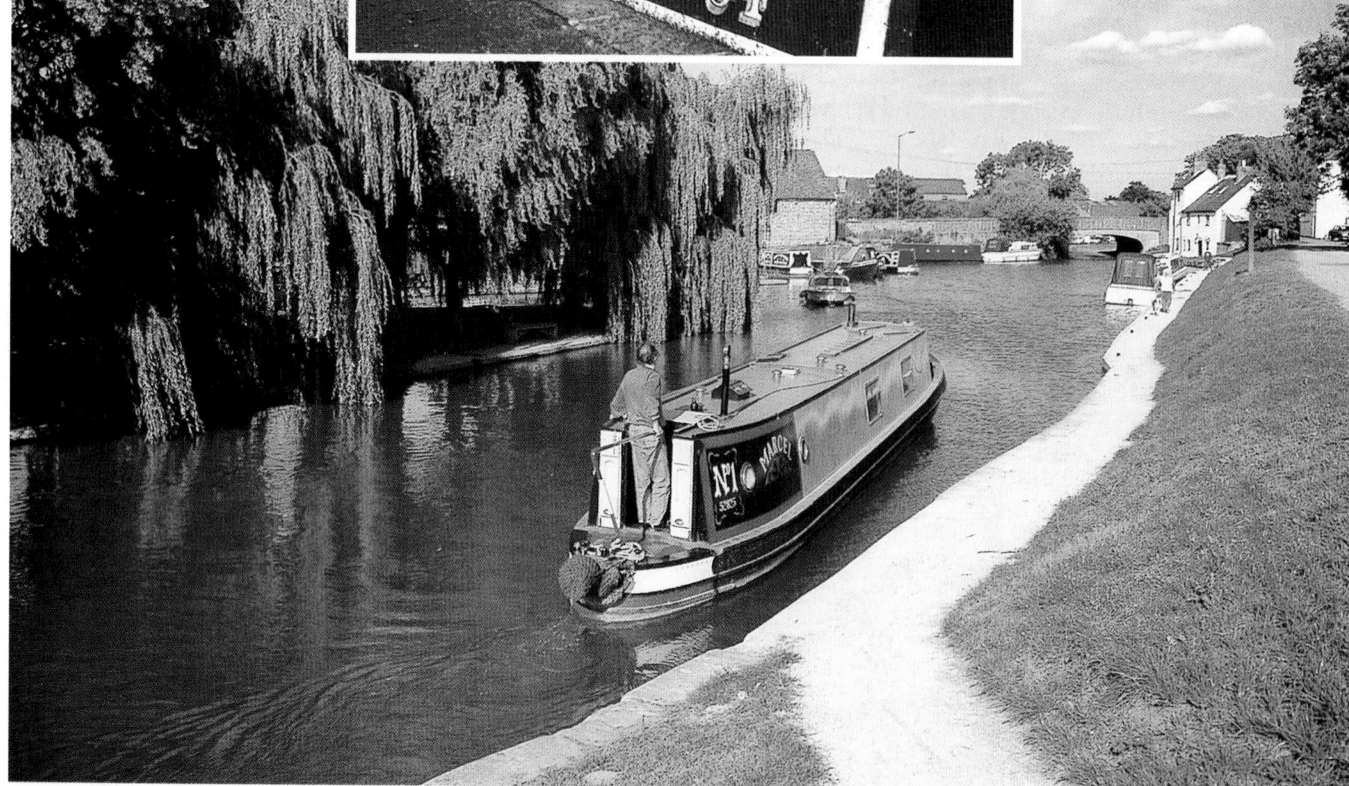

Bridgewater and the Trent and Mersey were his two greatest achievements.

The success of these canals encouraged the formation of joint stock companies to build others. Whilst this certainly led to a flurry of activity, it also created problems. These companies built their canals as they saw fit and according to local conditions. The lack of coordination meant that some canals were open to just about any size of craft, whilst others were restricted to narrow boats only. Nonetheless, it became clear that canals were at least of great use locally and construction continued until the 1830s, at which point nearly every town of any importance was within striking distance of a stretch of navigable water.

Central England and East Anglia were two of the areas where waterways were particularly important. The Midlands were at the heart of the Industrial Revolution, and there are still 130 miles (209.1km) of navigable canal in Birmingham and the Black Country alone. With Wolverhampton and Cannock to the north and Stourbridge to the south, in its great days this area had 212 working locks, with 550 factory side basins, forming the greatest concentration of industrial canals in the country. In its heyday canal transport carried eight million tons a year, and even as late as the 1950s a million tons a year were still being transported on the waterways.

The Grand Union Canal, 300 miles (482.8km) long and as important as its name suggests, links London with Birmingham, and had it not been for the outbreak of World War II might have seen wide boats of 66 tons pushing along its waters.

A spur breaks away from the Grand Union near Daventry in Northamptonshire and runs for 66 miles (106.3km) to link up with the River Trent.

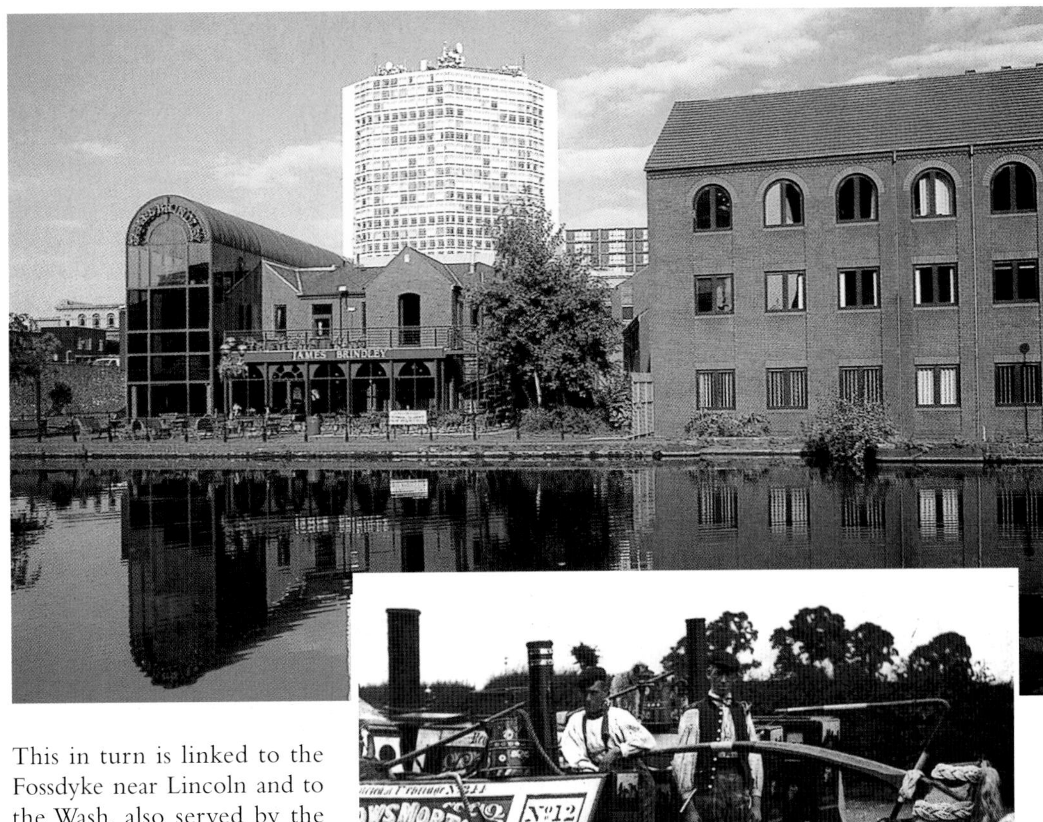

This in turn is linked to the Fossdyke near Lincoln and to the Wash, also served by the River Nene which is itself linked to the Grand Union via Northampton and Wellingborough.

DECLINE AND REBIRTH

Ironically, it was this very comprehensiveness of the canal system that led to the canal's downfall. Waterways were used to transport the coal that powered the steam locomotives on the railways, which were new, much faster and more efficient. Canals were gradually abandoned, and in some cases drained in order to become railbeds. With one or two major exceptions, commercial traffic has all but died and canals have assumed a new role as leisure amenities. And not only on the water – the old tow paths make excellent walk and cycle ways, and many tourist offices produce routes and trails to follow.

The greatest navigation in

Top: Birmingham's Gas Street Basin is part of a canal-side development; above: the traditional dress of the boatman, c1900–1910

Norfolk is that based on the Great Ouse, one of Britain's greatest rivers. It was first made navigable from the sea upstream to Bedford in the 17th century, when the surrounding land was drained by the Dutchman, Cornelius Vermuyden, creating new waterways. But its commercial usefulness had vanished by the late 19th century, and by the turn of the century much of it lay derelict. Today, after many vicissitudes, it has been reopened through the enthusiasm of the Great Ouse Restoration Society.

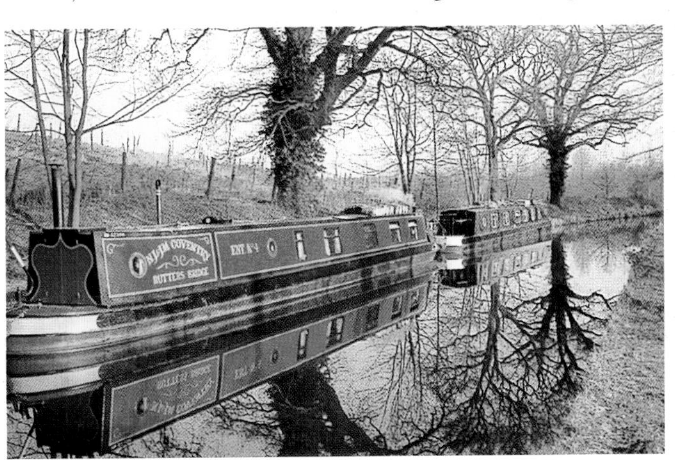

Colourful craft on the Shropshire Union Canal near Colemere

NEW TOWNS AND OLD TOWNS

Like many countries with long histories, Britain has had to adapt over the centuries to rapidly changing circumstances. Much that was taken for granted in the past has become redundant. Towns that were once prosperous have fallen on hard times as their once-famous products have become superfluous. New towns and communities have been planned and built, and their merits, or otherwise, continue to be debated.

Historically, with the exception of resort towns like Leamington Spa, towns have tended to grow organically. There was a moment of foundation in the sense that a family or a tribe settled at a particular place, which sometimes attracted others as time passed. Industries in turn grew according to need. The 20th century in Britain has seen the development of the 'new town', not a result of such serendipity but of philosophy.

VISIONS OF UTOPIA

Although visions of Utopia have been expressed in England since the Elizabethan era, to a large extent the ideas behind 'new' towns have been based on post-Victorian philanthropic reactions to urban poverty. The functions of towns were rationalised and organised, sorted and graded and then new ones were designed and laid out. Public buildings, entertainments and shops were to be in the centre, around this would be residential areas, and then, at the perimeter, the factories. From this grew the 'garden' towns of the early 20th century.

After World War II, the New Towns Act of 1946 promoted the construction of new towns, the first generation including Corby and the second including Peterborough and Milton Keynes. Such towns were noticeably less genteel than their 'garden city' predecessors and made much more use of strictly modern materials and designs; their planners also made provision for traffic. The express aim of the towns was to remove the poor from the slums of big cities, particularly London, to provide them with a more congenial and more humane environment. At the same time, it was hoped that they would divert potentially harmful pressure away from green belt areas.

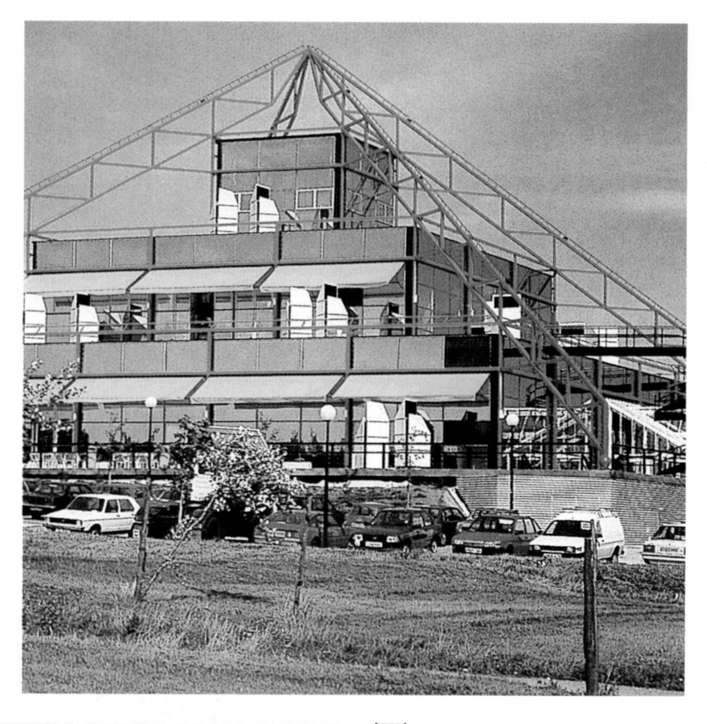

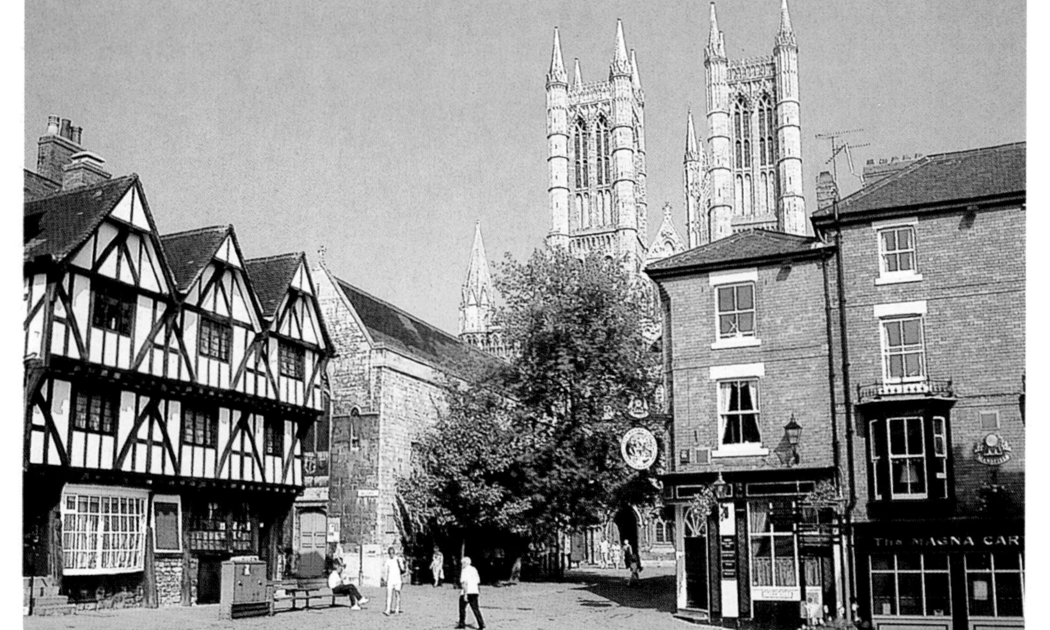

The adventurous architecture of The Point at Milton Keynes, above, contrasts sharply with Lincoln's medieval townscape, left

In many ways the new towns appear to have been a surprising success, at least economically, and indeed there is a steady lobby for the construction of more. Yet curiously, there is still a tendency to sneer at them. The principal accusation levelled is that they are 'soulless', an accusation that carries some weight when it is borne in mind that although it has been reasonably easy to attract business and employees to Milton Keynes, for example, it has proved a great deal harder to get their bosses to

buy homes for their families there.

The attraction of the leafy suburbs of old-fashioned cities or the traditional village green with pub is still very strong. In the case of Milton Keynes, founded in 1967, the business argument has been won – with a population in excess of 150,000, it has become the 13th-largest district in the country. The challenge now is to find other reasons for people to move there. Television campaigns emphasise the mix of old and new, whilst its proximity to Cambridge, Oxford and Stratford is cited as an advantage for the tourist.

IN EASY REACH

These days, perhaps, such arguments are almost superfluous. Milton Keynes, and others of the new towns, seem to be able to weather economic stagnation better than many of the older towns. One reason is location. The sites for the new towns were deliberately chosen with their relative position in mind, and Milton Keynes is rated as being the best centre for distribution in the whole country. The older towns are, of course, stuck with their location and have to choose industries that suit them, not the other way around –

although, should rail transport ever make a comeback, it could well be to the advantage of some of Britain's most historic towns.

A good general location results in a town that will attract a broad range of companies. Milton Keynes was chosen by Coca Cola some 25 years ago and since then at least another 3,000 businesses have followed, bringing with them over 65,000 jobs.

If, however, the accent appears to be purely on financial gain, that is not an entirely accurate impression. Another advantage to 'newness' is that heritage legislation, for the time being at least, is meaningless. Experiments can be made, therefore, and not just visual ones. The National Energy Foundation, for example, resides in Milton Keynes and as a result of the lessons learned in energy conservation there in the last 30 years, other towns are following its example. Soulless some of the new towns may be, but they are certainly not artless.

*A*ncient and modern are found all over Britain; shown here are splendid examples of both. Top right: a medieval building in Lincoln; middle right: the great façade of Peterborough Cathedral; bottom right and below: glass palaces in Milton Keynes

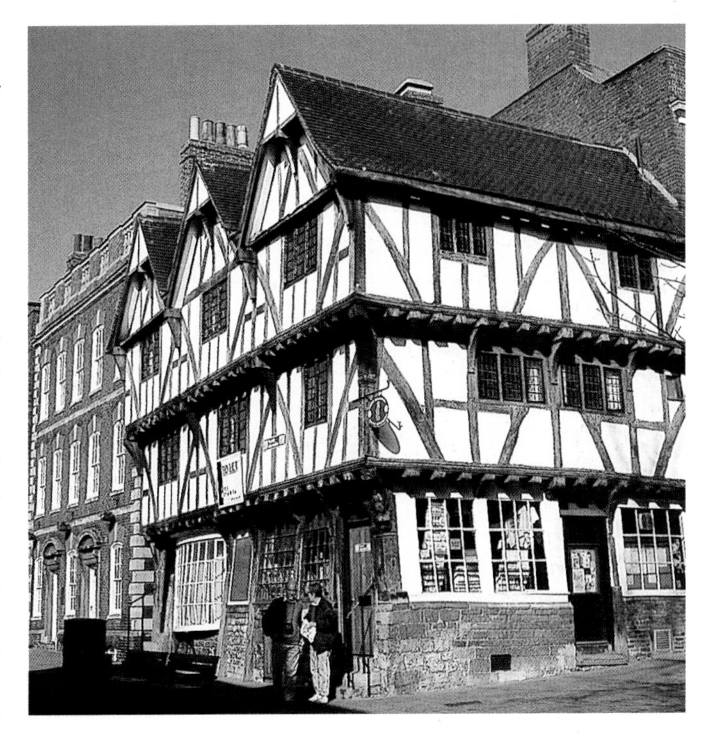

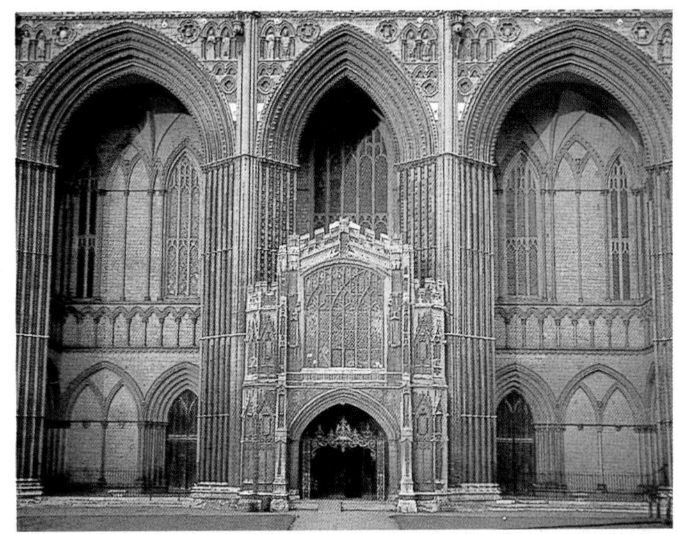

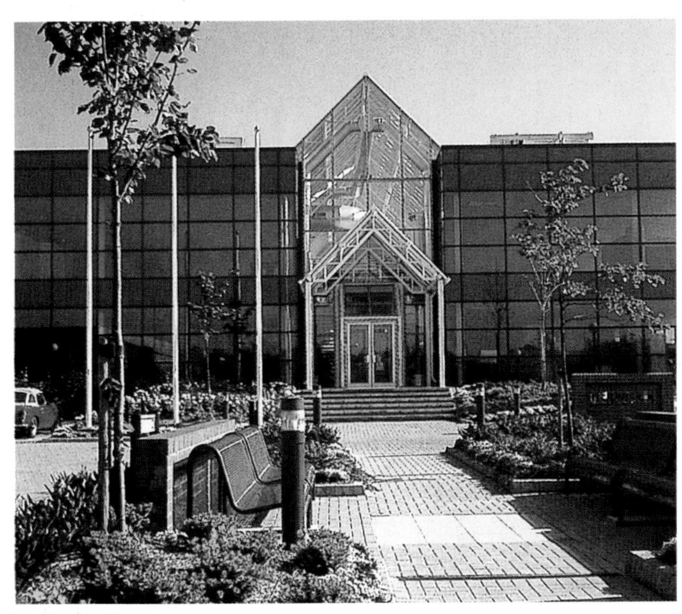

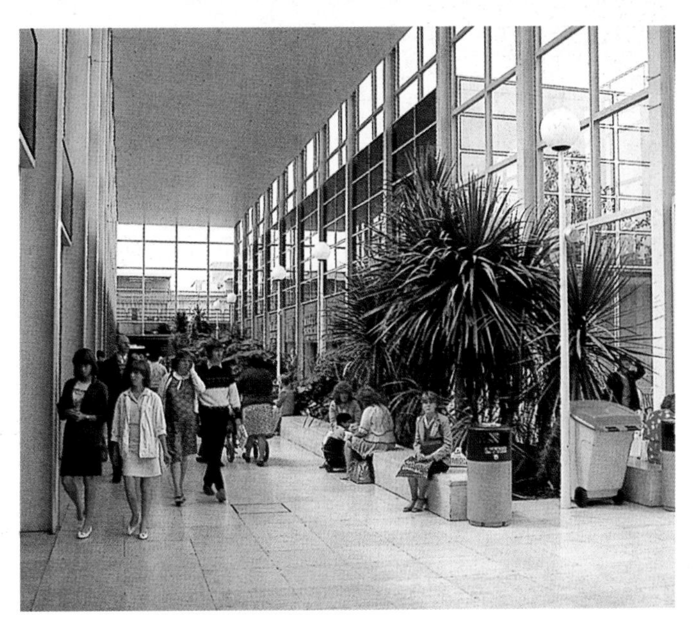

RARE BREEDS AND TRADITIONAL CROPS

Despite the Industrial Revolution and the proliferation of the great towns and cities that have become closely associated with the Midlands, England remains an essentially rural country. Gone, however, are the smallholdings that are still a significant feature of France and Italy; and gone, for the most part, are the meadows filled with orchids and other wild flowers that until recently seemed to fill summer horizons. England is one of the most advanced and efficient farming economies in the world, but it seems it has become so at the expense of a human dimension that has always appeared attractive to the romantically-inclined outsider.

The truth is that such changes have actually been taking place for centuries and resistance to them is not something new. Often it was not through the publication of letters in newspapers, but by riots and violence. The most famous example of this is the early 19th century Luddite movement which is supposed to have been named after a Leicestershire worker, Ned Ludd, who destroyed his machinery in anger.

CHANGING THE LANDSCAPE

Even as far back as the 17th century, the drainage scheme in the Norfolk fens instigated by the Duke of Bedford met with fierce opposition from local farmers who had previously made use of the marshes to rear geese, which were driven in their thousands as far away as London. Before the construction of the network of drainage ditches, the landscape of Norfolk had been essentially marshy, with rivers flowing aimlessly and with fickle unpredictability across it, ideal for geese but quite hopeless for crops.

Yet, even the construction of drainage ditches proved inadequate for the successful leaching of the fields, particularly of the peaty, black soil which tended to subside. Thus a way had to be found to pump the water from field to ditch and then from ditch to main channel. The windpump made its entry to enhance the popular vision of the Fenlands.

In the case of the Fens, a farming landscape has been created deliberately and although the sails of the windpumps no longer turn, modern pumps have taken their place. A flat landscape of hedgeless fields and farmsteads surrounded by dense, tall hedges as protection against the wind, seems to have become a permanent feature.

Norfolk and Leicestershire have both made several contributions to the changing aspect of English agriculture. The Norfolk Four Course Rotation is the foundation of modern farming, based on the principal of ploughing in compost instead of manure in sequence – roots, barley, seeds and wheat – which is said to bring the best out of the soil. Leicestershire's contribution was the development of modern sheep farming.

SELECTIVE BREEDING

There are some forty breeds of sheep still in existence in Britain, far more than in any other country in the world. Wool, after all, was the key to English prosperity in the Middle Ages, most notably in the Cotswolds and East Anglia. Yet, the breeds that provided the wool are no longer used and incredibly have come close to extinction. One reason for this is cross breeding, which is not entirely a modern phenomenon. The man behind this was Robert Bakewell, a farmer born in 1725 in the hamlet of Dishley, near Loughborough.

Below: not quite the prairies, but certainly the new face of farming, near Chelmsford; right: a Cotswold ewe, of the breed that brought so much wealth to the Cotswolds in medieval times; below right: rare breeds at Stratford's Shire Horse Centre

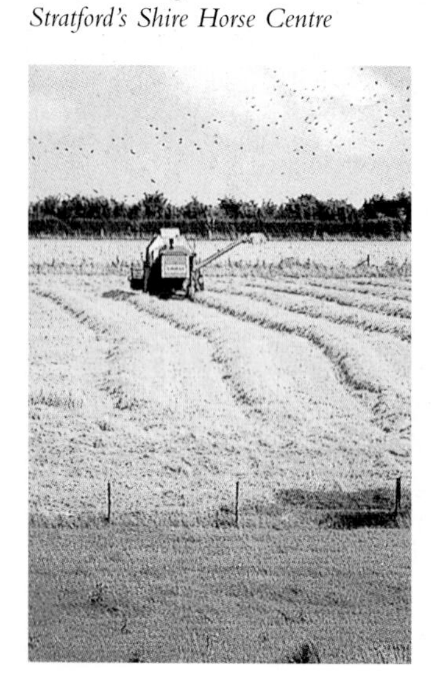

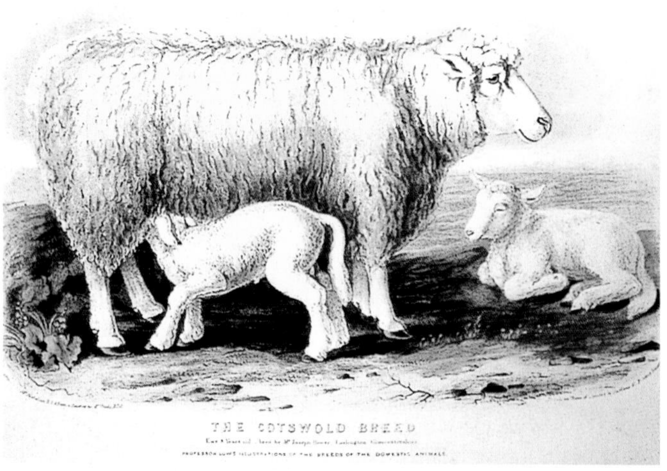

THE COTSWOLD BREED

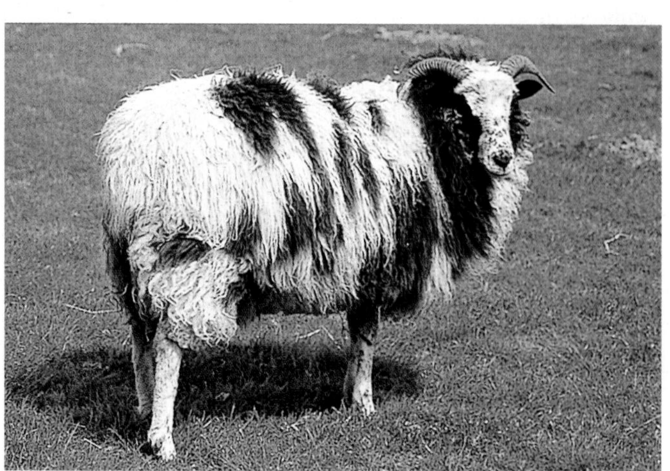

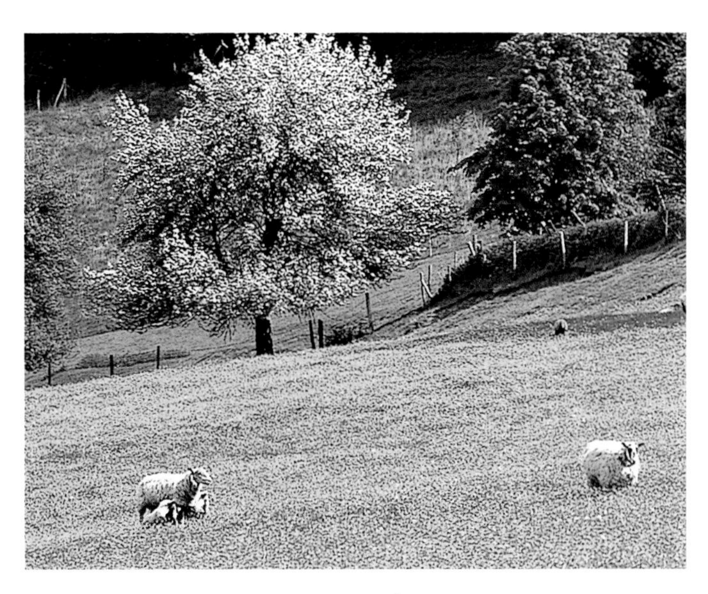

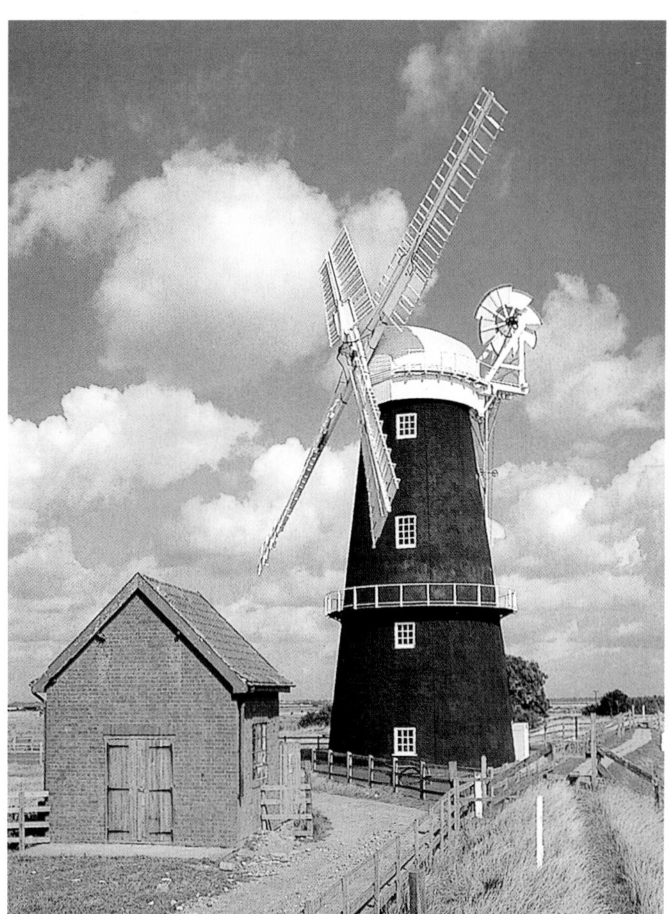

Before inheriting the family farm, Bakewell travelled extensively in England and Europe. By the time he started farming his own land, he had learnt the science of selective breeding, but instead of selecting the best from other herds he concentrated on inbreeding. He used his ideas for cattle rearing but his greatest successes came with sheep, the result of a programme based on the Leicester breed, which were similar to the old Lincoln and Cotswold sheep that had been the foundation of the medieval wool trade. The result was that he was able to produce early maturing sheep for the butcher. His Leicesters, and his ideas, made a vital contributions to sheep farming throughout the world.

Similarly, the Lincoln Long Wool breed was found all over the Midlands until it was later crossed with the ubiquitous Merino. Other local breeds of sheep have been less successful and are rarely found today – these include the Staffordshire Ryeland and the Norfolk Horn, although this latter is the ancestor of the Suffolk which is still sometimes crossed to pproduce fat lamb. Most of these local breeds of sheep, however, have disappeared from commercial farms.

The same is true of cattle, though once again breeds from

A field of buttercups and sheep near North Nibley; right: the Berney Arms Windpump in Norfolk, accessible by boat or rail, was used in draining the marshland and grinding clinker for cement; below right: a traditional rural landscape near Winchcombe in Gloucestershire

Lincolnshire and Suffolk have been important in producing modern strains. Sometimes the demise of a breed may be put down to vainglory – a strange case is that of the Lincolnshire Shorthorn, which was too often bred for its show qualities at the expense of its advantages as a producer.

As for pigs, local breeds such as the Essex Saddleback have lost out to fashion, overtaken by the popularity of the leaner Scandinavian varieties.

A certain monotony is therefore evident in the breeds which graze the landscape of our farms. But the developments that have led to this state of affairs are the fruition of centuries of striving as much as to the technocratic notions of our own time.

However, even if the old meadow flowers have gone, they have been replaced by the dazzle of yellow rape and the milky blue of flax; and no doubt the world will in due course regard them as much a part of the traditional rural panorama as were once upon a time poppies and cowslips.

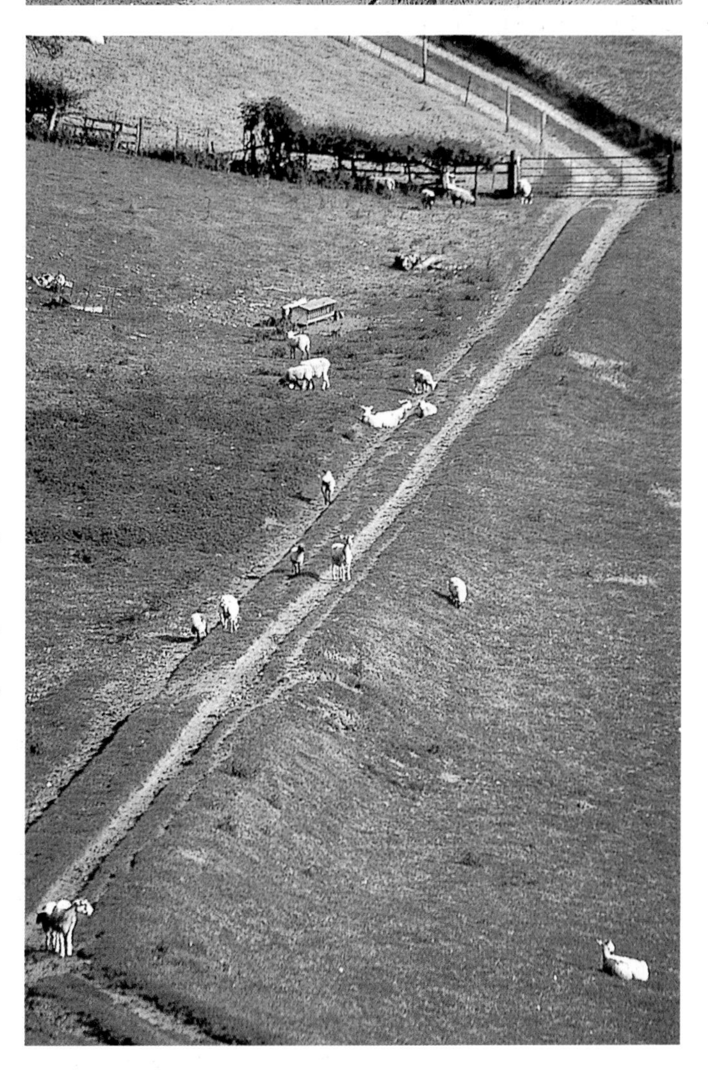

THE WELSH MARCHES – A FRONTIER LAND

A glance at Sheet 137 of the Ordnance Survey's 1:50,000 Landranger series, covering Ludlow and Wenlock Edge and the western edge of Shropshire, shows a landscape shaped by conflict and war.

Here in the heart of the troubled borderland of the Welsh Marches, many examples of of the defensive structures built at various times in the region's history are still visible. Ludlow's great red sandstone keep, built by Roger Montgomery, Earl of Shrewsbury, in the 11th century to repel Welsh raiders, was succeeded by many smaller castles of the 'motte and bailey' design, such as those scattered along Offa's Dyke. A classic example can be found at New Radnor.

Later, the fortified manors of Stokesay Castle, Bromfield, and Richard's Castle tell of more settled times, while the manors of Wilderhope and Croft Castle show the gradual trend away from defence towards the country houses found in more peaceful areas.

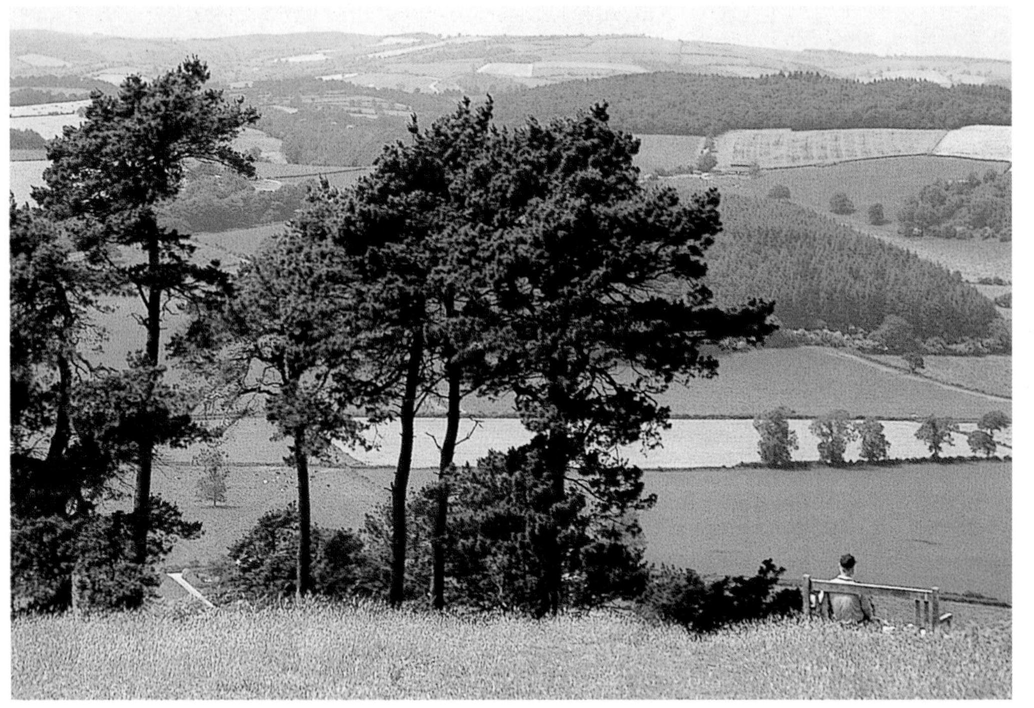

EARLY TIMES

In prehistoric times, the slopes of every major hill formed their own frontier with everything below, and settlers fortified their summits with banks, ditches and palisades, within which they enjoyed the best possible coigns of vantage. One of the most striking features of the above-mentioned map is the number of these 'forts,' 'camps' and 'earthworks' – over 20 of them – marked in the Gothic typeface which the OS uses, rather imprecisely, to indicate a 'non-Roman antiquity.'

The better-known examples include Croft Ambrey, south-west of Ludlow, where hundreds of regularly placed huts have been traced; and Caer Caradoc, overlooking the Church Stretton valley, where Caractacus is alleged to have made his last stand against the Romans. But there are many other lesser-known examples. Some, like Burfa Camp, Bury Ditches and Bagbury, are now hidden under blanket forestry plantations, but many others command the same sweeping views over the countryside which first attracted their builders over 2,000 years ago.

Magnificent views for miles around can be enjoyed from high up on Croft Ambrey Iron-Age hillfort – it is said that 14 counties are visible

Radio-carbon dating has shown that most British hillforts were built between 750 and 500 BC, though many were still in use up to the Roman invasion in the first century AD. The name 'hillfort' can be misleading, although many must have had a defensive purpose. But the idea that they were all the last outposts of the native Britons who fled there in the face of the invading Romans is one which is no longer in favour with modern archaeologists. Some believe that hillforts were the spiritual or religious centres of the Iron Age, and temples have been found in some of them. But there is no doubt that many others were settlements which were perhaps used only in the summer to watch over grazing stock, or as administrative or market centres.

AFTER THE ROMANS

Winding up from south to north through the western side of the said map is the ancient earthwork known as Offa's Dyke – now followed by the 177mile (285km) Offa's Dyke Path, which opened in 1971. Built in the last quarter of the 8th century by King Offa of Mercia to mark the western edge of his kingdom and to control Welsh incursions, Offa's Dyke is the longest continuous earthwork in Britain, and links the Severn and Dee estuaries.

There can be little doubt from its method of construction that Offa's Dyke was primarily defensive in nature, and there is some evidence that it may once have had a permanently manned stockade along its crest. It was said to have been instigated by Offa in ad 782, but the first reference to this monumental earthwork is

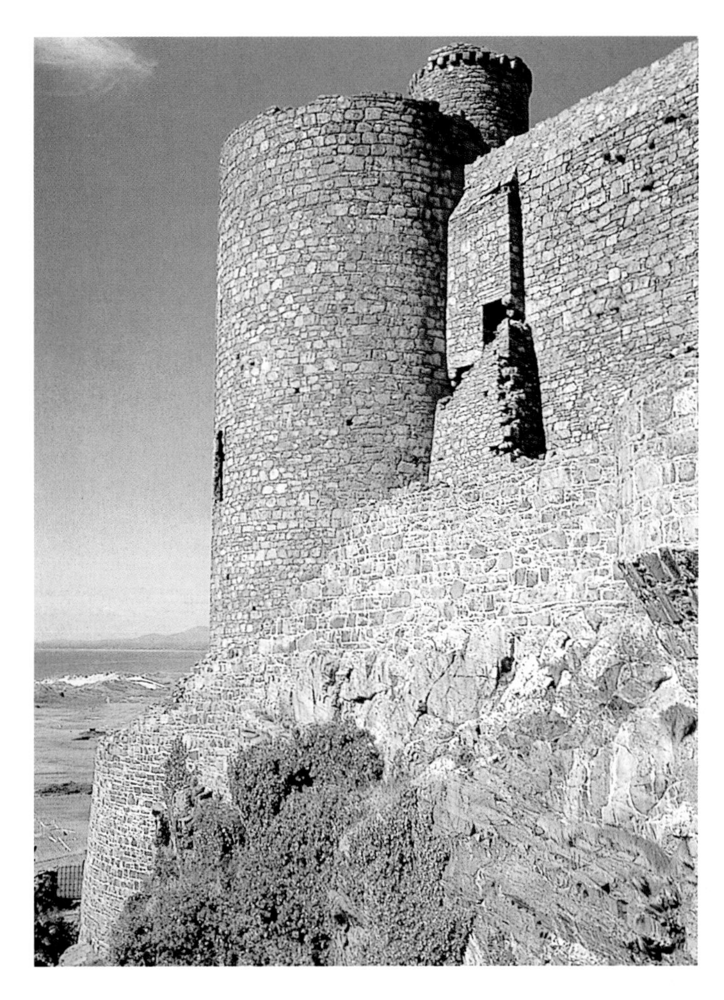

When Harlech Castle was built it had a sheer drop to the sea on one side. Though the sea has receded, it still has one of the most impressive situations of all Edward I's Welsh castles. The defence of its walls during the Wars of the Roses inspired the stirring song 'Men of Harlech'

English yoke, and after he evaded taking the oath of loyalty to Edward I, he was soon in open conflict with the king's army, commanded by Roger de Mortimer, Earl of Shrewsbury. Mortimer was just one of the immensely powerful Marcher Lords. Others of these included Roger de Lacy of Ludlow and Robert de Say of Clun.

Llywelyn was eventually defeated by the King in 1282, and to confirm his conquest, Edward built a series of massive fortresses throughout Wales. These castles, such as Conwy, Caernarfon, Harlech and Beaumaris, were at the forefront of medieval military architecture and even today stand as impressive ruins.

Welsh opposition was not finally stamped out until the defeat in 1410 of another great hero of nationalism, Owain Glyndwr. In 1472, in an attempt to subdue the powerful Marcher Lords as much as the still warring Welsh, Edward IV set up a Lord President and Council of the Marches, who were to supervise the affairs of Wales and the border for the next two centuries. The Council usually sat at Ludlow or Shrewsbury castles.

AFTER THE TUDORS

It was not until the reign of Henry VIII that the boundary between England and Wales was finally settled. One of the most impressive remains is Roger Montgomery's red sandstone castle towering above the River Teme at Ludlow. Started in 1085 during the first wave of castle-building, during its history it has been the prison for Edward IV's sons – 'the Princes in the Tower' – and the place where Henry VIII's elder brother, Arthur, died. On a different note, it was the scene in 1634 of the first production of John Milton's masque, *Comus*, and is still the regular venue for open-air Shakespearean productions.

Monmouth, with its rare portcullised gatehouse over the River Monnow, boasts the ruins of its 11th-century castle, where Henry V was born in 1387. Chepstow's great Norman castle still dominates the town's medieval streets, and across the border at Goodrich an almost perfectly preserved 13th-century castle still frowns down over the River Wye. At Rhuddlan, near Rhyl on the coast of north Wales, Edward I is said to have made his famous move to win over the Welsh by proclaiming his infant son as the first Prince of Wales.

Chepstow Castle is the first recorded Norman stone castle; it was used as a base for advances into Wales

not recorded until 100 years later, when Bishop Asser notes that Offa ordered the dyke to be built between Wales and Mercia 'from sea to sea'.

Following the decline of Mercia, the usually bickering Welsh princes united under Gruffydd ap Llywelyn and began serious incursions across the Dyke into England. These were eventually thwarted by Harold, who was later to become the short-lived King of England, in a vicious campaign of retaliation in 1063.

NORMAN BARONS AND WELSH PRINCES

The next chapter in the much-troubled history of the Marches begins with the Norman conquest of 1066. William set about subduing his new nation by making grants

of land to favoured 'Marcher' barons, who ruled by right of conquest and claimed special rights, not subject to the usual restraint of the law. It was these autocratic barons who built the string of earth mounds and wooden forts known as 'motte and bailey' castles, such as that still visible at New Radnor. The word 'Marches' has the same origin as 'mark', meaning a boundary.

The great stone castles of the Marches, such as Ludlow, Monmouth, Chepstow, Rhuddlan and Shrewsbury, came later, as the English overlords tried to stamp their authority over an unwilling populace. A double, and sometimes triple, line of castles were erected along the border, such as Grosmont, Skenfrith and White Castles in Monmouthshire.

But the Welsh princes like Gruffydd, now known as Llywelyn the Last, were still unwilling to bow under the

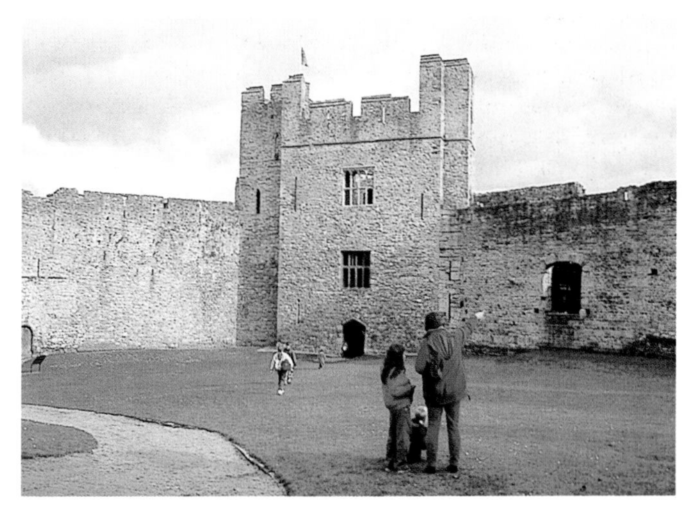

THE NATIONAL PARKS OF WALES

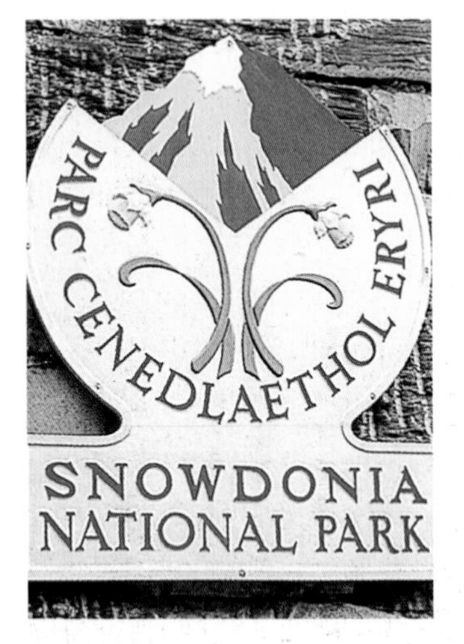

The three National Parks of Wales – Snowdonia, the Brecon Beacons and the Pembrokeshire Coast – could hardly offer greater scenic contrasts. From the jagged volcanic peaks of Snowdonia, which includes the highest ground south of Scotland, to the sweeping sandstone escarpments of the Brecon Beacons and the dramatic cliffs and bays of the Pembrokeshire Coast, the variety is breathtaking. In their tightly controlled protected areas, the parks encapsulate the very best of the unspoilt landscapes in the Principality.

A proposal for a fourth Welsh national park in the Cambrian Mountains of mid-Wales, centred on Plynlimon and the source of the Rivers Severn and Wye, was thwarted as a result of local opposition, mainly from farmers and landowners, in the mid 1970s.

There are several well-established routes to the summit, some of which have had to be extensively restored because of overuse. If the climb is too much, you can take the rack-and-pinion railway which winds up from Llanberis to the summit, where there is a café.

Slate and forestry have been the traditional industries in Snowdonia, but tourism is now as important in the slate-built villages of Llanberis, Capel Curig, Betws-y-Coed and Blaenau Ffestiniog.

SNOWDONIA

Snowdonia, at 827sq miles (2,142sq km), is the second largest national park in Britain after the Lake District, and was the first of the three to be designated (in 1951). Outdoor campaigners such as Sir Clough Williams Ellis, who built the Italianate fantasy village of Portmeirion, had long pressed for the proper protection of this unique and precious landscape.

It was medieval English sailors crossing the Irish Sea who gave Snowdon and Snowdonia its name – the wild, rocky landscape beyond Anglesey always seemed to them to be brushed with snow. To the Welsh, though, this mountainous region had always been known as *Eryri*, the 'abode of eagles', and it was the place where their leaders, from the legendary Arthur through to the historical figures of Llywelyn the Great and Owain Glyndwr, traditionally sought refuge from the invading English.

There is still an indefinable air of nostalgia and 'Welshness' in these sometimes savage hills, where Welsh speakers are still in the majority.

The physical shape of the national park is best described as a large diamond split into three by valleys which run north-east to south-west. These deep gashes neatly separate the main mountain groups of Snowdon, the Glynders and Carneddau in the north; the rugged Rhinogs and Arenig in the centre; Cadair Idris and the Arans to the south. Most visitors gravitate to the area around Snowdon, which at 3,560ft (1,085m) is a natural magnet to the peak-bagger.

THE BRECON BEACONS

The Brecon Beacons National Park, straddling the borders of Powys, Dyfed, Gwent and Mid Glamorgan, takes its name from, and is centred on the triple peaks of the Beacons themselves, which dominate the lush valley of the River Usk. These Old Red Sandstone mountains, the highest of which is Pen-y-Fan at 2,907ft (886m), stand like a petrified wave about to break over the ancient county town of Brecon, where the Romans had a fort at Y Gaer. The ascent of Pen-y-Fan is most easily achieved from the Storey Arms on the A470; those who make the climb are rewarded with spectacular views.

There is much more to the 522sq mile (1,352sq km) park, established in 1957, than the Beacons. Two other distinct mountain masses make up the area, both of which confusingly carry the name 'Black'. The Black Mountains (plural) are a range of sandstone hills running north–south from Hay-on-Wye to Abergavenny.

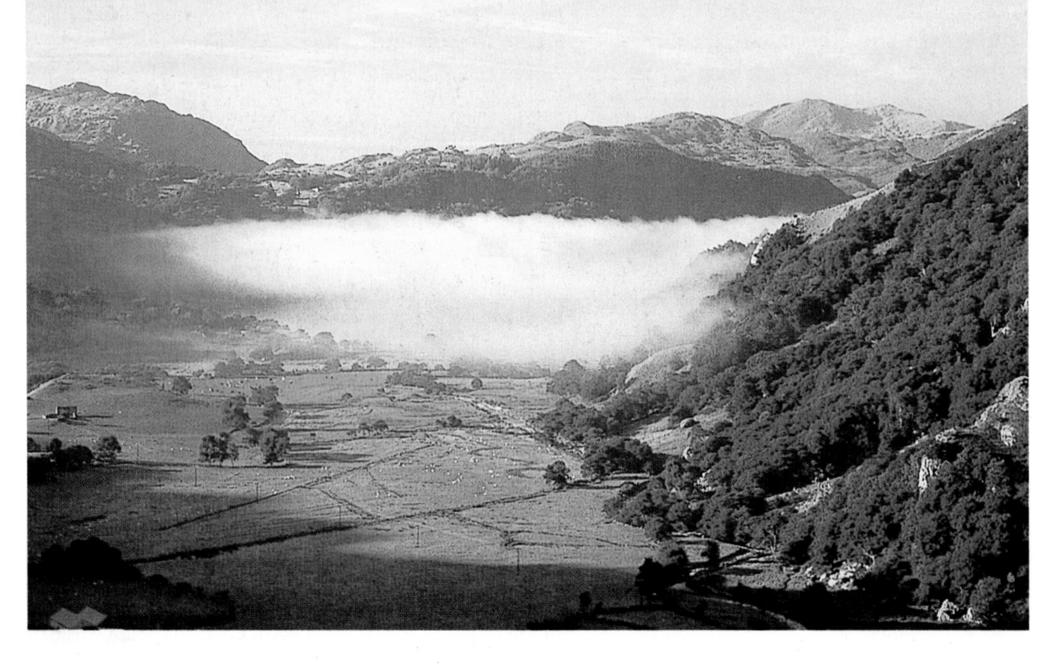

In the heart of Snowdonia – the view from Beddgelert towards Nantgwynant

Offa's Dyke, the 8th-century boundary embankment and ditch which separated England and Wales, runs along its crest and makes a fine walk. The Black Mountain (singular) is a wilder, less-visited area to the west of the A406 Sennybridge to Ystradgynlais road. It is centred on the sweeping crest of Carmarthen Van, at 2,631 ft (802 m) the highest point in the Black Mountain, which has the mysterious little glacial lake of Llyn y Fan Fach at its feet. Further west, near the boundary of the national park, remote Carreg Cennen Castle has one of the most spectacular situations of any castle in Wales.

There is another, altogether different landscape which dominates the south of the park. The area of Carboniferous rocks which stretches across the southern boundary has created a landscape of tumbling waterfalls, huge caves and potholes and beautiful woodlands which are a major attraction to visitors, and is easily accessible from the valleys of South Wales. A pleasant way to view the scenery is on the Brecon Mountain Railway from Pant Station, north of Merthyr Tydfil.

The Mellte and Hepste valleys, between Ystradfellte and Pont-neddfechan, are the centre of the Beacons caving country. Dan-yr-Ogof Showcaves system, north of Abercraf, has the largest chamber in any British showcave, and in Bone Cave evidence was found of human occupation 3,000 years ago. The caves are now part of a tourist complex with a number of attractions.

THE PEMBROKESHIRE COAST

This area of Dyfed is sometimes known as 'Little England beyond Wales' and the

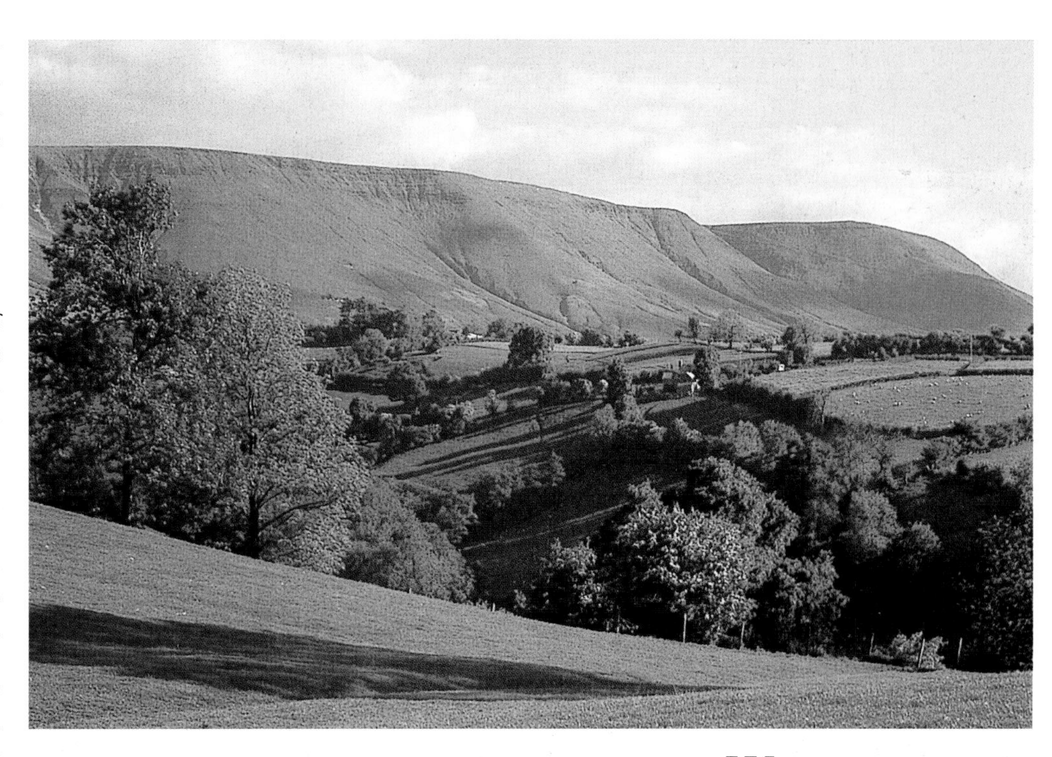

popularity of resorts like Tenby and St David's is undeniable. But the epithet has its basis in history, since a string of castles were erected by the Norman invaders, along a line from Newgale in the west to Amroth in the east, to subdue the native Welsh. The line – known by the Norse word *landsker*, meaning frontier – can still be traced in placenames. South of the line, many places have anglicised names and English is still the most common language, but north of the *landsker*, Welsh is more commonly spoken and Welsh names abound.

The Pembrokeshire Coast National Park – at 225sq miles (583sq km) one of the smallest British national parks – is the only one which is largely coastal, and it is not hard to see why. Its main glory is its superb 230-mile (370-km) coastline, followed for most of its way by the Pembrokeshire Coast Path, a wonderful rollercoaster of a walk with rugged cliffs, sandy bays and a number of ever-changing seascapes.

The 170 miles (274 km) of the Pembrokeshire Coast Path also offer a crash-course in geology, for the route shows at

a glance the story of the formation of the earth from the earliest pre-Cambrian rocks around the tiny cathedral city of St David's to the Ordovician volcanic structure of the north.

The only real uplands in this mainly coastal park are the Preseli Hills in the north, a self-contained moorland block of Ordovician rocks rising to 1,759 ft (536 m) at Foel Cwm Cerwym, south of Bryberian. The Preseli Hills are famous as the source of the blue stones which were somehow transported to far-off Wiltshire for the inner circle of Stonehenge.

Wild and remote it may be, but the reality of Black Mountain is far removed from the image of its name

The main attraction of Pembrokeshire will always be its coastline, and there are few more invigorating walking experiences in Britain than to stride along these cliffs in early spring, on a carpet of wild flowers, accompanied by the cries of the seabirds.

St David's Head separates the rocky coastline to the north from the sands of the aptly named Whitesand Bay to the south

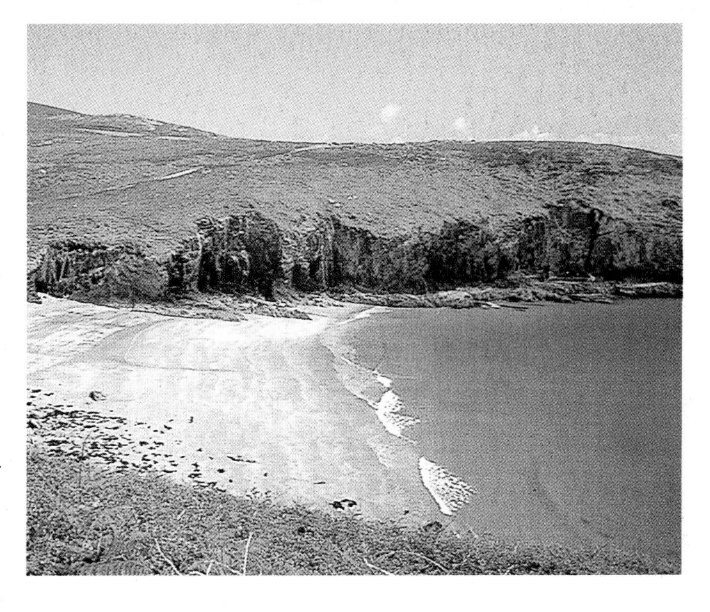

THE PEAK DISTRICT

The Peak District stands at the crossroads of Britain – linking the hard, uncompromising landscapes of the north and the lush greenness of the lowland south. As the southernmost extremity of the Pennine Chain, the Peak is the last knobbly vertebra in the backbone of England, and the first real hill country to be met by the traveller from the south and east. The change is quite sudden, as an early 18th-century traveller reflected on leaving Ashbourne to enter the Peak; 'at the summit of the hill it was a top coat colder'.

The landscape changes too, as you climb on to the limestone plateau in the south and centre, which is known as the White Peak. Gone are the neatly hedged fields of the Midlands, replaced by tumble-down drystone walls spreading up hill and down dale, seemingly with no regard for the swelling contours.

WILD FLOWERS OF THE PEAK

To the botanist, the Peak represents the best of both worlds. Here can be found southern types, like the nettle-leaved bell-flower, at their northern limit and northern types, like the cloudberry, at their southernmost extent. But to see the delicate white flowers of the cloudberry, you must travel north, leaving the limestone of the White Peak behind.

Enclosing the limestone plateau to the north, east and west is a mantle of bleak and sometimes forbidding, peat-covered moorland known, in contrast, as the Dark Peak. This is the home of hardy species such as the cloudberry which, as its name suggests, is frequently to be found in the clouds, and of the blue or mountain hare, which changes the colour of its coat to match the winter snows.

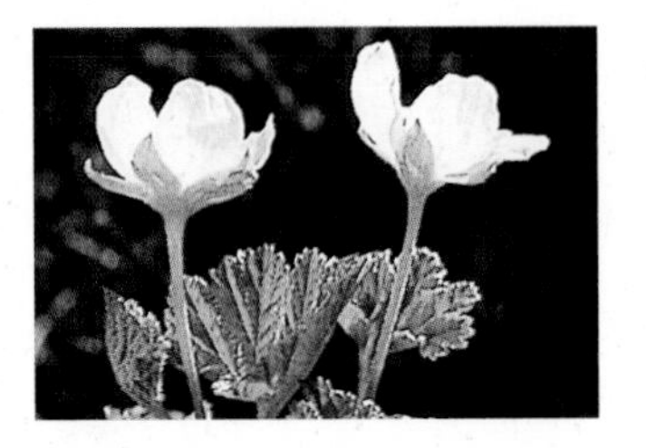

The cloudberry is equipped to survive on the high moors

THE ROCKS BENEATH

The predominant rock in the Dark Peak is millstone grit, a coarse sandstone which takes its name from the fact that it was once much in demand for mill and grindstones. Abandoned millstone quarries can be found beneath many gritstone edges, with piles of finished but now unwanted stones. The Peak National Park, which encompasses 555 sq miles (1,437.4sq km) and was the first in Britain to be set up in 1951, took the millstone symbol as its boundary marker and logo.

Both limestone and gritstone were laid down under tropical seas during the Carboniferous period, about 330 million years ago, and if you look carefully in a limestone wall or gatepost, you may just be able to make out the remains of the sea lilies and shells which created the rock. The grit was laid down later over the limestone under deltaic conditions not unlike those found in the Mississippi or Nile today.

EARLY SETTLERS

The Peak District, like any upland region, is the creation of its underlying geology, and the high and dry plateaux of the Peak were particularly attractive to the first settlers who made their way across the land bridge from Europe. The remoteness of the region has resulted in the survival of a surprising number of remains of these first hunter-gatherers, including perhaps the most spectacular – the stone circles of Arbor Low, near Youlgreave and the Nine Ladies on Stanton Moors. Almost every hilltop in the Peak seems to be marked by a burial mound or barrow, most dating from the Bronze Age and known by the local name of 'low.' Complete landscapes of the Bronze Age, including huts, stone circles, fields and barrows, have been identified on the now uninhabited moorlands to the east.

The Iron Age saw the construction of a number of apparently defensive hillforts, such as Mam Tor, commanding the upper Hope Valley near Castleton, and Fin Cop above Monsal Dale. Whether these defensive positions were ever the last resort of native Brigantians against the invading Romans will probably never be known, but the Imperial legions' chief interest in the Peak was in its abundant supplies of lead ore.

WEALTH FROM THE LAND

The Romans were the first to exploit the mineral wealth of the Peak District, and mining and quarrying has been a major local source of employment ever since. In the 18th and 19th centuries, lead production was a major source of Peak District wealth and over 10,000 miners were at work in the limestone area. Evidence of their passing can still be seen in White Peak meadows, where over 50,000 shafts have been identified.

The wealth won from lead and from the wool of their sheep gave landowners like the Dukes of Devonshire and Rutland the confidence to build

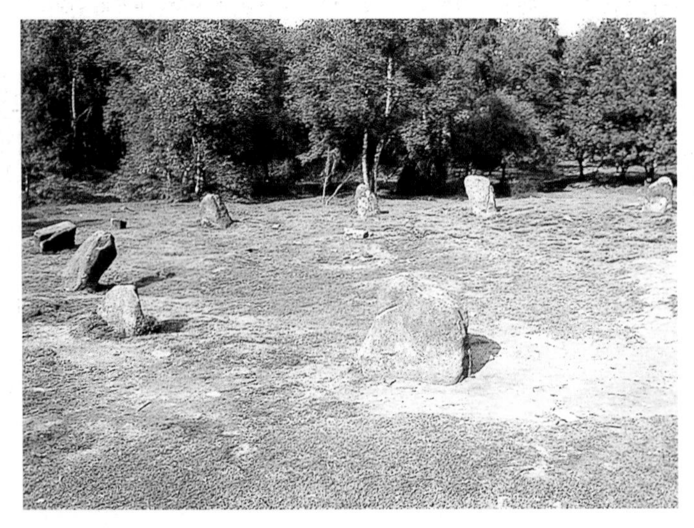

The Nine Ladies Stone Circle is evidence of the early occupation of Stanton Moor, amidst lovely countryside above the River Derwent

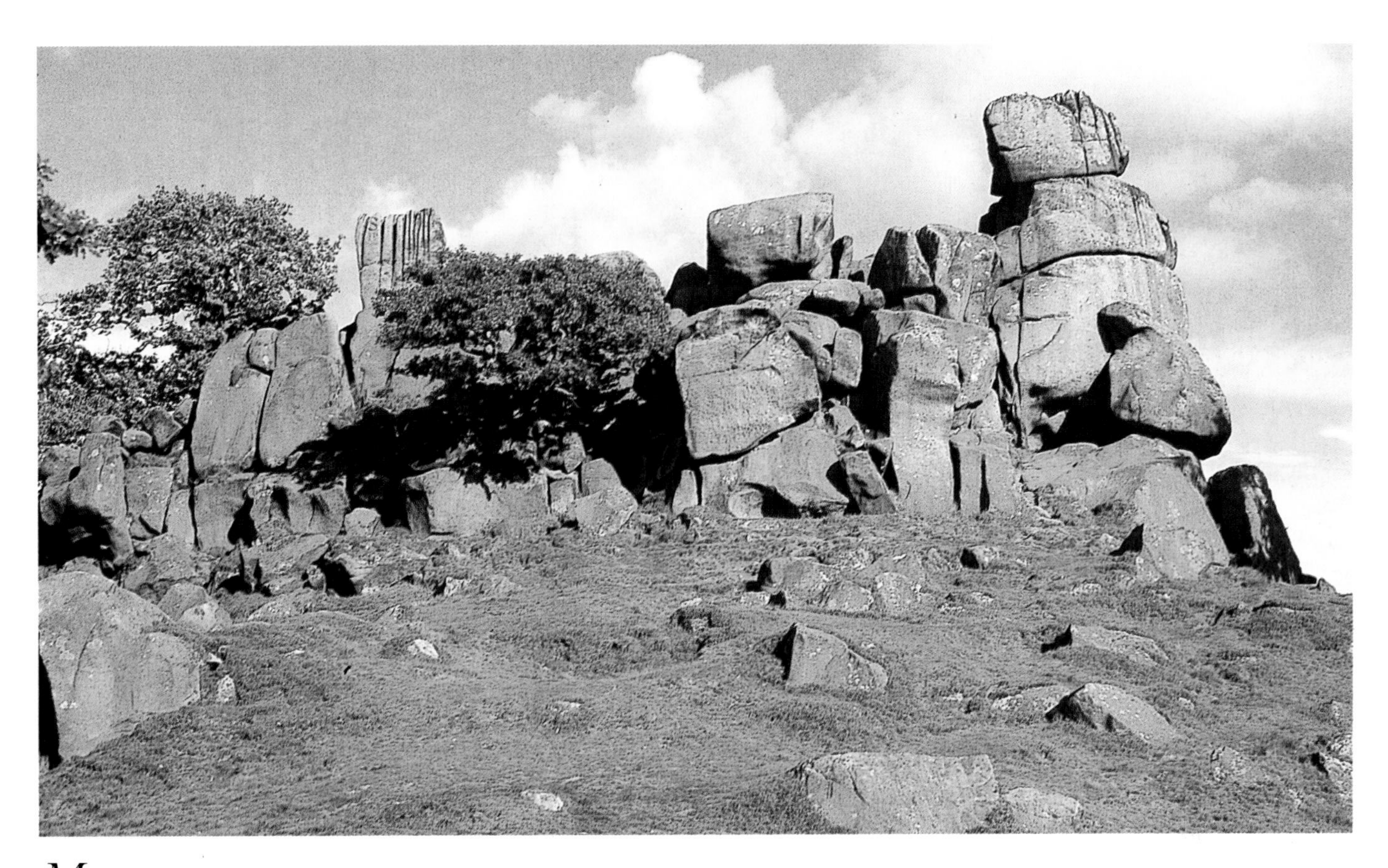

*M*ock Beggars Hall, above, is a natural rock formation, while Bakewell Pudding, bottom right, was an accidental creation

their magnificent houses of Chatsworth and Haddon Hall, both near Bakewell and superb but contrasting examples of the English country house.

Haddon Hall is the older and more intimate of the two, benefitting from the fact that it was abandoned for 200 years and therefore not significantly 'improved' since the late Middle Ages. It stands on a prominent bluff overlooking the River Wyel. Just over the hill in the Derwent Valley is Chatsworth, the palatial, Palladian-style seat of the Dukes of Devonshire, largely rebuilt in the 17th century and now a treasure house of works of art. It stands in extensive parkland landscaped by Lancelot 'Capability' Brown.

A much earlier seat of power in the Peak is the romantic ruin of Peveril Castle, high above the tiny township of Castleton in the Hope Valley. Peveril Castle was built by William Peveril shortly after the Norman Conquest as the administrative centre for the Royal Forest of the Peak – a hunting preserve for medieval kings and princes.

THE MOST VISITED NATIONAL PARK

Today, Castleton is a popular centre for the millions of visitors who throng to Britain's most-visited national park, many coming to visit the four famous caverns. Treak Cliff and the Blue John Cavern and Mine are where the rare semi-precious stone, Blue John, is found. Peak Cavern is the most spectacular, while Speedwell's flooded passages are explored by boat.

Matlock and Matlock Bath have family attractions such as Riber Castle Wildlife Park, the Heights of Abraham, with its cable cars, caverns, maze and water gardens, and its illuminations. Matlock Bath is also home to Temple Mine and the Peak District Mining Museum.

The 'capital' of the Peak is Bakewell, famous for the pudding (never known as a 'tart' here). The friendly little town is the natural centre, and has the biggest local livestock and street market every Monday.

Most of today's 22 million annual visitors to the Peak come from the surrounding towns and cities. Half the population of England live within day-trip distance of this precious island of unspoilt scenery. To them, the Peak District is a vital lung and breathing space – right on their doorstep.

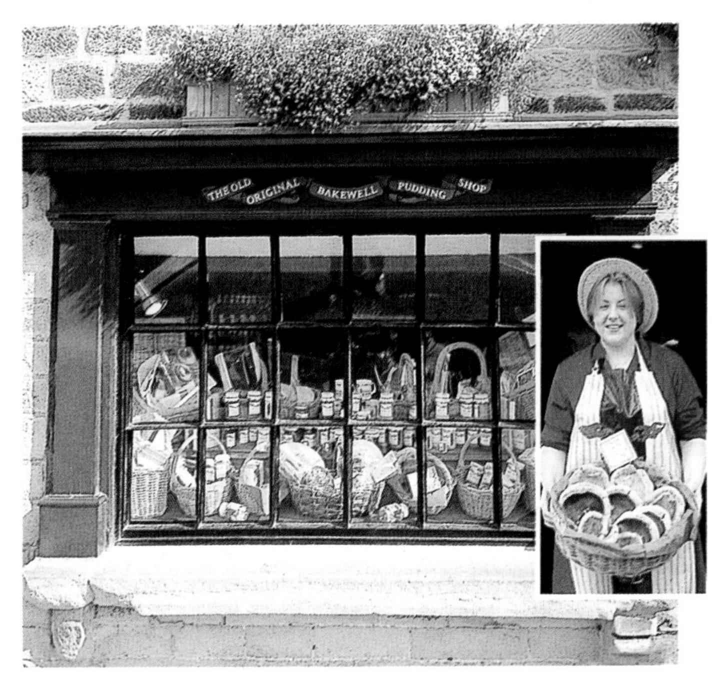

THE ABBEYS OF THE NORTH

EARLY CHRISTIANITY

St Paulinus (d. AD 644) was the first successful Christian missionary in the north, converting King Edwin, who made him Archbishop of York. Paulinus preached, baptised and encouraged the setting up of churches throughout the north, but when his patron was killed in battle, he returned to Kent and the north reverted to paganism.

The second wave of missionaries came from the Irish, rather than Roman tradition, and were spearheaded by St Columba (AD 521–97), who founded the monastery on Iona. His monks established churches throughout the north and one of them, St Aidan (d. AD 651), became the first Bishop of Lindisfarne (Holy Island), off the coast of Northumberland. The clash between the Celtic and Roman monasticism was finally resolved at the great Synod of Whitby, held at Whitby Abbey on the North Yorkshire coast, where it was decided to adopt Roman, Papal observances.

The most famous chronicler of these events was the Venerable Bede (AD 673–735), whose reputation has stood longer than the great abbey at Jarrow, where he lived and died. Bede was born into a Saxon family who sent him, at the age of seven, to be brought up as a monk at Wearmouth Abbey; he soon moved on to Jarrow where he spent the rest of his life. He learnt Latin, Greek and Hebrew and wrote treatises on theology, natural phenomena and orthography, but his most famous work was his *Ecclesiastical History of the English People*. Full of vividly told anecdotes, the work is also

From the very earliest days of Christianity, the remoteness and wildness of the northern English landscape attracted hermits and monastic communities alike, offering opportunities for retreat from the civilised world and the adoption of a life of self-sufficiency and poverty. It is ironic then that the success of these establishments resulted not only in the building of some of the finest and richest abbeys in the kingdom, but also in a transformation of their surroundings. The Cistercian brotherhood, in particular, by a combination of sheer hard work and technical expertise, turned unproductive land into fertile, well-drained fields which supported vast numbers of sheep. Though their grandiose abbeys are now reduced to ruins, the achievement of these medieval pioneers lives on in the oases of lush pasture which they created in the midst of moorland and fells.

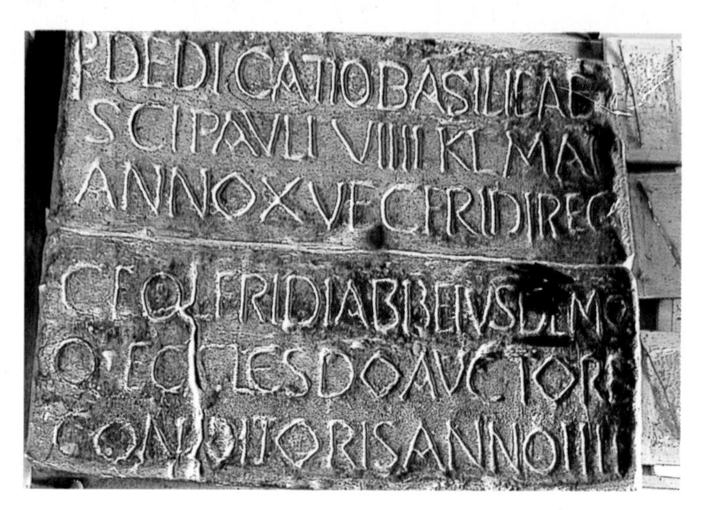

*T*he dedication stone of St Paul's Church in Jarrow, which contains the chapel where Bede worshipped. The church is now at the heart of the Bede's World exhibition, which tells of the former monastery here and of the life of the great chronicler

scholarly and accurate. Its extraordinary qualities were immediately recognised and it has remained the standard textbook on the early English Church for over 1200 years.

CISTERCIAN PIONEERS

It was the Cistercians who left the greatest legacy of monastic architecture. The oldest foundation, Rievaulx, was, as its name suggests, established by

French monks from Clairvaux, where the abbot, St Bernard (1091–1153), was one of the most influential of all medieval Christians. Rievaulx was founded in 1131 and by the end of the century there were said to be over 140 monks and 500 lay brothers living there. Its evocative ruins are set in a wooded valley in the Hambleton Hills of North Yorkshire. They are best seen from the vantage point of Rievaulx Terrace, which, with its Tuscan and Ionic Temples, was built specifically for that purpose in the mid-18th century.

On an even grander scale are the ruins of Fountains Abbey, founded a year after Rievaulx, but reconstructed in the second half of the century

after a disastrous fire. Built on a site once described as 'fit more for the dens of wild beasts than for the uses of man', the abbey became the wealthiest Cistercian house in England, a pre-eminence which is still evident from the sheer size of the remaining buildings and the rich beauty of their setting. Approached through the delightful water gardens of Studley Royal, the sight is breathtaking.

Between Rievaulx and Fountains are the ruins of Byland Abbey, founded in 1134, which boasts the longest Cistercian church in England. Its daughter house, Jervaulx, was, according to tradition, founded by a group of monks from Byland who lost their way on the banks of the River Yore and were guided to safety by a vision of the Virgin and Child, who declared 'Ye are late of Byland but now of Yorevale'.

The distinctive red sandstone remains of Furness Abbey in Cumbria, which was founded in 1123 but taken over by the Cistercians in 1147, testify to the fact that it came second only to Fountains in terms of wealth, owning extensive properties in northern England and the Isle of Man. In terms of size, it belittled even Fountains, having a dormitory twice as long.

The Cistercians were not the only monks to settle in this area. Two 12th-century Augustinian foundations have been preserved to some degree. One, Brinkburn Priory, despite its pretty setting by the River Coquet, always remained impoverished, but its church survived the Reformation because it served the parish; the church was completely restored in the 19th century and is regarded as the finest example of early Gothic

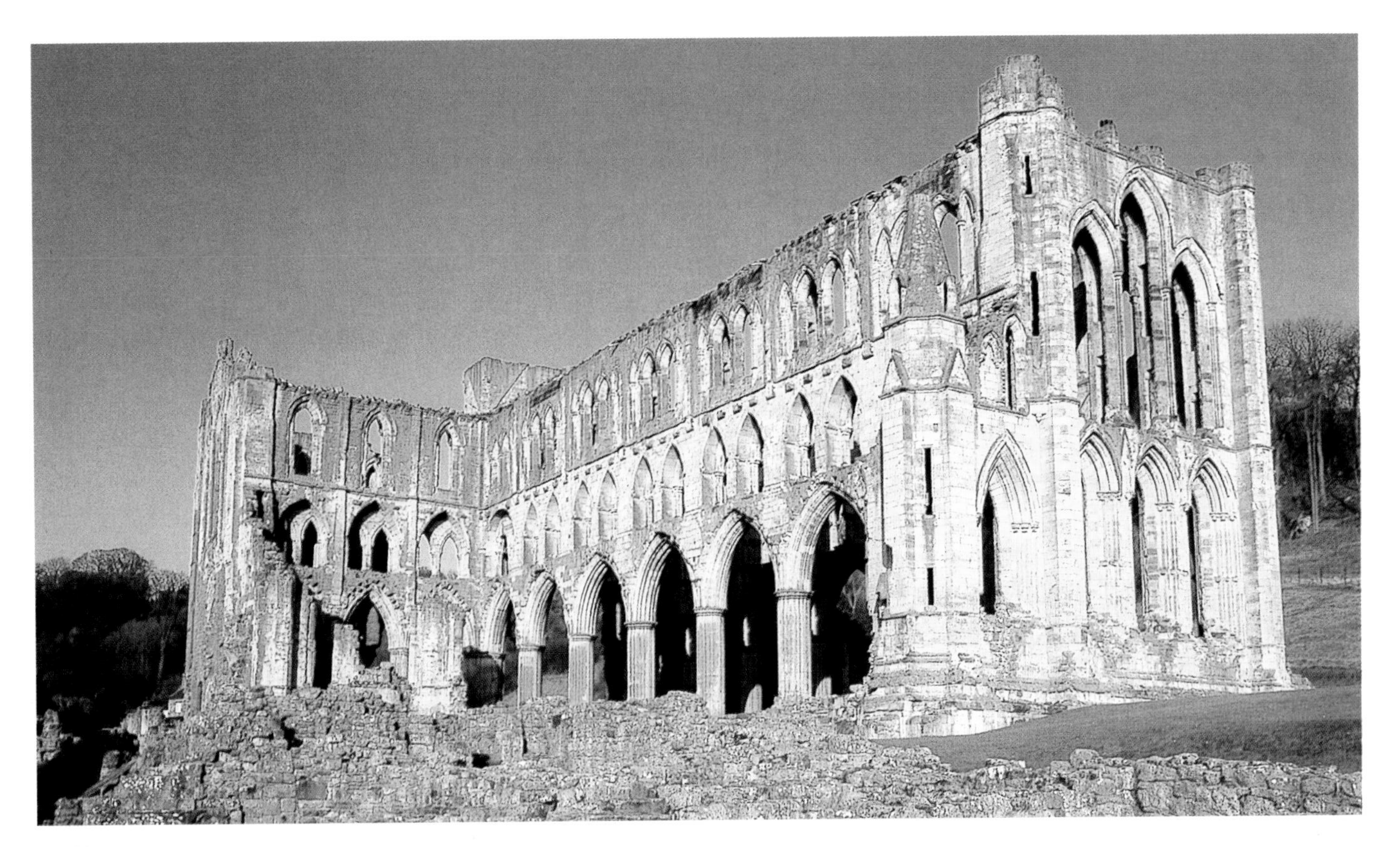

The remains of Rievaulx Abbey are still substantial, showing its former importance and prosperity. The nave, which dates back to 1135, is the earliest large Cistercian nave in Britain and the choir is a notable example of 13th-century work

architecture in Northumberland. Newburgh Priory in North Yorkshire lives on only because it was incorporated into the mansion built there by Henry VIII's chaplain; the house boasts possession of the tomb of that other destroyer of churches, Oliver Cromwell. The most unusual of all is Mount Grace Priory, founded in 1398, the best-preserved Carthusian charterhouse in England. Living in individual two-storey cells, each with its own garden, the Carthusians lived the life of hermits within the Priory precincts, reviving the Irish ideal which had inspired the very first monastic foundations in the area.

Fountains Abbey is the largest monastic ruin in Britain and is in a wonderful setting, surrounded by landscaped gardens. These were created in the 18th century and include water gardens, ornamental temples, follies and magnificent views

THE DISSOLUTION

Picturesque and tranquil though their ruins may be now, the great abbeys were once at the centre of religious, social and commercial life. This might have continued, had Henry VIII not divorced Katherine of Aragon so that he could marry Ann Boleyn. Because the Pope refused to approve of the arrangement, Henry VIII made himself Supreme Head of the Church in England, and the Dissolution of the Monasteries began in 1536, with around 800 monasteries suppressed. In the south of England there was little resistance, but in the north up to 40,000 men rallied to join the Pilgrimage of Grace, a peaceful protest which soon became an armed revolt, with finance, and even physical support, from the monks of Byland, Furness, Rievaulx and Whitby. With typical guile, Henry VIII persuaded the rebels to disband by promising that the monasteries would be saved, but then reneged and exacted a terrible revenge on all who had taken part. Monks were among the leaders whom he had executed, and every religious house was forcibly disbanded, its wealth seized and its lands sold.

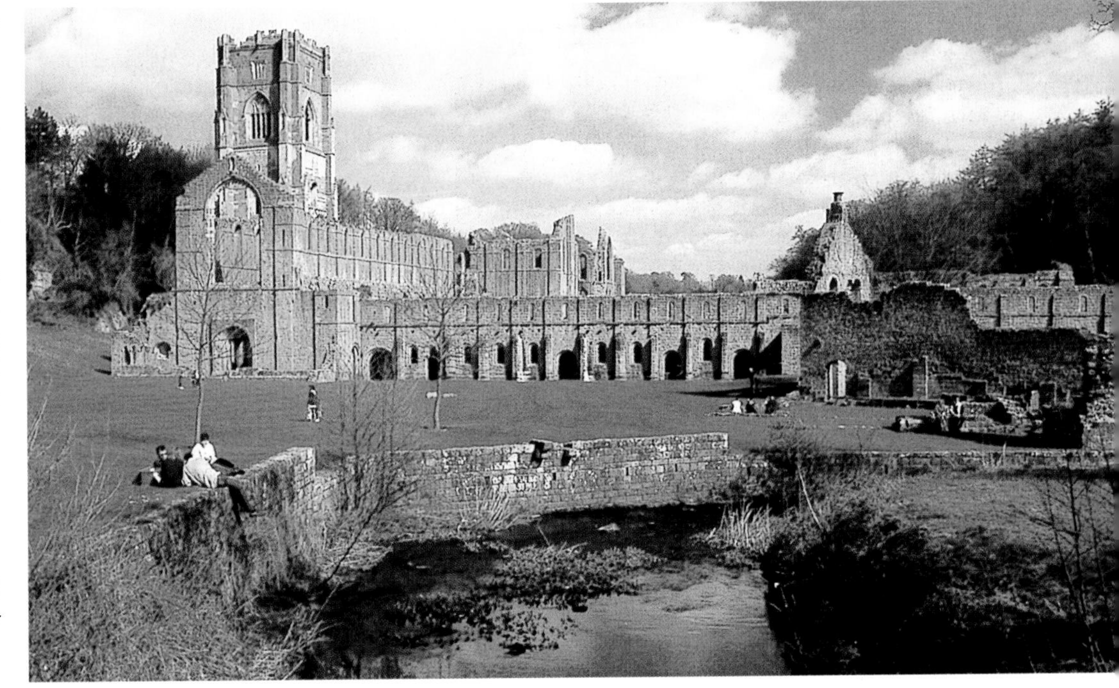

THE NORTH YORK MOORS

The most extensive area of moorland in England or Wales, the North York Moors covers 554 sq miles (892sq km) of glorious scenery. Rolling hills are ablaze with purple heather in late summer and there are pretty green valleys, with rock-strewn streams, and acres of forest. Apart from the busy seaside resorts, there are only a scattering of small market towns. Most settlements are villages, usually centred on a bridge over a river; the cottages are built of stone with distinctive red pantiled roofs. In the more remote dales and on the moortops, there are isolated farms and shooting lodges, reminders of the great estates which still own much of the land.

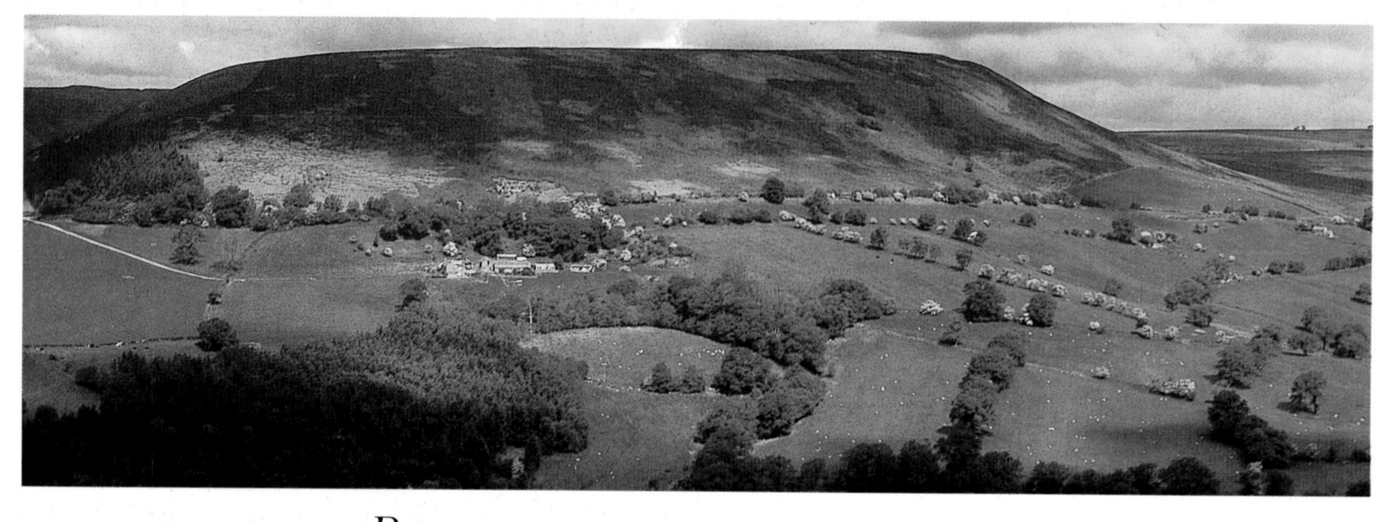

Bilsdale, near Hornby, is flanked on one side by the ridge of Easterside Hill

EARLY DAYS

The earliest man-made features on the North York Moors date from the Bronze Age and are appropriately mysterious. The 40 bridestones at Nab Ridge, on Nab End Moor in Bilsdale are the remains of a stone circle, 40 feet (12.2m) in diameter, which may once have formed the retaining wall of a burial chamber. Above Grosmont, at High and Low Bridestones, there are remains of stone circles and some standing stones. The most dramatic group is on Bridestones Moor, on the western edge of Dalby Forest, where the huge rocks have been weathered into fantastic and gravity-defying shapes by the wind and rain.

The Romans also left their mark. South of Goathland, stretching across Wheeldale Moor, is one of the best-preserved examples of a Roman road in Britain, built to connect the Roman fortress of Malton with Whitby on the coast. Its culverts, kerbstones and foundations, 16 feet (4.9m) wide, are visible for 16 miles (25.7km) over this remote moor. The road gave access to Roman forts, dating from AD 100, and their remains can be visited at Cawthorn Camps, to the north of Pickering. A Roman signal station, built on the cliffs at Scarborough in about AD 370, is the only one of five on the coast to have been excavated.

SAINTS AND POETS

Whitby holds a significant place in the history of early Christianity. The abbey, perched on the clifftop, was founded in AD 657 by St Hilda, and seven years later it hosted the Synod of Whitby, at which it was decided to adopt Roman, rather than Celtic practice in England. Caedmon, the first English Christian poet, appropriately had his home at the abbey. The dramatic ruins which command the coastline today are those of a much later, 13th-century foundation – on a dark night it is easy to see why Bram Stoker used it as the setting for his novel *Dracula*. St Mary's church, close by and reached by 199 steps from the harbour below, is a rare survivor from the 18th century, with its double-decker pulpit, galleries and box pews.

THE MIDDLE AGES

Originally a Celtic settlement founded in 270 BC, Pickering continued to thrive because it lay on the crossroads of the Malton to Whitby and Helmsley to Scarborough roads. The parish church is deservedly famous for its unusually complete set of medieval wall paintings, but it is the ruins of its motte and bailey castle which dominate this busy market town. Dating from the 12th century, the castle was reputedly used as a hunting lodge by every king from 1100 to 1400. Parts of the old Royal Forest of Pickering are still Crown Land, and there are forest drives, nature trails and picnic sites in nearby Dalby Forest.

The Normans built an even more impressive castle at Scarborough, with a curtain wall which envelopes the headland; its massive square keep, rising 80 feet (24.4m) high, is a landmark for miles around, though

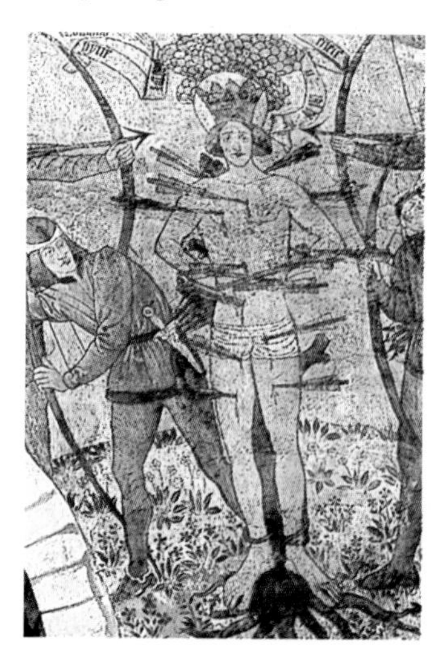

Pickering Church contains some remarkably well-preserved medieval wall-paintings

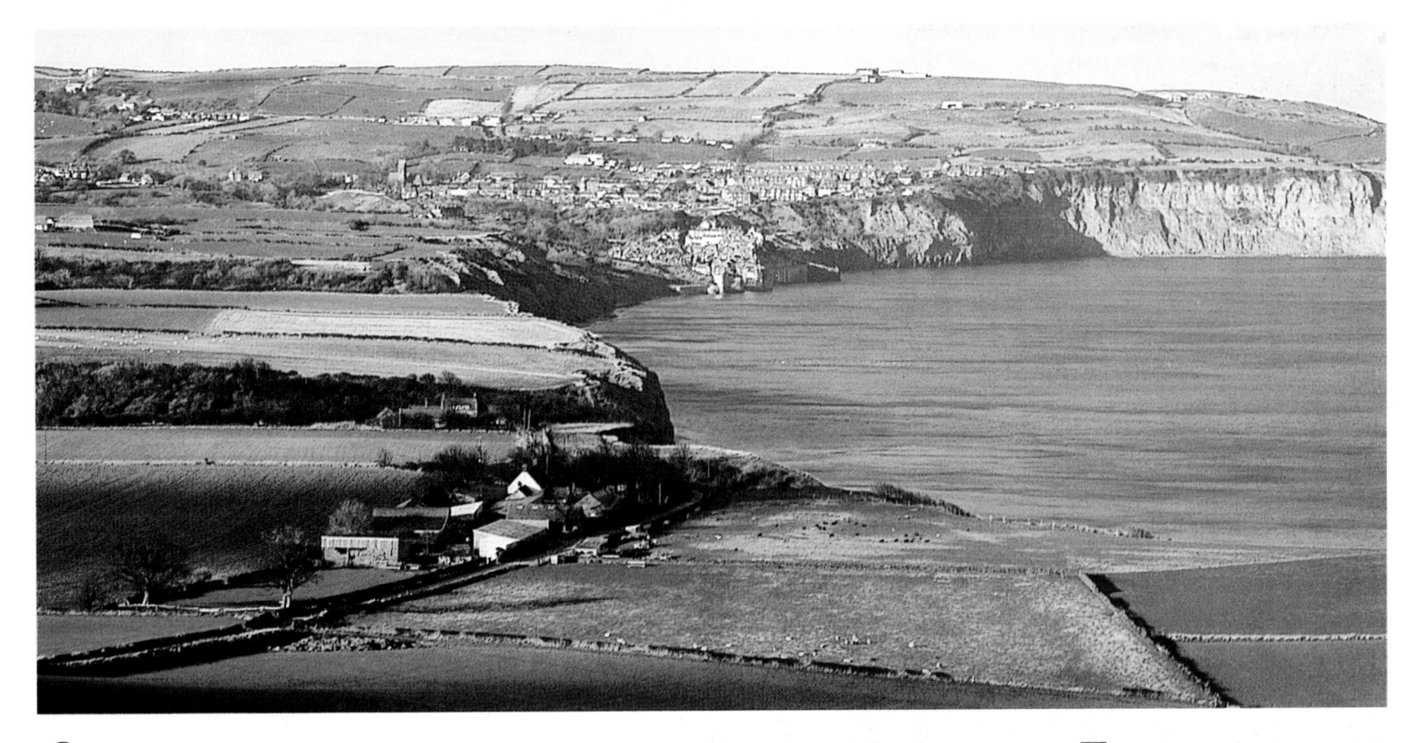

One of Britain's most picturesque villages, Robin Hood's Bay clings to the steep cliffs above the sea

the rest of the castle was almost completely destroyed during the Civil War.

SEAFARERS AND SMUGGLERS

The coastal towns of the North York Moors enjoyed their heydey in the 18th century. Whitby was then the base for a hugely successful whaling fleet, which is commemorated in Pannett Park Museum (there is a massive whalebone arch on the North cliff), and for colliers plying the North Sea. The Rev William Scoresby (1789–1857), son of a local whaling captain and explorer, unusually combined a career in the church with Arctic explorations, and became a leading authority on magnetism. Captain James Cook (1728–1779), the explorer and map-maker, also learnt his trade in Whitby. Though the town still has a fishing fleet and is famous for its shellfish, its importance as a port and harbour has declined.

Further down the coast, at Robin Hood's Bay, a more notorious trade was carried on. This quaint town, its cobbled

streets and tiny cottages crammed into the small gap between the sea and steep cliffs, was a haven for smugglers. The only access is on foot down a long, narrow and precipitous road, though there are plenty of cafés and inns in which to break the journey. The Smuggling Experience Museum is (fortunately) situated at the top of the hill, and recreates the atmosphere of those unruly times.

VICTORIAN SEASIDE SPAS

It was in the 19th century that the greatest changes came to the seaside towns of Scarborough and Whitby. Scarborough had claimed healing properties for its waters, taken from the stream flowing across the South Sands, for almost 200 years. They were said to cure asthma, skin diseases and melancholy as well as to cleanse the blood and stomach.

The town also lays claim to the invention of the bathing machine which enabled bathers to maintain their modesty. The craze for sea-bathing, another highly regarded cure for all manner of ills, swept the whole of the country. Anne Brontë (1820–1849) was one

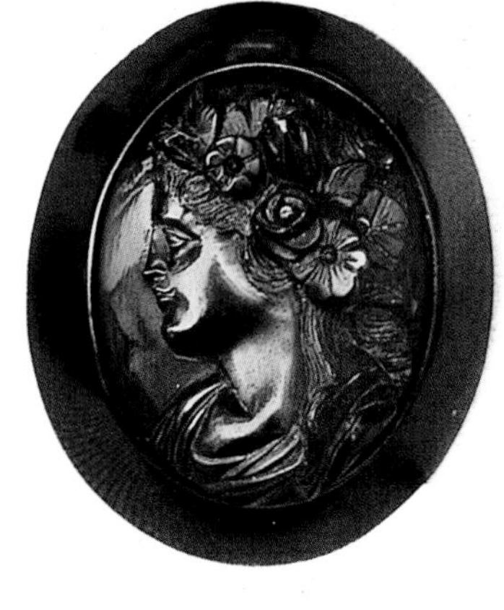

of many invalids who came to Scarborough for the sea-cure. She died here in 1849 and is buried in St Mary's churchyard.

Both Scarborough and Whitby were immensely fashionable in Victorian and Edwardian times, and many elegant buildings date from that time. Whitby's jet industry also thrived. The coal-black mineral was cut, polished and turned into mourning jewellery; it became an essential fashion item when adopted by the widowed Queen Victoria.

THE MOORS TODAY

The enduring popularity of the east coast owes much to the excellent long sandy beaches, while the lure of the

Examples of Whitby jet jewellery can be seen in the Whitby Museum

wild moorland and its communities never fades. Splendid views can be enjoyed from the steam trains of the North York Moors Railway, running 18 miles (28.9km) from Pickering to Grosmont; others can be seen along the 93 miles (149.6km) of the Cleveland Way footpath, which skirts the northern and western edges of the moors and then follows the coast towards Scarborough.

One major attraction of the moors is the Ryedale Folk Museum in Hutton-le-Hole, illustrating over 2,000 years of local history with an array of fascinating bygones. This is one of Britain's most remarkable open-air museums, with a reconstructed cruck house, Elizabethan manor and cottages from three different centuries. Here too are the oldest daylight photographic studio in England and a small glassmaking furnace of 1590 from Rosedale Abbey.

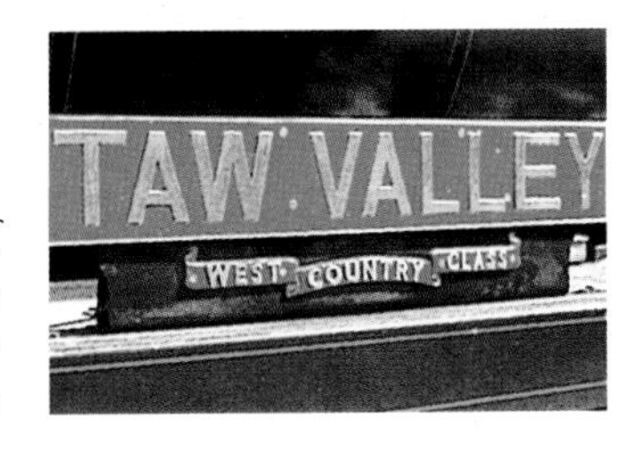

SCOTLAND'S STRONGHOLDS

Alone piper on the ramparts of Edinburgh Castle during the Military Tattoo is for many an enduring image of the Scottish castle – massively set on an impregnable rock, battlemented and guarded with cannon, manned by fierce Highlanders urged to deeds of heroism by the call of the pipes. For others, Eilean Donan on the road to Skye is the Scottish castle par excellence, an island-held fairytale reflected in ruffled waters of a loch and backed by dramatic mountains. Or it may be the pepperpot turrets and crow-stepped gables of towering Craigievar in the gentler country of Scotland's north-east. Such is the variety of Scottish castles, reflecting the troubled history of this determinedly independent country.

ROYAL FORTRESSES

The story of the Scottish castle really starts in the 13th century. Motte and bailey castles had been built to the Norman plan by the kings Alexander I and David I, who were brought up in Norman England, and these were gradually replaced by stone fortresses. Edinburgh, sitting on its volcanic rock, was an early example. Continually fought over by the Scots and English, little other than the chapel survives from its earliest days. It last saw action in 1745 when the Young Pretender failed to take it but was incarcerated there instead.

Another royal castle, Stirling, 'the key to Scotland', has an equally formidable setting, and many great battles, including Bannockburn in 1314, were fought near by. Most of

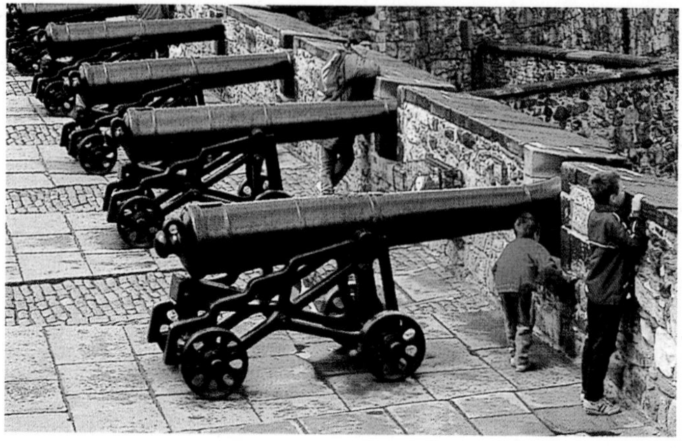

*C*annons on the battlements of Edinburgh's famous castle

the present buildings are late medieval, and Mary, Queen of Scots was crowned here as an infant in 1543. But it was not just monarchs who built great fortresses. Wherever a suitable site was available, and circumstances demanded, the great landowners of Scotland would build on it.

CLAN CASTLES

The MacLeods at Dunvegan in the west of the Isle of Skye still live in their ancestral castle beside a tongue of the sea. Enlarged and made more comfortable over the centuries, it tells of a lawless past. The family has additional protection from the Fairy Flag, possibly 7th century, which legend says will save the MacLeods from destruction on three occasions – it has already worked twice.

On the opposite side of the country St Andrews Castle was the stronghold for the powerful bishops, who were as involved in worldly politics as in prayer. As Scotland fought to retain (or recapture) its independence from England, the castle frequently changed hands, as its battered walls overlooking the sea testify.

One of the best of the early castles is set in wooded, rather undramatic country down on the Solway Firth, south of Dumfries. Caerlaverock is a wonderful triangular castle still surrounded by the waters of its moat – the very latest in military thinking when it was built in around 1280. Captured by the English king Edward I, 'the Hammer of the Scots', in 1300, it was constantly dismantled and besieged in the Middle Ages, yet managed to retain its splendour, and was later enhanced by a splendid Renaissance façade.

Not far away to the west is a much sterner castle – the massive 14th-century tower and walls of Threave. It sits on an island in the River Dee, and was built by the appropriately named Archibald the Grim, bastard son of Sir James Douglas. A later Douglas surrendered the castle to James II in 1455 after the king had bombarded it with the huge gun, 'Mons Meg', now in Edinburgh Castle. The Douglases also held the now-ruined Tantallon Castle on the southeast corner of the Firth of Forth, near North Berwick.

Some of the most impressive of Scottish castles are the result of careful restoration. Duart, on the Isle of Mull overlooking Loch Linnhe, retains 13th-century fragments, and was restored by Sir Fitzroy Maclean from 1911 onwards. It is now the home of the clan chief. The smaller castle of Eilean Donan on Loch Duich was in utter ruin after bombardment from an English warship in 1719 until it was restored in 1932.

*T*he high walls and round towers of Caerlaverock Castle, seat of the Maxwells, have stood firm since the 13th century, though the machicolations were added during the 15th century

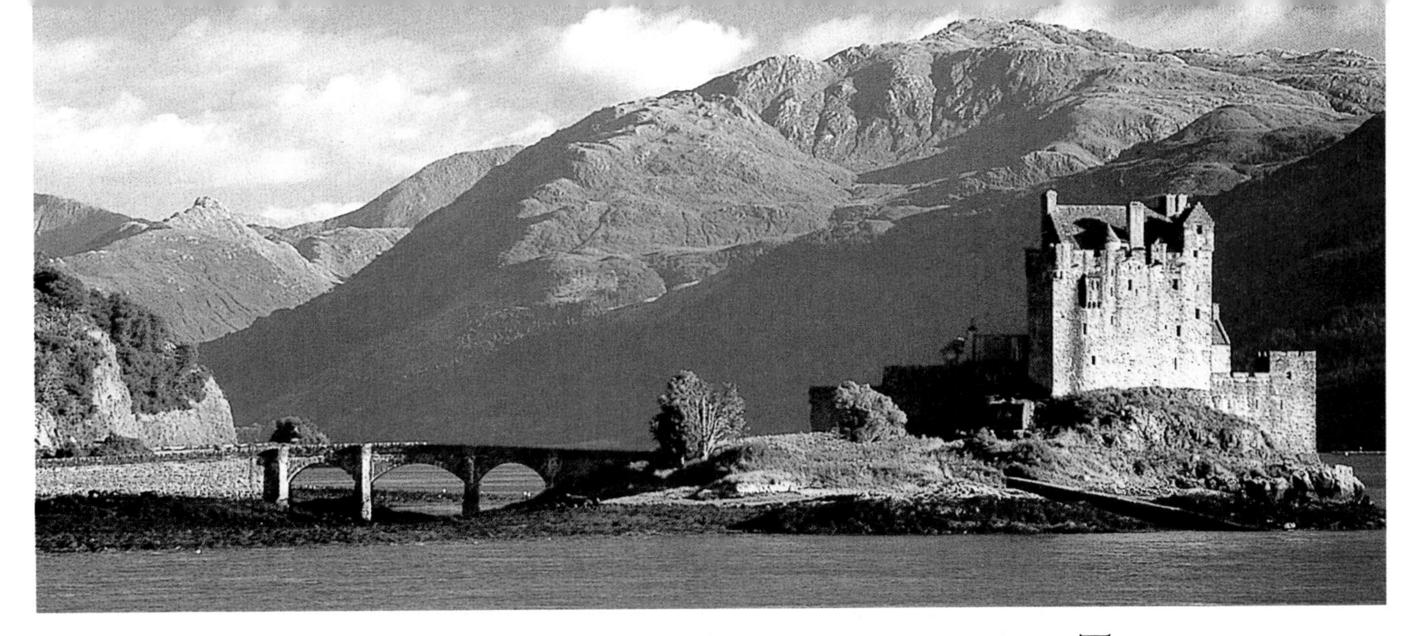

Eilean Donan Castle poses romantically on Loch Duich, amidst wonderful mountain scenery

THE CASTLES OF MAR

Once the crowns of England and Scotland had been united by King James VI & I, a new type of castle developed – the tower house. Times of increasing political stability demanded increasing comfort, without altogether abandoning a defensive role. These new towers are characterised by a plain lower storey – sometimes square, but more often L- or Z-shaped. On the upper floors they burst into a riot of corbelled-out

Craigevar Castle is perhaps the loveliest of all the Castles of Mar

towers and gables to increase the amount of accommodation, though access is still usually by spiral stairways.

Some of the best examples are found to the west of Aberdeen, between the Don and the Dee valleys – the former province of Mar. Among the best of the castles of Mar is Craigievar, unaltered since it was completed in 1626. Significantly, it was built not for a monarch or a clan chief, but for one of the Jacobean nouveau riche, the Aberdeen merchant William Forbes. The largest of the castles of Mar were Castle Fraser, Crathes and the extended Drum Castle. Glamis Castle, childhood home of Queen Elizabeth, the Queen Mother, has one of the most prickly rooflines, stiff with cone-topped towerlets.

At Drumlanrig, built in the 1680s, the Douglas Dukes of Queensberry built themselves a huge square palace, which succeeds in combining the appearance of a medieval stronghold with that of an early 17th-century mansion. Like many of the inhabited Scottish castles, its interiors are a luxurious contrast to its outward appearance.

SCOTTISH BARONIAL

It was not long before the style established by the castles of Mar began to influence architects. Inveraray Castle, rebuilt in the mid-18th century, uses the same vocabulary of turrets and battlements, though regulated with classical order,

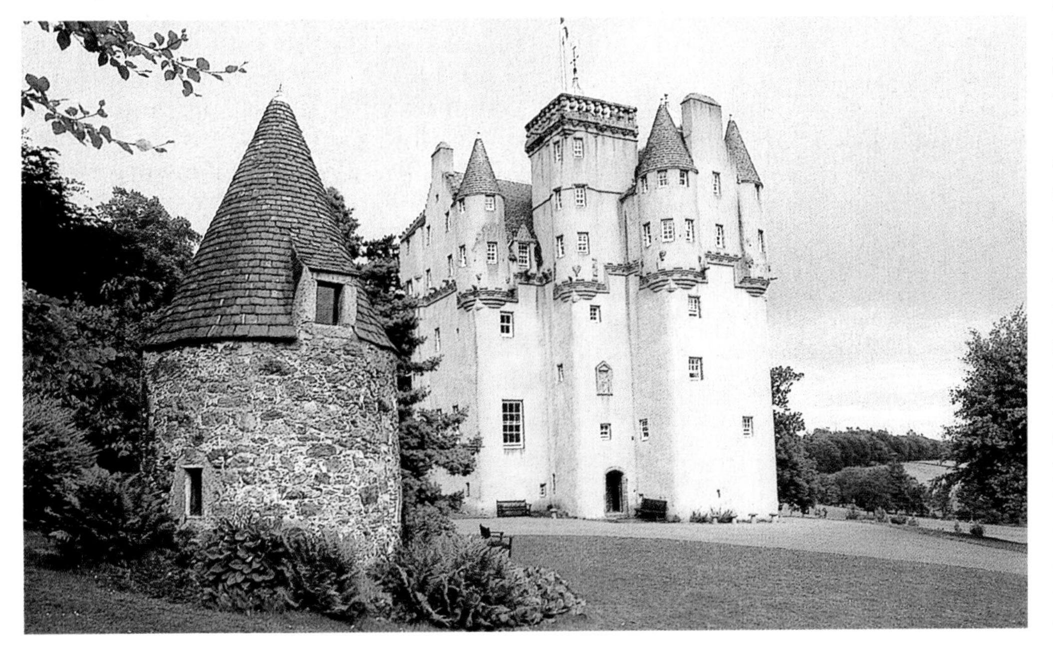
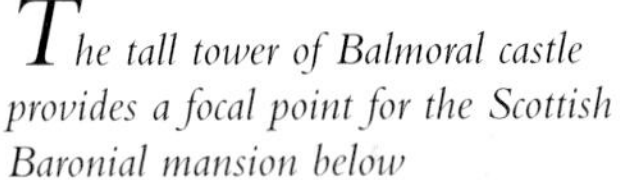

The tall tower of Balmoral castle provides a focal point for the Scottish Baronial mansion below

which also underpins superb Culzean on the Ayrshire coast, where Robert Adam's skills blend a castellated façade with wonderful Italianate interiors.

By the middle of the 19th century the 'Scottish Baronial' style was all the rage among the landed gentry. Blair Castle was reconstructed in the favoured style, and so was Dunrobin. The most famous achievement of all is Queen Victoria's Balmoral, where Prince Albert (with professional help, it must be said) provided a huge square keep with a more comfortable country house attached, with all its main apartments tricked out in tartan – the apotheosis of the Scottish castle.

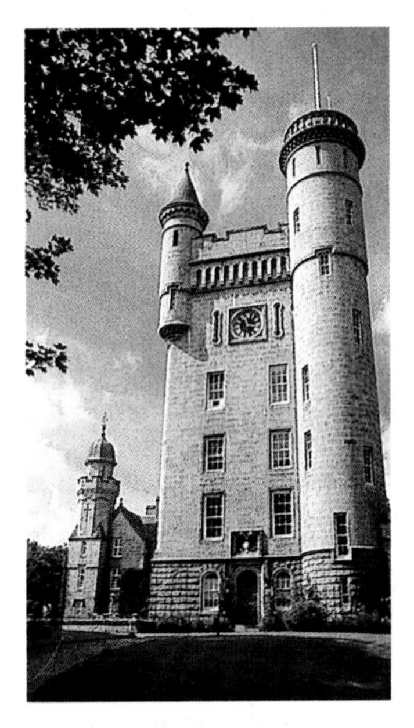

THE WILDLIFE OF SCOTLAND

From soaring crags to misty marshland, from mountain top to sea, from lowland plain to high moorland, the habitats of Scotland are about as varied as could be. Sub-tropical trees flourish less than 50 miles (80km) from the north coast in Inverewe gardens, warmed by the Gulf Stream. On the Cairngorm plateau genuine Arctic conditions, more typical of regions 1,000 (1,609km) miles north, prevail. Between these two extremes lie the high moorland, the lush glens, the rock-bound coasts and the gentle rivers that are home to many distinctive species.

Only the luckiest visitor will see some of Scotland's most precious treasures — the golden eagle, the osprey or the red squirrel, for example. Nor are the fierce wild cats easy to spot in moorland and forest. Otters, too, are seldom seen, though they hunt beside the seashore of the west coast and among the islands as well by inland burns. Despite their rarity, however, such species seem unlikely to go the way of others – wild reindeer died out here in the 12th century, the beaver probably in the 15th (though there are plans to reintroduce it), and the last wolf in Scotland was killed in 1743.

FORESTS OLD AND NEW

Many of the lost animals of Scotland needed the huge stretches of native pine forest which once covered much of the country. Now only one per cent of the Caledonian Forest survives, having fallen victim to man's greed for timber.

Eighteenth-century iron smelting accounted for the loss of many trees, which were felled and floated down the rivers to be burned for charcoal to fuel the furnaces. Others provided valuable timber, while deliberate clearance of forest (as well as of inhabitants) to introduce vast sheep runs accounted for many more. The bare, open, rocky landscape of much of the Highlands, although admired by visitors, is to a large extent the result of these predations.

Where there is forest today, much of it is the result of planting since the two world wars, and, although in recent years the ruler-straight edges have given way to more sensitive planting, the denseness, uniformity and blanketing effect of the trees have been much criticised. There has also been controversy over the commercial afforestation of large areas of open land, such as the unique bogland environment of the Flow Country of Sutherland and Caithness.

Where pockets of native pinewood survive – at the Black Wood of Rannoch, and Rothiemurchus Forest by the Cairngorms, for example – they are magical places, with mosses, blaeberries and junipers plentiful amid the trees, and wildflowers such as wintergreens and lady's tresses.

There are ancient oak woods, too, especially in the Argyll glens towards the Atlantic coast, where gnarled trees are hung with lichens and the forest floor is home to an amazing multitude of ferns and flowers. In places, too, are survivors of ancient birch forests – among the most accessible of them is the Birks of Aberfeldy.

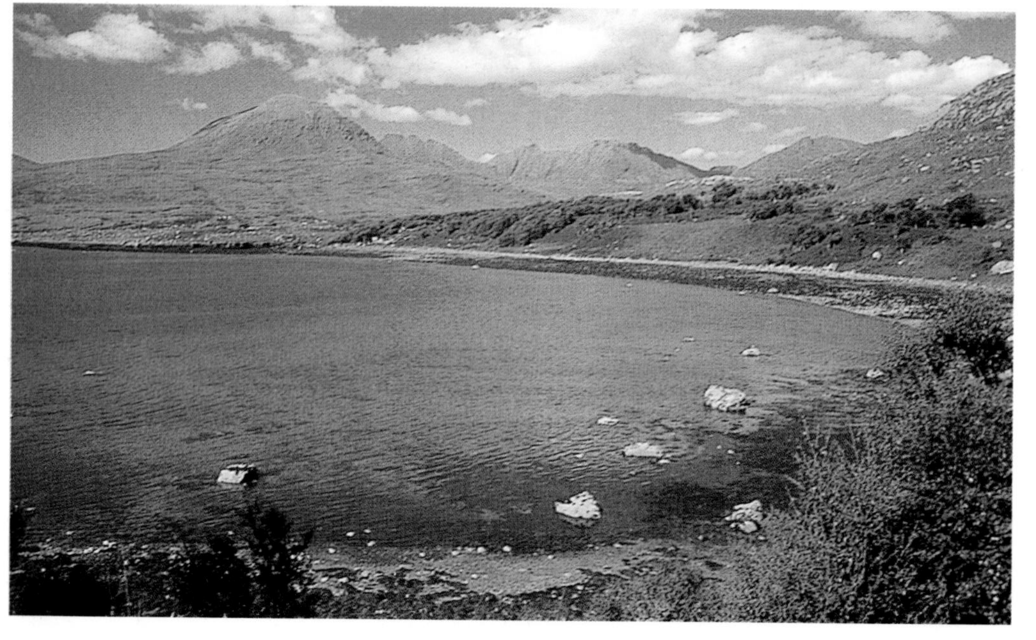

Upper Loch Torridon, a beautiful sea loch on the west coast, is bordered by magnificent Highland scenery

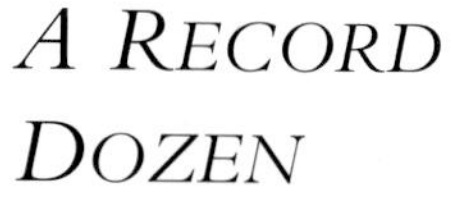

A RECORD DOZEN

The climate of Scotland is excellent for trees of all types – which may be why 12 of Britain's 30 tallest trees are here, among them a dead heat of two Douglas firs at the Hermitage in Perthshire and Dunans in Argyll, both of which measure 212ft (64.5m). Tayside also has the tallest holly and beech – both 150ft (46m) – at Hallyburton House, as well as a Sitka spruce measuring 200ft (61m) at Strathearn. Other giants are the 206ft (63m) grand fir at Strone in Argyll and a western hemlock 167ft (51m) near by at Benmore; and – a pigmy by comparison – the 98ft (30m) silver birch at Ballogie in Grampian. Scotland holds two sequoia records – for the tallest in Britain, 174ft (53m) at Strathpeffer, and for the largest, at Clunie Gardens in Tayside, with a diameter of 11ft 4in (3.5m). And as for age, the UK's oldest known tree still survives near Aberfeldy – the Fortingall Yew. It is thought to be around 1,500 years old.

At the other extreme are the miniature willow forests that clothe some Scottish mountains, high above the normal treeline. Cold and infertile, often covered with snow which may linger into the summer, this is inhospitable terrain for vegetation. But still

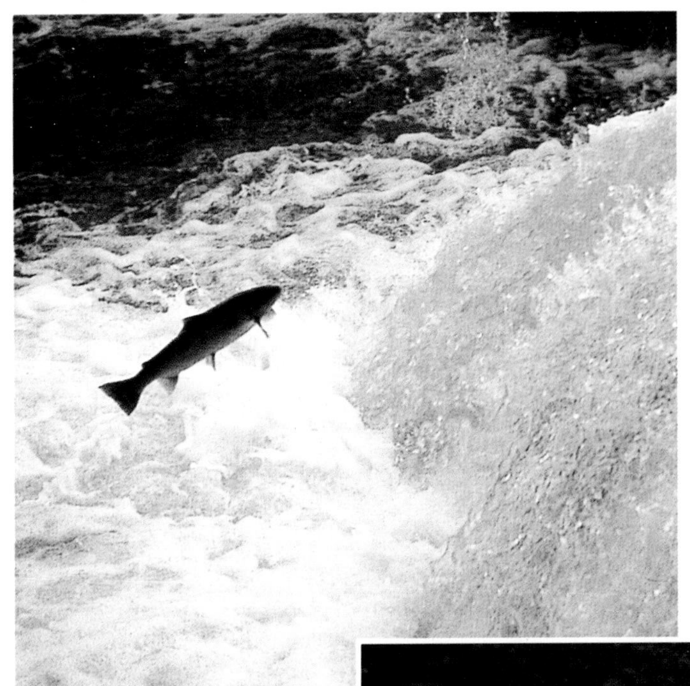

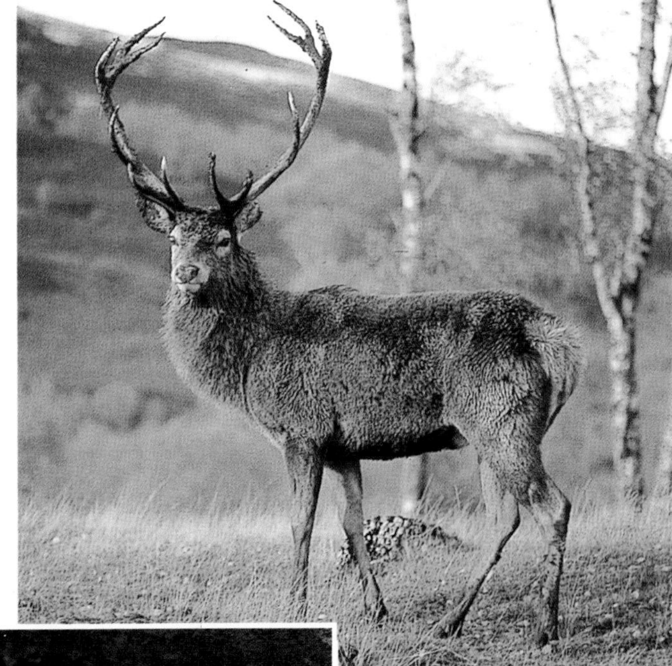

plants survive, often clustered in hollows or forming dense mats of green, which may suddenly burst into colourful flower in favourable conditions. Ben Lawers in Perthshire is particularly famous for the variety of its mountain flowers, including such rarities as the vivid blue alpine gentian and the drooping saxifrage.

Animals and birds, too, need to be hardy to survive the high mountain tops. The ptarmigan is one, often seen by skiers; its mottled brown plumage turns white in winter. A summer visitor, the dotterel, is much rarer; it breeds regularly in the eastern Highlands. Snow buntings also visit from their Arctic homes in the summer, but few stay to breed. The only butterfly regularly breeding here is the mountain ringlet. Mountain hares and stoats survive on the rocky slopes; they, too, turn white in the winter.

MOORS AND SHORES

On lower moorland two game species come into their own – the red deer and the grouse. Britain's largest wild animal,

the red deer was encouraged by Victorian landowners for sport, and stalking is still important in some areas. The sight of a magnificently antlered stag in a misty valley has been a favourite image of Scotland since before Landseer painted *The Monarch of the Glen*. The managed heather moors, where regular burning helps regenerate the plants, provide the habitat for many grouse – the red is the main target for sportsmen. Larger is the black grouse; each male has its territory – called a lek – where pinewoods meet moorland. The capercaillie, hunted to extinction in Scotland by 1800, was reintroduced in 1837 and is now found deep in the woodlands of the east of the country. Where bogland predominates – in the Flow

Country, for example, and on Rannoch Moor – domes of bog moss can provide striking colours in the landscape – from the brightest greens to stabbing orange and yellow. Where the bogs are wettest, plants such as the cranberry gain a foothold, as well as the insect-eating sundew. Glittering dragonflies are often seen fluttering over the bogland.

In extreme contrast are the flower-rich sea-meadows – the machair – which lie behind many Highland beaches, and are particularly spectacular on the shores of the Outer Hebrides, where the shell sand tempers the acidity of the peat soil. Here buttercups, orchids and gentians grow in colourful profusion. The primrose banks of Barra are an especially wonderful sight.

*E*nduring symbols of the wildlife of Scotland: leaping salmon, top left, red deer, above, and the well-camouflaged ptarmigan, left

Birds, too, congregate on the islands. Remote St Kilda has its own species of wren, while Foula in Shetland has vast numbers of great skuas, and in the friable mountainsides of Rum in the Inner Hebrides thousands of Manx sheerwaters have their burrows. On the mainland, the cliffs of Sutherland are thronged with colonies of fulmars, kittiwakes and guillemots, the mouth of the Tay is home to eider duck and the Solway estuary teems with barnacle geese.

The salmon, journeying upstream to its spawning grounds, is king of Scottish fish, but the more prosaic sea trout and trout cannot be disregarded. In mountain lochs the ferox trout – golden and spotted with black – lives alongside its red and black relative, the char. In the deepest of all – Loch Ness – may lurk the most mysterious of all Scotland's wildlife. If it does, it will add yet more to the rich diversity of the country's treasures.

Britain's Best Hotels

RED STAR AWARDS

Star classification is a quality scheme at five levels; the assessment rises from one star, denoting hotels with the simplest range of facilities, to five stars, denoting large, luxury hotels with a range of services and facilities that meet the best international standards. Every year a select number of hotels gain the AA's highest award – the **Red Star Award**. Only about 3 per cent of star-rated hotels in Britain and Ireland gain this accolade. All hotels with Red Stars usually have at least one **AA Rosette Award** for the quality of their cuisine. The AA's hotel and restaurant inspectors award rosettes annually on a rising scale of one to five.

Red Star Hotels
ENGLAND

CENTRAL LONDON

★★★★★❀❀
ATHENAEUM HOTEL
116 Piccadilly, W1
0171 499 3464
Overlooking Green Park, this elegant hotel remains one of the most popular and friendly hotels in London. There is an excellent range of bedrooms, all superbly appointed and thoughtfully equipped, including video and CD players. The Windsor Lounge serves afternoon tea and light meals, while the cosy, wood-panelled bar features a notable range of malt whiskies.

★★★★❀❀ **THE BERKELEY**
Wilton Place, Knightsbridge, SW1
0171 235 6000
In 1972 this hotel was built from scratch with the express purpose of providing the very best in hotel-keeping, and now offers an excellent range of bedrooms, some with outdoor balconies. Public rooms, which include the Lutyens writing room, are adorned with magnificent arrangements of flowers, and on the top floor there are top-rate leisure facilities, including a pool and a fitness suite. This is also the home of Vong restaurant, known for its innovative south-east Asian-inspired cuisine.

★★★★★❀❀❀❀
THE CAPITAL
Basil Street, Knightsbridge, SW3
0171 589 5171
The exclusive hotel is in the very heart of Knightsbridge, and the small, discreet dining-room, styled by Nina Campbell and Lord Linley, reflects the scale of the hotel. Two tasting menus provide a showcase for the star

dishes, which are served on Limoges china.

★★★★★❀❀ **CLARIDGE'S**
Brook St, W1
0171 629 8860
In its centenary year, this classic London hotel is still an example for others to follow. The stunning penthouses, generous corridors and opulent public areas have rarely looked so pristine and the overall impression is simply majestic. Not that one need be intimidated by the grandeur; there is a cheerful demeanour to much of the service (particularly in the restaurant), which encourages the guest to relax and make the most of the experience.

★★★★★❀❀❀
THE CONNAUGHT
Carlos Place, W1
0171 499 7070
The Connaught is famous for its measured service and quiet comfort (mobile phones and business meetings are banned). Modernisation is handled discreetly – air conditioning and a new telephone system have been installed with due respect for the elegance of the rooms. The Restaurant and The Grill Room share the same impeccable service and exhaustive menu.

★★★★★❀❀❀
THE DORCHESTER
Park Lane, W1
0171 629 8888
The Dorchester's individually designed bedrooms and suites are beautifully furnished and each of the sumptuous bathrooms features the Dorchester hallmark huge bath. The Promenade leading off the foyer is the perfect place for a drink or afternoon tea, and the bar, where live jazz is played in the evenings, specialises in

northern Italian dishes and cocktails. Both management and staff provide exceptional standards of service while retaining a reserved level of friendliness and decorum.

★★★★★ ❀❀
THE FOUR SEASONS HOTEL
Hamilton Place, Park Lane, W1
0171 499 0888
This Park Lane establishment combines high standards of professionalism with a warm and friendly style. The bedrooms have benefited from a programme of refurbishment and they offer excellent levels of comfort and facilities with tasteful design. Dining is a priority and the Lanes Dining Room should introduce an exciting new style of classical dishes in more contemporary surroundings.

★★★★❀❀ ❀
THE GORING HOTEL
Beeston Place, Grosvenor Gardens, SW1
0171 396 9000
Personally run by the Goring family since 1910, this hotel is a superb example of British hospitality. Bedrooms, although traditionally furnished, are bang up to date, providing all the facilities one would expect from such a highly regarded hotel. All have the benefit of air conditioning, while the beds are some of the most comfortable in the capital. Public area refurbishment has increased space in the garden bar and lounge, both popular for afternoon tea or cocktails.

★★★★❀❀ ❀
THE HALKIN HOTEL
Halkin Street, Belgravia, SW1
0171 333 1000
The Halkin is one of the more individual of the capital's top hotels, combining the best of modern Italian design and theattention to detail synonymous with the Far East.

Public spaces have a relaxed atmosphere and contemporary appeal. Bedrooms are equally modern, with state-of-the-art business communications, lighting and air-conditioning control systems.

★★★★★❀❀❀
LANDMARK HOTEL
222 Marylebone Road, NW1
0171 631 8000
At the heart of this magnificent hotel, housed in a Victorian building, is the spectacular Winter Garden, an eight-storey atrium fringed with high palm trees, where a pianist plays and delicious afternoon teas, drinks and light meals are served. Bedrooms are generously proportioned, with especially fine marble bathrooms offering deep tubs and separate shower cubicles. Guests can browse among multi-lingual TV channels and make use of three phone lines.

★★★★★ ❀❀
THE LANESBOROUGH
Hyde Park Corner, SW1
0171 259 5599
Formerly St George's Hospital, this famous London landmark occupies an enviable position on Hyde Park Corner. The superbly appointed and thoughtfully equipped bedrooms and suites offer the highest levels of comfort. Service from a personal butler, available 24 hours a day, underlines the hotel's commitment to the highest standard of customer care. Marble, rich fabrics and magnificent flower arrangements are the hallmarks of the delightful public areas, which include the popular cocktail bar.

★★★★★❀❀❀❀
MANDARIN ORIENTAL HYDE PARK
66 Knightsbridge, SW1
0171 235 2000
This celebrated hotel is conveniently positioned between Knightsbridge and Hyde Park. Bedrooms are individually decorated and spacious, and bathrooms modern. Marbled public areas include a popular cocktail lounge and the principal restaurant, The Park. The standard of the food is excellent throughout the hotel, and afternoon tea and breakfast should not be missed.

★★★★★❀❀❀❀ **THE SAVOY**
The Strand, WC2
0171 836 4343
The Savoy continues to provide high standards of comfort and quality, with quality linens and fabrics in all bedrooms, whilst meticulous care is taken to

preserve the famous art-deco design features, and the push-button bell system for summoning maid, valet or waiter. The new marble bathrooms with their celebrated showers are superb. The American bar maintains its popularity with the discerning, and The River Room restaurant is renowned for the flavours and precision of its menu. Afternoon tea deservedly remains a highlight.

★★★★❀❀ **STAFFORD**
16–18 St James's Place, SW1
0171 493 0111
Tucked discreetly away in exclusive St James's, this charming hotel has been completely refurbished; it boasts elegant, individually designed bedrooms and fine, cosy public rooms that include a comfortable drawing room and the bustling American Bar. Don't forget to ask the sommelier for a tour of the wonderful 350-year-old cellars, the ideal venue for private dinners, wine tastings, and small parties.

BERKSHIRE

★★★★❀❀❀
FREDRICK'S HOTEL
Shoppenhangers Road, Maidenhead
01628 635934
This delightful, personally run hotel is conveniently situated close to the railway station and the M4. Bedrooms are individual in style and each is well equipped with a number of welcome extras. Friendly, efficient service is provided by a team of enthusiastic staff, who make every effort to ensure guests enjoy their stay. A highlight of a visit is a meal in the restaurant, which serves memorable dishes in the modern style.

BUCKINGHAMSHIRE

★★★★❀❀❀
HARTWELL HOUSE
Oxford Road, Aylesbury
01296 747444
This grand country mansion stands in a 90-acre estate that includes a river and pleasant walks. Dating from 1600, the house was altered by Georgian architects, and noteworthy features such as delicate ceiling plasterwork and a Jacobean great staircase have been carefully preserved. Bedrooms are full of character and comfort, and those in a well-converted stable block have the advantage of being closer to the health centre complex, which also houses the Buttery coffee shop.

★★★★★❀❀❀❀
CLIVEDEN HOTEL, WALDO'S RESTAURANT
Cliveden, Taplow
01628 668561
Cliveden has a colourful past from its links with the influential Astor family. Visitors are treated as house guests and staff perpetuate the country house tradition of service. Bedrooms are steeped in quality and individual style. There is a range of reception rooms, for

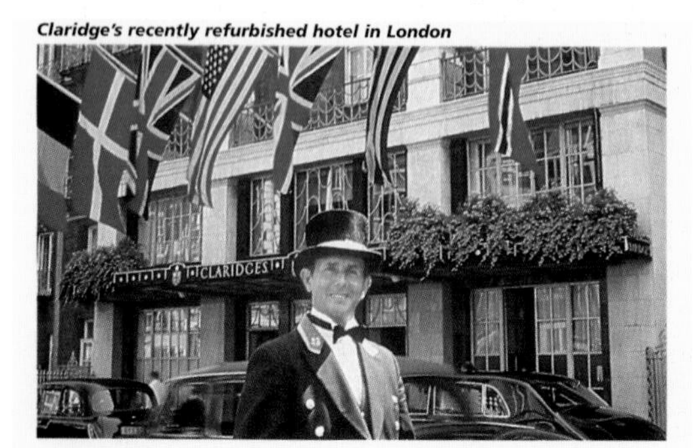
Claridge's recently refurbished hotel in London

PHONEDAY 2

Between June 1999 and Autumn 2000, more than 22 million telephone numbers will be altered as a result of PhoneDay2.

By 1 June 1999 all business systems must be able to accept numbers beginning 02. There will be a parallel running period during which the old 01 numbers can still be dialled. Full conversion of 01 to 02 must have taken place by 22 April 2000.

For example: for London numbers, the 020 code will replace 0171 and 0181, and local numbers will become eight-digit by adding 7 to the beginning of inner London numbers and 8 to outer London numbers.

These changes will affect some numbers printed in these pages.

quiet reflection, private dining and business purposes, with state-of-the-art facilities. Exceptional leisure facilites include cruises in the Astor electric canoe or the Thames Slipper Launch along Cliveden Reach.

CHESHIRE

★★★ ❀❀ **ROOKERY HALL**
Worleston, Nantwich
01270 610016
This imposing Regency mansion enjoys an enviable position in extensive gardens and grounds. Retaining much of its period charm and elegance, the hotel has nevertheless been modernised to appeal to both the corporate and leisure markets. Bedrooms are particularly spacious, each with a sumptuous bathroom and a range of thoughtful extras. Well-proportioned public rooms with real fires, fresh flowers and plenty of magazines, include an impressive hall and attractive drawing room.

★★★ ❀❀❀ **NUNSMERE HALL COUNTRY HOUSE**
Tarporley Road, Oakmere
01606 889100
Lovingly restored over the past ten years, this extended country house is peacefully situated in attractive gardens with a lake forming the boundary on three sides. Individually decorated and furnished rooms are very comfortable and thoughtfully equipped. The lounge, overlooking the garden, provides an appropriate setting for afternoon tea, while guests can also relax in the library or the oak-panelled bar.

CORNWALL & ISLES OF SCILLY

★★★ ❀❀❀ **WELL HOUSE**
St Keyne, Liskeard
01579 342001
This charming small hotel, in a valley setting between Liskeard and Looe, is the ideal location for a relaxing break. Bedrooms are tastefully furnished and well equipped, with personal touches such as fresh flowers to ensure a welcoming atmosphere. Public areas include an elegant sitting room, complete with log fire, and an intimate bar. There is an outdoor pool and tennis court, and afternoon tea with home-made biscuits is served on the terrace.

★★★ ❀❀❀ **ST MARTIN'S ON THE ISLE**
Lower Town, St Martin's
01720 422092
Designed in the 1980s and constructed from a cluster of cottages nestling in the hillside, this island hideaway is ideal for those looking for relaxation and tranquillity. The hotel has its own beach, jetty and yacht and enjoys unrivalled panoramic views of the sea and the surrounding islands. Individually decorated rooms have been named after local legends, places and events, and most have sea views. Public rooms have been cleverly designed with stone floors, split levels and refreshingly bold decor.

CUMBRIA

★★★ ❀❀ **FARLAM HALL HOTEL**
Hallbankgate, Brampton
016977 46234
This delightful country house, dating in part from the 16th century, stands in beautiful landscaped gardens. The lavish lounges promote relaxation with fine furnishings, open fires, reading material and a collection of traditional board games. Spacious bedrooms are opulently furnished and provide a myriad of thoughtful touches. The Victorian-style dining room is luxuriously elegant, with fine china and silver on crisp linen.

★★★ ❀❀❀ **MICHAEL'S NOOK COUNTRY HOUSE HOTEL**
Grasmere
015394 35496
Perched on the hills overlooking Grasmere, this fine, early Victorian Lakeland house offers the perfect retreat. The delightful bedrooms and day rooms are furnished with fine antique prints, rugs, furniture and porcelain, and provide every conceivable comfort, including blazing open fires in the elegant drawing room and the cosy bar. The service provided by the small team of dedicated staff is extremely friendly, discreet and professional.

★ ❀❀ **WHITE MOSS HOUSE**
Rydal Water, Grasmere
015394 35295
This traditional Lakeland house, close to Rydal Water, was once owned by William Wordsworth, but is now an intimate country hotel. Bedrooms are all individual, come in a variety of sizes and make excellent use of available space; they are also well equipped, enhanced by attractive fabrics. There is no bar, pre-dinner drinks being served in the lounge, with its books and coal fire. The five-course set dinner is served in the cosy cottage-style dining room.

★★★ ❀❀❀ **SHARROW BAY COUNTRY HOUSE**
near Pooley Bridge, Howtown
017684 86301
The enchanting Italianate Sharrow Bay sits in 12 acres of grounds on the shores of Lake Ullswater and has, arguably, the best views in England. Bedrooms are a delight, and whilst not all have en-suite facilities, they are all individually and thoughtfully furnished. Many are in the grounds, in cottages and also a lovely Elizabethan farmhouse, complete with its own lounge and breakfast room. Dinner at Sharrow is an occasion, the six-course meal being served by a smart and attentive team.

★ ❀❀ **SWINSIDE LODGE**
Newlands, Keswick
01768 72948
This delightful Victorian Lakeland house is surrounded by lush pasture, and enjoys delightful views; Derwentwater is just a five-minute stroll away. The house has a choice of

inviting lounges, packed with reading material and board games. In the bedrooms, decor is sparkling fresh, and the many extra touches include a supply of sweets, biscuits and a good range of toiletries. Set five-course dinners offer no choice until dessert, but are well thought out and imaginative. The house is unlicensed but guests are invited to bring their own wine.

★ ❀ **HIPPING HALL**
Cowan Bridge, Kirby Lonsdale
015242 71187
Set in four acres of beautiful grounds, complete with croquet lawns, this delightful country house offers an interesting and successful blend of architectural features, including a magnificent flagged baronial hall with minstrels' gallery. The well-equipped bedrooms are comfortable and offer many thoughtful touches.

★ ❀ **THE OLD CHURCH**
Old Church Bay, Watermillock
017684 86204
Commanding an enviable lakeside location, this splendid 18th-century country house enjoys stunning views of the lake and surrounding fells. Bedrooms come in three styles, but all excel in comfort, quality and equipment. Public areas are very relaxing. The lounge has a selection of board games and plenty of reading material, while the little bar is also inviting.

★★★ ❀❀❀ **GILPIN LODGE COUNTRY HOUSE HOTEL**
Crook Road, Windermere
015394 88818
This splendid Victorian residence nestles in 20 acres of woodlands, moors and gardens, so guests will find little difficulty relaxing once they arrive. Furnished with choice antiques and wonderful arrangements of fresh flowers, and warmed by real fires, the public rooms offer the perfect place to unwind and take afternoon tea. The stylishly decorated bedrooms are very comfortably furnished and some have four-poster beds or private sun terraces. Exceptional food, served in one of the three dining rooms, is another highlight of any stay.

★★★ ❀❀❀ **HOLBECK GHYLL**
Holbeck Lane, Windermere
015394 32375
Few hotels in the Lake District have views more dramatic than this delightful Victorian house: panoramic vistas stretch across Windermere Lake to the Langdale Fells beyond. The gently sloping grounds house a tennis court, and further leisure facilities have recently been added. Bedrooms are thoughtfully equipped and some have private balconies. Some rooms are in a separate cottage.

★★★ ❀❀ **MILLER HOWE HOTEL**
Rayrigg Road, Windermere
01534 42536
The delightfully furnished bedrooms of this popular hotel are generally spacious and share the wonderful views from

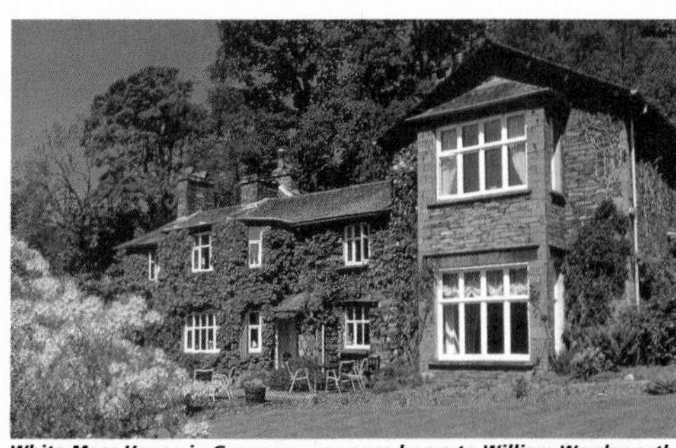
White Moss House in Grasmere was once home to William Wordsworth

the inviting lounges and the dining room, where many guests find themselves concentrating instead on the carefully prepared meals.

★ ❀❀ **THE OLD VICARAGE COUNTRY HOUSE HOTEL**
Church Road, Witherslack
015395 52381
Dating back to 1803, this delightful house retains many of its original features and is peacefully located in lovely gardens. Bedrooms in the main house are attractively decorated and furnished, with a number of fine antique pieces. Garden rooms are in modern buildings and tend to be larger. There is a choice of two lounges, one with an open log fire, and an intimate restaurant.

DERBYSHIRE

★★★ ❀❀ **THE CAVENDISH**
Baslow
01246 582311
This country house hotel enjoys an enviable position on the edge of the Chatsworth estate. Bedrooms are comfortably furnished and thoughtfully equipped with many extras, and the lounge provides a lovely setting in which to relax. Light meals are served all day in the Garden Room conservatory.

★★★ ❀❀❀ **FISCHER'S BASLOW HALL**
Calver Road, Baslow
01246 583259
Max and Susan Fischer's cosy country house hotel is ideal for business people and lovers of good food. This typical Derbyshire manor house has sumptuous bedrooms, and a few have kept their period bathroom fittings. Public rooms centre round the restaurant, and the slightly more casual Café-Max with its brasserie-style menu.

DEVON

★★ ❀❀ **BLAGDON MANOR COUNTRY HOTEL**
Ashwater
01409 211224
This delightful retreat, parts of which date back to the 16th century, is situated in rolling Devonshire countryside, and guests will find the atmosphere very relaxed. The seven bedrooms have luxury touches, such as bathrobes and superior quality bed linen. There is a choice of dayrooms: a soft-coloured Georgian lounge, a library, and a flagstoned bar with a snooker table. A magnificent table adorns the

elegant dining room, where guests enjoy a set dinner, based on fresh local produce.

★★ ❀❀ **HALMPSTONE MANOR**
Bishops Tawton, Barnstaple
01271 830321
This historic manor house is surrounded by the proprietors' working farm and land. The bedrooms, all individual, include two four-poster rooms, which are furnished with many personal touches, including sherry on arrival, fresh flowers, fruit and hot water bottles. The lounge, complete with log fire, is ideal to relax in after dinner, which is served in the candlelit panelled dining room.

★★★ ❀❀❀ **GIDLEIGH PARK**
Chagford
01647 432367
This well-kept mock Tudor house, set in 45 acres of the Dartmoor National Park, is the product of the tireless efforts of its owners, ably supported by a committed team of staff. Bedrooms vary in size and outlook but all guarantee the comforts expected of an hotel of such renown. The grounds contain running water, intriguing pools and banks, forests, peaceful retreats and a choice of sporting pursuits. Gourmets, bon viveurs and foodies are sure to find pleasure in the restaurant.

★★★ ❀❀ **LEWTRENCHARD MANOR**
Lewdown
01566 783256 & 783222
Surrounded by the lovely countryside of Dartmoor, the Jacobean manor of Lewtrenchard offers the highest standard of comfort but retains the atmosphere of a family home. Spacious bedrooms, each with its own personality, are equipped with modern facilities and have extensive views through leaded windows; fresh flowers, bottled waters and biscuits in every room are thoughtful touches. The public rooms feature ornate ceilings, oak panelling, carvings and large open fireplaces, combined with family antiques, warm colours and rich furnishings.

★ ❀❀ **HIGHCLIFFE HOUSE**
Sinai Hill, Lynton
01598 752235
This Victorian gentleman's residence has been made into a most delightful small hotel. Guests lucky enough to secure one of the six charming bedrooms will feel thoroughly

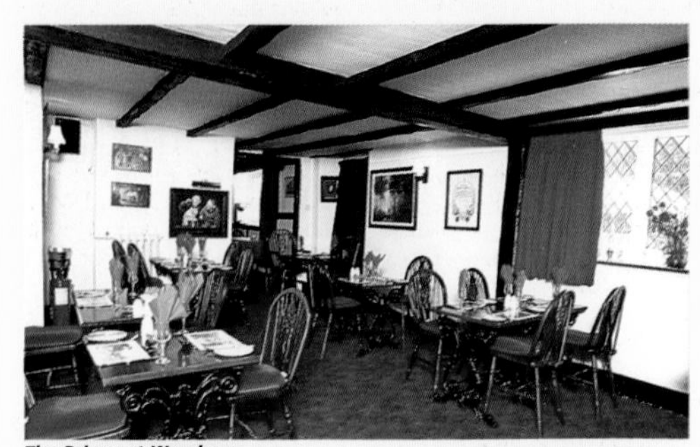
The Priory at Wareham

pampered. Situated 800 feet above the bay, the hotel enjoys spectacular views. There are two attractive lounges, both decorated entirely in keeping with the period of the house. Bedrooms are individually decorated with style and grace. Dinner in the elegant candlelit dining room is not to be missed. This hotel is totally non-smoking.

★★❀❀❀
WHITECHAPEL MANOR
South Molton
01769 573377
Situated in its own gardens and grounds on the edge of Exmoor, this delightful Grade I listed manor house is full of period character. Public areas include a choice of lounges with welcoming log fires during cooler months. The comfortable bedrooms are individually furnished and decorated and all rooms are well equipped. Whitechapel has gained a well deserved reputation for its cuisine and there is an interesting fixed-price menu of quality dishes.

★★❀ **WOODHAYES**
Whimple
01404 822237
Woodhayes is a charming Georgian house, tucked away in the country and yet only a short drive from either Exeter or Honiton, and set in four acres of lovely grounds. The owners offer a hospitable welcome and the cooking is of a very high standard. There are two tastefully decorated drawing rooms, with open fires in winter, and an attractive, well-stocked bar in farmhouse style. The comfortable, spacious bedrooms feature many extra personal touches and facilities.

DORSET
★★★❀❀❀
SUMMER LODGE
Evershot
01935 83424
Summer Lodge is situated in the centre of a picturesque Dorset village. The public rooms are comfortably furnished, and abundant floral arrangements, log fires and water colour paintings add to the genteel elegance. Bedrooms are individually furnished and decorated, and provided with thoughtful extras such as magazines, hot water bottles and fresh flowers. There is an interesting and imaginative daily set menu, with a seasonal carte also available.

★★★❀❀❀ **STOCK HILL COUNTRY HOUSE HOTEL**
Stock Hill, Gillingham
01747 823626
The beech-lined driveway gives a grand first impression of this delightful country house. The luxurious bedrooms are individually styled and furnished with a number of personal touches, antiques and ornaments. The hotel has eleven acres of mature grounds in which guests may wander freely, and a hard tennis court for those who wish to work off the calories. The restaurant cuisine combines modern ideas with traditional Austrian; the kitchen garden behind the hotel provides fresh ingredients.

★★★❀❀ **THE PRIORY**
Church Green, Wareham
01929 551666
Standing in four acres of beautiful gardens, this 16th-century former priory is situated on the banks of the River Frome. Steeped in history, the hotel offers luxurious bedrooms, all individually decorated with family antiques. Those in the adjacent boathouse are especially attractive. Throughout the public areas there is a relaxed atmosphere, with log fires and comfortable furnishings.

★★❀ **BEECHLEAS HOTEL**
17 Poole Road, Wimborne Minster
01202 841684
Within easy walking distance of the Minster, this elegant Georgian town house is located just to the south of the town centre. Furnished to a high standard, the spacious bedrooms are well equipped. The lounge is very comfortable and guests often take time to relax in the afternoons. The conservatory restaurant is bright and airy, and guests can choose from either the dinner or supper menus. Many of the ingredients are sourced from a local organic farm.

ESSEX
★★★❀❀
MAISON TALBOOTH
Stratford Road, Dedham
01206 322367
Overlooking tranquil Dedham Vale, this pretty Georgian hotel has always offered a warm welcome and attentive service. The spacious bedrooms are equipped with many thoughtful touches. There is a comfortable drawing room, with fresh flowers, period furniture and pictures, where guests may take

afternoon tea or snacks during the day. Excellent breakfasts are mainly served in the bedrooms. For dinner, Le Talbooth Restaurant is just down the road, a leisurely 15-minute walk in summer, though a courtesy car is provided.

GLOUCESTERSHIRE
★★★❀❀❀
BUCKLAND MANOR
Buckland, near Broadway
01386 852626
This 13th-century manor house stands on the edge of a secluded village, set on a hillside within extensive but impeccably maintained grounds. The welcoming public rooms have a wealth of fine period furniture, and bedrooms are spacious.

★★★❀❀
THE GREENWAY
Shurdington, Cheltenham
01242 862352
A charming Elizabethan manor house, the Greenway dates back to 1587 and is set amidst more than seven acres of well-tended gardens and beautiful countryside. The individually decorated bedrooms are divided between the main house and an adjacent Georgian coach house, and overlook a walled garden. The candlelit Conservatory Dining Room overlooks an illuminated sunken garden. Innovative recipes feature fresh local produce, herbs and spices, and the wine list has been carefully compiled to complement the food.

★★★❀❀
HOTEL ON THE PARK
38 Evesham Road, Cheltenham
01242 518898
A country house in style if not in location, this polished hotel offers quality throughout. Elegant ground floor public areas comprise a bar, restaurant and drawing room, with period furnishings and fine fabrics adding opulence to the relaxed comfort. Bedrooms are similarly appointed and include many pleasing touches such as sherry, mineral water and bath robes. The style of cuisine in the restaurant as distinctive as it is accomplished.

★★★❀❀
COTSWOLD HOUSE HOTEL & RESTAURANT
The Square, Chipping Campden
01386 840330
Proudly located in Chipping Campden's high street, this 17th-century house is now an elegant small hotel. Step inside and you will find charming public rooms, comfortably furnished with antiques and artworks. Log fires blaze invitingly in winter, and there are always pretty arrangements of fresh flowers. A choice of eating options is available with the informality of Forbes Brasserie supplementing the fine dining Garden Room Restaurant.

★★★❀❀❀
LOWER SLAUGHTER MANOR
Lower Slaughter
01451 820456
This country mansion stands in effortless tranquillity on the

edge of Lower Slaughter village. The immaculate stonework bears the mark of the Strong family, later responsible for St Paul's Cathedral. Such highly developed craftsmanship is reflected in the cooking, and ingredients are top-notch.

★★★❀❀ **CALCOT MANOR**
Calcot, Tetbury
01666 890391
Once a farmhouse belonging to Cistercian monks, this charming manor still has a 14th-century barn amongst its outbuildings. These days it is a beautifully appointed country house hotel offering high standards of accommodation guest care. The public areas include elegant and relaxing lounges where log fires burn in the winter, and a bright and modish restaurant which extends into a conservatory. Here one can sample some imaginative cooking with a Mediterranean bias and good robust flavours.

★★★❀❀ **THORNBURY CASTLE HOTEL**
Castle Street, Thornbury
01454 281182
This fine country house is unique in its adherence to the Tudor tradition. Food is an important pillar of the whole operation, and most dishes are a marriage of several carefully honed elements, with stuffing, parcelling and crusting being favoured techniques. The grounds feature classical gardens as well as a vineyard.

HAMPSHIRE
★★★❀❀❀ **HOLLINGTON COUNTRY HOUSE**
Woolton Hill, Highclere
01635 255100
Bedrooms at this charming country house are on two floors in the main house, with some in a nearby converted cottage. All are a fine size and decorated with great comfort, taste and an eye for detail. The public rooms have many architectural highlights, and the extensive grounds enjoy wonderful views and woodland walks. The excellent cuisine has some imaginative vegetarian dishes included among the modern British menus.

★★❀❀❀ **GORDLETON MILL**
Silver Street, Hordle, Lymington
01590 682219
Gordleton Mill is a little piece of Provence nestling in the Hampshire greenbelt, with lily-padded millponds, ivy-clad terracotta and sunny Mediterranean washes, and provençale tiles bordering a covered terrace. Themed evenings offer an excellent fixed-set menu with well-chosen accompanying wines.

★★★★❀❀❀
CHEWTON GLEN HOTEL
Christchurch Road, New Milton
01425 275341
Chewton Glen goes from strength to strength; sumptuous bathrooms and an abundance of comfort and quality are the result of continued investment and upgrading, particularly of the junior suites. High standards are complemented by

many thoughtful touches and efficient housekeeping. Good use is made of excellent raw ingredients in imaginative and innovative dishes. A comprehensive three course table d'hôte menu is offered at both lunch and dinner, as well as a lighter alternative at lunch.

★★★★❀❀ **TYLNEY HALL**
Rotherwick
01256 764881
Sixty-six acres of beautiful parkland surround Tylney Hall, a spacious Victorian country house with log fires and fine ceilings. The gardens (originally laid out by Gertrude Jekyll) are overlooked by the oak-panelled restaurant, a grand Victorian dining room where modern French cooking is the order of the day.

HEREFORDSHIRE
★❀❀
MARSH COUNTRY HOTEL
Eyton, Leominster
01568 613952
This 14th-century timber-framed house has an attractive 1½-acre garden, from where most of the vegetables and herbs for the table are produced. There is much character in the house, particularly in the splendid medieval great hall. The bedrooms, named after birds, are equally comfortable and welcoming. The overall effect is one of calm and tranquillity.

KENT
★★❀
KENNEL HOLT
Goudhurst Road, Cranbrook
01580 712032
This Elizabethan manor house is a charming oasis with five-acre gardens that are ideal for bird-watching or playing croquet. The relaxing public rooms are full of original features and historic charm, and there is a panelled library with a large collection of music and books. Individually styled bedrooms, some including four-poster beds, are comfortable and nicely furnished. Seasonal cuisine makes use of the best of local ingredients wherever possible.

LEICESTERSHIRE
★★★★❀❀
STAPLEFORD PARK
Melton Mowbray
01572 787522
Stapleford Park is the epitome of opulent English country living, and a sense of camaraderie and informality prevails which is more suggestive of a house party than a hotel. The dining room has magnificent 17th-century Grinling Gibbons carvings and is a suitably fine setting for the daily changing selection of dishes – which, in keeping with the whimsical notes found throughout the estate, always features at least one 'adult nursery' dish, such as deep-fried cod in yeast beer batter with home-made ketchup, or sausage and mash. Breakfasts are served on Beatrix Potter china.

LINCOLNSHIRE

★★❀❀❀
WINTERINGHAM FIELDS
Winteringham
01724 733096
This unassuming little hotel is superb. The house sits in the middle of a village a few hundred yards south of the Humber. There is a genuine warmth to the place and eating here is a pleasure. Swiss cuisine is combined with the local produce (Lincolnshire lamb, fish, home-grown salad leaves) and imaginative flair, to produce outstanding food.

NORFOLK

★★❀❀❀ **MORSTON HALL**
Blakeney
01263 741041
The flint-walled house, located in a small coastal village and dating from the 17th century, stands in delightful, well-tended gardens. The restaurant runs the width of the house, with garden views and well-spaced tables. The no-choice dinner is a fine, rewarding experience.

★★★❀❀
CONGHAM HALL HOTEL
Grimston
01485 600250
Secluded tree-lined gardens ensure privacy and tranquillity in this quintessentially English Georgian country retreat. Herbs and produce from the garden are used in the cooking. The menu, reflecting the chef's travels, reveals Mediterranean and Northern European influences.

OXFORDSHIRE

★★★★★❀❀❀❀
LE MANOIR AUX QUAT' SAISONS
Great Milton
0184 4278881
This delightful mellow stone 15th-century manor house, sympathetically restored and extended by Raymond Blanc, is peacefully positioned in immaculately maintained gardens, complete with interesting sculptures, and a traditional Japanese tea house. Bedrooms and suites, in both the main house and the converted stables, are beautifully appointed and offer a superb level of comfort. The highlight of any stay has to be the outstanding quality of the cuisine which earns the AA's supreme accolade of five rosettes.

RUTLAND

★★★★❀❀❀❀
HAMBLETON HALL
Oakham
01572 756991
The setting for Hambleton Hall is truly idyllic, surrounded by landscaped grounds and set against the backdrop of Rutland Water. Public rooms including the red lacquered bar and the elegant drawing room have stunning views of the lake. In the restaurant with its splendid silk wall coverings the menus change with the seasons; the desserts are particularly excellent.

SOMERSET

★★★★❀❀
THE QUEENSBERRY
Russel St, Bath
01225 447928
This carefully restored Bath-stone town house hotel is only a few minutes' walk from the city centre. Bedrooms are all individually furnished and tastefully decorated, boasting sofas and a number of thoughtful extras, such as fresh flowers, marble bathrooms with bath robes. On the ground floor there is a lounge and bar opening onto an enclosed courtyard garden. Hotel residents are advised to book in advance for the Olive Tree Restaurant, especially at weekends.

★★❀
ASHWICK HOUSE
Dulverton
01398 323868
Prepare to be pampered at this small Edwardian Hotel set in six acres on the edge of Exmoor. The atmosphere is relaxed and unhurried; guests can take tea or an aperitif on the terrace overlooking the grounds. Public areas are extensive, the main feature being the galleried hall with its welcoming log fire. Bedrooms are spacious and comfortable, with every conceivable facility, plus a few whimsical touches. Each evening a set menu is served using the finest of local produce.

★★★
HOMEWOOD PARK
Hinton Charterhouse
01225 723731
A model of small country house elegance, Homewood Park offers relaxed surroundings while still maintaining high standards of professionalism. Reached via a long drive, the mostly Georgian house is set in attractive grounds which include tennis courts and an outdoor heated swimming pool. Inside, the public areas are an invitation to sit back and take it easy, with welcoming sofas and roaring fires on winter days. In the kitchen the chef produces some masterful cooking based on classical foundations often with a inspired twist. The six-course tasting menu is an opportunity to sample the full range of his talents.

★★★❀❀
HUNSTRETE HOUSE HOTEL
Hunstrete
01761 490490
The 18th-century house stands in a 92-acre estate of park and woodland that can only be described as a haven of peace and tranquillity. The elegantly furnished public areas feature antiques, original paintings and and a collection of fine china. The cooking is highly creative with freshness and quality of ingredients of prime importance.

★★❀❀
THE OAKS
Porlock
01643 862265
Set in an elevated position, overlooking this charming village, The Oaks offers distant views of Porlock Bay. Bedrooms vary in size and have many thoughtful extras such as sherry, fresh fruit and flowers. The public rooms have been tastefully furnished with period pieces. During the summer, the garden is the perfect place to enjoy a drink before and after dinner. The cooking is another highlight of a stay here; the best of fresh local produce is carefully used in the preparation of some mouth-watering dishes.

★★★★❀❀
STON EASTON PARK
Ston Easton
01761 241631
Probably as authentic as surviving Palladian mansions get, Ston Easton rises majestically out of the classical parkland in which it is set. The grounds feature a man-made lake and plenty of scope for walking. Much effort has been devoted to refurbishment that chimes with the period. Food is taken seriously throughout the day, from breakfast-time croissants to excellent afternoon teas. Dinner offers a well-balanced menu and, while traditional British cuisine remains in the spotlight, it caters for a wide range of tastes.

★★★❀❀❀ **CASTLE HOTEL** Castle Green, Taunton
01823 272671
The setting of the Castle Hotel is remarkable: the wisteria-clad building is just a step from the town centre yet is tranquillity itself, sheltered by mature gardens. The restaurant is a lovely room, calm and serene. The cooking manages a balance between clever ideas and straightforwardness. Sourcing is all important and suppliers mostly hail from the West Country.

★★❀❀
LANGLEY HOUSE
Langley Marsh, Wiveliscombe
01984 623318
Parts of Langley House date back to the 16th century, while later additions bestow Georgian elegance. The property has been lovingly restored and refurbished, including the four-acre garden. There are deep armchairs in the boldly decorated sitting room where a log fire burns on colder evenings. Bedrooms vary in size and design, but all have thoughtful touches including fresh flowers, books, mineral water and hot water bottles in winter. The set menu makes use of the best of fresh and, whenever possible, local ingredients.

★❀❀
LITTLE BARWICK HOUSE
Barwick Village, Yeovil
01935 423902
Set amidst beautiful countryside on the edge of Yeovil, this charming, listed Georgian dower house enjoys the most peaceful of locations. The bedrooms are attractively decorated and feature many personal touches. Guests can enjoy afternoon tea in front of the fire in the cosy lounge or in the grounds of the secluded garden. Imaginative evening meals are served in the elegant dining room.

SUFFOLK

★★★★❀❀❀
HINTLESHAM HALL
Hintlesham
01473 652334
Hintlesham is a fine example of a country house hotel although its magnificent Georgian façade belies the Tudor origins of the house. The main dining room, The Salon, is elegant and grand, and noted for classical cuisine.

SURREY

★★❀ **LANGSHOTT MANOR**
Ladbroke Road, Horley
01293 786680
Set in beautiful gardens, this small Elizabethan manor house is a gem of a property. Day rooms include a cosy morning room/bar and a charming gallery sitting room. Bedrooms, some newly created in a separate mews house, combine modern comforts with great individuality. Dinner is served in the beamed dining room and makes good use of fresh, quality produce and sound cooking skills.

SUSSEX EAST

★★★❀❀
NETHERFIELD PLACE
Netherfield, Battle
01424 774455
Built in the 1920s in Georgian style, Netherfield Place is surrounded by fine gardens and 300 acres of parkland. This tranquil setting is matched by a peaceful atmosphere within: the lounge elegantly proportioned and civilised, the cocktail bar comfortable and welcoming. Accommodation varies from cosy rooms with dormer windows on the top floor to others where guests can luxuriate in spacious surroundings. The well balanced and interesting menu served in the panelled dining room makes good use of fresh produce from the hotel's own extensive kitchen garden.

★★★★❀❀
ASHDOWN PARK
Wych Cross, Forest Row
01342 824988
A splendid, vast country house overlooking a lake and set in fine grounds, Ashdown Park's previous roles have been as a home, a convent, and a management training centre. Today it is a very well-run hotel with a willing and friendly team of staff, many of whom have been there since it opened. There are some wonderful features, such as the chapel with stained glass windows and full working organ, in addition to excellent indoor and outdoor leisure facilities. One can enjoy refreshment on the terrace which overlooks the lake against a backdrop of stunning park and woodland. Bedrooms are spacious and decorated in traditional style.

★★★❀❀❀
HORSTED PLACE
Little Horsted, Uckfield
01825 750581
This magnificent Gothic-revival pile is surrounded by its own 100-acre estate, which includes the East Sussex National Golf Club. Inside is a splendid Pugin staircase and smart public rooms. Menus are assured and short, and offer a meeting point between traditional and contemporary ideas.

SUSSEX WEST

★★★★❀❀
AMBERLEY CASTLE
Amberley
01798 831992
Dating back to the 11th century, this castle is the real thing, complete with massive gate-house (with working portcullis) and high curtain walls concealing delightful gardens presided over by white peacocks. There are all sorts of discoveries to be made, from an ancient oubliette to garderobes (the last word in 14th-century sanitation). The castle has now been transformed into a luxury hotel with individually decorated bedrooms. Bathrooms, all with spa bathtubs, are reassuringly 20th-century. The Queens Room restaurant boasts a mural commemorating the visit here in 1685 of Catherine of Braganza, and sophisticated cooking based on carefully researched old English recipes.

★★★❀❀❀
GRAVETYE MANOR HOTEL
East Grinstead
01342 810567
A splendid Elizabethan manor house, this was one of the first of the grand post-war country house hotels, and it remains an exemplar of all that such a hotel should be. The walled kitchen garden is the source of much fresh produce, used to create an imaginative range of dishes.

★★★★❀❀❀
SOUTH LODGE HOTEL
Brighton Road, Lower Beeding
01403 891711
This beautifully restored Victorian mansion is the perfect

The impressive Georgian architecture of Netherfield Place

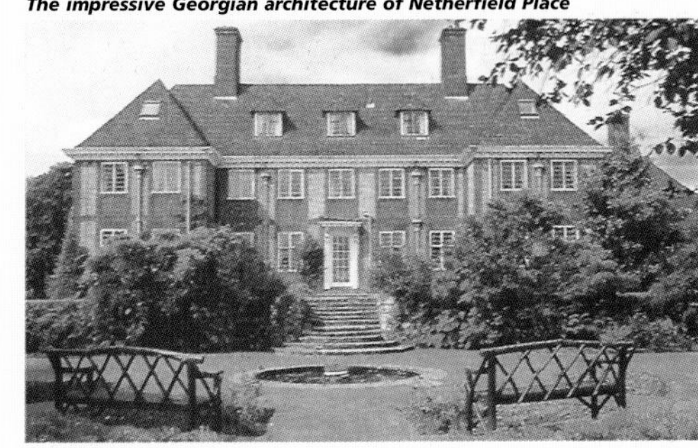

place for a quiet break. Escorted walks over the 90 acres of well-tended gardens are a good way to work up an appetite for the skilled, attentive cooking, pulling in influences from far and wide. Good use is made of produce grown in the hotel's walled garden.

★ ★ ★ ❀ ❀ ALEXANDER HOUSE
East St, Turners Hill
01342 714914
With its oldest part dating back to the 17th century, this is a particularly fine house set in 135 acres of well-tended gardens and grounds. Public rooms include the elegant and sunny south drawing room, and the oak-panelled library, warmed by a real log fire in winter months. Individually decorated bedrooms include six full suites, two with antique four-poster beds, one of which is believed to have been made for Napoleon. In the restaurant tail-coated waiters impress with highly polished service which complements the confident modern British cooking.

WARWICKSHIRE

★ ★ ★ ❀ ❀ ❀ MALLORY COURT HOTEL
Harbury Lane,
Bishop's Tachbrook,
Royal Leamington Spa
01926 330214
Study the carte over canapés in the comfortable lounge of this beautifully restored, chintzy English country house, set in 10 acres of landscaped grounds and lovely gardens. Move on to the panelled dining room or, in summer, the terrace, to enjoy the agreeably understated cooking. Service is friendly.

★ ❀ LANSDOWN HOTEL
87 Clarendon St, Royal
Leamington Spa
01926 450505
This Regency property is located just a short walk from the town centre. Bedrooms are individually decorated, attractively furnished and equipped with a good range of facilities. The comfortably appointed public rooms include a quiet lounge, a small bar and a pleasant dining room with a short and interesting set-priced carte, where quality fresh ingredients are carefully cooked and attractively presented.

WEST MIDLANDS

★ ★ ★ ❀ ❀ NUTHURST GRANGE HOTEL
Hockley Heath
01564 783972
Conveniently located close to the motorway network and just a short drive from Birmingham International airport, Nuthurst Grange lies secluded in seven acres of delightfully landscaped grounds and is approached by a long avenue. Imaginative menus embrace the best of modern and classical British and French cuisine, which is complemented by an interesting and varied fine wine list. Bedrooms are spacious and comfortable. A special feature is the heli-pad which is available for guests wishing to arrive by air.

★ ★ ★ ★ ❀ ❀ NEW HALL
Walmley Rd, Sutton Coldfield
0121 378 2442
Set in immaculate grounds and gardens, this beautifully restored hotel is reputedly the oldest moated manor house in England. The lovely grounds include a walled rose garden, a yew tree walk and an ornamental pool, as well as several leisure facilities. The day rooms retain many original features; the thoughtfully equipped bedrooms vary in size and are divided between the main house and a purpose-built wing. The delightful dining room is the showcase for the kitchen brigade to show off their care and dedication in creating fresh-tasting dishes.

WILTSHIRE

★ ★ ★ ★ ❀ ❀ MANOR HOUSE HOTEL
Castle Combe
01249 782206
Set in 26 acres of grounds with a romantic Italian garden, this 14th-century country house has been sympathetically extended to provide superbly furnished rooms. Public areas include a number of small lounge areas, some with roaring fires during the cooler months. Bedrooms situated in a row of original stone cottages within the grounds are currently being upgraded to the same standard as those in the main house. Service is both professional and friendly, while the meals continue to impress.

★ ★ ★ ★ ❀ ❀ ❀ LUCKNAM PARK
Colerne
01225 742777
This magnificent Palladian mansion boasts a mile-long, tree-lined drive, 500 acres of parkland, elegant public rooms, and extensive leisure facilities. The cooking includes the traditional – Dover sole with chips, pea purée and parsley sauce, for example – alongside the more complex.

WORCESTERSHIRE

★ ★ ★ ★ ❀ ❀ ❀ LYGON ARMS Broadway
01386 852255
Ideally situated in the centre of the ever popular village, this distinctive hotel has been sympathetically extended from an original 16th-century coaching inn. Bedrooms vary in style and layout, but each offers comfort and modern facilities plus some fine antique furniture. An air of quiet restfulness permeates the different lounge areas, some with open log fires, and the wine bar has a more informal atmosphere. The main restaurant is located in the Great Hall, featuring heraldic panels and a minstrels' gallery.

★ ★ ★ ❀ ❀ BROCKENCOTE HALL COUNTRY HOUSE HOTEL
Chaddesley Corbett
01562 777876
Set in the Worcestershire countryside, this Victorian mansion stands in its own extensive parkland, with a

Tudor dovecote, lake with varied waterfowl, and many fine specimen trees. There is an open fire in the lobby, a sunny conservatory lounge and a light and elegant dining room.

YORKSHIRE, NORTH

★ ★ ★ ❀ ❀ DEVONSHIRE ARMS COUNTRY HOUSE HOTEL
Bolton Abbey
01756 710441
Sedately situated in the picturesque Wharfe valley and bordered by the rolling hills of the Yorkshire Dales, this stylish country house hotel is owned by the Duke and Duchess of Devonshire, who take a personal interest in the operation and have loaned many pieces of furniture and art to adorn it. Leisure facilities are attractively located within a converted stone barn, and there is a choice of comfortable lounges. A new brasserie has recently been built and an eclectic range of dishes features local produce, some of it grown in the hotel's own kitchen garden.

★ ★ ★ ❀ ❀ THE GRANGE
1 Clifton, York
01904 644744
This bustling Regency town house is just a few minutes' walk from York's centre, and is furnished in country house style. The individually designed bedrooms have been thoughtfully equipped for the needs of business and leisure guests. There is a sunny morning room, a first-floor drawing room and a library, both licensed for wedding ceremonies and receptions. Dining options include a seafood bar, a popular and informal brasserie and the Ivy Restaurant, serving seasonal, rosette-worthy cuisine.

★ ★ ★ ❀ ❀ ❀ MIDDLETHORPE HALL
Bishopthorpe Road, York
01904 641241
This magnificent William III country house is located close to the city centre. Dinner is served in either the Oak or Marble dining room, with a more informal alternative offered by the Grill Room. Short menus are built on prime seasonal produce and usually include an interesting twist.

CHANNEL ISLANDS

★ ★ ★ ❀ ❀ CHATEAU LA CLAIRE
Rozel Bay, Jersey
01534 863354
High up over Rozel Bay, Chateau La Chaire is set on the side of a wooded valley and surrounded by five acres of terraced gardens; the higher you climb, the more striking the sea-views. Built as a gentleman's residence in 1843, the Chateau retains much of the atmosphere of a private country house, including some exquisite decorative plaster work in the drawing room. The oak-panelled dining room, with a conservatory extension, is a fine setting for some skilful and consistent cooking using the

best of local produce with many contemporary touches.

★ ★ ★ ★ ❀ ❀ ❀ LONGUEVILLE MANOR
St Saviour, Jersey
01534 25501
With parts of this prestigious estate dating back to the 13th century, it is not short of character or history. The twin dining rooms (one is reserved for non-smokers) feature ancient, heavily carved oak-panelling and provide an appropriately refined setting for the fine modern English cooking.

SCOTLAND

ABERDEENSHIRE

★ ★ ❀ ❀ BALGONIE COUNTRY HOUSE
Braemar Place, Ballater
013397 55482
A charming small country house, the hotel is Edwardian in style, set in four acres of mature gardens with superb views towards the hills of Glen Muick. Well maintained bedrooms offer two styles: the first-floor rooms are furnished in period character, while those on the top floor have a more modern feel. Public areas include a choice of inviting lounges, one with a bar. The elegant dining room is a perfect setting for the well produced food which is strong in local produce.

★ ★ ❀ THE OLD MANSE OF MARNOCH
Bridge of Marnoch
01466 780873
Standing on the bank of a river and set in mature gardens, this 200-year-old granite building has, as the proprietors describe it, 'a distinct churchy history'. Within, a relaxed atmosphere prevails, with an inviting lounge full of mementoes of the owners' travels. Not surprisingly, there's a good choice of malt whiskies.

★ ★ ★ ❀ KILDRUMMY CASTLE
Kildrummy
019755 71288
This Victorian country mansion overlooks the ruins of a nearby 13th-century castle, and stands in magnificent landscaped gardens. Inside, spacious reception rooms lead from the inviting hall and feature either oak or intricate plaster ceilings and walls hung with tapestries. The bedrooms are individually furnished, some with antiques, while others are of a more modern style.

ARGYLL & BUTE

★ ★ ★ ❀ ❀ ISLE OF ERISKA
Eriska
01631 720371
This is about as exclusive as a venue can get, on a private island. The building is an imposing baronial mansion, but the atmosphere unpretentious. The restaurant harvests many of its ingredients from the island, including wild garlic. The concise menu concentrates

on contemporary Scottish and French dishes.

★ ★ ❀ KILLIECHRONAN HOUSE
Killiechronan Estate, Isle of Mull
01680 300403
This small country house hotel is set within its own estate in one of Mull's many quieter corners at the head of Loch na Keal. All the comforts of a private house are provided with enthusiastic service. The two sitting rooms offer good levels of comfort and a host of reading material, and the two small and elegant dining rooms are where guests will enjoy the fine five-course dinners. The attractively decorated bedrooms are individual in style, many retaining the original period bathrooms.

★ ★ ★ ❀ ❀ ❀ AIRDS HOTEL
Port Appin
01631 730236
Elegant, luxurious and unpretentious are words that well describe this former inn on Loch Linnhe. As you enter, resist the temptation to sit and gaze over the garden and loch (you can do that from the dining room). Dishes are of the highest order, with the emphasis on local produce.

DUMFRIES & GALLOWAY

★ ❀ ❀ WELL VIEW
Ballplay Road, Moffat
01683 220184
This delightful Victorian house is set in gardens overlooking the town. It has a friendly and cosy atmosphere and one can relax in the lounge with board games or plenty to read, with a log fire in season. Bedrooms are individually decorated and thoughtfully equipped with little extra touches such as bathrobes and fruit. Most rooms are of good size and include a suite and mini-suite. The six-course dinner is cooked in a light, contemporary style.

★ ★ ★ ❀ ❀ ❀ KIRROUGHTREE HOUSE
Minnigaff, Newton Stewart
01671 402141
Standing in an elevated position about a mile north from the town, this impressive 17th-century mansion is set amid attractively landscaped gardens and eight acres of rolling forestry. Comfortable and spacious bedrooms are well equipped with modern facilities and offer many personal touches. The lounges are noted for their comfort and elegance, with deep sofas and tasteful antique furniture. There are two stately dining rooms serving fine dishes from an extensive range of local produce.

❀ ❀ ❀ KNOCKINAAM LODGE
Portpatrick
01776 810471
This small hotel has built a deserved reputation for both its hospitality and its fine cuisine. The secluded house is beautifully located in a cove at the end of a three-mile drive from the main road; it is bordered on three sides by

cliffs, while the lawns to the front lead down to the beach. Public areas include a morning room that overlooks the sea, an elegant drawing room and a cosy bar. Bedrooms vary in size, are brightly decorated and have many thoughtful touches including fine linens, the plumpest of pillows and warm electric blankets.

EAST LOTHIAN

★★★❀❀
GREYWALLS HOTEL
Muirfield, Gullane
01620 842144
Created as a hotel 50 years ago, Greywalls is a stunning Edwardian country house set in gardens laid out by Gertrude Jekyll. Within are enticing plump cushions and sumptuous furnishings, log fires and a grand piano, while the dining room has spectacular views over Muirfield golf course and the distant Firth of Forth.

FIFE

★★★★❀❀
BALBIRNIE HOUSE
Balbirnie Park, Markinch
01592 610066
A luxury hotel in the heart of the Kingdom of Fife, Balbirnie House is the centrepiece of a 416-acre estate where trees and rhododendrons abound. The Georgian mansion has been lovingly restored and attracts a loyal clientele. The magnificent day rooms, warmed by open fires and furnished with antiques, include a choice of three sitting rooms, one of which has a bar. The elegant restaurant is a relaxed yet formal environmnent for guests to enjoy the innovative cuisine.

★★❀❀❀ **THE PEAT INN**
Peat Inn
01334 840206
The dedicated owners have built up an enviable reputation for the excellence of their kitchen at this charming restaurant with rooms in rural Fife. The former old coaching inn stands at the cross-roads in the village to which it has given its name, just six miles from St Andrews. The restaurant is quite cosy, being arranged in sections so that if there are only a few diners they will not feel marooned. The inn also offers delicious home baking.

GLASGOW, CITY OF

★★★❀❀
ONE DEVONSHIRE GARDENS
Glasgow
0141 339 2001
Discreetly situated in a leafy terrace on the city's west side, this very individual hotel comprises three adjoining but not interconnecting town houses, each with bedrooms notable for their striking decor, sumptuous fabrics, subdued lighting and luxurious bathrooms. Each room has a music system, mini bar, and fresh flowers and fruit. In one house a stylish drawing room and bar are reserved for residents, whilst in another, an equally elegant cocktail lounge serves the restaurant.

HIGHLAND

★★★❀❀
ARISAIG HOUSE
Beasdale, Arisaig
01687 450622
A solid Scottish mansion set amongst oaks and rhododendrons. Its dining room is stately, with well-spaced tables and a set-price menu. The kitchen concentrates on getting the simple things right, and succeeds in mixing classical and modern ideas.

★★★★❀❀❀
INVERLOCHY CASTLE
Torlundy, Fort William
01397 702177
Exclusive and refined, but also offering a warm welcome, Inverlochy is one of the best hotels in Scotland. The restaurant is necessarily smart, with polished tables and superb views across the mountains to Fort William. The menu is dominated by Scottish produce.

★★❀ **DUNAIN PARK**
Inverness
01463 230512
Set in six acres of gardens, this delightful Georgian villa is superbly situated just outside Inverness. The individually designed and thoughtfully equipped bedrooms include a number of suites with small sitting rooms. The comfortable public rooms are filled with family photographs and fresh flowers, and on cooler evenings are warmed by open fires. Dinner is a highlight, and, as well as a good wine list, there are also over 200 malt whiskies on offer.

★❀❀❀ **HARLOSH HOUSE**
Harlosh, Isle of Skye
01470 521367
Harlosh House couldn't have a more perfect, tranquil setting: it's right on the shore of Loch Bracadale, with views to the Cuillin Hills. As might be expected, the sea provides most of the ingredients that appear at dinner, an inspired four-course meal with no choice until pudding; dedicated meat-eaters take heed.

★★❀❀❀ **THE CROSS**
Tweed Mill Brae, Kingussie
01540 661166
This converted tweed mill is set beside a stream and offers lovely accommodation with many thoughtful touches. The bright lounge provides comfortable seating with plenty of reading material and a television. There is an additional lounge where diners may enjoy an aperitif before the superb five-course fixed-price dinner. The dining room is spacious and comfortable and there is an excellent continental-style selection for breakfast.

★❀❀ **THE DOWER HOUSE**
Highfield, Muir of Ord
01463 870090
Just a few miles north of Inverness at the base of the Black Isle, this charming cottage hotel is an ideal location from which to explore the Highlands of Scotland. Lovingly and discreetly run, the house nestles

in four acres of secluded grounds. The dining room is small and intimate, which makes booking ahead essential.

★★❀❀ **KNOCKIE LODGE**
Whitebridge
01456 486276
Built as a shooting lodge over 200 years ago, Knockie Lodge enjoys a peaceful yet dramatic setting overlooking Loch nan Lann. Guests can enjoy afternoon tea in the comfortable lounge, with its log fire, honesty bar and periodicals, relax in the conservatory, or retire to the quieter lounge, which leads to the snooker room. The five-course set dinners are preceded by mouth-watering canapés in the lounge. Bedrooms, in a variety of sizes and styles, and are graced with personal touches, but don't expect TV.

PERTH & KINROSS

★★★★★❀❀❀
THE GLENEAGLES HOTEL
Auchterarder
01764 662231
Gleneagles may be a golfer's paradise but it also offers an outstanding range of other activities, even falconry. Afternoon tea is served in the drawing room, drinks in the cocktail bar, and the elegant Strathearn Restaurant, where a pianist plays, is the place for dinner. Using the finest ingredients, the kitchen places a modern, Scottish slant on traditional fare.

★★★❀❀❀ **KINLOCH HOUSE HOTEL**
Blairgowrie
01250 884237
An exceptional list of malt whiskies is one of the star attractions at this fine Scottish country residence, with its oak-panelled hall and first-floor galleries. A sign of the times, however, is the quality assurance printed on the back of the carte, which covers the sourcing of ingredients and guarantees nothing is made with genetically modified materials.

★★★❀❀❀ **KINNAIRD**
Kinnaird, Dunkeld
01796 482440
Kinnaird is a magnificent pile of a place, and the extensive grounds really do give meaning to the words 'Scottish baronial'. This is country house living on a grand scale, but without stuffiness, and the service is professional and friendly. Visitors tend to enthuse about the river valley view, enjoy the high level of cooking and look forward to returning.

SOUTH AYRSHIRE

★★★❀❀
LOCHGREEN HOUSE
Monkton Hill Rd, Southwood, Troon
01292 313343
Four dining rooms and two sumptuous sitting rooms are offered in this fine country house hotel. From the wooded and landscaped gardens visitors enjoy views over the golf course, the Firth of Clyde and Ailsa Craig. In addition to the

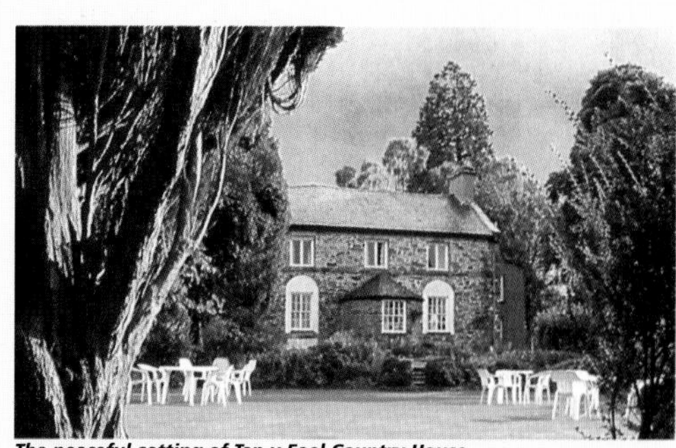
The peaceful setting of Tan-y-Foel Country House

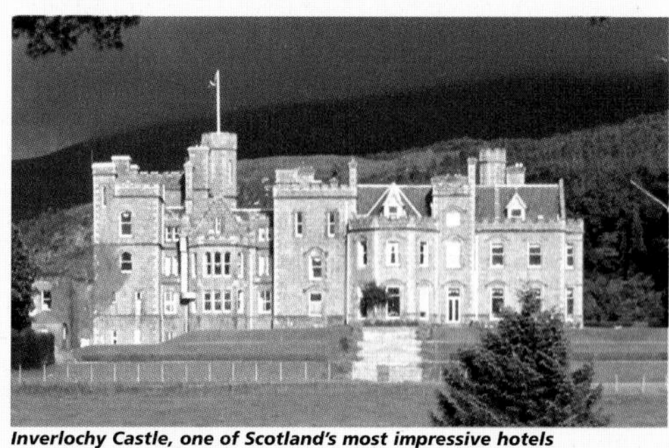
Inverlochy Castle, one of Scotland's most impressive hotels

option of the formal restaurant, guests can take meals in the library or in one of the two conservatories.

★★★★★❀❀ **TURNBERRY HOTEL, GOLF COURSES AND SPA**
Turnberry
01655 331000
Set in 800 acres of countryside with spectacular views over the Firth of Clyde, the hotel is world famous for its golf courses. The main restaurant (choose from three) has something of the time-warp air of an ocean-going liner, and serves dishes from a classic repertoire using prime Scottish ingredients.

STIRLING

★★★❀❀ **CROMLIX HOUSE**
Kinbuck, Dunblane
01786 822125
Set amid a 3,000-acre estate and surrounded by the gentle Perthshire countryside, Cromlix is a haven of tranquillity which is easily accessed off the A9. The diverse architectural styles of the interior are particularly evident in the wonderful day rooms, most of which are enhanced by roaring log fires and pretty floral displays. Deep-cushioned sofas and easy chairs in the morning room invite peaceful relaxation, while other inviting sitting areas are available in the hall and upstairs library. Bedrooms are very individual in style and most have their own private sitting rooms; all are furnished in period style.

★❀❀ **CREAGAN HOUSE**
Strathyre
01877 384638
This old 17th-century farmhouse, in the heart of the Queen Elizabeth Forest Park, has been converted into a most charming, cosy hotel. Carefully chosen antique pieces furnish the attractive bedrooms (including one with a hand-

made four-poster bed) that are equipped with many extra little comforts and individual touches. The sitting room is comfortable and amply provided with books and magazines; refreshments are willingly served here before or after an enjoyable meal in the impressive baronial-style restaurant.

WALES

CEREDIGION

★★★❀❀❀ **YNYSHIR HALL**
Eglwysfach
01654 781209
Set in 12 acres of mature gardens and surrounded by majestic scenery, this welcoming hotel offers a truly peaceful retreat. Individually designed bedrooms, varying in size, are delightfully furnished and equipped with a range of thoughtful extras. Both the bar and the drawing room are warmed by open fires during the cooler months and adorned by paintings of local views. The newly refurbished dining room provides the ideal setting for imaginative cuisine featuring a separate menu for vegetarians.

CONWY

★★❀❀ **TAN-Y-FOEL COUNTRY HOUSE HOTEL**
Capel Garmon, Betws-Y-Coed
01690 710507
This immaculately maintained 16th-century manor stands on a hillside with glorious views across the Conwy Valley towards the Snowdon mountain range. An abundance of reading material is provided within the two cosy lounges and both have cheerful log fires in the winter months. The dining room has been extended into a small conservatory area; cooking features the finest of Welsh produce. Individually decorated

and tastefully furnished bedrooms are all neatly presented; some have four-poster or brass bedsteads and most have delightful views.

★★ ◉ ◉
THE OLD RECTORY COUNTRY HOUSE
Llansanffraid Glan Conwy, Conwy
01492 580611
An oasis of calm and sums up this charming small hotel, with its delightful terraced gardens overlooking the Conwy Estuary and Snowdonia beyond. Inside, the intimate yet striking panelled public rooms are complemented by the classical interior design and antique pieces. Bedrooms are tastefully furnished in style with the building; two bedrooms are in a converted building in the grounds and can be used as a family suite if required. Dinner is served at individual tables but guests are seated at the same time, having enjoyed drinks and canapés together beforehand.

★★★ ◉ ◉
BODYSGALLEN HALL
Llandudno
01492 584466
Conwy Castle and Snowdonia provide the backdrop for this 17th-century country house set in 200 acres of parkland and superb formal gardens. The interior matches the magnificent surroundings, with wood panelled walls adorned with old masters. The spacious bedrooms are thoughtfully appointed; some are located in converted cottages in the grounds. The restaurant is the venue for some ambitious cooking with an emphasis on the best of local ingredients. The Spa leisure facilities offer guests the chance to burn off a few of the resulting calories.

★★ ◉ ◉ ◉
ST TUDNO
Promenade, Llandudno
01492 874411
For over 25 years, this famous seafront hotel has set the standard for other resort hotels. Although not the place for buckets and spades, toddlers will receive the same warm welcome as all the other guests. Bedrooms, some with sea views, offer a choice of sizes and individual styles. Public rooms include a non-smoking lounge, a convivial bar-lounge, and a small indoor swimming pool with good changing facilities. Menus in the air-conditioned Garden Room Restaurant specialise in local produce.

DENBIGHSHIRE
★★ ◉ ◉ ◉ **TYDDYN LLAN COUNTRY HOUSE HOTEL AND RESTAURANT**
Llandrillo
01490 440264
Set in landscaped gardens amongst fine scenery, this Georgian house provides an idyllic country retreat. The public rooms offer considerable comfort with a series of delightful lounges, warmed by roaring log fires during winter

months, and the elegantly appointed restaurant features an imaginative selection of dishes, created from quality local produce. Bedrooms are individually styled, each tastefully furnished.

GWYNEDD
★★ ◉ ◉ ◉
HOTEL MAES Y NEUADD
Talsarnau
01766 780200
This Welsh granite house sits in its own grounds, overlooking the kitchen gardens and Snowdonia National Park. Parts of the house date back to the 14th century, with granite walls some five feet thick. Attractively furnished bedrooms, four of which are in an adjacent coach house, boast many antique and period pieces.

POWYS
★★★ ◉ ◉
LAKE COUNTRY HOUSE
Llangammarsh Well
01591 620202
Perched on a hillside in verdant mid-Wales countryside, this special hotel offers warm hospitality and attentive service in elegant surroundings. Lavish afternoon teas are served in the lounge, where a log fire is a welcome comfort on winter days. In addition to the high-ceilinged restaurant there is a separate bar and also a billiard room. The bedrooms are mostly suite arrangements, individually decorated. The traditionally good standard of the hotel's cuisine is complemented by an extensive wine list.

★★★★ ◉ ◉ ◉
LLANGOED HALL
Llyswen
01874 754525
This imposing, largely Edwardian country house offers an exterior remodelled by Clough Williams-Ellis (of Portmeirion fame). Inside, Sir Bernard Ashley's uncompromising touch is responsible for a splendid balance between comfort, grandeur and interest. The bedrooms are appointed with a complementary mix of Laura Ashley designs and antiques, together with smart bathrooms. The opulent surroundings are matched by accomplished, imaginative cooking.

SWANSEA
★★ ◉ ◉ ◉ **FAIRYHILL**
Reynoldston
01792 390139
This impressive stone-built 18th-century mansion is delightfully set in 24 acres of wooded grounds, complete with stream and lake, in the heart of the Gower. The owners continue to improve the accommodation and share a desire to ensure that guests enjoy the best of care. Bedrooms are tastefully decorated and furnished in styles which accentuate the character of the house. There is a choice of comfortable sitting areas, and in season crackling log fires contribute to the atmosphere of warmth and relaxation.

IRELAND

CLARE
★★★ ◉ ◉
GREGANS CASTLE
Ballyvaughan
065 7077005
Standing at the foot of Corkscrew Hill with dramatic views over Galway Bay, the hotel is situated in an area rich in archaeological, geological and botanical interest. A high level of personal service and hospitality have earned special commendations in recent years, and the emphasis is on good food using fresh local produce.

CORK
★★★ ◉ ◉ ◉
LONGUEVILLE HOUSE HOTEL
Mallow
022 47156 & 47306
Set in a wooded estate, this 18th-century Georgian mansion has many fine features. The comfortable bedrooms overlook the river valley or a courtyard maze. The two elegant sitting rooms have fine examples of Italian plasterwork, and an Adam mantlepiece graces the President's Restaurant. The chef shows flair and sureness of touch in the preparation of an exciting range of dishes based on excellent fresh produce.

DUBLIN
★★★★ ◉ ◉ ◉
THE CLARENCE
6-8 Wellington Quay, Dublin
01 6709000
A resoundingly different and discerningly tasteful hotel, where the best architectural features of the 1850s have been combined with contemporary design. The bedrooms feature specially crafted American oak furniture and rich-coloured furnishings to superb effect, with all modern comforts provided. For sheer luxury, the two-bedroom penthouse suite is outstanding. Public areas include a long gallery with a baby grand piano and luxurious sofas, while an outdoor jacuzzi on the terrace has 360-degree views of the city. The bar is very smart, and the restaurant serves well-presented food.

GALWAY
★★★ ◉ ◉ **CASHEL HOUSE**
Cashel
095 31001
Award-winning gardens are the setting for this gracious country house hotel, which overlooks Cashel Bay. Rich fabrics and antique furnishings contribute to the atmosphere of luxury and peaceful elegance. The comfortable lounges have turf fires and antique furnishings, and the restaurant offers local produce such as Connemara lamb, skilfully prepared. Bedrooms are appealing, and luxury suites are available.

★★★★ ◉ ◉ **GLENLO ABBEY**
Bushypark, Galway
091 526666
Standing in a landscaped 134-acre estate, this restored 18th-century abbey overlooks the

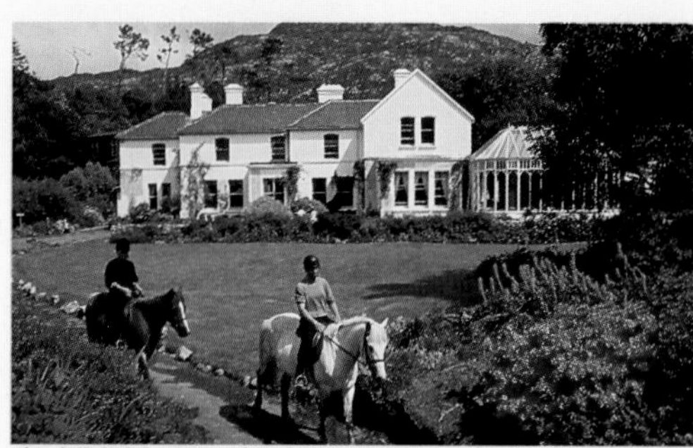
The delightful setting of Cashel House in County Galway

beautiful loch. The handsome original building now houses a boardroom, business centre, and conference and banqueting facilities. The bedrooms are housed in a well-designed modern wing with a library, restaurants, cocktail and cellar bars. Leisure facilities are situated in the grounds.

KERRY
★★★★ ◉ ◉ ◉
PARK HOTEL KENMARE
Kenmare
064 41200
The Park is synonymous with all the expectations of a luxurious country house hotel. On the famous Ring of Kerry, it stands above terraced gardens which overlook the estuary of the Kenmare River, with a glorious backdrop of mountains. Splendid antique furnishings, warm hospitality and sheer professionalism combine to draw guests back here time after time, and the restaurant offers good food and fine wines.

★★★★ ◉ ◉ ◉
SHEEN FALLS LODGE
Kenmare
064 41600
This beautifully appointed hotel, situated beside the Sheen River in 300 acres of glorious countryside, is surrounded by some of County Kerry's most stunning lake and mountain scenery. The cascading Sheen Falls are floodlit at night, creating a magical atmosphere which can be enjoyed from the public rooms and the restaurant, where menus featuring fresh local produce and home-grown herbs are a speciality. A luxurious lounge, well-stocked library, billiards room and cocktail bar are conducive to relaxation, and bedrooms, in three grades, are all spacious, comfortable and well equipped.

KILDARE
★★★★★ ◉ ◉ ◉
THE KILDARE HOTEL & COUNTRY CLUB
Straffan
01 6017200
In the heart of horse-breeding territory, in 330 acres of parkland beside the River Liffey, this very grand and luxurious hotel is known not only for its Arnold Palmer-designed golf course, and private fishing, but also for its country elegance and the quality of its decor and furnishings. Paintings, antiques and rugs enhance

the atmosphere, and bedrooms are well furnished and comfortable. The Arnold Palmer Conference and Banqueting Room and the new Clubhouse Restaurant for members provide fine facilities overlooking the course. The choice of menus features dishes cooked in French or speciality Irish style.

KILKENNY
★★★★ ◉ ◉ **MOUNT JULIET**
Thomastown
056 73000
Set in 1,500 acres of parkland, including a Jack Nicklaus-designed golf course where the Irish Opens were played in 1993 and 1994, this beautiful Palladian mansion is now a very special hotel. The elegant and spacious public rooms retain much of the original architectural features, including ornate plasterwork and fine Adam fireplaces in the cocktail bar, restaurant and drawing room.

WEXFORD
★★★ ◉ ◉
MARLFIELD HOUSE
Gorey
055 21124
This distinctive Regency house was once the residence of the Earl of Courtown, and today the hotel retains an atmosphere of elegance and luxury throughout its well-proportioned day rooms, which include an entrance foyer, library, drawing room and dining room leading into a fine conservatory, which looks out over the grounds as well as a wildlife preserve. Bedrooms are in keeping with the style of the downstairs rooms and there are some superb suites. Druids Glen and several other golf courses are within easy reach.

WICKLOW
★★★ ◉ ◉
TINAKILLY COUNTRY HOUSE & RESTAURANT
Rathnew
0404 69274
Built in 1870, this elegant house is set in seven acres of 19th-century gardens with breathtaking views of the sea. The highest standards of accommodation and hospitality are offered and the bedrooms are tastefully decorated with period furnishings; some of them feature four-poster beds. Country house cuisine is served, with the emphasis on fresh fish, local game and home-grown vegetables.

AA

ROAD ATLAS
OF THE
BRITISH
ISLES
2001

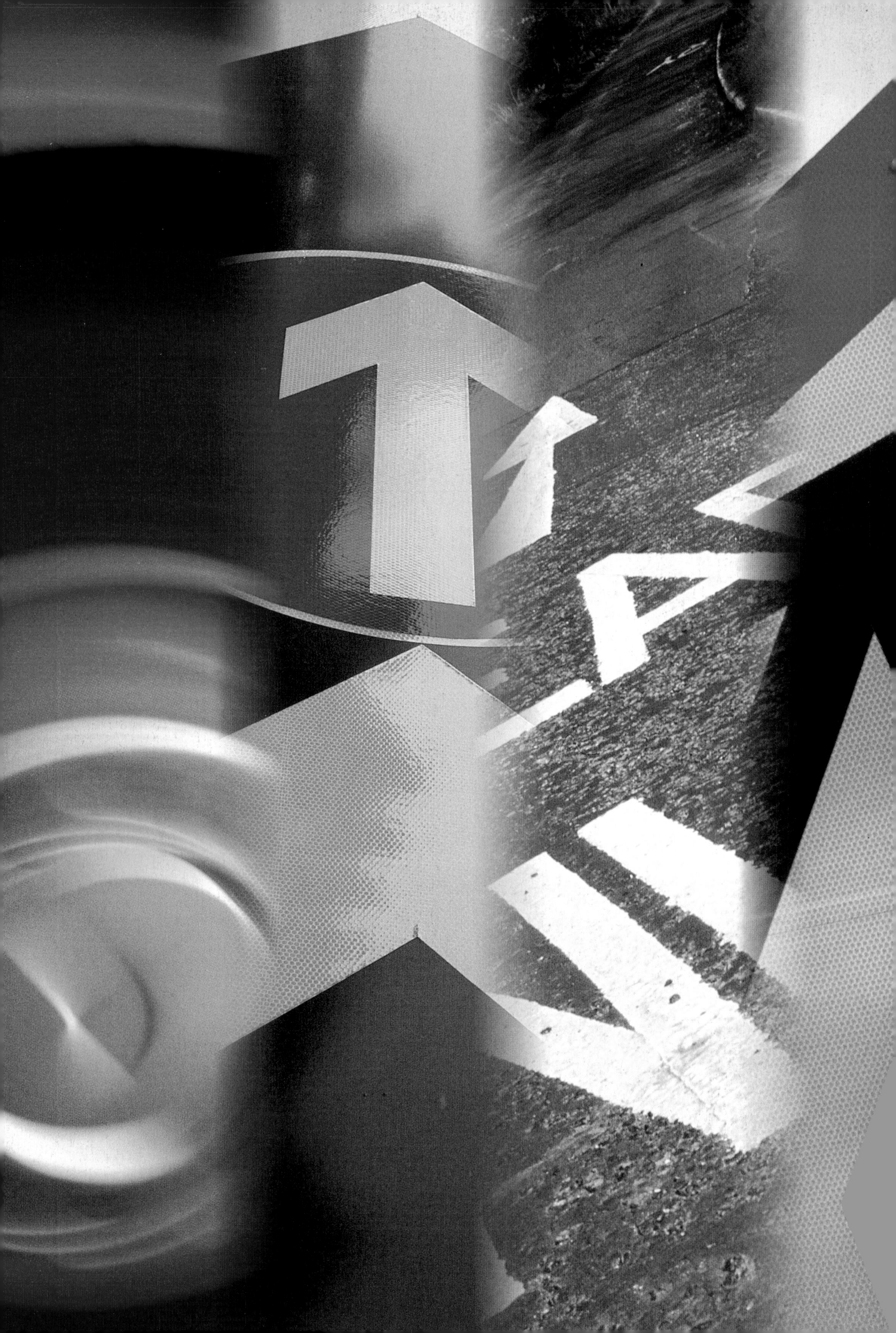

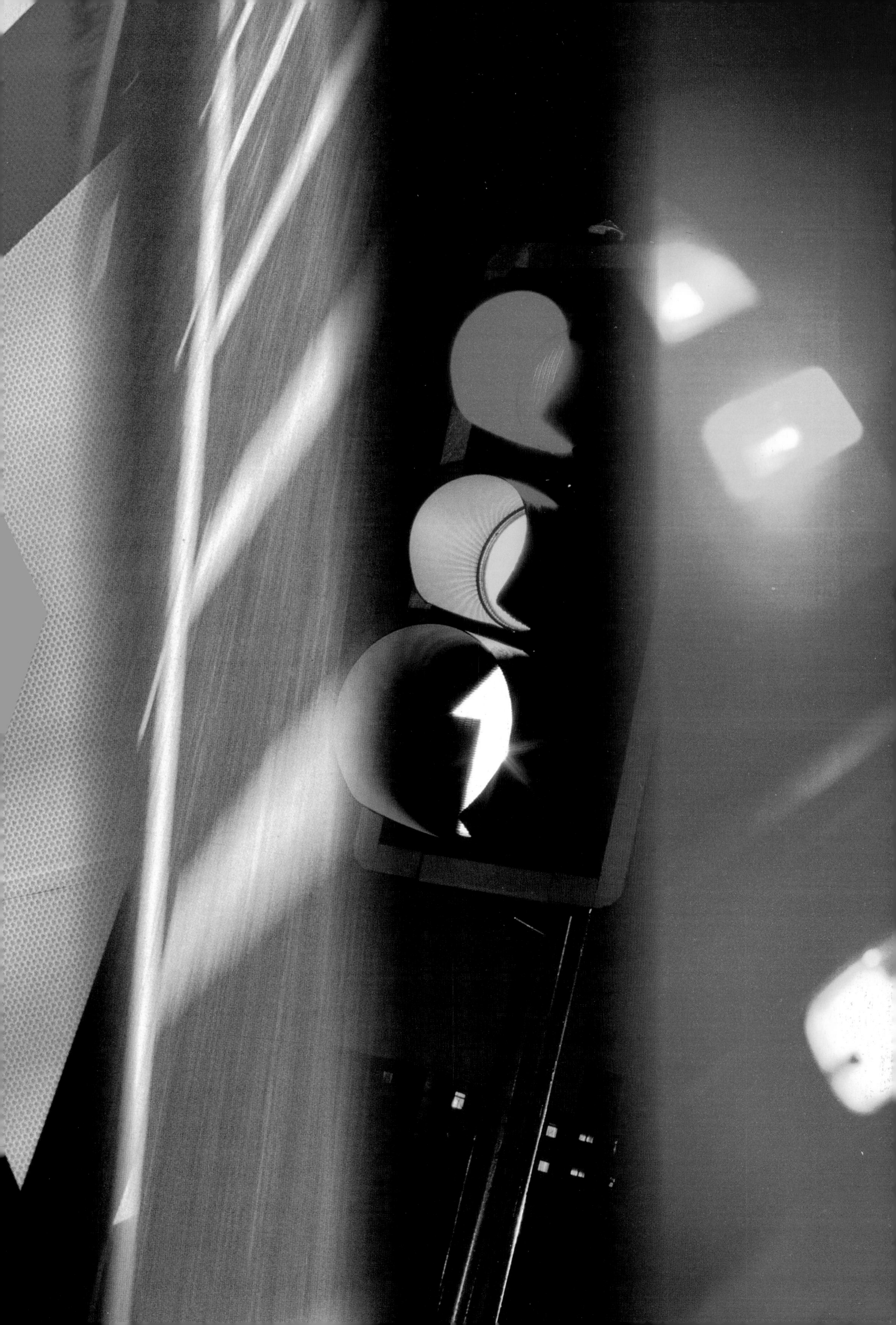

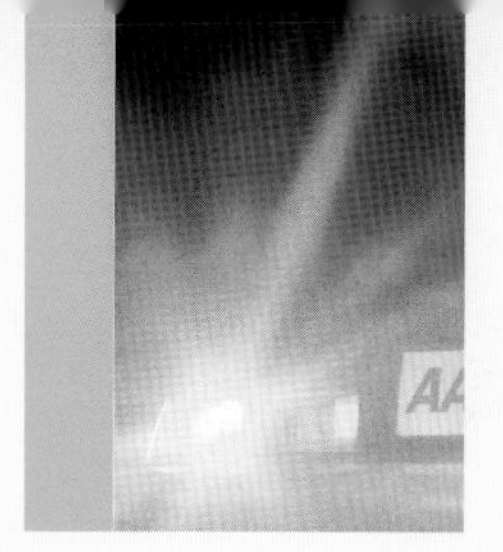

information for motorists

The AA is Britain's largest motoring organisation, providing accurate and up-to-date information services for all motorists – just give us a call

All 09003 prefixed numbers are charged at 60p per minute at all times (correct at time of going to press)

Traffic information

To check the latest road conditions before you travel call **08705 500 600** (AA members only) or visit our website at **www.theaa.co.uk** for more information.

AA Roadwatch on 09003 401 100 You can access one of the most detailed and accurate traffic reports available in the UK.

Select the latest traffic information for your local area or any other region of the UK. You can also request information on specific motorways and A-roads.

VODAFONE DIGITAL MOBILE USERS – call '1800' ... For an up-to-the-minute, location-specific traffic report, with the option to obtain information on a specific road or motorway. This service also gives you the opportunity to speak to an experienced AA Traffic and Travel Information Adviser for details about a particular incident or advice on an alternative route.

Calls to 1800 are charged at 45p per minute (59p per minute for Pay-as-you-Talk customers and operator service). Average call time 1 minute.

Need expert advice?

Access the expertise of the AA – **call 09003** followed by the numbers shown

Motoring hints and advice

401 505	Checks before you start, route planning and motorway driving	**401 509**	Motoring for disabled drivers
401 506	Child seats and harnesses	**401 522**	Towing: matching the vehicle to the load
401 508	Safe motorway driving	**401 526**	Motorway breakdowns

The material contained in these 09003 recorded information services has been researched by the AA. While every effort is made to ensure that it is accurate, no liability can be accepted arising from inaccuracies or omissions. © Automobile Association Developments Limited 2000.

Useful numbers

AA The Driving School 0800 60 70 80
Book your driving lessons anywhere in mainland Britain

Road User Information Line (Highways Agency) 0845 750 40 30
For information on motorways and trunk roads, to make a complaint or comment on road conditions or roadworks, for MoT and vehicle licence enquiries

Exclusive services for AA Members

All 08705 prefixed numbers are charged at BT's National Rate

AA Hotel Booking Service 08705 05 05 05 (9am–6pm, Mon–Fri; 9am–1pm, Sat)
Free reservation service for business or leisure travel covering over 8,000 AA-inspected establishments in Britain and Ireland

UK Route Planning visit **www.theaa.co.uk** or call **08705 500 600** (24 hours, 7 days a week) Free personalised itineraries for routes within Great Britain and Ireland

Special Offers and AA Services 08705 500 600 (24 hours, 7 days a week)
Expert advice and assistance on legal and technical aspects of motoring
Details of discounts on AA services and other exclusive offers and savings

AA Membership Administration 08705 444 444 (7am–11pm, 7 days a week)
For all Membership enquiries

**If you are not an AA Member and would like to be – call 0800 444 999
for details on how to join**

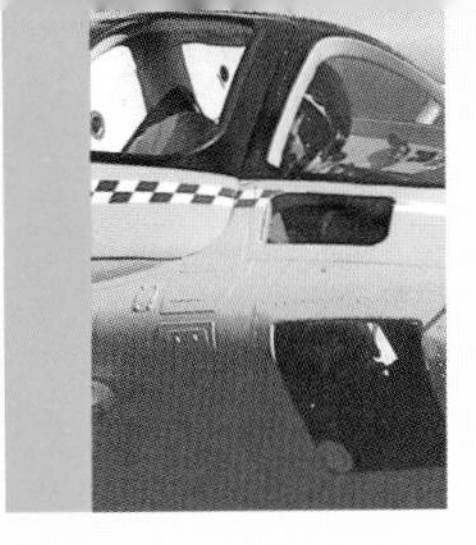

air ambulance

The Road User's Guide to Calling an Air Ambulance

Air ambulances are a vital part of emergency medical services, providing a rapid response and swift transfer from incident to hospital, free of traffic congestion. An airlift is of particular benefit in cases of head or spinal injuries, where a high level of patient comfort is necessary, or when a patient has to be taken to a specialist unit.

If you witness an accident, dial 999 and tell the operator an ambulance is needed.

Description of the incident: this information will help the ambulance control to decide whether an air ambulance is needed. For example: 'There are four cars involved in an accident, and it looks like there are three casualties.'

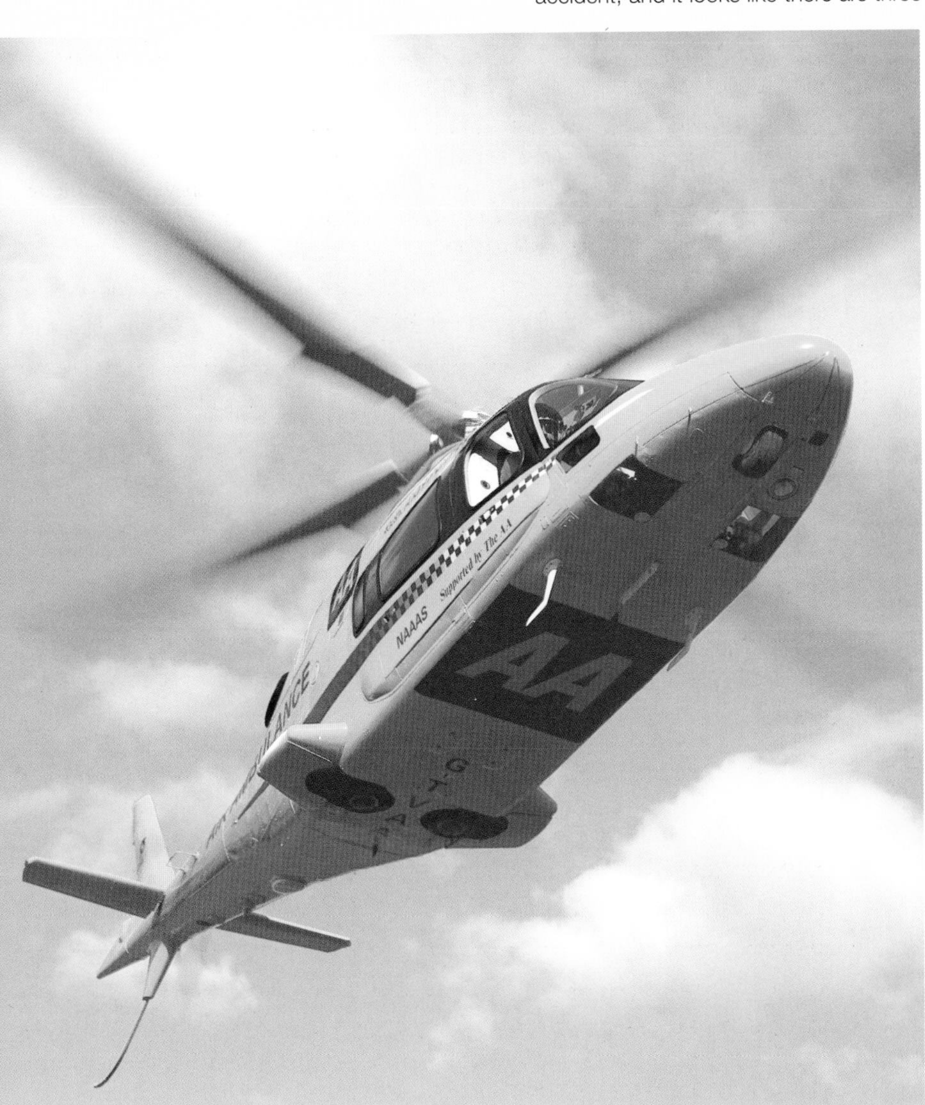

Location: try to give as accurate a location as you can. For example: 'A40 southbound carriageway, two miles south of the M50 exit for Ross-on-Wye.'

Relevant landmarks: look around for anything that might be visible from the air. For example: 'There's a petrol station near by.' or 'There's a farmhouse on the left.'

Dangers: try to spot potential hazards for an incoming aircraft, such as overhead wires, pylons and telegraph poles.

Other information: tell the operator other details that will help the crew locate you or that will help them to plan their landing. For example: 'We will be waving a red blanket.' or 'There is a flat field next to the road.'

The air ambulance pilot will use the information you provide to decide where to land. It might be necessary for the helicopter to land some distance from the accident, but this is to ensure the safety of the aircraft. You can assist the air ambulance by doing the following:

Wear something highly visible: a brightly coloured scarf, or anything that will make you easy to spot.

Stand with your back to the wind: it is very helpful to the pilot to know in which direction the wind is blowing as the helicopter must land into the wind.

Face the proposed landing area: choose somewhere as flat as possible. Air ambulances can manoeuvre very easily, but they need to land somewhere level.

Raise and outstretch your arms: if you have your back to the wind, this will indicate the wind direction and landing site to the crew. When the aircraft lands, stay well clear of the blades and tail rotor and wait for them to stop before approaching.

For more information about the work of the National Association of Air Ambulance Services, or to make a donation, please call **0800 3 899899**.

route planner

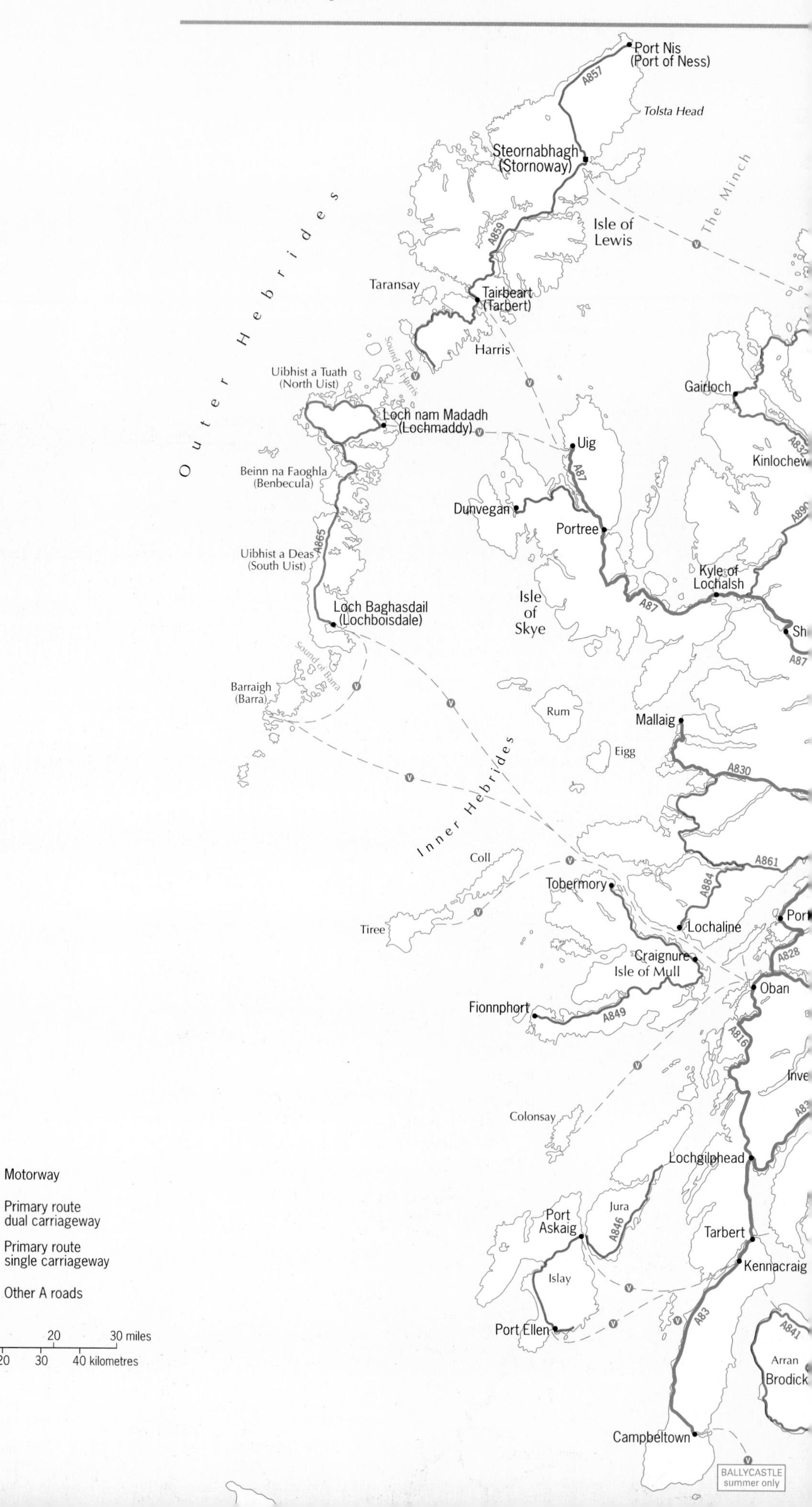

Legend:
- Motorway
- Primary route dual carriageway
- Primary route single carriageway
- Other A roads

Scale:
0 10 20 30 miles
0 10 20 30 40 kilometres

Place names on map:
Port Nis (Port of Ness), Tolsta Head, Steornabhagh (Stornoway), Isle of Lewis, The Minch, Outer Hebrides, Taransay, Tairbeart (Tarbert), Harris, Gairloch, Uibhist a Tuath (North Uist), Loch nam Madadh (Lochmaddy), Kinlochew, Uig, Beinn na Faoghla (Benbecula), Dunvegan, Portree, Uibhist a Deas (South Uist), Kyle of Lochalsh, Loch Baghasdail (Lochboisdale), Isle of Skye, Barraigh (Barra), Sound of Barra, Rum, Mallaig, Eigg, Inner Hebrides, Coll, Tobermory, Lochaline, Port, Tiree, Craignure Isle of Mull, Oban, Fionnphort, Colonsay, Inve, Lochgilphead, Port Askaig, Jura, Tarbert, Islay, Kennacraig, Port Ellen, Arran, Brodick, Campbeltown, BALLYCASTLE summer only

Road numbers: A857, A859, A865, A87, A830, A861, A884, A828, A849, A816, A846, A83, A841

VI

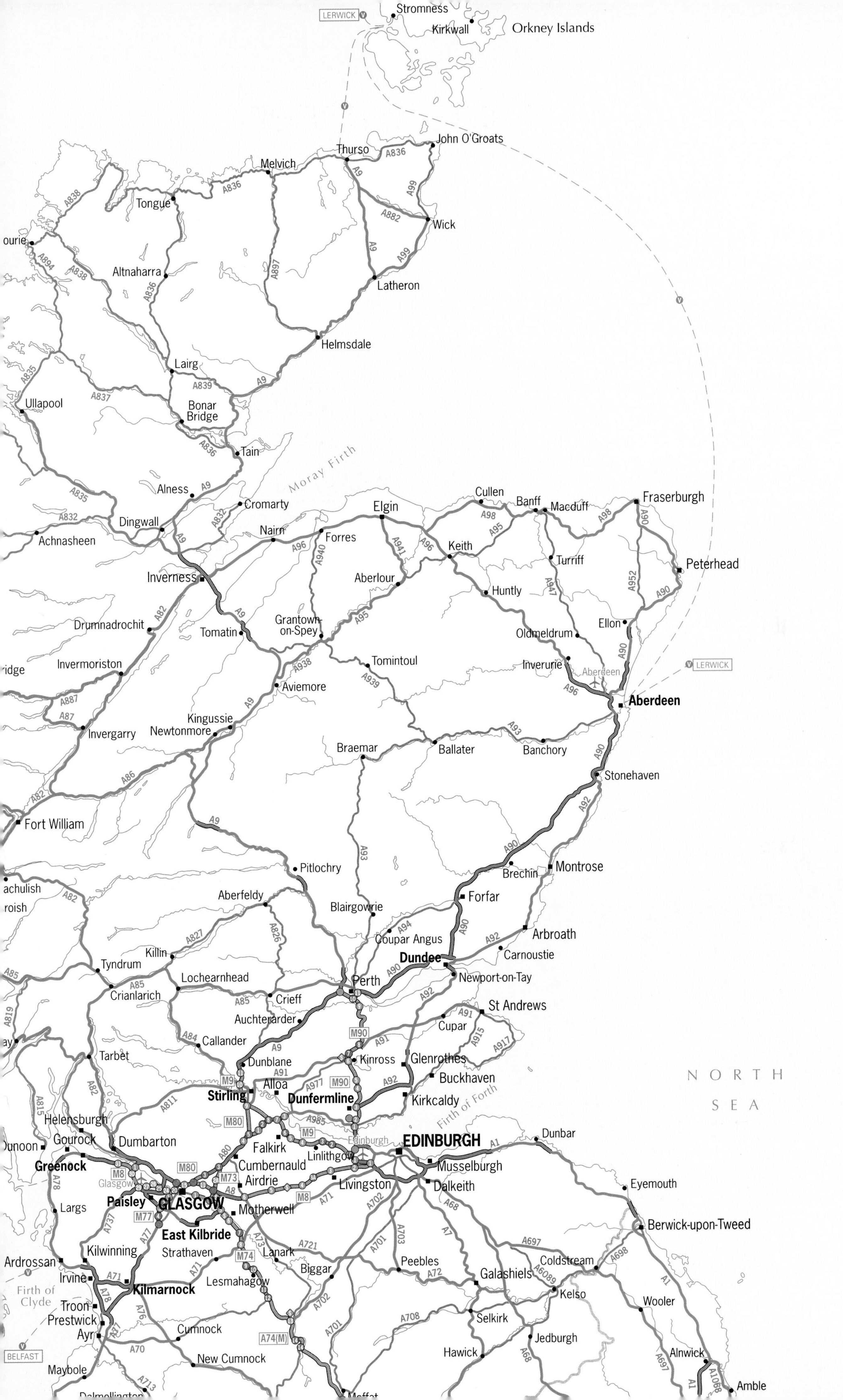

Stromness
Kirkwall
Orkney Islands
LERWICK
John O'Groats
Thurso
Melvich
Tongue
Wick
Altnaharra
Latheron
Helmsdale
Lairg
Bonar Bridge
Ullapool
Tain
Moray Firth
Alness
Cromarty
Dingwall
Achnasheen
Nairn
Forres
Elgin
Cullen
Banff
Macduff
Fraserburgh
Keith
Turriff
Peterhead
Inverness
Aberlour
Huntly
Drumnadrochit
Tomatin
Grantown-on-Spey
Ellon
Oldmeldrum
Invermoriston
Tomintoul
Inverurie
Aberdeen
Aviemore
Kingussie
Newtonmore
Invergarry
Braemar
Ballater
Banchory
Stonehaven
Fort William
Pitlochry
Brechin
Montrose
Aberfeldy
Forfar
Blairgowrie
Coupar Angus
Arbroath
Carnoustie
Killin
Tyndrum
Dundee
Newport-on-Tay
Lochearnhead
Perth
Crianlarich
Crieff
St Andrews
Auchterarder
Cupar
Callander
Kinross
Glenrothes
Tarbet
Dunblane
Buckhaven
Alloa
Stirling
Dunfermline
Kirkcaldy
Firth of Forth
NORTH SEA
Helensburgh
Gourock
Dumbarton
Falkirk
Linlithgow
EDINBURGH
Dunbar
Greenock
Cumbernauld
Musselburgh
Airdrie
Livingston
Dalkeith
Eyemouth
Largs
Paisley
GLASGOW
Motherwell
East Kilbride
Berwick-upon-Tweed
Kilwinning
Strathaven
Lanark
Peebles
Coldstream
Ardrossan
Irvine
Biggar
Galashiels
Kilmarnock
Lesmahagow
Kelso
Firth of Clyde
Troon
Prestwick
Ayr
Selkirk
Wooler
Cumnock
Jedburgh
BELFAST
Hawick
Alnwick
New Cumnock
Maybole
Amble
Moffat

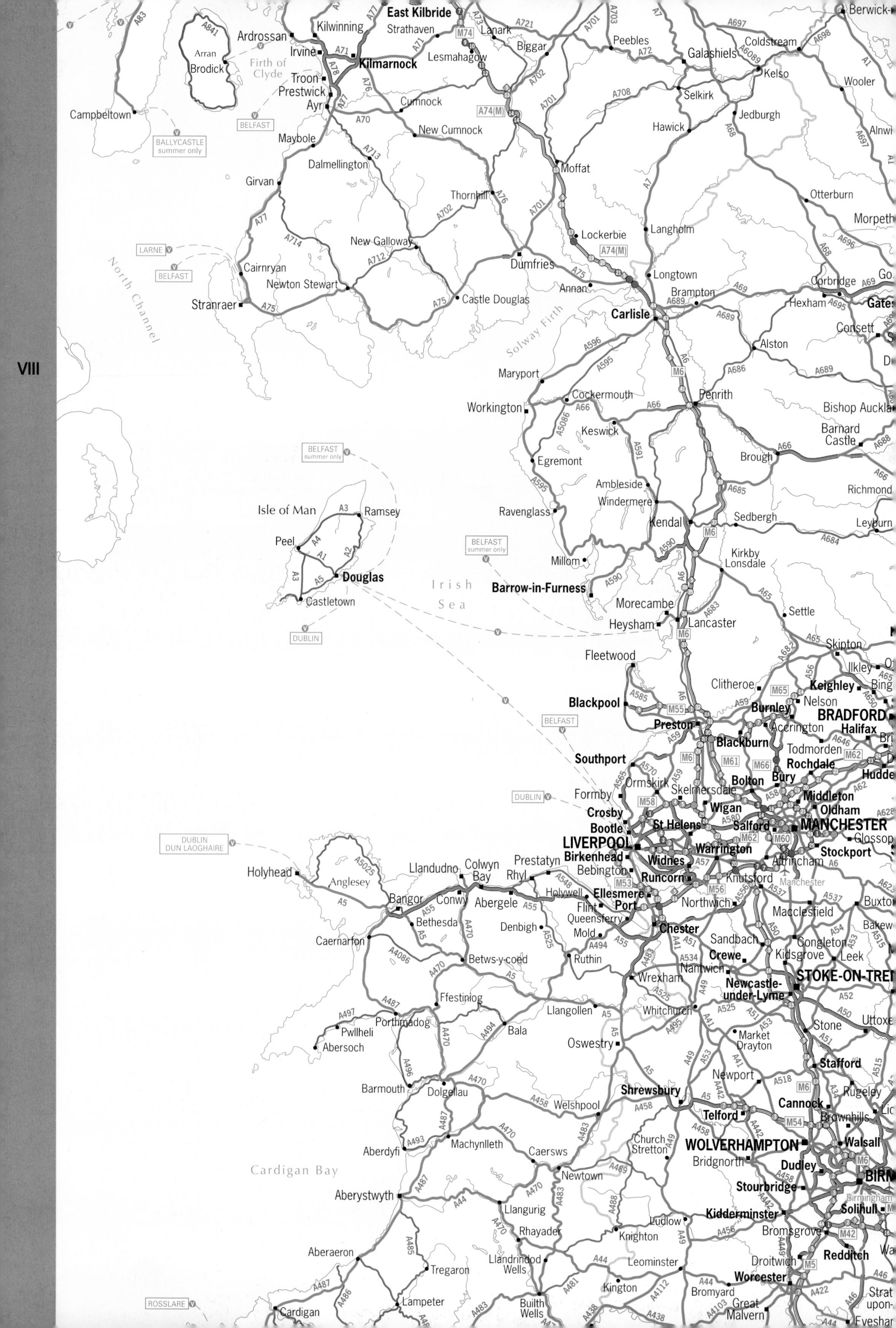
East Kilbride
Kilwinning
Strathaven
Lanark
Ardrossan
Arran
Brodick
Firth of Clyde
Irvine
Kilmarnock
Lesmahagow
Biggar
Peebles
Galashiels
Coldstream
Kelso
Wooler
Troon
Prestwick
Ayr
Cumnock
Selkirk
Jedburgh
Hawick
Campbeltown
BELFAST
BALLYCASTLE summer only
Maybole
New Cumnock
Dalmellington
Girvan
Moffat
Otterburn
Morpeth
Thornhill
Lockerbie
Langholm
LARNE
New Galloway
North Channel
Cairnryan
Newton Stewart
Dumfries
Longtown
Corbridge
Hexham
Annan
Brampton
Stranraer
Castle Douglas
Carlisle
Consett
Solway Firth
Alston
Maryport
Cockermouth
Penrith
Workington
Keswick
Bishop Auckland
Barnard Castle
Egremont
Brough
Ambleside
Richmond
Windermere
Isle of Man
Ramsey
Ravenglass
BELFAST summer only
Kendal
Sedbergh
Peel
Millom
Kirkby Lonsdale
Douglas
Irish Sea
Barrow-in-Furness
Castletown
Morecambe
Settle
Heysham
Lancaster
DUBLIN
Skipton
Fleetwood
Ilkley
Clitheroe
Keighley
Blackpool
Burnley
Nelson
BRADFORD
Preston
Accrington
Halifax
Blackburn
Todmorden
Southport
Rochdale
Bury
Ormskirk
Skelmersdale
Bolton
Formby
Middleton
Crosby
Wigan
Oldham
Bootle
St Helens
Salford
MANCHESTER
LIVERPOOL
Warrington
Glossop
Birkenhead
Widnes
Altrincham
Stockport
DUBLIN DUN LAOGHAIRE
Holyhead
Anglesey
Llandudno
Colwyn Bay
Prestatyn
Rhyl
Bebington
Runcorn
Knutsford
Manchester
Bangor
Conwy
Abergele
Holywell
Ellesmere Port
Northwich
Flint
Macclesfield
Bethesda
Denbigh
Queensferry
Chester
Caernarfon
Mold
Sandbach
Congleton
Crewe
Kidsgrove
Leek
Betws-y-coed
Ruthin
Nantwich
Wrexham
Newcastle-under-Lyme
Ffestiniog
Llangollen
Whitchurch
Pwllheli
Porthmadog
Bala
Stone
Abersoch
Oswestry
Market Drayton
Stafford
Newport
Barmouth
Dolgellau
Shrewsbury
Rugeley
Welshpool
Cannock
Telford
Brownhills
Church Stretton
Aberdyfi
Machynlleth
Caersws
WOLVERHAMPTON
Walsall
Bridgnorth
Cardigan Bay
Dudley
Newtown
Aberystwyth
Stourbridge
Birmingham
Llangurig
Kidderminster
Solihull
Ludlow
Rhayader
Knighton
Bromsgrove
Redditch
Aberaeron
Llandrindod Wells
Leominster
Droitwich
Tregaron
Worcester
Kington
Bromyard
ROSSLARE
Lampeter
Builth Wells
Great Malvern
Cardigan

weed

Amble

Ashington

Whitley Bay
Tynemouth
South Shields
NEWCASTLE UPON TYNE
Jarrow
SUNDERLAND
Chester-le-Street
A1(M)
A19
Spennymoor
Hartlepool
689
Stockton-on-Tees
Middlesbrough
Darlington
A66
A171
Scotch Corner
A19 A172
Guisborough
Stokesley
Whitby
A169
Northallerton A171
A684 Scalby
Thirsk Helmsley A170 Scarborough
A168 Pickering A170
 on Easingwold A64 Malton Filey
A61 A19 A166 A165 **Bridlington**
gate A59 A614
Driffield
York A614 A165
Wetherby Market A035
Weighton A164 Beverley
ey **LEEDS** A58 A163 A614 A1079 A164
dford A1(M) Selby A63 A19
A1 A65 Hessle **HULL**
se M1 M62 M62 A645 Goole Barton-upon-Humber
bury **Wakefield** Pontefract A15 Immingham
eld M62 Thorne **Scunthorpe** **Grimsby**
M1 M18 Cleethorpes
Barnsley A635 **Doncaster** M180 A18
616 Bawtry A159 A15 A631 Market A16 Louth
Rotherham A631 Rasen A16 Mablethorpe
FFIELD A1(M) Retford Gainsborough A46 A157 A16
nfield M1 Worksop A156 A46 A158 A52
Staveley A57 A158 Skegness
A619 **Chesterfield** A614 A57 Lincoln A158
A619 A60 A15 Horncastle
ck **Mansfield** A617
Alfreton A17 Sleaford Boston The Wash
nbourne A38 Newark-on-Trent A17 A52 A17 Sheringham Cromer
lkeston A6097 A1 A52 Grantham A52 A16 Hunstanton A149 A148
NOTTINGHAM A52 A17 King's A148 North Walsham
DERBY Long Eaton A607 Spalding Lynn Dersingham Fakenham Aylsham
A50 A606 A151 A1065 A148 A140 A1151 A149
rton upon Loughborough A46 Bourne A17 A1067 Dereham A47 **Norwich** Caister-on-Sea
Trent East Melton Mowbray A15 A1101 A11 A47 A146 **Great Yarmouth**
M1 Midlands A606 Stamford A16 Wisbech Downham A1122 Swaffham **Lowestoft**
M42 Oakham A6003 A47 Market A11 A143
amworth **LEICESTER** A606 **Peterborough** A141 Attleborough Bungay Beccles
M69 Wigston A47 March A134 A143 Diss A12
neaton Hinckley M1 Market A605 A1065 A1066 Southwold
GHAM Harborough A6003 Chatteris A11 Thetford A140
M6 **Corby** A605 A1(M) Ely A143 A1120 Aldeburgh
COVENTRY **Rugby** A14 Kettering A14 Huntingdon A10 A142 Bury St Edmunds
amington Spa M45 A508 A45 Stowmarket Woodbridge
A429 M40 A5 Daventry A45 St Neots A428 Newmarket A134 **Ipswich**
Banbury Towcester **Northampton** Biggleswade **Cambridge** Sudbury Haverhill
A423 M1 **Bedford** A11 A1307

▬▬▬	Motorway
▬▬▬	Primary route dual carriageway
▬▬▬	Primary route single carriageway
▬▬▬	Other A roads

0   10   20   30 miles
0   10   20   30   40 kilometres

X

Cardigan Bay

Bristol Channel

E N G L I S H

DUBLIN
DUN LAOGHAIRE

ROSSLARE
ROSSLARE
CORK

CHANNEL ISLANDS
ST MALO summer only

SANTANDER summer only
ROSCOFF
ST MALO winter only

Holyhead · Anglesey · Llandudno · Colwyn Bay · Rhyl · Prestatyn · **LIVERPOOL** · **Birkenhead** · Bebington · **Bootle** · **Crosby** · St Helens · **Wigan** · Salford · **MANCH** · Oldha · Stock · Knutsford · Manchester · Altrincham · A6

Bangor · Conwy · Abergele · Holywell · **Ellesmere Port** · Flint · **Runcorn** · **Widnes** · **Warrington** · Stock

Bethesda · Caernarfon · Denbigh · Mold · Queensferry · **Chester** · Northwich · Macclesfield · Sandbach · Congleton

Betws-y-coed · Ruthin · Wrexham · Nantwich · **Crewe** · Kidsgrove · **STOKE-O** · Stone

Ffestiniog · Bala · Llangollen · Oswestry · Whitchurch · **Newcastle-under-Lyme** · Market Drayton · **Staffo**

Porthmadog · Pwllheli · Abersoch · Welshpool · **Shrewsbury** · Newport · **M6** · **Cannock** · Brown

Barmouth · Dolgellau · Machynlleth · Caersws · **Telford** · **WOLVERHAMPTON** · **Dudley** · **Stourbridge** · **Staffo**

Aberdyfi · Newtown · Church Stretton · Bridgnorth · **Kidderminster**

Aberystwyth · Llangurig · Rhayader · Ludlow · Knighton · Leominster · **Bromsgrove** · Droitwich · **Redd**

Aberaeron · Tregaron · Llandrindod Wells · Kington · **Worcester** · Bromyard · Great Malvern

Cardigan · Lampeter · Builth Wells · Hay-on-Wye · Hereford · Ledbury · Tewkesbury · **Chel**

Newcastle Emlyn · Llandovery · Brecon · Ross-on-Wye · Monmouth · **Gloucester** · Stroud

Fishguard · St David's · Haverfordwest · Carmarthen · Llandeilo · Abergavenny · Chepstow · **M5**

Milford Haven · Pembroke Dock · Pembroke · St Clears · Llanelli · **M4** · Merthyr Tydfil · Ebbw Vale · Cwmbran

Tenby · Neath · **Swansea** · Port Talbot · Bridgend · **Newport** · Avonmouth · Clevedon · **BRISTOL** · Bath

CARDIFF · **Weston-super-Mare** · Cheddar · Frome · Trowbridge · Warminste

Ilfracombe · Lynton · Minehead · Watchet · Wells · Shepton Mallet · Glastonbury

Barnstaple · Bideford · Great Torrington · South Molton · Bridgwater · Taunton · Wincanton

Bude · Holsworthy · Hatherleigh · Tiverton · Yeovil · Sherborne · Shaftesbury

Okehampton · Crediton · Honiton · Chard · Crewkerne · Ilminster · Blandford Forum · Wimbor · Minste

Launceston · **Exeter** · Axminster · Bridport · Dorchester · **Poole**

Wadebridge · Tavistock · Exmouth · Dawlish · Teignmouth · Lyme Regis · Weymouth

Bodmin · Buckfastleigh · Newton Abbot · **Torquay** · Paignton · Fortuneswell

Newquay · Liskeard · Saltash · **PLYMOUTH** · Totnes · Dartmouth

Lostwithiel · St Austell · Torpoint · Kingsbridge

Redruth · Truro · Falmouth

Penzance · Helston · Lizard

Motorway
Primary route dual carriageway
Primary route single carriageway
Other A roads

0   10   20   30 miles
0 10 20 30 40 kilometres

C H A N N E L

road signs

Classes of signs

Our road system has a consistent and comprehensive set of road signs that provide you with information, instructions and warnings.

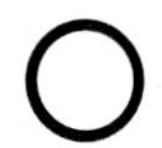

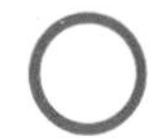

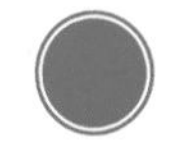

Circles order and prohibit   Triangles warn   Rectangles provide information

Junctions and roundabouts

These signs provide you with important information about the nature of the junction or the roundabout ahead.

| Distance to 'STOP' line ahead | Distance to 'GIVE WAY' line ahead | Give way to traffic on major road | Stop and give way | Crossroads | T-junction | Staggered junction | Roundabout | Mini-roundabout (roundabout circulation) | No through road |

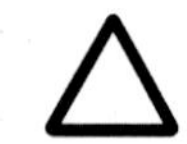

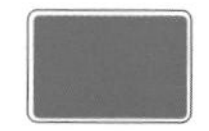

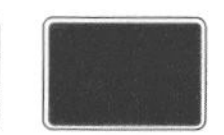

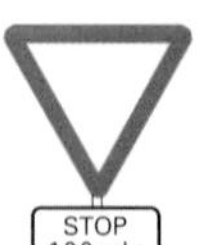

Traffic behaviour

Signs which must be obeyed. They indicate the speed or action you are required to take in particular situations.

| No stopping (clearway) | National speed limit applies | Maximum speed | Give priority to vehicles from opposite direction | No overtaking | Motor vehicles prohibited except for access | No entry for vehicular traffic | No U-turns | No right turn | No left turn |

| Turn left ahead | One-way traffic | Turn left | Vehicles may pass either side to reach same destination | Ahead only | Keep left |

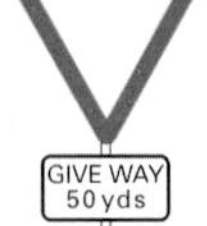

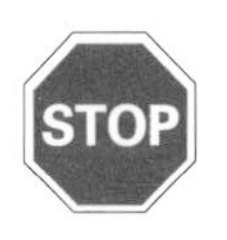

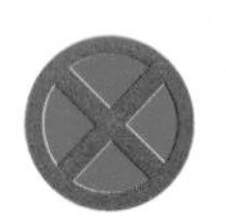

The road ahead

Advance warning of the road layout ahead enables you to plan a safe approach.

| Bend to left | Double bend, first to left | Bend to right | Double bend, first to right | Road hump or series of road humps ahead | Worded warning sign | Dual carriageway ahead | Steep hill downwards | Steep hill upwards |

| No goods vehicles over maximum gross weight shown (in tonnes) | No vehicles over width shown | No vehicles over height shown | Sharp deviation of route | Two-way traffic straight ahead | Traffic merges from left | Traffic merges from right | Road narrows on left | Road narrows on both sides |

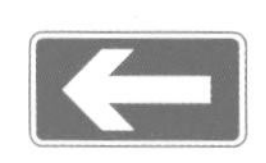

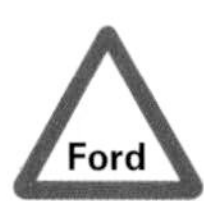

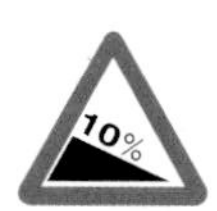

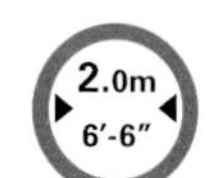

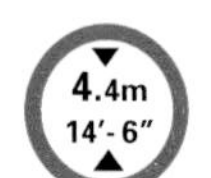

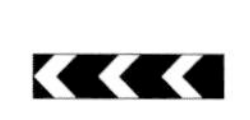

Hazards ahead

These signs warn you of potential hazards on the road ahead.

| Hospital ahead with accident and emergency facilities | Traffic queues likely ahead | Cycle route ahead | Slippery road | Road works | Uneven road | Wild animals | Falling or fallen rocks | Other danger |

| School crossing patrol ahead | School crossing patrol | Pedestrian crossing | Trams crossing ahead | Risk of grounding | Hump bridge | Opening or swing bridge ahead | Quayside or river bank |

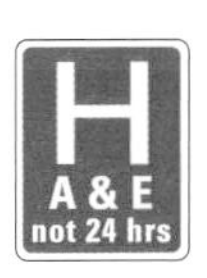

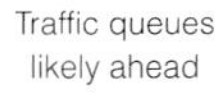

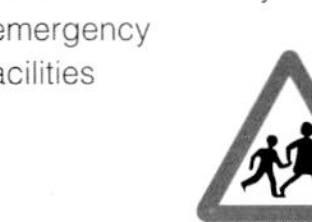

On the motorway

These signals are used to warn you of conditions ahead and the lanes affected. They may be located overhead, on the central reservation or over the nearside lane. Drivers must observe the advisory speed limits and should remember that the red circle means a mandatory speed control.

| Temporary maximum speed limit and information message | Change lane | Leave motorway at next exit | Do not proceed further in this lane |

| Reduced visibility ahead | Lane ahead closed | Temporary maximum speed limit | End of restriction | National speed limits apply | Traffic building up ahead. Reduce speed to a maximum of 60mph to help maintain flow | Traffic getting heavier ahead. Reduce speed to a maximum of 50mph or lower if incidents occur | Traffic improving. Maximum speed increased to 60mph | Traffic is lighter. Flow easier. Return to national speed limits. This will appear for 3 minutes before going blank |

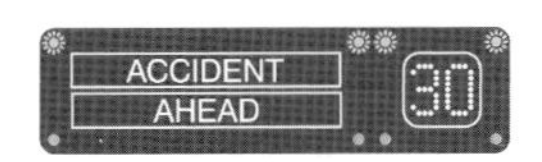

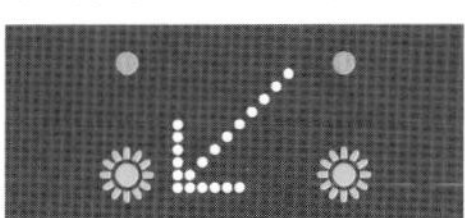

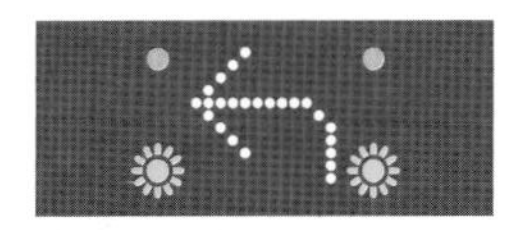

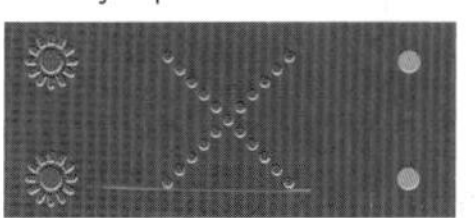

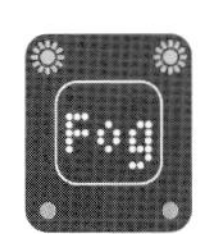

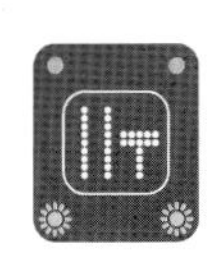

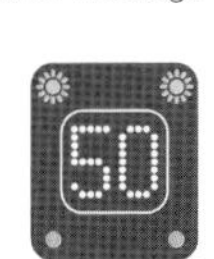

Motorway diversions

Where the motorway is closed, special signs advise you of the recommended diversion route around the incident.

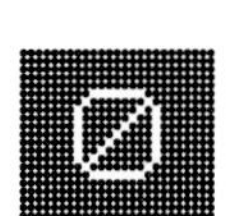

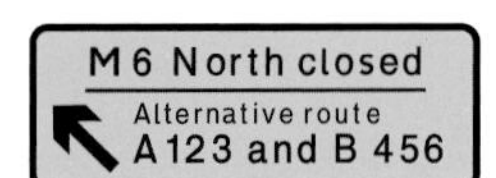

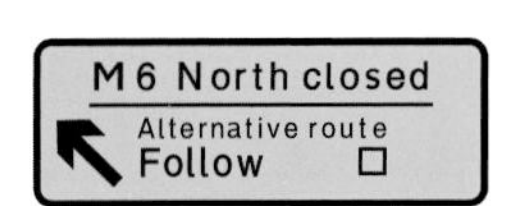

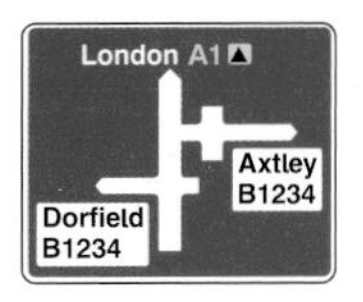

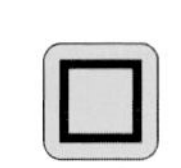

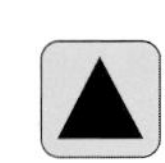

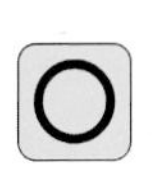

Symbols showing emergency diversion route
for motorway and other main road traffic

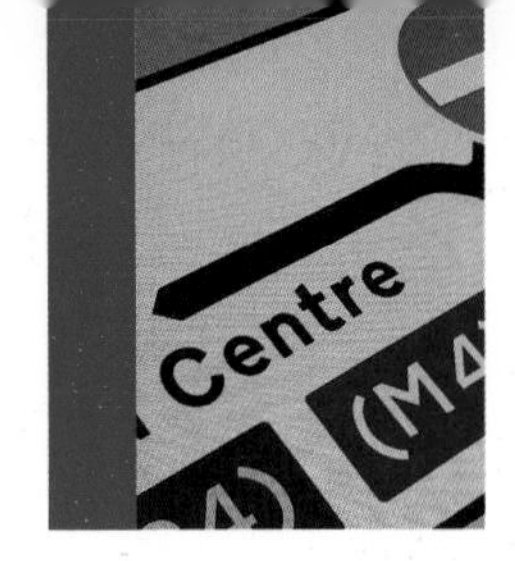

motorways – restricted junctions

Diagrams of selected motorway junctions which have entry and exit restrictions
(Motorways and Service Areas booklet also available tel: **08705 500 600**)

XIV

M1 London–Leeds

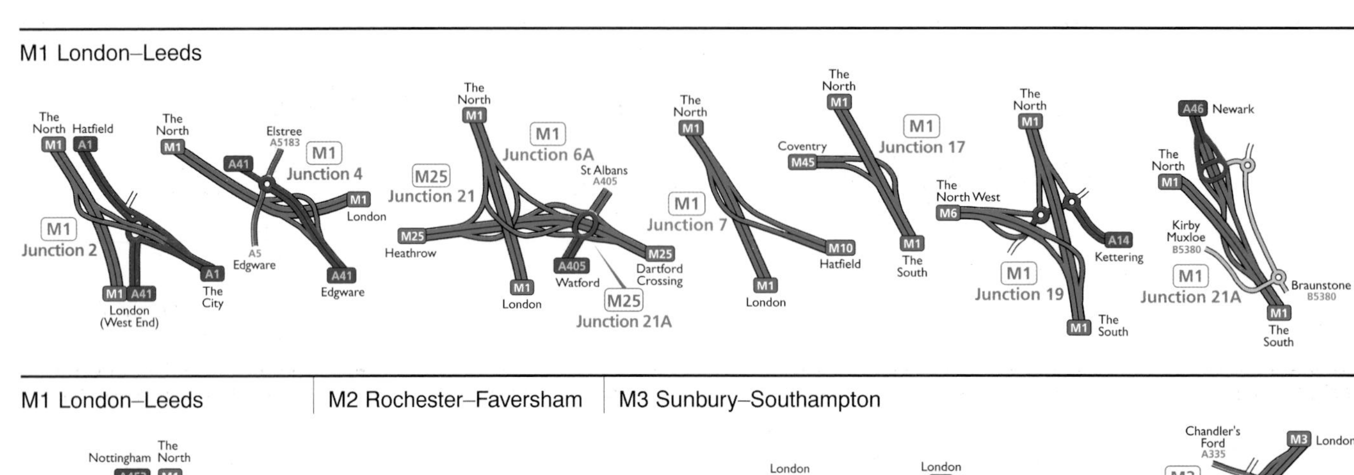

M1 London–Leeds | M2 Rochester–Faversham | M3 Sunbury–Southampton

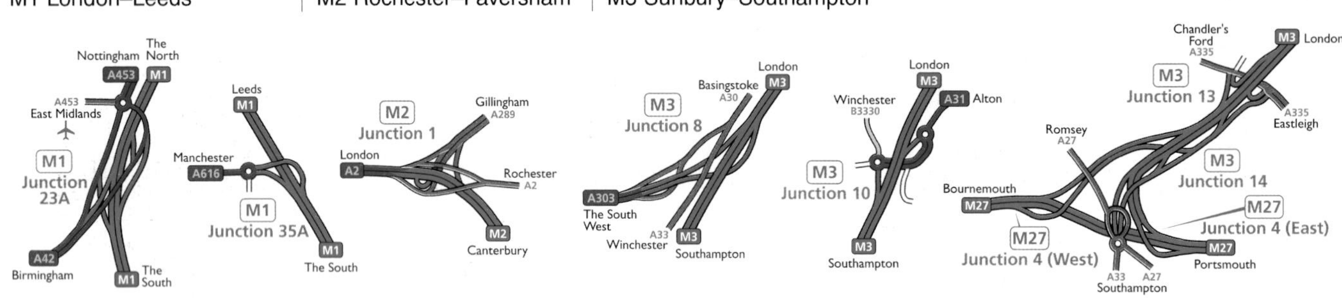

M4 London–South Wales | M5 Birmingham–Exeter

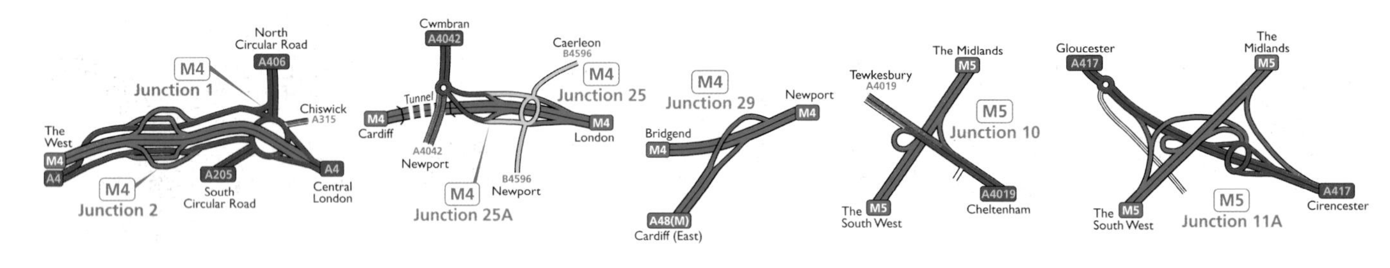

M5 Birmingham–Exeter | M6 Rugby–Carlisle

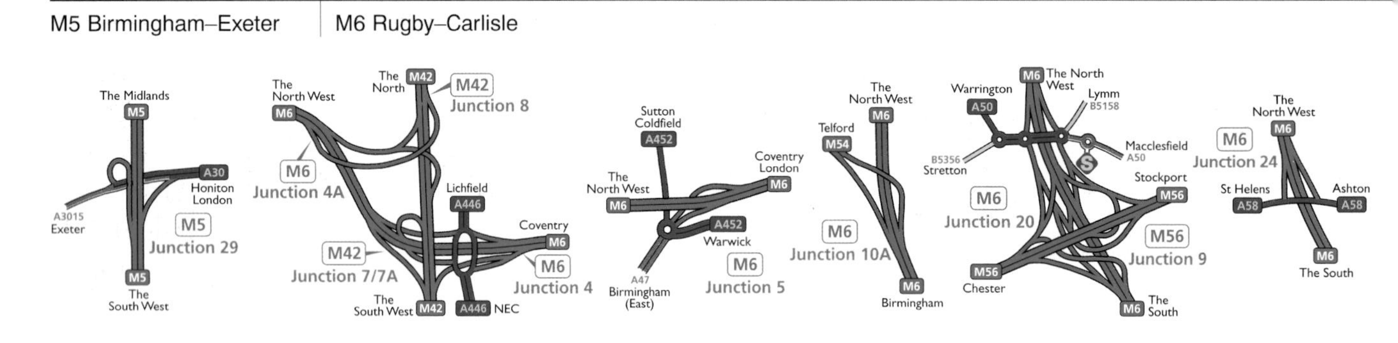

M6 Rugby–Carlisle | M8 Edinburgh–Bishopton

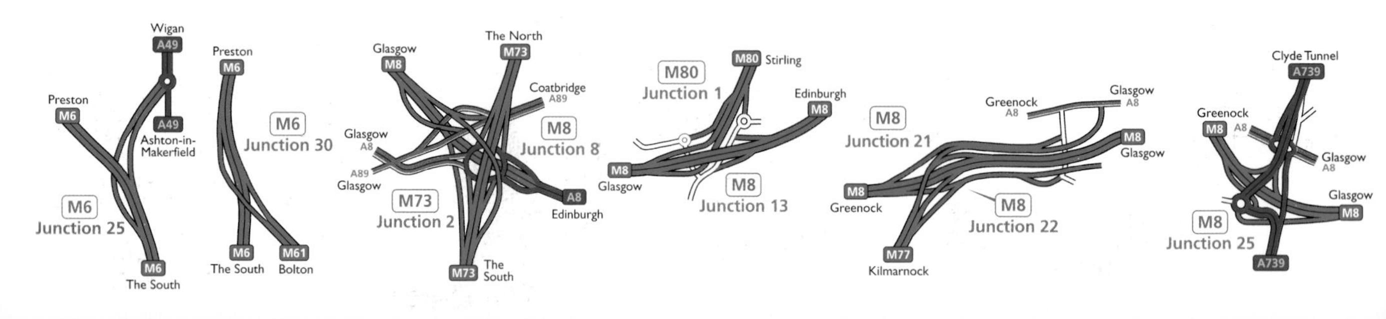

M8 Edinburgh–Bishopton

Glasgow ✈
Greenock
Erskine A726
M8
Glasgow
M8
M8
Junction 29
M8
Junction 28
M8
Junction 28A
Irvine
A737
A726
Paisley

M9 Edinburgh–Dunblane

Stirling
M9
Forth Road Bridge
A8000
Stirling
M9
Edinburgh
M9
M876
Glasgow
M9
Junction 8
B800
Kirkliston
M9
M9
Junction 1A
M9
Edinburgh

M11 London–Cambridge

M11
Cambridge
Newmarket
A11
Cambridge
A1301
Chigwell
A113
B184
Saffron Walden
A14
The North
M11
Cambridge
M11
A406
North Circular Road
A1400
Romford
Bedford
A428
M11
Junction 14
Newmarket
M11
Junction 4
A113
Wanstead
A406
North Circular Road
M11
Junction 9
M11
A1307
M11
London
Cambridge

M20 Swanley–Folkestone

M20
Junction 11A
Ashford
A20
A20
Tolls
Channel Tunnel Terminal
Dover
M20
M20
London
Channel Tunnel Terminal: Entry and exit is via the access roads at Junction 11a
M20
Junction 12
A20
Folkestone
London
M20
M20
Maidstone
M26
The West
M20
Junction 3

M25 London

Dartford Crossing
M25
M25
Maidstone
M26
M25
Junction 5
M25
Gatwick
(A21)
Sevenoaks
Esher
A244
A243
Kingston
Heathrow
M25
B2430
Leatherhead
M25
Junction 9
A243
A245
Leatherhead
A24
Epsom
M25
Dartford Crossing
B2122
Leatherhead
A24
Dorking

M25 London

The North (M1)
M25
Watford
(A41)
M25
Junction 19
M25
Heathrow

M27 Cadnam–Portsmouth

Southampton
Fareham
A27
M27
Waterlooville
(A3)
A27
Waterlooville
A397
M27
Junction 12
A27
Brighton
A3
Hillsea
M275
Portsmouth

M40 London–Birmingham

Birmingham
M40
Oxford
(A40)
A40
Thame
A329
M40
Junction 8
High Wycombe
A40
Wallingford
A329
M40
Junction 7
M40
London

M42 Bromsgrove–Measham

M5
Junction 4A
Birmingham
A38
Rednal
B4096
The North West
M5
London (M40)
M42
M5
M42
Junction 1
M5
The South West
B4096
Redditch
A38
Bromsgrove

M56 North Cheshire

A5103
Manchester
M56
Junction 2
Manchester
B5168
Altrincham
A560
M56
Stockport
A560
Cheadle
M56
Junction 3
M56
Chester

Ellesmere Port
M53
North Wales
M56
M53
Junction 11
Manchester
M56
M56
Junction 15
M53
Chester

M60 Greater Manchester

Preston (M61)
M60
M60
Junction 3
A34
Manchester
Stockport
M60
M56
Chester
M60
Junction 1
A34
Wilmslow

Manchester
A5103
Preston (M61)
M60
M60
Junction 5
Stockport
M60
A5103
Chester (M56)

M61
Junction 3
Bolton
(A666)
M61
Junction 2
M61
M61
Junction 1
Preston
M60
Leeds
M60
Junction 14
M60
Junction 15
A580
St Helens
Liverpool
M60
A580
Manchester

M60 Greater Manchester

M60
Junction 16
Bolton
A666
Leeds
M60
M60
Liverpool
A666
Swinton
M60
Junction 27
Manchester
A626
M60
Chester (M56)
A560
Cheadle
A626
Stockport
B6104
M60
Junction 26
Ashton-under-Lyne
M60
Denton
A6017
M60
Junction 25
A560
B6104
Bredbury

M62 Liverpool–Humberside

M62
Junction 23
Leeds
M62
Oldham
A640
A643
Brighouse
M62
Manchester
A640
Huddersfield

M73 East of Glasgow

M73
Junction 3
Stirling
A80
A80
Glasgow
M73
The South

M74 Glasgow–Gretna

Stirling
M73
M74
Junction 3
Glasgow
A74
M74
Glasgow (SE)
M73
Junction 1
Uddingston
A721
M74
Junction 4
M74
The South

M74, A74(M) Glasgow–Gretna

The North
A74(M)
Kirkpatrick Fleming
B7076
Gretna Green
A74(M)
A75
Dumfries
Longtown
A6071
B721
Gretna
B7076
A74
The South

M80 Glasgow–Stirling

Stirling
M80
M80
Junction 5
Kincardine Bridge
M876
M80
Junction 7
Stirling
A91
M80
Glasgow

M90 Forth Road Bridge–Perth

Perth
M90
B996
Tay Road Bridge
A91
M90
Junction 8
Perth
A912
Dundee
M90
B919
Glenrothes
M90
Junction 7
B996
Kinross
Inverness
(A9)
Stirling
A91
A911
Milnathort
M90
Junction 10
M90
Forth Road Bridge
A912
Bridge of Earn
M90
Forth Road Bridge

A1(M) Scotch Corner–Tyneside

Newcastle upon Tyne
A1(M)
Tyne Tunnel
A194(M)
Newcastle upon Tyne
B1288
Darlington
A66(M)
A1
A1(M)
Junction 65
A1(M)
Junction 57
A1(M)
Junction 65
A1231
Washington
B1288
Birtley
A1(M)
The South
A1(M)
The South

M25 London orbital motorway

Refer also to atlas pages 26–27

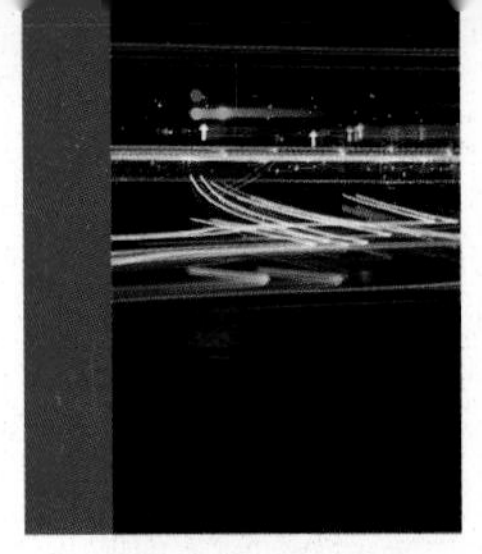

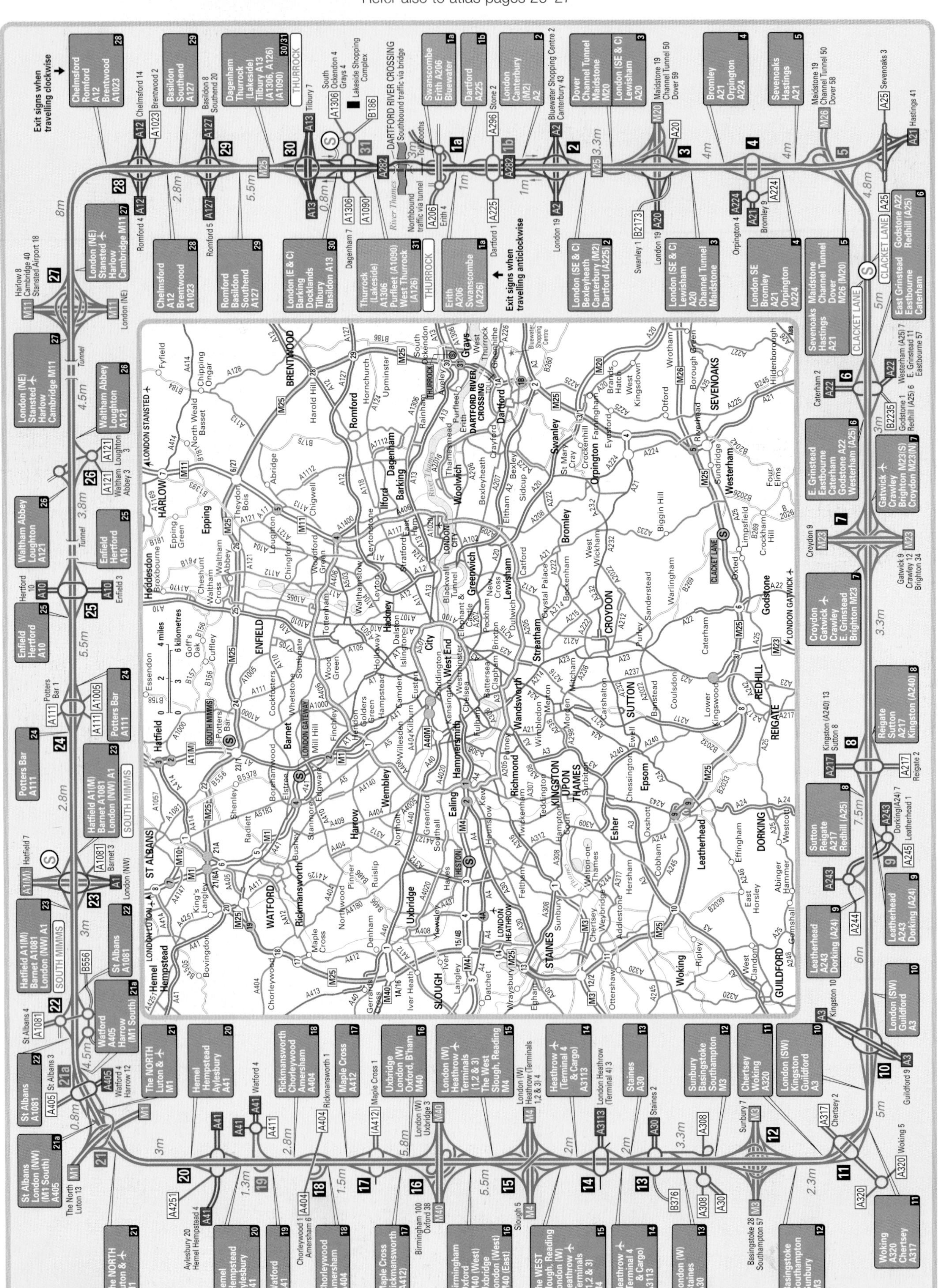

M60 Manchester orbital motorway

Refer also to atlas page 79

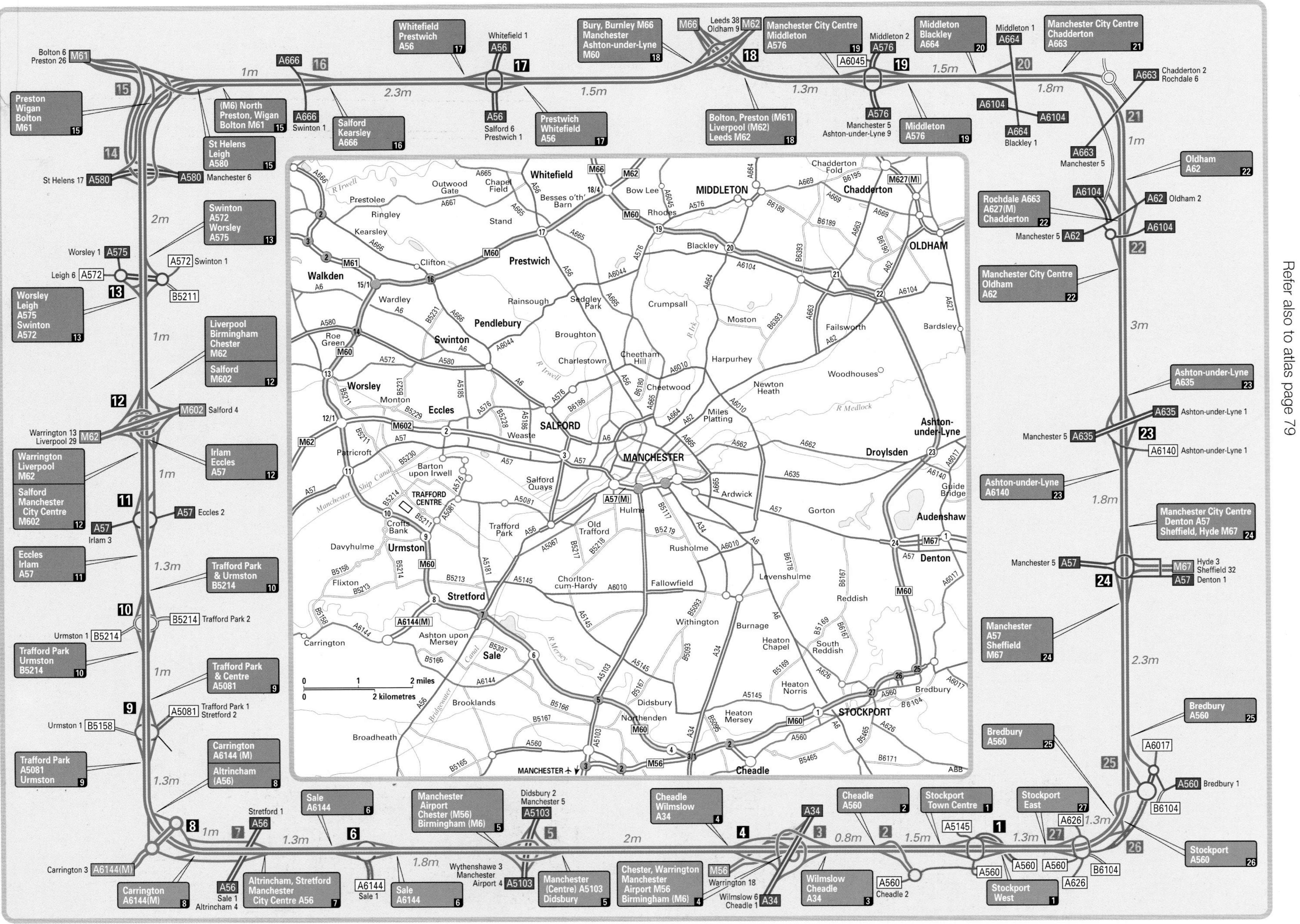

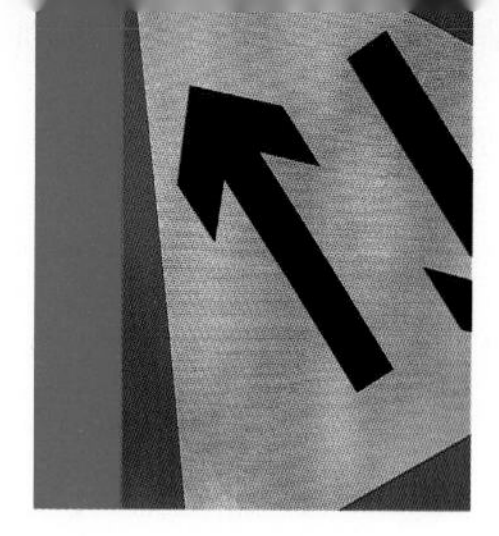

map symbols

Motoring information

M4	Motorway with number		Unclassified road single/dual carriageway	— **V**	Vehicle ferry – Great Britain
11	Motorway junction with and without number		Roundabout	BERGEN **V**	Vehicle ferry – continental
3	Restricted motorway junctions		Interchange		Railway line/in tunnel
S Fleet	Motorway service area		Narrow primary/other A/B road with passing places (Scotland)	—o—X—	Railway station and level crossing
	Motorway and junction under construction		Road under construction	++++++	Tourist railway
A3	Primary route single/dual carriageway	⊨=====	Road tunnel	⊕	Airport
S Grantham North	Primary route service area	→	Steep gradient (arrows point downhill)	Ⓗ	Heliport
BATH	Primary route destination	Toll	Road toll	Ⓕ	International freight terminal
A1123	Other A road single/dual carriageway	▼ 5 ▼	Distance in miles between symbols	★	Major shopping centre
B2070	B road single/dual carriageway				

P·R	7-day Park and Ride locations
☎	AA telephone
	Urban area and village
628 ▲	Spot height in metres
	River, canal, lake
	Sandy beach
	County/County Borough/Council Area boundary
	National boundary
85	Page overlap and number

Tourist information

Places of interest are also shown on town plans. See pages 159–232

							Ski slope – natural
ℹ	Tourist Information Centre		Agricultural showground		Prehistoric monument		Ski slope – artificial
ℹ	Tourist Information Centre (seasonal)		Theme park	✕ 1066	Battle site with year	NT	National Trust property
ℹ	Visitor or heritage centre		Farm or animal centre		Steam centre (railway)	NTS	National Trust for Scotland property
	Abbey, cathedral or priory		Zoological or wildlife collection		Cave	★	Other place of interest
	Ruined abbey, cathedral or priory		Bird collection		Windmill		Boxed symbols indicate attractions within urban areas
✗	Castle		Aquarium		Monument		National Park (England & Wales)
	Historic house or building		Nature reserve		Golf course		National Scenic Area (Scotland)
Ⓜ	Museum or art gallery	RSPB	RSPB site		County cricket ground		Forest Park
	Industrial interest	············	Forest drive		Rugby Union national stadium		Heritage Coast
	Aqueduct or viaduct	– – – – –	National trail		International athletics stadium		Little Chef Restaurant (7am–10pm)
❉	Garden	☀	Viewpoint		Horse racing		Travelodge
	Arboretum		Picnic site		Show jumping/equestrian circuit		Little Chef Restaurant and Travelodge
	Vineyard		Hill-fort		Motor-racing circuit	KING	Granada Burger King sites
	Country park		Roman antiquity		Air show venue	Ⓖ	Granada service area

XVIII

Ireland (see pages 154–157) For tourist information see opposite page

M1 — Motorway	N17 — National primary route (Republic of Ireland)	A4 — Primary route (Northern Ireland)	Road under construction
Motorway junction with and without number	N54 — National secondary route (Republic of Ireland)	A21 — A road (Northern Ireland)	5 — Distance in miles between symbols
Restricted motorway junctions	R182 — Regional road (Republic of Ireland)	B75 — B road (Northern Ireland)	International boundary

1

Central London (see pages 238–248)

Motorway	Restricted road (access only/private)	Banned turn (restricted periods only)	PO — Post Office
Primary route single/dual	Footpath	Ahead only	POL — Police station
Other A road single/dual	Track	Mini-roundabout	Steps
B road single/dual	Pedestrian street	Barrier	Church
Unclassified road single/dual	Railway line/in tunnel	Railway station	Tourist Information Centre
Unclassified road wide/narrow	One-way street	London Regional Transport (LRT) station	Tourist Information Centre (seasonal)
Road under construction	Compulsory turn	Docklands Light Railway (DLR) station	
Road tunnel wide/narrow	Banned turn	P — Parking	

Royal Parks (opening and closing times for traffic)
Green Park   Constitution Hill: closed Sundays, 08.00–dusk
Hyde Park   Open 05.00–midnight
Regent's Park   Open 05.00–midnight
St James's Park The Mall: closed Sundays, 08.00–dusk

Traffic regulations in the City of London include security checkpoints and restrict the number of entry and exit points.

Note: Oxford Street is closed to through-traffic (except buses & taxis) 07.00–19.00, Monday–Saturday. Restricted parts of Frith Street/Old Compton Street are closed to vehicles 12.00–01.00 daily.

District maps (see pages 256–267) For tourist information see opposite page

Motorway	Unclassified road single/dual	Inner London Regional Transport (LRT) station	H — Hospital
Motorway under construction	Road under construction	Outer London Regional Transport (LRT) station	Crem — Crematorium
Primary route single/dual	Restricted road	Railway station/LRT interchange	
Other A road single/dual	Railway line/in tunnel	Light railway/tramway station	
B road single/dual	Railway station	Sports stadium	

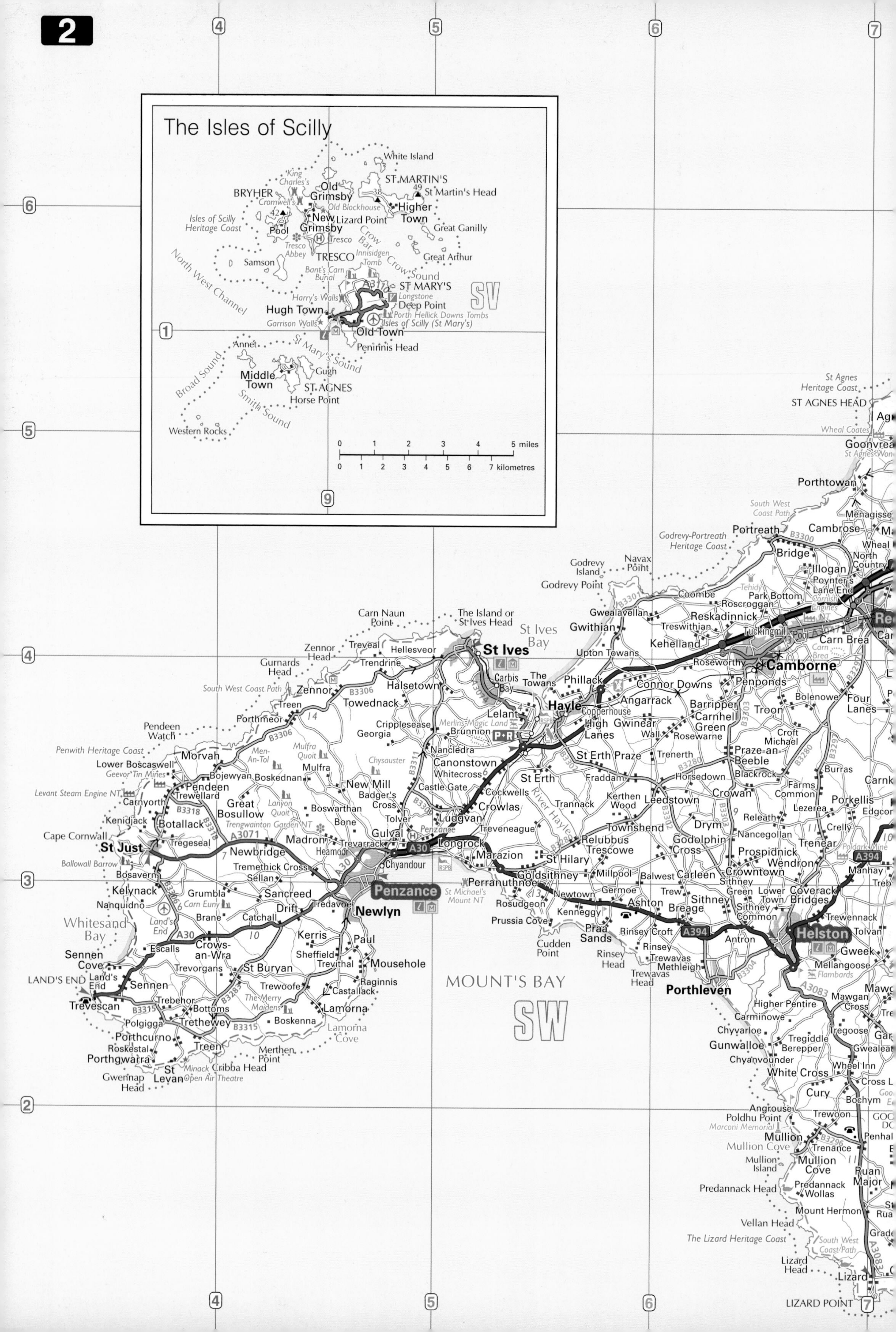

The Isles of Scilly

White Island

ST.MARTIN'S
38
49 St Martin's Head

BRYHER
'King Charles's Castle
Cromwell's Castle
Old Grimsby
Old Blockhouse
Higher Town

42
New Grimsby
Lizard Point

Isles of Scilly Heritage Coast
Pool
Tresco
(H) Tresco
Great Ganilly

Tresco Abbey

TRESCO
Innisidgen Tomb
Great Arthur

Samson
Bant's Carn Burial

Crow Sound

Crow Bar

St Mary's Sound

Harry's Walls

ST MARY'S
Longstone

Deep Point
Porth Hellick Downs Tombs

Hugh Town
Isles of Scilly (St Mary's)

Garrison Walls
Old Town

Peninnis Head

Annet

St Mary's Sound

Middle Town
Gugh

Broad Sound
ST.AGNES
Horse Point

Smith Sound

Western Rocks

SV

| 0 | 1 | 2 | 3 | 4 | 5 miles |
| 0 | 1 | 2 | 3 | 4 | 5 | 6 | 7 kilometres |

St Agnes Heritage Coast
ST AGNES HEAD
Ag

Wheal Coates
Goonvrea

Porthtowan

Menagisse
Cambrose

South West Coast Path

Godrevy-Portreath Heritage Coast
Portreath
B3300
Wheal
Bridge
North
Country
Illogan
Poynter's
Lane End

Godrevy Island
Navax Point

Godrevy Point

Coombe
Park Bottom
Roscroggan
Reskadinnick
Treswithian
Tuckingmill
Pool

Re

Carn Brea
Camborne

Carn Naun Point

The Island or St Ives Head

St Ives Bay

Gwealavellan
Kehelland
Upton Towans

Roseworthy

Penponds

Zennor Head
Treveal
Hellesveor
St Ives

Trendrine
Carbis Bay
The Towans
Phillack
Gwithian

Connor Downs
Barripper
Carnhell Green
Rosewarne

Bolenowe
Four Lanes

Gurnards Head
Zennor
Halsetown
Lelant
Hayle
Angarrack
Copperhouse

Troon
Croft Michael

South West Coast Path
B3306
Towednack
Merlin's Magic Land
High Gwinear
Wall

Praze-an-Beeble
Burras

Pendeen Watch
Treen
14
Cripplesease
Brunnion
St Erth Praze
Trenerth

Carnk

Penwith Heritage Coast
Porthmeor
Georgia
Nancledra
Fraddam
Horsedown
Blackrock

Morvah
Men-An-Tol
Mulfra Quoit
Canonstown
St Erth
Kerthen Wood
Crowan
Common

Lower Boscaswell
Geevor Tin Mines
Mulfra
Chysauster
Whitecross
Leedstown
Lezerea
Porkellis

Bojewyan
Boskednan
New Mill
Castle Gate
Cockwells
Trannack
Releath
Nancegollan
Edgcor

Pendeen
Trewellard
Badger's Cross
Tolver
Crowlas
Townshend
Godolphin Cross
Drym
Trenear

Levant Steam Engine NT
Great Bosullow
Lanyon Quoit
Bone
Ludgvan
Prospidnick
Crenver

Carnyorth
Boswarthen
Penzance
Treveneague
Drym
Wendron
Manhay

Kenidjack
Botallack
Madron
Gulval
Trevarrack
Longrock
Trescowe
Crowntown
Sithney

Cape Cornwall
Tregeseal
A3071
Newbridge
Heamoor
Marazion
St Hilary
Carleen
Green Lower Coverack

Ballowall Barrow
St Just
Tremethick Cross
Chyandour
St Michael's
Goldsithney
Millpool
Balwest
Sithney
Bridges

Bosavern
Sellan
Mount NT
Perranuthnoe
Newtown
Germoe
Trew
Breage
Sithney Common
Helston

Kelynack
Grumbla
Carn Euny
Sancreed
Drift
Newlyn
Rosudgeon
Kenneggy
Ashton
Antron

Nanquidno
Brane
Catchall
Prussia Cove
Praa Sands
Rinsey Croft
Trewennack

Whitesand Bay
Land's End
A30
Kerris
Paul
Cudden Point
Newtown
Rinsey
Methleigh
Trewavas
Head

Sennen Cove
Escalls
Crows-an-Wra
Sheffield
Trevithal
Mousehole
MOUNT'S BAY
Porthleven

LAND'S END
Land's End
Sennen
Trevorgans
St Buryan
Trewoofe
Raginnis
SW
Higher Pentire

Trevescan
Trebehor
Bottoms
The Merry Maidens
Castallack
Lamorna
Carminowe
Tregiddle
Tregoose

Polgigga
Trethewey
Treen
Boskenna
Lamorna Cove
Gunwalloe
Berepper
Gwealear

Porthcurno
Merthen Point
Chyanvounder
White Cross
Wheel Inn

Roskestal
Cribba Head
Cury
Bochym

Porthgwarra
Minack Open Air Theatre
St Levan
Gwennap Head

Angrouse
Poldhu Point
Marconi Memorial
Trewoon
GOO
DO
Penhal

Mullion
Mullion Cove
Trenance

Mullion Island
Mullion Cove
Ruan Major

Predannack Head
Predannack Wollas
Mount Hermon
St Rua

Vellan Head
The Lizard Heritage Coast

Lizard Head
South West Coast Path
Grade
A3083

LIZARD POINT
Lizard

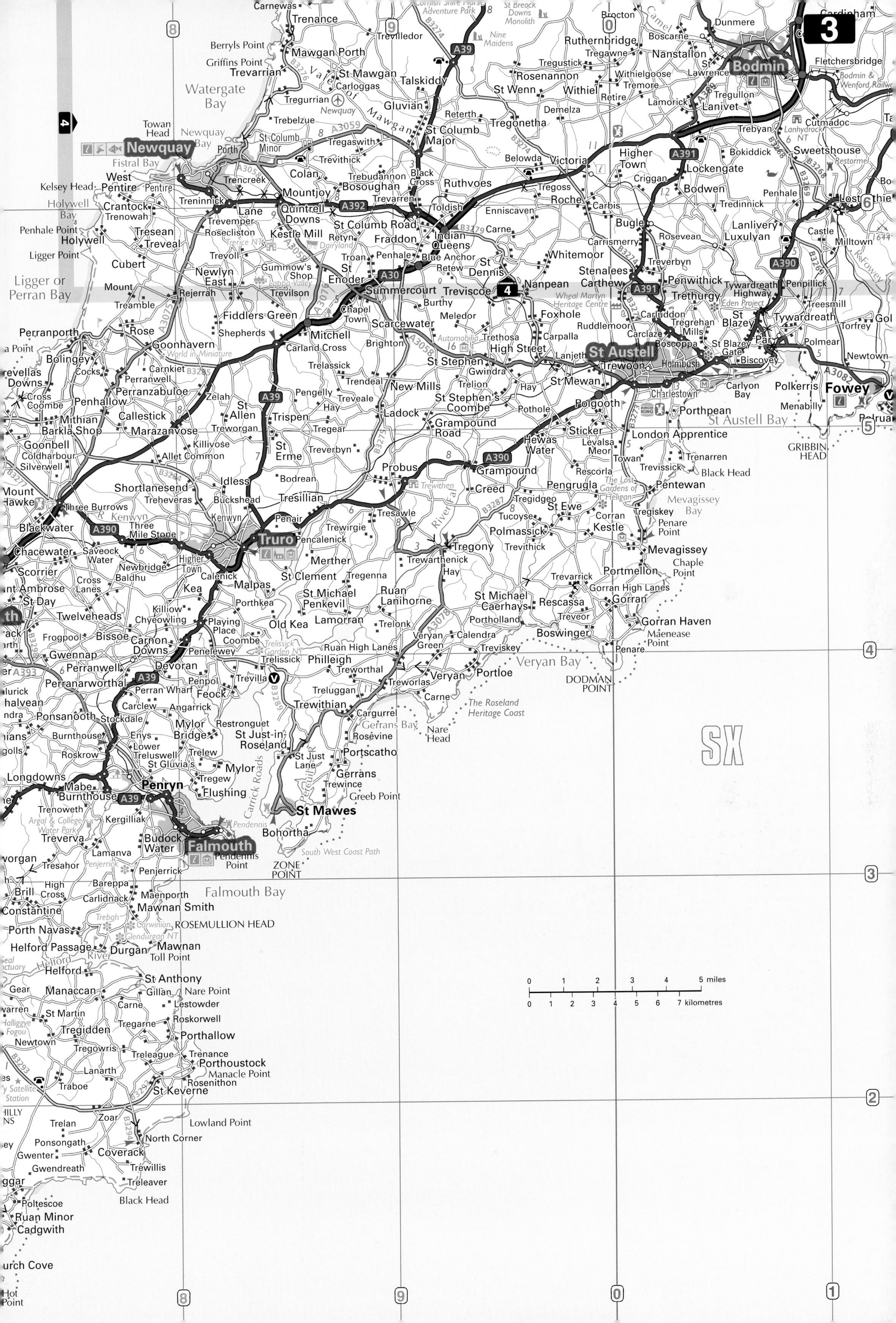

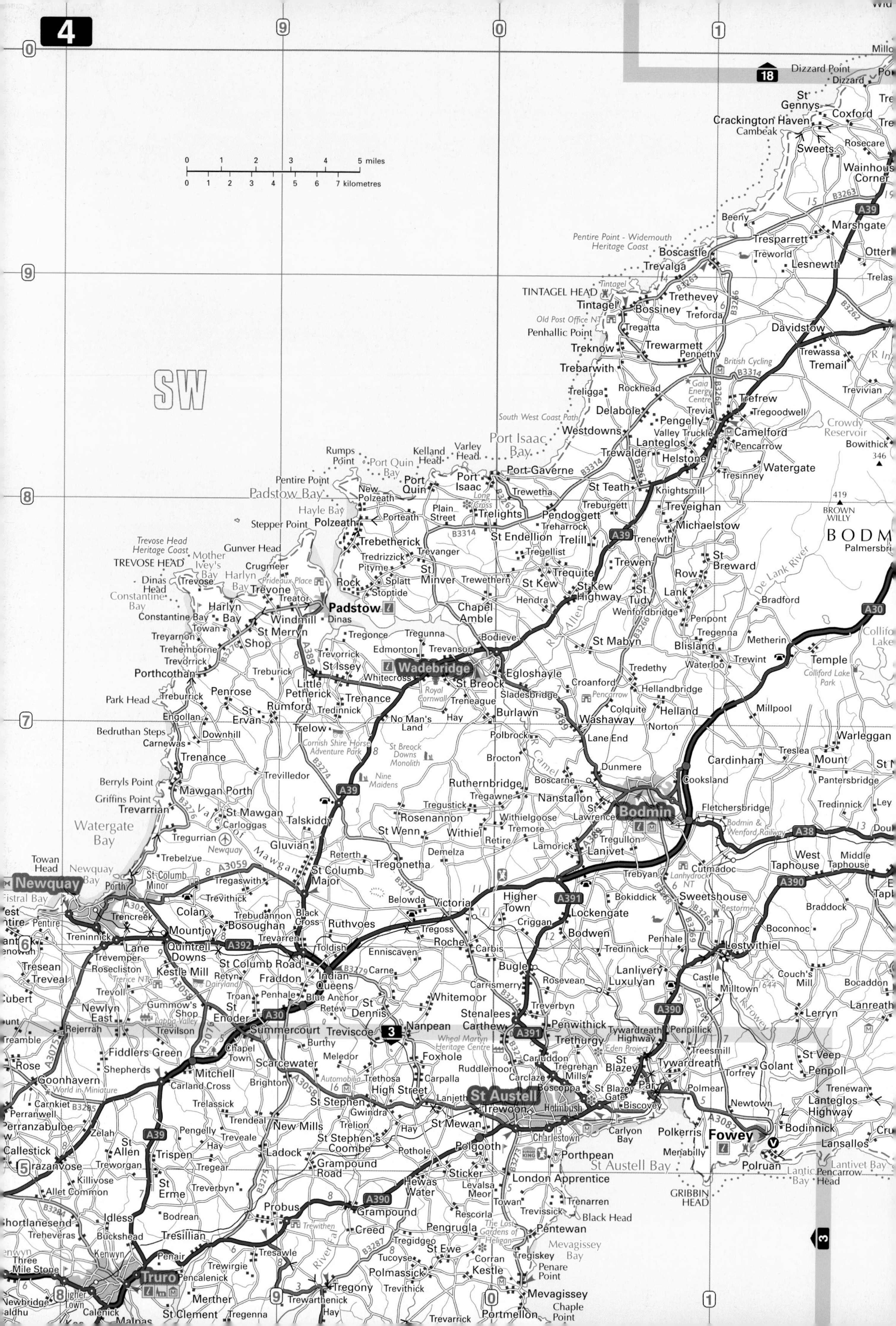

0 1 2 3 4 5 miles
0 1 2 3 4 5 6 7 kilometres
SW
18
Dizzard Point
Dizzard
St Gennys
Crackington Haven
Cambeak
Coxford
Sweets
Rosecare
Wainhouse Corner
B3263
A39
Beeny
Marshgate
Pentire Point - Widemouth Heritage Coast
Tresparrett
Boscastle
Treworld
Otterham
Trevalga
Lesnewth
Trelash
TINTAGEL HEAD
Tintagel
Trethevey
Bossiney
Treforda
B3266
Old Post Office NT
Tregatta
Davidstow
B3262
Penhallic Point
Treknow
Trewarmett
Trewassa
Tremail
Penpethy
British Cycling
Trebarwith
B3314
Gaia Energy Centre
Treligga
Rockhead
Trefrew
Trevivian
Delabole
Trevia
Tregoodwell
Crowdy Reservoir
South West Coast Path
Pengelly
Westdowns
Valley Truckle
Camelford
Bowithick
Lanteglos
Pencarrow
346
Port Isaac Bay
Rumps Point
Kelland Head
Varley Head
Trewalder
Helstone
Port Quin Bay
Port Gaverne
Watergate
Tresinney
Pentire Point
Port Quin
Port Isaac
St Teath
Knightsmill
Padstow Bay
New Polzeath
Long Cross
Trewetha
419
BROWN WILLY
Hayle Bay
Plain Street
Treburgett
Treveighan
Stepper Point
Polzeath
Porteath
Trelights
Pendoggett
Treharrock
Michaelstow
B3314
BODMIN
Trevose Head Heritage Coast
Trebetherick
St Endellion
Trelill
Trenewth
Palmersbridge
Mother Ivey's Bay
Gunver Head
Tredrizzick
Trevanger
Tregellist
TREVOSE HEAD
Crugmeer
Pityme
St Minver
Trewen
St Breward
Dinas Head
Trevose
Harlyn Bay
Prideaux Place
Splatt
Trequite
Row
De Lank River
Constantine Bay
Trevone
Rock
Trewethern
St Kew
St Kew Highway
St Tudy
Lank
Bradford
Treator
Stoptide
Hendra
Harlyn Bay
Padstow
Chapel Amble
Wenfordbridge
Penpont
A30
Constantine Bay
Windmill
Dinas
Towan
St Merryn
Tregonce
Tregunna
Bodieve
R. Allen
Tregenna
Metherin
Colliford Lake
Treyarnon
Shop
St Mabyn
Blisland
Trehemborne
Trevorrick
Edmonton
Trevanson
Temple
Trevorrick
St Issey
Wadebridge
Egloshayle
Waterloo
Trewint
Colliford Lake Park
Porthcothan
Treburick
Whitecross
St Breock
Tredethy
Croanford
Hellandbridge
Little Petherick
Royal Cornwall
Sladesbridge
Pencarrow
Park Head
Treburrick
Penrose
Trenance
Treneague
Colquite
Helland
Millpool
St Ervan
Rumford
Tredinnick
Hay
Burlawn
Washaway
Engollan
No Man's Land
Norton
Bedruthan Steps
Downhill
Trelow
Polbrock
Lane End
Warleggan
Carnewas
Cornish Shire Horse Adventure Park
St Breock Downs Monolith
Treslea
Trenance
Brocton
Cardinham
Mount
R. Camel
Dunmere
Trevilledor
Nine Maidens
Cooksland
Berryls Point
Boscarne
Pantersbridge
Mawgan Porth
Ruthernbridge
Griffins Point
Tregawne
Nanstallon
Fletchersbridge
Tredinnick
Trevarrian
Tregustick
St Lawrence
Bodmin
Vale of Mawgan
St Mawgan
Talskiddy
Withielgoose
Bodmin & Wenford Railway
Watergate Bay
Carloggas
Rosenannon
Tremore
A38
St Wenn
Withiel
Tregurrian
Retire
Lamorick
Tregullon
Newquay
Gluvian
Lanivet
West Taphouse
Middle Taphouse
Trebelzue
Reterth
Demelza
Towan Head
Newquay Bay
A3059
St Columb Major
Tregonetha
Trebyan
Cutmadoc
Lanhydrock NT
Newquay
St Columb Minor
Tregaswith
A390
Porth
Higher Town
Sweetshouse
Fistral Bay
Trevithick
Belowda
Victoria
A391
Bokiddick
Restormel
Braddock
Pentire
Colan
Trebudannon
Black Cross
Criggan
Lockengate
Trencreek
Bosoughan
Ruthvoes
Tregoss
Boconnoc
Treninnick
Mountjoy
Trevarren
Bodwen
Penhale
Lane
Quintrell Downs
A392
Toldish
Roche
Carbis
Tredinnick
Lostwithiel
Trevemper
Enniscaven
Tresean
Rosecliston
Kestle Mill
St Columb Road
Carne
Bugle
Lanlivery
Couch's Mill
Treveal
Trerice NT
Dairyland
Retyn
Fraddon
Indian Queens
Castle
Luxulyan
Bocaddon
Trevoll
Troan
Penhale
Blue Anchor
Carrismerry
Rosevean
Milltown
Cubert
Gummow's Shop
St Enoder
Whitemoor
R. Fowey
Lanreath
Newlyn East
Lappa Valley
St Dennis
Treverbyn
Retew
Stenalees
A390
Lerryn
Rejerrah
Trevilson
A30
Summercourt
Treviscoe
3
Nanpean
Carthew
Penwithick
Tywardreath Highway
Penpillick
Chapel Town
Burthy
Wheal Martyn Heritage Centre
Trethurgy
Eden Project
Treesmill
Fiddlers Green
Meledor
Foxhole
Carluddon
St Veep
Rose
Shepherds
Mitchell
Scarcewater
Ruddlemoor
Tregrehan Mills
St Blazey
Tywardreath
Golant
Penpoll
Goonhavern
Carland Cross
Brighton
Automobilia
Trethosa
Carpalla
Carclaze
Torfrey
World in Miniature
A3058
High Street
Boscoppa
St Blazey Gate
Par
Polmear
Trenewan
Carnkief
Trelassick
St Stephen
Lanjeth
St Austell
Holmbush
Biscovey
Newtown
Lanteglos Highway
Perranwell
Trendeal
Gwindra
Trewoon
Perranzabuloe
Zelah
New Mills
Trelion
Hay
St Mewan
Carlyon Bay
Polkerris
Bodinnick
A39
St Allen
Treveale
St Stephen's Coombe
Charlestown
Fowey
Callestick
Trispen
Ladock
Pothole
Polgooth
Porthpean
Menabilly
Lansallos
Lantivet Bay
Hay
Grampound Road
St Austell Bay
Polruan
Lantic Bay
Pencarrow Head
Treworgan
Tregear
Sticker
London Apprentice
Killivose
St Erme
Hewas Water
Levalsa Meor
GRIBBIN HEAD
Allet Common
Treverbyn
B3273
Probus
Town
Trenarren
Grampound
A390
Rescorla
Trevissick
Black Head
Shortlanesend
Idless
Bodrean
Trewithen
Creed
Pengrugla
The Lost Gardens of Heligan
Pentewan
Treheveras
Buckshead
Tresillian
Tregidgeo
Mevagissey Bay
Kenwyn
Penair
Tresawle
River Fal
B3287
St Ewe
Tregiskey
Three Mile Stone
Trewirgie
Tucoyse
Corran
Penare Point
Truro
Pencalenick
Polmassick
Kestle
Tregony
Trevithick
Mevagissey
Newbridge
Higher Town
Merther
Trewarthenick
Chapel Point
Calenick
St Clement
Tregenna
Hay
Trevarrick
Portmellon
Malpas

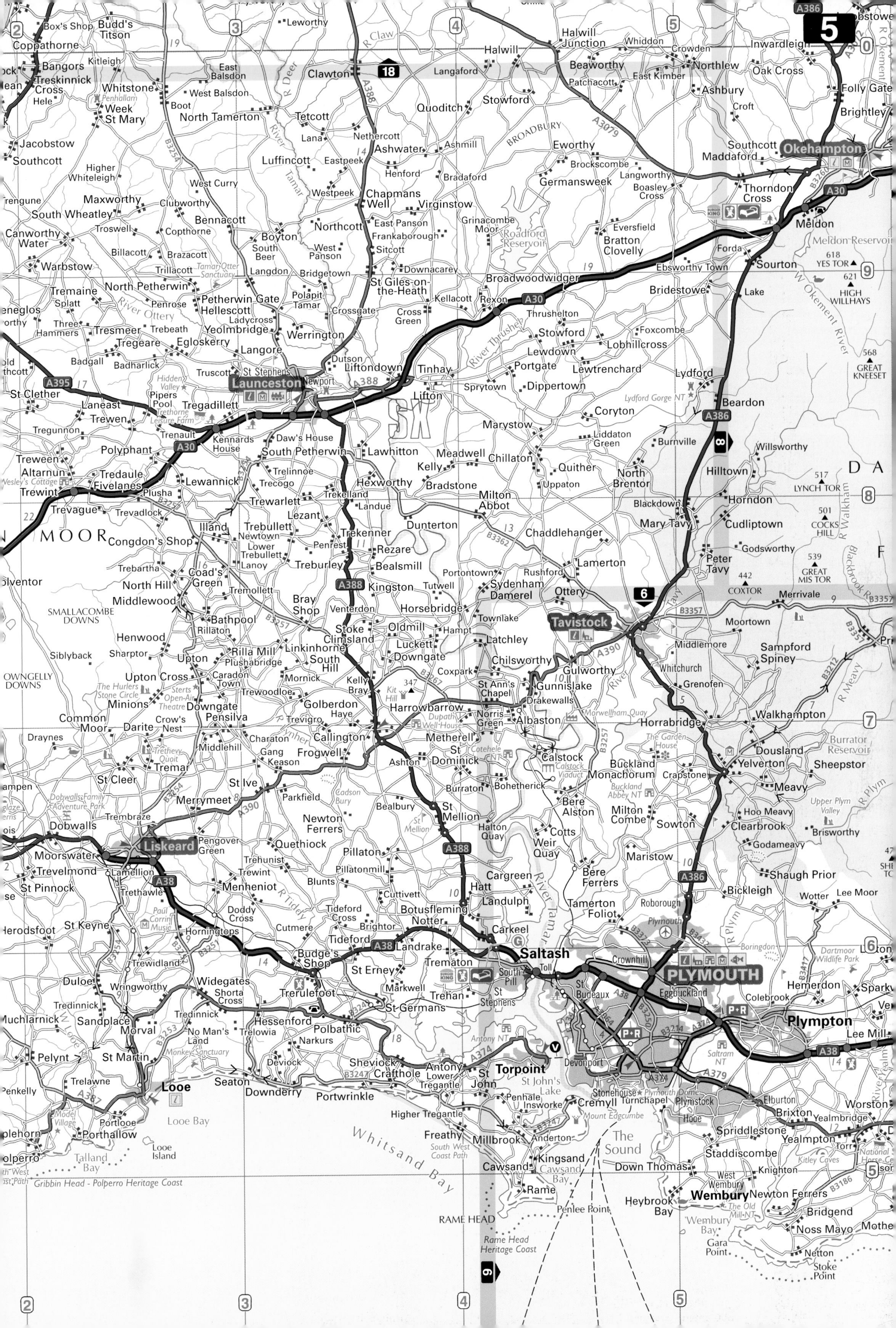

5
A386
Box's Shop
Budd's Titson
Leworthy
Coppathorne
Halwill Junction
Whiddon
Crowden
Inwardleigh
Bangors
Kitleigh
East Balsdon
Clawton
18
Langaford
Halwill
Beaworthy
Northlew
Oak Cross
Treskinnick Cross
Whitstone
West Balsdon
R Claw
R Deer
East Kimber
Patchacott
Ashbury
Folly Gate
Hele
Penhallam
Week St Mary
Boot
North Tamerton
Quoditch
Stowford
Croft
Brightley
Tetcott
A388
A3079
BROADBURY
Jacobstow
Lana
Nethercott
Ashwater
Ashmill
Eworthy
Southcott
Maddaford
Okehampton
Southcott
Luffincott
Eastpeek
Henford
Brockscombe
Langworthy
Higher Whiteleigh
River Tamar
Bradaford
Germansweek
Boasley Cross
Thorndon Cross
B3260
A30
West Curry
Westpeek
Chapmans Well
Virginstow
Meldon
Crengune
Maxworthy
Clubworthy
South Wheatley
Bennacott
Northcott
East Panson
Grinacombe Moor
Eversfield
Canworthy Water
Troswell
Copthorne
Boyton
Frankaborough
Roadford Reservoir
Bratton Clovelly
Meldon Reservoir
Billacott
Brazacott
South Beer
West Panson
Sitcott
Forda
618 YES TOR
Warbstow
Trillacott
Tamar Otter Sanctuary
Langdon
Bridgetown
Downacarey
Ebsworthy Town
Sourton
621 HIGH WILLHAYS
Tremaine
North Petherwin
Penrose
St Giles-on-the-Heath
Broadwoodwidger
Bridestowe
Lake
Splatt
River Ottery
Petherwin Gate
Hellescott
Polapit Tamar
Kellacott
Rexon
Thrushelton
W Okement River
Eneglos
Three Hammers
Ladycross
Crossgate
Cross Green
Foxcombe
Tresmeer
Trebeath
Yeolmbridge
Werrington
River Thrushel
Stowford
Lobhillcross
568 GREAT KNEESET
Tregeare
Egloskerry
Langore
Lewdown
Badgall
Badharlick
Dutson
Liftondown
Tinhay
Portgate
Lewtrenchard
Lydford
Hidden Valley
Truscott
St Stephens
Launceston
Newport
A388
Sprytown
Dippertown
A395
St Clether
Pipers Pool
Lifton
Lydford Gorge NT
Beardon
Laneast
Tregadillett
Trethorne Leisure Farm
Coryton
A386
Trewen
SX
Marystow
Tregunnon
Trenault
Kennards House
Daw's House
Liddaton Green
Burnville
8
Willsworthy
Polyphant
A30
South Petherwin
Lawhitton
Meadwell
Chillaton
Treween
Kelly
Quither
Hilltown
517 LYNCH TOR
Altarnun
Tredaule
Trelinnoe
Hexworthy
North Brentor
DA
Wesley's Cottage
Fivelanes
Lewannick
Trecogo
Bradstone
Uppaton
Trewint
Plusha
Trekelland
Milton Abbot
Blackdown
Horndon
8
Trevague
Trevadlock
Trewarlett
Landue
Mary Tavy
Cudliptown
501 COCKS HILL
R Walkham
B3254
Lezant
Dunterton
MOOR
Congdon's Shop
Illand
Trebullett
Newtown
Trekenner
13
Chaddlehanger
Lower Trebullett
Penrest
Rezare
B3362
Peter Tavy
Godsworthy
539 GREAT MIS TOR
Blackbrook R
Trebartha
Lanoy
Treburley
Bealsmill
Portontown
Rushford
Lamerton
Coad's Green
442 COXTOR
Olventor
North Hill
Tremollett
A388
Kingston
Tutwell
Sydenham Damerel
Ottery
6
Merrivale
B3357
Middlewood
Bray Shop
Venterdon
Horsebridge
R Tavy
SMALLACOMBE DOWNS
Bathpool
B3257
Townlake
Tavistock
B3357
Moortown
Rillaton
Stoke Climsland
Oldmill
Hampt
Henwood
Latchley
A390
Middlemore
Sampford Spiney
Siblyback
Sharptor
Rilla Mill
Linkinhorne
Luckett
Downgate
Whitchurch
Upton
Plushabridge
South Hill
Chilsworthy
Gulworthy
B3212
R Meavy
DOWNGELLY DOWNS
Upton Cross
Caradon Town
Mornick
Coxpark
Kelly Bray
St Ann's Chapel
Gunnislake
Grenofen
The Hurlers Stone Circle
Sterts Open-Air Theatre
Trewoodloe
Kit Hill
347
Drakewalls
River Tavy
Minions
Downgate
Golberdon
Harrowbarrow
Albaston
Walkhampton
Common Moor
Crow's Nest
Pensilva
Trevigro
Haye
Dupath Well-House
Norris Green
Morwellham Quay
Horrabridge
Darite
Callington
Metherell
The Garden House
Draynes
Charaton
R Lynher
Cotehele NT
B3257
Dousland
Burrator Reservoir
Trethevy Quoit
Middlehill
Gang
Frogwell
St Dominick
Calstock
Calstock Viaduct
Buckland Monachorum
Crapstone
Yelverton
Sheepstor
Tremar
Keason
Ashton
Tremar
St Cleer
Bohetherick
Buckland Abbey NT
Meavy
Campen
Dobwalls Family Adventure Park
St Ive
Parkfield
Cadson Bury
Burraton
Bere Alston
Milton Combe
Upper Plym Valley
R Plym
Merrymeet
B3254
A390
Bealbury
St Mellion
Hoo Meavy
Clearbrook
Trembraze
Newton Ferrers
Halton Quay
Cotts
Sowton
Dobwalls
St Mellion
Brisworthy
Weir Quay
Godameavy
Liskeard
Pengover Green
Quethiock
A388
Moorswater
Pillaton
Maristow
Trehunist
Lamellion
Pillatonmill
Trevelmond
Trewint
Cargreen
Bere Ferrers
A386
Shaugh Prior
St Pinnock
A38
Menheniot
Blunts
Hatt
River Tamar
Trethawle
R Tiddy
Cuttivett
10
Landulph
Tamerton Foliot
Bickleigh
Wotter
Lee Moor
Paul Corin's Music
Doddy Cross
Tideford Cross
Botusfleming
Roborough
Herodsfoot
St Keyne
Notter
Plymouth
R Plym
Horningtops
Cutmere
Brighton
Carkeel
Boringdon
Dartmoor Wildlife Park
B3254
B3251
Tideford
A38
Landrake
Saltash
Crownhill
Trewidland
14
Budge's Shop
Trematon
Toll
PLYMOUTH
Hemerdon
Duloe
St Erney
South Pill
Eggbuckland
B3417
Sparkw
Wringworthy
Widegates
Shorta Cross
Markwell
St Budeaux
A38
Colebrook
Tredinnick
Trerulefoot
Trehan
St Stephens
P+R
Plympton
Muchlarnick
Sandplace
Tredinnick
Hessenford
St Germans
B3250
Lee Mill
Morval
B3253
No Man's Land
Trelowia
Polbathic
B3396
B3214
A374
Narkurs
18
Antony NT
A38
Monkey Sanctuary
Pelynt
St Martin
Deviock
Sheviock
Antony
Devonport
Saltram NT
R Looe
Trelawne
Looe
Seaton
B3247
Crafthole
A374
St John
Torpoint
A374
A379
Lower Tregantle
St John's Lake
Stonehouse
Plymouth Dome
Turnchapel
Plymstock
Elburton
Worston
Penkelly
A387
Downderry
Portwrinkle
Penhale
Inswork
Cremyll
Brixton
Yealmbridge
Model Village
Portlooe
Looe Bay
Higher Tregantle
Mount Edgcumbe
Hooe
Spriddlestone
Yealmpton
Polperro
Porthallow
Whitsand Bay
Freathy
Millbrook
Anderton
The Sound
Staddiscombe
Torr
Looe Island
South West Coast Path
Kingsand
National Shire Horse Ce
Talland Bay
Cawsand
Cawsand Bay
Down Thomas
Kitley Caves
West Wembury
Knighton
South West Coast Path
Gribbin Head - Polperro Heritage Coast
Rame
B3186
Wembury
Newton Ferrers
Heybrook Bay
Penlee Point
The Old Mill NT
Bridgend
RAME HEAD
Wembury Bay
Noss Mayo
Rame Head Heritage Coast
Gara Point
Netton
Stoke Point
9
2
3
4
5
6
7
8
9
0

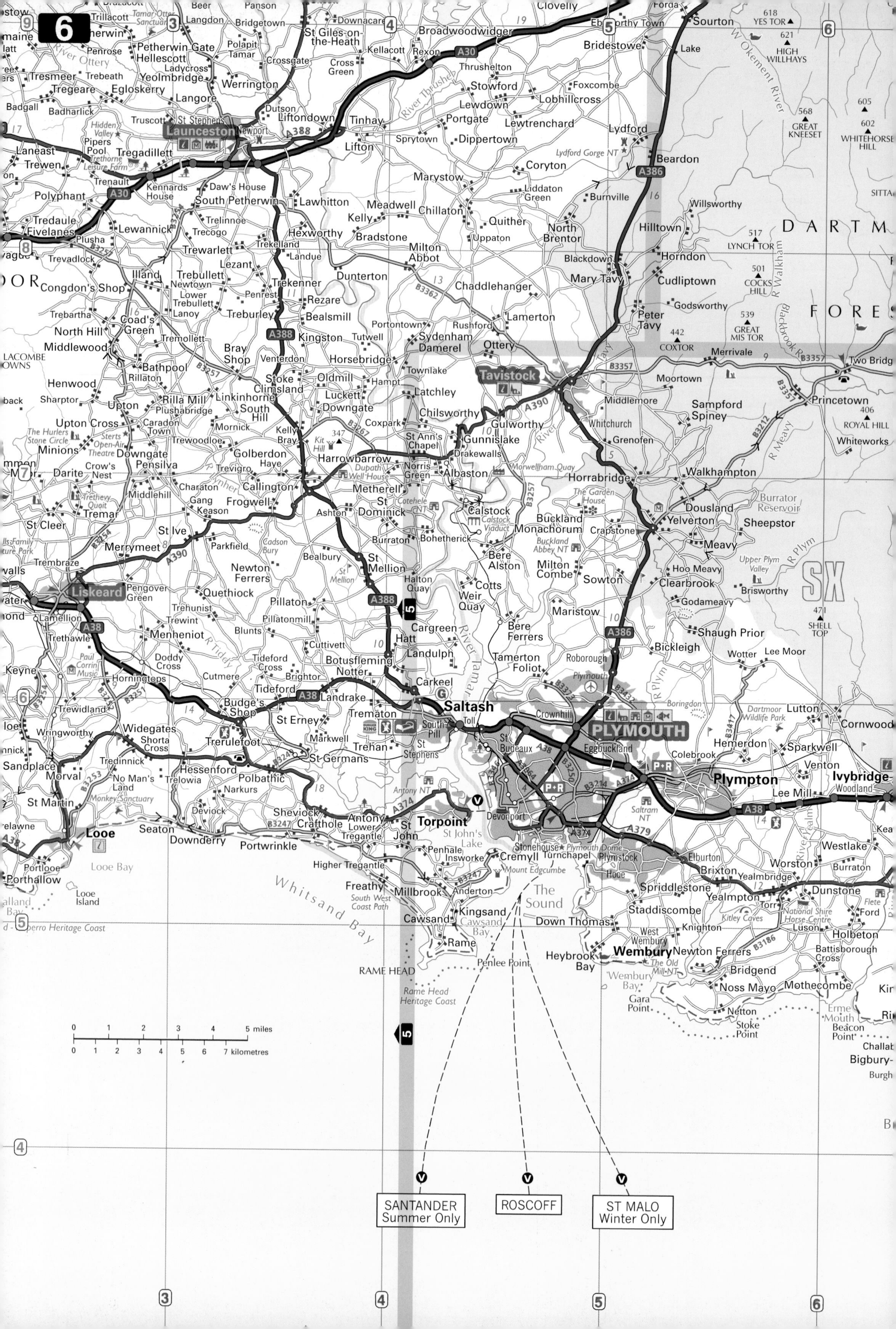

Launceston
Liskeard
Tavistock
Saltash
PLYMOUTH
Plympton
Ivybridge
Torpoint
Looe
Callington
Gunnislake
Lifton
Lydford
Bridestowe
Sourton
Broadwoodwidger
St Giles-on-the-Heath
Werrington
Egloskerry
Tresmeer
Tregeare
Langore
Yeolmbridge
Petherwin Gate
Hellescott
Ladycross
Polapit Tamar
Crossgate
Cross Green
Kellacott
Rexon
Thrushelton
Stowford
Lewdown
Lobhillcross
Foxcombe
Portgate
Lewtrenchard
Sprytown
Dippertown
Tinhay
Dutson
Liftondown
Newport
St Stephens
Truscott
Hidden Valley
Pipers Pool
Tregadillett
Trethorne Leisure Farm
Laneast
Trewen
Trenault
Kennards House
Daw's House
South Petherwin
Lawhitton
Polyphant
Tredaule
Fivelanes
Plusha
Lewannick
Trelinnoe
Trecogo
Trewarlett
Trekelland
Hexworthy
Landue
Bradstone
Kelly
Meadwell
Chillaton
Quither
Uppaton
Milton Abbot
Marystow
Coryton
Liddaton Green
Burnville
North Brentor
Blackdown
Mary Tavy
Beardon
Willsworthy
Hilltown
Horndon
Cudliptown
Godsworthy
Peter Tavy
Trevadlock
Lezant
Illand
Trebullett
Newtown
Lower Trebullett
Lanoy
Penrest
Trekenner
Rezare
Treburley
Bealsmill
Dunterton
Chaddlehanger
Lamerton
Rushford
Portontown
Sydenham Damerel
Ottery
Congdon's Shop
Trebartha
Coad's Green
North Hill
Middlewood
Tremollett
Bathpool
Rillaton
Bray Shop
Venterdon
Kingston
Tutwell
Horsebridge
Townlake
Hampt
Oldmill
Luckett
Stoke Climsland
Linkinhorne
Rilla Mill
Plushabridge
South Hill
Henwood
Sharptor
Upton
Upton Cross
Caradon Town
Mornick
The Hurlers Stone Circle
Minions
Sterts Open-Air Theatre
Trewoodloe
Kelly Bray
Downgate
Pensilva
Golberdon
Kit Hill
Harrowbarrow
Coxpark
Latchley
Chilsworthy
Gulworthy
St Ann's Chapel
Drakewalls
Darite
Crow's Nest
Middlehill
Trevigro
Haye
Charaton
Gang
Keason
Frogwell
Trethevy Quoit
Tremar
St Cleer
St Ive
Merrymeet
Parkfield
Cadson Bury
Dupath Well House
Norris Green
Albaston
Metherell
St Dominick
Cotehele NT
Calstock
Calstock Viaduct
Morwellham Quay
Ashton
Burraton
Bohetherick
Bealbury
St Mellion
Halton Quay
Newton Ferrers
Trembraze
Pengover Green
Quethiock
Trehunist
Pillaton
Pillatonmill
Trewint
Blunts
Menheniot
Lamellion
Trethawle
Doddy Cross
Paul Corrin Music
Cutmere
Tideford Cross
Tideford
Brighton
Cuttivett
Botusfleming
Notter
Hatt
Landulph
Cargreen
Weir Quay
Cotts
Bere Alston
Bere Ferrers
Tamerton Foliot
Roborough
Maristow
Milton Combe
Buckland Abbey NT
Buckland Monachorum
Crapstone
Sowton
Horrabridge
The Garden House
Grenofen
Whitchurch
Middlemore
Moortown
Merrivale
Sampford Spiney
Princetown
Two Bridges
Royal Hill
Whiteworks
Walkhampton
Dousland
Yelverton
Sheepstor
Burrator Reservoir
Meavy
Hoo Meavy
Clearbrook
Upper Plym Valley
Briswworthy
Godameavy
Shaugh Prior
Bickleigh
Wotter
Lee Moor
Boringdon
Dartmoor Wildlife Park
Lutton
Cornwood
Hemerdon
Sparkwell
Venton
Colebrook
Lee Mill
Woodland
Horningtops
Trewidland
Wringworthy
Widegates
Shorta Cross
Trerulefoot
Budge's Shop
Landrake
St Erney
Trematon
Markwell
Trehan
St Stephens
St Germans
South Pill
Carkeel
Tredinnick
Hessenford
Trelowia
Polbathic
Narkurs
Sandplace
Morval
No Man's Land
Monkey Sanctuary
St Martin
Deviock
Sheviock
Crafthole
Antony
Antony NT
Lower Tregantle
St John
St John's Lake
Seaton
Downderry
Portwrinkle
Portlooe
Porthallow
Looe Bay
Looe Island
Whitsand Bay
Higher Tregantle
Penhale
Inswork
Freathy
South West Coast Path
Millbrook
Anderton
Kingsand
Cawsand
Cawsand Bay
Rame
Rame Head
Rame Head Heritage Coast
Penlee Point
Cremyll
Mount Edgcumbe
The Sound
Stonehouse
Plymouth Dome
Turnchapel
Plymstock
Hooe
Devonport
St Budeaux
Crownhill
Eggbuckland
Saltram NT
Elburton
Brixton
Spriddlestone
Staddiscombe
Down Thomas
West Wembury
Wembury
Knighton
Heybrook Bay
The Old Mill NT
Wembury Bay
Gara Point
Yealmpton
Yealmbridge
Worston
Westlake
Burraton
Dunstone
Torr
Kitley Caves
National Shire Horse Centre
Luson
Flete
Ford
Holbeton
Battisborough Cross
Newton Ferrers
Bridgend
Noss Mayo
Mothecombe
Netton
Stoke Point
Erme Mouth
Beacon Point
Bigbury-
Burgh
Challab
DARTMOOR FOREST
SX
YES TOR 618
HIGH WILLHAYS 621
GREAT KNEESET 568
WHITEHORSE HILL 602
LYNCH TOR 517
COCKS HILL 501
GREAT MIS TOR 539
COXTOR 442
SHELL TOP 471
W Okement River
River Thrushel
River Ottery
River Tamar
R Tavy
R Walkham
R Meavy
R Plym
R Tiddy
R Lynher
River Yealm
Lydford Gorge NT
A30
A38
A388
A386
A390
A374
A379
B3257
B3254
B3251
B3252
B3253
B3247
B3362
B3357
B3212
B3373
B3432
B3417
B3250
B3214
B3186
P+R
SANTANDER Summer Only
ROSCOFF
ST MALO Winter Only
0 1 2 3 4 5 miles
0 1 2 3 4 5 6 7 kilometres

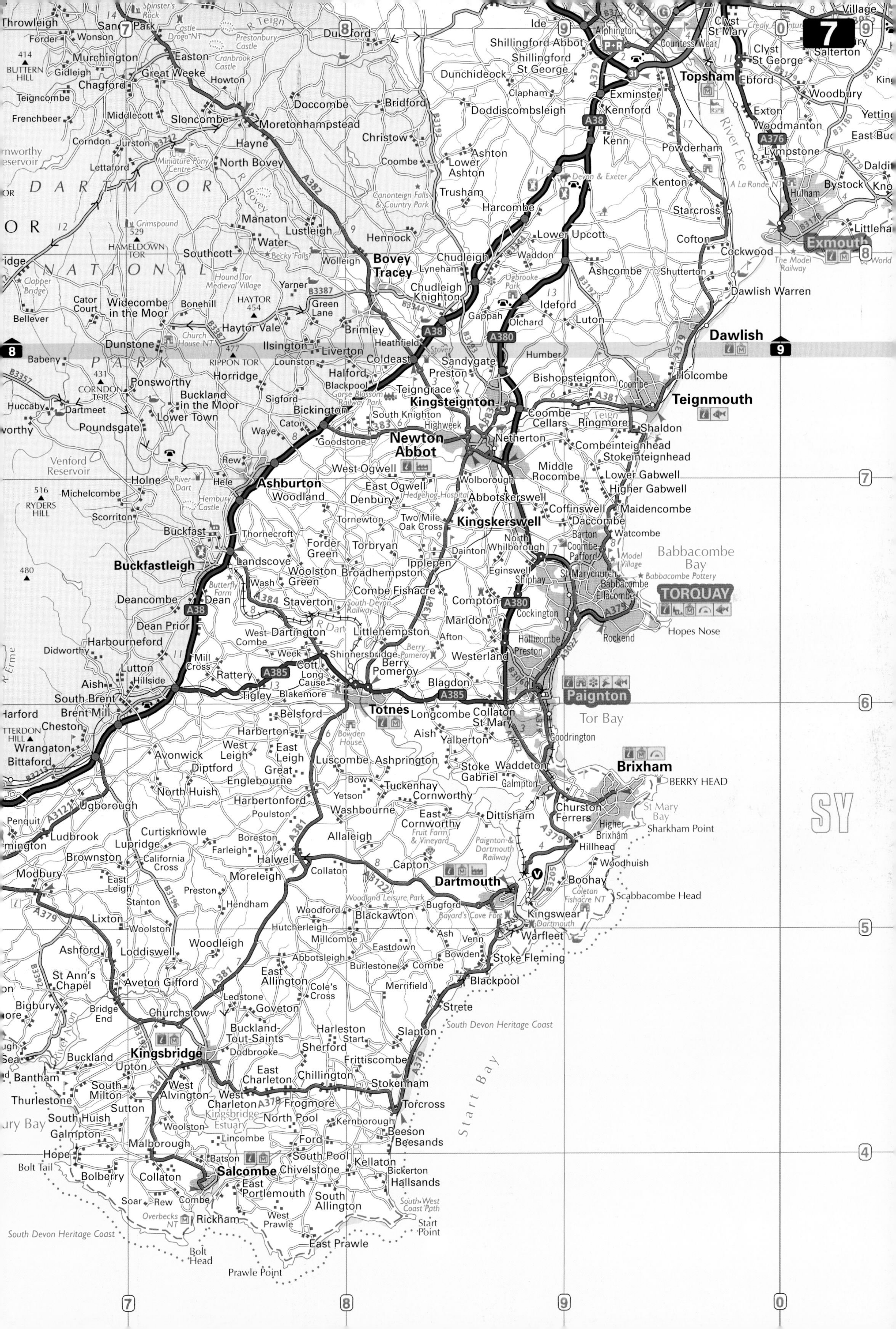

7
Throwleigh
Spinster's Rock
Sandy Park
Castle Drogo NT
R Teign
Prestonbury Castle
Dunsford
Ide
Alphington
P+R
Countess Wear
Clyst St Mary
Salterton
Forder
Wonson
Murchington
Easton
Cranbrook Castle
Shillingford Abbot
Shillingford St George
Topsham
Clyst St George
Ebford
BUTTERN HILL
Gidleigh
Great Weeke
Howton
Dunchideock
Exminster
Woodbury
Teigncombe
Chagford
Doccombe
Bridford
Clapham
Kennford
Exton
Frenchbeer
Middlecott
Sloncombe
Moretonhampstead
Doddiscombsleigh
Woodmanton
Corndon
Jurston
Hayne
Christow
Kenn
Powderham
River Exe
East Budleigh
Miniature Pony Centre
North Bovey
Coombe
Ashton
Lower Ashton
Lympstone
Lettaford
Devon & Exeter
Kenton
A La Ronde NT
Bystock
DARTMOOR
R Bovey
Canonteign Falls & Country Park
Trusham
Hulham
Harcombe
Starcross
Grimspound
Manaton
Lustleigh
Hennock
Lower Upcott
Cofton
Exmouth
HAMELDOWN TOR
Water
Becky Falls
Southcott
Wolleigh
Bovey Tracey
Chudleigh
Waddon
Cockwood
The Model Railway
NATIONAL
Hound Tor Medieval Village
Lyneham
Ashcombe
Shutterton
Clapper Bridge
Yarner
Chudleigh Knighton
Ugbrooke Park
Dawlish Warren
Cator Court
Widecombe in the Moor
Bonehill
HAYTOR
Green Lane
Ideford
Bellever
Haytor Vale
Gappah
Olchard
Luton
Church House NT
Brimley
Dawlish
Dunstone
Ilsington
Liverton
Heathfield
Stover
Babeny
PARK
RIPPON TOR
Lounston
Coldeast
Sandygate
Humber
CORNDON TOR
Ponsworthy
Horridge
Halford
Preston
Bishopsteignton
Holcombe
Buckland in the Moor
Blackpool
Gorse Blossom Railway Park
Teigngrace
Kingsteignton
Coombe
Teignmouth
Huccaby
Dartmeet
Sigford
Bickington
Lower Town
South Knighton
Coombe Cellars
Ringmore
R Teign
Shaldon
Poundsgate
Caton
Highweek
Waye
Goodstone
Newton Abbot
Netherton
Combeinteignhead
Stokeinteignhead
Venford Reservoir
Rew
West Ogwell
Middle Rocombe
Lower Gabwell
Holne
River Dart
Hele
Ashburton
Wolborough
Higher Gabwell
RYDERS HILL
Michelcombe
Hembury Castle
Woodland
East Ogwell
Denbury
Hedgehog Hospital
Abbotskerswell
Coffinswell
Maidencombe
Scorriton
Tornewton
Two Mile Oak Cross
Kingskerswell
Daccombe
Buckfast
Thornecroft
Forder Green
Torbryan
North Whilborough
Barton
Watcombe
Babbacombe Bay
Buckfastleigh
Landscove
Ipplepen
Dainton
Coombe Pafford
Model Village
Woolston Green
Broadhempston
Eginswell
St Marychurch
Babbacombe Pottery
Butterfly Farm
Wash
Shiphay
Babbacombe
Deancombe
Dean
Staverton
Combe Fishacre
Compton
Ellacombe
TORQUAY
South Devon Railway
Marldon
Cockington
Dean Prior
West Combe
Dartington
R Dart
Littlehempston
Afton
Rockend
Hopes Nose
Harbourneford
Hollicombe
Preston
Didworthy
Mill Cross
Week
Shinnersbridge
Berry Pomeroy
Westerland
Lutton
Rattery
Cott
Long Cause
Berry Pomeroy
Aish
Hillside
Blagdon
Paignton
South Brent
Tigley
Blakemore
Harford
Brent Mill
Belsford
Totnes
Longcombe
Collaton St Mary
Tor Bay
Cheston
Harberton
Bowden House
Aish
Yalberton
Goodrington
Wrangaton
West Leigh
East Leigh
Bittaford
Avonwick
Diptford
Great Englebourne
Luscombe
Ashprington
Stoke Gabriel
Waddeton
Brixham
Galmpton
BERRY HEAD
North Huish
Bow
Tuckenhay
Ugborough
Harbertonford
Yetson
Cornworthy
Churston Ferrers
St Mary Bay
SY
Penquit
Poulston
Washbourne
East Cornworthy
Dittisham
Higher Brixham
Sharkham Point
Curtisknowle
Ludbrook
Lupridge
Boreston
Allaleigh
Fruit Farm & Vineyard
Paignton & Dartmouth Railway
Hillhead
Brownston
California Cross
Farleigh
Halwell
Woodhuish
Modbury
East Leigh
Moreleigh
Collaton
Capton
Dartmouth
Boohay
Coleton Fishacre NT
Scabbacombe Head
Preston
Stanton
Hendham
Woodland Leisure Park
Bugford
Woodford
Blackawton
Bayard's Cove Fort
Kingswear
Dartmouth
Lixton
Woolston
Hutcherleigh
Millcombe
Warfleet
Ashford
Loddiswell
Woodleigh
Eastdown
Ash
Venn
Bowden
Abbotsleigh
Stoke Fleming
St Ann's Chapel
Aveton Gifford
East Allington
Burlestone
Combe
Blackpool
Merrifield
Cole's Cross
Bigbury
Bridge End
Ledstone
Goveton
Strete
River Avon
Churchstow
South Devon Heritage Coast
Buckland-Tout-Saints
Harleston
Start
Slapton
Kingsbridge
Dodbrooke
Sherford
Start Bay
Buckland
Frittiscombe
Upton
Bantham
East Charleton
Chillington
Stokenham
West Alvington
South Milton
Thurlestone
West Charleton
Frogmore
Torcross
Sutton
Kingsbridge Estuary
North Pool
South Huish
Woolston
Kernborough
Bigbury Bay
Galmpton
Beeson
Beesands
Lincombe
Marlborough
Ford
Hope
Batson
South Pool
Kellaton
Bolt Tail
Salcombe
Chivelstone
Bickerton
Bolberry
Collaton
Hallsands
East Portlemouth
South Allington
Soar
Rew
Combe
South West Coast Path
Overbecks NT
Rickham
West Prawle
Start Point
South Devon Heritage Coast
East Prawle
Bolt Head
Prawle Point
7
8
9
0

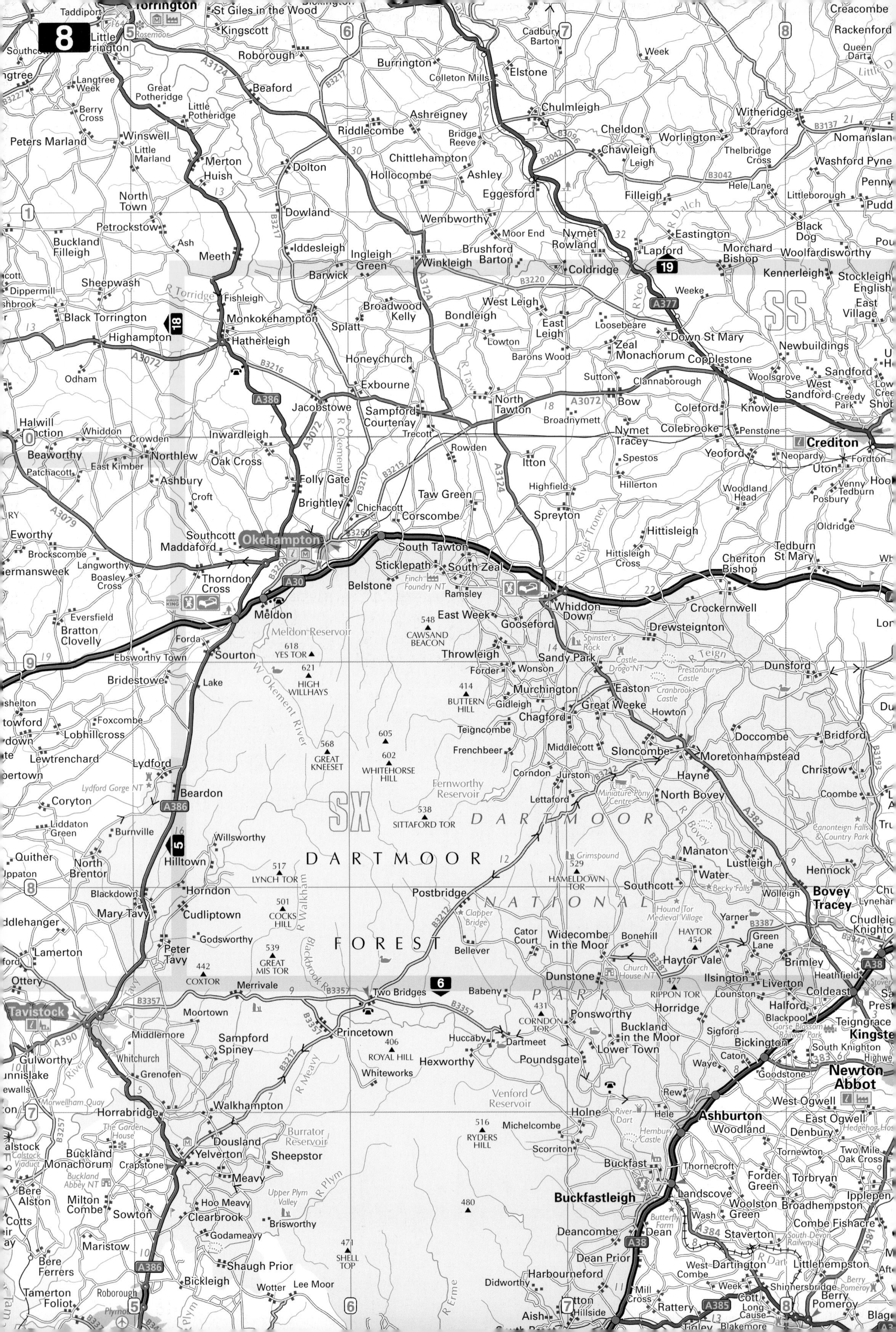
8
Taddiport
Torrington
St Giles in the Wood
Kingscott
Roborough
Little Torrington
Rosemoor
Southcott
Langtree Week
Great Potheridge
Little Potheridge
Berry Cross
Beaford
Burrington
Colleton Mills
Cadbury Barton
Elstone
Week
Creacombe
Rackenford
Queen Dart
Chulmleigh
Witheridge
Ashreigney
Riddlecombe
Bridge Reeve
Cheldon
Worlington
Drayford
Nomansland
Chawleigh
Leigh
Thelbridge Cross
Washford Pyne
Peters Marland
Winswell
Little Marland
Merton
Huish
Dolton
Chittlehampton
Hollocombe
Ashley
Eggesford
Filleigh
Hele Lane
Littleborough
Penny
Pudd
North Town
Dowland
Wembworthy
Petrockstow
Buckland Filleigh
Ash
Meeth
Iddesleigh
Ingleigh Green
Moor End
Nymet Rowland
Brushford Barton
Eastington
Lapford
Morchard Bishop
Black Dog
Woolfardisworthy
R Dalch
Barwick
Winkleigh
Coldridge
Kennerleigh
Stockleigh English
East Village
Sheepwash
R Torridge
Fishleigh
Dippermill
Black Torrington
Monkokehampton
Broadwood Kelly
Bondleigh
West Leigh
East Leigh
Weeke
Loosebeare
Down St Mary
Highampton
Hatherleigh
Splatt
Lowton
Zeal Monachorum
Copplestone
Newbuildings
Odham
Honeychurch
Barons Wood
Sutton
Clannaborough
Woolsgrove
West Sandford
Sandford
Creedy Park
Exbourne
Jacobstowe
Sampford Courtenay
North Tawton
Bow
Coleford
Knowle
Halwill Junction
Whiddon
Crowden
Inwardleigh
Trecott
Broadnymett
Nymet Tracey
Colebrooke
Penstone
Crediton
Beaworthy
Northlew
Oak Cross
Patchacott
East Kimber
Ashbury
Folly Gate
Rowden
Itton
Spestos
Yeoford
Neopardy
Fordton
Uton
Hillerton
Highfield
Woodland Head
Venny Tedburn
Posbury
Croft
Brightley
Chichacott
Taw Green
Corscombe
Spreyton
Oldridge
Eworthy
Southcott
Maddaford
Okehampton
South Tawton
Hittisleigh
Brockscombe
Germansweek
Langworthy
Boasley Cross
Thorndon Cross
Sticklepath
South Zeal
Hittisleigh Cross
River Troney
Cheriton Bishop
Tedburn St Mary
Belstone
Finch Foundry NT
Ramsley
Whiddon Down
Crockernwell
Eversfield
Bratton Clovelly
Meldon
East Week
Gooseford
Drewsteignton
Meldon Reservoir
548 CAWSAND BEACON
Forda
618 YES TOR
Throwleigh
Spinster's Rock
Castle Drogo NT
R Teign
Sandy Park
Dunsford
Prestonbury Castle
Sourton
Ebsworthy Town
621 HIGH WILLHAYS
Forder
Wonson
Bridestowe
Lake
W Okement River
414 BUTTERN HILL
Murchington
Gidleigh
Easton
Cranbrook Castle
Chagford
Great Weeke
Howton
Foxcombe
Lobhillcross
605
Teigncombe
Doccombe
Bridford
568 GREAT KNEESET
602 WHITEHORSE HILL
Frenchbeer
Middlecott
Sloncombe
Moretonhampstead
Lewtrenchard
Lydford
Jurston
Hayne
Christow
Corndon
Fernworthy Reservoir
Lydford Gorge NT
Beardon
Lettaford
Miniature Pony Centre
North Bovey
Coombe
Coryton
SX
538 SITTAFORD TOR
DARTMOOR
Liddaton Green
Burnville
Canonteign Falls & Country Park
Willsworthy
Grimspound
R Bovey
Manaton
Lustleigh
Hilltown
Quither
North Brentor
517 LYNCH TOR
DARTMOOR
529 HAMELDOWN TOR
Water
Hennock
Bovey Tracey
Horndon
Postbridge
NATIONAL
Southcott
Becky Falls
Wolleigh
Blackdown
Mary Tavy
501 COCKS HILL
Cudliptown
R Walkham
Clapper Bridge
Hound Tor Medieval Village
Yarner
Godsworthy
Cator Court
Widecombe in the Moor
Bonehill
HAYTOR 454
Green Lane
Chudleigh Knighton
Lamerton
Peter Tavy
539 GREAT MIS TOR
Blackbrook R
FOREST
Bellever
Haytor Vale
Brimley
Heathfield
Ottery
442 COXTOR
Dunstone
Church House NT
477 RIPPON TOR
Ilsington
Liverton
Coldeast
Merrivale
Two Bridges
Babeny
PARK
Lounston
Tavistock
Moortown
431 CORNDON TOR
Ponsworthy
Horridge
Halford
Blackpool
Teigngrace
Middlemoor
Sampford Spiney
Princetown
Huccaby
Dartmeet
Buckland in the Moor
Sigford
Gorse Blossom Railway Park
Kingsteignton
Gulworthy
Whitchurch
406 ROYAL HILL
Hexworthy
Poundsgate
Lower Town
Bickington
South Knighton
Caton
Waye
Goodstone
Newton Abbot
Grenofen
R Meavy
Whiteworks
Venford Reservoir
Morwellham Quay
Rew
West Ogwell
Horrabridge
Walkhampton
Holne
River Dart
Hele
Ashburton
East Ogwell
Woodland
Denbury
Hedgehog Hospital
The Garden House
Burrator Reservoir
516 RYDERS HILL
Michelcombe
Hembury Castle
Dousland
Yelverton
Sheepstor
Scorriton
Tornewton
Two Mile Oak Cross
Calstock
Buckland Monachorum
Crapstone
Buckfast
Thornecroft
Buckland Abbey NT
Meavy
R Plym
Forder Green
Torbryan
Bere Alston
Milton Combe
Hoo Meavy
Upper Plym Valley
480
Buckfastleigh
Landscove
Ipplepen
Sowton
Clearbrook
Brisworthy
Butterfly Farm
Woolston Green
Broadhempston
Wash
Cotts
Godameavy
Dean
Deancombe
Staverton
Combe Fishacre
South Devon Railway
Maristow
471 SHELL TOP
Bere Ferrers
Shaugh Prior
Dean Prior
West Combe
Dartington
R Dart
Littlehempston
Harbourneford
Berry Pomeroy
Bickleigh
Wotter
Lee Moor
Didworthy
Week
Shinnersbridge
Tamerton Foliot
Roborough
R Erme
Mill Cross
Rattery
Cott
Long Cause
Berry Pomeroy
Aish
Hillside
Tigley
Blakemore
Plymouth
SS
A3124
A3072
A386
A30
A377
A382
A38
A385
A384
A390
A3079
B3217
B3220
B3215
B3216
B3260
B3212
B3357
B3387
B3344
B3193
B3096
B3042
B3137
B3227
B3257
19
18
5
6
7
9
10
1
0

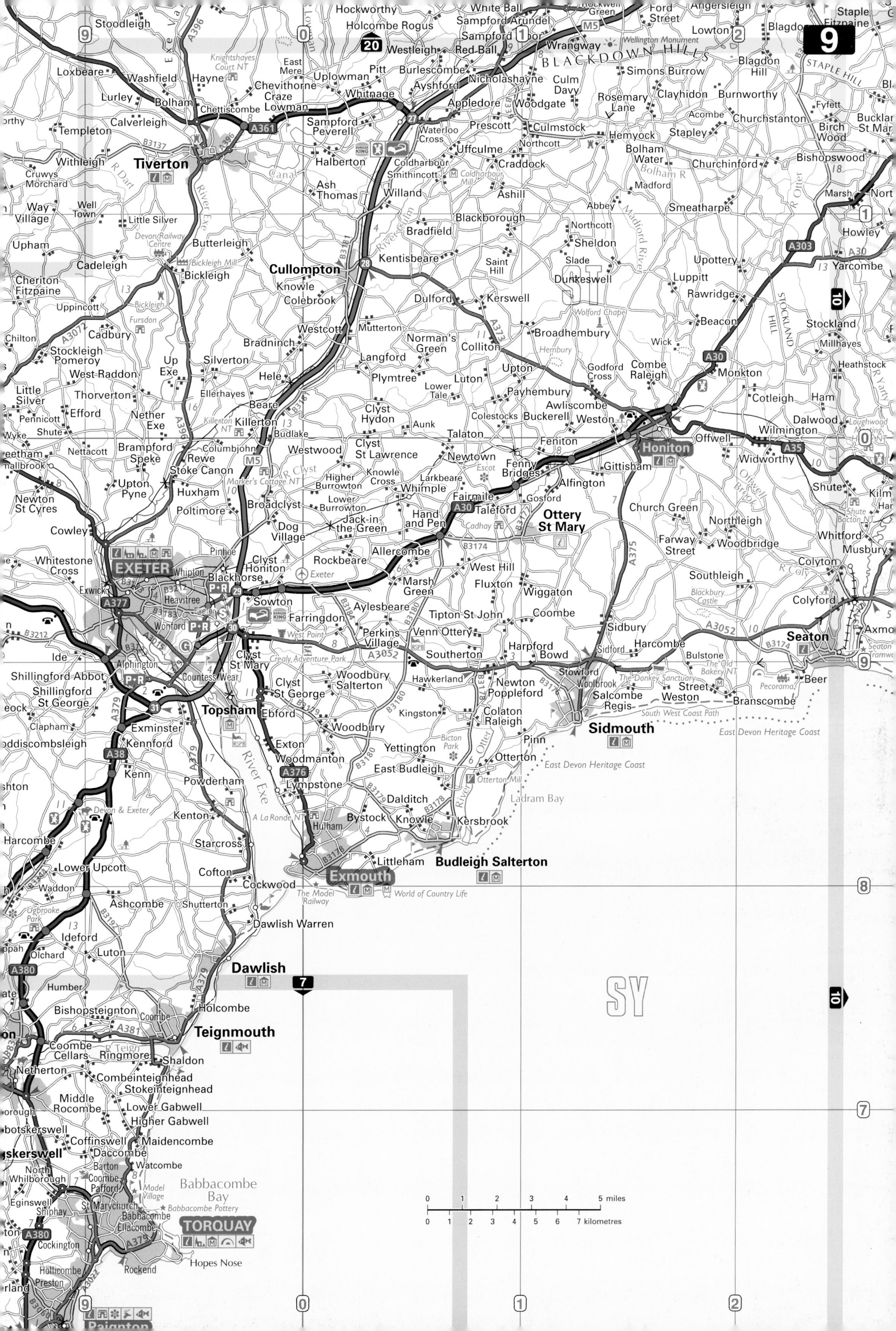
Hockworthy
Holcombe Rogus
White Ball
Sampford Arundel
Sampford
Ford Street
Angersleigh
Lowton
Blagdon
Staple Fitzpaine
Stoodleigh
Westleigh
Red Ball
Wrangway
Wellington Monument
BLACKDOWN HILLS
Knightshayes Court NT
East Mere
Pitt
Burlescombe
Nicholashayne
Simons Burrow
Blagdon Hill
STAPLE HILL
Loxbeare
Washfield
Hayne
Chevithorne
Uplowman
Craze Lowman
Whitnage
Ayshford
Culm Davy
Clayhidon
Burnworthy
Rosemary Lane
Lurley
Bolham
Chettiscombe
Appledore
Woodgate
Fyfett
Acombe
Churchstanton
Bucklar St Mar
Calverleigh
Templeton
Sampford Peverell
Waterloo Cross
Prescott
Culmstock
Hemyock
Stapley
Birch Wood
Tiverton
Withleigh
Cruwys Morchard
Halberton
Uffculme
Northcott
Bolham Water
Churchinford
Bishopswood
Coldharbour
Smithincott
Coldharbour Mill
Craddock
Bolham R
Madford
Canal
Ash Thomas
Willand
Ashill
Abbey
Smeatharpe
Marsh
Way Village
Well Town
Little Silver
Devon Railway Centre
Blackborough
Northcott
Howley
Upham
Butterleigh
Bradfield
Sheldon
River Culm
Kentisbeare
Saint Hill
Slade
Upottery
Yarcombe
Cadeleigh
Bickleigh Mill
Bickleigh
Cullompton
Dunkeswell
Luppitt
Cheriton Fitzpaine
Knowle
Colebrook
Rawridge
Dulford
Kerswell
Wolford Chapel
Uppincott
Fursdon
Beacon
Stockland
Westcott
Mutterton
STOCKLAND HILL
Chilton
Cadbury
Broadhembury
Millhayes
Stockleigh Pomeroy
Bradninch
Norman's Green
Colliton
Hembury
Wick
West Raddon
Up Exe
Silverton
Langford
Upton
Godford Cross
Combe Raleigh
Monkton
Heathstock
Little Silver
Thorverton
Hele
Plymtree
Luton
Lower Tale
Payhembury
Cotleigh
Ham
Ellerhayes
Beare
Clyst Hydon
Awliscombe
Efford
Nether Exe
Killerton NT
Killerton
Colestocks
Buckerell
Weston
Dalwood
Loughwood Meeting
Pennicott
Shute
Budlake
Aunk
Wilmington
Wyke
Talaton
Feniton
Offwell
Brampford Speke
Columbjohn
Westwood
Clyst St Lawrence
Honiton
Nettacott
Rewe
Newtown
Fenny Bridges
Widworthy
Stoke Canon
R Clyst
Higher Burrowton
Knowle Cross
Larkbeare
Escot
Gittisham
Upton Pyne
Marker's Cottage NT
Whimple
Alfington
Shute
Newton St Cyres
Huxham
Lower Burrowton
Fairmile
Gosford
Church Green
Kilm
Poltimore
Broadclyst
Talaford
Ottery St Mary
Shute Barton NT
Cowley
Dog Village
Jack-in-the-Green
Hand and Pen
Cadhay
Northleigh
Whitford
Pinhoe
Allercombe
Farway Street
Woodbridge
Musbury
Whitestone Cross
EXETER
Whipton
Clyst Honiton
Rockbeare
West Hill
Colyton
Blackhorse
Exeter
Southleigh
Exwick
Heavitree
Sowton
Marsh Green
Fluxton
Wiggaton
Blackbury Castle
Colyford
Aylesbeare
Farringdon
Tipton St John
Coombe
Wonford
West Point
Perkins Village
Venn Ottery
Sidbury
Seaton
Axmo
Ide
Alphington
Clyst St Mary
Crealy Adventure Park
Southerton
Harpford
Bowd
Sidford
Harcombe
Bulstone
Seaton Tramway
Shillingford Abbot
Countess Wear
Woodbury Salterton
Hawkerland
Newton Poppleford
Stowford
Woolbrook
The Donkey Sanctuary
The Old Bakery NT
Beer
Shillingford St George
Clyst St George
Street
Pecorama
Topsham
Ebford
Salcombe Regis
Weston
Branscombe
Clapham
Exminster
Kingston
Colaton Raleigh
South West Coast Path
Sidmouth
Doddiscombsleigh
Kennford
Woodbury
East Devon Heritage Coast
Exton
Yettington
Bicton Park
Pinn
Woodmanton
Otterton
Kenn
River Exe
East Budleigh
Otterton Mill
Powderham
Lympstone
Dalditch
Ladram Bay
Devon & Exeter
Kenton
A La Ronde NT
Bystock
Knowle
River Otter
Kersbrook
Harcombe
Starcross
Hulham
Cofton
Littleham
Budleigh Salterton
Lower Upcott
Exmouth
Cockwood
Waddon
The Model Railway
World of Country Life
Ugbrooke Park
Ashcombe
Shutterton
Dawlish Warren
Ideford
Olchard
Luton
Dawlish
Humber
SY
Bishopsteignton
Holcombe
Coombe
Teignmouth
R Teign
Coombe Cellars
Ringmore
Shaldon
Netherton
Combeinteignhead
Stokeinteignhead
Middle Rocombe
Lower Gabwell
Higher Gabwell
Coffinswell
Maidencombe
Daccombe
Barton
Watcombe
North Whilborough
Coombe Pafford
Model Village
Babbacombe Bay
Babbacombe Pottery
Eginswell
Shiphay
St Marychurch
Babbacombe
Ellacombe
TORQUAY
Cockington
Hopes Nose
Rockend
Hollicombe
Preston
Paignton
M5
A396
A361
A3137
A3072
A396
B3181
A373
A30
A303
A35
A377
A379
A38
A376
A3052
B3174
B3180
B3178
B3179
B3184
A375
A380
A381
A3022
B3192
0 1 2 3 4 5 miles
0 1 2 3 4 5 6 7 kilometres

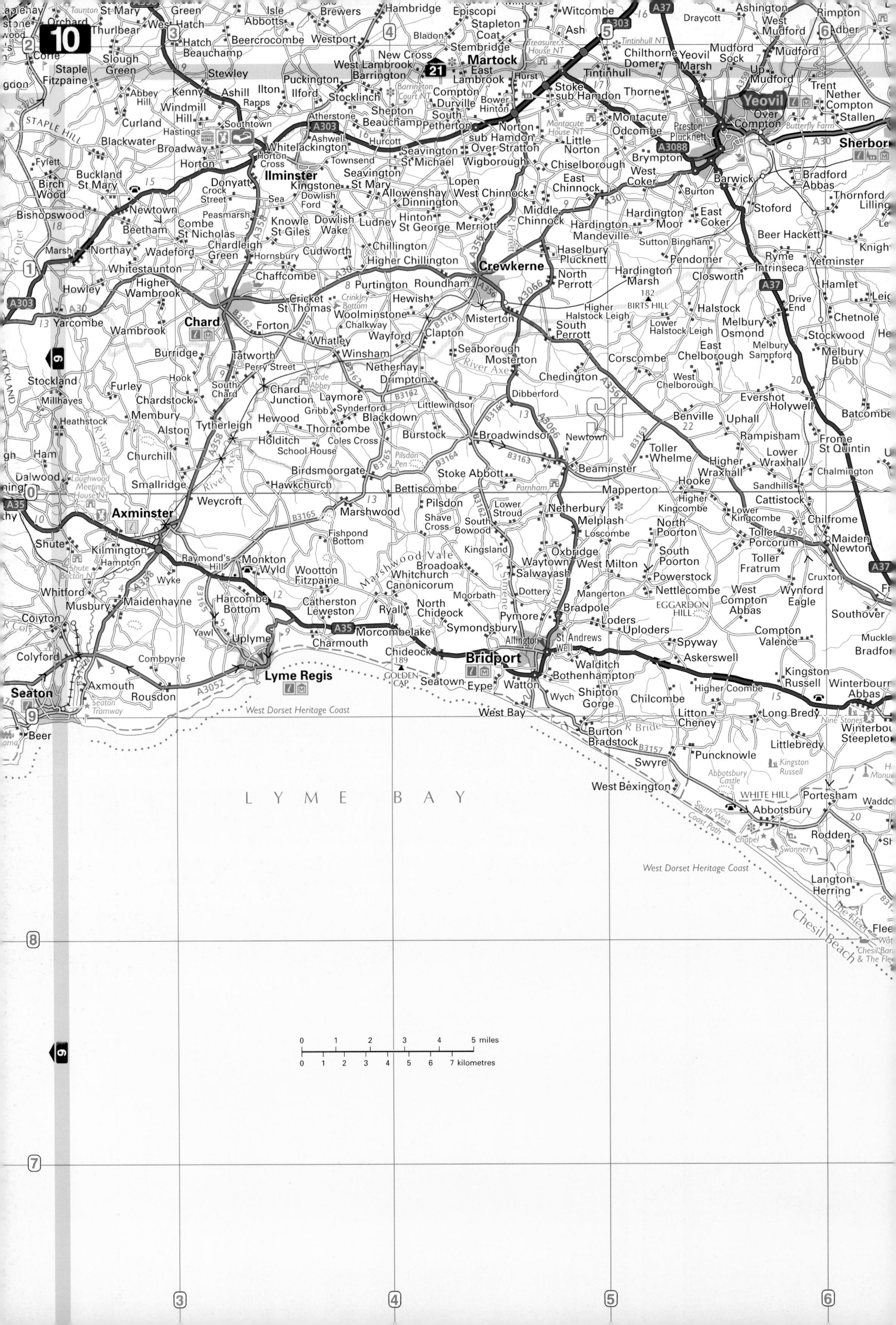
10
Taunton
Staple Fitzpaine
Thurlbear
Orchard
Hatch Beauchamp
West Hatch
Slough Green
Beercrocombe
Isle Abbotts
Westport
Hambridge
Brewers
Episcopi
Witcombe
Ash
Stapleton
Coat
Stembridge
Bladon
Martock
New Cross
West Lambrook
Barrington
East Lambrook
Treasurer's House NT
Tintinhull NT
Tintinhull
Chilthorne Domer
Yeovil Marsh
Mudford Sock
Mudford
Up Mudford
Ashington
West Mudford
Rimpton
Adber
Draycott
Trent
Nether Compton
Stallen
Yeovil
Over Compton
Butterfly Farm
Sherborne
Stewley
Kenny
Ashill
Ilton
Rapps
Ilford
Puckington
Stocklinch
Barrington Court NT
Compton Durville
South Petherton
Shepton Beauchamp
Hurst
Bower Hinton
Stoke sub Hamdon
Thorne
Montacute
Montacute House NT
Odcombe
Preston Plucknett
Abbey Hill
Windmill Hill
Curland
Staple Hill
Blackwater
Hastings
Southtown
Broadway
Horton
Whitelackington
Horton Cross
Atherstone
Ashwell
Hurcott
Seavington St Michael
Norton sub Hamdon
Over Stratton
Little Norton
Brympton
Townsend
Wigborough
Chiselborough
West Coker
Barwick
Ilminster
Seavington St Mary
Kingstone
Lopen
West Chinnock
East Chinnock
Burton
Bradford Abbas
Thornford
Fyfett
Buckland St Mary
Birch Wood
Donyatt
Crock Street
Sea
Dowlish Ford
Allowenshay
Dinnington
Middle Chinnock
Hardington Mandeville
Hardington Moor
East Coker
Stoford
Bishopswood
Newtown
Beetham
Combe St Nicholas
Peasmarsh
Knowle St Giles
Dowlish Wake
Ludney
Hinton St George
Merriott
Haselbury Plucknett
Sutton Bingham
Beer Hackett
Marsh
Northay
Wadeford
Chardleigh Green
Hornsbury
Cudworth
Chillington
Higher Chillington
Crewkerne
Pendomer
Ryme Intrinseca
Yetminster
Whitestaunton
Howley
Higher Wambrook
Chaffcombe
Purtington
Roundham
North Perrott
Hardington Marsh
Closworth
Hamlet
A303
A30
Yarcombe
Wambrook
Chard
Cricket St Thomas
Crinkley Bottom
Woolminstone
Hewish
Misterton
Higher Halstock Leigh
Birts Hill
Halstock
Melbury Osmond
Drive End
Chetnole
Forton
Chalkway
Wayford
Clapton
South Perrott
Lower Halstock Leigh
East Chelborough
Melbury Sampford
Stockwood
Melbury Bubb
Stockland
Burridge
Tatworth
Perry Street
Whatley
Winsham
Seaborough
Mosterton
River Axe
Corscombe
West Chelborough
Chedington
Furley
Hook
South Chard
Chard Junction
Forde Abbey
Netherhay
Drimpton
Dibberford
Evershot
Holywell
Batcombe
Millhayes
Chardstock
Laymore
Gribb
Synderford
Littlewindsor
Membury
Heathstock
Alston
Tytherleigh
Hewood
Blackdown
Thorncombe
Broadwindsor
Benville
Uphall
Rampisham
Frome St Quintin
Newtown
Burstock
Holditch
Coles Cross
School House
Toller Whelme
Lower Wraxhall
Churchill
Ham
Pilsdon Pen
Higher Wraxhall
Birdsmoorgate
Stoke Abbott
Beaminster
Chalmington
Dalwood
Loughwood Meeting House NT
Smallridge
Hawkchurch
Bettiscombe
Parnham
Mapperton
Hooke
Sandhills
Weycroft
Pilsdon
Higher Kingcombe
Cattistock
Axminster
Marshwood
Lower Stroud
Netherbury
Melplash
North Poorton
Lower Kingcombe
Chilfrome
Shave Cross
South Bowood
Loscombe
Toller Porcorum
Maiden Newton
Shute
Kilmington
Hampton
Fishpond Bottom
Kingsland
Oxbridge
South Poorton
Toller Fratrum
Raymond's Hill
Monkton Wyld
Marshwood Vale
Broadoak
Waytown
Salwayash
West Milton
Powerstock
Cruxton
Shute Barton NT
Wyke
Wootton Fitzpaine
Whitchurch Canonicorum
Nettlecombe
West Compton Abbas
Wynford Eagle
Whitford
Musbury
Maidenhayne
Harcombe Bottom
Catherston Leweston
North Chideock
Moorbath
Dottery
Mangerton
Bradpole
Eggardon Hill
Southover
Colyton
Ryall
Symondsbury
Pymore
Loders
Uploders
Compton Valence
Yawl
Uplyme
Morcombelake
Allington
St Andrews Well
Spyway
Colyford
Combpyne
Charmouth
Chideock
Bridport
Askerswell
Kingston Russell
Winterbourne Abbas
Golden Cap
Seatown
Eype
Watton
Walditch
Bothenhampton
Higher Coombe
Axmouth
Rousdon
Lyme Regis
Wych
Shipton Gorge
Chilcombe
Litton Cheney
Long Bredy
Nine Stones
Winterbourne Steepleton
Seaton
Seaton Tramway
West Dorset Heritage Coast
West Bay
Beer
Burton Bradstock
R Bride
Littlebredy
Swyre
Puncknowle
Kingston Russell
West Bexington
Abbotsbury Castle
White Hill
Portesham
Abbotsbury
South West Coast Path
Chapel
Swannery
Rodden
LYME BAY
West Dorset Heritage Coast
Langton Herring
The Fleet
Chesil Beach
0 1 2 3 4 5 miles
0 1 2 3 4 5 6 7 kilometres

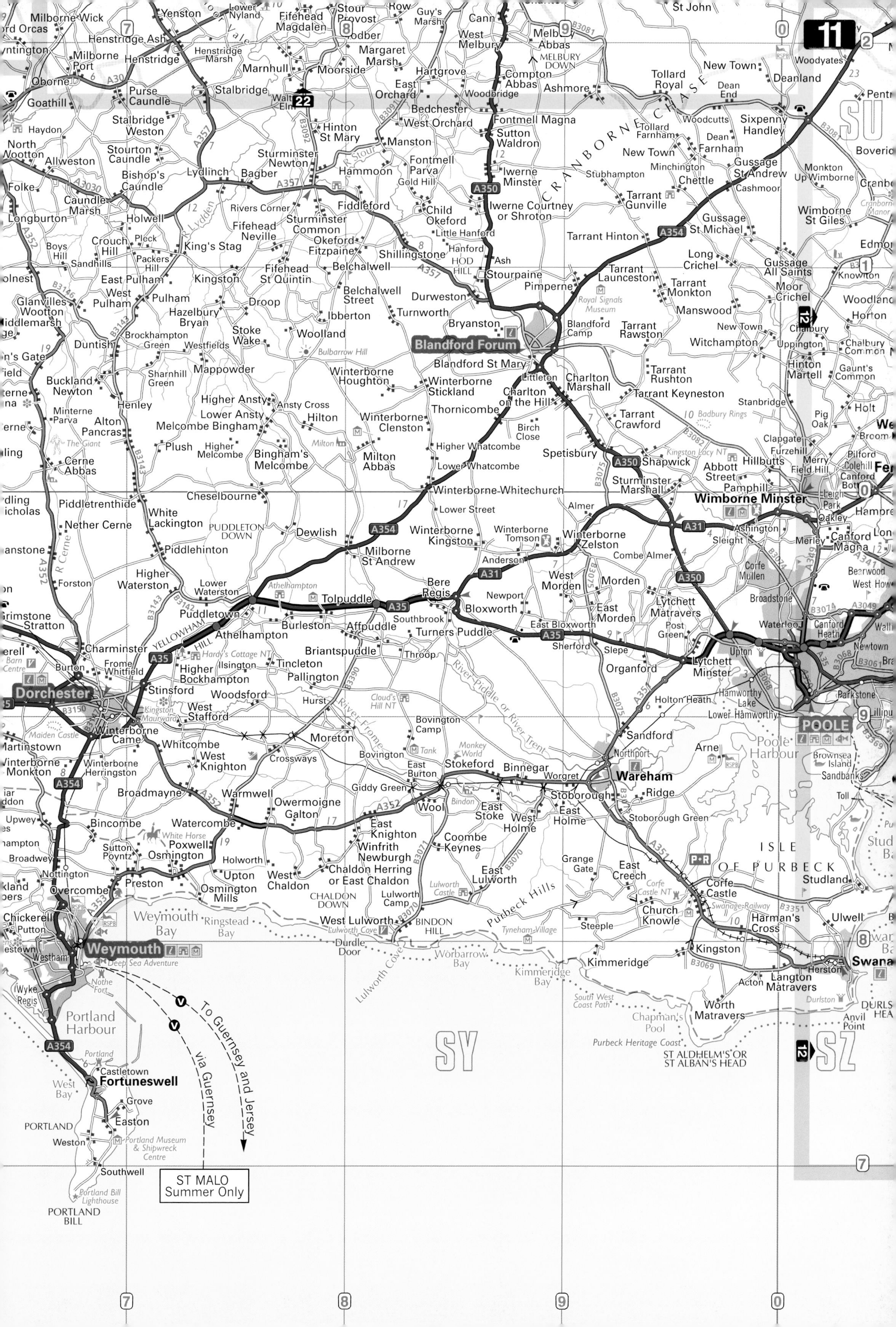
Milborne Wick
Yenston
Lower Nyland
Fifehead Magdalen
Stour Provost
Row
Guy's Marsh
Cann
St John
Henstridge Ash
Henstridge Marsh
Todber
Margaret Marsh
West Melbury
Melbury Abbas
MELBURY DOWN
Woodyates
Milborne Port
Henstridge
Marnhull
Moorside
Hartgrove
Compton Abbas
Ashmore
Tollard Royal
New Town
Deanland
Oborne
Purse Caundle
Stalbridge
Walton Elm
East Orchard
Woodbridge
Dean End
Goathill
Bedchester
West Orchard
Fontmell Magna
CRANBORNE CHASE
Tollard Farnham
Woodcutts
Sixpenny Handley
Haydon
Stalbridge Weston
Hinton St Mary
Sutton Waldron
Dean
Farnham
North Wootton
Stourton Caundle
Manston
Allweston
Sturminster Newton
R Stour
Fontmell Parva
New Town
Minchington
Gussage St Andrew
Monkton Up Wimborne
Boveridge
Bishop's Caundle
Lydlinch
Bagber
Hammoon
Gold Hill
Iwerne Minster
Stubhampton
Chettle
Cashmoor
Cranborne
Folke
A3030
A357
A350
Tarrant Gunville
Cranborne Manor
Caundle Marsh
Rivers Corner
Fiddleford
Child Okeford
Iwerne Courtney or Shroton
Wimborne St Giles
Longburton
Holwell
R Lydden
Sturminster Common
Gussage St Michael
A354
Fifehead Neville
Little Hanford
Tarrant Hinton
Boys Hill
Crouch Hill
Pleck
King's Stag
Okeford Fitzpaine
Hanford
Shillingstone
HOD HILL
Ash
Long Crichel
Gussage All Saints
Edmondsham
Sandhills
Packers Hill
Fifehead St Quintin
Belchalwell
Stourpaine
Tarrant Launceston
Knowlton
East Pulham
Kingston
Pimperne
Tarrant Monkton
Moor Crichel
Glanvilles Wootton
West Pulham
Pulham
Belchalwell Street
Durweston
Royal Signals Museum
Woodlands
Hazelbury Bryan
Droop
Ibberton
Turnwoth
Manswood
Horton
Middlemarsh
Bryanston
Blandford Camp
Tarrant Rawston
New Town
Chalbury
Stoke Wake
Woolland
Witchampton
Uppington
Chalbury Common
Duntish
Brockhampton Green
Westfields
Bulbarrow Hill
Blandford Forum
Hinton Martell
Gaunt's Common
Blandford St Mary
Tarrant Rushton
Buckland Newton
Sharnhill Green
Mappowder
Winterborne Houghton
Winterborne Stickland
Littleton
Charlton Marshall
Charlton on the Hill
Tarrant Keyneston
Stanbridge
Holt
Henley
Higher Ansty
Ansty Cross
Thornicombe
Tarrant Crawford
Badbury Rings
Minterne Parva
Alton Pancras
Lower Ansty
Hilton
Winterborne Clenston
Birch Close
Pig Oak
Melcombe Bingham
Clapgate
Furzehill
Broom Hill
The Giant
Milton
Higher Whatcombe
Kingston Lacy NT
Pilford
Plush
Higher Melcombe
Bingham's Melcombe
Milton Abbas
Spetisbury
A350
Shapwick
Abbott Street
Hillbutts
Merry Field Hill
Colehill
Cerne Abbas
Lower Whatcombe
Canford Bottom
Sturminster Marshall
Pamphill
Ferndown
Cheselbourne
Winterborne Whitechurch
Wimborne Minster
Leigh Park
Piddletrenthide
White Lackington
Lower Street
Almer
Oakley
Hampreston
Nether Cerne
PUDDLETON DOWN
Dewlish
A354
Winterborne Kingston
Winterborne Tomson
Winterborne Zelston
A31
Ashington
Sleight
Merley
Canford Magna
Longham
R Cerne
Piddlehinton
Milborne St Andrew
Anderson
Combe Almer
Corfe Mullen
Bearwood
West Howe
Higher Waterston
West Morden
Morden
A350
Forston
Lower Waterston
Athelhampton
Tolpuddle
Bere Regis
Newport
Lytchett Matravers
Broadstone
Grimstone
Stratton
Puddletown
A35
Southbrook
Bloxworth
East Morden
Burleston
Affpuddle
Turners Puddle
East Bloxworth
Post Green
Waterloo
Canford Heath
Athelhampton
YELLOWHAM HILL
Sherford
Slepe
Upton
Newtown
Charminster
Hardy's Cottage NT
Briantspuddle
Throop
Lytchett Minster
Bournemouth
Burton
Frome Whitfield
Higher Bockhampton
Ilsington
Tincleton
Pallington
River Piddle or River Trent
Organford
Dorchester
Stinsford
Woodsford
Cloud's Hill NT
Holton Heath
Hamworthy
Lake
Parkstone
Kingston Maurward
West Stafford
Hurst
River Frome
Bovington Camp
Lower Hamworthy
POOLE
Maiden Castle
Winterborne Came
Moreton
Sandford
Poole Harbour
Martinstown
Whitcombe
Tank
Monkey World
Arne
Brownsea Island
Winterborne Monkton
Winterborne Herringston
West Knighton
Crossways
Bovington
Stokeford
Binnegar
Northport
Wareham
Sandbanks
East Burton
Worgret
A354
Broadmayne
Warmwell
Giddy Green
Bindon
Stoborough
Ridge
Toll
Owermoigne
Galton
A352
Wool
East Stoke
West Holme
East Holme
Stoborough Green
Upwey
Bincombe
Watercombe
East Knighton
White Horse
Coombe Keynes
ISLE OF PURBECK
Studland
Sutton Poyntz
Poxwell
Winfrith Newburgh
Broadwey
Osmington
Holworth
Grange Gate
East Creech
Nottington
Upton
West Chaldon
Chaldon Herring or East Chaldon
East Lulworth
Corfe Castle
Overcombe
Preston
Osmington Mills
CHALDON DOWN
Lulworth Castle
Corfe Castle NT
Lulworth Camp
Purbeck Hills
Church Knowle
Swanage Railway
Chickerell
Weymouth Bay
Ringstead Bay
West Lulworth
BINDON HILL
Tyneham Village
Steeple
Harman's Cross
Ulwell
Putton
Lulworth Cove
Durdle Door
Westham
Weymouth
Deep Sea Adventure
Worbarrow Bay
Kingston
Swanage
Kimmeridge
Kimmeridge Bay
Herston
Nothe Fort
Langton Matravers
Acton
Wyke Regis
South West Coast Path
Durlston
DURLSTON HEAD
To Guernsey and Jersey
Worth Matravers
Chapman's Pool
Anvil Point
Portland Harbour
via Guernsey
Purbeck Heritage Coast
SY
ST ALDHELM'S OR ST ALBAN'S HEAD
SZ
A354
Portland
Castletown
Fortuneswell
West Bay
Grove
Easton
PORTLAND
Weston
Portland Museum & Shipwreck Centre
Southwell
ST MALO Summer Only
Portland Bill Lighthouse
PORTLAND BILL
SU

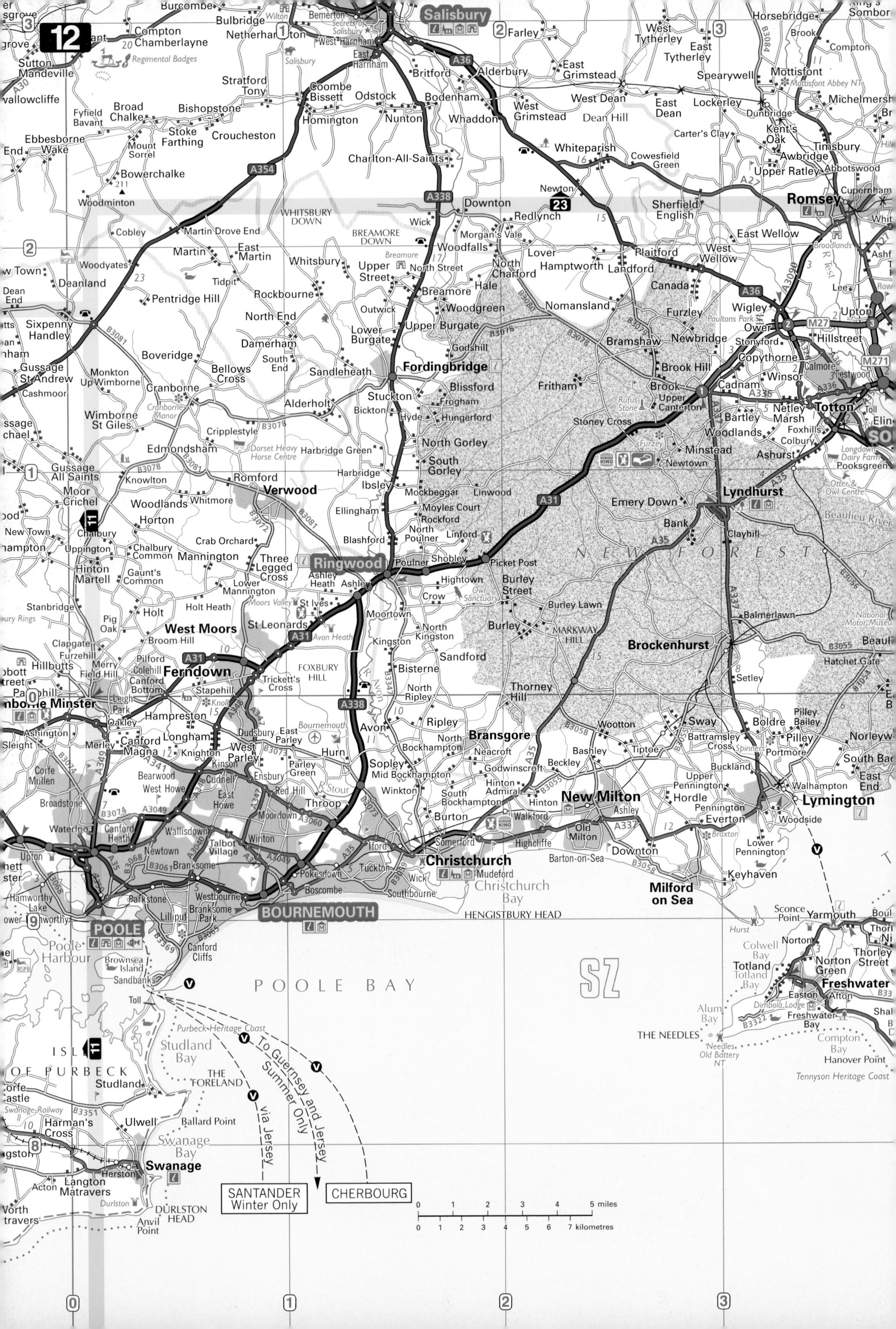
12
Salisbury
Burcombe
Bulbridge
Wilton
Netherhampton
Bemerton
Secrets of Salisbury
West Harnham
East Harnham
Salisbury
Compton Chamberlayne
Regimental Badges
Sutton Mandeville
Swallowcliffe
Fyfield Bavant
Broad Chalke
Stratford Tony
Bishopstone
Coombe Bissett
Homington
Odstock
Nunton
Britford
Bodenham
Alderbury
Whaddon
Farley
West Tytherley
East Tytherley
East Grimstead
West Grimstead
Spearywell
West Dean
East Dean
Dean Hill
Lockerley
Horsebridge
Mottisfont
Mottisfont Abbey NT
Michelmersh
Dunbridge
Kent's Oak
Carter's Clay
Timsbury
Awbridge
Abbotswood
Upper Ratley
Compton
Brook
Ebbesborne Wake
Mount Sorrel
Stoke Farthing
Croucheston
Bowerchalke
Woodminton
Charlton-All-Saints
Whiteparish
Cowesfield Green
Newton
Downton
Redlynch
Sherfield English
Romsey
Cupernham
Broadlands
East Wellow
West Wellow
Plaitford
Landford
Hamptworth
Lover
North Charford
Hale
Morgan's Vale
Woodfalls
Wick
WHITSBURY DOWN
BREAMORE DOWN
Breamore
Cobley
Martin Drove End
Martin
East Martin
Woodyates
Deanland
Dean End
Tidpit
Pentridge Hill
Whitsbury
Upper Street
North Street
Rockbourne
Breamore
Woodgreen
Nomansland
Canada
Wigley
Paultons Park
Furzley
Ower
Upton
Sixpenny Handley
North End
Outwick
Lower Burgate
Upper Burgate
Godshill
Bramshaw
Newbridge
Stonyford
Copythorne
Hillstreet
Calmore
Testwood
Totton
Eling
Damerham
South End
Boveridge
Bellows Cross
Sandleheath
Fordingbridge
Fritham
Brook Hill
Brook
Cadnam
Winsor
Netley Marsh
Gussage St Andrew
Monkton Up Wimborne
Cashmoor
Cranborne
Cranborne Manor
Alderholt
Stuckton
Bickton
Blissford
Frogham
Hyde
Hungerford
Rufus Stone
Upper Canterton
Stoney Cross
Bartley
Woodlands
Foxhills
Colbury
Ashurst
Longdown Dairy Farm
Pooksgreen
Wimborne St Giles
Cripplestyle
Edmondsham
Dorset Heavy Horse Centre
Harbridge Green
Harbridge
Ibsley
North Gorley
South Gorley
Furzey
Minstead
Newtown
Lyndhurst
Otter & Owl Centre
Gussage All Saints
Knowlton
Romford
Verwood
Moor Crichel
Woodlands
Whitmore
Horton
Mockbeggar
Linwood
Moyles Court
Rockford
Ellingham
Emery Down
Bank
Beaulieu River
New Town
Chalbury
Uppington
Chalbury Common
Crab Orchard
Mannington
Blashford
North Poulner
Linford
Clayhill
Hinton Martell
Gaunt's Common
Three Legged Cross
Ringwood
Poulner
Shobley
Picket Post
NEW FOREST
Ashley Heath
Ashley
Lower Mannington
Hightown
Burley Street
Owl Sanctuary
Crow
Burley Lawn
Stanbridge
Holt Heath
Moors Valley
St Ives
Moortown
Pig Oak
Holt
West Moors
St Leonards
Avon Heath
North Kingston
Kingston
Burley
MARKWAY HILL
Balmerlawn
National Motor Museum
Clapgate
Furzehill
Broom Hill
Pilford
Colehill
Merry Field Hill
Hillbutts
Ferndown
FOXBURY HILL
Sandford
Brockenhurst
Beaulieu
Hatchet Gate
Canford Bottom
Stapehill
Knoll
Trickett's Cross
Bisterne
North Ripley
Thorney Hill
Setley
Wimborne Minster
Leigh Park
Hampreston
Oakley
Ashington
Merley
Canford Magna
Longham
Dudsbury
East Parley
Bournemouth
Avon
Ripley
North Bransgore
Bransgore
Wootton
Sway
Boldre
Pilley Bailey
Pilley
Norleywood
Corfe Mullen
Bearwood
Knighton
Kinson
West Parley
Hurn
Bockhampton
Neacroft
Bashley
Tiptoe
Battramsley Cross
Spinners
Portmore
South Baddesley
West Howe
Cudnell
Ensbury
Parley Green
Sopley
Mid Bockhampton
Godwinscroft
Beckley
Buckland
Upper Pennington
Walhampton
East End
Broadstone
East Howe
Red Hill
Stour
Throop
Winkton
Hinton Admiral
Hinton
New Milton
Ashley
Hordle
Lymington
Pennington
Everton
Woodside
Waterloo
Canford Heath
Wallisdown
Moordown
Winton
South Bockhampton
Burton
Walkford
Old Milton
Upton
Newtown
Talbot Village
Iford
Somerford
Highcliffe
Downton
Braxton
Lower Pennington
Branksome
Pokesdown
Tuckton
Christchurch
Mudeford
Barton-on-Sea
Keyhaven
Hamworthy
Lake
Parkstone
Westbourne
Branksome Park
Boscombe
Wick
Southbourne
Christchurch Bay
Milford on Sea
BOURNEMOUTH
HENGISTBURY HEAD
Lilliput
POOLE
Poole Harbour
Brownsea Island
Canford Cliffs
Sandbanks
POOLE BAY
SZ
Hurst
Sconce Point
Yarmouth
Colwell Bay
Norton
Totland
Totland Bay
Norton Green
Thorley Street
Freshwater
Easton
Afton
Dimbola Lodge
Freshwater Bay
Alum Bay
THE NEEDLES
Needles Old Battery NT
Compton Bay
Hanover Point
Tennyson Heritage Coast
Toll
Purbeck Heritage Coast
Studland Bay
ISLE OF PURBECK
THE FORELAND
Studland
Corfe Castle
Swanage Railway
Harman's Cross
Ulwell
Ballard Point
Swanage Bay
Swanage
Herston
Langton Matravers
Acton
Durlston
DURLSTON HEAD
Anvil Point
Worth Matravers
To Guernsey and Jersey Summer Only
via Jersey
SANTANDER Winter Only
CHERBOURG
A36
A354
A338
A27
A3090
M27
M271
A336
A337
A35
A31
A341
A348
A347
A3049
A3060
B3081
B3078
B3080
B3079
B3072
B3073
B3074
B3068
B3061
B3065
B3369
B3351
B3347
B3058
B3055
B3054
B3056
B3322
0 1 2 3 4 5 miles
0 1 2 3 4 5 6 7 kilometres
0
1
2
3

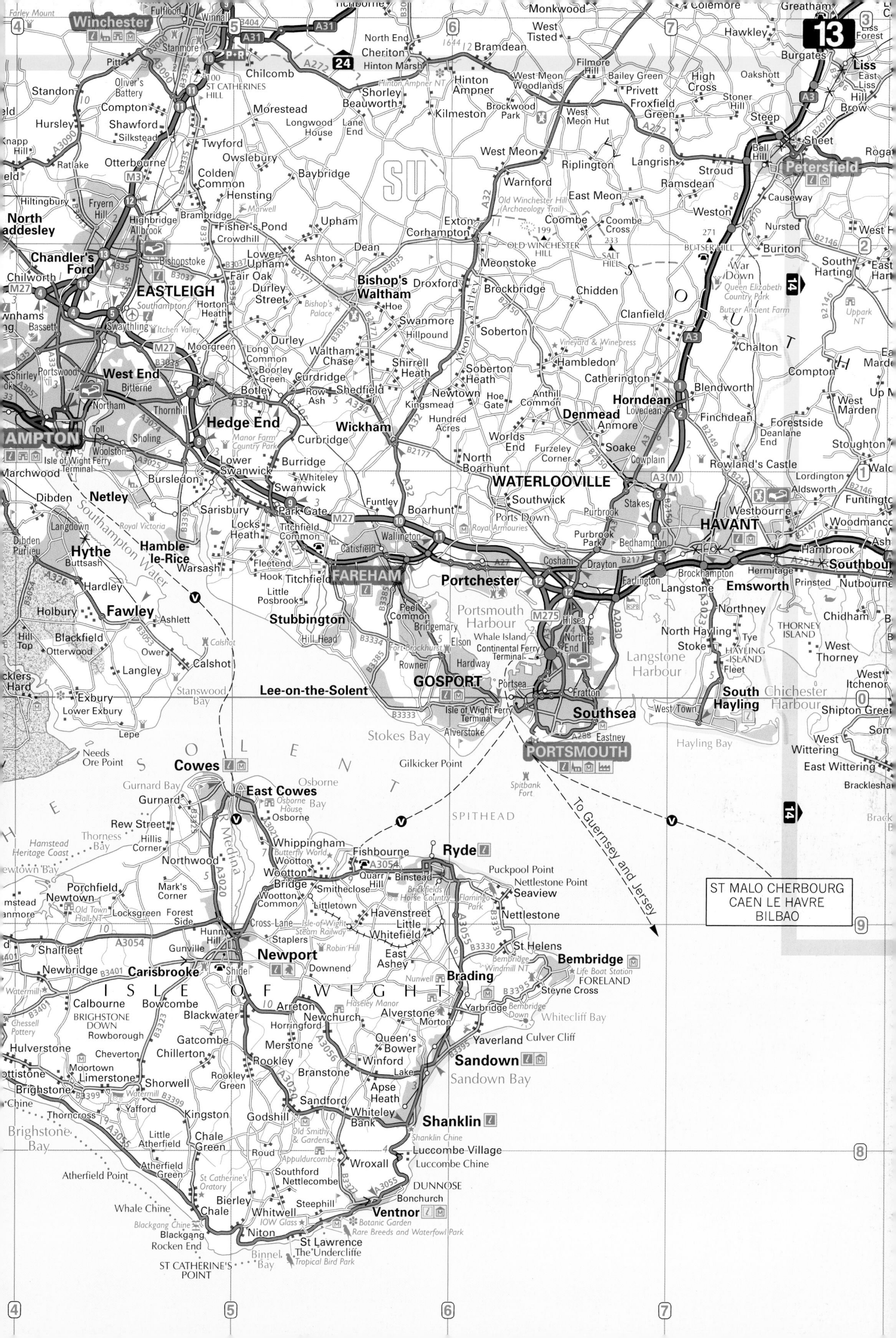
Winchester
Petersfield
EASTLEIGH
West End
Hedge End
Bishop's Waltham
Wickham
WATERLOOVILLE
HAVANT
Horndean
FAREHAM
Portchester
GOSPORT
Southsea
PORTSMOUTH
Emsworth
South Hayling
Hythe
Fawley
Netley
Hamble-le-Rice
Stubbington
Lee-on-the-Solent
Cowes
East Cowes
Ryde
Newport
Bembridge
Brading
Sandown
Shanklin
Ventnor
ISLE OF WIGHT
THE SOLENT
SPITHEAD
Southampton Water
Portsmouth Harbour
Langstone Harbour
Chichester Harbour
Hayling Bay
Stokes Bay
Sandown Bay
Brighstone Bay
To Guernsey and Jersey
ST MALO CHERBOURG
CAEN LE HAVRE
BILBAO

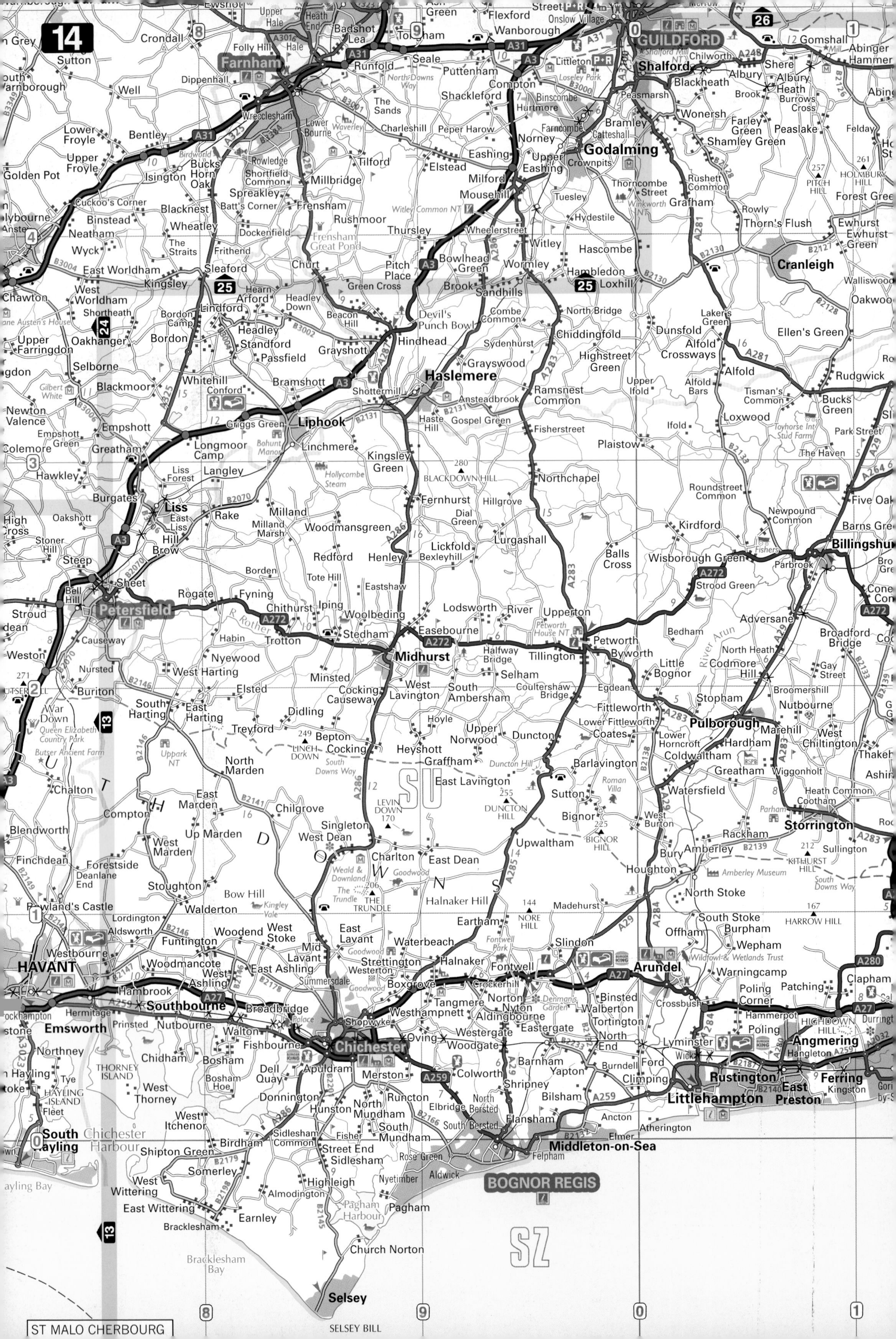

14
Crondall
Sutton
Farnham
Upper Hale
Heath End
Badshot Lea
Folly Hill
Hale
Tongham
Seale
Runfold
Puttenham
Ash Green
Flexford
Wanborough
Onslow Village
GUILDFORD
Shalford
Chilworth
Albury
Shere
Gomshall
Abinger Hammer
Dippenhall
Well
Wrecclesham
Lower Bourne
Waverley
The Sands
Charleshill
North Downs Way
Compton
Littleton
Loseley Park
Binscombe
Hurtmore
Shackleford
Peper Harow
Farncombe
Catteshall
Norney
Eashing
Upper Eashing
Godalming
Crownpits
Peasmarsh
Bramley
Blackheath
Wonersh
Brook
Albury Heath
Burrows Cross
Farley Green
Peaslake
Shamley Green
Felday
Lower Froyle
Bentley
Upper Froyle
Golden Pot
Isington
Birdworld
Bucks Horn Oak
Rowledge
Shortfield Common
Spreakley
Batt's Corner
Millbridge
Tilford
Elstead
Milford
Mousehill
Frensham
Rushmoor
Thursley
Witley Common NT
Wheelerstreet
Tuesley
Hydestile
Thorncombe Street
Winkworth NT
Rushett Common
Grafham
Pitch Hill
Holmbury Hill
Forest Green
Rowly
Thorn's Flush
Ewhurst
Ewhurst Green
Cuckoo's Corner
Binstead
Blacknest
Wheatley
Neatham
Dockenfield
Frensham Great Pond
Wyck
The Straits
Frithend
Churt
Pitch Place
Bowlhead Green
Witley
Hascombe
Cranleigh
East Worldham
Sleaford
Kingsley
Green Cross
Brook
Sandhills
Wormley
Hambledon
Loxhill
Chawton
West Worldham
Hearn
Arford
Headley Down
Lindford
Beacon Hill
Devil's Punch Bowl
Combe Common
North Bridge
Walliswood
Oakwood
Shortheath
Jane Austen's House
Bordon Camp
Headley
Standford
Passfield
Hindhead
Grayshott
Sydenhurst
Chiddingfold
Dunsfold
Alfold Crossways
Laker's Green
Ellen's Green
Upper Farringdon
Oakhanger
Bordon
Selborne
Gilbert White
Blackmoor
Whitehill
Conford
Bramshott
Shottermill
Haslemere
Grayswood
Highstreet Green
Upper Ifold
Alfold
Alfold Bars
Rudgwick
Newton Valence
Empshott
Empshott Green
Griggs Green
Liphook
Haste Hill
Ansteadbrook
Gospel Green
Ramsnest Common
Fisherstreet
Tisman's Common
Bucks Green
Loxwood
Ifold
Toyhorse Int Stud Farm
Park Street
Colemore
Greatham
Longmoor Camp
Bohunt Manor
Linchmere
Kingsley Green
Plaistow
The Haven
Hawkley
Liss Forest
Langley
Hollycombe Steam
280
Blackdown Hill
Northchapel
Roundstreet Common
Burgates
Liss
Oakshott
Rake
Milland
Fernhurst
Hillgrove
Dial Green
Five Oak
Newpound Common
High Cross
East Liss
Hill Brow
Milland Marsh
Woodmansgreen
Lickfold
Lurgashall
Kirdford
Barns Green
Stoner Hill
Steep
Redford
Henley
Bexleyhill
Balls Cross
Wisborough Green
Fishers
Billingshurst
Parbrook
Bell Hill
Sheet
Borden
Tote Hill
Eastshaw
Strood Green
Petersfield
Rogate
Fyning
Chithurst
Iping
Lodsworth
River
Upperton
Stroud
R Rother
Woolbeding
Stedham
Easebourne
Petworth House NT
Petworth
Byworth
Adversane
Causeway
Habin
Trotton
Midhurst
Halfway Bridge
Tillington
Bedham
River Arun
North Heath
Broadford Bridge
Weston
Nyewood
West Harting
Selham
Little Bognor
Codmore Hill
Gay Street
271
Nursted
Buriton
Elsted
Minsted
Cocking Causeway
West Lavington
South Ambersham
Coultershaw Bridge
Egdean
Stopham
Broomershill
Nutbourne
War Down
Queen Elizabeth Country Park
South Harting
East Harting
Didling
Hoyle
Fittleworth
Lower Fittleworth
Coates
Pulborough
Marehill
West Chiltington
Butser Ancient Farm
Treyford
249
Bepton
Linch Down
Cocking
Heyshott
Upper Norwood
Duncton
Lower Horncroft
Coldwaltham
Hardham
Uppark NT
Graffham
South Downs Way
Duncton Hill
Barlavington
Greatham
Wiggonholt
Thakeham
Chalton
North Marden
East Lavington
Roman Villa
Watersfield
Heath Common
Cootham
East Marden
Chilgrove
Levin Down
170
255
Duncton Hill
Sutton
Bignor
Storrington
Compton
Singleton
225
West Burton
Parham
Blendworth
West Marden
Up Marden
West Dean
Upwaltham
Bignor Hill
Rackham
Sullington
Finchdean
Forestside
Charlton
East Dean
Bury
Amberley
212
Kithurst Hill
Deanlane End
Weald & Downland
Goodwood
Houghton
Amberley Museum
South Downs Way
Stoughton
The Trundle
206
Bow Hill
Kingley Vale
Halnaker Hill
North Stoke
Rowland's Castle
Walderton
144
Nore Hill
Madehurst
167
Harrow Hill
Lordington
Eartham
South Stoke
Burpham
Aldsworth
Woodend
West Stoke
East Lavant
Offham
Funtington
Mid Lavant
Waterbeach
Fontwell Park
Slindon
Wepham
Wildfowl & Wetlands Trust
Westbourne
Goodwood
Strettington
Halnaker
Fontwell
Arundel
HAVANT
Woodmancote
Westerton
Warningcamp
Clapham
West Ashling
East Ashling
Summersdale
Boxgrove
Crockerhill
Binsted
Poling Corner
Patching
Hambrook
Goodwood
Tangmere
Norton
Nyton
Denmans Garden
Walberton
Crossbush
Southbourne
Broadbridge
Westhampnett
Aldingbourne
Tortington
Hammerpot
Highdown Hill
Durrington
Hermitage
Prinsted
Nutbourne
Palace
Shopwyke
Poling
Emsworth
Walton
Oving
Westergate
Eastergate
North End
Lyminster
Angmering
Fishbourne
Chichester
Woodgate
Northney
Chidham
Bosham
Apuldram
Barnham
Ford
Wick
Hangleton
Hayling
Tye
Thorney Island
Dell Quay
Merston
Colworth
Yapton
Burndell
Climping
Rustington
East Preston
Ferring
Kingston
Goring-by-Sea
Hayling Island
Fleet
West Thorney
Bosham Hoe
Donnington
North Runcton
Shripney
Bilsham
Littlehampton
West Itchenor
Hunston
North Mundham
Elbridge
North Bersted
Flansham
Ancton
South Hayling
Chichester Harbour
Sidlesham Common
Fisher
South Mundham
South Bersted
Elmer
Atherington
Birdham
Shipton Green
Street End
Sidlesham
Rose Green
Middleton-on-Sea
Felpham
Hayling Bay
Somerley
Aldwick
BOGNOR REGIS
West Wittering
Highleigh
Almodington
Nyetimber
Pagham Harbour
Pagham
East Wittering
Bracklesham
Earnley
Church Norton
Bracklesham Bay
SZ
SU
SOUTH DOWNS
Selsey
SELSEY BILL
ST MALO CHERBOURG
A31
A3
A325
A287
A286
A283
A281
A272
A29
A264
A27
A259
A280
A284
A285
A3023
A2032
B3000
B3001
B3004
B3006
B3002
B3384
B2131
B2130
B2127
B2128
B2133
B2070
B2146
B2141
B2145
B2178
B2179
B2198
B2147
B2149
B2166
B2132
B2233
B2187
B2140
B2139
B2138
B2126
B2248
A248
8
9
0
1
2
3
4
13
24
25
26

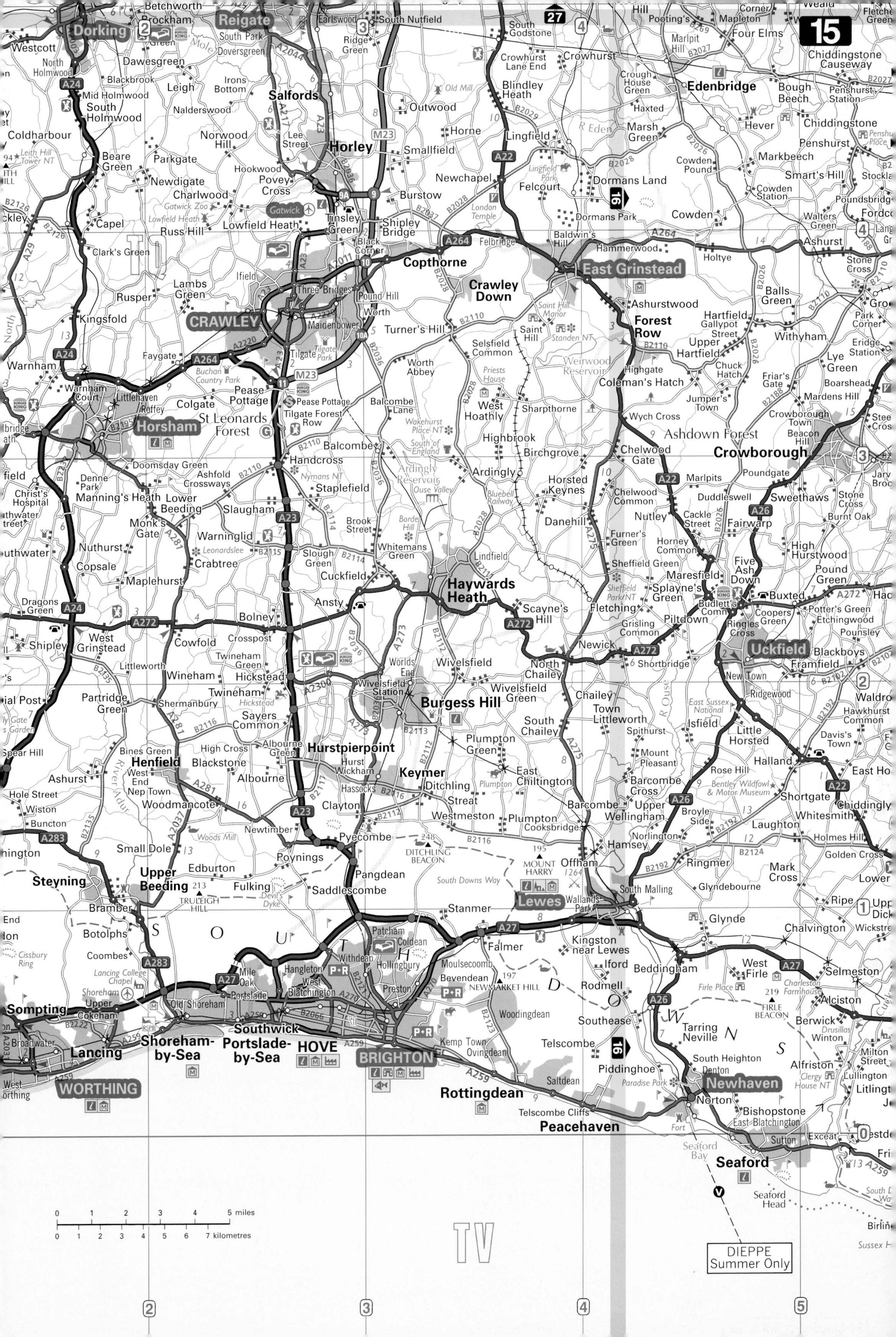
Betchworth
Brockham
Dorking
Reigate
Westcott
North Holmwood
Dawesgreen
South Park
Doversgreen
Earlswood
South Nutfield
Ridge Green
South Godstone
Crowhurst Lane End
Crowhurst
Hill
Pooting's
Mapleton
Four Elms
Marlpit Hill
Chiddingstone Causeway
Edenbridge
Bough Beech
Penshurst Station
Crouch House Green
Haxted
Marsh Green
Hever
Chiddingstone
Penshurst
Markbeech
Cowden Pound
Smart's Hill
Cowden Station
Poundsbridge
Cowden
Walters Green
Ashurst
Blackbrook
Mid Holmwood
Leigh
Irons Bottom
Salfords
Old Mill
Outwood
Blindley Heath
South Holmwood
Nalderswood
Coldharbour
Leith Hill Tower NT
Norwood Hill
Lee Street
Horley
Horne
Smallfield
Lingfield
Beare Green
Parkgate
Hookwood
Povey Cross
Newchapel
Felcourt
Lingfield Park
Dormans Land
Newdigate
Charlwood
Gatwick Zoo
Gatwick
Burstow
Dormans Park
Capel
Lowfield Heath
Russ Hill
Tinsley Green
Shipley Bridge
London Temple
Clark's Green
Black Corner
Copthorne
Felbridge
Baldwin's Hill
Hammerwood
Holtye
Stone Cross
Ifield
Lambs Green
Rusper
Three Bridges
Pound Hill
Crawley Down
East Grinstead
Ashurstwood
Balls Green
Kingsfold
CRAWLEY
Maidenbower
Worth
Turner's Hill
Saint Hill Manor
Saint Hill
Standen NT
Forest Row
Hartfield
Gallypot Street
Upper Hartfield
Withyham
Park Corner
Eridge Station
Warnham
Faygate
Tilgate
Tilgate Park
Selsfield Common
Weirwood Reservoir
Highgate
Coleman's Hatch
Chuck Hatch
Lye Green
Friar's Gate
Boarshead
Warnham Court
Littlehaven
Buchan Country Park
Pease Pottage
Worth Abbey
Priests House
Roffey
Colgate
Tilgate Forest Row
Balcombe Lane
West Hoathly
Sharpthorne
Jumper's Town
Mardens Hill
Crowborough Town
Horsham
St Leonards Forest
Wakehurst Place NT
Wych Cross
Ashdown Forest
Beacon Hill
Balcombe
South of England
Highbrook
Chelwood Gate
Crowborough
Doomsday Green
Handcross
Ardingly Reservoir
Birchgrove
Denne Park
Ashfold Crossways
Nymans NT
Ardingly
Horsted Keynes
Marlpits
Poundgate
Christ's Hospital
Manning's Heath
Lower Beeding
Staplefield
Ouse Valley
Bluebell Railway
Chelwood Common
Duddleswell
Sweethaws
Stone Cross
Slaugham
Brook Street
Borde Hill
Danehill
Nutley
Cackle Street
Fairwarp
Burnt Oak
Monk's Gate
Warninglid
Furner's Green
Horney Common
Nuthurst
Leonardslee
Slough Green
Whitemans Green
Lindfield
High Hurstwood
Crabtree
Sheffield Green
Five Ash Down
Pound Green
Copsale
Maplehurst
Cuckfield
Haywards Heath
Maresfield
Sheffield Park NT
Splayne's Green
Buxted
Dragons Green
Ansty
Scayne's Hill
Fletching
Budlett's Common
Potter's Green
Coopers Green
Etchingwood
Bolney
Piltdown
Grisling Common
Ringles Cross
Pounsley
West Grinstead
Shipley
Crosspost
Cowfold
Newick
Uckfield
Blackboys
Twineham Green
Worlds End
Wivelsfield
North Chailey
Shortbridge
Framfield
Littleworth
Wineham
Hickstead
Wivelsfield Station
New Town
Partridge Green
Twineham
Wivelsfield Green
Chailey
Ridgewood
Waldron
Shermanbury
Burgess Hill
Town Littleworth
East Sussex National
Hawkhurst Common
Sayers Common
South Chailey
Spithurst
Isfield
Little Horsted
Davis's Town
Spear Hill
Bines Green
High Cross
Albourne Green
Hurstpierpoint
Plumpton Green
Mount Pleasant
Henfield
Blackstone
Hurst Wickham
Keymer
Rose Hill
Halland
Ashurst
West End
Albourne
East Chiltington
Barcombe Cross
Bentley Wildfowl & Motor Museum
East Hoathly
Hole Street
Nep Town
Hassocks
Ditchling
Plumpton
Shortgate
Wiston
Woodmancote
Clayton
Street
Westmeston
Plumpton
Cooksbridge
Barcombe
Upper Wellingham
Broyle Side
Whitesmith
Chiddingly
Buncton
Newtimber
Laughton
Woods Mill
Pyecombe
Ditchling Beacon
Norlington
Hamsey
Holmes Hill
Small Dole
Poynings
Mount Harry
Offham
Ringmer
Golden Cross
Steyning
Upper Beeding
Edburton
Pangdean
South Downs Way
Mark Cross
Fulking
Devil's Dyke
Saddlescombe
South Malling
Glyndebourne
Bramber
Truleigh Hill
Lewes
Wallands Park
Ripe
Stanmer
Botolphs
Patcham
Glynde
Chalvington
Coombes
Coldean
Falmer
Kingston near Lewes
Cissbury Ring
Withdean
Hollingbury
Iford
Beddingham
West Firle
Selmeston
Lancing College Chapel
Mile Oak
Hangleton
Moulsecoomb
Firle Place
Charleston Farmhouse
Shoreham
Upper Cokeham
West Blatchington
Bevendean
Newmarket Hill
Rodmell
Firle Beacon
Alciston
Sompting
Old Shoreham
Portslade
Preston
Woodingdean
Southease
Tarring Neville
Berwick
Broadwater
Lancing
Shoreham-by-Sea
Southwick
Portslade-by-Sea
Hove
Kemp Town
Ovingdean
Telscombe
Drusillas
Winton
Brighton
South Heighton
Denton
Alfriston
Milton Street
West Worthing
Worthing
Piddinghoe
Paradise Park
Saltdean
Newhaven
Clergy House NT
Lullington
Litlington
Rottingdean
Norton
Telscombe Cliffs
Bishopstone
Peacehaven
Fort
East Blatchington
Sutton
Exceat
Seaford Bay
Seaford
Seaford Head
South Downs Way
Birling
Sussex
TD
TV
DIEPPE Summer Only
0 1 2 3 4 5 miles
0 1 2 3 4 5 6 7 kilometres
2
3
4
5

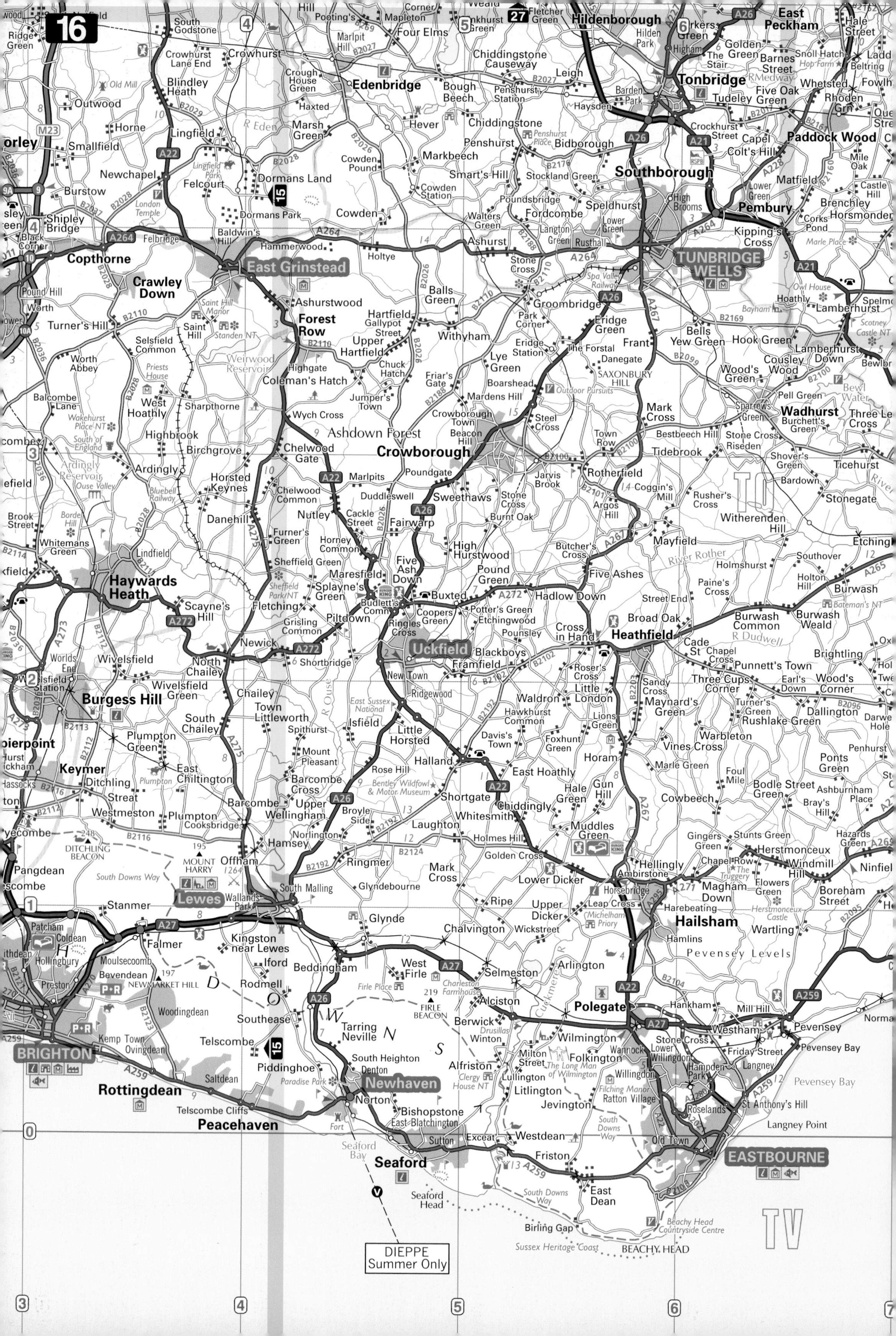

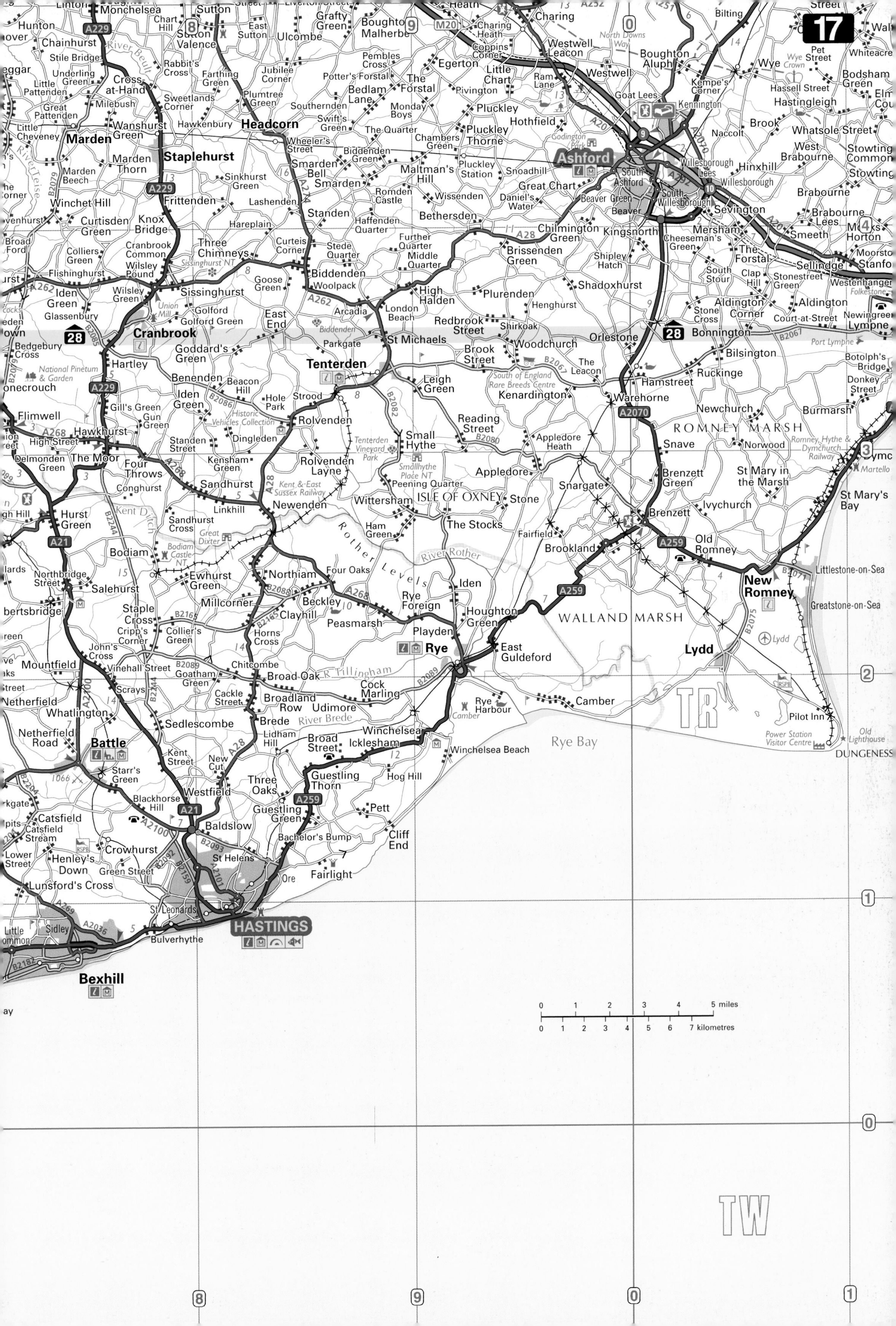
17
Charing
Westwell Leacon
Westwell
Boughton Aluph
Wye
Pet Street
Whiteacre
Bodsham Green
Hassell Street
Hastingleigh
Brook
Naccolt
Whatsole Street
West Brabourne
Stowting Common
Stowting
Brabourne
Brabourne Lees
Smeeth
Monks Horton
Sellindge
Stanford
Westenhanger
Folkestone
Kennington
Goat Lees
Ashford
South Ashford
Willesborough Lees
Willesborough
South Willesborough
Hinxhill
Sevington
Mersham
Kingsnorth
Beaver Green
Beaver
Great Chart
Chilmington Green
Daniel's Water
Bethersden
Brissenden Green
Shipley Hatch
Shadoxhurst
Cheeseman's Green
The Forstal
South Stour
Clap Hill
Stonestreet Green
Aldington Corner
Aldington
Stone Cross
Court-at-Street
Newingreen
Lympne
Port Lympne
Bonnington
Bilsington
Ruckinge
Hamstreet
Warehorne
Orlestone
Woodchurch
Shirkoak
Henghurst
Plurenden
High Halden
London Beach
Redbrook Street
Brook Street
The Leacon
South of England Rare Breeds Centre
Kenardington
Botolph's Bridge
Donkey Street
Burmarsh
Newchurch
ROMNEY MARSH
Snave
Norwood
Romney, Hythe & Dymchurch Railway
Dymchurch
Martello
Brenzett Green
St Mary in the Marsh
St Mary's Bay
Brenzett
Ivychurch
Old Romney
New Romney
Littlestone-on-Sea
Greatstone-on-Sea
Lydd
WALLAND MARSH
Pilot Inn
Power Station Visitor Centre
Old Lighthouse
DUNGENESS
Camber
Rye Harbour
Rye Bay
TR
TW
Brookland
Fairfield
Snargate
Appledore
Appledore Heath
Reading Street
Stone
ISLE OF OXNEY
Wittersham
The Stocks
Ham Green
River Rother
Rother Levels
Iden
Rye Foreign
Houghton Green
Playden
Rye
East Guldeford
Peasmarsh
Beckley
Four Oaks
Northiam
Clayhill
Horns Cross
Broad Oak
Cock Marling
Udimore
Broadland Row
Brede
River Brede
Winchelsea
Winchelsea Beach
Icklesham
Broad Street
Lidham Hill
Guestling Thorn
Hog Hill
Three Oaks
Guestling Green
Pett
Cliff End
Fairlight
Ore
St Helens
Hastings
St Leonards
Bulverhythe
Sidley
Little Common
Bexhill
Baldslow
Westfield
Blackhorse Hill
New Cut
Kent Street
Sedlescombe
Starr's Green
Battle
Catsfield
Catsfield Stream
Crowhurst
Henley's Down
Green Street
Lower Street
Lunsford's Cross
Netherfield Road
Netherfield
Whatlington
Scrays
Vinehall Street
John's Cross
Mountfield
Cackle Street
Goatham Green
Chitcombe
Cripp's Corner
Collier's Green
Staple Cross
Salehurst
Robertsbridge
Northbridge Street
Ewhurst Green
Millcorner
Bodiam
Bodiam Castle NT
Great Dixter
Hurst Green
Sandhurst Cross
Kent Ditch
Linkhill
Newenden
Sandhurst
Kent & East Sussex Railway
Conghurst
Four Throws
The Moor
Hawkhurst
Highgate
Delmonden Green
Flimwell
Standen Street
Kensham Green
Dingleden
Rolvenden
Rolvenden Layne
Historic Vehicles Collection
Hole Park
Strood
Iden Green
Gun Green
Gill's Green
Benenden
Beacon Hill
Hartley
Goddard's Green
Tenterden
Tenterden Vineyard Park
Small Hythe
Smallhythe Place NT
Peening Quarter
Leigh Green
St Michaels
Parkgate
Biddenden
Woolpack
Arcadia
East End
Cranbrook
Golford
Golford Green
Union Mill
Sissinghurst
Sissinghurst NT
Goose Green
Wilsley Green
Wilsley Pound
Iden Green
Glassenbury
Bedgebury Cross
National Pinetum & Garden
Flishinghurst
Colliers Green
Cranbrook Common
Three Chimneys
Knox Bridge
Curtisden Green
Winchet Hill
Marden Beech
Marden Thorn
Marden
Staplehurst
Frittenden
Sinkhurst Green
Lashenden
Hareplain
Curteis Corner
Stede Quarter
Further Quarter
Middle Quarter
Standen
Haffenden Quarter
Romden Castle
Smarden
Smarden Bell
Maltman's Hill
Wissenden
Pluckley Station
Snoadhill
Biddenden Green
Wheeler's Street
Headcorn
Hawkenbury
Sweetlands Corner
Plumtree Green
Southernden
Swift's Green
The Quarter
Chambers Green
Pluckley Thorne
Pluckley
Hothfield
Godington Park
Monday Boys
Bedlam Lane
Forstal
Pivington
Little Chart
Ram Lane
Egerton
Potter's Forstal
Pembles Cross
Coppins Corner
Charing Heath
Boughton Malherbe
Grafty Green
Ulcombe
East Sutton
Sutton Valence
Chart Hill
Rabbit's Cross
Farthing Green
Jubilee Corner
Chainhurst
Hunton
Stile Bridge
Underling Green
Little Pattenden
Great Pattenden
Cross-at-Hand
Milebush
Wanshurst Green
Little Cheveney
River Beult
River Teise
Monchelsea
0 1 2 3 4 5 miles
0 1 2 3 4 5 6 7 kilometres

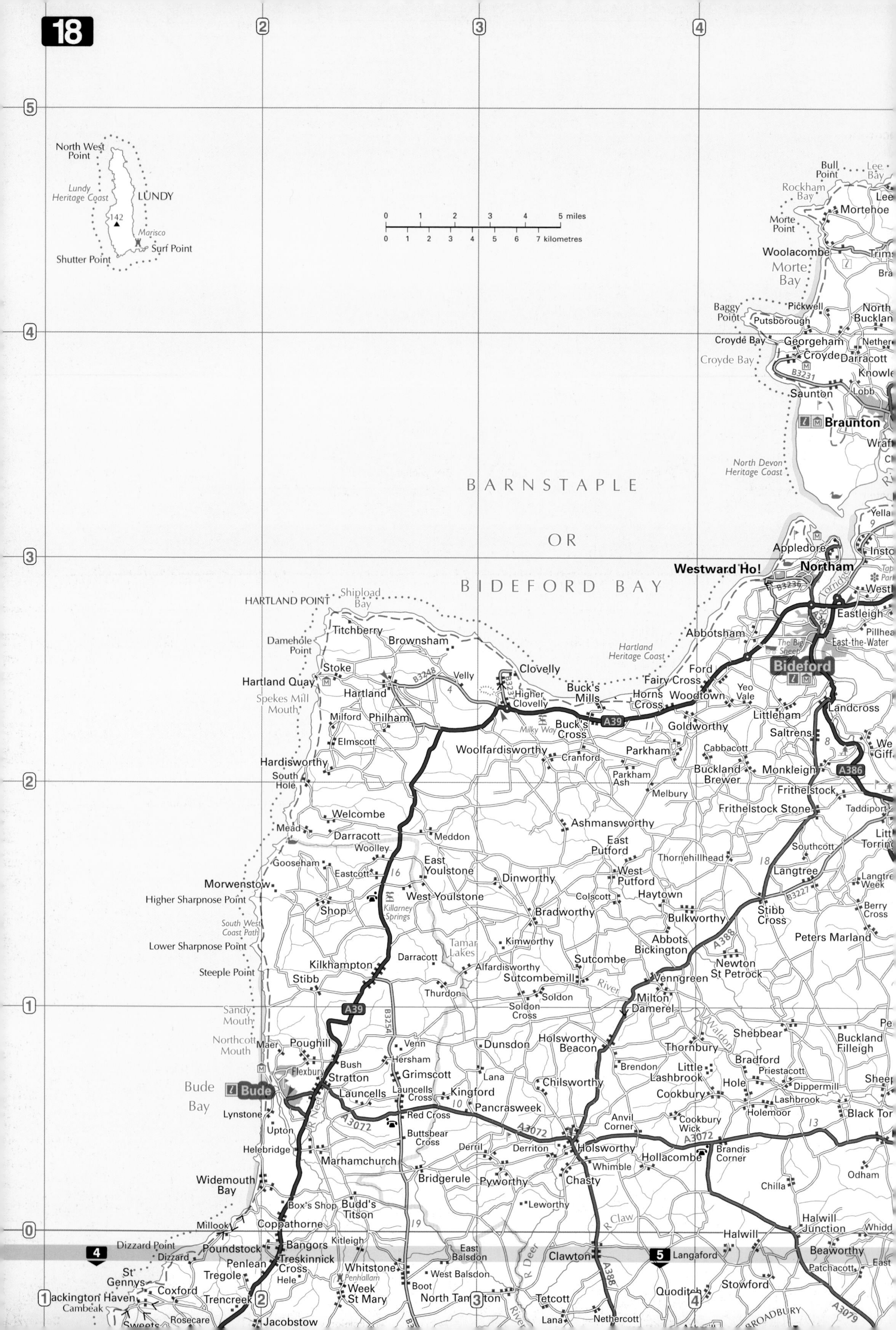

North West Point

Lundy Heritage Coast

LUNDY

▲142

Marisco

Surf Point

Shutter Point

0 1 2 3 4 5 miles
0 1 2 3 4 5 6 7 kilometres

B A R N S T A P L E

O R

B I D E F O R D   B A Y

Bull Point
Lee Bay
Rockham Bay
Lee
Morte Point
Mortehoe
Bra
Woolacombe
Morte Bay

Baggy Point
Pickwell
North Bucklan
Putsborough
Croyde Bay
Georgeham
Croyde
Darracott
Croyde Bay
Knowle
Saunton
Lobb

North Devon Heritage Coast

Braunton
Wra

Appledore
Insto
Westward Ho!
Northam
Tap Par
West
Eastleigh
Pillhea
East-the-Water

HARTLAND POINT
Shipload Bay
Titchberry
Brownsham
Abbotsham
The Big Sheep
Bideford
Damehole Point
Stoke
Velly
Clovelly
Hartland Heritage Coast
Ford
Fairy Cross
Hartland Quay
Hartland
Higher Clovelly
Buck's Mills
Horns Cross
Woodtown
Yeo Vale
Littleham
Landcross
Spekes Mill Mouth
Milford
Philham
Buck's Cross
A39
Goldworthy
Cabbacott
Saltrens
We Giff
Elmscott
Woolfardisworthy
Cranford
Parkham
Buckland Brewer
Monkleigh
A386
Hardisworthy
Parkham Ash
Melbury
Frithelstock
South Hole
Melbury
Frithelstock Stone
Taddipor
Welcombe
Ashmansworthy
Thornehillhead
Langtree
Litt Torring
Mead
Darracott
East Putford
Langtre Week
Woolley
Meddon
Gooseham
East Youlstone
Dinworthy
West Putford
Southcott
Eastcott
16
Haytown
18
Morwenstow
West Youlstone
Colscott
Langtree
Higher Sharpnose Point
Killarney Springs
Bradworthy
B3227
Berry Cross
Shop
Kimworthy
Bulkworthy
Stibb Cross
Peters Marland
South West Coast Path
Darracott
Alfardisworthy
Abbots Bickington
Newton St Petrock
Lower Sharpnose Point
Tamar Lakes
Sutcombe
A388
Steeple Point
Kilkhampton
Sutcombemill
Venngreen
Stibb
Thurdon
Soldon
River
Milton Damerel
Sandy Mouth
Soldon Cross
Pe
Waldon
Northcott Mouth
Maer
Poughill
Venn
Dunsdon
Holsworthy Beacon
Shebbear
Buckland Filleigh
Bude Bay
Bush
Hersham
Thornbury
Flexbury
Stratton
Grimscott
Lana
Brendon
Little Lashbrook
Bradford
Priestacott
Hole
Dippermill
Sheep
Bude
Launcells
Chilsworthy
Cookbury
Lashbrook
Lynstone
Launcells Cross
Kingford
10
Pancrasweek
A3072
Anvil Corner
Cookbury Wick
Holemoor
Black Tor
Upton
A3072
Red Cross
Derril
Holsworthy
Hollacombe
Brandis Corner
13
Helebridge
Buttsbear Cross
Derriton
Whimble
Chilla
Odham
Widemouth Bay
Marhamchurch
Bridgerule
Pyworthy
Chasty
Box's Shop
Budd's Titson
Leworthy
R Claw
Halwill Junction
Whidd
Millook
Coppathorne
19
Halwill
Dizzard Point
Kitleigh
East Balsdon
Clawton
Langaford
Beaworthy
Dizzard
Poundstock
Bangors
Treskinnick Cross
Whitstone
West Balsdon
A386
Quoditch
Stowford
Patchacott
East
St Gennys
Penlean
Hele
Penhallam
Boot
Nethercott
BROADBURY
A3079
ackington Haven
Tregole
Coxford
Week St Mary
North Tan ton
Tetcott
Cambeak
Trencreek
Jacobstow
Lana
Sweets
Rosecare

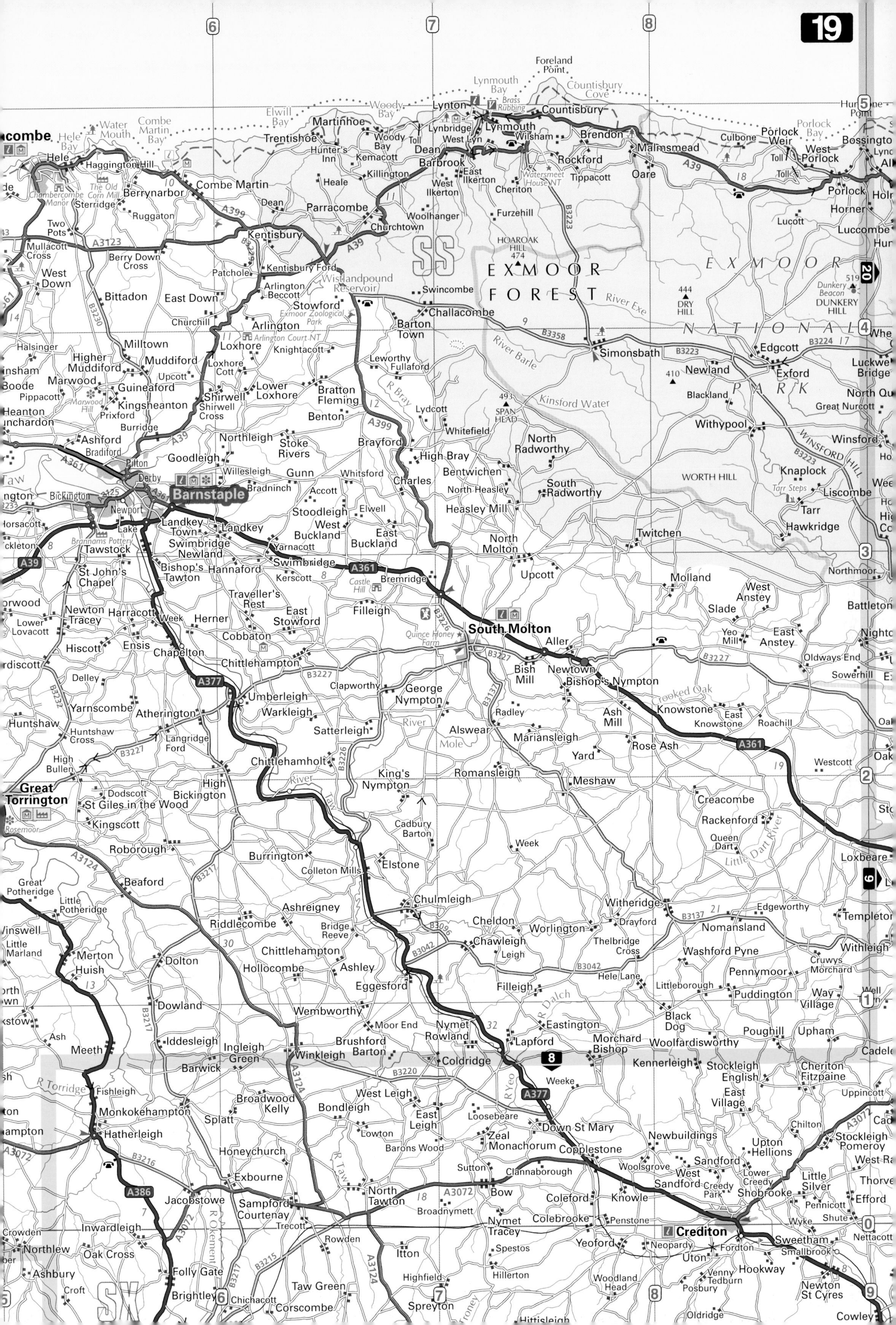
6
7
8
Foreland Point
Lynmouth Bay
Countisbury Cove
Brass Rubbing
Elwill Bay
Woody Bay
Lynton
Countisbury
Hurlstone Point
Water Mouth
Combe Martin Bay
Hele Bay
Martinhoe
Trentishoe
Woody Bay
Toll
Lynbridge
West Lyn
Lynmouth
Wilsham
Brendon
Culbone
Porlock Weir
Porlock Bay
Bossington
Hele
Haggington Hill
Hunter's Inn
Kemacott
Dean
Barbrook
Malmsmead
Rockford
West Porlock
Toll
A39
Chambercombe Manor
The Old Corn Mill
Sterridge
Berrynarbor
Combe Martin
Heale
Killington
East Ilkerton
West Ilkerton
Watersmeet House NT
Cheriton
Tippacott
Oare
Porlock
Ruggaton
Dean
Parracombe
Woolhanger
Furzehill
B3223
Horner
Lucott
Two Pots
A399
Kentisbury
Churchtown
Luccombe
Mullacott Cross
A3123
Berry Down Cross
B3229
A39
SS
HOAROAK HILL 474
EXMOOR FOREST
EXMOOR
NATIONAL PARK
West Down
Patcholes
Kentisbury Ford
Wistlandpound Reservoir
Swincombe
River Exe
444 DRY HILL
Dunkery Beacon
519
DUNKERY HILL
20
Bittadon
East Down
B3230
Arlington Beccott
Stowford
Exmoor Zoological Park
Challacombe
Churchill
Arlington
Arlington Court NT
Barton Town
B3358
Simonsbath
B3223
Edgcott
B3224
Halsinger
Milltown
Knightacott
River Barle
Exford
Luckwell Bridge
Higher Muddiford
Muddiford
Loxhore
Loxhore Cott
Lewworthy
Fullaford
410
Newland
Marwood
Upcott
Guineaford
Shirwell
Lower Loxhore
Bratton Fleming
R Bray
493 SPAN HEAD
Kinsford Water
Blackland
North Quarme
Boode
Pippacott
Marwood Hill
Kingsheanton
Prixford
Shirwell Cross
Benton
Lydcott
Withypool
Great Nurcott
Heanton Punchardon
Burridge
A399
Whitefield
North Radworthy
Winsford
Ashford
Bradiford
Northleigh
Stoke Rivers
Brayford
High Bray
Bentwichen
WINSFORD HILL
Pilton
Goodleigh
Willesleigh
Gunn
Whitsford
Charles
North Heasley
South Radworthy
WORTH HILL
Knaplock
Tarr Steps
Liscombe
Taw
Derby
Barnstaple
Bradninch
Accott
Heasley Mill
Tarr
Bickington
A361
Newport
Stoodleigh
Elwell
Hawkridge
Horsacott
Lake
Landkey Town
Landkey
West Buckland
East Buckland
North Molton
Twitchen
Brannams Pottery
Tawstock
Swimbridge Newland
Yarnacott
Swimbridge
A361
A39
St John's Chapel
Bishop's Tawton
Hannaford
Kerscott
Castle Hill
Bremridge
Upcott
Northmoor
Molland
West Anstey
Battleton
Newton Tracey
Harracott
Traveller's Rest
Filleigh
Slade
Lower Lovacott
Week
Herner
East Stowford
B3226
South Molton
Aller
Yeo Mill
East Anstey
Hiscott
Ensis
Cobbaton
Quince Honey Farm
Chapelton
B3227
Bish Mill
Newtown
B3227
Oldways End
Sowerhill
Chittlehampton
Delley
Clapworthy
George Nympton
Bishop's Nympton
B3227
A377
B3137
Crooked Oak
Knowstone
East Knowstone
Roachill
B3232
Umberleigh
Yarnscombe
Atherington
Warkleigh
Radley
Ash Mill
Huntshaw
Huntshaw Cross
Langridge Ford
Satterleigh
River Mole
Alswear
Mariansleigh
Rose Ash
A361
B3227
Yard
High Bullen
Chittlehamholt
B3226
Westcott
Great Torrington
High Bickington
King's Nympton
Romansleigh
Meshaw
Dodscott
St Giles in the Wood
River Taw
Creacombe
Rosemoor
Kingscott
Cadbury Barton
Rackenford
Little Dart River
Queen Dart
Roborough
Week
A3124
Burrington
Loxbeare
Elstone
Colleton Mills
B3217
Great Potheridge
Beaford
9
Little Potheridge
Chulmleigh
Witheridge
Edgeworthy
Ashreigney
B3137
Templeton
Winswell
Riddlecombe
Bridge Reeve
Cheldon
Drayford
Nomansland
B3096
Worlington
Chawleigh
Little Marland
Merton
30
Chittlehampton
Leigh
Thelbridge Cross
Washford Pyne
Withleigh
B3042
Cruwys Morchard
Dolton
Huish
Hollocombe
Ashley
B3042
Pennymoor
Eggesford
Hele Lane
Filleigh
Littleborough
R Dalch
Puddington
Way Village
Dowland
B3217
Wembworthy
Well Town
Black Dog
Ash
Moor End
Nymet Rowland
Eastington
Meeth
32
Poughill
Upham
Iddesleigh
Ingleigh Green
Brushford Barton
Lapford
Morchard Bishop
Woolfardisworthy
Cadeleigh
Barwick
Winkleigh
Coldridge
8
Kennerleigh
Stockleigh English
Cheriton Fitzpaine
B3220
Weeke
R Torridge
Fishleigh
A3124
West Leigh
R Yeo
A377
East Village
Uppincott
Broadwood Kelly
Monkokehampton
Bondleigh
East Leigh
Loosebeare
Splatt
Lowton
Down St Mary
Chilton
A3072
Hatherleigh
Zeal Monachorum
Newbuildings
Upton Hellions
Stockleigh Pomeroy
A3072
Honeychurch
Barons Wood
Copplestone
B3216
R Taw
Sutton
Sandford
West Raddon
Exbourne
Clannaborough
Woolsgrove
West Sandford
Lower Creedy
Creedy Park
Little Silver
Thorverton
A386
North Tawton
18
A3072
Bow
Shobrooke
Jacobstowe
Sampford Courtenay
Broadnymett
Coleford
Knowle
Pennicott
Efford
A3072
R Okement
Trecott
Nymet Tracey
Colebrooke
Penstone
Wyke
Shute
Inwardleigh
Crediton
Sweetham
Nettacott
Crowden
Northlew
Rowden
Neopardy
Fordton
Smallbrook
Oak Cross
B3215
Itton
Spestos
Yeoford
Uton
Hookway
Ashbury
Folly Gate
A3124
Hillerton
Venny Tedburn
Croft
B3217
Highfield
Woodland Head
Posbury
Newton St Cyres
SX
Brightley
Chichacott
Taw Green
Corscombe
Spreyton
Hittisleigh
Oldridge
Cowley
0
1
2
3
4
5

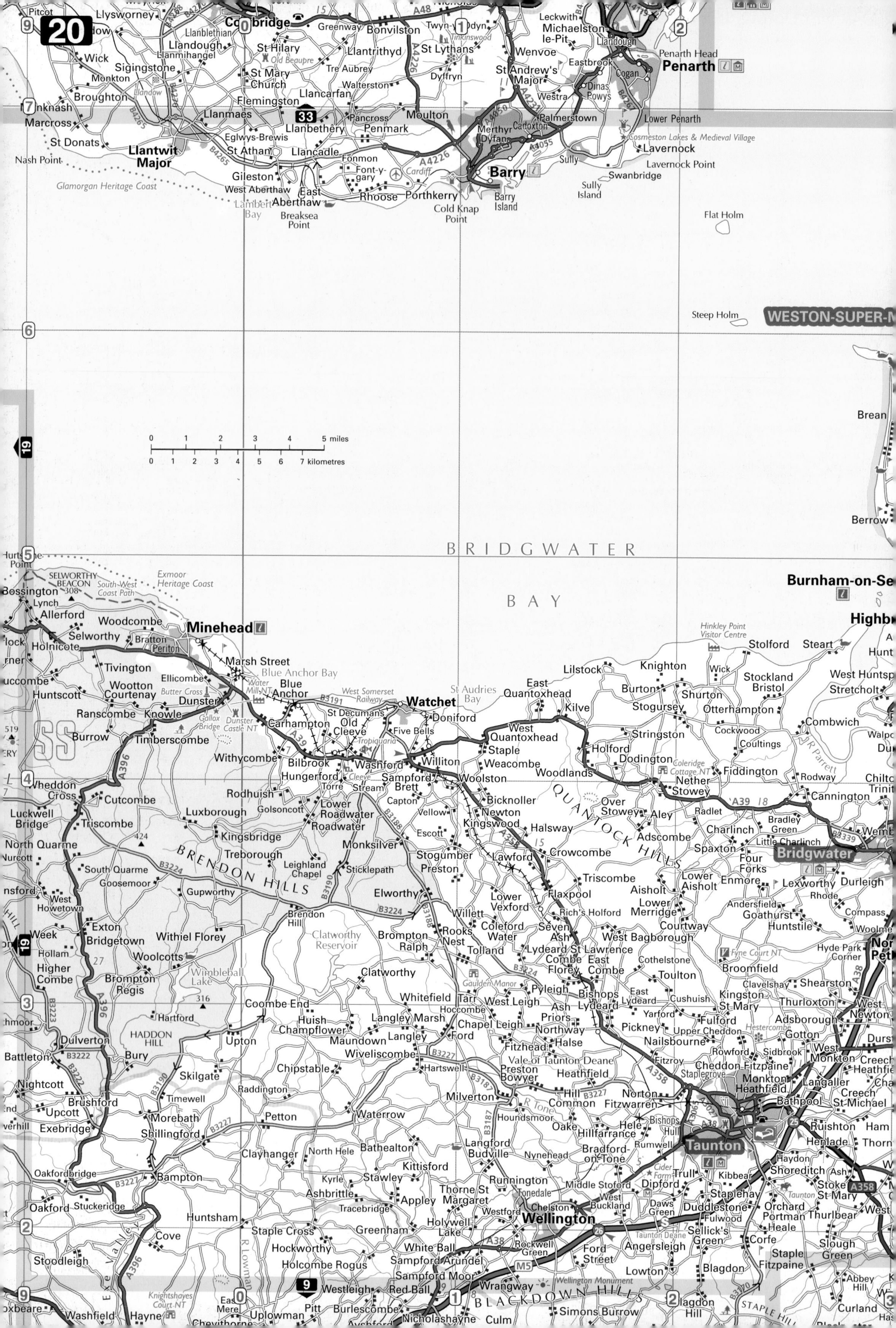

20
Pitcot
Llysworney
Cowbridge
Llanblethian
Llandough
Llanmihangel
Wick
Sigingstone
Monkton
Broughton
Marcross
St Donats
Nash Point
Llantwit Major
Llanmaes
Eglwys-Brewis
St Athan
Gileston
West Aberthaw
East Aberthaw
Lambert Bay
Breaksea Point
Glamorgan Heritage Coast
St Hilary
Old Beaupre
St Mary Church
Flemingston
Llancarfan
Llanbethery
Llancadle
Greenway
Bonvilston
Llantrithyd
Tre Aubrey
Walterston
Pancross
Penmark
Fonmon
Font-y-gary
Rhoose
Porthkerry
Cardiff
Cold Knap Point
Twyn-yr-Odyn
Tinkinswood
St Lythans
Dyffryn
Moulton
Wenvoe
St Andrew's Major
Merthyr Dyfan
Cadoxton
Barry
Barry Island
Leckwith
Michaelston-le-Pit
Llandough
Eastbrook
Dinas Powys
Westra
Palmerstown
Sully
Sully Island
Swanbridge
Penarth Head
Penarth
Cogan
Lower Penarth
Cosmeston Lakes & Medieval Village
Lavernock
Lavernock Point
Flat Holm
Steep Holm
WESTON-SUPER-M
Brean
Berrow
BRIDGWATER BAY
Burnham-on-Se
Highb
0 1 2 3 4 5 miles
0 1 2 3 4 5 6 7 kilometres
Hurlstone Point
SELWORTHY BEACON 308
South West Coast Path
Exmoor Heritage Coast
Bossington
Lynch
Allerford
Woodcombe
Selworthy
Holnicote
Minehead
Bratton
Periton
Marsh Street
Blue Anchor Bay
Tivington
Ellicombe
Wootton Courtenay
Huntscott
Luccombe
Butter Cross
Dunster
Water Mill NT
Blue Anchor
West Somerset Railway
Watchet
St Audries Bay
Ranscombe
Knowle
Gallox Bridge
Dunster Castle NT
Carhampton
St Decumans
Old Cleeve
Doniford
Five Bells
Tropiquaria
Burrow
Timberscombe
Withycombe
Bilbrook
Washford
Williton
Hungerford
Cleeve
Sampford Brett
Torre
Stream
Capton
Wheddon Cross
Cutcombe
Rodhuish
Luxborough
Golsoncott
Lower Roadwater
Roadwater
Luckwell Bridge
Triscombe
North Quarme
Kingsbridge
Treborough
BRENDON HILLS
Leighland Chapel
Monksilver
Sticklepath
South Quarme
Goosemoor
Gupworthy
West Howetown
Exton
Bridgetown
Week
Hollam
Higher Combe
Withiel Florey
Woolcotts
Brompton Regis
Wimbleball Lake
Brendon Hill
Clatworthy Reservoir
Elworthy
Brompton Ralph
Clatworthy
Hartford
HADDON HILL
Dulverton
Battleton
Bury
Coombe End
Huish Champflower
Upton
Maundown
Langley Marsh
Langley
Wiveliscombe
Chipstable
Skilgate
Raddington
Timewell
Nightcott
Brushford
Upcott
Exebridge
Morebath
Shillingford
Petton
Waterrow
Clayhanger
North Hele
Bathealton
Oakfordbridge
Bampton
Oakford
Stuckeridge
Kittisford
Kyrle
Stawley
Ashbrittle
Tracebridge
Appley
Huntsham
Cove
Staple Cross
Hockworthy
Greenham
Holcombe Rogus
Stoodleigh
Exe Valley
R Lowman
Knightshayes Court NT
East Mere
Washfield
Hayne
Uplowman
Chevithorne
Westleigh
Pitt
Burlescombe
Ayshford
Red Ball
Sampford Moor
Sampford Arundel
White Ball
Nicholashayne
Culm
Wrangway
Wellington Monument
BLACKDOWN HILLS
Simons Burrow
Lilstock
East Quantoxhead
Kilve
West Quantoxhead
Staple
Weacombe
Woolston
Bicknoller
Newton
Kingswood
Vellow
Escott
Stogumber
Preston
Halsway
Lawford
Crowcombe
Woodlands
Holford
Dodington
Over Stowey
Aley
QUANTOCK HILLS
Triscombe
Flaxpool
Lower Vexford
Willett
Coleford Water
Rooks Nest
Tolland
Rich's Holford
Seven Ash
West Bagborough
Lydeard St Lawrence
Combe Florey
East Combe
Gaulden Manor
Pyleigh
Bishops Lydeard
Ash Priors
West Leigh
Tarr
Hoccombe
Chapel Leigh
Ford
Northway
Halse
Fitzhead
Vale of Taunton Deane
Hartswell
Preston Bowyer
Heathfield
Milverton
Hill Common
R Tone
Houndsmoor
Oake
Langford Budville
Nynehead
Runnington
Thorne St Margaret
Tonedale
Westford
Holywell Lake
Chelston
Wellington
Rockwell Green
Ford Street
Hinkley Point Visitor Centre
Knighton
Stolford
Steart
Wick
Stockland Bristol
Burton
Shurton
Stogursey
Otterhampton
Stringston
Cockwood
Coultings
Coleridge Cottage NT
Nether Stowey
Fiddington
Rodway
Radlet
Cannington
Combwich
Charlinch
Bradley Green
Adscombe
Little Charlinch
Spaxton
Four Forks
Bridgwater
Lower Aisholt
Aisholt
Enmore
Lexworthy
Durleigh
Lower Merridge
Andersfield
Goathurst
Huntstile
Courtway
Cothelstone
Fyne Court NT
Broomfield
Toulton
East Lydeard
Kingston St Mary
Clavelshay
Shearston
Cushuish
Yarford
Fulford
Thurloxton
Pickney
Upper Cheddon
Hestercombe
Adsborough
Gotton
Nailsbourne
Rowford
Sidbrook
Fitzroy
Cheddon Fitzpaine
West Monkton
Staplegrove
Monkton Heathfield
Langaller
Norton Fitzwarren
Bathpool
Creech St Michael
Hele
Bishops Hull
Hillfarrance
Rumwell
Taunton
Ruishton
Henlade
Bradford-on-Tone
Cider Farm
Trull
Kibbear
Haydon
Shoreditch
Ash
Stoke St Mary
Middle Stoford
Dipford
Staplehay
West Buckland
Daws Green
Duddlestone
Fulwood
Orchard Portman
Thurlbear
Sellick's Green
Heale
Taunton Deane
Angersleigh
Corfe
Slough Green
Staple Fitzpaine
Lowton
Blagdon
Abbey Hill
Blagdon Hill
STAPLE HILL
Curland
A48
A4226
A4231
A4050
A4055
A39
A396
A358
A38
A361
M5
B3191
B3190
B3188
B3224
B3222
B3223
B3227
B3187
B3339
B4265
B4270
B4267
B4268
B3170

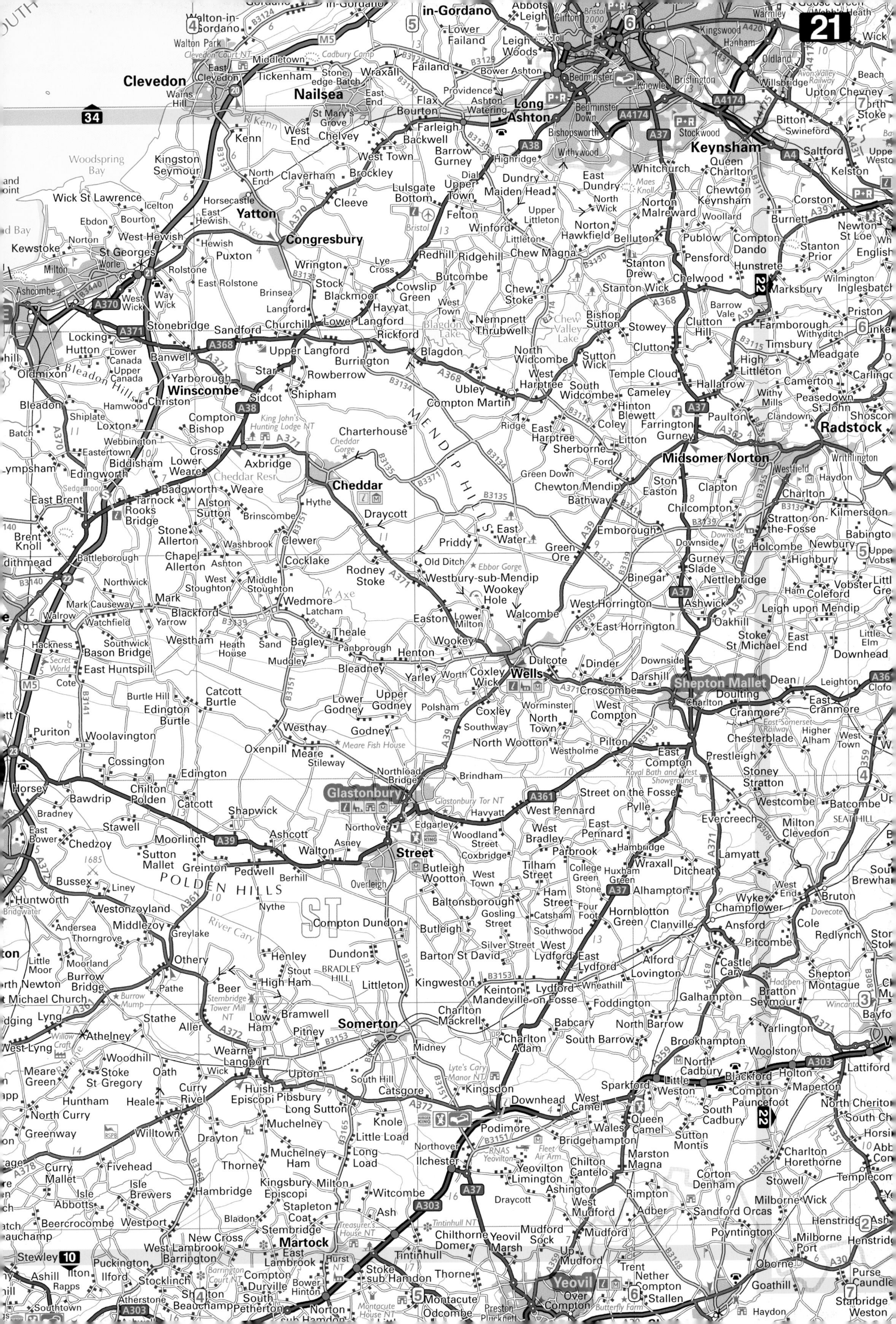

Walton-in-Gordano
in-Gordano
Abbots Leigh
Clifton
Bristol 2000
Warmley
Walton Park
Clevedon Court NT
Middletown
Cadbury Camp
Lower Failand
Leigh Woods
Kingswood
Hanham
Oldland
Wick
Clevedon
East Clevedon
Tickenham
Stone-edge-Batch
Wraxall
Failand
Bower Ashton
Bedminster
Knowle
Brislington
Willsbridge
Avon Valley Railway
Beach
Upton Cheyney
Wains Hill
Nailsea
East End
Providence
Ashton Watering
Long Ashton
Bedminster Down
North Stoke
Flax Bourton
St Mary's Grove
Farleigh
Backwell
Bishopsworth
Stockwood
Keynsham
Bitton
Swineford
Saltford
Kelston
Kenn
R Kenn
West End
Chelvey
West Town
Barrow Gurney
Highridge
Withywood
Whitchurch
Queen Charlton
Woodspring Bay
Kingston Seymour
North End
Claverham
Brockley
Lulsgate Bottom
Dial
Upper Town
Dundry
Maiden Head
East Dundry
Maes Knoll
North Wick
Chewton Keynsham
Corston
Newton St Loe
Wick St Lawrence
Icelton
Horsecastle
Yatton
Cleeve
Felton
Bristol
Upper Littleton
Norton Malreward
Woollard
Burnett
Ebdon
Bourton
East Hewish
Congresbury
Winford
Norton Hawkfield
Belluton
Publow
Compton Dando
Stanton Prior
English
Kewstoke
Norton
West Hewish
R Yeo
Hewish
Puxton
Littleton
Chew Magna
Pensford
Hunstrete
St Georges
Milton
Worle
Rolstone
Wrington
Lye Cross
Redhill
Ridgehill
Stanton Drew
Chelwood
Marksbury
Wilmington
Inglesbatch
Ashcombe
East Rolstone
Brinsea
Stock
Blackmoor
Cowslip Green
Butcombe
Chew Stoke
Stanton Wick
Barrow Vale
West Wick
Way Wick
Langford
Havyat
West Town
Nempnett Thrubwell
Blagdon Lake
Chew Valley Lake
Bishop Sutton
Stowey
Clutton Hill
Farmborough
Withyditch
Priston
Locking
Hutton
Stonebridge
Sandford
Churchill
Lower Langford
Rickford
Clutton
Timsbury
Lower Canada
Upper Canada
Banwell
Upper Langford
Burrington
Blagdon
North Widcombe
Sutton Wick
High Littleton
Meadgate
Oldmixon
Bleadon Hills
Yarborough
Star
Rowberrow
Ubley
West Harptree
Temple Cloud
Camerton
Carlingcott
Winscombe
Sidcot
Shipham
South Widcombe
Cameley
Hallatrow
Withy Mills
Peasedown St John
Shoscombe
Bleadon
Hamwood
Christon
Compton Martin
Hinton Blewett
Paulton
Clandown
Radstock
Shiplate
Loxton
Compton Bishop
King John's Hunting Lodge NT
Charterhouse
MENDIP HILLS
Ridge
East Harptree
Coley
Farrington Gurney
Batch
Webbington
Cheddar Gorge
Litton
Sherborne
Midsomer Norton
Writhlington
Eastertown
Cross
Axbridge
Ford
Westfield
Haydon
Lympsham
Edingworth
Biddisham
Lower Weare
Cheddar Resr
Cheddar
Green Down
Chewton Mendip
Ston Easton
Clapton
Charlton
Sedgemoor
Badgworth
Weare
Bathway
Chilcompton
Kilmersdon
East Brent
Tarnock
Alston Sutton
Hythe
Draycott
Stratton-on-the-Fosse
Rooks Bridge
Brinscombe
East Water
Emborough
Babington
Brent Knoll
Stone Allerton
Washbrook
Clewer
Priddy
Green Ore
Downside
Holcombe
Newbury
Battleborough
Chapel Allerton
Ashton
Cocklake
Old Ditch
Ebbor Gorge
Gurney Slade
Highbury
Northwick
West Stoughton
Middle Stoughton
Rodney Stoke
Westbury-sub-Mendip
Binegar
Nettlebridge
Vobster
Mark Causeway
Mark
R Axe
Wookey Hole
Ham
Coleford
Walrow
Watchfield
Blackford
Wedmore
Latcham
Walcombe
West Horrington
Ashwick
Leigh upon Mendip
Yarrow
Theale
Easton
Lower Milton
East Horrington
Oakhill
Hackness
Southwick
Westham
Heath House
Sand
Bagley
Panborough
Henton
Wookey
Stoke St Michael
East End
Little Elm
Bason Bridge
Secret World
East Huntspill
Mudgley
Bleadney
Yarley
Worth
Coxley Wick
Wells
Dulcote
Dinder
Downside
Downhead
Cote
Darshill
Shepton Mallet
Dean
Leighton
Burtle Hill
Catcott Burtle
Edington Burtle
Lower Godney
Upper Godney
Polsham
Worminster
Croscombe
Doulting
Charlton
East Cranmore
Cranmore
Coxley
West Compton
East Somerset Railway
Puriton
Woolavington
Westhay
Godney
Southway
North Town
Higher Alham
West Town
Meare Fish House
North Wootton
Westholme
Pilton
Chesterblade
Oxenpill
Meare
Stileway
East Compton
Prestleigh
Cossington
Northload Bridge
Brindham
Royal Bath and West Showground
Stoney Stratton
Edington
Street on the Fosse
Horsey
Chilton Polden
Glastonbury
Glastonbury Tor NT
Havyatt
Pylle
Westcombe
Batcombe
Bawdrip
Catcott
West Pennard
Evercreech
SEAT HILL
Bradney
Shapwick
Northover
Edgarley
East Pennard
Milton Clevedon
Stawell
West Bradley
East Bower
Chedzoy
Moorlinch
Ashcott
Woodland Street
Hambridge
Lamyatt
Asney
Walton
Street
Coxbridge
Parbrook
Sutton Mallet
Greinton
Pedwell
Tilham Street
College Green
Huxham Green
Wraxall
Ditcheat
Butleigh Wootton
Sou Brewham
Bussex
Liney
Berhill
POLDEN HILLS
Overleigh
West Town
Stone
Alhampton
West End
Huntworth
Ham Street
Bruton
Westonzoyland
Nythe
Baltonsborough
Four Foot
Hornblotton Green
Wyke Champflower
Bridgwater
Andersea
Middlezoy
River Cary
Compton Dundon
Gosling Street
Catsham
Clanville
Ansford
Dovecote
Cole
Thorngrove
Greylake
Butleigh
Southwood
Redlynch
Silver Street
West Lydford
Pitcombe
Little Moor
Othery
Henley
Dundon
Barton St David
East Lydford
Alford
Castle Cary
Moorland
Stout
BRADLEY HILL
Lovington
Shepton Montague
Burrow Bridge
High Ham
Wheathill
Hadspen
North Newton
Pathe
Beer
Littleton
Kingweston
Keinton Mandeville
Lydford on Fosse
Bratton Seymour
Burrow Mump
Stembridge Tower Mill NT
Foddington
Galhampton
Wincanton
St Michael Church
Low Ham
Bramwell
Charlton Mackrell
Babcary
North Barrow
Bayford
Lyng
Stathe
Aller
Pitney
Somerton
Yarlington
Willow Craft
Athelney
Wearne
Charlton Adam
South Barrow
West Lyng
Langport
Midney
Lyte's Cary Manor NT
Brookhampton
Woolston
Woodhill
Oath
Wick
North Cadbury
Lattiford
Meare Green
Stoke St Gregory
Curry Rivel
Upton
South Hill
Little Weston
Blackford
Holton
Huish Episcopi
Sparkford
Maperton
Huntham
Heale
Pibsbury
Catsgore
Kingsdon
Downhead
West Camel
Compton Pauncefoot
North Cheriton
Long Sutton
Queen Camel
South Cadbury
South Cheriton
North Curry
Muchelney
Knole
Podimore
Wales
Horsington
Greenway
Willtown
Drayton
Little Load
Bridgehampton
Sutton Montis
Abbas Combe
Northover
RNAS Yeovilton
Fleet Air Arm
Marston Magna
Curry Mallet
Fivehead
Thorney
Muchelney Ham
Long Load
Ilchester
Yeovilton
Chilton Cantelo
Charlton Horethorne
Isle Brewers
Kingsbury Episcopi
Milton
Limington
Corton Denham
Stowell
Templecombe
Isle Abbotts
Hambridge
Witcombe
Ashington
Rimpton
Milborne Wick
Stapleton
Ash
Draycott
West Mudford
Beercrocombe
Westport
Coat
Adber
Sandford Orcas
Bladon
Stembridge
Tintinhull NT
Mudford Sock
Henstridge Ash
Treasurer's House NT
Chilthorne Domer
Yeovil Marsh
Mudford
Poyntington
Beauchamp
New Cross
Martock
Milborne Port
Henstridge
Stewley
West Lambrook
Barrington
East Lambrook
Hurst
Tintinhull
Up Mudford
Trent
Oborne
Purse Caundle
Ashill
Ilton
Puckington
Ilford
Barrington Court NT
Compton Durville
Stoke sub Hamdon
Thorne
Yeovil
Nether Compton
Goathill
Rapps
Stocklinch
Shepton Beauchamp
South Petherton
Bower Hinton
Over Compton
Stallen
Stalbridge Weston
Southtown
Atherstone
Norton sub Hamdon
Montacute
Montacute House NT
Odcombe
Preston Plucknett
Butterfly Farm
Haydon
M5
A370
A371
A368
A38
A39
A37
A361
A372
A303
A359
A4
A4174
A420
A431
A3440
B3124
B3128
B3129
B3130
B3133
B3134
B3135
B3139
B3140
B3141
B3151
B3153
B3165
B3168
B3114
B3115
B3116
B3355
B3136
B3081
B3148
B3151
22
34
10

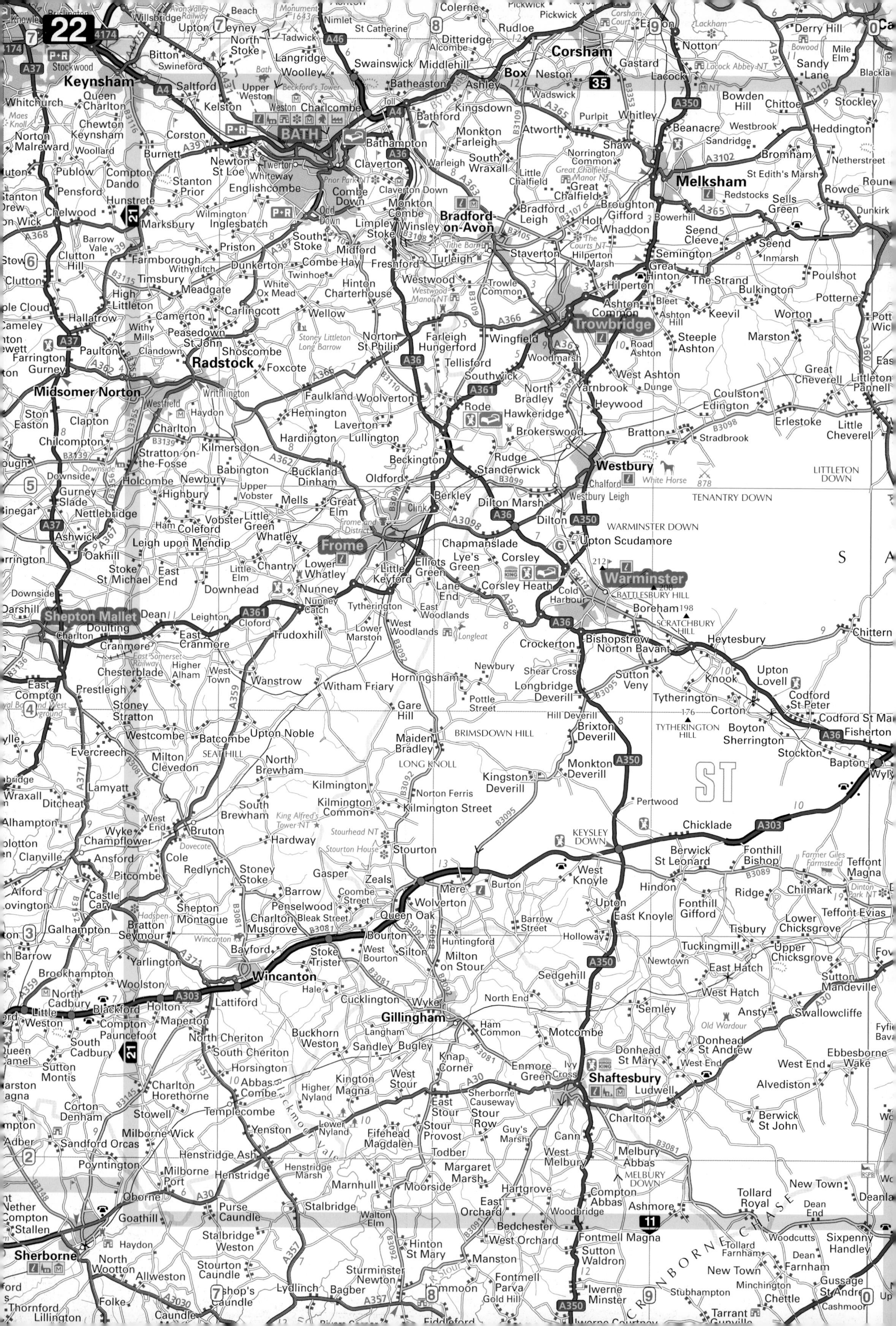
22
Keynsham
Bitton
Swineford
Saltford
Kelston
Upton Cheyney
North Stoke
Langridge
Woolley
Tadwick
Nimlet
Beach
Swainswick
St Catherine
Colerne
Ditteridge
Alcombe
Middlehill
Rudloe
Pickwick
Corsham
Gastard
Notton
Lacock
Derry Hill
Sandy Lane
Bowden Hill
Chittoe
Stockley
Heddington
Box
Neston
Batheaston
Ashley
Wadswick
Kingsdown
Bathford
Upper Weston
Weston
Charlcombe
BATH
Bathampton
Claverton
Monkton Farleigh
South Wraxall
Atworth
Purlpit
Whitley
Shaw
Beanacre
Westbrook
Sandridge
Bromham
Netherstreet
Melksham
St Edith's Marsh
Rowde
Whitchurch
Queen Charlton
Chewton Keynsham
Norton Malreward
Woollard
Corston
Burnett
Newton St Loe
Twerton
Whiteway
Englishcombe
Stanton Prior
Compton Dando
Publow
Pensford
Hunstrete
Marksbury
Wilmington
Inglesbatch
Combe Down
Odd Down
Monkton Combe
Limpley Stoke
Winsley
Bradford-on-Avon
Bradford Leigh
Little Chalfield
Great Chalfield
Norrington Common
Broughton Gifford
Holt
Whaddon
Bowerhill
Redstocks
Sells Green
Seend Cleeve
Seend
Inmarsh
Semington
Chelwood
Barrow Vale
Clutton Hill
Clutton
Farmborough
Withyditch
Priston
South Stoke
Midford
Dunkerton
Combe Hay
Freshford
Turleigh
Staverton
Hilperton Marsh
Great Hinton
Hilperton
The Strand
Poulshot
Bulkington
Potterne
Timsbury
Meadgate
High Littleton
Twinhoe
White Ox Mead
Hinton Charterhouse
Westwood
Trowle Common
Ashton Common
Bleet
Ashton Hill
Keevil
Worton
Hallatrow
Camerton
Carlingcott
Wellow
Trowbridge
Withy Mills
Peasedown St John
Stoney Littleton Long Barrow
Norton St Philip
Farleigh Hungerford
Wingfield
Road Ashton
Steeple Ashton
Marston
Farrington Gurney
Paulton
Clandown
Shoscombe
Radstock
Foxcote
Tellisford
Woodmarsh
West Ashton
Great Cheverell
Littleton Pannell
Midsomer Norton
Westfield
Writhlington
Haydon
Faulkland
Woolverton
Southwick
North Bradley
Yarnbrook
Dunge
Coulston
Edington
Heywood
Rode
Hawkeridge
Ston Easton
Clapton
Charlton
Hemington
Laverton
Lullington
Hardington
Brokerswood
Bratton
Stradbrook
Erlestoke
Little Cheverell
Chilcompton
Kilmersdon
Stratton-on-the-Fosse
Babington
Buckland Dinham
Beckington
Rudge
Standerwick
Westbury
Chalford
White Horse
LITTLETON DOWN
Downside
Holcombe
Newbury
Oldford
Berkley
Dilton Marsh
Westbury Leigh
TENANTRY DOWN
Gurney Slade
Highbury
Upper Vobster
Mells
Great Elm
Clink
Binegar
Nettlebridge
Ham
Vobster
Coleford
Little Green
Whatley
Frome
Dilton
WARMINSTER DOWN
Ashwick
Oakhill
Leigh upon Mendip
Chapmanslade
Upton Scudamore
Lye's Green
Corsley
Elliots Green
Stoke St Michael
East End
Little Elm
Chantry
Lower Whatley
Little Keyford
Warminster
Downhead
Nunney
Lane End
Corsley Heath
Cold Harbour
BATTLESBURY HILL
Shepton Mallet
Dean
Leighton
Nunney Catch
Tytherington
East Woodlands
Boreham
Doulting
Cloford
West Woodlands
Longleat
SCRATCHBURY HILL
Heytesbury
Chitterne
Cranmore
East Cranmore
Trudoxhill
Lower Marston
Crockerton
Bishopstrow
Norton Bavant
East Somerset Railway
Chesterblade
Higher Alham
West Town
Wanstrow
Newbury
Shear Cross
Sutton Veny
Knook
Upton Lovell
Prestleigh
East Compton
Witham Friary
Horningsham
Longbridge Deverill
Tytherington
Codford St Peter
Corton
Stoney Stratton
Pottle Street
Gare Hill
Hill Deverill
Brixton Deverill
TYTHERINGTON HILL
Boyton
Sherrington
Codford St Mary
Fisherton
Westcombe
Batcombe
Upton Noble
Maiden Bradley
BRIMSDOWN HILL
Stockton
Bapton
Evercreech
SEAT HILL
Milton Clevedon
North Brewham
LONG KNOLL
Monkton Deverill
Kingston Deverill
Lamyatt
Kilmington
Norton Ferris
Wraxall
Ditcheat
South Brewham
Kilmington Common
Kilmington Street
Pertwood
West End
King Alfred's Tower NT
Stourhead NT
Wyke Champflower
Bruton
Hardway
Chicklade
Stourton
KEYSLEY DOWN
Berwick St Leonard
Fonthill Bishop
Teffont Magna
Farmer Giles Farmstead
Clanville
Ansford
Cole
Dovecote
Redlynch
Stoney Stoke
Gasper
Zeals
Mere
Burton
West Knoyle
Hindon
Ridge
Chilmark
Pitcombe
Castle Cary
Barrow
Coombe Street
Alford
Lovington
Shepton Montague
Penselwood
Wolverton
Upton
Fonthill Gifford
Teffont Evias
Lower Chicksgrove
East Knoyle
Hadspen
Charlton Musgrove
Bleak Street
Queen Oak
Barrow Street
Tisbury
Galhampton
Bratton Seymour
Wincanton
Bourton
Holloway
Tuckingmill
Upper Chicksgrove
Bayford
Stoke Trister
West Bourton
Silton
Huntingford
Milton on Stour
Newtown
East Hatch
Sutton Mandeville
Yarlington
Brookhampton
North Cadbury
Woolston
Wincanton
Hale
Sedgehill
West Hatch
Little Weston
Blackford
Holton
Lattiford
Cucklington
Wyke
North End
Semley
Ansty
Swallowcliffe
Compton Pauncefoot
Maperton
Gillingham
Langham
Ham Common
Motcombe
Old Wardour
South Cadbury
North Cheriton
Buckhorn Weston
South Cheriton
Sandley
Bugley
Donhead St Andrew
Donhead St Mary
Ebbesborne Wake
Sutton Montis
Horsington
Knap Corner
Enmore Green
Ivy Cross
West End
Charlton Horethorne
Abbas Combe
Higher Nyland
Kington Magna
West Stour
Shaftesbury
Ludwell
Alvediston
Corton Denham
Templecombe
East Stour
Sherborne Causeway
Stour Row
Charlton
Berwick St John
Stowell
Blackmore Vale
Lower Nyland
Stour Provost
Guy's Marsh
Cann
Milborne Wick
Yenston
Fifehead Magdalen
Todber
West Melbury
Melbury Abbas
Sandford Orcas
Henstridge Ash
Poyntington
Henstridge Marsh
Margaret Marsh
MELBURY DOWN
Milborne Port
Henstridge
Marnhull
Moorside
Hartgrove
Compton Abbas
New Town
Tollard Royal
Oborne
Purse Caundle
Stalbridge
Walton Elm
East Orchard
Woodbridge
Ashmore
Dean End
Deanland
Nether Compton
Stallen
Goathill
Bedchester
West Orchard
Fontmell Magna
Woodcutts
Sixpenny Handley
Stalbridge Weston
Hinton St Mary
Sutton Waldron
Tollard Farnham
Dean
Sherborne
Haydon
North Wootton
Allweston
Stourton Caundle
Manston
Farnham
New Town
Gussage St Andrew
Sturminster Newton
Fontmell Parva
Minchington
Bishop's Caundle
Lydlinch
Bagber
Hammoon
Gold Hill
Iwerne Minster
Stubhampton
Chettle
Cashmoor
Thornford
Folke
Caundle
Lillington
Tarrant Gunville
CRANBORNE CHASE
A36
A37
A39
A4
A46
A350
A361
A362
A365
A366
A367
A368
A303
A371
A357
A359
A30
A3030
A3098
A3102
A342
A360
B3098
B3099
B3092
B3095
B3081
B3089
B3109
B3110
B3115
B3116
B3139
B3145
B3148
B3352
B3353
B3355
B3356
B3414
B3091
B3108
B3107
B3105
B3135
B3136
B3151

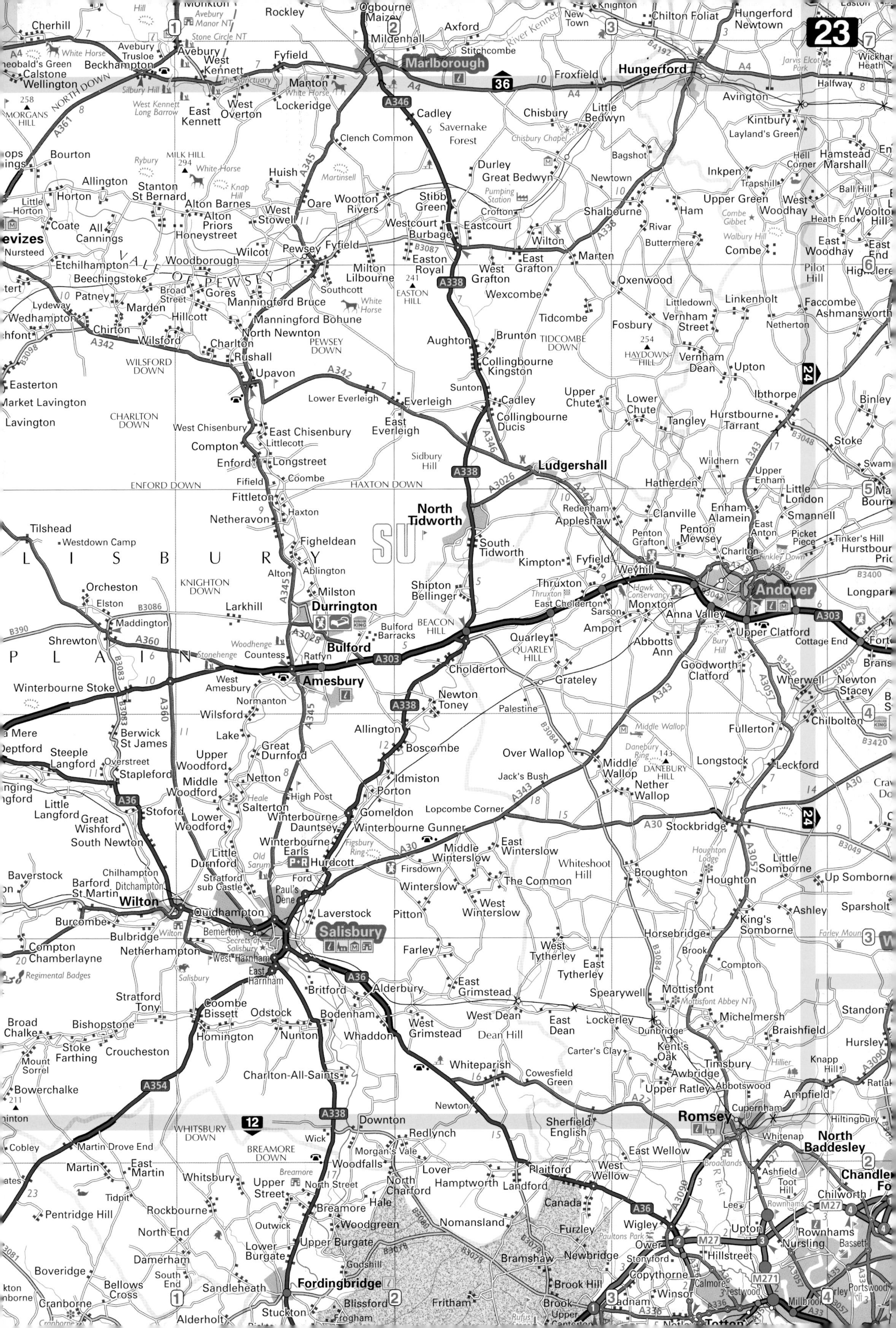

23
Cherhill
Avebury
Avebury Trusloe
Beckhampton
West Kennett
East Kennett
West Overton
Rockley
Ogbourne Maizey
Mildenhall
Marlborough
Axford
Stitchcombe
Manton
Fyfield
Lockeridge
Chilton Foliat
Hungerford Newtown
Hungerford
Froxfield
Avington
Kintbury
Little Bedwyn
Chisbury
Cadley
Savernake Forest
Clench Common
Calstone Wellington
Bourton
Allington
Horton
Stanton St Bernard
Alton Barnes
Alton Priors
Honeystreet
All Cannings
Coate
Huish
Oare
Wootton Rivers
West Stowell
Durley
Great Bedwyn
Bagshot
Inkpen
Stibb Green
Crofton
Westcourt
Burbage
Eastcourt
Shalbourne
Ham
Upper Green
West Woodhay
Rivar
Buttermere
Combe
East Woodhay
Wilton
Marten
East Grafton
West Grafton
Easton Royal
Milton Lilbourne
Pewsey
Fyfield
Wilcot
Woodborough
Etchilhampton
VALE OF PEWSEY
Beechingstoke
Broad Street
Gores
Manningford Bruce
Manningford Bohune
Patney
Marden
Hillcott
Chirton
Wilsford
Charlton
Rushall
North Newnton
Upavon
Oxenwood
Wexcombe
Tidcombe
Littledown
Vernham Street
Linkenholt
Faccombe
Ashmansworth
Fosbury
Vernham Dean
Upton
Brunton
Aughton
Collingbourne Kingston
Sunton
Cadley
Collingbourne Ducis
Everleigh
East Everleigh
Lower Everleigh
Upper Chute
Lower Chute
Tangley
Hurstbourne Tarrant
Ibthorpe
Easterton
Market Lavington
Lavington
East Chisenbury
West Chisenbury
Littlecott
Compton
Enford
Longstreet
Coombe
Fifield
Fittleton
Haxton
Netheravon
Ludgershall
Wildhern
Hatherden
Upper Enham
Little London
Redenham
Appleshaw
Clanville
Enham-Alamein
Smannell
North Tidworth
South Tidworth
Penton Grafton
Penton Mewsey
East Anton
Charlton
Tilshead
Westdown Camp
SALISBURY PLAIN
Figheldean
Ablington
Alton
Milston
Orcheston
Elston
Maddington
Shrewton
Larkhill
Durrington
Bulford
Bulford Barracks
Shipton Bellinger
Kimpton
Fyfield
Weyhill
Thruxton
East Cholderton
Sarson
Monxton
Amport
Anna Valley
Andover
Upper Clatford
Abbotts Ann
Quarley
Cholderton
Grateley
Goodworth Clatford
Wherwell
Newton Stacey
Chilbolton
Stonehenge
Countess
Ratfyn
Amesbury
West Amesbury
Winterbourne Stoke
Normanton
Wilsford
Lake
Newton Toney
Allington
Boscombe
Palestine
Fullerton
Berwick St James
Steeple Langford
Stapleford
Upper Woodford
Great Durnford
Middle Woodford
Netton
Salterton
Lower Woodford
Over Wallop
Middle Wallop
Nether Wallop
Jack's Bush
Longstock
Leckford
Idmiston
Porton
Gomeldon
Winterbourne Dauntsey
Winterbourne Gunner
Lopcombe Corner
Stockbridge
Little Langford
Great Wishford
South Newton
Stoford
Little Durnford
Winterbourne Earls
Hurdcott
Firsdown
Middle Winterslow
East Winterslow
Whiteshoot Hill
Broughton
Houghton
Little Somborne
Up Somborne
Baverstock
Barford St Martin
Chilhampton
Ditchampton
Wilton
Stratford sub Castle
Ford
Paul's Dene
Laverstock
Winterslow
The Common
West Winterslow
Pitton
Ashley
Sparsholt
King's Somborne
Burcombe
Quidhampton
Bemerton
Salisbury
Bulbridge
Netherhampton
Compton Chamberlayne
West Harnham
East Harnham
Farley
West Tytherley
East Tytherley
Horsebridge
Brook
Compton
Stratford Tony
Coombe Bissett
Odstock
Britford
Alderbury
East Grimstead
Spearywell
Mottisfont
Broad Chalke
Bishopstone
Homington
Nunton
Bodenham
West Dean
West Grimstead
Whaddon
Dean Hill
East Dean
Lockerley
Dunbridge
Michelmersh
Braishfield
Stoke Farthing
Croucheston
Mount Sorrel
Bowerchalke
Charlton-All-Saints
Whiteparish
Carter's Clay
Kent's Oak
Awbridge
Timsbury
Cowesfield Green
Upper Ratley
Abbotswood
Ampfield
Newton
Downton
Redlynch
Sherfield English
Romsey
North Baddesley
Martin Drove End
Whitsbury Down
Breamore Down
Wick
Morgan's Vale
Woodfalls
East Wellow
West Wellow
Plaitford
Martin
East Martin
Whitsbury
Upper Street
North Street
North Charford
Lover
Hamptworth
Landford
Canada
Pentridge Hill
Rockbourne
Breamore
Hale
Nomansland
Wigley
Furzley
Lee
Upton
Nursling
Rownhams
Chilworth
North End
Outwick
Woodgreen
Lower Burgate
Upper Burgate
Godshill
Bramshaw
Newbridge
Ower
Hillstreet
Damerham
Boveridge
South End
Bellows Cross
Sandleheath
Fordingbridge
Brook Hill
Copythorne
Calmore
Testwood
Cranborne
Stuckton
Blissford
Frogham
Fritham
Brook
Cadnam
Winsor
Totton
Alderholt

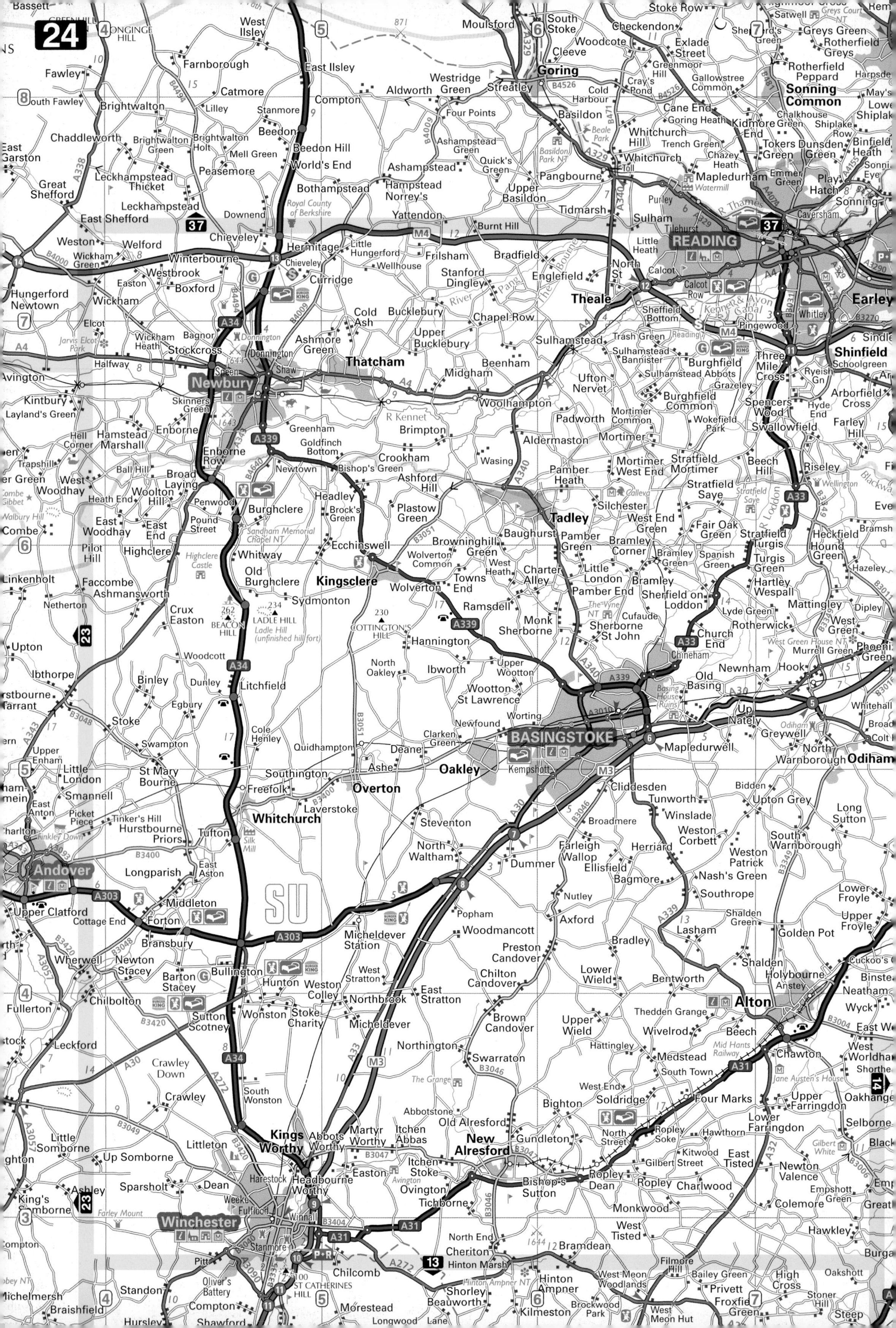
Newbury
Thatcham
READING
Theale
Tadley
Kingsclere
BASINGSTOKE
Overton
Oakley
Whitchurch
Andover
Winchester
Alton
New Alresford
Kings Worthy
Goring
Pangbourne
Earley
Shinfield
Odiham
Sonning Common
SU

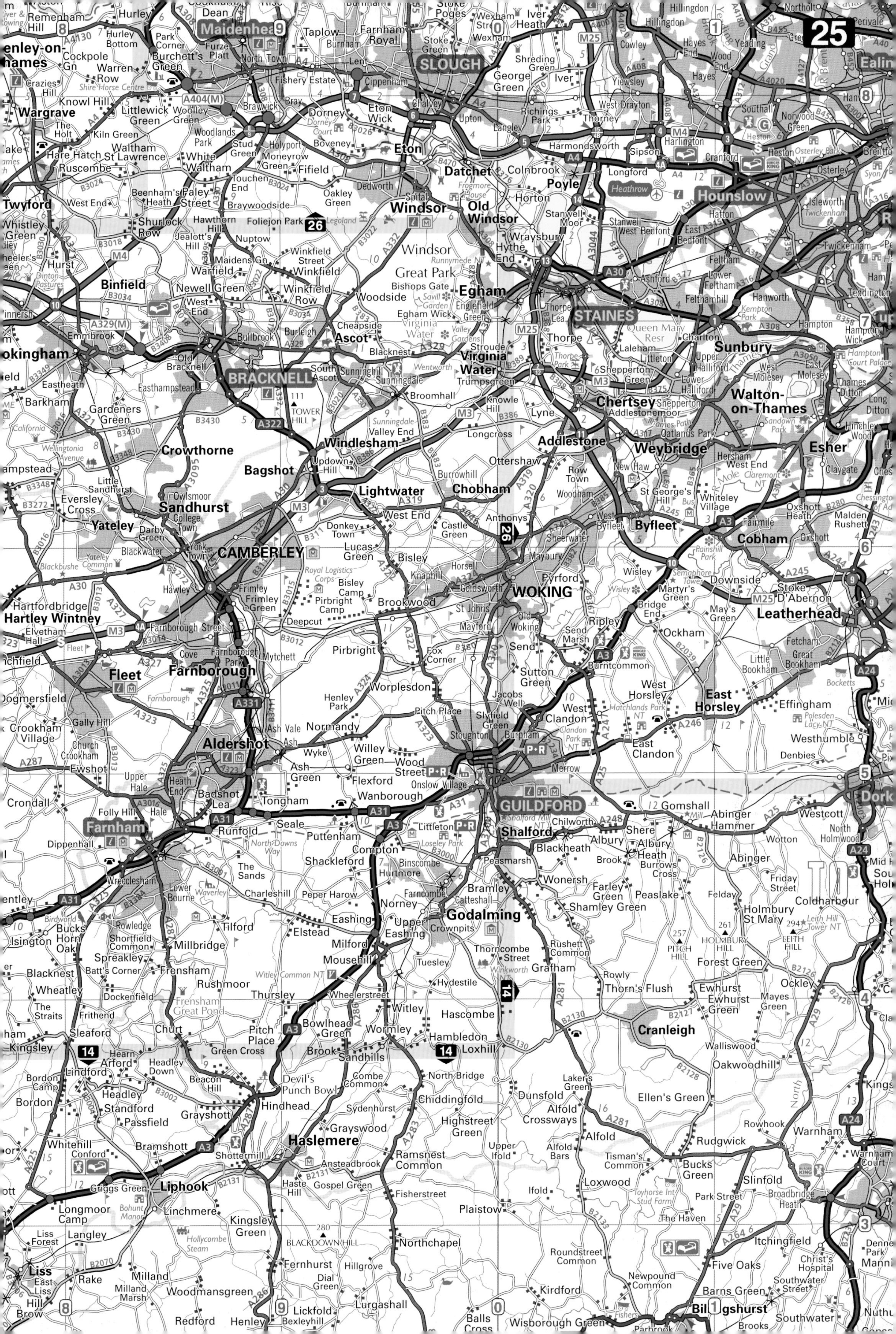

25
Remenham Hill
Hurley
Maidenhead
Taplow
Farnham Royal
Stoke Poges
Wexham Street
Iver Heath
Hillingdon
Northolt
Perivale
Henley-on-Thames
Hurley Bottom
Park Corner
Burchett's Green
Furze Platt
North Town
Burnham
Stoke Green
SLOUGH
Shreding Green
Cowley
Hayes End
Yeading
Ealing
Cockpole Green
Warren Row
Crazies Hill
Shire Horse Centre
Lent
Fishery Estate
Cippenham
George Green
Iver
Yiewsley
Wood End
Hayes
Southall
Hanwell
Knowl Hill
Wargrave
Littlewick Green
Woolley Green
Braywick
Bray
Dorney
Eton Wick
Chalvey
Upton
Richings Park
West Drayton
Thorney
Norwood Green
The Holt
Kiln Green
Waltham St Lawrence
Woodlands Park
Stud Green
Holyport
Dorney Court
Boveney
Eton
Langley
Harmondsworth
Sipson
Harlington
Heston
Osterley Park
Brentford
Hare Hatch
Ruscombe
White Waltham
Moneyrow Green
Fifield
Datchet
Colnbrook
Poyle
Longford
Cranford
Hounslow
Osterley
Syon
Twyford
West End
Beenham's Heath
Paley Street
Touchen End
Braywoodside
Oakley Green
Dedworth
Spital
Frogmore House
Heathrow
Windsor
Old Windsor
Horton
Stanwell Moor
Stanwell
Isleworth
Twickenham
Whistley Green
Shurlock Row
Hawthorn Hill
Foliejon Park
Legoland
Wraysbury
West Bedfont
East Bedfont
Hatton
Hurst
Jealott's Hill
Nuptow
Maidens Gn
Winkfield Street
Winkfield
Windsor Great Park
Hythe End
Runnymede NT
Ashford
Feltham
Dinton Pastures
Binfield
Warfield
Newell Green
Winkfield Row
Bishops Gate
Savill Garden
Egham
Englefield Green
Egham Wick
Lower Feltham
Hanworth
Teddington
Feltham hill
Kempton Park
Hampton
West End
Woodside
Thorpe Lea
STAINES
Queen Mary Resr
Hampton Wick
Winnersh
Emmbrook
Burleigh
Bullbrook
Cheapside
Ascot
Virginia Water
Valley Gardens
Thorpe
Charlton
Sunbury
Wokingham
Old Bracknell
Blacknest
Stroude
Laleham
Upper Halliford
Hampton Court Palace
BRACKNELL
South Ascot
Sunninghill
Sunningdale
Wentworth
Virginia Water
Trumpsgreen
Thorpe Park
Chertsey
Shepperton Green
Littleton
West Molesey
East Molesey
Eastheath
Easthampstead
Lower Halliford
Walton-on-Thames
Thames Ditton
Barkham
Gardeners Green
TOWER HILL
Broomhall
Knowle Hill
Lyne
Addlestonemoor
Shepperton
Long Ditton
California
B3430
Valley End
Sunningdale
Longcross
Thames Path
Oatlands Park
Sandown Park
Hinchley Wood
Wellingtonia Avenue
Crowthorne
Windlesham
Addlestone
Weybridge
Esher
Finchampstead
Bagshot
Updown Hill
Burrowhill
Ottershaw
Row Town
New Haw
Hersham
West End
Claremont NT
Claygate
Little Sandhurst
Owlsmoor
Lightwater
Chobham
Woodham
St George's Hill
River Mole
Whiteley Village
Eversley Cross
Sandhurst
College Town
West End
Anthonys
West Byfleet
Byfleet
Oxshott Heath
Malden Rushett
Yateley
Darby Green
Donkey Town
Castle Green
Sheerwater
Fairmile
Cobham
Oxshott
Blackwater
York Town
CAMBERLEY
Lucas Green
Bisley
Maybury
Rainshill Park
Yateley Common
Blackbushe
Royal Logistics Corps
Horsell
Pyrford
Wisley
Downside
Stoke D'Abernon
Hawley
Frimley
Knaphill
Goldsworth
WOKING
Semaphore Tower
Martyr's Green
Hartfordbridge
Hartley Wintney
Frimley Green
Bisley Camp
Pirbright Camp
Brookwood
St Johns
Bridge End
May's Green
Leatherhead
Deepcut
Old Woking
Ripley
Ockham
Elvetham Hall
Farnborough Street
Mayford
Send Marsh
Fetcham
Fleet
Cove
Farnborough Park
Mytchett
Pirbright
Fox Corner
Send
Little Bookham
Great Bookham
Farnborough
Burntcommon
Dogmersfield
Sutton Green
West Horsley
East Horsley
Effingham
Bocketts
Henley Park
Worplesdon
Jacobs Well
West Clandon
Hatchlands Park NT
Crookham Village
Gally Hill
Pitch Place
Slyfield Green
Burpham
Clandon Park NT
Polesden Lacey NT
Church Crookham
Ash Vale
Normandy
Stoughton
East Clandon
Westhumble
Ewshot
Upper Hale
Aldershot
Ash
Wyke
Willey Green
Wood Street
Denbies
Heath End
Ash Green
Flexford
Onslow Village
Merrow
Crondall
Badshot Lea
Tongham
Wanborough
GUILDFORD
Gomshall
Abinger Hammer
Westcott
Dorking
Folly Hill
Hale
Farnham
Runfold
Seale
Littleton
Shalford Mill
Chilworth
Shere
North Holmwood
Dippenhall
North Downs Way
Puttenham
Loseley Park
Shalford
Blackheath
Albury
Albury Heath
Wotton
Compton
Binscombe
Peasmarsh
Brook
Burrows Cross
Abinger
Mid Holmwood
The Sands
Shackleford
Hurtmore
Wonersh
Farley Green
Friday Street
Wrecclesham
Lower Bourne
Waverley
Charleshill
Peper Harow
Farncombe
Catteshall
Bramley
Peaslake
Feldy
Coldharbour
Bentley
Birdworld
Norney
Shamley Green
Holmbury St Mary
Leith Hill Tower NT
Bucks Horn Oak
Rowledge
Tilford
Elstead
Eashing
Upper Eashing
Godalming
Crownpits
Isington
Shortfield Common
Millbridge
Milford
Thorncombe Street
Rushett Common
PITCH HILL
HOLMBURY HILL
LEITH HILL
Spreakley
Batt's Corner
Frensham
Mousehill
Tuesley
Winkworth
Grafham
Forest Green
Blacknest
Witley Common NT
Hydestile
Rowly
Thorn's Flush
Ewhurst
Ockley
Wheatley
Rushmoor
Dockenfield
Frensham Great Pond
Thursley
Wheelerstreet
Witley
Hascombe
Ewhurst Green
Mayes Green
The Straits
Frithend
Bowlhead Green
Cranleigh
Sleaford
Churt
Pitch Place
Wormley
Hambledon
Kingsley
Hearn
Arford
Headley Down
Green Cross
Brook
Sandhills
Loxhill
Walliswood
Lindford
Beacon Hill
Devil's Punch Bowl
Combe Common
North Bridge
Laker's Green
Oakwoodhill
Bordon Camp
Headley
Hindhead
Sydenhurst
Chiddingfold
Dunsfold
Ellen's Green
Kingsfold
Bordon
Standford
Grayshott
Alfold Crossways
Passfield
Grayswood
Highstreet Green
Alfold
Rowhook
Warnham
Whitehill
Conford
Bramshott
Haslemere
Ramsnest Common
Upper Ifold
Alfold Bars
Rudgwick
Warnham Court
Shottermill
Ansteadbrook
Tisman's Common
Bucks Green
Griggs Green
Liphook
Haste Hill
Gospel Green
Loxwood
Slinfold
Fisherstreet
Ifold
Park Street
Broadbridge Heath
Longmoor Camp
Bohunt Manor
Linchmere
Toyhorse Int Stud Farm
Plaistow
The Haven
Liss Forest
Langley
Kingsley Green
BLACKDOWN HILL
Northchapel
Itchingfield
Dennes Park
Hollycombe Steam
Roundstreet Common
Christ's Hospital
Liss
Rake
Fernhurst
Hillgrove
Five Oaks
Mannings Heath
East Liss
Milland
Dial Green
Newpound Common
Southwater Street
Milland Marsh
Woodmansgreen
Kirdford
Barns Green
Hill Brow
Lickfold
Lurgashall
Billingshurst
Southwater
Redford
Henley
Bexleyhill
Balls Cross
Wisborough Green
Fishers
Brooks
Parbrook
Nuthurst

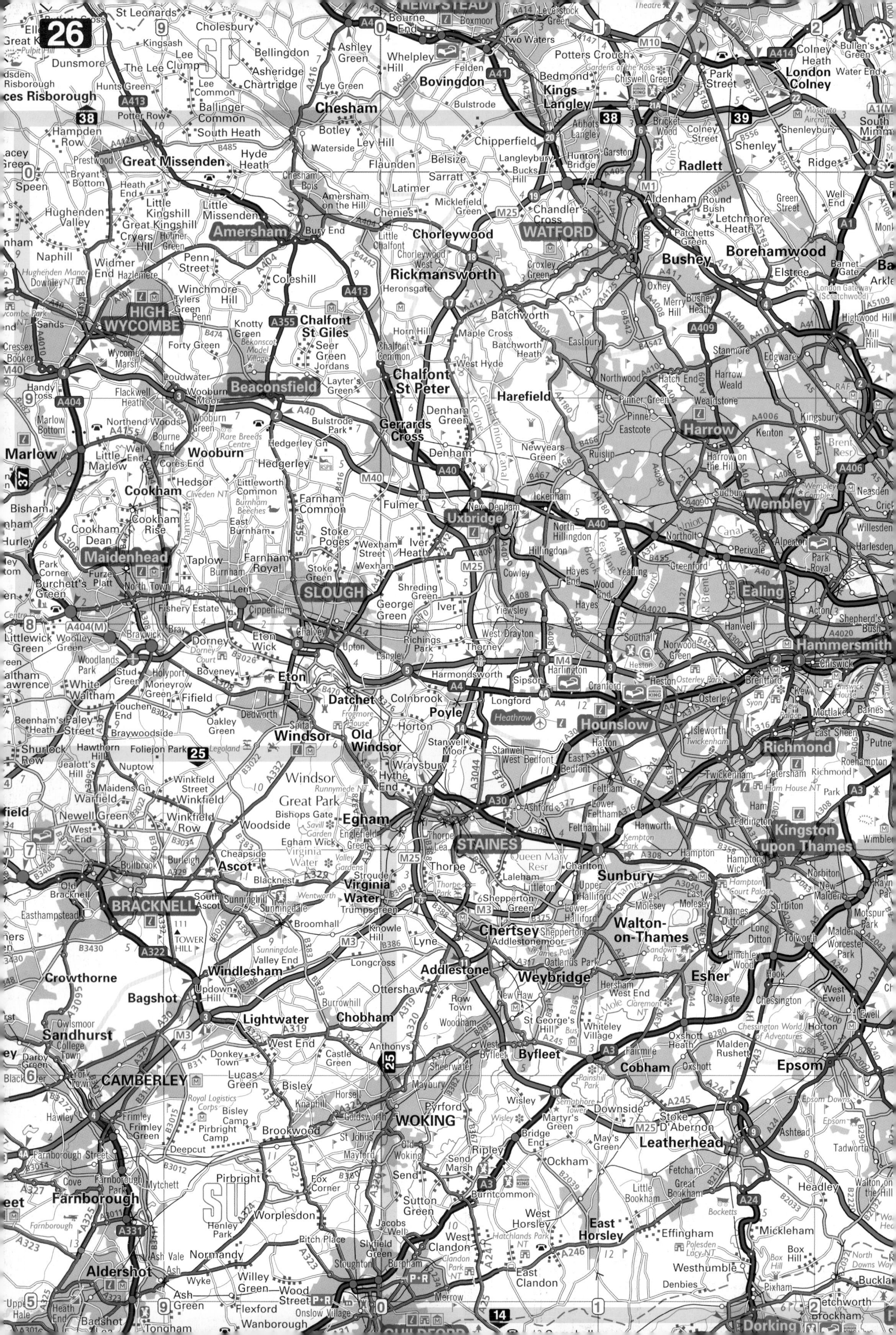

26
HEMPSTEAD
St Leonards
Cholesbury
Bellingdon
Asheridge
Chartridge
Lee
The Lee Clump
Lee Common
Ballinger Common
South Heath
Great Missenden
Little Missenden
Amersham
Chesham
Chesham Bois
Amersham on the Hill
Ashley Green
Bourne End
Boxmoor
Whelpley Hill
Bovingdon
Felden
Two Waters
Leverstock Green
Potters Crouch
Bedmond
Kings Langley
Abbots Langley
Chipperfield
Belsize
Sarratt
Flaunden
Latimer
Chenies
Botley
Ley Hill
Lye Green
Waterside
Bucks Hill
Langleybury
Hunton Bridge
Garston
WATFORD
Chandler's Cross
Micklefield Green
Chorleywood
Chorleywood West
Little Chalfont
Rickmansworth
Croxley Green
Heronsgate
Batchworth
Batchworth Heath
Maple Cross
West Hyde
Harefield
Eastbury
Northwood
Pinner Green
Pinner
Eastcote
Ruislip
Hatch End
Harrow Weald
Wealdstone
Harrow
Harrow on the Hill
Stanmore
Edgware
Kingsbury
Kenton
Wembley
Neasden
Sudbury
Northolt
Perivale
Alperton
Park Royal
Ealing
Greenford
Hanwell
Acton
Hammersmith
Chiswick
Brentford
Kew
Osterley
Isleworth
Richmond
Twickenham
Petersham
Ham
Teddington
Kingston upon Thames
Hampton Wick
Hampton
Sunbury
Hanworth
Feltham
Lower Feltham
Hounslow
Heston
Cranford
Hatton
East Bedfont
Stanwell
West Bedfont
Heathrow
Harlington
Sipson
Longford
Harmondsworth
Hayes
Hayes End
Yeading
Southall
Norwood Green
Yiewsley
West Drayton
Hillingdon
North Hillingdon
Ickenham
Uxbridge
New Denham
Denham
Denham Green
Cowley
Iver
Iver Heath
Richings Park
Thorney
Langley
SLOUGH
George Green
Shreding Green
Wexham
Wexham Street
Stoke Poges
Stoke Green
Farnham Royal
Farnham Common
Burnham
East Burnham
Fulmer
Gerrards Cross
Chalfont St Peter
Chalfont St Giles
Chalfont Common
Horn Hill
Seer Green
Jordans
Layter's Green
Beaconsfield
Hedgerley
Hedgerley Gn
Bulstrode Park
Coleshill
Winchmore Hill
Penn
Penn Street
Tylers Green
Knotty Green
Forty Green
Loudwater
Wooburn
Wooburn Green
Wooburn Moor
Bourne End
Cores End
Hedsor
Littleworth Common
Flackwell Heath
HIGH WYCOMBE
Wycombe Marsh
Hazlemere
Widmer End
Great Kingshill
Little Kingshill
Cryers Hill
Holmer Green
Hughenden Valley
Naphill
Downley
Hughenden Manor NT
Sands
Cressex
Booker
Handy Cross
Marlow
Marlow Bottom
Little Marlow
Well End
Northend Woods
Cookham
Cookham Dean
Cookham Rise
Bisham
Hurley
Maidenhead
Furze Platt
Taplow
Park Corner
Burchett's Green
North Town
Lent
Cippenham
Fishery Estate
Bray
Braywick
Dorney
Dorney Reach
Boveney
Eton
Eton Wick
Chalvey
Upton
Datchet
Windsor
Old Windsor
Colnbrook
Poyle
Horton
Wraysbury
Stanwell Moor
Hythe End
Egham
Englefield Green
Egham Wick
Virginia Water
Thorpe
Thorpe Lea
STAINES
Laleham
Littleton
Charlton
Upper Halliford
Lower Halliford
Shepperton
Shepperton Green
Chertsey
Addlestone
Addlestonemoor
Weybridge
Walton-on-Thames
West Molesey
East Molesey
Thames Ditton
Long Ditton
Surbiton
Tolworth
Hinchley Wood
Esher
Claygate
Hersham
West End
Chessington
Hook
Epsom
Ewell
West Ewell
Oxshott
Cobham
Fairmile
Downside
Stoke D'Abernon
Leatherhead
Fetcham
Great Bookham
Little Bookham
Effingham
Westhumble
Mickleham
Box Hill
Dorking
Ashtead
Headley
Tadworth
Byfleet
West Byfleet
Wisley
Ripley
Send
Send Marsh
Ockham
East Horsley
West Horsley
East Clandon
West Clandon
Burntcommon
WOKING
Pyrford
Maybury
Sheerwater
Knaphill
Horsell
Goldsworth
St Johns
Brookwood
Bisley
Chobham
Ottershaw
Lyne
Longcross
Lightwater
Windlesham
Bagshot
Camberley
Frimley
Sandhurst
Crowthorne
BRACKNELL
Ascot
South Ascot
Sunninghill
Sunningdale
Winkfield
Winkfield Row
Warfield
Farnborough
Aldershot
Pirbright
Worplesdon
Normandy
Ash
Ash Vale
Wood Street
Flexford
Wanborough
Tongham
GUILDFORD
Radlett
Aldenham
Bushey
Bushey Heath
Borehamwood
Elstree
Shenley
London Colney
Colney Heath
Park Street
Colney Street
Ridge
Letchmore Heath
Patchetts Green
Round Bush
Oxhey
Merry Hill
Barnet Gate
Arkley
Mill Hill

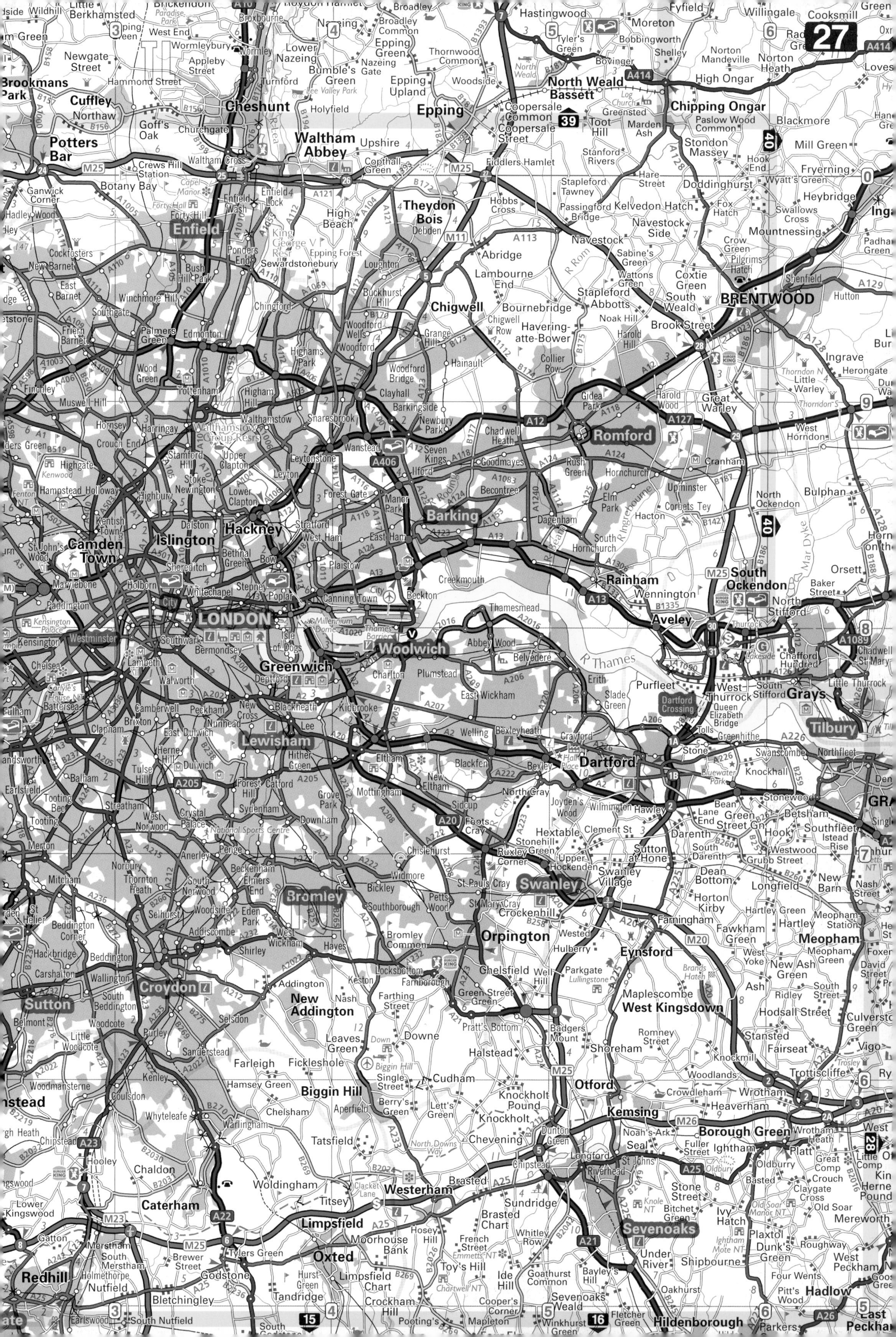

Little Berkhamsted
Newgate Street
Brookmans Park
Cuffley
Northaw
Potters Bar
Goff's Oak
Churchgate
Cheshunt
Wormleybury
Wormley
Broxbourne
Turnford
Hammond Street
West End
Appleby Street
Lower Nazeing
Nazeing
Bumble's Green
Nazeing Gate
Lee Valley Park
Holyfield
Waltham Abbey
Upshire
Waltham Cross
Crews Hill Station
Botany Bay
Ganwick Corner
Hadley Wood
Enfield
Enfield Wash
Enfield Lock
Forty Hill
Capel Manor
Copthall Green
Epping
Epping Green
Epping Upland
Broadley Common
Thornwood Common
Woodside
Hastingwood
Tyler's Green
Moreton
Bobbingworth
Bovinger
Shelley
North Weald Bassett
Coopersale Common
Coopersale Street
Greensted
Toot Hill
Marden Ash
Chipping Ongar
High Ongar
Norton Mandeville
Norton Heath
Willingale
Cooksmill Green
Fyfield
Paslow Wood Common
Blackmore
Stondon Massey
Mill Green
Hook End
Fryerning
Wyatt's Green
Heybridge
Ingatestone
Fiddlers Hamlet
Stanford Rivers
Hare Street
Doddinghurst
Stapleford Tawney
Passingford Bridge
Kelvedon Hatch
Fox Hatch
Swallows Cross
Navestock
Navestock Side
Mountnessing
Theydon Bois
Hobbs Cross
Debden
High Beach
Abridge
Lambourne End
Loughton
Epping Forest
King George V Resr
Ponders End
Sewardstonebury
Bush Hill Park
Cockfosters
New Barnet
East Barnet
Winchmore Hill
Southgate
Friern Barnet
Palmers Green
Edmonton
Chingford
Buckhurst Hill
Woodford Wells
Woodford
Woodford Bridge
Grange Hill
Chigwell
Chigwell Row
Hainault
Bournebridge
Havering-atte-Bower
Stapleford Abbotts
Sabine's Green
Wattons Green
Noak Hill
Harold Hill
Coxtie Green
Crow Green
Pilgrims Hatch
South Weald
Brook Street
Brentwood
Shenfield
Hutton
Ingrave
Herongate
Thorndon N
Little Warley
Great Warley
Harold Wood
Collier Row
Gidea Park
Romford
Highams Park
Finchley
Muswell Hill
Wood Green
Tottenham
Higham Hill
Walthamstow
Hornsey
Harringay
Crouch End
Highgate
Kenwood
Hampstead
Holloway
Stamford Hill
Upper Clapton
Stoke Newington
Highbury
Lower Clapton
Kentish Town
Camden Town
Islington
Dalston
Hackney
Leyton
Leytonstone
Snaresbrook
Wanstead
Barkingside
Newbury Park
Seven Kings
Ilford
Goodmayes
Chadwell Heath
Rush Green
Hornchurch
Upminster
Cranham
West Horndon
Bulphan
North Ockendon
Corbets Tey
Becontree
Barking
Dagenham
Elm Park
Hacton
South Hornchurch
Rainham
Wennington
South Ockendon
Orsett
Baker Street
North Stifford
Aveley
Thurrock
Lakeside
Chafford Hundred
Chadwell St Mary
Little Thurrock
Grays
Tilbury
West Thurrock
South Stifford
Purfleet
Dartford Crossing
Queen Elizabeth II Bridge
Forest Gate
Manor Park
Stratford
West Ham
East Ham
Plaistow
Bow
Bethnal Green
Shoreditch
Whitechapel
Stepney
Poplar
Canning Town
Beckton
Creekmouth
Thamesmead
St John's Wood
Marylebone
Paddington
Holborn
City
London
Westminster
Kensington
Kensington Palace
Chelsea
Carlyle's House NT
Battersea
Fulham
Southwark
Bermondsey
Lambeth
Millennium Dome
Isle of Dogs
Thames Barrier
Woolwich
Greenwich
Deptford
Charlton
Plumstead
Abbey Wood
Belvedere
Erith
East Wickham
Slade Green
Walworth
Camberwell
Peckham
New Cross
Blackheath
Kidbrooke
Lee
Lewisham
Welling
Bexleyheath
Crayford
Dartford
Stone
Greenhithe
Swanscombe
Northfleet
Knockhall
Bluewater Park
Brixton
Clapham
East Dulwich
Nunhead
Herne Hill
Dulwich
Tulse Hill
Balham
Tooting
Tooting Bec
Earlsfield
Streatham
West Norwood
Crystal Palace
National Sports Centre
Forest Hill
Catford
Hither Green
Sydenham
Eltham
Mottingham
Grove Park
Blackfen
New Eltham
Bexley
North Cray
Sidcup
Foots Cray
Joyden's Wood
Wilmington
Hawley
Lane End
Bean
Green Street Green
Betsham
Southfleet
Stonewood
Dareth
South Darenth
Hextable
Clement St
Sutton at Hone
Downham
Penge
Anerley
Beckenham
Elmers End
Bromley
Chislehurst
Widmore
Bickley
Southborough
Petts Wood
St Pauls Cray
St Mary Cray
Ruxley Corner
Stonehill Green
Upper Hockenden
Swanley
Swanley Village
Crockenhill
Wested
Orpington
Farningham
Horton Kirby
Dean Bottom
Longfield
Hartley Green
Hartley
Fawkham Green
Meopham
Meopham Station
Meopham Green
West Yoke
New Ash Green
Ash
Ridley
South Street
Hodsall Street
Culverstone Green
Vigo
Trottiscliffe
Grubb Street
Westwood
Istead Rise
New Barn
Nash Street
Merton
Mitcham
Norbury
Thornton Heath
South Norwood
Selhurst
Woodside
Eden Park
Addiscombe
Shirley
West Wickham
Hayes
Bromley Common
Locksbottom
Farnborough
Keston
Chelsfield
Well Hill
Hulberry
Parkgate
Lullingstone
Eynsford
Maplescombe
West Kingsdown
Brands Hatch
St Helier
Beddington Corner
Beddington
Hackbridge
Carshalton
Wallington
Croydon
Sutton
South Beddington
Belmont
Woodcote
Little Woodcote
Purley
Selsdon
Sanderstead
Addington
New Addington
Nash
Farthing Street
Downe
Leaves Green
Green Street Green
Pratt's Bottom
Badgers Mount
Halstead
Shoreham
Romney Street
Stansted
Fairseat
Knockmill
Woodlands
Crowdleham
Wrotham
Wrotham Heath
Heaverham
Kemsing
Otford
Farleigh
Fickleshole
Biggin Hill
Single Street
Cudham
Berry's Green
Aperfield
Lett's Green
Knockholt Pound
Knockholt
Chevening
Dunton Green
Hamsey Green
Chelsham
Woodmansterne
Kenley
Coulsdon
Whyteleafe
Warlingham
Tatsfield
Chipstead
Hooley
Chaldon
Caterham
Woldingham
Titsey
Westerham
Brasted
Sundridge
Brasted Chart
Riverhead
Longford
Seal
Noah's Ark
Borough Green
Ightham
Fuller Street
Platt
Great Comp
Crouch
Basted
Oldbury
Stone Street
Bitchet Green
Ivy Hatch
Claygate Cross
Old Soar
Mereworth
Plaxtol
Dunk's Green
Roughway
West Peckham
Shipbourne
Hadlow
Oakhurst
Four Wents
Pitt's Wood
Sevenoaks
Knole NT
Ightham Mote NT
Under River
Sevenoaks Weald
Bayley's Hill
Hildenborough
Fletcher Green
Ide Hill
Goathurst Common
Toy's Hill
French Street
Emmetts NT
Chartwell NT
Whitley Row
Hosey Hill
Limpsfield
Limpsfield Chart
Oxted
Moorhouse Bank
Hurst Green
Tandridge
Crockham Hill
Cooper's Corner
Mapleton
Pooting's
Winkhurst Green
Kingswood
Lower Kingswood
Gatton
Merstham
South Merstham
Redhill
Holmethorpe
Nutfield
South Nutfield
Bletchingley
Godstone
Tylers Green
Brewer Street
Earlswood
Parkers
East Peckham
R Thames
R Rom
R Roding
M25
M11
M20
M26
M23
A12
A13
A127
A406
A20
A21
A22
A23
A25
A205
A2
A414
A128
A1089

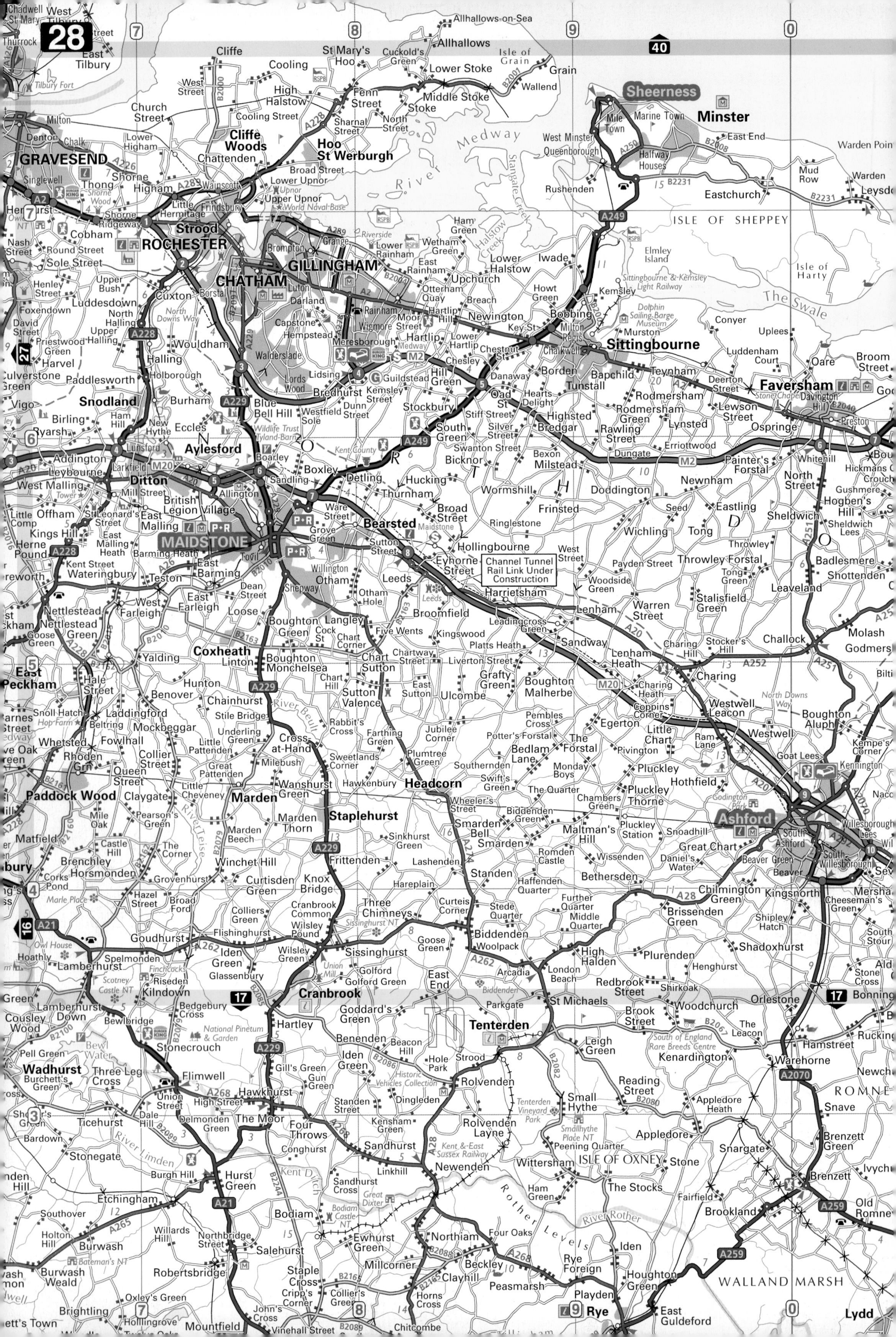

28
7
8
9
0
40
27
16
17
17
Allhallows-on-Sea
Allhallows
St Mary's Hoo
Cuckold's Green
Isle of Grain
Grain
Wallend
Cliffe
Cooling
West Street
High Halstow
Fenn Street
Lower Stoke
Middle Stoke
Stoke
Sheerness
Minster
Mile Town
Marine Town
East End
Warden Point
Warden
Leysdown
Mud Row
West Minster
Queenborough
Halfway Houses
Rushenden
Eastchurch
ISLE OF SHEPPEY
Elmley Island
Isle of Harty
The Swale
River Medway
Stangate Creek
Halstow Creek
Church Street
Cooling Street
Sharnal Street
North Street
Cliffe Woods
Hoo St Werburgh
Milton
Denton
Chalk
Lower Higham
GRAVESEND
Chattenden
Broad Street
Lower Upnor
Upnor
Upper Upnor
World Naval Base
Singlewell
Thong
Shorne
Higham
Wainscott
Frindsbury
Little Hermitage
Shorne Ridgeway
Henhurst
Nash Street
Cobham
Round Street
Sole Street
Strood
ROCHESTER
Riverside
Lower Rainham
Wetham Green
Ham Green
Lower Halstow
Iwade
Brompton
Grange
GILLINGHAM
CHATHAM
East Rainham
Upchurch
Otterham Quay
Breach
Howt Green
Kemsley
Sittingbourne & Kemsley Light Railway
Dolphin Sailing Barge Museum
Henley Street
Upper Bush
Luddesdown
Cuxton
Borstal
Luton
Darland
Rainham
Moor Street
Wigmore
Hartlip Hill
Newington
Bobbing
Key St
Milton Regis
Murston
Conyer
Uplees
Foxendown
North Halling
North Downs Way
David Street
Upper Halling
Priestwood Green
Harvel
Culverstone Green
Paddlesworth
Capstone
Hempstead
Meresborough
Hartlip
Lower Hartlip
Chestnut St
Chalkwell
Sittingbourne
Luddenham Court
Oare
Broom Street
Wouldham
Halling
Holborough
Walderslade
Lidsing
Lords Wood
Guildstead
Kemsley Street
Chesley
Danaway
Borden
Tunstall
Bapchild
Teynham
Deerton Street
Faversham
Davington Hill
Preston
Snodland
Vigo
Birling
Ryarsh
Burham
Blue Bell Hill
Bredhurst
Dunn Street
Westfield Sole
Hill Green
Stockbury
Oad St
Hearts Delight
Highsted
Rodmersham
Rodmersham Green
Lewson Street
Ospringe
Lynsted
Stone Chapel
Ham Hill
New Hythe
Eccles
Aylesford
Wildlife Trust Tyland Barn
Kent County
South Green
Stiff Street
Silver Street
Bredgar
Rawling Street
Erriottwood
Addington
Leybourne
Lunsford
Larkfield
Ditton
Boarley
Sandling
Boxley
Detling
Swanton Street
Bicknor
Bexon
Milstead
Dungate
Painter's Forstal
Whitehill
Hickmans Cross
Crouch
West Malling
Tower
Mill Street
Allington
Hucking
Thurnham
Wormshill
Doddington
Newnham
North Street
Gushmere
Hogben's Hill
Little Comp
Offham
St Leonard's Street
East Malling
British Legion Village
Ware Street
Bearsted
Broad Street
Ringlestone
Frinsted
Seed
Eastling
Sheldwich
Sheldwich Lees
Kings Hill
Herne Pound
MAIDSTONE
Barming Heath
Malling Heath
Grove Green
Sutton Street
Hollingbourne
Wichling
Tong
Throwley
Kent Street
Wateringbury
Fovil
East Barming
Willington
Otham
Eyhorne Street
Channel Tunnel Rail Link Under Construction
West Street
Payden Street
Throwley Forstal
Tong Green
Badlesmere
Shottenden
Teston
Dean Street
Shepway
Leeds
Otham Hole
Harrietsham
Woodside Green
Leaveland
Nettlestead
Nettlestead Green
West Farleigh
East Farleigh
Loose
Broomfield
Lenham
Warren Street
Stalisfield Green
Goose Green
Boughton Green
Cock St
Langley
Chart Corner
Five Wents
Kingswood
Leadingcross Green
Sandway
Lenham Heath
Charing Hill
Stocker's Hill
Challock
Molash
Godmersham
Yalding
Coxheath
Linton
Boughton Monchelsea
Chart Sutton
Chartway Street
Platts Heath
Liverton Street
Grafty Green
Charing
Charing Heath
East Peckham
Hale Street
Hunton
Chart Hill
Sutton Valence
East Sutton
Ulcombe
Boughton Malherbe
Westwell Leacon
North Downs Way
Boughton Aluph
Benover
Chainhurst
Snoll Hatch
Hop Farm
Laddingford
Beltring
Stile Bridge
River Beult
Rabbit's Cross
Pembles Cross
Egerton
Coppins Corner
Little Chart
Westwell
Ram Lane
Kempe's Corner
Mockbeggar
Underling Green
Cross-at-Hand
Farthing Green
Jubilee Corner
Potter's Forstal
The Forstal
Pivington
Goat Lees
Kennington
Whetsted
Fowlhall
Rhoden Grn
Collier Street
Little Pattenden
Great Pattenden
Milebush
Sweetlands Corner
Plumtree Green
Bedlam Lane
Southernden
Monday Boys
Pluckley
Hothfield
Paddock Wood
Queen Street
Claygate
Little Cheveney
Marden
Wanshurst Green
Hawkenbury
Headcorn
Swift's Green
The Quarter
Chambers Green
Pluckley Thorne
Godinton Park
Ashford
Mile Oak
Pearson's Green
Marden Thorn
Staplehurst
Wheeler's Street
Biddenden Green
Smarden Bell
Smarden
Maltman's Hill
Pluckley Station
Snoadhill
Great Chart
South Ashford
Willesborough Lees
Matfield
Castle Hill
The Corner
Marden Beech
Sinkhurst Green
Romden Castle
Wissenden
Daniel's Water
Beaver Green
Beaver
South Willesborough
Brenchley
Horsmonden
Winchet Hill
Frittenden
Lashenden
Standen
Bethersden
Chilmington Green
Kingsnorth
Mersham
Corks Pond
Grovenhurst
Curtisden Green
Knox Bridge
Hareplain
Haffenden Quarter
Further Quarter
Brissenden Green
Cheeseman's Green
Marle Place
Hazel Street
Broad Ford
Colliers Green
Cranbrook Common
Three Chimneys
Curteis Corner
Stede Quarter
Middle Quarter
Shipley Hatch
South Stour
Goudhurst
Flishinghurst
Wilsley Pound
Sissinghurst NT
Goose Green
Biddenden
Woolpack
High Halden
Plurenden
Shadoxhurst
Owl House
Hoathly
Lamberhurst
Spelmonden
Iden Green
Wilsley Green
Sissinghurst
Arcadia
London Beach
Henghurst
Aldington
Finchcocks
Scotney Castle NT
Riseden
Glassenbury
Union Mill
Golford
Golford Green
East End
Redbrook Street
Shirkoak
Stone Cross
Kilndown
Cranbrook
Biddenden
Parkgate
St Michaels
Brook Street
Woodchurch
Orlestone
Bonnington
Lamberhurst Down
Cousley Wood
Bedgebury Cross
Bewlbridge
National Pinetum & Garden
Hartley
Goddard's Green
Benenden
Tenterden
The Leacon
South of England Rare Breeds Centre
Hamstreet
Ruckinge
Bewl Water
Pell Green
Stonecrouch
Beacon Hill
Hole Park
Iden Green
Strood
Leigh Green
Kenardington
Warehorne
Newchurch
Wadhurst
Burchett's Green
Three Leg Cross
Flimwell
Gill's Green
Gun Green
Historic Vehicles Collection
Rolvenden
Reading Street
ROMNEY
Union Street
High Street
Hawkhurst
Standen Street
Dingleden
Tenterden Vineyard Park
Small Hythe
Appledore Heath
Snave
Shover's Green
Ticehurst
Dale Hill
Delmonden Green
The Moor
Four Throws
Kensham Green
Rolvenden Layne
Smallhythe Place NT
Appledore
Brenzett Green
Bardown
River Limden
Conghurst
Sandhurst
Kent & East Sussex Railway
Peening Quarter
Snargate
Ivychurch
Stonegate
Wittersham
ISLE OF OXNEY
Stone
Kent Ditch
Linkhill
Newenden
Brenzett
Burgh Hill
Hurst Green
Sandhurst Cross
Ham Green
The Stocks
Fairfield
Etchingham
Great Dixter
Rother Levels
River Rother
Brookland
Old Romney
Southover
Bodiam
Bodiam Castle NT
Holton Hill
Burwash
Willards Hill
Northbridge Street
Ewhurst Green
Northiam
Four Oaks
Iden
Salehurst
Bateman's NT
Millcorner
Beckley
Rye Foreign
Burwash Weald
Robertsbridge
Staple Cross
Clayhill
Peasmarsh
Houghton Green
WALLAND MARSH
Oxley's Green
Collier's Green
Horns Cross
Cripp's Corner
Playden
Brightling
Hollingrove
John's Cross
Mountfield
Vinehall Street
Chitcombe
Rye
East Guldeford
Lydd
West Tilbury
Tilbury
East Tilbury
Tilbury Fort
Thurrock
Chadwell St Mary
Street
A228
A229
A249
A2
M2
M20
A20
A21
A26
A262
A268
A274
A252
A251
A28
A2070
A259
A265
A250
B2000
B2001
B2231
B2008
B2163
B2010
B2162
B2160
B2079
B2086
B2082
B2080
B2067
B2085
B2099
B2100
B2089
B2165
B2088
B2244
B2040

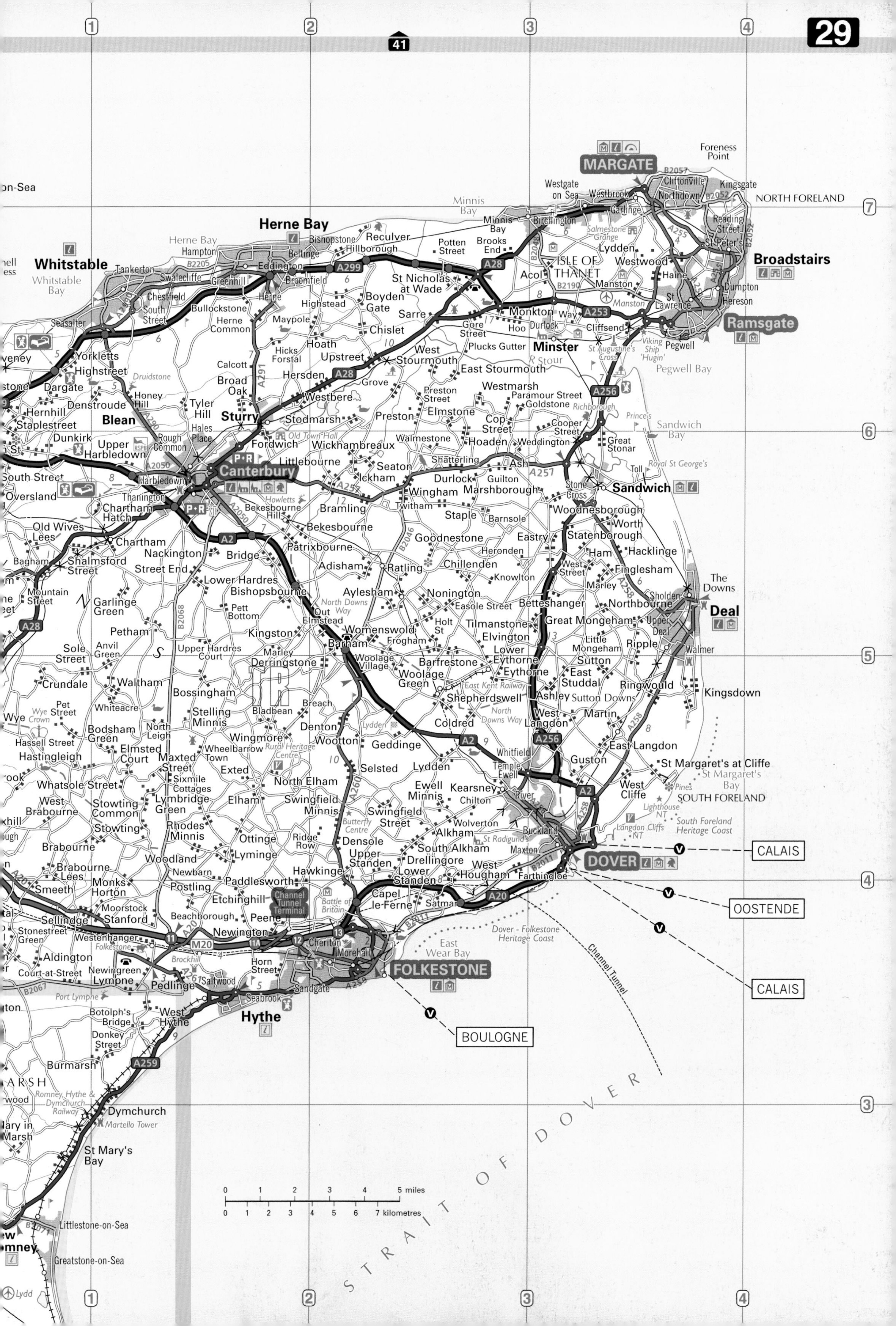
29
41
MARGATE
Foreness Point
Westgate on Sea
Westbrook
Cliftonville
Northdown
Kingsgate
NORTH FORELAND
Garlinge
Birchington
Minnis Bay
Reading Street
St Peter's
Broadstairs
Salmestone Grange
Lydden
Westwood
Haine
Dumpton
Hereson
ISLE OF THANET
Acol
Manston
St Lawrence
Ramsgate
Monkton
Way
Cliffsend
Pegwell
Pegwell Bay
Viking Ship 'Hugin'
St Augustine's Cross
Minster
Durlock
Hoo
Gore Street
Plucks Gutter
R Stour
Herne Bay
Bishopstone
Reculver
Hillborough
Beltinge
Potten Street
Brooks End
Herne Bay
Hampton
Eddington
Whitstable
Whitstable Bay
Tankerton
Swalecliffe
Greenhill
Broomfield
Herne
St Nicholas at Wade
Highstead
Boyden Gate
Sarre
Chislet
Maypole
Chestfield
South Street
Bullockstone
Herne Common
Seasalter
Yorkletts
Highstreet
Dargate
Druidstone
Hicks Forstal
Hoath
Upstreet
West Stourmouth
East Stourmouth
Calcott
Broad Oak
Hersden
Grove
Westbere
Preston Street
Westmarsh
Paramour Street
Goldstone
Richborough
Honey Hill
Hernhill
Denstroude
Staplestreet
Blean
Tyler Hill
Sturry
Hales Place
Stodmarsh
Preston
Elmstone
Cop Street
Cooper Street
Great Stonar
Sandwich Bay
Prince's
Dunkirk
Upper Harbledown
Rough Common
Fordwich
Old Town Hall
Wickhambreaux
Walmestone
Hoaden
Weddington
Littlebourne
Seaton
Shatterling
Ash
Royal St George's
Toll
Canterbury
Harbledown
South Street
Oversland
Ickham
Durlock
Guilton
Wingham
Marshborough
Stone Cross
Sandwich
Thanington
Chartham Hatch
Howletts
Bekesbourne Hill
Bramling
Twitham
Staple
Barnsole
Woodnesborough
Worth
Old Wives Lees
Chartham
Bekesbourne
Goodnestone
Eastry
Statenborough
Bagham
Shalmsford Street
Nackington
Bridge
Patrixbourne
Heronden
Ham
Hacklinge
Street End
Adisham
Ratling
Chillenden
West Street
Finglesham
The Downs
Mountain Street
Lower Hardres
Bishopsbourne
Knowlton
Marley
Garlinge Green
Pett Bottom
North Downs Way
Aylesham
Nonington
Easole Street
Betteshanger
Northbourne
Sholden
Deal
Elmstead
Holt St
Tilmanstone
Great Mongeham
Upper Deal
Petham
Kingston
Womenswold
Elvington
Little Mongeham
Ripple
Walmer
Sole Street
Anvil Green
Upper Hardres Court
Marley
Barham
Frogham
Lower Eythorne
Derringstone
Woolage Village
Barfrestone
Eythorne
Sutton
East Studdal
Crundale
Waltham
Woolage Green
East Kent Railway
Ringwould
Kingsdown
Bossingham
Breach
Shepherdswell
Ashley
Sutton Downs
Wye
Pet Street
Whiteacre
Stelling Minnis
Bladbean
West Langdon
Martin
Coldred
North Downs Way
Bodsham Green
North Leigh
Denton
Lydden
Hassell Street
Elmsted Court
Wingmore
Wootton
Geddinge
Whitfield
East Langdon
Hastingleigh
Wheelbarrow Town
Rural Heritage Centre
Temple Ewell
Guston
St Margaret's at Cliffe
St Margaret's Bay
Maxted Street
Exted
Selsted
Lydden
Sixmile Cottages
North Elham
Ewell Minnis
Kearsney
River
West Cliffe
Pines
SOUTH FORELAND
Whatsole Street
Elham
Swingfield Minnis
Chilton
Lighthouse NT
West Brabourne
Stowting Common
Lymbridge Green
Swingfield Street
South Foreland Heritage Coast
Langdon Cliffs NT
Stowting
Rhodes Minnis
Butterfly Centre
Wolverton
Alkham
Buckland
Brabourne
Ottinge
Ridge Row
Densole
South Alkham
St Radigund's
Maxton
Woodland
Lyminge
Upper Standen
Drellingore
West Hougham
DOVER
CALAIS
Brabourne Lees
Newbarn
Hawkinge
Lower Standen
Farthingloe
Smeeth
Monks Horton
Postling
Paddlesworth
Capel le-Ferne
Satmar
Moorstock
Etchinghill
Channel Tunnel Terminal
Battle of Britain
OOSTENDE
Sellindge
Stanford
Beachborough
Peene
Dover - Folkestone Heritage Coast
Stonestreet Green
Westenhanger
Newington
Cheriton
Channel Tunnel
Folkestone
Aldington
Brockhill
Morehall
East Wear Bay
CALAIS
Court-at-Street
Newingreen
Horn Street
FOLKESTONE
Lympne
Pedlinge
Saltwood
Sandgate
Port Lympne
Seabrook
Hythe
Botolph's Bridge
West Hythe
BOULOGNE
Donkey Street
Burmarsh
Romney, Hythe & Dymchurch Railway
Dymchurch
Martello Tower
St Mary's Bay
STRAIT OF DOVER
0 1 2 3 4 5 miles
0 1 2 3 4 5 6 7 kilometres
Littlestone-on-Sea
Greatstone-on-Sea
Lydd

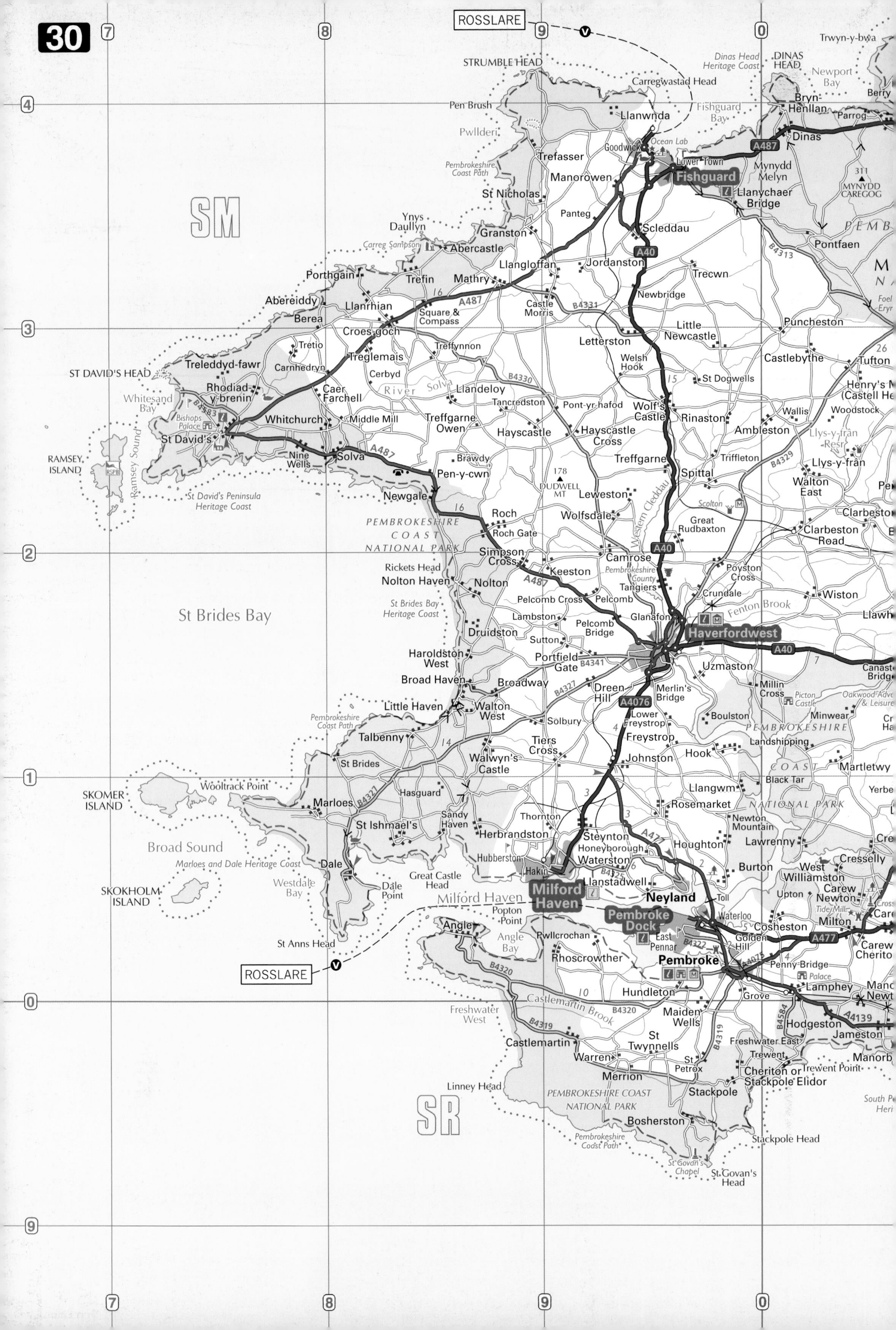
ROSSLARE
STRUMBLE HEAD
Carregwastad Head
Dinas Head Heritage Coast
DINAS HEAD
Newport Bay
Trwyn-y-bwa
Pen Brush
Llanwnda
Fishguard Bay
Bryn-Henllan
Berry
Parrog
Dinas
Pwllderi
Goodwick
Ocean Lab
Lower Town
A487
Fishguard
Mynydd Melyn
MYNYDD CAREGOG
Pembrokeshire Coast Path
Trefasser
Manorowen
Llanychaer Bridge
St Nicholas
Panteg
SM
Ynys Daullyn
Granston
Scleddau
Pontfaen
Carreg Sampson
Abercastle
A40
B4313
Llangloffan
Jordanston
Porthgain
Trefin
Mathry
Trecwn
Abereiddy
Llanrhian
A487
Castle Morris
Newbridge
B4331
Berea
Square & Compass
Croes-goch
Little Newcastle
Puncheston
Tretio
Letterston
Treffynnon
Treglemais
Welsh Hook
Castlebythe
Tufton
ST DAVID'S HEAD
Treleddyd-fawr
Carnhedryn
Cerbyd
B4330
St Dogwells
Henry's Moat (Castell Hendre)
Whitesand Bay
Rhodiad-y-brenin
Caer Farchell
River Solva
Llandeloy
Tancredston
Pont-yr-hafod
Wolf's Castle
Woodstock
Wallis
Bishops Palace
B4583
Whitchurch
Middle Mill
Treffgarne Owen
Hayscastle
Hayscastle Cross
Rinaston
Ambleston
Llys-y-frân Resr
St David's
RAMSEY ISLAND
Ramsey Sound
Nine Wells
Solva
A487
Brawdy
Treffgarne
Triffleton
B4329
Llys-y-frân
Pen-y-cwn
178
DUDWELL MT
Spittal
Walton East
St David's Peninsula Heritage Coast
Newgale
Leweston
Western Cleddau
Scolton
Roch
Wolfsdale
Great Rudbaxton
Clarbeston
PEMBROKESHIRE COAST NATIONAL PARK
Roch Gate
Clarbeston Road
A40
Simpson Cross
Camrose
Keeston
Poyston Cross
Rickets Head
Nolton Haven
Nolton
Pembrokeshire County
Tangiers
A487
Crundale
Wiston
St Brides Bay Heritage Coast
Pelcomb Cross
Pelcomb
Fenton Brook
St Brides Bay
Lambston
Glanafon
Druidston
Pelcomb Bridge
Haverfordwest
Sutton
A40
Haroldston West
Portfield Gate
B4341
Uzmaston
Canaston Bridge
Broad Haven
Broadway
B4327
Dreen Hill
Merlin's Bridge
Millin Cross
Picton Castle
Oakwood Adventure & Leisure
Little Haven
Walton West
A4076
Pembrokeshire Coast Path
Boulston
Minwear
Lower Freystrop
Solbury
PEMBROKESHIRE
Talbenny
Freystrop
Tiers Cross
Hook
Landshipping
St Brides
Walwyn's Castle
Johnston
COAST
Martletwy
Wooltrack Point
Black Tar
SKOMER ISLAND
Hasguard
Llangwm
Marloes
B4327
Thornton
Rosemarket
NATIONAL PARK
St Ishmael's
Sandy Haven
Newton Mountain
Herbrandston
Steynton
Broad Sound
Honeyborough
Lawrenny
Hubberston
Waterston
Houghton
Marloes and Dale Heritage Coast
A477
Dale
Hakin
B4325
Burton
West Williamston
Cresselly
Great Castle Head
Llanstadwell
SKOKHOLM ISLAND
Westdale Bay
Dale Point
Milford Haven
Neyland
Toll
Upton
Carew
Newton
Tide Mill
Milford Haven
Popton Point
Pembroke Dock
Waterloo
Cosheston
Milton
Angle
Pwllcrochan
East Pennar
Golden Hill
A477
Carew Cheriton
Angle Bay
B4322
St Anns Head
Rhoscrowther
Pembroke
Penny Bridge
Palace
ROSSLARE
B4320
Lamphey
Hundleton
Grove
Freshwater West
Castlemartin Brook
B4320
B4584
Maiden Wells
A4139
Hodgeston
Jameston
B4319
St Twynnells
B4319
Castlemartin
Freshwater East
Trewent
Manorbier
Warren
St Petrox
Cheriton or Stackpole Elidor
Trewent Point
Merrion
Linney Head
Stackpole
PEMBROKESHIRE COAST NATIONAL PARK
SR
Bosherston
Stackpole Head
Pembrokeshire Coast Path
St Govan's Chapel
St Govan's Head

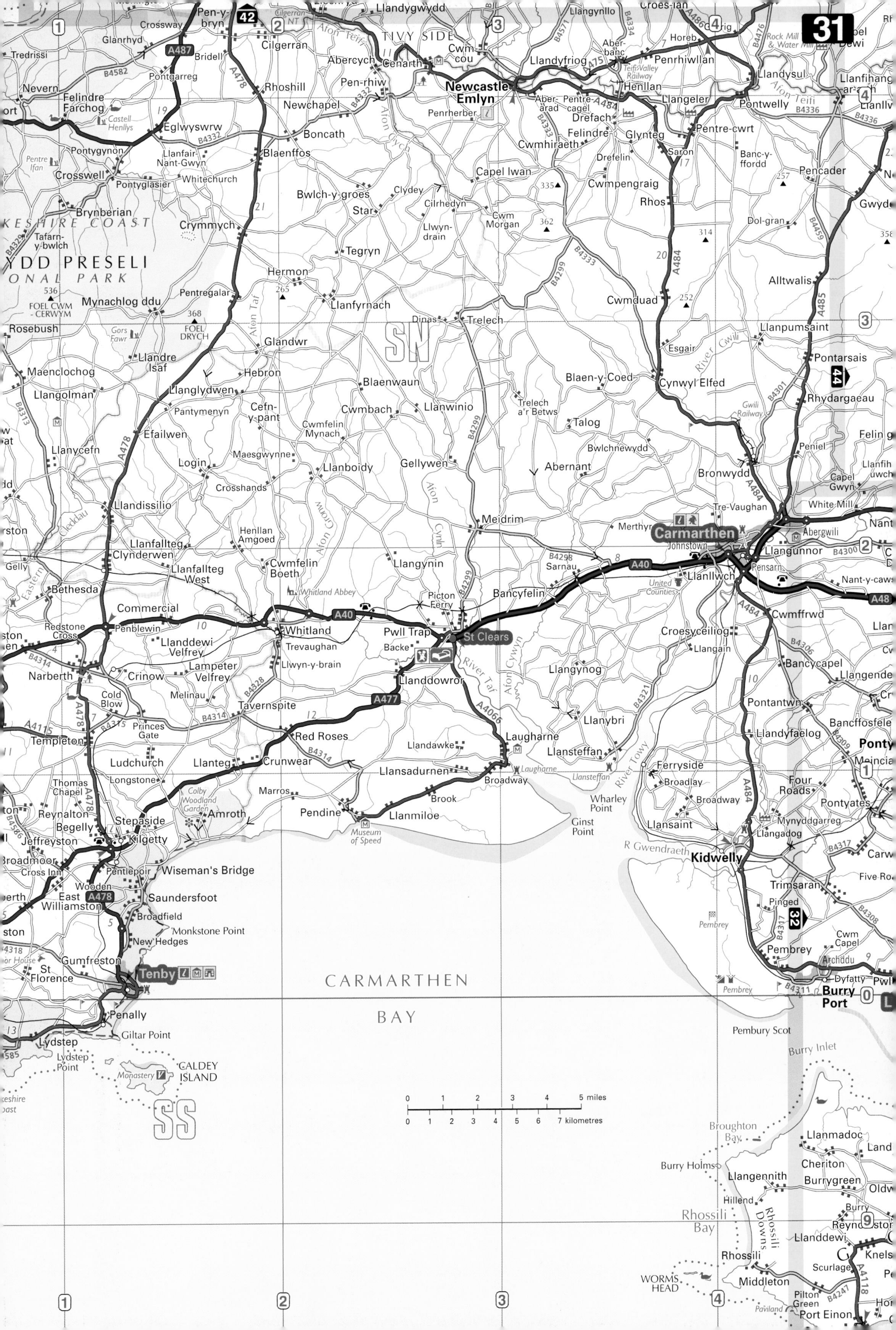
Pen-y-bryn
Cilgerran
Llandygwydd
Llangynllo
Croes-lan
Crossway
Glanrhyd
Tredrissi
Bridell
Pontgarreg
Nevern
Felindre Farchog
Castell Henllys
Eglwyswrw
Rhoshill
Newchapel
Boncath
Abercych
Cenarth
Pen-rhiw
TIVY SIDE
Cwm-cou
Newcastle Emlyn
Penrherber
Llandyfriog
Aber-banc
Horeb
Penrhiwllan
Teifi Valley Railway
Henllan
Llandysul
Aber-arad
Pentre-cagel
Drefach
Llangeler
Pontwelly
Felindre
Glynteg
Pentre-cwrt
Cwmhiraeth
Drefelin
Saron
Banc-y-ffordd
Pencader
Pontygynon
Pentre Ifan
Llanfair-Nant-Gwyn
Blaenffos
Crosswell
Pontyglasier
Whitechurch
Capel Iwan
Cwmpengraig
Rhos
Brynberian
Bwlch-y-groes
Clydey
Cilrhedyn
Star
Cwm Morgan
Llwyn-drain
Dol-gran
PEMBROKESHIRE COAST
Crymmych
Tafarn-y-bwlch
PRESELI
NATIONAL PARK
Tegryn
Hermon
Alltwalis
Foel Cwm Cerwyn
Mynachlog ddu
Pentregalar
Foel Drych
Llanfyrnach
Cwmduad
Rosebush
Gors Fawr
Glandwr
Dinas
Trelech
Llanpumsaint
Esgair
River Gwili
Pontarsais
Llandre Isaf
Maenclochog
Hebron
SN
Blaenwaun
Blaen-y-Coed
Cynwyl Elfed
Llangolman
Llanglydwen
Pantymenyn
Cefn-y-pant
Cwmbach
Llanwinio
Trelech a'r Betws
Gwili Railway
Rhydargaeau
Talog
Efailwen
Cwmfelin Mynach
Llanycefn
Bwlchnewydd
Peniel
Maesgwynne
Login
Llanboidy
Gellywen
Abernant
Bronwydd
Capel Gwyn
Crosshands
Llandissilio
Meidrim
Tre-Vaughan
White Mill
Merthyr
Carmarthen
Johnstown
Abergwili
Llangunnor
Henllan Amgoed
Llanfallteg
Clynderwen
Llangynin
Sarnau
Pensarn
Nant-y-caws
Cwmfelin Boeth
Llanfallteg West
Whitland Abbey
Llanllwch
United Counties
Bethesda
Picton Ferry
Bancyfelin
Commercial
Cwmffrwd
Redstone Cross
Penblewin
Whitland
Pwll Trap
St Clears
Croesyceiliog
Llanddewi Velfrey
Trevaughan
Backe
Llangain
Lampeter Velfrey
Llwyn-y-brain
River Taf
Afon Cywyn
Bancycapel
Narberth
Crinow
Llanddowror
Llangynog
Cold Blow
Melinau
Tavernspite
Pontantwn
Princes Gate
Llanybri
Templeton
Red Roses
Laugharne
Llandyfaelog
Llandawke
Llansteffan
Ludchurch
Llanteg
Crunwear
Llansadurnen
Ferryside
Four Roads
Longstone
Broadway
Laugharne
Llansteffan
Broadlay
Thomas Chapel
Marros
Colby Woodland Garden
Brook
River Towy
Broadway
Pontyates
Reynalton
Amroth
Pendine
Llanmiloe
Whartley Point
Mynyddgarreg
Begelly
Stepaside
Ginst Point
Llansaint
Llangadog
Jeffreyston
Kilgetty
Museum of Speed
R Gwendraeth
Kidwelly
Broadmoor
Cross Inn
Pentlepoir
Wiseman's Bridge
Trimsaran
Wooden
East Williamston
Saundersfoot
Pinged
Broadfield
Pembrey
Monkstone Point
New Hedges
Cwm Capel
Gumfreston
Pembrey
St Florence
Tenby
CARMARTHEN
Archddu
Dyfatty
Burry Port
Penally
BAY
Pembury Scot
Lydstep
Gilltar Point
Burry Inlet
Lydstep Point
Monastery
CALDEY ISLAND
0 1 2 3 4 5 miles
0 1 2 3 4 5 6 7 kilometres
SS
Broughton Bay
Llanmadoc
Burry Holms
Cheriton
Llangennith
Burrygreen
Hillend
Burry
Rhossili Bay
Rhossili Downs
Llanddewi
Rhossili
Scurlage
Worms Head
Middleton
Pilton Green
Paviland
Port Einon
A487
A478
A484
A475
A486
B4582
B4332
B4333
B4571
B4334
B4476
B4336
B4329
B4313
B4299
B4298
B4459
B4485
A485
B4301
A40
A48
A477
A4066
B4314
B4328
B4315
A4115
B4321
B4306
B4309
B4317
B4308
B4311
B4300
B4586
B4318
B4247
A4118
42
44
32

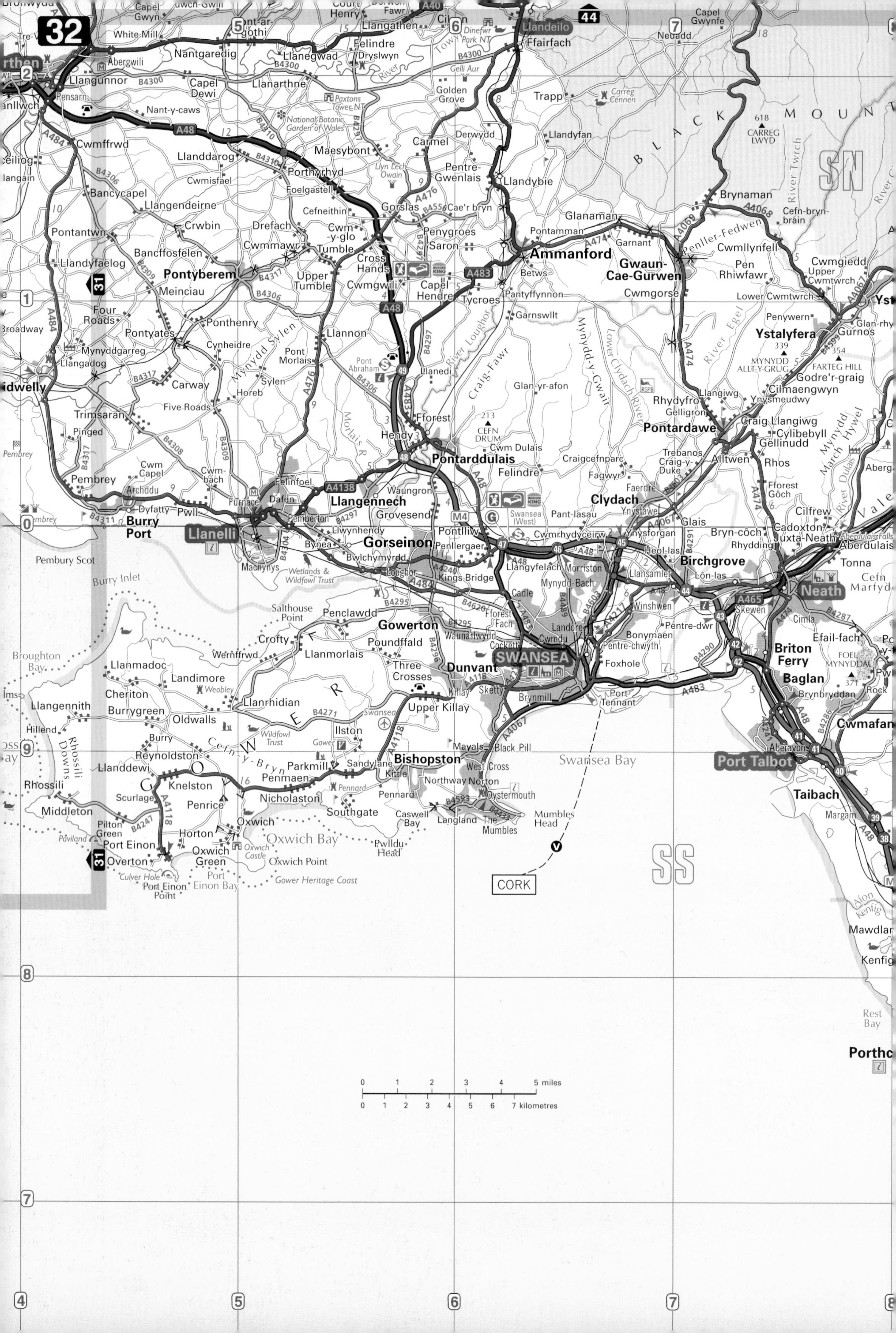
32
44
Capel Gwyn
White Mill
Nantgaredig
Abergwili
Llangunnor
Pensarn
Nant-y-caws
Capel Dewi
Llanarthne
Llanegwad
Felindre
Dryslwyn
Llangathen
Dinefwr Park NT
Llandeilo
Ffairfach
Capel Gwynfe
Neuadd
Paxtons Tower NT
National Botanic Garden of Wales
Golden Grove
Gelli Aur
Trapp
Carreg Cennen
BLACK MOUNTAIN
618 CARREG LWYD
SN
River Twrch
Cwmffrwd
Llanddarog
Porthyrhyd
Maesybont
Carmel
Derwydd
Llandyfan
Cwmisfael
Foelgastell
Llyn Llech Owain
Pentre-Gwenlais
Llandybie
Bancycapel
Llangendeirne
Cefneithin
Gorslas
Cae'r bryn
Crwbin
Drefach
Cwm-y-glo
Penygroes
Saron
Pontamman
Glanaman
Brynaman
Cefn-bryn-brain
Pontantwn
Bancffosfelen
Cwmmawr
Tumble
Cross Hands
Ammanford
Garnant
Gwaun-Cae-Gurwen
Penller-Fedwen
Cwmllynfell
Pen Rhiwfawr
Cwmgiedd
Upper Cwmtwrch
Lower Cwmtwrch
Llandyfaelog
Pontyberem
Meinciau
Upper Tumble
Cwmgwili
Capel Hendre
Betws
Tycroes
Pantyffynnon
Cwmgorse
Four Roads
Ponthenry
Pontyates
Mynydd Sylen
Llannon
Garnswllt
Penywern
Ystalyfera
Glan-rhyd
Gurnos
Broadway
Mynyddgarreg
Cynheidre
Pont Morlais
Pont Abraham
Llangadog
Llanedi
River Loughor
Craig-Fawr
Mynydd-y-Gwair
Lower Clydach River
River Egel
339 MYNYDD ALLT-Y-GRUG
354 FARTEG HILL
Godre'r-graig
Kidwelly
Carway
Sylen
Horeb
Glan-yr-afon
Cilmaengwyn
Ynysmeudwy
Llangiwg
Rhydyfro
Gelligron
Five Roads
Trimsaran
Morlais R.
Fforest
213 CEFN DRUM
Pontardawe
Craig Llangiwg
Cylibebyll
Gellinudd
Mynydd March Hywel
Pinged
Hendy
Cwm Dulais
Pontarddulais
Craigcefnparc
Trebanos
Craig-y-Duke
Alltwen
Rhos
Pembrey
Cwm Capel
Cwm-bach
Felinfoel
Felindre
Fagwyr
Faerdre
Fforest Gôch
Aberglais
River Dulais
Llangennech
Waungron
Clydach
Ynystawe
Cilfrew
Archddu
Dyfatty
Pwll
Furnace
Dafen
Pemberton
Grovesend
Pant-lasau
Glais
Cadoxton-Juxta-Neath
Aberdulais Falls
Burry Port
Llanelli
Llwynhendy
Pontlliw
Swansea (West)
Cwmrhydyceirw
Ynysforgan
Bryn-côch
Rhydding
Aberdulais
Vale
Pembury Scot
Bynea
Gorseinon
Penllergaer
Llangyfelach
Morriston
Heol-las
Birchgrove
Tonna
Machynys
Bwlchymyrdd
Wetlands & Wildfowl Trust
Loughor
Kings Bridge
Mynydd-Bach
Llansamlet
Lôn-las
Neath
Cefn Marfyd
Burry Inlet
Salthouse Point
Penclawdd
Cadle
Winshwen
Skewen
Cimla
Gowerton
Fforest Fach
Landore
Pentre-dwr
Efail-fach
Broughton Bay
Crofty
Wernffrwd
Llanmorlais
Poundffald
Waunarlwydd
Cockett
Cwmdu
Bonymaen
Pentre-chwyth
Briton Ferry
FOEL MYNYDDAU
Llanmadoc
Three Crosses
SWANSEA
Foxhole
Landimore
Dunvant
Baglan
Weobley
Cheriton
Llanrhidian
Killay
Sketty
Brynmill
Port Tennant
Brynbryddan
Llangennith
Burrygreen
Oldwalls
Upper Killay
Swansea
Cwmafan
Hillend
Wildfowl Trust
Ilston
Burry
Gower
Rhossili Downs
Reynoldston
Cefn-y-Bryn
GOWER
Bishopston
Mayals
Black Pill
Aberavon
Port Talbot
Llanddewi
Parkmill
Sandylane
Kittle
West Cross
Swansea Bay
Rhossili
Knelston
Penmaen
Northway
Norton
Scurlage
Penrice
Nicholaston
Pennard
Oystermouth
Taibach
Middleton
Oxwich
Southgate
Caswell Bay
Langland
The Mumbles
Mumbles Head
Margam
Pilton Green
Horton
Paviland
Port Einon
Oxwich Bay
Pwlldu Head
Overton
Oxwich Green
Oxwich Castle
Oxwich Point
SS
Culver Hole
Port Einon Bay
Gower Heritage Coast
Port Einon Point
CORK
Afon Kenfig
Mawdlam
Kenfig
Rest Bay
Porthcawl
0 1 2 3 4 5 miles
0 1 2 3 4 5 6 7 kilometres
A40
A48
A484
A476
A483
A474
A4069
A4068
A4067
A4138
A4240
A4118
A465
A4241
M4
B4300
B4310
B4306
B4309
B4317
B4308
B4311
B4304
B4297
B4295
B4296
B4620
B4271
B4489
B4603
B4217
B4290
B4291
B4287
B4286
B4436
B4593
B4433
B4247
B4556
A4217
A4230
A4599
31
4
5
6
7
8
9
0
1
2

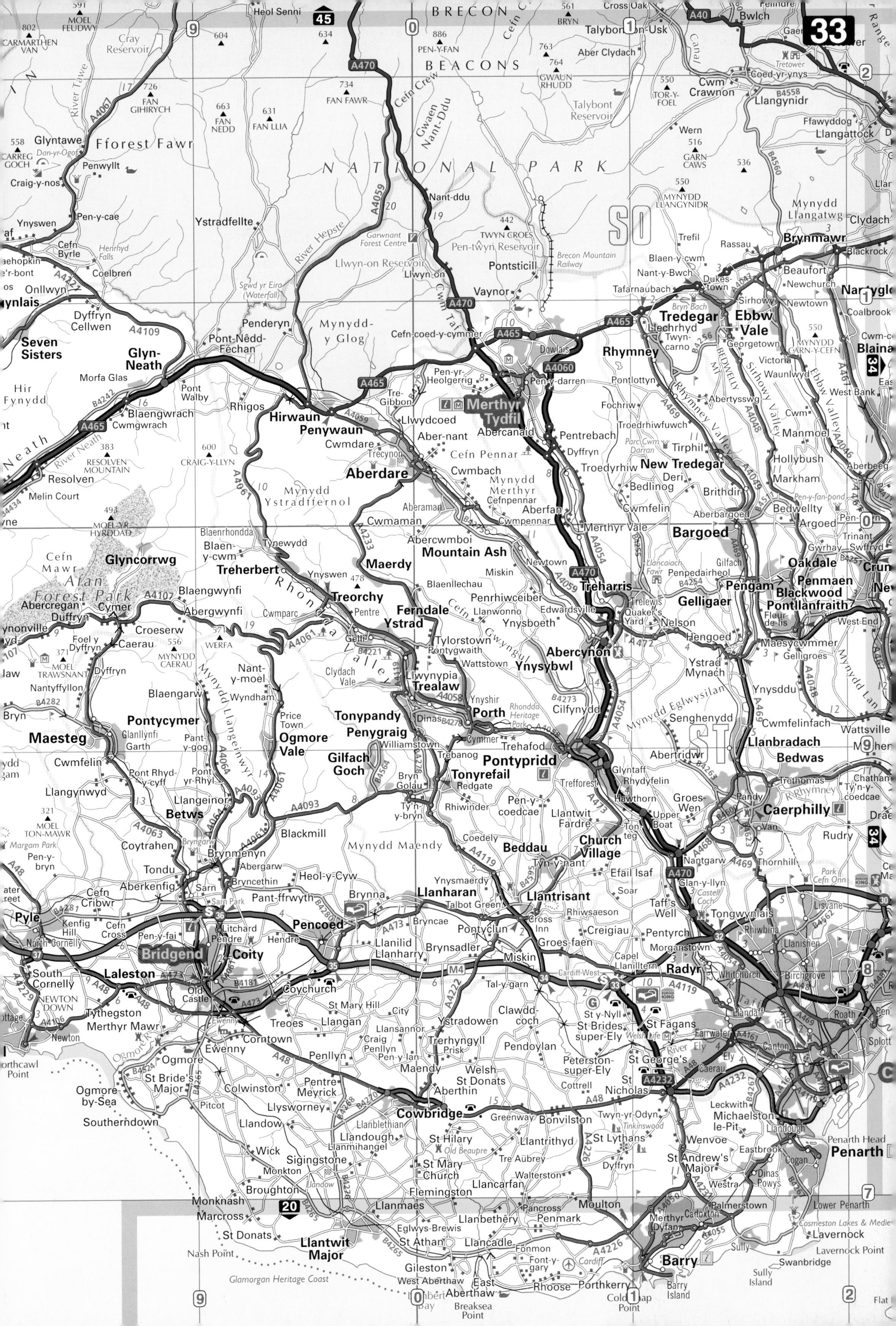
33
BRECON
BEACONS
NATIONAL PARK
Heol Senni
45
Talybont-on-Usk
Bwlch
Cross Oak
BRYN
PEN-Y-FAN
FAN FAWR
FAN GIHIRYCH
FAN NEDD
FAN LLIA
Cray Reservoir
MOEL FEUDWY
CARMARTHEN VAN
Cefn Crew
Gwaen Nant-Ddu
Aber Clydach
GWAUN RHUDD
TOR-Y-FOEL
Talybont Reservoir
Cwm Crawnon
Coed-yr-ynys
Tretower
Llangynidr
Ffawyddog
Llangattock
Wern
GARN CAWS
MYNYDD LLANGYNIDR
Mynydd Llangatwg
Clydach
Glyntawe
Fforest Fawr
CARREG GOCH
Dan-yr-Ogof
Penwyllt
Craig-y-nos
Ynyswen
Pen-y-cae
Ystradfellte
River Tawe
River Hepste
Nant-ddu
Garwnant Forest Centre
TWYN CROES
Pen-twyn Reservoir
Brecon Mountain Railway
Llwyn-on Reservoir
Llwyn-on
Pontsticill
Vaynor
Cwm Taf
Trefil
Rassau
Brynmawr
Blackrock
Blaen-y-cwm
Beaufort
Nant-y-Bwch
Dukestown
Newchurch
Tafarnaubach
Bryn Bach
Sirhowy
Newtown
Nantyglo
Coalbrook
Cefn Byrle
Henrhyd Falls
Coelbren
Onllwyn
Sgwd yr Eira (Waterfall)
Penderyn
Mynydd-y Glog
Cefn-coed-y-cymmer
Dowlais
Tredegar
Llechrhyd
Twyn-carno
Ebbw Vale
Georgetown
MYNYDD CARN-Y-CEFN
Blaina
Dyffryn Cellwen
Seven Sisters
Glyn-Neath
Pont-Nêdd-Fechan
Rhymney
Pen-yr-Heolgerrig
Pen-y-darren
Morfa Glas
Hir Fynydd
Pont Walby
Blaengwrach
Cwmgwrach
Rhigos
Hirwaun
Penywaun
Tre-Gibbon
Merthyr Tydfil
Llwydcoed
Aber-nant
Abercanaid
Pontlottyn
Fochriw
Victoria
Waunlwyd
West Bank
Abertysswg
Rhymney Valley
Sirhowy Valley
Ebbw Valley
Cwm
Manmoel
Neath
River Neath
RESOLVEN MOUNTAIN
Resolven
Melin Court
CRAIG-Y-LLYN
Cwmdare
Trecynon
Aberdare
Cefn Pennar
Cwmbach
Mynydd Merthyr
Pentrebach
Dyffryn
Troedyrhiw
Troedrhiwfuwch
Parc Cwm Darran
Tirphil
New Tredegar
Deri
Bedlinog
Brithdir
Hollybush
Markham
Aberbeeg
Mynydd Ystradffernol
Cefnpennar
Aberfan
Cwmfelin
Aberbargoed
Bedwellty
Pen-y-fan pond
Argoed
MOEL-YR-HYRDDAD
Blaenrhondda
Blaen-y-cwm
Tynewydd
Aberaman
Cwmaman
Cwmpennar
Abercwmboi
Mountain Ash
Merthyr Vale
Bargoed
Trinant
Gwrhay
Swffryd
Cefn Mawr
Glyncorrwg
Afan Forest Park
Treherbert
Ynyswen
Maerdy
Miskin
Llancaiach Fawr
Gilfach
Penpedairheol
Oakdale
Crumlin
Treharris
Pengam
Penmaen
Blackwood
Abercregan
Cymer
Duffryn
Blaengwynfi
Abergwynfi
Cwmparc
Treorchy
Pentre
Rhondda Valley
Ferndale
Ystrad
Blaenllechau
Penrhiwceiber
Llanwonno
Edwardsville
Trelewis
Quaker's Yard
Gelligaer
Nelson
Pontllanfraith
Fleur-de-lis
West End
Croeserw
Caerau
Foel y Dyffryn
MOEL TRAWSNANT
MYNYDD CAERAU
WERFA
Nant-y-moel
Wyndham
Clydach Vale
Gelli
Tylorstown
Pontygwaith
Wattstown
Cefn Gwyngul
Ynysboeth
Abercynon
Ynysybwl
Hengoed
Maesycwmmer
Gelligroes
Ystrad Mynach
Mynydd Lan
Nantyffyllon
Dyffryn
Blaengarw
Mynydd Llangeinwyr
Price Town
Llwynypia
Trealaw
Ynyshir
Porth
Rhondda Heritage Park
Cilfynydd
Mynydd Eglwysilan
Senghenydd
Ynysddu
Cwmfelinfach
Wattsville
Maesteg
Pontycymer
Garth
Garnllynfi
Pant-y-gog
Ogmore Vale
Tonypandy
Penygraig
Dinas
Williamstown
Cymmer
Trehafod
Pontypridd
Abertridwr
Llanbradach
Bedwas
Cwmfelin
Pont Rhyd-y-cyff
Pont-yr-Rhyl
Gilfach Goch
Trebanog
Tonyrefail
Bryn Golau
Redgate
Trefforest
Glyntaff
Rhydyfelin
Trethomas
Chatham
Ty'n-y-coedcae
Llangynwyd
Llangeinor
Betws
Tyn-y-bryn
Rhiwinder
Pen-y-coedcae
Llantwit Fardre
Hawthorn
Groes-Wen
Pandy
Caerphilly
Upper Boat
Van
Rudry
MOEL TON-MAWR
Margam Park
Pen-y-bryn
Coytrahen
Bryngarw
Blackmill
Mynydd Maendy
Coedely
Beddau
Church Village
Tonteg
Thornhill
Nantgarw
Park Cefn Onn
Tondu
Brynmenyn
Abergarw
Heol-y-Cyw
Ynysmaerdy
Tyn-y-nant
Efail Isaf
Glan-y-llyn
Castell Coch
Aberkenfig
Bryncethin
Sarn
Brynna
Llanharan
Llantrisant
Soar
Cefn Cribwr
Sarn Park
Pant-ffrwyth
Talbot Green
Taff's Well
Tongwynlais
Lisvane
Pyle
Kenfig Hill
Cefn Cross
Litchard
Pendre
Pencoed
Bryncae
Cross Inn
Rhiwsaeson
Rhiwbina
North Cornelly
Pen-y-fai
Bridgend
Coity
Hendre
Llanilid
Llanharry
Pontyclun
Creigiau
Pentyrch
Morganstown
Llanishen
Brynsadler
Groes-faen
Capel Llanilltern
Radyr
Whitchurch
South Cornelly
Laleston
Miskin
Cardiff West
Birchgrove
NEWTON DOWN
Old Castle
Coychurch
Tal-y-garn
Llandaff
Roath
Tythegston
Merthyr Mawr
Ewenny
St Mary Hill
Llangan
City
Ystradowen
Clawdd-coch
St y-Nyll
St Brides super-Ely
Welsh Life
St Fagans
Fairwater
Canton
Splott
Newton
Treoes
Corntown
Llansannor
Craig Penllyn
Trerhyngyll
Prisk
Pendoylan
River Ely
Caerau
Ely
Porthcawl Point
Ogmore
Ogmore River
Penllyn
Pen-y-lan
Maendy
Welsh St Donats
Peterston-super-Ely
St George's
St Nicholas
Ogmore-by-Sea
St Bride's Major
Colwinston
Pentre Meyrick
Aberthin
Cottrell
Leckwith
Michaelston-le-Pit
Llandough
Penarth Head
Penarth
Southerndown
Pitcot
Llysworney
Cowbridge
Greenway
Bonvilston
Twyn-yr-Odyn
Llandow
Llanblethian
Llandough
Llanmihangel
St Hilary
Old Beaupre
Llantrithyd
St Lythans
Tinkinswood
Wenvoe
Eastbrook
Cogan
Wick
Sigingstone
Monkton
St Mary Church
Tre Aubrey
Dyffryn
St Andrew's Major
Dinas Powys
Broughton
Walterston
Llancarfan
Flemingston
Westra
Monknash
Marcross
20
Llanmaes
Pancross
Penmark
Moulton
Palmerstown
Cadoxton
Lower Penarth
Cosmeston Lakes & Medieval Village
Eglwys-Brewis
Llanbethery
Merthyr Dyfan
Lavernock
St Donats
Llantwit Major
St Athan
Llancadle
Fonmon
Font-y-gary
Cardiff
Barry
Sully
Swanbridge
Lavernock Point
Nash Point
Gileston
Sully Island
Glamorgan Heritage Coast
West Aberthaw
East Aberthaw
Rhoose
Porthkerry
Cold Knap Point
Barry Island
Limpert Bay
Breaksea Point
Flat

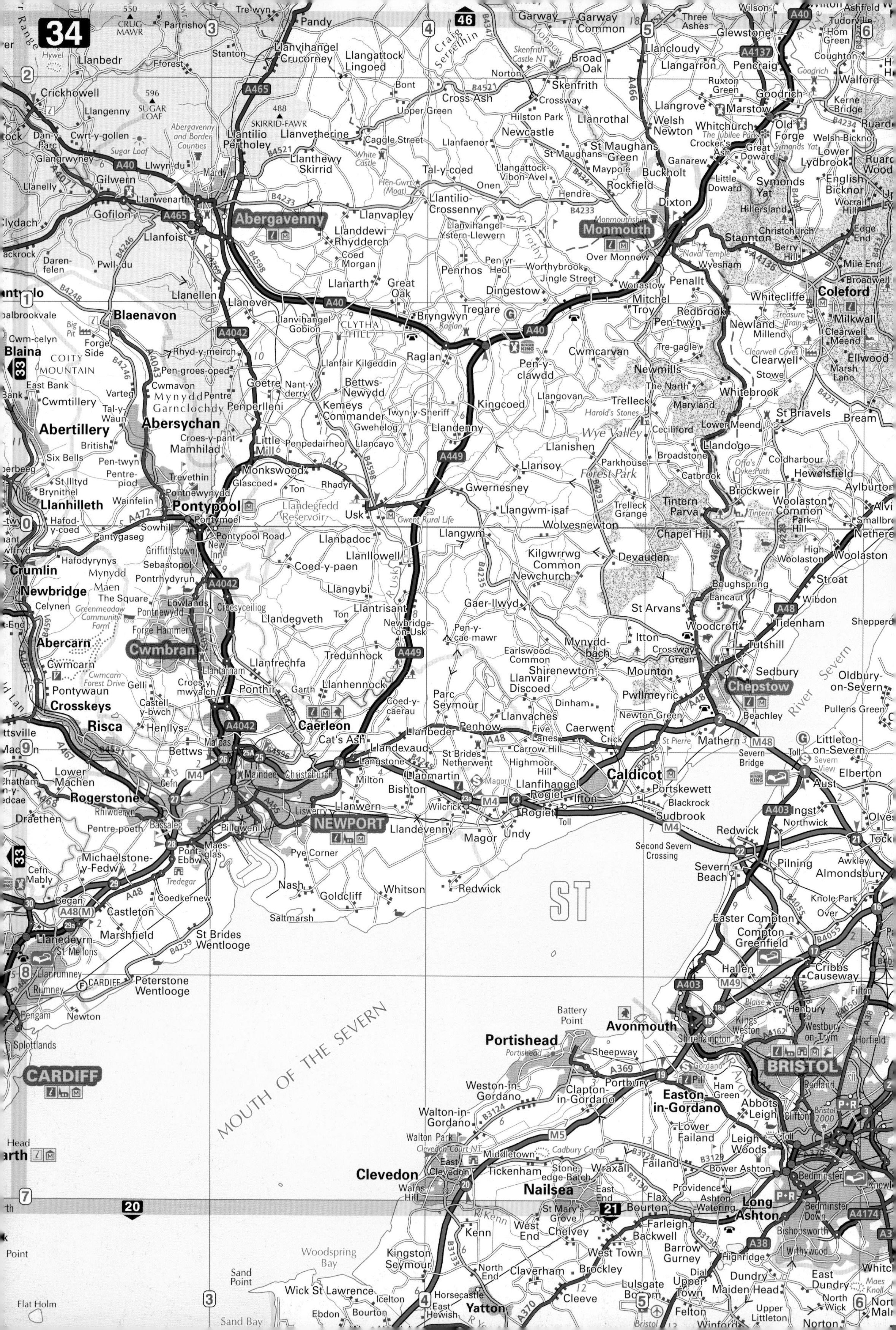
34
46
Crug Mawr
Partrishow
Tre-wyn
Pandy
Garway
Garway Common
Three Ashes
Wilson
Ashfield
Tudorville
Hom Green
Hywel
Llanbedr
Stanton
Llanvihangel Crucorney
Llangattock Lingoed
Craig Serrethin
Skenfrith Castle NT
Broad Oak
Llancloudy
Llangarron
Glewstone
Pencraig
Coughton
Walford
Fforest
Norton
Skenfrith
Ruxton Green
Goodrich
Kerne Bridge
Crickhowell
Llangenny
Sugar Loaf
Bont
Cross Ash
Crossway
Llangrove
Marstow
Skirrid-Fawr
Upper Green
Hilston Park
Llanrothal
Welsh Newton
Whitchurch
Old Forge
Welsh Bicknor
Ruardean
Dan-y-Parc
Cwrt-y-gollen
Abergavenny and Border Counties
Llantilio Pertholey
Llanvetherine
Caggle Street
Llanfaenor
Newcastle
St Maughans
St Maughans Green
Crocker's Ash
Great Doward
The Jubilee Park
Symonds Yat
Lower Lydbrook
Glangrwyney
Sugar Loaf
Llwyn-du
Llanthewy Skirrid
White Castle
Tal-y-coed
Llangattock-Vibon-Avel
Maypole
Buckholt
Ganarew
Little Doward
Symonds Yat
English Bicknor
Llanelly
Gilwern
Mardy
Hen-Gwrt (Moat)
Onen
Rockfield
Hendre
Dixton
Hillersland
Worrall Hill
Llanwenarth
Llantilio-Crossenny
Llanvapley
Abergavenny
Monmouth
Clydach
Gofilon
Llanfoist
Llanddewi Rhydderch
Llanvihangel Ystern-Llewern
Monmouthshire
Over Monnow
Staunton
Christchurch
Berry Hill
Edge End
Naval Temple
Wyesham
Mile End
Coed Morgan
Daren-felen
Pwll-du
Penrhos
Pen-yr-Heol
Worthybrook
Jingle Street
Llanarth
Great Oak
Dingestow
Wonastow
Penallt
Broadwell
Coleford
Llanellen
Llanover
Tregare
Mitchel Troy
Redbrook
Whitecliffe
Blaenavon
Llanvihangel Gobion
Clytha Hill
Bryngwyn
Raglan
Pen-twyn
Newland
Millend
Treasure Train
Milkwall
Clearwell
Meend
Cwm-celyn
Big Pit
Forge Side
Coity Mountain
Blaina
Rhyd-y-meirch
Llanfair Kilgeddin
Pen-y-clawdd
Cwmcarvan
Tre-gagle
Clearwell Caves
Clearwell
Ellwood
Pen-groes-oped
Newmills
Stowe
Marsh Lane
East Bank
Cwmtillery
Varteg
Cwmavon
Mynydd Garnclochdy
Pentre
Goetre
Nant-y-derry
Bettws-Newydd
Kingcoed
Llangovan
Trelleck
The North
Whitebrook
Tal-y-Waun
Penperlleni
Kemeys Commander
Twyn-y-Sheriff
Harold's Stones
Maryland
Abertillery
Abersychan
Gwehelog
Llandenny
St Briavels
Bream
Croes-y-pant
Mamhilad
Little Mill
Penpedairheol
Llancayo
Wye Valley
Ceciliford
Lower Meend
Llanishen
Llandogo
British
Six Bells
Pen-twyn
Pentre-piod
Trevethin
Monkswood
Glascoed
Ton
Rhadyr
Llansoy
Parkhouse
Broadstone
Forest Park
Coldharbour
Offa's Dyke Path
Hewelsfield
Catbrook
St Illtyd
Brynithel
Pontnewynydd
Gwernesney
Brockweir
Aylburton
Llanhilleth
Wainfelin
Pontypool
Llandegfedd Reservoir
Usk
Gwent Rural Life
Llangwm-isaf
Trelleck Grange
Tintern Parva
Tintern
Woolaston Common
Park Hill
Hafod-y-coed
Sowhill
Pontymoel
Wolvesnewton
Smallbrook
Pantygaseg
Pontypool Road
Llanbadoc
Llangwm
Chapel Hill
Netherend
Griffithstown
New Inn
Kilgwrrwg Common
Devauden
High Woolaston
Woolaston
Crumlin
Hafodyrynys
Sebastopol
Llanllowell
Coed-y-paen
Newchurch
Mynydd Maen
Pontrhydyrun
Stroat
Newbridge
Llangybi
Boughspring
Lancaut
Wibdon
Celynen
The Square
Lowlands
Croesyceiliog
Llantrisant
Gaer-llwyd
St Arvans
Greenmeadow Community Farm
Pontnewydd
Llandegveth
Newbridge-on-Usk
Pen-y-cae-mawr
Woodcroft
Tidenham
Shepperdine
Forge Hammer
Itton
Mynydd-bach
Abercarn
Cwmbran
Tredunhock
Earlswood Common
Crossway Green
Tutshill
Cwmcarn
Cwmcarn Forest Drive
Llantarnam
Llanfrechfa
Shirenewton
Mounton
Sedbury
Oldbury-on-Severn
Gelli
Croes-y-mwyalch
Llanvair Discoed
Chepstow
River Severn
Pontywaun
Ponthir
Garth
Llanhennock
Coed-y-caerau
Parc Seymour
Pwllmeyric
Crosskeys
Castell-y-bwch
Dinham
Newton Green
Beachley
Pullens Green
Risca
Henllys
Caerleon
Llanvaches
Penhow
Five Lanes
Caerwent
Crick
Mathern
Littleton-on-Severn
Malpas
Bettws
Cat's Ash
Llanbeder
Llandevaud
Carrow Hill
St Pierre
Severn Bridge
Toll
Severn View
Lower Machen
Langstone
St Brides Netherwent
Highmoor Hill
Caldicot
Maindee
Christchurch
Milton
Llanmartin
Magor
Llanfihangel Rogiet
Portskewett
Aust
Elberton
Cefn
Rogerstone
Bishton
Wilcrick
Rogiet
Ifton
Blackrock
Ingst
Northwick
Olveston
Rhiwderin
Liswerry
Llanwern
Toll
Sudbrook
Draethen
Bassaleg
Pentre-poeth
Pillgwenlly
Newport
Llandevenny
Magor
Undy
Redwick
Tockington
Second Severn Crossing
Maes-glas
Pont-Ebbw
Pye Corner
Michaelstone-y-Fedw
Tredegar
Severn Beach
Pilning
Awkley
Almondsbury
Cefn Mably
Nash
Goldcliff
Whitson
Redwick
ST
Coedkernew
Began
Castleton
Knole Park
Over
Saltmarsh
Easter Compton
Llanedeyrn
St Mellons
Marshfield
St Brides Wentlooge
Compton Greenfield
Cribbs Causeway
Llanrumney
Cardiff
Peterstone Wentlooge
Hallen
Filton
Rumney
Pengam
Newton
Blaise
Henbury
Battery Point
Avonmouth
Kings Weston
Westbury-on-Trym
Horfield
Splottlands
Mouth of the Severn
Portishead
Shirehampton
Sheepway
Cardiff
Gordano
Pill
Bristol
Redland
Weston-in-Gordano
Portbury
Clapton-in-Gordano
Easton-in-Gordano
Ham Green
Abbots Leigh
Clifton
Bristol 2000
Walton-in-Gordano
Lower Failand
Leigh Woods
Walton Park
Clevedon Court NT
Middletown
Cadbury Camp
Failand
Bower Ashton
Head
Clevedon
East Clevedon
Tickenham
Stone-edge-Batch
Wraxall
Bedminster
Knowle
Wains Hill
Nailsea
East End
Flax Bourton
Providence
Ashton Watering
Long Ashton
Bedminster Down
St Mary's Grove
Kenn
West End
Chelvey
Farleigh
Backwell
Barrow Gurney
Bishopsworth
Woodspring Bay
Kingston Seymour
West Town
Highridge
Withywood
Point
Sand Point
North End
Claverham
Brockley
Dundry
East Dundry
Maes Knoll
Whitchurch
Wick St Lawrence
Lulsgate Bottom
Upper Town
Maiden Head
Cleeve
North Wick
Flat Holm
Icelton
Horsecastle
East Hewish
Yatton
Felton
Winford
Upper Littleton
Norton
Sand Bay
Ebdon
Bourton
20
33
Elidir
Mouth of the Severn

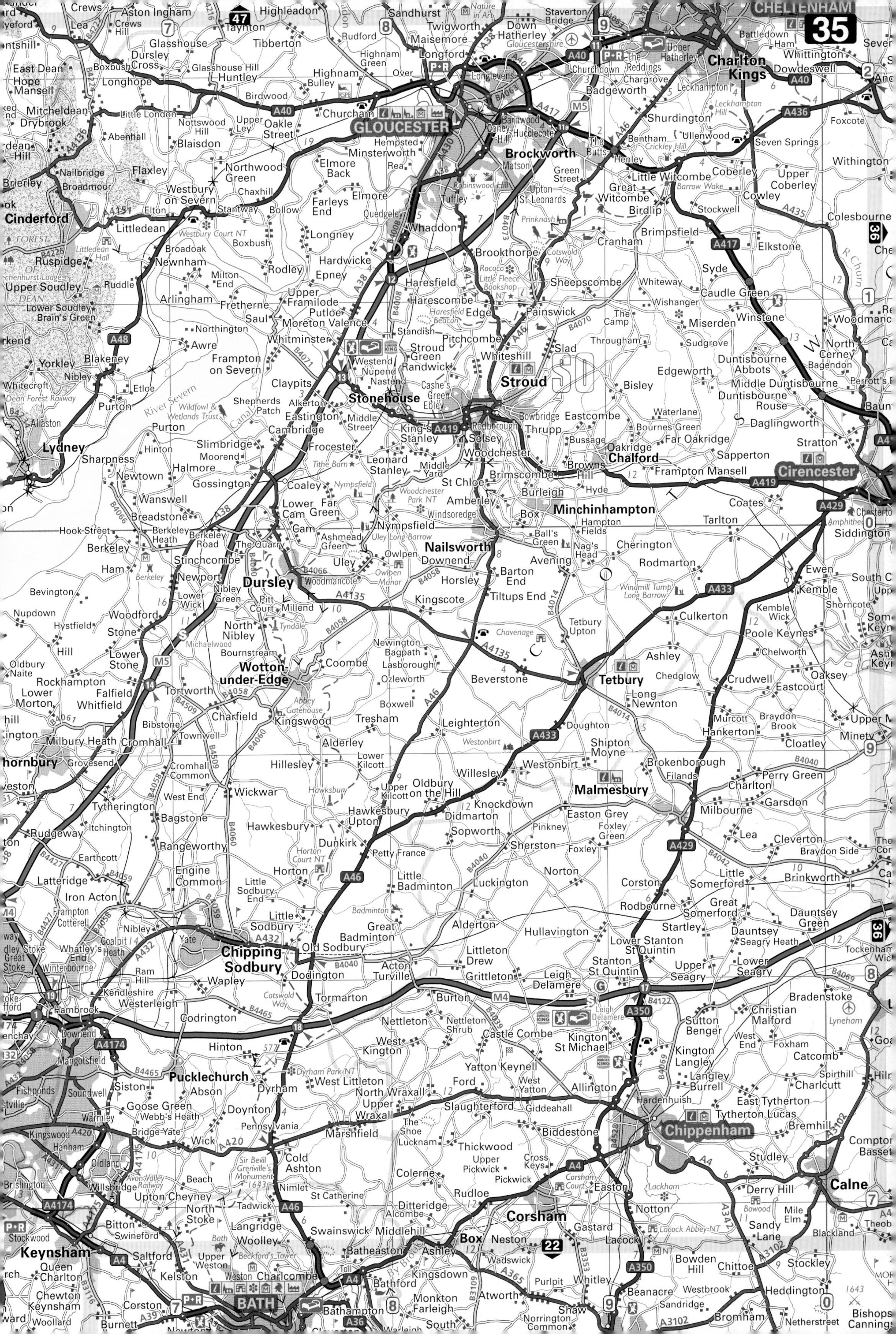
35
CHELTENHAM
GLOUCESTER
Charlton Kings
Brockworth
Cinderford
Lydney
Stroud
Stonehouse
Nailsworth
Minchinhampton
Chalford
Cirencester
Dursley
Wotton-under-Edge
Tetbury
Malmesbury
Chipping Sodbury
Yate
Pucklechurch
Chippenham
Calne
Corsham
Keynsham
BATH
Thornbury
River Severn
36
47
22

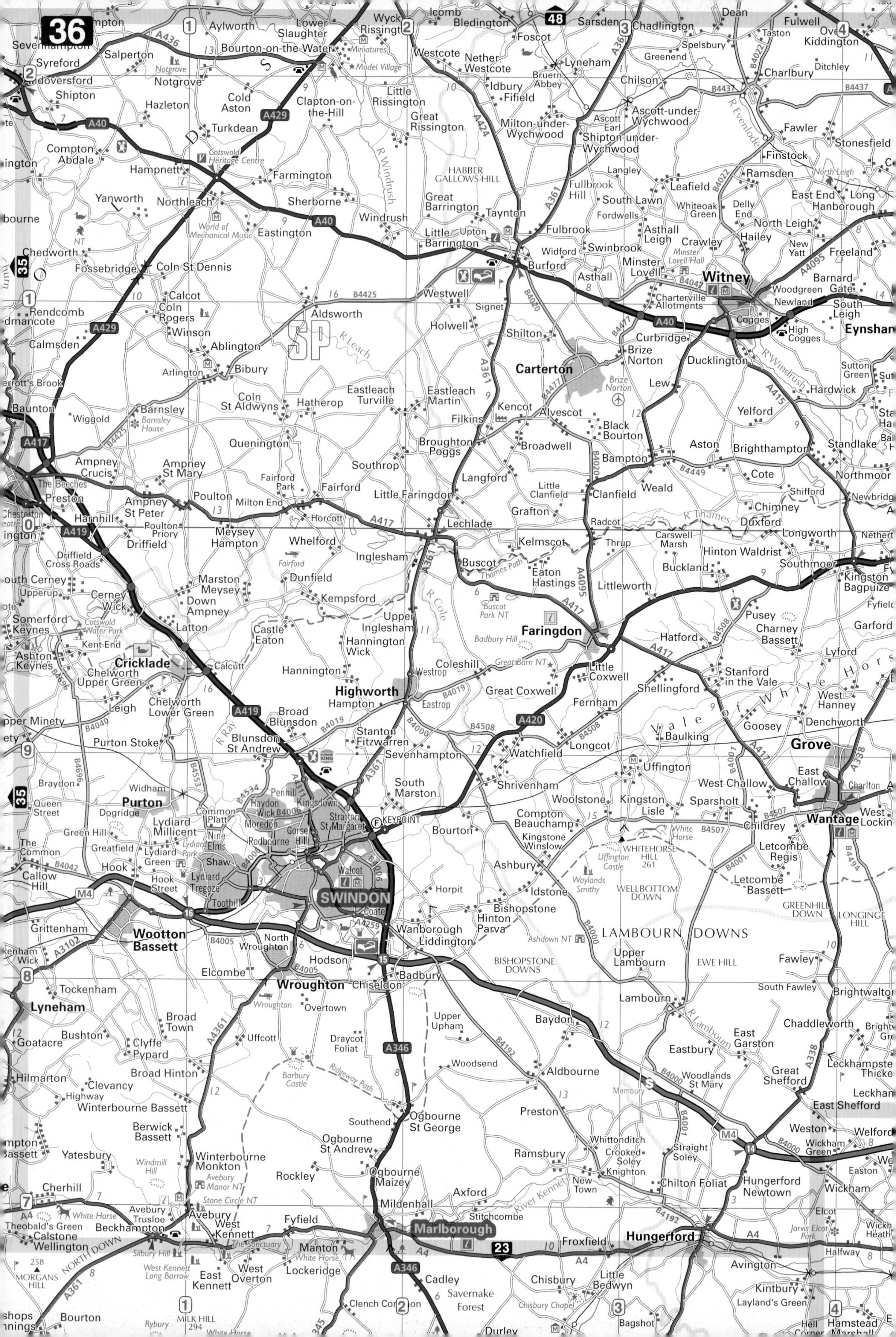
48
Aylworth
Lower Slaughter
Bourton-on-the-Water
Miniatures
Model Village
Wyck Rissington
Icomb
Bledington
Sarsden
Chadlington
Dean
Fulwell
Over Kiddington
Taston
Spelsbury
Syreford
Salperton
Notgrove
Andoversford
Shipton
Hazleton
Cold Aston
Turkdean
Clapton-on-the-Hill
Little Rissington
Great Rissington
Westcote
Nether Westcote
Foscot
Lyneham
Idbury
Fifield
Bruern Abbey
Greenend
Chilson
Ascott-under-Wychwood
Ascott Earl
Milton-under-Wychwood
Shipton-under-Wychwood
Charlbury
Ditchley
Fawler
Stonesfield
Finstock
Compton Abdale
Hampnett
Cotswold Heritage Centre
Farmington
Yanworth
Northleach
World of Mechanical Music
Sherborne
Windrush
Eastington
HABBER GALLOWS HILL
Great Barrington
Taynton
Little Barrington
Upton
Langley
Fullbrook Hill
South Lawn
Fordwells
Leafield
Whiteoak Green
Ramsden
Delly End
North Leigh
East End
Long Hanborough
Hailey
New Yatt
Freeland
Crawley
Asthall Leigh
Minster Lovell Hall
Minster Lovell
Swinbrook
Fulbrook
Widford
Burford
Asthall
Witney
Barnard Gate
Woodgreen
Newland
South Leigh
Eynsham
Chedworth
Fossebridge
Coln St Dennis
Calcot
Coln Rogers
Rendcomb
Winson
Calmsden
Ablington
Bibury
Arlington
Aldsworth
Westwell
Signet
Holwell
Shilton
Charterville Allotments
Cogges
High Cogges
Curbridge
Brize Norton
Ducklington
Carterton
Lew
Sutton Green
Hardwick
Baunton
Wiggold
Barnsley
Barnsley House
Coln St Aldwyns
Hatherop
Eastleach Turville
Eastleach Martin
Kencot
Alvescot
Black Bourton
Filkins
Broadwell
Broughton Poggs
Quenington
Yelford
Aston
Brighthampton
Standlake
Bampton
Cote
Weald
Northmoor
Ampney Crucis
Ampney St Mary
The Beeches
Preston
Ampney St Peter
Poulton
Fairford Park
Fairford
Southrop
Little Faringdon
Langford
Little Clanfield
Clanfield
Shifford
Chimney
Duxford
Harnhill
Milton End
Horcott
Poulton Priory
Driffield
Meysey Hampton
Lechlade
Grafton
Radcot
Longworth
Whelford
Inglesham
Kelmscot
Thrup
Carswell Marsh
Hinton Waldrist
Driffield Cross Roads
Buscot
Eaton Hastings
Buckland
Southmoor
Kingston Bagpuize
South Cerney
Upperup
Marston Meysey
Dunfield
Kempsford
Cerney Wick
Down Ampney
Littleworth
Buscot Park NT
Fyfield
Pusey
Somerford Keynes
Cotswold Water Park
Latton
Upper Inglesham
Castle Eaton
Hannington Wick
Faringdon
Charney Bassett
Garford
Ashton Keynes
Kent End
Badbury Hill
Hatford
Lyford
Cricklade
Chelworth Upper Green
Calcutt
Hannington
Coleshill
Great Barn NT
Little Coxwell
Stanford in the Vale
Highworth
Westrop
Great Coxwell
Shellingford
West Hanney
Chelworth Lower Green
Leigh
Hampton
Eastrop
Fernham
Vale of White Horse
Upper Minety
Broad Blunsdon
Stanton Fitzwarren
Baulking
Goosey
Denchworth
Purton Stoke
Blunsdon St Andrew
Sevenhampton
Watchfield
Longcot
Grove
Uffington
Braydon
Widham
South Marston
Shrivenham
West Challow
East Challow
Charlton
Queen Street
Purton
Dogridge
Haydon Wick
Penhill
Kingsdown
Stratton St Margaret
Woolstone
Kingston Lisle
Sparsholt
Wantage
West Lockinge
Lydiard Millicent
Common Platt
Moredon
Gorse Hill
Keypoint
Bourton
Compton Beauchamp
Childrey
Green Hill
Greatfield
Lydiard Green
Nine Elms
Rodbourne
Kingstone Winslow
White Horse
Whitehorse Hill 261
The Common
Shaw
Uffington Castle
Letcombe Regis
Callow Hill
Hook
Hook Street
Lydiard Tregoze
Toothill
Walcot
SWINDON
Ashbury
Waylands Smithy
Letcombe Bassett
Horpit
Idstone
Wellbottom Down
Greenhill Down
Longinge Hill
Grittenham
Wootton Bassett
Coate
Wanborough
Liddington
Bishopstone
Hinton Parva
Ashdown NT
Lambourn Downs
North Wroughton
Upper Lambourn
Ewe Hill
Fawley
Hodson
Badbury
Bishopstone Downs
Elcombe
Tockenham
Wroughton
Chiseldon
South Fawley
Brightwalton
Lyneham
Overtown
Lambourn
Broad Town
Upper Upham
Baydon
Chaddleworth
Goatacre
Bushton
Clyffe Pypard
Uffcott
Draycot Foliat
East Garston
Eastbury
Broad Hinton
Woodsend
Aldbourne
Great Shefford
Leckhampstead Thicket
Hilmarton
Clevancy
Barbury Castle
Ridgeway Path
Woodlands St Mary
Highway
Winterbourne Bassett
Membury
Leckhampstead
East Shefford
Berwick Bassett
Southend
Ogbourne St George
Preston
Weston
Welford
Ogbourne St Andrew
Whittonditch
Crooked Soley
Knighton
Straight Soley
Wickham Green
Yatesbury
Windmill Hill
Winterbourne Monkton
Ramsbury
Avebury Manor NT
Rockley
Ogbourne Maizey
New Town
Chilton Foliat
Hungerford Newtown
Easton
Cherhill
Stone Circle NT
Mildenhall
Axford
River Kennet
Wickham
White Horse
Avebury Trusloe
Avebury
West Kennett
Fyfield
Stitchcombe
Elcot
Theobald's Green
Calstone Wellington
Beckhampton
Marlborough
Jarvis Elcot Park
Wickham Heath
The Sanctuary
Manton
White Horse
Froxfield
Hungerford
Halfway
North Down
Silbury Hill
23
Morgans Hill 258
West Kennett Long Barrow
East Kennett
West Overton
Lockeridge
Cadley
Avington
Savernake Forest
Chisbury
Little Bedwyn
Kintbury
Layland's Green
Chisbury Chapel
Clench Common
Milk Hill 294
Rybury
Bourton
Bagshot
Durley
Hamstead
SP
R Windrush
R Evenlode
R Leach
R Thames
Thames Path
R Cole
R Ray
R Lambourn
A40
A429
A424
A361
A417
A419
A420
A415
A4095
A338
A4361
A346
A3102
A4
M4
A436
A44
B4425
B4020
B4477
B4449
B4047
B4022
B4437
B4019
B4000
B4508
B4507
B4001
B4192
B4005
B4006
B4553
B4534
B4696
B4040
B4042
B4696
A4259
A4311
B4494
35
1
2
3
4
7
8
9

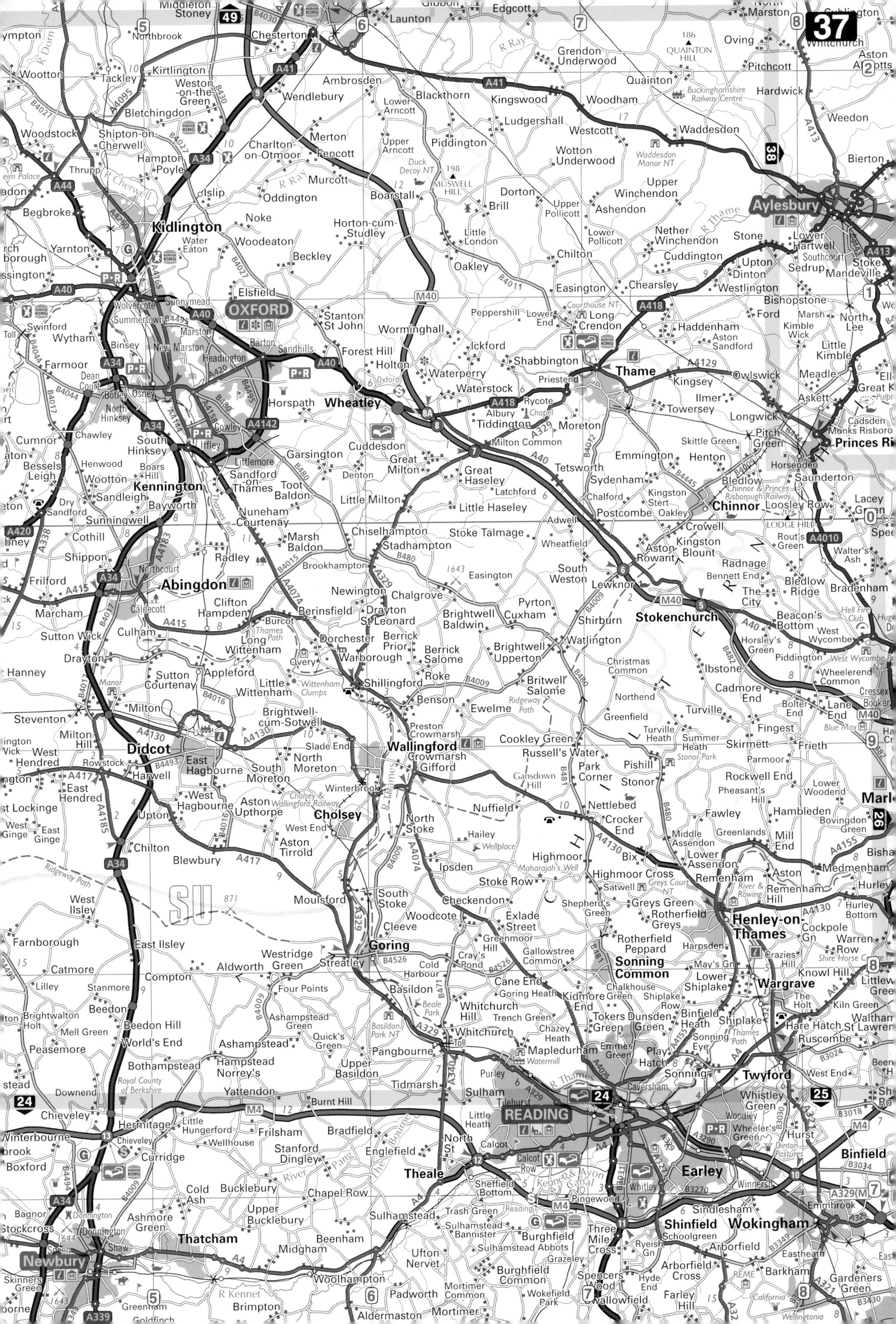

37
Middleton Stoney
Northbrook
Chesterton
Launton
Gibbon
Edgcott
Marston
Cublington
Whitchurch
Aston Abbotts
Oving
Pitchcott
Quainton Hill
Grendon Underwood
Kirtlington
Tackley
Wootton
Weston-on-the-Green
Ambrosden
Wendlebury
Blackthorn
Lower Arncott
Kingswood
Woodham
Quainton
Buckinghamshire Railway Centre
Hardwick
Weedon
Bletchingdon
Woodstock
Shipton-on-Cherwell
Hampton Poyle
Thrupp
Charlton-on-Otmoor
Merton
Fencott
Upper Arncott
Piddington
Ludgershall
Westcott
Waddesdon
Waddesdon Manor NT
Wotton Underwood
Bierton
Duck Decoy NT
Muswell Hill
Murcott
Boarstall
Islip
Oddington
Dorton
Brill
Upper Winchendon
Ashendon
Upper Pollicott
Aylesbury
Begbroke
Kidlington
Noke
Horton-cum-Studley
Little London
Lower Pollicott
Nether Winchendon
Stone
Lower Hartwell
Yarnton
Water Eaton
Woodeaton
Beckley
Oakley
Chilton
Cuddington
Southcourt
Stoke Mandeville
Upton
Dinton
Sedrup
Westlington
Bishopstone
Easington
Chearsley
Elsfield
Sunnymead
Wolvercote
Summertown
OXFORD
Stanton St John
Worminghall
Peppershill
Lower End
Courthouse NT
Long Crendon
Haddenham
Aston Sandford
Ford
Marsh
Kimble Wick
North Lee
Little Kimble
Swinford
Wytham
Binsey
Marston
New Marston
Barton
Sandhills
Headington
Forest Hill
Holton
Ickford
Shabbington
Thame
Kingsey
Owlswick
Meadle
Great Kimble
Farmoor
Dean Court
Botley
Osney
North Hinksey
Horspath
Wheatley
Waterperry
Waterstock
Priestend
Ilmer
Towersey
Longwick
Askett
Albury
Rycote Chapel
Tiddington
Moreton
Cowley
Iffley
South Hinksey
Cumnor
Chawley
Littlemore
Cuddesdon
Milton Common
Skittle Green
Pitch Green
Monks Risborough
Princes Risborough
Cadsden
Henwood
Boars Hill
Garsington
Great Milton
Great Haseley
Tetsworth
Emmington
Henton
Horsenden
Saunderton
Bessels Leigh
Wootton
Sandford-on-Thames
Denton
Toot Baldon
Latchford
Sydenham
Bledlow
Kingston Stert
Chalford
Chinnor
Loosley Row
Lacey Green
Sandleigh
Kennington
Dry Sandford
Bayworth
Sunningwell
Nuneham Courtenay
Little Milton
Little Haseley
Postcombe
Oakley
Lodge Hill
Cothill
Marsh Baldon
Chiselhampton
Stoke Talmage
Adwell
Wheatfield
Crowell
Aston Rowant
Kingston Blount
Rout's Green
Walter's Ash
Shippon
Radley
Northcourt
Stadhampton
Brookhampton
Easington
South Weston
Lewknor
Radnage
Bennett End
Bledlow Ridge
Bradenham
Frilford
Abingdon
Caldecott
Clifton Hampden
Newington
Chalgrove
Berinsfield
Drayton St Leonard
Brightwell Baldwin
Cuxham
Pyrton
Shirburn
Stokenchurch
The City
Beacon's Bottom
West Wycombe
Marcham
Culham
Burcot
Thames Path
Long Wittenham
Dorchester
Berrick Prior
Berrick Salome
Brightwell Upperton
Watlington
Horsley's Green
Piddington
Hell Fire Club
Sutton Wick
Drayton
Overy
Warborough
Christmas Common
Ibstone
Wheelerend Common
Hanney
Sutton Courtenay
Appleford
Little Wittenham
Wittenham Clumps
Shillingford
Roke
Britwell Salome
Ridgeway Path
Northend
Cadmore End
Bolter End
Lane End
Cressex
Steventon
Milton
Brightwell-cum-Sotwell
Benson
Ewelme
Greenfield
Turville
Fingest
Blue Max
Milton Hill
West Hendred
Didcot
Slade End
Preston Crowmarsh
Wallingford
Cookley Green
Turville Heath
Summer Heath
Skirmett
Frieth
Rowstock
East Hagbourne
North Moreton
South Moreton
Crowmarsh Gifford
Russell's Water
Stonor Park
Parmoor
Harwell
East Hendred
Gangsdown Hill
Park Corner
Pishill
Stonor
Rockwell End
Lower Woodend
Pheasant's Hill
West Hagbourne
Aston Upthorpe
Cholsey & Wallingford Railway
Winterbrook
Cholsey
Nuffield
Nettlebed
Fawley
Hambleden
Marlow
East Lockinge
Upton
West End
North Stoke
Crocker End
Middle Assendon
Greenlands
Mill End
Bovingdon Green
West Ginge
East Ginge
Chilton
Aston Tirrold
Hailey
Wellplace
Highmoor
Maharajah's Well
Bix
Lower Assendon
Medmenham
Blewbury
Ipsden
Highmoor Cross
Remenham
Aston
Ridgeway Path
Stoke Row
Satwell
Greys Court NT
River & Rowing
Remenham Hill
Hurley
West Ilsley
SU
Moulsford
South Stoke
Checkendon
Shepherd's Green
Greys Green
Rotherfield Greys
Henley-on-Thames
Hurley Bottom
Woodcote
Exlade Street
Cockpole Gn
Farnborough
Cleeve
Greenmoor Hill
Rotherfield Peppard
Harpsden
Warren Row
East Ilsley
Westridge Green
Goring
Streatley
Cray's Pond
Gallowstree Common
Sonning Common
Crazies Hill
Shire Horse Centre
Catmore
Aldworth
Cold Harbour
May's Green
Knowl Hill
Compton
Four Points
Cane End
Goring Heath
Lower Shiplake
Chalkhouse Green
Wargrave
Littlewick Green
Lilley
Stanmore
Basildon
Beale Park
Whitchurch Hill
Kidmore End
Shiplake Row
The Holt
Kiln Green
Brightwalton Holt
Beedon
Ashampstead Green
Trench Green
Tokers Green
Dunsden Green
Binfield Heath
Shiplake
Waltham St Lawrence
Mell Green
Beedon Hill
Quick's Green
Basildon Park NT
Chazey Heath
Thames Path
Hare Hatch
Peasemore
World's End
Ashampstead
Pangbourne
Whitchurch
Mapledurham
Watermill
Emmer Green
Play Hatch
Sonning Eye
Ruscombe
Bothampstead
Hampstead Norrey's
Upper Basildon
Tidmarsh
Purley
Sonning
Twyford
West End
Royal County of Berkshire
Downend
Yattendon
Burnt Hill
Sulham
Tilehurst
Caversham
Whistley Green
Woodley
Chieveley
Hermitage
Little Hungerford
Frilsham
Bradfield
Little Heath
READING
Wheeler's Green
Hurst
Winterbourne
Chieveley
Wellhouse
Stanford Dingley
Englefield
North St
Calcot
Dinton Pastures
Binfield
Curridge
Calcot Row
Theale
Earley
Winnersh
Boxford
Cold Ash
Bucklebury
Chapel Row
Sheffield Bottom
Kennet & Avon Canal
Whitley
Pingewood
Upper Bucklebury
Trash Green
Sulhamstead
Sulhamstead Bannister
Burghfield
Sindlesham
Emmbrook
Bagnor
Donnington
Ashmore Green
Thatcham
Beenham
Sulhamstead Abbots
Three Mile Cross
Ryeish Gn
Shinfield
Schoolgreen
Wokingham
Stockcross
Shaw
Midgham
Ufton Nervet
Grazeley
Arborfield
Eastheath
Newbury
Burghfield Common
Spencers Wood
Hyde End
Arborfield Cross
Barkham
Skinners Green
Woolhampton
Mortimer Common
REME
Gardeners Green
Greenham
R Kennet
Brimpton
Padworth
Wokefield Park
Swallowfield
Farley Hill
California
Aldermaston
Mortimer
Goldfinch
Wellington

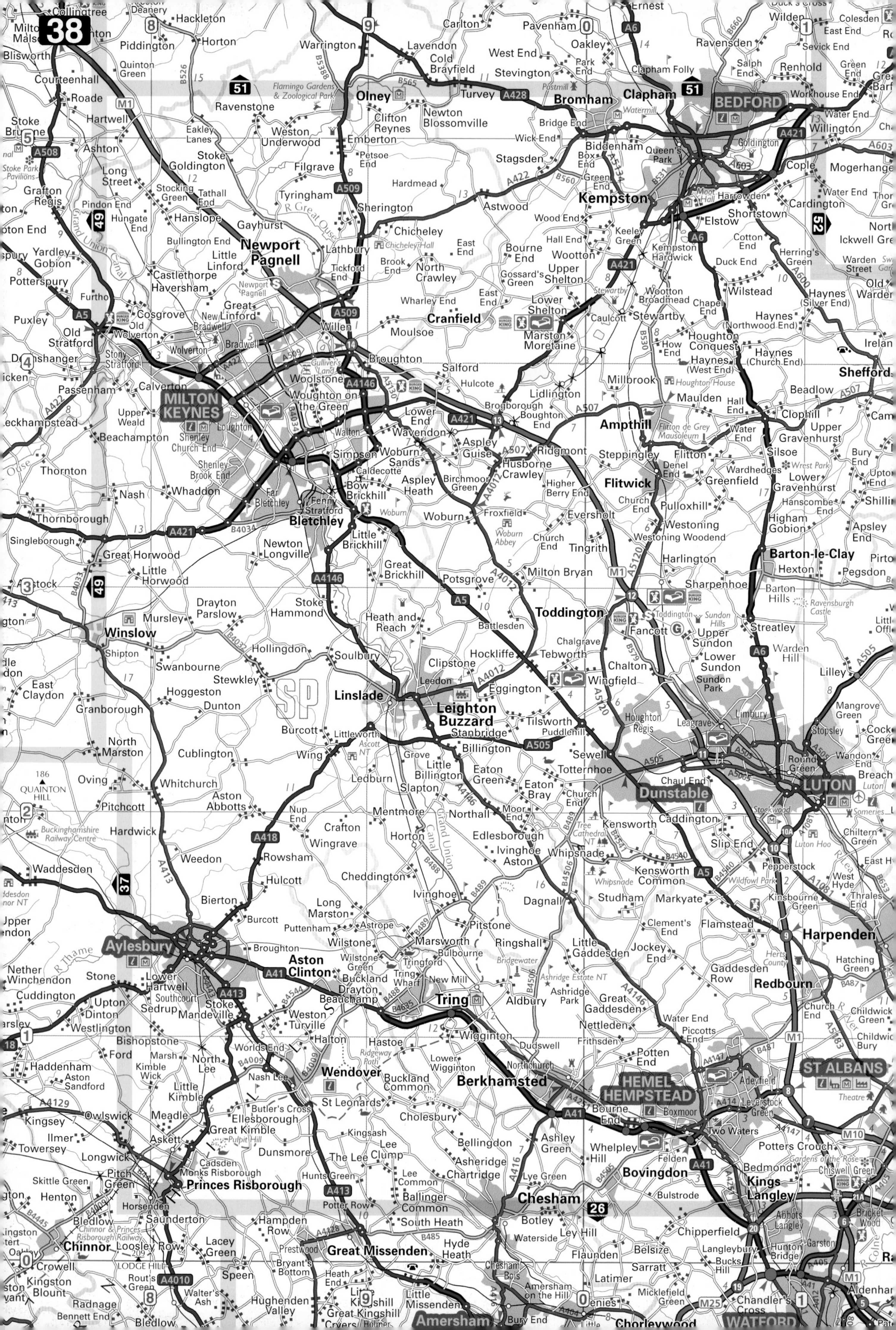

38
Hackleton
Horton
Piddington
Quinton Green
Blisworth
Courteenhall
Roade
Hartwell
Stoke Bruerne
Ashton
Long Street
Grafton Regis
Pindon End
Hungate End
Hanslope
Yardley Gobion
Potterspury
Castlethorpe
Haversham
Little Linford
Cosgrove
Puxley
Old Stratford
Stony Stratford
Passenham
Calverton
Upper Weald
Beachampton
Thornton
Nash
Whaddon
Thornborough
Singleborough
Great Horwood
Little Horwood
Mursley
Drayton Parslow
Winslow
Shipton
Swanbourne
East Claydon
Granborough
Hoggeston
Dunton
North Marston
Oving
Pitchcott
Hardwick
Whitchurch
Cublington
Aston Abbotts
Weedon
Waddesdon
Aylesbury
Stone
Lower Hartwell
Nether Winchendon
Cuddington
Upton
Dinton
Westlington
Bishopstone
Ford
Haddenham
Aston Sandford
Kingsey
Ilmer
Towersey
Longwick
Owlswick
Meadle
Askett
Princes Risborough
Monks Risborough
Skittle Green
Henton
Bledlow
Saunderton
Chinnor
Loosley Row
Lacey Green
Crowell
Kingston Blount
Speen
Radnage
Bennett End
Bledlow
Walter's Ash
Hughenden Valley
Great Kingshill
Little Kingshill
Great Missenden
Prestwood
Hampden Row
Little Missenden
Amersham
Chesham
Chesham Bois
Botley
Ley Hill
Latimer
Flaunden
Sarratt
Belsize
Chipperfield
Chorleywood
Bovingdon
Kings Langley
Abbots Langley
WATFORD
Garston
ST ALBANS
HEMEL HEMPSTEAD
Boxmoor
Two Waters
Potters Crouch
Bedmond
Berkhamsted
Northchurch
Wigginton
Tring
Aldbury
Dudswell
Ashridge Park
Ringshall
Little Gaddesden
Great Gaddesden
Nettleden
Frithsden
Potten End
Water End
Redbourn
Harpenden
Flamstead
Markyate
Kensworth
Caddington
Slip End
Studham
Whipsnade
Dagnall
Ivinghoe
Ivinghoe Aston
Pitstone
Marsworth
Bulbourne
Wilstone
Long Marston
Puttenham
Astrope
Cheddington
Aston Clinton
Buckland
Drayton Beauchamp
Weston Turville
Halton
Hastoe
Wendover
Buckland Common
St Leonards
Cholesbury
Lee Clump
The Lee
Ballinger Common
South Heath
Hyde Heath
Rowsham
Hulcott
Bierton
Burcott
Wingrave
Crafton
Mentmore
Horton
Northall
Edlesborough
Eaton Bray
Totternhoe
Dunstable
LUTON
Stopsley
Leagrave
Limbury
Houghton Regis
Chalton
Wingfield
Tebworth
Chalgrave
Toddington
Fancott
Sundon Park
Upper Sundon
Lower Sundon
Streatley
Barton-le-Clay
Hexton
Pegsdon
Lilley
Harlington
Sharpenhoe
Westoning
Flitwick
Flitton
Silsoe
Shillington
Clophill
Upper Gravenhurst
Lower Gravenhurst
Greenfield
Pulloxhill
Ampthill
Maulden
Millbrook
Lidlington
Marston Moretaine
Cranfield
Moulsoe
Salford
Hulcote
Brogborough
Ridgmont
Husborne Crawley
Aspley Guise
Woburn Sands
Aspley Heath
Woburn
Eversholt
Tingrith
Milton Bryan
Potsgrove
Battlesden
Hockliffe
Eggington
Tilsworth
Stanbridge
Billington
Leighton Buzzard
Linslade
Soulbury
Stoke Hammond
Great Brickhill
Little Brickhill
Bletchley
Newton Longville
Heath and Reach
Wing
Ledburn
Slapton
Cheddington
MILTON KEYNES
Woolstone
Broughton
Newport Pagnell
Gayhurst
Lathbury
Tyringham
Sherington
Chicheley
North Crawley
Olney
Emberton
Weston Underwood
Ravenstone
Lavendon
Cold Brayfield
Turvey
Stevington
Bromham
Clapham
BEDFORD
Kempston
Elstow
Wilstead
Cardington
Cople
Shefford
Stagsden
Astwood
Wootton
Houghton Conquest
Haynes
Pavenham
Oakley
Carlton
Harrold
Warrington
Ravensden
Renhold
Willington
Woburn Abbey

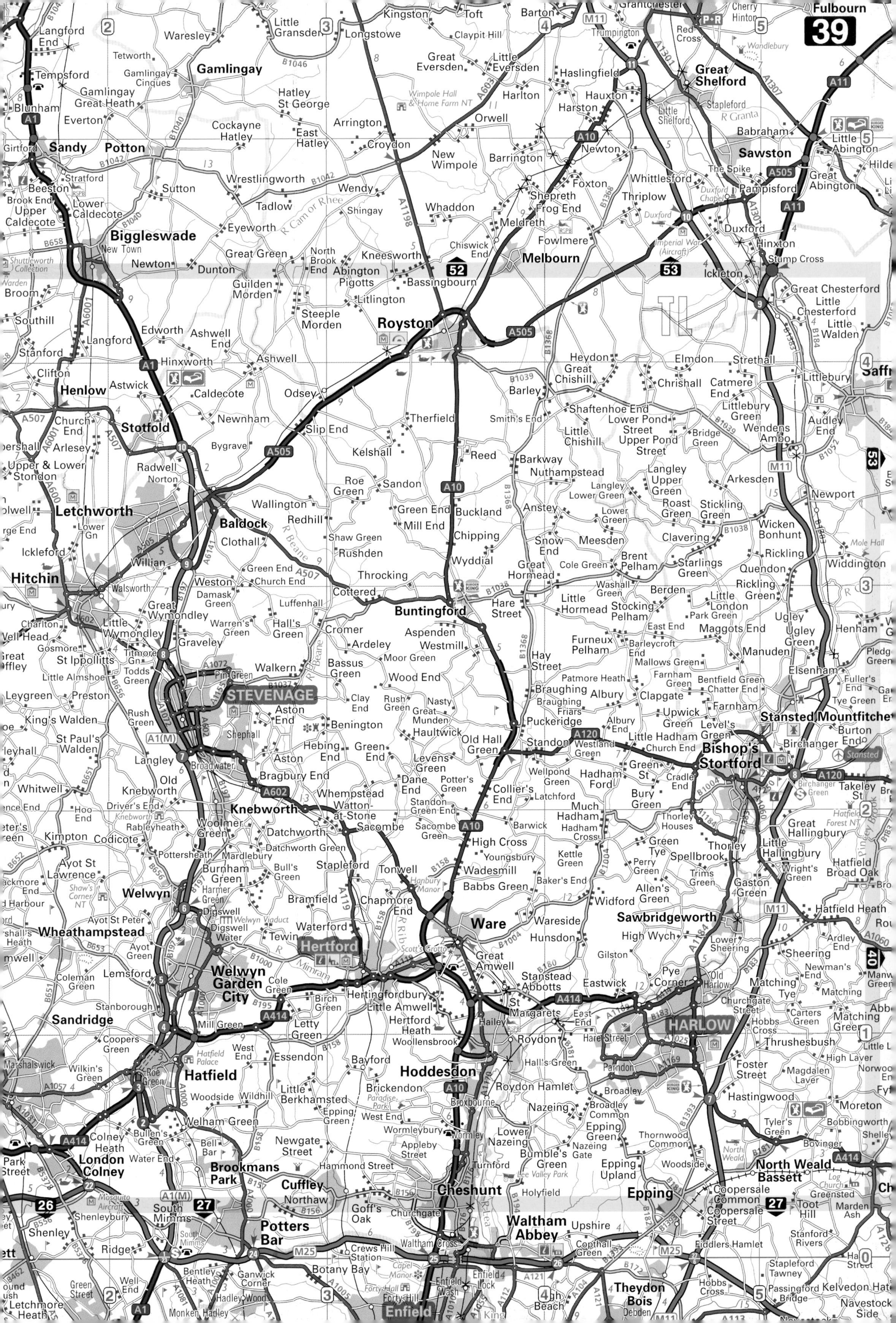
39
Fulbourn
Langford End
Waresley
Little Gransden
Longstowe
Kingston
Toft
Barton
Grantchester
Trumpington
Cherry Hinton
Red Cross
Wandlebury
Tetworth
Gamlingay
Gamlingay Cinques
Gamlingay Great Heath
Tempsford
Blunham
Everton
Hatley St George
Cockayne Hatley
East Hatley
Arrington
Croydon
Great Eversden
Little Eversden
Wimpole Hall & Home Farm NT
Haslingfield
Harlton
Hauxton
Harston
Orwell
Great Shelford
Little Shelford
Stapleford
Babraham
Little Abington
Sawston
Great Abington
Girtford
Sandy
Potton
Stratford
Beeston
Brook End
Upper Caldecote
Lower Caldecote
Sutton
Wrestlingworth
Wendy
Tadlow
Shingay
New Wimpole
Barrington
Newton
Foxton
Shepreth
Frog End
Whittlesford
Thriplow
The Spike
Pampisford
Duxford Chapel
Duxford
Whaddon
Meldreth
Fowlmere
Melbourn
Chiswick End
Imperial War (Aircraft)
Hinxton
Stump Cross
Ickleton
Biggleswade
New Town
Newton
Dunton
Eyeworth
Great Green
North Brook End
Abington Pigotts
Kneesworth
Bassingbourn
Shuttleworth Collection
Warden
Broom
Southill
Langford
Stanford
Guilden Morden
Steeple Morden
Litlington
Royston
Great Chesterford
Little Chesterford
Little Walden
TL
Edworth
Ashwell End
Ashwell
Hinxworth
Heydon
Great Chishill
Elmdon
Strethall
Chrishall
Catmere End
Littlebury
Clifton
Henlow
Astwick
Caldecote
Odsey
Barley
Shaftenhoe End
Little Chishill
Lower Pond Street
Upper Pond Street
Littlebury Green
Wendens Ambo
Audley End
Bridge Green
Church End
Stotfold
Arlesey
Newnham
Slip End
Therfield
Smith's End
Upper & Lower Stondon
Bygrave
Radwell
Norton
Kelshall
Reed
Barkway
Nuthampstead
Langley Upper Green
Langley Lower Green
Arkesden
Newport
Letchworth
Roe Green
Sandon
Green End
Buckland
Anstey
Lower Green
Roast Green
Stickling Green
Wicken Bonhunt
Lower Gn
Wallington
Baldock
Redhill
Mill End
Chipping
Snow End
Meesden
Clavering
Brent Pelham
Rickling
Ickleford
Clothall
Shaw Green
Rushden
Wyddial
Cole Green
Great Hormead
Starlings Green
Quendon
Mole Hall
Widdington
Hitchin
Willian
Walsworth
Green End
Church End
Weston
Throcking
Washall Green
Rickling Green
Damask Green
Luffenhall
Cottered
Hare Street
Little Hormead
Stocking Pelham
Berden
Little London
Park Green
Charlton
Great Wymondley
Little Wymondley
Warren's Green
Hall's Green
Buntingford
Aspenden
Westmill
Cromer
Ardeley
East End
Maggots End
Ugley
Ugley Green
Henham
Gosmore
Graveley
Furneux Pelham
Barleycroft End
Manuden
Pledgdon Green
St Ippollitts
Titmore Gn
Todds Green
Walkern
Bassus Green
Moor Green
Hay Street
Mallows Green
Elsenham
Little Almshoe
Pin Green
Wood End
Patmore Heath
Farnham Green
Bentfield Green
Chatter End
Fuller's End
Leygreen
Preston
STEVENAGE
Clay End
Rush Green
Nasty
Braughing
Braughing Friars
Albury
Clapgate
Tye Green
King's Walden
Rush Green
Aston End
Benington
Great Munden
Haultwick
Puckeridge
Albury End
Upwick Green
Farnham
Stansted Mountfitchet
St Paul's Walden
Shephall
Hebing End
Green End
Old Hall Green
Standon
Westland Green
Little Hadham
Level's Green
Burton End
Langley
Aston
Levens Green
Church End
Bishop's Stortford
Birchanger
Stansted
Broadwater
Old Knebworth
Bragbury End
Dane End
Potter's Green
Wellpond Green
Hadham Ford
Green St
Cradle End
Whitwell
Knebworth
Driver's End
Knebworth
Whempstead
Watton-at-Stone
Standon Green End
Collier's End
Latchford
Bury Green
Much Hadham
Hadham Cross
Thorley Houses
Takeley
Birchanger Green
Hoo End
Rableyheath
Woolmer Green
Datchworth
Sacombe
Sacombe Green
Barwick
Great Hallingbury
Hatfield Forest NT
Kimpton
Codicote
Datchworth Green
High Cross
Youngsbury
Green Tye
Thorley
Little Hallingbury
Ayot St Lawrence
Pottersheath
Mardlebury
Stapleford
Tonwell
Wadesmill
Kettle Green
Perry Green
Spellbrook
Trims Green
Wright's Green
Hatfield Broad Oak
Burnham Green
Bull's Green
Hanbury Manor
Babbs Green
Baker's End
Allen's Green
Gaston Green
Shaw's Corner NT
Harmer Green
Welwyn
Bramfield
Chapmore End
Widford
Hatfield Heath
Digswell
Welwyn Viaduct
Ware
Wareside
Sawbridgeworth
Ayot St Peter
Digswell Water
Waterford
Tewin
Hunsdon
High Wych
Ardley End
Wheathampstead
Ayot Green
Hertford
Scott's Grotto
Great Amwell
Lower Sheering
Sheering
Lemsford
Welwyn Garden City
Cole Green
Stanstead Abbotts
Gilston
Pye Corner
Old Harlow
Newman's End
Coleman Green
Hertingfordbury
Eastwick
Matching Tye
Matching
Stanborough
Birch Green
Little Amwell
St Margarets
Churchgate Street
Carters Green
Matching Green
Sandridge
Mill Green
Letty Green
Hertford Heath
Hailey
East End
HARLOW
Hobbs Cross
Thrushesbush
Coopers Green
West End
Woollensbrook
Roydon
Hare Street
Little Laver
High Laver
Marshalswick
Hatfield Palace
Hatfield
Essendon
Bayford
Hoddesdon
Hall's Green
Parndon
Foster Street
Magdalen Laver
Roe Green
Wilkin's Green
Woodside
Wildhill
Little Berkhamsted
Brickendon
Paradise Park
Broxbourne
Roydon Hamlet
Broadley
Hastingwood
Moreton
Epping Green
West End
Nazeing
Broadley Common
Tyler's Green
Bobbingworth
Colney Heath
Bullen's Green
Welham Green
Wormleybury
Wormley
Lower Nazeing
Epping Green
Thornwood Common
Bovinger
Newgate Street
Appleby Street
Nazeing Gate
Bumble's Green
Epping Upland
Woodside
North Weald
London Colney
Water End
Bell Bar
Brookmans Park
Hammond Street
Turnford
Lee Valley Park
North Weald Bassett
Park Street
Cuffley
Northaw
Cheshunt
Holyfield
Epping
Coopersale Common
Coopersale Street
Greensted
Toot Hill
Marden Ash
Mosquito Aircraft
South Mimms
Goff's Oak
Churchgate
Shenleybury
Potters Bar
Waltham Abbey
Upshire
Shenley
South Mimms
Crews Hill Station
Waltham Cross
Copthall Green
Fiddlers Hamlet
Stanford Rivers
Ridge
Botany Bay
Capel Manor
Enfield Lock
Enfield Wash
Stapleford Tawney
Bentley Heath
Ganwick Corner
Forty Hall
Forty Hill
Hobbs Cross
Theydon Bois
Passingford Bridge
Kelvedon Hatch
Navestock Side
Green Street
Well End
Hadley Wood
Monken Hadley
Enfield
Debden
Letchmore Heath
A1
A1(M)
A505
A10
A120
A414
A602
A11
A1307
A1301
A603
B1042
B1040
B1046
B1039
B1038
B1368
B158
B1000
B197
B1004
B1383
A1184
A1060
A1170
A1169
A1025
M11
M25
A1057
A1081
A6141
A507
A600
A6001
A1072
A1155
A119
B1037
B656
B651
B653
B195
B156
B157
B181
B183
B1393
B172
A121
A104
A112
A1005
A1000
B5378
B556
B462
R Cam or Rhee
R Granta
R Beane
R Rib
R Mimram
52
53
27
26
40
2
3
4
5

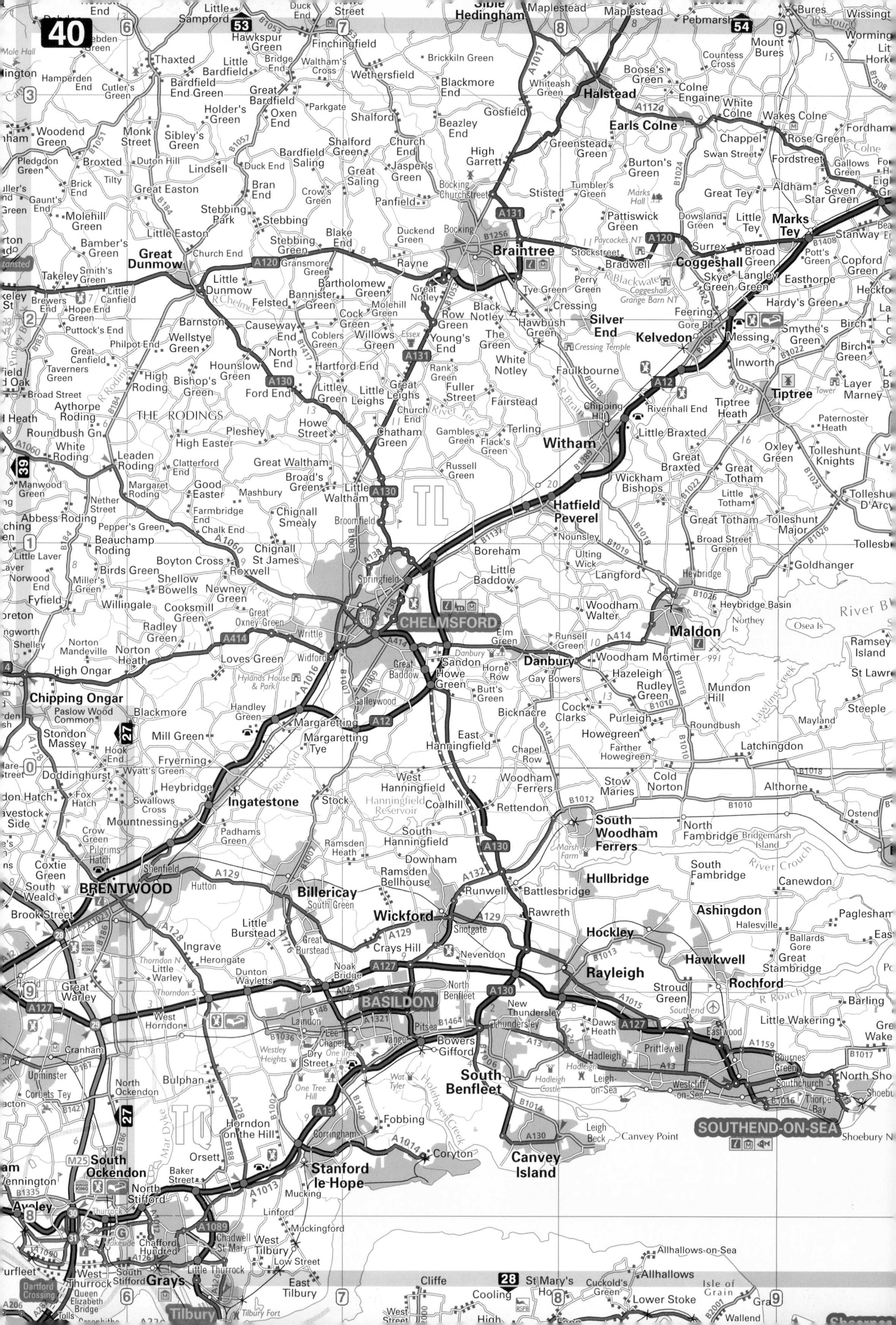
Thaxted
Great Dunmow
Braintree
Halstead
Earls Colne
Coggeshall
Kelvedon
Witham
Tiptree
Hatfield Peverel
Maldon
CHELMSFORD
Danbury
Ingatestone
Chipping Ongar
BRENTWOOD
Billericay
Wickford
BASILDON
South Woodham Ferrers
Hullbridge
Rayleigh
Rochford
SOUTHEND-ON-SEA
South Benfleet
Canvey Island
Stanford le Hope
Grays
Tilbury
South Ockendon
Marks Tey
Silver End
THE RODINGS
TL
TQ

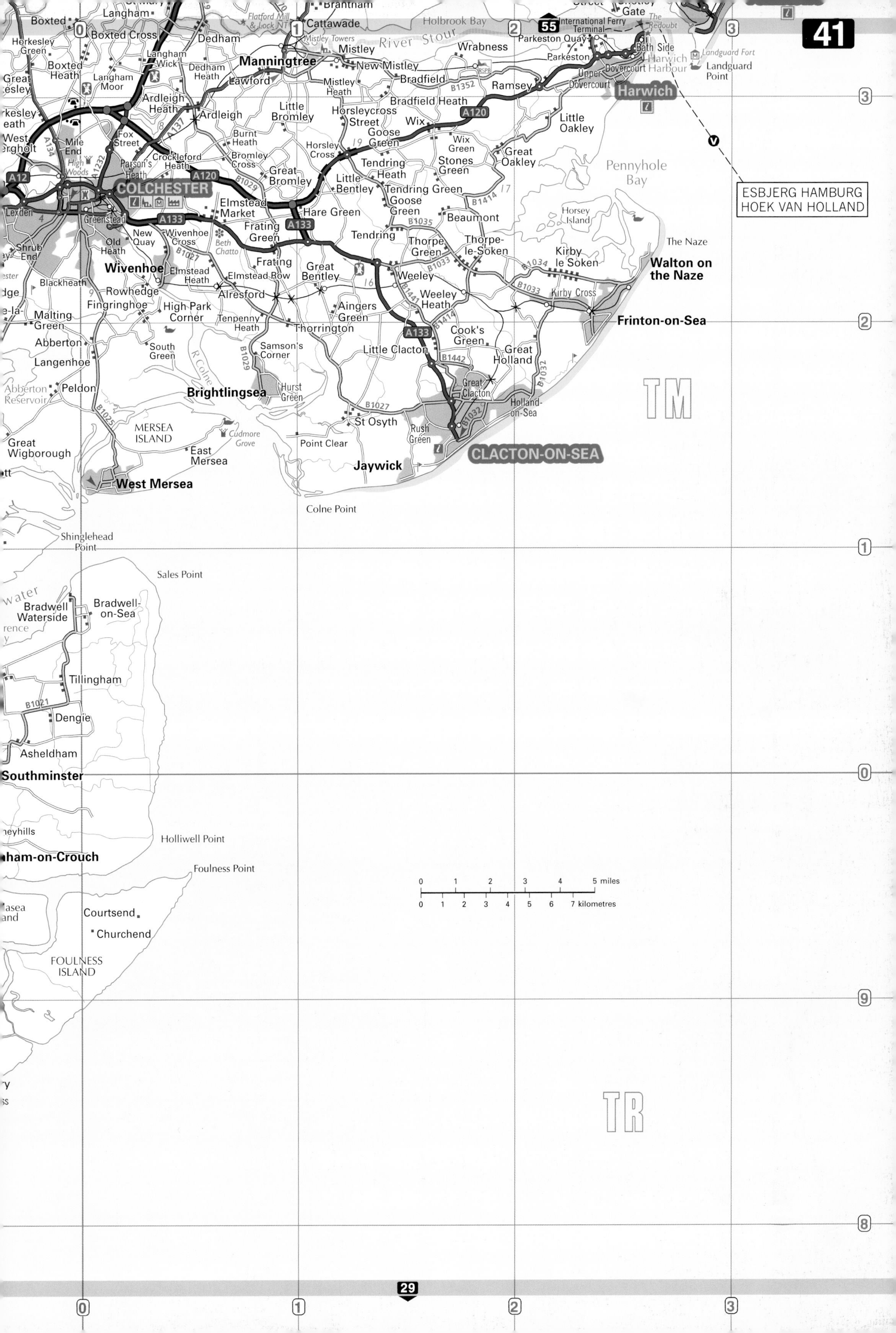
Langham
Boxted
Boxted Cross
Dedham
Cattawade
Holbrook Bay
International Ferry Terminal
Gate
The Redoubt
Horkesley Green
Boxted Heath
Langham Wick
Dedham Heath
Manningtree
Mistley
River Stour
Wrabness
Parkeston Quay
Parkeston
Bath Side
Harwich Harbour
Landguard Fort
Landguard Point
Langham Moor
Lawford
New Mistley
Mistley Heath
Bradfield
Ramsey
Upper Dovercourt
Dovercourt
Harwich
Ardleigh Heath
Ardleigh
Little Bromley
Horsleycross Street
Bradfield Heath
Wix
Little Oakley
Fox Street
Mile End
High Woods
Burnt Heath
Bromley Cross
Crockleford Heath
Horsley Cross
Goose Green
Wix Green
Stones Green
Great Oakley
Pennyhole Bay
Parson's Heath
COLCHESTER
Great Bromley
Tendring Heath
Little Bentley
Tendring Green
Goose Green
ESBJERG HAMBURG
HOEK VAN HOLLAND
Lexden
Greenstead
Elmstead Market
Hare Green
Beaumont
Horsey Island
Old Heath
New Quay
Wivenhoe Cross
Beth Chatto
Frating Green
Tendring
Thorpe Green
Thorpe-le-Soken
The Naze
Kirby le Soken
Walton on the Naze
Shrub End
Wivenhoe
Elmstead Heath
Frating
Great Bentley
Weeley
Blackheath
Elmstead Row
Alresford
Weeley Heath
Kirby Cross
Rowhedge
Fingringhoe
High Park Corner
Tenpenny Heath
Aingers Green
Thorrington
Frinton-on-Sea
Malting Green
Abberton
South Green
Samson's Corner
Little Clacton
Cook's Green
Great Holland
Langenhoe
R Colne
Great Clacton
Abberton Reservoir
Peldon
Brightlingsea
Hurst Green
Holland-on-Sea
TM
MERSEA ISLAND
Cudmore Grove
St Osyth
Rush Green
Great Wigborough
East Mersea
Point Clear
CLACTON-ON-SEA
Jaywick
West Mersea
Colne Point
Shinglehead Point
Sales Point
Bradwell Waterside
Bradwell-on-Sea
Tillingham
Dengie
Asheldham
Southminster
Holliwell Point
ham-on-Crouch
Foulness Point
Courtsend
Churchend
FOULNESS ISLAND
TR
A12
A134
A1232
A137
A120
A133
B1029
B1027
B1025
B1352
B1035
B1414
B1033
B1034
B1441
B1442
B1032
B1021
55
0 1 2 3 4 5 miles
0 1 2 3 4 5 6 7 kilometres

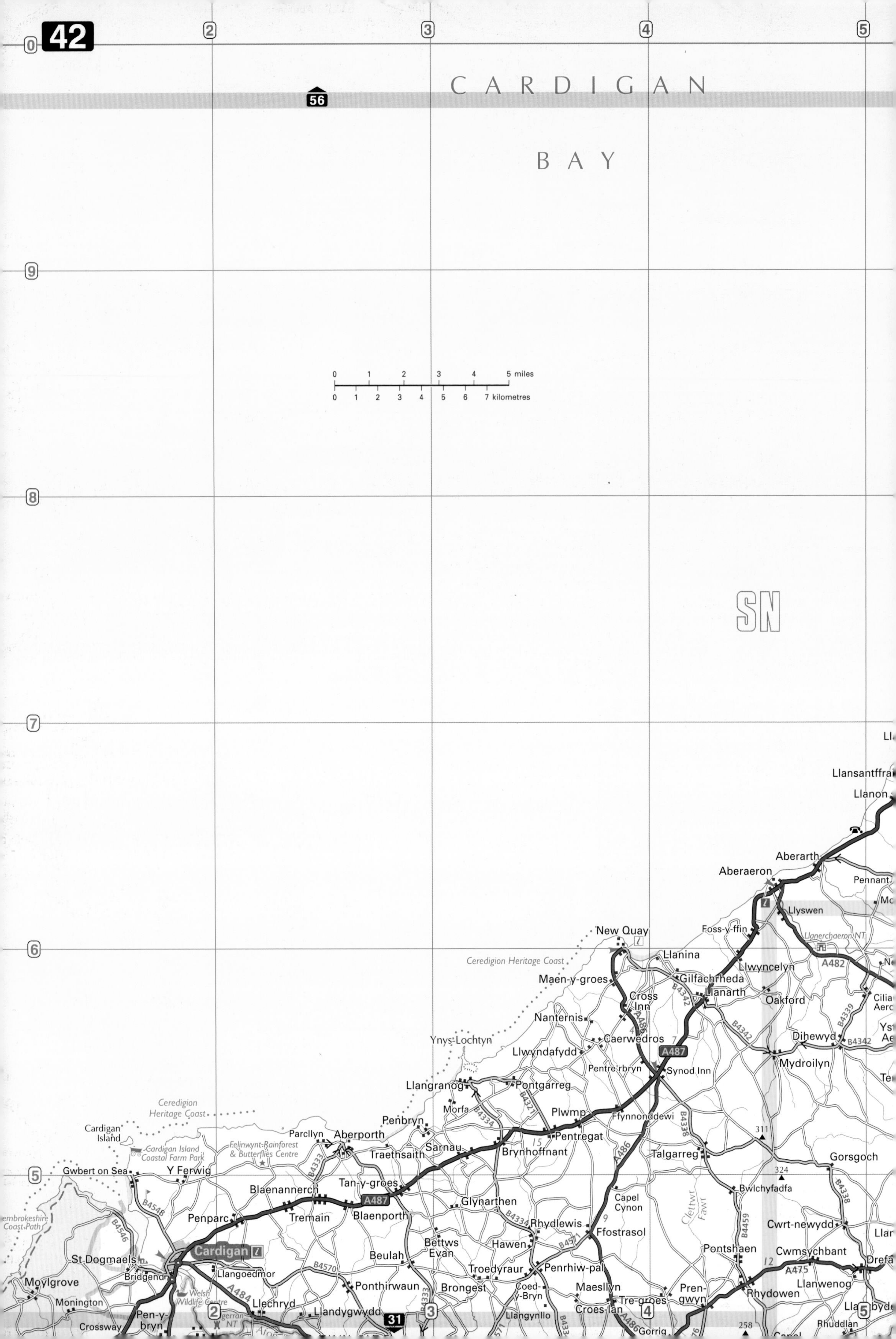

CARDIGAN

BAY

SN

0 1 2 3 4 5 miles

0 1 2 3 4 5 6 7 kilometres

Llansantffrai

Llanon

Aberarth

Aberaeron

Pennant

Llyswen

New Quay

Foss-y-ffin

Mo

Ceredigion Heritage Coast

Llanerchaeron NT

Llanina

A482

Ne

Llwyncelyn

Maen-y-groes

Gilfachrheda

Cross
Inn

Llanarth

Oakford

Cilia
Aero

Nanternis

Caerwedros

7

Dihewyd

Mydroilyn

Te

Ynys-Lochtyn

Llwyndafydd

Pentre'rbryn

Synod Inn

A487

Llangranog

Pontgarreg

Morfa

Plwmp

Ffynnonddewi

311

Penbryn

Pentregat

15

Flostrasol

Talgarreg

Gorsgoch

Sarnau

Brynhoffnant

Parcllyn

Aberporth

Traethsaith

324

Bwlchyfadfa

Cardigan
Island

Felinwynt Rainforest
& Butterflies Centre

Cardigan Island
Coastal Farm Park

Tan-y-groes

B4338

Gwbert on Sea

Y Ferwig

Blaenannerch

A487

Glynarthen

Capel
Cynon

Ffostrasol

Cwrt-newydd

Penparc

Tremain

Blaenporth

Rhydlewis

9

B4459

Llar

embrokeshire
Coast Path

Pembrokeshire
Coast Path

St Dogmaels

Cardigan

Beulah

Bettws
Evan

Hawen

Cwmsychbant

Drefa

Moylgrove

Bridgend

Llangoedmor

Troedyraur

Penrhiw-pal

Maesllyn

Prengwyn

Rhydowen

Llanwenog

Lla

Monington

Welsh
Wildlife
Centre

Llechryd

Ponthirwaun

Brongest

Coed-
y-Bryn

Tre-groes

258

Rhuddlan

Crossway

Pen-y-
bryn

Llandygwydd

Llangynllo

Croes-lan

Gorrig

Cilla

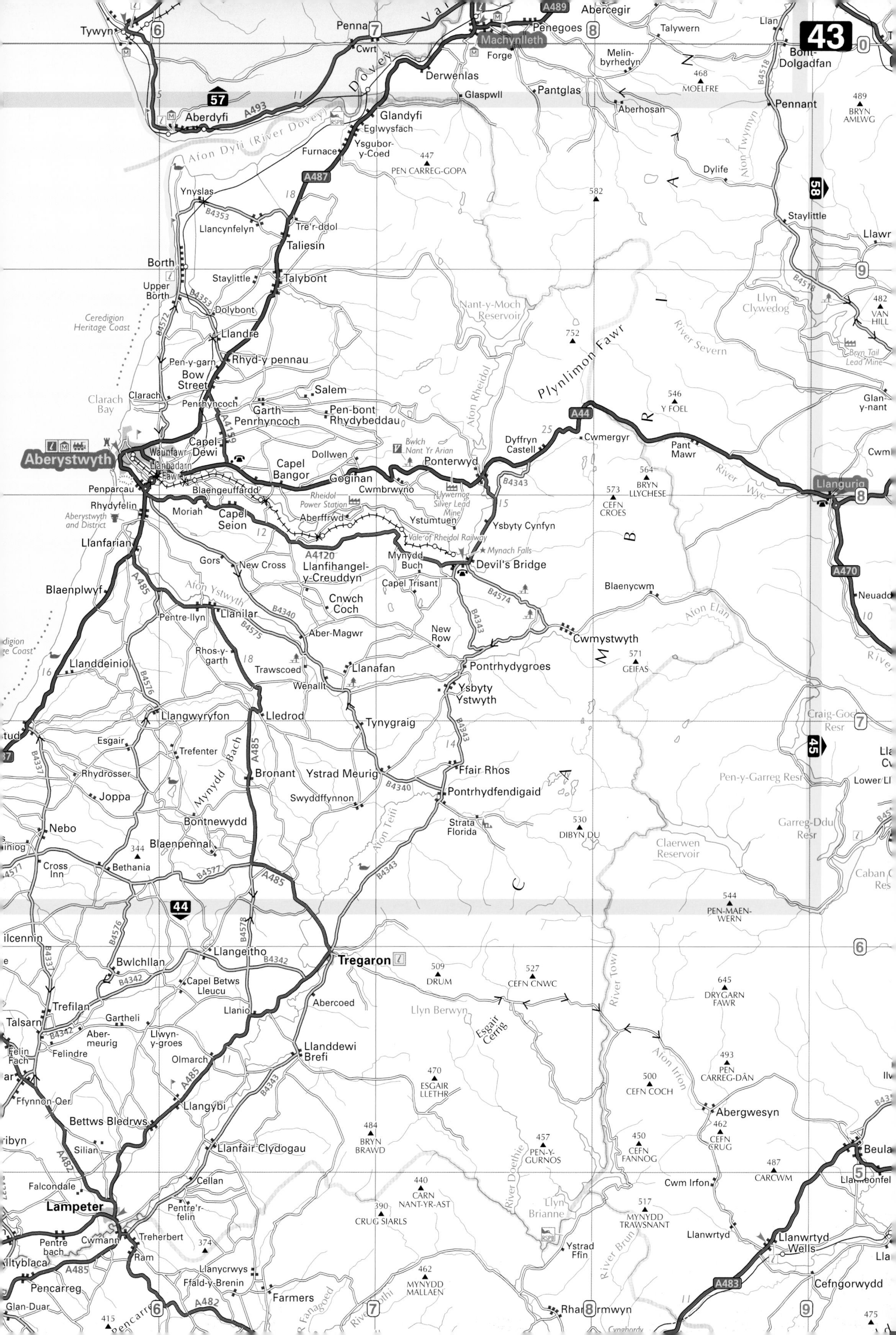

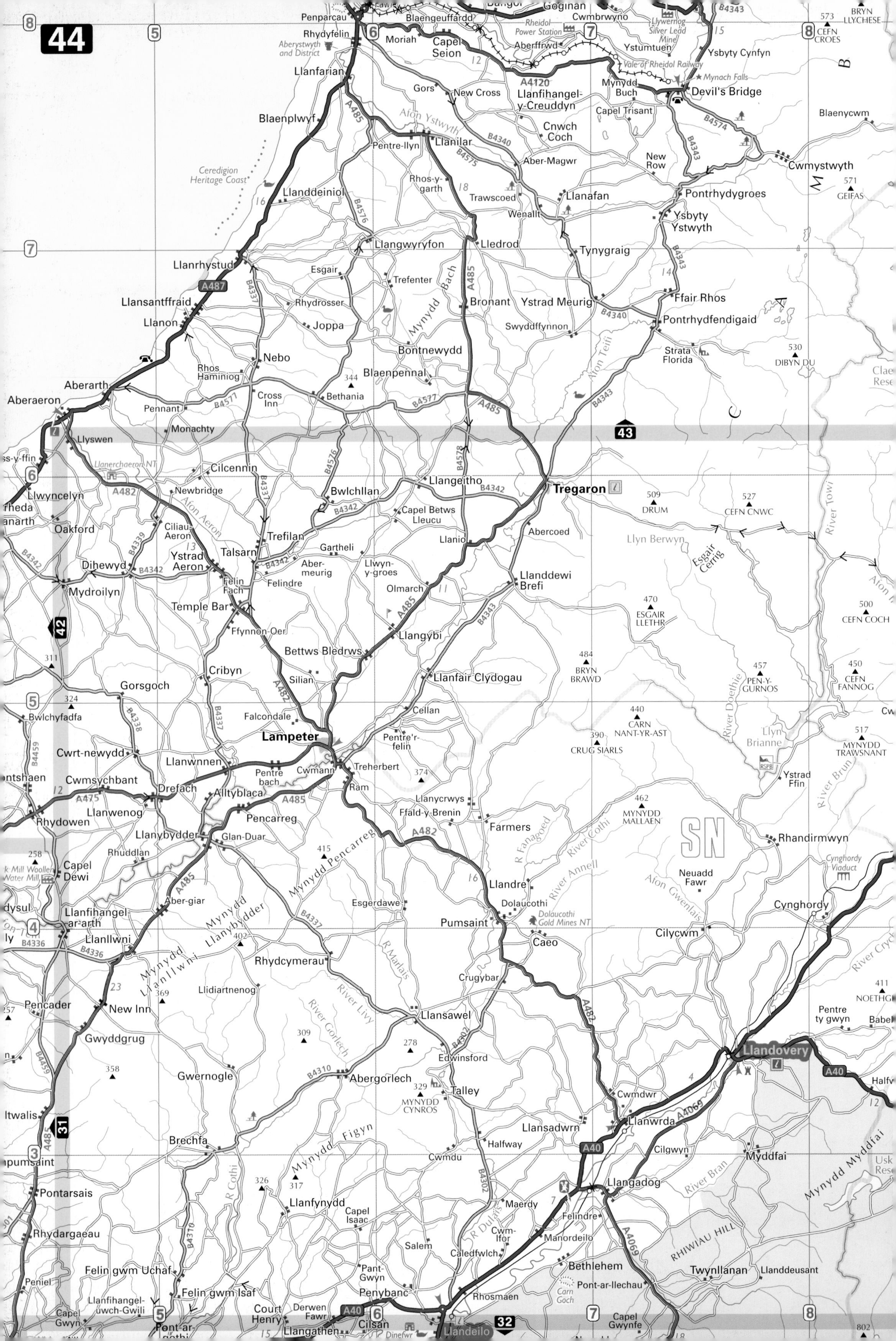

Penparcau
Rhydyfelin
Aberystwyth and District
Blaengeuffardd
Moriah
Capel Seion
Rheidol Power Station
Aberffrwd
Goginan
Cwmbrwyno
Llywernog Silver Lead Mine
Ystumtuen
Vale of Rheidol Railway
Mynach Falls
Ysbyty Cynfyn
B4343
CEFN CROES
BRYN LLYCHESE
573
Llanfarian
Gors
New Cross
A4120
Llanfihangel-y-Creuddyn
Mynydd Buch
Devil's Bridge
Capel Trisant
Blaenplwyf
A485
Afon Ystwyth
Cnwch Coch
B4574
Blaenycwm
Pentre-llyn
Llanilar
B4340
B4575
Aber-Magwr
New Row
Cwmystwyth
Ceredigion Heritage Coast
Rhos-y-garth
Trawscoed
Llanafan
Pontrhydygroes
571
GEIFAS
Llanddeiniol
B4576
Wenallt
Ysbyty Ystwyth
Llangwyryfon
Lledrod
Tynygraig
Llanrhystud
Esgair
Trefenter
Mynydd Bach
B4343
A487
B4337
Llansantffraid
Rhydrosser
Bronant
Ystrad Meurig
Ffair Rhos
Llanon
Joppa
B4340
Pontrhydfendigaid
Swyddffynnon
Bontnewydd
Strata Florida
530
DIBYN DU
Nebo
Rhos Haminiog
Afon Teifi
Aberarth
344
Blaenpennal
Cross Inn
Bethania
Aberaeron
Pennant
B4571
B4577
A485
B4343
43
Monachty
Llyswen
Llanerchaeron NT
Cilcennin
B4576
B4578
B4337
Llangeitho
Tregaron
B4342
509
DRUM
527
CEFN CNWC
Llwyncelyn
A482
Newbridge
Bwlchllan
Oakford
Ciliau-Aeron
Afon Aeron
B4342
Capel Betws Lleucu
Trefilan
Abercoed
Llyn Berwyn
Esgair Cerrig
River Towi
B4339
Ystrad Aeron
Talsarn
Llanio
Dihewyd
B4342
B4342
Gartheli
Aber-meurig
Llwyn-y-groes
Llanddewi Brefi
Felin Fach
Felindre
Mydroilyn
Olmarch
470
ESGAIR LLETHR
500
CEFN COCH
Temple Bar
A485
B4343
42
Ffynnon-Oer
Llangybi
484
BRYN BRAWD
457
PEN-Y-GURNOS
450
CEFN FANNOG
Bettws Bledrws
311
Cribyn
A482
Silian
Llanfair Clydogau
River Doethie
Gorsgoch
324
Bwlchyfadfa
B4338
B4337
Falcondale
Cellan
440
CARN NANT-YR-AST
517
MYNYDD TRAWSNANT
Lampeter
Pentre'r-felin
390
CRUG SIARLS
Llyn Brianne
Cwrt-newydd
B4459
Llanwnnen
Treherbert
RSPB
Pentre bach
Cwmann
374
Ystrad Ffin
Cwmsychbant
Drefach
Ram
Llanycrwys
462
MYNYDD MALLAEN
River Brun
A475
Alltyblaca
A485
Ffald-y-Brenin
Rhydowen
Llanwenog
Pencarreg
Farmers
R Fanagoed
River Cothi
SN
Rhandirmwyn
Llanybydder
Glan-Duar
A482
258
Rhuddlan
415
Mynydd Pencarreg
River Annell
Cynghordy Viaduct
Capel Dewi
Neuadd Fawr
A485
Afon Gwenlais
Llanfihangel-ar-arth
Aber-giar
Mynydd Llanybydder
Esgerdawe
Llandre
Dolaucothi
Dolaucothi Gold Mines NT
Cynghordy
B4337
Pumsaint
Cilycwm
Llanllwni
B4336
402
R Marlais
Caeo
Mynydd Llanllwni
Rhydcymerau
River Crychan
River Livy
Crugybar
411
NOETHGEN
369
Llidiartnenog
A482
Pencader
New Inn
River Gorlech
Llansawel
Pentre ty gwyn
309
278
B4302
Gwyddgrug
Edwinsford
Llandovery
358
B4310
Gwernogle
Abergorlech
329
MYNYDD CYNROS
Talley
A40
B4459
Cwmdwr
A4069
A485
31
Brechfa
Llansadwrn
Llanwrda
Halfway
A40
Cilgwyn
Myddfai
Mynydd Figyn
Mynydd Myddfai
Cwmdu
326
317
Llangadog
Pontarsais
R Cothi
B4302
River Bran
Llanfynydd
Maerdy
Felindre
Capel Isaac
R Dulais
Cwm-Ifor
Manordeilo
A4069
RHIWIAU HILL
Rhydargaeau
B4310
Salem
Caledfwlch
Bethlehem
Felin gwm Uchaf
Peniel
Pant-Gwyn
Twynllanan
Llanddeusant
Pont-ar-llechau
Carn Goch
Llanfihangel-uwch-Gwili
Felin gwm Isaf
Penybanc
Rhosmaen
Capel Gwyn
Court Henry
Derwen Fawr
A40
Cilsan
32
Llandeilo
Dinefwr
Llangathen
Capel Gwynfe
802

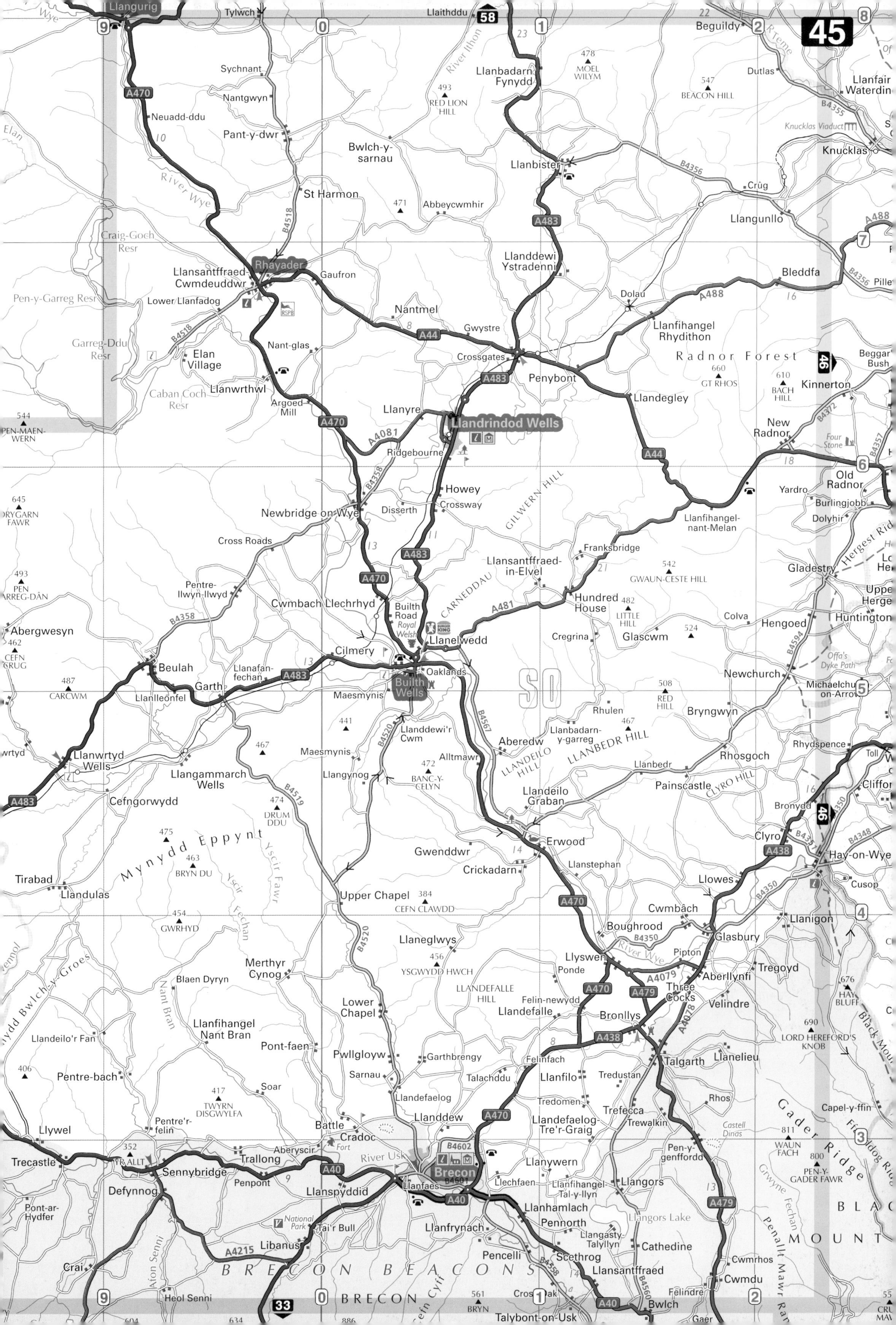

45
Llangurig
Tylwch
Llaithddu
58
Beguildy
R. Teme
Wye
Sychnant
Nantgwyn
Neuadd-ddu
Pant-y-dwr
A470
River Ithon
Llanbadarn Fynydd
478 MOEL WILYM
493 RED LION HILL
547 BEACON HILL
Dutlas
Llanfair Waterdine
B4355
Knucklas Viaduct
Knucklas
Elan
Bwlch-y-sarnau
Llanbister
B4356
Crûg
River Wye
St Harmon
471
Abbeycwmhir
A483
Llangunllo
A488
Craig-Goch Resr
B4518
Llansantffraed-Cwmdeuddwr
Rhayader
Gaufron
Llanddewi Ystradenni
Bleddfa
Pilleth
Pen-y-Garreg Resr
Lower Llanfadog
RSPB
Dolau
Nantmel
Llanfihangel Rhydithon
Garreg-Ddu Resr
Elan Village
Nant-glas
A44
Gwystre
Crossgates
Radnor Forest
660 GT RHOS
610 BACH HILL
46
Beggar's Bush
Kinnerton
Caban Coch Resr
Llanwrthwl
Penybont
Llandegley
Argoed Mill
Llanyre
Llandrindod Wells
544 PEN-MAEN-WERN
A4081
Ridgebourne
New Radnor
Four Stones
B4372
B4357
Old Radnor
645 DRYGARN FAWR
Howey
Crossway
GILWERN HILL
Yardro
Burlingjobb
Dolyhir
Newbridge on Wye
Disserth
B4358
Llanfihangel-nant-Melan
Hergest Ridge
Cross Roads
Franksbridge
542 GWAUN-CESTE HILL
Llansantffraed-in-Elvel
Gladestry
493 PEN GARREG-DÂN
Pentre-llwyn-llwyd
CARNEDDAU
Hundred House
482 LITTLE HILL
Cwmbach Llechrhyd
Builth Road
Royal Welsh
A481
Colva
Hengoed
Huntington
Abergwesyn
462 CEFN CRUG
Cregrina
Glascwm
524
Llanelwedd
Cilmery
B4594
Offa's Dyke Path
Beulah
Llanafan-fechan
Oakland
Newchurch
487 CARCWM
Garth
Builth Wells
SO
Michaelchurch-on-Arrow
Llanlleonfel
Maesmynis
508 RED HILL
Rhulen
Bryngwyn
441
Llanddewi'r Cwm
B4567
467
Llanbadarn-y-garreg
Aberedw
LLANBEDR HILL
Rhydspence
Llanwrtyd Wells
467
Maesmynis
Alltmawr
LLANDEILO HILL
Llanbedr
Rhosgoch
Llangammarch Wells
Llangynog
472 BANC-Y-CELYN
Painscastle
CLYRO HILL
Clifford
B4520
B4519
Llandeilo Graban
Bronydd
Cefngorwydd
474 DRUM DDU
B4350
475
Mynydd Eppynt
Erwood
Clyro
B4348
463 BRYN DU
Ysgir Fawr
Gwenddwr
Crickadarn
Llanstephan
A438
Hay-on-Wye
Tirabad
Llandulas
Ysgir Fechan
Llowes
Cusop
Upper Chapel
384 CEFN CLAWDD
Cwmbâch
454 GWRHYD
Boughrood
Llanigon
Llaneglwys
Glasbury
Llyswen
Pipton
456 YSGWYDD HWCH
Ponde
River Wye
Tregoyd
Merthyr Cynog
A4079
Aberllynfi
Blaen Dyryn
Nant Bran
LLANDEFALLE HILL
A470
A479
Three Cocks
676 HAY BLUFF
Lower Chapel
Felin-newydd
Velindre
Llanfihangel Nant Bran
Llandefalle
Bronllys
A4078
Llandeilo'r Fan
Pont-faen
A438
690 LORD HEREFORD'S KNOB
Pwllgloyw
Garthbrengy
Felinfach
Talgarth
Llanelieu
406
Pentre-bach
Sarnau
Talachddu
Llanfilo
Tredustan
Soar
417 TWYRN DISGWYLFA
Llandefaelog
Tredomen
Rhos
Llanddew
Trefecca
Trewalkin
Gader Ridge
Capel-y-ffin
Llywel
Pentre'r-felin
Battle
Llandefaelog-Tre'r-Graig
Castell Dinas
Cradoc
Fort
811 WAUN FACH
352 YR ALLT
Aberyscir
Pen-y-genfforddd
800 PEN-Y-GADER FAWR
Trecastle
Trallong
River Usk
B4602
Llanywern
Sennybridge
A40
Brecon
Grwyne Fechan
Defynnog
Penpont
Llanfaes
B4601
Llechfaen
Llanfihangel-Tal-y-llyn
Llangors
Llanspyddid
Pont-ar-Hydfer
A40
Llanhamlach
Llangors Lake
BLACK MOUNTAINS
National Park
Tai'r Bull
Llanfrynach
Pennorth
Llangasty-Talyllyn
Cathedine
A4215
Libanus
Afon Senni
Pencelli
Scethrog
Cwmrhos
Crai
BRECON BEACONS
B4558
Llansantffraed
Cwmdu
B4560
Felindre
Heol Senni
33
BRECON
Cefn Cyff
561 BRYN
Cross Oak
A40
Bwlch
Talybont-on-Usk
Gaer

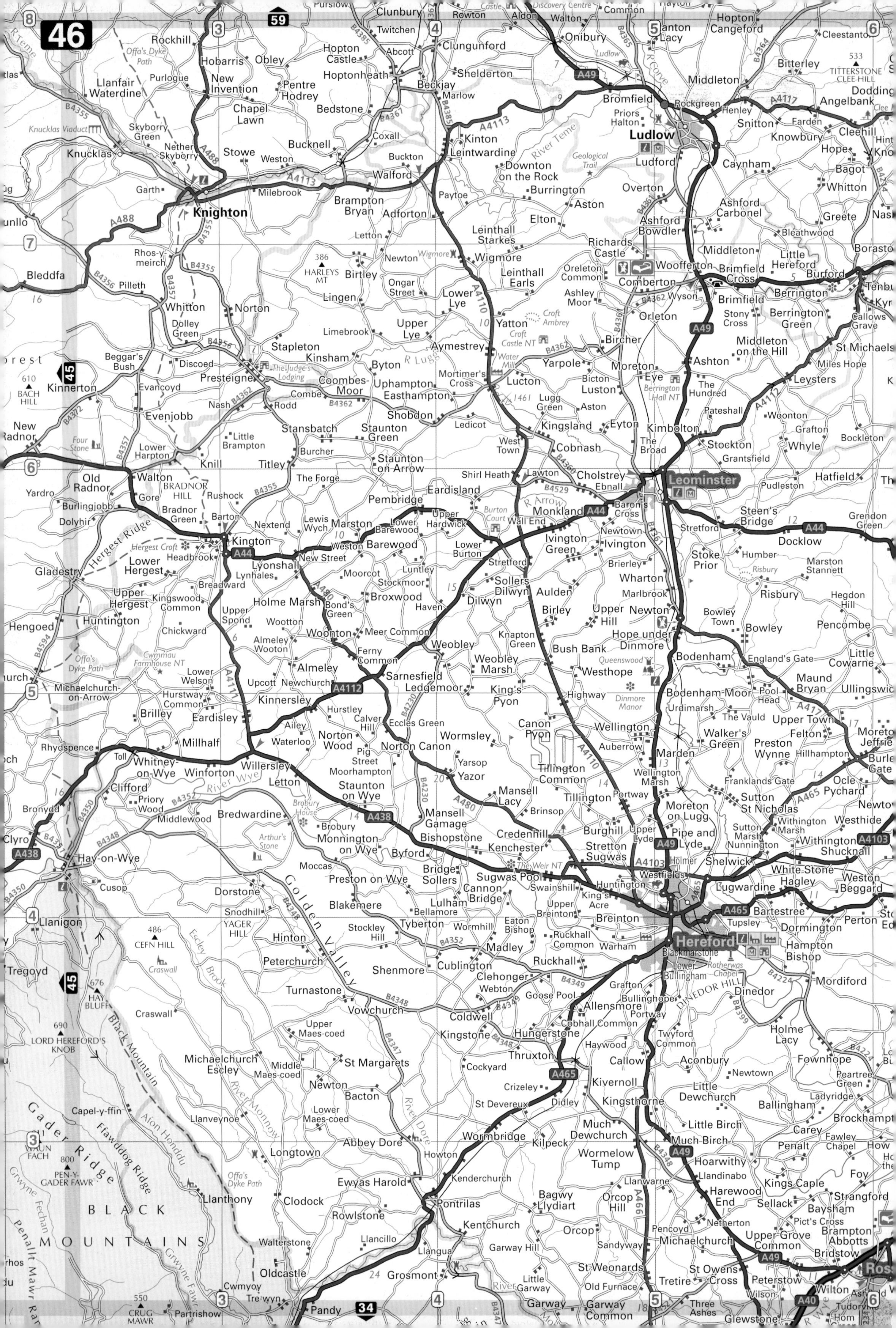
59
Clunbury
Twitchen
Rowton
Aldon
Walton
Onibury
Stanton Lacy
Hopton Cangeford
Cleestanton
Rockhill
Offa's Dyke Path
Hobarris
Obley
Hopton Castle
Abcott
Clungunford
Ludlow
Bitterley
533 TITTERSTONE CLEE HILL
Llanfair Waterdine
Purlogue
New Invention
Pentre Hodrey
Hoptonheath
Shelderton
Middleton
Dodding
Beckjay
Marlow
Bromfield
Priors Halton
Rockgreen
Henley
Angelbank
Chapel Lawn
Bedstone
Snitton
Farden
Cleehill
Knucklas Viaduct
Skyborry Green
Coxall
Kinton
Ludlow
Knowbury
Hope
Nether Skyborry
Bucknell
Leintwardine
River Teme
Geological Trail
Knucklas
Stowe
Weston
Buckton
Downton on the Rock
Ludford
Caynham
Bagot
Garth
Walford
Whitton
Knighton
Milebrook
Burrington
Overton
Brampton Bryan
Paytoe
Aston
Ashford Carbonel
Adforton
Elton
Ashford Bowdler
Greete
Bleathwood
Letton
Leinthall Starkes
Richards Castle
Middleton
Little Hereford
Rhos-y-meirch
386 HARLEYS MT
Newton
Wigmore
Wigmore
Bleddfa
Birtley
Ongar Street
Leinthall Earls
Oreleton Common
Woofferton
Brimfield Cross
Burford
Pilleth
Ashley Moor
Comberton
Wyson
Brimfield
Berrington
Whitton
Norton
Lingen
Lower Lye
Croft Ambrey
Orleton
Stony Cross
Berrington Green
Dolley Green
Limebrook
Upper Lye
Yatton
Croft Castle NT
Callows Grave
Stapleton
Aymestrey
Bircher
Middleton on the Hill
St Michaels
Forest
Beggar's Bush
Discoed
Kinsham
R Lugg
Water Mill
Yarpole
Moreton
Ashton
Miles Hope
610 BACH HILL
Kinnerton
Presteigne
The Judge's Lodging
Coombes-Moor
Byton
Mortimer's Cross
Lucton
Bicton
Eye
Leysters
Evancoyd
Uphampton
Luston
Berrington Hall NT
The Hundred
Combe
Easthampton
1461
Lugg Green
Aston
Pateshall
Nash
Rodd
Shobdon
Evenjobb
Woonton
New Radnor
Little Brampton
Stansbatch
Staunton Green
Ledicot
Kingsland
Eyton
Kimbolton
Grafton
Four Stone
Lower Harpton
West Town
The Broad
Whyle
Bockleton
Stockton
Burcher
Cobnash
Grantsfield
Knill
Titley
Staunton on Arrow
Old Radnor
Walton
Shirl Heath
Lawton
Cholstrey
Leominster
Hatfield
BRADNOR HILL
The Forge
Ebnall
Yardro
Gore
Rushock
Eardisland
Pudleston
Burlingjobb
Bradnor Green
Pembridge
Upper Hardwick
Burton Court
R Arrow
Monkland
Baron's Cross
Steen's Bridge
Grendon Green
Dolyhir
Barton
Nextend
Lewis Wych
Marston
Lower Barewood
Wall End
Stretford
Hergest Ridge
Hergest Croft
Kington
Weston
Barewood
Lower Burton
Ivington Green
Newtown
Ivington
Docklow
Headbrook
New Street
Stoke Prior
Humber
Marston Stannett
Lower Hergest
Lyonshall
Lynhales
Luntley
Stretford
Brierley
Wharton
Risbury
Gladestry
Moorcot
Breadward
Stockmoor
Sollers Dilwyn
Risbury
Upper Hergest
Kingswood Common
Holme Marsh
Bond's Green
Broxwood
Dilwyn
Aulden
Marlbrook
Hegdon Hill
Huntington
Upper Spond
Haven
Birley
Upper Hill
Newton
Bowley Town
Pencombe
Hengoed
Chickward
Wootton
Bowley
Almeley Wooton
Woonton
Meer Common
Knapton Green
Hope under Dinmore
Offa's Dyke Path
Cwmmau Farmhouse NT
Ferny Common
Weobley
Bush Bank
Bodenham
England's Gate
Little Cowarne
Lower Welson
Almeley
Weobley Marsh
Westhope
Queenswood
Maund Bryan
Michaelchurch-on-Arrow
Upcott
Newchurch
Sarnesfield
Ledgemoor
King's Pyon
Dinmore Manor
Bodenham Moor
Pool Head
Ullingswick
Hurstway Common
Kinnersley
Hurstley
Highway
Urdimarsh
Brilley
Eardisley
Calver Hill
Eccles Green
Canon Pyon
Wellington
The Vauld
Upper Town
Ailey
Norton Wood
Wormsley
Walker's Green
Felton
Moreton Jeffries
Rhydspence
Millhalf
Waterloo
Pig Street
Norton Canon
SO
Auberrow
Preston Wynne
Toll
Whitney-on-Wye
Winforton
Willersley
Moorhampton
Yarsop
Marden
Hillhampton
Burley Gate
Letton
Yazor
Tillington Common
Wellington Marsh
Clifford
River Wye
Staunton on Wye
Frankland's Gate
Ocle Pychard
Priory Wood
Mansell Lacy
Tillington
Portway
Sutton St Nicholas
Bronydd
Middlewood
Bredwardine
Brobury House
Mansell Gamage
Brinsop
Moreton on Lugg
Withington Marsh
Westhide
Brobury
Arthur's Stone
Monnington on Wye
Bishopstone
Credenhill
Burghill
Upper Lyde
Pipe and Lyde
Sutton Marsh
Nunnington
Withington
Clyro
Kenchester
Stretton Sugwas
Shucknall
Hay-on-Wye
Byford
Holmer
Shelwick
Moccas
Bridge Sollers
The Weir NT
Sugwas Pool
Westfields
White Stone
Weston Beggard
Cusop
Preston on Wye
Swainshill
Huntington
Lugwardine
Hagley
Golden Valley
Dorstone
Cannon Bridge
King's Acre
Upper Breinton
Bartestree
Blakemere
Lulham
Breinton
Tupsley
Snodhill
Bellamore
Dormington
Perton
Llanigon
YAGER HILL
Stockley Hill
Tyberton
Wormhill
Eaton Bishop
Ruckhall Common
Hereford
Hampton Bishop
486 CEFN HILL
Hinton
Madley
Warham
Blackmarstone
Craswall
Peterchurch
Cublington
Ruckhall
Lower Bullingham
Rotherwas Chapel
Tregoyd
Escley Brook
Shenmore
Clehonger
Mordiford
676 HAY BLUFF
Turnastone
Webton
Goose Pool
Grafton
Bullinghope
DINEDOR HILL
Dinedor
Vowchurch
Allensmore
Portway
Black Mountain
Craswall
Coldwell
Cobhall Common
Holme Lacy
Upper Maes-coed
690 LORD HEREFORD'S KNOB
Kingstone
Hungerstone
Twyford Common
Haywood
Fownhope
Michaelchurch Escley
Middle Maes-coed
St Margarets
Thruxton
Callow
Aconbury
Cockyard
Newtown
Peartree Green
Kivernoll
Newton
Crizeley
Little Dewchurch
Ladyridge
Bacton
Gader Ridge
Capel-y-ffin
Afon Honddu
St Devereux
Didley
Kingsthorne
Ballingham
Lower Maes-coed
Brockhampton
Llanveynoe
River Monnow
River Dore
Much Dewchurch
Little Birch
Carey
Wormbridge
Kilpeck
Fawley Chapel
WAUN FACH
Abbey Dore
Much Birch
Penalt
Longtown
Howton
Wormelow Tump
800 PEN-Y-GADER FAWR
Hoarwithy
Ffawddog Ridge
Llandinabo
Foy
Kenderchurch
Kings Caple
Offa's Dyke Path
Ewyas Harold
Harewood End
Strangford
Llanthony
Clodock
Pontrilas
Bagwy Llydiart
Orcop Hill
Llanwarne
Sellack
Baysham
BLACK MOUNTAINS
Rowlstone
Kentchurch
Pencoyd
Netherton
Pict's Cross
Grwyne Fechan
Llancillo
Orcop
Michaelchurch
Upper Grove Common
Brampton Abbotts
Walterstone
Garway Hill
Sandyway
Penallt Mawr
Llangua
Bridstow
Oldcastle
Grosmont
Little Garway
St Weonards
Tretire
St Owens Cross
Peterstow
Wilton
Ross
Cwmyoy
Grwyne Fawr
Old Furnace
Wilson
550 CRUG MAWR
Tre-wyn
Pandy
Garway
Garway Common
Three Ashes
Tudorville
Patrishow
34
Glewstone
R Wye
A49
A4113
A488
A4110
A4117
A4112
A44
A480
A4111
A438
A4103
A465
A466
A417
A40
B4385
B4367
B4365
B4364
B4361
B4355
B4356
B4357
B4362
B4372
B4529
B4360
B4594
B4350
B4351
B4352
B4348
B4349
B4230
B4224
B4399
B4347
B4521
B4352
B4348
45
45

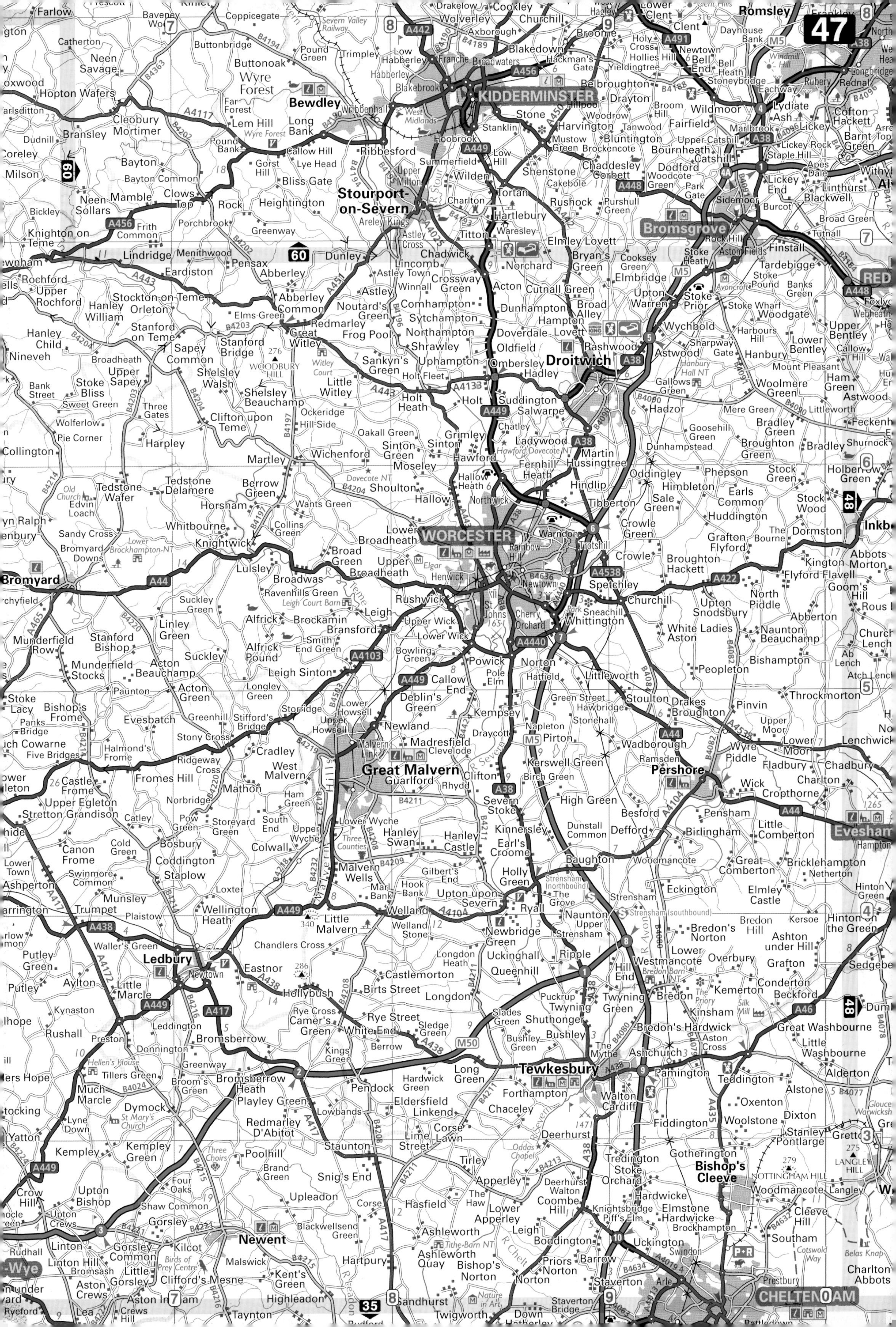
47
Farlow
Bayeney Wood
Coppicegate
Severn Valley Railway
Drakelow
Cookley
Wolverley
Churchill
Axborough
Hagley
Lower Clent
Clent
Romsley
Dayhouse Bank
Catherton
Buttonbridge
Pound Green
Trimpley
Low Habberley
Franche
Broadwaters
Blakedown
Broome
Holy Cross
Hollies Hill
Newtown
Bell End
Bell Heath
Neen Savage
Buttonoak
Wyre Forest
Habberley
Hackman's Gate
Yieldingtree
Stoneybridge
Rubery
Rednal
Longbridge
Hopton Wafers
Bewdley
Blakebrook
KIDDERMINSTER
Belbroughton
Eachway
Cleobury Mortimer
Far Forest
Lem Hill
Long Bank
Wribbenhall
West Midlands
Drayton
Broom Hill
Wildmoor
Lydiate Ash
Cofton Hackett
Bransley
Dudnill
Wyre Forest
Pound Bank
Callow Hill
Ribbesford
Hoobrook
Stanklin
Stone
Woodrow
Harvington
Tanwood
Fairfield
Marlbrook
Lickey
Barnt Green
Coreley
Bayton
Gorst Hill
Lye Head
Summerfield
Low Hill
Mustow Green
Bluntington
Brockencote
Upper Catshill
Catshill
Lickey Rock
Staple Hill
Milson
Bayton Common
Bliss Gate
Upper Milton
Wilden
Shenstone
Chaddesley Corbett
Bournheath
Dodford
Woodcote Green
Park Gate
Apes Dale
Withybed
Lickey End
Linthurst
Neen Sollars
Mamble
Clows Top
Rock
Heightington
Stourport-on-Severn
Charlton
Tortan
Cakebole
Rushock
Purshull Green
Sidemoor
Burcot
Blackwell
Bickley
Hartlebury
Areley Kings
Broad Green
Knighton on Teme
Frith Common
Porchbrook
Greenway
Astley Cross
Titton
Waresley
Elmley Lovett
Bromsgrove
Rock Hill
Finstall
Tutnall
Newnham
Lindridge
Menithwood
Pensax
Dunley
Chadwick
Bryan's Green
Cooksey Green
Stoke Heath
Aston Fields
Tardebigge
Eardiston
Abberley
Lincomb
Astley Town
Norchard
Elmbridge
Rochford
Upper Rochford
Winnall
Crossway Green
Acton
Cutnall Green
Upton Warren
Stoke Prior
Stoke Pound
Banks Green
Avoncroft
Hanley William
Stockton on Teme
Orleton
Abberley Common
Astley
Noutard's Green
Comhampton
Dunhampton
Broad Alley
Hampton Lovett
Stoke Wharf
Woodgate
Webheath
Elms Green
Sytchampton
Upper Bentley
Hanley Child
Stanford on Teme
Redmarley
Frog Pool
Northampton
Doverdale
Wychbold
Harbours Hill
Lower Bentley
Great Witley
Shrawley
Oldfield
Rashwood
Sharpway Gate
Callow Hill
Nineveh
Sapey Common
Stanford Bridge
Woodbury Hill
Witley Court
Sankyn's Green
Uphampton
Ombersley
Droitwich
Astwood
Hanbury
Hanbury Hall NT
Mount Pleasant
Broadheath
Upper Sapey
Shelsley Walsh
Holt Fleet
Hadley
Gallows Green
Woolmere Green
Ham Green
Bank Street
Stoke Bliss
Little Witley
Holt Heath
Holt
Suddington
Salwarpe
Hadzor
Astwood
Sweet Green
Three Gates
Shelsley Beauchamp
Ockeridge
Mere Green
Littleworth
Wolferlow
Clifton upon Teme
Hill Side
Chatley
Goosehill Green
Bradley Green
Feckenham
Pie Corner
Oakall Green
Grimley
Ladywood
Dunhampstead
Broughton Green
Bradley
Shurnock
Collington
Harpley
Sinton Green
Sinton
Hawford
Hawford Dovecote NT
Martin Hussingtree
Martley
Wichenford
Moseley
Fernhill Heath
Oddingley
Phepson
Stock Green
Holberrow Green
Old Church
Edvin Loach
Tedstone Wafer
Tedstone Delamere
Berrow Green
Dovecote NT
Shoulton
Hallow Heath
Hindlip
Himbleton
Earls Common
Horsham
Wants Green
Hallow
Northwick
Tibberton
Sale Green
Stock Wood
Huddington
Whitbourne
Collins Green
Lower Broadheath
WORCESTER
Warndon
Crowle Green
Grafton Flyford
The Bourne
Dormston
Inkberrow
Sandy Cross
Knightwick
Lower Brockhampton NT
Bromyard Downs
Broad Green
Upper Broadheath
Rainbow Hill
Trotshill
Crowle
Broughton Hackett
Abbots Morton
Kington
Flyford Flavell
Bromyard
Lulsley
Elgar
Henwick
Newtown
Spetchley
North Piddle
Goom's Hill
Broadwas
Ravenhills Green
Leigh Court Barn
Rushwick
St Johns
Cherry Orchard
Sneachill
Whittington
Churchill
Upton Snodsbury
Rous Lench
Suckley Green
Alfrick
Brockamin
Leigh
Bransford
Upper Wick
Lower Wick
White Ladies Aston
Naunton Beauchamp
Abberton
Church Lench
Munderfield Row
Stanford Bishop
Linley Green
Alfrick Pound
Smith End Green
Bowling Green
Powick
Norton
Peopleton
Bishampton
Ab Lench
Munderfield Stocks
Acton Beauchamp
Suckley
Leigh Sinton
Callow End
Pole Elm
Hatfield
Littleworth
Atch Lench
Paunton
Acton Green
Longley Green
Deblin's Green
Green Street
Hawbridge
Stoulton
Drakes Broughton
Pinvin
Throckmorton
Stoke Lacy
Bishop's Frome
Panks Bridge
Evesbatch
Greenhill
Stifford's Bridge
Storridge
Lower Howsell
Upper Howsell
Kempsey
Napleton
Stonehall
Upper Moor
Much Cowarne
Five Bridges
Halmond's Frome
Stony Cross
Cradley
Newland
Malvern Link
Madresfield
Draycott
Clevelode
Pirton
Wadborough
Wyre Piddle
Lower Moor
Lenchwick
Castle Frome
Fromes Hill
Ridgeway Cross
West Malvern
Great Malvern
Guarlford
Clifton
Kerswell Green
Ramsden
Pershore
Fladbury
Chadbury
Upper Egleton
Mathon
Norbridge
Ham Green
Rhydd
Birch Green
Charlton
Cropthorne
Stretton Grandison
Catley
Pow Green
Storeyard Green
South End
Upper Wyche
Lower Wyche
Hanley Swan
Severn Stoke
High Green
Besford
Pensham
Evesham
Hampton
Canon Frome
Cold Green
Bosbury
Colwall
Three Counties
Hanley Castle
Kinnersley
Dunstall Common
Defford
Birlingham
Little Comberton
Lower Town
Swinmore Common
Coddington
Malvern Wells
Earl's Croome
Baughton
Woodmancote
Great Comberton
Bricklehampton
Netherton
Ashperton
Staplow
Loxter
Marl Bank
Hook Bank
Gilbert's End
Holly Green
Strensham
Eckington
Elmley Castle
Hinton Green
Trumpet
Munsley
Wellington Heath
Welland
Upton upon Severn
Ryall
The Grove
Naunton
Upper Strensham
Bredon's Norton
Bredon Hill
Kersoe
Ashton under Hill
Hinton on the Green
Plaistow
Little Malvern
Welland Stone
Newbridge Green
Ripple
Westmancote
Lower Westmancote
Overbury
Grafton
Sedgeberrow
Waller's Green
Chandlers Cross
Longdon Heath
Uckinghall
Hill End
Bredon Barn NT
Putley Green
Ledbury
Eastnor
Castlemorton
Queenhill
Kemerton
Conderton
Putley
Aylton
Little Marcle
Hollybush
Birts Street
Longdon
Puckrup
Twyning
Twyning Green
Bredon
The Priory
Beckford
Kynaston
Rye Cross
Camer's Green
Rye Street
Sledge Green
Slades Green
Shuthonger
Kinsham
Silk Mill
Dumbleton
Rushall
Preston
Leddington
Bromsberrow
White End
Berrow
Bushley
Bushley Green
Bredon's Hardwick
Aston Cross
Great Washbourne
Little Washbourne
Donnington
Kings Green
The Mythe
Ashchurch
Hellen's House
Greenway
Tillers Green
Broom's Green
Bromsberrow Heath
Playley Green
Pendock
Hardwick Green
Long Green
Tewkesbury
Pamington
Teddington
Alderton
Much Marcle
Dymock
St Mary's Church
Lowbands
Redmarley D'Abitot
Eldersfield
Linkend
Forthampton
Chaceley
Walton Cardiff
Oxenton
Alstone
Gloucestershire Warwickshire Railway
Lyne Down
Kempley
Kempley Green
Three Choirs
Staunton
Lime Street
Corse Lawn
Deerhurst
Odda's Chapel
Fiddington
Woolstone
Dixton
Stanley Pontlarge
Gretton
Yatton
Poolhill
Brand Green
Snig's End
Tirley
Apperley
Tredington
Stoke Orchard
Gotherington
Bishop's Cleeve
Langley Hill
Nottingham Hill
Four Oaks
Upleadon
Deerhurst Walton
Coombe Hill
Hardwicke
Woodmancote
Langley
Crow Hill
Upton Bishop
Shaw Common
Gorsley
Corse
Hasfield
The Haw
Lower Apperley
Knightsbridge
Piff's Elm
Elmstone Hardwicke
Brockhampton
Cleeve Hill
Upton Crews
Newent
Blackwellsend Green
Ashleworth
Tithe Barn NT
Leigh
Boddington
Uckington
Swindon
Southam
Cotswold Way
Belas Knap
Linton
Gorsley Common
Kilcot
Birds of Prey Centre
Malswick
Hartpury
Ashleworth Quay
Bishop's Norton
Priors Norton
Barrow
Staverton
Arle
Prestbury
Charlton Abbots
Rudhall
Linton Hill
Bromsash
Little Gorsley
Clifford's Mesne
Kent's Green
Aston Crews
Aston Ingham
Highleadon
Sandhurst
Twigworth
Nature in Art
Staverton Bridge
Down Hatherley
CHELTENHAM
Ross-on-Wye
Weston under Penyard
Ryeford
Lea
Crews Hill
Taynton
Rudford
A442
A456
A449
A450
A448
A38
A491
M5
A4025
A443
A451
A4133
A4538
A422
A44
A4440
A4103
A4104
A449
A438
A4172
A417
A4104
M50
A46
A435
A4019
A40
B4194
B4190
B4189
B4363
B4117
B4202
B4188
B4096
B4091
B4193
B4203
B4204
B4197
B4090
B4214
B4220
B4084
B4082
B4503
B4219
B4211
B4232
B4208
B4209
B4218
B4080
B4079
B4077
B4078
B4216
B4024
B4221
B4215
B4213
B4634
B4632
60
48
35

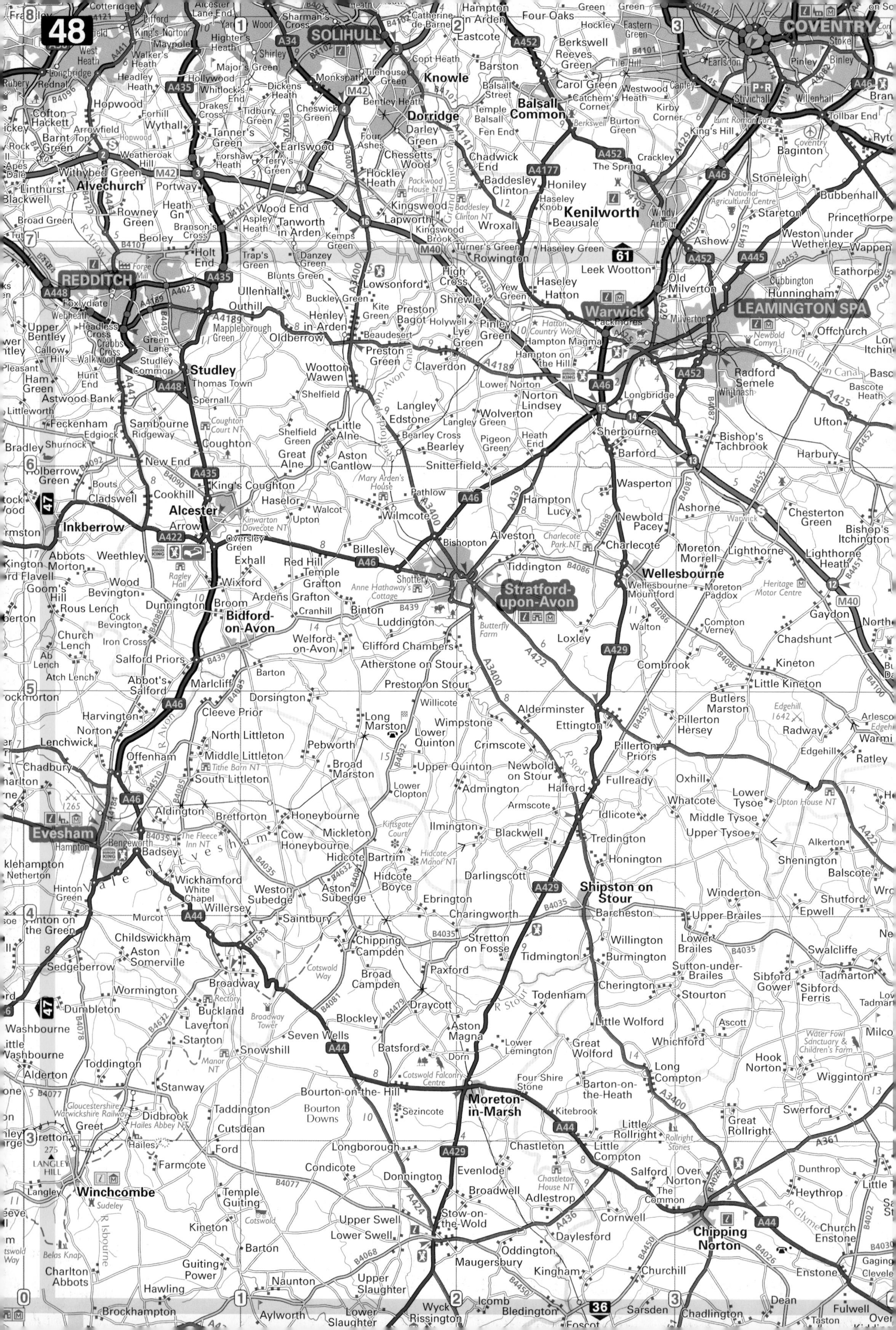

48
Cotteridge
Lifford
King's Norton
Maypole
West Heath
Walker's Heath
Longbridge
Rubery
Rednal
Headley Heath
Hopwood
Cofton Hackett
Arrowfield
Barnt Green
Withybed Green
Alvechurch
Linthurst
Blackwell
Broad Green
Weatheroak Hill
Forhill
Wythall
Rowney Green
Beoley
Heath Gn
REDDITCH
Foxlydiate
Webheath
Headless Cross
Crabbs Cross
Walkwood
Upper Bentley
Callow Hill
Hunt End
Ham Green
Astwood Bank
Feckenham
Edgiock
Shurnock
Bradley
Holberrow Green
Bouts
Cladswell
Inkberrow
Abbots Morton
Weethley
Kington
Flavell
Goom's Hill
Rous Lench
Church Lench
Ab Lench
Atch Lench
Iron Cross
Salford Priors
Abbot's Salford
Harvington
Norton
Lenchwick
Chadbury
Offenham
Evesham
Hampton
Bengeworth
Badsey
Netherton
Hinton Green
Hinton on the Green
Childswickham
Aston Somerville
Sedgeberrow
Wormington
Dumbleton
Washbourne
Alderton
Toddington
Stanway
Didbrook
Greet
Gretton
Hailes
Farmcote
Langley Hill
Winchcombe
Sudeley
Belas Knap
Charlton Abbots
Hawling
Brockhampton
Acocks Green
Lane End
Yardley Wood
Highter's Heath
Major's Green
Hollywood
Whitlock's End
Drakes Cross
Tanner's Green
Forshaw Heath
Portway
Wood End
Aspley Heath
Tanworth in Arden
Holt End
Trap's Green
Danzey Green
Blunts Green
Ullenhall
Outhill
Mappleborough Green
Studley
Thomas Town
Spernall
Sambourne
Ridgeway
Coughton
Coughton Court NT
New End
Cookhill
King's Coughton
Alcester
Arrow
Kinwarton Dovecote NT
Oversley Green
Exhall
Ragley Hall
Wixford
Dunnington
Broom
Bidford-on-Avon
Marlcliff
Cleeve Prior
North Littleton
Middle Littleton
South Littleton
Tithe Barn NT
Aldington
Bretforton
The Fleece Inn NT
Vale of Evesham
Wickhamford
Murcot
Willersey
Broadway
Broadway Tower
Buckland
Laverton
Stanton
Snowshill
Taddington
Cutsdean
Ford
Temple Guiting
Kineton
Barton
Guiting Power
Naunton
Aylworth
SOLIHULL
Shirley
Dickens Heath
Monkspath
Tidbury Green
Cheswick Green
Earlswood
Terry's Green
Hockley Heath
Packwood House NT
Kingswood
Lapworth
Kemps Green
Lowsonford
Buckley Green
Henley-in-Arden
Beaudesert
Oldberrow
Preston Green
Wootton Wawen
Shelfield
Shelfield Green
Little Alne
Great Alne
Aston Cantlow
Haselor
Walcot
Upton
Wilmcote
Mary Arden's House
Pathlow
Billesley
Red Hill
Temple Grafton
Ardens Grafton
Binton
Cranhill
Welford-on-Avon
Barton
Dorsington
Pebworth
Long Marston
Broad Marston
Honeybourne
Cow Honeybourne
Mickleton
Weston Subedge
Aston Subedge
Saintbury
Chipping Campden
Broad Campden
Cotswold Way
Blockley
Seven Wells
Batsford
Bourton-on-the-Hill
Bourton Downs
Sezincote
Longborough
Condicote
Donnington
Upper Swell
Lower Swell
Upper Slaughter
Lower Slaughter
Catherine-de-Barnes
Copt Heath
Tilehouse Green
Knowle
Bentley Heath
Dorridge
Four Ashes
Darley Green
Chessetts Wood
Preston Bagot
Kite Green
Claverdon
Holywell
Lye Green
Langley
Edstone
Bearley Cross
Bearley
Snitterfield
Wolverton
Langley Green
Pigeon Green
Heath End
Bishopton
Shottery
Anne Hathaway's Cottage
Stratford-upon-Avon
Butterfly Farm
Luddington
Clifford Chambers
Atherstone on Stour
Preston on Stour
Willicote
Wimpstone
Lower Quinton
Upper Quinton
Lower Clopton
Admington
Crimscote
Ilmington
Kiftsgate Court
Hidcote Manor NT
Hidcote Bartrim
Hidcote Boyce
Ebrington
Charingworth
Stretton on Fosse
Paxford
Draycott
Aston Magna
Dorn
Cotswold Falconry Centre
Moreton-in-Marsh
Evenlode
Broadwell
Stow-on-the-Wold
Maugersbury
Wyck Rissington
Icomb
Hampton in Arden
Eastcote
Barston
Balsall Street
Temple Balsall
Fen End
Balsall Common
Chadwick End
Baddesley Clinton
Baddesley Clinton NT
Wroxall
Kingswood Brook
Turner's Green
Rowington
High Cross
Shrewley
Yew Green
Pinley Green
Hatton Country World
Hampton Magna
Hampton on the Hill
Lower Norton
Norton Lindsey
Alveston
Tiddington
Charlecote Park NT
Hampton Lucy
Alderminster
Ettington
Newbold on Stour
Armscote
Blackwell
Halford
Darlingscott
Tidmington
Todenham
Lower Lemington
Four Shire Stone
Great Wolford
Little Wolford
Barton-on-the-Heath
Kitebrook
Chastleton
Chastleton House NT
Adlestrop
Oddington
Daylesford
Kingham
Bledington
Foscot
Four Oaks
Berkswell
Reeves Green
Carol Green
Catchem's Corner
Burton Green
Westwood Heath
Honiley
Haseley Knob
Kenilworth
Beausale
Haseley Green
Leek Wootton
Haseley
Hatton
Warwick
Packmores
Longbridge
Sherbourne
Barford
Wasperton
Newbold Pacey
Charlecote
Wellesbourne
Wellesbourne Mountford
Loxley
Walton
Combrook
Pillerton Hersey
Pillerton Priors
Fullready
Idlicote
Tredington
Honington
Shipston on Stour
Barcheston
Willington
Burmington
Cherington
Stourton
Whichford
Long Compton
Little Rollright
Rollright Stones
Little Compton
Salford
Over Norton
The Common
Cornwell
Chipping Norton
Churchill
Sarsden
Chadlington
Hockley
Eastern Green
Tile Hill
Westwood
Canley
Kirby Corner
Lunt Roman Fort
King's Hill
The Spring
Crackley
Windy Arbour
National Agricultural Centre
Stoneleigh
Ashow
Old Milverton
Milverton
LEAMINGTON SPA
Newbold Comyn
Radford Semele
Whitnash
Bishop's Tachbrook
Ashorne
Moreton Morrell
Moreton Paddox
Compton Verney
Kineton
Little Kineton
Butlers Marston
Edgehill 1642
Radway
Oxhill
Whatcote
Lower Tysoe
Middle Tysoe
Upper Tysoe
Upton House NT
Winderton
Upper Brailes
Lower Brailes
Sutton-under-Brailes
Sibford Gower
Sibford Ferris
Ascott
Hook Norton
Great Rollright
Swerford
Dunthrop
Heythrop
Church Enstone
Enstone
Dean
COVENTRY
Stoke
Earlsdon
Pinley
Binley
Stivichall
Willenhall
Tollbar End
Baginton
Coventry
Bubbenhall
Stareton
Princethorpe
Weston under Wetherley
Wappenbury
Cubbington
Hunningham
Eathorpe
Offchurch
Grand Union Canal
Bascote Heath
Ufton
Harbury
Chesterton Green
Bishop's Itchington
Lighthorne
Lighthorne Heath
Heritage Motor Centre
Gaydon
Chadshunt
Arlescot
Edgehill
Ratley
Alkerton
Shenington
Balscote
Shutford
Epwell
Swalcliffe
Tadmarton
Water Fowl Sanctuary & Children's Farm
Wigginton
Fulwell
Taston
M42
M40
A34
A435
A441
A448
A4189
A422
A46
A3400
A4177
A452
A429
A445
A439
A44
A424
A436
A361
61
47
36

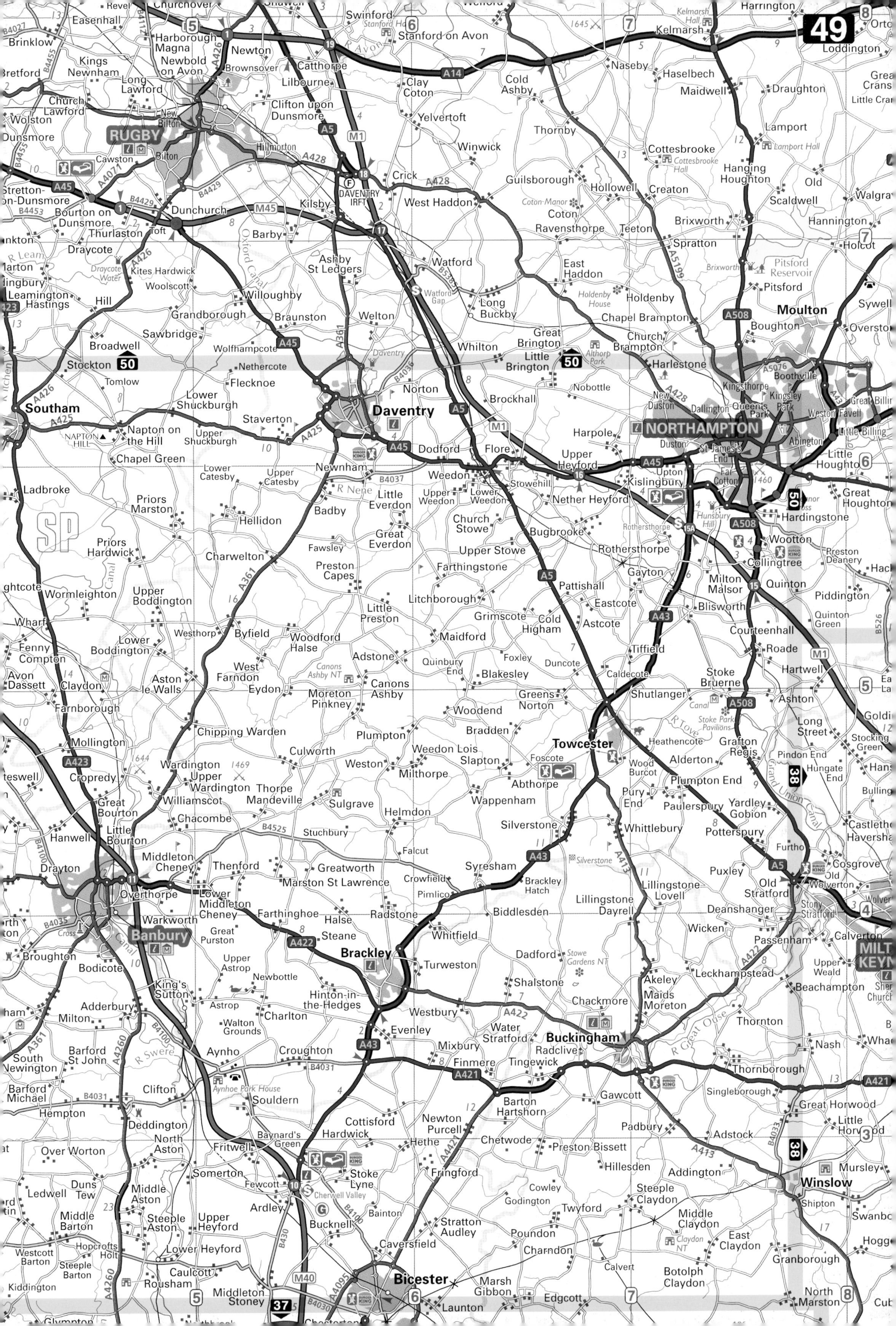

49
Churchover
Easenhall
Brinklow
Harborough Magna
Newton
Swinford
Stanford Hall
Stanford on Avon
Kelmarsh
Kelmarsh Hall
Harrington
Loddington
Kings Newnham
Newbold on Avon
Brownsover
Catthorpe
Lilbourne
Naseby
Haselbech
Maidwell
Draughton
Bretford
Long Lawford
Church Lawford
Clifton upon Dunsmore
Clay Coton
Cold Ashby
Yelvertoft
Thornby
Wolston
Dunsmore
RUGBY
New Bilton
Bilton
Hillmorton
Cawston
Winwick
Cottesbrooke
Cottesbrooke Hall
Lamport
Lamport Hall
Hanging Houghton
Old
Crick
DAVENTRY IRFT
Guilsborough
Hollowell
Creaton
Stretton-on-Dunsmore
Bourton on Dunsmore
Dunchurch
Kilsby
West Haddon
Coton Manor
Coton
Scaldwell
Walgrave
Thurlaston
Toft
Barby
Ravensthorpe
Teeton
Brixworth
Hannington
Draycote
Draycote Water
Kites Hardwick
Woolscott
Ashby St Ledgers
Watford
Watford Gap
East Haddon
Spratton
Holcot
Pitsford Reservoir
Pitsford
Leamington Hastings
Hill
Willoughby
Long Buckby
Holdenby House
Holdenby
Sywell
Grandborough
Braunston
Welton
Chapel Brampton
Moulton
Boughton
Overstone
Sawbridge
Broadwell
Wolfhampcote
Whilton
Great Brington
Church Brampton
Althorp Park
Little Brington
Stockton
Nethercote
Flecknoe
Daventry
Harlestone
Boothville
Kingsthorpe
Kingsley Park
Tomlow
Norton
Nobottle
Southam
Lower Shuckburgh
Brockhall
New Duston
Dallington
Queen's Park
Weston Favell
Great Billing
Napton on the Hill
Staverton
Upper Shuckburgh
Harpole
NORTHAMPTON
Duston
Little Billing
Abington
Chapel Green
Dodford
Flore
Upper Heyford
St James's End
Little Houghton
Newnham
Lower Catesby
Upper Catesby
Weedon
Kislingbury
Upton
Far Cotton
Ladbroke
Priors Marston
Little Everdon
Upper Weedon
Lower Weedon
Stowehill
Nether Heyford
Great Houghton
Badby
Hardingstone
Hellidon
Church Stowe
Bugbrooke
Rothersthorpe
Hunsbury Hill
Wootton
Great Everdon
Fawsley
Priors Hardwick
Charwelton
Upper Stowe
Preston Deanery
Preston Capes
Farthingstone
Gayton
Collingtree
Hackleton
Wormleighton
Upper Boddington
Pattishall
Milton Malsor
Quinton
Eastcote
Litchborough
Little Preston
Piddington
Blisworth
Grimscote
Cold Higham
Astcote
Quinton Green
Wharf
Westhorp
Byfield
Woodford Halse
Maidford
Courteenhall
Fenny Compton
Lower Boddington
Adstone
Foxley
Tiffield
Roade
Canons Ashby NT
Quinbury End
Duncote
Stoke Bruerne
Hartwell
Avon Dassett
Claydon
West Farndon
Aston le Walls
Eydon
Canons Ashby
Blakesley
Caldecote
Moreton Pinkney
Greens Norton
Shutlanger
Ashton
Farnborough
Woodend
Stoke Park Pavilions
Long Street
Chipping Warden
Plumpton
Bradden
Towcester
Heathencote
Grafton Regis
Stocking Green
Mollington
Culworth
Weedon Lois
Slapton
Pindon End
Hungate End
Wardington
Weston
Foscote
Wood Burcot
Alderton
Cropredy
Upper Wardington
Thorpe Mandeville
Milthorpe
Abthorpe
Plumpton End
Great Bourton
Williamscot
Wappenham
Pury End
Paulerspury
Yardley Gobion
Sulgrave
Helmdon
Chacombe
Silverstone
Whittlebury
Potterspury
Castlethorpe
Hanwell
Little Bourton
Stuchbury
Haversham
Middleton Cheney
Thenford
Falcut
Furtho
Drayton
Greatworth
Syresham
Brackley Hatch
Puxley
Cosgrove
Marston St Lawrence
Crowfield
Lillingstone Lovell
Old Stratford
Old Wolverton
Overthorpe
Lower Middleton Cheney
Pimlico
Lillingstone Dayrell
Deanshanger
Stony Stratford
Warkworth
Farthinghoe
Biddlesden
Halse
Radstone
Wicken
Banbury
Great Purston
Steane
Whitfield
Passenham
Calverton
Brackley
Dadford
Stowe Gardens NT
Broughton
Upper Astrop
Turweston
Bodicote
Newbottle
Shalstone
Akeley
Leckhampstead
Upper Weald
King's Sutton
Hinton-in-the-Hedges
Chackmore
Maids Moreton
Beachampton
Adderbury
Astrop
Westbury
Thornton
Milton
Walton Grounds
Charlton
Evenley
Water Stratford
Buckingham
South Newington
Barford St John
Aynho
Croughton
Mixbury
Radclive
Nash
Finmere
Tingewick
Thornborough
Barford St Michael
Clifton
Aynhoe Park House
Souldern
Barton Hartshorn
Gawcott
Singleborough
Great Horwood
Hempton
Deddington
Cottisford
Hardwick
Newton Purcell
Padbury
Little Horwood
Over Worton
North Aston
Fritwell
Baynard's Green
Hethe
Chetwode
Preston Bissett
Adstock
Hillesden
Mursley
Somerton
Fewcott
Stoke Lyne
Fringford
Addington
Winslow
Ledwell
Duns Tew
Middle Aston
Cherwell Valley
Cowley
Godington
Steeple Claydon
Middle Barton
Steeple Aston
Upper Heyford
Ardley
Bainton
Twyford
Middle Claydon
Shipton
Swanbourne
Bucknell
Stratton Audley
Claydon NT
East Claydon
Hopcrofts Holt
Westcott Barton
Steeple Barton
Lower Heyford
Caversfield
Poundon
Charndon
Granborough
Hoggeston
Calvert
Botolph Claydon
Kiddington
Rousham
Caulcott
Middleton Stoney
Bicester
Marsh Gibbon
Edgcott
North Marston
Launton
Chesterton
Glympton
37
38
50
5
6
7
8
3
4
A14
A45
A428
A5
M1
M45
A426
A4071
A361
A425
A423
A43
A508
A5076
A5199
A422
A421
A413
A4421
A4260
A4095
A4100
B4525
B4031
B4030
B4037
B4038
B4035
B4100
B4429
B4453
B4027
B4455
B5385
B4036
B4100
B430
B526
B4033
M40
SP
NAPTON HILL
R Avon
R Leam
R Nene
R Tove
R Great Ouse
R Swere
Oxford Canal
Grand Union Canal
1645
1644
1469
1460

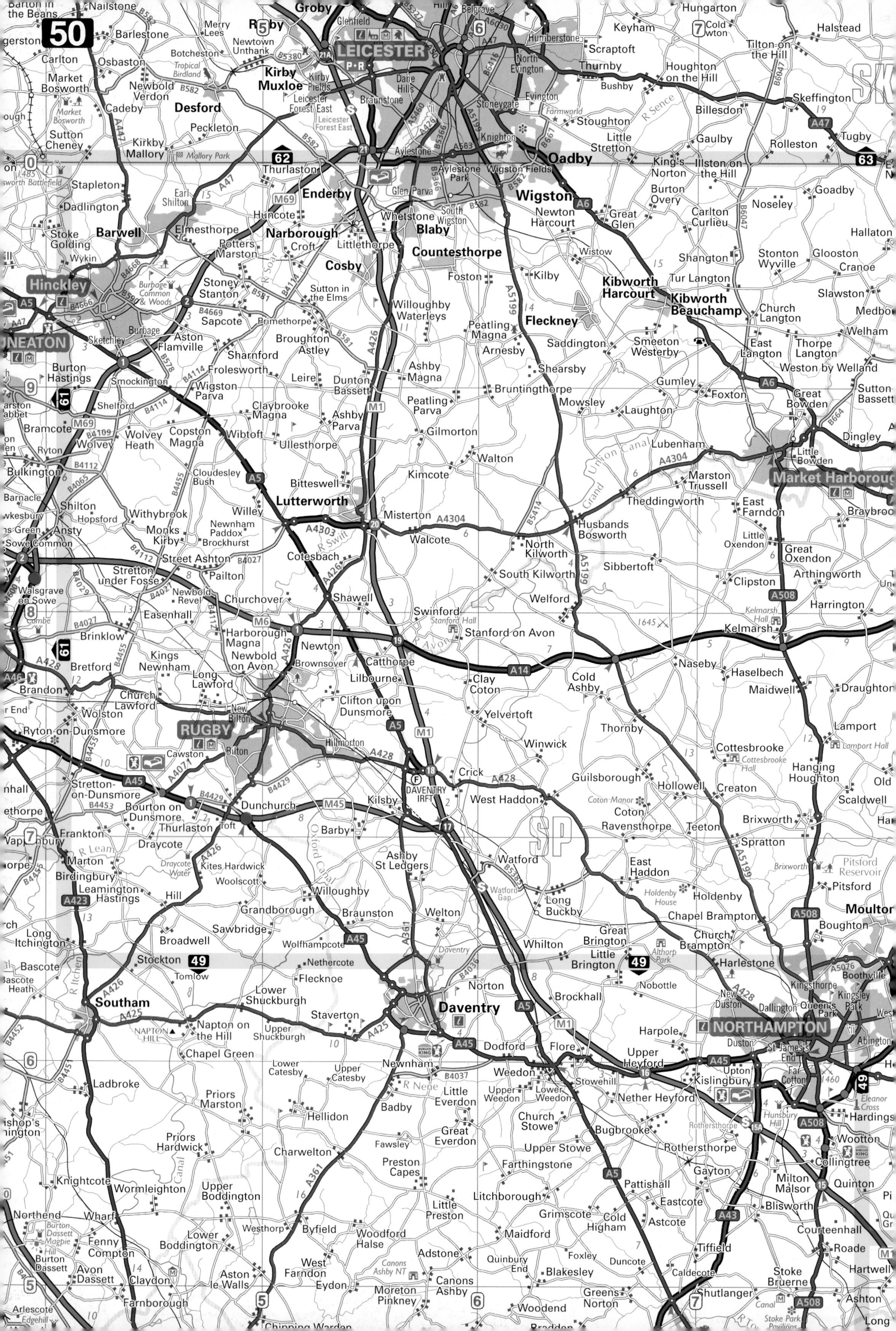

50
Barton in the Beans
Nailstone
Barlestone
Merry Lees
Ratby
Groby
Glenfield
Belgrave
Hungarton
Keyham
Cold Newton
Halstead
Carlton
Osbaston
Botcheston
Newtown Unthank
LEICESTER
Humberstone
Scraptoft
Tilton on the Hill
Market Bosworth
Tropical Birdland
Kirby Muxloe
Kirby Fields
Dane Hills
North Evington
Thurnby
Houghton on the Hill
Newbold Verdon
Desford
Leicester Forest East
Braunstone
Evington
Bushby
Market Bosworth
Cadeby
Stoneygate
Farmworld
Billesdon
Skeffington
Sutton Cheney
Peckleton
Stoughton
R Sence
Kirkby Mallory
Mallory Park
Knighton
Little Stretton
Gaulby
Rolleston
Tugby
Aylestone
Oadby
King's Norton
Illston on the Hill
Thurlaston
Aylestone Park
Wigston Fields
Bosworth Battlefield
Stapleton
Earl Shilton
Enderby
Glen Parva
Wigston
Burton Overy
Goadby
Dadlington
Noseley
Huncote
Whetstone
South Wigston
Newton Harcourt
Great Glen
Carlton Curlieu
Stoke Golding
Barwell
Elmesthorpe
Narborough
Blaby
Hallaton
Potters Marston
Croft
Littlethorpe
Countesthorpe
Wistow
Shangton
Stonton Wyville
Glooston
Wykin
Cosby
Cranoe
Hinckley
Burbage Common & Woods
Stoney Stanton
Sutton in the Elms
Foston
Kilby
Kibworth Harcourt
Tur Langton
Kibworth Beauchamp
Slawston
Willoughby Waterleys
Church Langton
Medbourne
Sapcote
Primethorpe
Fleckney
Burbage
Aston Flamville
Peatling Magna
Saddington
Smeeton Westerby
Welham
NUNEATON
Sketchley
Broughton Astley
Arnesby
East Langton
Thorpe Langton
Sharnford
Shearsby
Weston by Welland
Burton Hastings
Smockington
Frolesworth
Leire
Dunton Bassett
Ashby Magna
Gumley
Foxton
Sutton Bassett
Wigston Parva
Bruntingthorpe
Great Bowden
Shelford
Claybrooke Magna
Peatling Parva
Mowsley
Laughton
Ashby Parva
Bramcote
Wolvey
Wolvey Heath
Copston Magna
Wibtoft
Ullesthorpe
Gilmorton
Dingley
Lubenham
Ryton
Walton
Little Bowden
Union Canal
Bulkington
Cloudesley Bush
Kimcote
Marston Trussell
Market Harborough
Barnacle
Bitteswell
Grand
Theddingworth
Shilton
Hopsford
Withybrook
Willey
Lutterworth
East Farndon
Braybrooke
Ansty
Monks Kirby
Newnham Paddox
Brockhurst
Misterton
Husbands Bosworth
Walcote
Little Oxendon
Sowe Common
North Kilworth
Great Oxendon
R Swift
Street Ashton
Cotesbach
Sibbertoft
Arthingworth
Stretton under Fosse
Pailton
South Kilworth
Clipston
Walsgrave on Sowe
Newbold Revel
Churchover
Shawell
Welford
Harrington
Easenhall
Swinford
Stanford Hall
Kelmarsh Hall
Combe
Brinklow
Harborough Magna
Stanford on Avon
Kelmarsh
Newbold on Avon
Newton
R Avon
Naseby
Kings Newnham
Brownsover
Catthorpe
Cold Ashby
Haselbech
Bretford
Long Lawford
Lilbourne
Clay Coton
Maidwell
Draughton
Brandon
Church Lawford
Clifton upon Dunsmore
Wolston
New Bilton
Yelvertoft
Thornby
Lamport
Ryton-on-Dunsmore
RUGBY
Hillmorton
Winwick
Cottesbrooke
Lamport Hall
Cawston
Bilton
Cottesbrooke Hall
Hanging Houghton
Crick
Guilsborough
Hollowell
Creaton
Old
Stretton-on-Dunsmore
DAVENTRY IRFT
West Haddon
Coton Manor
Scaldwell
Bourton on Dunsmore
Dunchurch
Kilsby
Coton
Thurlaston
Toft
Barby
Ravensthorpe
Teeton
Brixworth
Frankton
Draycote
Spratton
R Leam
Oxford Canal
Ashby St Ledgers
Watford
Marton
Draycote Water
Kites Hardwick
East Haddon
Pitsford Reservoir
Birdingbury
Woolscott
Watford Gap
Brixworth
Leamington Hastings
Willoughby
Long Buckby
Holdenby House
Holdenby
Pitsford
Hill
Moulton
Grandborough
Braunston
Welton
Chapel Brampton
Long Itchington
Sawbridge
Great Brington
Boughton
Broadwell
Wolfhampcote
Whilton
Church Brampton
Daventry
Little Brington
Althorp Park
Stockton
Nethercote
Harlestone
Bascote
Tomlow
Flecknoe
Norton
Nobottle
Boothville
Bascote Heath
R Itchen
Lower Shuckburgh
Kingsthorpe
Kingsley Park
Southam
Brockhall
New Duston
Dallington
Queen's Park
Staverton
Daventry
Napton on the Hill
NAPTON HILL
Upper Shuckburgh
Harpole
NORTHAMPTON
Chapel Green
Dodford
Flore
Upper Heyford
Duston
St James's End
Abington
Lower Catesby
Upper Catesby
Newnham
Weedon
Stowehill
Upton
Far Cotton
Ladbroke
R Nene
Little Everdon
Upper Weedon
Lower Weedon
Nether Heyford
Kislingbury
Eleanor Cross
Priors Marston
Badby
Hunsbury Hill
Hardings
Bishop's Itchington
Hellidon
Church Stowe
Bugbrooke
Rothersthorpe
Wootton
Great Everdon
Priors Hardwick
Fawsley
Upper Stowe
Rothersthorpe
Collingtree
Charwelton
Preston Capes
Farthingstone
Gayton
Knightcote
Milton Malsor
Quinton
Wormleighton
Upper Boddington
Litchborough
Pattishall
Eastcote
Little Preston
Blisworth
Northend
Wharf
Grimscote
Cold Higham
Astcote
Burton Dassett Magpie Hill
Westhorp
Byfield
Woodford Halse
Maidford
Courteenhall
Fenny Compton
Lower Boddington
Roade
Burton Dassett
Avon Dassett
West Farndon
Adstone
Quinbury End
Foxley
Duncote
Tiffield
Aston le Walls
Canons Ashby NT
Canons Ashby
Blakesley
Caldecote
Stoke Bruerne
Hartwell
Claydon
Eydon
Moreton Pinkney
Greens Norton
Shutlanger
Ashton
Arlescote
Farnborough
Woodend
Canal
Stoke Park Pavilions
Edgehill
Chipping Warden
Long

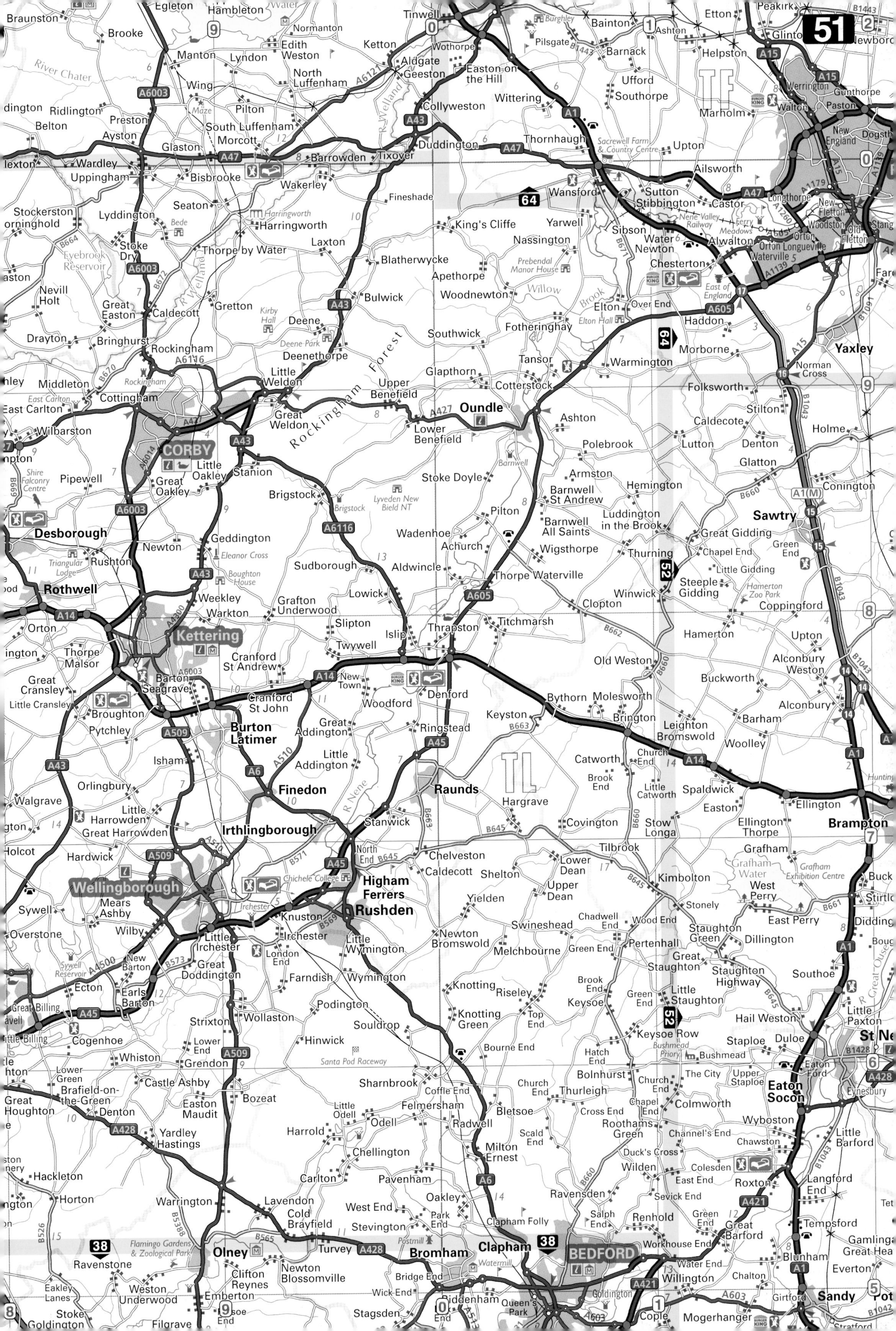

51
Braunston
Egleton
Hambleton
Normanton
Tinwell
Peakirk
Etton
Bainton
Ashton
Glinton
Newborough
Brooke
Edith Weston
Ketton
Wothorpe
Burghley
Pilsgate
Barnack
Helpston
Manton
Lyndon
Aldgate
Geeston
Easton-on-the-Hill
Ufford
Southorpe
River Chater
North Luffenham
Werrington
Gunthorpe
Wing
Walton
Paston
Ridlington
Pilton
Collyweston
Wittering
Marholm
Belton
Preston
Maze
South Luffenham
Ayston
Morcott
Duddington
Thornhaugh
Sacrewell Farm & Country Centre
Upton
New England
Dogsthorpe
Glaston
Wardley
Barrowden
Tixover
Ailsworth
Uppingham
Bisbrooke
Wakerley
Fineshade
Wansford
Sutton
Stibbington
Castor
Longthorpe
Stockerston
Seaton
Harringworth
Nene Valley Railway
Ferry Meadows
Woodston
Old Fletton
New Fletton
Lyddington
Bede
King's Cliffe
Yarwell
Sibson
Water Newton
Alwalton
Orton Longueville
Orton Waterville
Eyebrook Reservoir
Stoke Dry
Thorpe by Water
Laxton
Nassington
Prebendal Manor House
Chesterton
Blatherwycke
Apethorpe
East of England
Nevill Holt
Great Easton
Caldecott
Gretton
Kirby Hall
Bulwick
Woodnewton
Willow Brook
Elton
Over End
Elton Hall
Haddon
Drayton
Bringhurst
Rockingham
Deene
Deene Park
Deenethorpe
Southwick
Fotheringhay
Morborne
Yaxley
Tansor
Warmington
Norman Cross
Middleton
Rockingham Forest
Little Weldon
Upper Benefield
Glapthorn
Cotterstock
Folksworth
East Carlton
Cottingham
Great Weldon
Oundle
Lower Benefield
Ashton
Stilton
Caldecote
Holme
Wilbarston
CORBY
Polebrook
Lutton
Denton
Little Oakley
Stanion
Barnwell
Armston
Glatton
Shire Falconry Centre
Pipewell
Great Oakley
Stoke Doyle
Barnwell St Andrew
Hemington
Conington
Brigstock
Lyveden New Bield NT
Pilton
Barnwell All Saints
Luddington in the Brook
Sawtry
Desborough
Newton
Geddington
Eleanor Cross
Wadenhoe
Achurch
Wigsthorpe
Great Gidding
Green End
Chapel End
Thurning
Little Gidding
Triangular Lodge
Rushton
Boughton House
Sudborough
Aldwincle
Thorpe Waterville
Steeple Gidding
Hamerton Zoo Park
Rothwell
Lowick
Winwick
Clopton
Coppingford
Weekley
Warkton
Grafton Underwood
Slipton
Islip
Thrapston
Titchmarsh
Orton
Kettering
Twywell
Hamerton
Upton
Thorpe Malsor
Cranford St Andrew
Old Weston
Alconbury Weston
Great Cransley
Little Cransley
Barton Seagrave
New Town
Denford
Buckworth
Bythorn
Molesworth
Alconbury
Broughton
Cranford St John
Woodford
Keyston
Brington
Barham
Pytchley
Burton Latimer
Great Addington
Ringstead
Leighton Bromswold
Woolley
Isham
Little Addington
Catworth
Church End
Brook End
Orlingbury
Finedon
Raunds
Hargrave
Little Catworth
Spaldwick
Ellington
Walgrave
Little Harrowden
Great Harrowden
Irthlingborough
Stanwick
Covington
Stow Longa
Easton
Ellington Thorpe
Brampton
Holcot
Hardwick
North End
Chelveston
Tilbrook
Lower Dean
Upper Dean
Grafham
Grafham Water
Grafham Exhibition Centre
Buckden
Wellingborough
Chichele College
Higham Ferrers
Caldecott
Shelton
Kimbolton
West Perry
Sywell
Mears Ashby
Irchester
Rushden
Yielden
Stonely
East Perry
Wilby
Knuston
Chadwell End
Wood End
Overstone
Little Irchester
Irchester
Little Wymington
Newton Bromswold
Swineshead
Melchbourne
Green End
Pertenhall
Staughton Green
Dillington
Sywell Reservoir
New Barton
Great Doddington
London End
Great Staughton
Staughton Highway
Southoe
Ecton
Earls Barton
Farndish
Wymington
Knotting
Riseley
Brook End
Keysoe
Green End
Little Staughton
Great Billing
Podington
Knotting Green
Top End
Hail Weston
Little Paxton
Strixton
Wollaston
Souldrop
Keysoe Row
Bushmead Priory
Bushmead
Staploe
Duloe
St Neots
Cogenhoe
Lower End
Hinwick
Bourne End
Hatch End
Eaton Ford
Whiston
Grendon
Santa Pod Raceway
Bolnhurst
The City
Upper Staploe
Lower Green
Castle Ashby
Sharnbrook
Coffle End
Church End
Thurleigh
Eaton Socon
Eynesbury
Brafield-on-the-Green
Bozeat
Little Odell
Felmersham
Chapel End
Colmworth
Great Houghton
Denton
Easton Maudit
Odell
Radwell
Bletsoe
Cross End
Roothams Green
Wyboston
Harrold
Scald End
Channel's End
Little Barford
Yardley Hastings
Chellington
Milton Ernest
Chawston
Duck's Cross
Wilden
Colesden
Hackleton
Carlton
Pavenham
East End
Roxton
Langford End
Horton
Oakley
Ravensden
Sevick End
Warrington
Lavendon
Cold Brayfield
West End
Park End
Clapham Folly
Salph End
Renhold
Green End
Great Barford
Tempsford
Stevington
Flamingo Gardens & Zoological Park
Olney
Turvey
Postmill
Bromham
Clapham
Workhouse End
Gamlingay Great Heath
Ravenstone
Watermill
BEDFORD
Blunham
Clifton Reynes
Newton Blossomville
Bridge End
Water End
Willington
Chalton
Everton
Eakley Lanes
Weston Underwood
Emberton
Wick End
Biddenham
Goldington
Sandy
Stoke Goldington
Filgrave
Petsoe End
Stagsden
Queen's Park
Cople
Mogerhanger
Girtford
Stratford

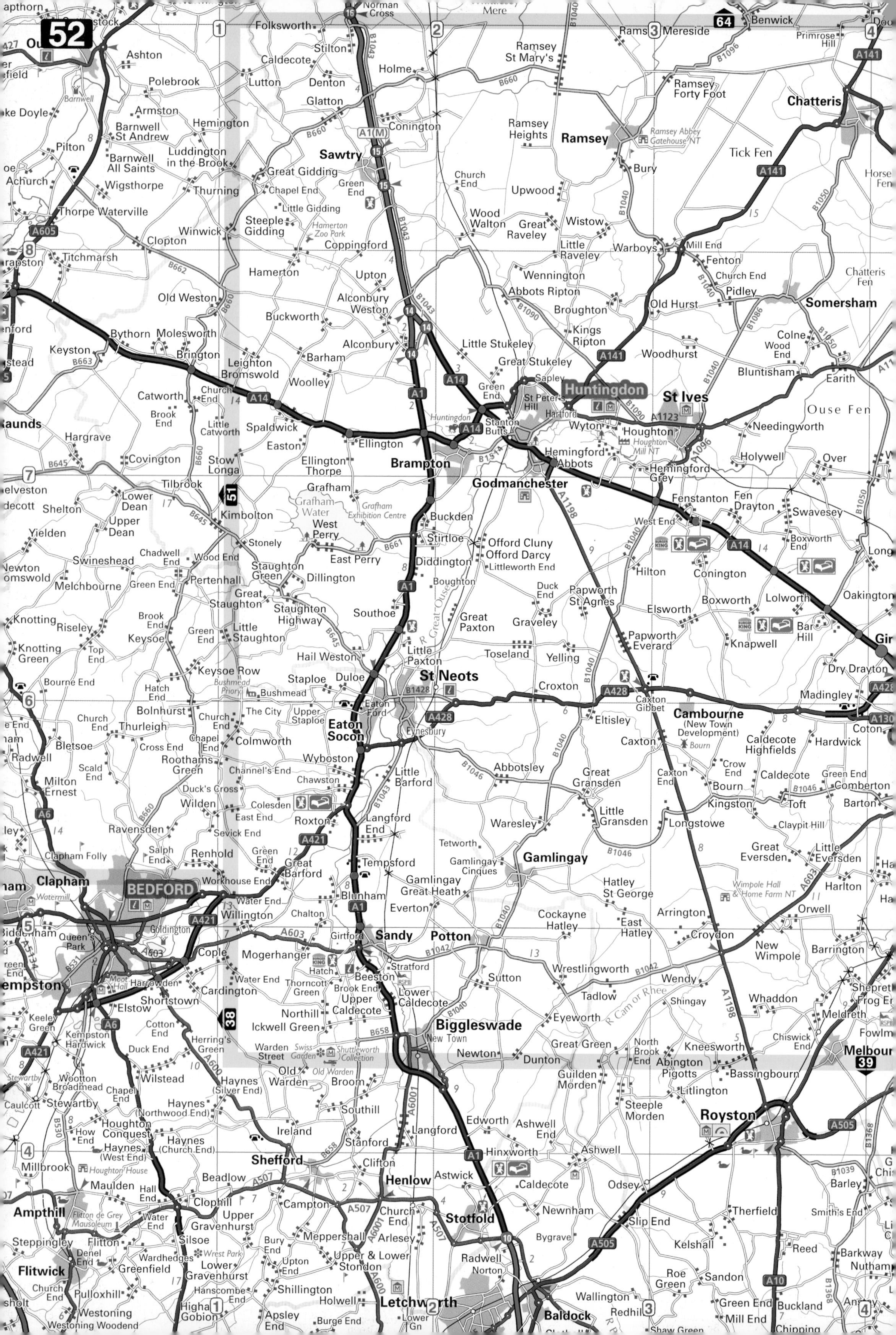

52
64
51
38
39
Folksworth
Norman Cross
Stilton
Caldecote
Holme
Ramsey St Mary's
Rams
Mereside
Benwick
Primrose Hill
Ashton
Polebrook
Lutton
Denton
Glatton
Ramsey Forty Foot
Chatteris
Armston
Barnwell
Hemington
Barnwell St Andrew
Conington
Ramsey Heights
Ramsey
Ramsey Abbey Gatehouse NT
Barnwell All Saints
Luddington in the Brook
Sawtry
Tick Fen
Pilton
Great Gidding
Bury
Achurch
Wigsthorpe
Chapel End
Green End
Church End
Upwood
Thurning
Little Gidding
Thorpe Waterville
Steeple Gidding
Hamerton Zoo Park
Wood Walton
Great Raveley
Wistow
Winwick
Clopton
Coppingford
Little Raveley
Warboys
Mill End
Titchmarsh
Fenton
Hamerton
Upton
Wennington
Church End
Chatteris Fen
Old Weston
Alconbury Weston
Abbots Ripton
Pidley
Buckworth
Broughton
Old Hurst
Somersham
Bythorn
Molesworth
Kings Ripton
Colne
Keyston
Brington
Alconbury
Little Stukeley
Wood End
Barham
Woodhurst
Leighton Bromswold
Great Stukeley
Bluntisham
Woolley
Sapley
Earith
Catworth
Church End
Green End
Huntingdon
St Ives
Brook End
St Peter's Hill
Hartford
Ouse Fen
Little Catworth
Spaldwick
Stanton Butts
Wyton
Houghton
Needingworth
Hargrave
Easton
Ellington
Houghton Mill NT
Covington
Stow Longa
Ellington Thorpe
Brampton
Hemingford Abbots
Holywell
Over
Hemingford Grey
Tilbrook
Godmanchester
Grafham
Fenstanton
Fen Drayton
Lower Dean
Grafham Water
Grafham Exhibition Centre
Swavesey
Shelton
Upper Dean
Kimbolton
West Perry
Buckden
West End
Yielden
Stonely
Stirtloe
Offord Cluny
Boxworth End
Chadwell End
Wood End
Offord Darcy
Swineshead
Staughton Green
East Perry
Diddington
Littleworth End
Hilton
Conington
Melchbourne
Green End
Pertenhall
Dillington
Boughton
Duck End
Papworth St Agnes
Boxworth
Lolworth
Oakington
Great Staughton
Staughton Highway
Southoe
Elsworth
Knotting
Brook End
Riseley
Little Staughton
Great Paxton
Graveley
Papworth Everard
Bar Hill
Keysoe
Green End
Knotting Green
Top End
Hail Weston
Little Paxton
Toseland
Yelling
Knapwell
Keysoe Row
Dry Drayton
Bourne End
Bushmead Priory
Staploe
Duloe
St Neots
Croxton
Bushmead
Hatch End
Eaton Ford
Caxton Gibbet
Madingley
Bolnhurst
The City
Upper Staploe
Eaton Socon
Eynesbury
Cambourne
Eltisley
Church End
Church End
Thurleigh
(New Town Development)
Coton
Chapel End
Caxton
Bourn
Caldecote Highfields
Hardwick
Bletsoe
Cross End
Colmworth
Wyboston
Radwell
Roothams Green
Channel's End
Little Barford
Abbotsley
Crow End
Great Gransden
Caxton End
Caldecote
Green End
Scald End
Chawston
Bourn
Comberton
Milton Ernest
Duck's Cross
Kingston
Toft
Barton
Wilden
Colesden
Little Gransden
Longstowe
East End
Langford End
Waresley
Claypit Hill
Ravensden
Roxton
Sevick End
Tetworth
Great Eversden
Little Eversden
Salph End
Renhold
Green End
Tempsford
Gamlingay Cinques
Gamlingay
Clapham Folly
Great Barford
Harlton
Clapham
Workhouse End
Gamlingay Great Heath
Hatley St George
BEDFORD
Watermill
Water End
Blunham
Wimpole Hall & Home Farm NT
Willington
Chalton
Everton
Arrington
Orwell
Cockayne Hatley
Biddenham
Queen's Park
Goldington
Girtford
Sandy
Potton
East Hatley
Croydon
Copley
Mogerhanger
New Wimpole
Barrington
Hatch
Stratford
Beeston
Wrestlingworth
Kempston
Harrowden
Water End
Thorncott Green
Brook End
Sutton
Wendy
Shepreth
Moot Hall
Cardington
Lower Caldecote
Shortstown
Upper Caldecote
Tadlow
Shingay
Whaddon
Frog End
Elstow
Northill
Eyeworth
Meldreth
Keeley Green
Cotton End
Biggleswade
Kempston Hardwick
Ickwell Green
New Town
Chiswick End
Fowlmere
Herring's Green
Swiss Garden
Shuttleworth Collection
Great Green
North Brook End
Kneesworth
Melbourn
Duck End
Warden Street
Newton
Dunton
Abington Pigotts
Old Warden
Guilden Morden
Bassingbourn
Wootton Broadmead
Wilstead
Haynes (Silver End)
Broom
Stewartby
Chapel End
Litlington
Caulcott
Haynes (Northwood End)
Southill
Steeple Morden
Royston
How End
Houghton Conquest
Edworth
Ashwell End
Ireland
Langford
Haynes (West End)
Haynes (Church End)
Stanford
Millbrook
Shefford
Hinxworth
Ashwell
Houghton House
Clifton
Barley
Beadlow
Maulden
Henlow
Astwick
Caldecote
Odsey
Hall End
Clophill
Ampthill
Campton
Church End
Therfield
Smith's End
Upper Gravenhurst
Stotfold
Newnham
Flitton de Grey Mausoleum
Water End
Slip End
Steppingley
Flitton
Silsoe
Meppershall
Arlesey
Bygrave
Kelshall
Reed
Denel End
Wrest Park
Bury End
Wardhedges
Upper & Lower Stondon
Radwell
Barkway
Flitwick
Lower Gravenhurst
Upton End
Norton
Nuthampstead
Greenfield
Shillington
Roe Green
Sandon
Church End
Hanscombe End
Letchworth
Pulloxhill
Holwell
Wallington
Green End
Buckland
Higham Gobion
Baldock
Redhill
Westoning
Apsley End
Burge End
Lower Gn
Mill End
Westoning Woodend
Shaw Green
Chipping
A1(M)
A1
A14
A141
A1123
A1096
A1198
A428
A421
A6
A603
A600
A6001
A507
A505
A10
A605
A5134
B1043
B1040
B1090
B1086
B1050
B1096
B660
B662
B663
B645
B1514
B1428
B1046
B1042
B658
B1039
B1368
B531
B530
R Great Ouse
R Cam or Rhee

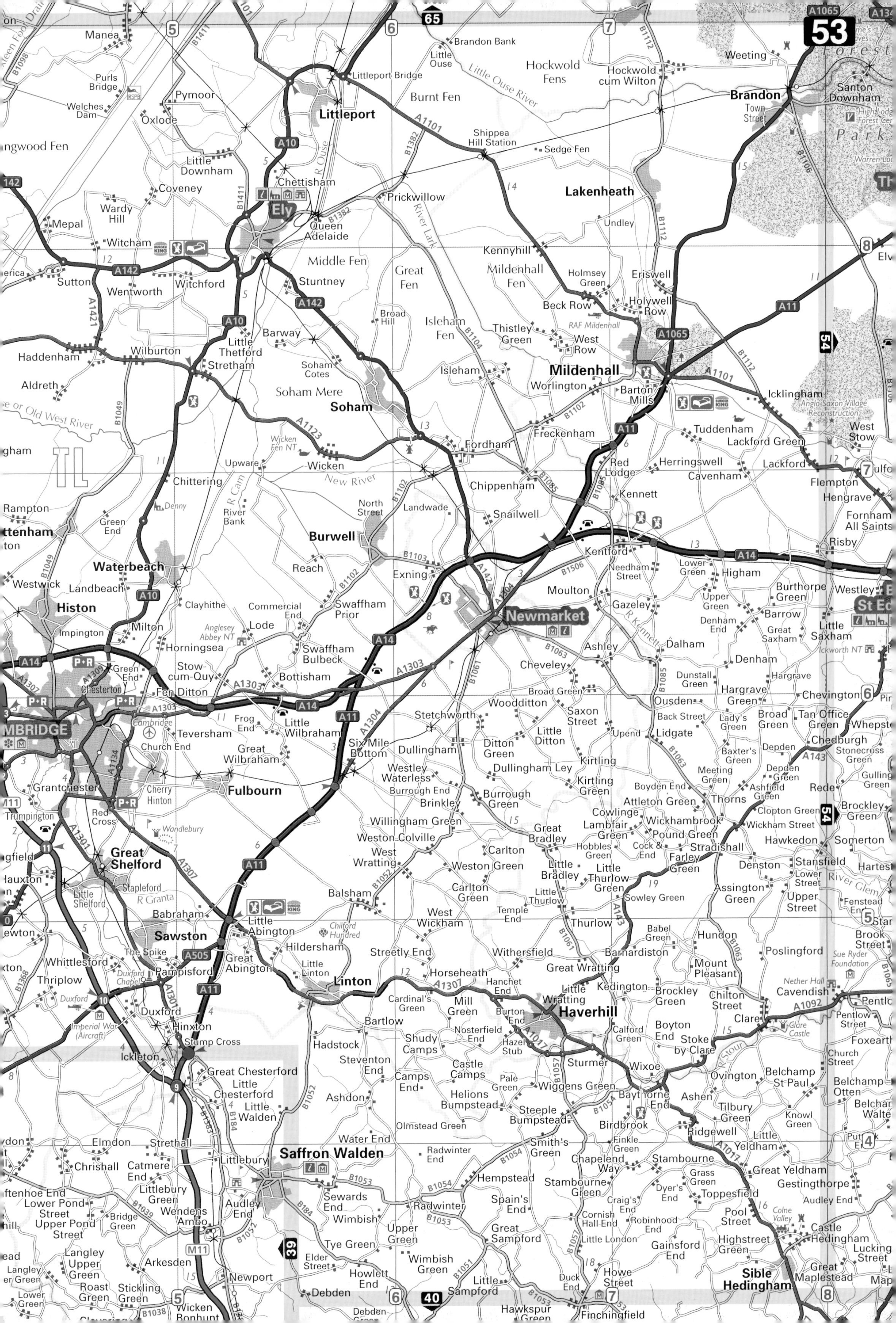
53
65
A1065
Manea
Purls Bridge
Welches Dam
Pymoor
Oxlode
ngwood Fen
Little Downham
Coveney
Wardy Hill
Mepal
Witcham
Sutton
Wentworth
Witchford
A142
A1421
Haddenham
Aldreth
Wilburton
Little Thetford
Stretham
Old West River
B1049
TL
Chittering
Denny
Rampton
Green End
Cottenham
Waterbeach
Westwick
Landbeach
Histon
Impington
Milton
Horningsea
Clayhithe
Stow-cum-Quy
Fen Ditton
Chesterton
CAMBRIDGE
Teversham
Church End
Cherry Hinton
Grantchester
Trumpington
Red Cross
Wandlebury
Great Shelford
Stapleford
Little Shelford
R Granta
Hauxton
Newton
Babraham
Sawston
The Spike
Whittlesford
Thriplow
Duxford
Duxford Chapel
Imperial War (Aircraft)
Pampisford
Great Abington
Little Abington
Hinxton
Stump Cross
Ickleton
Great Chesterford
Little Chesterford
Little Walden
Elmdon
Strethall
Chrishall
Catmere End
Littlebury
Littlebury Green
Wendens Ambo
Audley End
Saffron Walden
Arkesden
Newport
Langley Upper Green
Roast Green
Stickling Green
Wicken Bonhunt
Littleport
Littleport Bridge
Ely
Chettisham
Queen Adelaide
Prickwillow
Burnt Fen
Brandon Bank
Little Ouse
Little Ouse River
Hockwold Fens
Hockwold cum Wilton
Weeting
Brandon
Town Street
Santon Downham
Shippea Hill Station
Sedge Fen
Lakenheath
Undley
Kennyhill
Mildenhall Fen
Holmsey Green
Eriswell
Beck Row
Holywell Row
RAF Mildenhall
Thistley Green
West Row
Mildenhall
Worlington
Barton Mills
Icklingham
Anglo-Saxon Village Reconstruction
West Stow
Tuddenham
Lackford Green
Lackford
Herringswell
Cavenham
Flempton
Hengrave
Fornham All Saints
Risby
Middle Fen
Great Fen
Stuntney
Broad Hill
Isleham Fen
Isleham
Barway
Soham Cotes
Soham Mere
Soham
Wicken Fen NT
Wicken
Upware
New River
Fordham
Freckenham
Red Lodge
Kennett
Chippenham
Snailwell
North Street
Landwade
Burwell
Reach
Exning
Swaffham Prior
Commercial End
Lode
Anglesey Abbey NT
Swaffham Bulbeck
Bottisham
Newmarket
Moulton
Kentford
Needham Street
Gazeley
Lower Green
Higham
Upper Green
Denham End
Burthorpe Green
Barrow
Westley
Great Saxham
Little Saxham
Ickworth NT
Dalham
Denham
Ashley
Cheveley
Dunstall Green
Hargrave
Hargrave Green
Chevington
Broad Green
Ousden
Woodditton
Saxon Street
Stetchworth
Dullingham
Little Wilbraham
Great Wilbraham
Frog End
Six Mile Bottom
Fulbourn
Westley Waterless
Burrough End
Brinkley
Ditton Green
Little Ditton
Dullingham Ley
Kirtling
Kirtling Green
Burrough Green
Upend
Lidgate
Back Street
Lady's Green
Broad Green
Tan Office Green
Whepstead
Depden
Chedburgh
Baxter's Green
Stonecross Green
Meeting Green
Depden Green
Boyden End
Ashfield Green
Rede
Thorns
Attleton Green
Cowlinge
Lambfair Green
Wickhambrook
Pound Green
Great Bradley
Hobbles Green
Cock & End
Stradishall
Farley Green
Clopton Green
Wickham Street
Brockley Green
Hawkedon
Somerton
Willingham Green
Weston Colville
West Wratting
Carlton
Weston Green
Little Bradley
Little Thurlow
Little Thurlow Green
Carlton Green
Sowley Green
Denston
Stansfield
Lower Street
Upper Street
Assington Green
Hartest
Fenstead End
River Glem
Balsham
Chilford Hundred
Temple End
Thurlow
West Wickham
Hildersham
Little Linton
Linton
Streetly End
Withersfield
Babel Green
Hundon
Great Wratting
Barnardiston
Mount Pleasant
Poslingford
Brook Street
Sue Ryder Foundation
Horseheath
Hanchet End
Little Wratting
Haverhill
Kedington
Brockley Green
Chilton Street
Nether Hall
Cavendish
Pentlow
Pentlow Street
Clare
Clare Castle
Cardinal's Green
Mill Green
Bartlow
Burton End
Nosterfield End
Shudy Camps
Hazel Stub
Calford Green
Boyton End
Stoke by Clare
Hadstock
Steventon End
Castle Camps
Camps End
Sturmer
Wixoe
Ovington
Belchamp St Paul
Belchamp Otten
Belchamp Walter
Foxearth
Church Street
Pale Green
Wiggens Green
Helions Bumpstead
Steeple Bumpstead
Baythorne End
Ashen
Tilbury Green
Knowl Green
Ashdon
Olmstead Green
Birdbrook
Ridgewell
Little Yeldham
Water End
Radwinter End
Smith's Green
Finkle Green
Chapelend Way
Stambourne
Grass Green
Great Yeldham
Gestingthorpe
Sewards End
Hempstead
Stambourne Green
Dyer's End
Toppesfield
Audley End
Radwinter
Wimbish
Spain's End
Craig's End
Cornish Hall End
Robinhood End
Pool Street
Colne Valley
Castle Hedingham
Upper Green
Great Sampford
Little London
Gainsford End
Highstreet Green
Lucking Street
Tye Green
Elder Street
Wimbish Green
Howlett End
Howe Street
Sible Hedingham
Great Maplestead
Debden
Little Sampford
Duck End
Hawkspur Green
Finchingfield
Debden Green
Lower Green
Langley Lower Green
Forest
Park
Warren Lodge
High Lodge Forest Centre
Thetford
Elveden
Stowlangtoft
St Edmundsbury
A10
A11
A14
A142
A1101
A1123
A1303
A1304
A1307
A1309
A1301
A1134
A505
A1017
A1092
A143
M11
B1098
B1411
B1382
B1112
B1106
B1104
B1102
B1103
B1085
B1506
B1063
B1061
B1052
B1054
B1053
B1051
B1057
B1383
B1184
B1039
B1038
B1368
39
40
54
1
2
3
4
5
6
7
8
9
10
11
12
13
14
15
16
17
18
19

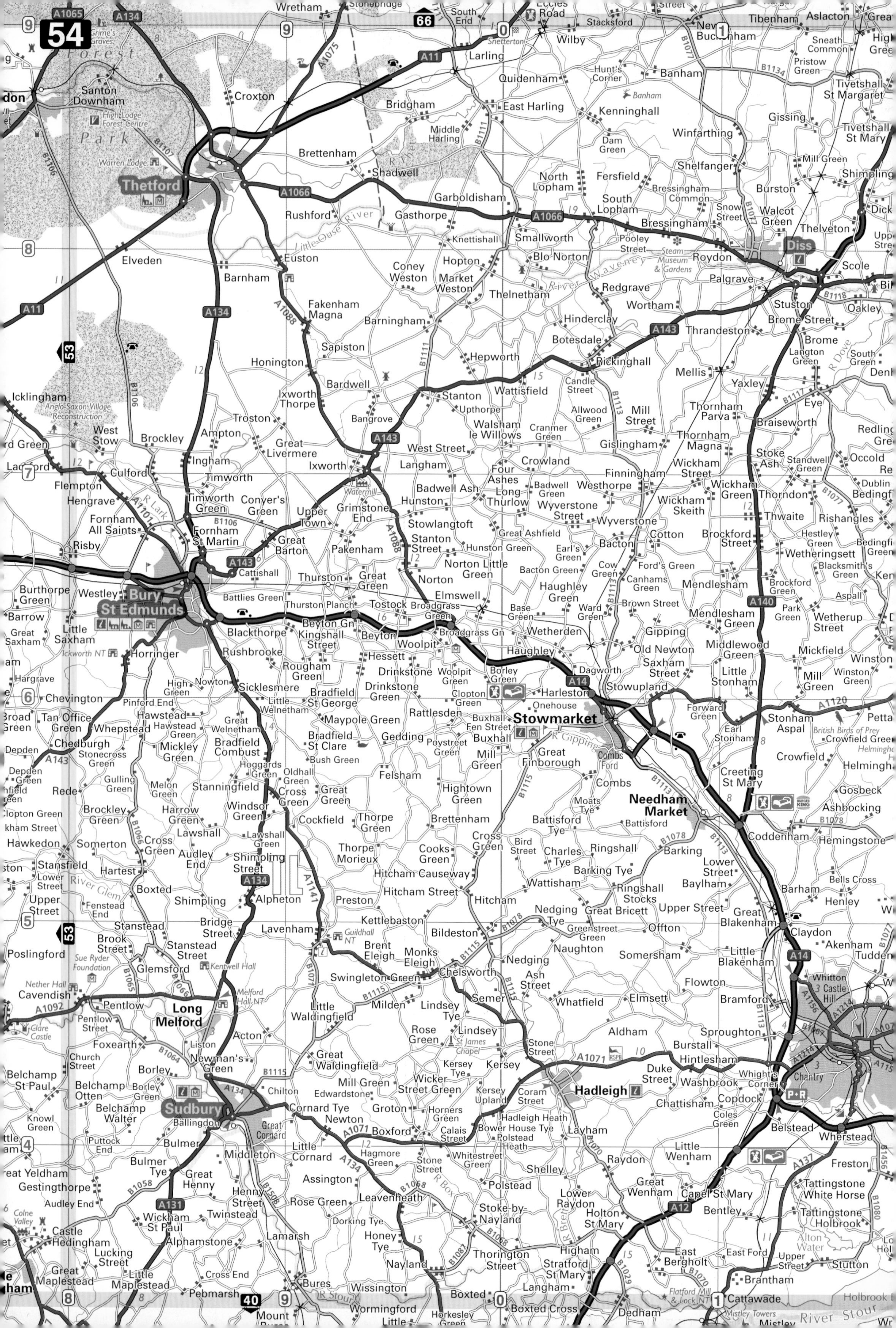
54
A1065
A134
Grime's Graves
Forest
Wretham
Stonebridge
66
South End
Eccles Road
Snetterton
Wilby
Stacksford
New Buckenham
Tibenham
Aslacton
Santon Downham
High Lodge Forest Centre
Park
Warren Lodge
Thetford
Croxton
A11
Larling
Quidenham
Hunt's Corner
Banham
Sneath Common
Pristow Green
Tivetshall St Margaret
Bridgham
East Harling
Kenninghall
Gissing
Middle Harling
Dam Green
Winfarthing
Tivetshall St Mary
Brettenham
Shadwell
North Lopham
Fersfield
Shelfanger
Mill Green
Shimpling
Bressingham Common
Burston
Garboldisham
South Lopham
A1066
A1066
Rushford
Gasthorpe
Little Ouse River
Knettishall
Smallworth
Bressingham
Snow Street
Walcot Green
Dickleburgh
Thelveton
Pooley Street
Steam Museum & Gardens
Diss
Elveden
Euston
Hopton
Blo Norton
Roydon
Scole
Barnham
Coney Weston
Market Weston
Thelnetham
River Waveney
Redgrave
Palgrave
Stuston
Brome Street
Oakley
Fakenham Magna
Wortham
Hinderclay
A143
Thrandeston
Barningham
Botesdale
Brome
Sapiston
Hepworth
Rickinghall
Langton Green
South Green
Honington
Mellis
Yaxley
Bardwell
Stanton
Wattisfield
Candle Street
Eye
Icklingham
Anglo-Saxon Village Reconstruction
Ixworth Thorpe
Upthorpe
Allwood Green
Mill Street
Thornham Parva
Braiseworth
Troston
Bangrove
Walsham le Willows
Cranmer Green
West Stow
Brockley
Ampton
Great Livermere
West Street
Gislingham
Thornham Magna
Redlingfield
Ingham
Langham
Crowland
Stoke Ash
Standwell Green
Occold
Lackford
Culford
Ixworth
Timworth
Four Ashes
Finningham
Wickham Street
Flempton
Watermill
Badwell Ash
Long Thurlow
Badwell Green
Westhorpe
Wickham Green
Thorndon
Dublin
Bedingfield
Hengrave
Timworth Green
Conyer's Green
Grimstone End
Hunston
Wyverstone Street
Wickham Skeith
Fornham All Saints
Upper Town
Stowlangtoft
Wyverstone
Thwaite
Rishangles
Fornham St Martin
Great Barton
Great Ashfield
Cotton
Brockford Street
Hestley Green
Risby
Pakenham
Stanton Street
Hunston Green
Earl's Green
Bacton
Wetheringsett
Bedingfield Green
Cattishall
Norton Little Green
Bacton Green
Cow Green
Ford's Green
Blacksmith's Green
Burthorpe Green
Westley
Thurston
Great Green
Norton
Canhams Green
Mendlesham
Brockford Green
Bury St Edmunds
Battlies Green
Thurston Planch
Tostock
Elmswell
Haughley Green
Brown Street
Aspall
Barrow
Beyton Gn
Broadgrass Green
Base Green
Ward Green
Mendlesham Green
Park Green
Wetherup Street
Great Saxham
Little Saxham
Blackthorpe
Kingshall Street
Beyton
Broadgrass Gn
Wetherden
Gipping
Ickworth NT
Horringer
Rushbrooke
Woolpit
Haughley
Old Newton
Middlewood Green
Mickfield
Winston
Hessett
Rougham Green
Drinkstone
Woolpit Green
Borley Green
Dagworth
Saxham Street
Little Stonham
Winston Green
Hargrave
High Green
Nowton
Sicklesmere
Bradfield St George
Drinkstone Green
Clopton Green
A14
Harleston
Stowupland
Mill Green
Chevington
Pinford End
Little Welnetham
Onehouse
Forward Green
A1120
Broad Green
Tan Office Green
Hawstead
Hawstead Green
Great Welnetham
Maypole Green
Rattlesden
Buxhall Fen Street
Stowmarket
Earl Stonham
Stonham Aspal
British Birds of Prey
Crowfield Green
Whepstead
Bradfield Combust
Bradfield St Clare
Gedding
Poystreet Green
Buxhall
R Gipping
Great Finborough
Combs Ford
Crowfield
Depden
Chedburgh
Mickley Green
Stonecross Green
Bush Green
Mill Green
Helmingham
Depden Green
Gulling Green
Hoggards Green
Oldhall Green
Felsham
Combs
Needham Market
Creeting St Mary
Gosbeck
Rede
Melon Green
Stanningfield
Cross Green
Great Green
Hightown Green
Moats Tye
Battisford
Ashbocking
Clopton Green
Brockley Green
Harrow Green
Windsor Green
Cockfield
Thorpe Green
Brettenham
Battisford Tye
Hemingstone
Hawkedon
Somerton
Cross Green
Lawshall
Lawshall Green
Cross Green
Bird Street
Charles Tye
Ringshall
Barking
Coddenham
Stansfield
Hartest
Audley End
Shimpling Street
Thorpe Morieux
Cooks Green
Barking Tye
Lower Street
Bells Cross
Lower Street
River Glem
Boxted
Hitcham Causeway
Wattisham
Ringshall Stocks
Baylham
Barham
Upper Street
Fenstead End
Shimpling
Alpheton
Preston
Hitcham Street
Hitcham
Great Bricett
Upper Street
Great Blakenham
Henley
Stanstead
Bridge Street
Lavenham
Kettlebaston
Nedging Tye
Greenstreet Green
Offton
Claydon
Brook Street
Stanstead Street
Guildhall NT
Brent Eleigh
Bildeston
Naughton
Somersham
Little Blakenham
Akenham
Tuddenham
Poslingford
Sue Ryder Foundation
Glemsford
Kentwell Hall
Monks Eleigh
Nedging
Swingleton Green
Chelsworth
Ash Street
Flowton
Whitton
Castle Hill
Nether Hall
Cavendish
Pentlow
Long Melford
Melford Hall NT
Milden
Lindsey Tye
Semer
Whatfield
Elmsett
Bramford
A1092
Pentlow Street
Little Waldingfield
Clare Castle
Foxearth
Acton
Liston
Rose Green
Lindsey
St James Chapel
Aldham
Sproughton
Church Street
Newman's Green
Great Waldingfield
Stone Street
Burstall
Belchamp St Paul
Borley
Kersey Tye
Kersey
A1071
Duke Street
Hintlesham
Whight's Corner
Belchamp Otten
Borley Green
Chilton
Mill Green
Wicker Street Green
Kersey Upland
Coram Street
Hadleigh
Washbrook
Chantry
Belchamp Walter
Sudbury
Edwardstone
Groton
Horners Green
Chattisham
Copdock
Ballingdon
Great Cornard
Cornard Tye
Newton
Hadleigh Heath
Bower House Tye
Coles Green
Belstead
Knowl Green
Bulmer
Boxford
Calais Street
Polstead Heath
Layham
Wherstead
Puttock End
Middleton
Little Cornard
Hagmore Green
Stone Street
Whitestreet Green
Little Wenham
Freston
Bulmer Tye
Great Henny
Assington
R Box
Shelley
Raydon
Great Yeldham
Gestingthorpe
Henny Street
Leavenheath
Polstead
Great Wenham
Capel St Mary
Tattingstone White Horse
Audley End
Wickham St Paul
Twinstead
Rose Green
Dorking Tye
Stoke-by-Nayland
Lower Raydon
Holton St Mary
Bentley
Tattingstone
Holbrook
Colne Valley
Castle Hedingham
Alphamstone
Lamarsh
Honey Tye
A12
Alton Water
Lucking Street
Nayland
Thorington Street
Higham
Stratford St Mary
East Bergholt
East Ford
Upper Street
Stutton
Great Maplestead
Little Maplestead
Cross End
Pebmarsh
Bures
Wissington
Langham
Brantham
40
R Stour
Boxted
Flatford Mill & Lock NT
Cattawade
Holbrook Creek
Mount Bures
Wormingford
Boxted Cross
Dedham
Mistley Towers
Mistley
River Stour
Little Horkesley
Horkesley Green
53
53
A134
A1075
A1088
A1101
A143
A1141
A131
A137
A140
A1156
A1214
A1071
A1088
B1106
B1107
B1111
B1077
B1134
B1118
B1117
B1113
B1078
B1115
B1071
B1066
B1065
B1064
B1058
B1508
B1068
B1087
B1070
B1029
B1080
B1456

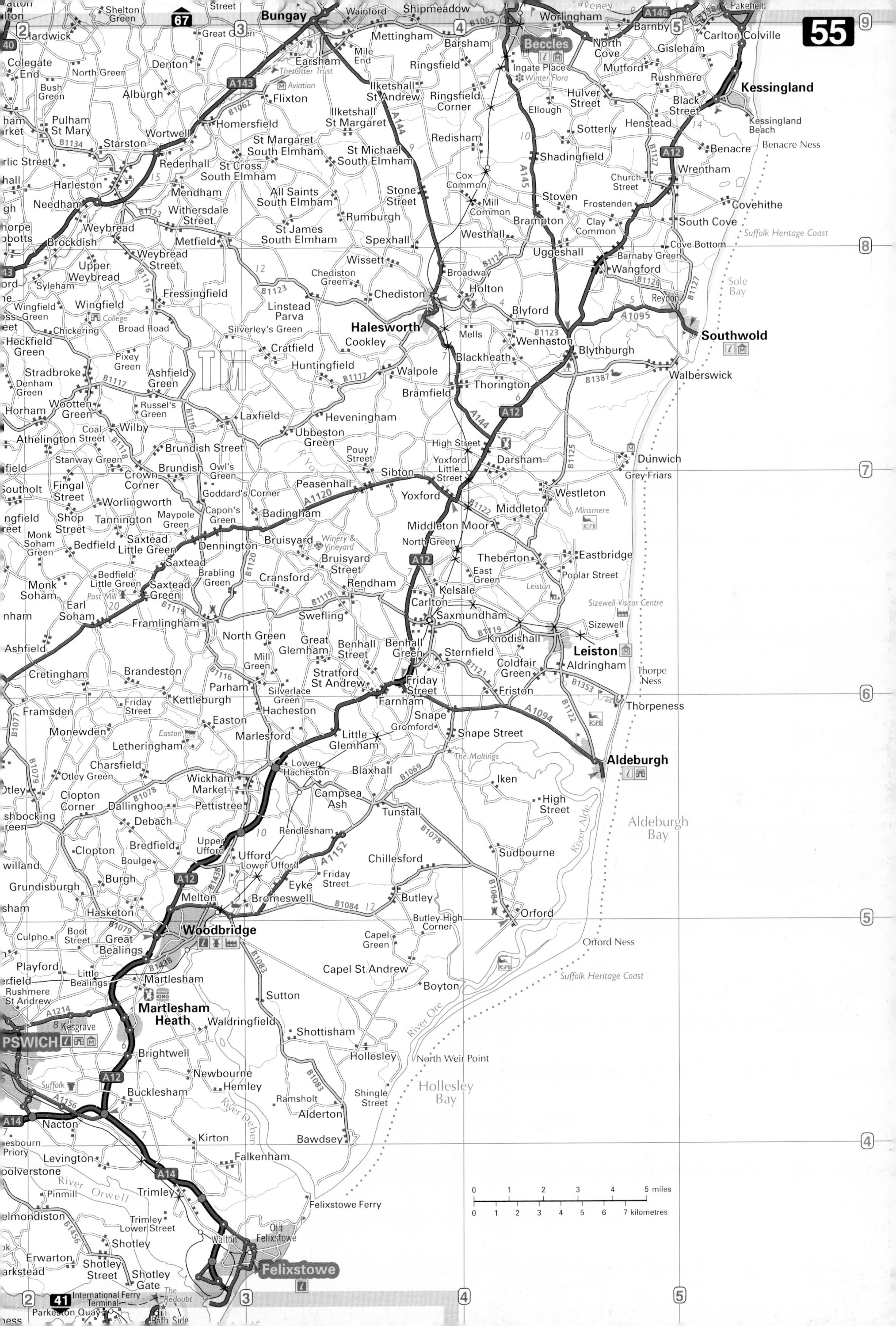
55
Bungay
Shelton Green
Street
67
Great Green
Wainford
Shipmeadow
Worlingham
A146
Pakefield
Hardwick
Mettingham
Barsham
Beccles
Barnby
Carlton Colville
Colegate End
North Green
Denton
Earsham
Mile End
Ringsfield
North Cove
Gisleham
The Otter Trust
Ingate Place
Mutford
Rushmere
Bush Green
A143
Aviation
Ilketshall St Andrew
Ringsfield Corner
Winter Flora
Hulver Street
Kessingland
Alburgh
Flixton
Ellough
Black Street
Pulham St Mary
B1062
Ilketshall St Margaret
Henstead
Kessingland Beach
Wortwell
Homersfield
A144
Redisham
Sotterly
B1134
Starston
St Margaret South Elmham
St Michael South Elmham
Shadingfield
A12
Benacre
Benacre Ness
Redenhall
St Cross South Elmham
Cox Common
A145
B1127
Wrentham
Harleston
Mendham
All Saints South Elmham
Stone Street
Mill Common
Church Street
Needham
Withersdale Street
Rumburgh
Stoven
Frostenden
Covehithe
Weybread
B1123
St James South Elmham
Brampton
Clay Common
South Cove
Brockdish
Metfield
Spexhall
Westhall
Suffolk Heritage Coast
Weybread Street
Uggeshall
Cove Bottom
Upper Weybread
Wissett
Barnaby Green
Syleham
Chediston Green
Broadway
B1124
Wangford
Sole Bay
B1116
Fressingfield
Chediston
Holton
B1126
Reydon
Wingfield
Linstead Parva
Blyford
A1095
Wingfield Green
College
Chickering
Broad Road
Silverley's Green
Halesworth
Mells
Wenhaston
Southwold
Heckfield Green
Cookley
Blythburgh
Cratfield
Blackheath
Pixey Green
Huntingfield
Walpole
B1387
Walberswick
Stradbroke
Ashfield Green
B1117
Denham Green
Thorington
Bramfield
Wootten Green
Russel's Green
Horham
Laxfield
Heveningham
Coal Street
Wilby
Ubbeston Green
Athelington
B1118
Brundish Street
High Street
Darsham
Dunwich
Pouy Street
B1125
Stanway Green
Yoxford
Little Street
Brundish
Owl's Green
Sibton
Grey Friars
Crown Corner
Fingal Street
Peasenhall
Westleton
Goddard's Corner
Worlingworth
A1120
Yoxford
Middleton
Capon's Green
Maypole Green
B1122
Minsmere
Shop Street
Tannington
Badingham
Middleton Moor
RSPB
Monk Soham Green
Saxtead Little Green
Bruisyard
Winery & Vineyard
North Green
Theberton
Eastbridge
Bedfield
Dennington
Bruisyard Street
East Green
Poplar Street
Saxtead
Brabling Green
Cransford
Leiston
Bedfield Little Green
Saxtead Green
Rendham
Kelsale
Monk Soham
Post Mill
Carlton
Sizewell Visitor Centre
Earl Soham
B1119
Swefling
Saxmundham
Sizewell
Framlingham
Knodishall
North Green
Great Glemham
Benhall Street
Benhall Green
Sternfield
Leiston
Ashfield
Mill Green
Coldfair Green
Aldringham
Thorpe Ness
Cretingham
Brandeston
Stratford St Andrew
B1121
B1116
Parham
Friday Street
Friston
B1353
Friday Street
Silverlace Green
Kettleburgh
Farnham
Thorpeness
Framsden
Hacheston
Snape
A1094
B1077
Easton
Monewden
Little Glemham
Gromford
Snape Street
Letheringham
Marlesford
The Maltings
Aldeburgh
Charsfield
Lower Hacheston
Blaxhall
B1069
Iken
B1079
Otley Green
Wickham Market
Otley
Clopton Corner
B1078
Dallinghoo
Campsea Ash
High Street
Pettistree
Tunstall
Debach
Aldeburgh Bay
Rendlesham
Clopton
Bredfield
Upper Ufford
A1152
Sudbourne
Boulge
Ufford
River Alde
Lower Ufford
Chillesford
Grundisburgh
Burgh
Friday Street
Eyke
B1438
Butley
B1084
Melton
Bromeswell
Hasketon
Orford
Butley High Corner
Culpho
Boot Street
Great Bealings
Woodbridge
Capel Green
Orford Ness
B1083
Playford
Little Bealings
Capel St Andrew
Martlesham
Rushmere St Andrew
Suffolk Heritage Coast
Boyton
Sutton
A1214
Martlesham Heath
Waldringfield
Kesgrave
River Ore
Shottisham
IPSWICH
Brightwell
Hollesley
North Weir Point
Newbourne
Hemley
Suffolk
Bucklesham
Hollesley Bay
A1156
Ramsholt
Shingle Street
River Deben
Alderton
A14
Nacton
Kirton
Bawdsey
Levington
Falkenham
River Orwell
Trimley
Pinmill
Felixstowe Ferry
Trimley Lower Street
B1456
Walton
Old Felixstowe
Shotley
Erwarton
Shotley Street
Shotley Gate
Felixstowe
International Ferry Terminal
The Redoubt
41
Parkeston Quay
Bath Side
0 1 2 3 4 5 miles
0 1 2 3 4 5 6 7 kilometres
TM

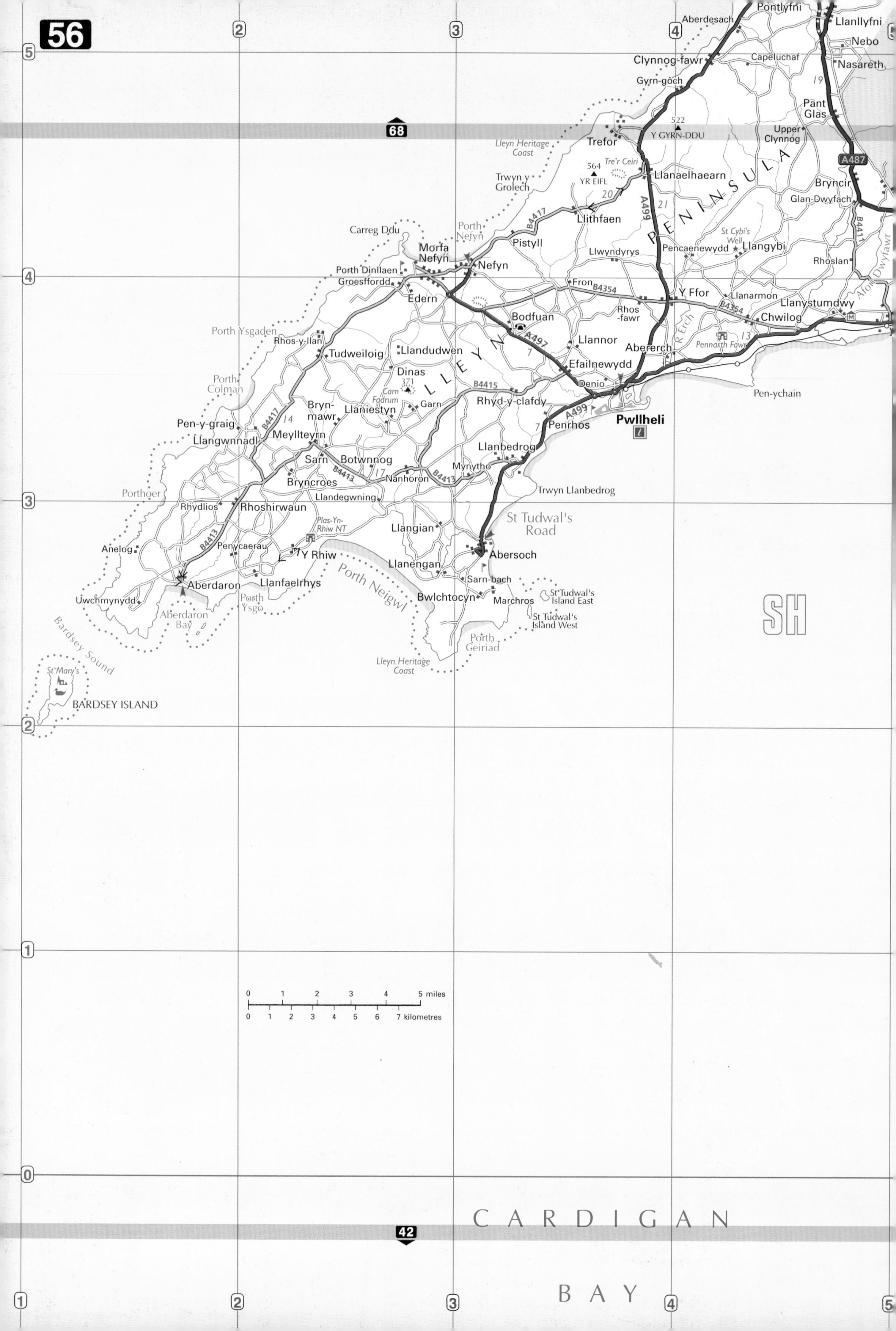
Pontlyfni
Aberdesach
Llanllyfni
Nebo
Clynnog-fawr
Capeluchaf
Nasareth
Gyrn-gôch
Pant Glas
522
Y GYRN-DDU
Upper Clynnog
Trefor
Lleyn Heritage Coast
A487
Tre'r Ceiri
564
YR EIFL
Llanaelhaearn
Trwyn y Grolech
PENINSULA
Bryncir
Glan-Dwyfach
A499
B4417
Llithfaen
B4411
Carreg Ddu
Porth Nefyn
St Cybi's Well
Pistyll
Llwyndyrys
Pencaenewydd
Llangybi
Morfa Nefyn
Rhoslan
Porth Dinllaen
Nefyn
Groesffordd
Fron
B4354
Y Ffor
Llanarmon
Afon Dwyfawr
Edern
Llanystumdwy
Rhos-fawr
B4354
Chwilog
Bodfuan
Porth Ysgaden
A497
Rhos-y-llan
R Erch
Pennarth Fawr
Tudweiloig
Llandudwen
LLEYN
Llannor
Abererch
Dinas
Efailnewydd
Porth Colman
371
Carn Fadrum
B4415
Denio
Pen-ychain
Bryn-mawr
Garn
Rhyd-y-clafdy
Llaniestyn
A499
Pen-y-graig
B4417
Penrhos
Pwllheli
Llangwnnadl
Meyllteyrn
Llanbedrog
Sarn
Botwnnog
B4413
Mynytho
Nanhoron
B4413
Porthoer
Bryncroes
Trwyn Llanbedrog
Llandegwning
Rhydlios
Rhoshirwaun
St Tudwal's Road
Plas-Yn-Rhiw NT
Llangian
Anelog
B4413
Penycaerau
Y Rhiw
Abersoch
Llanengan
Porth Neigwl
Aberdaron
Llanfaelrhys
Sarn-bach
St Tudwal's Island East
Uwchmynydd
Porth Ysgo
Bwlchtocyn
Marchros
St Tudwal's Island West
SH
Aberdaron Bay
Porth Ceiriad
Bardsey Sound
Lleyn Heritage Coast
St Mary's
BARDSEY ISLAND
68
42
0 1 2 3 4 5 miles
0 1 2 3 4 5 6 7 kilometres
CARDIGAN
BAY

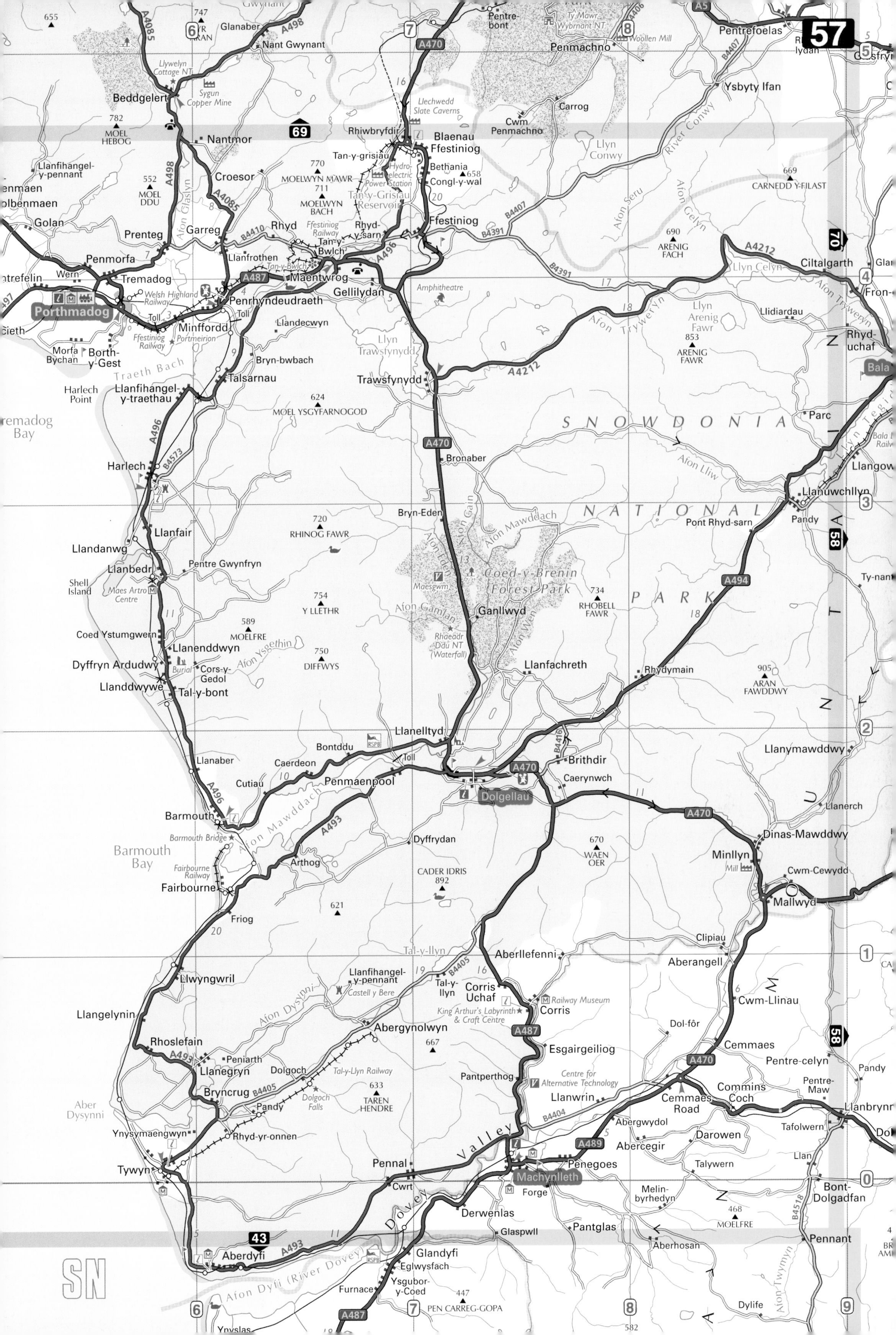
Beddgelert
Llywelyn Cottage NT
Sygun Copper Mine
Nant Gwynant
Glanaber
MOEL HEBOG
Nantmor
Llanfihangel-y-pennant
MOEL DDU
Croesor
Golan
Prenteg
Garreg
Rhyd
Penmorfa
Tremadog
Wern
Porthmadog
Welsh Highland Railway
Ffestiniog Railway
Minffordd
Portmeirion
Morfa Bychan
Borth-y-Gest
Traeth Bach
Harlech Point
Llanfihangel-y-traethau
Talsarnau
Bryn-bwbach
Llandecwyn
Penrhyndeudraeth
Llanfrothen
Maentwrog
Gellilydan
Tan-y-Bwlch
Rhyd-y-sarn
Tan-y-grisiau
Tan-y-Grisiau Reservoir
Hydro-electric Power Station
MOELWYN MAWR
MOELWYN BACH
Rhiwbryfdir
Llechwedd Slate Caverns
Blaenau Ffestiniog
Bethania
Congl-y-wal
Ffestiniog
Amphitheatre
Llyn Trawsfynydd
Trawsfynydd
MOEL YSGYFARNOGOD
Pentre-bont
Ty Mawr Wybrnant NT
Penmachno
Woollen Mill
Cwm Penmachno
Carrog
Llyn Conwy
Afon Serw
Afon Gelyn
River Conwy
Pentrefoelas
Ysbyty Ifan
CARNEDD Y FILAST
ARENIG FACH
Llyn Celyn
Ciltalgarth
Fron-goch
Afon Tryweryn
Llidiardau
Llyn Arenig Fawr
ARENIG FAWR
Rhyd-uchaf
Bala
Parc
S N O W D O N I A
N A T I O N A L
P A R K
Afon Lliw
Llanuwchllyn
Pandy
Pont Rhyd-sarn
Harlech
Tremadog Bay
Bronaber
Bryn-Eden
RHINOG FAWR
Afon Mawddach
Afon Gain
Afon Eden
Maesgwm
Coed-y-Brenin Forest Park
Ganllwyd
RHOBELL FAWR
Afon Gamlan
Rhaeadr Ddu NT (Waterfall)
Afon Wen
Llanfachreth
Rhydymain
ARAN FAWDDWY
Llanfair
Llandanwg
Llanbedr
Pentre Gwynfryn
Shell Island
Maes Artro Centre
Y LLETHR
Coed Ystumgwern
MOELFRE
Llanenddwyn
Afon Ysgethin
DIFFWYS
Dyffryn Ardudwy
Cors-y-Gedol
Burial
Llanddwywe
Tal-y-bont
Llanelltyd
Bontddu
Llanaber
Caerdeon
Cutiau
Penmaenpool
Toll
Brithdir
Caerynwch
Dolgellau
Llanymawddwy
Barmouth
Barmouth Bridge
Barmouth Bay
Fairbourne Railway
Fairbourne
Arthog
Dyffrydan
CADER IDRIS
WAEN OER
Llanerch
Dinas-Mawddwy
Minllyn
Mill
Cwm-Cewydd
Mallwyd
Friog
Tal-y-llyn
Aberllefenni
Clipiau
Aberangell
Llwyngwril
Llanfihangel-y-pennant
Castell y Bere
Tal-y-llyn
Corris Uchaf
Railway Museum
Corris
King Arthur's Labyrinth & Craft Centre
Cwm-Llinau
Llangelynin
Afon Dysynni
Abergynolwyn
Dol-fôr
Rhoslefain
Peniarth
Llanegryn
Esgairgeiliog
Cemmaes
Pentre-celyn
Dolgoch
Tal-y-Llyn Railway
Pantperthog
Centre for Alternative Technology
Commins Coch
Cemmaes Road
Pentre-Maw
Llanbrynmair
Bryncrug
TAREN HENDRE
Dolgoch Falls
Llanwrin
Aber Dysynni
Pandy
Abergwydol
Tafolwern
Ynysymaengwyn
Rhyd-yr-onnen
Darowen
Abercegir
Tywyn
Pennal
Machynlleth
Penegoes
Talywern
Llan
Bont-Dolgadfan
Cwrt
Dovey Valley
Forge
Derwenlas
Melin-byrhedyn
MOELFRE
Glaspwll
Pantglas
Aberhosan
Pennant
Aberdyfi
Glandyfi
Eglwysfach
Afon Dyfi (River Dovey)
Furnace
Ysgubor-y-Coed
PEN CARREG-GOPA
Afon Twymyn
Dylife
Ynyslas
SN

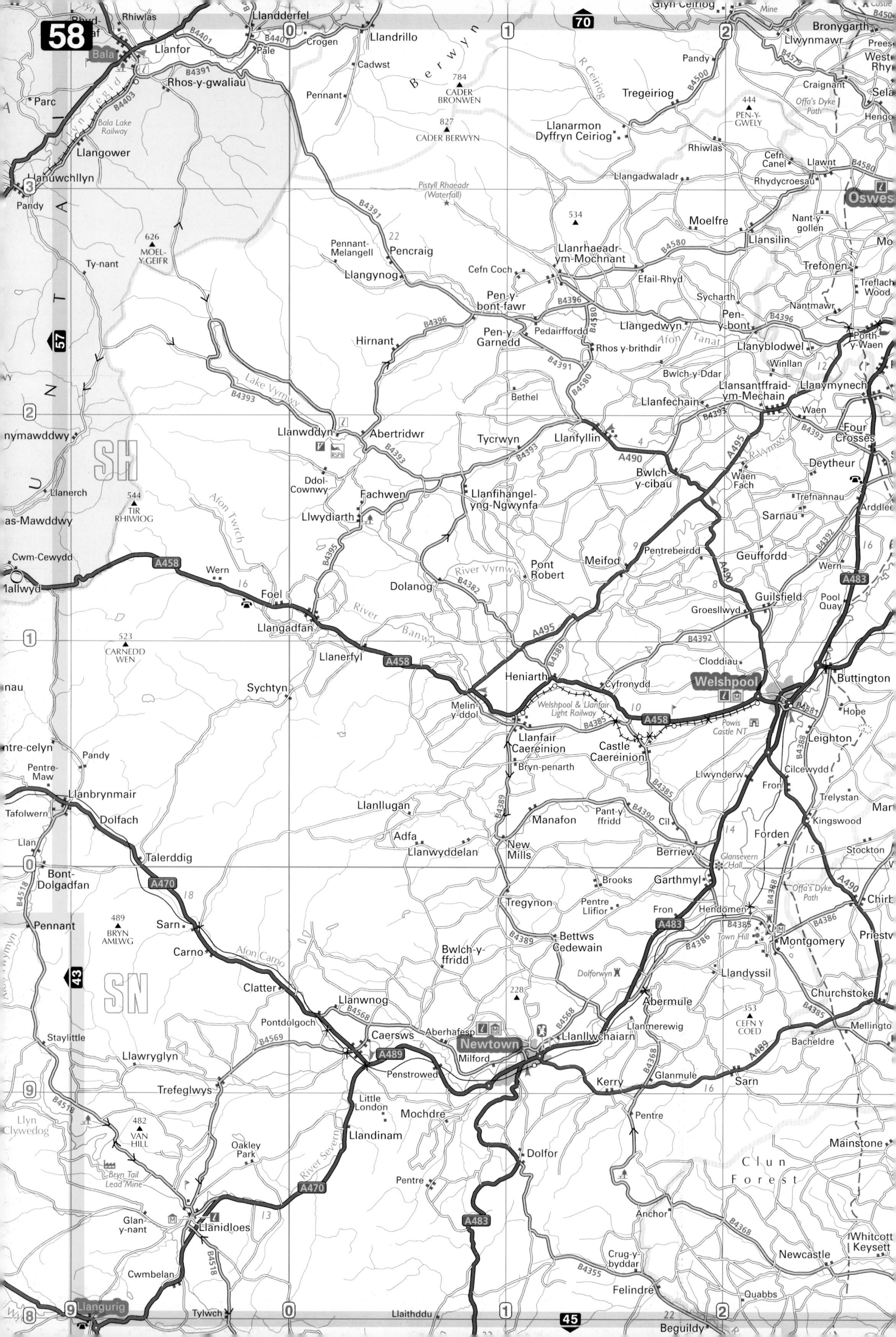
Bala
Llanfor
Llandderfel
Llandrillo
Berwyn
CADER BRONWEN
CADER BERWYN
Llanarmon Dyffryn Ceiriog
Tregeiriog
Bala Lake Railway
Llangower
Llanuwchllyn
Pistyll Rhaeadr (Waterfall)
Llanrhaeadr-ym-Mochnant
Llangynog
Pencraig
Lake Vyrnwy
Llanwddyn
Abertridwr
Llanfyllin
Llansantffraid-ym-Mechain
Llanymynech
Oswestry
Llansilin
Meifod
Welshpool
Welshpool & Llanfair Light Railway
Llanfair Caereinion
Castle Caereinion
Powis Castle NT
Montgomery
Newtown
Caersws
Llanidloes
Llangurig
Carno
Llanbrynmair
Mallwyd
Kerry
Dolfor
Clun Forest
Offa's Dyke Path
Beguildy
Felindre
Llandinam
Garthmyl
Berriew
Churchstoke
Sarn
SH
SN
70
57
43
45

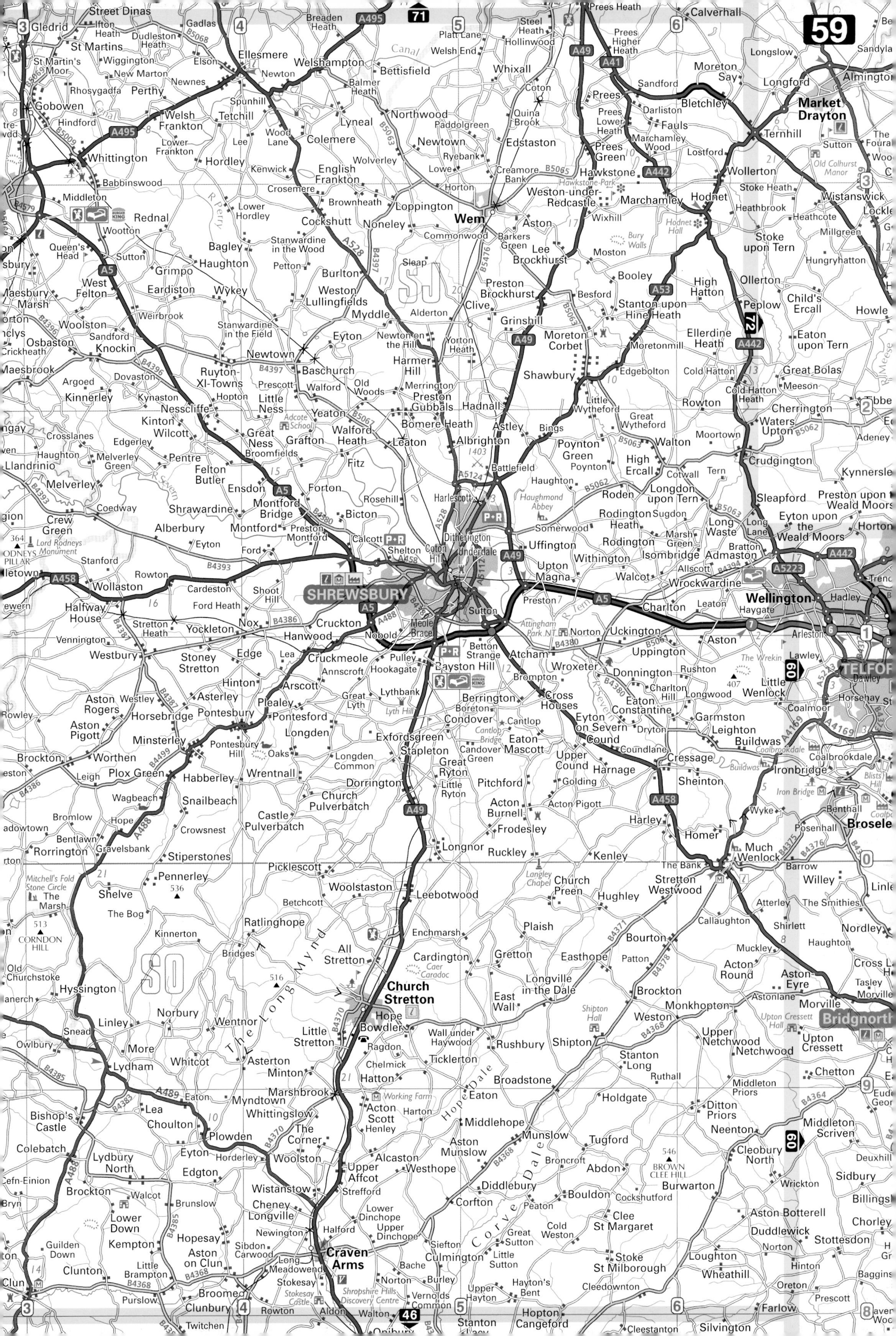

Street Dinas
Gledrid
Ifton Heath
Gadlas
Breaden Heath
A495
71
Steel Heath
Hollinwood
Prees Heath
Calverhall
St Martins
Dudleston Heath
Platt Lane
Whixall
Prees Higher Heath
Longslow
Sandyla
St Martin's Moor
Wiggington
Elson
Ellesmere
Welshampton
Welsh End
A49
A41
Moreton Say
Almington
New Marton
Newton
Bettisfield
Sandford
Longford
Market Drayton
Rhosygadfa
Perthy
Newnes
Balmer Heath
Coton
Prees
Darliston
Bletchley
Gobowen
Welsh Frankton
Spunhill
Tetchill
Lyneal
Northwood
Quina Brook
Prees Lower Heath
Fauls
Ternhill
Hindford
Paddolgreen
Sutton
A495
Lower Frankton
Lee
Wood Lane
Colemere
Newtown
Edstaston
Prees Green
Marchamley Wood
Lostford
Whittington
Hordley
Kenwick
Wolverley
Ryebank
English Frankton
Lowe
Creamore Bank
B5065
Hawkstone
A442
Wollerton
Old Colhurst Manor
Babbinswood
Crosemere
Horton
Hawkstone Park
Weston-under-Redcastle
Stoke Heath
Middleton
Brownheath
Loppington
Marchamley
Hodnet
Wistanswick
Rednal
Lower Hordley
Cockshutt
Noneley
Wem
Aston
Wixhill
Heathbrook
Hodnet Hall
Heathcote
Wootton
Commonwood
Barkers Green
Bury Walls
Millgreen
Queen's Head
Bagley
Stanwardine in the Wood
Lee Brockhurst
Moston
Stoke upon Tern
Sutton
Grimpo
Haughton
Petton
Sleap
Hungryhatton
West Felton
A5
Burlton
SJ
Booley
Eardiston
Wykey
Weston Lullingfields
Preston Brockhurst
Besford
High Hatton
Ollerton
Woolston
Weirbrook
Myddle
Alderton
Clive
A53
Stanton upon Hine Heath
Peplow
Child's Ercall
Howle
Sandford
Stanwardine in the Field
Grinshill
Osbaston
Knockin
Eyton
Newton on the Hill
Yorton Heath
Moreton Corbet
Ellerdine Heath
72
Eaton upon Tern
Newtown
A49
Moretonmill
A442
Maesbrook
Baschurch
Harmer Hill
Shawbury
Edgebolton
Cold Hatton
Great Bolas
Argoed
Dovaston
Ruyton-XI-Towns
Prescott
Kinnerley
Kynaston
Walford
Old Woods
Merrington
Preston Gubbals
Meeson
Hopton
Little Ness
Cold Hatton Heath
Nesscliffe
Hadnall
Little Wytheford
Rowton
Cherrington
Adcote School
Yeaton
Kinton
Wilcott
B5067
Bomere Heath
Astley
Great Wytheford
Waters Upton
Crosslanes
Great Ness
Walford Heath
Bings
B5062
Edgerley
Grafton
Leaton
Albrighton
Poynton Green
Moortown
Haughton
Melverley Green
Pentre
Broomfields
Walton
Adeney
1403
Poynton
High Ercall
Llandrinio
Fitz
Battlefield
Crudgington
A5124
Felton Butler
Haughton
Cotwall
Tern
Kynnersley
Melverley
Ensdon
Forton
Roden
Longdon upon Tern
Sleapford
Harlescott
Haughmond Abbey
Preston upon the Weald Moors
Coedway
Shrawardine
Montford Bridge
Rosehill
P+R
Rodington Heath
Sugdon
B5063
Crew Green
Bicton
Long Waste
Long Lane
Eyton upon the Weald Moors
Horton
364
Lord Rodneys Monument
Alberbury
Montford
Preston Montford
Calcott
Ditherington
Somerwood
Marsh Green
Bratton
Eyton
Uffington
Rodington
Ford
Shelton
Coton Hill
Underdale
A49
Withington
Isombridge
Admaston
A442
Stanford
B4393
Upton Magna
Allscott
A5223
Rowton
Cardeston
Shoot Hill
Walcot
Wrockwardine
A458
Wollaston
SHREWSBURY
Preston
Halfway House
Ford Heath
Sutton
Charlton
Leaton
Wellington
Hadley
Nox
A5
A488
Meole Brace
Attingham Park NT
Haygate
Stretton Heath
Yockleton
B4386
Cruckton
Norton
Uckington
Arleston
Vennington
Hanwood
Nobold
Betton Strange
Westbury
Lea
Edge
Cruckmeole
Pulley
Atcham
Uppington
Aston
Lawley
Stoney Stretton
Annscroft
Hookagate
Bayston Hill
Wroxeter
Donnington
Rushton
The Wrekin
TELFORD
Dawley
Hinton
Arscott
Brompton
Charlton Hill
407
Little Wenlock
Aston Rogers
Westley
Asterley
Great Lyth
Lythbank
Berrington
Cross Houses
Eaton Constantine
Longwood
Horsehay
Horsebridge
Pontesbury
Plealey
Lyth Hill
Boreton
Condover
Cantlop
Eyton on Severn
Garmston
Coalmoor
Aston Pigott
Pontesford
Cantlop Bridge
Dryton
Leighton
A4169
Minsterley
Longden
Exfordsgreen
Eaton Mascott
Cound
Buildwas
Brockton
Worthen
Pontesbury Hill
Oaks
Stapleton
Candover Green
Upper Cound
Coundlane
Coalbrookdale
Longden Common
Great Ryton
Harnage
Cressage
Coalbrookdale
Leigh
Plox Green
Habberley
Wrentnall
Dorrington
Pitchford
Golding
Sheinton
Ironbridge
Little Ryton
Blists Hill
Wagbeach
Snailbeach
Church Pulverbatch
Acton Burnell
Acton Pigott
A458
Iron Bridge
Benthall
Bromlow
Hope
Castle Pulverbatch
Harley
Broseley
Crowsnest
A49
Frodesley
Wyke
Posenhall
Bentlaw
A488
Homer
Rorrington
Gravelsbank
Longnor
Ruckley
Much Wenlock
Stiperstones
Kenley
The Bank
Barrow
Mitchell's Fold Stone Circle
Picklescott
Langley Chapel
Church Preen
Stretton Westwood
Willey
Pennerley
Woolstaston
Leebotwood
Linley
Shelve
536
Hughley
The Marsh
The Bog
Betchcott
Atterley
The Smithies
513
Ratlinghope
Plaish
Shirlett
CORNDON HILL
Kinnerton
Enchmarsh
Callaughton
Bourton
Nordley
Bridges
Mucklev
Haughton
SO
All Stretton
Cardington
Gretton
Easthope
Patton
Acton Round
Old Churchstoke
Caer Caradoc
Cross Lane
The Long Mynd
516
Longville in the Dale
Aston Eyre
Tasley
Hyssington
Church Stretton
Brockton
Astonlane
Morville
East Wall
Monkhopton
Norbury
Shipton Hall
Upton Cressett Hall
Bridgnorth
Linley
Wentnor
Hope Bowdler
Weston
Snead
Little Stretton
Wall under Haywood
Upper Netchwood
Upton Cressett
Owlbury
More
Ragdon
Rushbury
Shipton
Netchwood
Lydham
Whitcot
Asterton
Chelmick
Ticklerton
Stanton Long
Chetton
B4385
Minton
Ruthall
Hope Dale
Broadstone
Middleton Priors
A489
Eaton
Hatton
Marshbrook
Eaton
Holdgate
Bishop's Castle
Lea
Myndtown
Working Farm
Acton Scott
Harton
Ditton Priors
Choulton
Whittingslow
Henley
Middlehope
Neenton
Middleton Scriven
The Corner
Munslow
Colebatch
Plowden
Aston Munslow
Tugford
Lydbury North
Eyton
Horderley
Woolston
Alcaston
546
Cleobury North
Edgton
Upper Affcot
Westhope
Broncroft
Abdon
BROWN CLEE HILL
Deuxhill
Corve Dale
Sidbury
Wistanstow
Strefford
Diddlebury
Burwarton
Wrickton
Brockton
Walcot
Cheney Longville
Corfton
Bouldon
Cockshutford
Billings
Brunslow
Lower Down
Lower Dinchope
Peaton
Clee St Margaret
Aston Botterell
Newington
Halford
Upper Dinchope
Great Sutton
Cold Weston
Dudlewick
Chorley
Guilden Down
Kempton
Hopesay
Sibdon Carwood
Craven Arms
Siefton
Norton
Stottesdon
Aston on Clun
Long Meadowend
Culmington
Little Sutton
Stoke St Milborough
Loughton
Clunton
Little Brampton
B4368
Bache
Hinton
Stokesay
Norton
Burley
Hayton's Bent
Wheathill
Baggins
Clun
Stokesay Castle
Shropshire Hills Discovery Centre
Vernolds Common
Upper Hayton
Cleedownton
Oreton
Broome
Purslow
Clunbury
Rowton
Aldon
Walton
Hopton Cangeford
Prescott
Farlow
Twitchen
46
Onibury
Stanton Lacy
Cleestanton
Silvington

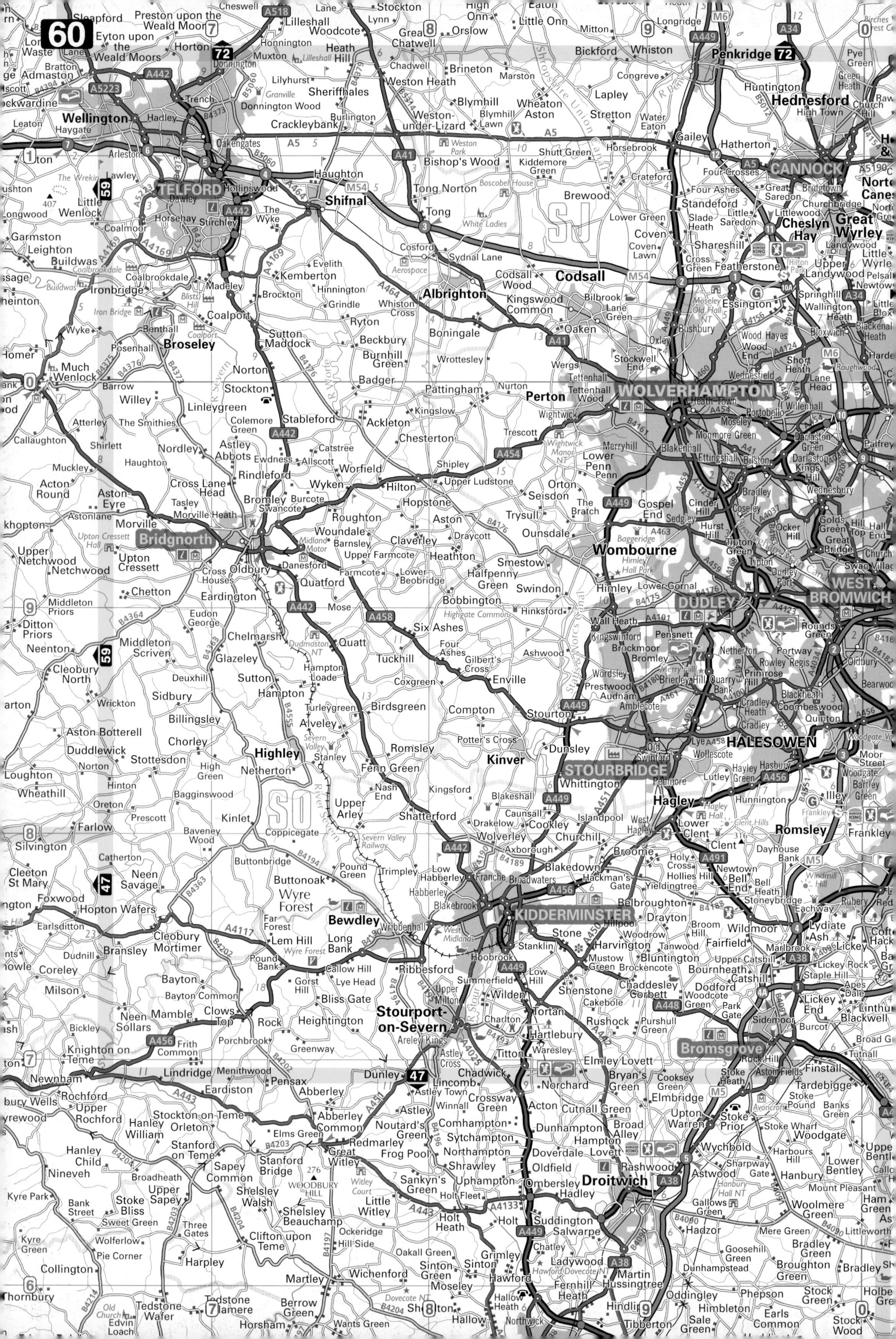
Wellington
TELFORD
Shifnal
Albrighton
Codsall
Penkridge
72
Hednesford
CANNOCK
Cheslyn Hay
Great Wyrley
WOLVERHAMPTON
Perton
Wombourne
DUDLEY
WEST BROMWICH
HALESOWEN
STOURBRIDGE
Hagley
Romsley
Kinver
Bridgnorth
Broseley
Much Wenlock
Ironbridge
Highley
Bewdley
Wyre Forest
KIDDERMINSTER
Stourport-on-Severn
Cleobury Mortimer
Droitwich
Bromsgrove
47
59
Tong
Brewood
Worfield
Claverley
Alveley
Chelmarsh
Kingswinford
Brierley Hill
Belbroughton
Hartlebury
Ombersley
Great Witley
Abberley
Tenbury Wells
Newnham
Kemberton
Oldbury
Quatt
Shatterford
Cookley
Wolverley
Chaddesley Corbett
Stoke Prior
Hanbury
SJ
SO

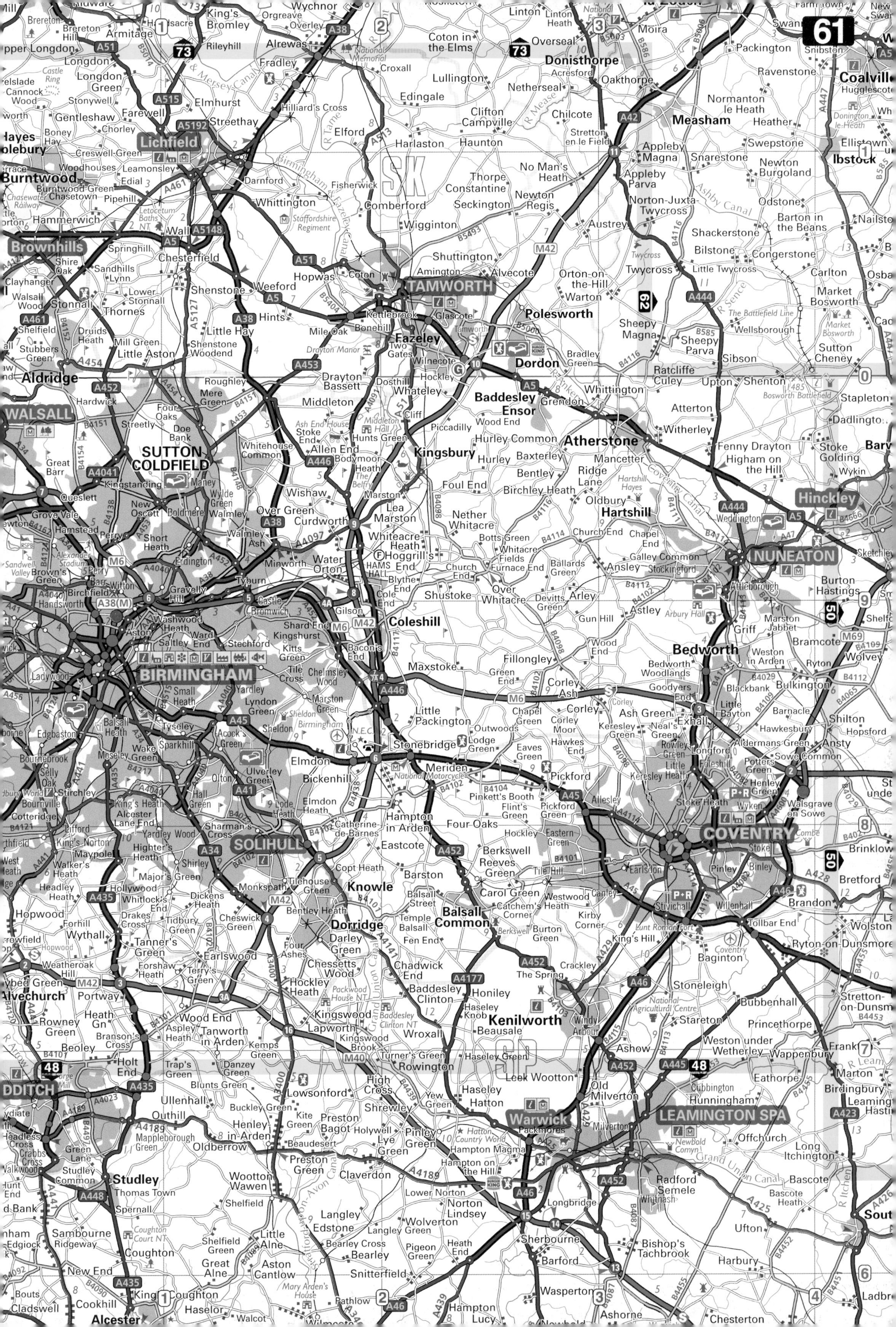
61
73
62
50
48
SK
SP
Lichfield
Brownhills
Burntwood
Aldridge
WALSALL
SUTTON COLDFIELD
BIRMINGHAM
SOLIHULL
TAMWORTH
Fazeley
Polesworth
Dordon
Atherstone
Hinckley
NUNEATON
Bedworth
COVENTRY
Kenilworth
Warwick
LEAMINGTON SPA
DDITCH
Alvechurch
Studley
Alcester
Coleshill
Kingsbury
Knowle
Dorridge
Balsall Common
Measham
Coalville
Ibstock
Donisthorpe
Moira
Sheepy Magna
Market Bosworth
Lapworth
Wellesbourne
Hopwood
Wythall
Meriden
Stonebridge
Kingstanding
Erdington
Castle Bromwich
Shard End
Chelmsley Wood
Marston Green
Elmdon
Hampton in Arden
Shirley
Whittington
Hopwas
Shenstone
Wall
Armitage
Alrewas
Fradley
Elford
Harlaston
Clifton Campville
No Man's Heath
Newton Regis
Austrey
Twycross
Appleby Magna
Snarestone
Barton in the Beans
Shackerstone
Congerstone
Carlton
Sibson
Ratcliffe Culey
Witherley
Fenny Drayton
Higham on the Hill
Stoke Golding
Burbage
Bulkington
Ansty
Binley
Baginton
Stoneleigh
Ryton-on-Dunsmore
Wolston
Princethorpe
Weston under Wetherley
Cubbington
Radford Semele
Bishop's Tachbrook
Barford
Sherbourne
Hampton Magna
Hatton
Shrewley
Rowington
Claverdon
Henley-in-Arden
Wootton Wawen
Tanworth in Arden
Earlswood
Hockley Heath
Chadwick End
Honiley
Leek Wootton
Berkswell
Fillongley
Corley
Arley
Ansley
Hartshill
Mancetter
Baxterley
Middleton
Drayton Bassett
Curdworth
Minworth
Water Orton
Wishaw
Great Barr
Streetly
Tyseley
Sparkhill
Moseley
Edgbaston
Selly Oak
Bournville
Stirchley
Kings Norton
Hollywood
Olton
Acocks Green
Bickenhill
National Motorcycle Museum
N.E.C.
Birmingham
Coventry
Bosworth Battlefield
The Battlefield Line
Ashby Canal
Coventry Canal
Grand Union Canal
Stratford-upon-Avon Canal
Birmingham & Fazeley Canal
Trent & Mersey Canal
R Tame
R Anker
R Mease
R Sence
R Arrow
R Leam
R Itchen
M6
M42
M40
M69
A5
A38
A38(M)
A45
A46
A444
A446
A452
A453
A435
A441
A3400
A4177
A429
A423
A425
A51
A513
A515
A5192
A5148
A454
A4041
A4040
A4097
A4189
A448
A47
A426
A428

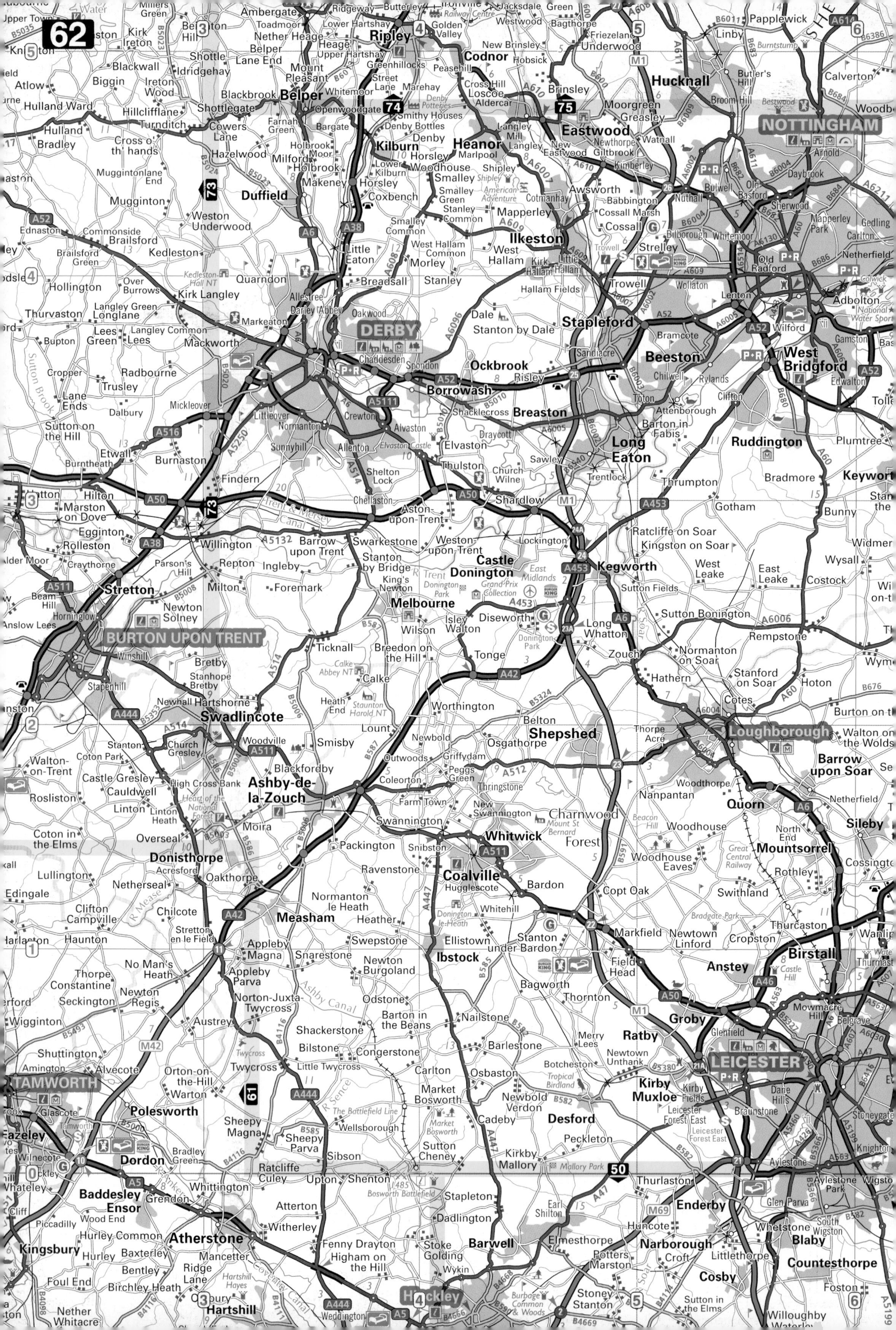
Ambergate
Ridgeway
Butterley
Ironville
Jacksdale
Westwood
Bagthorpe
Selston Green
Papplewick
Linby
Toadmoor
Lower Hartshay
Golden Valley
Ripley
Nether Heage
Heage
Upper Hartshay
Greenhillocks
Belper
Lane End
Shottle
Idridgehay
Blackwall
Kirk Ireton
Atlow
Biggin
Ireton Wood
Hulland Ward
Hillcliffane
Hulland
Bradley
Turnditch
Cowers Lane
Cross o' th' hands
Hazelwood
Muggintonlane End
Mugginton
Weston Underwood
Duffield
Milford
Holbrook
Holbrook Moor
Makeney
Farnah Green
Bargate
Blackbrook
Shottlegate
Mount Pleasant
Whitemoor
Openwoodgate
Street Lane
Marehay
Denby Potteries
Smithy Houses
Denby Bottles
Denby
Kilburn
Lower Kilburn
Horsley
Horsley Woodhouse
Coxbench
Codnor
Peasehill
Cross Hill
Loscoe
Aldercar
Heanor
Marlpool
Langley Mill
Langley
Shipley
Smalley
Smalley Green
Smalley Common
Stanley Common
American Adventure
Mapperley
Cotmanhay
Ilkeston
West Hallam
West Hallam Common
Morley
Little Eaton
Breadsall
Stanley
Kirk Hallam
Little Hallam
Hallam Fields
New Brinsley
Hobsick
Brinsley
Westwood
Friezeland
Underwood
Moorgreen
Greasley
Eastwood
Newthorpe
New Eastwood
Giltbrook
Kimberley
Watnall
Awsworth
Babbington
Cossall Marsh
Cossall
Strelley
Trowell
Hucknall
Butler's Hill
Broom Hill
Bestwood
Calverton
Woodborough
NOTTINGHAM
Arnold
Daybrook
Bulwell
Old Basford
Nuthall
Sherwood
Mapperley Park
Gedling
Carlton
Netherfield
Bilborough
Whitemoor
Old Radford
Radford
Wollaton
Lenton
Colwick
Adbolton
National Water Sports
Gamston
Wilford
West Bridgford
Edwalton
Bramcote
Beeston
Chilwell
Rylands
Stapleford
Sandiacre
Toton
Attenborough
Clifton
Barton in Fabis
Long Eaton
Ruddington
Plumtree
Keyworth
Ednaston
Commonside
Brailsford
Brailsford Green
Kedleston
Kedleston Hall NT
Quarndon
Hollington
Over Burrows
Kirk Langley
Thurvaston
Langley Green
Longlane
Lees Green
Lees
Langley Common
Mackworth
Markeaton
Bupton
Cropper
Radbourne
Trusley
Lane Ends
Dalbury
Sutton on the Hill
Etwall
Burnaston
Burntheath
Mickleover
Littleover
Normanton
Sunnyhill
Allenton
Alvaston
Crewton
Allestree
Darley Abbey
Oakwood
DERBY
Chaddesden
Spondon
Borrowash
Ockbrook
Dale
Stanton by Dale
Risley
Shacklecross
Breaston
Draycott
Elvaston
Elvaston Castle
Thulston
Church Wilne
Sawley
Trentlock
Shelton Lock
Chellaston
Aston-upon-Trent
Shardlow
Findern
Hilton
Marston on Dove
Egginton
Rolleston
Willington
Trent & Mersey Canal
Barrow upon Trent
Swarkestone
Weston-upon-Trent
Stanton by Bridge
Castle Donington
Lockington
Kegworth
Ratcliffe on Soar
Kingston on Soar
Thrumpton
Gotham
Bradmore
Bunny
West Leake
East Leake
Costock
Wysall
Widmerpool
Alder Moor
Craythorne
Parson's Hill
Repton
Ingleby
Foremark
Milton
Stretton
Beam Hill
Horninglow
Anslow Lees
Newton Solney
BURTON UPON TRENT
Winshill
Bretby
Stanhope Bretby
Stapenhill
Newhall
Hartshorne
Swadlincote
King's Newton
Melbourne
Donington Park
East Midlands
Grand Prix Collection
Diseworth
Isley Walton
Wilson
Breedon on the Hill
Ticknall
Calke Abbey NT
Calke
Staunton Harold NT
Heath End
Tonge
Long Whatton
Zouch
Sutton Fields
Sutton Bonington
Rempstone
Normanton on Soar
Hathern
Stanford on Soar
Hoton
Cotes
Burton on the Wolds
Loughborough
Walton on the Wolds
Thorpe Acre
Worthington
Belton
Shepshed
Osgathorpe
Newbold
Griffydam
Lount
Smisby
Woodville
Church Gresley
Stanton
Castle Gresley
Blackfordby
Ashby-de-la-Zouch
Outwoods
Coleorton
Peggs Green
Thringstone
Farm Town
Walton-on-Trent
Coton Park
Rosliston
Cauldwell
Linton
Linton Heath
High Cross Bank
Heart of the National Forest
Moira
Overseal
Coton in the Elms
Donisthorpe
Acresford
Oakthorpe
Lullington
Netherseal
Edingale
Chilcote
Clifton Campville
Haunton
Harlaston
Stretton en le Field
Measham
Packington
Ravenstone
Swannington
New Swannington
Snibston
Whitwick
Charnwood Forest
Mount St Bernard
Coalville
Hugglescote
Bardon
Whitehill
Donington le Heath
Heather
Swepstone
Snarestone
Newton Burgoland
Appleby Magna
Appleby Parva
Ellistown
Ibstock
Stanton under Bardon
Copt Oak
Markfield
Field Head
Nanpantan
Woodthorpe
Beacon Hill
Woodhouse
Woodhouse Eaves
Quorn
Great Central Railway
Mountsorrel
North End
Rothley
Swithland
Barrow upon Soar
Sileby
Cossington
Bradgate Park
Newtown Linford
Cropston
Thurcaston
Anstey
Birstall
Castle Hill
Thurmaston
Wanlip
No Man's Heath
Thorpe Constantine
Newton Regis
Seckington
Wigginton
Norton-Juxta-Twycross
Austrey
Ashby Canal
Odstone
Barton in the Beans
Shackerstone
Nailstone
Bagworth
Thornton
Groby
Ratby
Glenfield
Barlestone
Bilstone
Congerstone
Shuttington
Amington
Alvecote
Orton-on-the-Hill
Warton
Twycross
Little Twycross
Carlton
Market Bosworth
Osbaston
Botcheston
Tropical Birdland
Merry Lees
Newtown Unthank
Kirby Muxloe
Kirby Fields
Leicester Forest East
TAMWORTH
Glascote
Polesworth
Fazeley
Wilnecote
Sheepy Magna
Sheepy Parva
Wellsborough
The Battlefield Line
Sutton Cheney
Newbold Verdon
Desford
Cadeby
Peckleton
Kirkby Mallory
Mallory Park
Dordon
Bradley Green
Ratcliffe Culey
Upton
Shenton
Sibson
Bosworth Battlefield
Stapleton
Dadlington
Thurlaston
Earl Shilton
Enderby
Huncote
Narborough
Croft
Elmesthorpe
Potters Marston
Barwell
Stoke Golding
Wykin
Hinckley
Burbage Common & Woods
Stoney Stanton
Cosby
Sutton in the Elms
Littlethorpe
Whetstone
South Wigston
Blaby
Countesthorpe
Foston
Willoughby Waterleys
LEICESTER
Mowmacre Hill
Belgrave
Dane Hills
Braunstone
Stoneygate
Aylestone
Aylestone Park
Knighton
Glen Parva
Wigston
Whittington
Grendon
Baddesley Ensor
Atherstone
Atterton
Witherley
Fenny Drayton
Higham on the Hill
Mancetter
Ridge Lane
Hartshill Hayes
Hartshill
Oldbury
Coventry Canal
Weddington
Whateley
Cliff
Piccadilly
Wood End
Hurley Common
Kingsbury
Hurley
Baxterley
Bentley
Foul End
Birchley Heath
Nether Whitacre
Upper Town
Kirk Ireton
M1
A38
A6
A52
A50
A42
A453
A511
A512
A514
A444
A447
A46
A5
A60
A453
A6006
A610
A609
A608
A6096
A5111
A5010
A516
A5250
A5132
M42
M69
B5023
B5024
B5020
B6540
B6002
B5008
B5006
B587
B5324
B585
B582
B586
B5003
B4116
B585
B5000
B5493
B4098
B4111
B4669
B4668
B676
B6011
B6386
B684
B686
B680
B5380
B5327
B5366
A6007
A6002
A6005
A6004
A6030
A563
A5199
A426
A5460
A47
A612
A614
A611
A608
A6514
A6130
B6004
B682
B683
B6009
B600
B5010
B5004
B5035

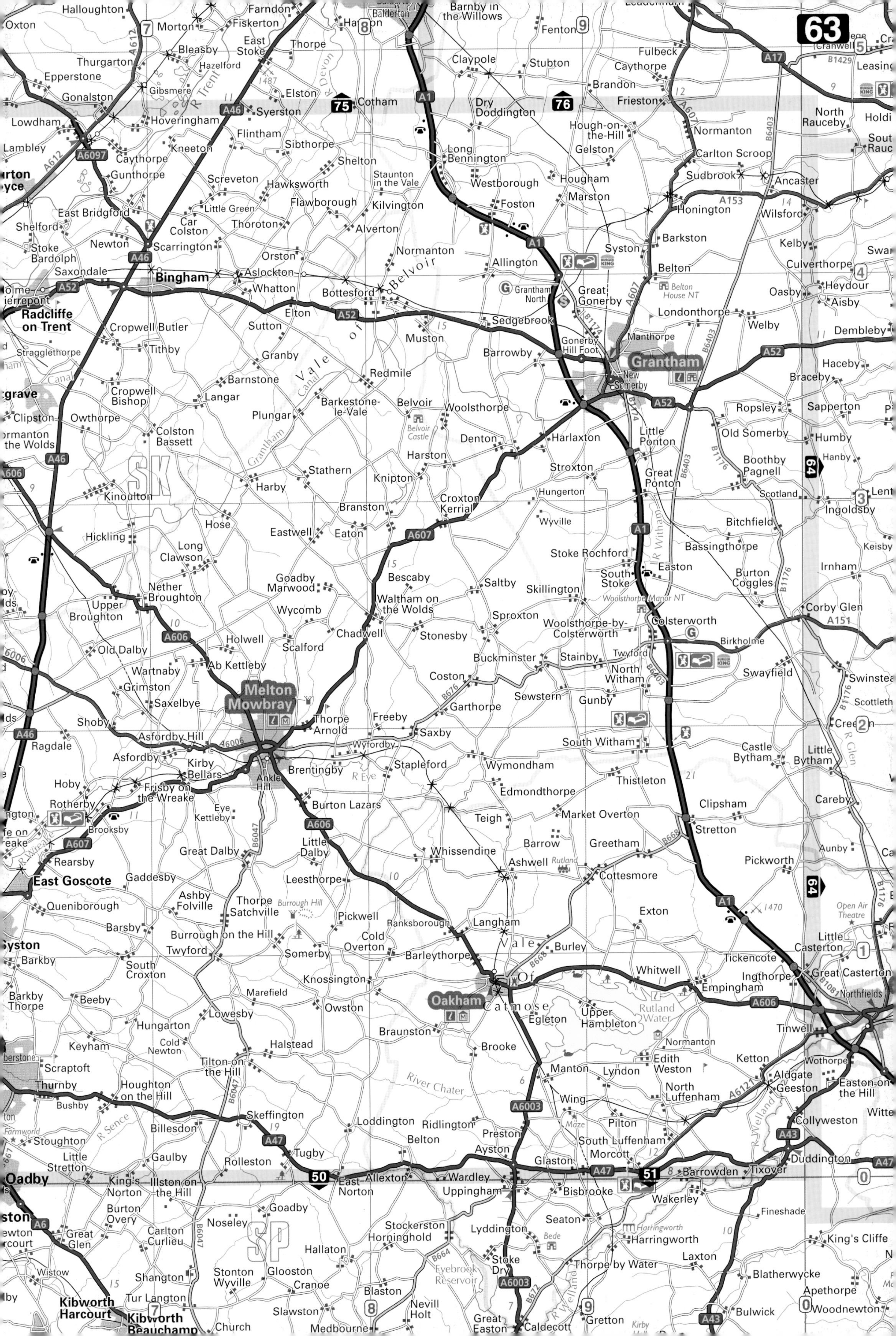
Halloughton
Oxton
Morton
Farndon
Fiskerton
Balderton
Hawton
Barnby in the Willows
Fenton
Thurgarton
Bleasby
East Stoke
Thorpe
Hazelford
Claypole
Stubton
Fulbeck
Caythorpe
Epperstone
Gibsmere
R Trent
Elston
R Devon
Cotham
Dry Doddington
Brandon
Frieston
Gonalston
Syerston
Hoveringham
Lowdham
Flintham
Hough-on-the-Hill
Normanton
North Rauceby
Lambley
Kneeton
Caythorpe
Sibthorpe
Shelton
Long Bennington
Gelston
Carlton Scroop
Gunthorpe
Screveton
Hawksworth
Staunton in the Vale
Westborough
Hougham
Sudbrook
Ancaster
Flawborough
Kilvington
Marston
Foston
Honington
Wilsford
Little Green
East Bridgford
Shelford
Car Colston
Thoroton
Alverton
Barkston
Kelby
Stoke Bardolph
Newton
Scarrington
Orston
Normanton
Syston
Allington
Belton
Culverthorpe
Saxondale
Bingham
Aslockton
Whatton
Belvoir
Bottesford
Grantham North
Belton House NT
Heydour
Oasby
Aisby
Radcliffe on Trent
Elton
Great Gonerby
Londonthorpe
Welby
Cropwell Butler
Sutton
Sedgebrook
Dembleby
Muston
Manthorpe
Stragglethorpe
Tithby
Granby
Barrowby
Gonerby Hill Foot
Grantham
Haceby
Redmile
New Somerby
Braceby
Cropwell Bishop
Barnstone
Vale of Belvoir
Langar
Barkestone-le-Vale
Belvoir
Woolsthorpe
Ropsley
Sapperton
Clipston
Owthorpe
Plungar
Belvoir Castle
Little Ponton
Old Somerby
Humby
Normanton on the Wolds
Colston Bassett
Grantham Canal
Denton
Harlaxton
Boothby Pagnell
Hanby
Stathern
Harston
Stroxton
Great Ponton
Kinoulton
Harby
Knipton
Hungerton
Scotland
Ingoldsby
Croxton Kerrial
Branston
Wyville
Bitchfield
Hose
Eastwell
Eaton
Hickling
Long Clawson
Stoke Rochford
Bassingthorpe
Keisby
Easton
Irnham
Bescaby
South Stoke
Burton Coggles
Goadby Marwood
Saltby
Skillington
Nether Broughton
Woolsthorpe Manor NT
Corby Glen
Upper Broughton
Waltham on the Wolds
Wycomb
Sproxton
Woolsthorpe-by-Colsterworth
Colsterworth
Chadwell
Stonesby
Birkholme
Holwell
Old Dalby
Scalford
Buckminster
Stainby
Twyford
North Witham
Swayfield
Wartnaby
Ab Kettleby
Coston
Grimston
Melton Mowbray
Sewstern
Gunby
Swinstead
Saxelbye
Garthorpe
Scottlethorpe
Creeton
Shoby
Thorpe Arnold
Freeby
Saxby
Asfordby Hill
Ragdale
Wyfordby
South Witham
Castle Bytham
Little Bytham
Asfordby
Kirby Bellars
Stapleford
Wymondham
R Glen
Brentingby
Hoby
Frisby on the Wreake
R Eye
Thistleton
Ankle Hill
Edmondthorpe
Rotherby
Eye Kettleby
Burton Lazars
Clipsham
Carebу
Brooksby
Teigh
Market Overton
Stretton
R Wreake
Little Dalby
Barrow
Greetham
Aunby
Rearsby
Great Dalby
Whissendine
Pickworth
Ashwell
Rutland
East Goscote
Gaddesby
Leesthorpe
Cottesmore
Queniborough
Ashby Folville
Thorpe Satchville
Burrough Hill
Exton
Open Air Theatre
Pickwell
Ranksborough
Langham
Barsby
Cold Overton
Syston
Burrough on the Hill
Little Casterton
Twyford
Somerby
Barleythorpe
Vale
Burley
Barkby
Tickencote
South Croxton
Whitwell
Ingthorpe
Great Casterton
Knossington
Empingham
Northfields
Barkby Thorpe
Marefield
Oakham
Vale of Catmose
Upper Hambleton
Rutland Water
Beeby
Owston
Lowesby
Egleton
Tinwell
Hungarton
Braunston
Normanton
Keyham
Cold Newton
Halstead
Brooke
Edith Weston
Ketton
Scraptoft
Tilton on the Hill
Manton
Lyndon
Wothorpe
River Chater
Thurnby
Houghton on the Hill
North Luffenham
Aldgate
Geeston
Easton-on-the-Hill
Wing
Bushby
Skeffington
Collyweston
Billesdon
Loddington
Ridlington
R Welland
Preston
Maze
Pilton
Stoughton
R Sence
Tugby
Belton
Ayston
South Luffenham
Gaulby
Little Stretton
Rolleston
Glaston
Morcott
Duddington
Oadby
King's Norton
Illston on the Hill
East Norton
Allexton
Wardley
Uppingham
Bisbrooke
Barrowden
Tixover
Wakerley
Goadby
Fineshade
Burton Overy
Noseley
Stockerston
Horninghold
Lyddington
Seaton
Great Glen
Carlton Curlieu
Harringworth
Bede
King's Cliffe
Hallaton
Wistow
Shangton
Stonton Wyville
Glooston
Eyebrook Reservoir
Stoke Dry
Thorpe by Water
Laxton
Blatherwycke
Cranoe
Apethorpe
Kibworth Harcourt
Tur Langton
Blaston
Nevill Holt
Woodnewton
Kibworth Beauchamp
Slawston
Great Easton
Caldecott
Gretton
Bulwick
Church Langton
Medbourne
Kirby
SK
SP
A1
A46
A52
A17
A607
A153
A606
A6097
A612
A151
A47
A43
A6003
A6
B1174
B6403
B1176
B676
B6047
B668
B664
B672
A6121
B1081
B1429
A6006
75
76
64
50
51
8
9
7
5
4
3
2
0

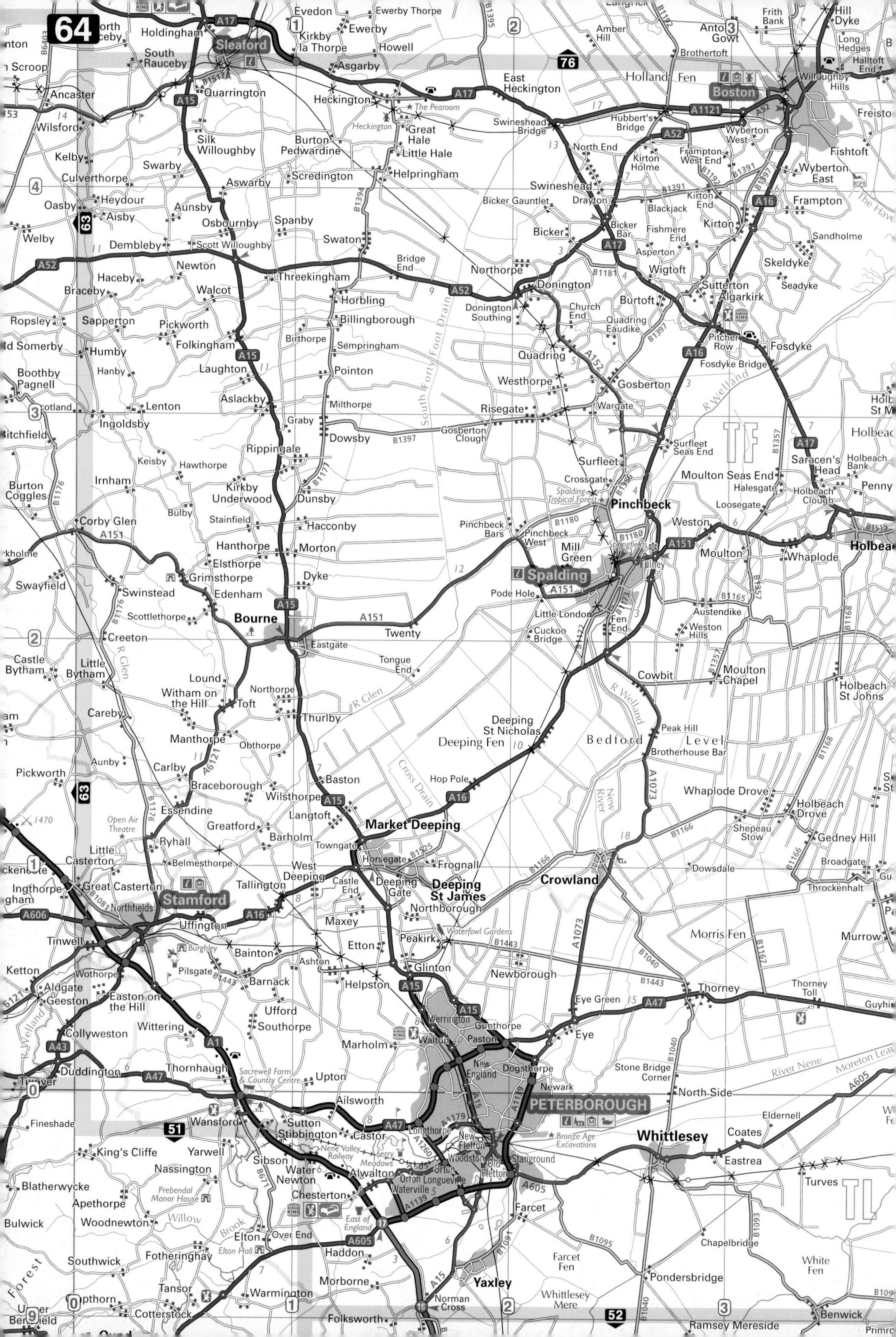

Sleaford
Holdingham
South Rauceby
Ancaster
Quarrington
Wilsford
Evedon
Kirkby la Thorpe
Ewerby Thorpe
Ewerby
Howell
Asgarby
Heckington
The Pearoom
Great Hale
Little Hale
Burton Pedwardine
Silk Willoughby
Kelby
Culverthorpe
Swarby
Aswarby
Scredington
Helpringham
Oasby
Heydour
Aisby
Aunsby
Osbournby
Spanby
Swaton
Welby
Dembleby
Scott Willoughby
Newton
Haceby
Braceby
Walcot
Threekingham
Bridge End
Horbling
Billingborough
Birthorpe
Sempringham
Pointon
Ropsley
Sapperton
Pickworth
Folkingham
Humby
Hanby
Laughton
Boothby Pagnell
Lenton
Ingoldsby
Aslackby
Milthorpe
Graby
Dowsby
Rippingale
Keisby
Hawthorpe
Irnham
Burton Coggles
Kirkby Underwood
Dunsby
Bulby
Stainfield
Hacconby
Corby Glen
Hanthorpe
Morton
Elsthorpe
Grimsthorpe
Swayfield
Swinstead
Edenham
Dyke
Scottlethorpe
Bourne
Eastgate
Creeton
Castle Bytham
Little Bytham
Lound
Witham on the Hill
Toft
Northorpe
Thurlby
Careby
Manthorpe
Obthorpe
Aunby
Pickworth
Carlby
Braceborough
Baston
Wilsthorpe
Langtoft
Essendine
Greatford
Barholm
Ryhall
Little Casterton
Belmesthorpe
Great Casterton
Stamford
Northfields
Tallington
West Deeping
Uffington
Tinwell
Ketton
Wothorpe
Burghley
Bainton
Pilsgate
Barnack
Aldgate
Geeston
Easton on the Hill
Ufford
Southorpe
Collyweston
Wittering
Duddington
Thornhaugh
Sacrewell Farm & Country Centre
Upton
Fineshade
Wansford
Sutton
Stibbington
Ailsworth
Castor
King's Cliffe
Yarwell
Nassington
Sibson
Water Newton
Blatherwycke
Apethorpe
Prebendal Manor House
Chesterton
Woodnewton
Bulwick
Elton
Elton Hall
Over End
Haddon
Southwick
Fotheringhay
Tansor
Morborne
Warmington
Cotterstock
Folksworth
East of England
Nene Valley Railway
Ferry Meadows
Alwalton
Orton Longueville
Orton Waterville
Market Deeping
Towngate
Horsegate
Frognall
Castle End
Deeping Gate
Deeping St James
Northborough
Maxey
Etton
Peakirk
Waterfowl Gardens
Helpston
Ashton
Glinton
Newborough
Marholm
Werrington
Walton
Gunthorpe
Paston
New England
Dogsthorpe
Newark
PETERBOROUGH
Longthorpe
New Fletton
Woodston
Old Fletton
Stanground
Bronze Age Excavations
Farcet
Yaxley
Norman Cross
Whittlesey Mere
Farcet Fen
Pondersbridge
Ramsey Mereside
Whittlesey
Eastrea
Coates
Eldernell
Turves
Chapelbridge
White Fen
Benwick
North Side
Stone Bridge Corner
Eye
Eye Green
Thorney
Thorney Toll
Guyhirn
Morris Fen
Murrow
Crowland
Dowsdale
Throckenholt
Shepeau Stow
Gedney Hill
Broadgate
Whaplode Drove
Holbeach Drove
Brotherhouse Bar
Peak Hill
Bedford Level
Deeping St Nicholas
Deeping Fen
Hop Pole
Cross Drain
New River
Cowbit
Moulton Chapel
Holbeach St Johns
Weston Hills
Austendike
Fen End
Little London
Cuckoo Bridge
Pode Hole
Spalding
Fulney
Mill Green
Pinchbeck West
Pinchbeck Bars
Springfields
Pinchbeck
Spalding Tropical Forest
Crossgate
Surfleet
Surfleet Seas End
Moulton
Whaplode
Weston
Loosegate
Holbeach Clough
Halesgate
Moulton Seas End
Saracen's Head
Holbeach Bank
Penny
Twenty
Tongue End
Gosberton Clough
Risegate
Westhorpe
Quadring
Gosberton
Wargate
South Forty Foot Drain
Donington
Donington Southing
Church End
Quadring Eaudike
Burtoft
Northorpe
Bicker
Bicker Gauntlet
Bicker Bar
Drayton
Swineshead
Swineshead Bridge
East Heckington
Holland Fen
Amber Hill
Frith Bank
Anton's Gowt
Brothertoft
Boston
Hubbert's Bridge
North End
Kirton Holme
Frampton West End
Wyberton West
Wyberton East
Fishtoft
Freiston
Willoughby Hills
Hill Dyke
Long Hedges
Halltoft End
Blackjack
Kirton End
Kirton
Frampton
Fishmere End
Asperton
Wigtoft
Sutterton
Algarkirk
Pitcher Row
Fosdyke
Fosdyke Bridge
Skeldyke
Seadyke
Sandholme
The Haven
R Welland
R Glen
River Nene
Moreton Leam
Holbeach St Marks
Holbeach
A17
A15
A52
A151
A16
A1121
A1073
A47
A605
A1139
A1179
A1260
A6121
A606
A43
A1
A152
B1395
B1192
B1394
B1397
B1177
B1176
B1181
B1391
B1180
B1356
B1165
B1357
B1168
B1166
B1443
B1040
B1167
B1095
B1091
B1093
B1525
B1081
B1172
B1173
B671
TF
TL
76
63
51
52

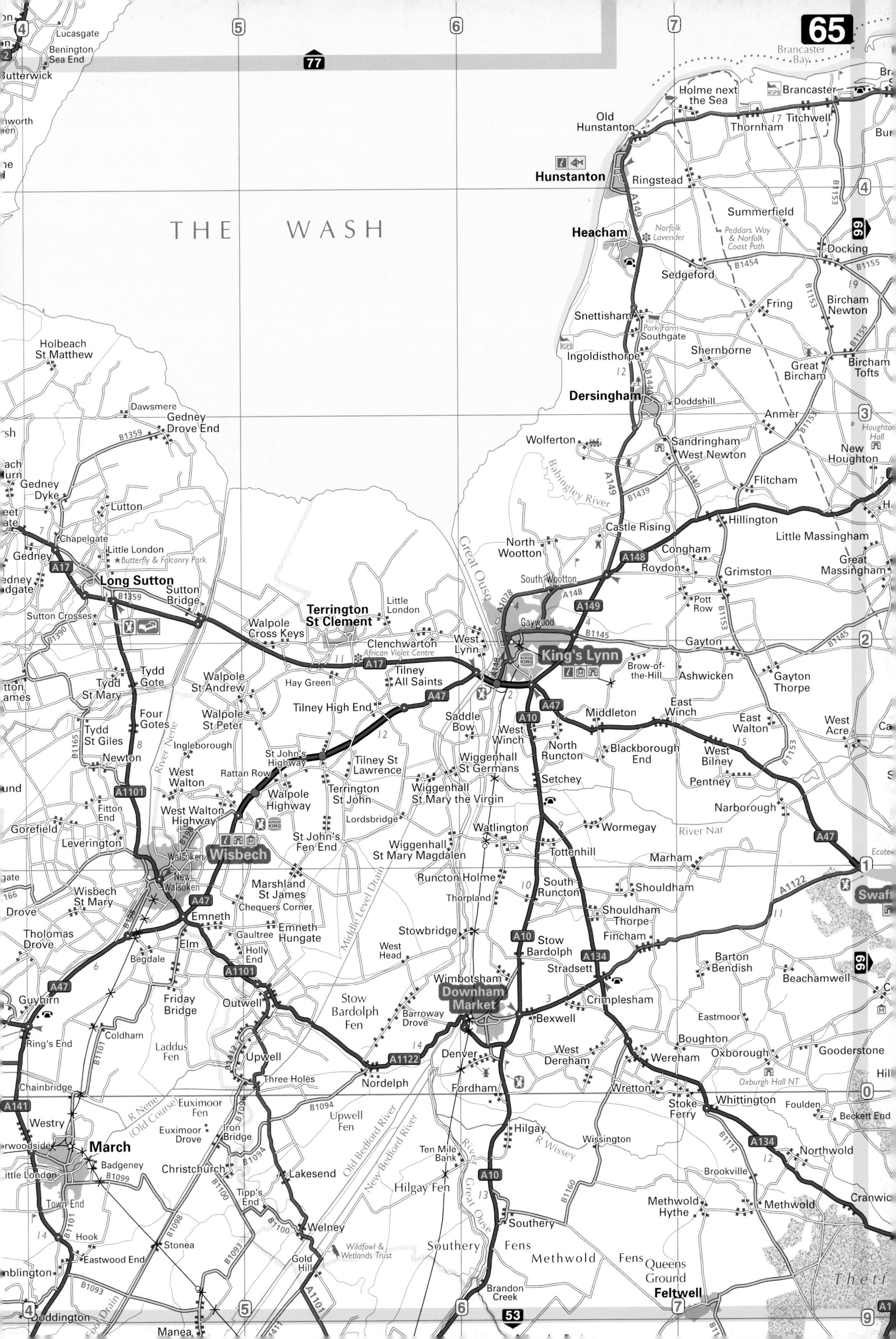

65
77
53
THE WASH
Lucasgate
Benington Sea End
Butterwick
Brancaster Bay
Holme next the Sea
Brancaster
Titchwell
Thornham
Old Hunstanton
Hunstanton
Ringstead
Summerfield
Heacham
Norfolk Lavender
Peddars Way & Norfolk Coast Path
Docking
Sedgeford
Fring
Bircham Newton
Snettisham
Park Farm
Southgate
Ingoldisthorpe
Shernborne
Great Bircham
Bircham Tofts
Dersingham
Doddshill
Anmer
Houghton Hall
Wolferton
Sandringham
West Newton
New Houghton
Babingley River
Flitcham
Hillington
Castle Rising
Little Massingham
North Wootton
Congham
Roydon
Grimston
Great Massingham
South Wootton
Pott Row
Gaywood
Gayton
King's Lynn
Brow-of-the-Hill
Ashwicken
Gayton Thorpe
Great Ouse
West Lynn
Holbeach St Matthew
Dawsmere
Gedney Drove End
Gedney Dyke
Lutton
Chapelgate
Little London
Butterfly & Falconry Park
Gedney
Long Sutton
Sutton Bridge
Sutton Crosses
Terrington St Clement
Little London
Walpole Cross Keys
Clenchwarton
African Violet Centre
Tilney All Saints
Tydd Gote
Tydd St Mary
Walpole St Andrew
Hay Green
Tilney High End
Four Gotes
Walpole St Peter
Tydd St Giles
Ingleborough
Newton
River Nene
St John's Highway
Tilney St Lawrence
Saddle Bow
West Winch
North Runcton
Middleton
East Winch
East Walton
West Acre
Blackborough End
West Bilney
Pentney
Narborough
West Walton
Rattan Row
Terrington St John
Wiggenhall St Germans
Wiggenhall St Mary the Virgin
Setchey
Fitton End
West Walton Highway
Walpole Highway
Lordsbridge
Watlington
Wormegay
River Nar
Gorefield
Leverington
Walsoken
Wisbech
St John's Fen End
Wiggenhall St Mary Magdalen
Tottenhill
Marham
New Walsoken
Marshland St James
Runcton Holme
South Runcton
Shouldham
Wisbech St Mary
Chequers Corner
Thorpland
Shouldham Thorpe
Emneth
Emneth Hungate
Middle Level Drain
Stowbridge
Fincham
Tholomas Drove
Elm
Gaultree
Holly End
West Head
Stow Bardolph
Barton Bendish
Begdale
Stradsett
Beachamwell
Wimbotsham
Friday Bridge
Outwell
Stow Bardolph Fen
Downham Market
Crimplesham
Guyhirn
Barroway Drove
Bexwell
Eastmoor
Coldham
Ring's End
Laddus Fen
Upwell
Denver
Boughton
West Dereham
Wereham
Oxborough
Gooderstone
Three Holes
Nordelph
Fordham
Chainbridge
Wretton
Oxburgh Hall NT
Stoke Ferry
Whittington
Foulden
Beckett End
Euximoor Fen
R Nene (Old Course)
Upwell Fen
Old Bedford River
New Bedford River
Westry
Euximoor Drove
Iron Bridge
Hilgay
R Wissey
Wissington
Northwold
March
Badgeney
Christchurch
Ten Mile Bank
River Great Ouse
Lakesend
Hilgay Fen
Brookville
Little London
Town End
Tipp's End
Methwold Hythe
Methwold
Southery
Welney
Hook
Stonea
Wildfowl & Wetlands Trust
Southery
Fens
Methwold
Fens
Queens Ground
Eastwood End
Gold Hill
Feltwell
Brandon Creek
Doddington
Manea
Swaffham
Cranwich
Ecotech
Thetford
A17
A47
A10
A134
A148
A149
A1101
A1122
A141
B1359
B1454
B1153
B1155
B1145
B1440
B1439
B1165
B1390
B1094
B1098
B1100
B1099
B1101
B1093
B1112
B1160
A1078

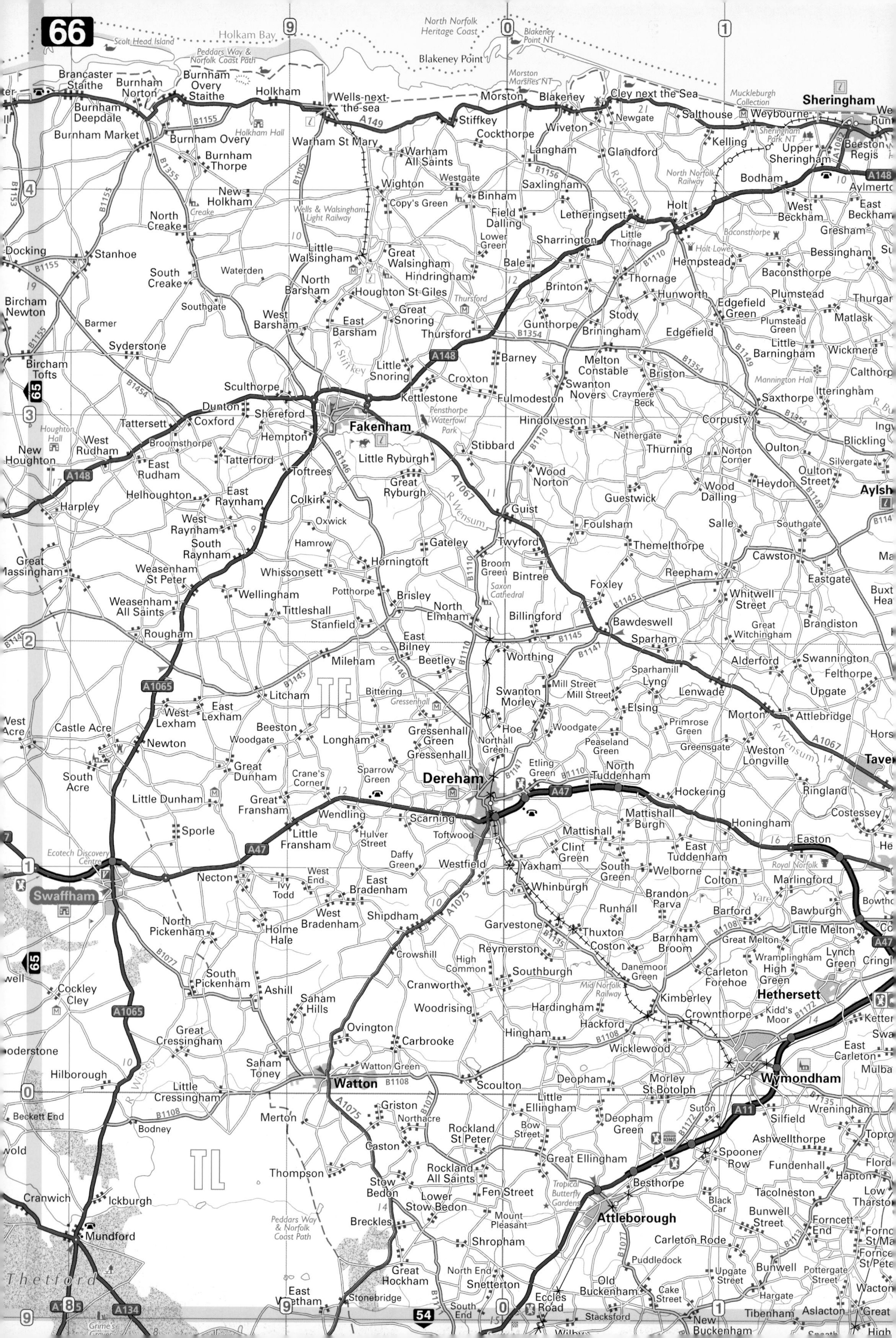
Scolt Head Island
Holkam Bay
Peddars Way & Norfolk Coast Path
North Norfolk Heritage Coast
Blakeney Point NT
Blakeney Point
Morston Marshes NT
Brancaster Staithe
Burnham Norton
Burnham Overy Staithe
Holkham
Wells-next-the-sea
Morston
Blakeney
Cley next the Sea
Muckleburgh Collection
Sheringham
Burnham Deepdale
Burnham Market
Burnham Overy
Holkham Hall
Warham St Mary
Stiffkey
Cockthorpe
Wiveton
Newgate
Salthouse
Weybourne
Sheringham Park NT
Upper Sheringham
Beeston Regis
Burnham Thorpe
Warham All Saints
Langham
Glandford
Kelling
North Norfolk Railway
Bodham
Aylmerton
New Holkham
Wighton
Westgate
Saxlingham
Binham
Copy's Green
Wells & Walsingham Light Railway
Field Dalling
Letheringsett
Holt
West Beckham
East Beckham
North Creake
Creake
R Glaven
Little Thornage
Baconsthorpe
Gresham
Docking
Stanhoe
Little Walsingham
Great Walsingham
Lower Green
Sharrington
Holt Lowes
Hempstead
Bessingham
Bale
South Creake
Waterden
Hindringham
Thornage
Baconsthorpe
Bircham Newton
North Barsham
Houghton St Giles
Thursford
Brinton
Hunworth
Edgefield Green
Plumstead
Thurgarton
Southgate
West Barsham
Great Snoring
Stody
Plumstead Green
Matlask
Barmer
East Barsham
Thursford
Gunthorpe
Briningham
Edgefield
Little Barningham
Wickmere
Syderstone
R Stiffkey
Barney
Melton Constable
Briston
Calthorpe
Bircham Tofts
Little Snoring
Croxton
Swanton Novers
Mannington Hall
Itteringham
Sculthorpe
Kettlestone
Fulmodeston
Craymere Beck
Saxthorpe
Dunton
Shereford
Pensthorpe Waterfowl Park
Corpusty
Tattersett
Coxford
Fakenham
Hindolveston
Houghton Hall
West Rudham
Broomsthorpe
Hempton
Stibbard
Nethergate
Thurning
Norton Corner
Blickling
Oulton
New Houghton
Tatterford
Little Ryburgh
Silvergate
East Rudham
Toftrees
Great Ryburgh
Wood Norton
Oulton Street
Heydon
Aylsham
Helhoughton
East Raynham
Colkirk
R Wensum
Guestwick
Wood Dalling
Harpley
Guist
Salle
Southgate
West Raynham
Oxwick
Foulsham
South Raynham
Hamrow
Gateley
Twyford
Themelthorpe
Cawston
Great Massingham
Broom Green
Weasenham St Peter
Whissonsett
Horningtoft
Bintree
Reepham
Eastgate
Saxon Cathedral
Foxley
Wellingham
Potthorpe
Brisley
Whitwell Street
Weasenham All Saints
Tittleshall
North Elmham
Billingford
Bawdeswell
Stanfield
Brandiston
Great Witchingham
Rougham
East Bilney
Sparham
Mileham
Beetley
Worthing
Alderford
Swannington
Felthorpe
Sparhamill
Lyng
Mill Street
Mill Street
Litcham
Bittering
Gressenhall
Swanton Morley
Lenwade
Upgate
East Lexham
West Lexham
Elsing
Morton
Attlebridge
West Acre
Castle Acre
Beeston
Woodgate
Primrose Green
Newton
Woodgate
Longham
Gressenhall Green
Hoe
Peaseland Green
Greensgate
Weston Longville
Northall Green
R Wensum
Gressenhall
Great Dunham
Crane's Corner
Sparrow Green
Etling Green
North Tuddenham
South Acre
Dereham
Hockering
Ringland
Little Dunham
Great Fransham
Wendling
Scarning
Mattishall Burgh
Costessey
Sporle
Little Fransham
Hulver Street
Toftwood
Mattishall
Honingham
Clint Green
East Tuddenham
Easton
Ecotech Discovery Centre
Daffy Green
Westfield
Yaxham
South Green
Welborne
Royal Norfolk
Necton
West End
Ivy Todd
East Bradenham
Whinburgh
Colton
Marlingford
Swaffham
Brandon Parva
R Yare
Runhall
Barford
Bawburgh
West Bradenham
Shipdham
North Pickenham
Holme Hale
Garvestone
Thuxton
Barnham Broom
Great Melton
Little Melton
Crowshill
Reymerston
Coston
Wramplingham
Lynch Green
High Common
Southburgh
Danemoor Green
Carleton Forehoe
High Green
South Pickenham
Cranworth
Mid Norfolk Railway
Cockley Cley
Ashill
Saham Hills
Woodrising
Hardingham
Kimberley
Hethersett
Crownthorpe
Kidd's Moor
Hackford
Great Cressingham
Ovington
Carbrooke
Hingham
Wicklewood
East Carleton
Oderstone
Saham Toney
Watton Green
Hilborough
R Wissey
Watton
Scoulton
Deopham
Morley St Botolph
Wymondham
Little Cressingham
Little Ellingham
Beckett End
Merton
Griston
Northacre
Suton
Silfield
Wreningham
Bodney
Rockland St Peter
Bow Street
Deopham Green
Ashwellthorpe
Caston
Spooner Row
Great Ellingham
Thompson
Rockland All Saints
Fundenhall
Stow Bedon
Tropical Butterfly Gardens
Besthorpe
Hapton
Cranwich
Ickburgh
Lower Stow Bedon
Fen Street
Black Car
Tacolneston
Mount Pleasant
Attleborough
Bunwell Street
Forncett End
Peddars Way & Norfolk Coast Path
Breckles
Shropham
Carleton Rode
Mundford
Puddledock
Great Hockham
North End
Snetterton
Upgate Street
Bunwell
Pottergate Street
Thetford
Old Buckenham
Cake Street
Hargate
East Wretham
Stonebridge
South End
Eccles Road
Stacksford
New Buckenham
Tibenham
Aslacton
Grime's Graves
A149
A148
A1067
A1065
A47
A1075
A11
A134
A1082
B1155
B1355
B1105
B1153
B1156
B1110
B1354
B1149
B1454
B1146
B1145
B1147
B1135
B1108
B1077
B1172
B1113
TF
TL
65
54

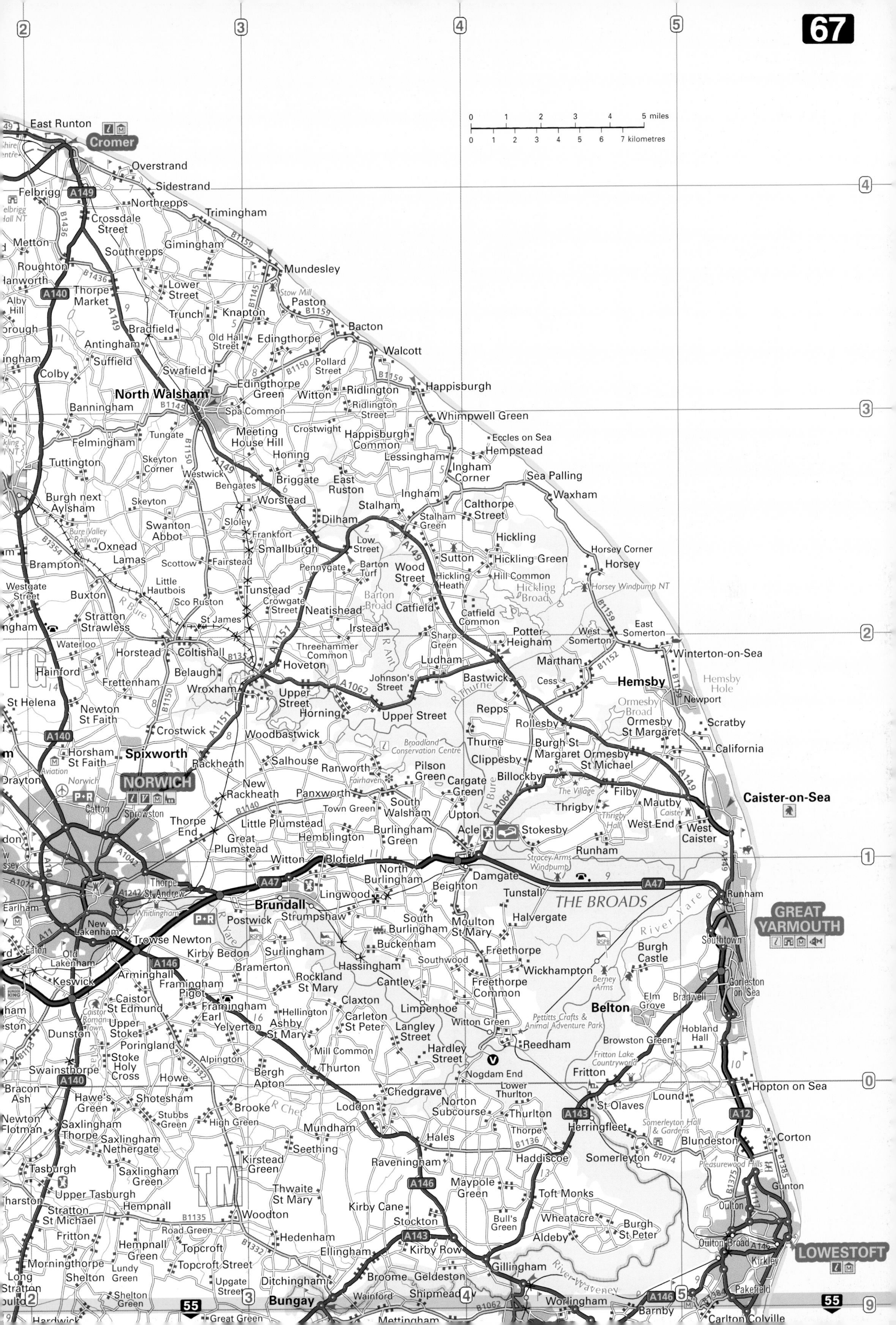

0 1 2 3 4 5 miles
0 1 2 3 4 5 6 7 kilometres
East Runton
Cromer
Overstrand
Sidestrand
Felbrigg
Northrepps
Trimingham
Crossdale Street
Metton
Southrepps
Gimingham
Roughton
Mundesley
Lower Street
Thorpe Market
Stow Mill
Paston
Trunch
Knapton
Bacton
Bradfield
Old Hall Street
Edingthorpe
Antingham
Walcott
Suffield
Pollard Street
Colby
Swafield
Edingthorpe Green
Witton
Ridlington
Happisburgh
North Walsham
Banningham
Spa Common
Ridlington Street
Whimpwell Green
Meeting House Hill
Crostwight
Happisburgh Common
Eccles on Sea
Felmingham
Tungate
Hempstead
Honing
Lessingham
Tuttington
Skeyton Corner
Ingham Corner
Westwick
Briggate
East Ruston
Sea Palling
Bengates
Ingham
Waxham
Burgh next Aylsham
Skeyton
Worstead
Stalham
Calthorpe Street
Dilham
Stalham Green
Swanton Abbot
Sloley
Hickling
Bure Valley Railway
Frankfort
Low Street
Oxnead
Smallburgh
Sutton
Hickling Green
Horsey Corner
Brampton
Lamas
Scottow
Fairstead
Pennygate
Barton Turf
Wood Street
Horsey
Hickling Heath
Hill Common
Hickling Broad
Horsey Windpump NT
Westgate Street
Little Hautbois
Tunstead
Buxton
Barton Broad
Sco Ruston
Crowgate Street
Neatishead
Catfield
Catfield Common
Stratton Strawless
R Bure
St James
Irstead
East Somerton
Sharp Green
Potter Heigham
West Somerton
Waterloo
Horstead
Coltishall
Threehammer Common
Winterton-on-Sea
Ludham
Martham
Hainford
Belaugh
Hoveton
R Ant
Frettenham
Johnson's Street
Bastwick
Cess
Hemsby
Hemsby Hole
Wroxham
R Thurne
A1062
Upper Street
Ormesby Broad
Newport
St Helena
Newton St Faith
Repps
Horning
Upper Street
Rollesby
Ormesby St Margaret
Scratby
Crostwick
Woodbastwick
Thurne
Burgh St Margaret
Ormesby St Michael
California
Horsham St Faith
Spixworth
Broadland Conservation Centre
Clippesby
Aviation
Salhouse
Rackheath
Ranworth
Pilson Green
Norwich
NORWICH
Fairhaven
Cargate Green
Billockby
Filby
Caister-on-Sea
Drayton
New Rackheath
Panxworth
South Walsham
The Village
Mautby
Catton
Town Green
Thrigby
Caister
Sprowston
Thorpe End
Little Plumstead
Upton
Thrigby Hall
West End
West Caister
Burlingham Green
Acle
Stokesby
Great Plumstead
Hemblington
Runham
Stracey Arms Windpump
Witton
Blofield
North Burlingham
Damgate
Thorpe St Andrew
Beighton
Tunstall
THE BROADS
Runham
Brundall
Lingwood
Earlham
Whitlingham
Postwick
Strumpshaw
South Burlingham
Halvergate
GREAT YARMOUTH
Moulton St Mary
River Yare
New Lakenham
Trowse Newton
Southtown
Buckenham
Eaton
Kirby Bedon
Surlingham
Freethorpe
Burgh Castle
Old Lakenham
Bramerton
Southwood
Hassingham
Wickhampton
Arminghall
Berney Arms
Keswick
Framingham Pigot
Rockland St Mary
Cantley
Freethorpe Common
Gorleston on Sea
Elm Grove
Bradwell
Caistor St Edmund
Claxton
Framingham Earl
Hellington
Limpenhoe
Belton
Caistor Roman Town
Upper Stoke
Carleton St Peter
Pettitts Crafts & Animal Adventure Park
Yelverton
Ashby St Mary
Witton Green
Dunston
Langley Street
Hobland Hall
Browston Green
Poringland
Reedham
Stoke Holy Cross
Mill Common
Hardley Street
Fritton Lake Countryworld
Alpington
Swainsthorpe
Thurton
Howe
Bergh Apton
Nogdam End
Fritton
Bracon Ash
Lower Thurlton
Hopton on Sea
Hawe's Green
Shotesham
Chedgrave
Lound
Newton Flotman
Stubbs Green
Brooke
R Chet
Loddon
Norton Subcourse
Thurlton
St Olaves
Saxlingham Thorpe
High Green
Mundham
Herringfleet
Somerleyton Hall & Gardens
Saxlingham Nethergate
Thorpe
Hales
Blundeston
Corton
Seething
Kirstead Green
Ravenningham
Haddiscoe
Somerleyton
Tasburgh
Saxlingham Green
Pleasurewood Hills
Maypole Green
Gunton
Upper Tasburgh
Thwaite St Mary
Toft Monks
Hempnall
Oulton
Stratton St Michael
Kirby Cane
Woodton
Road Green
Stockton
Bull's Green
Wheatacre
Burgh St Peter
Fritton
Hempnall Green
Topcroft
Hedenham
Aldeby
Oulton Broad
Ellingham
Kirby Row
Morningthorpe
LOWESTOFT
Lundy Green
Topcroft Street
Gillingham
Kirkley
Long Stratton
Shelton
Upgate Street
Ditchingham
Broome
Geldeston
River Waveney
Pakefield
Shelton Green
Bungay
Wainford
Shipmeadow
Worlingham
Barnby
Hardwick
Great Green
Mettingham
Carlton Colville
TG
TM

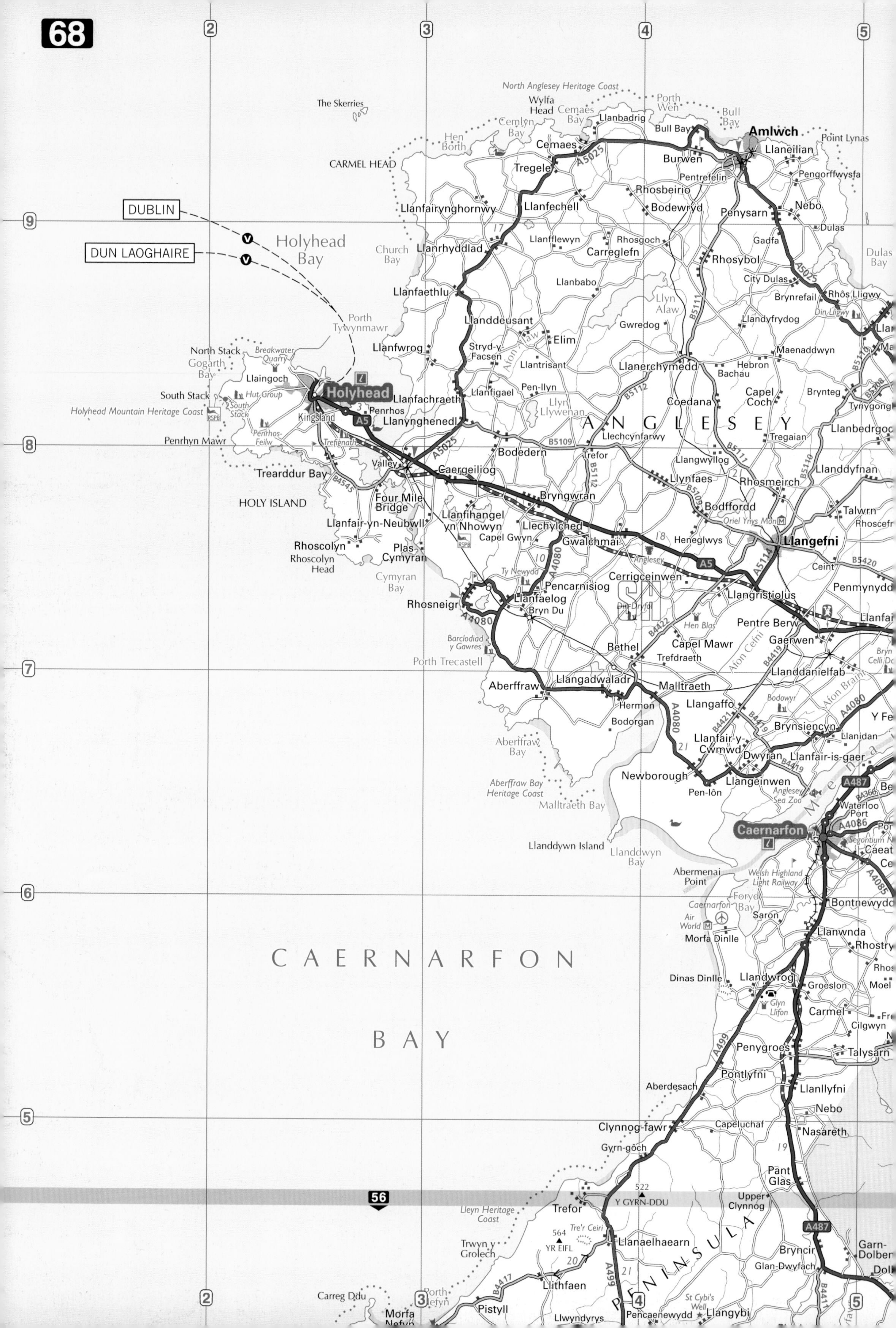
North Anglesey Heritage Coast
The Skerries
Wylfa Head
Cemaes Bay
Porth Wen
Bull Bay
Amlwch
Point Lynas
Cemlyn Bay
Hen Borth
Llanbadrig
Bull Bay
Llaneilian
CARMEL HEAD
Cemaes
Burwen
Tregele
Pengorffwysfa
Pentrefelin
Rhosbeirio
DUBLIN
Llanfairynghornwy
Llanfechell
Bodewryd
Penysarn
Nebo
DUN LAOGHAIRE
Holyhead Bay
Llanfflewyn
Rhosgoch
Dulas
Church Bay
Llanrhyddlad
Carreglefn
Gadfa
Dulas Bay
Rhosybol
City Dulas
Llanbabo
Llanfaethlu
Llyn Alaw
Brynrefail
Rhôs Lligwy
Porth Tywynmawr
Llanddeusant
Gwredog
Llandyfrydog
Elim
North Stack
Breakwater Quarry
Llanfwrog
Stryd-y-Facsen
Maenaddwyn
Gogarth Bay
Llantrisant
Llanerchymedd
Hebron
Bachau
Llaingoch
Holyhead
Pen-llyn
South Stack
Hut Group
Llanfachraeth
Llanfigael
Capel Coch
Brynteg
Holyhead Mountain Heritage Coast
Penrhos
Llyn Llywenan
Coedana
Tynygongl
Kingsland
Llanynghenedl
ANGLESEY
Llanbedrgoch
Penrhos-Feilw
Penrhyn Mawr
Bodedern
Llechcynfarwy
Tregaian
Trefignath
Trefor
Llangwyllog
Valley
Caergeiliog
Llanddyfnan
Trearddur Bay
Llynfaes
Rhosmeirch
HOLY ISLAND
Four Mile Bridge
Bryngwran
Bodffordd
Talwrn
Oriel Ynys Môn
Rhoscefn
Llanfair-yn-Neubwll
Llanfihangel yn Nhowyn
Llechylched
Capel Gwyn
Gwalchmai
Heneglwys
Llangefni
Rhoscolyn
Rhoscolyn Head
Plas Cymyran
Cymyran Bay
Ty Newydd
Anglesey
Ceint
Cerrigceinwen
Penmynydd
Pencarnisiog
Rhosneigr
Llanfaelog
Din Dryfol
Llangristiolus
Bryn Du
Hen Blas
Pentre Berw
Llanfair
Barclodiad y Gawres
Gaerwen
Bethel
Capel Mawr
Afon Cefni
Bryn Celli Ddu
Porth Trecastell
Trefdraeth
Llanddanielfab
Aberffraw
Llangadwaladr
Malltraeth
Hermon
Llangaffo
Bodowyr
Afon Braint
Bodorgan
Y Fe
Brynsiencyn
Aberffraw Bay
Llanfair-y-Cwmwd
Llanidan
Dwyran
Llanfair-is-gaer
Aberffraw Bay Heritage Coast
Newborough
Llangeinwen
Malltraeth Bay
Pen-lôn
Anglesey Sea Zoo
Waterloo Port
Caernarfon
Segontium
Llanddwyn Island
Llanddwyn Bay
Caeat
Abermenai Point
Welsh Highland Light Railway
Foryd Bay
Bontnewydd
Caernarfon Air World
Saron
Morfa Dinlle
Llanwnda
Rhostry
CAERNARFON BAY
Dinas Dinlle
Llandwrog
Groeslon
Moel
Glyn Llifon
Carmel
Cilgwyn
Penygroes
Talysarn
Pontlyfni
Aberdesach
Llanllyfni
Nebo
Clynnog-fawr
Capeluchaf
Nasareth
Gyrn-goch
Pant Glas
522
Y GYRN-DDU
Upper Clynnog
Lleyn Heritage Coast
Trefor
Tre'r Ceiri
564
YR EIFL
Llanaelhaearn
Trwyn y Gorlech
Bryncir
Garn-Dolbenmaen
Glan-Dwyfach
Llithfaen
Carreg Ddu
Porth Nefyn
Pistyll
PENINSULA
St Cybi's Well
Pencaenewydd
Llangybi
Morfa Nefyn
Llwyndyrys
56

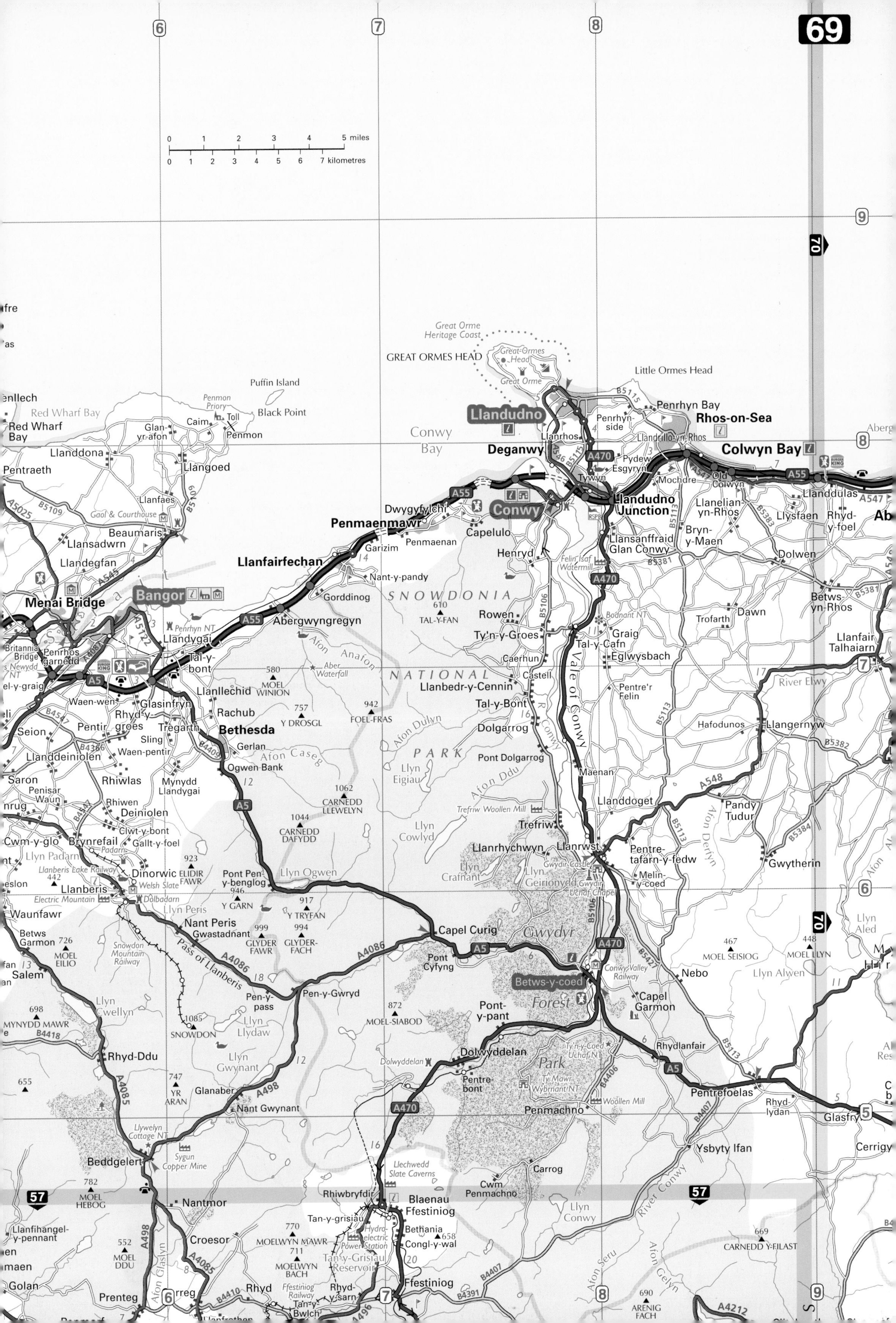

Great Orme Heritage Coast
GREAT ORMES HEAD
Little Ormes Head
Puffin Island
Black Point
Penmon
Red Wharf Bay
Conwy Bay
Llandudno
Deganwy
Penrhyn Bay
Rhos-on-Sea
Colwyn Bay
Conwy
Llandudno Junction
Penmaenmawr
Llanfairfechan
Dwygyfylchi
Beaumaris
Llangoed
Menai Bridge
Bangor
Abergwyngregyn
Bethesda
SNOWDONIA NATIONAL PARK
Vale of Conwy
Llanrwst
Trefriw
Capel Curig
Betws-y-coed
Gwydyr Forest
Dolwyddelan
Llanberis
Dinorwic
Nant Peris
Pass of Llanberis
Pen-y-Gwryd
Pen-y-pass
SNOWDON
Rhyd-Ddu
Beddgelert
Nantmor
Blaenau Ffestiniog
Ffestiniog
Tan-y-grisiau
Penmachno
Pentrefoelas
Ysbyty Ifan
Nebo
Llangernyw
Gwytherin
Llanddulas
Llysfaen
Abergele
Betws-yn-Rhos
Llyn Ogwen
Llyn Padarn
Llyn Cwellyn
Llyn Gwynant
Llyn Conwy
Llyn Alwen
0 1 2 3 4 5 miles
0 1 2 3 4 5 6 7 kilometres

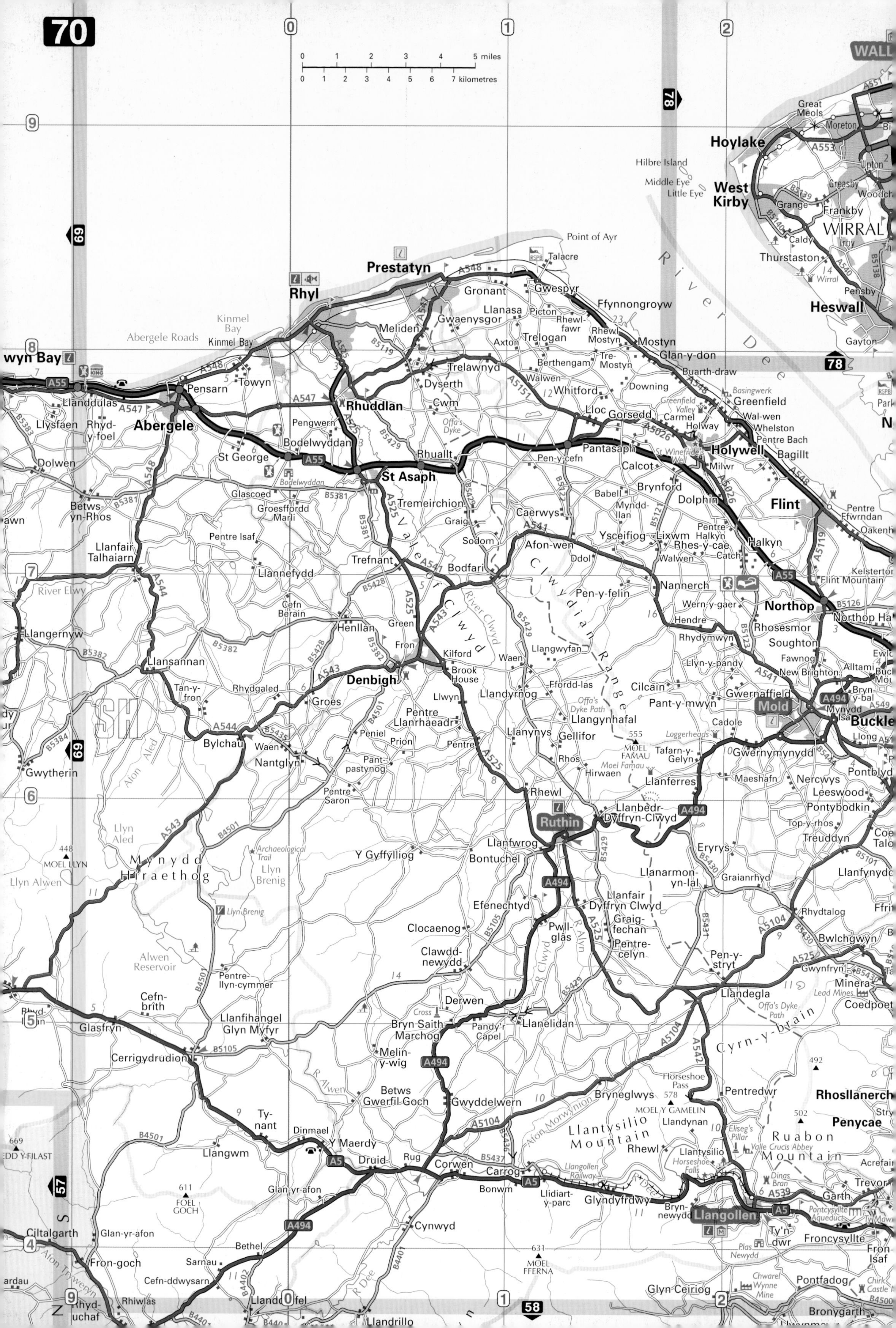
0 1 2 3 4 5 miles
0 1 2 3 4 5 6 7 kilometres
WALL
78
Great Meols
Moreton
Hoylake
Hilbre Island
Middle Eye
Little Eye
West Kirby
A553
Upton
Greasby
Woodch
Grange
Frankby
WIRRAL
Caldy
Irby
Thurstaston
Wirral
Pensby
Heswall
Gayton
River Dee
Point of Ayr
Talacre
RSPB
Prestatyn
A548
Rhyl
Gronant
Gwespyr
Ffynnongroyw
Llanasa
Picton
Rhewl-fawr
Rhewl Mostyn
Mostyn
Glan-y-don
Gwaenysgor
Meliden
Axton
Trelogan
Tre-Mostyn
Berthengam
Kinmel Bay
Abergele Roads
wyn Bay
A55
Llanddulas
A547
Pensarn
Towyn
Trelawnyd
Dyserth
Walwen
Whitford
Downing
Buarth-draw
Basingwerk
Greenfield
Greenfield Valley
Carmel
Holway
Wal-wen
Whelston
Pentre Bach
Bagillt
Llysfaen
Rhyd-y-foel
Abergele
Rhuddlan
Cwm
Offa's Dyke
Lloc
Gorsedd
A5026
St Winefride's Well
Holywell
Milwr
Pengwern
Bodelwyddan
St George
Rhuallt
Pantasaph
Pen-y-cefn
Calcot
Brynford
Dolphin
Flint
Dolwen
St Asaph
B5381
Glascoed
Groesffordd Marli
Tremeirchion
Caerwys
Babell
Myndd-llan
Betws-yn-Rhos
Graig
A541
Yscefiog
Lixwm
Pentre Halkyn
Rhes-y-cae
Catch
Halkyn
Pentre Ffwrndan
Oakenh
Llanfair Talhaiarn
Pentre Isaf
Sodom
Afon-wen
Walwen
Ddol
Trefnant
Bodfari
Vale of Clwyd
Clwydian Range
Kelsterton
Flint Mountain
Nannerch
A5119
Llannefydd
River Elwy
A544
B5428
Pen-y-felin
Wern-y-gaer
Northop
Northop Ha
Cefn Berain
Henllan
Green
A525
River Clwyd
B5429
Hendre
Rhosesmor
Llangernyw
Rhydymwyn
Soughton
B5382
Fron
A543
Kilford
Llangwyfan
Llyn-y-pandy
Fawnog
Alltami
New Brighton
Llansannan
Denbigh
Brook House
Waen
Cilcain
Bryn-y-bal
Tan-y-fron
Rhydgaled
Groes
Llwyn
Llandyrnog
Ffordd-las
Offa's Dyke Path
Pant-y-mwyn
Gwernaffield
Mold
Mynydd Isa
Buckle
Pentre Llanrhaeadr
Llangynhafal
Cadole
Loggerheads
Llong
SH
Bylchau
B5435
Waen
Peniel
Prion
Pentre
Llanynys
Gellifor
555 MOEL FAMAU
Moel Famau
Tafarn-y-Gelyn
Gwernymynydd
Nantglyn
Pant-pastynog
Rhos
Hirwaen
Llanferres
Maeshafn
Nercwys
Pontblyd
Gwytherin
Afon Aled
Pentre Saron
Rhewl
Leeswood
Ruthin
Llanbedr-Dyffryn-Clwyd
A494
Pontybodkin
Top-y-rhos
Treuddyn
Llyn Aled
A543
B4501
Archaeological Trail
Llanfwrog
Y Gyffylliog
Bontuchel
Eryrys
448 MOEL LLYN
Mynydd Hiraethog
Llyn Brenig
B5430
Llanarmon-yn-Ial
Graianrhyd
Llanfynydd
Llyn Alwen
B5101
Llanfair Dyffryn Clwyd
Efenechtyd
Llyn Brenig
Rhydtalog
Pwll-glas
Graig-fechan
Clocaenog
B5105
Pentre-celyn
A5104
Bwlchgwyn
Alwen Reservoir
Clawdd-newydd
Pen-y-stryt
Gwynfryn
Minera
Pentre-llyn-cymmer
Cefn-brith
Derwen
Llandegla
Lead Mines
Coedpoet
Offa's Dyke Path
Cyrn-y-brain
Rhyd-lydan
Glasfryn
Llanfihangel Glyn Myfyr
Cross
Bryn Saith Marchog
Pandy'r Capel
Llanelidan
B5105
Cerrigydrudion
Melin-y-wig
R Alwen
492
Betws Gwerfil Goch
Gwyddelwern
Bryneglwys
Horseshoe Pass
578 MOEL Y GAMELIN
Llandynan
Pentredwr
Rhosllanerch
Ty-nant
Afon Morwynion
Llantysilio Mountain
Eliseg's Pillar
Valle Crucis Abbey
502
Penycae
B4501
Dinmael
Y Maerdy
Rhewl
Llantysilio
Ruabon Mountain
669 EDD Y-FILAST
Llangwm
Druid
Rug
Corwen
B5437
Carrog
Horseshoe Falls
Llangollen Railway
Acrefair
57
611 FOEL GOCH
Glan-yr-afon
Bonwm
Lliidiart-y-parc
Glyndyfrdwy
Bryn-newydd
Dinas Bran
A539
Trevor
Garth
Llangollen
Pontcysyllte Aqueduct
Ciltalgarth
Glan-yr-afon
A494
Cynwyd
Ty'n-dwr
Froncysyllte
Bethel
631 MOEL FFERNA
Plas Newydd
Fron-isaf
Afon Tryweryn
Fron-goch
Sarnau
Cefn-ddwysarn
B4401
Chwarel Wynne Mine
Pontfadog
Chirk Castle
ardau
R Dee
B4402
Glyn Ceiriog
Rhyd-uchaf
Rhiwlas
Llandderfel
58
Llandrillo
Bronygarth
B4500
69

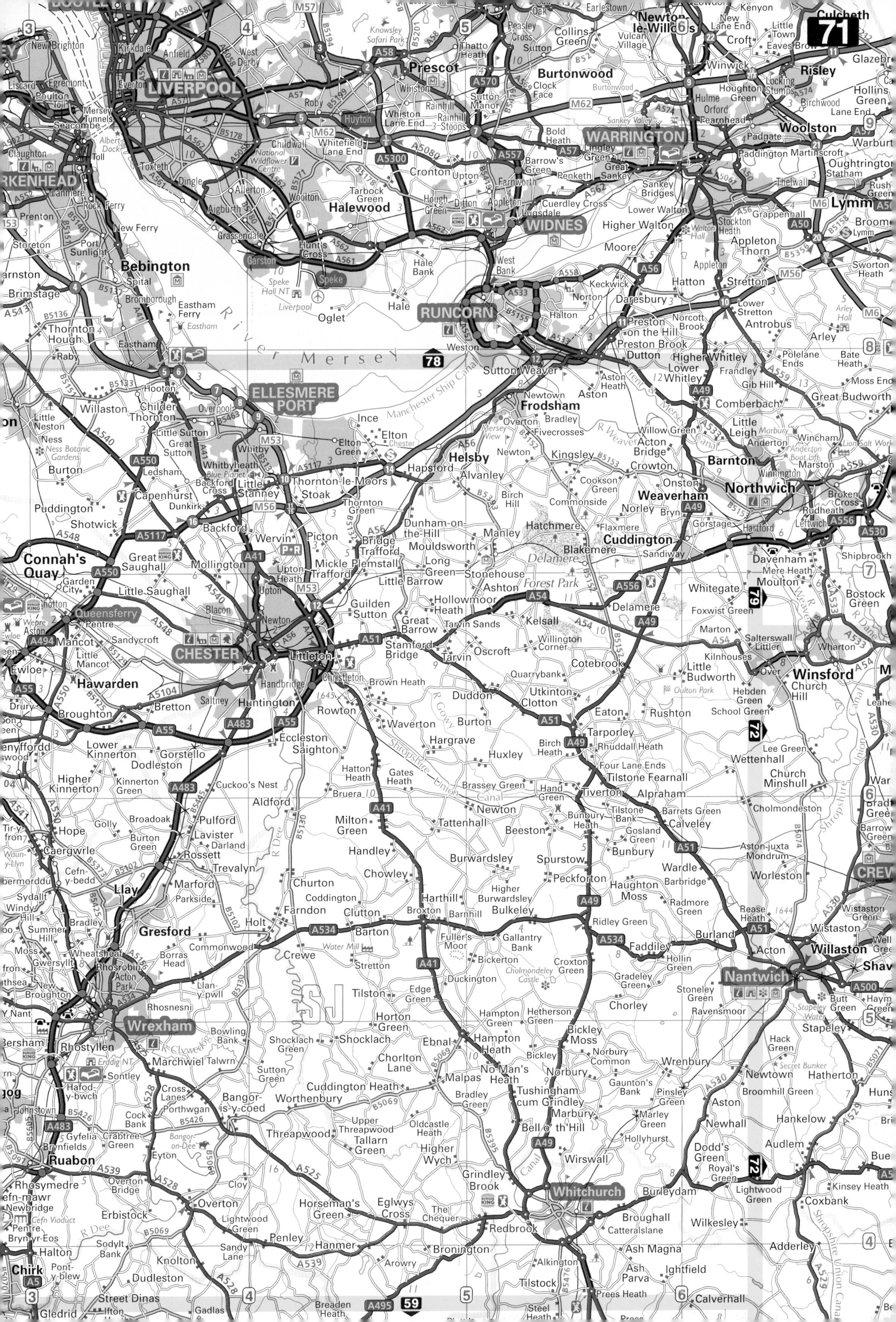
LIVERPOOL
New Brighton
Kirkdale
Anfield
West Derby
Knowsley Safari Park
Prescot
Thatto Heath
Peasley Cross
Sutton
Collins Green
Earlestown
Newton-le-Willows
Kenyon
New Lane End
Culcheth
Little Town
Croft
Eaves Brow
Glazebury
Winwick
Risley
Burtonwood
Liscard
Egremont
Poulton
Seacombe
Mersey Tunnels
Everton
Roby
Huyton
Whiston
Rainhill
Sutton Manor
Clock Face
Houghton Green
Locking Stumps
Hulme
Orford
Birchwood
Hollins Green
Lane End
Fearnhead
Sankey Valley
Woolston
Warburton
Claughton
Albert Dock
Toll
Childwall
National Wildflower Centre
Whitefield Lane End
Whiston Lane End
Rainhill Stoops
Bold Heath
WARRINGTON
Padgate
Martinscroft
Paddington
Oughtrington
Statham
Thelwall
Lymm
Rush Green
BIRKENHEAD
Tranmere
Toxteth
Dingle
Allerton
Woolton
Tarbock Green
Cronton
Upton
Farnworth
Barrow's Green
Penketh
Lingley Green
Great Sankey
Sankey Bridges
Halewood
Hough Green
Ditton
Appleton
Cuerdley Cross
Lugsdale
WIDNES
Lower Walton
Higher Walton
Walton Hall
Grappenhall
Stockton Heath
Appleton Thorn
Broomedge
Rock Ferry
Prenton
New Ferry
Storeton
Port Sunlight
Aigburth
Grassendale
Garston
Hunts Cross
Speke
Speke Hall NT
Liverpool
Hale Bank
Hale
Oglet
West Bank
Moore
Hatton
Stretton
Swarton Heath
Bebington
Spital
Bromborough
Eastham Ferry
Eastham
River Mersey
Keckwick
Norton
Halton
Daresbury
RUNCORN
Weston
Preston on the Hill
Preston Brook
Norcott Brook
Lower Stretton
Antrobus
Arley Hall
Arley
Thornton Hough
Brimstage
Raby
Dutton
Higher Whitley
Lower Whitley
Polelane Ends
Bate Heath
Frandley
Gib Hill
Moss End
Great Budworth
Sutton Weaver
Aston Heath
Aston
Newtown
Frodsham
Overton
Bradley
Fivecrosses
Comberbach
Little Leigh
Marbury
Anderton
Anderton Boat Lift
Wincham
Lion Salt Works
Marston
Barnton
Winnington
Willow Green
Acton Bridge
Crowton
Onston
Northwich
Weaverham
Broken Cross
Rudheath
Leftwich
Hooton
Childer Thornton
Overpool
ELLESMERE PORT
Manchester Ship Canal
Little Neston
Willaston
Little Sutton
Great Sutton
Ince
Elton
Elton Green
Chester
Ness
Ness Botanic Gardens
Whitby
Whitbyheath
Blue Planet
Helsby
Hapsford
Alvanley
Newton
Kingsley
Cookson Green
Burton
Ledsham
Capenhurst
Backford Cross
Little Stanney
Thornton-le-Moors
Stoak
Thornton Green
Birch Hill
Commonside
Norley
Bryn
Gorstage
Hartford
Puddington
Shotwick
Dunkirk
Backford
Wervin
Picton
Bridge Trafford
Dunham-on-the-Hill
Manley
Mouldsworth
Hatchmere
Flaxmere
Cuddington
Blakemere
Sandiway
Davenham
Shipbrook
Mere Heath
Moulton
Connah's Quay
Great Saughall
Mollington
Upton Heath
Upton
Mickle Trafford
Plemstall
Long Green
Little Barrow
Stonehouse
Ashton
Delamere Forest Park
Delamere
Whitegate
Foxwist Green
Bostock Green
Garden City
Little Saughall
Blacon
Queensferry
Pentre
Shotton
Aston
Mancot
Sandycroft
Little Mancot
CHESTER
Newton
Littleton
Guilden Sutton
Great Barrow
Hollowmoor Heath
Tarvin Sands
Kelsall
Willington Corner
Marton
Salterswall
Littler
Kilnhouses
Wharton
Ewloe
Hawarden
Saltney
Handbridge
Christleton
Stamford Bridge
Tarvin
Oscroft
Quarrybank
Cotebrook
Little Budworth
Oulton Park
Over
Winsford
Church Hill
Drury
Broughton
Bretton
Huntington
Brown Heath
Rowton
Duddon
Utkinton
Clotton
Eaton
Rushton
Hebden Green
School Green
Lower Kinnerton
Dodleston
Gorstello
Eccleston
Saighton
Waverton
Burton
Hargrave
Huxley
Birch Heath
Tarporley
Rhuddall Heath
Lee Green
Wettenhall
Higher Kinnerton
Kinnerton Green
Cuckoo's Nest
Aldford
Hatton Heath
Gates Heath
Bruera
Shropshire Union Canal
Brassey Green
Hand Green
Four Lane Ends
Tilstone Fearnall
Tiverton
Alpraham
Church Minshull
Hope
Golly
Broadoak
Pulford
Lavister
Darland
Burton Green
Rossett
Trevalyn
Caergwrle
Cefn-y-bedd
Milton Green
Newton
Tattenhall
Beeston
Bunbury Heath
Tilstone Bank
Barrets Green
Calveley
Cholmondeston
Gosland Green
Bunbury
Handley
Chowley
Burwardsley
Spurstow
Peckforton
Aston-juxta Mondrum
Wardle
Barbridge
Worleston
Llay
Marford
Parkside
Churton
Coddington
Farndon
Clutton
Harthill
Broxton
Barnhill
Higher Burwardsley
Bulkeley
Haughton Moss
Radmore Green
Rease Heath
Wistaston Green
Gresford
Holt
Barton
Fuller's Moor
Gallantry Bank
Ridley Green
Faddiley
Burland
Acton
Willaston
Wistaston
Wheatsheaf
Gwersyllt
Rhosrobin
Acton Park
Borras Head
Commonwood
Crewe
Water Mill
Stretton
Bickerton
Cholmondeley Castle
Croxton Green
Hollin Green
Gradeley Green
Nantwich
Stoneley Green
Butt Green
Shavington
New Broughton
Llan-y-pwll
Rhosnesni
Tilston
Edge Green
Duckington
Hampton Green
Hetherson Green
Chorley
Ravensmoor
Stapeley Water
Stapeley
Wrexham
Bowling Bank
Horton Green
Shocklach Green
Shocklach
Ebnal
Hampton Heath
Bickley Moss
Norbury Common
Bickley
Rhostyllen
Marchwiel
Talwrn
Erddig NT
Sontley
Sutton Green
Chorlton Lane
No Man's Heath
Norbury
Wrenbury
Gaunton's Bank
Secret Bunker
Newtown
Hatherton
Hafod-y-bwch
Cross Lanes
Porthwgan
Bangor-is-y-coed
Cuddington Heath
Worthenbury
Malpas
Bradley Green
Tushingham cum Grindley
Marbury
Pinsley Green
Marley Green
Aston
Broomhill Green
Johnstown
Cock Bank
Crabtree Green
Gyfelia
Brynfields
Bangor-on-Dee
Upper Threapwood
Threapwood
Tallarn Green
Oldcastle Heath
Higher Wych
Bell o' th' Hill
Hollyhurst
Newhall
Hankelow
Dodd's Green
Royal's Green
Audlem
Ruabon
Eyton
Wirswall
Grindley Brook
Whitchurch
Burleydam
Lightwood Green
Kinsey Heath
Coxbank
Rhosymedre
Cefn-mawr
Newbridge
Cefn Viaduct
Pentre
Bryn-yr-Eos
Overton Bridge
Cloy
Overton
Lightwood Green
Horseman's Green
Eglwys Cross
The Chequer
Redbrook
Broughall
Catteralslane
Wilkesley
Adderley
Halton
Chirk
Pont-y-blew
Sodylt Bank
Sandy Lane
Penley
Hanmer
Arowry
Bronington
Alkington
Ash Magna
Ash Parva
Ightfield
Knolton
Dudleston
Street Dinas
Tilstock
Prees Heath
Calverhall
Gledrid
Ifton
Gadlas
Breaden Heath
Steel Heath
Shropshire Union Canal
Liverpool Airport
78
79
72
59

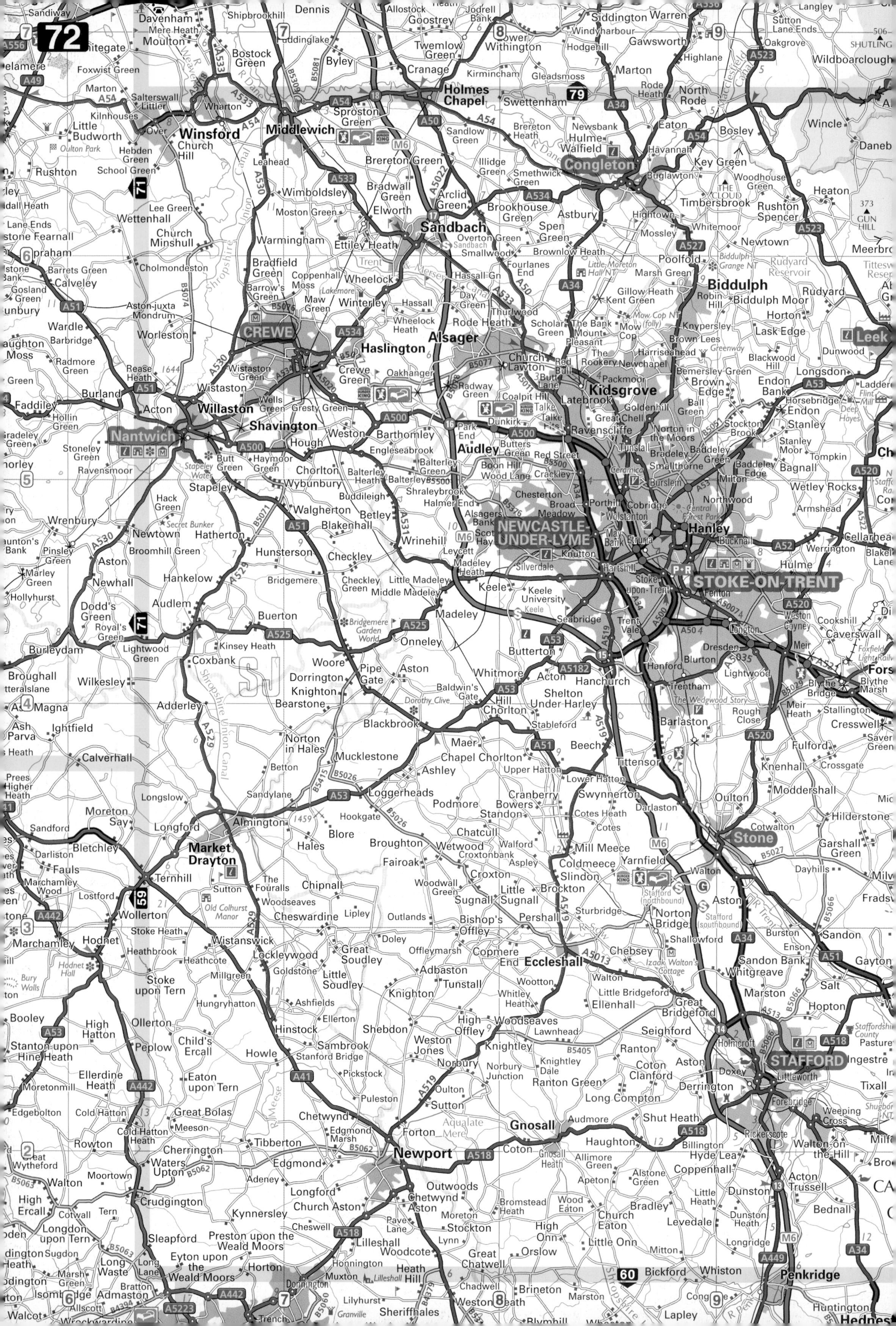
Sandiway
Davenham
Shipbrookhill
Dennis
Allostock
Goostrey
Jodrell Bank
Siddington
Warren
Langley
Mere Heath
Moulton
Whitegate
Byley
Twemlow Green
Lower Withington
Windyharbour
Hodgehill
Gawsworth
Sutton Lane Ends
Oakgrove
Wildboarclough
Bostock Green
Foxwist Green
Cranage
Kirmincham
Gleadsmoss
Highlane
Marton
Rode Heath
North Rode
Holmes Chapel
Swettenham
Salterswall
Littler
Wharton
Sproston Green
Kilnhouses
Little Budworth
Over
Winsford
Church Hill
Middlewich
Sandlow Green
Brereton Heath
Newsbank
Hulme Walfield
Eaton
Bosley
Wincle
Oulton Park
Hebden Green
School Green
Rushton
Leahead
Brereton Green
Illidge Green
Smethwick Green
Congleton
Havannah
Key Green
Woodhouse Green
Buglawton
The Cloud
Heaton
Timbersbrook
Rushton Spencer
Gun Hill
Wimboldsley
Bradwall Green
Arclid Green
Brookhouse Green
Astbury
Lee Green
Wettenhall
Moston Green
Elworth
Sandbach
Spen Green
Hightown
Mossley
Whitemoor
Newtown
Church Minshull
Warmingham
Overton Green
Smallwood
Brownlow Heath
Ettiley Heath
Meerbrook
Poolfold
Biddulph
Biddulph Grange NT
Rudyard Reservoir
Tittesworth Reservoir
Cholmondeston
Barrets Green
Calveley
Bradfield Green
Coppenhall Moss
Wheelock
Hassall Green
Fourlanes End
Little Moreton Hall NT
Marsh Green
Gosland Green
Barrow's Green
Lakemore
Winterley
Hassall
Day Green
Gillow Heath
Kent Green
Robin Hill
Biddulph Moor
Rudyard
Aston-juxta Mondrum
Maw Green
Wheelock Heath
Thurlwood
Horton
Wardle
Barbridge
Worleston
Crewe
Alsager
Rode Heath
Scholar Green
The Bank
Mow Cop
Mount Pleasant
Knypersley
Lask Edge
Leek
Radmore Green
Haslington
Brown Lees
Greenway
Dunwood
Rease Heath
Wistaston Green
Crewe Green
Church Lawton
Red Bull
The Rookery
Harriseahead
Newchapel
Blackwood Hill
Burland
Wistaston
Oakhanger
Radway Green
Butt Lane
Packmoor
Kidsgrove
Bemersley Green
Brown Edge
Endon Bank
Longsdon
Faddiley
Acton
Willaston
Coalpit Hill
Talke
Latebrook
Goldenhill
Ball Green
Horsebridge
Endon
Deep Hayes
Hollin Green
Shavington
Wells Green
Gresty Green
Dunkirk
Talke Pits
Great Chell
Nantwich
Weston
Barthomley
Park End
Ravenscliffe
Norton in the Moors
Stockton Brook
Stanley
Hough
Audley
Butters Green
Tunstall
Bradeley
Baddeley Green
Stanley Moor
Stoneley Green
Butt Green
Engleseabrook
Red Street
Ravensmoor
Stapeley Water
Haymoor Green
Chorlton
Balterley Heath
Balterley Green
Boon Hill
Wood Lane
Crackley
Ceramica
Smallthorne
Baddeley Edge
Bagnall
Tompkin
Stapeley
Wybunbury
Shraleybrook
Burslem
Milton
Wetley Rocks
Hack Green
Buddileigh
Halmer End
Chesterton
Porthill
Cobridge
Northwood
Central Forest Park
Armshead
Wrenbury
Secret Bunker
Walgherton
Betley
Broad Meadow
Wolstanton
Blakenhall
Alsagers Bank
Newcastle-under-Lyme
Hanley
Newtown
Hatherton
Wrinehill
Scot Hay
Etruria
May Bank
Bucknall
Cellarhead
Pinsley Green
Broomhill Green
Hunsterson
Checkley
Leycett
Knutton
Werrington
Aston
Madeley Heath
Silverdale
Hartshill
Hulme
Marley Green
Newhall
Bridgemere
Checkley Green
Little Madeley
Middle Madeley
Keele
Keele University
Stoke-upon-Trent
Stoke-on-Trent
Fenton
Hankelow
Hollyhurst
Audlem
Dodd's Green
Madeley
Seabridge
Weston Coyney
Cookshill
Royal's Green
Buerton
Bridgemere Garden World
Trent Vale
Longton
Caverswall
Burleydam
Lightwood Green
Kinsey Heath
Onneley
Butterton
Dresden
Meir
Coxbank
Woore
Pipe Gate
Aston
Whitmore
Acton
Hanchurch
Blurton
Lightwood
Broughall
Wilkesley
Dorrington
Knighton
Baldwin's Gate
Hanford
Trentham
Blythe Bridge
Blythe Marsh
Bearstone
Dorothy Clive
Hill Chorlton
Shelton Under Harley
The Wedgwood Story
Meir Heath
Stallington
Adderley
Blackbrook
Stableford
Barlaston
Rough Close
Cresswell
Ightfield
Calverhall
Norton in Hales
Maer
Beech
Fulford
Mucklestone
Chapel Chorlton
Upper Hatton
Tittensor
Knenhall
Crossgate
Betton
Ashley
Lower Hatton
Swynnerton
Moddershall
Longslow
Sandylane
Loggerheads
Cranberry
Bowers
Oulton
Moreton Say
Podmore
Standon
Cotes Heath
Darlaston
Hilderstone
Sandford
Longford
Almington
Hookgate
Cotes
Cotwalton
Stone
Bletchley
Blore
Hales
Chatcull
Mill Meece
Garshall Green
Darliston
Market Drayton
Broughton
Wetwood
Walford
Croxtonbank
Aspley
Coldmeece
Yarnfield
Fauls
Ternhill
Fairoak
Slindon
Walton
Dayhills
Marchamley Wood
The Fourlans
Sutton
Chipnall
Woodwall Green
Croxton
Little Sugnall
Brockton
Stafford (northbound)
Lostford
Old Colhurst Manor
Woodseaves
Sugnall
Sturbridge
Norton Bridge
Aston
Wollerton
Cheswardine
Lipley
Outlands
Bishop's Offley
Pershall
Stafford (southbound)
Stoke Heath
Marchamley
Hodnet
Heathbrook
Wistanswick
Lockleywood
Great Soudley
Doley
Offleymarsh
Copmere End
Eccleshall
Chebsey
Shallowford
Burston
Sandon
Enson
Izaak Walton's Cottage
Hodnet Hall
Heathcote
Goldstone
Little Soudley
Adbaston
Walton
Sandon Bank
Whitgreave
Gayton
Bury Walls
Stoke upon Tern
Millgreen
Knighton
Tunstall
Wootton
Little Bridgeford
Whitley Heath
Ellenhall
Great Bridgeford
Marston
Salt
Hungryhatton
Ashfields
Ellerton
Hopton
Booley
High Hatton
Ollerton
Hinstock
Shebdon
High Offley
Woodseaves
Lawnhead
Seighford
Staffordshire County Showground
Weston Jones
Stanton upon Hine Heath
Peplow
Child's Ercall
Sambrook
Howle
Knightley
Ranton
Holmcroft
Stafford
Ingestre
Stanford Bridge
Norbury
Knightley Dale
Aston
Coton Clanford
Doxey
Littleworth
Ellerdine Heath
Eaton upon Tern
Pickstock
Norbury Junction
Ranton Green
Moretonmill
Tixall
Oulton
Derrington
Forebridge
Shugborough NT
Edgebolton
Cold Hatton
Great Bolas
Puleston
Sutton
Long Compton
Meeson
Chetwynd
Aqualate Mere
Gnosall
Audmore
Shut Heath
Weeping Cross
Cold Hatton Heath
Edgmond Marsh
Forton
Haughton
Rickerscote
Rowton
Cherrington
Tibberton
Billington
Walton-on-the-Hill
Great Wytheford
Waters Upton
Edgmond
Newport
Coton
Gnosall Heath
Hyde Lea
Allimore Green
Coppenhall
Acton Trussell
Moortown
Adeney
Outwoods
Apeton
Alstone Green
Walton
High Ercall
Cotwall
Tern
Crudgington
Longford
Chetwynd Aston
Bromstead Heath
Wood Eaton
Bradley
Dunston
Little Heath
Bednall
Kynnersley
Church Aston
Moreton
Church Eaton
Dunston Heath
Longdon upon Tern
Cheswell
Pave Lane
Stockton
High Onn
Levedale
Sleapford
Preston upon the Weald Moors
Lilleshall
Lynn
Little Onn
Longridge
Sugdon
Long Waste
Woodcote
Great Chatwell
Orslow
Mitton
Eyton upon the Weald Moors
Long Lane
Honnington
Horton
Bickford
Whiston
Penkridge
Marsh Green
Isombridge
Admaston
Bratton
Donnington
Muxton
Lilleshall
Heath Hill
Chadwell
Brineton
Marston
Cong
Allscott
Lilyhurst
Weston Heath
Sheriffhales
Granville
Huntington
Walcot
Wrockwardine
Trench
Lapley
Hednesford
Shropshire Union Canal
Macclesfield Canal
Trent & Mersey Canal
R Weaver
R Dane
R Trent
R Meese
R Sow
R Penk
A556
A49
A54
A533
A530
A51
A534
A5022
A50
A5020
A500
A5011
A34
A527
A53
A523
A520
A52
A5007
A5035
A521
A529
A525
A5182
A519
A41
A442
A518
A5013
A513
A449
A5223
B5081
B5309
B5074
B5076
B5077
B5078
B5071
B5500
B5367
B5051
B5026
B5415
B5062
B5063
B5405
B5066
B5027
B4394
B5060
B4379
B5029
B5063
M6
SJ
P+R
71
79
59
60
1644
1459
506
373

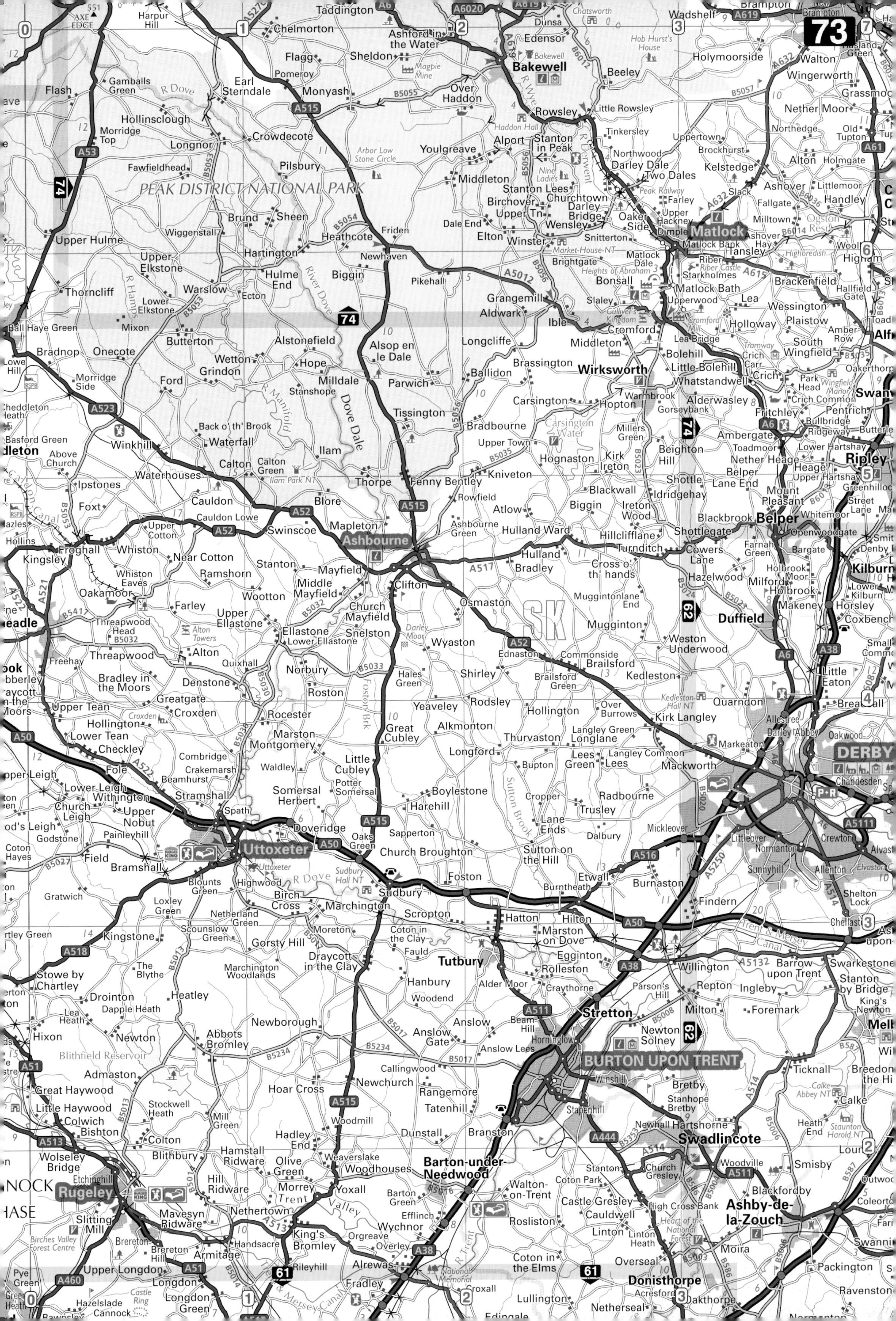

73
AXE EDGE
Harpur Hill
Taddington
Chelmorton
Ashford in the Water
A6020
Chatsworth
Dunsa
Edensor
Wadshelf
Brampton
A619
Hob Hurst's House
Holymoorside
Walton
Flagg
Sheldon
Magpie Mine
Bakewell
Beeley
Wingerworth
Flash
Gamballs Green
R Dove
Earl Sterndale
Pomeroy
Monyash
Over Haddon
B5055
Rowsley
Little Rowsley
B5057
Grassmoor
Nether Moor
A515
Haddon Hall
Hollinsclough
Morridge Top
Crowdecote
Longnor
Arbor Low Stone Circle
Youlgreave
Alport
Stanton in Peak
Tinkersley
Northwood
Uppertown
Brockhurst
Northedge
Old Tupton
A53
Fawfieldhead
Pilsbury
Nine Ladies
Darley Dale
Two Dales
Kelstedge
Alton
Holmgate
A61
B5053
PEAK DISTRICT NATIONAL PARK
Middleton
Stanton Lees
Peak Railway
Ashover
Littlemoor
Birchover
Churchtown
Farley
Slack
Fallgate
Handley
Brund
Sheen
Upper Tn
Darley Bridge
Upper Hackney
Oaker
Milltown
Ogston Resr
Wiggenstall
B5054
Friden
Dale End
Wensley
Side
Dimple
Matlock
Upper Hulme
Heathcote
Elton
Winster
Snitterton
Matlock Bank
Tansley
Ashover Hay
Woolley
Upper Elkstone
Hartington
Newhaven
Market House NT
Matlock Dale
Brightgate
Riber
Riber Castle
Highoredish
Higham
Hulme End
Biggin
River Dove
Pikehall
A5012
Heights of Abraham
Starkholmes
A615
Brackenfield
Thorncliff
R Hamps
Warslow
Ecton
Bonsall
Matlock Bath
Hallfield Gate
Lower Elkstone
Grangemill
Slaley
Upperwood
Lea
Wessington
Ball Haye Green
Mixon
74
Aldwark
Gulliver's Kingdom
Ible
Cromford
Cromford Mill
Holloway
Plaistow
Amber Row
Alfreton
Bradnop
Onecote
Butterton
Alstonefield
Alsop en le Dale
Longcliffe
Middleton
Lea Bridge
South Wingfield
Lowe Hill
Wetton
Hope
Brassington
Wirksworth
Little Bolehill
Bolehill
Tramway
Crich
Carr
Oakerthorpe
Morridge Side
Grindon
Ford
Milldale
Stanshope
Parwich
Ballidon
Whatstandwell
Crich Common
Park Head
Wingfield Manor
Swanwick
Cheddleton Heath
A523
R Manifold
Dove Dale
Tissington
B5056
Carsington
Hopton
Warmbrook
Gorseybank
Alderwasley
Fritchley
Pentrich
Bullbridge
Ridgeway
Butterley
Basford Green
Winkhill
Back o' th' Brook
Waterfall
Bradbourne
Carsington Water
Millers Green
Ambergate
Toadmoor
Lower Hartshay
Cheddleton
Above Church
Ilam
Calton
Calton Green
Ilam Park NT
Upper Town
B5035
Hognaston
Kirk Ireton
Beighton Hill
Nether Heage
Heage
Ripley
Waterhouses
Ipstones
Thorpe
Fenny Bentley
Kniveton
Shottle
Belper
Lane End
Upper Hartshay
Greenhillocks
Foxt
Cauldon
Blore
Rowsfield
Blackwall
Biggin
Ireton Wood
Idridgehay
Mount Pleasant
Street Lane
Hazles
Cauldon Lowe
Upper Cotton
A52
Swinscoe
Mapleton
Ashbourne
Ashbourne Green
Atlow
Hulland Ward
Hillcliffane
Blackbrook
Shottlegate
Whitemoor
Openwoodgate
Hollins
Froghall
Whiston
Kingsley
Near Cotton
Stanton
Mayfield
Hulland
Bradley
Turnditch
Cross o' th' hands
Cowers Lane
Farnah Green
Bargate
Denby
Kilburn
Whiston Eaves
Ramshorn
Middle Mayfield
Clifton
A517
Hazelwood
Holbrook Moor
Milford
Oakamoor
Wootton
Farley
Church Mayfield
Osmaston
Muggintonlane End
Holbrook
Makeney
Horsley
Cheadle
B5417
Threapwood Head
Alton Towers
Upper Ellastone
Darley Moor
SK
Mugginton
Duffield
Coxbench
Ellastone
Lower Ellastone
Snelston
Weston Underwood
Threapwood
Alton
Wyaston
Ednaston
Commonside
Brailsford
Freehay
Quixhall
Norbury
B5033
Hales Green
Shirley
Brailsford Green
Kedleston
Little Eaton
Bradley in the Moors
Denstone
Roston
Foston Brk
Kedleston Hall NT
Quarndon
Breadsall
Upper Tean
Greatgate
Croxden
Rocester
Yeaveley
Rodsley
Hollington
Over Burrows
Kirk Langley
Allestree
Darley Abbey
Oakwood
Hollington
Lower Tean
Checkley
Marston Montgomery
Great Cubley
Alkmonton
Thurvaston
Langley Green
Longlane
Markeaton
DERBY
A50
Combridge
Crakemarsh
Waldley
Little Cubley
Longford
Bupton
Lees Green
Langley Common
Lees
Mackworth
Chaddesden
Fole
A522
Beamhurst
Somersal Herbert
Potter Somersal
Boylestone
Cropper
Radbourne
Lower Leigh
Withington
Stramshall
Harehill
Sutton Brook
Trusley
Church Leigh
Upper Nobut
Spath
Doveridge
Lane Ends
Dalbury
Mickleover
Littleover
Crewton
A5111
Godstone
Painleyhill
Uttoxeter
Oaks Green
Sapperton
Normanton
Alvaston
Coton Hayes
Field
B5027
Bramshall
Church Broughton
Sutton on the Hill
A516
Sunnyhill
Allenton
Elvaston
Uttoxeter
Highwood
R Dove
Sudbury Hall NT
Sudbury
Foston
Etwall
Burnaston
Burntheath
Blounts Green
Birch Cross
Marchington
Gratwich
Loxley Green
Netherland Green
Scropton
Hatton
Hilton
Findern
Shelton Lock
Chellaston
Kingstone
Scounslow Green
Moreton
Coton in the Clay
Fauld
Marston on Dove
Egginton
Willington
Trent & Mersey Canal
A5132
Barrow upon Trent
Swarkestone
A518
Gorsty Hill
Draycott in the Clay
Tutbury
Rolleston
A38
Stanton by Bridge
The Blythe
Marchington Woodlands
Hanbury
Alder Moor
Craythorne
Parson's Hill
Repton
Ingleby
Stowe by Chartley
Drointon
Heatley
Woodend
A511
Stretton
Milton
Foremark
King's Newton
Dapple Heath
Lea Heath
Newborough
B5017
Anslow
Anslow Gate
Beam Hill
B5008
Newton Solney
Melbourne
Hixon
Newton
Abbots Bromley
Horninglow
Blithfield Reservoir
B5234
Anslow Lees
BURTON UPON TRENT
A51
Admaston
Callingwood
Winshill
Ticknall
Breedon on the Hill
Great Haywood
Hoar Cross
Newchurch
Rangemore
Bretby
Stanhope Bretby
Calke Abbey NT
Calke
Little Haywood
Stockwell Heath
Tatenhill
Stapenhill
Colwich
Bishton
Mill Green
Woodmill
Heath End
Staunton Harold NT
A513
Colton
Hadley End
Dunstall
Branston
Newhall
Hartshorne
Swadlincote
Wolseley Bridge
Blithbury
Hamstall Ridware
Olive Green
Weaverslake
A444
Lount
Etchinghill
Woodhouses
Barton-under-Needwood
Stanton
Church Gresley
Woodville
Smisby
CANNOCK
Rugeley
Hill Ridware
Morrey
Yoxall
Barton Green
Walton-on-Trent
Coton Park
Blackfordby
Coleorton
CHASE
Trent Valley
Castle Gresley
High Cross Bank
Ashby-de-la-Zouch
Slitting Mill
Mavesyn Ridware
Nethertown
Efflinch
Wychnor
Rosliston
Cauldwell
Heart of the National Forest
Birches Valley Forest Centre
Brereton
Brereton Hill
Armitage
Handsacre
King's Bromley
Orgreave
Overley
Linton
Linton Heath
Moira
Swannington
Pye Green
Upper Longdon
Rileyhill
Alrewas
National Memorial
R Trent
Coton in the Elms
Overseal
Packington
Longdon
Fradley
Croxall
Donisthorpe
Acresford
Oakthorpe
Ravenstone
Hazelslade
Cannock
Castle Ring
Longdon Green
Trent & Mersey Canal
Lullington
Netherseal
Edingale
61
62

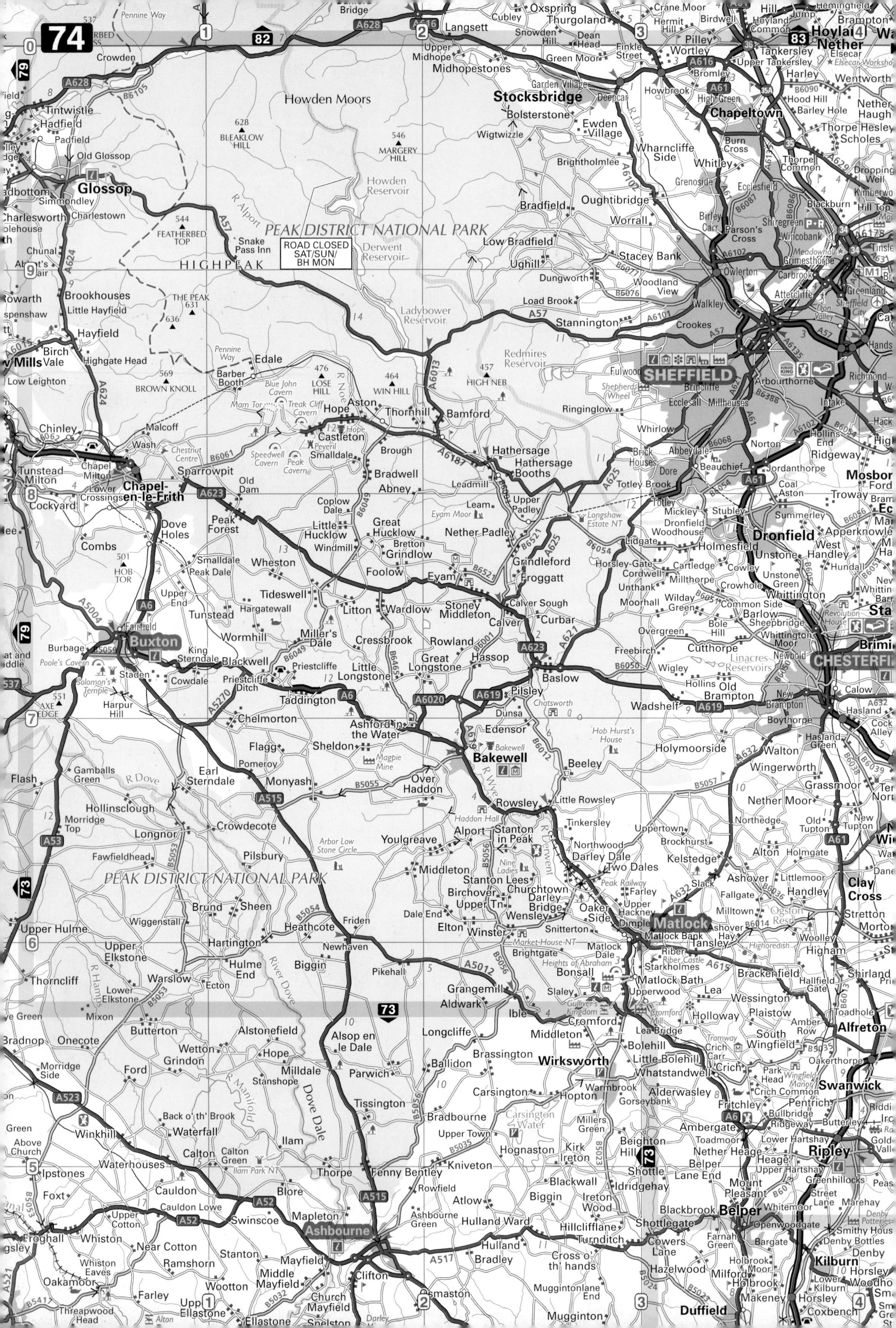

82
83
79
73
Pennine Way
Crowden
Langsett
Upper Midhope
Midhopestones
Oxspring
Thurgoland
Cubley
Snowden Hill
Dean Head
Green Moor
Finkle Street
Crane Moor
Hermit Hill
Birdwell
Pilley
Wortley
Hoyland Common
Hoyland Nether
Tankersley
Upper Tankersley
Elsecar
Bromley
Harley
Wentworth
Howbrook
High Green
Chapeltown
Hood Hill
Barley Hole
Nether Haugh
Thorpe Hesley
Scholes
Burn Cross
Thorpe Common
Brampton
Tintwistle
Hadfield
Padfield
Old Glossop
Glossop
Simmondley
Charlesworth
Charlestown
Chunal
Brookhouses
Little Hayfield
Hayfield
Birch Vale
Highgate Head
Low Leighton
Howden Moors
628 BLEAKLOW HILL
546 MARGERY HILL
Howden Reservoir
Derwent Reservoir
Ladybower Reservoir
544 FEATHERBED TOP
Snake Pass Inn
ROAD CLOSED SAT/SUN/ BH MON
PEAK DISTRICT NATIONAL PARK
HIGH PEAK
THE PEAK 631
636
Stocksbridge
Garden Village
Deepcar
Bolsterstone
Ewden Village
Wigtwizzle
Wharncliffe Side
Whitley
Grenoside
Ecclesfield
Brightholmlee
Bradfield
Oughtibridge
Worrall
Low Bradfield
Stacey Bank
Ughill
Dungworth
Woodland View
Load Brook
Stannington
Birley Carr
Parson's Cross
Shiregreen
Wincobank
Blackburn
Hill Top
Meadowhall
Grimesthorpe
Owlerton
Carbrook
Attercliffe
Walkley
Crookes
Greenland
Sheffield City
Darnall
Handsworth
Richmond
SHEFFIELD
Fulwood
Shepherd Wheel
Brincliffe
Ecclesall
Millhouses
Arbourthorne
Intake
Ringinglow
Redmires Reservoir
457 HIGH NEB
Whirlow
Norton
Hollins End
Ridgeway
Brick Houses
Abbeydale
Beauchief
Dore
Totley Brook
Jordanthorpe
Mosborough
Coal Aston
Troway
Totley
Mickley
Dronfield Woodhouse
Stubley
Summerley
Dronfield
Apperknowle
Lidgate
Holmesfield
Unstone
West Handley
Edale
Barber Booth
Blue John Cavern
Mam Tor
Treak Cliff Cavern
476 LOSE HILL
464 WIN HILL
569 BROWN KNOLL
Hope
Aston
Thornhill
Bamford
Castleton
Peveril
Smalldale
Brough
Hathersage
Hathersage Booths
Bradwell
Abney
Leadmill
Chinley
Malcoff
Wash
Chestnut Centre
Chapel Milton
Tunstead Milton
Chapel-en-le-Frith
Lower Crossings
Cockyard
Sparrowpit
Speedwell Cavern
Peak Cavern
Old Dam
Peak Forest
Dove Holes
Combs
501 HOB TOR
Coplow Dale
Little Hucklow
Great Hucklow
Bretton
Grindlow
Windmill
Eyam Moor
Leam
Upper Padley
Longshaw Estate NT
Nether Padley
Grindleford
Froggatt
Horsley Gate
Cordwell
Cartledge
Cowley
Unthank
Millthorpe
Crowhole
Unstone Green
Whittington
Smalldale
Peak Dale
Wheston
Foolow
Eyam
Upper End
Tideswell
Hargatewall
Tunstead
Litton
Wardlow
Stoney Middleton
Calver Sough
Curbar
Calver
Moorhall
Wilday Green
Barlow
Common Side
Sheepbridge
Whittington Moor
Newbold
Revolution House
Fairfield
Buxton
Wormhill
Miller's Dale
Cressbrook
Rowland
Great Longstone
Hassop
Overgreen
Freebirch
Cutthorpe
Bole Hill
Linacres Reservoirs
CHESTERFIELD
Burbage
Poole's Cavern
King Sterndale
Blackwell
Priestcliffe
Little Longstone
Wigley
Hollins
Old Brampton
Staden
Cowdale
Priestcliffe Ditch
Taddington
Baslow
Pilsley
Chatsworth
Dunsa
Wadshelf
New Brampton
Calow
Boythorpe
Hasland
Solomon's Temple
Harpur Hill
551 AXE EDGE
Chelmorton
Ashford in the Water
Edensor
Hob Hurst's House
Hasland Green
Holymoorside
Walton
Flagg
Sheldon
Bakewell
Beeley
Wingerworth
Gamballs Green
Flash
R Dove
Earl Sterndale
Pomeroy
Magpie Mine
Monyash
Over Haddon
Grassmoor
Hollinsclough
Morridge Top
Rowsley
Little Rowsley
Nether Moor
Longnor
Crowdecote
Haddon Hall
Alport
Stanton in Peak
Tinkersley
Uppertown
Northedge
Old Tupton
New Tupton
Fawfieldhead
Pilsbury
Arbor Low Stone Circle
Youlgreave
Nine Ladies
Northwood
Darley Dale
Brockhurst
Kelstedge
Alton
Holmgate
PEAK DISTRICT NATIONAL PARK
Middleton
Stanton Lees
Two Dales
Peak Railway
Ashover
Littlemoor
Clay Cross
Birchover
Upper Tn
Churchtown
Darley Bridge
Farley
Slack
Fallgate
Handley
Brund
Sheen
Wiggenstall
Heathcote
Friden
Dale End
Elton
Wensley
Oaker Side
Upper Hackney
Milltown
Ogston Resr
Stretton
Upper Hulme
Hartington
Winster
Snitterton
Dimple
Matlock
Ashover Hay
Woolley
Upper Elkstone
Newhaven
Market House NT
Brightgate
Matlock Dale
Matlock Bank
Tansley
Higham
Riber
Riber Castle
Heights of Abraham
Starkholmes
Thorncliff
Warslow
Hulme End
Biggin
Pikehall
Bonsall
Matlock Bath
Brackenfield
Shirland
Lower Elkstone
Ecton
River Dove
Grangemill
Slaley
Upperwood
Lea
Hallfield Gate
Aldwark
Wessington
Mixon
Ible
Gulliver's Kingdom
Cromford
Cromford Mill
Holloway
Plaistow
Toadhole
Butterton
Alstonefield
Longcliffe
Middleton
Lea Bridge
Amber Row
Alfreton
Bradnop
Onecote
Wetton
Hope
Alsop en le Dale
Brassington
Wirksworth
Bolehill
Tramway
South Wingfield
Crich Carr
Crich
Little Bolehill
Whatstandwell
Oakerthorpe
Morridge Side
Grindon
Ford
Milldale
Stanshope
R Manifold
Parwich
Ballidon
Park Head
Wingfield Manor
Swanwick
Dove Dale
Carsington
Warmbrook
Hopton
Gorseybank
Alderwasley
Crich Common
Pentrich
Back o' th' Brook
Waterfall
Tissington
Bradbourne
Carsington Water
Millers Green
Fritchley
Bullbridge
Ridgeway
Butterley
Winkhill
Ilam
Upper Town
Hognaston
Kirk Ireton
Beighton Hill
Ambergate
Toadmoor
Lower Hartshay
Nether Heage
Heage
Ripley
Above Church
Waterhouses
Calton
Calton Green
Ilam Park NT
Thorpe
Fenny Bentley
Kniveton
Shottle
Belper Lane End
Upper Hartshay
Greenhillocks
Ipstones
Foxt
Cauldon
Cauldon Lowe
Blore
Rowfield
Blackwall
Idridgehay
Ireton Wood
Mount Pleasant
Street Lane
Marehay
Upper Cotton
Swinscoe
Mapleton
Ashbourne
Ashbourne Green
Atlow
Biggin
Hulland Ward
Hillcliff Lane
Blackbrook
Belper
Whitemoor
Openwoodgate
Denby Pottery
Smithy Houses
Froghall
Whiston
Near Cotton
Ramshorn
Stanton
Hulland
Bradley
Cross o' th' hands
Turnditch
Shottlegate
Cowers Lane
Farnah Green
Bargate
Denby Bottles
Denby
Kilburn
Whiston Eaves
Oakamoor
Mayfield
Middle Mayfield
Wootton
Clifton
Hazelwood
Holbrook Moor
Milford
Holbrook
Lower Kilburn
Horsley
Horsley Woodhouse
Farley
Upper Ellastone
Church Mayfield
Snelston
Osmaston
Mugginton Lane End
Makeney
Duffield
Threapwood Head
Alton
Ellastone
Darley
Mugginton
Coxbench
A628
A616
A61
A629
A6102
A6178
A57
A6101
A6135
A621
A625
A6013
A6187
B6001
B6049
B6061
A623
A6
A5004
A5270
A6020
A619
A632
A624
A515
A53
A5012
B5053
B5054
B5055
B5056
B5057
A615
B5035
A610
A523
A52
A517
B5023
B5032
B6014
B6036
B6013
A38
B6105

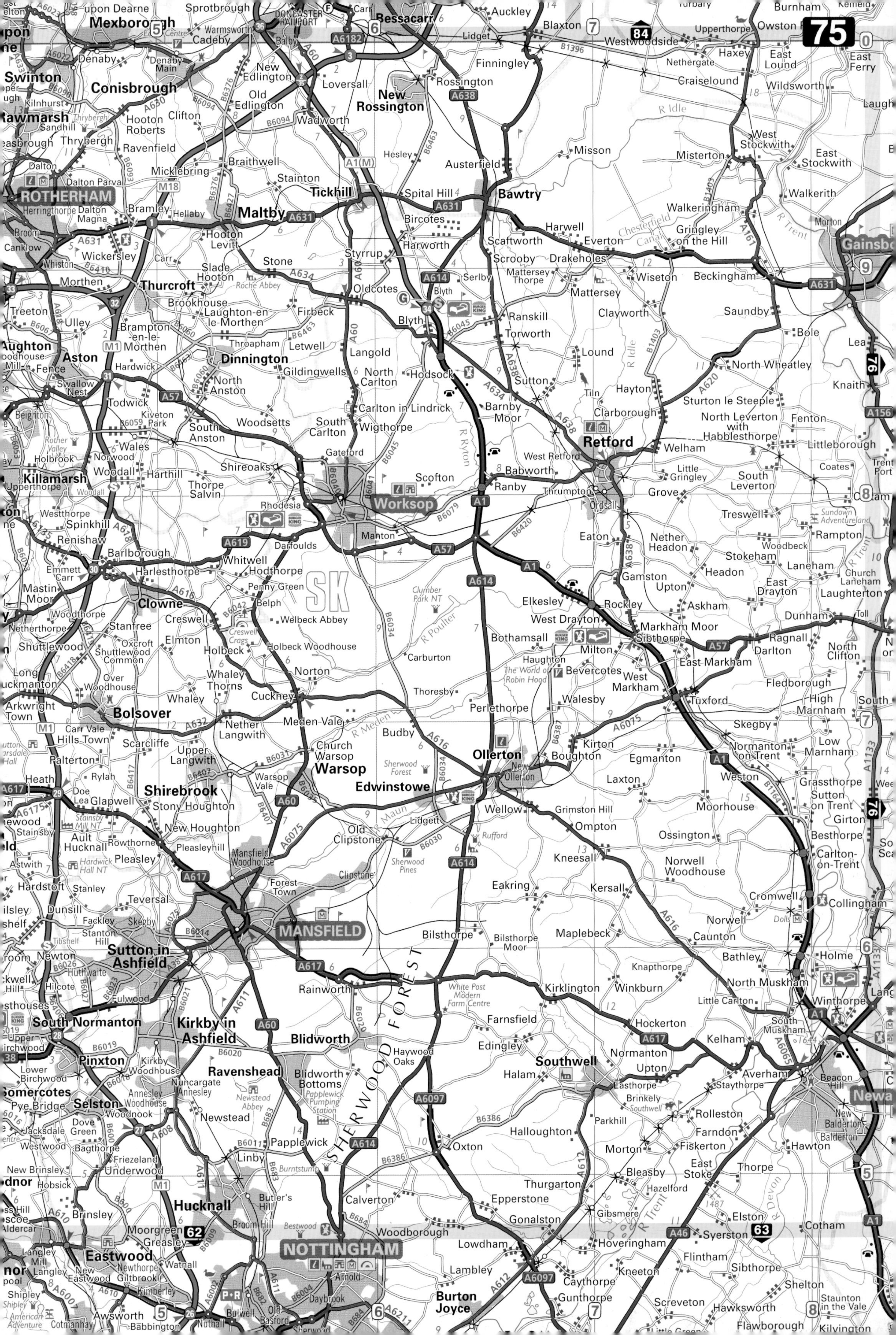

Mexborough
Sprotbrough
DONCASTER RAILPORT
Bessacarr
Auckley
Blaxton
Burnham
Cadeby
Warmsworth
Lidget
Westwoodside
Upperthorpe
Owston Ferry
Denaby
Denaby Main
New Edlington
Old Edlington
Loversall
Finningley
Haxey
Nethergate
East Lound
East Ferry
Swinton
Conisbrough
Rossington
New Rossington
Graiseleund
Wildsworth
Laughton
Kilnhurst
Rawmarsh
Sandhill
Thrybergh
Hooton Roberts
Clifton
Wadworth
R Idle
Parkgate
Ravenfield
Hesley
Misson
West Stockwith
Misterton
East Stockwith
Dalton
Braithwell
Austerfield
Micklebring
Stainton
Dalton Parva
ROTHERHAM
Herringthorpe
Dalton Magna
Bramley
Hellaby
Maltby
Tickhill
Spital Hill
Bawtry
Walkerith
Walkeringham
Gringley on the Hill
Morton
Gainsborough
Broom
Canklow
Wickersley
Hooton Levitt
Bircotes
Harworth
Harwell
Everton
Chesterfield Canal
Scaftworth
Scrooby
Drakeholes
Mattersey Thorpe
Mattersey
Wiseton
Beckingham
Whiston
Morthen
Thurcroft
Slade Hooton
Stone
Styrrup
Oldcotes
Roche Abbey
Serlby
Blyth
Treeton
Ulley
Brookhouse
Laughton-en-le-Morthen
Firbeck
Clayworth
Saundby
Bole
Brampton-en-le-Morthen
Letwell
Langold
Ranskill
Torworth
Lound
Aughton
Aston
Fence
Throapham
Dinnington
Gildingwells
North Carlton
Hodsock
Sutton
North Wheatley
Lea
Knaith
Swallow Nest
Hardwick
North Anston
Todwick
Kiveton Park
South Anston
Carlton in Lindrick
Barnby Moor
Hayton
Tiln
Clarborough
Sturton le Steeple
North Leverton with Habblesthorpe
Fenton
Beighton
Woodsetts
South Carlton
Wigthorpe
R Ryton
Retford
Welham
Littleborough
Wales
Rother Valley
Holbrook
Norwood
Gateford
Shireoaks
Babworth
West Retford
Little Gringley
South Leverton
Coates
Trent Port
Killamarsh
Woodall
Harthill
Thorpe Salvin
Scofton
Ranby
Thrumpton
Grove
Upperthorpe
Rhodesia
Worksop
Ordsall
Treswell
Sundown Adventureland
Westthorpe
Spinkhill
Manton
Eaton
Nether Headon
Woodbeck
Rampton
Renishaw
Darfoulds
Stokeham
Laneham
Church Laneham
Barlborough
Whitwell
Emmett Carr
Hodthorpe
Headon
Gamston
Upton
East Drayton
Laughterton
Mastin Moor
Harlesthorpe
Penny Green
Clumber Park NT
Elkesley
Rockley
Clowne
Belph
West Drayton
Askham
Dunham
Woodthorpe
Welbeck Abbey
Markham Moor
Sibthorpe
Ragnall
Netherthorpe
Stanfree
Creswell
Creswell Crags
R Poulter
Bothamsall
Milton
Darlton
North Clifton
Shuttlewood
Oxcroft
Elmton
Holbeck
Holbeck Woodhouse
Carburton
Shuttlewood Common
Haughton
The World of Robin Hood
Bevercotes
East Markham
West Markham
Long Duckmanton
Over Woodhouse
Norton
Whaley Thorns
Whaley
Thoresby
Cuckney
Walesby
Tuxford
Fledborough
High Marnham
South
Arkwright Town
Bolsover
Perlethorpe
Carr Vale
Hills Town
Nether Langwith
Meden Vale
R Meden
Budby
Skegby
Low Marnham
Scarcliffe
Upper Langwith
Church Warsop
Warsop
Kirton
Egmanton
Normanton on Trent
Palterton
Sherwood Forest
Ollerton
Boughton
New Ollerton
Laxton
Weston
Heath
Rylah
Shirebrook
Warsop Vale
Edwinstowe
Grassthorpe
Sutton on Trent
Doe Lea
Glapwell
Stony Houghton
Wellow
Grimston Hill
Moorhouse
Girton
Stainsby Mill NT
New Houghton
Old Clipstone
R Maun
Lidgett
Ompton
Besthorpe
Ault Hucknall
Rowthorne
Pleasleyhill
Rufford
Ossington
Astwith
Hardwick Hall NT
Pleasley
Mansfield Woodhouse
Sherwood Pines
Kneesall
Carlton-on-Trent
Norwell Woodhouse
Hardstoft
Stanley
Forest Town
Clipstone
Eakring
Kersall
Teversal
Cromwell
Collingham
Tibshelf
Dunsill
Fackley
Skegby
MANSFIELD
Norwell
Stanton Hill
Bilsthorpe
Bilsthorpe Moor
Maplebeck
Caunton
Dolls
Newton
Sutton in Ashfield
Bathley
Holme
Huthwaite
Rainworth
FOREST
White Post Modern Farm Centre
Knapthorpe
Kirklington
Winkburn
North Muskham
Blackwell
Hilcote
Fulwood
Little Carlton
Winthorpe
South Normanton
Kirkby in Ashfield
Blidworth
Farnsfield
Hockerton
South Muskham
Kelham
Lower Birchwood
Pinxton
Kirkby Woodhouse
Haywood Oaks
Edingley
Normanton
Southwell
Upton
Averham
Staythorpe
Beacon Hill
Somercotes
Pye Bridge
Selston
Ravenshead
Nuncargate
Annesley
Annesley Woodhouse
Blidworth Bottoms
Papplewick Pumping Station
Newstead Abbey
Halam
Easthorpe
Brinkely
Newark
Woodnook
Newstead
Rolleston
New Balderton
Balderton
Jacksdale
Dove Green
Westwood
Bagthorpe
Papplewick
SHERWOOD
Oxton
Halloughton
Parkhill
Farndon
Fiskerton
Morton
Hawton
Friezeland
Underwood
Linby
Burntstump
East Stoke
Thorpe
New Brinsley
Hobsick
Bleasby
Hazelford
Brinsley
Hucknall
Butler's Hill
Calverton
Thurgarton
Epperstone
Gibsmere
R Trent
R Devon
Elston
Broom Hill
Bestwood
Gonalston
Moorgreen
Greasley
Woodborough
Syerston
Cotham
Langley Mill
Eastwood
Newthorpe
NOTTINGHAM
Lowdham
Hoveringham
Flintham
Watnall
Giltbrook
Arnold
Lambley
Kneeton
Sibthorpe
Langley
New Eastwood
Kimberley
Caythorpe
Shelton
Shipley
Daybrook
Burton Joyce
Gunthorpe
Screveton
Hawksworth
Staunton in the Vale
American Adventure
Cotmanhay
Awsworth
Babbington
Nuthall
Bulwell
Old Basford
Flawborough
Kilvington
Sherwood

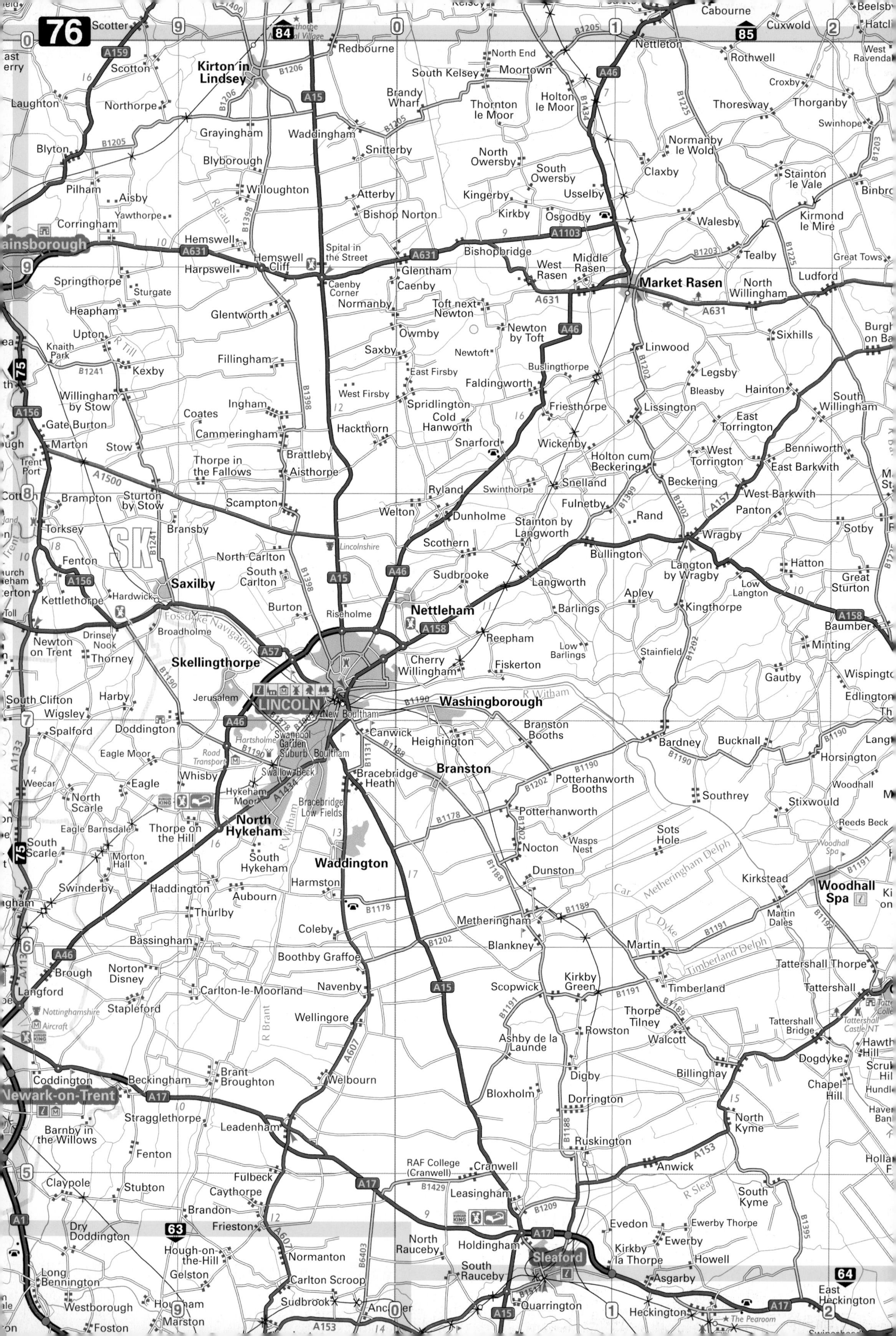
84
85
Scotter
Redbourne
Cabourne
Cuxwold
Nettleton
Rothwell
Kirton in Lindsey
Scotton
South Kelsey
North End
Moortown
Brandy Wharf
Thornton le Moor
Holton le Moor
Croxby
Thoresway
Thorganby
Swinhope
Laughton
Northorpe
Grayingham
Waddingham
Snitterby
North Owersby
Normanby le Wold
Claxby
Blyton
Blyborough
South Owersby
Stainton le Vale
Pilham
Aisby
Willoughton
Atterby
Kingerby
Usselby
Kirkby
Osgodby
Bishop Norton
Walesby
Kirmond le Mire
Yawthorpe
Corringham
Gainsborough
Hemswell
Harpswell
Hemswell Cliff
Spital in the Street
Glentham
Bishopbridge
West Rasen
Middle Rasen
Tealby
Great Tows
Market Rasen
North Willingham
Ludford
Springthorpe
Sturgate
Caenby Corner
Caenby
Normanby
Toft next Newton
Heapham
Glentworth
Upton
Owmby
Newton by Toft
Linwood
Sixhills
Knaith Park
Saxby
Newtoft
Kexby
Fillingham
East Firsby
Buslingthorpe
Legsby
Faldingworth
Bleasby
Hainton
West Firsby
Spridlington
Friesthorpe
Lissington
South Willingham
Willingham by Stow
Ingham
Coates
Cold Hanworth
East Torrington
Gate Burton
Cammeringham
Hackthorn
Snarford
Wickenby
West Torrington
Benniworth
Marton
Stow
Brattleby
Holton cum Beckering
East Barkwith
Trent Port
Thorpe in the Fallows
Aisthorpe
Snelland
Beckering
Ryland
Swinthorpe
West Barkwith
Brampton
Sturton by Stow
Scampton
Welton
Dunholme
Fulnetby
Panton
Rand
Torksey
Bransby
Stainton by Langworth
Wragby
Sotby
Scothern
Lincolnshire
Bullington
Fenton
North Carlton
South Carlton
Langton by Wragby
Hatton
Saxilby
Sudbrooke
Langworth
Great Sturton
Low Langton
Apley
Kettlethorpe
Hardwick
Burton
Riseholme
Nettleham
Barlings
Kingthorpe
Baumber
Fossdyke Navigation
Broadholme
Reepham
Minting
Newton on Trent
Drinsey Nook
Low Barlings
Stainfield
Thorney
Skellingthorpe
Cherry Willingham
Fiskerton
Gautby
Wispington
Harby
Jerusalem
LINCOLN
Washingborough
R Witham
Edlington
South Clifton
Wigsley
New Boultham
Spalford
Doddington
Canwick
Branston Booths
Bardney
Bucknall
Hartsholme
Swanpool Garden Suburb
Boultham
Heighington
Eagle Moor
Road Transport
Horsington
Weecar
Whisby
Swallow Beck
Bracebridge Heath
Branston
Potterhanworth Booths
Southrey
Woodhall
North Scarle
Eagle
Hykeham Moor
Bracebridge Low Fields
Potterhanworth
Stixwould
Eagle Barnsdale
Thorpe on the Hill
North Hykeham
Sots Hole
Reeds Beck
South Scarle
Morton Hall
South Hykeham
Nocton
Wasps Nest
Woodhall Spa
Waddington
Dunston
Metheringham Delph
Kirkstead
Swinderby
Haddington
Harmston
Aubourn
Car Dyke
Martin Dales
Thurlby
Metheringham
Coleby
Bassingham
Blankney
Martin
Timberland Delph
Tattershall Thorpe
Brough
Norton Disney
Boothby Graffoe
Kirkby Green
Tattershall
Langford
Carlton-le-Moorland
Navenby
Scopwick
Timberland
Nottinghamshire
Stapleford
Thorpe Tilney
Tattershall Bridge
Tattershall Castle NT
Aircraft
Wellingore
R Brant
Rowston
Walcott
Ashby de la Launde
Dogdyke
Digby
Billinghay
Coddington
Beckingham
Brant Broughton
Welbourn
Chapel Hill
Newark-on-Trent
Bloxholm
Dorrington
Stragglethorpe
Leadenham
North Kyme
Barnby in the Willows
Fenton
Ruskington
RAF College (Cranwell)
Cranwell
Anwick
Claypole
Stubton
Fulbeck
Caythorpe
Leasingham
R Slea
South Kyme
Brandon
Evedon
Ewerby Thorpe
63
64
Dry Doddington
Frieston
North Rauceby
Holdingham
Ewerby
Hough-on-the-Hill
Normanton
Kirkby la Thorpe
Howell
Sleaford
South Rauceby
Asgarby
Long Bennington
Gelston
Carlton Scroop
East Heckington
Westborough
Hougham
Sudbrook
Ancaster
Quarrington
Heckington
The Pearoom
Marston
Foston
A159
A15
A631
A1103
A46
A156
A1500
A57
A158
A157
A1434
A17
A607
A153
A1
A1133
B1205
B1206
B1398
B1434
B1225
B1203
B1241
B1202
B1399
B1190
B1178
B1131
B1188
B1189
B1191
B1192
B1429
B1209
B1188
B6403
B1395
SK

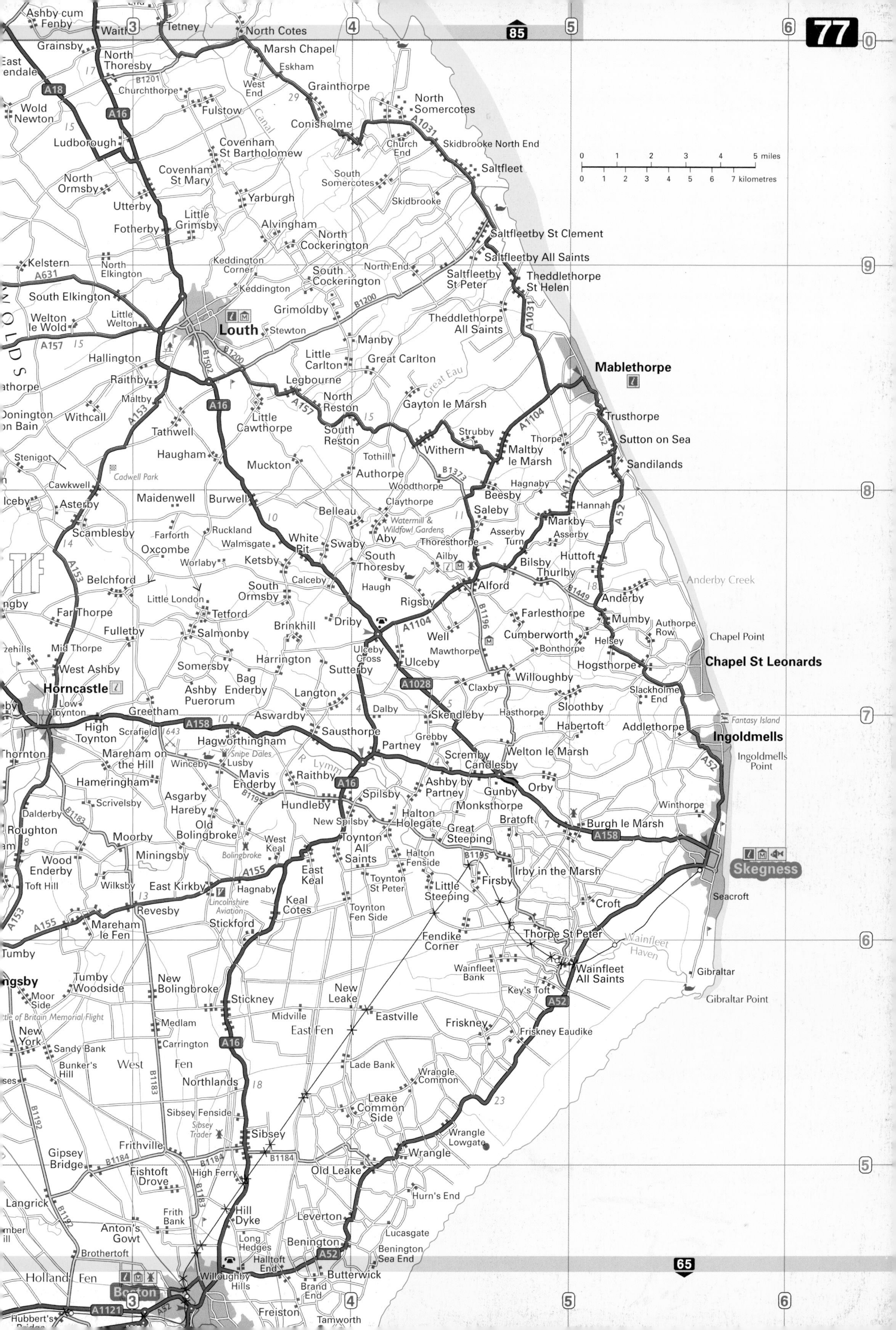
Ashby cum Fenby
Waith
Tetney
North Cotes
85
Grainsby
Marsh Chapel
North Thoresby
Eskham
B1201
West End
Grainthorpe
A18
Churchthorpe
Fulstow
29
North Somercotes
A16
Canal
Wold Newton
Conisholme
A1031
Ludborough
Covenham St Bartholomew
Church End
Skidbrooke North End
Saltfleet
Covenham St Mary
South Somercotes
North Ormsby
Yarburgh
Skidbrooke
Utterby
Little Grimsby
Alvingham
Fotherby
North Cockerington
Saltfleetby St Clement
Kelstern
North Elkington
Keddington Corner
Saltfleetby All Saints
A631
South Cockerington
North End
Saltfleetby St Peter
Theddlethorpe St Helen
South Elkington
Keddington
Grimoldby
B1200
Welton le Wold
Little Welton
Louth
Stewton
Theddlethorpe All Saints
A157
Manby
Hallington
B1502
B1200
Little Carlton
Great Carlton
Mablethorpe
Raithby
Legbourne
Great Eau
Maltby
North Reston
Gayton le Marsh
Donington on Bain
Withcall
A153
A16
Little Cawthorpe
A157
South Reston
Trusthorpe
A1104
Tathwell
Strubby
Thorpe
Sutton on Sea
A52
Stenigot
Haugham
Withern
Maltby le Marsh
Sandilands
Muckton
Tothill
Cadwell Park
Authorpe
B1373
Hagnaby
Cawkwell
Woodthorpe
Beesby
A1111
Maidenwell
Burwell
Hannah
Asterby
Claythorpe
Saleby
Belleau
Markby
Scamblesby
Farforth
Ruckland
Watermill & Wildfowl Gardens
Asserby Turn
Asserby
Walmsgate
White Pit
Swaby
Aby
Thoresthorpe
Oxcombe
South Thoresby
Ailby
Huttoft
Worlaby
Ketsby
Bilsby
Thurlby
Anderby Creek
Belchford
Calceby
Alford
South Ormsby
Haugh
B1449
Anderby
Little London
Rigsby
Far Thorpe
Tetford
B1196
Farlesthorpe
Mumby
Authorpe Row
Driby
A1104
Fulletby
Salmonby
Brinkhill
Well
Cumberworth
Helsey
Chapel Point
Mid Thorpe
Ulceby Cross
Mawthorpe
Bonthorpe
Chapel St Leonards
Harrington
Hogsthorpe
West Ashby
Somersby
Ulceby
Sutterby
Willoughby
Horncastle
Bag Enderby
A1028
Claxby
Slackholme End
Ashby Puerorum
Langton
Low Toynton
Greetham
Aswardby
Dalby
Skendleby
Hasthorpe
Sloothby
Fantasy Island
High Toynton
A158
Sausthorpe
Habertoft
Addlethorpe
Ingoldmells
Scrafield
Grebby
Hagworthingham
Partney
Scremby
Welton le Marsh
Thornton
Mareham on the Hill
Snipe Dales
Candlesby
Ingoldmells Point
Winceby
Lusby
R Lymn
A52
Hameringham
Mavis Enderby
Raithby
Ashby by Partney
Orby
A16
Gunby
Scrivelsby
Asgarby
B1195
Spilsby
Hundleby
Monksthorpe
Winthorpe
Dalderby
Hareby
B1183
Halton Holegate
Bratoft
Burgh le Marsh
Roughton
Old Bolingbroke
New Spilsby
Great Steeping
A158
Moorby
West Keal
Toynton All Saints
Wood Enderby
Miningsby
Bolingbroke
B1195
Halton Fenside
Skegness
East Keal
Irby in the Marsh
Toft Hill
A155
Toynton St Peter
Little Steeping
Firsby
Wilksby
East Kirkby
Hagnaby
Keal Cotes
Croft
Seacroft
Lincolnshire Aviation
Revesby
Toynton Fen Side
A153
A155
Mareham le Fen
Stickford
Fendike Corner
Thorpe St Peter
Wainfleet Haven
Tumby
Wainfleet Bank
Wainfleet All Saints
Gibraltar
Tumby Woodside
New Bolingbroke
New Leake
Key's Toft
Moor Side
Stickney
A52
Gibraltar Point
Midville
Eastville
Friskney
Medlam
East Fen
Friskney Eaudike
New York
Carrington
A16
Sandy Bank
Lade Bank
Bunker's Hill
West
Fen
Wrangle Common
B1183
Northlands
Leake Common Side
23
B1192
Sibsey Fenside
Sibsey Trader
Sibsey
Wrangle Lowgate
Frithville
Gipsey Bridge
B1184
B1184
B1184
Wrangle
Fishtoft Drove
High Ferry
Old Leake
B1183
Hurn's End
Langrick
Frith Bank
Hill Dyke
B1192
Anton's Gowt
Leverton
Lucasgate
Long Hedges
Benington
Brothertoft
Benington Sea End
Halltoft End
A52
65
Holland Fen
Butterwick
Boston
Brand End
A1121
Hubbert's Bridge
A52
Freiston
Tamworth
0 1 2 3 4 5 miles
0 1 2 3 4 5 6 7 kilometres
3
4
5
6
0
9
8
7
6
5
TF

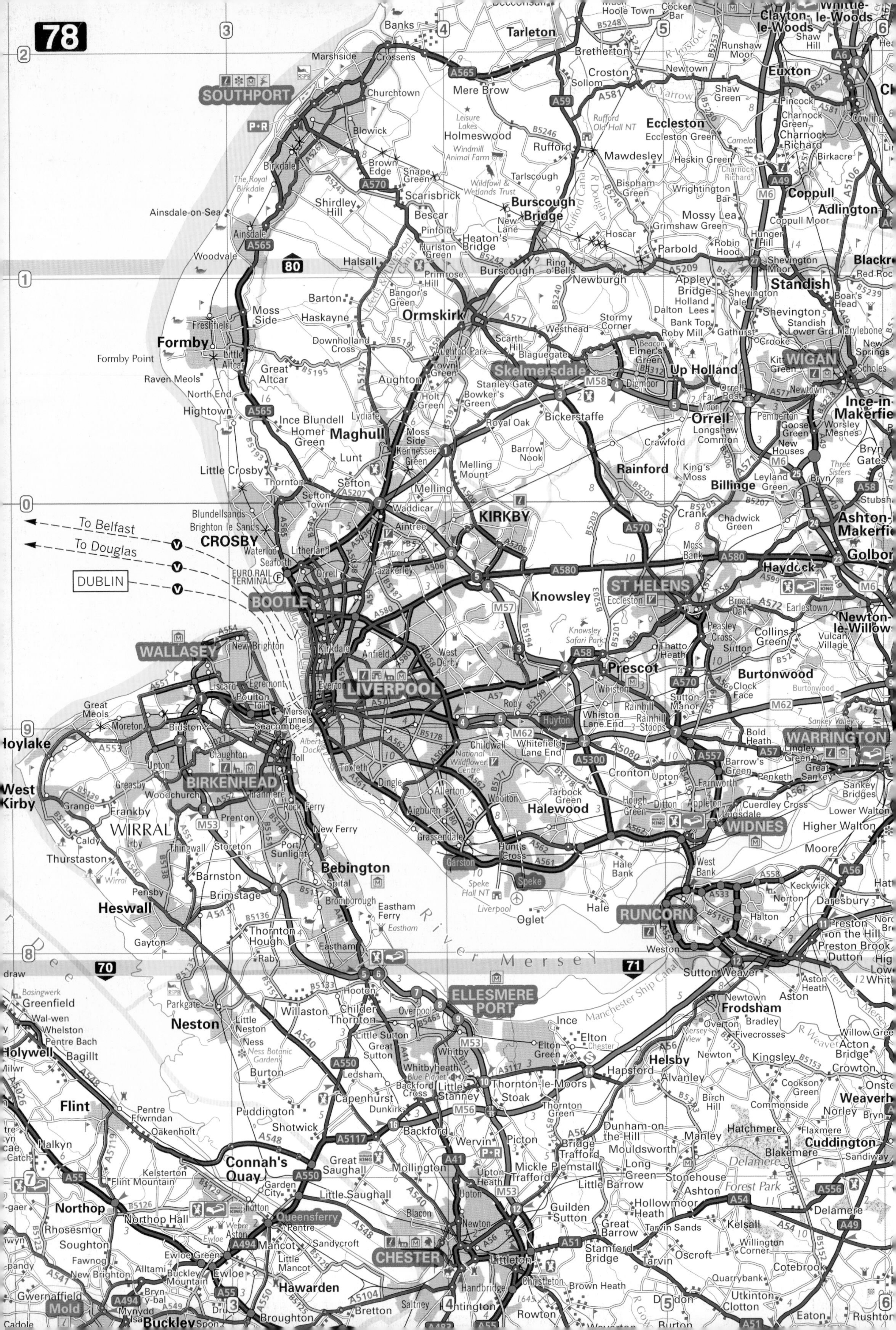

SOUTHPORT
Banks
Marshside
Crossens
Churchtown
Tarleton
Hoole Town
Bretherton
Croston
Sollom
Mere Brow
Holmeswood
Leisure Lakes
Windmill Animal Farm
Rufford
Rufford Old Hall NT
Eccleston
Eccleston Green
Mawdesley
Heskin Green
Clayton-le-Woods
Whittle-le-Woods
Shaw Hill
Runshaw Moor
Newtown
Euxton
Shaw Green
Pincock
Charnock Green
Charnock Richard
Birkacre
Cowling
Coppull
Adlington
Coppull Moor
Blowick
Birkdale
The Royal Birkdale
Brown Edge
Snape Green
Scarisbrick
Wildfowl & Wetlands Trust
Tarlscough
Burscough Bridge
New Lane
Bispham Green
Wrightington Bar
Mossy Lea
Grimshaw Green
Shirdley Hill
Bescar
Pinfold
Ainsdale-on-Sea
Ainsdale
Woodvale
Heaton's Bridge
Hurlston Green
Halsall
Burscough
Ring o'Bells
Hoscar
Parbold
Robin Hood
Hunger Hill
Shevington Moor
Standish
Blackrod
Red Rock
Primrose Hill
Newburgh
Appley Bridge
Shevington Vale
Holland Lees
Dalton
Bank Top
Roby Mill
Gathurst
Shevington
Standish Lower Ground
Boar's Head
Marylebone
Barton
Bangor's Green
Haskayne
Ormskirk
Westhead
Stormy Corner
Moss Side
Freshfield
Formby
Formby Point
Little Altcar
Downholland Cross
Aughton Park
Scarth Hill
Blaguegate
Skelmersdale
Beacon
Elmer's Green
Up Holland
Digmoor
Crooke
Kitt Green
WIGAN
New Springs
Scholes
Raven Meols
Great Altcar
Aughton
Town Green
Stanley Gate
Bowker's Green
Orrell Post
Far Moor
Newtown
Ince-in-Makerfield
North End
Hightown
Holt Green
Bickerstaffe
Orrell
Pemberton
Goose Green
Worsley Mesnes
Ince Blundell
Homer Green
Maghull
Lydiate
Moss Side
Royal Oak
Barrow Nook
Crawford
Longshaw Common
New Houses
Bryn Gates
Kennessee Green
Lunt
Little Crosby
Melling Mount
Rainford
King's Moss
Billinge
Leyland Green
Three Sisters
Bryn
Thornton
Sefton
Sefton Town
Melling
Waddicar
Stubshaw
Blundellsands
Brighton le Sands
CROSBY
KIRKBY
Crank
Chadwick Green
Ashton-in-Makerfield
To Belfast
To Douglas
DUBLIN
Waterloo
Seaforth
EURO RAIL TERMINAL
Litherland
Orrell
Aintree
Fazakerley
Moss Bank
Golborne
Haydock
Knowsley
ST HELENS
Eccleston
Broad Oak
Earlestown
Newton-le-Willows
BOOTLE
Knowsley Safari Park
Peasley Cross
Sutton
Collins Green
Vulcan Village
WALLASEY
New Brighton
Kirkdale
Anfield
West Derby
Thatto Heath
Prescot
Burtonwood
Liscard
Egremont
Everton
LIVERPOOL
Whiston
Clock Face
Poulton
Mersey Tunnels
Roby
Huyton
Rainhill
Sutton Manor
Great Meols
Moreton
Bidston
Seacombe
Whiston Lane End
Rainhill Stoops
Sankey Valley
Hoylake
Albert Dock
Childwall
Whitefield Lane End
Bold Heath
WARRINGTON
Claughton
Toll
Toxteth
National Wildflower Centre
Barrow's Green
Lingley Green
Upton
Dingle
Cronton
Penketh
Great Sankey
West Kirby
Greasby
BIRKENHEAD
Tranmere
Allerton
Woolton
Tarbock Green
Farnworth
Grange
Frankby
Woodchurch
Rock Ferry
Hough Green
Ditton
Appleton
Cuerdley Cross
Sankey Bridges
Prenton
Halewood
Lugsdale
WIDNES
Lower Walton
Higher Walton
WIRRAL
Irby
Caldy
Thingwall
Storeton
Aigburth
New Ferry
Port Sunlight
Thurstaston
Grassendale
Garston
Hunts Cross
Hale Bank
Moore
Barnston
Bebington
Speke
West Bank
Keckwick
Daresbury
Heswall
Pensby
Brimstage
Spital
Bromborough
Eastham Ferry
Eastham
River Mersey
Speke Hall NT
Liverpool
Oglet
Hale
RUNCORN
Norton
Halton
Preston on the Hill
Preston Brook
Dutton
Gayton
Thornton Hough
Raby
Weston
Sutton Weaver
Aston Heath
Aston
Dee
Basingwerk
Greenfield
Wal-wen
Whelston
Pentre Bach
Holywell
Bagillt
Parkgate
Neston
Little Neston
Ness
Ness Botanic Gardens
Burton
Willaston
Hooton
Childer Thornton
Overpool
ELLESMERE PORT
Little Sutton
Great Sutton
Whitby
Ince
Elton
Elton Green
Manchester Ship Canal
Newtown
Frodsham
Overton
Mersey View
Bradley
Fivecrosses
Willow Green
Acton Bridge
Crowton
Whitbyheath
Blue Planet
Ledsham
Capenhurst
Backford Cross
Little Stanney
Thornton-le-Moors
Stoak
Hapsford
Helsby
Alvanley
Newton
Kingsley
Cookson Green
Onston
Weaverham
Flint
Pentre Ffwrndan
Oakenholt
Puddington
Dunkirk
Shotwick
Backford
Wervin
Picton
Thornton Green
Dunham-on-the-Hill
Birch Hill
Commonside
Norley
Bryn
Hatchmere
Flaxmere
Cuddington
Halkyn
Kelsterton
Flint Mountain
Connah's Quay
Great Saughall
Mollington
Bridge Trafford
Mickle Trafford
Plemstall
Mouldsworth
Manley
Blakemere
Delamere
Sandiway
Long Green
Stonehouse
Ashton
Forest Park
Northop
Northop Hall
Shotton
Garden City
Queensferry
Little Saughall
Upton Heath
Upton
Little Barrow
Hollowmoor Heath
Kelsall
Rhosesmor
Soughton
Fawnog
Wepre
Ewloe
Aston
Pentre
Mancot
Sandycroft
Blacon
Guilden Sutton
Great Barrow
Tarvin Sands
Newton
Willington Corner
CHESTER
Little Mancot
Littleton
Stamford Bridge
Tarvin
Oscroft
Cotebrook
Alltami
New Brighton
Ewloe Green
Buckley Mountain
Hawarden
Quarrybank
Gwernaffield
Bryn-y-bal
Mold
Mynydd Isa
Buckley
Bretton
Saltney
Handbridge
Christleton
Brown Heath
Utkinton
Clotton
Broughton
Rowton
Duddon
Burton
Eaton
Rushton

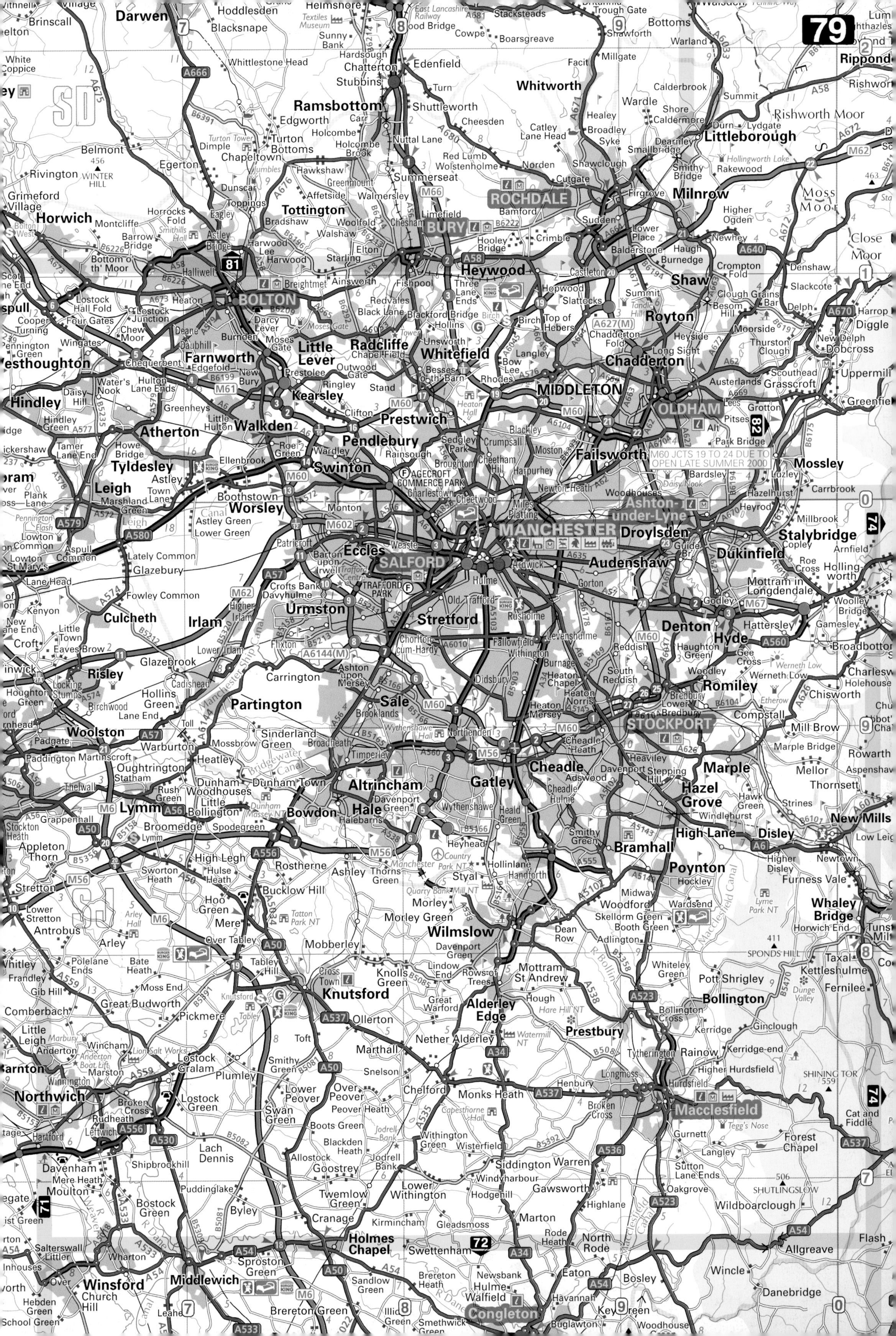

79
Darwen
Hoddlesden
Blacksnape
Helmshore
Textiles Museum
Sunny Bank
East Lancashire Railway
Stacksteads
Trough Gate
Bottoms
Brinscall
White Coppice
Whittlestone Head
Hardsough
Chatterton
Stubbins
Edenfield
Cowpe
Boarsgreave
Shawforth
Warland
Millgate
Facit
Rippond
Rishworth
Whitworth
Calderbrook
Summit
Wardle
Shore
Caldermore
Rishworth Moor
Turn
Ramsbottom
Shuttleworth
Edgworth
Carr
Holcombe
Cheesden
Catley Lane Head
Healey
Broadley
Syke
Durn
Lydgate
Littleborough
Dearnley
Smallbridge
Belmont
456 WINTER HILL
Rivington
Turton Tower
Dimple
Turton Bottoms
Chapeltown
Holcombe Brook
Nuttal Lane
Red Lumb
Wolstenholme
Norden
Shawclough
Hollingworth Lake
Smithy Bridge
Rakewood
Egerton
Hawkshaw
Greenmount
Summerseat
Grimeford Village
Dunscar
Toppings
Affetside
Walmersley
ROCHDALE
Cutgate
Firgrove
Milnrow
Moss Moor
Horwich
Montcliffe
Horrocks Fold
Eagley
Tottington
Bradshaw
Woolfold
Limefield
Bamford
Sudden
Higher Ogden
Close Moor
Smithills Hall
Barrow Bridge
Astley Bridge
Harwood Lee
Walshaw
BURY
Hooley Bridge
Crimble
Lower Place
Balderstone
Newhey
Haugh
Burnedge
Denshaw
Bottom o' th' Moor
Halliwell
Harwood
Starling
Elton
Heywood
Castleton
Crompton Fold
Shaw
Slackcote
Ainsworth
Breightmet
Fishpool
Three Lane Ends
Hopwood
Slattocks
Summit
Clough
Grains Bar
Delph
Harrop
Diggle
Lostock Hall Fold
Heaton
BOLTON
Redvales
Black Lane
Blackford Bridge
Birch
Top of Hebers
Royton
Besom Hill
Heyside
Moorside
New Delph
Dobcross
Cooper Turning
Four Gates
Lostock Junction
Chew Moor
Darcy Lever
Moses Gate
Hollins
Unsworth
Chadderton Fold
Long Sight
Thurston Clough
Pennington Green
Wingates
Deane
Daubhill
Burnden
Little Lever
Radcliffe
Chapel Field
Whitefield
Langley
Chadderton
Scouthead
Grasscroft
Uppermill
Westhoughton
Chequerbent
Farnworth
Edgefold
Prestolee
Outwood Gate
Bow Lee
Rhodes
Besses o' th' Barn
MIDDLETON
Austerlands
Lees
Greenfield
Hindley
Daisy Hill
Water's Nook
Hulton Lane Ends
New Bury
Ringley
Stand
Kearsley
Heaton Hall
OLDHAM
Grotton
Pitses
Alt
Hindley Green
Greenheys
Little Hulton
Walkden
Clifton
Prestwich
Blackley
Failsworth
Park Bridge
Atherton
Tamer Lane End
Howe Bridge
Roe Green
Wardley
Pendlebury
Rainsough
Sedgley Park
Crumpsall
Moston
M60 JCTS 19 TO 24 DUE TO OPEN LATE SUMMER 2000
Bardsley
Daisy Nook
Mossley
Luzley
Tyldesley
Astley
Ellenbrook
Swinton
Agecroft Commerce Park
Broughton
Cheetham Hill
Harpurhey
Newton Heath
Woodhouses
Hazelhurst
Carrbrook
Leigh
Town Lane
Charlestown
Cheetwood
Miles Platting
Ashton-under-Lyne
Heyrod
Plank Lane
Marshland Green
Boothstown
Worsley
Monton
Millbrook
Pennington Flash
Astley Green
Lower Green
MANCHESTER
Droylsden
Stalybridge
Lowton
Lowton Common
Patricroft
Weaste
Eccles
Guide Bridge
Copley
Arnfield
Lowton St Mary's
Aspull Common
Lately Common
Glazebury
Barton upon Irwell
SALFORD
Trafford Centre
Ardwick
Audenshaw
Dukinfield
Roe Cross
Hollingworth
Lane Head
Fowley Common
Crofts Bank
Davyhulme
Trafford Park
Hulme
Gorton
Mottram in Longdendale
Kenyon
Higher Irlam
Old Trafford
Rusholme
Godley
Woolley Bridge
Culcheth
Irlam
Urmston
Stretford
Denton
Hattersley
Gamesley
New Lane End
Little Town
Croft
Eaves Brow
Flixton
Chorlton-cum-Hardy
Fallowfield
Levenshulme
Hyde
Lower Irlam
Withington
Reddish
Haughton Green
Gee Cross
Broadbottom
Risley
Glazebrook
Ashton upon Mersey
Carrington
Burnage
Heaton Chapel
South Reddish
Werneth Low
Charlesworth
Holehouse
Locking Stumps
Cadishead
Didsbury
Heaton Norris
Woodley
Romiley
Houghton Green
Hollins Green
Birchwood
Lane End
Partington
Sale
Brooklands
Heaton Mersey
Bredbury
Lower Bredbury
Etherow
Chisworth
Compstall
Woolston
Padgate
Toll
Warburton
Sinderland Green
Broadheath
Wythenshawe Hall
Northenden
STOCKPORT
Cheadle Heath
Mill Brow
Paddington
Martinscroft
Oughtrington
Statham
Mossbrow
Heatley
Bridgewater Canal
Timperley
Heaviley
Marple Bridge
Rowarth
Thelwall
Dunham Woodhouses
Dunham Town
Altrincham
Gatley
Cheadle
Adswood
Davenport
Stepping Hill
Marple
Mellor
Aspenshaw
Thornsett
Rush Green
Lymm
Little Bollington
Dunham Massey NT
Bowdon
Hale
Davenport Green
Wythenshawe
Heald Green
Cheadle Hulme
Hazel Grove
Hawk Green
Strines
Grappenhall
Broomedge
Spodegreen
Halebarns
Windlehurst
New Mills
Stockton Heath
Appleton Thorn
Lymm
Heyhead
Smithy Green
Bramhall
High Lane
Disley
Low Leigh
High Legh
Rostherne
Ashley
Thorns Green
Manchester Airport
Country Park NT
Hollinlane
Handforth
Poynton
Higher Disley
Newtown
Swerton Heath
Hulse Heath
Styal
Hockley
Furness Vale
Stretton
Bucklow Hill
Quarry Bank Mill NT
Midway
Lyme Park NT
Lower Stretton
Antrobus
Hoo Green
Mere
Tatton Park NT
Morley
Morley Green
Woodford
Wardsend
Skellorm Green
Booth Green
Whaley Bridge
Horwich End
Arley Hall
Arley
Over Tabley
Wilmslow
Dean Row
Adlington
Mobberley
Davenport Green
411
SPONDS HILL
Taxal
Whitley
Polelane Ends
Bate Heath
Tabley Hill
Cross Town
Knolls Green
Lindow End
Rows of Trees
Mottram St Andrew
Whiteley Green
Pott Shrigley
Kettleshulme
Fernilee
Frandley
Gib Hill
Moss End
Knutsford
Great Warford
Alderley Edge
Hough
Hare Hill NT
Bollington
Dunge Valley
Comberbach
Great Budworth
Pickmere
Tabley
Ollerton
Bollington Cross
Kerridge
Gincluogh
Little Leigh
Marbury
Wincham
Lion Salt Works
Lostock Gralam
Anderton
Anderton Boat Lift
Marston
Toft
Nether Alderley
Watermill NT
Prestbury
Tytherington
Rainow
Kerridge-end
Marthall
Barnton
Winnington
Smithy Green
Snelson
Higher Hurdsfield
Shining Tor 559
Plumley
Lostock Green
Northwich
Lower Peover
Over Peover
Chelford
Monks Heath
Henbury
Longmoss
Hurdsfield
Broken Cross
Macclesfield
Cat and Fiddle
Rudheath
Leftwich
Swan Green
Peover Heath
Capesthorne Hall
Broken Cross
Tegg's Nose
Hartford
Boots Green
Jodrell Bank
Withington Green
Wisterfield
Gurnett
Forest Chapel
Davenham
Lach Dennis
Blackden Heath
Langley
Mere Heath
Shipbrookhill
Allostock
Goostrey
Siddington
Warren
Sutton Lane Ends
Moulton
Windyharbour
Gawsworth
506 SHUTLINGSLOW
Puddinglake
Twemlow Green
Lower Withington
Hodgehill
Oakgrove
Bostock Green
Byley
Cranage
Highlane
Wildboarclough
Kirmincham
Gleadsmoss
Marton
Rode Heath
North Rode
Allgreave
Flash
Salterswall
Littler
Wharton
Holmes Chapel
Swettenham
Sproston Green
Eaton
Newsbank
Winsford
Over
Middlewich
Sandlow Green
Brereton Heath
Hulme Walfield
Bosley
Wincle
Danebridge
Church Hill
Hebden Green
School Green
Leahe
Brereton Green
Congleton
Havannah
Key Green
Buglawton
Woodhouse
Smethwick Green
M60
M62
M61
M66
M602
M56
M6
M67
A6
A56
A34
A50
A54
A57
A58
A537
A523
A556
A533
A530
A559
A580
A579
A666
A627(M)
A6144(M)
A640
A670
A560
A5103

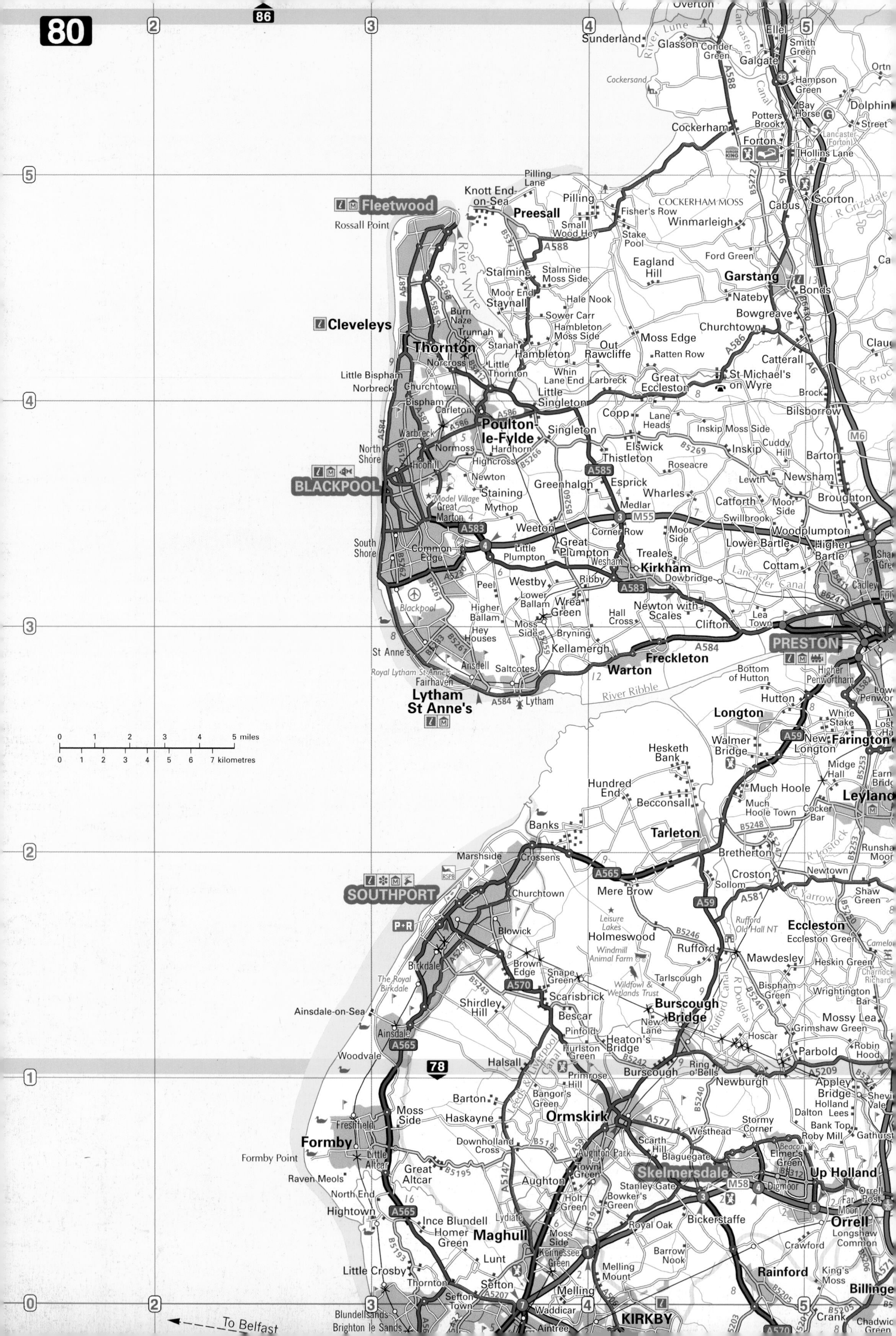
86
78
To Belfast
0 1 2 3 4 5 miles
0 1 2 3 4 5 6 7 kilometres
Overton
Sunderland
Glasson
Conder Green
Galgate
Ellel
Smith Green
Hampson Green
Lancaster Canal
River Lune
Cockersand
Cockerham
Potters Brook
Forton
Bay Horse
Lancaster (Forton)
Hollins Lane
Dolphin
Street
Orton
Pilling Lane
Knott End-on-Sea
Pilling
Preesall
Small Wood Hey
Fisher's Row
COCKERHAM MOSS
Winmarleigh
Stake Pool
Cabus
Scorton
R Grizedale
Fleetwood
Rossall Point
River Wyre
Stalmine
Stalmine Moss Side
Moor End
Staynall
Hale Nook
Eagland Hill
Ford Green
Garstang
Bonds
Nateby
Bowgreave
Churchtown
Cleveleys
Burn Naze
Trunnah
Stanah
Sower Carr
Hambleton Moss Side
Hambleton
Out Rawcliffe
Moss Edge
Ratten Row
Catterall
Thornton
Norcross
Little Thornton
Little Bispham
Norbreck
Churchtown
Bispham
Carleton
Whin Lane End
Larbreck
Great Eccleston
St Michael's on Wyre
Little Singleton
Brock
Bilsborrow
Poulton-le-Fylde
Warbreck
Singleton
Copp
Lane Heads
Inskip Moss Side
Inskip
Cuddy Hill
Barton
North Shore
Normoss
Hardhorn
Elswick
Thistleton
Roseacre
Lewth
Newsham
Highcross
BLACKPOOL
Hoohill
Newton
Staining
Greenhalgh
Esprick
Wharles
Catforth
Moor Side
Broughton
Model Village
Great Marton
Mythop
Medlar
Swillbrook
Woodplumpton
Weeton
Corner Row
Moor Side
Lower Bartle
Higher Bartle
South Shore
Common Edge
Little Plumpton
Great Plumpton
Wesham
Treales
Kirkham
Cottam
Peel
Westby
Ribby
Dowbridge
Lancaster Canal
Cadley
Blackpool
Higher Ballam
Lower Ballam
Wrea Green
Hall Cross
Newton with Scales
Clifton
Lea Town
Hey Houses
Moss Side
Bryning
Kellamergh
PRESTON
St Anne's
Ansdell
Saltcotes
Warton
Freckleton
Royal Lytham St Annes
Fairhaven
Bottom of Hutton
Higher Penwortham
Lytham St Anne's
Lytham
River Ribble
Hutton
Lower Penwortham
Longton
White Stake
Walmer Bridge
New Longton
Farington
Hesketh Bank
Midge Hall
Hundred End
Much Hoole
Becconsall
Much Hoole Town
Cocker Bar
Leyland
Banks
Tarleton
Bretherton
R Lostock
Runshaw Moor
Marshside
Crossens
Croston
Newtown
SOUTHPORT
RSPB
Churchtown
Mere Brow
Sollom
R Yarrow
Shaw Green
P+R
Leisure Lakes
Rufford Old Hall NT
Eccleston
Blowick
Holmeswood
Eccleston Green
Windmill Animal Farm
Rufford
Mawdesley
Brown Edge
Heskin Green
Birkdale
Snape Green
Tarlscough
The Royal Birkdale
Wildfowl & Wetlands Trust
Rufford Canal
R Douglas
Bispham Green
Wrightington Bar
Shirdley Hill
Scarisbrick
Burscough Bridge
Ainsdale-on-Sea
Bescar
New Lane
Mossy Lea
Grimshaw Green
Ainsdale
Pinfold
Heaton's Bridge
Hoscar
Woodvale
Hurlston Green
Parbold
Robin Hood
Halsall
Burscough
Ring o'Bells
Leeds & Liverpool Canal
Primrose Hill
Newburgh
Appley Bridge
Barton
Bangor's Green
Holland Lees
Moss Side
Haskayne
Ormskirk
Dalton
Stormy Corner
Freshfield
Westhead
Bank Top
Roby Mill
Gathurst
Formby
Little Altcar
Downholland Cross
Scarth Hill
Aughton Park
Blaguegate
Beacon
Elmer's Green
Formby Point
Great Altcar
Town Green
Skelmersdale
Up Holland
Raven Meols
Aughton
Stanley Gate
Digmoor
Orrell Post
North End
Holt Green
Bowker's Green
Far Moor
Hightown
Bickerstaffe
Orrell
Ince Blundell
Lydiate
Royal Oak
Homer Green
Maghull
Moss Side
Crawford
Longshaw Common
Lunt
Kennessee Green
Barrow Nook
Melling Mount
Little Crosby
Rainford
King's Moss
Billinge
Thornton
Sefton
Sefton Town
Melling
Waddicar
KIRKBY
Blundellsands
Brighton le Sands
Aintree
Crank
Chadwick Green

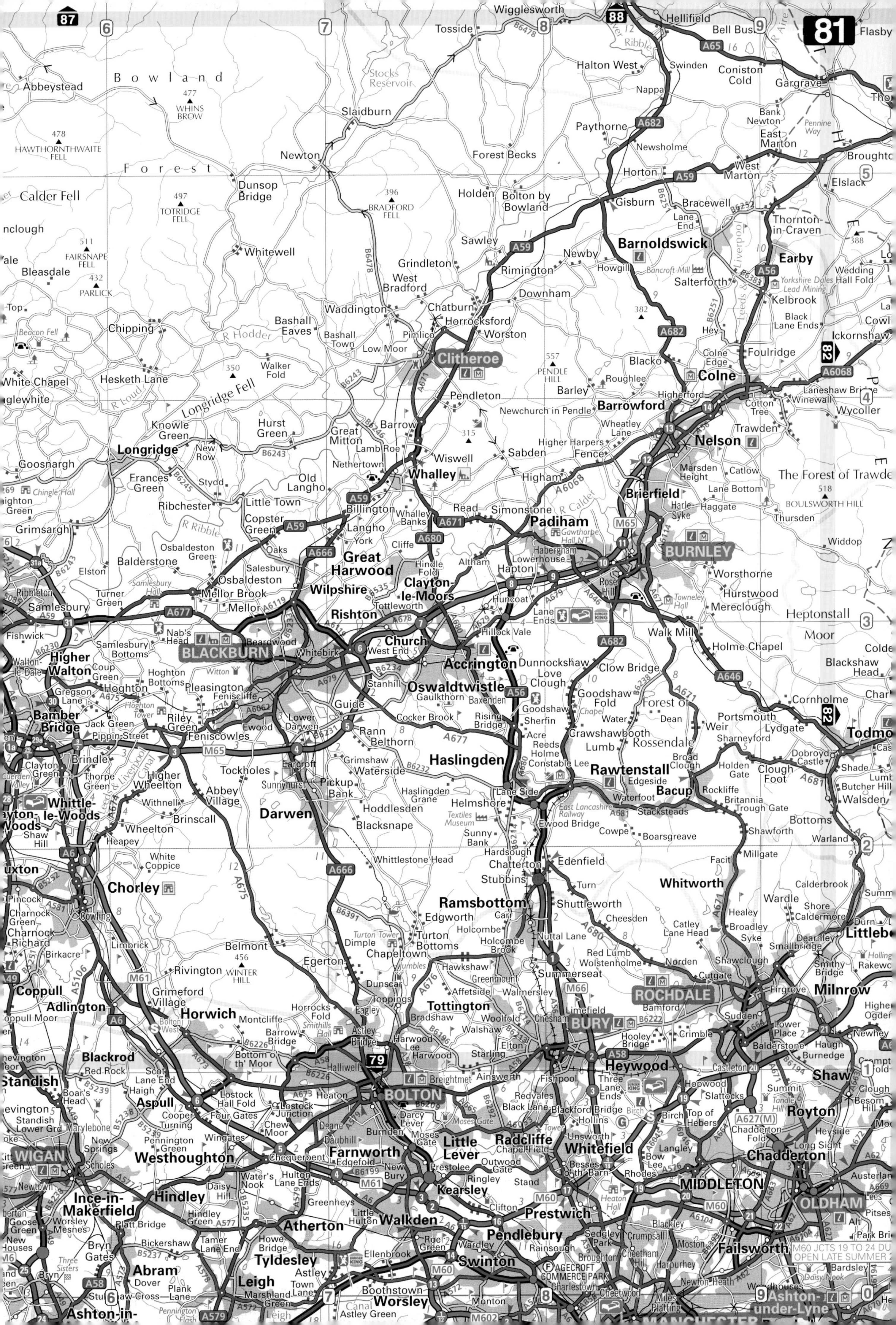

87
6
7
Wigglesworth
Tosside
8
88
Hellifield
Bell Busk
9
81
Flasby
Abbeystead
Bowland
Stocks Reservoir
Halton West
Swinden
Coniston Cold
Gargrave
477
WHINS BROW
Slaidburn
Nappa
Bank Newton
Pennine Way
Paythorne
A682
East Marton
478
HAWTHORNTHWAITE FELL
Newton
Forest Becks
Newsholme
Broughton
Forest
Horton
A59
West Marton
5
Elslack
Calder Fell
Dunsop Bridge
497
TOTRIDGE FELL
396
BRADFORD FELL
Holden
Bolton by Bowland
Gisburn
Bracewell
Lane End
Thornton-in-Craven
Sawley
Barnoldswick
Earby
Whitewell
511
FAIRSNAPE FELL
Grindleton
Rimington
Newby
Howgill
Bancroft Mill
Salterforth
A56
Yorkshire Dales Lead Mining
Wedding Hall Fold
Bleasdale
432
PARLICK
West Bradford
Downham
Kelbrook
Waddington
Chatburn
Horrocksford
382
Black Lane Ends
Cowl
Bashall Eaves
Bashall Town
Worston
Hey
Ickornshaw
Chipping
Beacon Fell
R Hodder
Pimlico
Low Moor
A682
82
Walker Fold
350
Clitheroe
557
PENDLE HILL
Blacko
Colne Edge
Foulridge
A6068
White Chapel
Hesketh Lane
Roughlee
Colne
Longridge Fell
R Loud
Pendleton
Barley
Laneshaw Bridge
Winewall
4
Higherford
Cotton Tree
Wycoller
Newchurch in Pendle
Barrowford
Knowle Green
Hurst Green
Great Mitton
Barrow
315
Wheatley Lane
Trawden
Nelson
Longridge
New Row
Lamb Roe
Wiswell
Sabden
Higher Harpers
Fence
Goosnargh
B6243
Nethertown
Whalley
Marsden Height
Catlow
The Forest of Trawden
Frances Green
Stydd
Old Langho
Higham
Lane Bottom
Chingle Hall
518
BOULSWORTH HILL
Ribchester
Little Town
Billington
Read
Simonstone
Brierfield
Harle Syke
Haggate
Thursden
Copster Green
R Ribble
Whalley Banks
A671
Padiham
Gawthorpe Hall NT
Grimsargh
Langho
York
Cliffe
A680
M65
BURNLEY
Widdop
Osbaldeston Green
Oaks
A666
Great Harwood
Habergham
Balderstone
Salesbury
Hindle Fold
Altham
Lowerhouse
10
Worsthorne
Elston
Samlesbury Hall
Osbaldeston
Wilpshire
Clayton-le-Moors
Hapton
Rose Hill
Hurstwood
Ribbleton
Turner Green
Mellor Brook
Mellor
A6119
Huncoat
A679
Towneley Hall
Samlesbury
Tottleworth
Rishton
Lane Ends
Mereclough
Heptonstall
3
A59
A677
A678
Hillock Vale
Walk Mill
Moor
Fishwick
Nab's Head
BLACKBURN
Beardwood
Church
A682
Samlesbury Bottoms
Whitebirk
West End
Holme Chapel
Higher Walton
Witton
Accrington
Dunnockshaw
Blackshaw Head
Walton-le-Dale
Coup Green
Hoghton Bottoms
B6234
Love Clough
Clow Bridge
Hoghton
Pleasington
Stanhill
Oswaldtwistle
A646
Gregson Lane
Feniscliffe
A679
Gaulkthorn
Baxenden
Goodshaw Fold
Forest of Dean
Cornholme
Bamber Bridge
Hoghton Tower
A6062
Lower Darwen
Guide
A56
Goodshaw Chapel
Water
Portsmouth
Lydgate
Jack Green
Riley Green
Ewood
Cocker Brook
Rising Bridge
Sherfin
Weir
82
Todmorden
Pippin Street
Feniscowles
Rann
Belthorn
A677
Acre
Crawshawbooth
Rossendale
Sharneyford
Clayton Green
Brindle
M65
4
Earcroft
Grimshaw
Reeds Holme
Lumb
Broad Clough
Dobroyd Castle
Cuerden Valley
Thorpe Green
Higher Wheelton
Tockholes
Waterside
Haslingden
Constable Lee
Rawtenstall
Holden Gate
Clough Foot
Shade
Leeds & Liverpool Canal
A674
Abbey Village
Sunnyhurst
Pickup Bank
Haslingden Grane
Edgeside
Bacup
Rockliffe
A681
Lumbutts
Butcher Hill
Whittle-le-Woods
Withnell
Lane Side
Waterfoot
Britannia
Trough Gate
Walsden
Brinscall
Darwen
Hoddlesden
Helmshore
Textiles Museum
East Lancashire Railway
Stacksteads
Wheelton
Blacksnape
Ewood Bridge
Cowpe
Boarsgreave
Bottoms
Shaw Hill
Heapey
Sunny Bank
Shawforth
Warland
A6
White Coppice
Whittlestone Head
Hardsough
Edenfield
Millgate
Facit
2
A666
Chatterton
Stubbins
Whitworth
Calderbrook
Chorley
A675
Turn
Ramsbottom
Shuttleworth
Wardle
Shore
Pincock
Carr
Cheesden
Healey
Caldermore
Charnock Green
Cowling
Edgworth
B6391
Catley Lane Head
Broadley
Durn
Littleborough
Charnock Richard
Holcombe
Nuttal Lane
Syke
Dearnley
Turton Tower
Turton Bottoms
A680
Smallbridge
Birkacre
Limbrick
Belmont
Dimple
Chapeltown
Holcombe Brook
Red Lumb
Hollingworth Lake
456
WINTER HILL
Egerton
Wolstenholme
Norden
Shawclough
Smithy Bridge
Rakewood
Rivington
Jumbles
Hawkshaw
Summerseat
Cutgate
Coppull
M61
A5106
Grimeford Village
Dunscar
Greenmount
M66
ROCHDALE
Firgrove
Milnrow
Adlington
Tottington
Affetside
Walmersley
Coppull Moor
A6
Horwich
Bolton West
Montcliffe
Horrocks Fold
Toppings
Eagley
Bradshaw
Woolfold
Limefield
Chesham
Bamford
Sudden
Higher Ogden
Smithills Hall
Astley Bridge
Walshaw
BURY
B6222
Crimble
Lower Place
Newhey
Barrow Bridge
Hooley Bridge
21
Blackrod
B6226
Harwood Lee
B6196
Elton
Balderstone
Haugh
Shevington Moor
Bottom o' th' Moor
Harwood
Starling
A58
Burnedge
Red Rock
Halliwell
79
Heywood
Castleton
Crompton Fold
Scot Lane End
Breightmet
Ainsworth
Fishpool
Three Lane Ends
Shaw
Standish
Boar's Head
Haigh
Lostock Hall Fold
Heaton
BOLTON
Redvales
Hopwood
Summit
Clough
Aspull
Lostock Junction
Black Lane
Slattocks
Tandle Hill
Besom Hill
Shevington
Cooper Turning
Four Gates
Darcy Lever
Moses Gate
Blackford Bridge
Birch
Top of Hebers
A627(M)
Royton
Standish Lower Ground
Marylebone
Chew Moor
Deane
Burnden
Tower
Hollins
Chadderton Fold
Heyside
New Springs
Wingates
Daubhill
Little Lever
Radcliffe
Langley
Long Sight
WIGAN
Pennington Green
Chequerbent
Farnworth
Chapel Field
Whitefield
Bow Lee
Chadderton
Scholes
Westhoughton
Edgefold
Prestolee
Outwood Gate
Besses o' th' Barn
Rhodes
Newtown
Water's Nook
Hulton Lane Ends
New Bury
Ringley
Stand
MIDDLETON
Austerlands
Ince-in-Makerfield
Hindley
Daisy Hill
M61
Kearsley
M60
Heaton Hall
OLDHAM
Hindley Green
Greenheys
Clifton
Prestwich
Goose Green
Worsley Mesnes
Platt Bridge
A577
Little Hulton
Walkden
Blackley
Failsworth
Atherton
Pendlebury
Crumpsall
Moston
Park Bridge
Bryn Gates
Bickershaw
Tamer Lane End
Howe Bridge
Wardley
Sedgley Park
Roe Green
Rainsough
Cheetham Hill
M60 JCTS 19 TO 24 DUE OPEN LATE SUMMER 2
New Houses
Three Sisters
B5237
Tyldesley
Ellenbrook
Swinton
Broughton
Harpurhey
Bardsley
Abram
Astley
Agecroft Commerce Park
Daisy Nook
Bryn
Dover
Plank Lane
Leigh
Town Lane
M60
Charlestown
Newton Heath
A58
Marshland Green
Boothstown
Cheetwood
Woodhouses
Stubshaw Cross
Worsley
Miles Platting
Ashton-under-Lyne
Ashton-in-Makerfield
Pennington Flash
A579
Monton
Astley Green
Canal

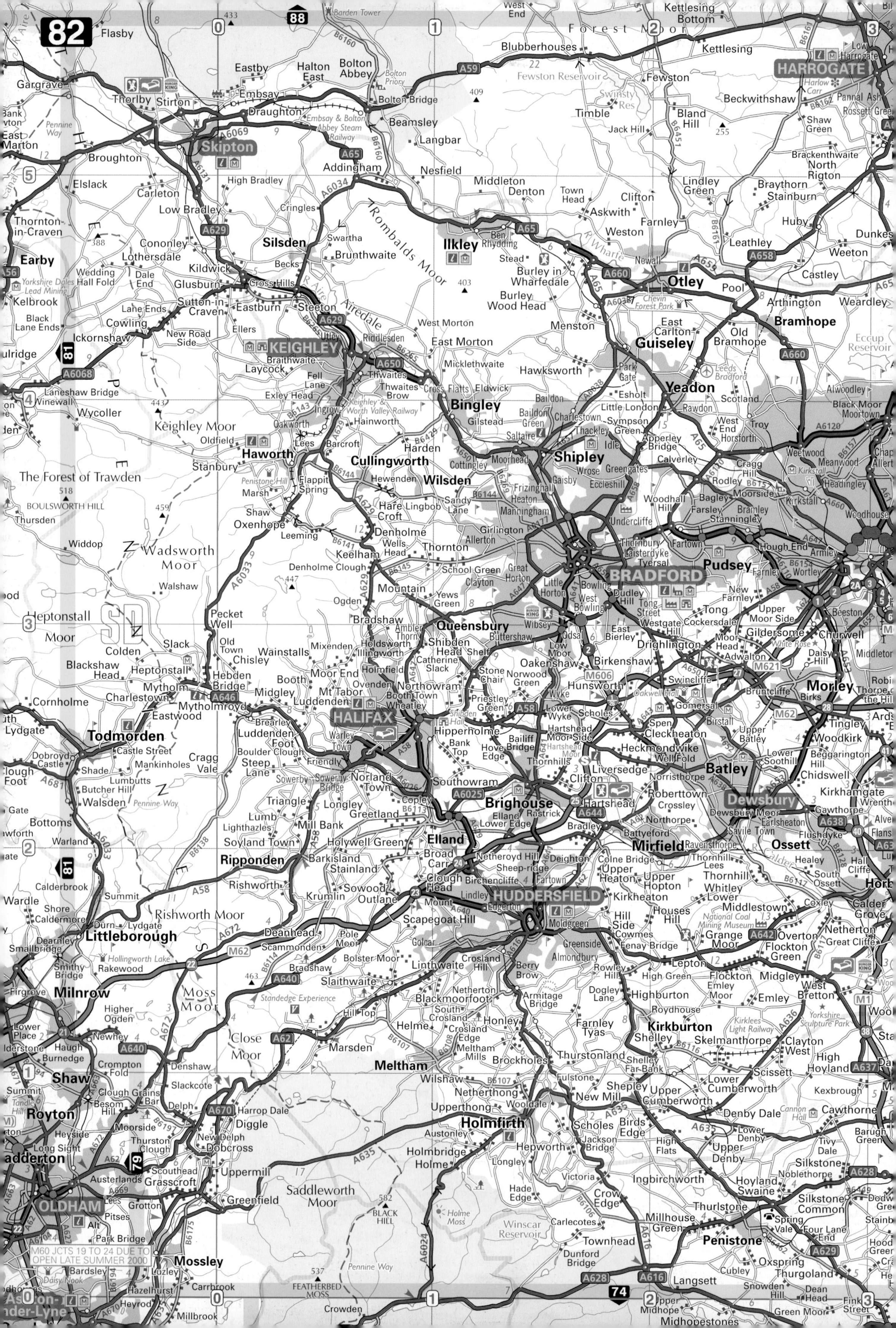
88
Flasby
Barden Tower
Forest Moor
Kettlesing Bottom
Kettlesing
Blubberhouses
Fewston Reservoir
Fewston
HARROGATE
Gargrave
Thorlby
Stirton
Embsay
Eastby
Halton East
Bolton Abbey
Bolton Priory
Bolton Bridge
Draughton
Embsay & Bolton Abbey Steam Railway
Beamsley
Langbar
Timble
Swinsty Res
Bland Hill
Beckwithshaw
Harlow Carr
Pannal Ash
Shaw Green
Skipton
Broughton
Addingham
Nesfield
Middleton
Denton
Town Head
Askwith
Clifton
Lindley Green
Braythorn
Stainburn
Brackenthwaite
North Rigton
Elslack
Carleton
High Bradley
Low Bradley
Cringles
Rombalds Moor
Ilkley
Ben Rhydding
Weston
Farnley
Huby
Thornton-in-Craven
Earby
Cononley
Lothersdale
Silsden
Swartha
Bunthwaite
Kildwick
Stead
Burley in Wharfedale
Newall
Otley
Pool
Leathley
Weeton
Castley
Dunkeswick
Wedding Hall Fold
Dale End
Glusburn
Cross Hills
Becks
Yorkshire Dales Lead Mining
Kelbrook
Sutton-in-Craven
Eastburn
Steeton
Airedale
Burley Wood Head
Chevin Forest Park
Menston
Arthington
Weardley
Bramhope
Black Lane Ends
Cowling
Lane Ends
Ellers
Utley
Riddlesden
West Morton
East Morton
East Carlton
Guiseley
Old Bramhope
Eccup Reservoir
Ickornshaw
New Road Side
KEIGHLEY
Braithwaite
Laycock
Fell Lane
Thwaites
Thwaites Brow
Micklethwaite
Hawksworth
Park Gate
Yeadon
Leeds Bradford
Alwoodley
Laneshaw Bridge
Winewall
Wycoller
Keighley Moor
Exley Head
Cross Flatts
Eldwick
Bingley
Baildon
Esholt
Little London
Rawdon
Scotland
Black Moor
Moortown
Keighley & Worth Valley Railway
Ingrow
Oakworth
Hainworth
Gilstead
Baildon Green
Charlestown
Saltaire
Thackley
Sympson Green
Idle
Apperley Bridge
West End
Horsforth
Troy
Oldfield
Haworth
Lees
Barcroft
Harden
Cullingworth
Moorhead
Shipley
Calverley
Weetwood
Meanwood
Kirkstall
Headingley
The Forest of Trawden
Stanbury
Penistone Hill
Marsh
Flappit Spring
Hewenden
Wilsden
Cottingley
Frizinghall
Gaisby
Wrose
Greengates
Eccleshill
Cragg Hill
Rodley
Moorside
BOULSWORTH HILL
Thursden
Shaw
Oxenhope
Hare Croft
Lingbob
Sandy Lane
Heaton
Manningham
Woodhall Hill
Bagley
Farsley
Bramley
Stanningley
Undercliffe
Woodhouse
Widdop
Wadsworth Moor
Leeming
Denholme
Wells Head
Thornton
Girlington
Allerton
Thornbury
Laisterdyke
Tyersal
Fartown
Hough End
Armley
Keelham
Denholme Clough
School Green
Clayton
Great Horton
BRADFORD
Pudsey
Farnley
Wortley
Walshaw
Mountain
Yews Green
Little Horton
Bowling
West Bowling
Dudley Hill
Tong Street
Tong
New Farnley
Heptonstall Moor
Pecket Well
Ogden
Bradshaw
Ambler Thorn
Queensbury
Buttershaw
Wibsey
Odsal
Westgate Hill
Cockersdale
Upper Moor Side
Beeston
Old Town
Slack
Colden
Chisley
Wainstalls
Mixenden
Holdsworth
Illingworth
Shibden Head
Catherine Slack
Shelf
Low Moor
East Bierley
Drighlington
Moor Head
Adwalton
Gildersome
White Rose
Churwell
Middleton
Daisy Hill
Blackshaw Head
Heptonstall
Hebden Bridge
Mytholm
Booth
Moor End
Holmfield
Stone Chair
Norwood Green
Oakenshaw
Birkenshaw
Swincliffe
Morley
Cornholme
Charlestown
Mytholmroyd
Midgley
Mt Tabor
Ovenden
Northowram
Hunsworth
Oakwell Hall
Gomersal
Bruntcliffe
Birks
Thorpe on the Hill
Eastwood
Luddenden
Booth Town
Priestley Green
Wyke
Lower Wyke
Scholes
Lydgate
Todmorden
Brearley
Luddenden Foot
HALIFAX
Wheatley
Shibden Hall
Hipperholme
Bailiff Bridge
Hartshead Moor Side
Spen
Cleckheaton
Birstall
Upper Batley
Tingley
Ardsley
Castle Street
Dobroyd Castle
Mankinholes
Cragg Vale
Boulder Clough
Warley Town
Bank Top
Hove Edge
Hartshead Moor
Heckmondwike
Woodkirk
Shade
Clough Foot
Lumbutts
Butcher Hill
Walsden
Pennine Way
Steep Lane
Friendly
Sowerby
Sowerby Bridge
Norland Town
Southowram
Thornhills
Liversedge
Wellfold
Batley
Lower Soothill
Beggarington Hill
Chidswell
Triangle
Longley
Copley
Greetland
Brighouse
Elland
Rastrick
Lower Edge
Clifton
Hartshead
Norristhorpe
Roberttown
Crossley
Dewsbury
Kirkhamgate
Gate
Bottoms
Lumb
Lighthazles
Mill Bank
Bradley
Battyeford
Northorpe
Dewsbury Moor
Earlsheaton
Gawthorpe
Wrenthorpe
Warland
Soyland Town
Holywell Green
Elland
Mirfield
Ravensthorpe
Savile Town
Ossett
Flushdyke
Ripponden
Barkisland
Stainland
Broad Carr
Netheroyd Hill
Sheep-ridge
Deighton
Colne Bridge
Upper Heaton
Upper Hopton
Thornhill
Thornhill Lees
Healey
Hall Cliffe
Calderbrook
Rishworth
Sowood
Clough Head
Birchencliffe
Fartown
Kirkheaton
Whitley Lower
South Ossett
Summit
Wardle
Shore
Caldermore
Krumlin
Outlane
Lindley
HUDDERSFIELD
Mount
Edgerton
Hill Side
Houses Hill
Middlestown
Coxley
Calder Grove
Rishworth Moor
Durn
Lydgate
Littleborough
Deanhead
Scapegoat Hill
Pole Moor
Golcar
Moldgreen
Cowmes
National Coal Mining Museum
Grange Moor
Netherton
Overton
Great Cliffe
Dearnley
Smallbridge
Scammonden
Bolster Moor
Crosland Hill
Greenside
Almondbury
Fenay Bridge
Flockton Green
Smithy Bridge
Hollingworth Lake
Rakewood
Moss Moor
Bradshaw
Slaithwaite
Linthwaite
Berry Brow
Rowley Hill
Lepton
High Green
Flockton
Midgley
West Bretton
Firgrove
Milnrow
Standedge Experience
Netherton
Blackmoorfoot
Armitage Bridge
Dogley Lane
Highburton
Emley Moor
Emley
Yorkshire Sculpture Park
Lower Place
Higher Ogden
Hill Top
South Crosland
Honley
Royd House
Farnley Tyas
Kirkburton
Kirklees Light Railway
Clayton West
Newhey
Haugh
Burnedge
Close Moor
Marsden
Helme
Crosland Edge
Meltham Mills
Thurstonland
Shelley
Skelmanthorpe
High Hoyland
Crompton Fold
Shaw
Denshaw
Meltham
Brockholes
Shelley Far Bank
Scissett
Summit
Clough
Grains Bar
Besom Hill
Royton
Slackcote
Delph
Wilshaw
Netherthong
Fulstone
New Mill
Shepley
Upper Cumberworth
Lower Cumberworth
Kexbrough
Harrop Dale
Diggle
Upperthong
Wooldale
Holmfirth
Scholes
Birds Edge
Denby Dale
Cannon Hall
Cawthorne
Heyside
Long Sight
Moorside
Thurston Clough
New Delph
Dobcross
Austonley
Hepworth
Jackson Bridge
High Flats
Lower Denby
Upper Denby
Tivy Dale
Barugh Green
Chadderton
Scouthead
Austerlands
Grasscroft
Uppermill
Holmbridge
Holme
Longley
Silkstone
Noblethorpe
OLDHAM
Lees
Pitses
Grotton
Greenfield
Saddleworth Moor
BLACK HILL
Victoria
Ingbirchworth
Hoyland Swaine
Silkstone Common
Alt
Park Bridge
Holme Moss
Hade Edge
Crow Edge
Millhouse Green
Thurlstone
Spring Vale
Four Lane End
Winscar Reservoir
Carlecotes
Penistone
M60 JCTS 19 TO 24 DUE TO OPEN LATE SUMMER 2000
Mossley
Townhead
Dunford Bridge
Oxspring
Bardsley
Daisy Nook
Luzley
Pennine Way
Cubley
Thurgoland
FEATHERBED MOSS
Carrbrook
Langsett
Snowden Hill
Dean Head
Hazelhurst
Heyrod
Ashton-under-Lyne
Crowden
Upper Midhope
Midhopestones
Green Moor
Fink Street
Millbrook
74
81
79
A59
A65
A6069
A629
A6034
A650
A660
A658
A6068
A646
A58
A6033
A641
A644
A62
A6025
A640
A672
A670
A635
A6024
A628
A616
A629
A636
A642
A638
M62
M606
M621
M1
A6120
A647
A6177

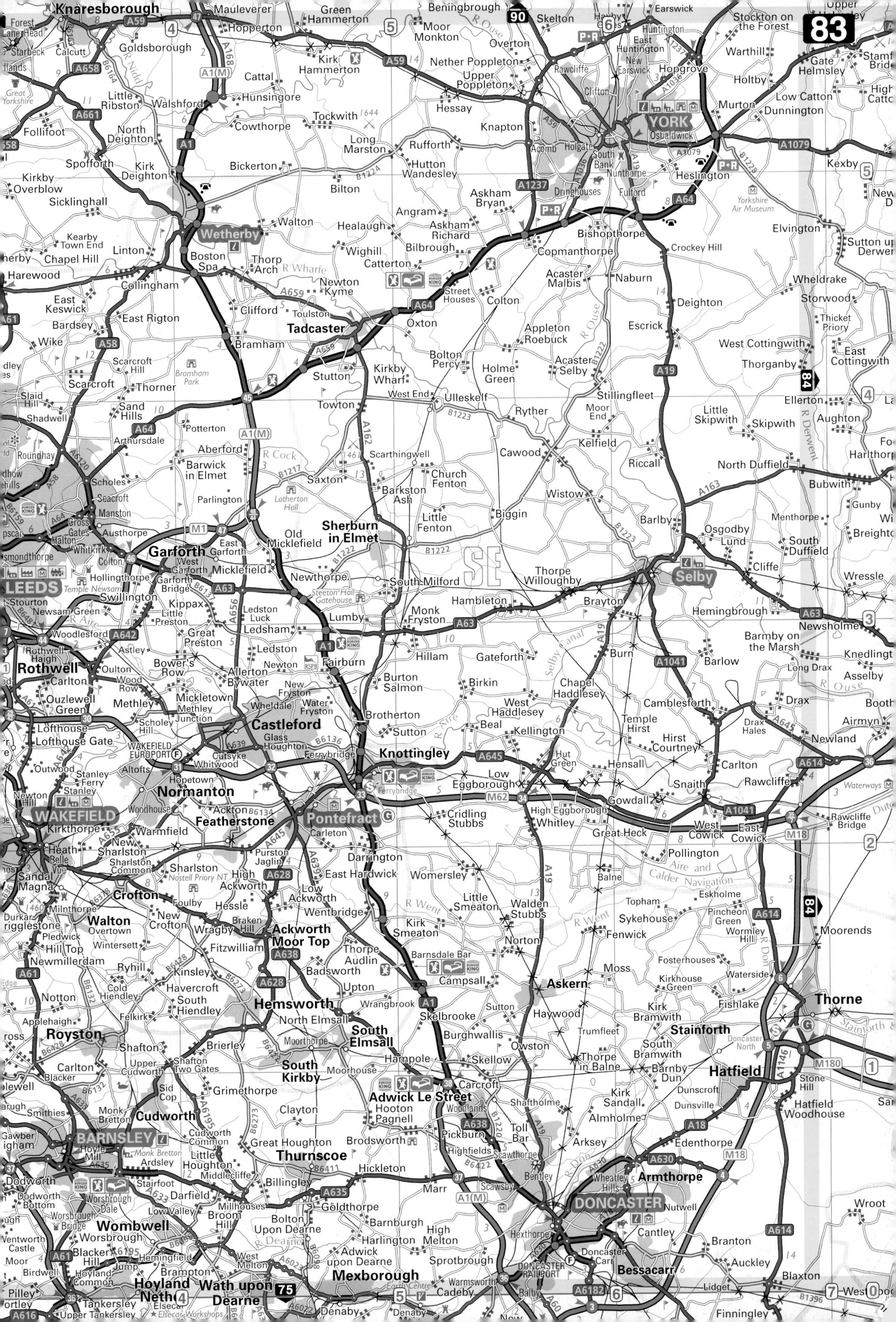
Knaresborough
Mauleverer
Green Hammerton
Beningbrough
90
Skelton
Haxby
Earswick
Stockton on the Forest
Upper Helmsley
Forest Lane Head
Starbeck
Calcutt
A59
Hopperton
5
Moor Monkton
Overton
P+R
Huntington
East Huntington
New Earswick
Warthill
Gate Helmsley
Stamford Bridge
Goldsborough
Kirk Hammerton
Nether Poppleton
Rawcliffe
Hopgrove
Holtby
A658
A1(M)
Cattal
Upper Poppleton
Clifton
Murton
Low Catton
High Catton
Great Yorkshire
Little Ribston
Walshford
Hunsingore
Hessay
Dunnington
A661
Tockwith
1644
YORK
Osbaldwick
Follifoot
North Deighton
Cowthorpe
Knapton
A1079
Kexby
Long Marston
Rufforth
Acomb
Holgate
South Bank
Spofforth
Kirk Deighton
Bickerton
Hutton Wandesley
Nunthorpe
Heslington
Kirkby Overblow
Bilton
B1224
A1237
Dringhouses
Fulford
Yorkshire Air Museum
Sicklinghall
Askham Bryan
A64
Angram
Walton
Askham Richard
Healaugh
Wetherby
Bishopthorpe
Elvington
Kearby Town End
Linton
Bilbrough
Wighill
Crockey Hill
Sutton upon Derwent
Chapel Hill
Boston Spa
Thorp Arch
R Wharfe
Catterton
Copmanthorpe
Harewood
Collingham
Newton Kyme
Acaster Malbis
Naburn
Wheldrake
East Keswick
A659
Street Houses
Colton
Storwood
Bardsey
East Rigton
Clifford
Toulston
Tadcaster
Deighton
Oxton
Appleton Roebuck
Escrick
Thicket Priory
Wike
A58
Bramham
R Ouse
West Cottingwith
East Cottingwith
Scarcroft Hill
Bramham Park
Bolton Percy
Holme Green
Acaster Selby
Thorganby
Scarcroft
Thorner
Stutton
Kirkby Wharf
B1222
A19
84
Slaid Hill
Sand Hills
West End
Ulleskelf
Stillingfleet
Ellerton
Shadwell
Towton
Moor End
Ryther
Little Skipwith
Skipwith
Aughton
Potterton
B1223
R Derwent
Roundhay
Arthursdale
Aberford
A1(M)
R Cock
Scarthingwell
Kelfield
Cawood
Harlthorpe
Barwick in Elmet
A162
1461
Church Fenton
Riccall
North Duffield
Scholes
B1217
Saxton
Barkston Ash
Wistow
A163
Bubwith
Parlington
Lotherton Hall
Seacroft
Manston
Little Fenton
Biggin
Gunby
Barlby
Osgodby
Menthorpe
Cross Gates
M1
Austhorpe
Old Micklefield
Sherburn in Elmet
Lund
Breighton
Halton
Whitkirk
Colton
Garforth
East Garforth
South Duffield
LEEDS
West Garforth
Micklefield
Cliffe
Osmondthorpe
Temple Newsam
Hollingthorpe
Garforth Bridge
Newthorpe
South Milford
SE
Thorpe Willoughby
Selby
Wressle
Stourton
Swillington
Kippax
Steeton Hall Gatehouse
Hambleton
Brayton
Newsam Green
Little Preston
A656
Ledston Luck
Lumby
Monk Fryston
Hemingbrough
Newsholme
R Aire
Ledsham
A63
Woodlesford
A642
Great Preston
Barmby on the Marsh
Rothwell Haigh
Astley
Ledston
A1
Hillam
Gateforth
Burn
Knedlington
Rothwell
Oulton
Bower's Row
Newton
Fairburn
A1041
Barlow
Long Drax
Carlton
Wood Row
Allerton Bywater
Burton Salmon
Birkin
Asselby
Ouzlewell Green
Methley
Mickletown
New Fryston
Selby Canal
Chapel Haddlesey
Camblesforth
Drax
Methley Junction
Wheldale
Water Fryston
West Haddlesey
Temple Hirst
Booth
Lofthouse
Scholey Hill
Castleford
Brotherton
Beal
Drax Hales
Airmyn
Lofthouse Gate
WAKEFIELD EUROPORT
Glass Houghton
Sutton
Kellington
Hirst Courtney
A645
Newland
Outwood
Cutsyke
B6136
Ferrybridge
Knottingley
Hut Green
Hensall
Carlton
A614
Stanley Ferry
Altofts
Whitwood
Low Eggborough
Rawcliffe
Stanley
Hopetown
Snaith
Waterways
Newton Hill
Normanton
M62
Gowdall
A1041
Rawcliffe Bridge
WAKEFIELD
Woodhouse
Ackton
Featherstone
Pontefract
Cridling Stubbs
High Eggborough
Whitley
West Cowick
East Cowick
M18
Kirkthorpe
Warmfield
Carleton
Great Heck
Heath
New Sharlston
Purston Jaglin
Darrington
Pollington
Sharlston
Sharlston Common
Aire and Calder Navigation
Sandal Magna
High Ackworth
A628
A639
East Hardwick
Womersley
Balne
Eskholme
Crofton
Nostell Priory NT
Low Ackworth
Topham
Pincheon Green
Milnthorpe
Foulby
Little Smeaton
Walden Stubbs
Sykehouse
Wormley Hill
Walton
Hessle
Wentbridge
R Went
A614
84
Overtown
New Crofton
Kirk Smeaton
Fenwick
Moorends
Pledwick
Braken Hill
Wragby
Ackworth Moor Top
Norton
Hill Top
Wintersett
Fitzwilliam
Thorpe Audlin
R Don
Newmillerdam
A638
Barnsdale Bar
Fosterhouses
Ryhill
Kinsley
Badsworth
Moss
Kirkhouse Green
Waterside
A61
Havercroft
A628
Campsall
Askern
Thorne
Notton
Cold Hiendley
South Hiendley
Upton
Wrangbrook
Sutton
Kirk Bramwith
Fishlake
Felkirk
Hemsworth
Skelbrooke
Haywood
Applehaigh
North Elmsall
Stainforth
Royston
South Elmsall
Trumfleet
Doncaster North
Shafton
Brierley
Moorthorpe
Burghwallis
Owston
South Bramwith
Carlton
Upper Cudworth
Shafton Two Gates
South Kirkby
Hampole
Skellow
Thorpe in Balne
M180
Blacker
Moorhouse
Barnby Dun
Hatfield
Stone Hill
Sid Cop
Grimethorpe
Carcroft
Kirk Sandall
Dunscroft
Smithies
Monk Bretton
Cudworth
Clayton
Adwick Le Street
Shaftholme
Dunsville
Hatfield Woodhouse
Hooton Pagnell
Woodlands
Almholme
BARNSLEY
Cudworth Common
A638
Toll Bar
A18
Hoyle Mill
Monk Bretton
Little Houghton
Great Houghton
Brodsworth
Pickburn
Arksey
Edenthorpe
Ardsley
Thurnscoe
Highfields
Scawthorpe
A630
M18
Dodworth
Stairfoot
Middlecliffe
B6411
Hickleton
Bentley
Wheatley Hills
Armthorpe
Dodworth Bottom
Darfield
Billingley
A635
Marr
Scawsby
Worsbrough Dale
Low Valley
Goldthorpe
A1(M)
DONCASTER
Nutwell
Wroot
Worsbrough Bridge
Wombwell
Millhouses
Broom Hill
Bolton Upon Dearne
Barnburgh
High Melton
Cantley
Worsbrough
Harlington
Hexthorpe
A614
Wentworth Castle
R Dearne
Adwick upon Dearne
Branton
Blacker Hill
Hemingfield
West Melton
Sprotbrough
Doncaster Carr
Auckley
Birdwell
Hoyland Common
Jump
Brampton
DONCASTER RAILPORT
Bessacarr
Blaxton
Pilley
Hoyland Nether
Wath upon Dearne
75
Mexborough
Earth Centre
Warmsworth
Cadeby
Balby
A6182
Lidget
West Moor
Tankersley
Elsecar
Denaby
B1396
Finningley
Upper Tankersley
Elsecar Workshops
A616

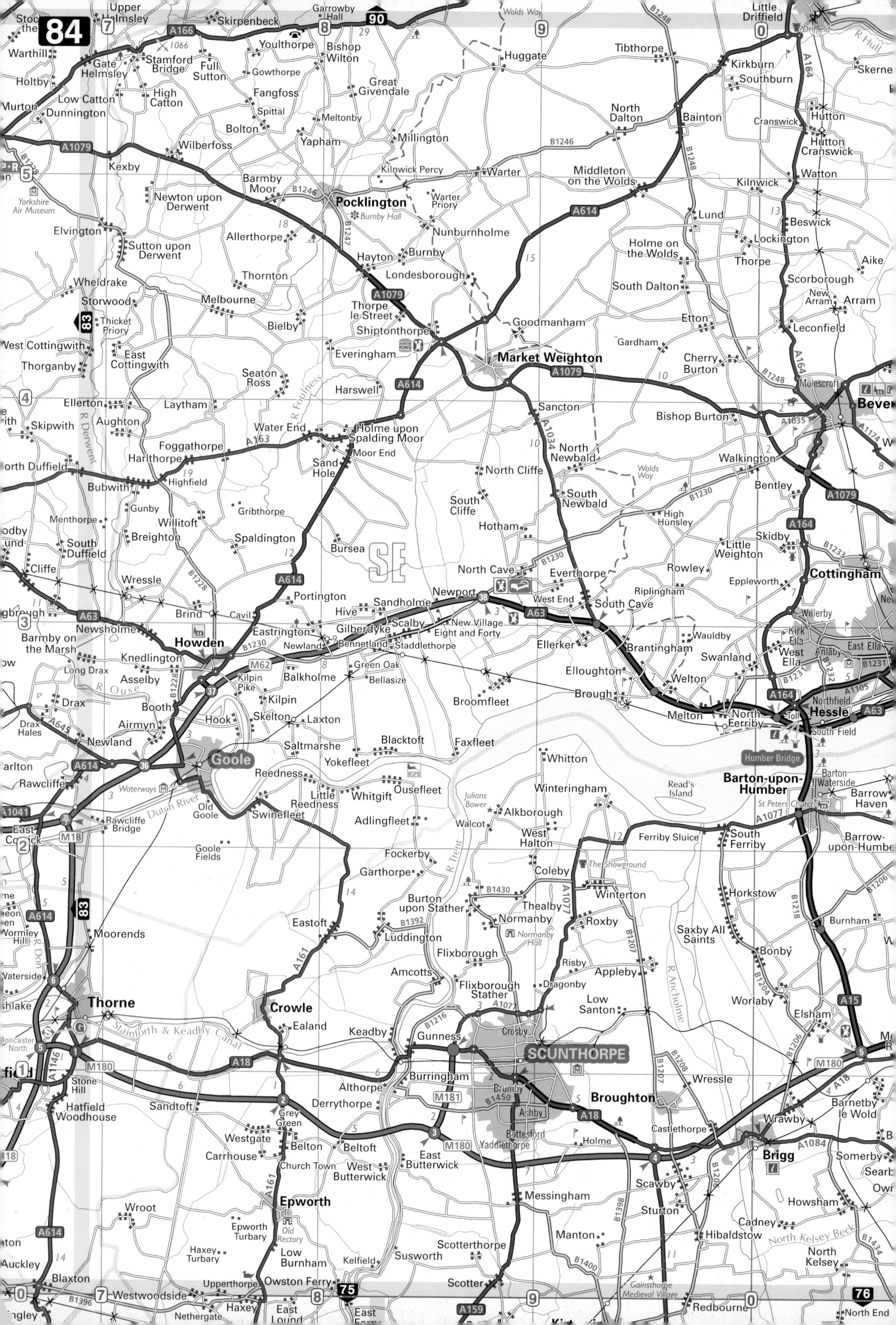

84
Stockton on the Forest
Upper Helmsley
Skirpenbeck
Garrowby Hall
90
Wolds Way
9
Little Driffield
Driffield
R Hull
Warthill
Gate Helmsley
1066
Stamford Bridge
Full Sutton
Youlthorpe
Bishop Wilton
29
Huggate
Tibthorpe
0
Kirkburn
Southburn
A164
Skerne
A166
Holtby
Gowthorpe
Great Givendale
High Catton
Low Catton
Fangfoss
Murton
Dunnington
Spittal
Meltonby
North Dalton
Bainton
Cranswick
Hutton
Hutton Cranswick
Bolton
Yapham
Millington
B1246
B1248
A1079
Wilberfoss
Kexby
Kilnwick Percy
Warter
Middleton on the Wolds
Kilnwick
Watton
5
B1228
Barmby Moor
B1246
Pocklington
Warter Priory
A614
Yorkshire Air Museum
Newton upon Derwent
Burnby Hall
Lund
13
Beswick
18
B1247
Nunburnholme
Elvington
Sutton upon Derwent
Allerthorpe
Holme on the Wolds
Lockington
Hayton
Burnby
15
Thorpe
Aike
Thornton
Londesborough
Scorborough
Wheldrake
A1079
South Dalton
New Arram
Arram
Storwood
Melbourne
Thorpe le Street
83
Thicket Priory
Bielby
Goodmanham
Etton
Leconfield
West Cottingwith
Shiptonthorpe
Gardham
East Cottingwith
Everingham
Market Weighton
A1079
Cherry Burton
Thorganby
Seaton Ross
R Foulness
Harswell
10
B1248
Molescroft
A164
4
A614
Beverley
Ellerton
Laytham
Sancton
Skipwith
Aughton
Water End
Holme upon Spalding Moor
Bishop Burton
A1035
R Derwent
A163
A1034
A1174
Foggathorpe
10
North Newbald
Walkington
Harlthorpe
Moor End
North Duffield
19
Sand Hole
North Cliffe
Wolds Way
Bentley
8
Highfield
Bubwith
South Cliffe
South Newbald
A1079
B1230
7
Gunby
Gribthorpe
Menthorpe
Willitoft
High Hunsley
A164
Hotham
Skidby
Breighton
Spaldington
Bursea
SE
Little Weighton
South Duffield
12
B1230
B1233
North Cave
Everthorpe
Rowley
Cottingham
Cliffe
A614
Wressle
Eppleworth
B1228
Riplingham
Portington
Newport
Sandholme
38
West End
South Cave
11
Willerby
Brind
Cavil
Hive
3
A63
A63
Barlby Brough
3
Newsholme
Gilberdyke
Scalby
New Village
Eight and Forty
Wauldby
Kirk Ella
Howden
Eastrington
Barmby on the Marsh
Newland
Bennetland
Staddlethorpe
Ellerker
Brantingham
West Ella
Anlaby
East Ella
B1230
Swanland
B1231
Knedlington
Long Drax
M62
Green Oak
8
Elloughton
B1232
Asselby
Kilpin Pike
Balkholme
Bellasize
Welton
A1105
B1228
R Ouse
37
Kilpin
Brough
A164
Northfield
Drax
Booth
Broomfleet
Melton
North Ferriby
Hessle
A63
Hook
Skelton
Laxton
Toll
Drax Hales
Airmyn
A645
3
South Field
Newland
Saltmarshe
Blacktoft
Faxfleet
Goole
Whitton
Humber Bridge
Carlton
A614
36
Yokefleet
Reedness
RSPB
Barton-upon-Humber
Barton Waterside
Rawcliffe
Waterways
3
Dutch River
Little Reedness
Whitgift
Ousefleet
Julians Bower
Winteringham
Read's Island
Barrow Haven
St Peters Church
Old Goole
Swinefleet
Alkborough
A1041
Rawcliffe Bridge
Adlingfleet
Walcot
West Halton
A1077
East Cowick
M18
2
12
Ferriby Sluice
South Ferriby
Barrow-upon-Humber
Goole Fields
Fockerby
R Trent
Coleby
The Showground
5
Garthorpe
B1430
14
Winterton
Horkstow
B1206
Burton upon Stather
Thealby
B1218
A614
83
A1077
Eastoft
Normanby
Roxby
Saxby All Saints
Burnham
B1392
Normanby Hall
Moorends
Luddington
B1207
Wormley Hill
A161
R Don
Flixborough
Risby
Bonby
R Ancholme
Appleby
Amcotts
Flixborough Stather
Dragonby
B1204
Waterside
6
Crowle
3
A1077
Low Santon
Worlaby
A15
Thorne
2
Ealand
Stainforth & Keadby Canal
B1216
Crosby
Elsham
G
Keadby
Gunness
SCUNTHORPE
5
Doncaster North
1
6
A18
1
M180
Stone Hill
6
Althorpe
Burringham
Brumby
B1207
B1208
Wressle
M180
A18
B1450
M181
Broughton
4
Barnetby le Wolf
A1146
Hatfield Woodhouse
Sandtoft
2
Grey Green
Derrythorpe
5
2
Ashby
A18
Castlethorpe
Wrawby
3
Bottesford
Westgate
Belton
Beltoft
M180
Yaddlethorpe
Holme
A1084
Brigg
Carrhouse
East Butterwick
4
3
Somerby
Church Town
West Butterwick
Searby
B1206
Owmby
Scawby
Messingham
A161
Epworth
Howsham
B1398
Sturton
Wroot
Epworth Turbary
Old Rectory
Cadney
North Kelsey Beck
A614
Manton
Hibaldstow
B1434
Haxey Turbary
Low Burnham
Scotterthorpe
North Kelsey
Auckley
14
Kelfield
Susworth
B1400
11
Blaxton
Upperthorpe
Owston Ferry
Scotter
Gainsthorpe Medieval Village
76
0
7
Westwoodside
75
8
9
0
B1396
Haxey
East Lound
A159
Redbourne
North End
Nethergate
East Ferry

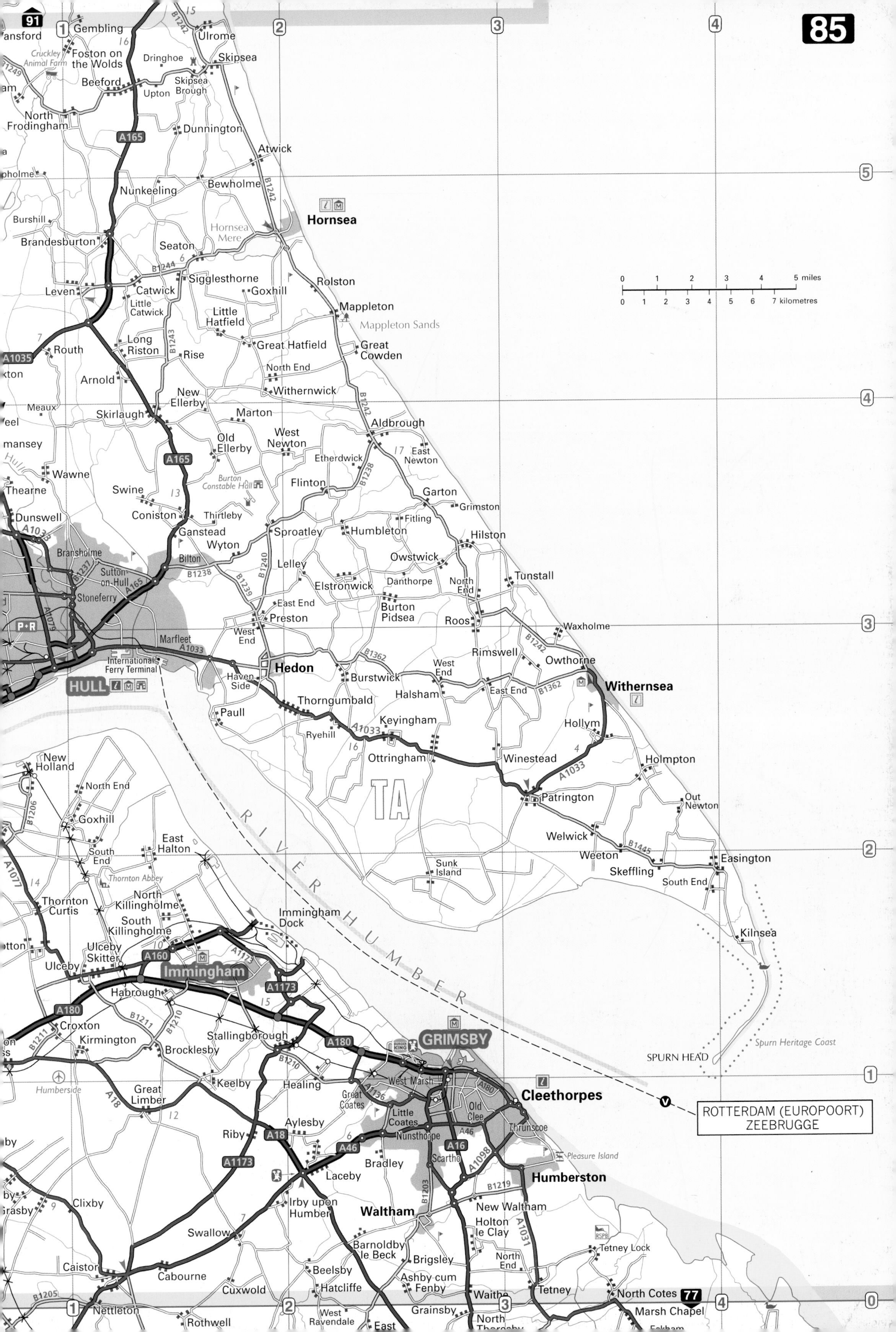
91
Gembling
Foston on the Wolds
Beeford
North Frodingham
Ulrome
Skipsea
Dringhoe
Skipsea Brough
Upton
Dunnington
Atwick
Nunkeeling
Bewholme
Hornsea
Hornsea Mere
Burshill
Brandesburton
Seaton
Sigglesthorne
Goxhill
Rolston
Leven
Catwick
Little Catwick
Little Hatfield
Mappleton
Mappleton Sands
Routh
Long Riston
Rise
Great Hatfield
Great Cowden
Arnold
North End
Withernwick
New Ellerby
Meaux
Skirlaugh
Marton
Aldbrough
Old Ellerby
West Newton
East Newton
Etherdwick
Wawne
Thearne
Swine
Burton Constable Hall
Flinton
Garton
Grimston
Dunswell
Coniston
Thirtleby
Fitling
Ganstead
Sproatley
Humbleton
Hilston
Wyton
Bransholme
Bilton
Owstwick
Lelley
Sutton-on-Hull
Stoneferry
Elstronwick
Danthorpe
North End
Tunstall
East End
Burton Pidsea
Preston
Roos
Waxholme
West End
Marfleet
Rimswell
International Ferry Terminal
Hedon
Owthorne
HULL
Haven Side
Burstwick
West End
Withernsea
East End
Halsham
Thorngumbald
Paull
Keyingham
Hollym
Ryehill
Ottringham
Winestead
Holmpton
New Holland
TA
Patrington
Out Newton
North End
Goxhill
East Halton
Welwick
South End
Weeton
Easington
Skeffling
Sunk Island
South End
Thornton Abbey
Thornton Curtis
North Killingholme
South Killingholme
Immingham Dock
RIVER HUMBER
Kilnsea
Ulceby Skitter
Ulceby
Immingham
Habrough
Croxton
Kirmington
Stallingborough
Brocklesby
GRIMSBY
Spurn Heritage Coast
SPURN HEAD
Humberside
Keelby
Healing
West Marsh
Great Limber
Great Coates
Little Coates
Old Clee
Cleethorpes
ROTTERDAM (EUROPOORT)
ZEEBRUGGE
Aylesby
Riby
Nunsthorpe
Thrunscoe
Scartho
Pleasure Island
Bradley
Laceby
Humberston
Clixby
Irby upon Humber
Waltham
New Waltham
Holton le Clay
Swallow
Barnoldby le Beck
Brigsley
Tetney Lock
North End
Caistor
Cabourne
Beelsby
Ashby cum Fenby
Hatcliffe
Cuxwold
Tetney
Waithe
North Cotes
77
Marsh Chapel
Nettleton
Rothwell
West Ravendale
Grainsby
East
North Thoresby
A165
B1242
A1035
A1033
A1079
B1238
B1240
B1239
B1362
B1445
A160
A1173
A180
B1211
B1210
A18
A46
A16
A1098
B1203
B1219
A1031
A1136
B1206
A1077
B1205
0 1 2 3 4 5 miles
0 1 2 3 4 5 6 7 kilometres

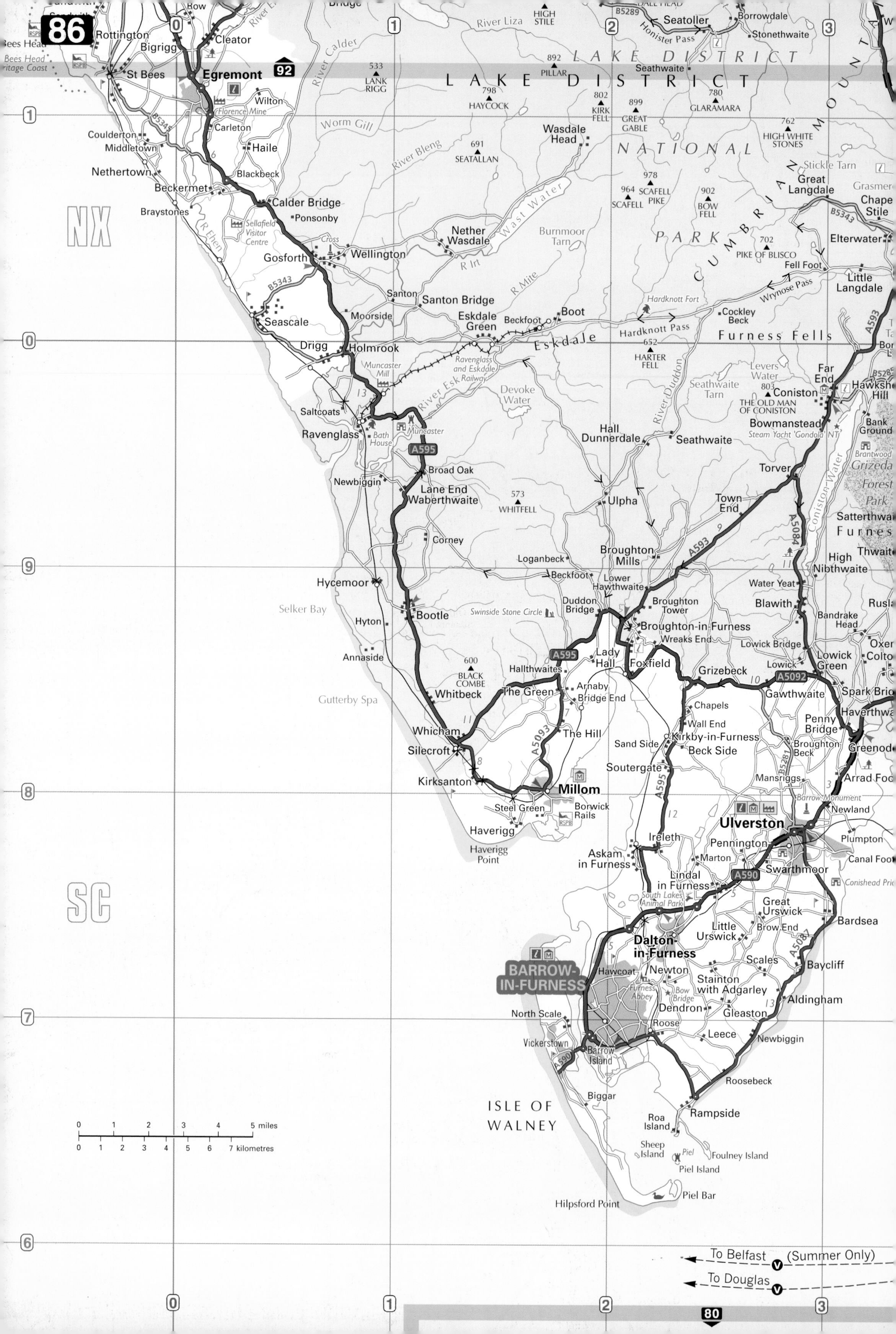
86
92
80
Rottington
Bigrigg
Cleator
St Bees
Egremont
Florence Mine
Wilton
Carleton
Coulderton
Middletown
Haile
Nethertown
Blackbeck
Beckermet
Braystones
Calder Bridge
Ponsonby
Sellafield Visitor Centre
Gosforth
Wellington
Seascale
Drigg
Holmrook
Saltcoats
Ravenglass
Muncaster Mill
Muncaster
Bath House
Newbiggin
Broad Oak
Lane End
Waberthwaite
Corney
Hycemoor
Selker Bay
Hyton
Bootle
Annaside
Gutterby Spa
Whitbeck
Whicham
Silecroft
Kirksanton
Millom
Steel Green
Haverigg
Haverigg Point
Borwick Rails
The Green
Hallthwaites
The Hill
Arnaby
Bridge End
Lady Hall
Foxfield
Duddon Bridge
Broughton-in-Furness
Broughton Tower
Wreaks End
Lower Hawthwaite
Beckfoot
Loganbeck
Broughton Mills
Swinside Stone Circle
Ulpha
Hall Dunnerdale
Seathwaite
Seathwaite Tarn
Devoke Water
Ravenglass and Eskdale Railway
Eskdale Green
Eskdale
Beckfoot
Boot
Hardknott Fort
Hardknott Pass
Wrynose Pass
Cockley Beck
Furness Fells
Santon
Santon Bridge
Moorside
Nether Wasdale
Wast Water
Burnmoor Tarn
Wasdale Head
River Calder
River Liza
River Bleng
Worm Gill
R Irt
R Mite
River Esk
River Duddon
R Ehen
LAKE DISTRICT NATIONAL PARK
CUMBRIAN MOUNTAINS
533 LANK RIGG
798 HAYCOCK
892 PILLAR
HIGH STILE
691 SEATALLAN
802 KIRK FELL
899 GREAT GABLE
978 SCAFELL PIKE
964 SCAFELL
902 BOW FELL
780 GLARAMARA
762 HIGH WHITE STONES
702 PIKE OF BLISCO
652 HARTER FELL
573 WHITFELL
600 BLACK COMBE
803 THE OLD MAN OF CONISTON
Seatoller
Borrowdale
Honister Pass
Stonethwaite
Seathwaite
Stickle Tarn
Great Langdale
Chapel Stile
Elterwater
Fell Foot
Little Langdale
Levers Water
Far End
Coniston
Hawkshead Hill
Bowmanstead
Steam Yacht 'Gondola' NT
Bank Ground
Brantwood
Grizedale Forest Park
Coniston Water
Torver
Town End
Satterthwaite
High Nibthwaite
Water Yeat
Blawith
Bandrake Head
Lowick Bridge
Lowick
Lowick Green
Grizebeck
Gawthwaite
Spark Bridge
Chapels
Wall End
Kirkby-in-Furness
Beck Side
Sand Side
Soutergate
Penny Bridge
Broughton Beck
Greenodd
Mansriggs
Arrad Foot
Barrow Monument
Newland
Ulverston
Pennington
Plumpton
Canal Foot
Swarthmoor
Conishead Priory
Ireleth
Askam in Furness
Marton
Lindal in Furness
South Lakes Animal Park
Great Urswick
Bardsea
Little Urswick
Brow End
Dalton-in-Furness
Scales
Baycliff
BARROW-IN-FURNESS
Hawcoat
Newton
Stainton with Adgarley
Furness Abbey
Bow Bridge
Dendron
Gleaston
Aldingham
North Scale
Roose
Leece
Newbiggin
Vickerstown
Barrow Island
Roosebeck
Biggar
Rampside
ISLE OF WALNEY
Roa Island
Sheep Island
Piel
Foulney Island
Piel Island
Piel Bar
Hilpsford Point
NX
SC
A595
A593
A5092
A5084
A590
A5087
B5281
B5345
B5343
B5289
0 1 2 3 4 5 miles
0 1 2 3 4 5 6 7 kilometres
To Belfast (Summer Only)
To Douglas

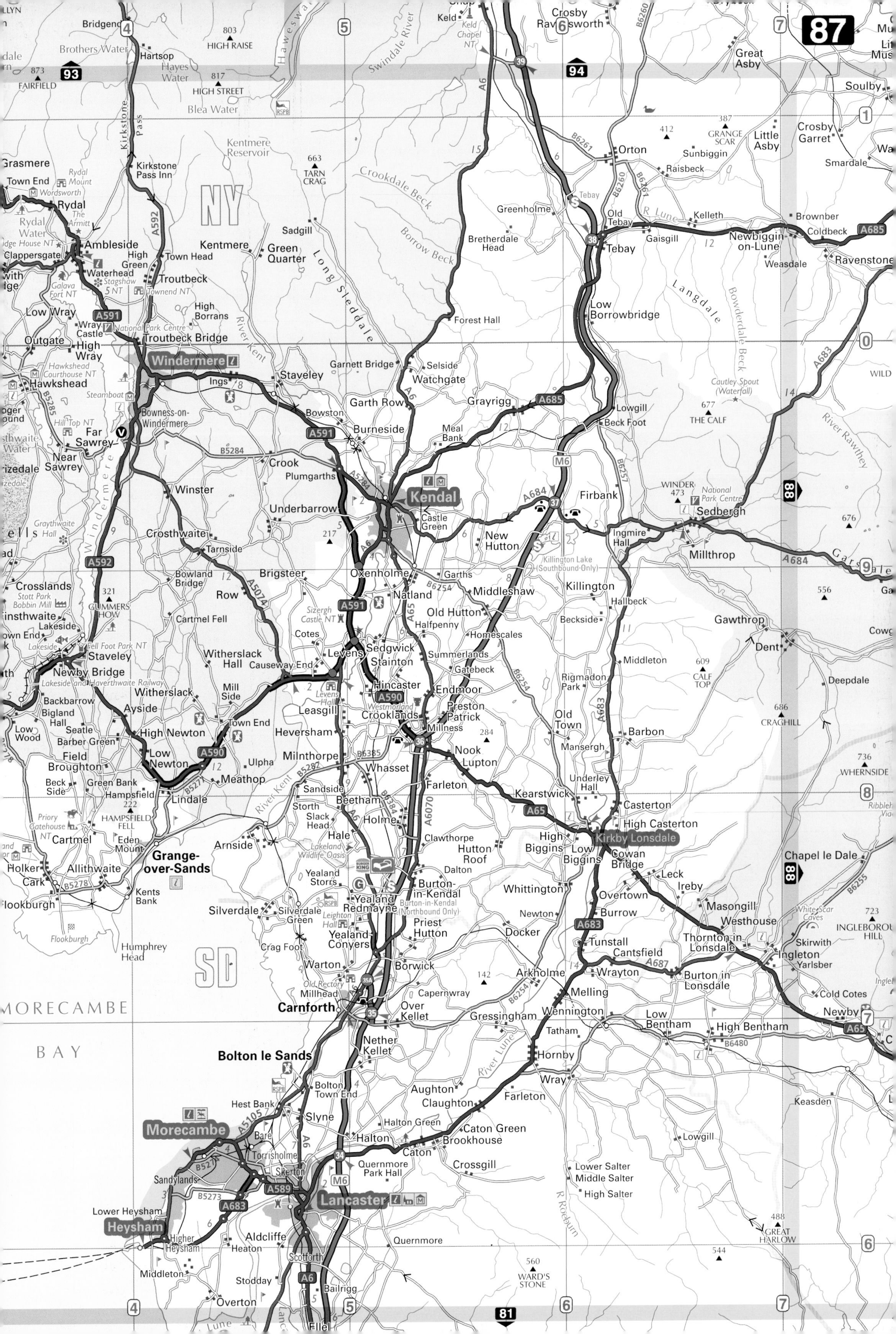
Bridgend
Brothers Water
Hartsop
803 HIGH RAISE
Hayes Water
873 FAIRFIELD
93
817 HIGH STREET
Blea Water
Haweswater
Swindale River
Keld
Keld Chapel NT
Crosby Ravensworth
94
B6260
Great Asby
Soulby
Kirkstone Pass
Kirkstone Pass Inn
Kentmere Reservoir
663 TARN CRAG
Crookdale Beck
NY
Grasmere
Rydal Mount
Town End
Wordsworth
Rydal
The Armitt
Rydal Water
Ambleside
Clappersgate
A592
Waterhead
Stagshaw NT
Galava Fort NT
Troutbeck
Townend NT
High Green
Town Head
Kentmere
Sadgill
Green Quarter
Long Sleddale
Borrow Beck
High Borrans
River Kent
Low Wray
Wray Castle
A591
National Park Centre
Troutbeck Bridge
Outgate
High Wray
Windermere
Hawkshead Courthouse NT
Hawkshead
B5285
Steamboat
Ings
Staveley
Garnett Bridge
Selside
Watchgate
Forest Hall
Bowston
Garth Row
A6
Burneside
Bowness-on-Windermere
Hill Top NT
Far Sawrey
Near Sawrey
B5284
Crook
Plumgarths
A5284
Winster
Underbarrow
Kendal
Castle Green
New Hutton
Crosthwaite
Tarnside
217
Graythwaite Hall
A592
Brigsteer
Oxenholme
Garths
B6254
Middleshaw
Bowland Bridge
Row
A5074
Crosslands
321 GUMMERS HOW
Stott Park Bobbin Mill
Cartmel Fell
Sizergh Castle NT
A591
Natland
Old Hutton
Halfpenny
A65
Lakeside
Cotes
Homescales
Fell Foot Park NT
Staveley
Witherslack Hall
Levens
Sedgwick
Stainton
Summerlands
Causeway End
Gatebeck
Newby Bridge
Lakeside and Haverthwaite Railway
Hincaster
Endmoor
A590
Preston Patrick
Backbarrow
Witherslack
Mill Side
Leasgill
Levens Hall
Westmorland
Crooklands
Millness
Bigland Hall
Ayside
Low Wood
Seatle
High Newton
Town End
Heversham
284
Barber Green
Low Newton
A590
Milnthorpe
B6385
Nook
Lupton
Field Broughton
Ulpha
B5282
Whasset
Beck Side
Green Bank
Meathop
Hampsfield
B5271
Lindale
Sandside
Farleton
222 HAMPSFIELD FELL
River Kent
Storth
Slack Head
Beetham
B6384
A6070
Priory Gatehouse NT
Cartmel
Eden Mount
Arnside
Hale
Holme
Clawthorpe
Hutton Roof
Grange-over-Sands
Lakeland Wildlife Oasis
Holker
Cark
Allithwaite
B5278
Yealand Storrs
Dalton
Burton-in-Kendal
Kents Bank
Flookburgh
Silverdale
Silverdale Green
Yealand Redmayne
Burton-in-Kendal (Northbound Only)
Leighton Hall
Priest Hutton
Yealand Conyers
Humphrey Head
Crag Foot
SD
Warton
Borwick
Old Rectory
Millhead
Capernwray
MORECAMBE
BAY
Carnforth
Over Kellet
Nether Kellet
Bolton le Sands
Bolton Town End
Hest Bank
Slyne
A5105
Morecambe
Bare
A6
Torrisholme
Halton Green
Halton
Caton
Aughton
Claughton
Caton Green
Brookhouse
Crossgill
Quernmore Park Hall
B5274
Sandylands
Skerton
M6
B5273
A589
A683
Lancaster
Lower Heysham
Heysham
Higher Heysham
Aldcliffe
Heaton
Scotforth
Quernmore
Middleton
Stodday
A6
Bailrigg
Overton
Lune
Ellel
81
Orton
B6261
412
387 GRANGE SCAR
Sunbiggin
Little Asby
Crosby Garrett
Smardale
Raisbeck
Tebay
B6260
Old Tebay
R. Lune
Kelleth
Brownber
Greenholme
Bretherdale Head
Gaisgill
Newbiggin-on-Lune
Coldbeck
A685
Tebay
Weasdale
Ravenstonedale
Langdale
Bowderdale Beck
Low Borrowbridge
A683
Cautley Spout (Waterfall)
677 THE CALF
Lowgill
Beck Foot
Grayrigg
A685
Meal Bank
River Rawthey
M6
B6257
WINDER 473
National Park Centre
Firbank
A684
Sedbergh
676
Ingmire Hall
Killington Lake (Southbound Only)
Millthrop
A684
Garsdale
Killington
556
Hallbeck
Beckside
Gawthrop
Dent
Middleton
609 CALF TOP
Deepdale
Rigmaden Park
B6254
686 CRAGHILL
Old Town
Barbon
Mansergh
736 WHERNSIDE
Underley Hall
Kearstwick
Casterton
High Casterton
A65
Kirkby Lonsdale
High Biggins
Low Biggins
Cowan Bridge
Chapel le Dale
Leck
Ireby
Whittington
Overtown
Masongill
B6255
Burrow
White Scar Caves
Newton
Westhouse
723 INGLEBOROUGH HILL
Docker
A683
Tunstall
Thornton-in-Lonsdale
Skirwith
Cantsfield
Ingleton
Yarlsber
A687
142
Arkholme
Wrayton
Burton in Lonsdale
B6254
Melling
Cold Cotes
Gressingham
Wennington
Low Bentham
Newby
Tatham
High Bentham
B6480
A65
Hornby
River Lune
Wray
Farleton
Keasden
Lowgill
Lower Salter
Middle Salter
High Salter
R Roeburn
488 GREAT HARLOW
560 WARD'S STONE
544
WILD

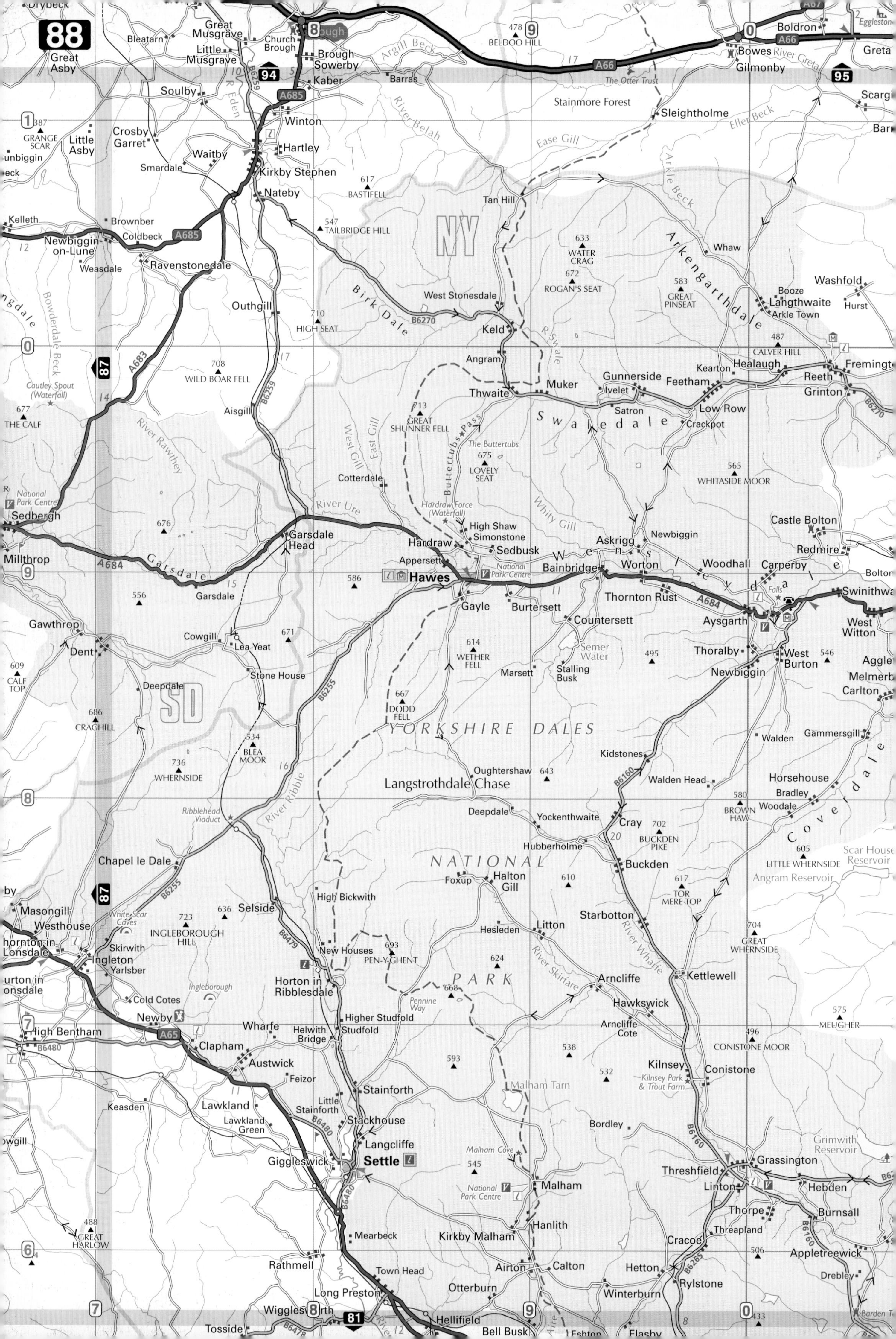
Great Musgrave
Little Musgrave
Church Brough
Brough
Brough Sowerby
Kaber
Barras
Bleatarn
Great Asby
Soulby
Winton
Hartley
Crosby Garret
Little Asby
Waitby
Smardale
Kirkby Stephen
Nateby
Kelleth
Brownber
Newbiggin-on-Lune
Coldbeck
Weasdale
Ravenstonedale
Outhgill
Aisgill
Bowes
Gilmonby
Boldron
Greta
Stainmore Forest
Sleightholme
The Otter Trust
BELDOO HILL
GRANGE SCAR
BASTIFELL
TAILBRIDGE HILL
Tan Hill
WATER CRAG
ROGAN'S SEAT
GREAT PINSEAT
Arkengarthdale
Whaw
Booze
Langthwaite
Arkle Town
Washfold
Hurst
West Stonesdale
Birk Dale
Keld
HIGH SEAT
WILD BOAR FELL
Angram
Thwaite
Muker
Gunnerside
Ivelet
Satron
Feetham
Kearton
Healaugh
Reeth
Grinton
Fremington
Low Row
Crackpot
CALVER HILL
Swaledale
GREAT SHUNNER FELL
Buttertubs Pass
The Buttertubs
LOVELY SEAT
WHITASIDE MOOR
Cotterdale
Cautley Spout (Waterfall)
THE CALF
National Park Centre
Sedbergh
Millthrop
Garsdale
Garsdale Head
Hardraw Force (Waterfall)
High Shaw
Simonstone
Hardraw
Sedbusk
Appersett
Hawes
Gayle
Burtersett
Askrigg
Newbiggin
Bainbridge
Worton
Woodhall
Carperby
Castle Bolton
Redmire
Bolton
Wensleydale
Thornton Rust
Aysgarth
Swinithwaite
West Witton
Countersett
Semer Water
Marsett
Stalling Busk
Thoralby
West Burton
Newbiggin
Carlton
Melmerby
Gawthrop
Dent
Cowgill
Lea Yeat
Stone House
Deepdale
CALF TOP
CRAGHILL
WETHER FELL
DODD FELL
YORKSHIRE DALES
NATIONAL
PARK
Kidstones
Walden
Gammersgill
Walden Head
Horsehouse
Bradley
Woodale
Coverdale
BLEA MOOR
WHERNSIDE
Oughtershaw
Langstrothdale Chase
Deepdale
Yockenthwaite
Cray
BUCKDEN PIKE
BROWN HAW
Hubberholme
Buckden
LITTLE WHERNSIDE
Scar House Reservoir
Angram Reservoir
Ribblehead Viaduct
River Ribble
Chapel le Dale
Foxup
Halton Gill
TOR MERE TOP
High Bickwith
Masongill
Westhouse
White Scar Caves
Selside
INGLEBOROUGH HILL
Thornton in Lonsdale
Ingleton
Skirwith
Yarlsber
Burton in Lonsdale
Hesleden
Litton
Starbotton
GREAT WHERNSIDE
New Houses
PEN-Y-GHENT
Horton in Ribblesdale
Ingleborough
Cold Cotes
Pennine Way
River Skirfare
River Wharfe
Arncliffe
Kettlewell
Hawkswick
Arncliffe Cote
Newby
High Bentham
Clapham
Wharfe
Helwith Bridge
Higher Studfold
Studfold
Austwick
MEUGHER
CONISTONE MOOR
Kilnsey
Kilnsey Park & Trout Farm
Conistone
Feizor
Stainforth
Little Stainforth
Malham Tarn
Keasden
Lawkland
Lawkland Green
Stackhouse
Langcliffe
Bordley
Grimwith Reservoir
Giggleswick
Settle
Malham Cove
Malham
National Park Centre
Threshfield
Grassington
Linton
Hebden
Thorpe
Burnsall
Threapland
GREAT HARLOW
Mearbeck
Kirkby Malham
Hanlith
Cracoe
Appletreewick
Drebley
Rathmell
Airton
Calton
Hetton
Rylstone
Town Head
Long Preston
Otterburn
Winterburn
Wigglesworth
Hellifield
Tosside
Bell Busk
Eshton
Flasby
Barden
NY
SD
A66
A685
A683
A684
A65
A67
B6259
B6270
B6255
B6479
B6480
B6160
B6265
B6478
94
95
87
81

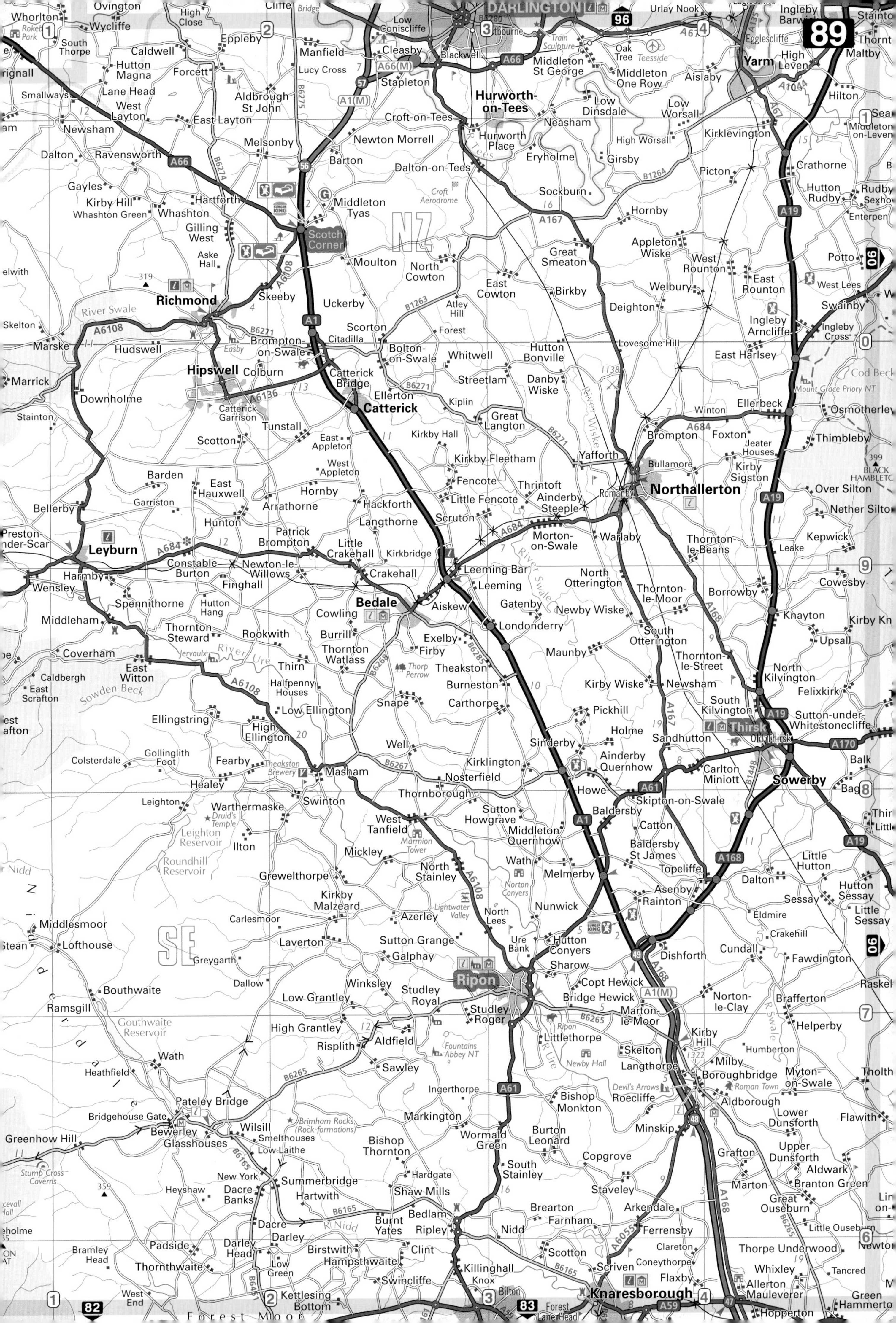
Whorlton
Ovington
Wycliffe
Rokeby Park
High Close
Cliffe
Bridge
DARLINGTON
Urlay Nook
Ingleby Barwick
Stainton
Thornaby
96
South Thorpe
Caldwell
Eppleby
Manfield
Low Coniscliffe
Cleasby
Blackwell
Cockerton
Haughton le Skerne
Bishopton
Sadberge
Middleton St George
Oak Tree
Teesside
Middleton One Row
Egglescliffe
Yarm
High Leven
Maltby
Hutton Magna
Forcett
Lucy Cross
A66(M)
A66
A67
A135
A1044
Aislaby
Lane Head
Aldbrough St John
Stapleton
A1(M)
Hurworth-on-Tees
Low Dinsdale
Low Worsall
Hilton
Smallways
West Layton
East Layton
B6275
Croft-on-Tees
Neasham
Kirklevington
Seamer
Middleton-on-Leven
Newsham
Melsonby
Newton Morrell
Hurworth Place
High Worsall
Dalton
Ravensworth
A66
B6274
Barton
Eryholme
Girsby
Crathorne
Dalton-on-Tees
Picton
B1264
Gayles
Croft Aerodrome
Sockburn
Hutton Rudby
Rudby
Sexhow
Kirby Hill
Hartforth
Middleton Tyas
Hornby
Enterpen
Whashton Green
Whashton
A167
A19
Gilling West
Scotch Corner
NZ
Appleton Wiske
Aske Hall
Moulton
North Cowton
Great Smeaton
West Rounton
Potto
Eltwith
319
A6108
East Rounton
West Lees
Richmond
Skeeby
East Cowton
Birkby
Welbury
Uckerby
Atley Hill
Deighton
Swainby
River Swale
B1263
Ingleby Arncliffe
Skelton
A6108
Scorton
Forest
Ingleby Cross
Marske
Hudswell
B6271
Brompton-on-Swale
Citadilla
Bolton-on-Swale
Whitwell
Hutton Bonville
Lovesome Hill
East Harlsey
Easby
Streetlam
Danby Wiske
Cod Beck
Hipswell
Colburn
Catterick Bridge
Ellerton
River Wiske
Mount Grace Priory NT
Marrick
Downholme
A6136
B6271
Kiplin
Winton
Ellerbeck
Osmotherley
Catterick Garrison
Catterick
Great Langton
A684
Stainton
Tunstall
Brompton
Foxton
Thimbleby
Kirkby Hall
Jeater Houses
Scotton
East Appleton
B6271
Yafforth
Bullamore
Kirkby Fleetham
West Appleton
Kirby Sigston
399
BLACK HAMBLETON
Barden
East Hauxwell
Hornby
Fencote
Thrintoft
Romanby
Northallerton
Over Silton
Garriston
Arrathorne
Hackforth
Little Fencote
Ainderby Steeple
A19
Bellerby
Hunton
Langthorne
Scruton
Nether Silton
Preston-under-Scar
Patrick Brompton
A684
Morton-on-Swale
Warlaby
Thornton-le-Beans
Kepwick
Leyburn
A684
Little Crakehall
Kirkbridge
River Swale
Leake
Constable Burton
Newton-le-Willows
Leeming Bar
North Otterington
Harmby
Wensley
Finghall
Crakehall
Leeming
Thornton-le-Moor
Borrowby
Cowesby
Spennithorne
Hutton Hang
Bedale
Aiskew
Gatenby
Newby Wiske
Middleham
Cowling
Londonderry
Knayton
Kirby Knowle
Thornton Steward
Rookwith
Burrill
Exelby
South Otterington
Upsall
A168
Coverham
River Ure
Jervaulx
Thornton Watlass
Firby
B6285
Maunby
Thornton-le-Street
North Kilvington
East Witton
Thirn
B6268
Thorp Perrow
Theakston
Caldbergh
East Scrafton
A6108
Halfpenny Houses
Burneston
Kirby Wiske
Newsham
Felixkirk
Sowden Beck
Carthorpe
South Kilvington
A19
Sutton-under-Whitestonecliffe
Ellingstring
Low Ellington
Snape
Pickhill
A167
Thirsk
High Ellington
Holme
Sandhutton
Old Thirsk
A170
Well
Sinderby
Colsterdale
Gollinglith Foot
Fearby
Theakston Brewery
Kirklington
Ainderby Quernhow
Carlton Miniott
Balk
Masham
B6267
Nosterfield
Sowerby
Healey
Thornborough
Howe
A61
B1448
Bagby
Leighton
Warthermaske
Swinton
Sutton Howgrave
Baldersby
Skipton-on-Swale
Druid's Temple
West Tanfield
Middleton Quernhow
Catton
Leighton Reservoir
A1
Ilton
Marmion Tower
Baldersby St James
A19
Mickley
Wath
A168
Little Hutton
Roundhill Reservoir
Topcliffe
Nidd
North Stainley
A6108
Melmerby
Grewelthorpe
Norton Conyers
Dalton
Hutton Sessay
Asenby
Rainton
Sessay
Kirkby Malzeard
Nunwick
Lightwater Valley
Little Sessay
Middlesmoor
Carlesmoor
Azerley
North Lees
Eldmire
Crakehill
SE
Hutton Conyers
Stean
Lofthouse
Laverton
Sutton Grange
Ure Bank
Cundall
Greygarth
Galphay
Dishforth
Fawdington
Sharow
A168
Ripon
Copt Hewick
Dallow
Winksley
Raskelf
Bouthwaite
Studley Royal
Bridge Hewick
A1(M)
Norton-le-Clay
Brafferton
Low Grantley
Marton-le-Moor
Ramsgill
Studley Roger
B6265
Helperby
Ripon
Littlethorpe
R Ure
Gouthwaite Reservoir
High Grantley
Aldfield
Kirby Hill
Skelton
Humberton
Risplith
Fountains Abbey NT
Newby Hall
Langthorpe
Milby
Wath
Sawley
1322
Boroughbridge
Myton-on-Swale
Tholthorpe
Heathfield
B6265
Devil's Arrows
Roman Town
Ingerthorpe
A61
Aldborough
Roecliffe
Bishop Monkton
Pateley Bridge
Bridgehouse Gate
Lower Dunsforth
Flawith
Brimham Rocks (Rock formations)
Markington
Bewerley
Wilsill
Burton Leonard
Minskip
Greenhow Hill
Glasshouses
Smelthouses
Wormald Green
Upper Dunsforth
Bishop Thornton
Grafton
Low Laithe
B6165
Stump Cross Caverns
South Stainley
Copgrove
Aldwark
New York
Summerbridge
Hardgate
Marton
Heyshaw
Dacre Banks
Shaw Mills
Staveley
Branton Green
Hartwith
359
B6165
Great Ouseburn
Arkendale
Brearton
Dacre
R Nidd
Burnt Yates
Bedlam
Farnham
Ferrensby
Little Ouseburn
Darley
Ripley
Nidd
A6055
B6265
Bramley Head
Padside
Darley Head
Clareton
Birstwith
Clint
Scotton
Thorpe Underwood
Newton
Hampsthwaite
Coneythorpe
Low Green
Killinghall
Scriven
Whixley
Thornthwaite
B6165
Tancred
B6451
Swincliffe
Flaxby
Knox
Allerton Mauleverer
West End
Kettlesing Bottom
Bilton
Knaresborough
A59
Green Hammerton
82
83
Forest Lane Head
Hopperton
Forest Moor

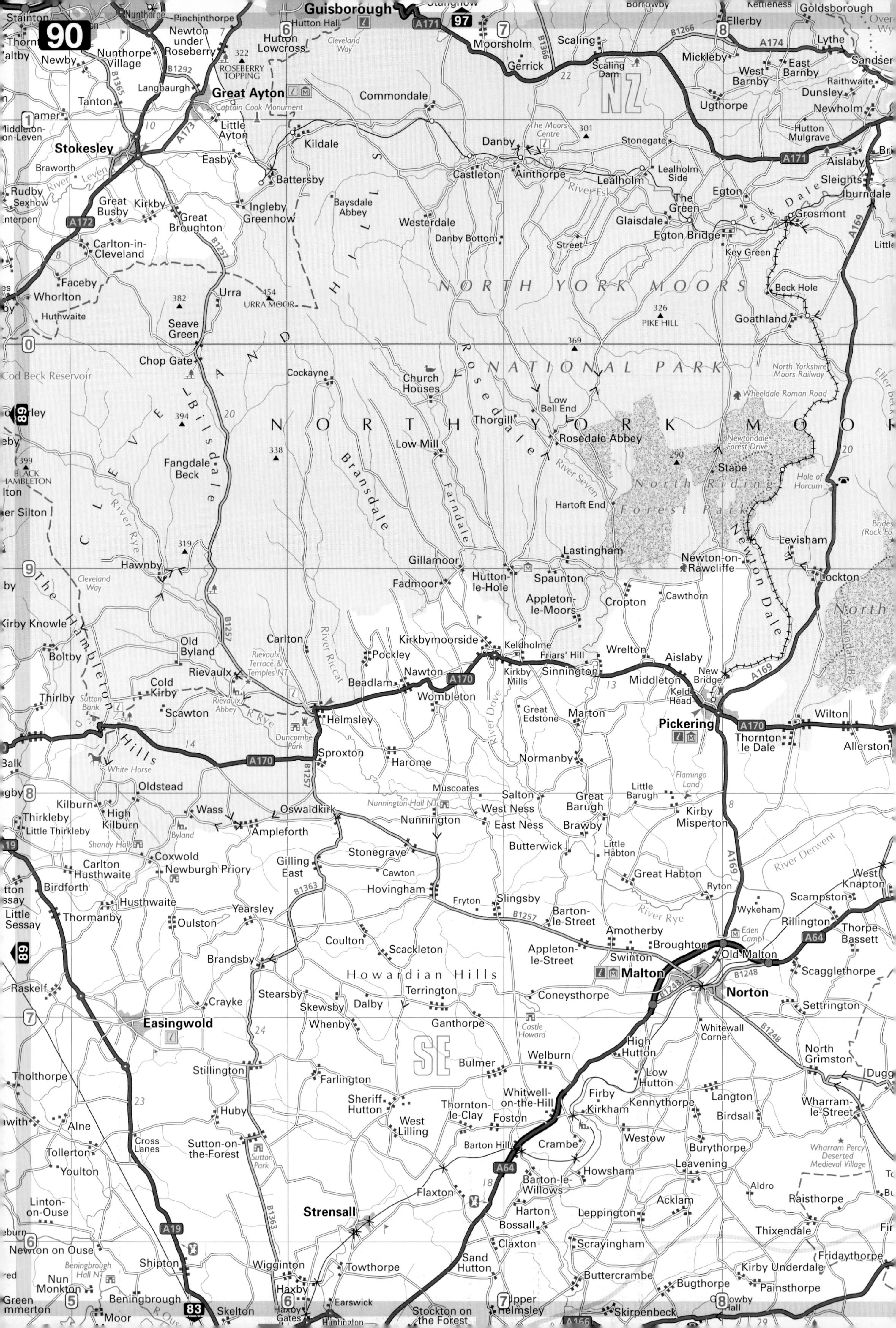

90
Guisborough
97
Stainton
Nunthorpe
Pinchinthorpe
Newton under Roseberry
Hutton Hall
Hutton Lowcross
Cleveland Way
Moorsholm
Gerrick
Scaling
Scaling Dam
Borrowby
Kettleness
Goldsborough
Ellerby
Lythe
Sandsend
Mickleby
East Barnby
West Barnby
Raithwaite
Dunsley
Newholm
Ugthorpe
Hutton Mulgrave
Newby
Nunthorpe Village
Roseberry Topping
322
Marton
Tanton
Langbaurgh
Great Ayton
Captain Cook Monument
Commondale
NZ
Little Ayton
Kildale
Stokesley
Easby
Battersby
Braworth
River Leven
Rudby
Sexhow
Great Busby
Kirkby
Great Broughton
Ingleby Greenhow
Baysdale Abbey
Westerdale
Danby
The Moors Centre
301
Castleton
Ainthorpe
Stonegate
Lealholm
Lealholm Side
River Esk
The Green
Egton
Glaisdale
Egton Bridge
Grosmont
Esk Dale
Sleights
Aislaby
Iburndale
Key Green
Danby Bottom
Street
Carlton-in-Cleveland
Faceby
Whorlton
Huthwaite
Urra
382
454
URRA MOOR
Seave Green
Chop Gate
Cod Beck Reservoir
NORTH YORK MOORS
NATIONAL PARK
326
PIKE HILL
Beck Hole
Goathland
369
North Yorkshire Moors Railway
Wheeldale Roman Road
Cockayne
Church Houses
Low Bell End
Thorgill
Rosedale
Rosedale Abbey
River Seven
CLEVELAND HILLS
Bilsdale
394
338
Fangdale Beck
Low Mill
Bransdale
Farndale
NORTH YORK MOORS
290
Stape
Newtondale Forest Drive
Hole of Horcum
North Riding Forest Park
Hartoft End
399
BLACK HAMBLETON
River Rye
319
Hawnby
Cleveland Way
Gillamoor
Lastingham
Levisham
Newton-on-Rawcliffe
Newton Dale
Lockton
Fadmoor
Hutton-le-Hole
Spaunton
Appleton-le-Moors
Cropton
Cawthorn
The Hambleton Hills
Kirby Knowle
Boltby
Old Byland
Carlton
River Riccal
Kirkbymoorside
Keldholme
Friars' Hill
Wrelton
Aislaby
Rievaulx
Rievaulx Terrace & Temples NT
Rievaulx Abbey
Pockley
Nawton
Beadlam
A170
Kirkby Mills
Sinnington
Middleton
New Bridge
Keld Head
Cold Kirby
Thirlby
Sutton Bank
Scawton
Helmsley
Wombleton
Great Edstone
Marton
Pickering
Wilton
Thornton le Dale
Allerston
Duncombe Park
Sproxton
Harome
River Dove
Normanby
White Horse
Oldstead
Kilburn
High Kilburn
Wass
Oswaldkirk
Ampleforth
Byland
Thirkleby
Little Thirkleby
Shandy Hall
Muscoates
Nunnington Hall NT
Nunnington
Salton
West Ness
East Ness
Great Barugh
Little Barugh
Flamingo Land
Kirby Misperton
Brawby
Butterwick
Little Habton
Great Habton
Coxwold
Newburgh Priory
Carlton Husthwaite
Birdforth
Gilling East
Stonegrave
Cawton
Hovingham
Fryton
Slingsby
River Derwent
West Knapton
Ryton
Wykeham
Scampston
Husthwaite
Thormanby
Little Sessay
Oulston
Yearsley
B1257
Barton-le-Street
River Rye
Amotherby
Eden Camp
Rillington
Thorpe Bassett
Coulton
Scackleton
Appleton-le-Street
Swinton
Broughton
Old Malton
A64
Brandsby
Howardian Hills
Malton
Scagglethorpe
Raskelf
Crayke
Stearsby
Skewsby
Dalby
Terrington
Coneysthorpe
Norton
Settrington
Easingwold
Whenby
Ganthorpe
Castle Howard
Whitewall Corner
SE
High Hutton
North Grimston
Tholthorpe
Stillington
Farlington
Bulmer
Welburn
Low Hutton
Duggleby
Sheriff Hutton
West Lilling
Thornton-le-Clay
Whitwell-on-the-Hill
Foston
Firby
Kirkham
Kennythorpe
Langton
Birdsall
Wharram-le-Street
Huby
Alne
Tollerton
Cross Lanes
Sutton-on-the-Forest
Sutton Park
Barton Hill
Crambe
Westow
Burythorpe
Wharram Percy Deserted Medieval Village
Youlton
Flaxton
Barton-le-Willows
Howsham
Leavening
Aldro
Raisthorpe
Linton-on-Ouse
Strensall
Harton
Leppington
Acklam
Bossall
Claxton
Scrayingham
Thixendale
Newton on Ouse
Beningbrough Hall NT
Shipton
Wigginton
Towthorpe
Sand Hutton
Buttercrambe
Kirby Underdale
Fridaythorpe
Nun Monkton
Haxby
Beningbrough
Bugthorpe
Painsthorpe
Green Hammerton
Moor
83
Skelton
Haxby Gates
Earswick
Huntington
Stockton on the Forest
Upper Helmsley
Skirpenbeck
Gowthorpe Hall
A166
A19
A169
A171
A172
A173
A174
B1248
B1257
B1363
B1365
B1366
B1266
B1292
89

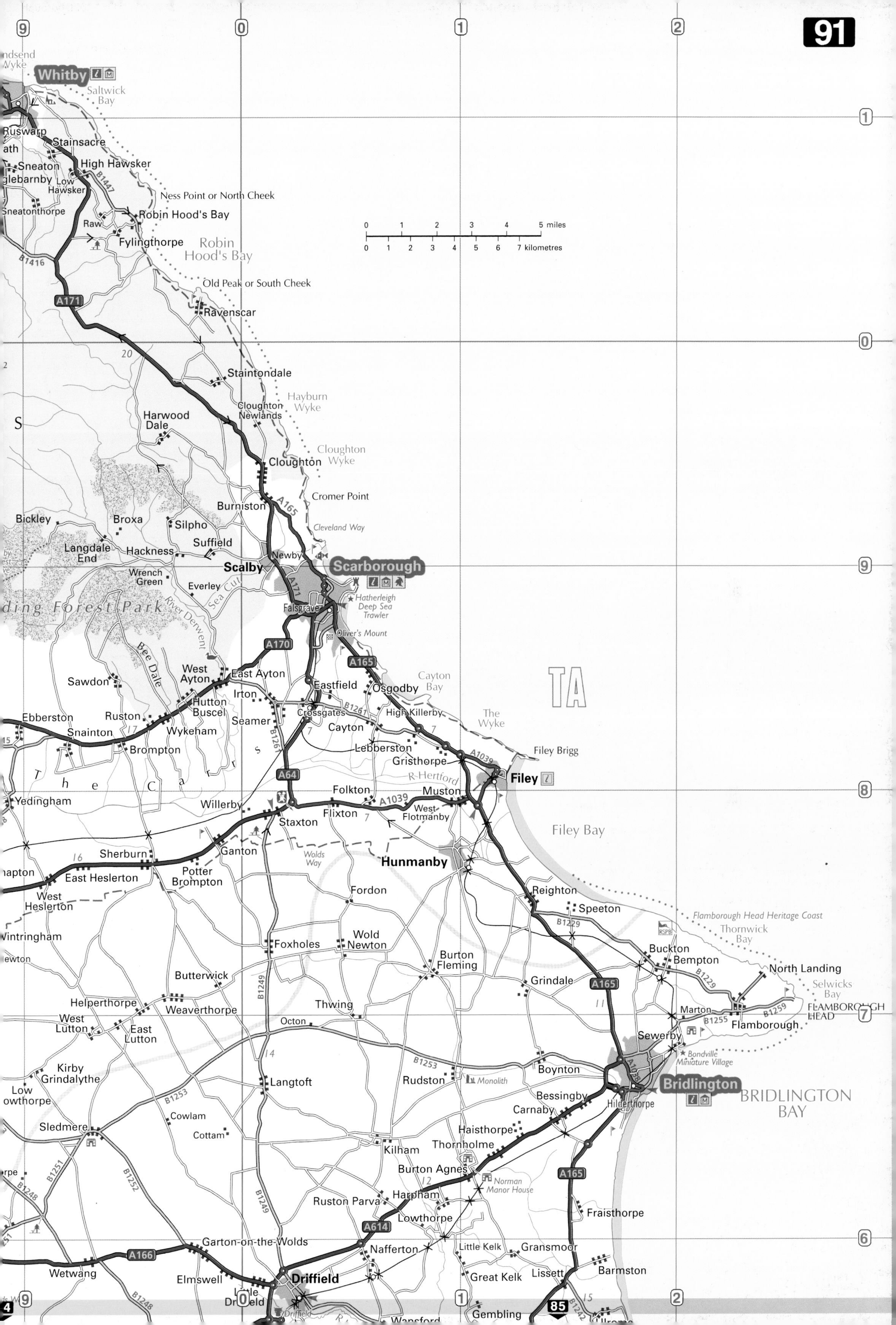
Whitby
Saltwick Bay
Ruswarp
Stainsacre
Sneaton
High Hawsker
Low Hawsker
Sneatonthorpe
Ness Point or North Cheek
Robin Hood's Bay
Raw
Fylingthorpe
Robin Hood's Bay
B1416
B1447
Old Peak or South Cheek
A171
Ravenscar
20
Staintondale
Hayburn Wyke
Cloughton Newlands
Harwood Dale
Cloughton Wyke
Cloughton
Cromer Point
Burniston
A165
Cleveland Way
Bickley
Broxa
Silpho
Suffield
Langdale End
Hackness
Newby
Scarborough
Scalby
Wrench Green
Everley
Sea Cut
River Derwent
Falsgrave
Hatherleigh Deep Sea Trawler
Oliver's Mount
A170
Bee Dale
A165
Cayton Bay
TA
West Ayton
East Ayton
Sawdon
Eastfield
Osgodby
Irton
Hutton Buscel
High Killerby
The Wyke
Ebberston
Ruston
Seamer
Crossgates
B1261
Cayton
Snainton
Wykeham
Lebberston
Filey Brigg
Brompton
Gristhorpe
A1039
R Hertford
Filey
The Carrs
A64
Folkton
Muston
Yedingham
Willerby
Flixton
A1039
West Flotmanby
Staxton
Filey Bay
Sherburn
Ganton
16
Wolds Way
Hunmanby
East Heslerton
Potter Brompton
West Heslerton
Fordon
Reighton
Speeton
B1229
Flamborough Head Heritage Coast
Thornwick Bay
Wintringham
Foxholes
Wold Newton
Buckton
Bempton
Burton Fleming
North Landing
Butterwick
B1249
Grindale
A165
B1229
Selwicks Bay
Helperthorpe
Weaverthorpe
Thwing
Marton
West Lutton
East Lutton
Octon
B1255
B1259
Flamborough
FLAMBOROUGH HEAD
Sewerby
Bondville Miniature Village
Kirby Grindalythe
B1253
Boynton
Rudston
Monolith
Langtoft
Bridlington
Hilderthorpe
BRIDLINGTON BAY
Bessingby
Carnaby
B1253
Cowlam
Cottam
Sledmere
Haisthorpe
Thornholme
Kilham
Burton Agnes
Norman Manor House
A165
B1251
B1252
B1249
Harpham
Ruston Parva
Fraisthorpe
A614
Lowthorpe
Garton-on-the-Wolds
A166
Nafferton
Little Kelk
Gransmoor
Wetwang
Elmswell
Driffield
Great Kelk
Lissett
Barmston
Little Driffield
Gembling
Wansford
B1248
85
5 miles
7 kilometres

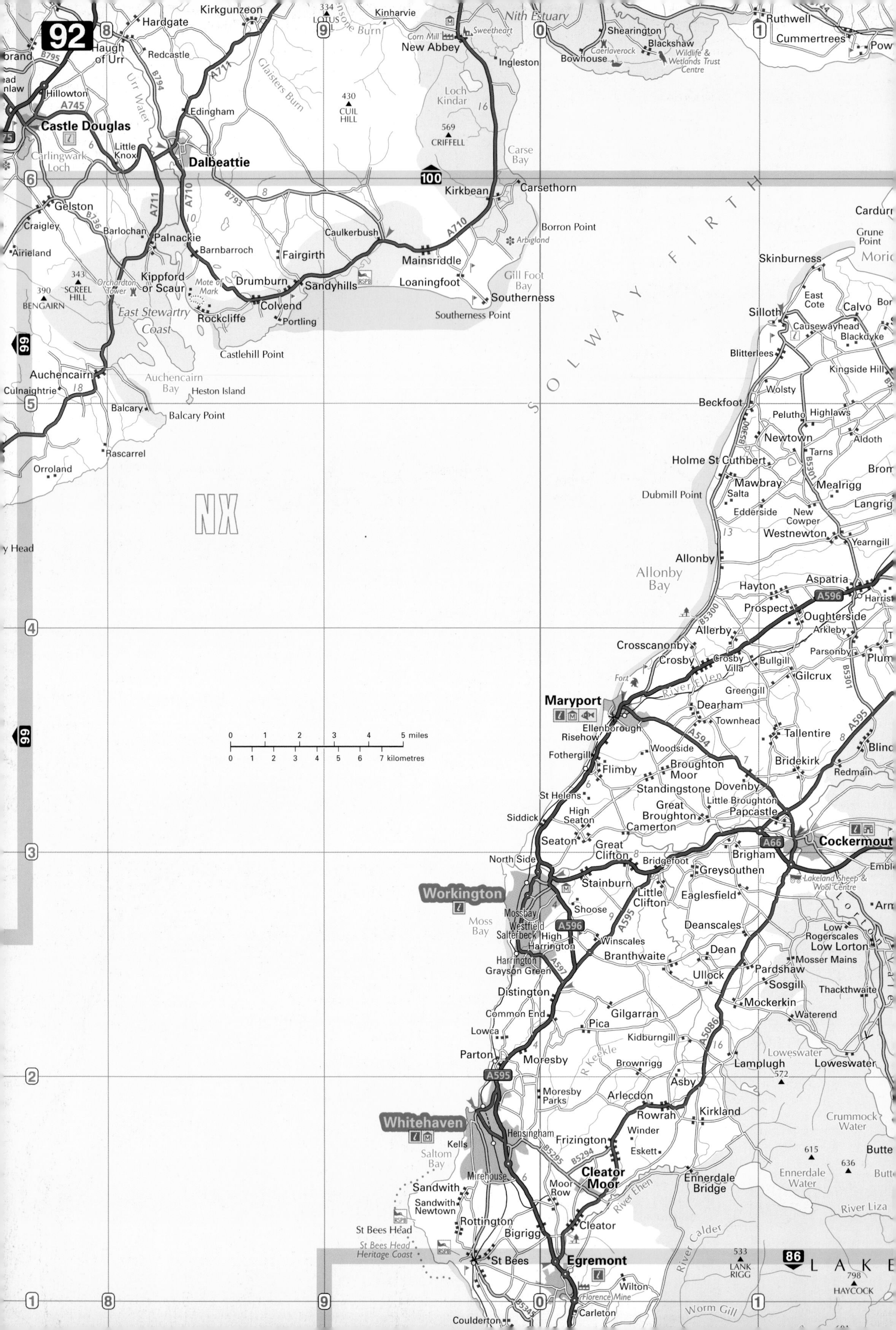

Kirkgunzeon
Hardgate
Haugh of Urr
Redcastle
Urr Water
Hillowton
A745
Castle Douglas
Carlingwark Loch
Little Knox
Edingham
Dalbeattie
Glaisters Burn
334 LOTUS
Kinharvie
New Abbey
Corn Mill
Sweetheart
Nith Estuary
Ingleston
430 CUIL HILL
Loch Kindar
569 CRIFFELL
Carse Bay
Shearington
Caerlaverock
Blackshaw
Wildlife & Wetlands Trust Centre
Bowhouse
Ruthwell
Cummertrees
Kirkbean
Carsethorn
Borron Point
Arbigland
Gelston
Craigley
Airieland
Barlochan
Palnackie
Barnbarroch
A711
A710
B793
B736
B794
B795
343 SCREEL HILL
390 BENGAIRN
Orchardton Tower
Kippford or Scaur
Mote of Mark
Drumburn
Rockcliffe
Colvend
Portling
Sandyhills
Fairgirth
Caulkerbush
Mainsriddle
Loaningfoot
Gill Foot Bay
Southerness
Southerness Point
East Stewartry Coast
Castlehill Point
Auchencairn
Auchencairn Bay
Heston Island
Culnaightrie
Balcary
Balcary Point
Rascarrel
Orroland
NX
SOLWAY FIRTH
Cardurnock
Grune Point
Skinburness
East Cote
Calvo
Silloth
Causewayhead
Blackdyke
Blitterlees
Kingside Hill
Wolsty
Beckfoot
Pelutho
Highlaws
Newtown
Aldoth
Tarns
Holme St Cuthbert
B5300
B5301
Mawbray
Salta
Mealrigg
Dubmill Point
Edderside
New Cowper
Langrigg
Westnewton
Yearngill
Allonby
Allonby Bay
Hayton
Aspatria
A596
Prospect
Oughterside
Allerby
Arkleby
Crosscanonby
Crosby
Crosby Villa
Bullgill
Parsonby
Gilcrux
Fort
River Ellen
Greengill
Maryport
Dearham
Townhead
Ellenborough
Risehow
A594
Tallentire
A595
Woodside
Fothergill
Flimby
Broughton Moor
Bridekirk
Redmain
Standingstone
Dovenby
St Helens
Little Broughton
Siddick
High Seaton
Great Broughton
Papcastle
Camerton
Seaton
Great Clifton
Bridgefoot
A66
Brigham
Cockermouth
North Side
Greysouthen
Stainburn
Lakeland Sheep & Wool Centre
Workington
Little Clifton
Eaglesfield
Shoose
Mossbay
Moss Bay
Westfield
Salterbeck
High Harrington
Harrington
Grayson Green
A597
Winscales
Branthwaite
Deanscales
Dean
Ullock
Low Rogerscales
Low Lorton
Mosser Mains
Pardshaw
Sosgill
Thackthwaite
Distington
Mockerkin
Waterend
Common End
Gilgarran
Pica
Lowca
Kidburngill
A5086
Parton
Moresby
R Keekle
Brownrigg
Lamplugh
572
Loweswater
A595
Asby
Moresby Parks
Arlecdon
Rowrah
Kirkland
Whitehaven
Crummock Water
Hensingham
Frizington
Winder
Kells
Saltom Bay
B5295
B5294
Eskett
615
636
Cleator Moor
Mirehouse
Moor Row
River Ehen
Ennerdale Bridge
Ennerdale Water
Sandwith
Sandwith Newtown
River Liza
Rottington
Cleator
St Bees Head
Bigrigg
River Calder
St Bees Head Heritage Coast
RSPB
St Bees
Egremont
533 LANK RIGG
LAKE
798 HAYCOCK
Wilton
Florence Mine
Worm Gill
Carleton
B5345
Coulderton
0 1 2 3 4 5 miles
0 1 2 3 4 5 6 7 kilometres
100
99
86

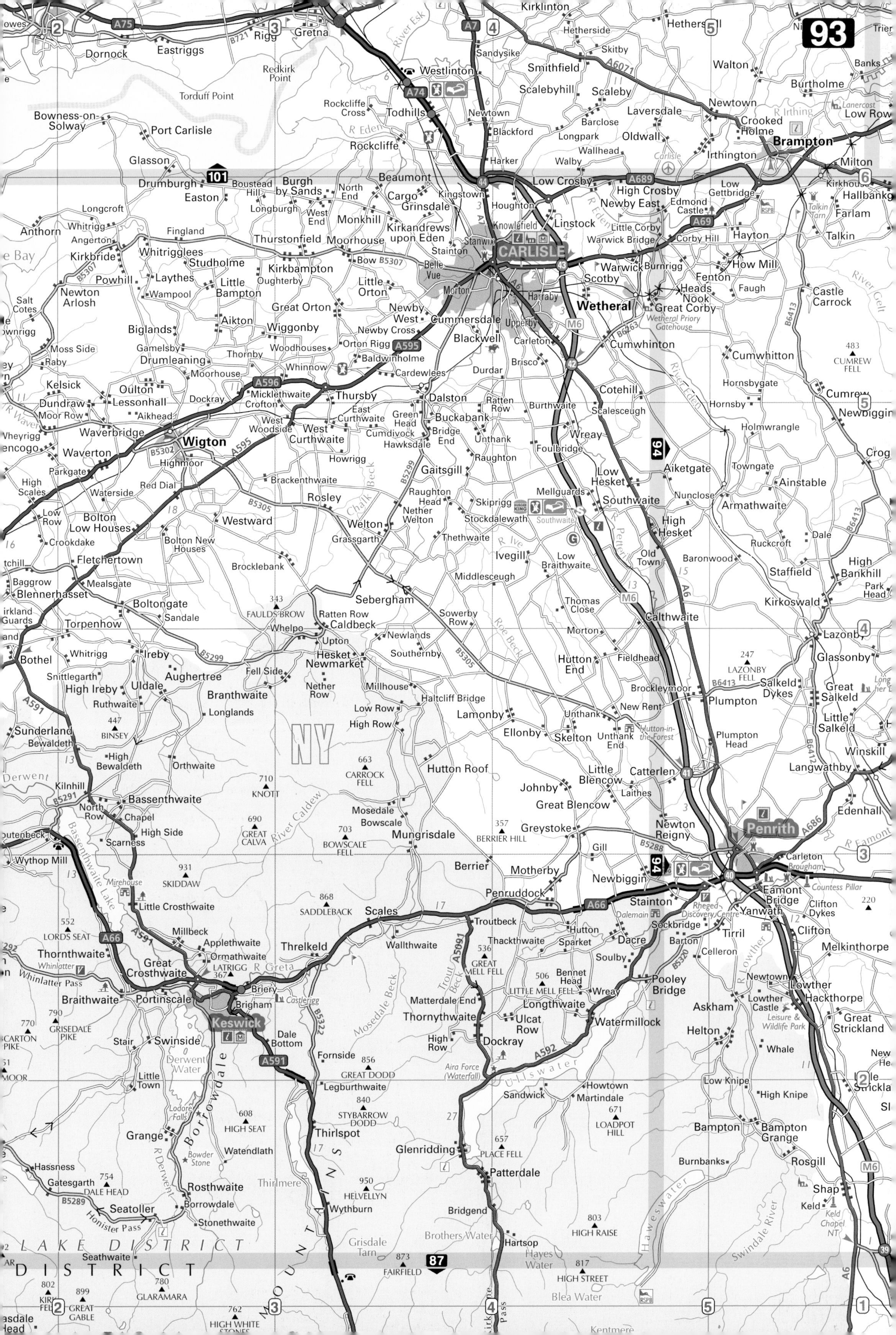
Dornock
Eastriggs
Rigg
Gretna
Redkirk Point
Torduff Point
Bowness-on-Solway
Port Carlisle
Glasson
Drumburgh
Boustead Hill
Easton
Burgh by Sands
Longburgh
North End
West End
Beaumont
Cargo
Grinsdale
Kingstown
Monkhill
Kirkandrews upon Eden
Rockcliffe Cross
Rockcliffe
R Eden
Todhills
Westlinton
River Esk
Kirklinton
Hetherside
Sandysike
Smithfield
Skitby
Scalebyhill
Scaleby
Newtown
Blackford
Harker
Laversdale
Barclose
Longpark
Oldwall
Wallhead
Walby
Hethersgill
Walton
Banks
Burtholme
Newtown
R Irthing
Lanercost
Crooked Holme
Low Row
Brampton
Irthington
Carlisle
Milton
Kirkhouse
Hallbankgate
Farlam
Talkin Tarn
Talkin
Low Gelt Bridge
Edmond Castle
Newby East
High Crosby
Low Crosby
Houghton
Knowlefield
Linstock
Little Corby
Warwick Bridge
Corby Hill
Hayton
How Mill
Fenton
Faugh
Heads Nook
Castle Carrock
River Gelt
Great Corby
Wetheral Priory Gatehouse
Wetheral
Scotby
Warwick
Burnrigg
Stanwix
Stainton
CARLISLE
Belle Vue
Morton
Harraby
Upperby
Carleton
Cummersdale
Newby West
Newby Cross
Blackwell
Longcroft
Anthorn
Whitrigg
Angerton
Fingland
Kirkbride
Whitrigglees
Studholme
Thurstonfield
Moorhouse
Bow
Kirkbampton
Oughterby
Little Orton
Powhill
Laythes
Wampool
Little Bampton
Newton Arlosh
Salt Cotes
Great Orton
Aikton
Biglands
Wiggonby
Orton Rigg
Baldwinholme
Gamelsby
Woodhouses
Thornby
Drumleaning
Moss Side
Raby
Whinnow
Moorhouse
Cardewlees
Kelsick
Oulton
Lessonhall
Dockray
Micklethwaite
Crofton
Thursby
Dundraw
Moor Row
Aikhead
East Curthwaite
West Woodside
West Curthwaite
Waverbridge
Wigton
Highmoor
Waverton
Parkgate
High Scales
Waterside
Red Dial
Low Row
Bolton Low Houses
Crookdake
Westward
Bolton New Houses
Brackenthwaite
Rosley
Howrigg
Chalk Beck
Cumdivock
Green Head
Hawksdale
Dalston
Buckabank
Bridge End
Gaitsgill
Durdar
Brisco
Ratten Row
Unthank
Raughton
Burthwaite
Foulbridge
Wreay
Cumwhinton
Cotehill
Scalesceugh
Cumwhitton
Cumrew Fell
Hornsbygate
Hornsby
Cumrew
Newbiggin
Holmwrangle
River Eden
Aiketgate
Towngate
Crog
Ainstable
Low Hesket
Nunclose
Armathwaite
Southwaite
Mellguards
Skiprigg
Stockdalewath
Raughton Head
Nether Welton
Welton
Grassgarth
Thethwaite
R Ive
Ivegill
Low Braithwaite
High Hesket
Old Town
Baronwood
Ruckcroft
Dale
High Bankhill
Park Head
Staffield
Kirkoswald
Fletchertown
Baggrow
Mealsgate
Blennerhasset
Brocklebank
Middlesceugh
Sebergham
Boltongate
Sandale
Faulds Brow
Ratten Row
Caldbeck
Whelpo
Sowerby Row
Roe Beck
Thomas Close
Calthwaite
Torpenhow
Bothel
Whitrigg
Ireby
Upton
Newlands
Hesket Newmarket
Southernby
Morton
Hutton End
Fieldhead
Lazonby
Glassonby
Lazonby Fell
Salkeld Dykes
Great Salkeld
Brockleymoor
Plumpton
Snittlegarth
High Ireby
Uldale
Aughertree
Fell Side
Nether Row
Millhouse
Haltcliff Bridge
Branthwaite
Ruthwaite
Longlands
Low Row
High Row
Lamonby
Unthank
New Rent
Hutton-in-the-Forest
Ellonby
Skelton
Unthank End
Plumpton Head
Little Salkeld
Winskill
Langwathby
Sunderland
Bewaldeth
Binsey
High Bewaldeth
Orthwaite
NY
Carrock Fell
Hutton Roof
Little Blencow
Catterlen
Johnby
Laithes
Great Blencow
Edenhall
Derwent
Kilnhill
Bassenthwaite
North Row
Chapel
High Side
Knott
Great Calva
River Caldew
Mosedale
Bowscale
Bowscale Fell
Mungrisdale
Berrier Hill
Greystoke
Newton Reigny
Penrith
Scarness
Wythop Mill
Bassenthwaite Lake
Skiddaw
Mirehouse
Berrier
Motherby
Gill
Newbiggin
Carleton
Brougham
Countess Pillar
Eamont Bridge
Penruddock
Stainton
Dalemain
Rheged Discovery Centre
Yanwath
Clifton Dykes
Little Crosthwaite
Saddleback
Scales
Troutbeck
Hutton
Sockbridge
Tirril
Clifton
Lords Seat
Millbeck
Applethwaite
Ormathwaite
Thornthwaite
Whinlatter
Whinlatter Pass
Threlkeld
Wallthwaite
Thackthwaite
Great Mell Fell
Sparket
Dacre
Barton
Soulby
Celleron
Melkinthorpe
Great Crosthwaite
Latrigg
R Greta
Briery
Brigham
Castlerigg
Little Mell Fell
Bennet Head
Wreay
Pooley Bridge
Newtown
R Lowther
Lowther
Hackthorpe
Lowther Castle
Leisure & Wildlife Park
Great Strickland
Braithwaite
Portinscale
Keswick
Mosedale Beck
Matterdale End
Trout Beck
Thornythwaite
Longthwaite
Ulcat Row
Watermillock
Askham
Helton
Grisedale Pike
Stair
Swinside
Dale Bottom
High Row
Dockray
Whale
Causey Pike
Derwent Water
Fornside
Great Dodd
Aira Force (Waterfall)
Ullswater
Low Knipe
High Knipe
Little Town
Borrowdale
Legburthwaite
Howtown
Sandwick
Martindale
Lodore Falls
High Seat
Stybarrow Dodd
Loadpot Hill
Bampton
Bampton Grange
Grange
R Derwent
Bowder Stone
Watendlath
Thirlspot
Glenridding
Place Fell
Hassness
Gatesgarth
Dale Head
Rosthwaite
Thirlmere
Patterdale
Burnbanks
Rosgill
Shap
Keld
Keld Chapel NT
Seatoller
Honister Pass
Borrowdale
Stonethwaite
Helvellyn
Wythburn
Bridgend
Haweswater
Swindale River
High Raise
Lake District
Brothers Water
Hartsop
Grisdale Tarn
Seathwaite
Fairfield
Hayes Water
High Street
Mountains
Kirk Pass
Glaramara
Great Gable
Blea Water
High White Stones
Kentmere

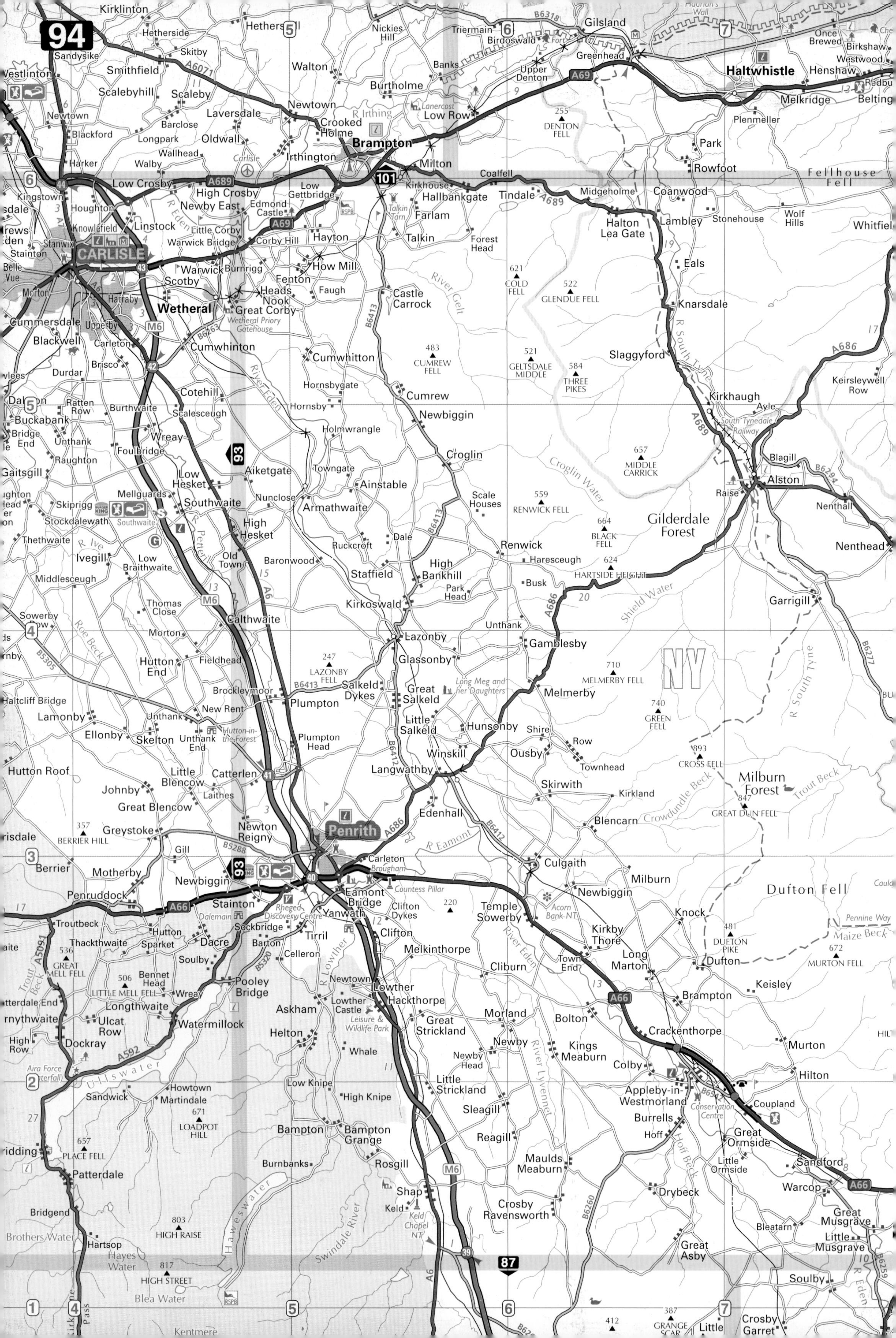
94
Kirklinton
Hetherside
Hethersgill
Nickies Hill
Triermain
Birdoswald
Gilsland
Hadrian's Wall
Greenhead
Once Brewed
Birkshaw
Westwood
Haltwhistle
Henshaw
Redburn
Melkridge
Belting
Sandysike
Skitby
Westlinton
Smithfield
Walton
Banks
Upper Denton
Burtholme
Scalebyhill
Scaleby
Newtown
Lanercost
Low Row
255
DENTON FELL
Plenmeller
Laversdale
Crooked Holme
R Irthing
Barclose
Blackford
Longpark
Oldwall
Brampton
Park
Wallhead
Irthington
Milton
Rowfoot
Harker
Walby
Carlisle
Coalfell
Fellhouse Fell
Low Crosby
A689
A6071
A69
101
Kingstown
High Crosby
Low Gettbridge
Kirkhouse
Hallbankgate
Tindale
Midgeholme
Coanwood
Houghton
Newby East
Edmond Castle
Talkin Tarn
Farlam
Halton Lea Gate
Lambley
Stonehouse
Wolf Hills
Whitfield
Knowlefield
Linstock
Little Corby
Stanwix
Warwick Bridge
Corby Hill
Hayton
Talkin
Forest Head
Stainton
CARLISLE
Warwick
Burnrigg
How Mill
Eals
Belle Vue
Scotby
Fenton
621
COLD FELL
522
GLENDUE FELL
Morton
Harraby
Heads Nook
Faugh
Castle Carrock
River Gelt
Wetheral
Great Corby
Knarsdale
Wetheral Priory Gatehouse
Cummersdale
Upperby
M6
Carleton
Cumwhinton
Blackwell
Cumwhitton
483
CUMREW FELL
521
GELTSDALE MIDDLE
584
THREE PIKES
Slaggyford
R South Tyne
A686
Keirsleywell Row
Brisco
Durdar
Hornsbygate
Cotehill
Cumrew
Kirkhaugh
Ayle
Dalston
Ratten Row
Hornsby
Burthwaite
Scalesceugh
Newbiggin
South Tynedale Railway
Buckabank
Bridge End
Unthank
Wreay
Holmwrangle
River Eden
Foulbridge
93
Croglin
Raughton
Blagill
Gaitsgill
Low Hesket
Aiketgate
Towngate
657
MIDDLE CARRICK
Alston
Mellguards
Ainstable
Croglin Water
Raise
Skiprigg
Southwaite
Nunclose
Scale Houses
559
RENWICK FELL
Nenthall
Stockdalewath
Armathwaite
High Hesket
Gilderdale Forest
664
BLACK FELL
Thethwaite
R Ive
Ruckcroft
Dale
Renwick
Haresceugh
Nenthead
Ivegill
Low Braithwaite
Old Town
Baronwood
High Bankhill
624
HARTSIDE HEIGHT
Middlesceugh
Staffield
Busk
Shield Water
Park Head
Garrigill
Thomas Close
Kirkoswald
Sowerby Row
Calthwaite
Unthank
Morton
Lazonby
Gamblesby
Roe Beck
247
LAZONBY FELL
Glassonby
710
MELMERBY FELL
NY
Hutton End
Fieldhead
B5305
B6413
B6412
B6277
Salkeld Dykes
Long Meg and her Daughters
Great Salkeld
Melmerby
Brockleymoor
Haltcliff Bridge
Plumpton
740
GREEN FELL
R South Tyne
Lamonby
Unthank
New Rent
Little Salkeld
Hunsonby
Ellonby
Skelton
Unthank End
Hutton-in-the-Forest
Plumpton Head
Shire
Row
893
CROSS FELL
Winskill
Ousby
Townhead
Milburn Forest
Hutton Roof
Little Blencow
Catterlen
Langwathby
Skirwith
Crowdundle Beck
Trout Beck
Johnby
Laithes
Kirkland
847
GREAT DUN FELL
Great Blencow
Edenhall
Blencarn
357
BERRIER HILL
Greystoke
Newton Reigny
Penrith
R Eamont
Berrier
Gill
B5288
Carleton
Culgaith
Motherby
Newbiggin
Brougham
Milburn
Dufton Fell
Penruddock
Stainton
Eamont Bridge
Countess Pillar
220
Newbiggin
A66
Dalemain
Rheged Discovery Centre
Yanwath
Clifton Dykes
Temple Sowerby
Acorn Bank NT
Knock
Pennine Way
Troutbeck
Hutton
Sockbridge
Tirril
Clifton
Kirkby Thore
481
DUFTON PIKE
Maize Beck
Thackthwaite
Sparket
Dacre
Barton
Celleron
Melkinthorpe
River Eden
Long Marton
672
MURTON FELL
536
GREAT MELL FELL
Soulby
B5320
R Lowther
Cliburn
Town End
Dufton
Trout Beck
A5091
506
LITTLE MELL FELL
Bennet Head
Wreay
Pooley Bridge
Newtown
Lowther
Keisley
Matterdale End
Longthwaite
Hackthorpe
Askham
Lowther Castle
Leisure & Wildlife Park
Morland
Bolton
Brampton
Ulcat Row
Watermillock
Great Strickland
Crackenthorpe
High Row
Dockray
Helton
Newby
Kings Meaburn
Murton
Aira Force
A592
Ullswater
Whale
Newby Head
River Lyvennet
Colby
Hilton
Howtown
Low Knipe
Little Strickland
Appleby-in-Westmorland
Sandwick
Martindale
High Knipe
Conservation Centre
Coupland
671
LOADPOT HILL
Sleagill
Burrells
Bampton
Bampton Grange
Reagill
Hoff
Hoff Beck
Great Ormside
657
PLACE FELL
Glenridding
Burnbanks
Rosgill
Maulds Meaburn
Little Ormside
Sandford
Patterdale
B6260
M6
Shap
Crosby Ravensworth
Drybeck
Warcop
Haweswater
Swindale River
Keld
Keld Chapel NT
Bridgend
803
HIGH RAISE
Great Musgrave
Brothers Water
Hartsop
Hayes Water
Bleatarn
Little Musgrave
Great Asby
39
87
817
HIGH STREET
A6
Soulby
R Eden
B6259
Blea Water
Kirkstone Pass
387
GRANGE SCAR
412
Little
Crosby Garrett
Kentmere
1
2
3
4
5
6
7

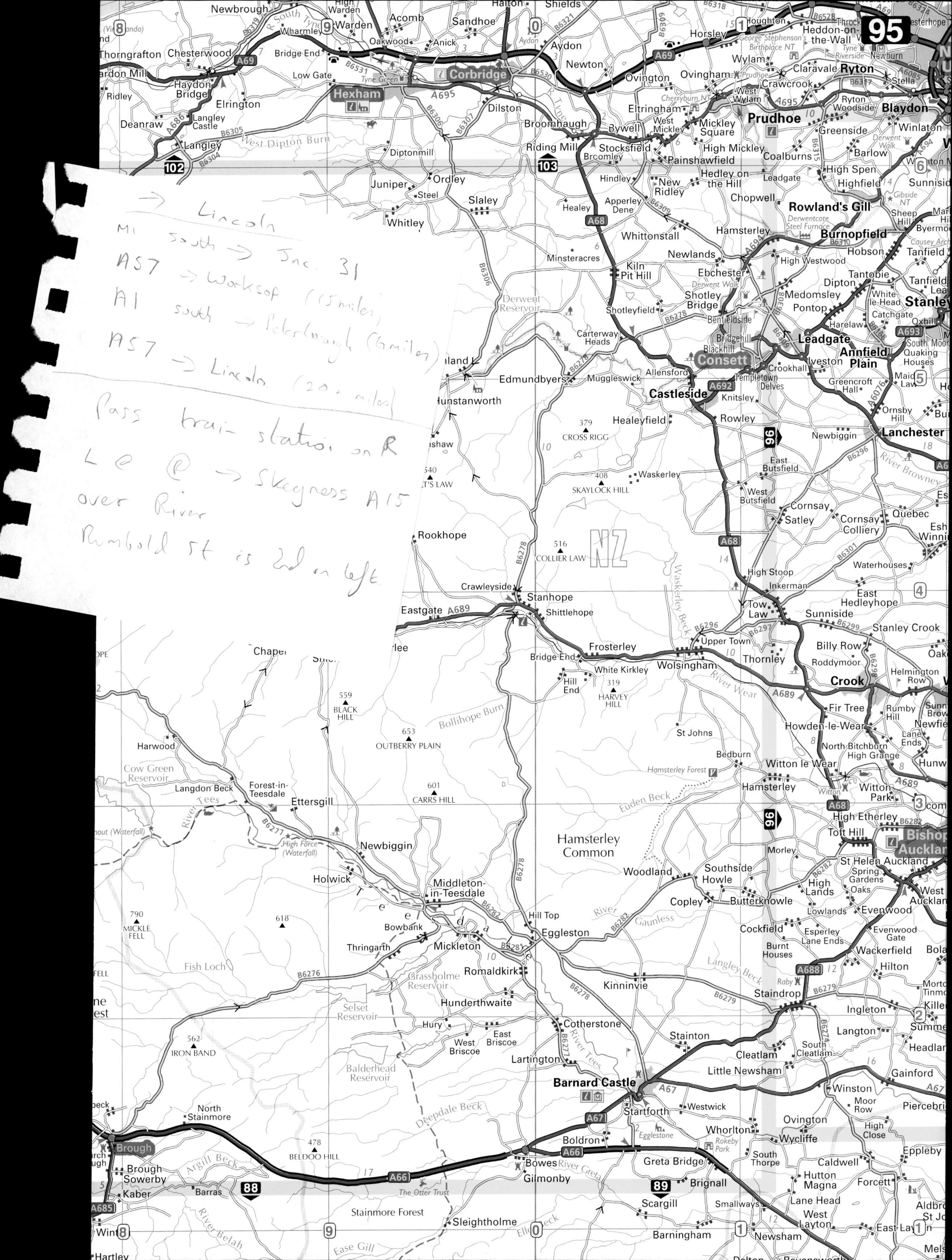

Handwritten note:

→ Lincoln

M1 south → Jnc. 31

A57 → Worksop (15 miles)

A1 south → Peterborough (6 miles)

A57 → Lincoln (20 miles)

Pass train station on R

L @ ℗ → Skegness A15

over River

Rumbold St is 2nd on left

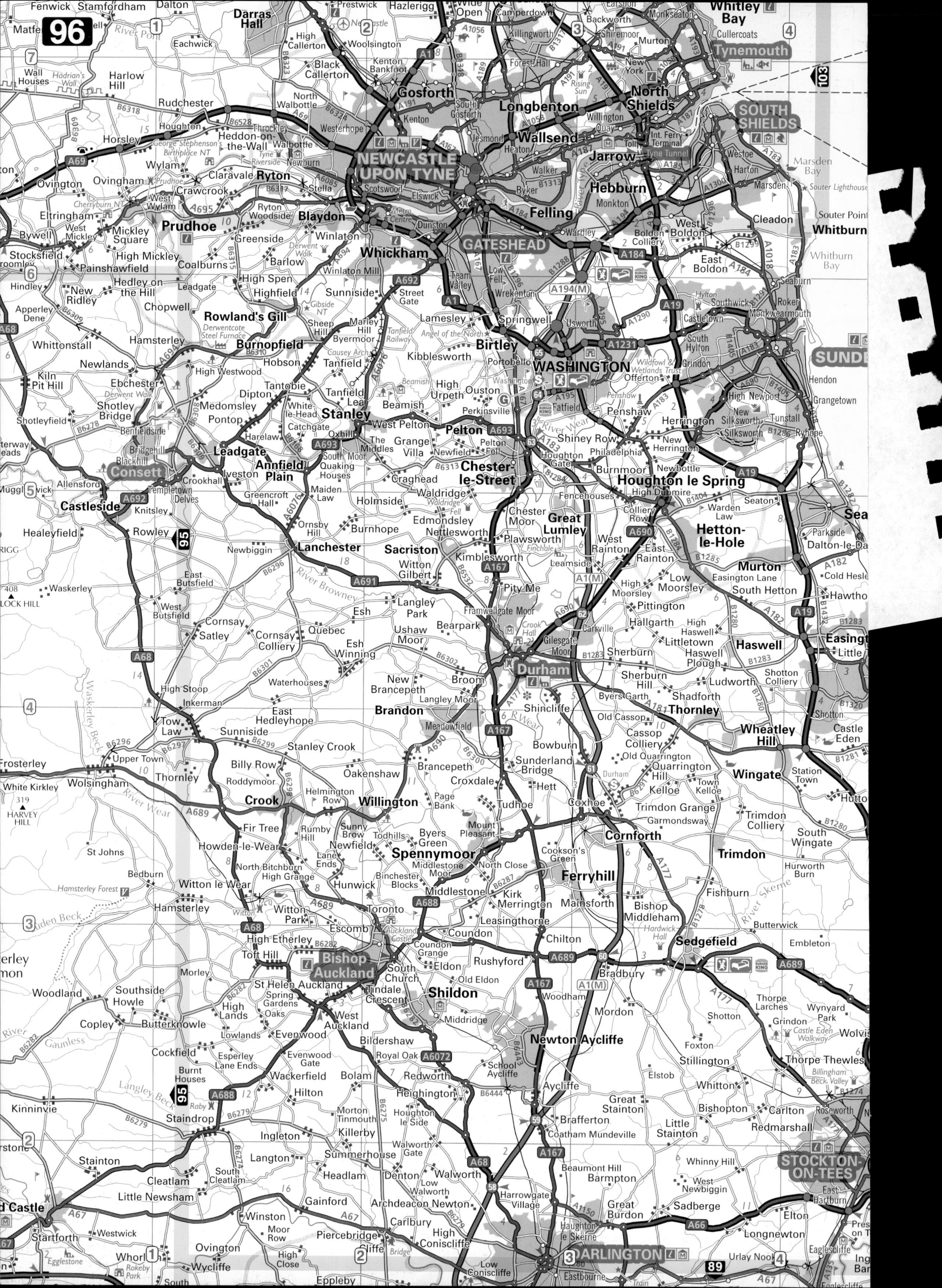

96
Fenwick
Stamfordham
Dalton
Darras Hall
Prestwick
Hazlerigg
Wide Open
Camperdown
Backworth
Monkseaton
Whitley Bay
Cullercoats
Tynemouth
103
Matfen
Eachwick
High Callerton
Woolsington
Black Callerton
Kenton Bankfoot
Killingworth
Forest Hall
Shiremoor
Murton
New York
North Shields
Wall
Houses
Hadrian's Wall
Harlow Hill
North Walbottle
Gosforth
South Gosforth
Kenton
Longbenton
Willington Quay
Rudchester
Houghton
Throckley
Westerhope
Jesmond
Wallsend
South Shields
Horsley
Heddon-on-the-Wall
Walbottle
George Stephenson's Birthplace NT
Newburn
Newcastle upon Tyne
Heaton
Jarrow
Tyne Tunnel
Westoe
Harton
Marsden Bay
A69
Wylam
Ovington
Ovingham
Claravale
Ryton
Stella
Crawcrook
Scotswood
Elswick
Walker
Byker
Hebburn
Marsden
Souter Lighthouse
Eltringham
Cherryburn NT
West Wylam
Prudhoe
Ryton Woodside
Blaydon
Metro Centre
Dunston
Felling
Monkton
Cleadon
Souter Point
Whitburn
Bywell
West Mickley
Mickley Square
Greenside
Winlaton
Whickham
Gateshead
Wardley
Boldon Colliery
West Boldon
Stocksfield
High Mickley
Coalburns
Barlow
Derwent Walk
Winlaton Mill
Low Fell
Team Valley
East Boldon
Whitburn Bay
Hindley
Painshawfield
Hedley on the Hill
Leadgate
High Spen
Highfield
Sunniside
Street Gate
A692
Wrekenton
A194(M)
Seaburn
Apperley Dene
New Ridley
Chopwell
Rowland's Gill
Gibside NT
A1
Lamesley
Springwell
Usworth
A19
Southwick
Roker
Monkwearmouth
Castletown
Derwentcote Steel Furnace
Sheep Hill
Marley Hill
Byermoor
Tanfield Railway
Angel of the North
Birtley
South Hylton
A1231
Hamsterley
Whittonstall
Burnopfield
Causey Arch
Tanfield
Kibblesworth
Portobello
Washington
Wildfowl & Wetlands Trust
Grindon
Sunderland
Newlands
Kiln Pit Hill
Hobson
High Westwood
Ebchester
Derwent Walk
Tantobie
Beamish
High Urpeth
Ouston
Offerton
Hendon
Shotley Bridge
Medomsley
Dipton
Tanfield Lea
Perkinsville
Fatfield
Penshaw
High Newport
Grangetown
Shotleyfield
Pontop
White-le-Head
Stanley
Catchgate
West Pelton
Pelton
A693
New Silksworth
Tunstall
Silksworth
Ryhope
Benfieldside
Harelaw
Oxhill
The Middles
Grange Villa
Pelton Fell
Shiney Row
Herrington
New Herrington
Philadelphia
Blackhill
Bridgehill
Leadgate
South Moor
Newfield
Houghton Gate
Consett
Annfield Plain
Quaking Houses
Chester-le-Street
Burnmoor
Newbottle
Houghton le Spring
Allensford
Iveston
Crookhall
Templetown
Delves
Greencroft Hall
Maiden Law
Craghead
Waldridge
Fencehouses
High Dubmire
Seaton
Castleside
A692
Knitsley
Holmside
Edmondsley
Chester Moor
Great Lumley
Colliery Row
Warden Law
Seaham
Healeyfield
Rowley
95
Ornsby Hill
Burnhope
Nettlesworth
West Rainton
Hetton-le-Hole
Parkside
Dalton-le-Dale
Newbiggin
Lanchester
Sacriston
Plawsworth
Finchale
East Rainton
Kimblesworth
A167
Leamside
Murton
Easington Lane
A182
Cold Hesledon
East Butsfield
Witton Gilbert
A1(M)
Waskerley
Lock Hill
A691
River Browney
Pity Me
High Moorsley
Low Moorsley
South Hetton
Hawthorn
West Butsfield
Esh
Langley Park
Framwellgate Moor
Pittington
Cornsay
Satley
Cornsay Colliery
Quebec
Ushaw Moor
Bearpark
Carrville
Hallgarth
High Haswell
Littletown
Haswell
Easington
Little
A68
Esh Winning
Gilesgate Moor
Sherburn
Haswell Plough
Durham
Sherburn Hill
Shotton Colliery
Waterhouses
New Brancepeth
Broom
Ludworth
High Stoop
Inkerman
Langley Moor
Byers Garth
Shadforth
Brandon
Shincliffe
Thornley
Tow Law
East Hedleyhope
Old Cassop
Shotton
Waskerley Beck
Sunniside
Meadowfield
Cassop Colliery
Wheatley Hill
Castle Eden
Frosterley
Upper Town
Stanley Crook
Bowburn
Old Quarrington
Billy Row
Oakenshaw
Brancepeth
Sunderland Bridge
Quarrington Hill
Wingate
Station Town
White Kirkley
Wolsingham
Thornley
Roddymoor
Croxdale
Hett
Town Kelloe
Kelloe
Hutton
Harvey Hill
River Wear
Crook
Helmington Row
Willington
Page Bank
Tudhoe
Coxhoe
Trimdon Grange
Trimdon Colliery
A689
Fir Tree
Rumby Hill
Sunny Brow
Todhills
Byers Green
Mount Pleasant
Garmondsway
Cornforth
South Wingate
Howden-le-Wear
Newfield
Spennymoor
Cookson's Green
St Johns
Lane Ends
North Close
Middlestone Moor
Trimdon
Ferryhill
Hurworth Burn
Bedburn
North Bitchburn
High Grange
Binchester Blocks
Hamsterley Forest
Witton le Wear
Hunwick
Middlestone
Kirk Merrington
Fishburn
Hamsterley
Witton Park
Toronto
Mainsforth
Bishop Middleham
Escomb
Auckland Castle
Leasingthorne
Hardwick Hall
Butterwick
High Etherley
Coundon
Coundon Grange
Chilton
Sedgefield
Embleton
Toft Hill
Bishop Auckland
Rushyford
Eldon
South Church
Old Eldon
Bradbury
Morley
St Helen Auckland
Woodland
Southside
Howle
Spring Gardens
Oaks
Tindale Crescent
Shildon
Woodham
Thorpe Larches
Wynyard Park
Mordon
High Lands
West Auckland
Middridge
Shotton
Grindon
Castle Eden Walkway
Copley
Butterknowle
Lowlands
Evenwood
Bildershaw
Newton Aycliffe
Foxton
Wolviston
Cockfield
Esperley Lane Ends
Evenwood Gate
Royal Oak
A6072
School Aycliffe
Stillington
Thorpe Thewles
Burnt Houses
Wackerfield
Bolam
Redworth
Elstob
Billingham Beck Valley
Hilton
Heighington
Aycliffe
Whitton
Langley Beck
Raby
A688
Great Stainton
Bishopton
Carlton
Roseworth
Kinninvie
Staindrop
Morton Tinmouth
Houghton le Side
Brafferton
Little Stainton
Redmarshall
Ingleton
Killerby
Coatham Mundeville
Walworth Gate
Stockton-on-Tees
Stainton
Langton
Summerhouse
Whinny Hill
Headlam
Denton
Walworth
Beaumont Hill
Barmpton
South Cleatlam
Cleatlam
Low Walworth
West Newbiggin
Little Newsham
Gainford
Archdeacon Newton
Harrowgate Village
Great Burdon
Sadberge
East Hartburn
Barnard Castle
A67
Winston
Carlbury
Haughton le Skerne
A66
Elton
Startforth
Westwick
Moor Row
Piercebridge
High Coniscliffe
Longnewton
Preston on Tees
Whorlton
Ovington
Cliffe
Bridge
Darlington
Urlay Nook
Egglescliffe
Egglestone
Rokeby Park
Wycliffe
High Close
Low Coniscliffe
Eastbourne
89
South
Eppleby

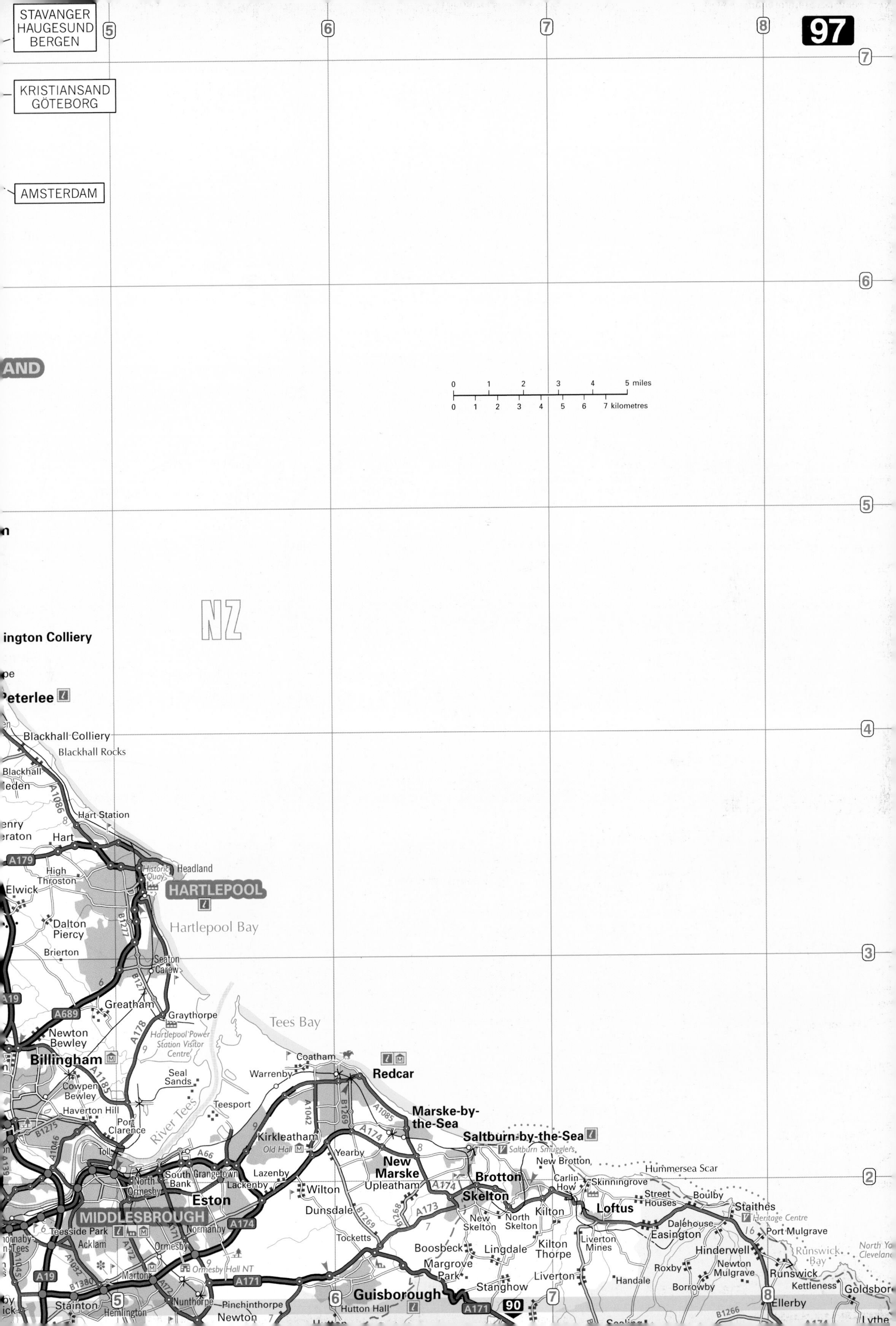
STAVANGER
HAUGESUND
BERGEN
KRISTIANSAND
GÖTEBORG
AMSTERDAM
0 1 2 3 4 5 miles
0 1 2 3 4 5 6 7 kilometres
NZ
Peterlee
Blackhall Colliery
Blackhall Rocks
Hart Station
Hart
A179
High Throston
Elwick
Headland
Historic Quay
HARTLEPOOL
Hartlepool Bay
Dalton Piercy
Brierton
Seaton Carew
Greatham
A689
Graythorpe
Hartlepool Power Station Visitor Centre
Tees Bay
Newton Bewley
Billingham
Cowpen Bewley
Seal Sands
Coatham
Redcar
Warrenby
Teesport
Haverton Hill
Port Clarence
River Tees
Marske-by-the-Sea
Saltburn-by-the-Sea
Saltburn Smugglers
Kirkleatham
Old Hall
Yearby
New Marske
Upleatham
Wilton
Dunsdale
Lazenby
Lackenby
South Bank
Grangetown
North Ormesby
Eston
MIDDLESBROUGH
Teesside Park
Acklam
Normanby
Ormesby
Ormesby Hall NT
Marton
Nunthorpe
Pinchinthorpe
Newton
Stainton
Hemlington
Tocketts
Guisborough
Hutton Hall
Boosbeck
Margrove Park
Stanghow
Lingdale
New Skelton
North Skelton
Skelton
Brotton
New Brotton
Carlin How
Skinningrove
Kilton
Kilton Thorpe
Liverton
Liverton Mines
Loftus
Hummersea Scar
Street Houses
Boulby
Dalehouse
Easington
Staithes
Heritage Centre
Port Mulgrave
Hinderwell
Newton Mulgrave
Roxby
Borrowby
Handale
Runswick Bay
Runswick
Kettleness
Goldsborough
Ellerby
Lythe
A174
A171
A173
A172
A19
A66
A1085
A1042
A178
A1185
A1086
B1277
B1269
B1268
B1266
B1380
B1275
90

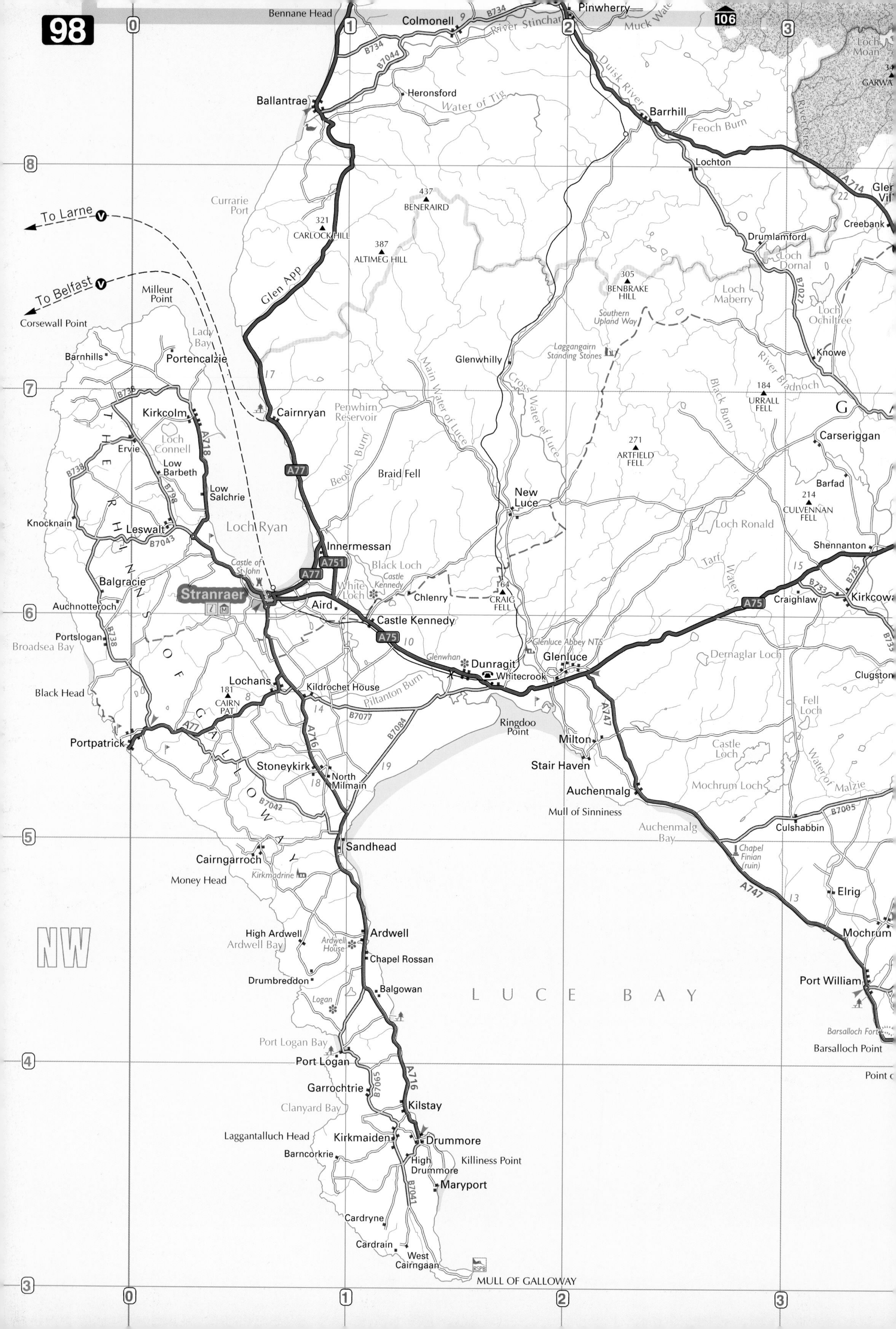

Bennane Head
Colmonell
Pinwherry
River Stinchar
Muck Water
106
Ballantrae
Heronsford
Water of Tig
Barrhill
Feoch Burn
Duisk River
Lochton
Currarie Port
437 BENERAIRD
321 CARLOCK HILL
387 ALTIMEG HILL
To Larne
To Belfast
Corsewall Point
Milleur Point
Glen App
Creebank
Drumlamford
Loch Dornal
305 BENBRAKE HILL
Southern Upland Way
Loch Maberry
Loch Ochiltree
Knowe
Lady Bay
Barnhills
Portencalzie
Glenwhilly
Laggangairn Standing Stones
Main Water of Luce
Cross Water of Luce
River Bladnoch
Black Burn
184 URRALL FELL
Kirkcolm
Cairnryan
Penwhirn Reservoir
Loch Connell
Ervie
Low Barbeth
Low Salchrie
THE RHINNS OF GALLOWAY
Beoch Burn
Braid Fell
271 ARTFIELD FELL
Carseriggan
Barfad
214 CULVENNAN FELL
New Luce
Knocknain
Leswalt
Loch Ryan
Innermessan
Loch Ronald
Shennanton
Balgracie
Castle of St John
Stranraer
Black Loch
Castle Kennedy
White Loch
Chlenry
164 CRAIG FELL
Tarf Water
Craighlaw
Kirkcowan
Auchnotteroch
Aird
Castle Kennedy
Portslogan
Broadsea Bay
Glenwhan
Dunragit
Whitecrook
Glenluce Abbey NTS
Glenluce
Dernaglar Loch
Clugston
Black Head
Lochans
181 CAIRN PAT
Kildrochet House
Piltanton Burn
Fell Loch
Ringdoo Point
Portpatrick
Milton
Castle Loch
Stair Haven
Stoneykirk
North Milmain
Water of Malzie
Mochrum Loch
Auchenmalg
Mull of Sinniness
Auchenmalg Bay
Culshabbin
Sandhead
Cairngarroch
Money Head
Kirkmadrine
Chapel Finian (ruin)
Elrig
Mochrum
High Ardwell
Ardwell Bay
Ardwell
Ardwell House
Chapel Rossan
Drumbreddon
Balgowan
Logan
LUCE BAY
Port William
Barsalloch Fort
Barsalloch Point
Port Logan Bay
Port Logan
Garrochtrie
Kilstay
Clanyard Bay
Laggantalluch Head
Kirkmaiden
Drummore
Barncorkrie
High Drummore
Killiness Point
Maryport
Cardryne
Cardrain
West Cairngaan
RSPB
MULL OF GALLOWAY
NW

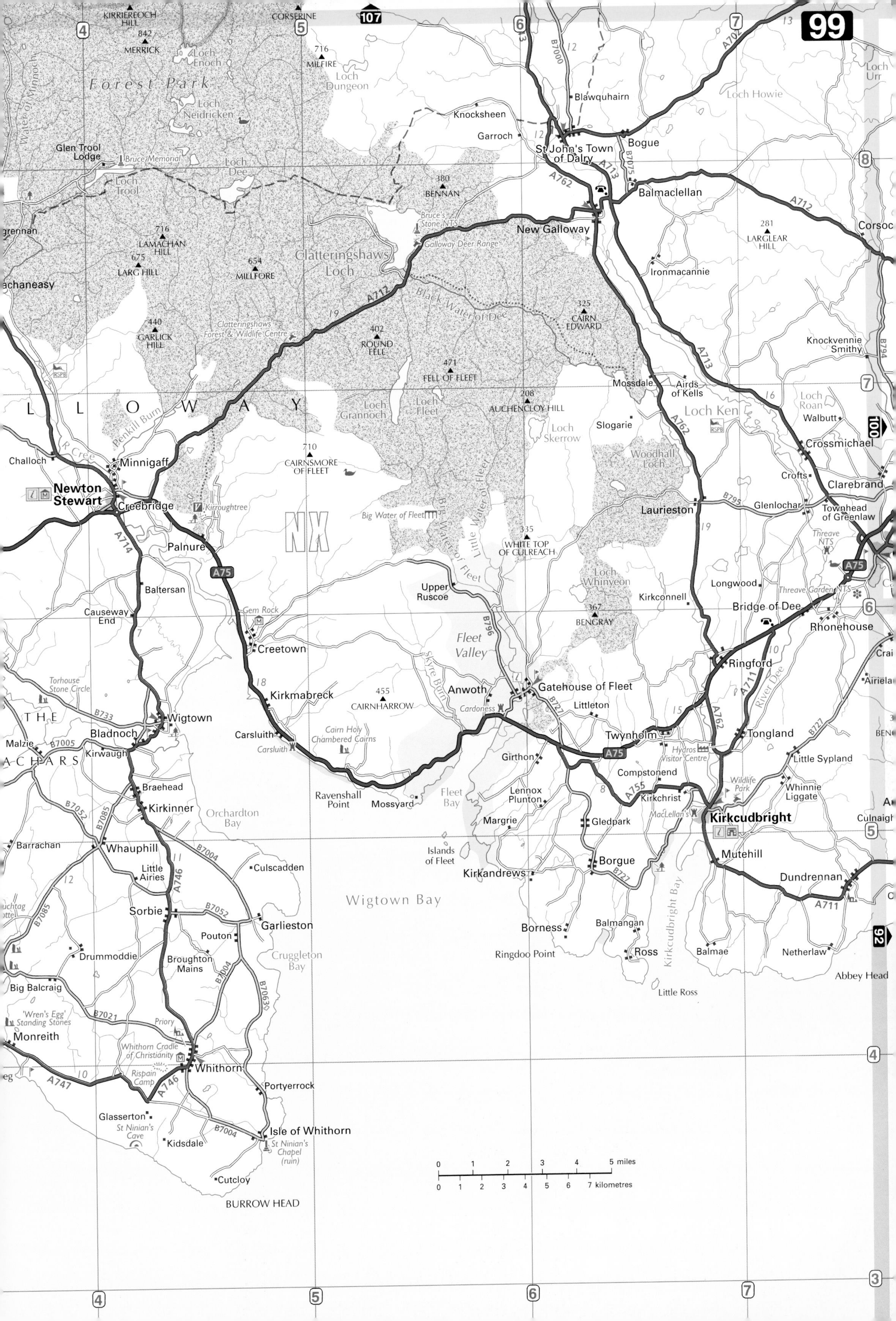
107
100
92
KIRRIEREOCH HILL
CORSERINE
842
MERRICK
Loch Enoch
716
MILFIRE
Loch Dungeon
Forest Park
Loch Neidricken
Water of Minnoch
Glen Trool Lodge
Bruce Memorial
Loch Trool
Loch Dee
380
BENNAN
Bruce's Stone NTS
Galloway Deer Range
Clatteringshaws Loch
716
LAMACHAN HILL
675
LARG HILL
654
MILLFORE
440
GARLICK HILL
Clatteringshaws Forest & Wildlife Centre
Black Water of Dee
402
ROUND FELL
471
FELL OF FLEET
325
CAIRN EDWARD
208
AUCHENCLOY HILL
Loch Grannoch
Loch Fleet
Loch Skerrow
Woodhall Loch
GALLOWAY
Penkill Burn
R Cree
Challoch
Minnigaff
Newton Stewart
Creebridge
Kirroughtree
710
CAIRNSMORE OF FLEET
NX
Big Water of Fleet
Little Water of Fleet
335
WHITE TOP OF CULREACH
Loch Whinyeon
367
BENGRAY
Palnure
Baltersan
Causeway End
Gem Rock
Creetown
Upper Ruscoe
Fleet Valley
Skyre Burn
Torhouse Stone Circle
Kirkmabreck
455
CAIRNHARROW
Anwoth
Cardoness
Gatehouse of Fleet
Littleton
Wigtown
Bladnoch
Malzie
Kirwaugh
MACHARS
Carsluith
Cairn Holy Chambered Cairns
Ravenshall Point
Mossyard
Fleet Bay
Girthon
Twynholm
Braehead
Kirkinner
Orchardton Bay
Lennox Plunton
Margrie
Islands of Fleet
Kirkandrews
Barrachan
Whauphill
Little Airies
Culscadden
Sorbie
Garlieston
Pouton
Wigtown Bay
Cruggleton Bay
Drummoddie
Broughton Mains
Big Balcraig
'Wren's Egg' Standing Stones
Monreith
Priory
Whithorn Cradle of Christianity
Whithorn
Rispain Camp
Portyerrock
Glasserton
St Ninian's Cave
Kidsdale
Isle of Whithorn
St Ninian's Chapel (ruin)
Cutcloy
BURROW HEAD
Blawquhairn
Knocksheen
Garroch
St John's Town of Dalry
Bogue
Balmaclellan
New Galloway
Loch Howie
Loch Urr
281
LARGLEAR HILL
Corsoc
Ironmacannie
Knockvennie Smithy
Mossdale
Airds of Kells
Loch Ken
Slogarie
Loch Roan
Walbutt
Crossmichael
Crofts
Clarebrand
Laurieston
Glenlochar
Townhead of Greenlaw
Threave NTS
Longwood
Threave Garden NTS
Kirkconnell
Bridge of Dee
Rhonehouse
Ringford
River Dee
Tongland
Hydros Visitor Centre
Compstonend
Wildlife Park
Little Sypland
Whinnie Liggate
Kirkchrist
MacLellan's
Kirkcudbright
Culnaigh
Gledpark
Borgue
Mutehill
Dundrennan
Kirkcudbright Bay
Borness
Balmangan
Ringdoo Point
Ross
Balmae
Netherlaw
Abbey Head
Little Ross
A712
A75
A714
A746
A747
A762
A713
A702
A711
A755
B7000
B7075
B794
B795
B796
B727
B733
B7005
B7052
B7085
B7004
B7063
B7021
0 1 2 3 4 5 miles
0 1 2 3 4 5 6 7 kilometres

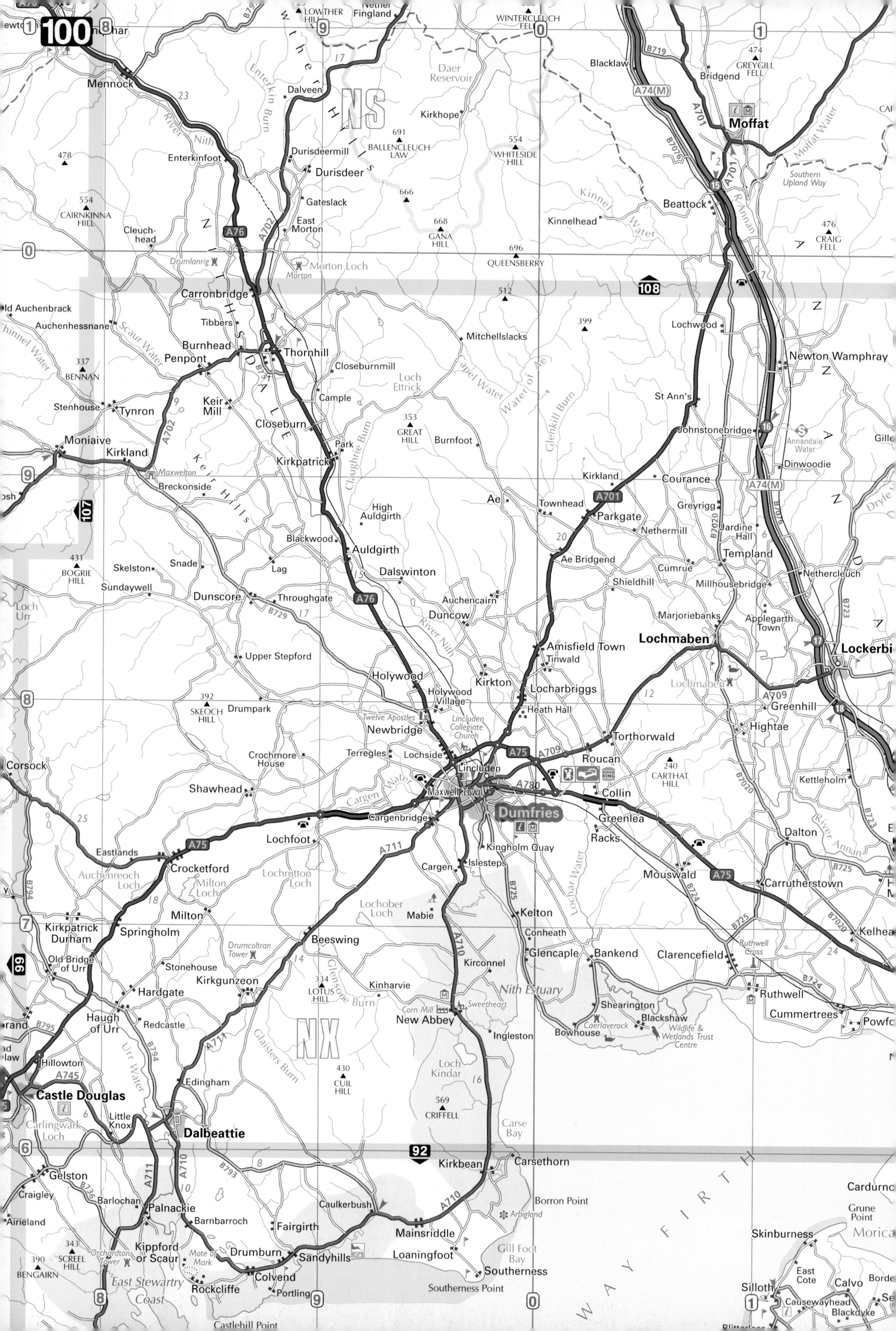
Mennock
Dalveen
Durisdeermill
Durisdeer
Gateslack
East Morton
Enterkinfoot
Cleuch-head
Drumlanrig
Morton Loch
Carronbridge
Tibbers
Thornhill
Closeburnmill
Burnhead
Penpont
Tynron
Stenhouse
Keir Mill
Closeburn
Moniaive
Kirkland
Maxwelton
Breckonside
Kirkpatrick
Park
Cample
Auldgirth
Blackwood
Lag
Dalswinton
Snade
Skelston
Dunscore
Throughgate
Sundaywell
Upper Stepford
Holywood
Holywood Village
Newbridge
Drumpark
Twelve Apostles
Lincluden Collegiate Church
Terregles
Lochside
Lincluden
Maxwell Town
Dumfries
Crochmore House
Shawhead
Cargenbridge
Lochfoot
Corsock
Eastlands
Crocketford
Auchenreoch Loch
Milton Loch
Milton
Lochrutton Loch
Cargen
Islesteps
Kingholm Quay
Lochober Loch
Mabie
Beeswing
Springholm
Kirkpatrick Durham
Old Bridge of Urr
Drumcoltran Tower
Stonehouse
Kirkgunzeon
Hardgate
Haugh of Urr
Redcastle
Kinharvie
Corn Mill
Sweetheart
New Abbey
Hillowton
Castle Douglas
Carlingwalk Loch
Little Knox
Edingham
Dalbeattie
Gelston
Craigley
Barlochan
Palnackie
Barnbarroch
Airieland
Kipplford or Scaur
Orchardton Tower
Mote of Mark
Drumburn
Sandyhills
Colvend
Rockcliffe
Portling
East Stewartry Coast
Castlehill Point
Fairgirth
Caulkerbush
Mainsriddle
Loaningfoot
Southerness
Southerness Point
Gill Foot Bay
Kirkbean
Carsethorn
Arbigland
Borron Point
Carse Bay
Loch Kindar
CRIFFELL
CUIL HILL
LOTUS HILL
Ingleston
Nith Estuary
Kirconnel
Glencaple
Conheath
Kelton
Bankend
Shearington
Blackshaw
Caerlaverock
Bowhouse
Wildlife & Wetlands Trust Centre
Clarencefield
Ruthwell Cross
Ruthwell
Cummertrees
Mouswald
Carrutherstown
Racks
Greenlea
Collin
Roucan
Torthorwald
CARTHAT HILL
Kettleholm
Dalton
Locharbriggs
Heath Hall
Kirkton
Amisfield Town
Tinwald
Duncow
Auchencairn
Lochmaben
Hightae
Greenhill
Lockerbie
Applegarth Town
Marjoriebanks
Millhousebridge
Templand
Shieldhill
Cumrue
Ae Bridgend
Ae
Parkgate
Townhead
Nethermill
Greyrigg
Jardine Hall
Courance
Kirkland
Johnstonebridge
Dinwoodie
Annandale Water
St Ann's
Newton Wamphray
Lochwood
Mitchellslacks
GREAT HILL
Burnfoot
High Auldgirth
Loch Ettrick
QUEENSBERRY
GANA HILL
WHITESIDE HILL
BALLENCLEUCH LAW
Kirkhope
Daer Reservoir
Kinnelhead
Beattock
Moffat
Bridgend
Blacklaw
GREYGILL FELL
CRAIG FELL
Southern Upland Way
CAIRNKINNA HILL
BENNAN
BOGRIE HILL
SKEOCH HILL
Auchenbrack
Auchenhessnane
LOWTHER HILL
Nether Fingland
WINTERCLEUCH FELL
NITHSDALE
ANNANDALE
Keir Hills
Lowther Hills
SOLWAY FIRTH
Skinburness
Silloth
East Cote
Calvo
Causewayhead
Blackdyke
Cardurnock
Grune Point
Kelhead
Powfoot
NS
NX
107
108
99
92
A76
A702
A701
A74(M)
A75
A709
A780
A710
A711
A745
B729
B725
B724
B7020
B7076
B794
B793
B736
B795
B719
B723
B729

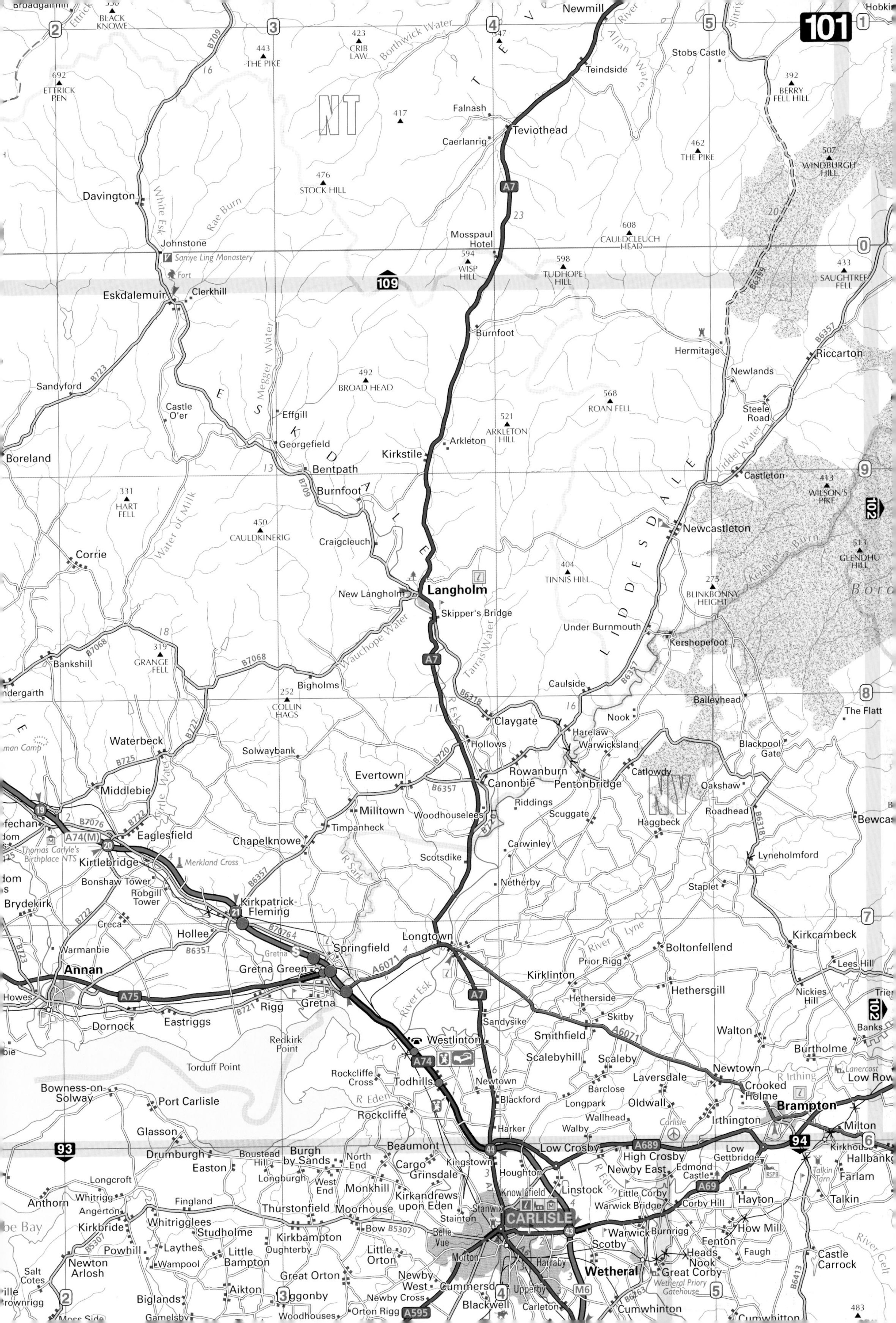

101
Newmill
Teindside
Allan Water
Stobs Castle
Borthwick Water
423 CRIB LAW
443 THE PIKE
692 ETTRICK PEN
BLACK KNOWE
392 BERRY FELL HILL
Falnash
Teviothead
Caerlanrig
417
NT
462 THE PIKE
507 WINDBURGH HILL
476 STOCK HILL
Davington
White Esk
Rae Burn
A7
Mosspaul Hotel
608 CAULDCLEUCH HEAD
Johnstone
Samye Ling Monastery
Fort
594 WISP HILL
598 TUDHOPE HILL
433 SAUGHTREE FELL
109
Eskdalemuir
Clerkhill
B709
B6399
Burnfoot
Hermitage
Riccarton
B6357
Newlands
Sandyford
B723
Megget Water
492 BROAD HEAD
568 ROAN FELL
Castle O'er
Effgill
521 ARKLETON HILL
Steele Road
Georgefield
Arkleton
Liddel Water
Boreland
Kirkstile
Bentpath
Castleton
ESKDALE
413 WILSON'S PIKE
331 HART FELL
Burnfoot
102
Water of Milk
450 CAULDKINERIG
Craigcleuch
Newcastleton
Corrie
LIDDESDALE
513 GLENDHU HILL
Kershope Burn
404 TINNIS HILL
275 BLINKBONNY HEIGHT
New Langholm
Langholm
Skipper's Bridge
Wauchope Water
Under Burnmouth
Kershopefoot
B7068
319 GRANGE FELL
Bankshill
Tarras Water
Bigholms
Caulside
252 COLLIN HAGS
Baileyhead
B6318
Claygate
The Flatt
R Esk
Nook
Harelaw
Waterbeck
Hollows
Warwicksland
Blackpool Gate
B725
Solwaybank
B720
Rowanburn
Catlowdy
Canonbie
Pentonbridge
Oakshaw
Evertown
B6357
NY
Middlebie
Kirtle Water
Milltown
Riddings
Woodhouselees
Roadhead
Scuggate
Bewcastle
Haggbeck
Eaglesfield
Timpanheck
A74(M)
Chapelknowe
Carwinley
Thomas Carlyle's Birthplace NTS
Kirtlebridge
Merkland Cross
Scotsdike
Lyneholmford
R Sark
Bonshaw Tower
Netherby
Staplet
Robgill Tower
B6357
Brydekirk
Kirkpatrick-Fleming
B722
Creca
Hollee
Longtown
Kirkcambeck
River Lyne
B7076
Warmanbie
B6357
Springfield
Boltonfellend
Gretna
Annan
Gretna Green
A6071
Prior Rigg
Lees Hill
Kirklinton
Howes
A75
Hethersgill
Hetherside
Nickies Hill
Rigg
Gretna
River Esk
B721
Eastriggs
Sandysike
Skitby
Dornock
Smithfield
Walton
A6071
Redkirk Point
Westlinton
Banks
Burtholme
Torduff Point
Scalebyhill
Scaleby
A74
Newtown
Lanercost
Rockcliffe Cross
Todhills
Laversdale
R Irthing
Low Row
Newtown
Crooked Holme
Bowness-on-Solway
Barclose
Blackford
R Eden
Port Carlisle
Longpark
Oldwall
Brampton
Rockcliffe
Irthington
Wallhead
Carlisle
Glasson
Harker
Walby
Milton
Beaumont
Low Crosby
A689
94
Kirkhouse
93
Drumburgh
Boustead Hill
Burgh by Sands
North End
Cargo
Kingstown
High Crosby
Low Gettbridge
Hallbank
Easton
Grinsdale
Houghton
Newby East
Edmond Castle
Longburgh
West End
Farlam
Longcroft
Monkhill
Talkin Tarn
Whitrigg
Knowlefield
Linstock
Little Corby
Anthorn
Fingland
Kirkandrews upon Eden
A69
Angerton
Warwick Bridge
Corby Hill
Hayton
Talkin
Thurstonfield
Moorhouse
Stanwix
Whitrigglees
CARLISLE
Stainton
Kirkbride
Studholme
Kirkbampton
Bow
B5307
Belle Vue
Warwick
Burnrigg
How Mill
Fenton
Powhill
Laythes
Oughterby
Little Orton
Morton
Scotby
Heads Nook
Faugh
Castle Carrock
Newton Arlosh
Wampool
Little Bampton
Harraby
Wetheral
Great Corby
Salt Cotes
Great Orton
Newby West
Wetheral Priory Gatehouse
Aikton
Cummersdale
Upperby
M6
B6413
Biglands
Oggonby
Newby Cross
Blackwell
Carleton
Cumwhinton
Cumwhitton
483
Orton Rigg
A595
Woodhouses
Gamelsby
Moss Side

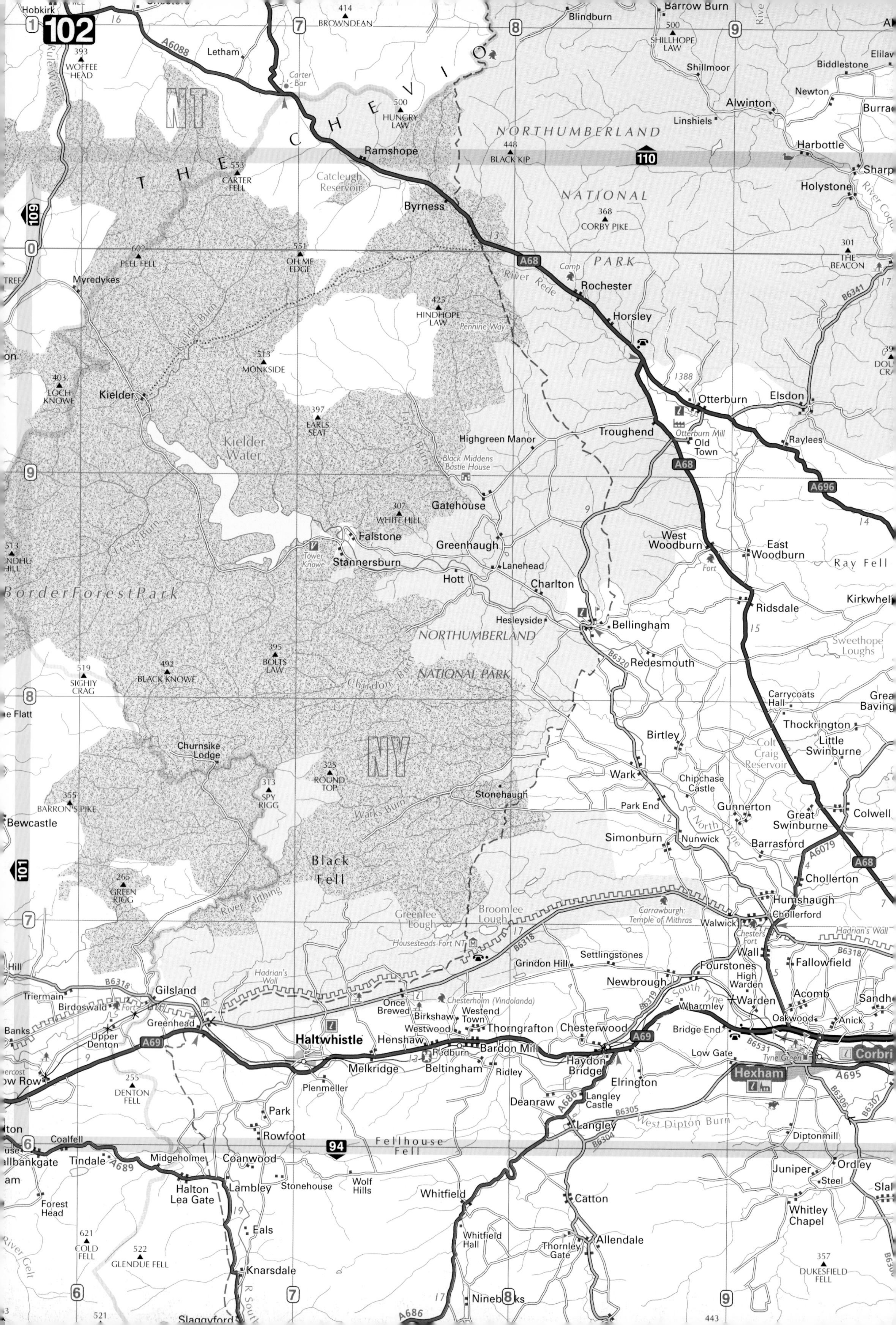
102
Hobkirk
Rule Water
393 WOFFEE HEAD
A6088
Letham
414 BROWNDEAN
Carter Bar
NT
THE CHEVIOT
500 HUNGRY LAW
Ramshope
553 CARTER FELL
Catcleugh Reservoir
Byrness
109
602 PEEL FELL
551 OH ME EDGE
Myredykes
Kielder Burn
425 HINDHOPE LAW
Pennine Way
513 MONKSIDE
403 LOCH KNOWE
Kielder
397 EARLS SEAT
Kielder Water
Tarset Burn
Black Middens Bastle House
Gatehouse
307 WHITE HILL
Falstone
Tower Knowe
Stannersburn
Greenhaugh
Lewis Burn
513 HINDHU HILL
Border Forest Park
Hott
Lanehead
Charlton
Hesleyside
NORTHUMBERLAND
NATIONAL PARK
395 BOLTS LAW
492 BLACK KNOWE
519 SIGHTY CRAG
Chirdon Burn
e Flatt
Churnsike Lodge
NY
325 ROUND TOP
313 SPY RIGG
355 BARRON'S PIKE
Bewcastle
Warks Burn
Stonehaugh
Black Fell
101
265 GREEN RIGG
River Irthing
Greenlee Lough
Broomlee Lough
Housesteads Fort NT
B6318
Hadrian's Wall
Gilsland
Triermain
Birdoswald
Fort
Banks
Upper Denton
Greenhead
A69
Haltwhistle
Once Brewed
Birkshaw
Westwood
Chesterholm (Vindolanda)
Westend Town
Thorngrafton
Henshaw
Redburn
Bardon Mill
Melkridge
Beltingham
Ridley
Plenmeller
255 DENTON FELL
Park
Rowfoot
Coalfell
Tindale
A689
Midgeholme
Coanwood
94
Fellhouse Fell
Halton Lea Gate
Lambley
Stonehouse
Wolf Hills
Forest Head
Eals
621 COLD FELL
522 GLENDUE FELL
River Gelt
Knarsdale
R South Tyne
Slaggyford
521
Blindburn
Barrow Burn
500 SHILLHOPE LAW
Shillmoor
Biddlestone
Elilaw
Newton
Alwinton
Burradon
Linshiels
NORTHUMBERLAND
448 BLACK KIP
110
Harbottle
Sharperton
Holystone
River Coquet
NATIONAL
368 CORBY PIKE
PARK
301 THE BEACON
A68
Camp
Rochester
River Rede
B6341
Horsley
1388
Otterburn
Elsdon
Troughend
Otterburn Mill
Old Town
Highgreen Manor
Raylees
A696
West Woodburn
East Woodburn
Fort
Ray Fell
Ridsdale
Kirkwhelpington
Bellingham
B6320
Redesmouth
Sweethope Loughs
Carrycoats Hall
Great Bavington
Thockrington
Birtley
Colt Crag Reservoir
Little Swinburne
Wark
Chipchase Castle
Park End
Gunnerton
Great Swinburne
Colwell
Simonburn
Nunwick
R North Tyne
Barrasford
A6079
Chollerton
Humshaugh
Carrawburgh: Temple of Mithras
Walwick
Chollerford
Chesters Fort
Hadrian's Wall
Wall
Settlingstones
Grindon Hill
Fourstones
Fallowfield
Newbrough
High Warden
B6319
R South Tyne
Warden
Acomb
Wharmley
Sandhoe
Oakwood
Anick
Chesterwood
Bridge End
Haydon Bridge
Low Gate
B6531
Tyne Green
Corbridge
Hexham
A695
Elrington
Langley Castle
Deanraw
A686
B6305
Langley
West Dipton Burn
B6304
B6306
B6307
Diptonmill
Juniper
Ordley
Steel
Whitfield
Catton
Whitley Chapel
Whitfield Hall
Allendale
Thornley Gate
357 DUKESFIELD FELL
Ninebanks
443
A686

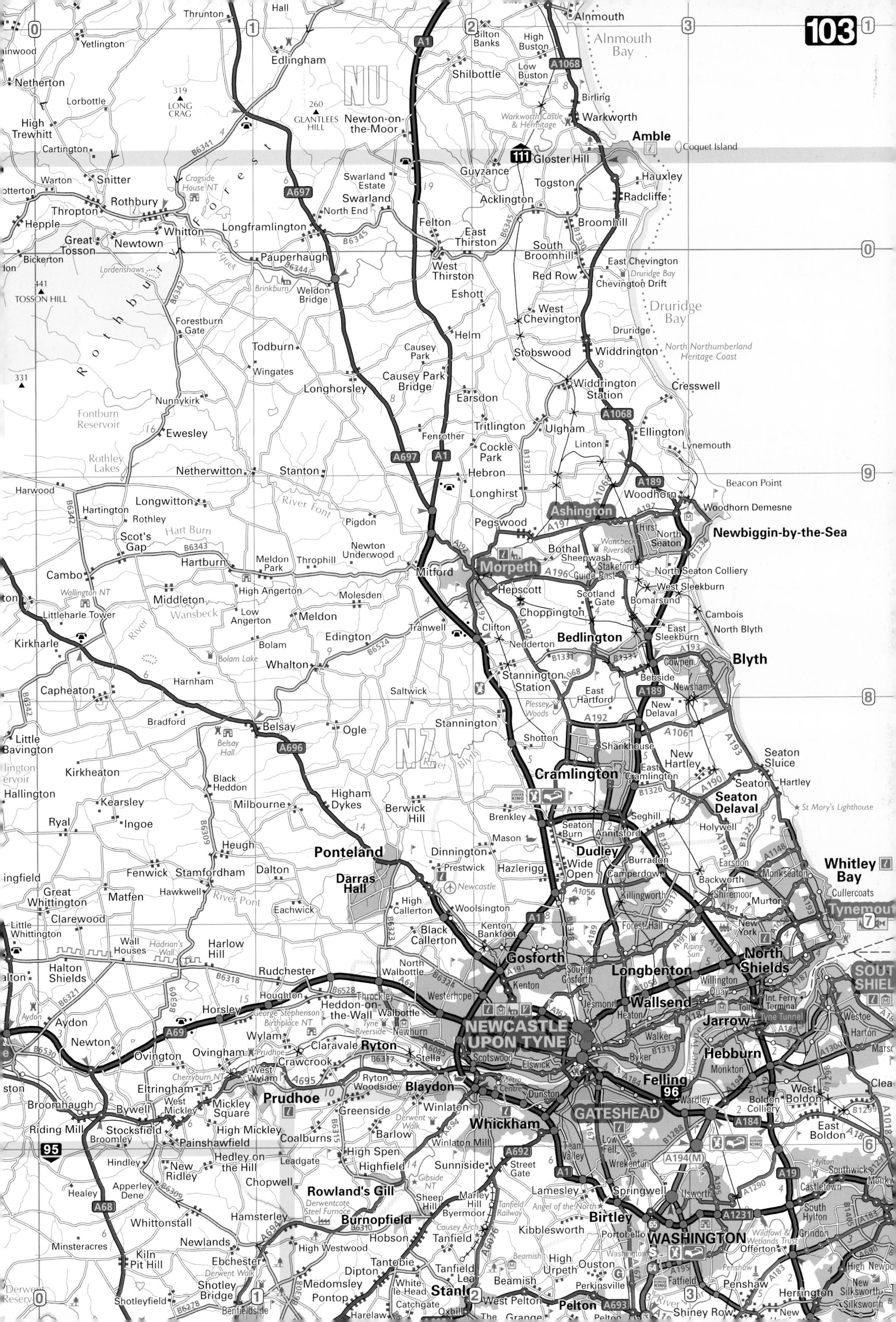
Thrunton
Hall
Alnmouth
Alnmouth Bay
Yetlington
Edlingham
Bilton Banks
High Buston
Low Buston
Shilbottle
A1
A1068
NU
Netherton
Lorbottle
319 LONG CRAG
260 GLANTLEES HILL
Newton-on-the-Moor
Birling
Warkworth
Warkworth Castle & Hermitage
Amble
Coquet Island
High Trewhitt
Cartington
B6341
111
Gloster Hill
Warton
Snitter
Cragside House NT
Swarland Estate
Guyzance
Hauxley
Togston
Radcliffe
Rothbury
Thropton
A697
Swarland
North End
Acklington
Hepple
Whitton
Longframlington
Felton
East Thirston
Broomhill
Great Tosson
Newtown
B6345
South Broomhill
Bickerton
Lordenshaws
Pauperhaugh
B6344
West Thirston
East Chevington
Druridge Bay
Red Row
Chevington Drift
441 TOSSON HILL
Brinkburn
Weldon Bridge
Eshott
Rothbury Forest
B6342
Forestburn Gate
West Chevington
Druridge Bay
Helm
Druridge
Todburn
Causey Park
Stobswood
Widdrington
North Northumberland Heritage Coast
Wingates
Causey Park Bridge
331
Longhorsley
Widdrington Station
Cresswell
Earsdon
Nunnykirk
Fontburn Reservoir
A1068
Ewesley
Tritlington
Ulgham
Ellington
Fenrother
Cockle Park
Linton
Lynemouth
Rothley Lakes
A697
B1337
Netherwitton
Stanton
Hebron
Beacon Point
Harwood
A189
Woodhorn
Longwitton
Longhirst
River Font
Ashington
Woodhorn Demesne
Hartington
Rothley
Pigdon
Pegswood
A197
Hart Burn
Hirst
North Seaton
Newbiggin-by-the-Sea
Scot's Gap
Newton Underwood
Bothal
Wansbeck Riverside
B6343
Hartburn
Meldon Park
Throphill
Sheepwash
Morpeth
Stakeford
North Seaton Colliery
Cambo
Mitford
A196
Guide Post
West Sleekburn
Wallington NT
High Angerton
Hepscott
Molesden
Scotland Gate
Bomarsund
Middleton
Choppington
Littleharle Tower
Wansbeck
Low Angerton
Meldon
Cambois
Tranwell
Clifton
East Sleekburn
North Blyth
Kirkharle
River
Edington
Bedlington
Bolam
Nedderton
B6524
B1331
Blyth
Cowpen
Bolam Lake
Whalton
Bebside
Harnham
Stannington Station
Capheaton
A1068
A189
Saltwick
Newsham
East Hartford
Plessey Woods
New Delaval
Bradford
Belsay
Ogle
Stannington
A192
A1061
Little Bavington
Belsay Hall
A696
Shotton
NZ
River Blyth
Shankhouse
Kirkheaton
Black Heddon
East Cramlington
New Hartley
Seaton Sluice
Cramlington
Hartley
Higham Dykes
Hallington
Seaton
Kearsley
Milbourne
Berwick Hill
Seaton Delaval
B1326
A190
St Mary's Lighthouse
Ryal
Ingoe
Brenkley
Seghill
B6309
Holywell
Seaton Burn
Annitsford
Heugh
Mason
Ponteland
Dinnington
Dudley
Whitley Bay
Darras Hall
Prestwick
Hazlerigg
Burradon
Earsdon
Fenwick
Stamfordham
Dalton
Wide Open
Monkseaton
Camperdown
Newcastle
Backworth
Cullercoats
Great Whittington
Matfen
Hawkwell
River Pont
High Callerton
Killingworth
Shiremoor
Murton
Tynemouth
Eachwick
Woolsington
A1056
Little Whittington
Clarewood
Forest Hall
New York
Kenton Bankfoot
Black Callerton
Wall Houses
Hadrian's Wall
Harlow Hill
Gosforth
North Shields
Rising Sun
Halton Shields
North Walbottle
Longbenton
Rudchester
South Gosforth
Kenton
Willington Quay
B6318
B6321
B6528
Houghton
Throckley
Westerhope
Wallsend
Int. Ferry Terminal
South Shields
Aydon
Horsley
Heddon-on-the-Wall
Walbottle
Jesmond
Heaton
Tyne Tunnel
Aydon
George Stephenson's Birthplace NT
Newburn
Tyne Riverside
NEWCASTLE UPON TYNE
Jarrow
Westoe
Harton
A69
Wylam
Walker
Newton
Claravale
Ryton
Hebburn
Ovington
Ovingham
Prudhoe
Crawcrook
Stella
Scotswood
Elswick
Byker
Monkton
Cherryburn NT
West Wylam
A695
Ryton Woodside
Blaydon
Metro Centre
Felling
Eltringham
96
Wardley
West Boldon
Broomhaugh
West Mickley
Mickley Square
Prudhoe
Dunston
Boldon Colliery
Bywell
Greenside
Winlaton
GATESHEAD
A184
B1299
Riding Mill
Stocksfield
High Mickley
Derwent Walk
Whickham
Broomley
Painshawfield
Barlow
East Boldon
95
Coalburns
Winlaton Mill
Low Fell
Hindley
New Ridley
Hedley on the Hill
Leadgate
High Spen
Team Valley
Wrekenton
A194(M)
Highfield
A692
Sunniside
Street Gate
A19
Southwick
Healey
Apperley Dene
Chopwell
Gibside NT
Springwell
Castletown
B6309
Rowland's Gill
Sheep Hill
Marley Hill
Lamesley
Usworth
A1290
A68
Derwentcote Steel Furnace
Byermoor
Tanfield Railway
Angel of the North
South Hylton
Whittonstall
Hamsterley
Burnopfield
Causey Arch
Birtley
A1231
Newlands
Hobson
Tanfield
Kibblesworth
Portobello
WASHINGTON
Wildfowl & Wetlands Trust
Grindon
Minsteracres
High Westwood
Beamish
Washington
Offerton
Kiln Pit Hill
Ebchester
Tantobie
High Urpeth
Ouston
Penshaw
Derwent Walk
Tanfield Lea
Beamish
Derwent Reservoir
Shotley Bridge
Medomsley
Dipton
White-le-Head
Perkinsville
Fatfield
Penshaw
Herrington
New Silksworth
Shotleyfield
Benfieldside
Pontop
Catchgate
Stanley
West Pelton
Pelton
A693
Shiney Row
Silksworth
Harelaw
Oxhill
The Grange
New

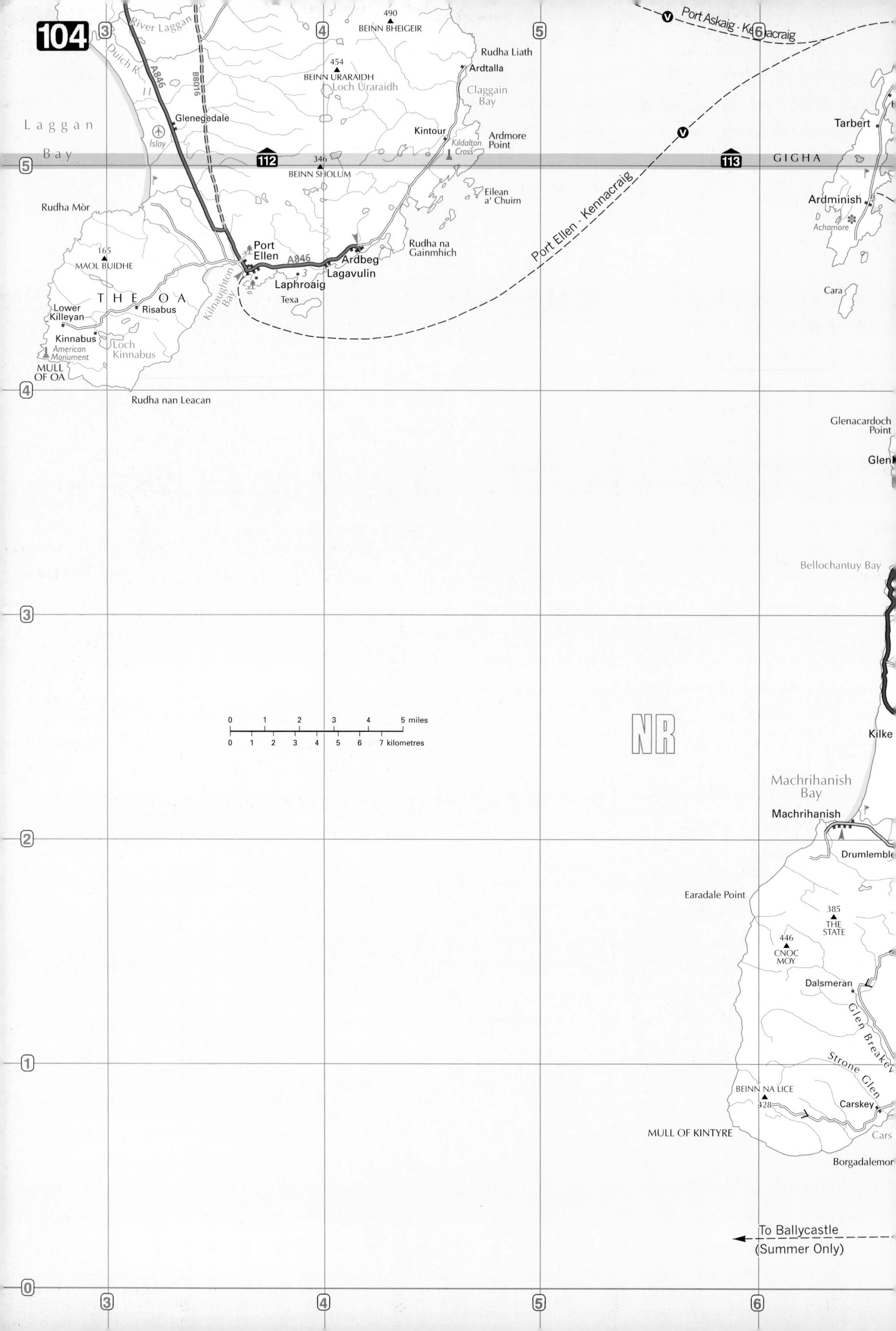

River Laggan

Dutch R

A846

B8016

490
BEINN BHEIGEIR

454
BEINN URARAIDH

Loch Uraraidh

Rudha Liath

Ardtalla

Claggain
Bay

Kintour

Ardmore
Point

Kildalton
Cross

Glenegedale

Islay

Laggan

Bay

112

346
BEINN SHOLUM

Eilean
a' Chuirn

Port Askaig · Kennacraig

GIGHA

113

Tarbert

Ardminish

Achamore

Port Ellen · Kennacraig

Rudha Mòr

165
MAOL BUIDHE

Port
Ellen

A846

Ardbeg
Lagavulin

Rudha na
Gainmhich

Cara

THE OA

Risabus

Kilnaughton Bay

Laphroaig

Texa

3

Lower
Killeyan

Kinnabus

American
Monument

Loch
Kinnabus

MULL
OF OA

Rudha nan Leacan

Glenacardoch
Point

Glen

Bellochantuy Bay

NR

Machrihanish
Bay

Machrihanish

Kilke

Drumlemble

Earadale Point

385
THE
STATE

446
CNOC
MOY

Dalsmeran

Glen Breakerie

Strone Glen

BEINN NA LICE

428

Carskey

Cars

MULL OF KINTYRE

Borgadalemor

| 0 | 1 | 2 | 3 | 4 | 5 miles |

| 0 | 1 | 2 | 3 | 4 | 5 | 6 | 7 kilometres |

To Ballycastle
(Summer Only)

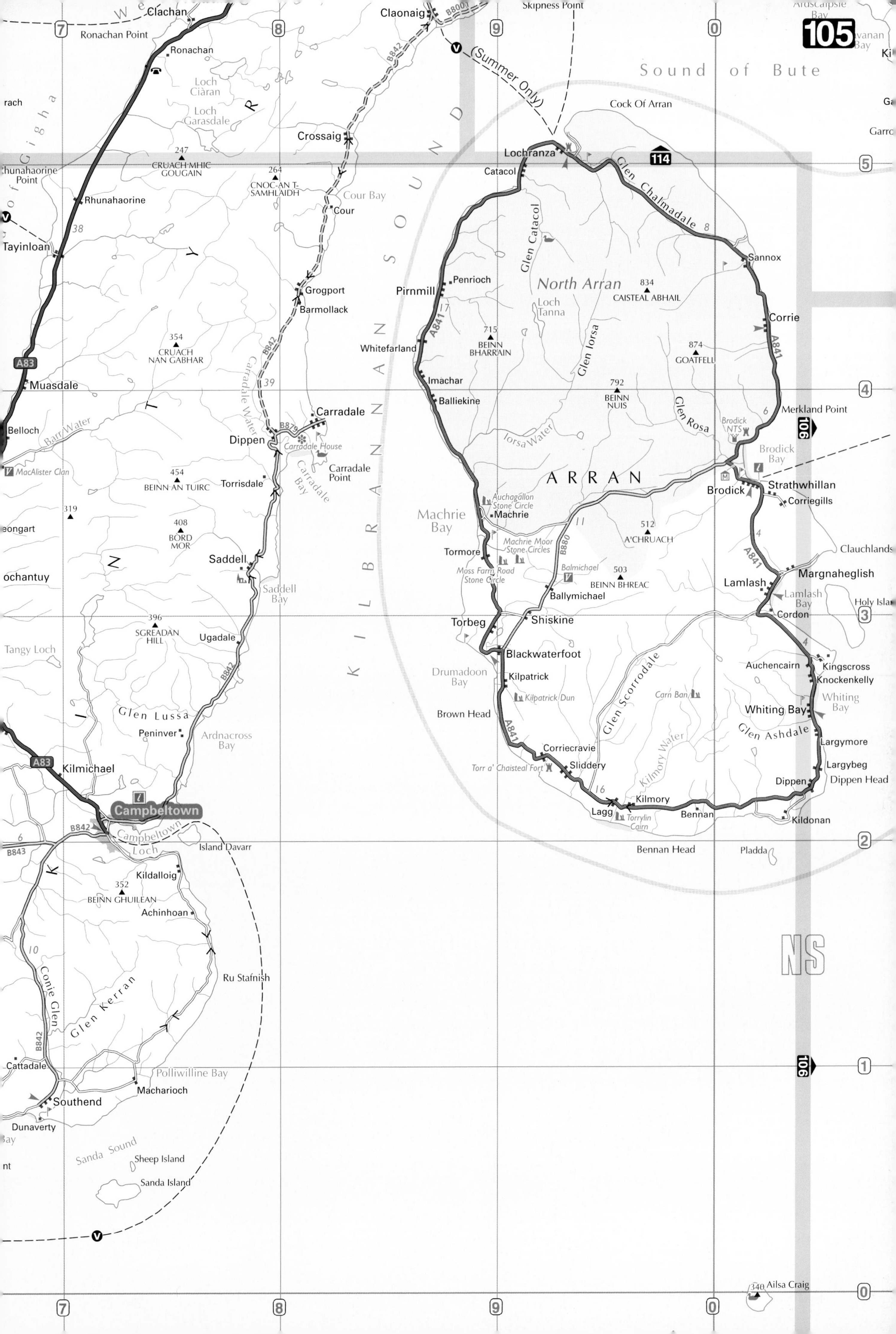
Sound of Bute
Cock Of Arran
Lochranza
Catacol
Glen Chalmadale
Sannox
Corrie
North Arran
CAISTEAL ABHAIL
GOATFELL
BEINN BHARRAIN
BEINN NUIS
Glen Catacol
Loch Tanna
Glen Iorsa
Glen Rosa
Iorsa Water
Pirnmill
Penrioch
Whitefarland
Imachar
Balliekine
Merkland Point
Brodick
Brodick Bay
Strathwhillan
Corriegills
ARRAN
Machrie Bay
Machrie
Auchagallon Stone Circle
Tormore
Machrie Moor Stone Circles
Moss Farm Road Stone Circle
Balmichael
Ballymichael
A'CHRUACH
BEINN BHREAC
Clauchlands
Lamlash
Lamlash Bay
Margnaheglish
Holy Isla
Cordon
Torbeg
Shiskine
Blackwaterfoot
Drumadoon Bay
Kilpatrick
Kilpatrick Dun
Brown Head
Glen Scorrodale
Carn Ban
Kilmory Water
Auchencairn
Kingscross
Knockenkelly
Whiting Bay
Glen Ashdale
Largymore
Largybeg
Dippen Head
Dippen
Corriecravie
Sliddery
Torr a' Chaisteal Fort
Kilmory
Lagg
Torrylin Cairn
Bennan
Kildonan
Bennan Head
Pladda
Ailsa Craig
NS
KILBRANNAN SOUND
Claonaig
Skipness Point
(Summer Only)
Crossaig
Cour Bay
Cour
Grogport
Barmollack
Carradale
Dippen
Carradale House
Carradale Point
Carradale Bay
Carradale Water
Torrisdale
Saddell
Saddell Bay
Ugadale
Ardnacross Bay
Peninver
Glen Lussa
Clachan
Ronachan Point
Ronachan
Loch Ciàran
Loch Garasdale
CRUACH MHIC GOUGAIN
CNOC-AN T-SAMHLAIDH
Rhunahaorine Point
Rhunahaorine
Tayinloan
CRUACH NAN GABHAR
Muasdale
Belloch
Barr Water
MacAlister Clan
BEINN AN TUIRC
BORD MOR
SGREADAN HILL
Tangy Loch
KINTYRE
Kilmichael
Campbeltown
Campbeltown Loch
Island Davarr
Kildalloig
BEINN GHUILEAN
Achinhoan
Ru Stafnish
Glen Kerran
Conie Glen
Cattadale
Polliwilline Bay
Southend
Macharioch
Dunaverty
Sanda Sound
Sheep Island
Sanda Island
A83
A841
B842
B880
B879
B8001
B843
114
106

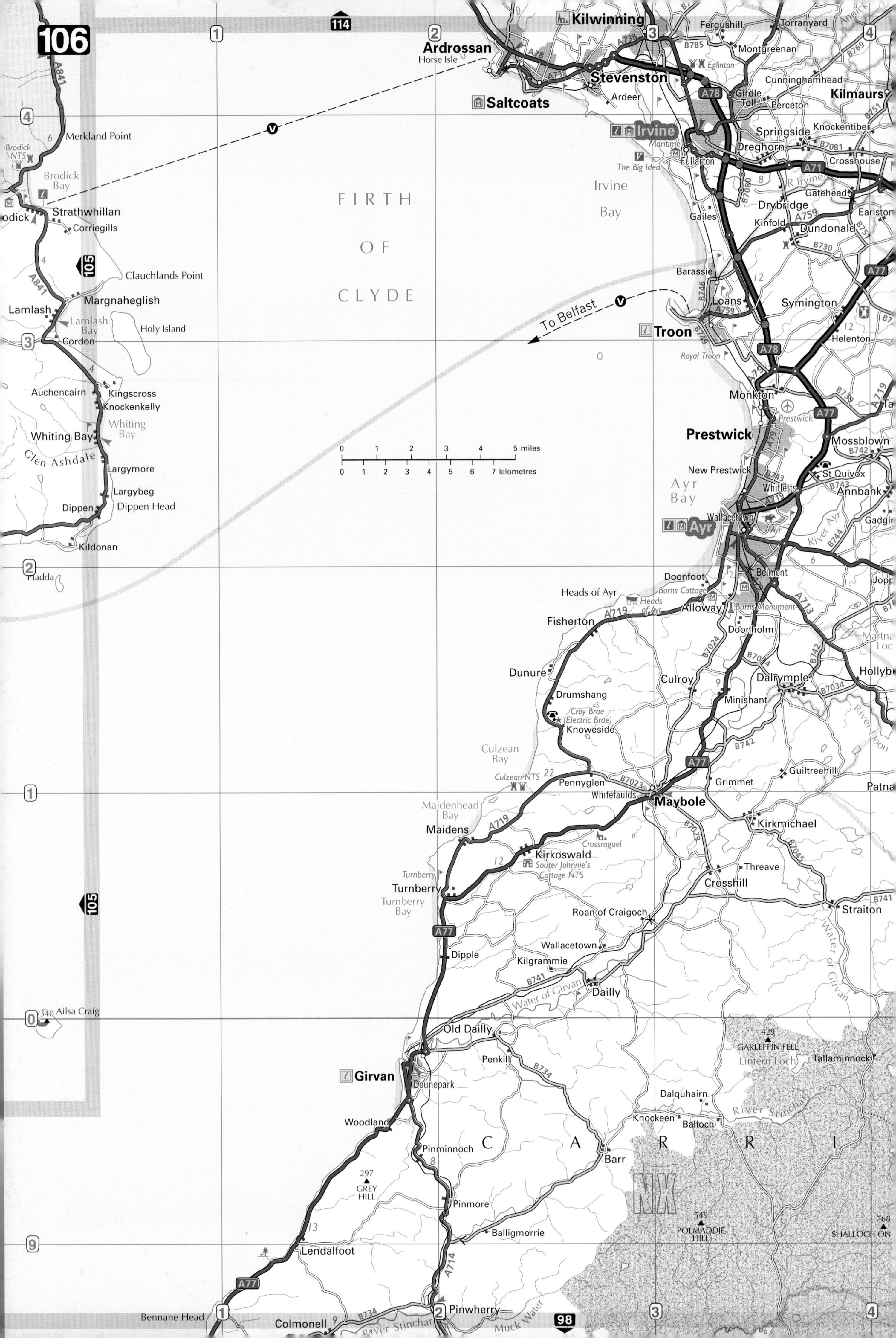

114
1
2
3
4
Kilwinning
Ardrossan
Horse Isle
Fergushill
Torranyard
Montgreenan
Eglinton
Stevenston
Saltcoats
Ardeer
Cunninghamhead
Kilmaurs
Girdle Toll
Perceton
Irvine
Maritime
Springside
Knockentiber
Dreghorn
Fullarton
The Big Idea
Crosshouse
Merkland Point
Brodick NTS
Brodick Bay
Strathwhillan
Corriegills
FIRTH
OF
CLYDE
Irvine Bay
Gatehead
Drybridge
Kinfold
Dundonald
Earlston
Gailes
Clauchlands Point
Margnaheglish
Lamlash
Lamlash Bay
Holy Island
Cordon
Barassie
Loans
Symington
To Belfast
Troon
Royal Troon
Helenton
Auchencairn
Kingscross
Knockenkelly
Whiting Bay
Whiting Bay
Glen Ashdale
Largymore
Largybeg
Dippen
Dippen Head
Kildonan
Pladda
Monkton
Prestwick
Prestwick
Mossblown
New Prestwick
St Quivox
Whitletts
Annbank
Ayr Bay
Wallacetown
Ayr
Gadgirth
River Ayr
Belmont
Doonfoot
Burns Cottage
Heads of Ayr
Heads of Ayr
Alloway
Burns Monument
Fisherton
Doonholm
Dunure
Culroy
Dalrymple
Hollybush
Drumshang
Minishant
Croy Brae (Electric Brae)
Knoweside
River Doon
Culzean Bay
Culzean NTS
Pennyglen
Whitefaulds
Maybole
Grimmet
Guiltreehill
Patna
Maidenhead Bay
Maidens
Kirkmichael
Crossraguel
Kirkoswald
Souter Johnnie's Cottage NTS
Threave
Turnberry
Turnberry
Turnberry Bay
Crosshill
Straiton
Roan of Craigoch
Wallacetown
Dipple
Kilgrammie
Water of Girvan
Dailly
Water of Girvan
340 Ailsa Craig
Old Dailly
429 GARLEFFIN FELL
Linfern Loch
Tallaminnock
Penkill
Girvan
Dounepark
Dalquhairn
Knockeen
Balloch
River Stinchar
Woodland
Pinminnoch
C A R R I
Barr
297 GREY HILL
NX
Pinmore
549 POLMADDIE HILL
768 SHALLOCH ON
Balligmorrie
Lendalfoot
Pinwherry
Muck Water
Bennane Head
Colmonell
River Stinchar
98
105
0 1 2 3 4 5 miles
0 1 2 3 4 5 6 7 kilometres
A78
A738
B785
B769
A759
A71
B7081
B751
B7080
R Irvine
B730
B746
A77
A719
B742
B743
B744
A713
B7024
B7034
B7023
B7045
B741
B734
A714
A841

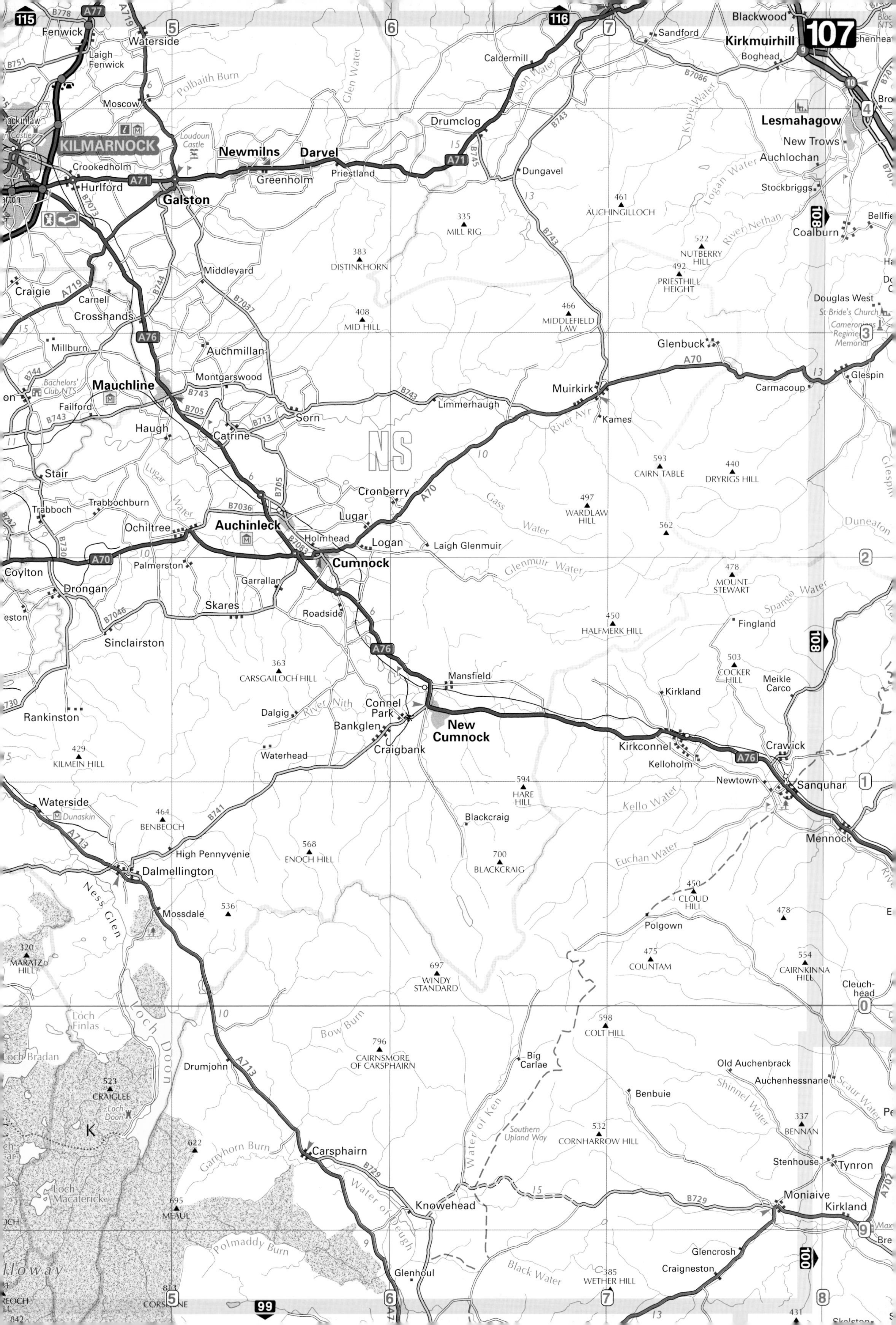

107
KILMARNOCK
Fenwick
Waterside
Laigh Fenwick
Moscow
Crookedholm
Hurlford
Galston
Newmilns
Darvel
Greenholm
Priestland
Drumclog
Caldermill
Sandford
Blackwood
Kirkmuirhill
Boghead
Lesmahagow
New Trows
Auchlochan
Stockbriggs
Coalburn
Dungavel
AUCHINGILLOCH
MILL RIG
DISTINKHORN
NUTBERRY HILL
PRIESTHILL HEIGHT
Middleyard
Craigie
Carnell
Crosshands
MID HILL
MIDDLEFIELD LAW
Douglas West
St Bride's Church
Cameronians Regiment Memorial
Glenbuck
Millburn
Auchmillan
Montgarswood
Mauchline
Bachelors' Club NTS
Failford
Haugh
Catrine
Sorn
Limmerhaugh
Muirkirk
Kames
Carmacoup
Glespin
NS
Stair
Trabboch
Trabbochburn
Ochiltree
Auchinleck
Cronberry
Lugar
Holmhead
Logan
Laigh Glenmuir
Cumnock
CAIRN TABLE
DRYRIGS HILL
WARDLAW HILL
Coylton
Drongan
Palmerston
Garrallan
Skares
Roadside
Sinclairston
MOUNT STEWART
HALFMERK HILL
Fingland
COCKER HILL
Meikle Carco
CARSGAILOCH HILL
Mansfield
Kirkland
Rankinston
Dalgig
Connel Park
Bankglen
Craigbank
New Cumnock
Kirkconnel
Kelloholm
Crawick
Newtown
Sanquhar
KILMEIN HILL
Waterhead
HARE HILL
Blackcraig
Mennock
Waterside
Dunaskin
BENBEOCH
High Pennyvenie
ENOCH HILL
BLACKCRAIG
Dalmellington
Ness Glen
Mossdale
CLOUD HILL
Polgown
MARATZ HILL
WINDY STANDARD
COUNTAM
CAIRNKINNA HILL
Cleuch-head
Loch Finlas
Loch Bradan
Loch Doon
Drumjohn
CAIRNSMORE OF CARSPHAIRN
COLT HILL
Big Carlae
Old Auchenbrack
Auchenhessnane
CRAIGLEE
Benbuie
BENNAN
Carsphairn
Southern Upland Way
CORNHARROW HILL
Stenhouse
Tynron
Loch Macaterick
MEAUL
Knowehead
Moniaive
Kirkland
Polmaddy Burn
Glencrosh
Craigneston
Glenhoul
WETHER HILL
CORSERINE
99
100
108
115
116

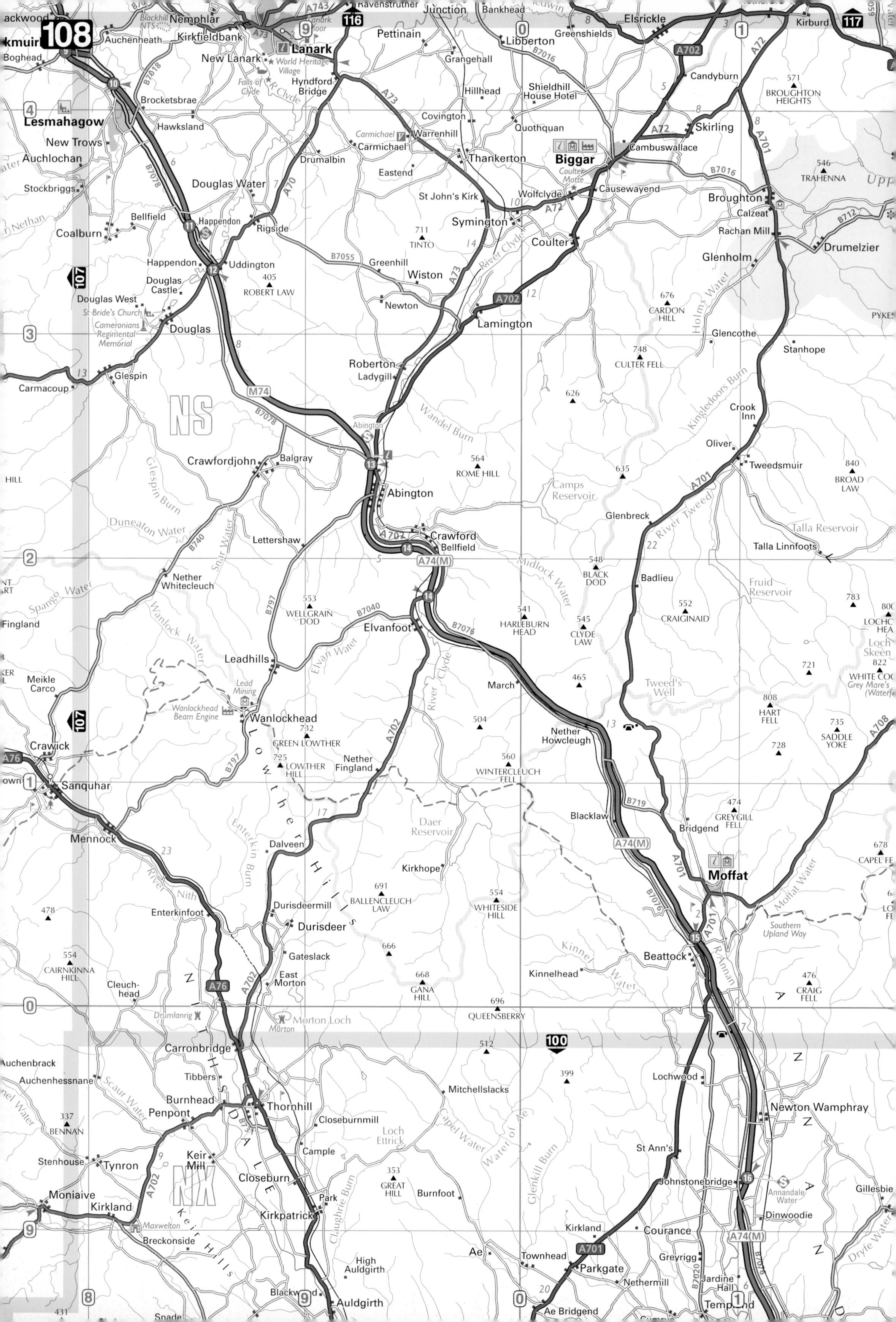

108
116
117
107
100
Lanark
New Lanark
World Heritage Village
Falls of Clyde
Hyndford Bridge
Pettinain
Libberton
Elsrickle
Kirkurd
Greenshields
Nemphlar
Kirkfieldbank
Auchenheath
Boghead
Lesmahagow
New Trows
Auchlochan
Brocketsbrae
Hawksland
Stockbriggs
Coalburn
Bellfield
Douglas Water
Happendon
Rigside
Uddington
Douglas Castle
Douglas West
St Bride's Church
Cameronians Regimental Memorial
Douglas
Glespin
Carmacoup
Grangehall
Hillhead
Shieldhill House Hotel
Quothquan
Covington
Carmichael
Warrenhill
Drumalbin
Eastend
Thankerton
Biggar
Coulter Motte
Cambuswallace
Candyburn
Skirling
Broughton Heights
Trahenna
Causewayend
Wolfclyde
St John's Kirk
Symington
Coulter
Broughton
Calzeat
Rachan Mill
Drumelzier
Glenholm
Tinto
Greenhill
Wiston
Robert Law
Newton
Lamington
Cardon Hill
Holms Water
Glencothe
Stanhope
Culter Fell
Roberton
Ladygill
Abington
NS
Crawfordjohn
Balgray
Glespin Burn
Wandel Burn
Rome Hill
Camps Reservoir
Kingledoors Burn
Crook Inn
Oliver
Tweedsmuir
Broad Law
Duneaton Water
Lettershaw
Crawford
Bellfield
Glenbreck
River Tweed
Talla Reservoir
Talla Linnfoots
Nether Whitecleuch
Snar Water
Spango Water
Wanlock Water
Fingland
Wellgrain Dod
Elvanfoot
Elvan Water
Harleburn Head
Black Dod
Midlock Water
Clyde Law
Badlieu
Fruid Reservoir
Craiginaid
Loch Skeen
White Coomb
Grey Mare's Tail (Waterfall)
Leadhills
Lead Mining
Wanlockhead
Wanlockhead Beam Engine
Green Lowther
Lowther Hill
Lowther Hills
Meikle Carco
Crawick
Sanquhar
Mennock
River Clyde
March
Tweed's Well
Nether Howcleugh
Hart Fell
Saddle Yoke
Nether Fingland
Wintercleuch Fell
Daer Reservoir
Blacklaw
Bridgend
Greygill Fell
Moffat
Moffat Water
Capel Fell
Southern Upland Way
Enterkin Burn
River Nith
Dalveen
Kirkhope
Ballencleuch Law
Whiteside Hill
Enterkinfoot
Durisdeermill
Durisdeer
Gateslack
East Morton
Kinnel Water
Kinnelhead
Beattock
R. Annan
Craig Fell
Cairnkinna Hill
Cleuch-head
Gana Hill
Queensberry
Drumlanrig
Morton Loch
Morton
Nithsdale
Annandale
Auchenbrack
Auchenhessnane
Scaur Water
Tibbers
Carronbridge
Mitchellslacks
Lochwood
Burnhead
Penpont
Thornhill
Closeburnmill
Loch Ettrick
Capel Water
Water of Ae
Newton Wamphray
Bennan
Stenhouse
Tynron
Keir Mill
Cample
Closeburn
Great Hill
Burnfoot
Glenkill Burn
St Ann's
Johnstonebridge
Annandale Water
Gillesbie
NX
Moniaive
Kirkland
Maxwelton
Breckonside
Keir Hills
Park
Kirkpatrick
Claughrie Burn
Dinwoodie
Courance
Greyrigg
Ae
Townhead
Parkgate
Nethermill
Jardine Hall
Dryfe Water
High Auldgirth
Blackwood
Auldgirth
Templand
Ae Bridgend
Snade
Ravenstruther
Junction
Bankhead
M74
A74(M)
A70
A72
A73
A76
A701
A702
A743
A708
B7016
B7018
B7055
B7078
B7040
B7076
B740
B797
B719
B712
B7020
B729

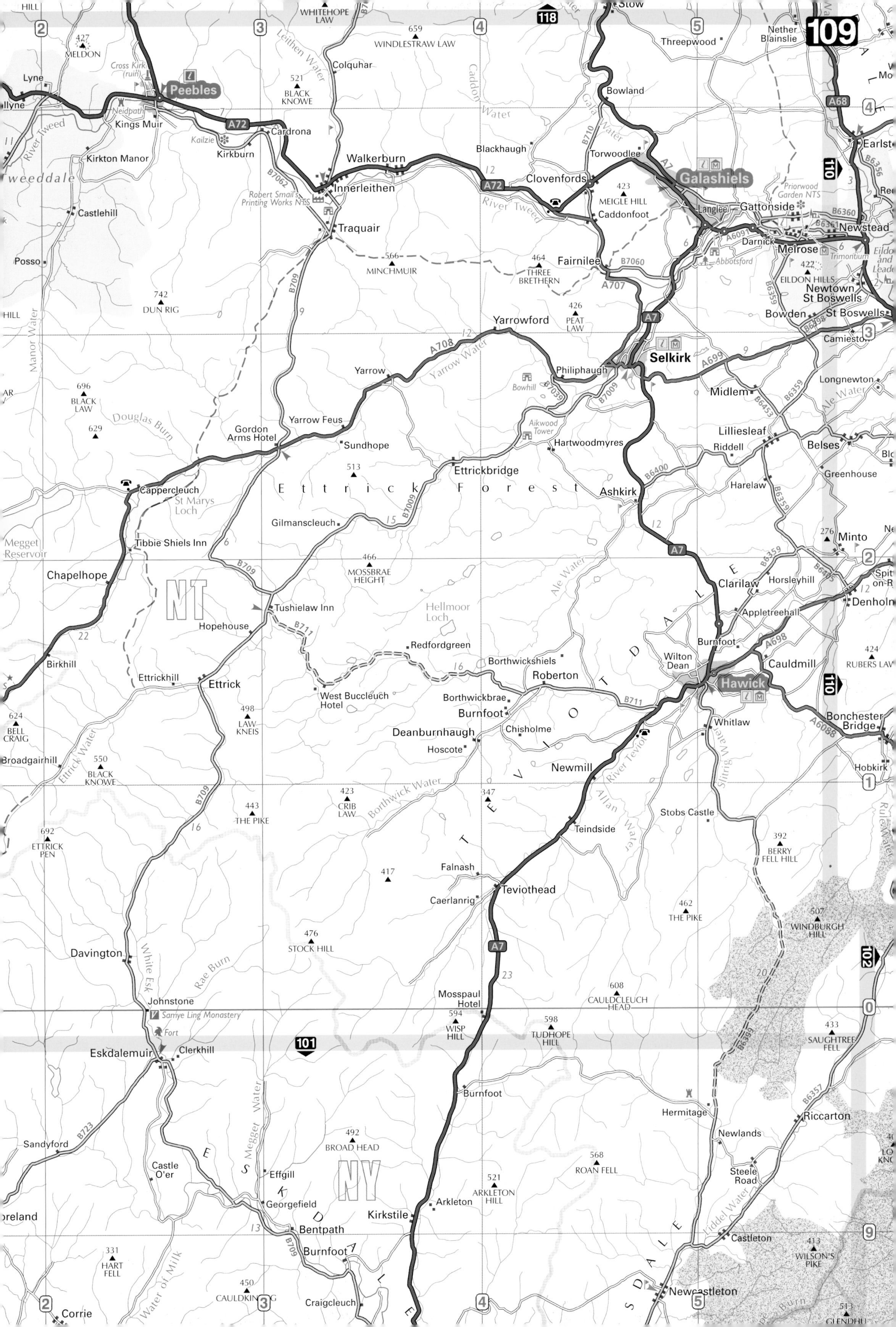
109
Peebles
Lyne
Cross Kirk (ruin)
Neidpath
Kings Muir
River Tweed
Kirkton Manor
Tweeddale
Castlehill
Posso
Manor Water
MELDON
BLACK LAW
Douglas Burn
DUN RIG
Kailzie
Kirkburn
Cardrona
A72
Walkerburn
Innerleithen
Robert Smail's Printing Works NTS
Traquair
B709
B7062
Leithen Water
Colquhar
WHITEHOPE LAW
WINDLESTRAW LAW
BLACK KNOWE
MINCHMUIR
Caddon Water
Blackhaugh
Clovenfords
River Tweed
Torwoodlee
Gala Water
Bowland
Stow
Threepwood
Nether Blainslie
Galashiels
MEIGLE HILL
Caddonfoot
Langlee
Gattonside
Priorwood Garden NTS
Darnick
Melrose
Newstead
Abbotsford
Fairnilee
B7060
A707
THREE BRETHERN
PEAT LAW
EILDON HILLS
Newtown St Boswells
Bowden
St Boswells
Trimontium
Earlston
A68
B6356
B6360
B6361
A6091
B6359
B6398
Camieston
Yarrowford
A708
Yarrow Water
Yarrow
Philiphaugh
Bowhill
B7039
Selkirk
A7
A699
Midlem
B6453
Longnewton
Ale Water
Yarrow Feus
Gordon Arms Hotel
Sundhope
Aikwood Tower
B7009
Hartwoodmyres
Lilliesleaf
Riddell
Belses
Greenhouse
B6400
Harelaw
Ettrickbridge
Ettrick Forest
Ashkirk
Cappercleuch
St Marys Loch
Megget Reservoir
Tibbie Shiels Inn
Chapelhope
Gilmanscleuch
MOSSBRAE HEIGHT
Hellmoor Loch
Ale Water
Minto
Horsleyhill
Clarilaw
Denholm
Spittal-on-Rule
NT
Tushielaw Inn
Hopehouse
B711
Redfordgreen
Appletreehall
Burnfoot
A698
Cauldmill
RUBERS LAW
Birkhill
Ettrickhill
Ettrick
West Buccleuch Hotel
Borthwickshiels
Roberton
Wilton Dean
Hawick
TEVIOTDALE
BELL CRAIG
LAW KNEIS
Borthwickbrae
Burnfoot
Deanburnhaugh
Chisholme
Hoscote
Whitlaw
Bonchester Bridge
A6088
Broadgairhill
Ettrick Water
BLACK KNOWE
Newmill
River Teviot
Slitrig Water
Hobkirk
THE PIKE
CRIB LAW
Borthwick Water
Allan Water
Teindside
Stobs Castle
Rule Water
ETTRICK PEN
BERRY FELL HILL
Falnash
Teviothead
Caerlanrig
THE PIKE
WINDBURGH HILL
Davington
STOCK HILL
White Esk
Rae Burn
Johnstone
Samye Ling Monastery
Fort
Mosspaul Hotel
WISP HILL
TUDHOPE HILL
CAULDCLEUCH HEAD
SAUGHTREE FELL
102
B6399
101
Eskdalemuir
Clerkhill
Burnfoot
Hermitage
Riccarton
B6357
Sandyford
B723
BROAD HEAD
Newlands
Megget Water
Castle O'er
Effgill
ESKDALE
NY
ARKLETON HILL
ROAN FELL
Steele Road
Georgefield
Arkleton
Kirkstile
Liddel Water
Bentpath
Castleton
WILSON'S PIKE
B709
Burnfoot
HART FELL
Water of Milk
CAULDKINE RIG
Craigcleuch
Newcastleton
LIDDESDALE
Corrie
GLENDHU
118
110

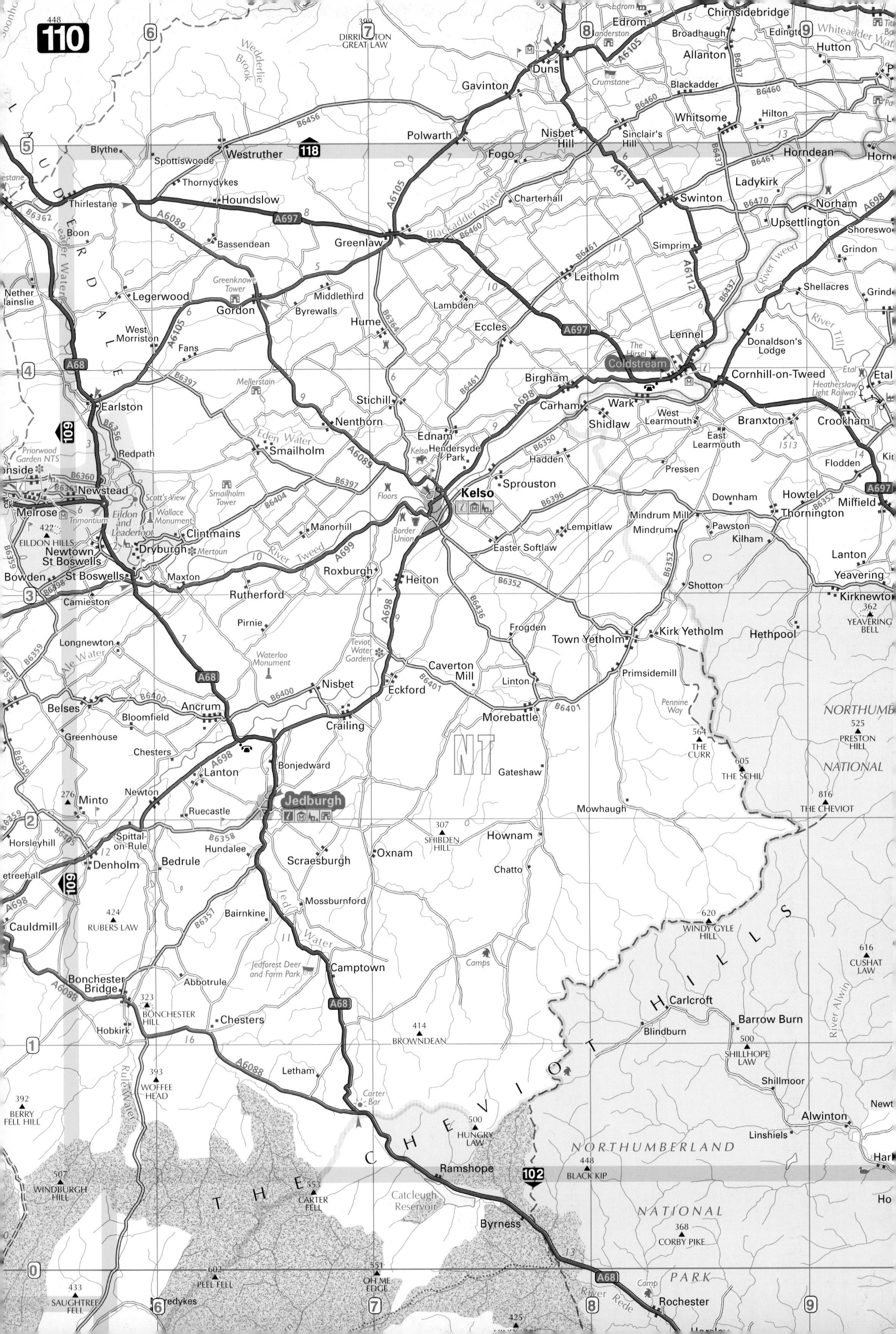

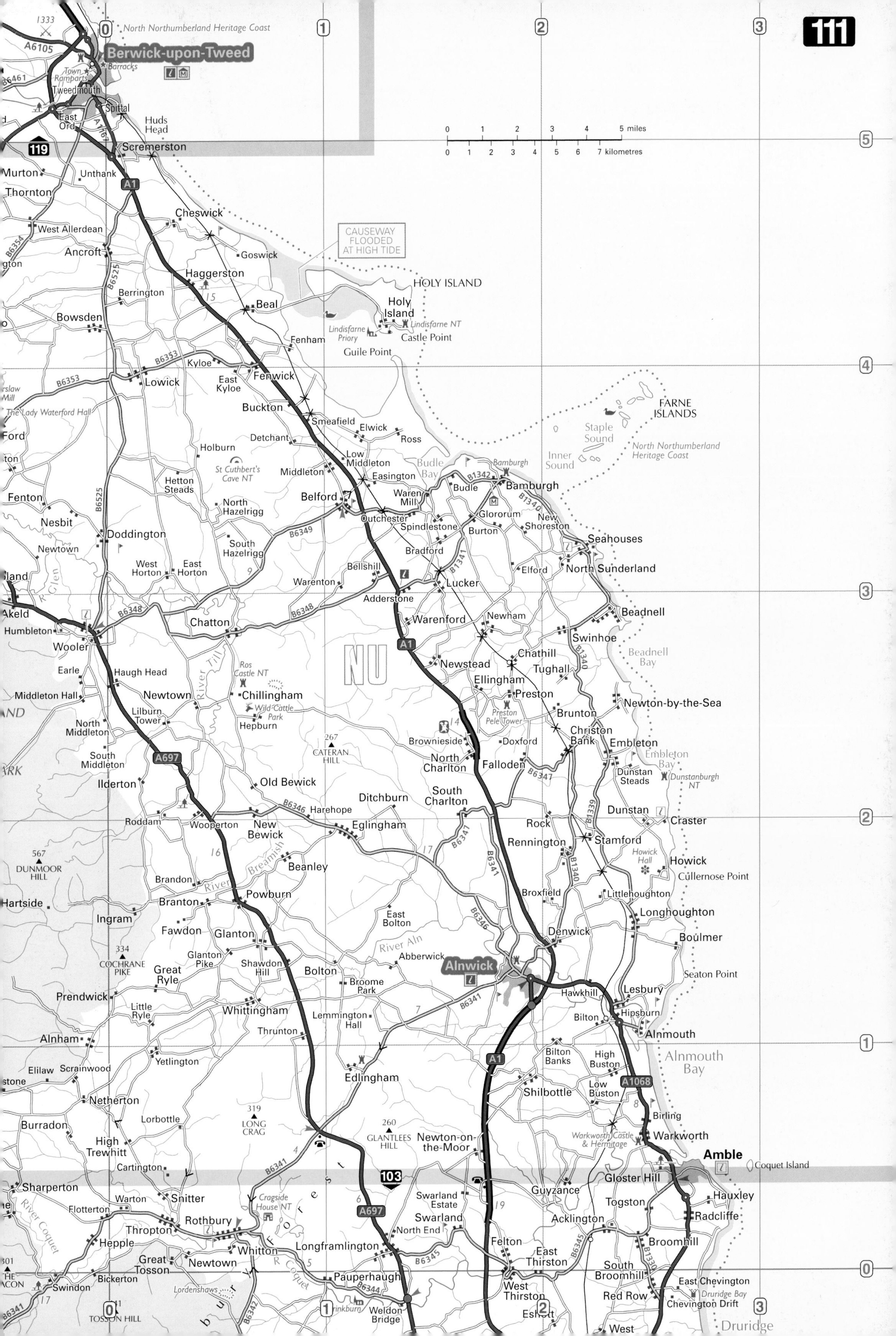
Berwick-upon-Tweed
North Northumberland Heritage Coast
Tweedmouth
Spittal
Scremerston
Cheswick
Goswick
Haggerston
Beal
CAUSEWAY FLOODED AT HIGH TIDE
HOLY ISLAND
Holy Island
Lindisfarne Priory
Lindisfarne NT
Castle Point
Guile Point
Fenham
Kyloe
East Kyloe
Fenwick
Lowick
Buckton
Smeafield
Elwick
Ross
Detchant
Holburn
Low Middleton
Middleton
Easington
Budle Bay
Bamburgh
Belford
Waren Mill
Outchester
Spindlestone
Glororum
Burton
New Shoreston
Seahouses
North Sunderland
FARNE ISLANDS
Staple Sound
Inner Sound
Bradford
Lucker
Elford
Bellshill
Warenton
Adderstone
Beadnell
Warenford
Newham
Swinhoe
Beadnell Bay
Chathill
Tughall
Newstead
Ellingham
Preston
Newton-by-the-Sea
Brunton
Christon Bank
Embleton
Embleton Bay
Dunstanburgh NT
Doxford
Brownieside
North Charlton
Falloden
South Charlton
Ditchburn
Rock
Dunstan
Craster
Rennington
Stamford
Howick
Cullernose Point
Eglingham
Harehope
Beanley
Broxfield
Littlehoughton
Longhoughton
Boulmer
Denwick
Alnwick
Abberwick
Hawkhill
Lesbury
Seaton Point
Hipsburn
Bilton
Alnmouth
Alnmouth Bay
Bilton Banks
High Buston
Low Buston
Shilbottle
Birling
Warkworth
Amble
Coquet Island
Gloster Hill
Hauxley
Togston
Radcliffe
Guyzance
Acklington
Broomhill
Felton
East Thirston
West Thirston
South Broomhill
East Chevington
Red Row
Chevington Drift
Druridge
Eshott
West
Wooler
Humbleton
Akeld
Chatton
Chillingham
Hepburn
Lilburn Tower
Newtown
Haugh Head
Earle
Middleton Hall
North Middleton
South Middleton
Ilderton
Old Bewick
New Bewick
Wooperton
Roddam
Brandon
Powburn
Branton
Ingram
Fawdon
Glanton
Glanton Pike
Shawdon Hill
Bolton
Broome Park
Whittingham
Lemmington Hall
Thrunton
Edlingham
Great Ryle
Little Ryle
Prendwick
Alnham
Yetlington
Netherton
Burradon
High Trewhitt
Lorbottle
Cartington
Sharperton
Snitter
Warton
Flotterton
Thropton
Rothbury
Hepple
Whitton
Great Tosson
Newtown
Bickerton
Swindon
Longframlington
Swarland Estate
Swarland
North End
Newton-on-the-Moor
Pauperhaugh
Weldon Bridge
Doddington
Nesbit
Fenton
Newtown
West Horton
East Horton
Hetton Steads
North Hazelrigg
South Hazelrigg
Bowsden
Berrington
Ancroft
West Allerdean
Thornton
Murton
Unthank
East Ord
Huds Head
Ford
Cragside House NT
5 miles
7 kilometres
NU

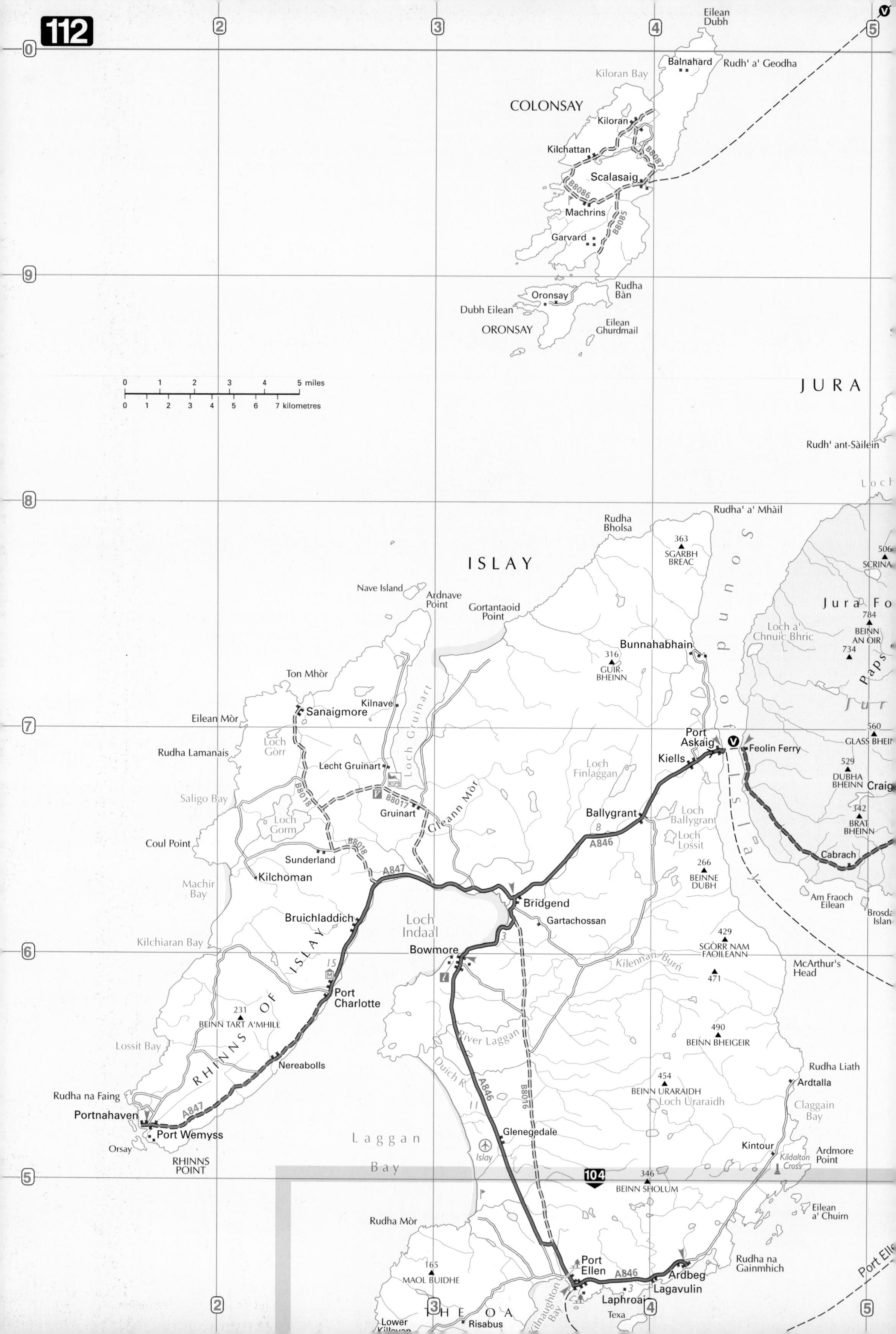

JURA

COLONSAY

Eilean
Dubh

Balnahard
Rudh' a' Geodha

Kiloran Bay

Kiloran

B8087

Kilchattan

Scalasaig

B8086

Machrins

B8085

Garvard

Oronsay

Rudha
Bàn

Dubh Eilean

ORONSAY

Eilean
Ghurdmail

Rudh' ant-Sàilein

| 0 | 1 | 2 | 3 | 4 | 5 miles |
| 0 | 1 2 3 | 4 5 | 6 | 7 kilometres |

ISLAY

Rudha
Bholsa

Rudha' a' Mhàil

363
▲ SGARBH
BREAC

506
▲ SCRINA

Nave Island

Ardnave
Point

Gortantaoid
Point

Bunnahabhain

316
▲ GUIR-
BHEINN

Jura Fo

784
▲ BEINN
AN OIR

734 ▲

Ton Mhòr

Kilnave

Loch a'
Chnuic Bhric

Eilean Mòr

Sanaigmore

Port
Askaig

Feolin Ferry

560
▲ GLASS BHEIN

Rudha Lamanais

Loch
Gorr

Loch Gruinart

Kiells

529
▲ DUBHA
BHEIN

Craig

Lecht Gruinart

RSPB

B8018

Loch
Finlaggan

Ballygrant

8

A846

Loch
Ballygrant

342 ▲
BRAT
BHEINN

Cabrach

Saligo Bay

B8017

Gruinart

Gleann Mòr

Loch
Lossit

Am Fraoch
Eilean

Brosda
Islan

Coul Point

Loch
Gorm

B8018

Sunderland

A847

266
▲ BEINNE
DUBH

Machir
Bay

Kilchoman

Bridgend

Gartachossan

429
▲ SGORR NAM
FAOILEANN

Kilchiaran Bay

Bruichladdich

Loch
Indaal

3

Bowmore

Kilennan Burn

471 ▲

McArthur's
Head

Port
Charlotte

15
M

490
▲ BEINN BHEIGEIR

RHINNS OF ISLAY

231 ▲
BEINN TART A'MHILL

Nereabolls

River Laggan

Duich R.

A846

B8016

454 ▲
BEINN URARAIDH
Loch Uraraidh

Rudha Liath

Ardtalla

Lossit Bay

Rudha na Faing

A847

Portnahaven

Port Wemyss

Orsay

RHINNS
POINT

Laggan

Bay

Islay

Rudha Mòr

Glenegedale

Claggain
Bay

Kintour

Ardmore
Point

Kildalton
Cross

104

346 ▲
BEINN SHOLUM

Eilean
a' Chuirn

Port Ell

THE OA

165 ▲
MAOL BUIDHE

Kilnaughton Bay

Port
Ellen

A846

Ardbeg

Lagavulin

Laphroa

Rudha na
Gainmhich

Texa

3

Lower
Killeyan

Risabus

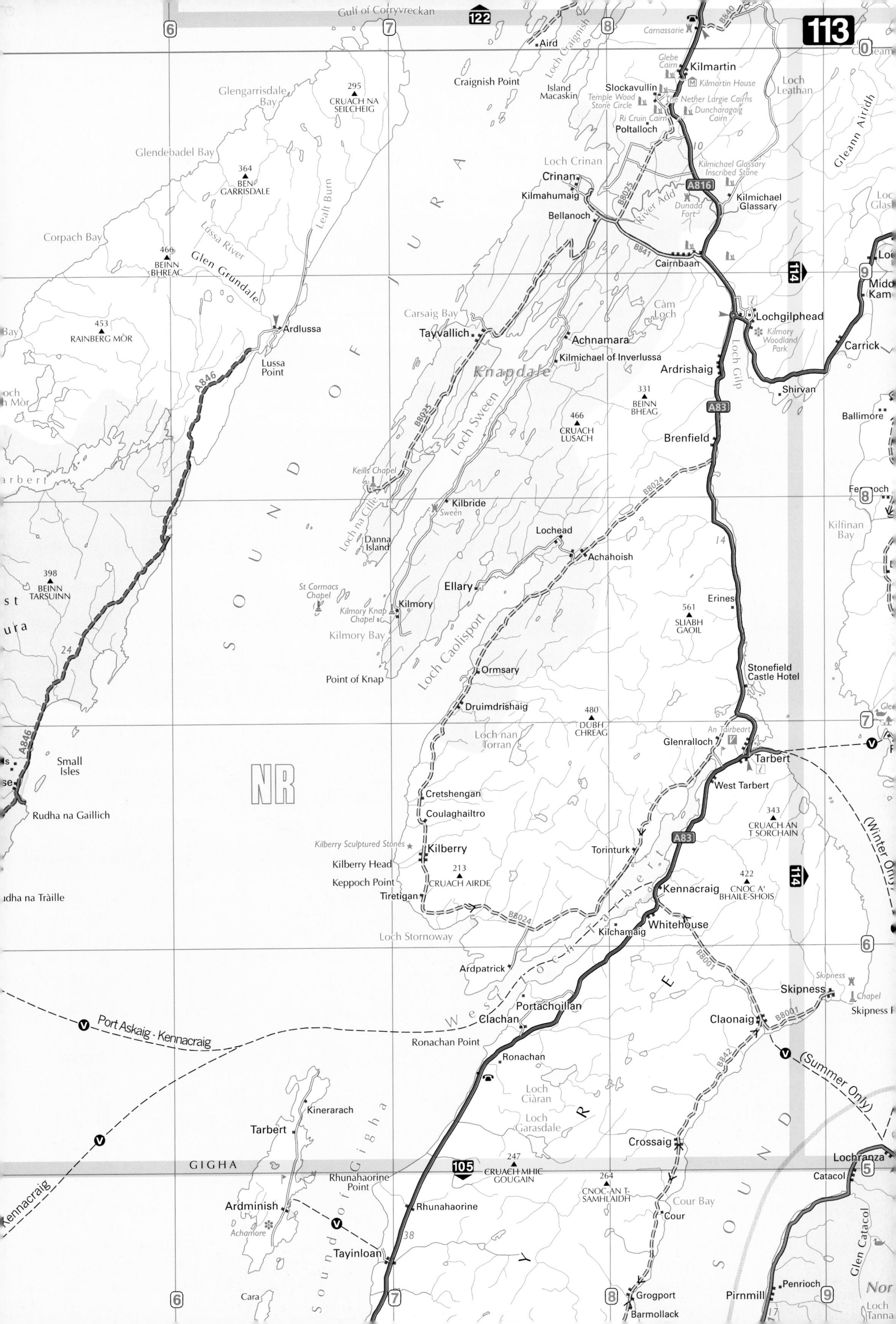
Gulf of Corryvreckan
122
Aird
Craignish Point
Carnassarie
Kilmartin
Glebe Cairn
Kilmartin House
Loch Leathan
Island Macaskin
Slockavullin
Temple Wood Stone Circle
The Nether Largie Cairns
Dunchraigaig Cairn
Ri Cruin Cairn
Poltalloch
Glengarrisdale Bay
CRUACH NA SEILCHEIG
Glendebadel Bay
BEN GARRISDALE
Lealt Burn
Loch Crinan
Crinan
Kilmahumaig
Bellanoch
River Add
Dunadd Fort
A816
Kilmichael Glassary Inscribed Stone
Kilmichael Glassary
Gleann Airidh
Corpach Bay
Lussa River
Glen Grundale
BEINN BHREAC
B841
Cairnbaan
114
Carsaig Bay
Càm Loch
Lochgilphead
Kilmory Woodland Park
Ardlussa
RAINBERG MÒR
Tayvallich
Achnamara
Kilmichael of Inverlussa
Lussa Point
Knapdale
Ardrishaig
Loch Gilp
Carrick
Shirvan
A846
BEINN BHEAG
CRUACH LUSACH
Loch Sween
B8025
A83
Brenfield
Ballimore
Keills Chapel
B8024
Kilbride
Sween
SOUND OF JURA
Loch na Cille
Danna Island
Lochead
Achahoish
Kilfinan Bay
BEINN TARSUINN
St Cormacs Chapel
Ellary
Kilmory
Kilmory Knap Chapel
Kilmory Bay
Erines
SLIABH GAOIL
Loch Caolisport
Ormsary
Point of Knap
Stonefield Castle Hotel
Druimdrishaig
DUBH CHREAG
Loch nan Torran
An Tairbeart
Glenralloch
Tarbert
West Tarbert
Small Isles
NR
Cretshengan
Coulaghailtro
Rudha na Gaillich
CRUACH AN T SORCHAIN
Kilberry Sculptured Stones
Kilberry
Kilberry Head
Keppoch Point
Tiretigan
CRUACH AIRDE
Torinturk
Kennacraig
CNOC A' BHAILE-SHOIS
(Winter Only)
West Loch Tarbert
Whitehouse
Kilchamaig
Loch Stornoway
B8001
Ardpatrick
Skipness
Chapel
Portachoillan
Clachan
Claonaig
Port Askaig - Kennacraig
Ronachan Point
Ronachan
B8842
(Summer Only)
Loch Ciàran
Loch Garasdale
Kinerarach
Tarbert
Crossaig
GIGHA
105
CRUACH MHIC GOUGAIN
Lochranza
Catacol
Rhunahaorine Point
Rhunahaorine
CNOC-AN T-SAMHLAIDH
Cour Bay
Cour
Ardminish
Achamore
Sound of Gigha
Tayinloan
Glen Catacol
Penrioch
Pirnmill
Grogport
Barmollack
Cara
Kennacraig

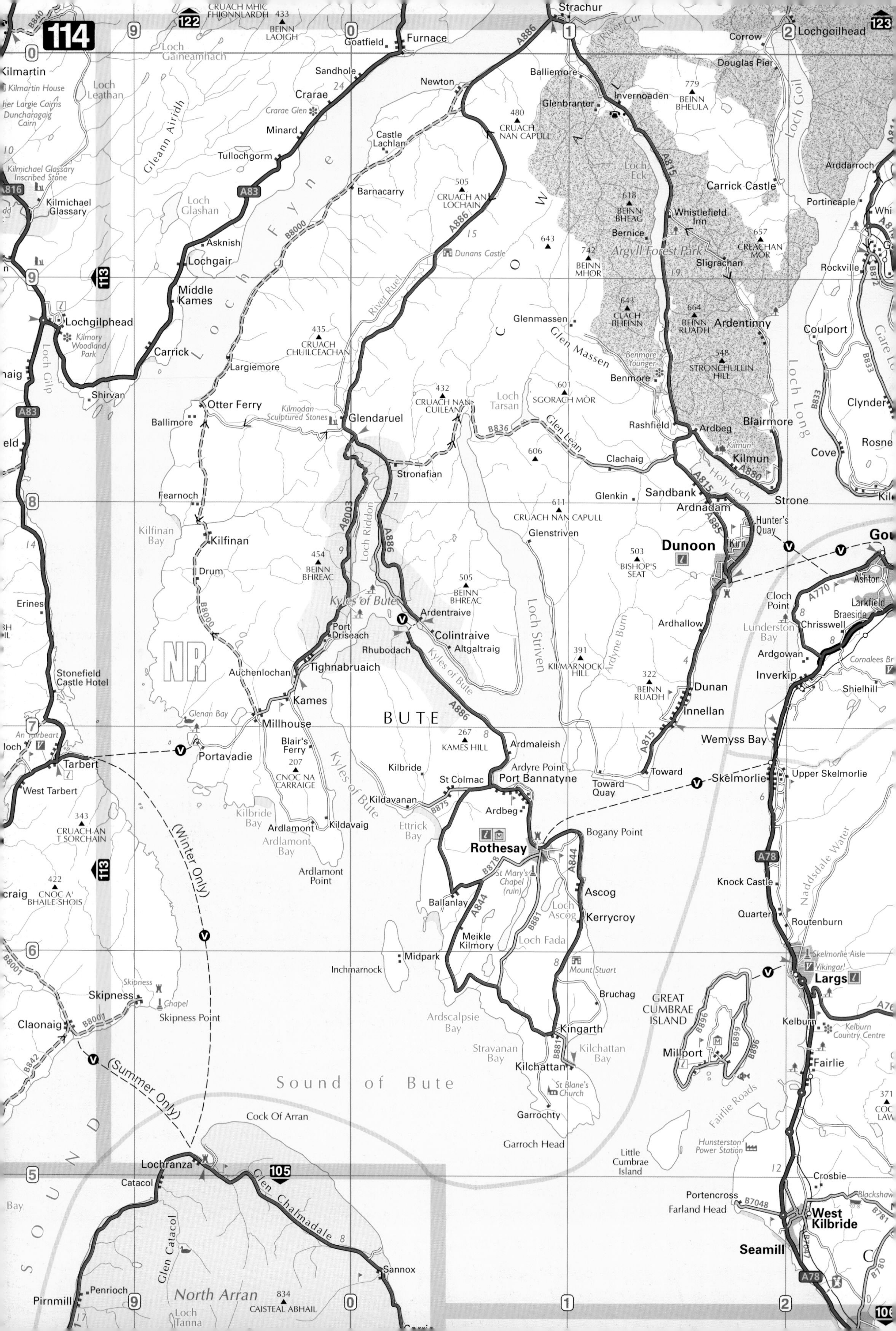

Strachur
Furnace
Goatfield
Lochgoilhead
Corrow
Douglas Pier
Loch Goil
Kilmartin
Kilmartin House
Loch Leathan
Loch Gaineamhach
Sandhole
Crarae
Crarae Glen
Minard
Newton
Castle Lachlan
Balliemore
Glenbranter
Invernoaden
BEINN BHEULA
CRUACH NAN CAPULL
Gleann Airidh
Tullochgorm
Kilmichael Glassary Inscribed Stone
Kilmichael Glassary
Loch Glashan
A83
Barnacarry
CRUACH AN LOCHAIN
Loch Eck
BEINN BHEAG
Whistlefield Inn
Carrick Castle
Arddarroch
Portincaple
Bernice
CREACHAN MOR
Argyll Forest Park
Asknish
Lochgair
Loch Fyne
Dunans Castle
BEINN MHOR
Sligrachan
Rockville
Middle Kames
Lochgilphead
Kilmory Woodland Park
River Ruel
Glenmassen
CLACH BHEINN
BEINN RUADH
Ardentinny
Coulport
Carrick
CRUACH CHUILCEACHAN
Largiemore
Glen Massen
Benmore Younger
Benmore
STRONCHULLIN HILL
Loch Long
Clynder
Shirvan
Loch Gilp
Otter Ferry
Ballimore
Kilmodan Sculptured Stones
Glendaruel
CRUACH NAN CUILEAN
Loch Tarsan
SGORACH MOR
Glen Lean
Rashfield
Ardbeg
Blairmore
Kilmun
Cove
Rosneath
Stronafian
Clachaig
Holy Loch
Fearnoch
Glenkin
Sandbank
Ardnadam
Strone
Kilfinan Bay
Kilfinan
CRUACH NAN CAPULL
Glenstriven
Hunter's Quay
Dunoon
Drum
BEINN BHREAC
Loch Riddon
BISHOP'S SEAT
Erines
Kyles of Bute
Ardentraive
Colintraive
Loch Striven
Cloch Point
Lunderston Bay
Ashton
Larkfield
Braeside
Chrisswell
Port Driseach
Rhubodach
Altgaltraig
Ardyne Burn
Ardhallow
Ardgowan
Inverkip
Cornalees
Shielhill
NR
Stonefield Castle Hotel
Auchenlochan
Tighnabruaich
Kames
KILMARNOCK HILL
BEINN RUADH
Dunan
Innellan
Glenan Bay
Millhouse
BUTE
An Tairbeart
Portavadie
Blair's Ferry
KAMES HILL
Ardmaleish
Wemyss Bay
Tarbert
West Tarbert
CNOC NA CARRAIGE
Kilbride
St Colmac
Ardyre Point
Port Bannatyne
Toward Quay
Toward
Skelmorlie
Upper Skelmorlie
CRUACH AN T SORCHAIN
Kilbride Bay
Ardlamont
Kildavaig
Kildavanan
Ettrick Bay
Ardbeg
Bogany Point
Ardlamont Bay
Rothesay
Naddsdale Water
(Winter Only)
CNOC A' BHAILE-SHOIS
Ardlamont Point
St Mary's Chapel (ruin)
Ascog
Loch Ascog
Knock Castle
Ballanlay
Kerrycroy
Quarter
Routenburn
Meikle Kilmory
Loch Fada
Skelmorlie Aisle
Vikingar!
Midpark
Inchmarnock
Mount Stuart
Largs
Skipness
Chapel
Skipness Point
Bruchag
GREAT CUMBRAE ISLAND
Claonaig
Ardscalpsie Bay
Kingarth
Kelburn
Kelburn Country Centre
Millport
Stravanan Bay
Kilchattan Bay
Kilchattan
Fairlie
(Summer Only)
Sound of Bute
St Blane's Church
Fairlie Roads
Garrochty
COCK LAW
Cock Of Arran
Garroch Head
Hunterston Power Station
Little Cumbrae Island
SOUND
Lochranza
Catacol
Glen Chalmadale
Crosbie
Portencross
Farland Head
West Kilbride
Blackshaw
Bay
Glen Catacol
Seamill
Sannox
Penrioch
North Arran
CAISTEAL ABHAIL
Pirnmill
Loch Tanna
A78
A815
A886
A8003
A844
B8000
B836
B875
B878
B881
B8001
B842
B7048
B896
B899
A885
A880
B833
A770
122
123
113
105

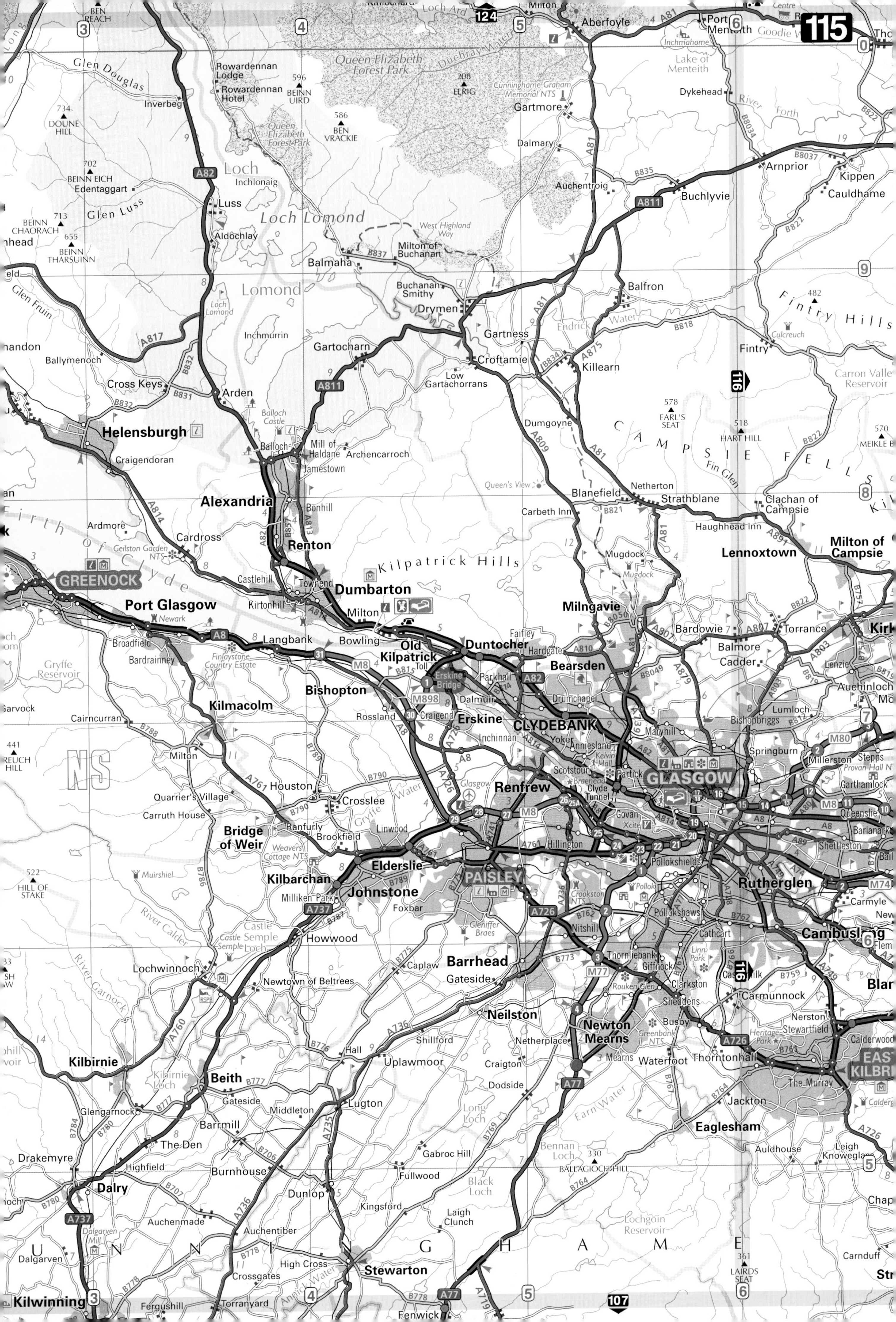
Aberfoyle
Port of Menteith
Lake of Menteith
Inchmahome
Loch Ard
Queen Elizabeth Forest Park
Duchray Water
Rowardennan Lodge
Rowardennan Hotel
596 BEINN UIRD
208 ELRIG
Cunninghame Graham Memorial NTS
Gartmore
Dykehead
River Forth
Glen Douglas
Inverbeg
734 DOUNE HILL
586 BEN VRACKIE
Dalmary
Arnprior
Kippen
Cauldhame
Buchlyvie
Auchentroig
702 BEINN EICH
Edentaggart
Loch Lomond
Inchlonaig
Luss
Glen Luss
713 BEINN CHAORACH
655 BEINN THARSUINN
Aldochlay
West Highland Way
Milton of Buchanan
Balmaha
Buchanan Smithy
Drymen
Balfron
Fintry Hills
482
Glen Fruin
Inchmurrin
Gartocharn
Gartness
Endrick Water
Fintry
Culcreuch
Ballymenoch
Croftamie
Killearn
Carron Valley Reservoir
Cross Keys
Arden
Low Gartachorrans
578 EARL'S SEAT
518 HART HILL
570 MEIKLE BIN
Balloch Castle
Helensburgh
Craigendoran
Balloch
Mill of Haldane
Archencarroch
Jamestown
Dumgoyne
CAMPSIE FELLS
Fin Glen
Alexandria
Bonhill
Queen's View
Blanefield
Netherton
Strathblane
Clachan of Campsie
Firth of Clyde
Ardmore
Cardross
Geilston Garden NTS
Renton
Kilpatrick Hills
Carbeth Inn
Haughhead Inn
Milton of Campsie
Lennoxtown
GREENOCK
Castlehill
Townend
Dumbarton
Mugdock
Port Glasgow
Newark
Kirtonhill
Milton
Milngavie
Bardowie
Torrance
Kirkintilloch
Broadfield
Bardrainney
Langbank
Bowling
Old Kilpatrick
Duntocher
Faifley
Hardgate
Bearsden
Balmore
Cadder
Lenzie
Auchinloch
Gryffe Reservoir
Finlaystone Country Estate
Bishopton
Erskine Bridge
Parkhall
Dalmuir
Drumchapel
Lumloch
Bishopbriggs
Garvock
Cairncurran
Kilmacolm
Rossland
Craigend
Erskine
CLYDEBANK
Maryhill
Springburn
Millerston
Stepps
Provan Hall NTS
Gartharnlock
441 CREUCH HILL
Milton
Inchinnan
Yoker
Anniesland
Kelvin Hall
Scotstoun
Partick
GLASGOW
NS
Quarrier's Village
Houston
Glasgow Airport
Renfrew
Braehead
Clyde Tunnel
Crosslee
Gryffe Water
Carruth House
Bridge of Weir
Ranfurly
Brookfield
Linwood
Govan
Xcite
Queenslie
Barlanark
Weavers Cottage NTS
Hillington
Shettleston
Muirshiel
Elderslie
Pollokshields
Kilbarchan
PAISLEY
Rutherglen
522 HILL OF STAKE
Johnstone
Milliken Park
Pollok
Crookston NTS
Carmyle
River Calder
Foxbar
Pollokshaws
Nitshill
Castle Semple Loch
Howwood
Gleniffer Braes
Cathcart
Cambuslang
Linn Park
Thornliebank
Giffnock
Lochwinnoch
Caplaw
Barrhead
Gateside
Clarkston
Castlemilk
River Garnock
Newtown of Beltrees
Rouken Glen
Sheddens
Carmunnock
Blantyre
RSPB
Neilston
Busby
Nerston
Stewartfield
Heritage Park
Calderwood
Kilbirnie
Shillford
Netherplace
Newton Mearns
Greenbank NTS
Mearns
Waterfoot
Thorntonhall
EAST KILBRIDE
Kilbirnie Loch
Hall
Uplawmoor
Craigton
The Murray
Beith
Dodside
Calderglen
Gateside
Lugton
Middleton
Earn Water
Jackton
Glengarnock
Long Loch
Eaglesham
Barrmill
Drakemyre
The Den
Auldhouse
Leigh Knowglass
Bennan Loch
330 BALLAGIOCH HILL
Gabroc Hill
Highfield
Burnhouse
Fullwood
Dalry
Black Loch
Dunlop
Kingsford
Laigh Clunch
Auchenmade
Lochgoin Reservoir
Auchentiber
Dalgarven Mill
CUNNINGHAME
Dalgarven
High Cross
Stewarton
361 LAIRDS SEAT
Carnduff
Crossgates
Annick Water
Kilwinning
Fergushill
Torranyard
Fenwick
A81
A811
A82
A817
A814
A8
M8
M898
A726
A761
A737
A736
A760
A735
A77
M77
M80
M74
A749
A803
A807
A879
A809
A875
A891
A739
A741
B8037
B835
B822
B818
B834
B837
B832
B831
B821
B8050
B8049
B815
B788
B789
B790
B786
B787
B775
B773
B762
B766
B759
B769
B776
B777
B780
B784
B706
B707
B778
B764
B8034
B822
124
116
107

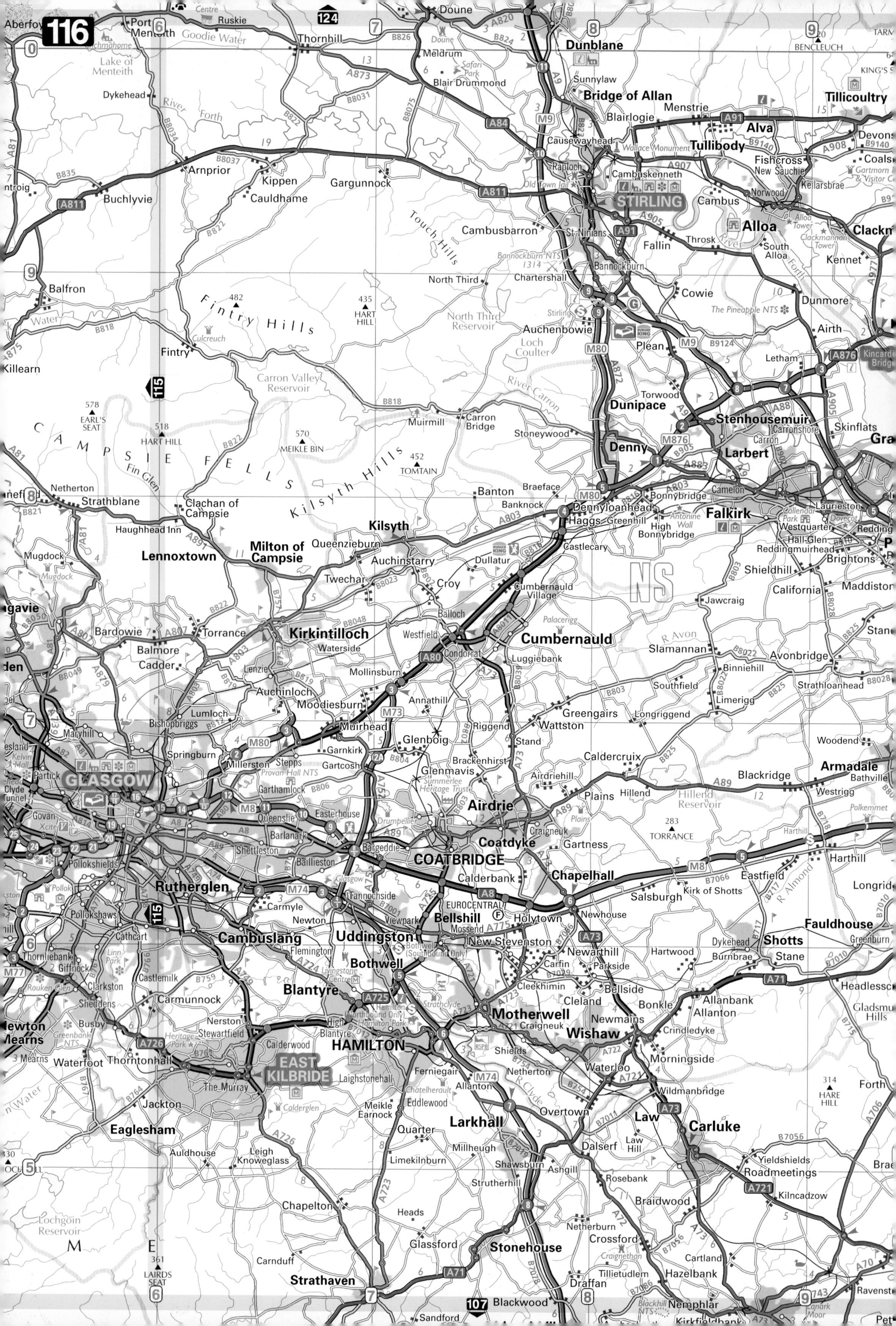
116
Aberfoyle
Port of Menteith
Ruskie
Goodie Water
Thornhill
Doune
Dunblane
Lake of Menteith
Meldrum
Safari Park
Blair Drummond
Dykehead
River Forth
Bridge of Allan
Sunnylaw
Menstrie
Tillicoultry
Blairlogie
Alva
Causewayhead
Wallace Monument
Tullibody
Devonside
Fishcross
Coalsnaughton
New Sauchie
Gartmorn
Raploch
Cambuskenneth
Arnprior
Kippen
Gargunnock
Buchlyvie
Cauldhame
Old Town Jail
STIRLING
Cambus
Norwood
Kellarsbrae
Touch Hills
Cambusbarron
St Ninians
Alloa
Alloa Tower
Clackmannan
Clackmannan Tower
Fallin
Throsk
South Alloa
Kennet
Bannockburn NTS 1314
Bannockburn
Chartershall
Balfron
North Third
Cowie
Dunmore
Fintry Hills
HART HILL
North Third Reservoir
Stirling
The Pineapple NTS
Auchenbowie
Airth
Water
Culcreuch
Loch Coulter
Plean
Fintry
Killearn
Carron Valley Reservoir
Letham
Kincardine Bridge
River Carron
Torwood
Dunipace
Stenhousemuir
578 EARL'S SEAT
518 HART HILL
Muirmill
Carron Bridge
Carronshore
Skinflats
CAMPSIE FELLS
570 MEIKLE BIN
Stoneywood
Carron
Fin Glen
Kilsyth Hills
452 TOMTAIN
Denny
Larbert
Netherton
Banton
Braeface
Camelon
Bonnybridge
Strathblane
Clachan of Campsie
Banknock
Dennyloanhead
Laurieston
Haggs
Greenhill
Falkirk
Callendar Park
Antonine Wall
Dovecot
High Bonnybridge
Westquarter
Redding
Haughhead Inn
Kilsyth
Hall-Glen
Milton of Campsie
Queenzieburn
Reddingmuirhead
Lennoxtown
Castlecary
Brightons
Mugdock
Auchinstarry
Dullatur
Shieldhill
Twechar
Croy
Cumbernauld Village
California
Maddiston
Balloch
Palacerigg
Bardowie
Torrance
Kirkintilloch
Westfield
Cumbernauld
Balmore
R Avon
Slamannan
Avonbridge
Waterside
Condorrat
Cadder
Lenzie
Luggiebank
Mollinsburn
Binniehill
Auchinloch
Annathill
Southfield
Strathloanhead
Moodiesburn
Limerigg
Lumloch
Greengairs
Longriggend
Bishopbriggs
Muirhead
Riggend
Wattston
Maryhill
Glenboig
Stand
Woodend
Garnkirk
Springburn
Caldercruix
Armadale
Millerston
Stepps
Gartcosh
Brackenhirst
Provan Hall NTS
Glenmavis
Summerlee Heritage Trust
Partick
GLASGOW
Airdriehill
Blackridge
Bathville
Garthamlock
Plains
Hillend
Westrigg
Hillend Reservoir
Airdrie
Easterhouse
Govan
Queenslie
Drumpellier
Polkemmet
Barlanark
Craigneuk
283 TORRANCE
Coatdyke
Gartness
Shettleston
Bargeddie
COATBRIDGE
Harthill
Pollokshields
Baillieston
Chapelhall
Eastfield
Calderbank
Rutherglen
Glasgow Zoo
Tannochside
Longridge
EUROCENTRAL
Salsburgh
Kirk of Shotts
Carmyle
Viewpark
Bellshill
Holytown
Newhouse
Pollokshaws
Newton
Mossend
Fauldhouse
Cambuslang
Uddingston
New Stevenston
Cathcart
Shotts
Greenburn
Thornliebank
Flemington
Bothwell
Newarthill
Hartwood
Dykehead
Burnbrae
Stane
Giffnock
Carfin
Parkside
Livingstone Centre
Castlemilk
Rouken Glen
Clarkston
Blantyre
Cleekhimin
Bellside
Headlesscross
Carmunnock
Cleland
Sheddens
Strathclyde
Bonkle
Allanbank
Allanton
Motherwell
Newmains
Gladsmuir Hills
Busby
Nerston
Hamilton Park
Craigneuk
Newton Mearns
Stewartfield
High Blantyre
Crindledyke
Wishaw
Greenbank NTS
Heritage Park
Calderwood
HAMILTON
Shields
Morningside
Mearns
Waterfoot
Thorntonhall
EAST KILBRIDE
Netherton
Waterloo
Ferniegair
Laighstonehall
Allanton
The Murray
Chatelherault
314 HARE HILL
Forth
Wildmanbridge
Eddlewood
Meikle Earnock
Overtown
Jackton
Calderglen
Larkhall
Law
Carluke
Eaglesham
Quarter
Law Hill
Auldhouse
Leigh Knoweglass
Millheugh
Dalserf
Yieldshields
Limekilnburn
Shawsburn
Ashgill
Roadmeetings
Rosebank
Strutherhill
Kilncadzow
Braidwood
Chapelton
Lochgoin Reservoir
Heads
Netherburn
Crossford
Glassford
Stonehouse
Craignethan
Cartland
361 LAIRDS SEAT
Carnduff
Tillietudlem
Hazelbank
Strathaven
Draffan
Blackwood
Nemphlar
Lanark Moor
Blackhill NTS
Kirkfieldbank
Sandford
NS
124
115
107

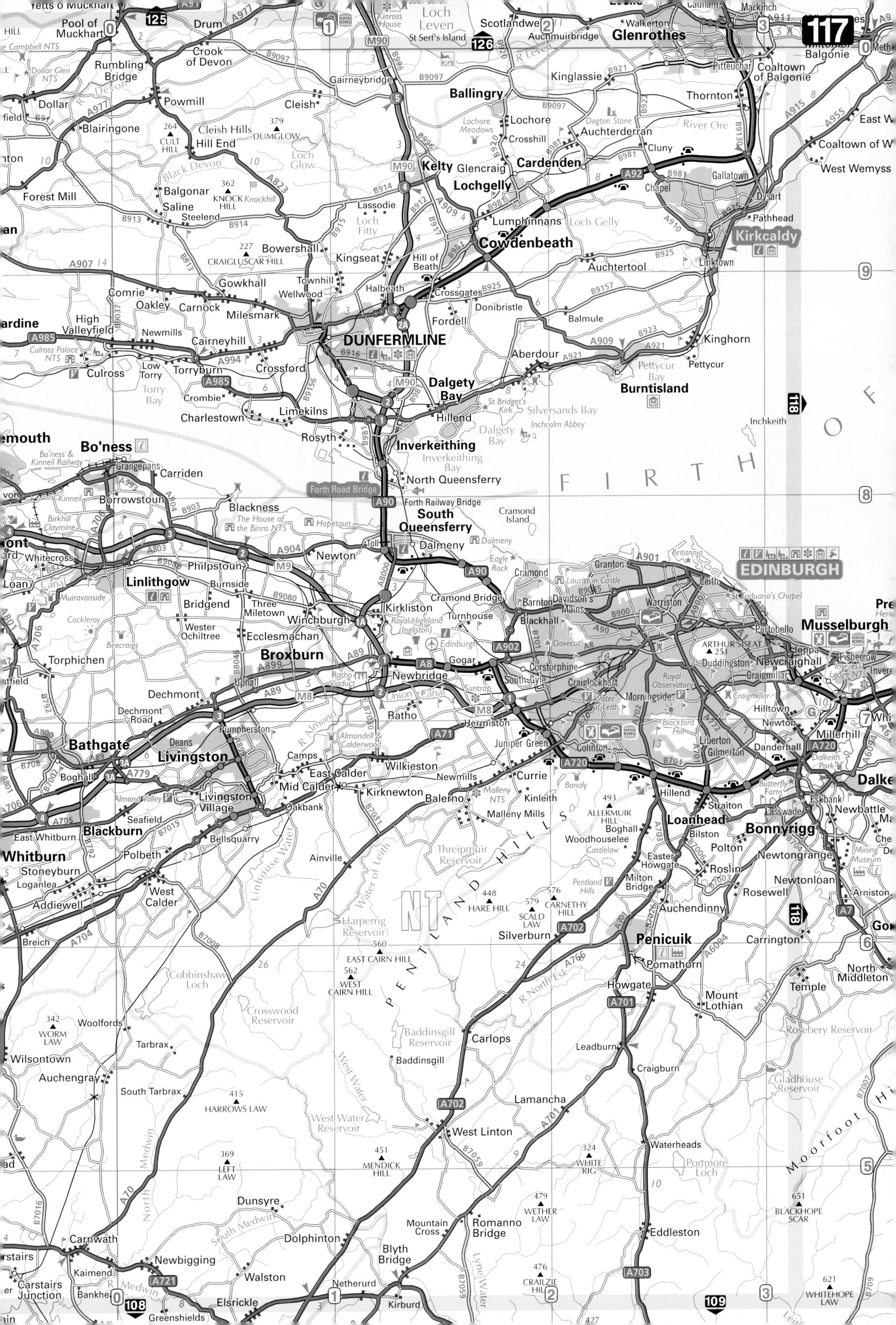
117
Pool of Muckhart
Drum
Crook of Devon
Loch Leven
Kinross House
St Serf's Island
Scotlandwell
Auchmuirbridge
Walkerton
Glenrothes
Markinch
Milton of Balgonie
Rumbling Bridge
Dollar
Powmill
Cleish
Gairneybridge
Ballingry
Kinglassie
Pitteuchar
Coaltown of Balgonie
Thornton
Blairingone
Cleish Hills
Hill End
Dumglow
Cult Hill
Loch Glow
Lochore
Lochore Meadows
Crosshill
Dogton Stone
Auchterderran
River Ore
Cluny
East Wemyss
Coaltown of Wemyss
West Wemyss
Black Devon
Kelty
Glencraig
Cardenden
Lochgelly
Gallatown
Chapel
Dysart
Pathhead
Forest Mill
Balgonar
Saline
Knock Hill
Steelend
Lassodie
Loch Fitty
Lumphinnans
Loch Gelly
Kirkcaldy
Bowershall
Craigluscar Hill
Kingseat
Hill of Beath
Cowdenbeath
Auchtertool
Linktown
Townhill
Gowkhall
Comrie
Oakley
Carnock
Milesmark
Wellwood
Halbeath
Crossgates
Donibristle
Fordell
Balmule
High Valleyfield
Newmills
Cairneyhill
Dunfermline
Culross Palace NTS
Culross
Low Torry
Torryburn
Crossford
Torry Bay
Crombie
Charlestown
Limekilns
Rosyth
Dalgety Bay
Hillend
Aberdour
St Bridget's Kirk
Silversands Bay
Inchcolm Abbey
Kinghorn
Pettycur Bay
Pettycur
Burntisland
Inchkeith
Bo'ness
Bo'ness & Kinneil Railway
Grangepans
Carriden
Inverkeithing
Inverkeithing Bay
North Queensferry
Forth Road Bridge
Forth Railway Bridge
Firth of
Borrowstoun
Kinneil
Blackness
The House of the Binns NTS
Hopetoun
South Queensferry
Cramond Island
Birkhill Claymine
Whitecross
Philpstoun
Newton
Dalmeny
Eagle Rock
Cramond
Granton
Britannia
Leith
Edinburgh
Linlithgow
Burnside
Lauriston Castle
Muiravonside
Bridgend
Three Miletown
Kirkliston
Cramond Bridge
Barnton
Davidson's Mains
Warriston
St Triduana's Chapel
Musselburgh
Cockleroy
Beecraigs
Wester Ochiltree
Ecclesmachan
Winchburgh
Royal Highland (Ingliston)
Turnhouse
Blackhall
Portobello
Arthur's Seat
Joppa
Fisherrow
Torphichen
Broxburn
Edinburgh
Gogar
Dovecot
Duddingston
Newcraighall
Inveresk Lodge NTS
Uphall
Ratho Viaduct
Newbridge
Corstorphine
South Gyle
Craiglockhart
Royal Observatory
Craigmillar
Dechmont
Union Canal
Suntrap
Water of Leith
Morningside
Hilltown
Dechmont Road
Ratho
Hermiston
Blackford Hill
Newton
Millerhill
Bathgate
Deans
Pumpherston
Almondell & Calderwood
Juniper Green
Colinton
Liberton
Gilmerton
Danderhall
Dalkeith Park
Livingston
Camps
Wilkieston
Boghall
East Calder
Mid Calder
Newmills
Currie
Kirknewton
Balerno
Malleny NTS
Kinleith
Bonaly
Hillend
Straiton
Eskbank
Dalkeith
Newbattle
Almond Valley
Livingston Village
Oakbank
Seafield
Malleny Mills
Allermuir Hill
Boghall
Loanhead
Bonnyrigg
Blackburn
East Whitburn
Bellsquarry
Bilston
Woodhouselee
Castlelaw
Polton
Whitburn
Polbeth
Ainville
Threipmuir Reservoir
Pentland Hills
Easter Howgate
Roslin
Newtongrange
Mining Museum
Stoneyburn
Loganlea
West Calder
Milton Bridge
Newtonloan
Rosewell
Arniston
Addiewell
Hare Hill
Carnethy Hill
Scald Law
Auchendinny
Harperrig Reservoir
Silverburn
Penicuik
Carrington
Breich
East Cairn Hill
West Cairn Hill
Pomathorn
North Middleton
Cobbinshaw Loch
River North Esk
Howgate
Temple
Mount Lothian
Crosswood Reservoir
Woolfords
Worm Law
Baddinsgill Reservoir
Carlops
Rosebery Reservoir
Tarbrax
Leadburn
Wilsontown
Baddinsgill
Craigburn
Auchengray
South Tarbrax
Harrows Law
Gladhouse Reservoir
West Water
Lamancha
West Water Reservoir
West Linton
Moorfoot Hills
Waterheads
Left Law
Mendick Hill
White Rig
Portmore Loch
Medwin
Dunsyre
South Medwin
Wether Law
Blackhope Scar
Mountain Cross
Romanno Bridge
Eddleston
Carnwath
Dolphinton
Newbigging
Blyth Bridge
Lyne Water
Kaimend
Walston
Crailzie Hill
Whitehope Law
Carstairs Junction
Bankhead
Netherurd
Elsrickle
Kirkburd
Greenshields

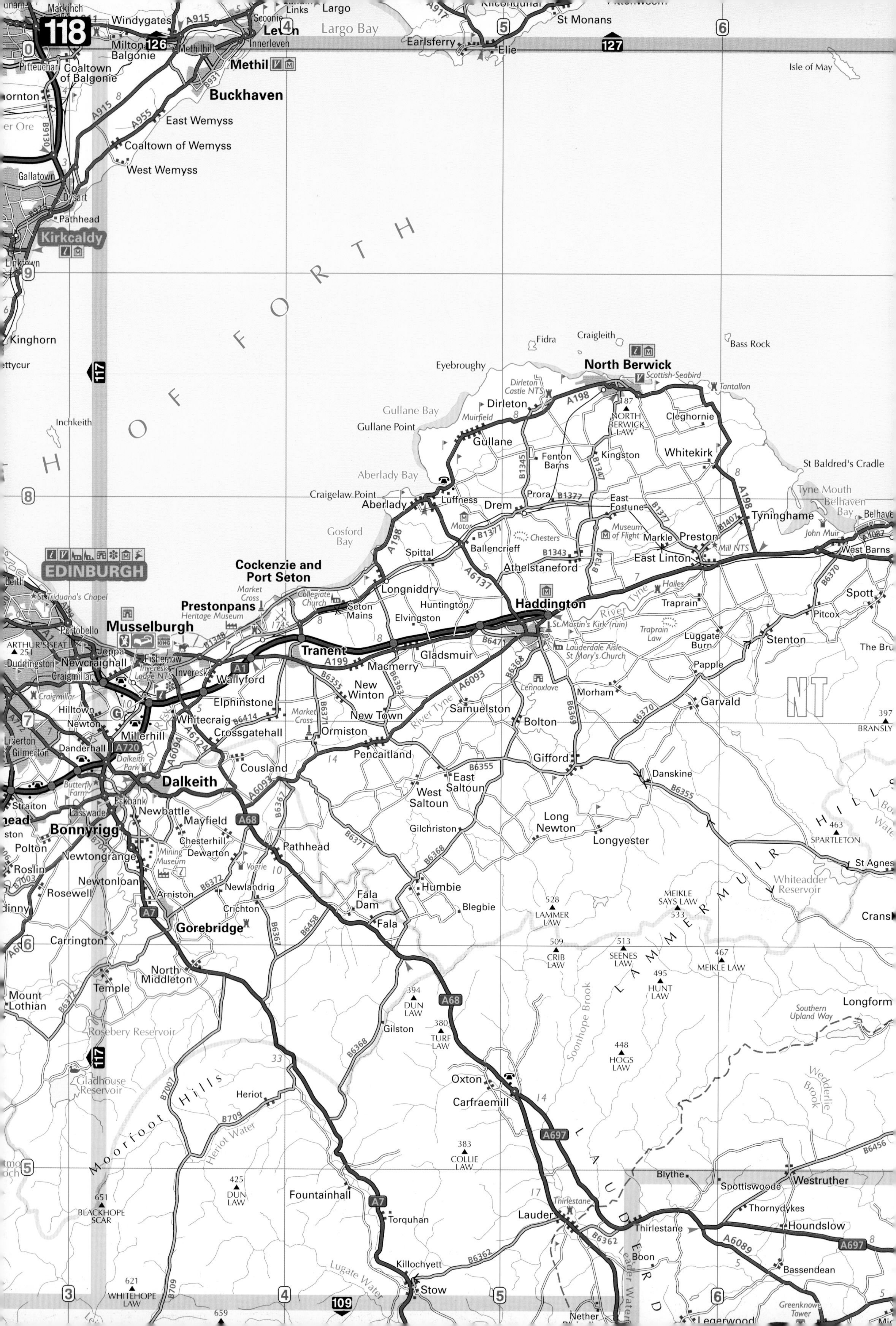
118
126
127
117
109
Markinch
Windygates
Links
Largo
Largo Bay
Leven
Scoonie
Innerleven
Methilhill
Milton
Balgonie
Pitteuchar
Coaltown of Balgonie
Methil
Buckhaven
East Wemyss
Coaltown of Wemyss
West Wemyss
Gallatown
Dysart
Pathhead
Kirkcaldy
Linktown
Kinghorn
Inchkeith
Earlsferry
Elie
St Monans
Isle of May
FIRTH OF FORTH
Fidra
Craigleith
Bass Rock
Eyebroughy
North Berwick
Scottish Seabird
Tantallon
Dirleton
Dirleton Castle NTS
NORTH BERWICK LAW
Cleghornie
Gullane Bay
Gullane Point
Muirfield
Gullane
Fenton Barns
Kingston
Whitekirk
St Baldred's Cradle
Aberlady Bay
Craigielaw Point
Aberlady
Luffness
Drem
Prora
East Fortune
Tyne Mouth
Belhaven Bay
Tyninghame
John Muir
Museum of Flight
Markle
Preston
Mill NTS
West Barns
Gosford Bay
Spittal
Ballencrieff
Chesters
Athelstaneford
East Linton
Hailes
Traprain
Spott
Pitcox
EDINBURGH
Leith
St Triduana's Chapel
Cockenzie and Port Seton
Market Cross
Collegiate Church
Seton Mains
Longniddry
Huntington
Haddington
Elvington
Prestonpans
Heritage Museum
Musselburgh
Portobello
Joppa
ARTHUR'S SEAT
Duddingston
Newcraighall
Craigmillar
Fisherrow
Inveresk
Inveresk Lodge NTS
Tranent
Gladsmuir
Macmerry
Wallyford
Elphinstone
New Winton
Samuelston
St Martin's Kirk (ruin)
Traprain Law
Lauderdale Aisle
St Mary's Church
Luggate Burn
Stenton
Papple
The Brunt
Lennoxlove
Morham
Garvald
NT
BRANSLY
Hilltown
Newton
Whitecraig
Crossgatehall
Market Cross
Ormiston
New Town
Bolton
Liberton
Gilmerton
Danderhall
Millerhill
Dalkeith Park
Pencaitland
Gifford
Danskine
Cousland
Dalkeith
Butterfly Farm
East Saltoun
West Saltoun
Straiton
Eskbank
Lasswade
Newbattle
Mayfield
Long Newton
Longyester
SPARTLETON
LAMMERMUIR HILLS
Bonnyrigg
Polton
Chesterhill
Dewarton
Gilchriston
Pathhead
Newtongrange
Mining Museum
Roslin
Vogrie
Whiteadder Reservoir
St Agnes
Newtonloan
Rosewell
Arniston
Newlandrig
Humbie
MEIKLE SAYS LAW
Crichton
Fala Dam
Fala
Blegbie
LAMMER LAW
Cranshaws
Gorebridge
Carrington
CRIB LAW
SEENES LAW
MEIKLE LAW
North Middleton
Temple
Mount Lothian
DUN LAW
HUNT LAW
Soonhope Brook
Longformacus
Southern Upland Way
Rosebery Reservoir
Gilston
TURF LAW
HOGS LAW
Gladhouse Reservoir
Moorfoot Hills
Heriot
Oxton
Carfraemill
Wedderlie Brook
Heriot Water
COLLIE LAW
LAUDERDALE
Blythe
Spottiswoode
Westruther
Thornydykes
DUN LAW
Fountainhall
BLACKHOPE SCAR
Torquhan
Lauder
Thirlestane
Thirlestane
Houndslow
Boon
Bassendean
Killochyett
Lugate Water
Leader Water
WHITEHOPE LAW
Stow
Nether
Legerwood
Greenknowe Tower
A915
A955
B9130
A917
A198
B1345
B1347
B1377
B1407
A1087
B1371
B1343
B6370
A6137
B1348
A1
A199
B6471
B6363
B6355
B6368
A6093
B6414
B6371
B6369
A720
A6094
A6124
A68
B6367
B6372
B6458
B7003
A7
B6362
B7007
B709
A697
A6089
B6456
B6355
187
251
397
463
528
533
509
513
467
394
495
380
448
383
425
651
621
659

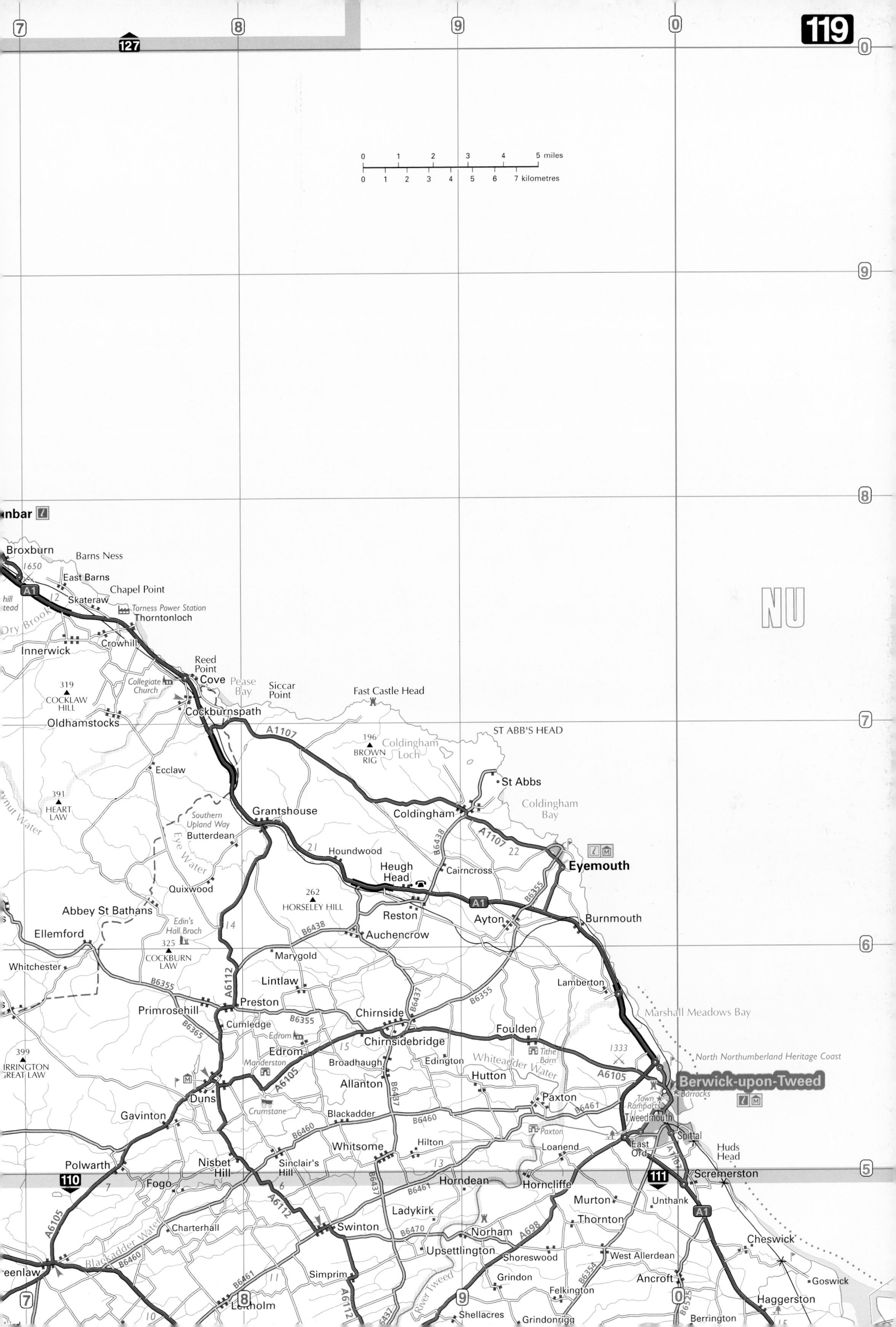

0

9

8

7

0 1 2 3 4 5 miles
0 1 2 3 4 5 6 7 kilometres

NU

Dunbar

Broxburn
1650
Barns Ness
A1
East Barns
Skateraw
Chapel Point
hill
stead
Dry Brook
Torness Power Station
Thorntonloch
Crowhill
Innerwick
319
COCKLAW HILL
Collegiate Church
Reed Point
Cove
Pease Bay
Siccar Point
Fast Castle Head
ST ABB'S HEAD
Oldhamstocks
Cockburnspath
A1107
196
BROWN RIG
Coldingham Loch
Ecclaw
St Abbs
391
HEART LAW
Southern Upland Way
Butterdean
Grantshouse
Coldingham
A1107
Coldingham Bay
nut Water
Eye Water
Quixwood
21
Houndwood
Heugh Head
B6438
22
Eyemouth
Abbey St Bathans
Edin's Hall Broch
262
HORSELEY HILL
Cairncross
A1
Reston
Ayton
Burnmouth
Ellemford
325
COCKBURN LAW
Marygold
Auchencrow
B6355
Whitchester
B6355
Lintlaw
A6112
Lamberton
Marshall Meadows Bay
399
RRINGTON GREAT LAW
Primrosehill
B6365
Cumledge
Preston
B6355
Chirnside
B6437
Foulden
B6355
North Northumberland Heritage Coast
Berwick-upon-Tweed
Edrom
15
Chirnsidebridge
Manderston
Broadhaugh
Edington
1333
Whiteadder Water
Tithe Barn
A6105
Town Ramparts
Barracks
Duns
Allanton
B6437
Hutton
Paxton
Tweedmouth
Spittal
Gavinton
Crumstane
Blackadder
B6460
Whitsome
Hilton
B6460
Loanend
East Ord
Huds Head
Polwarth
Fogo
Nisbet Hill
Sinclair's Hill
13
B6437
Horndean
Horncliffe
Murton
Unthank
Scremerston
110
7
A6112
6
B6461
Ladykirk
B6461
Thornton
A1
eenlaw
A6105
B6460
Charterhall
Swinton
B6470
Norham
A698
Shoreswood
West Allerdean
Cheswick
Simprim
Upsettlington
Grindon
Ancroft
Goswick
7
8
Letholm
10
9
A6112
River Tweed
Shellacres
Felkington
Grindonrigg
0
Berrington
Haggerston

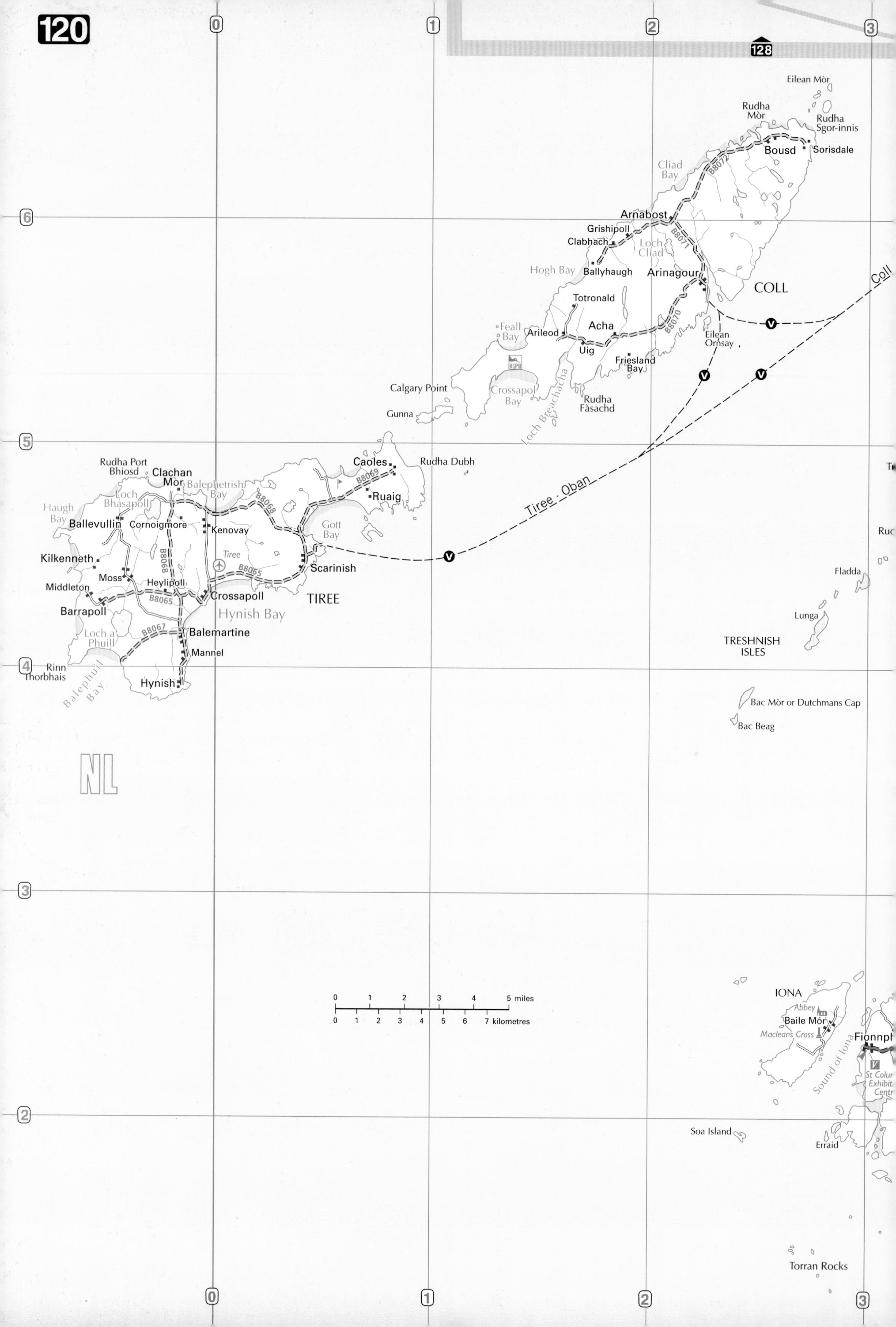

128

Eilean Mòr
Rudha Mòr
Rudha Sgor-innis
Bousd · Sorisdale

Cliad Bay

B8071

Arnabost
Grishipoll
Clabhach
Loch Cliad

Hogh Bay   Ballyhaugh
Arinagour

COLL

Coll

Totronald

B8071

Arileod   Acha
Feall Bay
Uig
Friesland Bay

Eilean Ornsay

Ⓥ

Ⓥ

Calgary Point
Crossapoll Bay
Rudha Fàsachd
Loch Breachacha

Gunna

Ⓥ

Tiree · Oban

Rudha Port Bhiosd
Clachan Mòr
Caoles
Rudha Dubh

Balephetrish Bay
B8069
Ruaig

Loch Bhasapoll
B8068

Haugh Bay
Ballevullin   Cornoigmore
Kenovay
Gott Bay

Tiree

Kilkenneth
B8068
Ⓥ

Moss   Heylipoll
B8065
Scarinish

Middleton
Crossapoll
TIREE

Barrapoll
B8065
Hynish Bay

Loch a Phuill
B8067
Balemartine

Rinn Thorbhais
Mannel

Balephuil Bay
Hynish

NL

T

Ruc

Fladda

Lunga

TRESHNISH ISLES

Bac Mòr or Dutchmans Cap

Bac Beag

0   1   2   3   4   5 miles
0 1 2 3 4 5 6   7 kilometres

IONA
Abbey
Baile Mòr
Macleans Cross
Fionnph

St Colur Exhibit Centr

Sound of Iona

Soa Island
Erraid

Torran Rocks

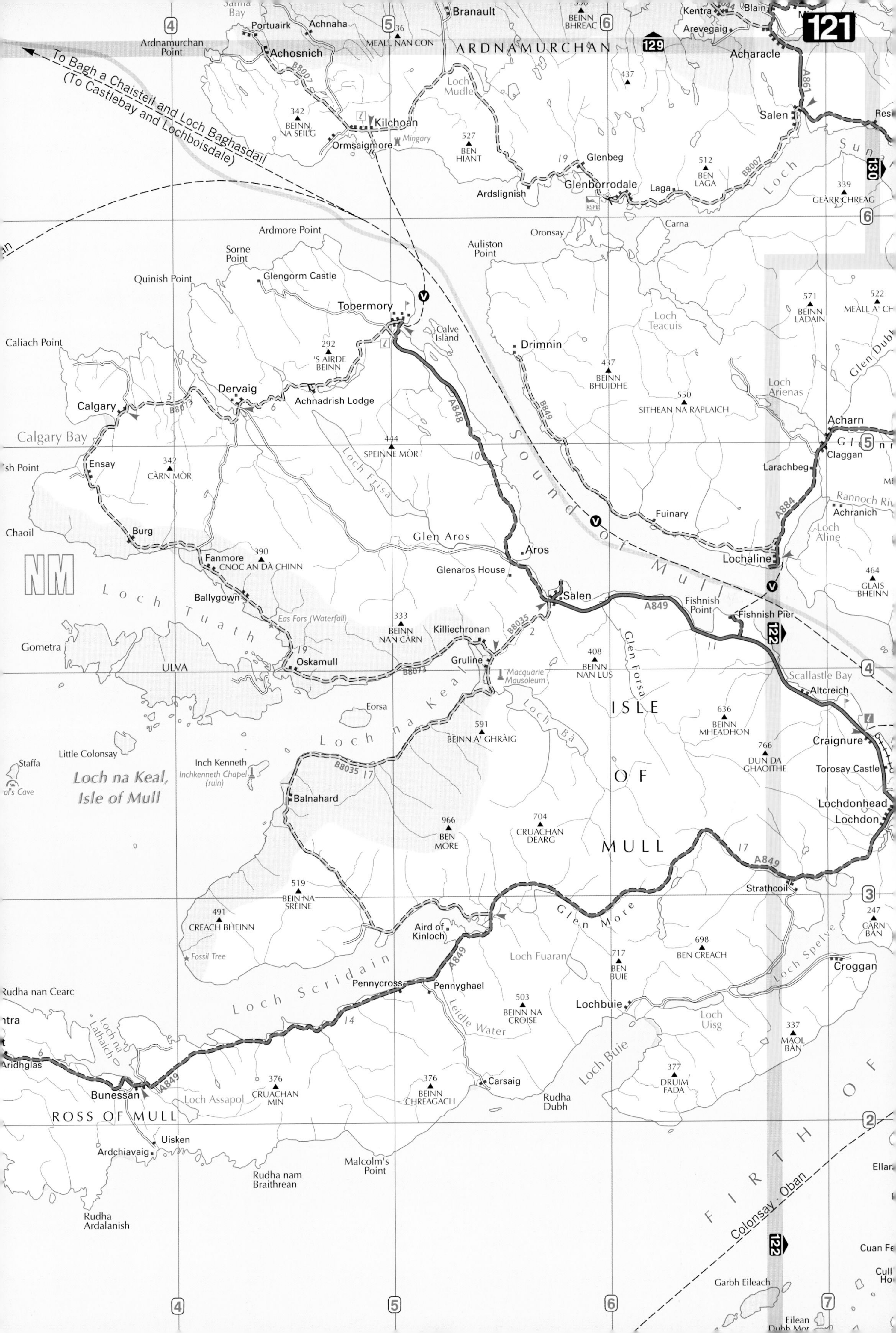

Sanna Bay

Portuairk
Achnaha
Achosnich
Ardnamurchan
Point
4

Branault
MEALL NAN CON
5 36
BEINN
BHREAC
6
Kentra
Arevegaig
Blain
129
Acharacle
A861

ARDNAMURCHAN

BEINN
NA SEIL'G
342
Kilchoan
Ormsaigmore
Mingary
Loch
Mudle
437
Glenbeg
BEN
HIANT
527
Salen
A861
B8007

To Bagh a Chaisteil and Loch Baghasdail
(To Castlebay and Lochboisdale)

Ardslignish
Glenborrodale
RSPB
Laga
19
BEN
LAGA
512
Loch Sun
B8007
130
6

Ardmore Point
Sorne
Point
Glengorm Castle
Auliston
Point
Oronsay
Carna
GEARR CHREAG
339

Quinish Point

Caliach Point

Tobermory
V
Calve
Island
Drimnin
Loch
Teacuis
BEINN
LADAIN
571
MEALL A' CH
522

's AIRDE
BEINN
292
Z
A848
BEINN
BHUIDHE
437
Loch
Arienas
Glen Dub

Dervaig
Achnadrish Lodge
SITHEAN NA RAPLAICH
550
Acharn
G   nr
5

Calgary
B8073
5
6
SPEINNE MÒR
444
Loch Frisa
B8049
10
Sound of Mull
Fuinary
Larachbeg
Claggan
A884
Rannoch Riv
Achranich
Loch
Aline
ME

Calgary Bay

Ensay
sh Point
CÀRN MÒR
342

Chaoil
Burg

NM
Loch Tuath
Fanmore
CNOC AN DÀ CHINN
390
Glen Aros
Aros
Glenaros House
V
Lochaline
GLAIS
BHEINN
464

Gometra
Ballygown
Eas Fors (Waterfall)
BEINN
NAN CÀRN
333
Killiechronan
B8035
Salen
A849
Fishnish
Point
Fishnish Pier
V
122
11
Scallastle Bay
4

Staffa
al's Cave
Little Colonsay
ULVA
Oskamull
B8073
19
Gruline
Macquarie
Mausoleum
BEINN
NAN LUS
408
Glen Forsa
BEINN
MHEADHON
636
Altcreich
Craignure
Z

Inch Kenneth
Inchkenneth Chapel
(ruin)
Eorsa
BEINN A' GHRÀIG
591
Loch Bà
DUN DA
GHAOITHE
766
Torosay Castle

ISLE

Balnahard
Loch na Keal,
Isle of Mull
B8035
17
BEN
MORE
966
CRUACHAN
DEARG
704
Lochdonhead
Lochdon

OF

BEIN NA
SREINE
519
CREACH BHEINN
491
Fossil Tree
Aird of
Kinloch
Glen More
17
A849
BEN CREACH
698
Strathcoil
CÀRN
BAN
247
3

Rudha nan Cearc
Loch na
Lathaich
Pennycross
A849
Pennyghael
Loch Fuaran
BEN
BUIE
717
Loch Scridain
Leidle Water
BEINN NA
CROISE
503
Lochbuie
Loch Spelve
Croggan

tra
Aridhglas
6
Bunessan
A849
Loch Assapol
CRUACHAN
MIN
376
BEINN
CHREAGACH
376
Carsaig
Rudha
Dubh
Loch Buie
Loch
Uisg
DRUIM
FADA
377
MAOL
BAN
337

ROSS OF MULL
Uisken
Ardchiavaig
Malcolm's
Point
2

Rudha nam
Braithrean
Colonsay · Oban
FIRTH OF

Rudha
Ardalanish
122
Garbh Eileach
Cuan Fe
Cull
Ho

Eilean
Dubh Mor
4
5
6
7

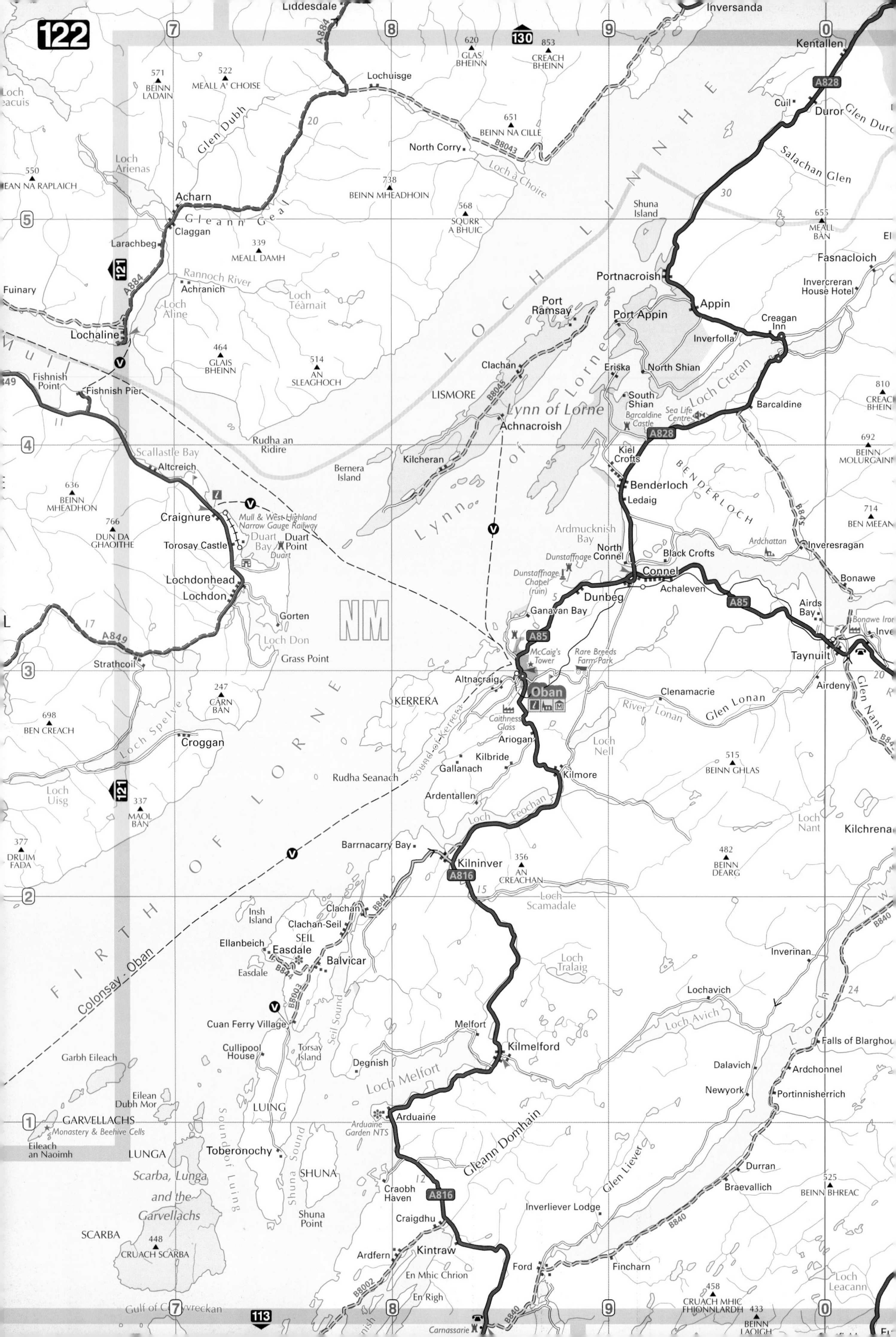

122
Liddesdale
Inversanda
130
Kentallen
A828
Cuil
Duror
Glen Duror
Salachan Glen
Lochuisge
620 GLAS BHEINN
853 CREACH BHEINN
571 BEINN LADAIN
522 MEALL A' CHOISE
Glen Dubh
Loch Arienas
550
Acharn
Gleann Geal
Claggan
Larachbeg
121
A884
Fuinary
Rannoch River
Achranich
Loch Aline
Lochaline
Loch Tèarnait
464 GLAIS BHEINN
514 AN SLEAGHOCH
651 BEINN NA CILLE
B8043
North Corry
Loch a' Choire
738 BEINN MHEADHOIN
339 MEALL DAMH
568 SGURR A BHUIC
LOCH LINNHE
Shuna Island
655 MEALL BAN
Fasnacloich
Invercreran House Hotel
Portnacroish
Appin
Port Ramsay
Port Appin
Creagan Inn
Inverfolla
Clachan
Eriska
North Shian
LISMORE
B8045
Lynn of Lorne
Achnacroish
South Shian
Barcaldine Castle
Sea Life Centre
Loch Creran
Barcaldine
810 CREACH BHEIN
692 BEINN MOLURGAINN
Mull
Fishnish Point
Fishnish Pier
Scallastle Bay
Altcreich
Rudha an Ridire
Bernera Island
Kilcheran
Kiel Crofts
A828
Benderloch
Ledaig
BENDERLOCH
B845
714 BEN MEEAN
636 BEINN MHEADHON
766 DUN DA GHAOITHE
Craignure
Mull & West Highland Narrow Gauge Railway
Duart Bay
Duart Point
Duart
Torosay Castle
Lochdonhead
Lochdon
Gorten
Loch Don
Grass Point
Lynn of Lorne
Ardmucknish Bay
North Connel
Dunstaffnage
Black Crofts
Ardchattan
Inveresragan
Bonawe
Connel
Achaleven
Dunbeg
Dunstaffnage Chapel (ruin)
Ganavan Bay
A85
Airds Bay
Bonawe Iron
Taynuilt
NM
A849
Strathcoil
247 CARN BAN
McCaig's Tower
Rare Breeds Farm Park
Altnacraig
Oban
Clenamacrie
River Lonan
Glen Lonan
Airdeny
Glen Nant
698 BEN CREACH
Loch Spelve
Croggan
KERRERA
Sound of Kerrera
Caithness Glass
Ariogan
Loch Nell
Kilbride
Gallanach
515 BEINN GHLAS
Rudha Seanach
Kilmore
Ardentallen
Loch Feochan
Loch Uisg
337 MAOL BAN
Loch Nant
Kilchrenan
377 DRUIM FADA
FIRTH OF LORNE
Barnacarry Bay
Kilninver
A816
356 AN CREACHAN
Loch Scamadale
482 BEINN DEARG
Insh Island
Clachan
Clachan-Seil
B844
SEIL
Ellanbeich
Easdale
Balvicar
Loch Tralaig
B840
Inverinan
Colonsay - Oban
B8003
Seil Sound
Lochavich
Loch Avich
Cuan Ferry Village
Melfort
Kilmelford
Loch Awe
Falls of Blarghour
Garbh Eileach
Cullipool House
Torsay Island
Degnish
Loch Melfort
Dalavich
Ardchonnel
Eilean Dubh Mor
LUING
Newyork
Portinnisherrich
GARVELLACHS
Monastery & Beehive Cells
Arduaine Garden NTS
Arduaine
Gleann Domhain
Eileach an Naoimh
LUNGA
Toberonochy
Sound of Luing
Shuna Sound
SHUNA
Glen Liever
Durran
Scarba, Lunga and the Garvellachs
Craobh Haven
Braevallich
525 BEINN BHREAC
Shuna Point
Inverliever Lodge
SCARBA
448 CRUACH SCARBA
Craigdhu
Kintraw
Ardfern
En Mhic Chrion
Ford
Fincharn
Loch Leacann
B8002
En Righ
458 CRUACH MHIC FHIONNLARDH
433 BEINN LAOIGH
Gulf of Corryvreckan
113
Carnassarie

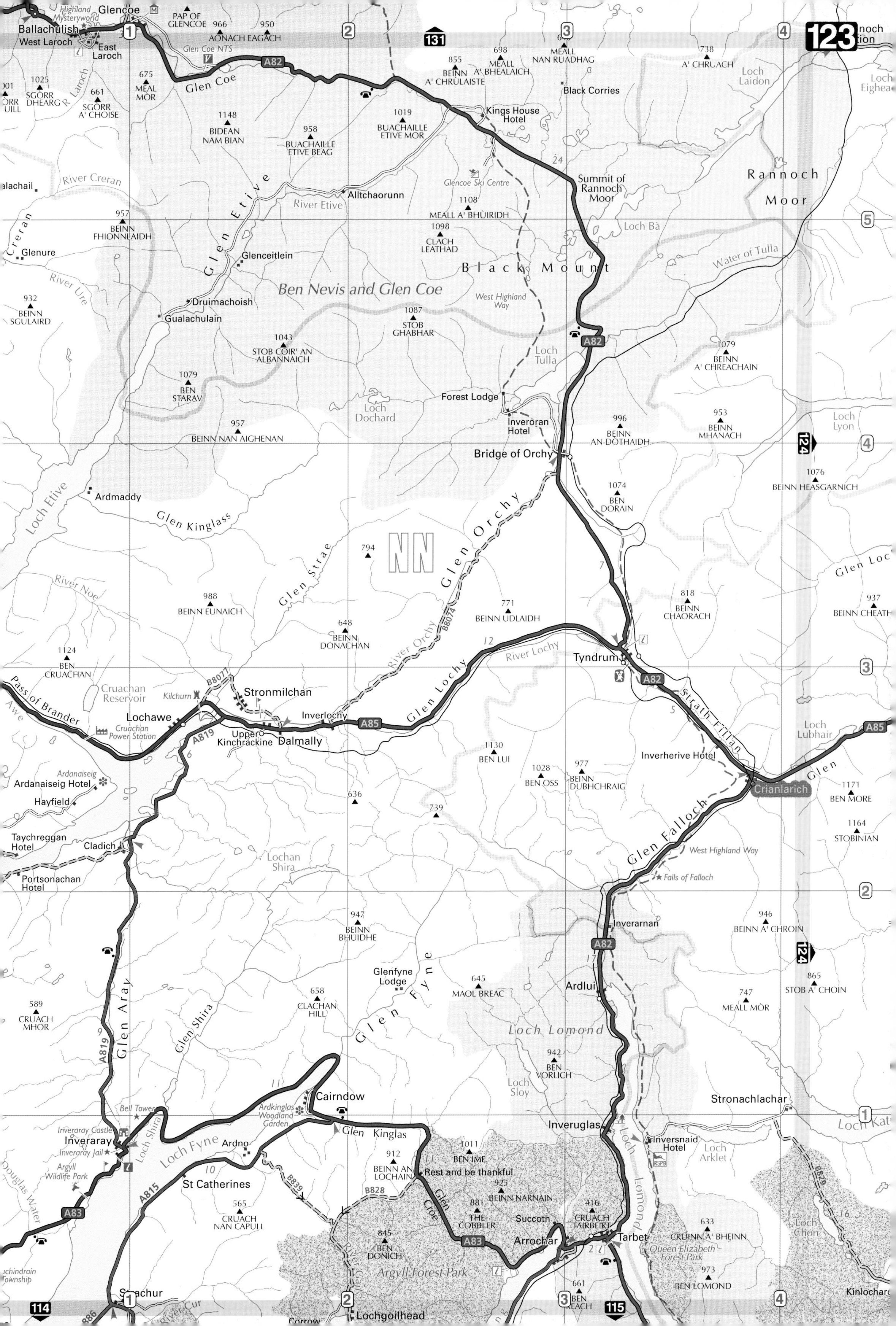
Glencoe
Ballachulish
West Laroch
East Laroch
Highland Mysteryworld
PAP OF GLENCOE
AONACH EAGACH
Glen Coe NTS
A82
Glen Coe
MEAL MÒR
SGÒRR DHEARG
SGÒRR A' CHOISE
BIDEAN NAM BIAN
BUACHAILLE ETIVE BEAG
BUACHAILLE ETIVE MOR
BEINN A' CHRULAISTE
MEALL A' BHEALAICH
MEALL NAN RUADHAG
Black Corries
Kings House Hotel
A' CHRUACH
Loch Laidon
Rannoch Moor
Summit of Rannoch Moor
Glencoe Ski Centre
MEALL A' BHÙIRIDH
CLACH LEATHAD
Loch Bà
Water of Tulla
Black Mount
Alltchaorunn
River Etive
Glen Etive
River Creran
BEINN FHIONNLAIDH
Glenure
Glenceitlein
River Ure
BEINN SGULAIRD
Druimachoish
Gualachulain
Ben Nevis and Glen Coe
West Highland Way
STOB GHABHAR
STOB COIR' AN ALBANNAICH
Loch Tulla
BEINN A' CHREACHAIN
BEN STARAV
Forest Lodge
Loch Dochard
Inveroran Hotel
BEINN NAN AIGHENAN
BEINN AN DOTHAIDH
BEINN MHANACH
Loch Lyon
Bridge of Orchy
BEN DORAIN
BEINN HEASGARNICH
Ardmaddy
Loch Etive
Glen Kinglass
Glen Orchy
Glen Strae
NN
River Noe
BEINN EUNAICH
BEINN UDLAIDH
BEINN CHAORACH
Glen Lochy
BEINN CHEATH
BEINN DONACHAN
River Orchy
B8074
River Lochy
Tyndrum
BEN CRUACHAN
Cruachan Reservoir
Pass of Brander
Kilchurn
B8077
Stronmilchan
Lochawe
Cruachan Power Station
Inverlochy
A85
Upper Kinchrackine
Dalmally
A819
Strath Fillan
Loch Lubhair
BEN LUI
BEN OSS
BEINN DUBHCHRAIG
Inverherive Hotel
Crianlarich
BEN MORE
Ardanaiseig
Ardanaiseig Hotel
Hayfield
Taychreggan Hotel
Cladich
Lochan Shira
Glen Falloch
West Highland Way
Falls of Falloch
STOBINIAN
Portsonachan Hotel
BEINN BHUIDHE
Inverarnan
BEINN A' CHROIN
Glenfyne Lodge
Glen Fyne
MAOL BREAC
Ardlui
STOB A' CHOIN
MEALL MÒR
CRUACH MHOR
CLACHAN HILL
Glen Shira
Glen Aray
Loch Lomond
BEN VORLICH
Loch Sloy
Cairndow
Ardkinglas Woodland Garden
Stronachlachar
Bell Tower
Inveraray Castle
Inveraray
Inveraray Jail
Argyll Wildlife Park
Loch Shira
Loch Fyne
Ardno
Glen Kinglas
Inveruglas
Inversnaid Hotel
RSPB
Loch Arklet
Loch Katrine
BEINN AN LOCHAIN
BEN IME
Rest and be thankful
BEINN NARNAIN
St Catherines
B839
B828
B829
A815
A83
Douglas Water
CRUACH NAN CAPULL
THE COBBLER
Glen Croe
Succoth
CRUACH TAIRBEIRT
Arrochar
Tarbet
CRUINN A' BHEINN
Queen Elizabeth Forest Park
Loch Chon
BEN DONICH
Argyll Forest Park
BEN LOMOND
Auchindrain Township
Strachur
River Cur
BEN REACH
Lochgoilhead
Corrow
Kinlochard
131
124
114
115

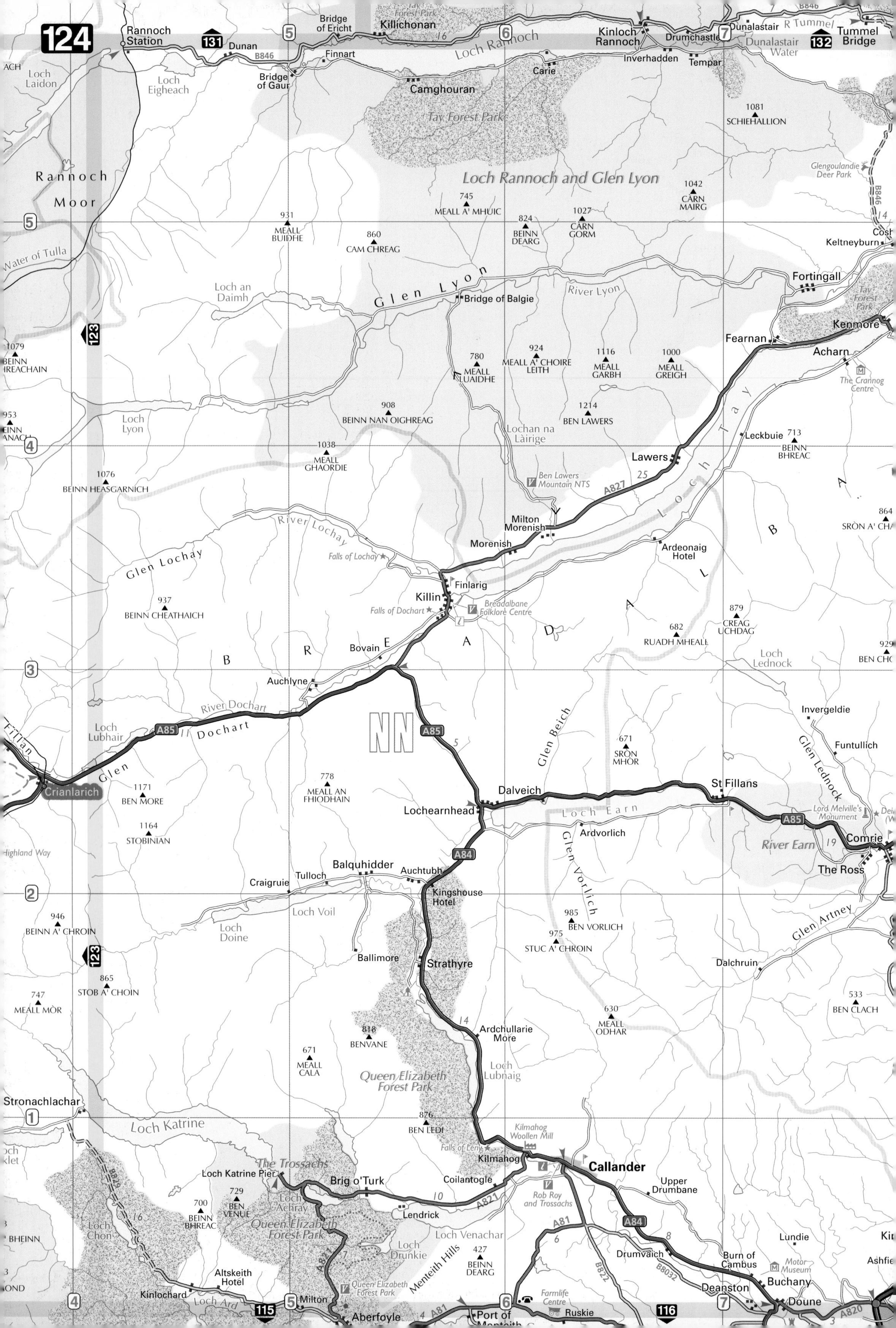

Rannoch Station
Dunan
Bridge of Ericht
Killichonan
Loch Rannoch
Kinloch Rannoch
Drumchastle
Dunalastair
Tummel Bridge
Dunalastair Water
Inverhadden
Tempar
Finnart
Bridge of Gaur
Carie
Camghouran
Loch Laidon
Loch Eigheach
Tay Forest Park
SCHIEHALLION
Rannoch Moor
Loch Rannoch and Glen Lyon
MEALL A' MHUIC
CARN MAIRG
CARN GORM
BEINN DEARG
MEALL BUIDHE
CAM CHREAG
Glengoulandie Deer Park
Keltneyburn
Water of Tulla
Loch an Daimh
Glen Lyon
Bridge of Balgie
River Lyon
Fortingall
Kenmore
Fearnan
Acharn
The Crannog Centre
MEALL LUAIDHE
MEALL A' CHOIRE LEITH
MEALL GARBH
MEALL GREIGH
BEINN NAN OIGHREAG
BEN LAWERS
Loch Lyon
Lochan na Làirige
Leckbuie
BEINN BHREAC
MEALL GHAORDIE
BEINN HEASGARNICH
Lawers
Ben Lawers Mountain NTS
Loch Tay
River Lochay
Milton Morenish
Morenish
Glen Lochay
Falls of Lochay
Ardeonaig Hotel
BREADALBANE
Finlarig
Killin
Breadalbane Folklore Centre
Falls of Dochart
BEINN CHEATHAICH
RUADH MHEALL
CREAG UCHDAG
Bovain
Loch Lednock
Auchlyne
River Dochart
Glen Dochart
Loch Lubhair
Crianlarich
NN
Glen Beich
SRON MHOR
Invergeldie
Funtullich
Glen Lednock
MEALL AN FHIODHAIN
BEN MORE
STOBINIAN
Dalveich
St Fillans
Lochearnhead
Loch Earn
Ardvorlich
Lord Melville's Monument
Comrie
River Earn
The Ross
Balquhidder
Auchtubh
Tulloch
Craigruie
Kingshouse Hotel
Loch Voil
Loch Doine
Glen Vorlich
BEN VORLICH
STUC A' CHROIN
Glen Artney
BEINN A' CHROIN
Ballimore
Strathyre
Dalchruin
STOB A' CHOIN
MEALL MÒR
MEALL ODHAR
BEN CLACH
Ardchullarie More
BENVANE
MEALL CALA
Queen Elizabeth Forest Park
Loch Lubnaig
Stronachlachar
Loch Katrine
BEN LEDI
Kilmahog Woollen Mill
Falls of Leny
Kilmahog
Callander
The Trossachs
Loch Katrine Pier
Brig o' Turk
Coilantogle
Upper Drumbane
BEINN BHREAC
BEN VENUE
Loch Achray
Lendrick
Rob Roy and Trossachs
Loch Chon
Loch Venachar
Loch Drunkie
BEINN DEARG
Menteith Hills
Drumvaich
Lundie
Burn of Cambus
Motor Museum
Altskeith Hotel
Kinlochard
Loch Ard
Milton
Aberfoyle
Farmlife Centre
Ruskie
Port of Menteith
Deanston
Buchany
Doune
A85
A84
A827
A821
A81
B846
B829
B822
B8032
A820

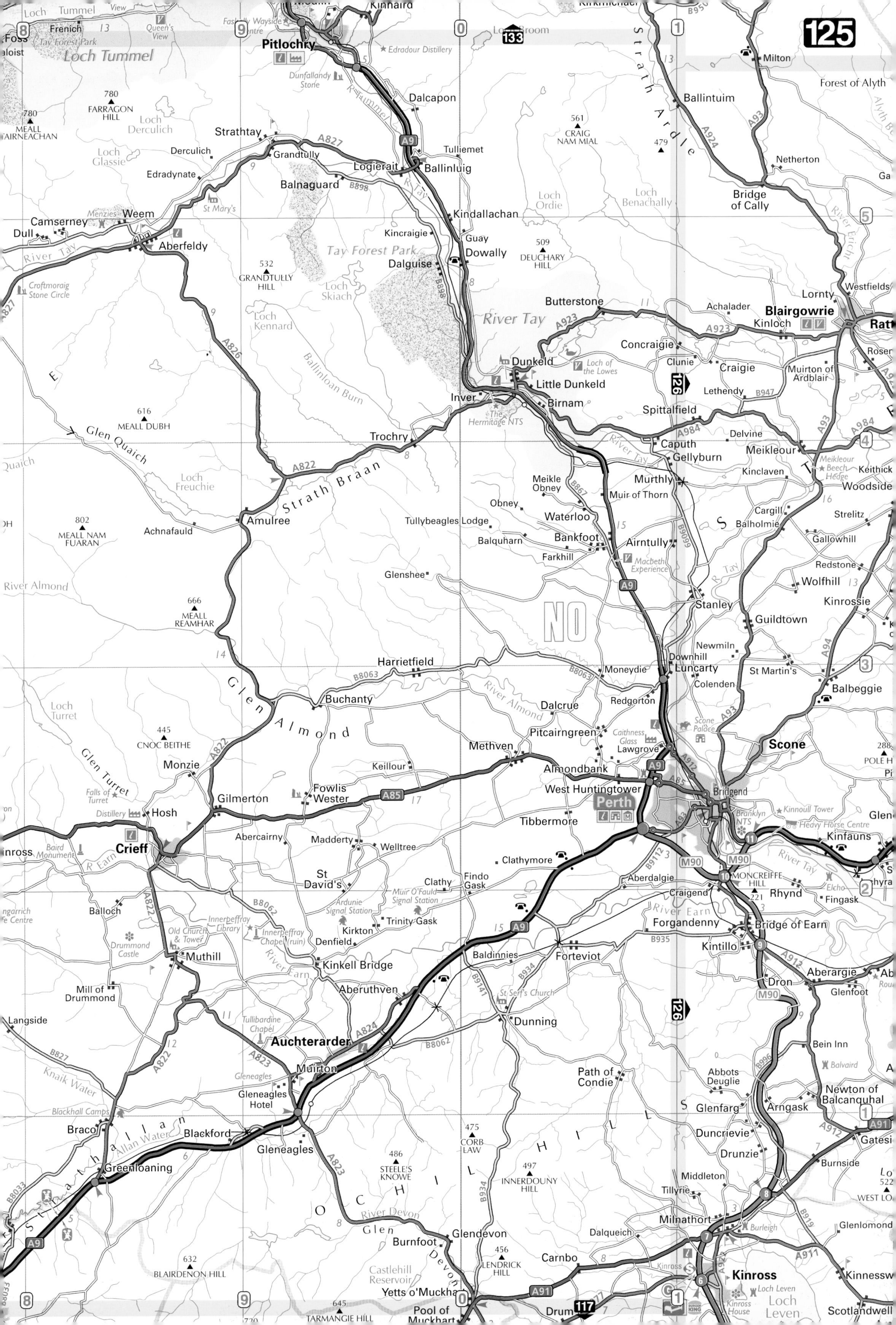
125
Loch Tummel
Pitlochry
Edradour Distillery
Dunfallandy Stone
Dalcapon
Kinnaird
Frenich
Queen's View
Tay Forest Park
780
FARRAGON HILL
MEALL AIRNEACHAN
Loch Derculich
Strathtay
Derculich
Loch Glassie
Edradynate
Grandtully
A827
Logierait
Tulliemet
Ballinluig
Balnaguard
B898
A9
561
CRAIG NAM MIAL
479
Strath Ardle
Ballintuim
Milton
Forest of Alyth
A93
A924
Netherton
Bridge of Cally
Loch Ordie
Loch Benachally
Kindallachan
Camserney
Menzies
Weem
St Mary's
Dull
Aberfeldy
River Tay
Kincraigie
Guay
Dowally
509
DEUCHARY HILL
Dalguise
532
GRANDTULLY HILL
Loch Skiach
Croftmoraig Stone Circle
Butterstone
A923
River Tay
Achalader
Blairgowrie
Kinloch
Lornty
Westfields
Loch Kennard
A826
Dunkeld
Loch of the Lowes
Concraigie
Clunie
Craigie
Muirton of Ardblair
Little Dunkeld
Lethendy
B947
Inver
Birnam
Ballinloan Burn
The Hermitage NTS
Spittalfield
A984
616
MEALL DUBH
Glen Quaich
Trochry
Caputh
Delvine
Meikleour
Gellyburn
Meikleour Beech Hedge
Kinclaven
Keithick
Woodside
A822
Loch Freuchie
Strath Braan
Meikle Obney
Murthly
Muir of Thorn
B867
Obney
Cargill
Balholmie
Strelitz
802
MEALL NAM FUARAN
Achnafauld
Amulree
Tullybeagles Lodge
Waterloo
Bankfoot
Balquharn
Airntully
B9099
Gallowhill
Farkhill
Macbeth Experience
Redstone
Wolfhill
River Almond
Glenshee
666
MEALL REAMHAR
NO
Stanley
Kinrossie
Guildtown
Newmiln
Downhill
Luncarty
St Martin's
Harrietfield
B8063
Moneydie
Colenden
Balbeggie
A94
Loch Turret
Glen Almond
Buchanty
River Almond
Dalcrue
Redgorton
445
CNOC BEITHE
Pitcairngreen
Caithness Glass
Scone Palace
Scone
Glen Turret
Monzie
Methven
Lawgrove
Falls of Turret
Keillour
Almondbank
A85
288
POLE HILL
Gilmerton
Fowlis Wester
West Huntingtower
Bridgend
Distillery
Hosh
Perth
Kinnoull Tower
Branklyn NTS
Heavy Horse Centre
Tibbermore
Kinfauns
Baird Monument
Crieff
Abercairny
Madderty
Welltree
Clathymore
M90
River Tay
R Earn
St David's
Clathy
Findo Gask
Aberdalgie
MONCREIFFE HILL
Rhynd
Elcho
Fingask
B9112
Craigend
Balloch
A822
Innerpeffray Library
Muir O'Fauld Signal Station
Ardunie Signal Station
Trinity Gask
River Earn
Forgandenny
Bridge of Earn
Old Church & Tower
Innerpeffray Chapel (ruin)
Kirkton
Drummond Castle
Denfield
B935
Kintillo
Muthill
Baldinnies
Forteviot
Kinkell Bridge
A912
Aberargie
Mill of Drummond
Aberuthven
B9141
B934
St Serf's Church
Dron
Glenfoot
Langside
Tullibardine Chapel
Dunning
Bein Inn
B827
Auchterarder
A824
B8062
Abbots Deuglie
Balvaird
A823
Muirton
Path of Condie
B996
Newton of Balcanquhal
Knaik Water
Gleneagles
Gleneagles Hotel
Glenfarg
Arngask
Blackhall Camps
OCHIL HILLS
A91
Braco
Blackford
Duncrievie
Gateside
Allan Water
Strathallan
Gleneagles
475
CORB LAW
Drunzie
Burnside
Greenloaning
486
STEELE'S KNOWE
497
INNERDOUNY HILL
Middleton
Tillyrie
WEST LOMOND
B8033
River Devon
Milnathort
Burleigh
Glenlomond
Glen Devon
Glendevon
Dalqueich
B919
A911
632
BLAIRDENON HILL
Burnfoot
456
LENDRICK HILL
Carnbo
Kinross
Castlehill Reservoir
Kinnesswood
Yetts o'Muckhart
Loch Leven
Kinross House
645
TARMANGIE HILL
Pool of Muckhart
Drum
Scotlandwell

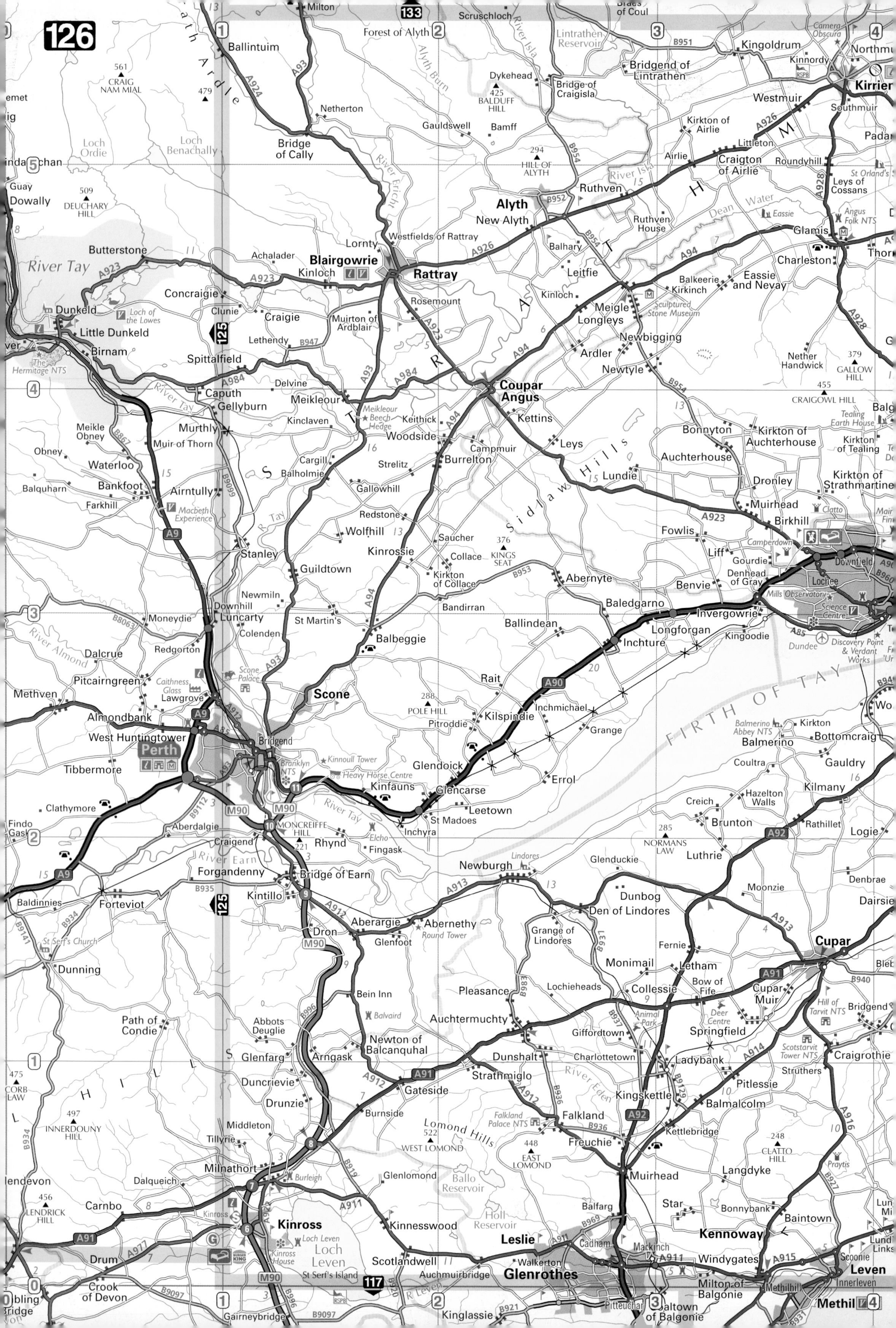
126
Milton
133
Scruschloch
Forest of Alyth
Lintrathen Reservoir
B951
Kingoldrum
Kinnordy
Northmuir
Kirriemuir
Ballintuim
River Ardle
A924
A93
561 CRAIG NAM MIAL
479
Bridgend of Lintrathen
Dykehead
Bridge of Craigisla
425 BALDUFF HILL
River Isla
Alyth Burn
Westmuir
Southmuir
Netherton
Gauldswell
Bamff
Kirkton of Airlie
A926
Littleton
Padanaram
Loch Ordie
Loch Benachally
Bridge of Cally
294 HILL OF ALYTH
B954
Airlie
Craigton of Airlie
Roundyhill
Guay
Dowally
509 DEUCHARY HILL
River Ericht
Ruthven
River Isla
St Orland's Stone
Leys of Cossans
A928
Alyth
New Alyth
B952
Ruthven House
Dean Water
Eassie
Angus Folk NTS
Glamis
Butterstone
Achalader
Lornty
Westfields of Rattray
Blairgowrie
Kinloch
Rattray
A926
Balhary
River Tay
A923
Leitfie
A94
Charleston
Balkeerie
Kirkinch
Eassie and Nevay
Concraigie
Clunie
Dunkeld
Loch of the Lowes
Craigie
Rosemount
Kinloch
Meigle
Sculptured Stone Museum
Longleys
Little Dunkeld
125
Muirton of Ardblair
A923
Birnam
The Hermitage NTS
Lethendy
B947
Newbigging
Ardler
Spittalfield
Nether Handwick
379 GALLOW HILL
A984
Delvine
Newtyle
Caputh
Gellyburn
Meikleour
Meikleour Beech Hedge
A93
A984
Coupar Angus
455 CRAIGOWL HILL
B954
Meikle Obney
Murthly
Kinclaven
Keithick
Kettins
Tealing Earth House
Muir of Thorn
Woodside
A94
Campmuir
Leys
Bonnyton
Kirkton of Auchterhouse
Kirkton of Tealing
Obney
Waterloo
B867
Burrelton
Sidlaw Hills
Auchterhouse
Cargill
Strelitz
Lundie
Balquharn
Bankfoot
Airntully
Balholmie
Gallowhill
Dronley
Kirkton of Strathmartine
Farkhill
B9099
Macbeth Experience
Redstone
Muirhead
Birkhill
Clatto
A9
R. Tay
Wolfhill
A923
Fowlis
Camperdown
Stanley
Saucher
376 KINGS SEAT
Kinrossie
Collace
Liff
Gourdie
Downfield
Guildtown
Kirkton of Collace
B953
Abernyte
Denhead of Gray
Benvie
Lochee
Newmiln
A94
Mills Observatory
Downhill
Bandirran
Baledgarno
Science Centre
Moneydie
Luncarty
St Martin's
Invergowrie
B8063
Colenden
Ballindean
Longforgan
Kingoodie
River Almond
Dalcrue
Redgorton
Balbeggie
Inchture
A85
Dundee
Discovery Point & Verdant Works
Pitcairngreen
Caithness Glass
Scone Palace
A93
Rait
A90
Methven
Lawgrove
Scone
288 POLE HILL
FIRTH OF TAY
Almondbank
A9
A912
Kilspindie
Inchmichael
Balmerino Abbey NTS
Kirkton
West Huntingtower
A85
Bridgend
Pitroddie
Grange
Balmerino
Bottomcraig
Perth
Tibbermore
Branklyn NTS
Kinnoull Tower
Heavy Horse Centre
Glendoick
Errol
Coultra
Gauldry
Kinfauns
Glencarse
Kilmany
Clathymore
M90
M90
River Tay
Leetown
Creich
Hazelton Walls
Findo Gask
Aberdalgie
B9112
MONCREIFFE HILL
St Madoes
Inchyra
285 NORMANS LAW
Brunton
Rathillet
Craigend
221
Rhynd
Elcho
Fingask
Luthrie
A92
Logie
River Earn
A9
Forgandenny
Bridge of Earn
Newburgh
Lindores
Glenduckie
Denbrae
B935
Kintillo
A913
Dunbog
Moonzie
Dairsie
Baldinnies
Forteviot
125
A912
Den of Lindores
B934
Aberargie
Abernethy Round Tower
Grange of Lindores
A913
B9141
St Serf's Church
Dron
Glenfoot
Fernie
Cupar
M90
B931
Dunning
Monimail
Letham
Bein Inn
Pleasance
Lochieheads
Collessie
A91
Bow of Fife
Cupar Muir
B940
Balvaird
B937
Deer Centre
Hill of Tarvit NTS
Bridgend
Path of Condie
Abbots Deuglie
B996
Newton of Balcanqhual
Auchtermuchty
Animal Park
Giffordtown
Springfield
Glenfarg
Arngask
Dunshalt
Charlottetown
Scotstarvit Tower NTS
Craigrothie
475 CORB LAW
Duncrievie
A912
A91
Strathmiglo
River Eden
Ladybank
A914
Struthers
Pitlessie
Drunzie
Gateside
A912
B936
Kingskettle
B9129
Balmalcolm
497 INNERDOUNY HILL
Burnside
Falkland Palace NTS
Falkland
A92
A916
Middleton
Lomond Hills
522 WEST LOMOND
B936
Kettlebridge
248 CLATTO HILL
Tillyrie
448 EAST LOMOND
Freuchie
Praytis
Milnathort
Burleigh
B919
Glenlomond
Ballo Reservoir
Muirhead
Langdyke
Glendevon
Dalqueich
B927
456 LENDRICK HILL
Carnbo
A911
Holl Reservoir
Balfarg
Star
Bonnybank
Baintown
Kinross
A922
Kinross
Kinnesswood
B969
A91
Loch Leven
Kinross House
Loch Leven
Leslie
A911
Cadham
Markinch
Kennoway
A977
A911
Windygates
A915
Scoonie
Drum
Scotlandwell
Walkerton
Leven
Crook of Devon
M90
St Serf's Island
117
Auchmuirbridge
Glenrothes
Milton of Balgonie
Methilhill
Innerleven
B9097
B996
B920
R. Leven
Methil
Gairneybridge
B9097
Kinglassie
B921
Pitteuchar
Baltown of Balgonie
Blebo Craigs
Dolbling Bridge

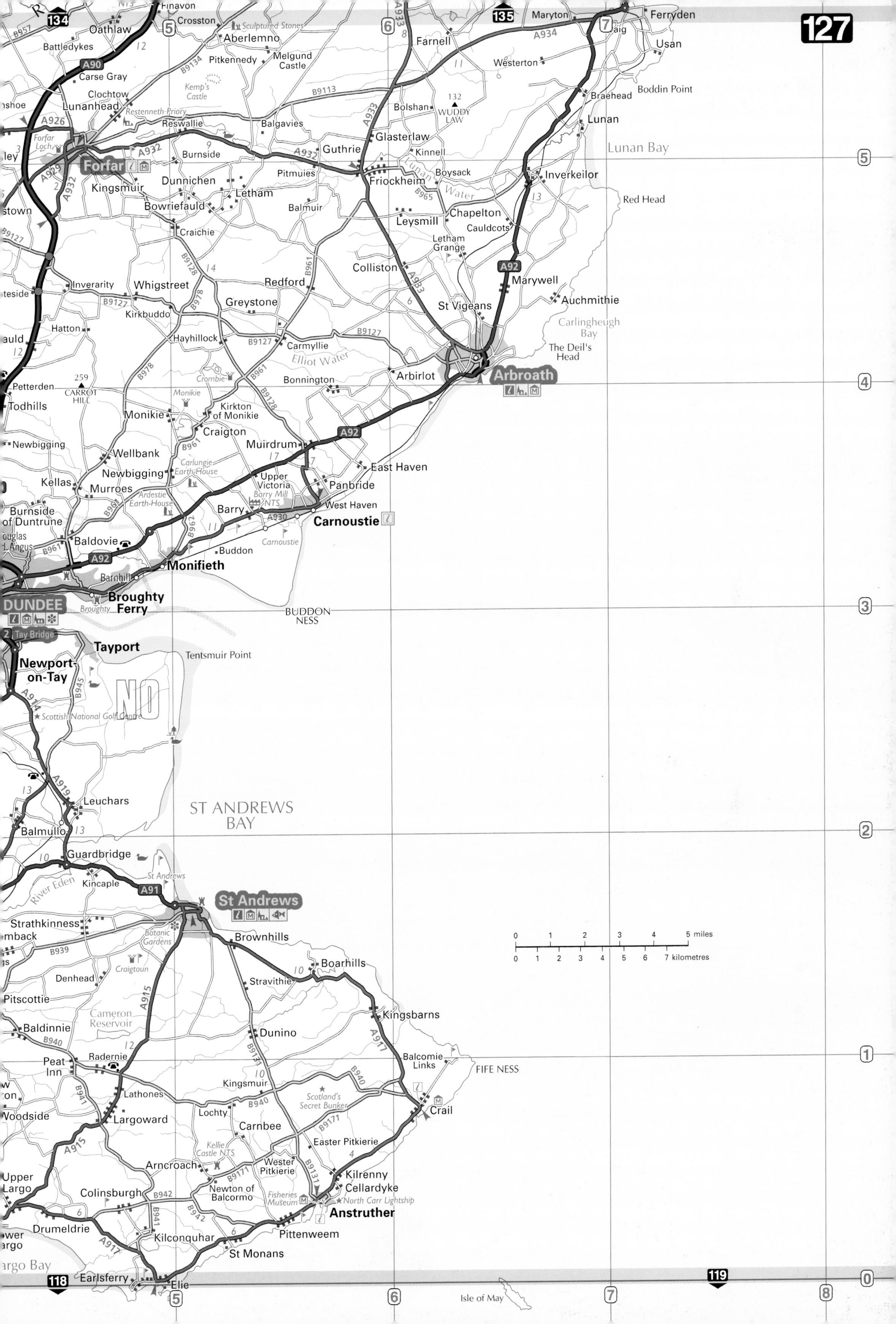
134
135
Finavon
Crosston
Oathlaw
Battledykes
Sculptured Stones
Aberlemno
Pitkennedy
Melgund Castle
Maryton
Ferryden
Craig
Usan
Farnell
A934
Westerton
A90
Carse Gray
Clochtow
Lunanhead
Restenneth Priory
Kemp's Castle
B9134
B9113
Bolshan
132
WUDDY LAW
Braehead
Boddin Point
Lunan
Lunan Bay
A926
Forfar Loch
Reswallie
Balgavies
A933
Glasterlaw
Kinnell
Forfar
A932
Burnside
Guthrie
A929
Kingsmuir
Dunnichen
Pitmuies
Friockheim
Boysack
Lunan Water
Inverkeilor
Letham
B965
Red Head
Bowriefauld
Balmuir
Leysmill
Chapelton
Cauldcots
Craichie
Letham Grange
B9127
B9128
Colliston
A92
Marywell
Inverarity
Whigstreet
Redford
B961
Auchmithie
Kirkbuddo
Greystone
B978
St Vigeans
Carlingheugh Bay
Hatton
Hayhillock
Carmyllie
The Deil's Head
Elliot Water
259
CARROT HILL
Petterden
Crombie
Bonnington
Arbirlot
Arbroath
Todhills
Monikie
Monikie
Kirkton of Monikie
Craigton
Newbigging
Muirdrum
Wellbank
Carlungie Earth House
East Haven
Newbigging
Upper Victoria
Panbride
Kellas
Murroes
Barry Mill NTS
Ardestie Earth-House
West Haven
Burnside of Duntrune
Barry
A930
Carnoustie
Baldovie
B962
Carnoustie
Buddon
B961
Monifieth
Barnhill
DUNDEE
Broughty Ferry
Broughty
BUDDON NESS
Tay Bridge
Tayport
Tentsmuir Point
Newport-on-Tay
B945
A914
NO
Scottish National Golf Centre
A919
Leuchars
ST ANDREWS BAY
Balmullo
Guardbridge
River Eden
Kincaple
St Andrews
A91
St Andrews
Strathkinness
Botanic Gardens
B939
Brownhills
Craigtoun
Boarhills
Denhead
Stravithie
Pitscottie
Cameron Reservoir
A915
Kingsbarns
Baldinnie
Dunino
B940
A917
Peat Inn
Radernie
Balcomie Links
FIFE NESS
B9131
Kingsmuir
Lathones
Scotland's Secret Bunker
Crail
Woodside
Largoward
Lochty
Carnbee
B9171
Easter Pitkierie
Kellie Castle NTS
Arncroach
Wester Pitkierie
Kilrenny
Upper Largo
Cellardyke
Colinsburgh
B942
Newton of Balcormo
Fisheries Museum
North Carr Lightship
Anstruther
B941
Drumeldrie
Kilconquhar
Pittenweem
St Monans
Largo Bay
118
Earlsferry
Elie
Isle of May
119
0 1 2 3 4 5 miles
0 1 2 3 4 5 6 7 kilometres

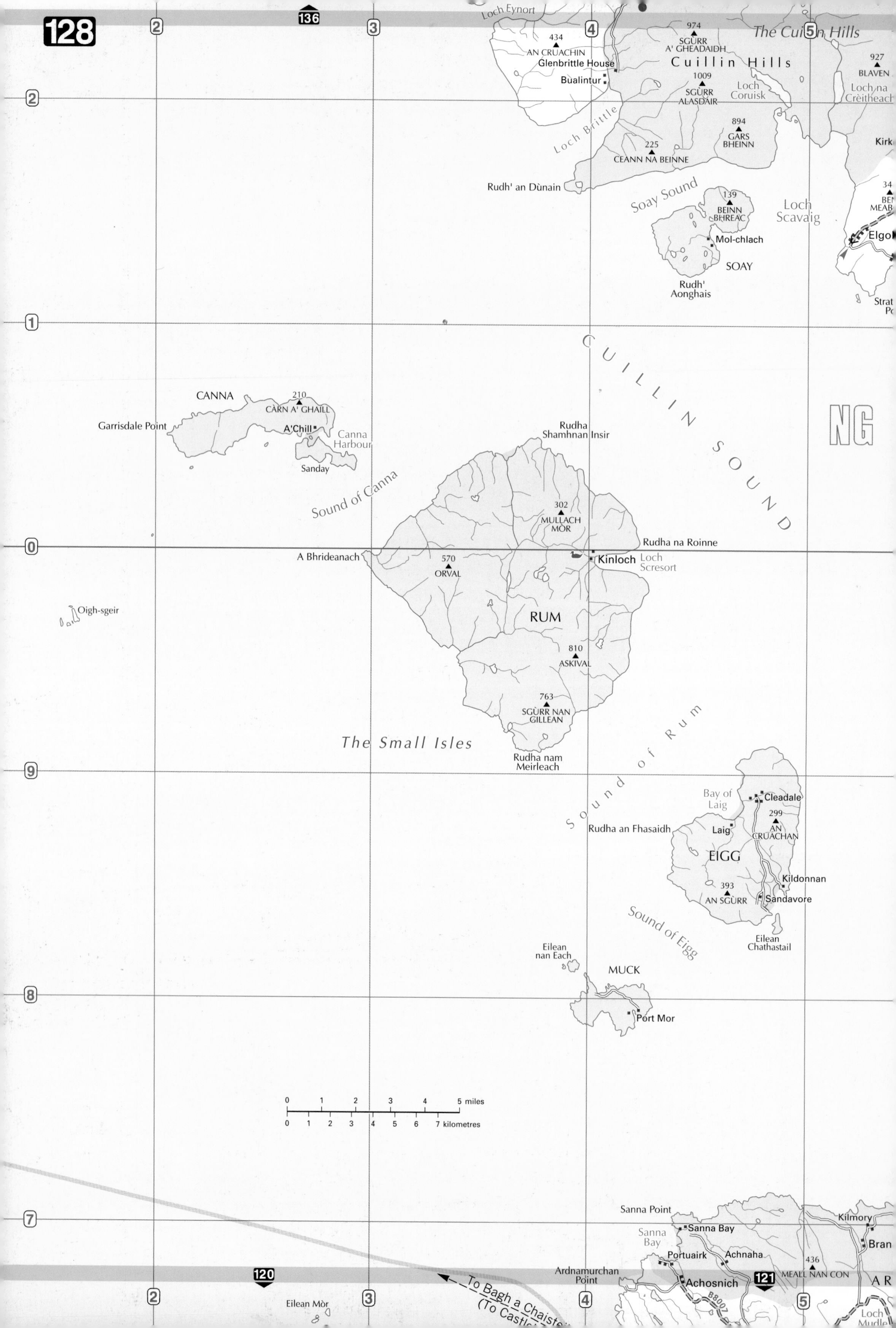

136
Loch Eynort
434 AN CRUACHIN
Glenbrittle House
Bualintur
974 SGÙRR A' GHEADAIDH
Cuillin Hills
The Cuillin Hills
1009 SGÙRR ALASDAIR
Loch Coruisk
927 BLAVEN
Loch na Crèitheach
Loch Brittle
894 GARS BHEINN
225 CEANN NA BEINNE
Kirk
Rudh' an Dùnain
Soay Sound
139 BEINN BHREAC
Loch Scavaig
Mol-chlach
SOAY
Rudh' Aonghais
Elgol
CUILLIN SOUND
NG
CANNA
210 CÀRN A' GHAILL
Garrisdale Point
A'Chill
Canna Harbour
Sanday
Rudha Shamhnan Insir
Sound of Canna
302 MULLACH MÒR
Rudha na Roinne
A Bhrideanach
570 ORVAL
Kinloch
Loch Scresort
Oigh-sgeir
RUM
810 ASKIVAL
763 SGÙRR NAN GILLEAN
The Small Isles
Rudha nam Meirleach
Sound of Rum
Bay of Laig
Cleadale
299 AN CRUACHAN
Laig
Rudha an Fhasaidh
EIGG
Kildonnan
393 AN SGÙRR
Sandavore
Sound of Eigg
Eilean Chathastail
Eilean nan Each
MUCK
Port Mor
0 1 2 3 4 5 miles
0 1 2 3 4 5 6 7 kilometres
Sanna Point
Kilmory
Sanna Bay
Bran
Portuairk
Achnaha
436 MEALL NAN CON
Ardnamurchan Point
Achosnich
B8007
120
121
To Bagh a Chaiste
(To Castle
Eilean Mòr

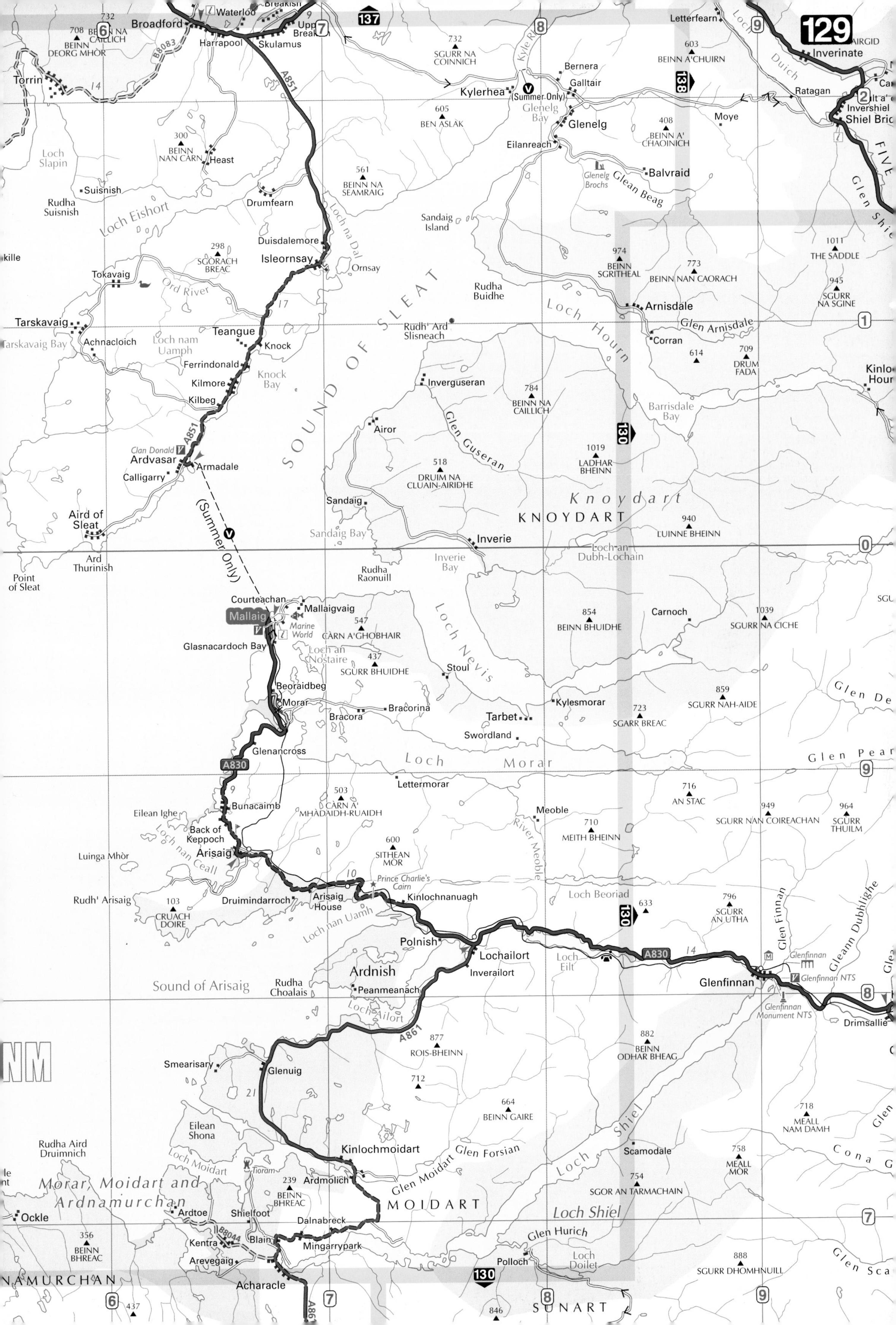
129
137
138
130
Broadford
Waterloo
Breakish
Upper Breakish
Harrapool
Skulamus
708 BEINN DEORG MHÒR
732 BEINN NA CAILLICH
Torrin
B8083
A851
Loch Slapin
300 BEINN NAN CARN
Heast
Suisnish
Rudha Suisnish
Loch Eishort
Drumfearn
Duisdalemore
Isleornsay
Ornsay
Loch na Dal
298 SGORACH BREAC
Tokavaig
Ord River
Tarskavaig
Tarskavaig Bay
Achnacloich
Loch nam Uamph
Teangue
Knock
Ferrindonald
Knock Bay
Kilmore
Kilbeg
Clan Donald
Ardvasar
Armadale
Calligarry
Aird of Sleat
Ard Thurinish
Point of Sleat
(Summer Only)
SOUND OF SLEAT
732 SGURR NA COINNICH
Kylerhea
Kyle Rhea
Bernera
Galltair
Glenelg Bay
Glenelg
605 BEN ASLAK
Eilanreach
561 BEINN NA SEAMRAIG
Glenelg Brochs
Glean Beag
Balvraid
408 BEINN A' CHAOINICH
Letterfearn
Loch Duich
603 BEINN A' CHUIRN
Invérinate
Ratagan
Moye
Inversheil
Shiel Bridge
Glen Shiel
Sandaig Island
Rudha Buidhe
974 BEINN SGRITHEAL
773 BEINN NAN CAORACH
1011 THE SADDLE
945 SGURR NA SGINE
Arnisdale
Glen Arnisdale
Loch Hourn
Corran
Rudh' Ard Slisneach
614
709 DRUM FADA
Inverguseran
784 BEINN NA CAILLICH
Barrisdale Bay
Airor
Glen Guseran
1019 LADHAR BHEINN
518 DRUIM NA CLUAIN-AIRIDHE
Knoydart
KNOYDART
Sandaig
Sandaig Bay
Inverie
940 LUINNE BHEINN
Loch an Dubh-Lochain
Inverie Bay
Rudha Raonuill
Courteachan
Mallaig
Mallaigvaig
Marine World
547 CÀRN A' GHOBHAIR
Glasnacardoch Bay
Loch an Nostaire
437 SGURR BHUIDHE
Loch Nevis
Stoul
854 BEINN BHUIDHE
Carnoch
1039 SGURR NA CICHE
Beoraidbeg
Morar
Bracora
Bracorina
Tarbet
Kylesmorar
723 SGARR BREAC
859 SGURR NAH-AIDE
Glen Dessary
Swordland
Glenancross
A830
Loch Morar
Glen Pean
Lettermorar
503 CÀRN A' MHADAIDH-RUAIDH
716 AN STAC
Meoble
Eilean Ighe
Bunacaimb
Back of Keppoch
Loch nan Ceall
Arisaig
710 MEITH BHEINN
River Meoble
949 SGURR NAN COIREACHAN
964 SGURR THUILM
Luinga Mhòr
600 SITHEAN MOR
Prince Charlie's Cairn
Rudh' Arisaig
103 CRUACH DOIRE
Druimindarroch
Arisaig House
Kinlochnanuagh
Loch Beoriad
633
796 SGURR AN UTHA
Glen Finnan
Gleann Dubhlighe
Loch nan Uamh
Polnish
Lochailort
Inverailort
Loch Eilt
Glenfinnan
Glenfinnan NTS
Glenfinnan Monument NTS
Drimsallie
Sound of Arisaig
Ardnish
Rudha Choalais
Peanmeanach
Loch Ailort
A861
877 ROIS-BHEINN
882 BEINN ODHAR BHEAG
NM
Smearisary
Glenuig
712
664 BEINN GAIRE
718 MEALL NAM DAMH
Eilean Shona
Rudha Aird Druimnich
Kinlochmoidart
Glen Forsian
Glen Moidart
Loch Shiel
Scamodale
Cona Glen
Loch Moidart
Tioram
239 BEINN BHREAC
Ardmolich
754 SGOR AN TARMACHAIN
758 MEALL MOR
Morar, Moidart and Ardnamurchan
MOIDART
Ockle
Ardtoe
Shielfoot
Dalnabreck
356 BEINN BHREAC
Kentra
B8044
Blain
Mingarrypark
Glen Hurich
Arevegaig
Polloch
Loch Doilet
888 SGURR DHOMHNUILL
Glen Scaddle
ARDNAMURCHAN
Acharacle
437
846
SUNART

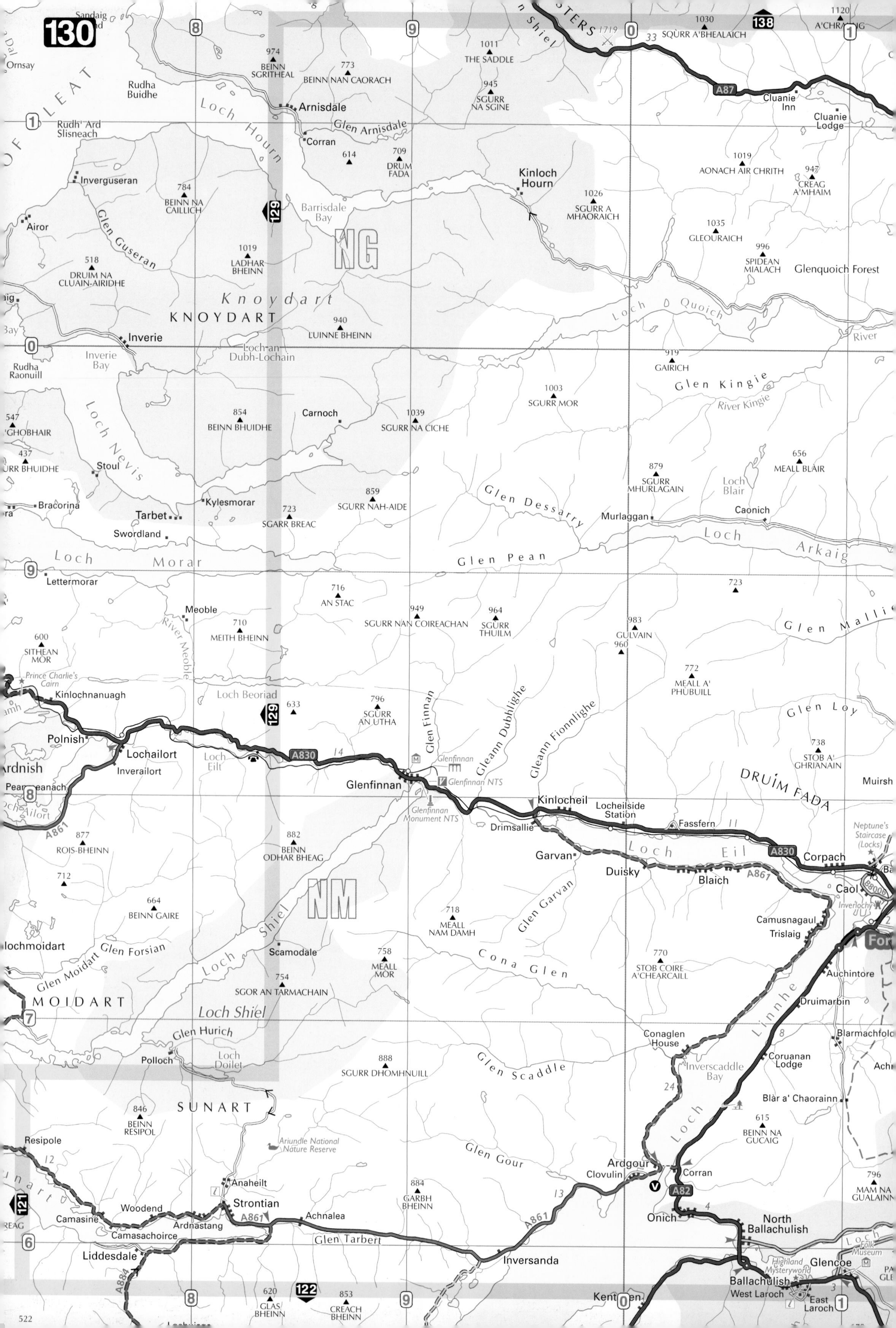
130
Sandaig
Ornsay
Rudha Buidhe
Rudh' Ard Slisneach
Inverguseran
Airor
Glen Guseran
Loch Hourn
974 BEINN SGRITHEAL
773 BEINN NAN CAORACH
Arnisdale
Glen Arnisdale
Corran
614
709 DRUM FADA
1011 THE SADDLE
945 SGURR NA SGINE
784 BEINN NA CAILLICH
Barrisdale Bay
NG
1019 LADHAR BHEINN
518 DRUIM NA CLUAIN-AIRIDHE
Knoydart
KNOYDART
Kinloch Hourn
1026 SGURR A MHAORAICH
A87
Cluanie Inn
Cluanie Lodge
1030 SGÙRR A' BHEALAICH
1120
1719
33
1019 AONACH AIR CHRITH
947 CREAG A' MHAIM
1035 GLEOURAICH
996 SPIDEAN MIALACH
Glenquoich Forest
Loch Quoich
River
940 LUINNE BHEINN
Inverie
Inverie Bay
Loch an Dubh-Lochain
Rudha Raonuill
919 GAIRICH
Glen Kingie
River Kingie
1003 SGURR MOR
854 BEINN BHUIDHE
Carnoch
1039 SGURR NA CICHE
547
437
Loch Nevis
Stoul
Bracorina
Tarbet
Kylesmorar
Swordland
723 SGARR BREAC
859 SGURR NAH-AIDE
879 SGURR MHURLAGAIN
656 MEALL BLAIR
Loch Blair
Glen Dessarry
Murlaggan
Caonich
Loch Arkaig
Loch Morar
Glen Pean
Lettermorar
716 AN STAC
723
Meoble
710 MEITH BHEINN
River Meoble
949 SGURR NAN COIREACHAN
964 SGURR THUILM
983 GULVAIN
960
Glen Mallie
600 SITHEAN MOR
Prince Charlie's Cairn
Kinlochnanuagh
Loch Beoriad
633
796 SGURR AN UTHA
772 MEALL A' PHUBUILL
Glen Loy
Glen Finnan
Gleann Dubhlighe
Gleann Fionnlighe
Polnish
Lochailort
Inverailort
Loch Eilt
A830
14
Glenfinnan
Glenfinnan NTS
Glenfinnan Monument NTS
738 STOB A' GHRIANAIN
DRUIM FADA
Muirsh
Ardnish
Kinlocheil
Locheilside Station
Drimsallie
Fassfern
11
Neptune's Staircase (Locks)
A861
877 ROIS-BHEINN
882 BEINN ODHAR BHEAG
Garvan
Duisky
Loch Eil
Blaich
A830
Corpach
Caol
B8006
Inverlochy
712
NM
664 BEINN GAIRE
718 MEALL NAM DAMH
Glen Garvan
Camusnagaul
Trislaig
Glen Forsian
Scamodale
758 MEALL MOR
Cona Glen
770 STOB COIRE A'CHEARCAILL
Auchintore
Glen Moidart
MOIDART
Loch Shiel
754 SGOR AN TARMACHAIN
Loch Linnhe
Druimarbin
Glen Hurich
Conaglen House
Blarmachfold
Polloch
Loch Doilet
888 SGURR DHOMHNUILL
Glen Scaddle
Inverscaddle Bay
Coruanan Lodge
24
846 BEINN RESIPOL
SUNART
Ariundle National Nature Reserve
Blàr a' Chaorainn
615 BEINN NA GUCAIG
Resipole
12
Glen Gour
Ardgour
Clovulin
Corran
A82
Anaheilt
884 GARBH BHEINN
796 MAM NA GUALAINN
Woodend
Strontian
Camasine
Ardnastang
A861
Achnalea
13
Onich
North Ballachulish
Camasachoirce
Glen Tarbert
Liddesdale
Inversanda
Highland Mysteryworld
Glencoe
Ballachulish
West Laroch
East Laroch
A884
620 GLAS BHEINN
853 CREACH BHEINN
Kentallen
8
9
0
1
7
6
129
138
121
122
522

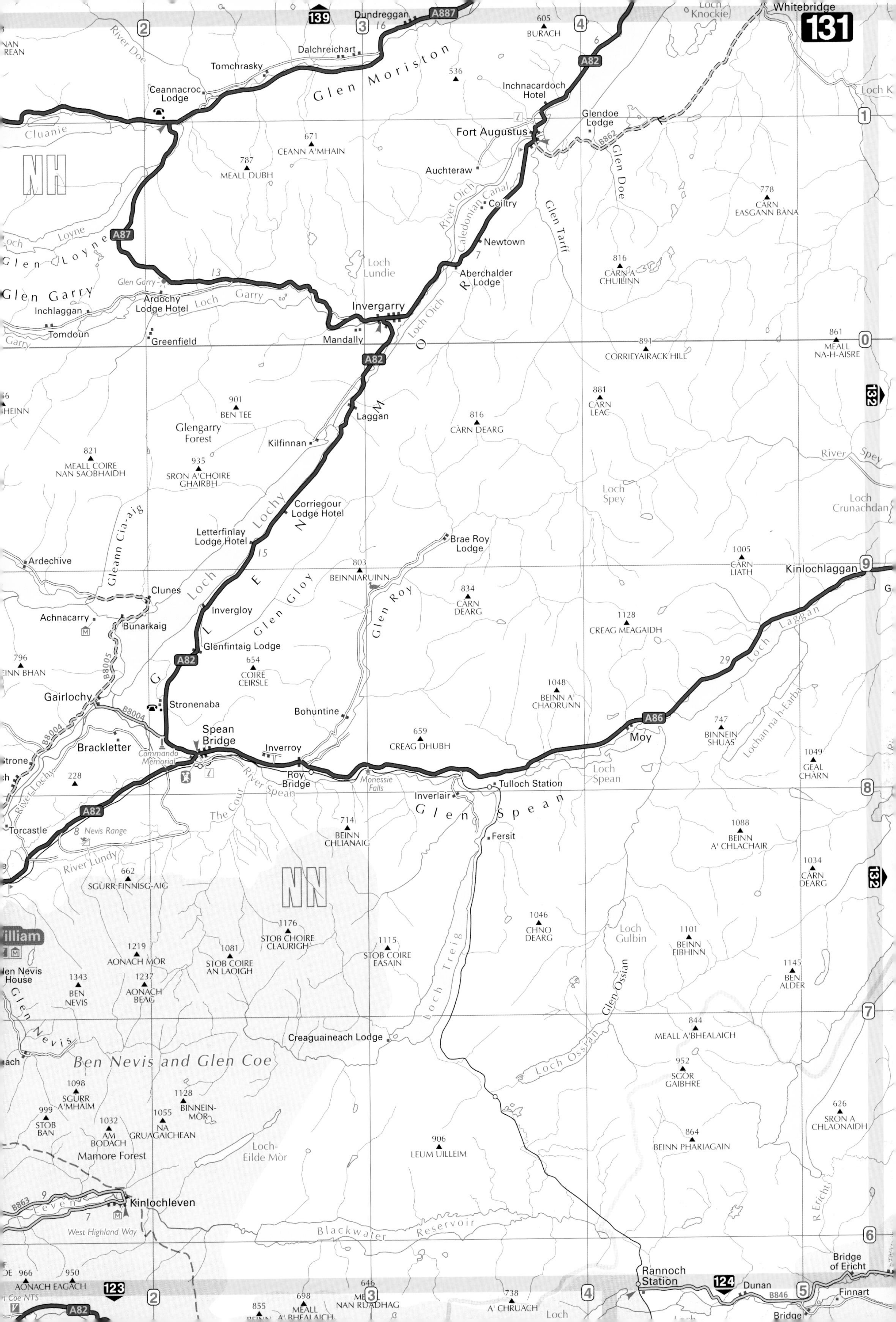

131
Whitebridge
Dundreggan
A887
Dalchreichart
Tomchrasky
Ceannacroc Lodge
Glen Moriston
Cluanie
NH
BURACH
Inchnacardoch Hotel
A82
Fort Augustus
Glendoe Lodge
B862
Glen Doe
CEANN A' MHAIN
MEALL DUBH
Auchteraw
Caledonian Canal
River Oich
Coiltry
Newtown
Glen Tarff
CARN EASGANN BANA
A87
Glen Loyne
Glen Garry
Loch Lundie
Aberchalder Lodge
CARN A' CHUILINN
Ardochy Lodge Hotel
Loch Garry
Inchlaggan
Tomdoun
Greenfield
Invergarry
Mandally
Loch Oich
CORRIEYAIRACK HILL
MEALL NA-H-AISRE
132
BEN TEE
Glengarry Forest
Laggan
CARN DEARG
CARN LEAC
Kilfinnan
MEALL COIRE NAN SAOBHAIDH
SRON A' CHOIRE GHAIRBH
River Spey
Loch Spey
Loch Crunachdan
Corriegour Lodge Hotel
Loch Lochy
Gleann Cia-aig
Letterfinlay Lodge Hotel
Brae Roy Lodge
Ardechive
BEINNIARUINN
CARN LIATH
Kinlochlaggan
Clunes
Glen Gloy
Glen Roy
CARN DEARG
Achnacarry
Bunarkaig
Invergloy
CREAG MEAGAIDH
Loch Laggan
Glenfintaig Lodge
B8005
COIRE CEIRSLE
BEINN A' CHAORUNN
Gairlochy
Stronenaba
B8004
Bohuntine
A86
Spean Bridge
Brackletter
Commando Memorial
Inverroy
Roy Bridge
CREAG DHUBH
Moy
BINNEIN SHUAS
Lochan na h-Earba
GEAL CHARN
River Lochy
Monessie Falls
River Spean
Tulloch Station
Loch Spean
Inverlair
Glen Spean
The Cour
Torcastle
Nevis Range
BEINN CHLIANAIG
Fersit
BEINN A' CHLACHAIR
River Lundy
SGÙRR FINNISG-AIG
NN
CARN DEARG
STOB CHOIRE CLAURIGH
STOB COIRE EASAIN
CHNO DEARG
Loch Gulbin
BEINN EIBHINN
AONACH MÒR
STOB COIRE AN LAOIGH
Loch Treig
Ben Nevis House
BEN NEVIS
AONACH BEAG
Glen Ossian
BEN ALDER
Glen Nevis
Creaguaineach Lodge
MEALL A' BHEALAICH
Ben Nevis and Glen Coe
Loch Ossian
SGOR GAIBHRE
SGURR A' MHAIMH
BINNEIN MÒR
STOB BAN
AM BODACH
NA GRUAGAICHEAN
SRON A CHLAONAIDH
Mamore Forest
Loch Eilde Mòr
LEUM UILLEIM
BEINN PHARIAGAIN
B863
Kinlochleven
West Highland Way
R Ericht
Blackwater Reservoir
Bridge of Ericht
AONACH EAGACH
123
Rannoch Station
124
Dunan
B846
Finnart
A' CHRUACH

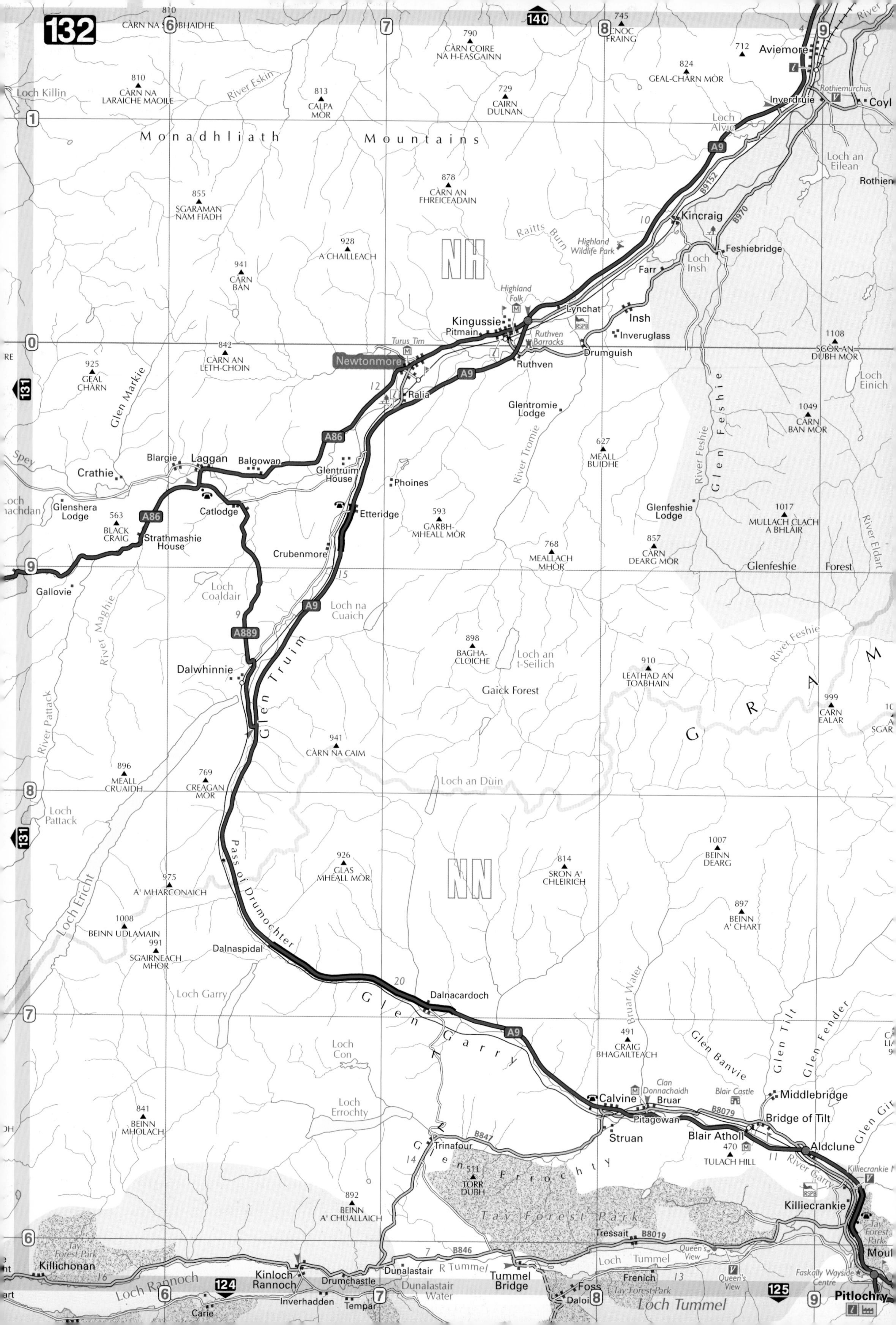
Monadhliath Mountains
Aviemore
Inverdruie
Rothiemurchus
Coylumbridge
Loch Alvie
Loch an Eilean
Kincraig
Feshiebridge
Loch Insh
Highland Wildlife Park
Farr
Kingussie
Highland Folk Museum
Lynchat
Insh
Inveruglass
Pitmain
Ruthven Barracks
Drumguish
Ruthven
Newtonmore
Ralia
Glentromie Lodge
Laggan
Balgowan
Blargie
Crathie
Glentruim House
Phoines
Catlodge
Glenshera Lodge
Strathmashie House
Etteridge
Glenfeshie Lodge
Crubenmore
Glenfeshie Forest
Gallovie
Loch Coaldair
Loch na Cuaich
Dalwhinnie
Gaick Forest
Glen Truim
Loch an t-Seilich
Loch an Dùin
Pass of Drumochter
Loch Ericht
Loch Pattack
Dalnaspidal
Loch Garry
Dalnacardoch
Glen Garry
Loch Con
Loch Errochty
Calvine
Clan Donnachaidh
Bruar
Blair Castle
Middlebridge
Bridge of Tilt
Pitagowan
Struan
Blair Atholl
Aldclune
Trinafour
Glen Errochty
Tay Forest Park
Killiecrankie
Tressait
Killichonan
Loch Rannoch
Kinloch Rannoch
Drumchastle
Dunalastair
Dunalastair Water
Tummel Bridge
Loch Tummel
Queen's View
Foss
Daloist
Faskally Wayside Centre
Pitlochry
Carie
Inverhadden
Tempar
Glen Feshie
River Feshie
Glen Tilt
Glen Fender
Glen Banvie
Bruar Water
River Tromie
River Eskin
River Pattack
River Maghie
Glen Markie
Loch Killin
Raitts Burn
A9
A86
A889
B9152
B970
B847
B846
B8019
B8079
810 CÀRN NA SAOBHAIDHE
790 CÀRN COIRE NA H-EASGAINN
745 CNOC FRAING
712
824 GEAL-CHARN MÒR
810 CÀRN NA LARAICHE MAOILE
813 CALPA MÒR
729 CAIRN DULNAN
878 CÀRN AN FHREICEADAIN
855 SGARAMAN NAM FIADH
928 A' CHAILLEACH
941 CÀRN BÀN
842 CÀRN AN LETH-CHOIN
925 GEAL CHÀRN
1108 SGOR AN DUBH MÒR
1049 CÀRN BAN MÒR
627 MEALL BUIDHE
563 BLACK CRAIG
593 GARBH-MHEALL MÒR
768 MEALLACH MHÒR
857 CÀRN DEARG MÒR
1017 MULLACH CLACH A BHLÀIR
898 BAGHA-CLOICHE
910 LEATHAD AN TOABHAIN
999 CARN EALAR
941 CÀRN NA CAIM
896 MEALL CRUAIDH
769 CREAGAN MÒR
926 GLAS MHEALL MÒR
814 SRON A' CHLEIRICH
1007 BEINN DEARG
975 A' MHARCONAICH
897 BEINN A' CHAIT
1008 BEINN UDLAMAIN
991 SGAIRNEACH MHÒR
491 CRAIG BHAGAILTEACH
470 TULACH HILL
841 BEINN MHOLACH
511 TORR DUBH
892 BEINN A' CHUALLAICH
NH
NN
GRAM
131
140
124
125

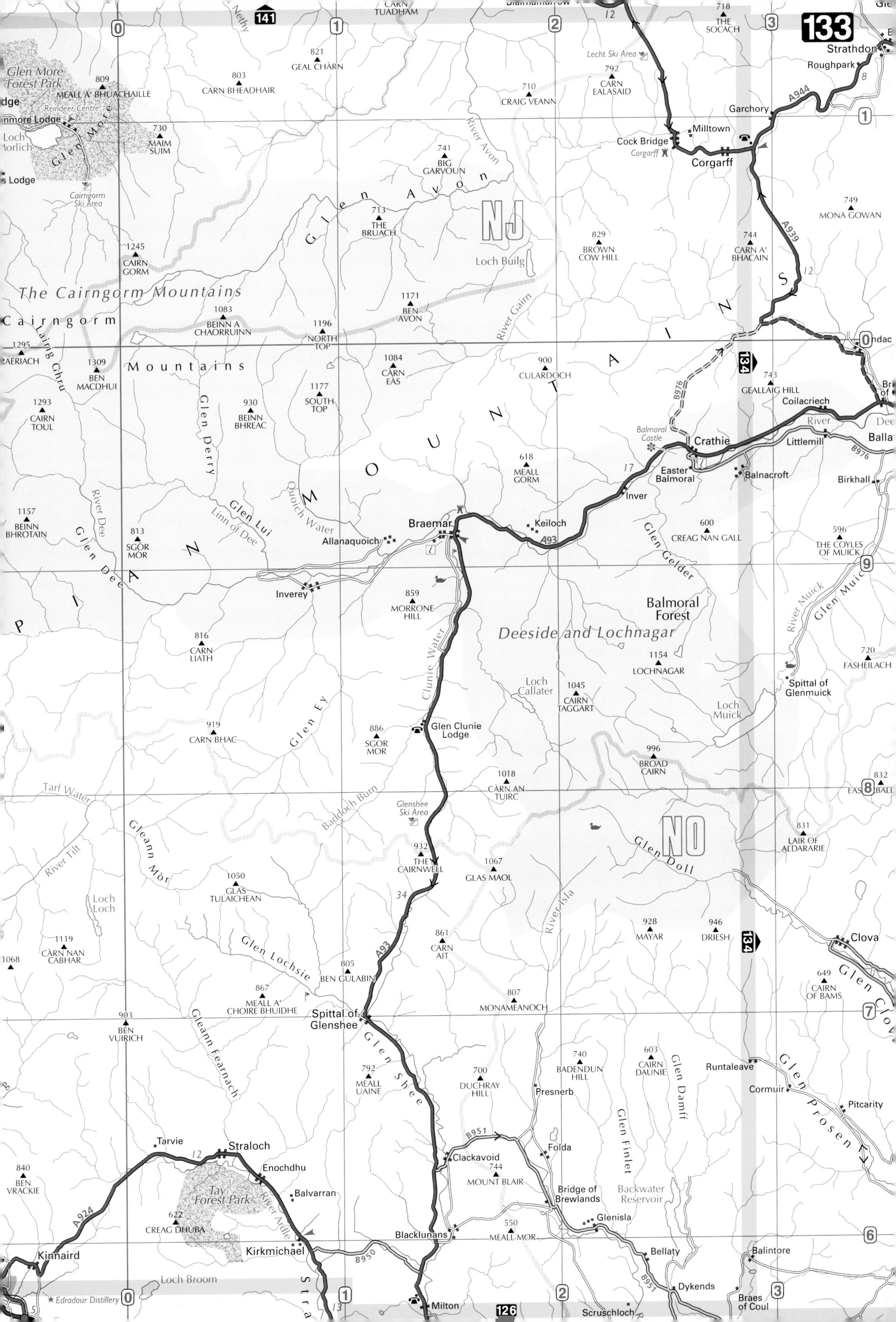
133
141
126
134
NJ
NO
Nethy
CARN TUADHAM
718 THE SOCACH
Strathdon
Roughpark
A944
Garchory
Lecht Ski Area
792 CARN EALASAID
710 CRAIG VEANN
821 GEAL CHÀRN
803 CARN BHEADHAIR
809 MEALL A' BHUACHAILLE
Glen More Forest Park
Reindeer Centre
Glen More
730 MAIM SUIM
Loch Morlich
Cairngorm Ski Area
Milltown
Cock Bridge
Corgarff
Corgarff
741 BIG GARVOUN
River Avon
Glen Avon
713 THE BRUACH
749 MONA GOWAN
829 BROWN COW HILL
744 CARN A' BHACAIN
A939
Loch Builg
1245 CAIRN GORM
The Cairngorm Mountains
Cairngorm Mountains
1171 BEN AVON
1083 BEINN A' CHAORRUINN
1196 NORTH TOP
River Gairn
1295 BRAERIACH
Lairig Ghru
1309 BEN MACDHUI
1084 CARN EAS
900 CULARDOCH
743 GEALLAIG HILL
B976
Coilacriech
1293 CAIRN TOUL
930 BEINN BHREAC
1177 SOUTH TOP
Glen Derry
Balmoral Castle
Crathie
River Dee
Littlemill
B976
618 MEALL GORM
Easter Balmoral
Balnacroft
Birkhall
PIAN MOUNTAINS
River Dee
Glen Dee
1157 BEINN BHROTAIN
813 SGÒR MÓR
Glen Lui
Linn of Dee
Quoich Water
Braemar
Allanaquoich
Keiloch
A93
Inver
Glen Gelder
600 CREAG NAN GALL
596 THE COYLES OF MUICK
Inverey
859 MORRONE HILL
Balmoral Forest
Deeside and Lochnagar
River Muick
Glen Muick
816 CARN LIATH
Clunie Water
1154 LOCHNAGAR
720 FASHEILACH
Spittal of Glenmuick
Loch Callater
1045 CAIRN TAGGART
Loch Muick
919 CARN BHAC
Glen Ey
886 SGOR MOR
Glen Clunie Lodge
996 BROAD CAIRN
1018 CÀRN AN TUIRC
832 EAST BALL
Tarf Water
Baddoch Burn
Glenshee Ski Area
Gleann Mòr
831 LAIR OF ALDARARIE
River Tilt
932 THE CAIRNWELL
1067 GLAS MAOL
Glen Doll
1050 GLAS TULAICHEAN
Loch Loch
34
River Isla
928 MAYAR
946 DRIESH
Clova
1119 CÀRN NAN CABHAR
Glen Lochsie
861 CARN AIT
1068
805 BEN GULABIN
649 CAIRN OF BAMS
Glen Clova
867 MEALL A' CHOIRE BHUIDHE
807 MONAMEANOCH
903 BEN VUIRICH
Spittal of Glenshee
Gleann Fearnach
Glen Shee
792 MEALL UAINE
700 DUCHRAY HILL
740 BADENDUN HILL
603 CAIRN DAUNIE
Glen Damff
Runtaleave
Cormuir
Glen Prosen
Pitcarity
Presnerb
Glen Finlet
B951
Folda
Tarvie
Straloch
Enochdhu
Clackavoid
744 MOUNT BLAIR
840 BEN VRACKIE
Balvarran
Tay Forest Park
River Ardle
Bridge of Brewlands
Backwater Reservoir
622 CREAG DHUBA
A924
Glenisla
550 MEALL MOR
Blacklunans
Kinnaird
Kirkmichael
B950
Bellaty
Balintore
Loch Broom
Edradour Distillery
Milton
Dykends
Scruschloch
Braes of Coul

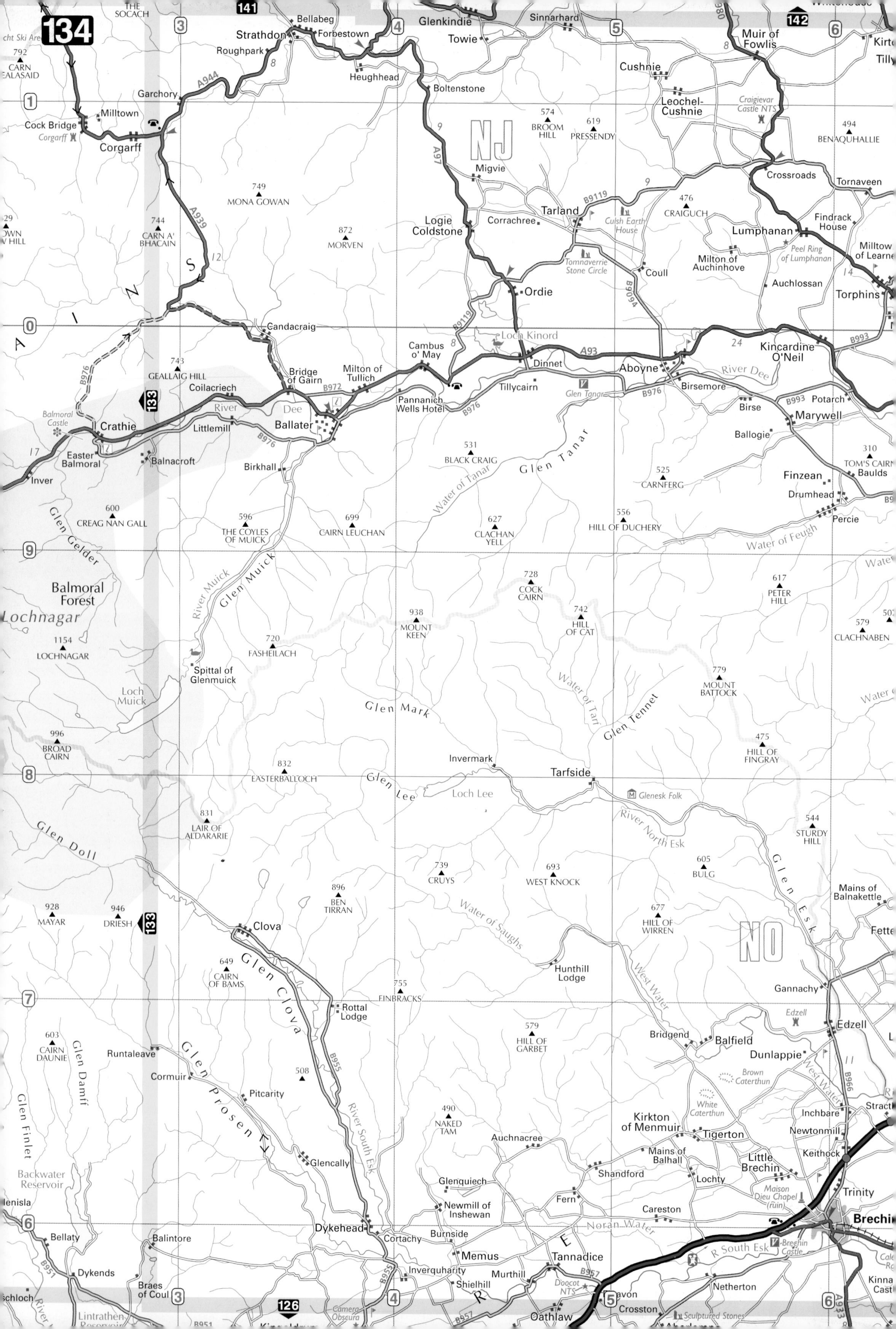
134
141
142
126
133
133
THE SOCACH
Bellabeg
Strathdon
Forbestown
Roughpark
Glenkindie
Towie
Sinnarhard
Muir of Fowlis
Kirk
Tilly
Cushnie
Leochel-Cushnie
Craigievar Castle NTS
792
CARN ELASAID
Heughhead
Boltenstone
Garchory
A944
Milltown
Cock Bridge
Corgarff
NJ
574
BROOM HILL
619
PRESSENDY
494
BENAQUHALLIE
A97
Migvie
Crossroads
Tornaveen
749
MONA GOWAN
Tarland
B9119
476
CRAIGUCH
Findrack House
744
CARN A' BHACAIN
A939
Logie Coldstone
Corrachree
Culsh Earth House
Lumphanan
Milltow of Learne
872
MORVEN
Peel Ring of Lumphanan
Tomnaverrie Stone Circle
Milton of Auchinhove
Coull
Auchlossan
Torphins
Ordie
B9094
Candacraig
B9119
Loch Kinord
Cambus o' May
A93
Dinnet
Kincardine O'Neil
B993
743
GEALLAIG HILL
Bridge of Gairn
Milton of Tullich
Aboyne
River Dee
Coilacriech
B972
Pannanich Wells Hotel
Tillycairn
Glen Tanar
B976
Birsemore
Potarch
B993
Birse
Balmoral Castle
Crathie
River
Dee
Ballater
Marywell
Littlemill
B976
Ballogie
17
Easter Balmoral
Balnacroft
531
BLACK CRAIG
310
TOM'S CAIRN
Inver
Birkhall
Glen Tanar
Water of Tanar
525
CARNFERG
Finzean
Baulds
Drumhead
600
CREAG NAN GALL
556
HILL OF DUCHERY
Percie
596
THE COYLES OF MUICK
699
CAIRN LEUCHAN
627
CLACHAN YELL
Water of Feugh
Glen Gelder
728
COCK CAIRN
617
PETER HILL
Balmoral Forest
River Muick
Glen Muick
938
MOUNT KEEN
742
HILL OF CAT
Lochnagar
579
CLACHNABEN
1154
LOCHNAGAR
720
FASHEILACH
Spittal of Glenmuick
779
MOUNT BATTOCK
Loch Muick
Water of Tarf
Glen Mark
Glen Tennet
996
BROAD CAIRN
475
HILL OF FINGRAY
Invermark
832
EASTERBALLOCH
Tarfside
Glen Lee
Loch Lee
Glenesk Folk
831
LAIR OF ALDARARIE
River North Esk
544
STURDY HILL
Glen Doll
739
CRUYS
693
WEST KNOCK
605
BULG
Glen Esk
Mains of Balnakettle
896
BEN TIRRAN
928
MAYAR
946
DRIESH
Water of Saughs
677
HILL OF WIRREN
Clova
NO
649
CAIRN OF BAMS
Glen Clova
Hunthill Lodge
West Water
755
FINBRACKS
Gannachy
Rottal Lodge
Edzell
Edzell
579
HILL OF GARBET
Bridgend
Balfield
603
CAIRN DAUNIE
Glen Damff
Runtaleave
Dunlappie
Glen Prosen
B955
Brown Caterthun
B966
Cormuir
508
Glen Finlet
Pitcarity
River South Esk
West Water
White Caterthun
490
NAKED TAM
Kirkton of Menmuir
Tigerton
Inchbare
Newtonmill
Keithock
Auchnacree
Mains of Balhall
Little Brechin
Glencally
Shandford
Backwater Reservoir
Glenquiech
Lochty
Trinity
Newmill of Inshewan
Fern
Maison Dieu Chapel (ruin)
Careston
Dykehead
Brechin
Bellaty
Cortachy
Burnside
Noran Water
Balintore
Memus
Tannadice
R South Esk
Brechin Castle
B951
Dykends
Inverquharity
Murthill
Shielhill
B957
Doocot NTS
Braes of Coul
Netherton
Tannadice
Crosston
Oathlaw
Lintrathen Reservoir
Camera Obscura
Sculptured Stones
B951
B957
A933

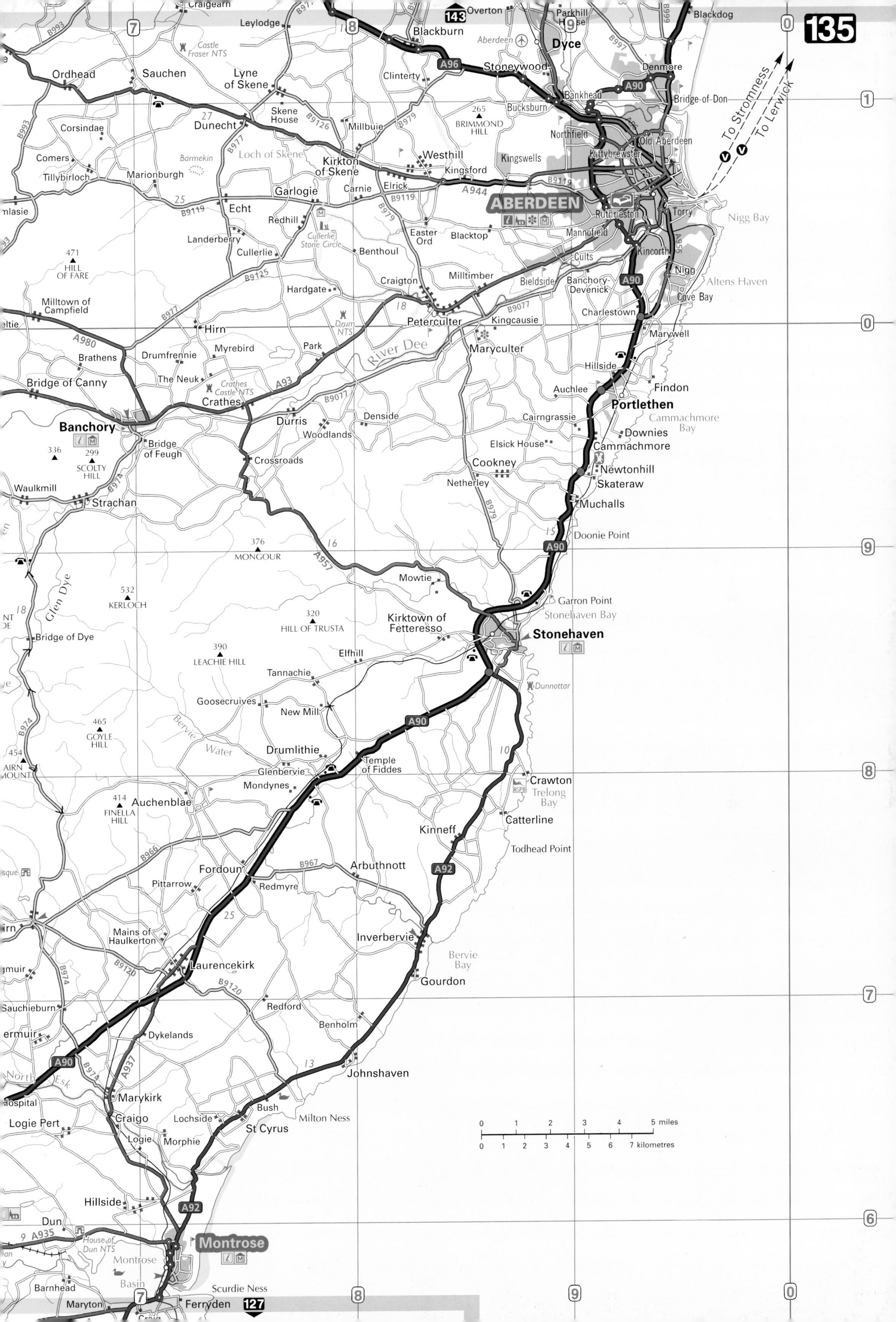
135
Craigearn
Leylodge
Overton
143
Blackburn
Parkhill House
Blackdog
Aberdeen
Dyce
Castle Fraser NTS
Ordhead
Sauchen
Lyne of Skene
Clinterty
A96
Stoneywood
Denmore
A90
Bankhead
Bridge-of-Don
To Stromness
To Lerwick
Skene House
B9126
Millbuie
265
BRIMMOND HILL
Bucksburn
Corsindae
Dunecht
Northfield
Old Aberdeen
Kittybrewster
Comers
Barmekin
Loch of Skene
Kirkton of Skene
Westhill
Kingswells
Tillybirloch
Marionburgh
Kingsford
Garlogie
Carnie
Elrick
A944
B9119
ABERDEEN
Echt
Redhill
Ruthrieston
Torry
Nigg Bay
Landerberry
Cullerlie Stone Circle
Easter Ord
Blacktop
Mannofield
Cullerlie
Benthoul
Kincorth
471
HILL OF FARE
Cults
Nigg
Milltimber
B9125
Craigton
Bieldside
Banchory-Devenick
Altens Haven
Cove Bay
Hardgate
Milltown of Campfield
Charlestown
Drum NTS
Peterculter
Kingcausie
B9077
Hirn
A980
Marywell
Maryculter
River Dee
Brathens
Drumfrennie
Myrebird
Park
Hillside
Bridge of Canny
The Neuk
Crathes Castle NTS
A93
Auchlee
Findon
Crathes
Portlethen
B9077
Cairngrassie
Cammachmore Bay
Banchory
Durris
Denside
Downies
Woodlands
Elsick House
Cammachmore
Bridge of Feugh
336
299
SCOLTY HILL
Crossroads
Cookney
Newtonhill
Netherley
Skateraw
Waulkmill
Strachan
Muchalls
B979
Doonie Point
376
MONGOUR
A957
Glen Dye
532
KERLOCH
Mowtie
Garron Point
Stonehaven Bay
320
HILL OF TRUSTA
Kirktown of Fetteresso
Stonehaven
Bridge of Dye
390
LEACHIE HILL
Elfhill
Tannachie
Dunnottar
Goosecruives
New Mill
465
GOYLE HILL
Bervie Water
Drumlithie
Temple of Fiddes
454
CAIRN MOUNT
Glenbervie
Crawton
Trelong Bay
Mondynes
414
FINELLA HILL
Auchenblae
Catterline
Kinneff
Todhead Point
B966
Fordoun
B967
Arbuthnott
A92
Pittarrow
Redmyre
Mains of Haulkerton
Inverbervie
Bervie Bay
B9120
Laurencekirk
B974
Gourdon
Redford
Sauchieburn
Benholm
Dykelands
A90
A937
North Esk
Johnshaven
Marykirk
Bush
Milton Ness
Craigo
Lochside
St Cyrus
Logie Pert
Logie
Morphie
0 1 2 3 4 5 miles
0 1 2 3 4 5 6 7 kilometres
Hillside
A92
Dun
A935
House of Dun NTS
Montrose
Montrose Basin
Barnhead
Scurdie Ness
Maryton
Ferryden
127

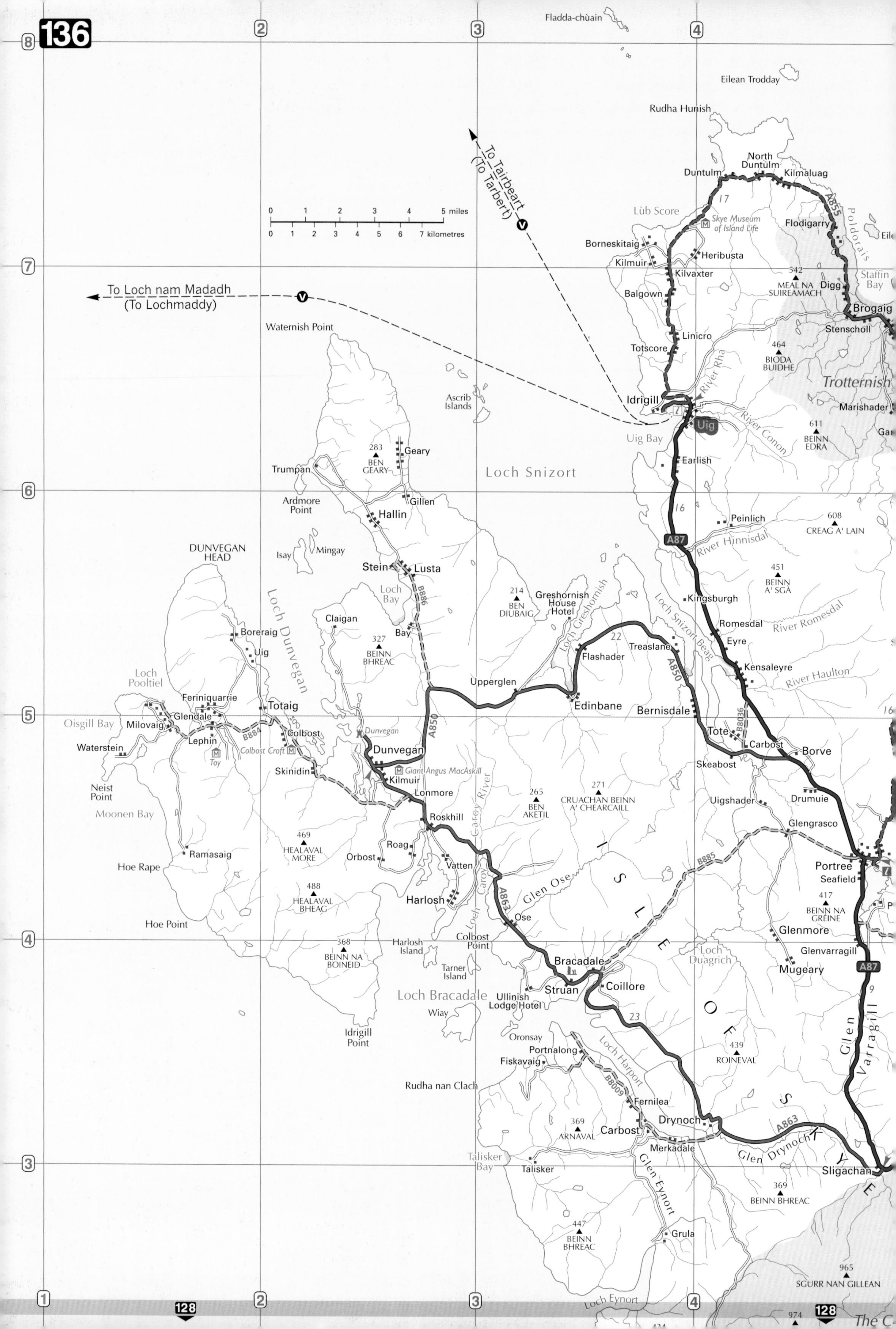

To Tairbeart (To Tarbert)
To Loch nam Madadh (To Lochmaddy)
0 1 2 3 4 5 miles
0 1 2 3 4 5 6 7 kilometres
Fladda-chùain
Eilean Trodday
Rudha Hunish
North Duntulm
Duntulm
Kilmaluag
Lùb Score
Skye Museum of Island Life
Flodigarry
Poldorais
Borneskitaig
Heribusta
Kilmuir
Kilvaxter
542 MEAL NA SUIREAMACH
Digg
Staffin Bay
Balgown
Brogaig
Stenscholl
Linicro
Totscore
464 BIODA BUIDHE
Trotternish
River Rha
Idrigill
Marishader
Uig
River Conon
Uig Bay
611 BEINN EDRA
Earlish
Loch Snizort
Waternish Point
Ascrib Islands
283 BEN GEARY
Geary
Trumpan
Ardmore Point
Gillen
Hallin
Peinlich
608 CREAG A' LAIN
River Hinnisdal
A87
DUNVEGAN HEAD
Isay
Mingay
Stein
Lusta
451 BEINN A' SGA
Loch Bay
B886
214 BEN DIUBAIG
Greshornish House Hotel
Loch Greshornish
Kingsburgh
Loch Snizort Beag
Romesdal
River Romesdal
Claigan
Bay
Boreraig
Uig
Loch Dunvegan
327 BEINN BHREAC
Eyre
Treaslane
Flashader
Kensaleyre
River Haulton
Loch Pooltiel
Upperglen
Feriniquarrie
Glendale
Totaig
Edinbane
Bernisdale
Oisgill Bay
Milovaig
Lephin
B884
Colbost
Dunvegan
A850
B8036
Tote
Carbost
Borve
Waterstein
Toy
Colbost Croft
Skinidin
Giant Angus MacAskill
Kilmuir
Skeabost
Neist Point
Lonmore
271 CRUACHAN BEINN A' CHEARCAILL
265 BEN AKETIL
Uigshader
Drumuie
Moonen Bay
Caroy River
Roskhill
Glengrasco
469 HEALAVAL MORE
Ramasaig
Roag
Orbost
B885
Portree
Hoe Rape
Vatten
Seafield
488 HEALAVAL BHEAG
Glen Ose
417 BEINN NA GRÈINE
Harlosh
A863
Ose
ISLE OF SKYE
Hoe Point
Loch Caroy
Glenmore
368 BEINN NA BOINEID
Harlosh Island
Colbost Point
Loch Duagrich
Glenvarragill
Bracadale
Mugeary
Tarner Island
Struan
Coillore
Loch Bracadale
Ullinish Lodge Hotel
Wiay
Glen Varragill
Idrigill Point
Oronsay
Portnalong
Loch Harport
439 ROINEVAL
Fiskavaig
B8009
Rudha nan Clach
Fernilea
369 ARNAVAL
Carbost
Drynoch
Merkadale
Glen Drynoch
Talisker Bay
Talisker
Glen Eynort
Sligachan
369 BEINN BHREAC
447 BEINN BHREAC
Grula
965 SGURR NAN GILLEAN
Loch Eynort
974

128
128

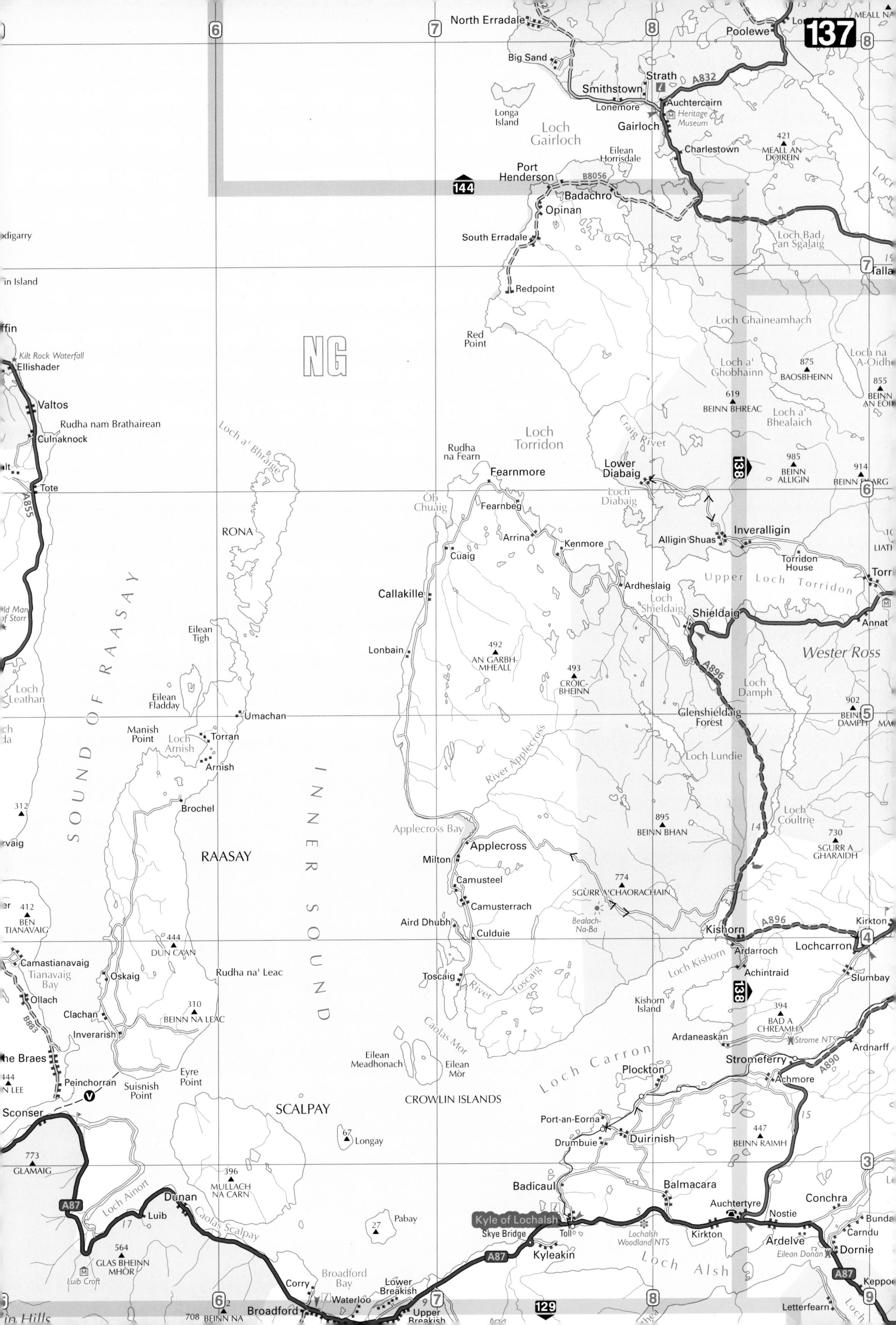
137
North Erradale
Poolewe
Big Sand
Strath
A832
Smithstown
Auchtercairn
Heritage Museum
Lonemore
Gairloch
Longa Island
Loch Gairloch
Eilean Horrisdale
Charlestown
421 MEALL AN DOIREIN
Port Henderson
B8056
144
Badachro
Opinan
South Erradale
Loch Bad an Sgalaig
Redpoint
Red Point
NG
Loch Ghaineamhach
Loch a' Ghobhainn
875 BAOSBHEINN
Loch na A-Oidhe
855 BEINN AN EOIN
619 BEINN BHREAC
Loch a' Bhealaich
Kilt Rock Waterfall
Ellishader
Valtos
Rudha nam Brathairean
Culnaknock
Tote
A855
Loch a' Bhràige
Loch Torridon
Craig River
Rudha na Fearn
Fearnmore
Lower Diabaig
Loch Diabaig
138
985 BEINN ALLIGIN
914 BEINN DEARG
Òb Chuaig
Fearnbeg
RONA
Arrina
Kenmore
Alligin Shuas
Inveralligin
Torridon House
Cuaig
SOUND OF RAASAY
Callakille
Ardheslaig
Upper Loch Torridon
Loch Shieldaig
Shieldaig
Annat
Eilean Tigh
Lonbain
492 AN GARBH-MHEALL
Wester Ross
A896
493 CROIC-BHEINN
Loch Damph
Loch Leathan
Eilean Fladday
Umachan
Glenshieldaig Forest
902
Manish Point
Loch Arnish
Torran
Arnish
River Applecross
Loch Lundie
INNER SOUND
Brochel
312
RAASAY
Applecross Bay
Applecross
895 BEINN BHAN
Loch Coultrie
730 SGURR A' GHARAIDH
Milton
Camusteel
774 SGÙRR A' CHAORACHAIN
Camusterrach
Bealach-Na-Ba
412 BEN TIANAVAIG
Aird Dhubh
Culduie
Kishorn
Kirkton
Lochcarron
444 DUN CAAN
Camastianavaig
Tianavaig Bay
Ardarroch
Loch Kishorn
Achintraid
Slumbay
Oskaig
Rudha na' Leac
Toscaig
River Toscaig
Ollach
Kishorn Island
394 BAD A' CHREAMHA
B883
310 BEINN NA LEAC
Clachan
Inverarish
Caolas Mòr
Ardaneaskan
Strome NTS
Ardnarff
Eilean Meadhonach
Eilean Mòr
Loch Carron
Stromeferry
The Braes
Peinchorran
Eyre Point
Suisnish Point
Plockton
A890
Achmore
Sconser
SCALPAY
CROWLIN ISLANDS
Port-an-Eorna
67 Longay
Drumbuie
Duirinish
447 BEINN RAIMH
773 GLAMAIG
396 MULLACH NA CARN
Badicaul
Balmacara
Conchra
Dunan
A87
Loch Ainort
Luib
Caolas Scalpay
27
Pabay
Kyle of Lochalsh
Auchtertyre
Nostie
Skye Bridge
Toll
Lochalsh Woodland NTS
Kirkton
Ardelve
Dornie
564 GLAS BHEINN MHÒR
Luib Croft
Kyleakin
Eilean Donan
Loch Alsh
Broadford Bay
Corry
Lower Breakish
Waterloo
Broadford
Upper Breakish
129
708 BEINN NA
Letterfearn
Keppoch

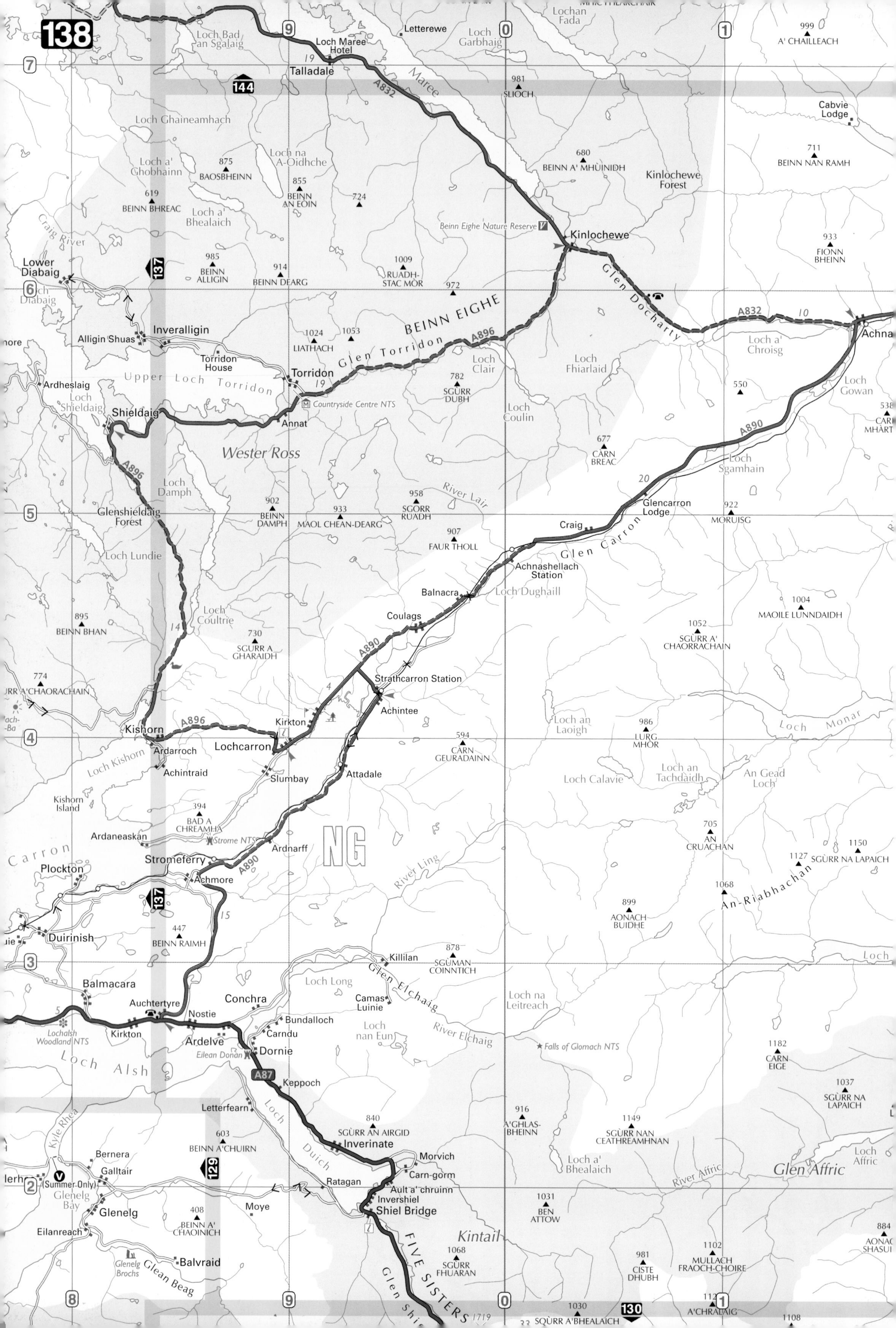
Loch Bad an Sgalaig
Letterewe
Loch Maree Hotel
Talladale
Loch Garbhaig
Lochan Fada
999 A' CHAILLEACH
144
A832
Maree
981 SLIOCH
Cabvie Lodge
Loch Ghaineamhach
Loch na A-Oidhche
Loch a' Ghobhainn
875 BAOSBHEINN
855 BEINN AN EOIN
680 BEINN A' MHÙINIDH
Kinlochewe Forest
711 BEINN NAN RAMH
619 BEINN BHREAC
Loch a' Bhealaich
724
Craig River
Beinn Eighe Nature Reserve
Kinlochewe
933 FIONN BHEINN
Lower Diabaig
137
985 BEINN ALLIGIN
914 BEINN DEARG
1009 RUADH-STAC MÒR
972
Loch Diabaig
Glen Docharty
BEINN EIGHE
A832
Achna
Inveralligin
Alligin Shuas
1024 LIATHACH
1053
Glen Torridon
A896
Loch a' Chroisg
Torridon House
Torridon
Loch Clair
Loch Fhiarlaid
Upper Loch Torridon
Ardheslaig
Loch Shieldaig
782 SGÙRR DUBH
550
Loch Gowan
Shieldaig
Countryside Centre NTS
Annat
Loch Coulin
538 CARN MHÀRT
Wester Ross
677 CARN BREAC
A890
Loch Sgamhain
A896
Loch Damph
River Lair
Glencarron Lodge
Glenshieldaig Forest
902 BEINN DAMPH
933 MAOL CHEAN-DEARG
958 SGORR RUADH
922 MORUISG
Craig
907 FAUR THOLL
Glen Carron
Loch Lundie
Achnashellach Station
Balnacra
Loch Dughaill
Loch Coultrie
Coulags
1004 MAOILE LUNNDAIDH
895 BEINN BHAN
730 SGURR A GHARAIDH
1052 SGÙRR A' CHAORRACHAIN
A890
774 SGURR A' CHAORACHAIN
Strathcarron Station
Achintee
A896
Kirkton
Kishorn
Loch an Laoigh
986 LURG MHOR
Loch Monar
Ardarroch
Lochcarron
594 CARN GEURADAINN
Loch Kishorn
Achintraid
Slumbay
Attadale
Loch Calavie
Loch an Tachdaidh
An Gead Loch
Kishorn Island
394 BAD A CHREAMHA
Ardaneaskan
Strome NTS
NG
705 AN CRUACHAN
Carron
Ardnarff
Stromeferry
A890
1150 SGÙRR NA LAPAICH
1127
Plockton
Achmore
River Ling
An-Riabhachan
137
1068
899 AONACH BUIDHE
447 BEINN RAIMH
Duirinish
878 SGÙMAN COINNTICH
Killilan
Loch
Balmacara
Loch Long
Glen Elchaig
Loch na Leitreach
Auchtertyre
Conchra
Camas-Luinie
Nostie
Bundalloch
Loch nan Eun
River Elchaig
Lochalsh Woodland NTS
Kirkton
Ardelve
Carndu
Eilean Donan
Dornie
Falls of Glomach NTS
1182 CARN EIGE
Loch Alsh
A87
Keppoch
1037 SGÙRR NA LAPAICH
Kyle Rhea
Letterfearn
Loch Duich
840 SGÙRR AN AIRGID
916 A'GHLAS-BHEINN
1149 SGÙRR NAN CEATHREAMHNAN
603 BEINN A'CHUIRN
Inverinate
Bernera
129
Morvich
Loch a' Bhealaich
Loch Affric
Galltair
Carn-gorm
River Affric
Glen Affric
Glenelg Bay
(Summer Only)
Ratagan
Ault a' chruinn
Inveshiel
Glenelg
Moye
Shiel Bridge
1031 BEN ATTOW
408 BEINN A' CHAOINICH
Eilanreach
Kintail
884 AONACH SHASUIN
1102 MULLACH FRAOCH-CHOIRE
981 CISTE DHUBH
1068 SGÙRR FHUARAN
Balvraid
Glenelg Brochs
Glean Beag
FIVE SISTERS
Glen Shiel
1030 SGÙRR A'BHEALAICH
130
A'CHRALAIG
1108

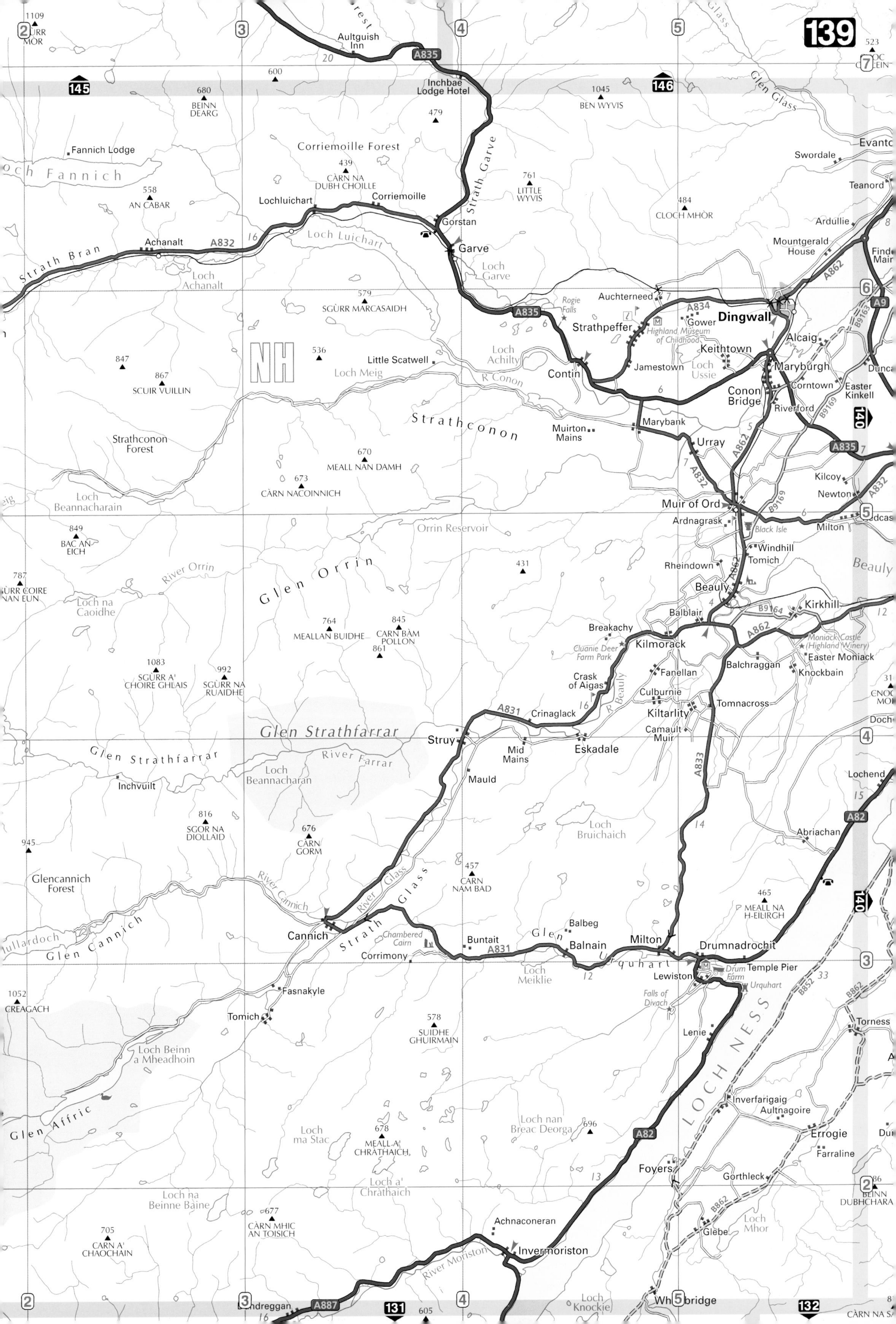

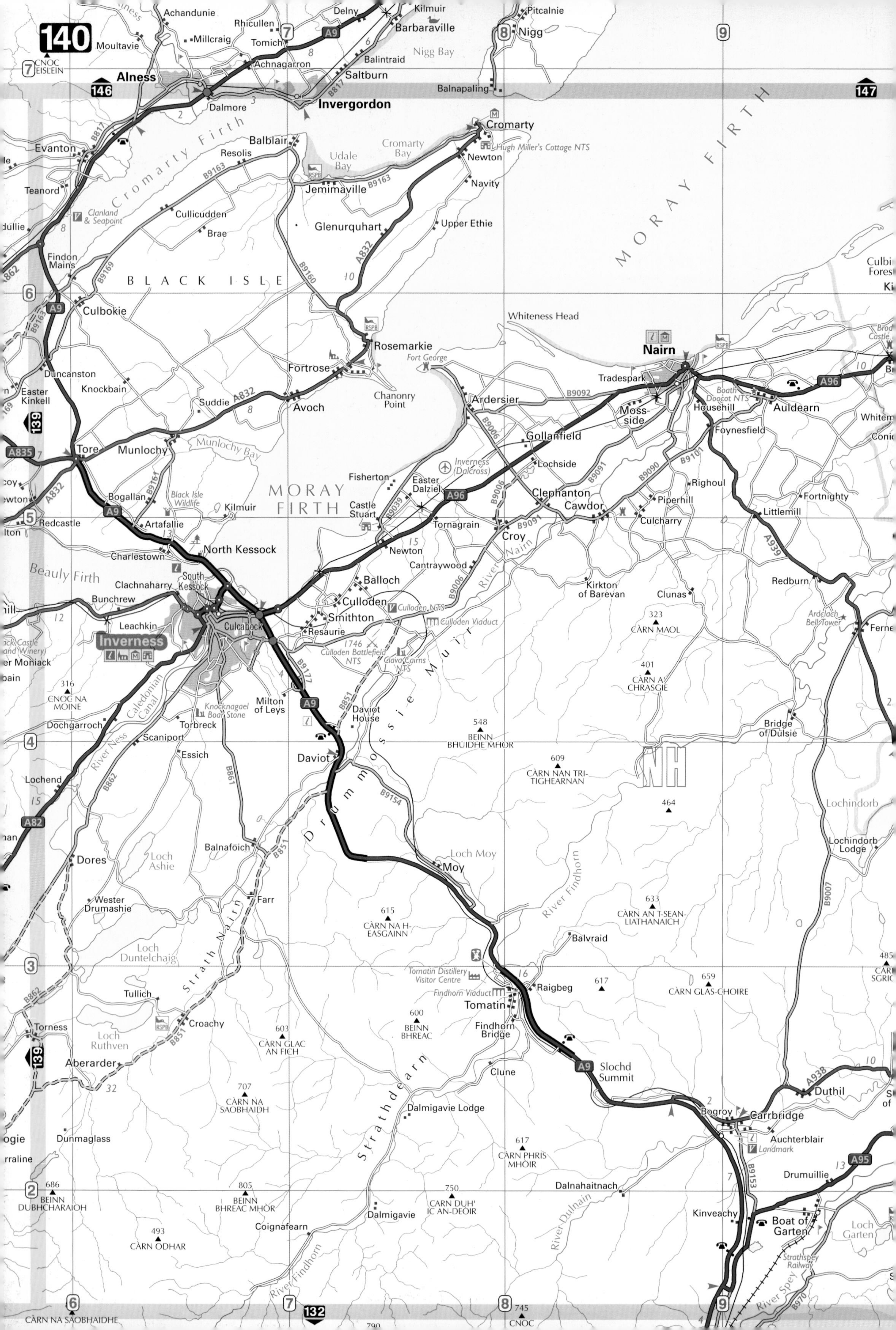
Alness
Invergordon
Cromarty
Cromarty Firth
BLACK ISLE
MORAY FIRTH
Nairn
Inverness
Culloden
Tomatin
Carrbridge
Boat of Garten
Dores
Moy
Slochd Summit
Rosemarkie
Fortrose
Avoch
North Kessock
Ardersier
Cawdor
Auldearn
Drummossie Muir
Strathdearn
Strath Nairn
NH
146
147
139
132

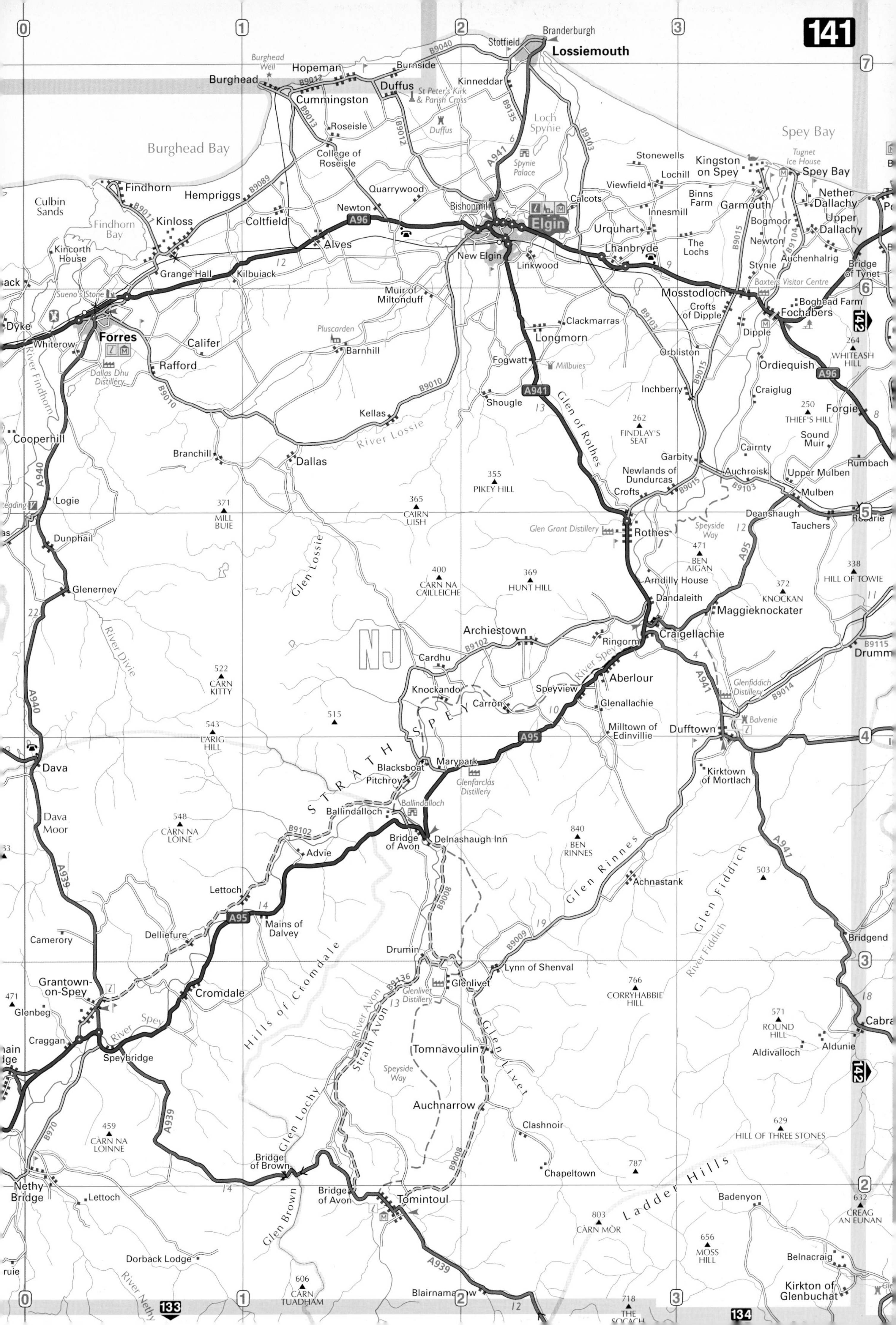
141
Branderburgh
Stotfield
Lossiemouth
Burghead Well
Hopeman
Burnside
Burghead
Kinneddar
Duffus
St Peter's Kirk & Parish Cross
Cummingston
Roseisle
Duffus
Loch Spynie
Burghead Bay
College of Roseisle
Spynie Palace
Spey Bay
Stonewells
Kingston on Spey
Tugnet Ice House
Spey Bay
Lochill
Findhorn
Hempriggs
Quarrywood
Viewfield
Culbin Sands
Findhorn Bay
Kinloss
Coltfield
Newton
Bishopmill
Calcots
Binns Farm
Garmouth
Nether Dallachy
Upper Dallachy
Elgin
Innesmill
Bogmoor
Urquhart
Newton
Kincorth House
Alves
Lhanbryde
The Lochs
Auchenhalrig
New Elgin
Linkwood
Stynie
Bridge of Tynet
Grange Hall
Kilbuiack
Baxters Visitor Centre
Sueno's Stone
Muir of Miltonduff
Mosstodloch
Crofts of Dipple
Boghead Farm
Fochabers
Dyke
Clackmarras
Dipple
Whiterow
Forres
Califer
Pluscarden
Barnhill
Longmorn
Orbliston
Whiteash Hill
Rafford
Dallas Dhu Distillery
Fogwatt
Millbuies
Ordiequish
River Findhorn
Shougle
Inchberry
Craiglug
Kellas
Thief's Hill
Forgie
Cooperhill
River Lossie
Findlay's Seat
Sound Muir
Branchill
Dallas
Glen of Rothes
Garbity
Cairnty
Rumbach
Pikey Hill
Newlands of Dundurcas
Auchroisk
Upper Mulben
Mulben
Logie
Mill Buie
Cairn Uish
Crofts
Deanshaugh
Tauchers
Glen Grant Distillery
Rothes
Speyside Way
Dunphail
Ben Aigan
Hill of Towie
Glen Lossie
Carn na Cailleiche
Hunt Hill
Ardilly House
Knockan
Glenerney
Dandaleith
Maggieknockater
River Divie
Archiestown
Ringorm
Craigellachie
NJ
Cardhu
River Spey
Aberlour
Carn Kitty
Knockando
Carron
Speyview
Glenallachie
Glenfiddich Distillery
Strath Spey
Larig Hill
Milltown of Edinvillie
Dufftown
Balvenie
Dava
Blacksboat
Marypark
Kirktown of Mortlach
Pitchroy
Glenfarclas Distillery
Ballindalloch
Ballindalloch
Dava Moor
Carn na Loine
Ben Rinnes
Bridge of Avon
Delnashaugh Inn
Advie
Glen Rinnes
Lettoch
Achnastank
Glen Fiddich
Mains of Dalvey
Delliefure
Camerory
Hills of Cromdale
Drumin
River Fiddich
Bridgend
Lynn of Shenval
Grantown-on-Spey
Glenlivet
Glenlivet Distillery
Corryhabbie Hill
Cromdale
Glenbeg
Round Hill
Craggan
River Spey
Aldivalloch
Aldunie
Speybridge
Tomnavoulin
Glen Livet
Strath Avon
River Avon
Speyside Way
Auchnarrow
Carn na Loinne
Glen Lochy
Clashnoir
Hill of Three Stones
Bridge of Brown
Chapeltown
Ladder Hills
Nethy Bridge
Lettoch
Bridge of Avon
Tomintoul
Badenyon
Creag an Eunan
Glen Brown
Carn Mor
Moss Hill
Dorback Lodge
Belnacraig
River Nethy
Carn Tuadham
Blairnamarrow
The Socach
Kirkton of Glenbuchat
133
134
142

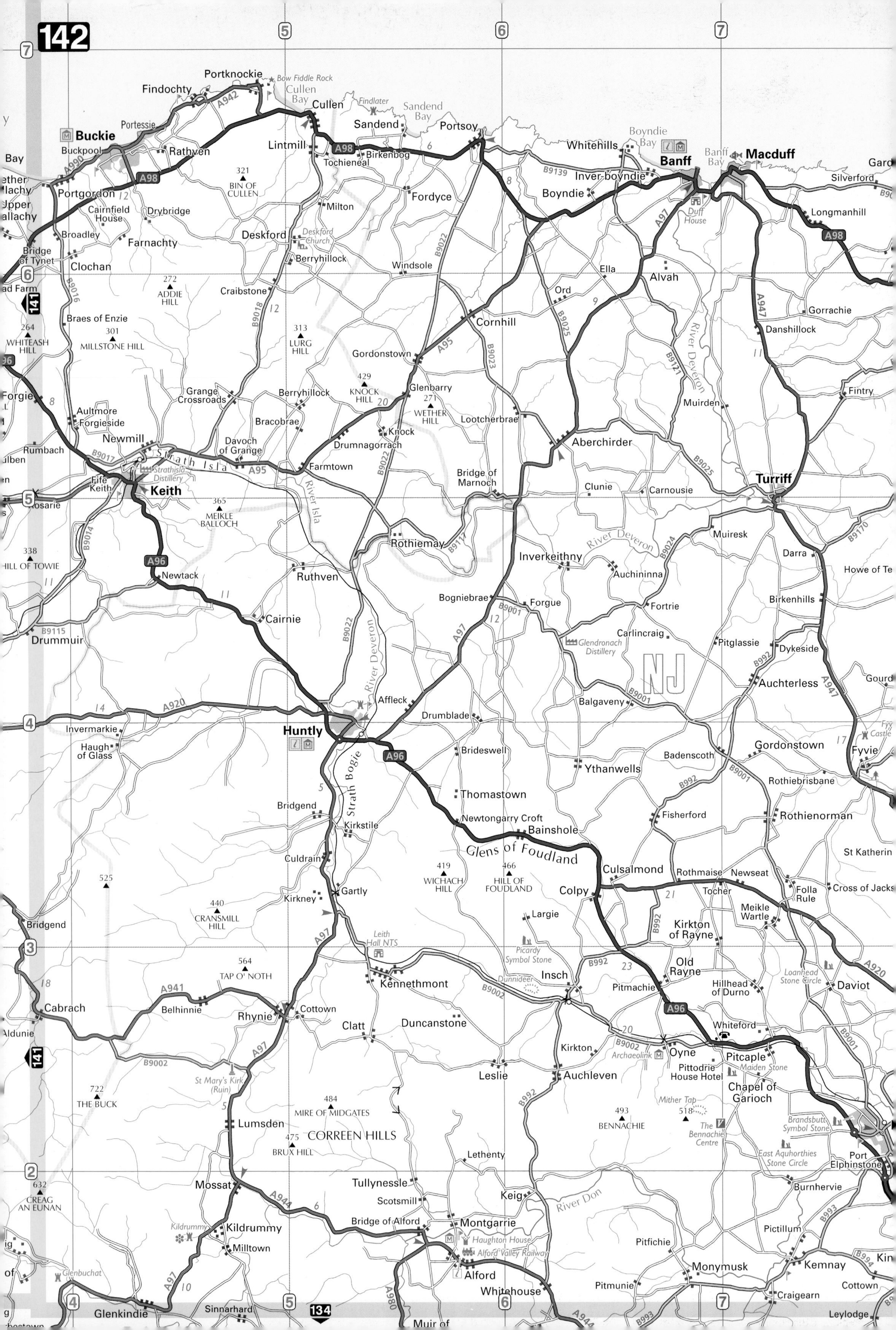
Portknockie
Bow Fiddle Rock
Cullen Bay
Findochty
Cullen
Findlater
Sandend Bay
Sandend
Portsoy
Boyndie Bay
Whitehills
Banff
Banff Bay
Macduff
Portessie
Buckie
Buckpool
Rathven
Lintmill
Tochieneal
Birkenbog
A98
A942
A990
321 BIN OF CULLEN
Inver-boyndie
B9139
Boyndie
Silverford
Longmanhill
Portgordon
Cairnfield House
Drybridge
Milton
Fordyce
Duff House
A97
Broadley
Farnachty
Deskford
Deskford Church
Bridge of Tynet
Clochan
Berryhillock
Windsole
B9022
Ella
Alvah
272 ADDIE HILL
Craibstone
Ord
B9016
B9018
B9025
Gorrachie
Danshillock
A947
Braes of Enzie
301 MILLSTONE HILL
264 WHITEASH HILL
313 LURG HILL
Cornhill
Gordonstown
A95
B9023
B9121
River Deveron
Forgie
Grange Crossroads
Berryhillock
429 KNOCK HILL
Glenbarry
271 WETHER HILL
Fintry
Muirden
Aultmore
Forgieside
Bracobrae
Knock
Lootcherbrae
Newmill
Davoch of Grange
Drumnagorrach
Aberchirder
Rumbach
B9017
Strath Isla
Strathisla Distillery
Farmtown
Fife Keith
Keith
River Isla
Bridge of Marnoch
Clunie
Carnousie
Turriff
365 MEIKLE BALLOCH
B9014
338 HILL OF TOWIE
Rothiemay
B9117
Muiresk
Darra
B9024
B9170
Howe of Te
Inverkeithny
Auchininna
A96
Newtack
Ruthven
Bogniebrae
Forgue
B9001
Fortrie
Birkenhills
Cairnie
B9115
Drummuir
Carlincraig
Glendronach Distillery
Pitglassie
Dykeside
B9022
NJ
B992
Auchterless
Gourd
A920
Affleck
Drumblade
Balgaveny
Invermarkie
Huntly
Haugh of Glass
Brideswell
Ythanwells
Badenscoth
Gordonstown
Fyvie
Fyvie Castle
Rothiebrisbane
Strath Bogie
Thomastown
Bridgend
Newtongarry Croft
Bainshole
Fisherford
Rothienorman
Kirkstile
Glens of Foudland
Culdrain
419 WICHACH HILL
466 HILL OF FOUDLAND
Culsalmond
Rothmaise
Newseat
St Katherin
525
Colpy
Tocher
Folla Rule
Cross of Jacks
Kirkney
Gartly
440 CRANSMILL HILL
Largie
Meikle Wartle
Bridgend
Kirkton of Rayne
Leith Hall NTS
Picardy Symbol Stone
564 TAP O' NOTH
Old Rayne
Loanhead Stone Circle
A941
Kennethmont
Dunnideer
Insch
Pitmachie
Hillhead of Durno
Daviot
B9002
Cabrach
Belhinnie
Rhynie
Cottown
Clatt
Duncanstone
Whiteford
Aldunie
Kirkton
Archaeolink
Oyne
Pitcaple
B9002
St Mary's Kirk (Ruin)
Leslie
Auchleven
Pittodrie House Hotel
Maiden Stone
Chapel of Garioch
722 THE BUCK
484 MIRE OF MIDGATES
Mither Tap
493 BENNACHIE
518
The Bennachie Centre
Brandsbutt Symbol Stone
Lumsden
475 BRUX HILL
CORREEN HILLS
Lethenty
East Aquhorthies Stone Circle
Port Elphinstone
632 CREAG AN EUNAN
Mossat
Tullynessle
Scotsmill
Keig
River Don
Burnhervie
A944
Kildrummy
Bridge of Alford
Montgarrie
Haughton House
Alford Valley Railway
Pictillum
B993
Milltown
Pitfichie
Glenbuchat
Alford
Monymusk
Kemnay
B994
Pitmunie
Whitehouse
Craigearn
Cottown
Glenkindie
Sinnarhard
A980
Muir of
Leylodge

141
141
134

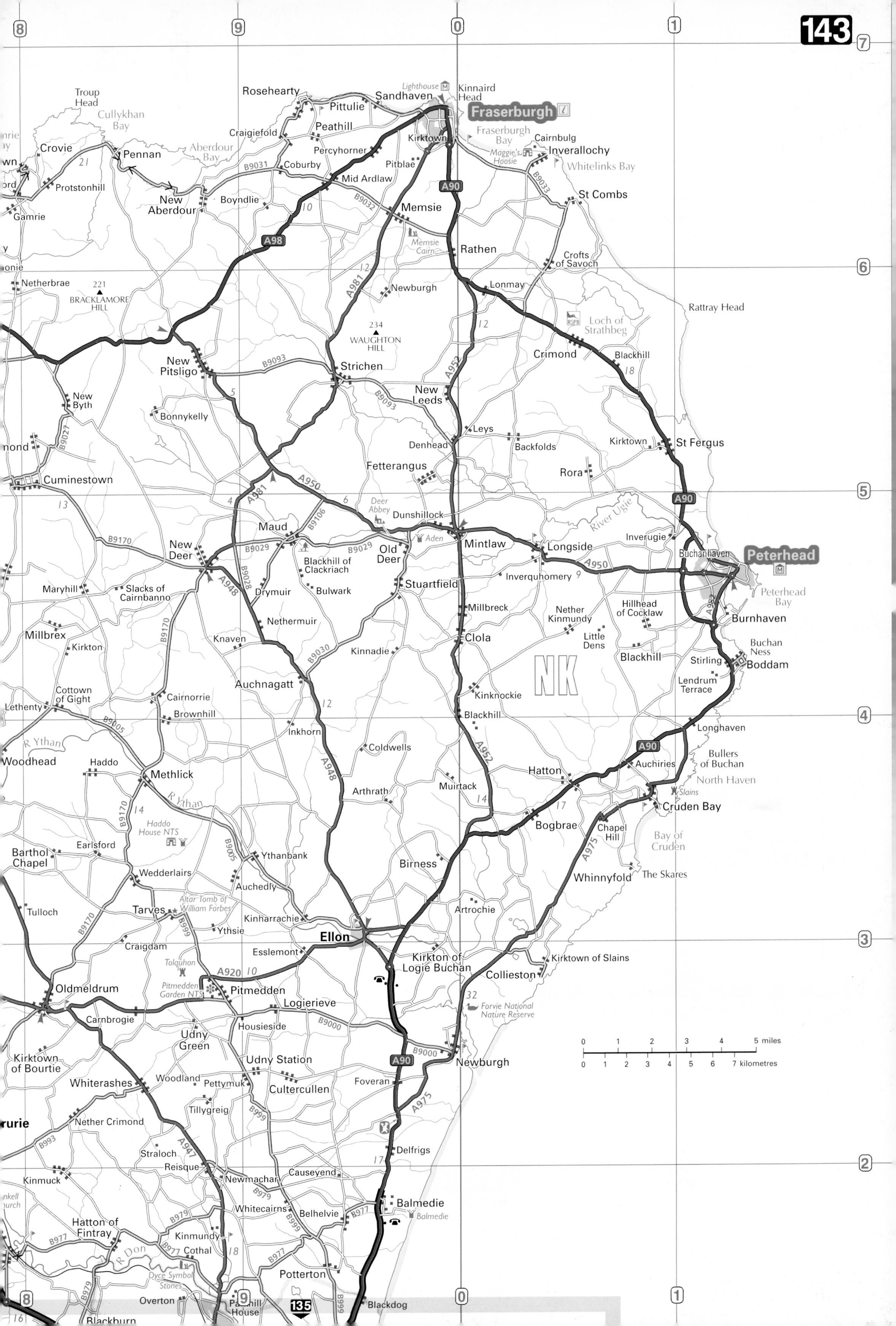
Troup Head
Cullykhan Bay
Crovie
Pennan
Protstonhill
Gamrie
New Aberdour
Aberdour Bay
Rosehearty
Pittulie
Sandhaven
Lighthouse
Kinnaird Head
Fraserburgh
Fraserburgh Bay
Kirktown
Cairnbulg
Inverallochy
Maggie's Hoosie
Whitelinks Bay
Craigiefold
Peathill
Percyhorner
Coburby
Pitblae
Mid Ardlaw
Boyndlie
Memsie
Memsie Cairn
St Combs
Rathen
Crofts of Savoch
Netherbrae
221
BRACKLAMORE HILL
Newburgh
Lonmay
234
WAUGHTON HILL
Loch of Strathbeg
Rattray Head
Crimond
Blackhill
New Pitsligo
Strichen
New Byth
Bonnykelly
New Leeds
Leys
Denhead
Backfolds
Kirktown
St Fergus
Cuminestown
Fetterangus
Rora
Deer Abbey
Dunshillock
River Ugie
Maud
New Deer
Old Deer
Aden
Mintlaw
Longside
Inverugie
Buchanhaven
Peterhead
Peterhead Bay
Blackhill of Clackriach
Bulwark
Stuartfield
Inverquhomery
Maryhill
Slacks of Cairnbanno
Drymuir
Millbreck
Nether Kinmundy
Hillhead of Cocklaw
Burnhaven
Millbrex
Kirkton
Nethermuir
Knaven
Clola
Little Dens
Blackhill
Buchan Ness
Stirling
Boddam
Kinnadie
NK
Auchnagatt
Cottown of Gight
Cairnorrie
Kinknockie
Lendrum Terrace
Lethenty
Brownhill
Blackhill
Longhaven
R Ythan
Inkhorn
Coldwells
Bullers of Buchan
Woodhead
Haddo
Methlick
Auchiries
Hatton
North Haven
Muirtack
Arthrath
Slains
Cruden Bay
Haddo House NTS
Bogbrae
Chapel Hill
Bay of Cruden
Barthol Chapel
Earlsford
Ythanbank
Birness
Whinnyfold
The Skares
Wedderlairs
Auchedly
Tulloch
Tarves
Altar Tomb of William Forbes
Kinharrachie
Artrochie
Ythsie
Ellon
Craigdam
Esslemont
Kirkton of Logie Buchan
Kirktown of Slains
Tolquhon
Collieston
Oldmeldrum
Pitmedden Garden NTS
Pitmedden
Forvie National Nature Reserve
Carnbrogie
Logierieve
Housieside
Udny Green
Newburgh
Kirktown of Bourtie
Udny Station
Whiterashes
Woodland
Pettymuk
Culterculien
Foveran
Tillygreig
Nether Crimond
Delfrigs
Straloch
Reisque
Kinmuck
Newmachar
Causeyend
Whitecairns
Belhelvie
Balmedie
Hatton of Fintray
Kinmundy
Cothal
R Don
Dyce Symbol Stones
Potterton
Overton
Parkhill House
Blackdog
Blackburn
A90
A98
A981
A952
A950
A948
A982
A975
A920
A947
B9031
B9032
B9033
B9093
B9027
B9170
B9029
B9028
B9106
B9030
B9005
B9000
B999
B977
B979
B993
135
0 1 2 3 4 5 miles
0 1 2 3 4 5 6 7 kilometres

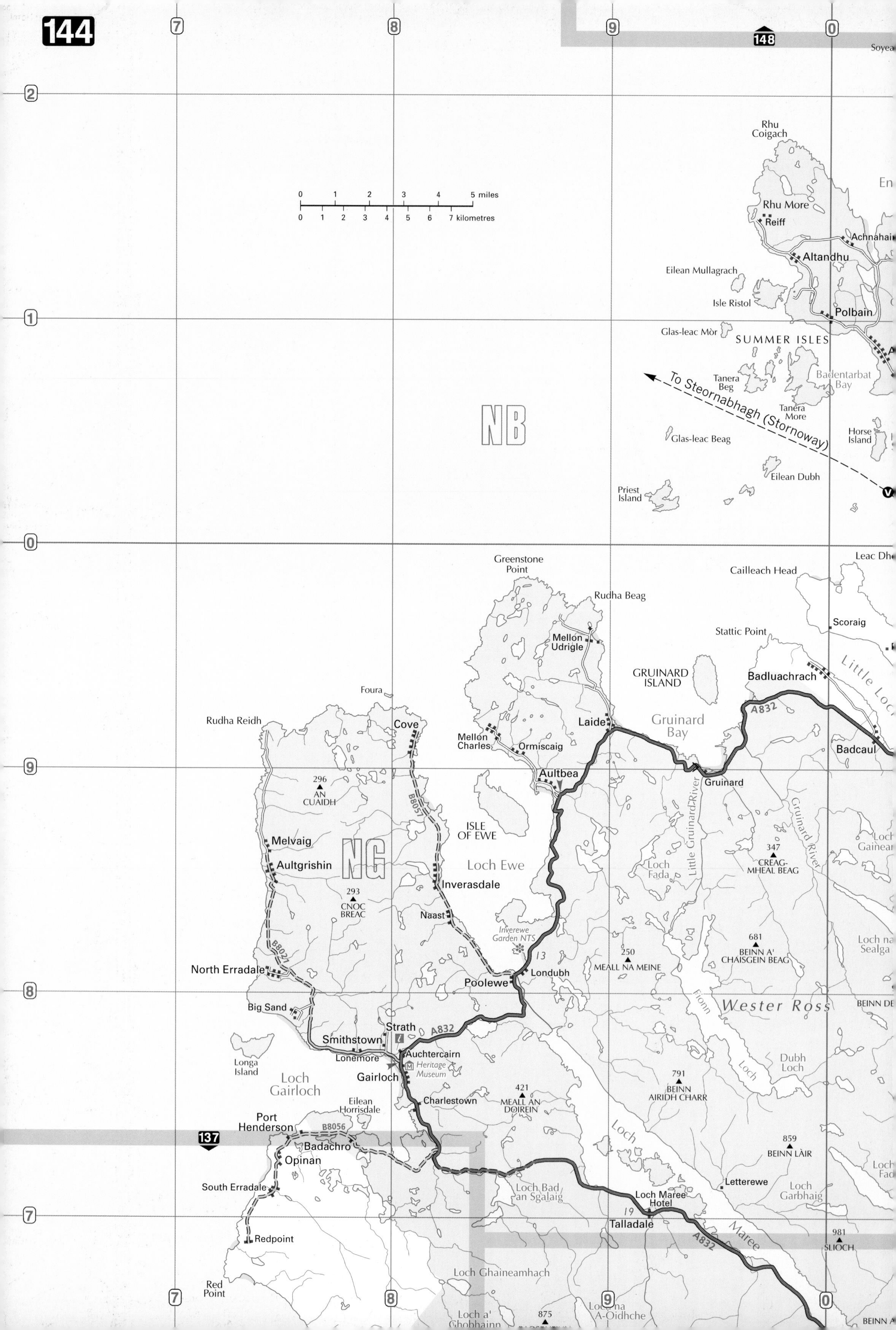

Soyea

7   8   9   148   0

2

Rhu
Coigach

Rhu More
Reiff   Achnahai

Altandhu

Eilean Mullagrach

Isle Ristol   Polbain

Glas-leac Mòr   SUMMER ISLES

1

NB

Tanera
Beg   Badentarbat
Bay

To Steornabhagh (Stornoway)

Tanera
More

Glas-leac Beag

Horse
Island

Priest
Island   Eilean Dubh   V

0

Greenstone
Point   Cailleach Head   Leac Dh

Rudha Beag   Scoraig

Mellon   Stattic Point
Udrigle

GRUINARD   Badluachrach   Little Loc
ISLAND

Foura   Laide   Gruinard   A832
Rudha Reidh   Cove   Bay

Mellon   Ormiscaig   Badcaul
Charles   Aultbea   Gruinard

9

296
AN
CUAIDH

Little Gruinard River

Melvaig   B8057   ISLE
OF EWE   Loch
Aultgrishin   NG   Loch Ewe   Fada   347   Loch
293   CREAG-   Gainea
CNOC   Inverasdale   MHEAL BEAG
BREAC   250
Naast   MEALL NA MEINE
B8021   681   Loch na
North Erradale   Inverewe   BEINN A'   Sealga
Garden NTS   CHAISGEIN BEAG
13
Big Sand   Poolewe   Londubh   Fionn   Wester Ross   BEINN DE

8

Longa   Strath   A832
Island   Smithstown   Loch   Dubh
Lonemore   Loch
Loch   Auchtercairn   791
Gairloch   Gairloch   Heritage   BEINN
Museum   AIRIDH CHARR
Eilean   Charlestown   421
Port   Horrisdale   MEALL AN
Henderson   B8056   DOIREIN   Loch
137   859
Badachro   BEINN LÀIR
Opinan   Loch Bad   Letterewe   Loch
an Sgalaig   Garbhaig   Loch
South Erradale   Fad

7

Redpoint   Loch Maree   19
Hotel   981
Talladale   A832   SLIOCH
Red   Loch Ghaineamhach   Maree
Point   875   Loch na
Loch a'   A-Oidhche
7   8   Chobhainn   9   0

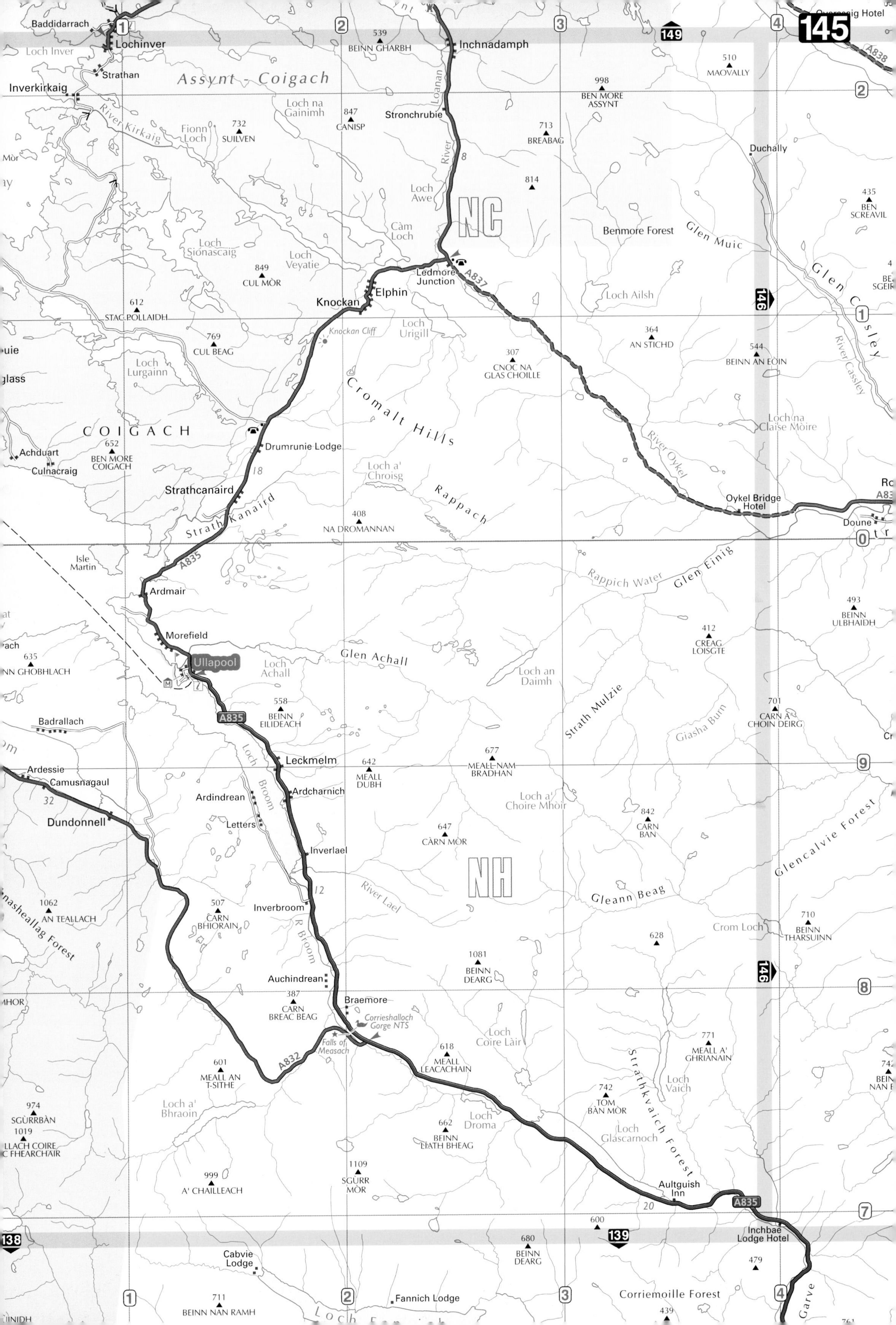
Baddidarrach
Lochinver
Loch Inver
Strathan
Inverkirkaig
River Kirkaig
Assynt - Coigach
539
BEINN GHARBH
Inchnadamph
Loch na Gainimh
847
CANISP
Fionn Loch
732
SUILVEN
Stronchrubie
River Loanan
998
BEN MORE ASSYNT
510
MAOVALLY
713
BREABAG
Duchally
814
Loch Awe
NC
Càm Loch
Benmore Forest
Glen Muic
435
BEN SCREAVIL
Loch Sionascaig
Loch Veyatie
849
CUL MOR
Ledmore Junction
A837
Elphin
Knockan
Loch Ailsh
Glen Cassley
612
STAC POLLAIDH
Knockan Cliff
Loch Urigill
364
AN STICHD
769
CUL BEAG
307
CNOC NA GLAS CHOILLE
544
BEINN AN EOIN
River Cassley
Loch Lurgainn
Cromalt Hills
Loch na Claise Mòire
COIGACH
Drumrunie Lodge
652
BEN MORE COIGACH
Achduart
Culnacraig
Loch a' Chroisg
River Oykel
Rappach
Strathcanaird
Strath Kanaird
Oykel Bridge Hotel
408
NA DROMANNAN
Doune
Isle Martin
A835
Rappich Water
Glen Einig
Ardmair
493
BEINN ULBHAIDH
Morefield
412
CREAG LOISGTE
635
Ullapool
Glen Achall
Loch Achall
Loch an Daimh
558
BEINN EILIDEACH
701
CARN A' CHOIN DEIRG
Badrallach
Strath Mulzie
Giasha Burn
677
MEALL NAM BRADHAN
Leckmelm
642
MEALL DUBH
Loch Broom
Ardessie
Camusnagaul
Ardcharnich
Ardindrean
Loch a' Choire Mhòir
Dundonnell
Letters
842
CARN BAN
Glencalvie Forest
647
CARN MOR
Inverlael
NH
River Lael
1062
AN TEALLACH
507
CARN BHIORAIN
Inverbroom
Gleann Beag
Crom Loch
710
BEINN THARSUINN
R Broom
628
1081
BEINN DEARG
Auchindrean
387
CARN BREAC BEAG
Braemore
Corrieshalloch Gorge NTS
Falls of Measach
Loch Coire Làir
771
MEALL A' GHRIANAIN
618
MEALL LEACACHAIN
A832
601
MEALL AN T-SITHE
Strathkvaich Forest
Loch Vaich
742
TOM BAN MOR
974
SGÙRR BÀN
Loch a' Bhraoin
Loch Droma
1019
Loch Glascarnoch
662
BEINN LIATH BHEAG
1109
SGÙRR MÒR
999
A' CHAILLEACH
Aultguish Inn
600
680
BEINN DEARG
Inchbae Lodge Hotel
479
Cabvie Lodge
Corriemoille Forest
Garve
711
BEINN NAN RAMH
Fannich Lodge
439
149
146
139
138

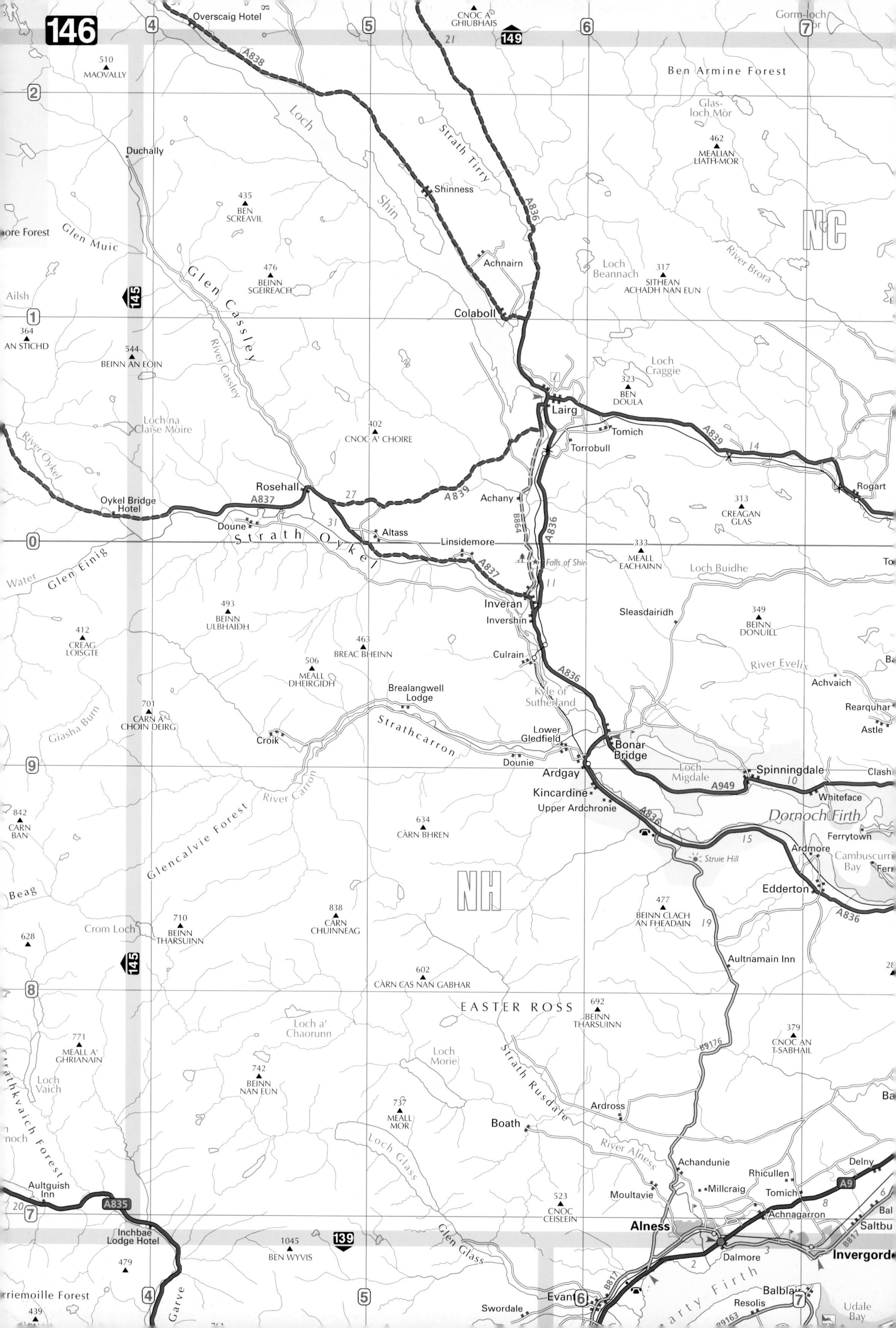
Overscaig Hotel
CNOC A' GHIUBHAIS
149
Gorm-loch Mòr
510 MAOVALLY
A838
Ben Armine Forest
Loch Shin
Strath Tirry
Glas-loch Mòr
462 MEALIAN LIATH-MOR
Duchally
Shinness
A836
435 BEN SCREAVIL
NC
Glen Muic
Achnairn
Loch Beannach
317 SITHEAN ACHADH NAN EUN
River Brora
476 BEINN SGEIREACH
Glen Cassley
Ailsh
145
Colaboll
364 AN STICHD
544 BEINN AN EOIN
River Cassley
Loch Craggie
323 BEN DOULA
Lairg
Tomich
Loch na Claise Mòire
402 CNOC A' CHOIRE
River Oykel
Torrobull
A839
Rosehall
Achany
313 CREAGAN GLAS
Rogart
Oykel Bridge Hotel
A837
Doune
Strath Oykel
Altass
B864
Linsidemore
333 MEALL EACHAINN
Loch Buidhe
Falls of Shin
Water
Glen Einig
Inveran
Invershin
Sleasdairidh
349 BEINN DONUILL
493 BEINN ULBHAIDH
412 CREAG LOISGTE
463 BREAC BHEINN
Culrain
506 MEALL DHEIRGIDH
River Evelix
Achvaich
Brealangwell Lodge
Kyle of Sutherland
701 CARN A' CHOIN DEIRG
Giasha Burn
Rearquhar
Strathcarron
Lower Gledfield
Astle
Croik
Bonar Bridge
Dounie
Ardgay
Loch Migdale
Spinningdale
A949
Clash
Kincardine
Whiteface
842 CARN BAN
River Carron
Upper Ardchronie
Dornoch Firth
634 CÀRN BHREN
Glencalvie Forest
Ferrytown
Struie Hill
Ardmore
Cambuscurrie Bay
NH
Edderton
Beag
477 BEINN CLACH AN FHEADAIN
838 CÀRN CHUINNEAG
Crom Loch
710 BEINN THARSUINN
628
Aultnamain Inn
602 CÀRN CAS NAN GHABHAR
EASTER ROSS
692 BEINN THARSUINN
Loch a' Chaorunn
771 MEALL A' GHRIANAIN
379 CNOC AN T-SABHAIL
B9176
Loch Morie
Loch Vaich
742 BEINN NAN EUN
Strath Rusdale
737 MEALL MOR
Strathvaich Forest
Ardross
Boath
Loch Glass
River Alness
Achandunie
Rhicullen
Delny
Millcraig
Tomich
A9
Aultguish Inn
Moultavie
A835
523 CNOC CEISLEIN
Achnagarron
Inchbae Lodge Hotel
Alness
Saltburn
1045 BEN WYVIS
139
Glen Glass
Dalmore
Invergordon
479
B817
Cromarty Firth
Balblair
Garve
Evanton
Resolis
Swordale
Udale Bay
B9163
439
Rriemoille Forest

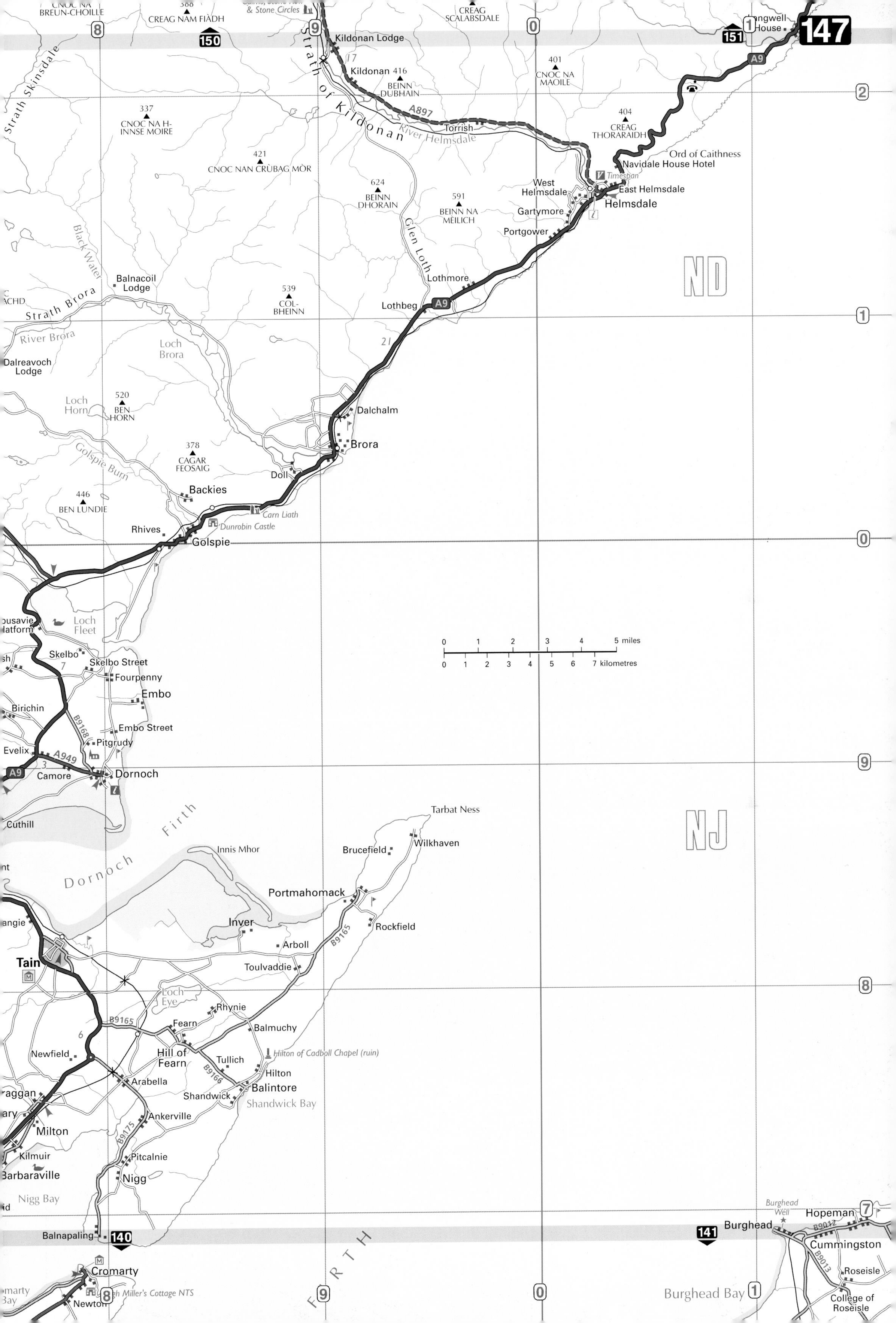
147
151
150
141
140
Kildonan Lodge
Kildonan
416 BEINN DUBHAIN
Strath of Kildonan
A897
Torrish
River Helmsdale
401 CNOC NA MAOILE
404 CREAG THORARAIDH
Ord of Caithness
Navidale House Hotel
Timespan
West Helmsdale
East Helmsdale
Helmsdale
Gartymore
Portgower
CREAG SCALABSDALE
CREAG NAM FIADH
CNOC NA BREUN-CHOILLE
& Stone Circles
Strath Skinsdale
337 CNOC NA H-INNSE MOIRE
421 CNOC NAN CRÙBAG MÒR
624 BEINN DHORAIN
591 BEINN NA MEILICH
Glen Loth
Lothmore
Lothbeg
A9
539 COL-BHEINN
Black Water
Balnacoil Lodge
Strath Brora
River Brora
Dalreavoch Lodge
Loch Brora
Loch Horn
520 BEN HORN
Dalchalm
Brora
378 CAGAR FEOSAIG
Doll
Golspie Burn
Backies
446 BEN LUNDIE
Carn Liath
Dunrobin Castle
Rhives
Golspie
ND
NJ
Loch Fleet
Skelbo
Skelbo Street
Fourpenny
Embo
Birichin
Embo Street
B9168
Pitgrudy
Evelix
A949
Camore
Dornoch
Cuthill
Dornoch Firth
Innis Mhor
Tarbat Ness
Wilkhaven
Brucefield
Portmahomack
Rockfield
Inver
Arboll
B9165
Toulvaddie
Tain
Loch Eye
Rhynie
Fearn
Balmuchy
Hilton of Cadboll Chapel (ruin)
Newfield
Hill of Fearn
Tullich
B9166
Hilton
Arabella
Balintore
Shandwick
Shandwick Bay
Ankerville
Milton
B9175
Kilmuir
Pitcalnie
Barbaraville
Nigg
Nigg Bay
Balnapaling
Cromarty
Hugh Miller's Cottage NTS
Newton
FIRTH
Burghead Bay
Burghead
Burghead Well
Hopeman
B9012
Cummingston
B9013
Roseisle
College of Roseisle
0 1 2 3 4 5 miles
0 1 2 3 4 5 6 7 kilometres

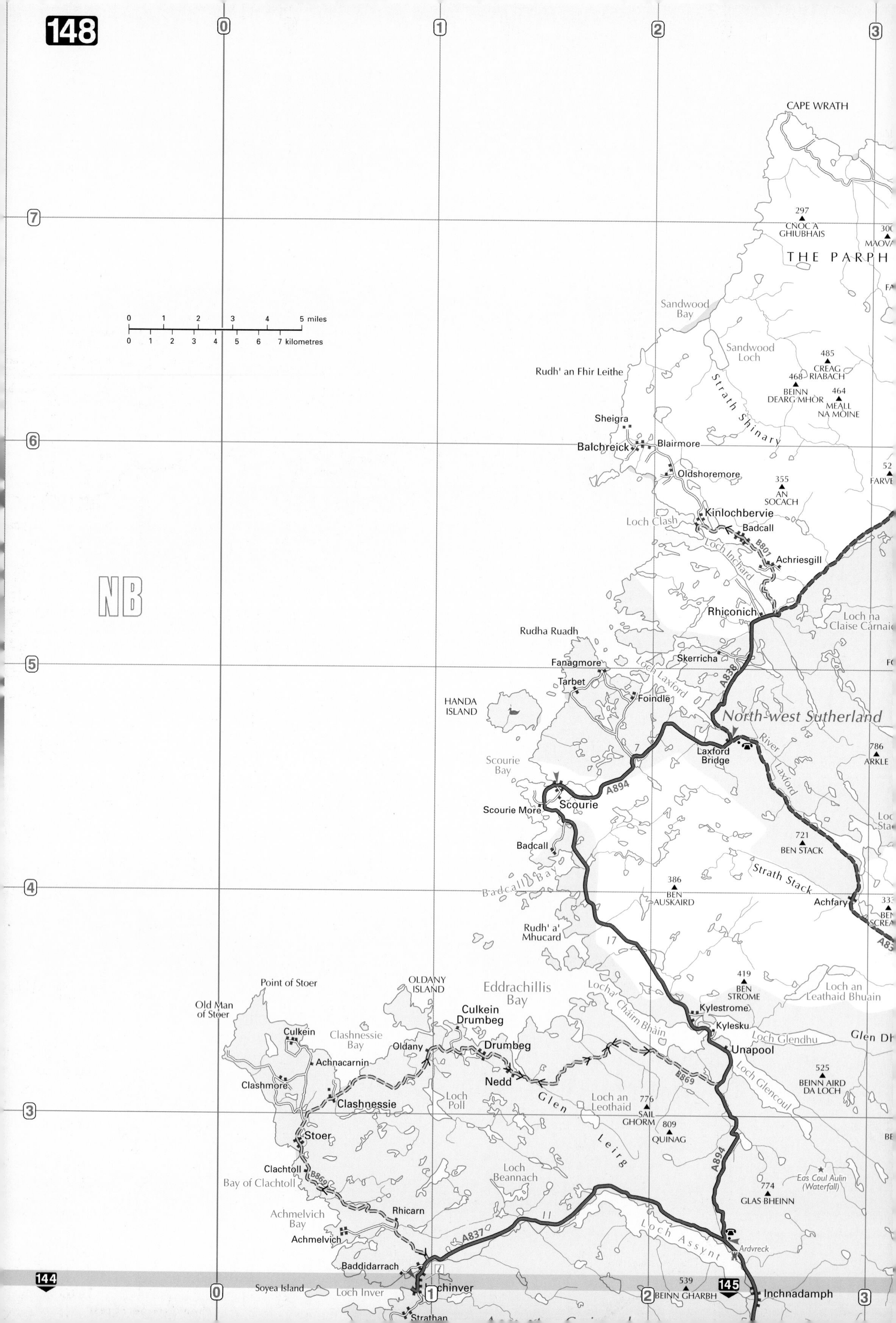

CAPE WRATH

297
CNOC A
GHIUBHAIS

300
MAOVA

THE PARPH

Sandwood
Bay

Sandwood
Loch

485
CREAG
RIABACH

468
BEINN
DEARG MHÒR

464
MEALL
NA MÒINE

Rudh' an Fhir Leithe

Strath Shinary

Sheigra

Balchreick — Blairmore

Oldshoremore

355
AN
SOCACH

52
FARVE

Loch Clash

Kinlochbervie

Badcall

B801

Achriesgill

Loch Inchard

Rhiconich

Loch na
Claise Càrnaic

NB

Rudha Ruadh

Skerricha

FO

Fanagmore

A838

Loch Laxford

North-west Sutherland

Tarbet

Foindle

HANDA
ISLAND

7

Laxford
Bridge

River Laxford

786
ARKLE

Scourie
Bay

A894

Scourie More — Scourie

721
BEN STACK

Strath Stack

Loc
Sta

Badcall

386
BEN
AUSKAIRD

Achfary

33
BEN
SCREA

A83

Badcall Bay

Rudh' a'
Mhucard

17

Point of Stoer

OLDANY
ISLAND

Eddrachillis
Bay

419
BEN
STROME

Loch an
Leathaid Bhuain

Glen DH

Old Man
of Stoer

Culkein
Drumbeg

Lochan Chàirn Bhàin

Kylestrome

Kylesku

Loch Glendhu

Culkein

Clashnessie
Bay

Oldany

Drumbeg

Unapool

B869

Loch Glencoul

525
BEINN AIRD
DA LOCH

BE

Achnacarnin

Nedd

Glen

Leirg

Loch an
Leothaid

776
SAIL
GHORM

809
QUINAG

Clashmore

Clashnessie

Loch
Poll

A894

Stoer

Loch
Beannach

774
GLAS BHEINN

Eas Coul Aulin
(Waterfall)

Clachtoll

B869

Bay of Clachtoll

Rhicarn

A837

11

Loch Assynt

Ardvreck

Achmelvich
Bay

Achmelvich

Baddidarrach

Soyea Island — Loch Inver — chinver

539
BEINN GHARBH

Inchnadamph

Strathan

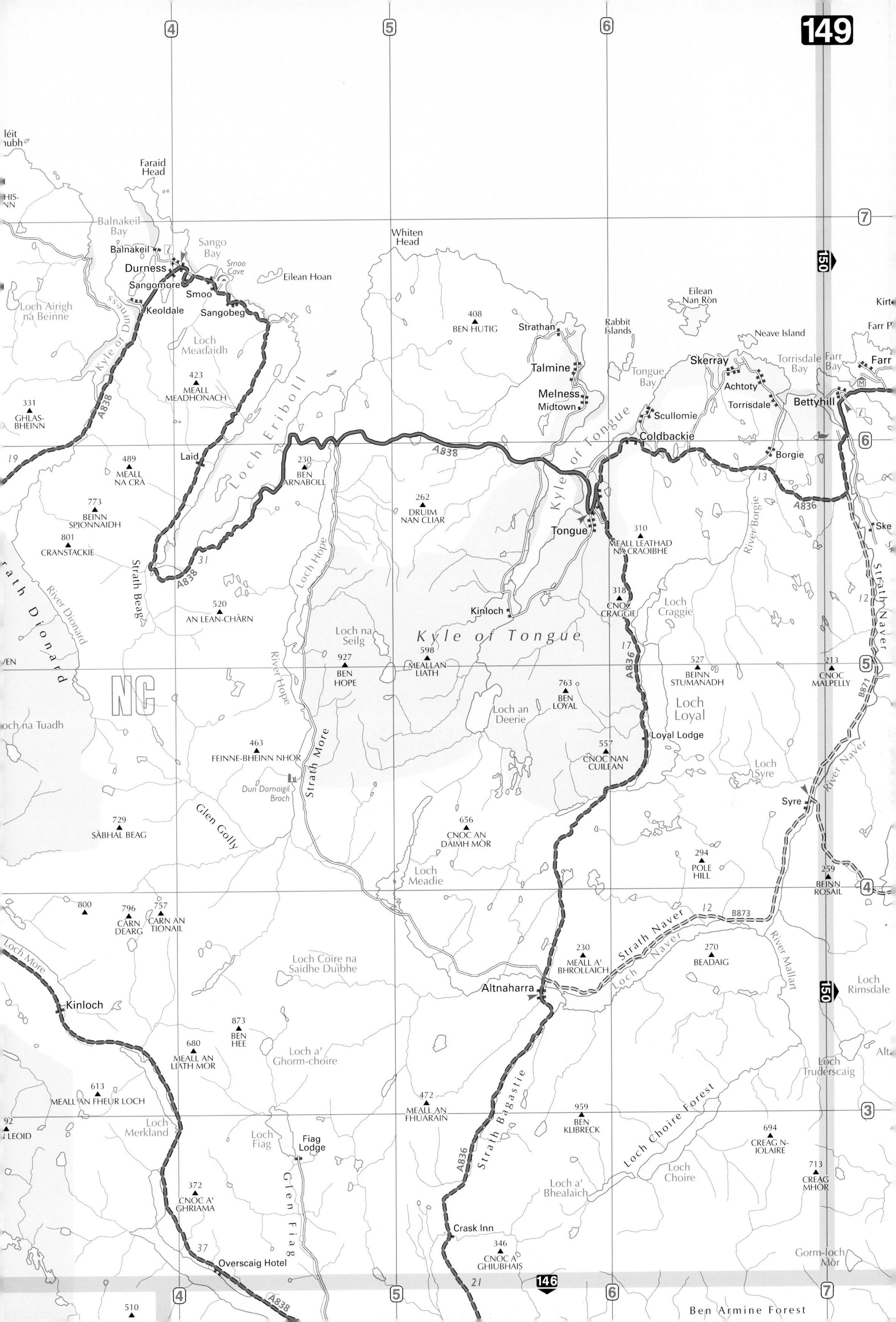
Faraid Head
Balnakeil Bay
Balnakeil
Durness
Sango Bay
Smoo Cave
Sangomore
Smoo
Keoldale
Sangobeg
Eilean Hoan
Whiten Head
Loch Airigh na Beinne
Kyle of Durness
Loch Meadaidh
423 MEALL MEADHONACH
Loch Eriboll
331 GHLAS-BHEINN
A838
Laid
489 MEALL NA CRÀ
773 BEINN SPIONNAIDH
801 CRANSTACKIE
230 BEN ARNABOLL
408 BEN HUTIG
Strathan
Rabbit Islands
Eilean Nan Ròn
Neave Island
Talmine
Melness
Midtown
Tongue Bay
Skerray
Achtoty
Torrisdale
Torrisdale Bay
Farr Bay
Farr
Bettyhill
Scullomie
Coldbackie
Borgie
Kyle of Tongue
262 DRUIM NAN CLIAR
Tongue
310 MEALL LEATHAD NA CRAOIBHE
River Borgie
A836
Strath Beag
Strath Dionard
River Dionard
520 AN LEAN-CHÀRN
Loch Hope
Kinloch
318 CNOC CRAGGIE
Loch Craggie
Strath Naver
Loch na Seilg
598 MEALLAN LIATH
927 BEN HOPE
River Hope
763 BEN LOYAL
527 BEINN STUMANADH
213 CNOC MALPELLY
B871
NC
Loch Loyal
Loch an Deerie
Loyal Lodge
Loch na Tuadh
463 FEINNE-BHEINN NHOR
Strath More
557 CNOC NAN CUILEAN
Loch Syre
River Naver
Dun Dornaigil Broch
Syre
Glen Golly
729 SÀBHAL BEAG
656 CNOC AN DAIMH MÒR
294 POLE HILL
Loch Meadie
259 BEINN ROSAIL
800
796 CARN DEARG
757 CARN AN TIONAIL
B873
Loch More
Loch Coire na Saidhe Duibhe
230 MEALL A' BHROLLAICH
270 BEADAIG
Loch Naver
River Mallart
Loch Rimsdale
Kinloch
Altnaharra
873 BEN HEE
680 MEALL AN LIATH MOR
Loch a' Ghorm-choire
Loch Truderscaig
613 MEALL AN FHEUR LOCH
472 MEALL AN FHUARAIN
959 BEN KLIBRECK
Strath Bagastie
Loch Choire Forest
694 CREAG N-IOLAIRE
Loch Merkland
Loch Fiag
Fiag Lodge
Glen Fiag
Loch Choire
Loch a' Bhealaich
713 CREAG MHOR
372 CNOC A' GHRIAMA
Crask Inn
346 CNOC A' GHIUBHAIS
Overscaig Hotel
Gorm-loch Mòr
510
Ben Armine Forest
150
146

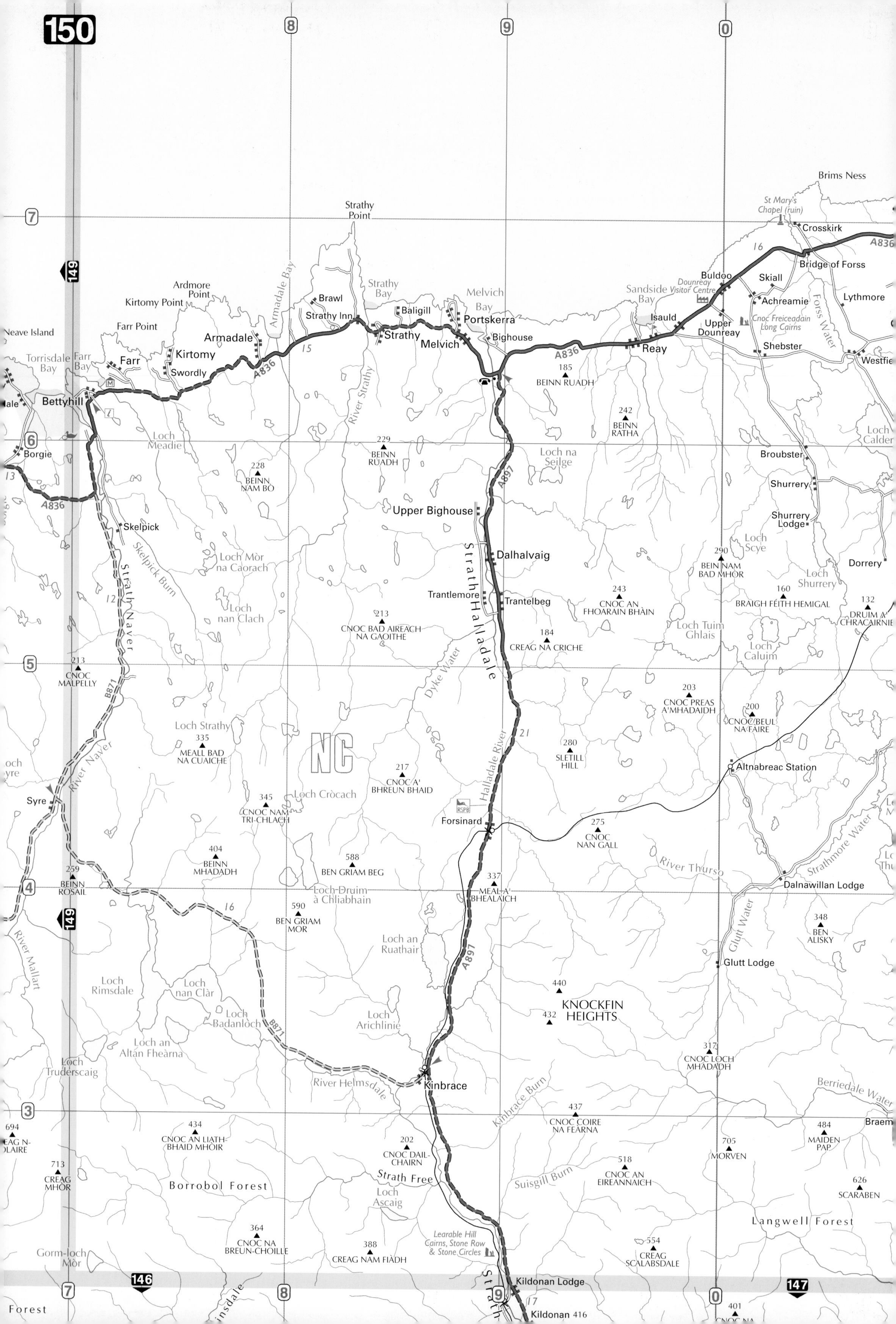
8
9
0
7
6
5
4
3
149
146
147
Brims Ness
St Mary's Chapel (ruin)
Crosskirk
A836
16
Bridge of Forss
Strathy Point
Buldoo
Skiall
Dounreay Visitor Centre
Sandside Bay
Lythmore
Achreamie
Ardmore Point
Kirtomy Point
Armadale Bay
Strathy Bay
Melvich Bay
Brawl
Baligill
Strathy Inn
Portskerra
Isauld
Upper Dounreay
Cnoc Freiceadain Long Cairns
Forss Water
Neave Island
Farr Point
Armadale
Strathy
Melvich
Bighouse
Reay
Shebster
Westfield
Torrisdale Bay
Farr Bay
Farr
Kirtomy
15
Swordly
185 BEINN RUADH
Bettyhill
242 BEINN RATHA
Loch Meadie
229 BEINN RUADH
River Strathy
Loch na Seilge
Loch Calder
Borgie
228 BEINN NAM BO
Broubster
A897
Shurrery
A836
Upper Bighouse
Shurrery Lodge
Skelpick
Loch Scye
Strath Halladale
Dalhalvaig
Loch Mòr na Caorach
290 BEIN NAM BAD MHOR
Dorrery
Skelpick Burn
Strath Naver
Loch nan Clach
Trantlemore
Trantelbeg
243 CNOC AN FHOARAIN BHÀIN
160 BRAIGH FÉITH HEMIGAL
Loch Shurrery
132 DRUIM A' CHRACAIRNIE
12
213 CNOC BAD AIREACH NA GAOITHE
Loch Tuim Ghlais
184 CREAG NA CRICHE
Loch Caluim
213 CNOC MALPELLY
Dyke Water
B871
203 CNOC PREAS A'MHADAIDH
200 CNOC BEUL NA FAIRE
Loch Strathy
21
River Naver
335 MEALL BAD NA CUAICHE
NC
280 SLETILL HILL
Halladale River
217 CNOC A' BHREUN BHAID
Altnabreac Station
345 CNOC NAM TRI-CHLACH
Loch Cròcach
Syre
RSPB
Forsinard
275 CNOC NAN GALL
404 BEINN MHADADH
588 BEN GRIAM BEG
River Thurso
Strathmore Water
259 BEINN ROSAIL
337 MEAL A' BHEALAICH
Loch Druim a' Chliabhain
Dalnawillan Lodge
16
590 BEN GRIAM MOR
348 BEN ALISKY
River Mallart
Loch an Ruathair
Glutt Water
A891
Glutt Lodge
Loch Rimsdale
Loch nan Clàr
440
KNOCKFIN HEIGHTS
Loch Badanloch
432
Loch Arichlinie
B871
Loch an Altan Fheàrna
317 CNOC LOCH MHADADH
Loch Truderscaig
Kinbrace
River Helmsdale
Kinbrace Burn
Berriedale Water
437 CNOC COIRE NA FEARNA
434 CNOC AN LIATH-BHAID MHÒIR
484 MAIDEN PAP
202 CNOC DAIL-CHAIRN
705 MORVEN
713 CREAG MHÒR
518 CNOC AN EIREANNAICH
Strath Free
Suisgill Burn
626 SCARABEN
Borrobol Forest
Loch Ascaig
Langwell Forest
364 CNOC NA BREUN-CHOILLE
Learable Hill Cairns, Stone Row & Stone Circles
388 CREAG NAM FIÀDH
554 CREAG SCALABSDALE
Gorm-loch Mòr
Kildonan Lodge
17
Kildonan 416
401
Forest

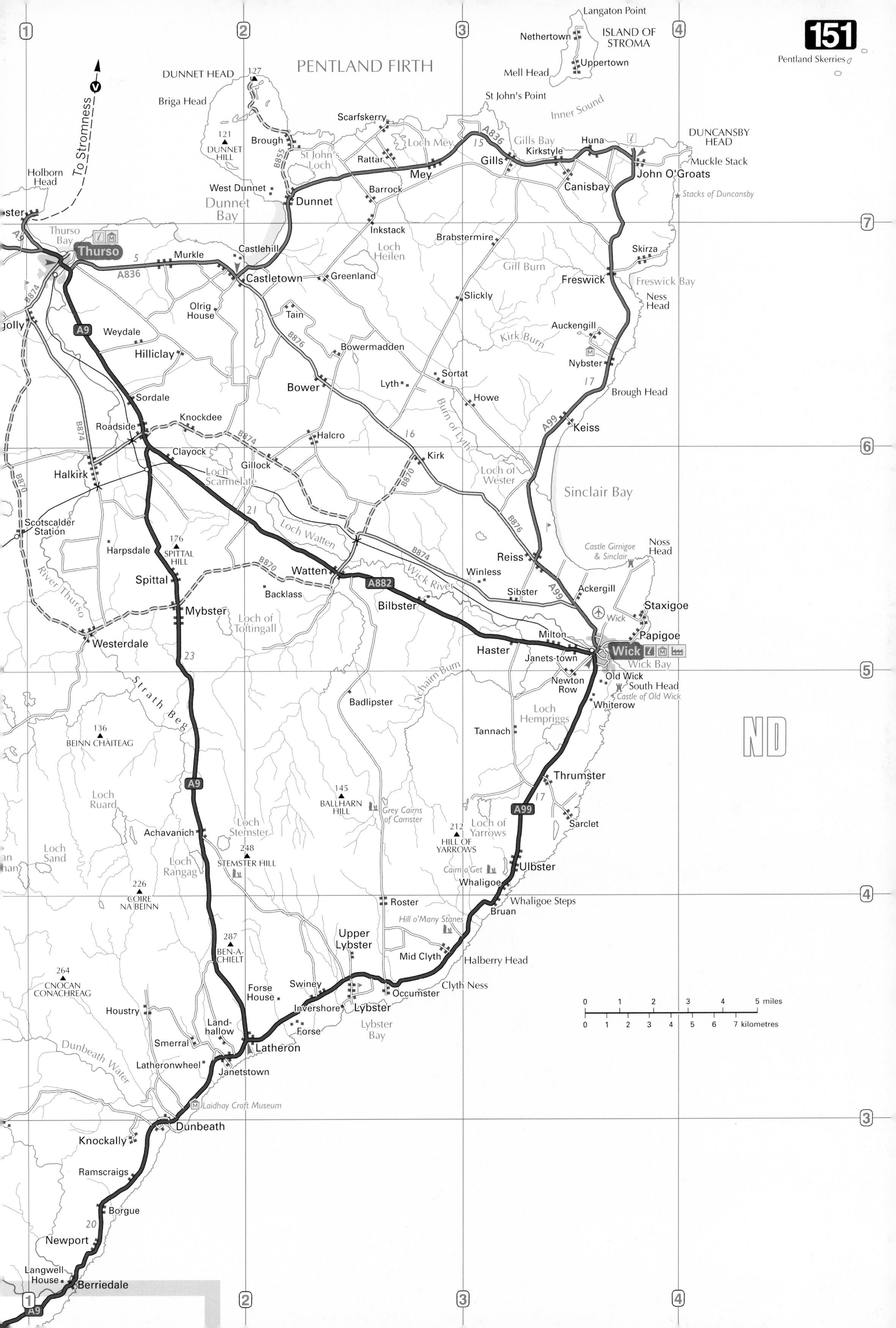
151
PENTLAND FIRTH
DUNNET HEAD
Briga Head
121 DUNNET HILL
Brough
St John's Loch
Scarfskerry
Loch Mey
Rattar
Mey
Barrock
Dunnet
West Dunnet
Dunnet Bay
Holborn Head
To Stromness
Thurso Bay
Thurso
Murkle
Castlehill
Castletown
Greenland
Inkstack
Loch Heilen
Brabstermire
Langaton Point
Nethertown
ISLAND OF STROMA
Uppertown
Mell Head
St John's Point
Inner Sound
Pentland Skerries
Gills Bay
Gills
Kirkstyle
Huna
Canisbay
DUNCANSBY HEAD
Muckle Stack
John O'Groats
Stacks of Duncansby
Skirza
Freswick
Freswick Bay
Ness Head
Gill Burn
Slickly
Auckengill
Kirk Burn
Nybster
Brough Head
Keiss
Sinclair Bay
Olrig House
Tain
Weydale
Hilliclay
Bowermadden
Sordale
Bower
Lyth
Sortat
Howe
Burn of Lyth
Knockdee
Roadside
Halcro
Kirk
Clayock
Halkirk
Gillock
Loch Scarmclate
Loch of Wester
Scotscalder Station
Harpsdale
176 SPITTAL HILL
Loch Watten
Spittal
River Thurso
Watten
Backlass
Bilbster
Wick River
Winless
Reiss
Sibster
Castle Girnigoe & Sinclair
Noss Head
Ackergill
Staxigoe
Wick
Papigoe
Mybster
Loch of Toftingall
Westerdale
Haster
Milton
Janets-town
Wick Bay
Newton Row
Old Wick
South Head
Castle of Old Wick
Whiterow
Strath Beg
Achairn Burn
Badlipster
Loch Hempriggs
Tannach
136 BEINN CHÀITEAG
ND
Thrumster
Loch Ruard
145 BALLHARN HILL
Grey Cairns of Camster
Sarclet
212 HILL OF YARROWS
Loch of Yarrows
Achavanich
Loch Stemster
248 STEMSTER HILL
Loch Sand
Loch Rangag
Cairn o'Get
Ulbster
Whaligoe
226 COIRE NA BEINN
Roster
Whaligoe Steps
Bruan
Hill o'Many Stanes
287 BEN-A-CHIELT
Upper Lybster
Mid Clyth
Halberry Head
264 CNOCAN CONACHREAG
Forse House
Swiney
Occumster
Clyth Ness
Houstry
Invershore
Lybster
Lybster Bay
Land-hallow
Forse
Smerral
Latheron
Dunbeath Water
Latheronwheel
Janetstown
Laidhay Croft Museum
Dunbeath
Knockally
Ramscraigs
Borgue
Newport
Langwell House
Berriedale
A9
A836
A99
A882
B855
B874
B876
B870
0 1 2 3 4 5 miles
0 1 2 3 4 5 6 7 kilometres

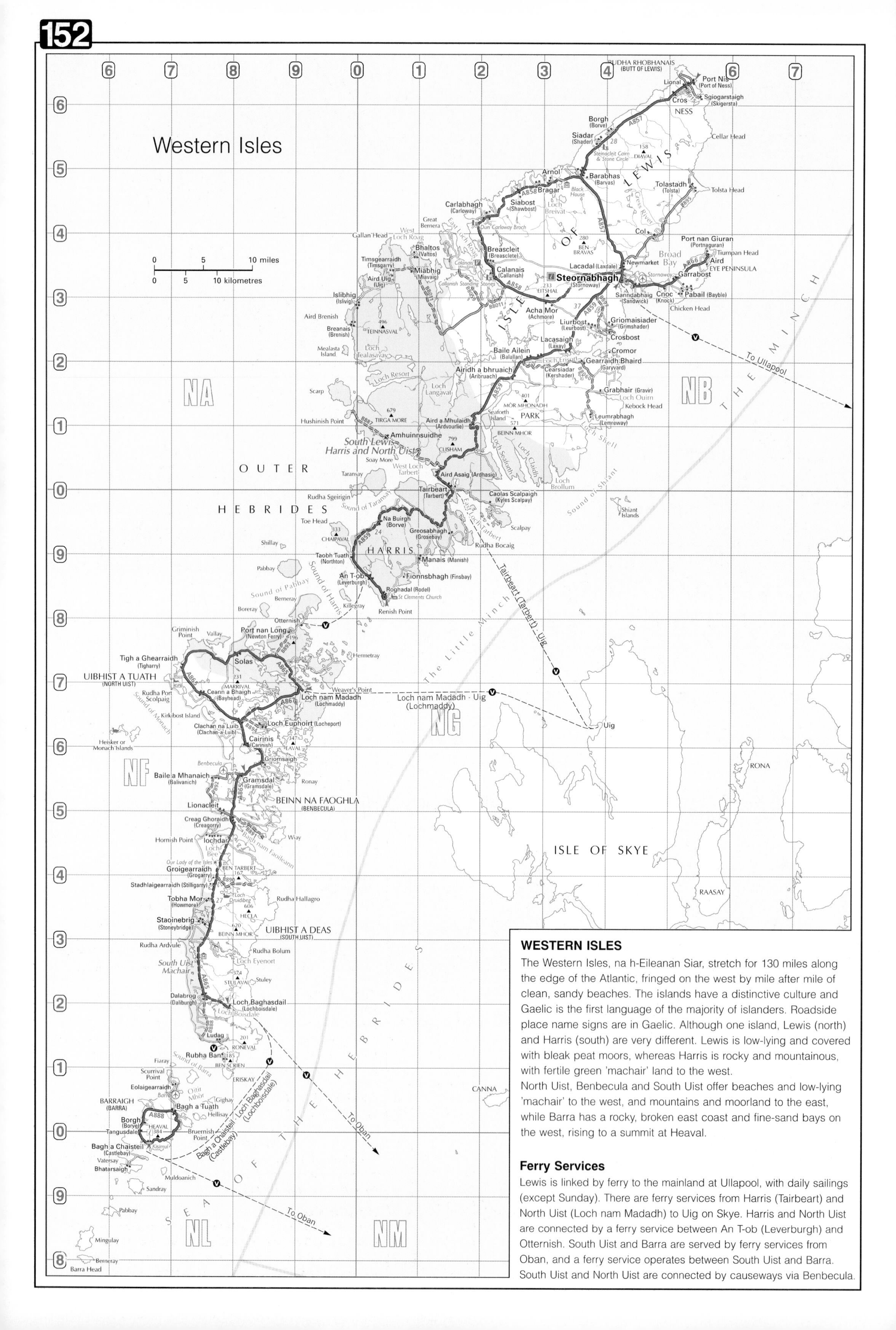

Western Isles

WESTERN ISLES

The Western Isles, na h-Eileanan Siar, stretch for 130 miles along the edge of the Atlantic, fringed on the west by mile after mile of clean, sandy beaches. The islands have a distinctive culture and Gaelic is the first language of the majority of islanders. Roadside place name signs are in Gaelic. Although one island, Lewis (north) and Harris (south) are very different. Lewis is low-lying and covered with bleak peat moors, whereas Harris is rocky and mountainous, with fertile green 'machair' land to the west.
North Uist, Benbecula and South Uist offer beaches and low-lying 'machair' to the west, and mountains and moorland to the east, while Barra has a rocky, broken east coast and fine-sand bays on the west, rising to a summit at Heaval.

Ferry Services

Lewis is linked by ferry to the mainland at Ullapool, with daily sailings (except Sunday). There are ferry services from Harris (Tairbeart) and North Uist (Loch nam Madadh) to Uig on Skye. Harris and North Uist are connected by a ferry service between An T-ob (Leverburgh) and Otternish. South Uist and Barra are served by ferry services from Oban, and a ferry service operates between South Uist and Barra. South Uist and North Uist are connected by causeways via Benbecula.

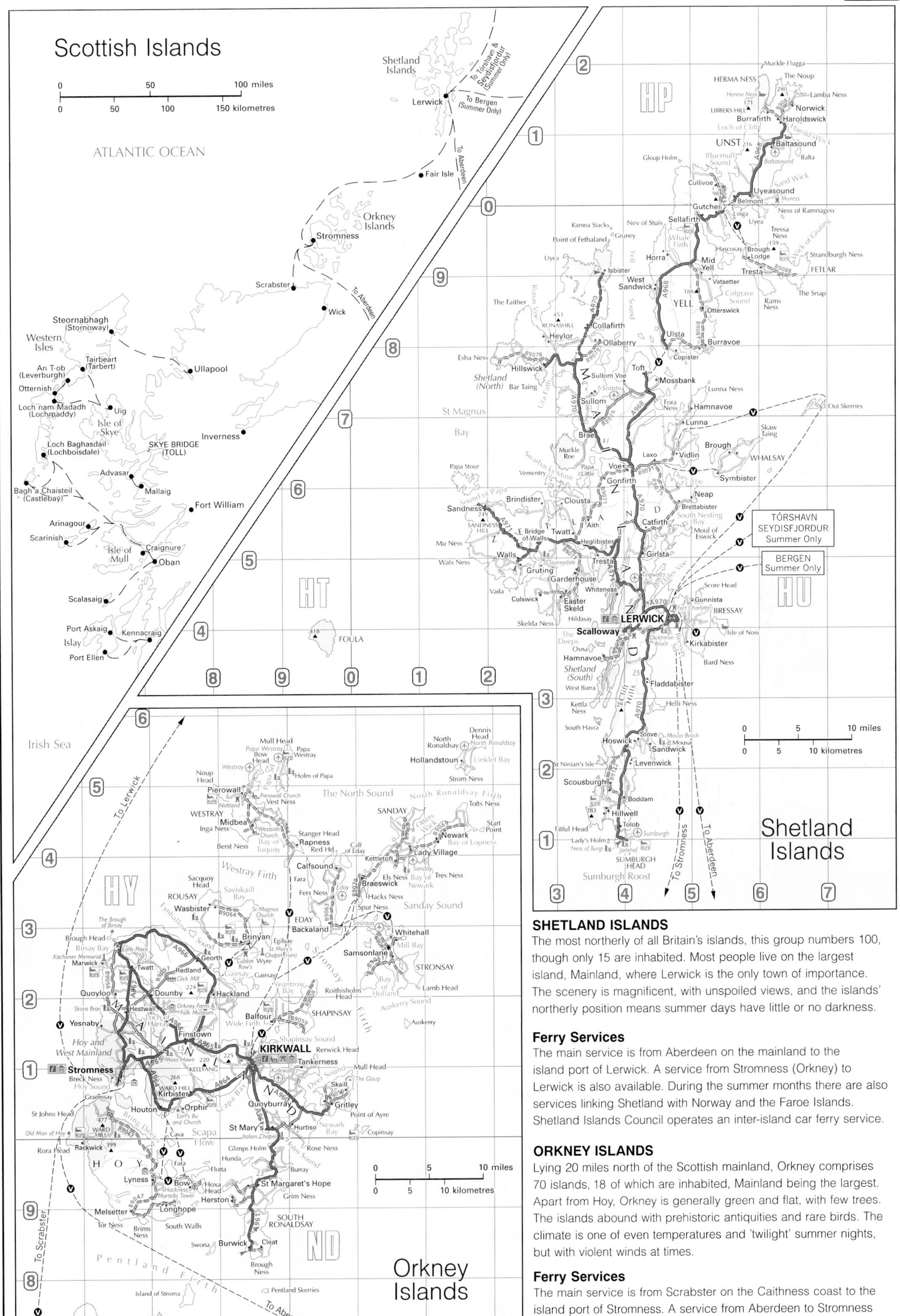

Scottish Islands

ATLANTIC OCEAN

SHETLAND ISLANDS
The most northerly of all Britain's islands, this group numbers 100, though only 15 are inhabited. Most people live on the largest island, Mainland, where Lerwick is the only town of importance. The scenery is magnificent, with unspoiled views, and the islands' northerly position means summer days have little or no darkness.

Ferry Services
The main service is from Aberdeen on the mainland to the island port of Lerwick. A service from Stromness (Orkney) to Lerwick is also available. During the summer months there are also services linking Shetland with Norway and the Faroe Islands. Shetland Islands Council operates an inter-island car ferry service.

ORKNEY ISLANDS
Lying 20 miles north of the Scottish mainland, Orkney comprises 70 islands, 18 of which are inhabited, Mainland being the largest. Apart from Hoy, Orkney is generally green and flat, with few trees. The islands abound with prehistoric antiquities and rare birds. The climate is one of even temperatures and 'twilight' summer nights, but with violent winds at times.

Ferry Services
The main service is from Scrabster on the Caithness coast to the island port of Stromness. A service from Aberdeen to Stromness provides a link to Shetland at Lerwick. Inter-island car ferry services are also operated (advance reservations recommended).

Shetland Islands

Orkney Islands

Ireland

Abbeydorney **B3**
Abbeyfeale **B3**
Abbeyleix **D3**
Adamstown **D3**
Adare **B3**
Adrigole **B2**
Ahascragh **C4**
Ahoghill **E6**
Allihies **A2**
Anascaul **A2**
Annalong **E5**
Annestown **D2**
Antrim **E6**
Ardagh **B3**
Ardara **C6**
Ardcath **E4**
Ardee **D5**
Ardfert **B3**
Ardfinnan **C3**
Ardglass **E5**
Ardgroom **A2**
Arklow **E3**
Arless **D3**
Armagh **D6**
Armoy **E7**
Arthurstown **D2**
Arvagh **D5**
Ashbourne **E4**
Ashford **E4**
Askeaton **B3**
Athboy **D5**
Athea **B3**
Athenry **C4**
Athleague **C4**
Athlone **C4**
Athy **D4**
Augher **D6**
Aughnacloy **D6**
Aughrim **E3**
Avoca **E3**

Bagenalstown **D3**
(Muine Bheag)
Bailieborough **D5**
Balbriggan **E4**
Balla **B5**
Ballacolla **D3**
Ballaghaderreen **C5**
Ballina **C3**
Ballina **B5**
Ballinafad **C5**
Ballinagh **D5**
Ballinakill **D3**
Ballinalee **C5**
Ballinamallard **D6**
Ballinamore **C5**
Ballinascarty **B2**
Ballinasloe **C4**
Ballindine **B5**
Ballineen **B2**
Ballingarry **C3**
Ballingarry **B3**
Ballingeary **B2**
(Béal Átha an Ghaorfthaidh)
Ballinhassig **C2**
Ballinlough **C5**
Ballinrobe **B5**
Ballinspittle **C2**
Ballintober **C5**
Ballintra **C6**
Ballivor **D4**
Ballon **D3**
Ballybaun **C4**
Ballybay **D5**
Ballybofey **C6**
Ballybunion **B3**
Ballycanew **E3**
Ballycarry **E6**
Ballycastle **B6**
Ballycastle **E7**
Ballyclare **E6**
Ballyconneely **A4**
Ballycotton **C2**
Ballycumber **C4**
Ballydehob **B1**
Ballydesmond **B2**
Ballyduff **C2**
Ballyduff **B3**
Ballyfarnan **C5**
Ballygalley **E6**
Ballygar **C4**
Ballygawley **D6**
Ballygowan **E6**
Ballyhaise **D5**
Ballyhale **D3**
Ballyhaunis **C5**
Ballyhean **B5**
Ballyheige **B3**
Ballyjamesduff **D5**
Ballykeeran **C4**
Ballylanders **C3**
Ballylongford **B3**
Ballylooby **C3**
Ballylynan **D3**
Ballymahon **C4**
Ballymakeery **B2**
Ballymena **E6**
Ballymoe **C5**
Ballymoney **D7**
Ballymore **C4**
Ballymore Eustace **D4**
Ballymote **C5**
Ballynahinch **E6**
Ballynure **E6**
Ballyporeen **C3**
Ballyragget **D3**
Ballyroan **D4**
Ballyronan **D6**
Ballysadare **C5**
Ballyshannon **C6**
Ballyvaughan **B4**
Ballywalter **E6**
Balrothery **E4**
Baltimore **B1**
Baltinglass **D3**
Banagher **C4**
Banbridge **E6**
Bandon **B2**
Bangor **E6**
Bangor Erris **B5**
Bansha **C3**
Banteer **B2**
Bantry **B2**
Beaufort **B2**
Belcoo **C6**
Belfast **E6**
Belgooly **C2**
Bellaghy **D6**
Belleek **C6**
Belmullet **B6**
(Béal an Mhuirhead)
Belturbet **D5**
Benburb **D6**
Bennett's Bridge **D3**
Beragh **D6**
Birr **C4**
Blacklion **C6**
Blackwater **E3**
Blarney **C2**
Blessington **D4**
Boherbue **B2**
Borris **D3**
Borris-in-Ossory **C4**
Borrisokane **C4**
Borrisoleigh **C3**
Boyle **C5**
Bracknagh **D4**
Bray **E4**
Bridgetown **D2**
Brittas **D4**
Broadford **C3**
Broadford **B3**
Broughshane **E6**
Bruff **C3**
Bruree **C3**
Bunclody **D3**
Buncrana **D7**
Bundoran **C6**
Bunmahon **D2**
Bunnahowen **B6**
Bunnyconnellan **B5**
Burnfort **C2**
Bushmills **D7**
Butler's Bridge **D5**
Buttevant **B2**

Cadamstown **C4**
Caherconlish **C3**
Caherdaniel **A2**
Cahersiveen **A2**
Cahir **C3**
Caledon **D6**
Callan **D3**
Caltra **C4**
Camp **A3**
Cappagh White **C3**
Cappamore **C3**
Cappoquin **C2**
Carlanstown **D5**
Calingford **E5**
Carlow **D3**
Carndonagh **D7**
Carnew **D3**
Carnlough **E7**
Carracastle **C5**
Carrick **C6**
(An Charraig)
Carrickfergus **E6**
Carrickmacross **D5**
Carrickmore **D6**
Carrick-on-Shannon **C5**
Carrick-on-Suir **D3**
Carrigahorig **C4**
Carrigaline **C2**
Carrigallen **D5**
Carriganimmy **B2**
Carrigans **D7**
Carrigart **C7**
(Carraig Airt)
Carrigtohill **C2**
Carrowkeel **D7**
Carryduff **E6**
Cashel **C3**
Castlebar **B5**
Castlebellingham **E5**
Castleblayney **D5**
Castlebridge **D3**
Castlecomer **D3**
Castlederg **D6**
Castledermot **D3**
Castleisland **B3**
Castlemaine **B2**
Castlemartyr **C2**
Castleplunket **C5**
Castlepollard **D5**
Castlerea **C5**
Castlerock **D7**
Castleshane **D5**
Castletown **D4**
Castletown Bearhaven **A2**
Castletownroche **C2**
Castletownshend **B1**
Castlewellan **E5**
Causeway **B3**
Cavan **D5**
Celbridge **D4**
Charlestown **C5**
Charleville **B3**
(Rath Luirc)
Clady **D6**
Clane **D4**
Clara **C4**
Clarecastle **B3**
Claremorris **B5**
Clarinbridge **B4**
Clashmore **C2**
Claudy **D7**
Clifden **A4**
Cliffoney **C6**
Clogh **D3**
Cloghan **C4**
Clogheen **C3**
Clogher **D6**
Clohamon **D3**
Clonakilty **B2**
Clonard **D4**
Clonbulloge **D4**
Clonbur **B5**
(An Fhairche)
Clondalkin **E4**
Clones **D5**
Clonmany **D7**
Clonmel **C3**
Clonmellon **D5**
Clonmore **C3**
Clonony **C4**
Clonoulty **C3**
Clonroche **D3**
Clontibret **D5**
Cloondara **C5**
Cloonlara **C3**
Clough **E6**
Cloughjordan **C4**
Cloyne **C2**
Coagh **D6**
Coalisland **D6**
Cobh **C2**
Coleraine **D7**
Collinstown **D5**
Collon **D5**
Collooney **C5**
Comber **E6**
Cong **B5**
Conna **C2**
Cookstown **D6**
Coole **D5**
Cooraclare **B3**
Cootehill **D5**
Cork **C2**
Cornamona **B4**
Corofin **B4**
Courtmacsherry **B2**
Courtown Harbour **E3**
Craigavon **E6**
Craughwell **C4**
Creeslough **C7**
Creggs **C5**
Croagh **B3**
Crolly (Croithlí) **C7**
Crookenwood **D4**
Crookhaven **B1**
Crookstown **B2**
Croom **B3**
Crossakeel **D5**
Cross Barry **B2**
Crosshaven **C2**
Crossmaglen **D5**
Crossmolina **B5**
Crumlin **E6**
Crusheen **B4**
Culdaff **D7**
Culleybackey **E6**
Curracloe **D3**
Curraghboy **C4**
Curry **C5**
Cushendall **E7**

Daingean **D4**
Delvin **D5**
Derrygonnelly **C6**
Derrylin **D5**
Dervock **E7**
Dingle **A2**
(An Daingean)
Doagh **E6**
Donaghadee **E6**
Donaghmore **C3**
Donegal **C6**
Doneraile **C2**
Doon **C4**
Doonbeg **B3**
Douglas **C2**
Downpatrick **E6**
Dowra **C5**
Draperstown **D6**
Drimoleague **B2**
Dripsey **B2**
Drogheda **E5**
Dromahair **C6**
Dromcolliher **B3**
Dromod **C5**
Dromore **E6**
Dromore **D6**
Dromore West **C6**
Drum **D5**
Drumcliff **C6**
Drumconrath **D5**
Drumkeeran **C5**
Drumlish **C5**
Drumquin **D6**
Drumshanbo **C5**
Drumsna **C5**
Duagh **B3**
Dublin **E4**
Duleek **E5**
Dunboyne **D4**
Duncormick **D2**
Dundalk **E5**
Dunderrow **C2**
Dundrum **E5**
Dunfanaghy **C7**
Dungannon **D6**
Dungarvan **C2**
Dungarvan **D3**
Dungiven **D7**
Dungloe **C7**
(An Clochan Liath)
Dungourney **C2**
Dunkineely **C6**
Dun Laoghaire **E4**
Dunlavin **D4**
Dunleer **E5**
Dunloy **E7**
Dunmanway **B2**
Dunmore **C5**
Dunmore East **D2**
Dunmurry **E6**
Dunshaughlin **D4**
Durrow **D3**
Durrus **B2**
Dysart **C4**

Easky **B6**
Edenderry **D4**
Edgeworthstown **D5**
Eglinton **D7**
Elphin **C5**
Emyvale **D6**
Enfield **D4**
Ennis **B3**
Enniscorthy **D3**
Enniscrone **B6**
Enniskean **B2**
Enniskillen **D6**
Ennistymon **B4**
Eyrecourt **C4**

Farnaght **C5**
Farranfore **B2**
Feakle **C4**
Fenagh **C5**
Ferbane **C4**
Fermoy **C2**
Ferns **D3**
Fethard **D2**
Fethard **C3**
Finnea **D5**
Fintona **D6**
Fivemiletown **D6**
Fontstown **D4**
Foxford **B5**
Foynes **B3**
Freemount **B3**
Frenchpark **C5**
Freshford **D3**
Fuerty **C5**

Galbally **C3**
Galway **B4**
Garrison **C6**
Garristown **E4**
Garvagh **D7**
Geashill **D4**
Gilford **E6**
Glandore **B1**
Glanworth **C2**
Glaslough **D6**
Glassan **C4**
Glenamaddy **C5**
Glenarm **E7**
Glenavy **E6**
Glenbeigh **A2**
Glencolumbkille **C6**
(Gleann Cholm Cille)
Glendalough **E4**
Glenealy **E3**
Glengarriff **B2**
Glenmore **D3**
Glenties **C6**
Glin **B3**
Glinsk **B4**
(Glinsce)
Golden **C3**
Goleen **B1**
Goresbridge **D3**
Gorey **E3**
Gort **B4**
Gortin **D6**
Gowran **D3**
Graiguenamanagh **D3**
Granard **D5**
Grange **C6**
Greyabbey **E6**
Greystones **E4**
Gulladuff **D6**

Hacketstown **D3**
Headford **B4**
Herbertstown **C3**
Hillsborough **E6**
Hilltown **E5**
Hospital **C3**
Holycross **C3**
Holywood **E6**
Howth **E4**

Inch **A2**
Inchigeelagh **B2**
Inishannon **B2**
Irvinestown **D6**

Johnstown **C3**

Kanturk **B2**
Keadue **C5**
Keady **D5**
Keel **A5**
Keenagh **C5**
Kells **E6**
Kells **D5**
Kenmare **B2**
Kesh **C6**
Kilbeggan **D4**
Kilberry **D5**
Kilbrittain **B2**
Kilcar **C6**
(Cill Charthaigh)
Kilcock **D4**
Kilcolgan **B4**
Kilconnell **C4**
Kilcoole **E4**
Kilcormac **C4**
Kilcullen **D4**
Kilcurry **E5**
Kildare **D4**
Kildavin **D3**
Kildorrery **C2**
Kilfenora **B4**
Kilgarvan **B2**
Kilkee **B3**
Kilkeel **E5**
Kilkelly **C5**
Kilkenny **D3**
Kilkieran **B4**
Kilkinlea **B3**
Kill **D2**
Killadysert **B3**
Killala **B6**
Killaloe **C3**
Killarney **B2**
Killashee **C5**
Killeigh **D4**
Killenaule **C3**
Killashandra **D5**
Killimer **B3**
Killimor **C4**
Killiney **E4**
Killinick **D2**
Killorglin **B2**
Killough **E5**
Killucan **D4**
Killybegs **C6**
Killyleagh **E6**
Kilmacanoge **E4**
Kilmacrenan **C7**
Kilmacthomas **D2**
Kilmaganny **D3**
Kilmaine **B5**
Kilmallock **C3**
Kilmanagh **D3**
Kilmeadan **D2**
Kilmeage **D4**
Kilmeedy **B3**
Kilmichael **B2**
Kilmore Quay **D2**
Kilnaleck **D5**
Kilrea **D7**
Kilrush **B3**
Kilsheelan **C3**
Kiltealy **D3**
Kiltegan **D3**
Kiltimagh **B5**
Kiltoom **C4**
Kingscourt **D5**
Kinlough **C6**
Kinnegad **D4**
Kinnitty **C4**
Kinsale **C2**
Kinvarra **B4**
Kircubbin **E6**
Knock **B5**
Knockcroghery **C4**
Knocklofty **C3**
Knocktopher **D3**

Lahinch **B4**
Laragh **E4**
Larne **E6**
Lauragh **A2**
Laurencetown **C4**
Leap **B2**
Leenane **B5**
Leighlinbridge **D3**
Leitrim **C5**
Leixlip **D4**
Lemybrien **C2**
Letterfrack **B5**
Letterkenny **D7**
Lifford **D6**
Limavady **D7**
Limerick **C3**
Lisbellaw **D6**
Lisburn **E6**
Liscanor **B4**
Liscarroll **B3**
Lisdoonvarna **B4**
Lismore **C2**
Lisnaskea **D6**
Lisryan **D5**
Listowel **B3**
Loghill **B3**
Londonderry **D7**
Longford **C5**
Loughbrickland **E6**
Loughgall **D6**
Loughglinn **C5**
Loughrea **C4**
Louisburgh **B5**
Lucan **D4**
Lurgan **E6**
Lusk **E4**

Macroom **B2**
Maghera **E5**
Maghera **D6**
Magherafelt **D6**
Maguiresbridge **D6**
Malahide **E4**
Malin **D7**
Malin More **C6**
Mallow **C2**
Manorhamilton **C6**
Markethill **D6**
Maynooth **D4**
Mazetown **E6**
Middletown **D6**
Midleton **C2**
Milford **D7**
Millstreet **B2**
Milltown **B2**
Milltown Malbay **B3**
Mitchelstown **C3**
Moate **C4**
Mohill **C5**
Monaghan **D5**
Monasterevin **D4**
Moneygall **C3**
Moneymore **D6**
Monivea **C4**
Mooncoin **D2**
Moorfields **E6**
Mount Bellew **C4**
Mount Charles **C6**
Mountmellick **D4**
Mountrath **D4**
Mountshannon **C4**
Moville **D7**
Moy **D6**
Moynalty **D5**
Moyvore **C4**
Muckross **B2**
Muff **D7**
Mullinavat **D3**
Mullingar **D4**
Mulrany **B5**
Myshall **D3**

Naas **D4**
Naul **E4**
Navan **D5**
Neale **B5**
Nenagh **C3**
Newbliss **D5**
Newbridge **D4**
(Droichead Nua)
Newcastle **E5**
Newcastle West **B3**
Newinn **C3**
Newmarket **B2**
Newmarket-on Fergus **B3**
Newport **C3**
Newport **B5**
New Ross **D3**
Newry **E5**
Newtown **D3**
Newtownabbey **E6**
Newtownards **E6**
Newtownbutler **D5**
Newtownhamilton **D5**
Newtown-mountkennedy **E4**
Newtownstewart **D6**
Newtown Forbes **C5**
Nobber **D5**

Oilgate **D3**
Oldcastle **D5**
Omagh **D6**
Omeath **E5**
Oola **C3**
Oranmore **B4**
Oughterard **B4**
Ovens **B2**

Pallas Grean **C3**
Parknasilla **A2**
Partry **B5**
Passage East **D2**
Passage West **C2**
Patrickswell **C3**
Paulstown **D3**
Pettigo **C6**
Plumbridge **D6**
Pomeroy **D6**
Portadown **E6**
Portaferry **E6**
Portarlington **D4**
Portavogie **E6**
Portglenone **E6**
Portlaoise **D4**
Portmarnock **E4**
Portrane **E4**
Portroe **C3**
Portrush **D7**
Portstewart **D7**
Portumna **C4**
Poulgorm Bridge **B2**
Poyntzpass **E6**

Raharney **D4**
Randalstown **E6**
Rasharkin **E7**
Rathangan **D4**
Rathcoole **D4**
Rathcormack **C2**
Rathdowney **C3**
Rathdrum **E3**
Rathfriland **E5**
Rathkeale **B3**
Rathmelton **D7**
Rathmolyon **D4**
Rathmore **B2**
Rathmullan **D7**
Rathnew **E4**
Rathowen **D5**
Rathvilly **D3**
Ratoath **D4**
Ray **D7**
Ring (An Rinn) **C2**
Ringaskiddy **C2**
Rockcorry **D5**
Roosky **C5**
Rosapenna **C7**
Rosbercon **D3**
Roscommon **C5**
Roscrea **C4**
Ross Carbery **B1**
Rosscor **C6**
Rosses Point **C6**
Rosslare Harbour **D2**
Rosslea **D5**
Rostrevor **E5**
Roundstone **B4**
Roundwood **E4**
Rush **E4**

St Johnstown **D7**
Saintfield **E6**
Sallins **D4**
Scarriff **C4**
Scartaglen **B2**
Scarva **E6**
Schull **B1**
Scramoge **C5**
Seskinore **D6**
Shanagarry **C2**
Shanagolden **B3**
Shannonbridge **C4**
Shercock **D5**
Shillelagh **D3**
Shinrone **C4**
Shrule **B4**
Silvermines **C3**
Sion Mills **D6**
Sixmilebridge **B3**
Skerries **E4**
Skibbereen **B1**
Slane **D5**
Sligo **C6**
Smithborough **D5**
Sneem **A2**
Spiddal **B4**
(An Spideal)
Stewartstown **D6**
Stonyford **D3**
Strabane **D6**
Stradbally **D4**
Stradone **D5**
Strandhill **C6**
Strangford **E6**
Stranorlar **C6**
Strokestown **C5**
Summerhill **D4**
Swanlinbar **C5**
Swatragh **D6**
Swinford **B5**
Swords **E4**

Taghmon **D3**
Tagoat **D2**
Tahilla **A2**
Tallaght **E4**
Tallow **C2**
Tallowbridge **C2**
Tandragee **E6**
Tang **C4**
Tarbert **B3**
Templemore **C3**
Templetouhy **C3**
Termonfeckin **E5**
Thomastown **D3**
Thurles **C3**
Timahoe **D4**
Timoleague **B2**
Tinahely **D3**
Tipperary **C3**
Tobercurry **C5**
Tobermore **D6**
Toomyvara **C3**
Toormore **B1**
Tralee **B3**
Tramore **D2**
Trim **D4**
Tuam **B4**
Tuamgraney **C3**
Tulla **B3**
Tullamore **D4**
Tullow **D3**
Tulsk **C5**
Turlough **B5**
Tyrellspass **D4**

Urlingford **C3**

Virginia **D5**

Warrenpoint **E5**
Waterford **D2**
Watergrasshill **C2**
Waterville **A2**
Westport **B5**
Wexford **D3**
Whitegate **C2**
Whitehead **E6**
Wicklow **E4**
Woodenbridge **E3**
Woodford **C4**

Youghal **C2**

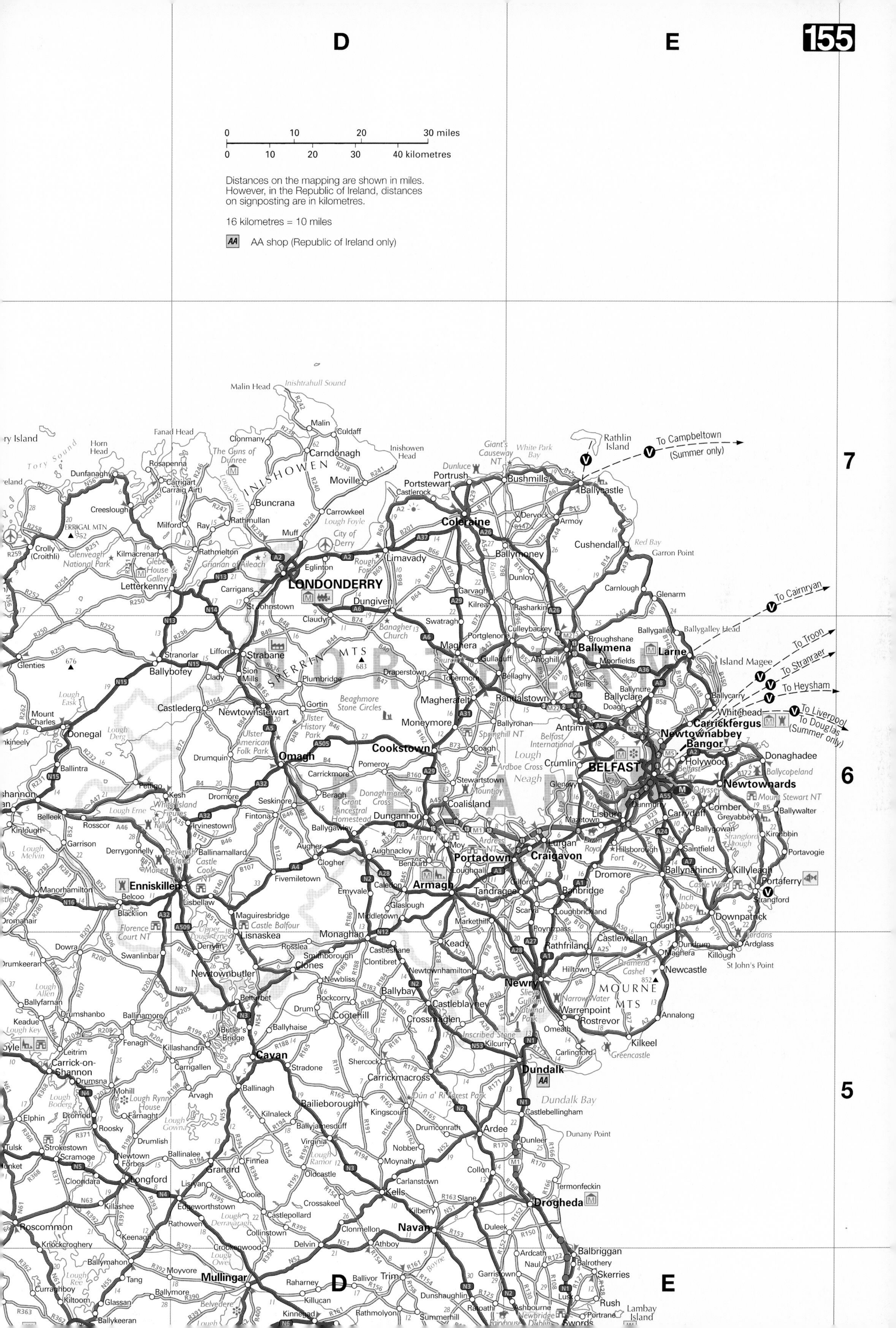
D
E
0 10 20 30 miles
0 10 20 30 40 kilometres
Distances on the mapping are shown in miles. However, in the Republic of Ireland, distances on signposting are in kilometres.
16 kilometres = 10 miles
AA shop (Republic of Ireland only)
7
6
5
NORTHERN IRELAND
SPERRIN MTS
MOURNE MTS
INISHOWEN
Malin Head
Rathlin Island
To Campbeltown (Summer only)
To Cairnryan
To Troon
To Stranraer
To Heysham
To Liverpool
To Douglas (Summer only)
LONDONDERRY
BELFAST
Coleraine
Ballymena
Larne
Carrickfergus
Newtownabbey
Bangor
Newtownards
Lisburn
Craigavon
Portadown
Armagh
Dungannon
Cookstown
Omagh
Strabane
Enniskillen
Newry
Dundalk
Drogheda
Cavan
Monaghan
Longford
Mullingar
Navan
Letterkenny
Donegal
Lough Neagh
Dundalk Bay
D
E

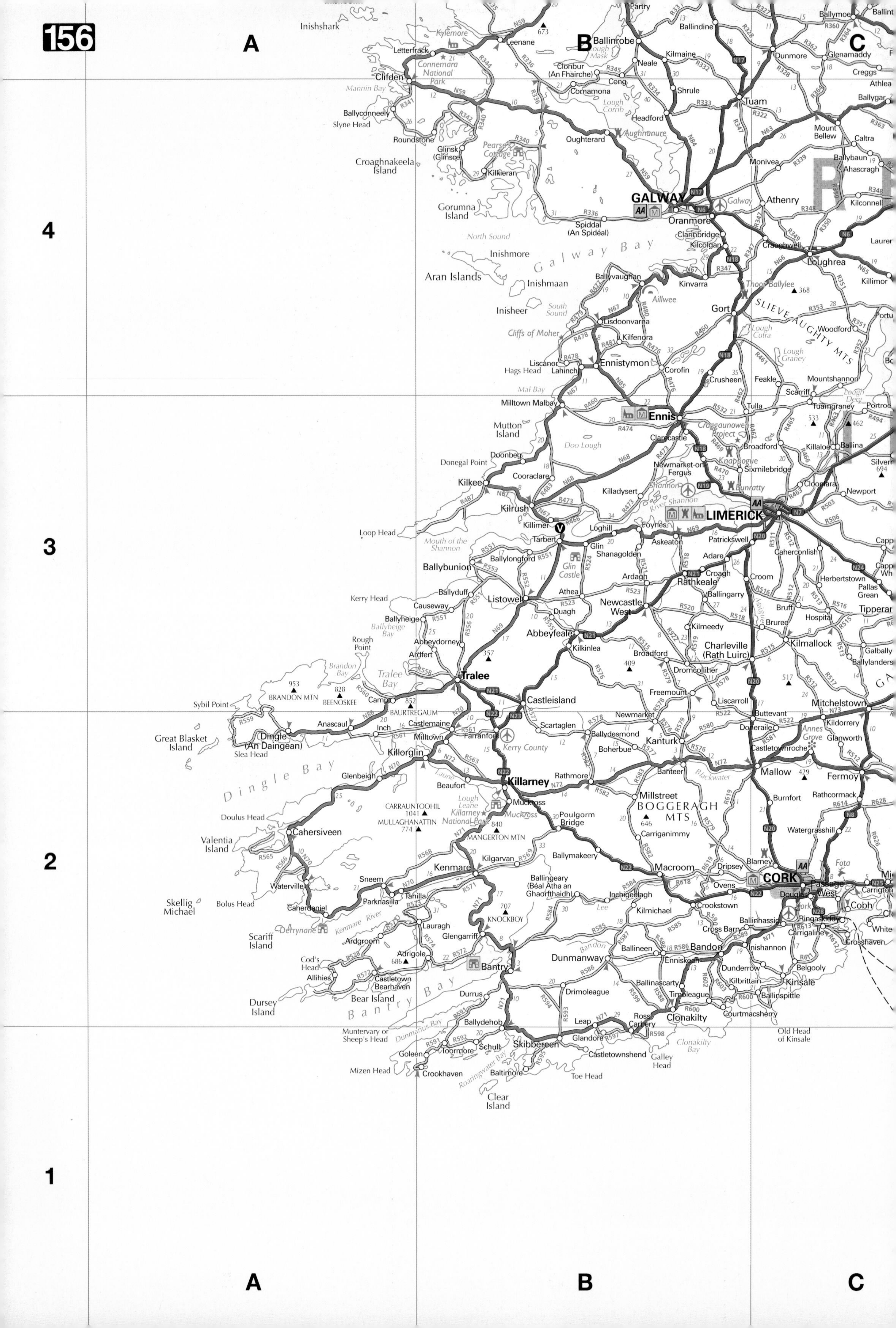
A
B
C
4
3
2
1
Inishshark
Kylemore
Leenane
673
Letterfrack
Connemara National Park
Clifden
Mannin Bay
Ballyconneely
Slyne Head
Roundstone
Glinsk (Glinsce)
Pearse's Cottage
Kilkieran
Croaghnakeela Island
Gorumna Island
Partry
Ballinrobe
Lough Mask
Clonbur (An Fhairche)
Cong
Cornamona
Lough Corrib
Oughterard
Aughnanure
Ballindine
Kilmaine
Neale
Shrule
Headford
Tuam
Ballymoe
Dunmore
Glenamaddy
Creggs
Athlea
Ballygar
Mount Bellew
Caltra
Monivea
Ballybaun
Ahascragh
Kilconnell
Athenry
GALWAY
Galway
Oranmore
Spiddal (An Spidéal)
Clarinbridge
Kilcolgan
Craughwell
Loughrea
Killimor
North Sound
Inishmore
Galway Bay
Aran Islands
Inishmaan
Inisheer
South Sound
Ballyvaughan
Aillwee
Kinvarra
Thoor Ballylee
368
Gort
SLIEVE AUGHTY MTS
Lisdoonvarna
Kilfenora
Cliffs of Moher
Lough Cutra
Lough Graney
Woodford
Liscanor
Hags Head
Lahinch
Ennistymon
Corofin
Crusheen
Feakle
Mountshannon
Scarriff
Lough Derg
Tuamgraney
Portroe
533
462
Mal Bay
Milltown Malbay
Ennis
Tulla
Craggaunowen Project
Clarecastle
Broadford
Killaloe
Ballina
Mutton Island
Doo Lough
Doonbeg
Donegal Point
Kilkee
Cooraclare
Newmarket-on-Fergus
Knappogue
Sixmilebridge
Bunratty
Cloonlara
Newport
694
Shannon
River Shannon
Killadysert
Kilrush
LIMERICK
Killimer
Loop Head
Mouth of the Shannon
Tarbert
Loghill
Foynes
Glin
Askeaton
Patrickswell
Shanagolden
Caherconlish
Glin Castle
Ballylongford
Ballybunion
Adare
Croom
Ardagh
Rathkeale
Croagh
Herbertstown
Pallas Grean
Ballyduff
Listowel
Athea
Kerry Head
Causeway
Newcastle West
Ballingarry
Bruff
Duagh
Ballyheige
Ballyheige Bay
Bruree
Hospital
Abbeyfeale
Kilmeedy
Abbeydorney
Rough Point
Ardfert
Kilkinlea
Charleville (Rath Luirc)
Kilmallock
Galbally
Ballylanders
357
409
Broadford
Dromcolliher
Brandon Bay
Tralee Bay
Tralee
517
953 BRANDON MTN
828 BEENOSKEE
Camp
852 BAURTREGAUM
Castleisland
Freemount
Liscarroll
Mitchelstown
Sybil Point
Buttevant
Anascaul
Scartaglen
Newmarket
Kildorrery
Dingle (An Daingean)
Inch
Castlemaine
Farranfore
Ballydesmond
Kanturk
Doneraile
Annes Grove
Glanworth
Great Blasket Island
Slea Head
Milltown
Kerry County
Boherbue
Castletownroche
Killorglin
Dingle Bay
Glenbeigh
Killarney
Rathmore
Banteer
Blackwater
Mallow
Fermoy
429
Beaufort
Millstreet
Burnfort
Rathcormack
Lough Leane
Muckross
Killarney National Park
BOGGERAGH MTS
Doulus Head
CARRAUNTOOHIL 1041
MULLAGHANATTIN 774
840 MANGERTON MTN
Poulgorm Bridge
646
Carriganimmy
Watergrasshill
Cahersiveen
Valentia Island
Kilgarvan
Ballymakeery
Kenmare
Macroom
Dripsey
Blarney
CORK
Fota
Sneem
Waterville
Ballingeary (Béal Atha an Ghaorfthaidh)
Inchigeelagh
Ovens
Douglas
Passage West
Cobh
Tahilla
Parknasilla
Skellig Michael
Bolus Head
Caherdaniel
707 KNOCKBOY
Lee
Kilmichael
Crookstown
Ballinhassig
Ringaskiddy
Derrynane
Kenmare River
Lauragh
Cross Barry
Carrigaline
Crosshaven
Scariff Island
Ardgroom
Glengarriff
Ballineen
Bandon
Innishannon
Cod's Head
Adrigole
686
Dunmanway
Enniskean
Dunderrow
Belgooly
Allihies
Castletown Bearhaven
Bantry
Kilbrittain
Kinsale
Bear Island
Bantry Bay
Durrus
Drimoleague
Ballinascarty
Timoleague
Ballinspittle
Dursey Island
Courtmacsherry
Ballydehob
Leap
Ross Carbery
Clonakilty
Muntervary or Sheep's Head
Dunmanus Bay
Schull
Toormore
Skibbereen
Glandore
Old Head of Kinsale
Goleen
Castletownshend
Clonakilty Bay
Galley Head
Mizen Head
Crookhaven
Roaringwater Bay
Baltimore
Toe Head
Clear Island

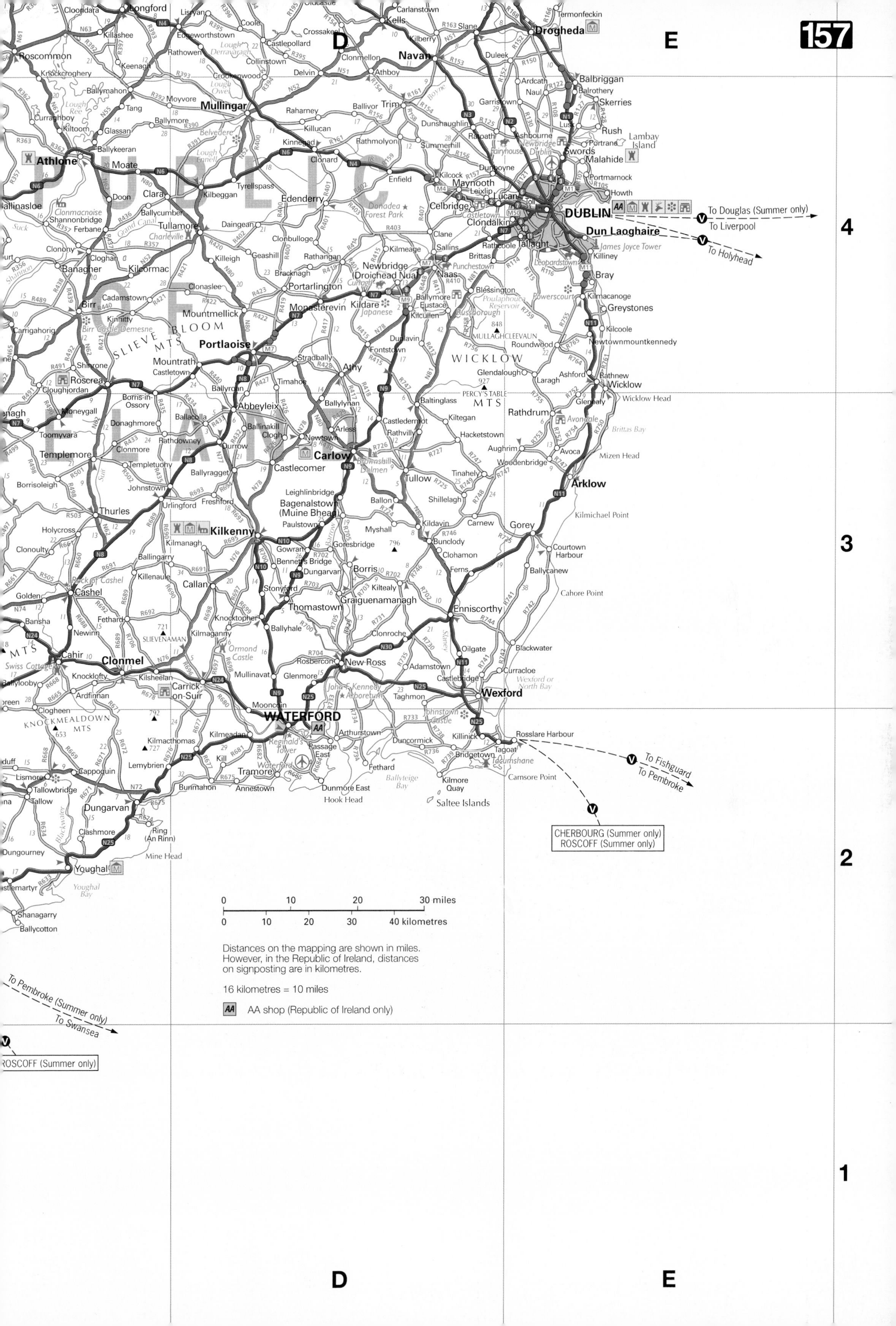
D
E
4
3
2
1
REPUBLIC OF IRELAND
DUBLIN
Dun Laoghaire
To Douglas (Summer only)
To Liverpool
To Holyhead
James Joyce Tower
Drogheda
Termonfeckin
Balbriggan
Balrothery
Skerries
Rush
Lambay Island
Lusk
Swords
Portrane
Malahide
Portmarnock
Howth
Killiney
Bray
Kilmacanoge
Greystones
Kilcoole
Newtownmountkennedy
Rathnew
Wicklow
Wicklow Head
Ashford
Glenealy
Brittas Bay
Mizen Head
Arklow
Kilmichael Point
Gorey
Courtown Harbour
Ballycanew
Cahore Point
Blackwater
Curracloe
Wexford or North Bay
Wexford
Rosslare Harbour
Tagoat
Tacumshane
Carnsore Point
To Fishguard
To Pembroke
CHERBOURG (Summer only)
ROSCOFF (Summer only)
Kilmore Quay
Saltee Islands
Ballyteige Bay
Bridgetown
Killinick
Johnstown Castle
Duncormick
Fethard
Hook Head
Dunmore East
Passage East
Arthurstown
Waterford
WATERFORD
Reginald's Tower
Tramore
Annestown
Bunmahon
Kill
Kilmeadan
Mooncoin
Lemybrien
Kilmacthomas
Dungarvan
Ring (An Rinn)
Mine Head
Clashmore
Youghal
Youghal Bay
Shanagarry
Ballycotton
Castlemartyr
Dungourney
Tallow
Tallowbridge
Lismore
Cappoquin
KNOCKMEALDOWN MTS
Clogheen
Ardfinnan
Cahir
Clonmel
Carrick-on-Suir
Kilsheelan
Knocklofty
Swiss Cottage
Newinn
Fethard
Bansha
Golden
Cashel
Rock of Cashel
SLIEVENAMAN
Kilmaganny
Ormond Castle
Mullinavat
Glenmore
New Ross
Rosbercon
John F. Kennedy Arboretum
Taghmon
Castlebridge
Oilgate
Adamstown
Enniscorthy
Clonroche
Ballyhale
Thomastown
Stonyford
Knocktopher
Callan
Kilkenny
Kilmanagh
Ballingarry
Killenaule
Holycross
Clonoulty
Thurles
Urlingford
Freshford
Johnstown
Templetuohy
Templemore
Borrisoleigh
Toomyvara
Moneygall
Roscrea
Cloughjordan
Shinrone
Birr
Birr Castle Demesne
Kinnitty
Cadamstown
Banagher
Cloghan
Ferbane
Shannonbridge
Clonmacnoise
Ballinasloe
Athlone
Moate
Doon
Clara
Tullamore
Charleville
Kilcormac
Killeigh
Daingean
Clonbulloge
Edenderry
Rathangan
Portarlington
Monasterevin
Mountmellick
Portlaoise
SLIEVE BLOOM MTS
Mountrath
Castletown
Borris-in-Ossory
Abbeyleix
Ballacolla
Durrow
Donaghmore
Rathdowney
Clonmore
Ballyragget
Ballyroan
Timahoe
Stradbally
Athy
Ballinakill
Ballylynan
Arless
Carlow
Castlecomer
Leighlinbridge
Bagenalstown (Muine Bheag)
Paulstown
Gowran
Goresbridge
Bennettsbridge
Dungarvan
Borris
Graiguenamanagh
Kiltealy
Myshall
Ballon
Tullow
Rathvilly
Castledermot
Kildavin
Bunclody
Clohamon
Ferns
Carnew
Shillelagh
Tinahely
Hacketstown
Kiltegan
Baltinglass
Aughrim
Woodenbridge
Avoca
Rathdrum
Avondale
Laragh
Glendalough
PERCY'S TABLE
WICKLOW MTS
MULLAGHCLEEVAUN
Roundwood
Powerscourt
Blessington
Poulaphouca Reservoir
Russborough
Dunlavin
Fontstown
Kilcullen
Ballymore Eustace
Naas
Punchestown
Kildare
Japanese Gardens
Curragh
Newbridge (Droichead Nua)
Kilmeage
Clane
Sallins
Celbridge
Castletown
Clondalkin
Brittas
Rathcoole
Tallaght
Leopardstown
Lucan
Leixlip
Maynooth
Kilcock
Enfield
Donadea Forest Park
Dunboyne
Ratoath
Ashbourne
Fairyhouse
Newbridge
Dunshaughlin
Summerhill
Rathmolyon
Trim
Ballivor
Clonard
Kinnegad
Killucan
Raharney
Mullingar
Belvedere
Lough Ennell
Tyrellspass
Kilbeggan
Moyvore
Ballymore
Ballymahon
Tang
Glassan
Ballykeeran
Kiltoom
Curraghboy
Lough Ree
Knockcroghery
Roscommon
Killashee
Longford
Cloondara
Lisryan
Edgeworthstown
Rathowen
Coole
Castlepollard
Lough Derravaragh
Collinstown
Crookedwood
Lough Owel
Keenagh
Delvin
Clonmellon
Athboy
Crossakeel
Kells
Carlanstown
Kilberry
Navan
Slane
Duleek
Ardcath
Naul
Garristown
0 10 20 30 miles
0 10 20 30 40 kilometres
Distances on the mapping are shown in miles.
However, in the Republic of Ireland, distances on signposting are in kilometres.
16 kilometres = 10 miles
AA shop (Republic of Ireland only)
To Pembroke (Summer only)
To Swansea
ROSCOFF (Summer only)

The Isle of Man

POINT OF AYRE

NX

MAN

SC

To Heysham
To Liverpool
Belfast (Summer Only)
DUBLIN

5 miles
6 kilometres

Cranstal
Bride
Point Cranstal (Shellag Point)
Ramsey
Ramsey Bay
Maughold
Maughold Head
Port Mooar
Ayres
Rue Point
The Lhen
Jurby
Jurby Head
Andreas
Sandygate
St Jude's
Sulby
Lezayre
Glen Auldyn
Dhoon Bay
Old Laxey
Laxey
Laxey Bay
Clay Head
Baldrine
Garwick Bay
Onchan Head
The Crook
Ballaugh
Orrisdale
Orrisdale Head
Kirk Michael
Ravensdale
The Bungalow
SNAEFELL
Sulby Reservoir
Baldwin
Crosby
Glen Mona
Strang
Union Mills
Onchan
DOUGLAS
Douglas Bay
Douglas Head
St John's
Crosby
St Marks
Santon
Port Soderick
Greeba
Glen Maye
Foxdale
Lower Foxdale
SOUTH BARRULE
Ballasalla
Derbyhaven
St Patrick's Isle
Peel
Contrary Head
Kirkpatrick
Dalby
Niarbyl
Niarbyl Bay
Grenaby
Ballabeg
Colby
Ballabeg
Castletown
Castletown Bay
Scarlett Point
Dreswick Point
Langness Point
Fleshwick
Port Erin
Howe
Cregneash
St Mary
Port St Mary
Spanish Head
Calf Sound
CALF OF MAN
Calgher Point

The Channel Islands

FRANCE
ALDERNEY
St Anne
HERM
SARK
GUERNSEY
St Peter Port
JERSEY
St Helier

10 mls
20 km

Guernsey

2 miles
2 kilometres

To Weymouth
To Portsmouth
To Poole (Summer Only)
To Jersey
ST MALO Summer Only

Fort le Marchant
Fort le Marchant
La Fontenelle
Clos du Valle
Bordeaux
L'Ancresse
L'Ancresse Bay
St Sampson
Belle Grève Bay
St Peter Port
Havelet
Les Terres Point
Putron Village
Jerbourg
St Martins Point
Moulin Huet Bay
Icart Point
Petit Bot Bay
Grande Havre
Vale
Islet Village
Capelles
Les Quartiers
La Rousaillerie
La Bellieuse
La Fosse
Fermain Bay
Saline Bay
Plein Heaume
Le Bourg
Villaze
Forest
Les Nicolles
Les Villets
Point de la Moye
Grandes Rocques
Cobo
Cobo Bay
Vazon Bay
King's Mills
St Andrew
St Martin
Les Hubits
Les Lohiers
Le Gron
Le Bigard
Richmond Fort
Perelle Bay
Vazon Bay
Perelle
Mont Saint
St Saviour
St Pierre's
Les Murchez
Perelle Bay
Pleinmont Point
Grosnez Point
Lihou Island
Roquaine Bay
La Houguette
St Peter's
Les Sages
Les Arquets
Torteval
Fort Grey
Fort Hommet

Jersey

2 miles
2 kilometres

ST MALO Summer Only
To Guernsey
To Weymouth
To Poole (Summer Only)
To Portsmouth

Royal Bay of Grouville
Nez du Guet
St Catherine's Bay
Verclut Point
Flicquet Bay
Archirondel
Faldouet
Gorey
La Rocque
La Rocque Point
Plat Rocque Point
Rozel Bay
Rozel
St Martin
La Hougue Bie
Maufant
Grouville
Le Pontac
Le Hocq
St Clements Bay
Le Croc
Bouley Bay
Trinity
Grand Chemins
Five Oaks
Longueville
St Saviour
Becquet Vincent
Vallée des Vaux
St Helier
St Clement
Les Houguais
Vicard Point
La Columbière
Belle Hougue Point
Haute Croix
Bellozanne Valley
St Aubin's Bay
Sorel Point
Ronez Point
St John's Bay
St John
Carrefour
Trois Bois
Millbrook
Beaumont
St Aubin
St Aubin's Bay
Elizabeth Castle
Mourier Valley
Fremont Point
La Mare
Six Rues
St Lawrence
St Peter's Valley
Belcroute Bay
Plemont Point
Plemont
Portinfer
Rouge Nez
La Grève de Lecq
Leoville
St Ouen
St Peter
St Mary
Quennevais
St Brelade
St Brelade's Bay
St Brelade's Bay
Point La Fret
Portelet Bay
Grosnez Point
Ville la Bas
Millais
L'Etacq
St Ouen's Bay
La Pulente
Corbière
Corbière Point
La Moye
Point La Moye
Kempt Tower

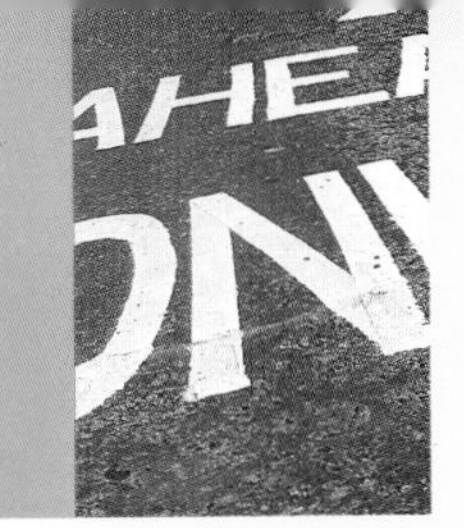

key to town plans

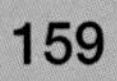

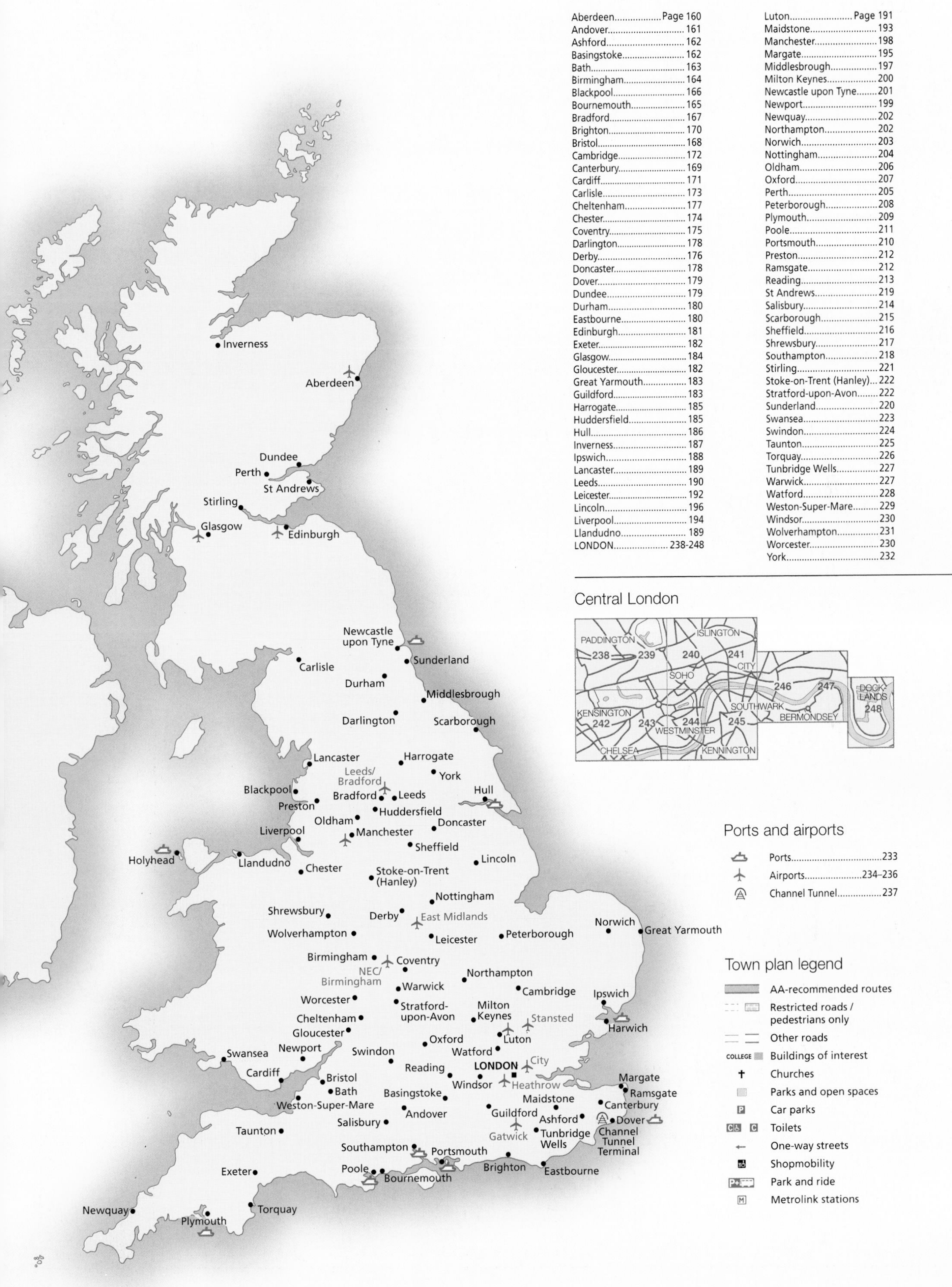

159

Central London

Ports and airports

⌂	Ports................................233	
✈	Airports.....................234–236	
Ⓐ	Channel Tunnel................237	

Town plan legend

▨	AA-recommended routes
⬚ ▨	Restricted roads / pedestrians only
═ ═	Other roads
COLLEGE ▪	Buildings of interest
†	Churches
▫	Parks and open spaces
ℙ	Car parks
C& C	Toilets
←	One-way streets
▥	Shopmobility
ℙ	Park and ride
Ⓜ	Metrolink stations

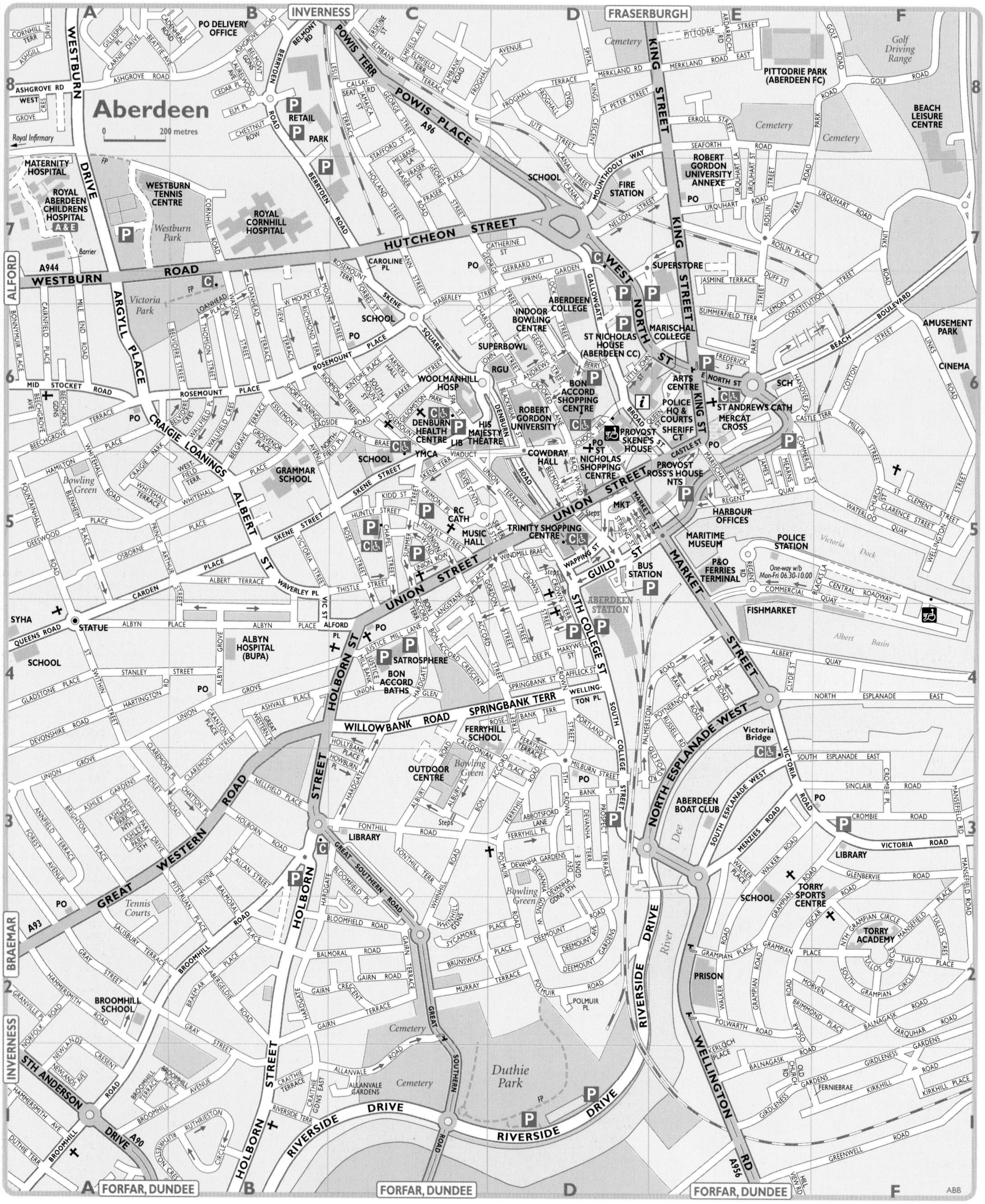
Aberdeen
200 metres
INVERNESS
FRASERBURGH
ALFORD
BRAEMAR
INVERNESS
FORFAR, DUNDEE
FORFAR, DUNDEE
FORFAR, DUNDEE
A
B
C
D
E
F
1
2
3
4
5
6
7
8
PO DELIVERY OFFICE
RETAIL
PARK
Royal Infirmary
MATERNITY HOSPITAL
ROYAL ABERDEEN CHILDRENS HOSPITAL
A & E
Barrier
WESTBURN TENNIS CENTRE
Westburn Park
ROYAL CORNHILL HOSPITAL
HUTCHEON STREET
POWIS PLACE
POWIS TERR
A96
WESTBURN DRIVE
WESTBURN ROAD
A944
ARGYLL PLACE
Victoria Park
CRAIGIE LOANINGS
ROSEMOUNT PLACE
SKENE SQUARE
SCHOOL
PO
Cemetery
PITTODRIE PARK (ABERDEEN FC)
Golf Driving Range
BEACH LEISURE CENTRE
KING STREET
MERKLAND ROAD
ERROLL STREET
SEAFORTH ROAD
ROBERT GORDON UNIVERSITY ANNEXE
URQUHART ROAD
FIRE STATION
MOUNTHOOLY WAY
WEST NORTH ST
SUPERSTORE
JASMINE TERRACE
SUMMERFIELD TERR
ABERDEEN COLLEGE
INDOOR BOWLING CENTRE
SUPERBOWL
ST NICHOLAS HOUSE (ABERDEEN CC)
MARISCHAL COLLEGE
BEACH BOULEVARD
AMUSEMENT PARK
CINEMA
RGU
WOOLMANHILL HOSP
BON ACCORD SHOPPING CENTRE
ARTS CENTRE
POLICE HQ & COURTS
SHERIFF CT
ST ANDREWS CATH
MERCAT CROSS
PROVOST SKENE'S HOUSE
ST NICHOLAS SHOPPING CENTRE
PROVOST ROSS'S HOUSE NTS
CASTLE ST
SCH
DENBURN HEALTH CENTRE
LIB
HIS MAJESTY'S THEATRE
ROBERT GORDON UNIVERSITY
COWDRAY HALL
YMCA
VIADUCT
GRAMMAR SCHOOL
SKENE STREET
UNION STREET
RC CATH
MUSIC HALL
TRINITY SHOPPING CENTRE
MKT
HARBOUR OFFICES
MARITIME MUSEUM
P&O FERRIES TERMINAL
POLICE STATION
Victoria Dock
One-way w/b Mon-Fri 06.30-10.00
COMMERCIAL QUAY
CENTRAL ROADWAY
FISHMARKET
Albert Basin
BUS STATION
GUILD ST
ABERDEEN STATION
STH COLLEGE ST
MARKET STREET
ALBERT ST
SKENE PLACE
ALBYN PLACE
SYHA
STATUE
QUEENS ROAD
SCHOOL
ALBYN HOSPITAL (BUPA)
HOLBORN ST
SATROSPHERE
BON ACCORD BATHS
WILLOWBANK ROAD
SPRINGBANK TERR
FERRYHILL SCHOOL
OUTDOOR CENTRE
Bowling Green
NORTH ESPLANADE WEST
NORTH ESPLANADE EAST
Victoria Bridge
ABERDEEN BOAT CLUB
VICTORIA ROAD
LIBRARY
TORRY SPORTS CENTRE
TORRY ACADEMY
GREAT WESTERN ROAD
A93
Tennis Courts
LIBRARY
GREAT SOUTHERN ROAD
HOLBORN STREET
BROOMHILL SCHOOL
Cemetery
Duthie Park
RIVERSIDE DRIVE
River Dee
PRISON
WELLINGTON RD
A956
STH ANDERSON DRIVE
A90
ABB

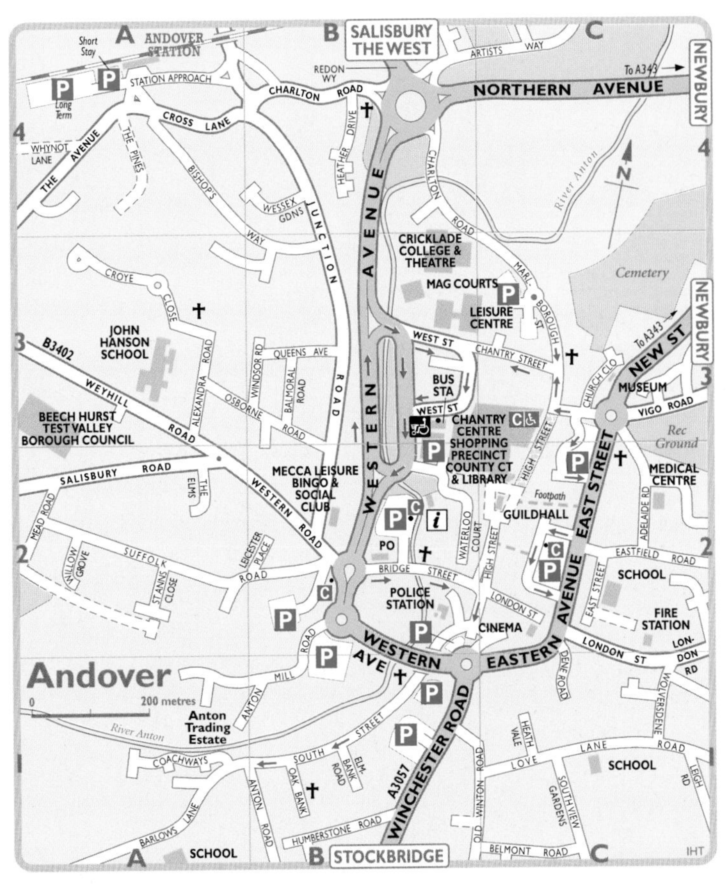

Andover

Andover is found on atlas page **23**,
grid reference **3645**

Adelaide Road	C2-C3	High Street	B2-C2-C3	The Avenue	A4
Alexandra Road	A3	Humberstone Road	B1	The Elms	A2
Anton Mill Road	A1-B1-B2	Junction Road	B2-B3-B4	The Pines	A4
Anton Road	B1	Leicester Place	B2	Vigo Road	C3
Artists Way	B4-C4	Leigh Road	C1	Waterloo Court	B2
Balmoral Road	B3	London Road	C1	Wessex Gardens	B4
Barlows Lane	A1	London Street	C1	Western Avenue	B1-B2-B3
Belmont Road	B1-C1	Love Lane	C1-C2	Western Road	A2-B2
Bishop's Way	A4-B4-B3	Marlborough Street	C3	West Street	B2-B3
Bridge Street	B2	Mead Road	A2	Weyhill Road	A3
Chantry Street	B3-C3	New Street	C3	Whynot Lane	A4
Charlton Road	B4-B3-C3	Northern Avenue	B4-C4	Winchester Road	B1
Church Close	C3	Oak Bank Road	B1	Windsor Road	B3
Coachways	A1	Old Winton Road	B1-C1	Willow Grove	A2
Cross Lane	A4	Osborne Road	A3-B3	Wolversdene Road	C1
Croye Close	A3	Queens Avenue	B3		
Dene Road	C1	Redon Way	B4		
Eastfield Road	C2	St Anns Close	A2		
East Street	C2-C3	Salisbury Road	A2		
Eastern Avenue	C1-C2	South Street	B1-B2		
Elmbank Road	B1	Southview Gardens	C1		
Heath Vale	C1	Station Approach	A4		
Heather Drive	B4	Suffolk Road	A2-B2		

Aberdeen

Aberdeen is found on atlas page **135**,
grid reference **9306**

Abbotsford Lane	D3	Belvidere Crescent	B6	Claremont Street	B3-B4	Fonthill Terrace	C3
Abergeldie Road	B2	Belvidere Street	B6	Clarence Street	F5	Forest Avenue	A2-A3
Affleck Street	D4	Berry Street	D6	Clyde Street	E4	Forbes Street	C6-C7
Albert Quay	E4-F4	Berryden Road	B8-B7-C7	Commerce Street	E5-E6	Fountainhall Road	A4-A5
Albert Street	B5	Blackfriar Street	D6	Commercial Quay	E5-F5-F4	Fraser Place	C7-C8
Albert Terrace	B5	Blacks Lane	F5	Constitution Street	E6-E7-F7	Fraser Road	C7
Albury Place	C3	Blenheim Place	A5	Cornhill Road	B7	Fraser Street	C7
Albury Road	C3-C4	Bloomfield Place	C2-C3	Cotton Street	F6	Frederick Street	E6
Albyn Grove	B4	Bloomfield Road	B2-C2	Craigie Loanings	A6-B6-B5	Froghall Avenue	C8-D8
Albyn Place	A4-B4	Bon Accord Crescent	C4	Craigie Park	A5-A6	Froghall Road	D8
Alford Place	B4-C4	Bon Accord Street	C3-D4-C4-C5	Craithie Gardens East	B1	Froghall Terrace	D8
Allan Street	B3	Bon Accord Terrace	C4-C5	Craithie Terrace	B1	Gairn Crescent	B2-C2
Allanvale Gardens	C1	Bonnymuir Place	A6	Crimon Place	C5	Gairn Road	C2
Allanvale Road	B1-C1-C2	Braemar Place	B2	Crombie Place	F3	Gairn Terrace	B2-C2
Ann Street	C7	Brighton Place	A3	Crombie Road	F3	Gallowgate	D6-D7
Annfield Terrace	A3	Brimmond Place	E2-F2	Crooked Lane	D6	George Street	C8-C7-D7-D6
Ardarroch Road	E8	Broad Street	D6-E6	Crown Street	D3-D4-D5	Gerrard Street	D7
Argyll Place	A6-A7	Broomhill Avenue	A1-B1	Crown Terrace	D4-D5	Gillespie Place	A8
Ashgill Drive	A8	Broomhill Place	A1-B1	Dee Place	D4	Gilsomston Park	C6
Ashgrove Road	A8-B8	Broomhill Road	A1-A2-B2-B3	Dee Street	D4-D5	Girdleness Gardens	E1-F1-F2
Ashgrove Road West	A8	Broomhill Terrace	A1	Deemount Avenue	D2	Gladstone Place	A4
Ashley Gardens	A3	Brunswick Place	C2-D2	Deemount Gardens	D2	Glenbervie Road	F3
Ashley Park Drive	A3	Cadenhead Road	A8-B8	Deemount Road	D2	Golf Road	F8
Ashley Park North	A3	Cairnfield Place	A6-A7	Deeswood Place	A5	Gordon Street	D4-D5-C5
Ashley Park South	A3	Caledonian Place	C4-C3-D3	Denburn Road	D5-D6	Grampian Place	E2-F2
Ashley Road	A3-B3	Calsay Seat Road	C8	Devanha Gardens	D3	Grampian Road	E2-E3-F3
Ashvale Place	B4	Canal Place	D7	Devanha Gardens East	D3	Granton Place	B4
Back Wynd	D5-D6	Canal Street	D7-D8	Devanha Gardens South	D3	Granville Place	A2
Baker Street	C6	Carden Place	A4-A5-B5	Devanha Gardens West	D2-D3	Gray Street	A2-B2-B1
Balmoral Place	B2-B3	Carnie Drive	A8	Devanha Terrace	D3	Great Southern Road	C1-C3-B3
Balmoral Road	B2-C2	Caroline Place	C7	Devonshire Road	A3-A4	Great Western Place	B4
Balnagask Road	E1-F2	Castle Street	E5-E6	Duff Street	E7	Great Western Road	A2-A3-B3-B4
Bank Street	D3	Castle Terrace	E6-F6	East North Street	E6	Greenwell Road	E1-F1
Beach Boulevard	E6-F6-F7	Catherine Street	C7-D7	Elm Place	B8	Grosvenor Place	B6
Beattie Avenue	A8-B8	Cedar Place	B8	Elmbank Road	C8	Grove Crescent	A8
Beechgrove Avenue	A6	Central Roadway	F5	Elmbank Terrace	C8	Guild Street	D5-E5
Beechgrove Gardens	A6	Chapel Street	C5	Elmfield Avenue	C8	Hamilton Place	A5-A6
Beechgrove Terrace	A5-A6	Charlotte Street	C7-C6-D6	Elmfield Terrace	C8	Hammersmith Avenue	A1
Belgrave Terrace	B5-B6	Chatton Place	B3	Erroll Street	E8	Hammersmith Road	A2
Belmont Gardens	B8	Chestnut Row	B8	Erskine Street	E8	Hanover Street	E6
Belmont Road	B8	Church Street	F5	Esslemont Avenue	B6-B5-C5	Hardgate	B2-B3-C3-C4
Belmont Street	D5	Claremont Place	A4-A3-B3	Exchange Street	D5	Hartington Road	A4
				Farmers Hall	C6	Holborn Road	B3
				Farquhar Road	F2	Holborn Street	B1-B2-B3-C4
				Ferniebrae	E1-F1	Holland Street	C7
				Ferryhill Place	D3	Hollybank Place	C3-C4
				Ferryhill Road	D3	Howburn Place	C3
				Ferryhill Terrace	D3-D4	Huntly Street	C5
				Fonthill Road	C3	Hutcheon Street	C7-D7

Irvine Place	B3	Loanhead Place	B6-B7	St Swithin Street	A4
Jack's Brae	C6	Loanhead Terrace	B6-B7	Salisbury Terrace	A2-B2
Jamaica Street	C8	Lock Street	D6-D7	School Hill	D6
James Street	E5	Maberley Street	C7-D7	Seaforth Road	E8
Jasmine Terrace	E7	Mansfield Place	F2-F3	Shore Lane	E5
John Street	C6-D6	Mansfield Road	F2-F3	Short Loanings	B6
Justice Mill Lane	C4	Marischal Street	E5-E6	Silver Street North	C5
Justice Mill Bank	C4	Market Street	D5-E5-E4	Silver Street South	D5
Jute Street	D8	Marywell Street	D4	Sinclair Road	E3-F3
Kerloch Place	E1-E2	Mearns Street	E5	Skene Square	C6-C7
Kidd Street	C5	Menzies Road	E3	Skene Street	B5-C5
King Street	E6-E7-E8-D8	Merkland Road	D8	Skene Terrace	C5
Kintore Place	C6	Merkland Road East	E8	South Anderson Drive	A1
Kirkhill Place	F1	Mid Stocket Road	A6	South College Street	D3-D4-D5
Kirkhill Road	E1-F1	Milburn Street	D3	South Crown Street	D3
Langstane Place	C4-C5	Mile End Road	A6-A7	South Esplanade East	E3-F3
Laurelwood Avenue	B8	Millbank Lane	C7-C8	South Esplanade West	E3
Leadside Road	B6-C6	Miller Street	F5-F6	South Grampian Circle	F2
Lemon Street	E6-E7	Morven Place	E2-F2	South Mount Street	C6
Leslie Terrace	C8	Mount Street	B7-C6	Spa Street	C6
Links Road	F6-F7	Mounthooly Way	D7-D8-E8	Spital Kings Crescent	D7-D8
Little John Street	D6	Murray Terrace	C2-D2	Spring Garden	D7
		Nellfield Place	B3	Springbank Street	D4
		Nelson Street	D7-E7	Springbank Terrace	C4-D4
		Newlands Avenue	A1	Stafford Street	C7-C8
		Newlands Crescent	A1-A2	Stanley Street	A4-B4
		Norfolk Road	A1-A2	Stell Road	E4
		North Esplanade East	E4-F4	Stirling Street	D5
		North Esplanade West	E3-E4	Summer Street	C5
		North Grampian Circle	F2	Summerfield Terrace	E6
		Northfield Place	B5-C6	Sycamore Place	C2-D2
		Old Church Road	E1	Thistle Street	C5
		Old Ford Road	E3-E4	Thomson Street	B6
		Osborne Place	A5-B5	Tullos Circle	F2
		Oscar Road	E2-F2-F3	Tullos Crescent	F2
		Palmerston Road	D3-D4-E4	Tullos Place	F2
		Park Road	E7-E8-F8	Union Glen	C4
		Park Street	E6-E7	Union Grove	A3-A4-B4-C4
		Pitstruan Place	A3-B3-B2	Union Row	C5
		Pittodrie Street	E8	Union Street	C4-C5-D5
		Polmuir Place	D2	Union Terrace	C5-D5
		Polmuir Road	D2-D3	Union Wynd	C5
		Polwarth Road	E2	Urquhart Lane	E7-E8
		Portland Street	D4	Urquhart Road	E7-F7
		Powis Place	C8-D7	Urquhart Street	E7-E8
		Powis Terrace	C8	Victoria Road	E4-E3-F3
		Poynernook Road	E4	Victoria Street	B4-B5
		Prince Arthur Street	A5-B5-B4	View Terrace	B6-B7
		Prospect Terrace	D2-D3	Walker Place	E3
		Queen Street	D6-E6	Walker Road	E2-E3
		Queens Road	A4	Wallfield Crescent	B6
		Raik Road	E4	Wallfield Place	B6
		Regent Quay	E5	Wapping Street	D5
		Regent Road	E5	Waterloo Quay	F5
		Richmond Street	B6-C6	Watson Street	B6-B7
		Richmond Terrace	B6-B7	Waverley Place	B5
		Riverside Drive	B1-C1-D1-E2	Wellington Place	D4
		Riverside Terrace	B1	Wellington Road	E1-E2-E3
		Rose Street	C4-C5	Wellington Street	F5-F6
		Rosebank Terrace	C4-D4	West Mount Street	B7
		Rosemount Place	A6-B6-C6	West North Street	D7-D6-E6
		Rosemount Terrace	C7	Westburn Drive	A7-A8
		Rosemount Viaduct	C6-C5	Westburn Road	A7-B7-C7
		Roslin Place	E7-F7	Westfield Terrace	B5
		Roslin Street	E7-E8	Whinhill Gardens	C2
		Russell Road	E4	Whinhill Road	C2-C3
		Ruthrieston Circle	B1	Whitehall Place	A5-B5-B6
		Ruthrieston Crescent	A1-B1	Whitehall Road	A5-A6
		St Andrew Street	D6	Whitehall Terrace	A5
		St Clement Street	F5	Willowbank Road	C4
		St Peter Street	D8	Windmill Brae	D5

161

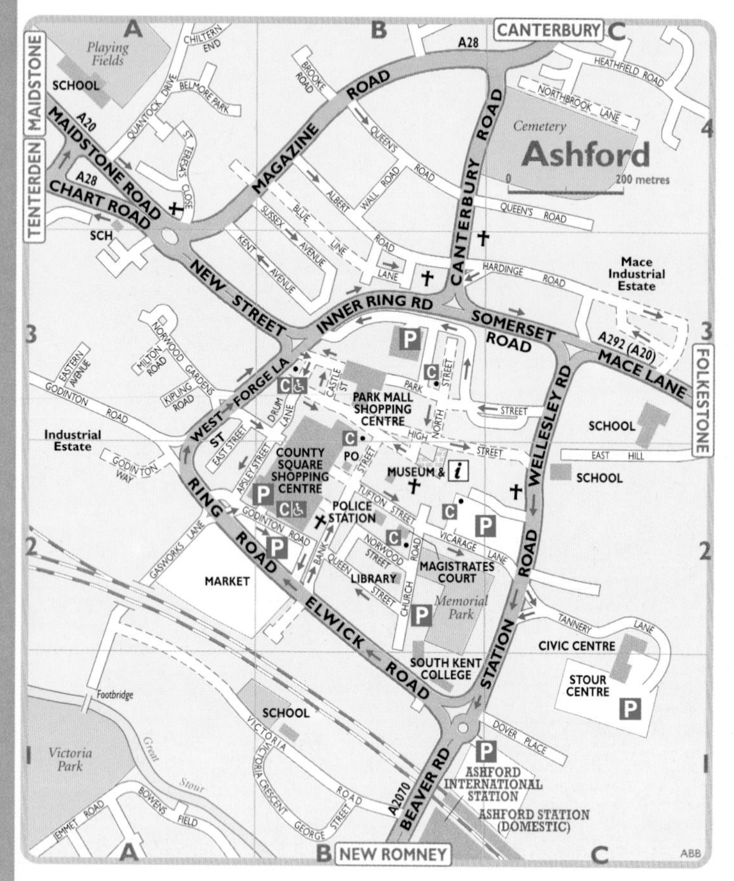

Ashford

Ashford is found on atlas page **28**, grid reference **0142**

Albert Road	B3-B4		St Teresa's Close	A4
Apsley Street	A2-B2		Somerset Road	B3-C3
Bank Street	B2-B3		Station Road	B1-C1-C2
Beaver Road	B1		Sussex Avenue	A4-B4-B3
Belmore Park	A4		Tannery Lane	C1-C2
Blue Line Lane	B3-B4		Tufton Street	B2
Bowens Field	A1		Vicarage Lane	B2-C2
Brooke Road	B4		Victoria Crescent	B1
Canterbury Road	B3-B4-C4		Victoria Road	A1-B1
Castle Street	B3		Wall Road	B4
Chart Road	A4		Wellesley Road	C2-C3
Chiltern End	A4		West Street	A2-A3
Church Road	B2			
Dover Place	B1-C1			
Drum Lane	B3			
East Hill	C2			
East Street	A2-A3			
Eastern Avenue	A3			
Elwick Road	B1-B2			
Forge Lane	A3-B3			
Gasworks Lane	A2			
George Street	B1			
Godinton Road	A3-A2-B2			
Godinton Way	A2			
Hardinge Road	B3-C3			
Heathfield Road	C4			
High Street	B3-B2-C2			
Inner Ring Road	B3			
Jemmet Road	A1			
Kent Avenue	A4-A3-B3			
Kipling Road	A3			
Mace Lane	C3			
Magazine Road	A4-B4			
Maidstone Road	A4			
Milton Road	A3			
New Street	A3-B3			
North Street	B3			
Northbrook Lane	C4			
Norwood Gardens	A3			
Norwood Street	B2			
Park Street	B3-C3			
Quantock Drive	A4			
Queen Street	B2			
Queen's Road	B4-C4			
Ring Road	A2-B2			

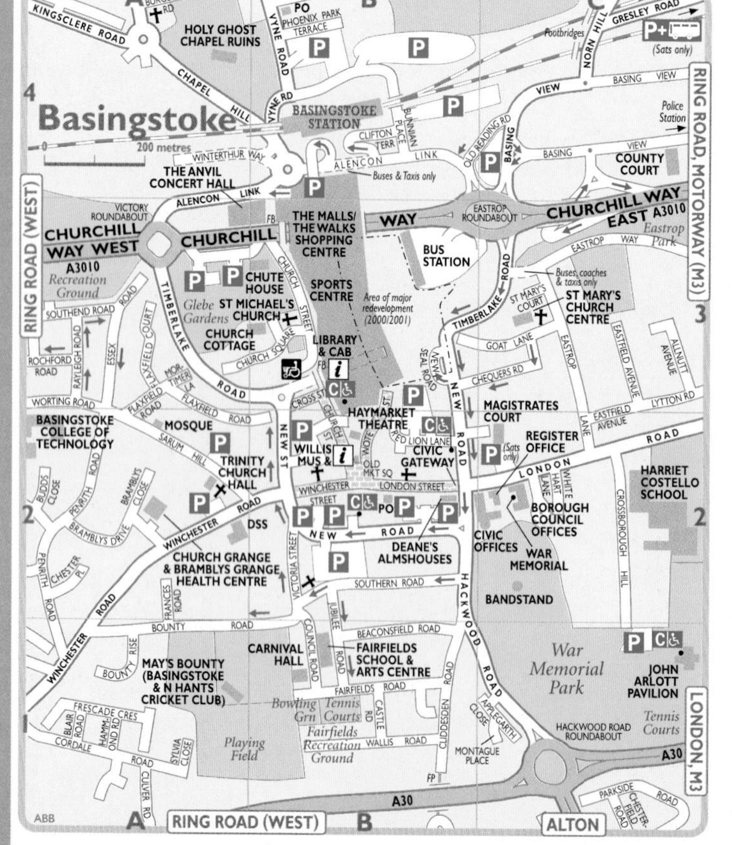

Basingstoke

Basingstoke is found on atlas page **24**, grid reference **6352**

Alencon Link	A3-A4-B4		London Road	B2-C2
Allnutt Avenue	C3		London Street	B2
Applegarth Close	C1		Lytton Road	C3
Basing View	C4		Montague Place	C1
Beaconsfield Road	B1		Mortimer Lane	A3
Blair Road	A1		New Road	B2-B3
Bounty Rise	A1		New Seal Road	B3
Bounty Road	A1-B1-B2		New Street	B2-B3
Bramblys Close	A2		Norn Hill	C4
Bramblys Drive	A2		Old Market Square	B2
Budds Close	A2		Old Reading Road	B4-C4
Bunnian Place	B4		Parkside Road	C1
Burgess Road	A4		Penrith Road	A1-A2
Castle Road	B1		Phoenix Park Terrace	B4
Chapel Hill	A4-B4		Rayleigh Road	A3
Chequers Road	B3-C3		Red Lion Lane	B2
Chester Place	A2		Rochford Road	A3
Chesterfield Road	C1		St Mary's Court	C3
Church Square	A3-B3		Sarum Hill	A2
Church Street	B2-B3		Southend Road	A3
Churchill Way	A3-B3		Southern Road	B2
Churchill Way East	C3-C4		Sylvia Close	A1
Churchill Way West	A3		Timberlake Road	A3-B3-C3
Cliddesden Road	B1		Victoria Street	B2
Clifton Terrace	B4		Vyne Road	B4
Cordale Road	A1		Wallis Road	B1
Council Road	B1-B2		White Hart Lane	C2
Cross Street	B3		Winchester Road	A1-A2-B2
Crossborough Hill	C1-C2		Winchester Street	B2
Culver Road	A1		Winterthur Way	A4-B4
Eastfield Avenue	C2-C3		Worting Road	A3
Eastrop Lane	C2-C3		Wote Street	B2-B3
Eastrop Way	C3			
Essex Road	A3			
Fairfields Road	B1			
Flaxfield Court	A3			
Flaxfield Road	A3-A2-B2			
Frances Road	A1-A2			
Frescade Crescent	A1			
Goat Lane	B3-C3			
Gresley Road	C4			
Hackwood Road	B1-B2-C1			
Hammond Road	A1			
Jubilee Road	B1-B2			
Kingsclere Road	A4			

162

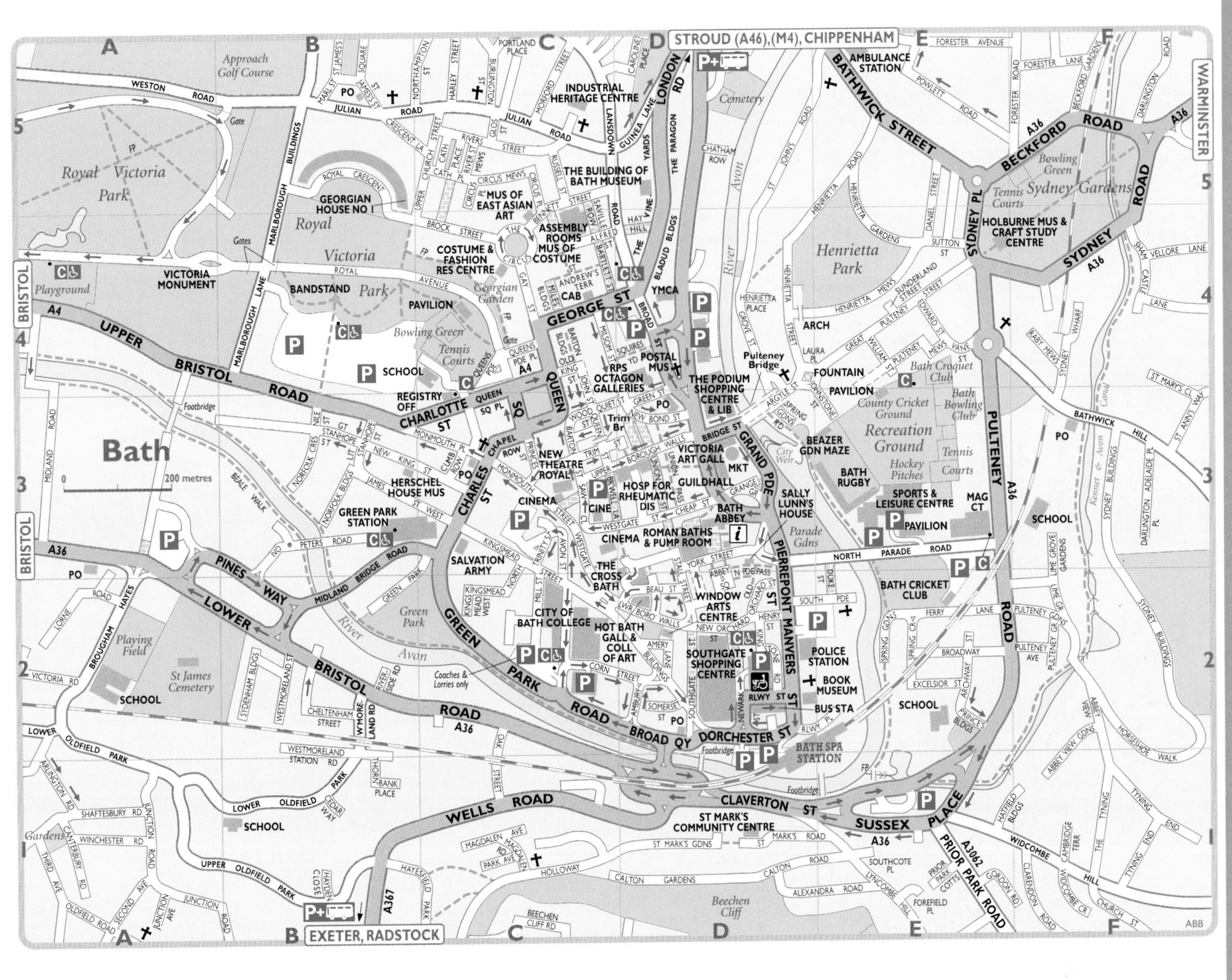

Bath

Bath is found on atlas page **22**,
grid reference **7464**

Abbey Square	D2-D3	Cambridge Terrace	F1	Gordon Road	E1-F1
Abbey View	F2	Canterbury Road	A1	Grand Parade	D3
Abbey View Gardens	F1-F2	Caroline Place	D5	Grange Grove	D3
Adelaide Place	F3	Catherine Place	C5	Great Pulteney Street	E4
Alexandra Road	D1-E1	Cedar Way	B1	Great Stanhope Street	B3
Alfred Street	C4	Chapel Row	C3	Green Park	B2-C3
Ambury	D2	Charles Street	C3	Green Park Road	C2-C3
Amery Lane Buildings	D2	Charlotte Street	B3-C3	Green Street	D3-D4
Archway Street	E2	Chatham Row	D5	Grove Street	D3
Argyle Street	D3-D4	Cheap Street	D3	Guinea Lane	D5
Arlington Road	A1	Cheltenham Street	B2	Harley Street	C5
Avon Street	C2-C3	Church Street	F1	Hatfield Buildings	E1-F1
Bartlett Street	C4	Circus Mews	C5	Hay Hill	D4
Barton Buildings	C4	Circus Place	C5	Hayden Close	B1
Barton Street	C3	Clarendon Road	F1	Hayesfield Park	B1-C1
Bath Street	D3	Claverton Street	D1	Henrietta Gardens	E4-E5
Bathwick Hill	E4-F4-F3	Corn Street	C2-D2	Henrietta Mews	D4-E4
Bathwick Street	E5	Crescent Lane	B5-C5	Henrietta Place	D4
Beau Street	D2	Cumberland Row	C3	Henrietta Road	D4-E5
Beckford Gardens	F5	Daniel Street	E4-E5	Henrietta Street	D4
Beckford Road	E5-F5	Darlington Place	F3	Henry Street	D2
Beechen Cliff Road	C1	Darlington Road	F5	Holloway	C1
Bennett Street	C4-C5	Dorchester Street	D2	Horseshoe Walk	F1-F2
Bladud Buildings	D4	Duke Street	E2-E3	Ivo Peters Road	B3
Bridge Street	D3	Edward Street	E4	James Street West	B3-C3
Bridgewell Lane	C3	Excelsior Street	E2	John Street	C3-C4
Broad Quay	D2	Ferry Lane	E2	Johnstone Street	E3
Broad Street	D4	Forefield Place	E1	Julian Road	B5-C5
Broadway	E2	Forester Avenue	E5-F5	Junction Avenue	A1
Brock Street	B4-C4	Forester Lane	F5	Junction Road	A1-B1
Brougham Hayes	A2-A3	Forester Road	F5	Kingsmead North	C2-C3
Burlington Street	C5	Gay Street	C4	Kingsmead Street	C3-C2
Calton Gardens	C1-D1	George Street	C4-D4	Kingsmead West	C2
Calton Road	D1-E1	Gloucester Street	C5	Kingstone Road	D2
				Lansdown Road	C5-D5-D4
				Laura Place	D4
				Lime Grove	F2
				Lime Grove Gardens	F2-F3
				Little Stanhope Street	B3
				London Road	D5
				Lorne Road	A2
				Lower Borough Walls	D2

Lower Bristol Road	A3-B2-C2-C1	Pulteney Gardens	F2	Sunderland Street	E4
Lower Oldfield Park	A2-A1-B2	Pulteney Grove	F2	Sussex Place	E1
Lyncombe Hill	E1	Pulteney Mews	E4	Sutton Street	E4
Magdalen Avenue	C1	Pulteney Road	E2-E3-E4	Sydenham Buildings	B2
Magdalen Road	C1	Queen Square	C3-C4	Sydney Buildings	F2-F3
Manvers Street	D2	Queen Square Place	C3-C4	Sydney Place	E4-E5
Marlborough Buildings	B4-B5	Queen Street	C3	Sydney Road	E4-F4-F5
Marlborough Lane	B4	Queens Parade	C4	Sydney Wharf	F3-F4
Midland Bridge Road	B2-B3-C3	Queens Parade Place	C4	The Circus	C4
Midland Road	A3-A4	Quiet Street	C3-D3	The Paragon	D5
Miles Buildings	C4	Raby Mews	F4	The Tyning	F1
Mill Street	C2	Railway Place	D2-E2	The Vineyards	D4-D5
Milsom Street	C4-D4	Railway Street	D2	Third Avenue	A1
Monmouth Place	B3-C3	River Street Mews	C5	Thornbank Place	B1
Monmouth Street	C3	Rivers Street	C5	Trim Street	C3-D3
Morford Street	C5	Riverside Road	B2	Trinity Street	C3
New Bond Street	D3	Royal Avenue	B4-C4	Tyning End	F1
New King Street	B3-C3	Royal Crescent	B5	Union Pass	D3
New Orchard Street	D2	Russell Street	C5	Union Street	D3
Newark Street	D2	St Andrew's Terrace	C4	Upper Borough Walls	C3-D3
Nile Street	B3	St Ann's Way	F3	Upper Bristol Road	A4-B4-B3
Norfolk Buildings	B3	St James's Square	B5	Upper Church Street	C5
Norfolk Crescent	B3	St James's Street	B5	Upper Oldfield Park	A1-B1
North Parade Passage	D2-D3	St John's Road	D4-D5-E5	Vane Street	E4
North Parade Road	D3-E3	St Mark's Gardens	D1	Vellore Lane	F4
Northampton Street	B5-C5	St Mark's Road	D1-E1	Victoria Road	A2
Oak Street	C1-C2	St Mary's Close	F3-F4	Wells Road	B1-C1-D1
Old King Street	C4	Savile Row	C4-C5	Westgate	C3
Old Orchard Street	D2	Saw Close	C3	Westgate Street	C3-D3
Oldfield Road	A1	Second Avenue	A1	Westmoreland Road	B2
Park Avenue	C1	Shaftesbury Road	A1	Westmoreland Station Road	B1-B2
Pierrepont Street	D2-D3	Sham Castle Lane	F4	Westmoreland Street	B2
Pines Way	A3-B3-B2	Somerset Street	D2	Weston Road	A5-B5
Portland Place	C5	South Parade	D2-E2	Widcombe Crescent	F1
Powlett Road	E5	Southcote Place	E1	Widcombe Hill	E1-F1
Prince's Buildings	E2	Southgate Street	D2	William Street	E4
Princes Street	C3	Spring Crescent	E2	Winchester Road	A1
Prior Park Cottages	E1	Spring Gardens	E2	Wood Street	C3
Prior Park Road	E1	Spring Gardens Road	D3	York Street	D3
Pulteney Avenue	F2	Squires Yard	D4		
		Stall Street	D2-D3		

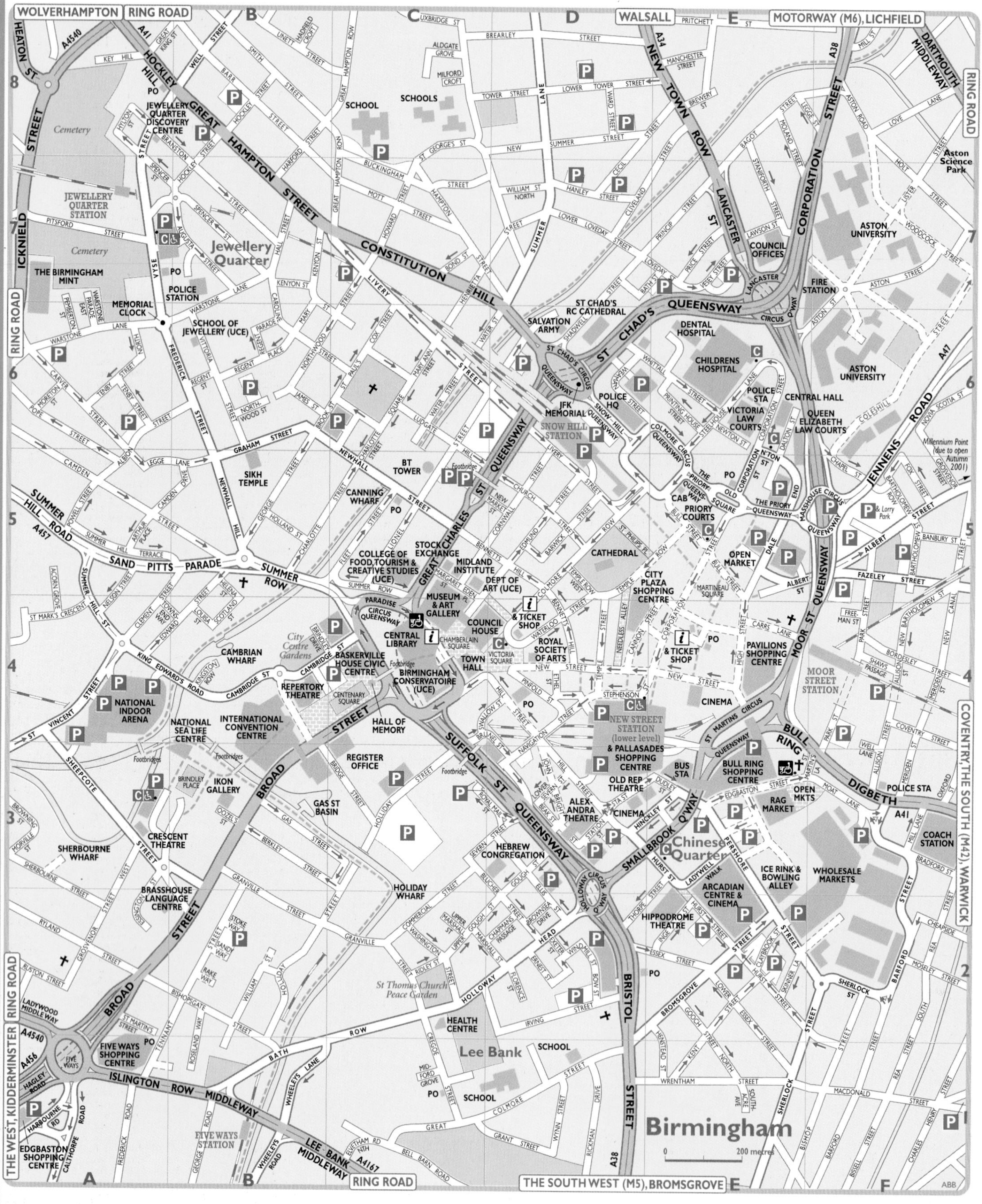

WOLVERHAMPTON RING ROAD — A4540 — A41 — WALSALL — A34 — MOTORWAY (M6), LICHFILD — A38

Jewellery Quarter

Cemetery

JEWELLERY QUARTER DISCOVERY CENTRE
JEWELLERY QUARTER STATION
THE BIRMINGHAM MINT
MEMORIAL CLOCK
POLICE STATION
SCHOOL OF JEWELLERY (UCE)

SCHOOL
SCHOOLS

CONSTITUTION HILL

ST CHAD'S RC CATHEDRAL
SALVATION ARMY
DENTAL HOSPITAL
CHILDRENS HOSPITAL
ASTON UNIVERSITY
ASTON SCIENCE PARK
FIRE STATION
COUNCIL OFFICES

JFK MEMORIAL
SNOW HILL STATION
POLICE HQ
VICTORIA LAW COURTS
QUEEN ELIZABETH LAW COURTS
CENTRAL HALL
POLICE STA
Millennium Point (due to open Autumn 2001)

SIKH TEMPLE
BT TOWER
CANNING WHARF
COLLEGE OF FOOD, TOURISM & CREATIVE STUDIES (UCE)
STOCK EXCHANGE
MIDLAND INSTITUTE
DEPT OF ART (UCE)
CATHEDRAL
THE PRIORY QUEENSWAY
PRIORY COURTS
CAB WAY
OPEN MARKET
CITY PLAZA SHOPPING CENTRE
PAVILIONS SHOPPING CENTRE

PARADISE CIRCUS QUEENSWAY
MUSEUM & ART GALLERY
CENTRAL LIBRARY
COUNCIL HOUSE
TOWN HALL
ROYAL SOCIETY OF ARTS
& TICKET SHOP
MARTINEAU SQUARE

CAMBRIAN WHARF
City Centre Gardens
BASKERVILLE HOUSE CIVIC CENTRE
BIRMINGHAM CONSERVATOIRE (UCE)
VICTORIA SQUARE
CHAMBERLAIN SQUARE
REPERTORY THEATRE
CENTENARY SQUARE
MOOR STREET STATION

NATIONAL INDOOR ARENA
NATIONAL SEA LIFE CENTRE
INTERNATIONAL CONVENTION CENTRE
HALL OF MEMORY
REGISTER OFFICE
CINEMA
NEW STREET STATION (lower level) & PALLASADES SHOPPING CENTRE
ST MARTINS CIRCUS
BULL RING
BULL RING SHOPPING CENTRE
OLD REP THEATRE
BUS STA

IKON GALLERY
BRINDLEY PLACE
GAS ST BASIN
HOLIDAY WHARF
ALEXANDRA THEATRE
CINEMA
Chinese Quarter
RAG MARKET
OPEN MKTS
ICE RINK & BOWLING ALLEY
WHOLESALE MARKETS
POLICE STA
COACH STATION

CRESCENT THEATRE
SHERBOURNE WHARF
BRASSHOUSE LANGUAGE CENTRE
HEBREW CONGREGATION
ARCADIAN CENTRE & CINEMA
HIPPODROME THEATRE

St Thomas Church Peace Garden
HEALTH CENTRE
Lee Bank
SCHOOL
SCHOOL

FIVE WAYS
LADYWOOD MIDDLE WAY
FIVE WAYS SHOPPING CENTRE
EDGBASTON SHOPPING CENTRE
FIVE WAYS STATION
ISLINGTON ROW MIDDLEWAY
LEE BANK MIDDLEWAY

Birmingham

0   200 metres

THE WEST, KIDDERMINSTER RING ROAD — A4540 — A456 — A4167 — RING ROAD
THE SOUTH WEST (M5), BROMSGROVE
COVENTRY, THE SOUTH (M42), WARWICK — A41

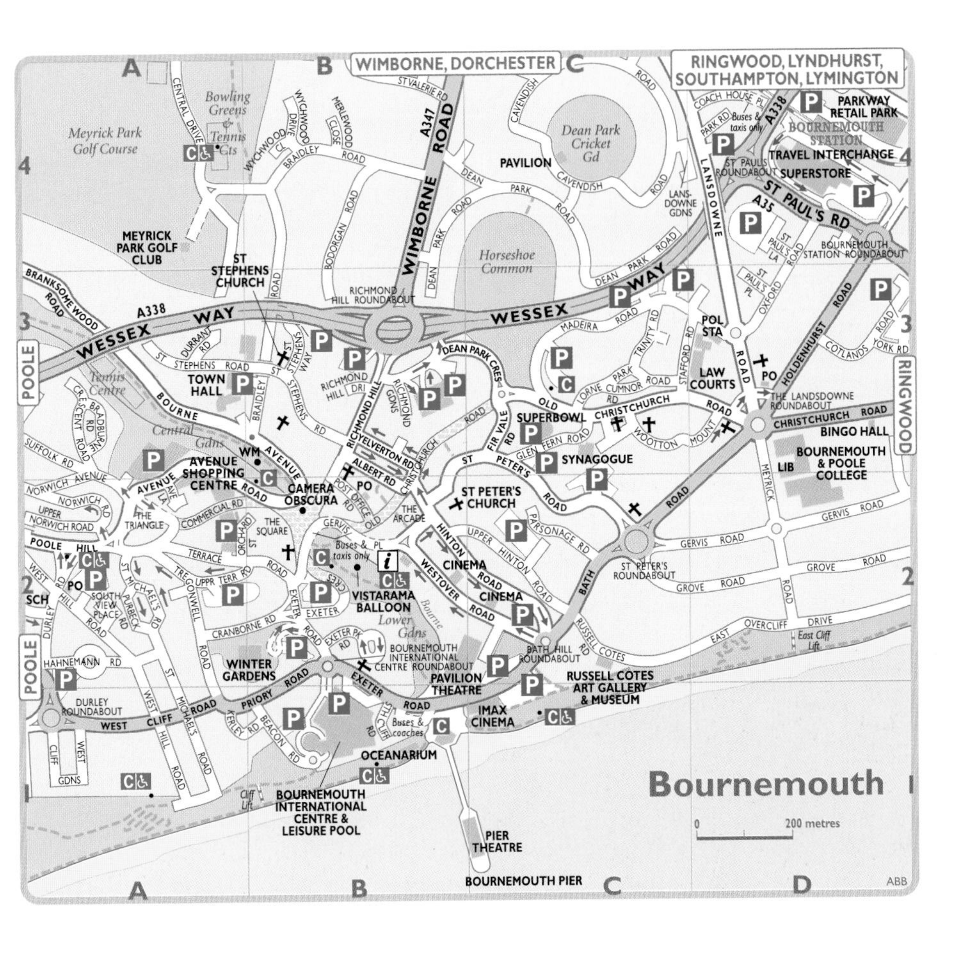

Bournemouth

Bournemouth

Bournemouth is found on atlas page 12,
grid reference 0890

Albert Road	B2-B3	Orchard Street	A2-B2
Avenue Lane	A2	Oxford Road	D3-D4
Avenue Road	A2-A3-B2	Park Road	D4
Bath Road	C2-D2-D3	Parsonage Road	C2
Beacon Road	B1	Poole Hill	A2
Bodorgan Road	B3-B4	Post Office Road	B2
Bourne Avenue	A3-B3-B2	Priory Road	A1-B1-B2
Bradburne Road	A3	Purbeck Road	A2
Braidley Road	B3-B4	Richmond Gardens	B3
Branksome Wood Road	A3-A4	Richmond Hill	B3
Cavendish Road	C4	Richmond Hill Drive	B3
Central Drive	A3-A4	Russell Cotes Road	C2
Christchurch Road	D3	St Michael's Road	A1-A2
Coach House Place	D4	St Paul's Lane	D4
Commercial Road	A2-B2	St Paul's Place	D3
Cumnor Road	C3	St Paul's Road	D4
Cotlands Road	D3	St Peter's Road	B2-B3-C3-C2
Cranborne Road	A2-B2	St Stephens Road	A3-B3
Crescent Road	A3	St Stephens Way	B3
Dean Park Crescent	B3-C3	St Valerie Road	B4
Dean Park Road	B3-B4-C4	South Cliff Road	B1
Durley Road	A2	South View Place	A2
Durrant Road	A2	Stafford Road	C3-D3
East Overcliff Drive	C2-D2	Suffolk Road	A3
Exeter Crescent	B2	Terrace Road	A2-B2
Exeter Park Road	B2	The Square	B2
Exeter Road	B1-B2	The Triangle	A2
Fir Vale Road	C3	Tregonwell Road	A1-A2
Gervis Place	B2	Trinity Road	C3
Gervis Road	C2-D2	Upper Hinton Road	B2-C2
Glen Fern Road	C3	Upper Norwich Road	A2
Grove Road	C2-D2	Upper Terrace Road	A2
Hahnemann Road	A2	Wessex Way	A3-B3-C3-D4
Hinton Road	B2-C2	West Cliff Gardens	A1
Holdenhurst Road	D3-D4	West Cliff Road	A1
Kerley Road	A1-B1	West Hill Road	A1-A2
Lansdowne Gardens	C4-D4	Westover Road	B2-C2
Lansdowne Road	C4-D4-D3	Wimborne Road	B3-B4
Lorne Park Road	C3	Wootton Mount	C3-D3
Madeira Road	C3	Wychwood Close	B4
Merlewood Close	B4	Wychwood Drive	B4
Meyrick Road	D2-D3	Yelverton Road	B3
Norwich Avenue	A2-A3	York Road	D3
Norwich Road	A2		
Old Christchurch Road	B2-C3-D3		

165

Birmingham

Birmingham is found on atlas page 61,
grid reference 0786

Acorn Grove	A4-A5	Cambridge Street	B4-C4	Five Ways	A1	Kent Street	E1-E2	Newhall Hill	B5	Smith Street	B8
Albert Street	E5-F5	Camden Drive	A5-B5	Fleet Street	C5	Kenyon Street	B7	Newhall Street	B6-C6-C5	Snow Hill Queensway	D6
Albion Street	A5-A6-B6	Camden Street	A6-A5-B5	Florence Street	D2	Key Hill	A8	Newton Street	E6-E5	Southacre Avenue	E1
Aldgate Grove	C8	Cannon Street	D4-E4	Fox Street	F5	King Edward's Road	A4-B4	Northwood Street	B6-C6-C7	Spencer Street	A7-B7
Allison Street	F3-F4	Caroline Street	B7-B6-C6	Frederick Road	A1	Kingston Row	B4	Nova Scotia Street	F6	Staniforth Street	E7-E8
Arthur Place	A5	Carrs Lane	E4	Frederick Street	A6-B6	Ladywell Walk	E3	Old Square	E5	Station Street	D3
Aston Road	F8	Carver Street	A5-A6	Freeman Street	F4	Ladywood Middleway	A1-A2	Oozel's Street	B3	Steelhouse Lane	E6
Aston Street	E6-F6-F7	Cecil Street	D7-D8-E8	Gas Street	B3-C3	Lancaster Circus Q'way	E6-E7	Oxford Street	F3	Stephenson Street	D4-E4
Augusta Street	B7	Centenary Square	C4	George Road	B1	Lancaster Street	E7	Paradise Circus Q'way	C4-C5	Stoke Way	B2
Bagot Street	E7-E8	Chamberlain Square	C4	George Street	B5-B6	Lawson Street	E7	Park Street	F4-F5	Suffolk Street Q'way	C4-C3-D3
Banbury Street	F5	Chapel Street	F5	Gooch Street North	E1-E2	Lee Bank Middleway	B1-C1	Pemberton Street	A6-A7	Summer Hill Road	A5
Barford Street	F1-F2-F3	Chapmans Passage	D2	Gough Street	D3	Legge Lane	A5-B5	Pershore Street	E3-E2-F2	Summer Hill Street	A4-A5
Barr Street	A8-B8-B7-C7	Charles Henry Street	F1-F2	Graham Street	B5-B6	Legge Street	E8-F8	Pinfold Street	D4	Summer Hill Terrace	A5-B5
Bartholomew Row	F5	Charlotte Street	B5-C5-C6	Grant Street	C1-D1	Lionel Street	C5-C6	Pitsford Street	A7	Summer Lane	D7-D8
Bartholomew Street	F5	Cheapside	F2	Granville Street	B3-B2-C2	Lister Street	F7-F8	Pope Street	A5-A6	Summer Row	B5-C5
Barwick Street	D5	Church Street	D5	Great Charles Street Q'way	C5	Livery Street	C7-C6-D5	Powell Street	A5	Swallow Street	C4-D4
Bath Row	B1-C2	Claybrook Street	E2	Great Colmore Street	C1-D1	Louisa Street	B4	Price Street	E7	Temple Row	D5-E5
Bath Street	D7-E7	Clement Street	A4-A5-B5	Great Hampton Row	C7-C8	Love Lane	F8	Princip Street	D7-E7	Temple Row West	D5
Beak Street	D3	Cleveland Street	D7-E7-D8	Great Hampton Street	B8-B7	Loveday Street	D7-E7	Printing House Street	E6	Temple Street	D4
Bell Barn Road	C1	Coleshill Street	F6-F7	Great King Street	A8-B8	Lower Essex Street	E1-E2	Pritchett Street	E8	Tenby Street	A6
Bennetts Hill	C5-D5-D4	Colmore Circus Q'way	D5-E6	Grosvenor Street	F5-F6	Lower Loveday Street	D7	Rake Way	B2	Tenby Street North	A6
Berkley Street	B3-C3	Colmore Row	D4-D5	Grosvenor Street West	A2-A3	Lower Severn Street	D3	Rea Street	F2-F3	Tennant Street	A1-B2-B3
Bishop Street	E1-F1-F2	Commercial Street	C2-C3	Hadfield Croft	B8	Lower Tower Street	D8-E8	Rea Street South	F1-F2	The Priory Queensway	E5
Bishopsgate Street	A2-B2-B1	Constitution Hill	C7-D7	Hagley Road	A1	Ludgate Hill	C5-C6	Regent Parade	B6	Thorpe Street	D2-E2-E3
Bissell Street	F1	Cornwall Street	C5-D5-D6	Hall Street	B7	Macdonald Street	E1-F1	Regent Place	B6	Tower Street	C8-D8
Blucher Street	C3-D3-D2	Corporation Street	E4-E5-E6	Hampton Street	C7-D7	Manchester Street	E8	Regent Street	B6	Townsend Way	A4-B4
Bond Street	C7	Corporation Street	E7-F8	Hanley Street	C5	Margaret Street	C5	Rickman Drive	D1	Unett Street	B8-C8
Bordesley Street	F4	Coventry Street	F4	Harbourne Road	A1	Marshall Street	C2-D2	Ridley Street	C2	Upper Gough Street	C2-D2
Bow Street	D2	Cox Street	C6	Harford Street	B7-B8	Martineau Square	E5	Roseland Way	B1-B2	Upper Marshall Street	C2
Bradford Street	F3	Cregoe Street	C1-C2	Heaton Street	A8	Mary Ann Street	C7	Royal Mail Street	C3-D3	Uxbridge Street	C8
Branston Street	A8-B8-B7	Dale End	E5	Helena Street	B5	Mary Street	B6-B7-C6	Ruston Street	A2	Vesey Street	E7
Brearley Street	C8-D8	Dalton Street	E6	Henrietta Street	C6-C7-D7	Masshouse Circus Q'way	E5-F5	Ryland Street	A2	Victoria Square	D4
Brewery Street	E8	Dartmouth Middleway	F8	Henstead Street	E1-E2	Meriden Street	F3-F4	St Chad's Circus Q'way	D6	Vittoria Street	B6
Bridge Street	B3-C3	Digbeth	F3	High Street	E4	Midford Grove	C1	St Chad's Queensway	D6-E7-E7	Vyse Street	A6-A7-A8
Brindley Drive	B4	Dudley Street	E3	Hill Street	C4-D4-D4	Midford Croft	C8	St George's Street	C7-C8	Ward Street	D8
Brindley Place	B3	Eden Place	C4-C5	Hinckley Street	D3-E3	Mill Lane	F3	St Mark's Crescent	A4	Warstone Lane	A6-B6-B7
Bristol Street	D1-D2	Edgbaston Street	E3	Hockley Hill	A8	Mill Street	F8	St Martin's Lane	E3-F3	Warstone Parade East	A6-A7
Broad Street	A2-B2-B4-C4	Edmund Street	D5	Hockley Street	B7-B8	Moat Lane	F3	St Martin's Street	A2	Washington Street	C2
Bromsgrove Street	D1-D2-E2	Edward Street	A4-B4-B5	Holland Street	B5	Moland Street	E7-E8	St Martins Circus Q'way	E3-E4	Water Street	C6-D6
Brook Street	B6-C6	Ellis Street	D2-D3	Holliday Street	B2-C2-C3	Moor Street Q'way	E4-F4-F5	St Paul's Square	C6	Waterloo Street	D4
Browning Street	A3	Elvetham Road North	C1	Holloway Circus Q'way	D2-D3	Moreton Street	A6	St Philips Place	D5-E5	Weaman Street	D6
Brownsea Drive	D2	Ernest Street	D2	Holloway Head	C2-D2	Morville Street	A3	St Vincent Street	A3-A4	Well Lane	F4
Brunel Street	C4-D4-D3	Essex Street	D2-E2	Holt Street	F7-F8	Moseley Street	F2	Sand Pitts Parade	A5-B5	Well Street	B8
Buckingham Street	C7-C8	Essington Street	A2-A3	Howard Street	C7	Mott Street	C7	Sandy Way	B2	Wheeleys Lane	B1-C1
Bull Ring	E4	Ethel Street	D4	Hurst Street	E2-F2-F1	Navigation Street	D3-D4	Scotland Street	B4	Wheeleys Road	B1
Bull Street	E5	Exeter Street	D2	Hylton Street	A8	Needless Alley	D4	Severn Street	C3-D3	Whittal Street	D6-E6
Calthorpe Road	A1	Fazeley Street	F5	Icknield Street	A6-A7-A8	Nelson Street	A4-A5	Shadwell Street	D6-D7	William Street	B1-B2
				Inge Street	E2	New Bartholomew Street	F4-F5	Shaws Passage	F4	William Street North	D7
				Irving Street	D2	New Canal Street	F4-F5	Sheepcote Street	A4-A3-B3-B2	Windmill Street	D2
				Islington Row Middleway	A1-B1	New Market Street	C5-D5	Sherbourne Street	A2-A3	Woodcock Street	F7-F8
				James Street	B6	New Street	D4-E4	Sherlock Street	E1-E2-F2	Wrentham Street	D1-E1
				Jennens Road	F5-F6	New Summer Street	C8-D8	Skinner Lane	E2	Wynn Street	D1
				John Bright Street	D3	New Town Row	D8-E8	Smallbrook Queensway	D3-E3		

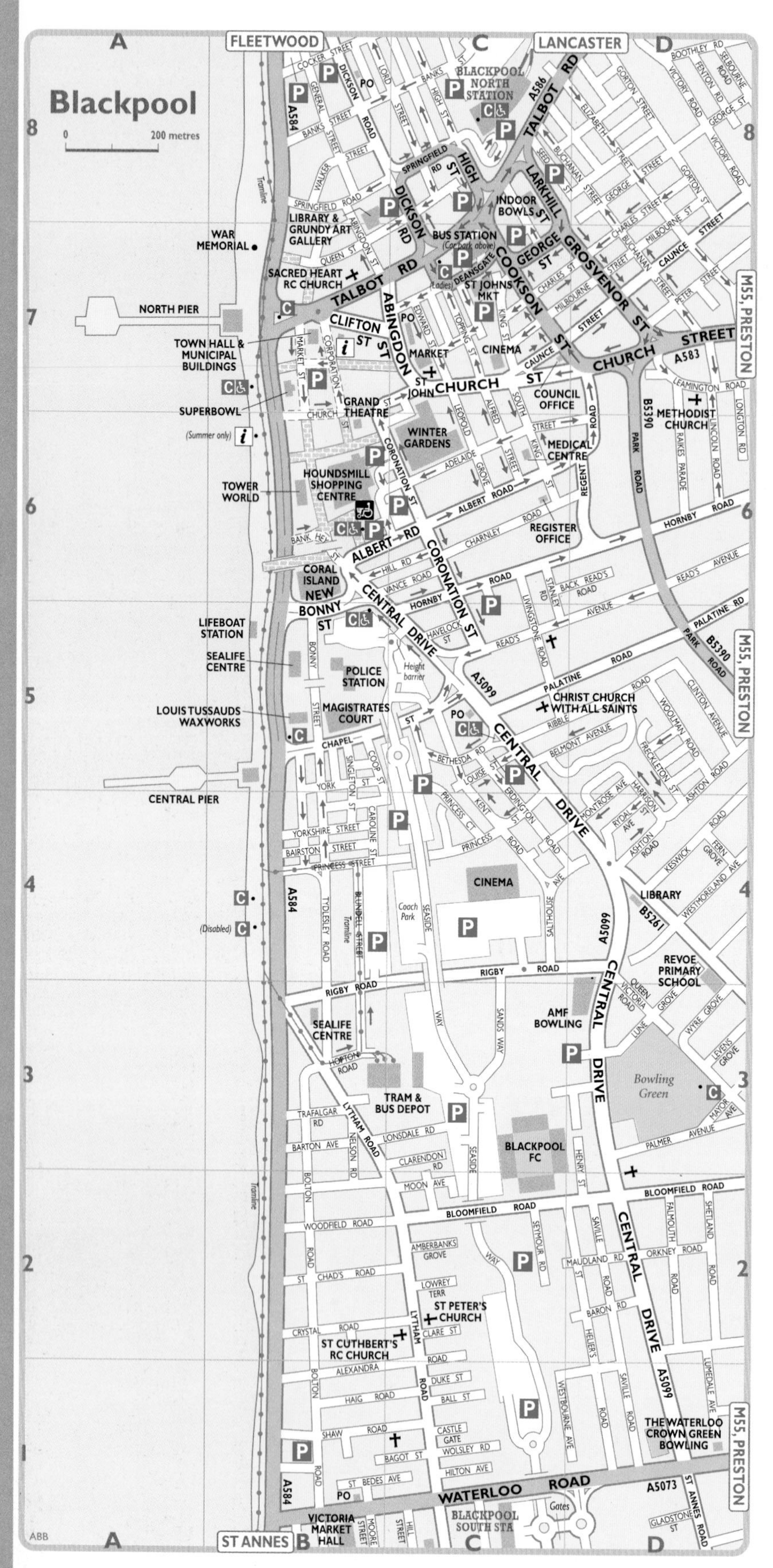

Blackpool

Blackpool is found on atlas page **80**,
grid reference **3036**

Abingdon Street	B8-B7-C7
Adelaide Street	C6-D6
Albert Road	B6-C6
Alexandra Road	B1-C1-C2
Alfred Street	C6-C7
Amberbanks Grove	C2
Ashton Road	D4-D5
Back Read's Road	C6-D6
Bagot Street	B1-C1
Bairston Street	B4
Ball Street	C1
Bank Hey Street	B6
Banks Street	B8-C8
Baron Road	D2
Barton Avenue	C5-D5
Belmont Avenue	C5-D5
Bethesda Road	C5
Bloomfield Road	C2-D2
Blundell Street	B4
Bolton Road	B1-B2-B3
Bonny Street	B5
Boothley Road	D8
Buchanan Street	C8-D8-D7
Caroline Street	B4
Castle Gate	C1
Caunce Street	C7-D7-D8
Central Drive	B6-C5-D4-D1
Chapel Street	B5-C5
Charles Street	C7-D7-D8
Charnley Road	C6-D6
Church Street	B6-B7-C7-D7
Clare Street	C2
Clarendon Road	C3
Clifton Street	B7
Clinton Avenue	D5
Cocker Street	B8
Cookson Street	C7
Coop Street	B4-B5
Coronation Street	B6-C6-C5
Corporation Street	B6-B7
Crystal Road	B2-C2
Deansgate	C7
Dickson Road	B8-C8-C7
Duke Street	C1
Edward Street	C7
Elizabeth Street	C8-D8
Erdington Road	C4-C5
Falmouth Road	D2
Fenton Road	D8
Fern Grove	D4
Freckleton Street	D4-D5
General Street	B8
George Street	C7-D8
Gladstone Street	D1
Gorton Street	D8
Grosvenor Street	C7-D7
Haig Road	B1-C1
Harrison Street	D4-D5
Havelock Street	C5
Henry Street	D2-D3
High Street	C8
Hill Road	B6-C6
Hill Street	C1
Hilton Avenue	C1
Hopton Road	B3
Hornby Road	C5-C6-D6
Kent Road	C4-C5
Keswick Road	D4-D5
King Street	C7
Larkhill Street	C8
Leamington Road	D7
Leopold Grove	C6-C7
Levens Grove	D3
Lincoln Road	D6-D7
Livingstone Road	C5-C6
Longton Road	D6-D7
Lonsdale Road	B3-C3
Lord Street	B8-C8
Louise Street	C5
Lowrey Terrace	C2
Lumedale Avenue	D1-D2
Lune Grove	D3-D4
Lytham Road	B3-C2-C1
Market Street	B7
Maudland Road	C2-D2
Mayor Avenue	D3
Milbourne Street	C7-D7-D8
Montrose Avenue	D4-D5
Moon Avenue	C2
Moore Street	B1
Nelson Road	B2-B3
New Bonny Street	B5-B6
Orkney Road	D2
Palatine Road	C5-D5-D6
Palmer Avenue	D3
Park Road	D5-D6-D7
Peter Street	D7
Princess Court	C4-C5

Princess Street	B4-C4
Queen Street	B7
Queen Victoria Road	D3-D4
Raikes Parade	D6-D7
Read's Avenue	C5-D5-D6
Regent Road	D6-D7
Ribble Road	C5-D5
Rigby Road	B3-C4-D4
Rydal Avenue	D4
St Annes Road	D1
St Bedes Avenue	B1-C1
St Chad's Road	B2-C2
St Helier's Road	D1-D2
Salthouse Avenue	C4-D4
Sands Way	C3-C4
Saville Road	D1-D2
Seaside Way	C1-C3-C5-C8
Seed Street	C8
Selbourne Road	D8
Seymour Road	C2
Shaw Road	B1-C1
Shetland Road	D2
Singleton Street	B4-B5
South King Street	C6-C7
Springfield Road	B8-C8
Stanley Road	C5-C6
Talbot Road	B7-C7-C8
Topping Street	C7
Trafalgar Road	B3
Tydlesley Road	B3-B4
Vance Road	B6-C6
Victory Road	D8
Walker Street	B8
Waterloo Road	B1-C1-D1
Westbourne Avenue	C1-D1
Westmoreland Avenue	D4
Wolsley Road	C1
Woodfield Road	B2-C2
Woolman Road	D5
Wyre Grove	D3
York Street	B5
Yorkshire Street	B4

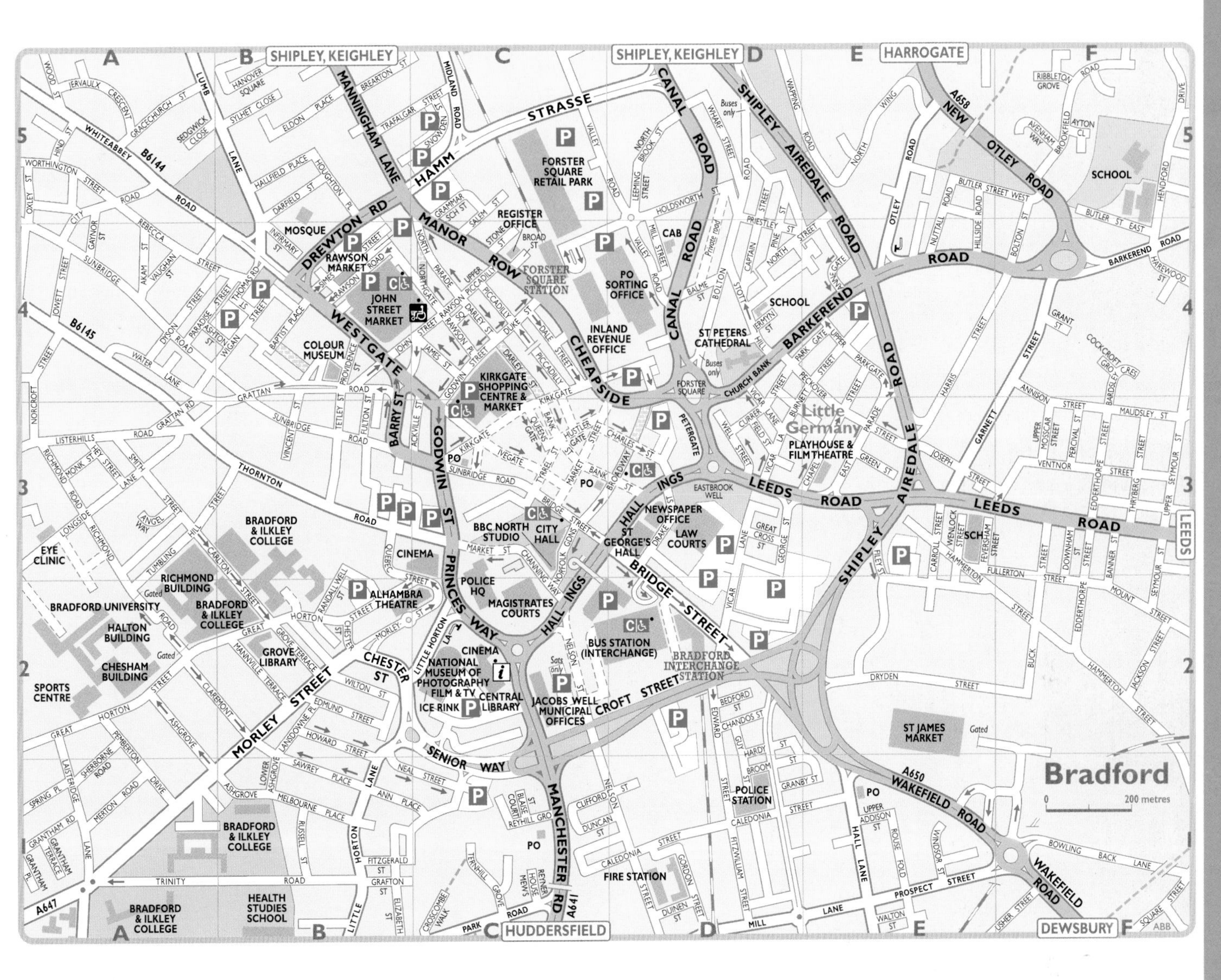

Bradford

Bradford is found on atlas page **82**,
grid reference 1632

Ackville Street	C3-C4	Carroll Street	E2-E3	Fitzgerald Street	B1	Ivegate	C3	Northgate	C4	Snowden Street	C5
Akam Street	A4	Chandos Street	D2	Fitzwilliam Street	D1	Jackson Street	F2	Nuttall Road	E4-E5	Spring Place	A1
Angel Way	A3	Channing Way	C2-C3	Fullerton Street	E3-F2	James Street	C4	Otley Road	E4-E5	Square Street	F1
Ann Place	B1-C1	Chapel Street	D3-E3-E4	Fulton Street	B3-B4	Jermyn Street	D4	Oxley Street	A4-A5	Stone Street	C4
Anne Gate	E4	Charles Street	C3-D3	Garnett Street	E3-F3-F4	Jervaulx Crescent	A5	Paradise Street	A4-B4	Stott Hill	D4
Annison Street	F3-F4	Cheapside	C4-D4-D3	Gaynor Street	A4-A5	John Street	B4-C4	Park Gate	D4-E4	Sunbridge Road	A4-B4-C3
Ashgrove	A2-A1-B1	Chester Street	B2	George Street	D3	Joseph Street	E3-F3	Park Road	C1	Sylhet Close	B5
Ashton Street	A4-B4	Church Bank	D3-D4	Godwin Street	C3-C4	Jowett Street	A4	Peckover Street	D4-E4-E3	Ternhill Grove	C1
Avenham Way	F5	City Road	A4-A5	Gordon Street	D1	Kirkgate	C3-C4	Pemberton Drive	A1-A2	Tetley Street	B3-B4
Ayton Close	F5	Claremont	A2-B2	Gracechurch Street	A5	Laisteridge Lane	A1-A2	Percival Street	F3	Thornton Road	A3-B3-C3
Balme Street	C3-D3	Clifford Street	C1-D1	Grafton Street	B1	Lansdowne Place	B2	Petergate	D3	Thryberg Street	F3
Bank Street	C3-D3	Cockcroft Grove	F4	Grammar School Street	C5	Leeds Road	D3-E3-F3	Piccadilly	C4	Trafalgar Street	B5-C5
Banner Street	F2-F3	Croft Street	C2-D2	Granby Street	D1-E1	Leeming Street	D5	Pine Street	D4-D5	Trinity Road	A1-B1
Baptist Place	B4	Croscombe Walk	C1	Grant Street	F4	Listerhills Road	A3	Priestley Street	D4-D5	Tumbling Street	A2-A3-B3
Bardsley Crescent	F3-F4	Currer Street	D3-D4	Grantham Place	A1	Little Horton Lane	B1-B2-C2	Princes Way	C2-C3	Tyrrel Street	C3
Barkerend Road	D4-E4-F4	Dale Street	C4	Grantham Road	A1	Longside Lane	A3	Prospect Street	E1-F1	Upper Addison Street	E1
Barry Street	B3-B4	Darfield Street	B5	Grantham Terrace	A1	Lower Ashgrove	B1	Providence Street	B4	Upper Mosscar Street	F3
Bedford Street	D2	Darley Street	C4	Grattan Road	A3-B3-B4	Lumb Lane	A5-B5	Quebec Street	B3-C2	Upper Parkgate	E4
Bolton Road	D4-D5	Downham Street	F3	Great Cross Street	D3	Manchester Road	C1	Queens Gate	C3	Upper Piccadilly	C4
Bolton Street	F4-F5	Drake Street	D3	Green Street	E3	Mannville Terrace	B2	Randall Well Street	B2-B3	Upper Seymour Street	F3-F4
Bowling Back Lane	F1	Drewton Road	B4-B5	Great Horton Road	A2-B2-C2	Manor Row	B5-C4	Rawson Place	C4	Usher Street	E1-F1
Brearton Street	B5-C5	Dryden Street	E2-F2	Grove Terrace	B2	Market Street	C3	Rawson Road	B4	Valley Road	C5-D5-D4
Bridge Street	C3-D3-D2	Duinen Street	D1	Guy Street	D1-D2	Maudsley Street	F3	Rawson Square	C4	Vaughan Street	A4
Broad Street	C4	Duke Street	B5	Hall Ings	C2-C3-D3	Melbourne Place	B1	Rebecca Street	A5-A4-B4	Ventnor Street	F3
Broadway	C3-D3	Duncan Street	C1-D1	Hall Lane	E1	Merton Road	A1	Reyhill Grove	C1	Vicar Lane	D2-D3-D4
Brookfield Road	F5	Dyson Street	A4	Hallfield Place	B5	Midland Road	C5	Reyner House Mews	C1	Vincent Street	B3-B4
Broom Street	D1	East Parade	E3-E4	Hamm Strasse	B5-C5-D5	Mill Lane	D1-E1	Ribbleton Grove	F5	Wakefield Road	E1-F1
Buck Street	F2-F3	Edderthorpe Street	F2-F3	Hammerton Street	E3-E2-F2-F1	Mill Street	D4	Richmond Road	A2-A3	Walton Street	E1
Burnett Street	D3-E4	Edmund Street	B2	Hanover Square	B5	Monk Street	B1	Rouse Fold	E1	Wapping Road	D5-E5
Butler Street East	F4-F5	Edward Street	D1-D2	Hardy Street	D2	Morley Street	A1-B1-B2-C2	Russell Street	B1	Water Lane	A4
Butler Street West	E5-F5	Eldon Place	B5	Harewood Street	F4	Mount Street	B2	St Blaise Court	C1	Well Street	D3
Caledonia Street	C1-D1-E1	Elizabeth Street	B1	Harris Street	E3-E4-F4	Neal Street	B2-B1-C1	St Thomas Road	B4	Wenlock Street	C4
Canal Road	D4-D5	Feversham Street	E3	Hendford Drive	F4-F5	Nelson Street	C2-C1-D1	Salem Street	C4-C5	Westgate	B4-C4
Captain Street	D4-D5	Field Street	D3	Hey Street	A3	New Otley Road	E5-F5-F4	Sawrey Place	B1-B2	Wharf Street	D5
Carlton Street	A3-B3-B2	Filey Street	E3	Hillside Road	E4-E5	Norcroft Street	A3-A4	Sedgwick Close	A5	Whiteabbey Road	A5-B4
				Hind Street	A5	Norfolk Gardens	C2-C3	Senior Way	C1-C2	Wigan Street	A4-B4
				Holdsworth Street	D5	North Brook Street	D5	Seymour Street	F2-F3	Wilton Street	B2
				Houghton Place	B5	North Parade	C4	Sherborne Road	A1-A2	Windsor Street	E1
				Howard Street	B2	North Street	D4-E4-E5	Shipley Airedale Road	D5-E5-E3-E2	Wood Street	A5
				Hustler Gate	C3	North Wing	E5	Simes Street	B4	Worthington Street	A5
				Infirmary Street	B4			Smith Street	A3		

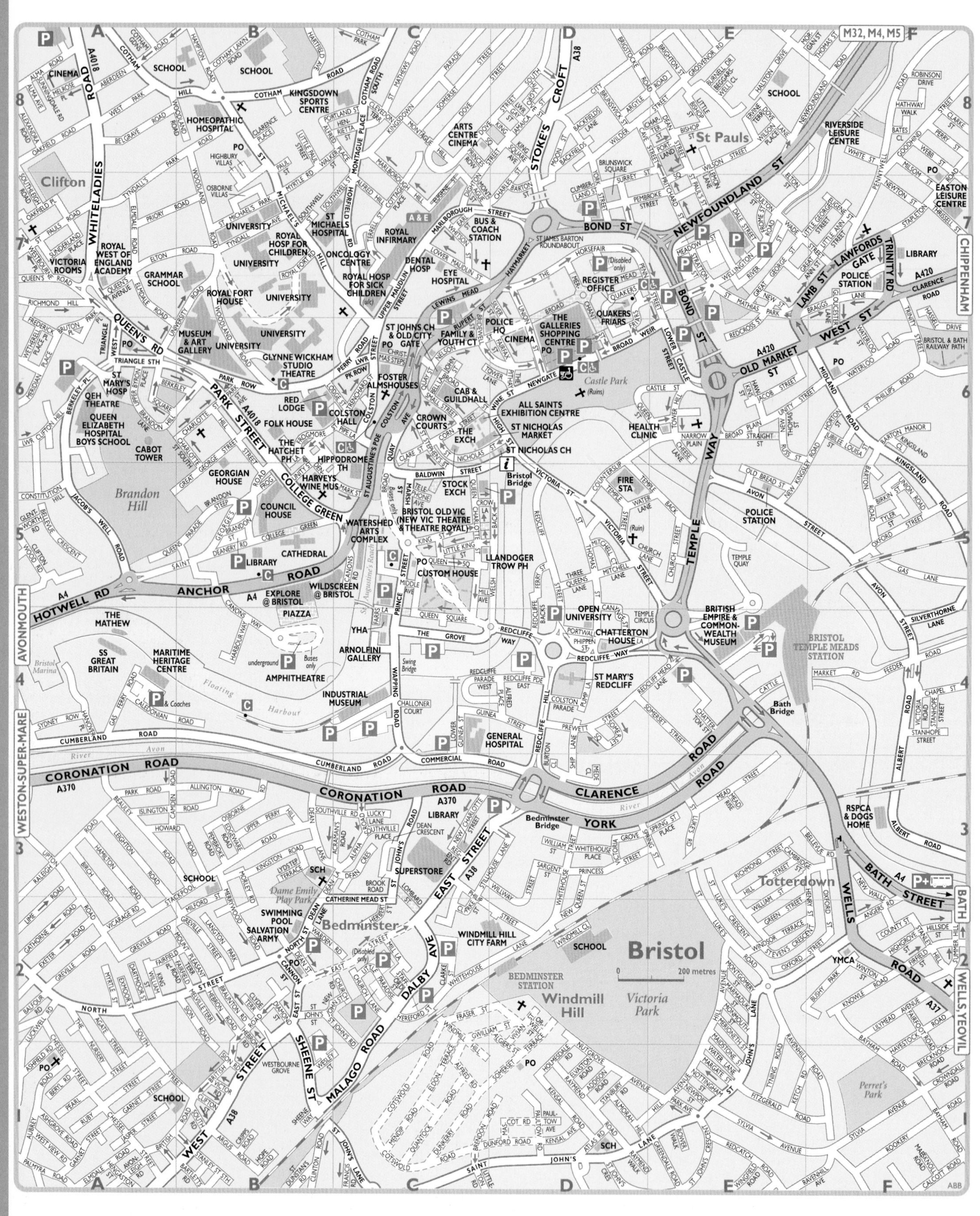
M32, M4, M5
CHIPPENHAM
AVONMOUTH
WESTON-SUPER-MARE
BATH
WELLS,YEOVIL
Clifton
St Pauls
Bristol
Bedminster
Totterdown
Windmill Hill
Victoria Park
Brandon Hill
Castle Park (Ruins)
Dame Emily Play Park
Perret's Park
Floating Harbour
River Avon
Bristol Marina
BRISTOL TEMPLE MEADS STATION
BEDMINSTER STATION
200 metres
WHITELADIES ROAD
QUEEN'S RD
PARK STREET
COLLEGE GREEN
ANCHOR ROAD
HOTWELL RD
CORONATION ROAD
CUMBERLAND ROAD
CLARENCE ROAD
YORK ROAD
BATH STREET
WELLS ROAD
TEMPLE WAY
BOND ST
NEWFOUNDLAND ST
STOKE'S CROFT
OLD MARKET ST
WEST ST
LAWFORDS GATE
EAST STREET
WEST STREET
NORTH STREET
MALAGO ROAD
DALBY AVE
SHEENE ST
COTHAM HILL
ST MICHAEL'S HILL
MARLBOROUGH STREET
HAYMARKET
REDCLIFFE WAY
VICTORIA STREET
PRINCE STREET
CINEMA
SCHOOL
HOMEOPATHIC HOSPITAL
KINGSDOWN SPORTS CENTRE
ARTS CENTRE CINEMA
UNIVERSITY
ROYAL WEST OF ENGLAND ACADEMY
VICTORIA ROOMS
GRAMMAR SCHOOL
ST MICHAELS HOSPITAL
ROYAL HOSP FOR CHILDREN
ROYAL INFIRMARY
ONCOLOGY CENTRE
DENTAL HOSP
EYE HOSPITAL
BUS & COACH STATION
ROYAL HOSP FOR SICK CHILDREN
ROYAL FORT HOUSE
MUSEUM & ART GALLERY
GLYNNE WICKHAM STUDIO THEATRE
ST MARY'S HOSP
QEH THEATRE
QUEEN ELIZABETH HOSPITAL BOYS SCHOOL
CABOT TOWER
RED LODGE
FOLK HOUSE
COLSTON HALL
FOSTER ALMSHOUSES
ST JOHNS CH & OLD CITY GATE
FAMILY & YOUTH CT
POLICE HQ
CINEMA
THE GALLERIES SHOPPING CENTRE
REGISTER OFFICE
QUAKERS FRIARS
CAB & GUILDHALL
CROWN COURTS
THE EXCH
ALL SAINTS EXHIBITION CENTRE
ST NICHOLAS MARKET
ST NICHOLAS CH
HEALTH CLINIC
THE HATCHET PH
HIPPODROME TH
GEORGIAN HOUSE
HARVEYS WINE MUS
COUNCIL HOUSE
WATERSHED ARTS COMPLEX
STOCK EXCH
BRISTOL OLD VIC (NEW VIC THEATRE & THEATRE ROYAL)
Bristol Bridge
FIRE STA
POLICE STATION
CATHEDRAL
LIBRARY
CUSTOM HOUSE
LLANDOGER TROW PH
EXPLORE @ BRISTOL
WILDSCREEN @ BRISTOL
PIAZZA
THE MATHEW
SS GREAT BRITAIN
MARITIME HERITAGE CENTRE
YHA
ARNOLFINI GALLERY
AMPHITHEATRE
INDUSTRIAL MUSEUM
OPEN UNIVERSITY
CHATTERTON HOUSE
ST MARY'S REDCLIFF
BRITISH EMPIRE & COMMON-WEALTH MUSEUM
Bath Bridge
GENERAL HOSPITAL
RIVERSIDE LEISURE CENTRE
EASTON LEISURE CENTRE
BRISTOL & BATH RAILWAY PATH
RSPCA & DOGS HOME
Bedminster Bridge
SUPERSTORE
SWIMMING POOL
SALVATION ARMY
WINDMILL HILL CITY FARM
YMCA
A4018
A38
A420
A4
A370
A37
ABB

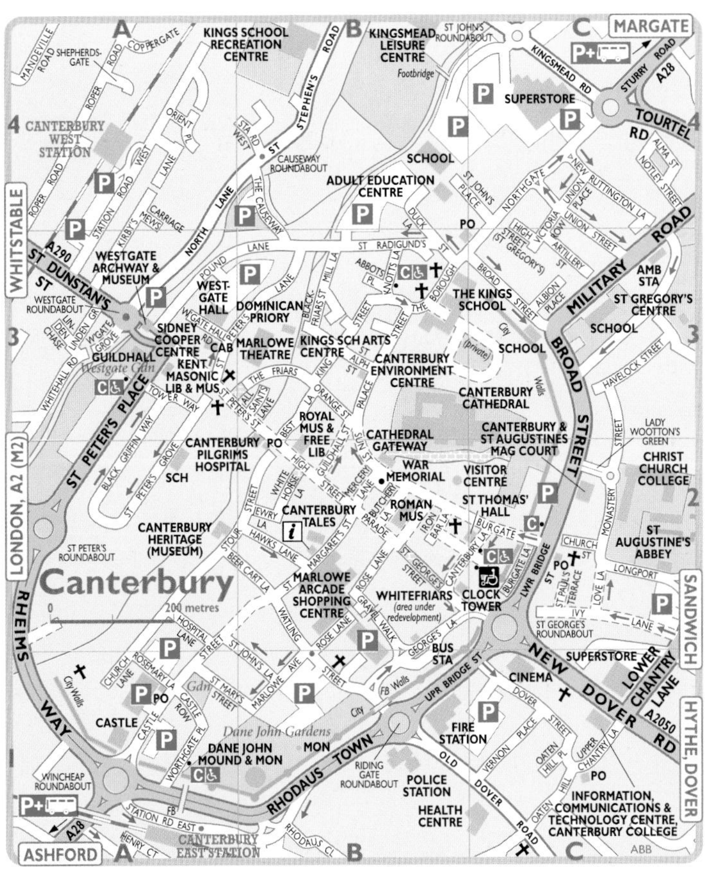

Canterbury

Canterbury is found on atlas page **29**,
grid reference **1457**

Abbots Place	B3	Kingsmead Road	C4	St Dunstan's Street	A3-A4
Albion Place	C3	Kirby's Lane	A3-A4	St George's Street	B2
All Saints Lane	B3	Knotts Lane	B3	St John's Lane	A2-B1
Alma Street	C4	Lady Wootton's Green	C2	St John's Place	B4-C4
Artillery Street	C3	Linden Chase	A3	St Margaret's Street	B2
Beer Cart Lane	A2-B2	Linden Green	A3	St Mary's Street	A1-B1
Best Lane	B3	Longport	C2	St Paul's Terrace	C2
Black Griffin Way	A2-A3	Love Lane	C2	St Peter's Grove	A2-A3
Blackfriars Street	B3	Lower Bridge Street	C2	St Peter's Lane	A3-B3
Broad Street	C2-C3	Lower Chantry Lane	C1-C2	St Peter's Place	A2-A3
Burgate	C2	Mandeville Road	A4	St Peter's Street	A3-B3
Burgate Lane	C2	Marlowe Avenue	B1	St Radigund's Street	B3
Butchery Lane	B2	Mercery Lane	B2	St Stephen's Road	B4
Canterbury Lane	B2-C2	Military Road	C3-C4	Shepherd's Gate	A4
Carriage Mews	A4	Mill Lane	B3	Station Road East	A2-B1
Castle Row	A1	Monastery Street	C2-C3	Station Road West	A3-A4-B4
Castle Street	A1-A2	New Dover Road	C1-C2	Stour Street	A2-B2
Church Lane	A1	New Ruttington Lane	C4	Sturry Road	C4
Church Street	C2	North Lane	A3-A4-B4	Sun Street	B2-B3
Coppergate	A4	Northgate	C3-C4	The Borough	B3
Cossington Road	C1	Notley Street	C4	The Causeway	B3-B4
Dover Street	C1	Oaten Hill	C1	The Friars	B3
Duck Lane	B4	Oaten Hill Place	C1	Tourtel Road	C4
George's Lane	B2	Old Dover Road	B1-C1	Tower Way	A3
Gravel Walk	B2	Orange Street	B3	Union Place	C4
Guildhall Street	B2-B3	Orient Place	A4	Union Street	C3-C4
Havelock Street	C3	Palace Street	B3	Upper Bridge Street	B1-B2
Hawks Lane	B2	Parade	B2	Upper Chantry Lane	C1
Henry Court	A1	Pound Lane	A3-B4	Vernon Place	C1
High Street	B2	Rheims Way	A1-A2	Victoria Row	C3-C4
High Street (St Gregory's)	C4	Rhodaus Close	B1	Watling Street	B1-B2
Hospital Lane	A2	Rhodaus Town	B1	Westgate Grove	A3
Iron Bar Lane	B2	Roper Road	A4	Westgate Hall Road	A3
Ivy Lane	C2	Rose Lane	B2	White Horse Lane	B2
Jewry Lane	B2	Rosemary Lane	A1	Whitehall Road	A3
King Street	B3	St Alphege Street	B3	Worthgate Place	A1

Bristol

Bristol is found on atlas page **34**,
grid reference **5972**

Aberdeen Road	A8-B8	Castle Street	D6-E6	Elmdale Road	A1	Kingsland Road	F5-F6	Paultow Road	D1	Spring Street	D3-E3
Agate Street	A1-A2	Catherine Mead Street	B2-C2	Elmdale Road	A6-A7	Kingston Road	B3	Pearl Street	A1	Stackpool Road	A2-B3
Albert Road	F3-F4	Cattle Market Road	E4-F4	Elton Road	A7-B7	Knowle Road	F2	Pembroke Street	D7-E7	Stafford Street	C2
Alfred Hill	C7	Cave Street	D8-E8	Elton Street	E7-E8	Lamb Street	E7-F7	Penn Street	D7-E7	Stanley Hill	F2
Alfred Place	B8-C8	Chapel Street	F4	Eugene Street	F7	Lawfords Gate	F7	Pennywell Road	F7-F8	Stanley Street South	B1
Alfred Place	D4	Charles Street	D7-D8	Exeter Road	A2	Leighton Road	A3	Perry Road	C6	Stapleton Road	F7-F8
Allington Road	B3	Charlotte Street	B6	Fairfax Street	D6	Lewins Mead	C7-D7	Philip Street	C3-C2-D2	Steven's Crescent	E2-F2
Alma Road	A8	Charlotte Street South	B6	Farrs Lane	C4-C5	Lilymead Avenue	F2	Portland Square	E7-E8	Stillhouse Lane	C3-D3
Almorah Hill	D1	Chatterton Street	E4	Feeder Road	F4	Lime Road	A2-A3	Portland Street	B8-C8	Stoke's Croft	D7-D8
Alpha Road	C3	Chessel Street	A1-A2	Ferry Street	D5	Little Ann Street	F7	Portwall Lane	D4	Stratton Street	E7
Anchor Road	A5-B5-C5	Christmas Steps	C6	Firfield Street	F2	Little Bishop Street	E8	Prewett Street	D4	Summer Hill	F2
Angers Road	F2-F3	Church Lane	C2	Fitzgerald Road	E1-F1	Little George Street	E7-F7	Prince Street	C4-C5	Surrey Street	D7-D8-E8
Argus Road	B1	Church Street	E5	Fraser Street	C1-D1	Little King Street	C5	Princess Street	D3	Sydney Row	A4
Atlas Road	D1	City Road	D8-E8	Frog Lane	B5-B6	Little Paradise	C2	Priory Road	A7-B7	Sylvia Avenue	E1-F1
Aubrey Road	A1	Clare Street	C6	Frogmore Street	B6-C6	Lodge Street	B6-C6	Pritchard Street	E7	Temple Back	D5-E5
Avon Street	E5-F5-F4	Clarence Road	D3-E3-E4	Garnet Street	A1	Lombard Street	C2-C3	Pump Lane	D4	Temple Quay	E5
Backfields	D8	Clarence Road	F7	Gas Ferry Road	A4	Louisa Street	F6	Quakers Friars	D6-D7	Temple Street	D5
Baldwin Street	C5-D6	Clevedon Terrace	C8	Gas Lane	F5	Lower Castle Street	E6	Quay Street	C6	Temple Way	E5-E6
Barton Road	F5-F6	Clifton Street	B1	Gathorne Road	A2	Lower Clifton Hill	A6	Queen Charlotte Street	C4-C5	Terrell Street	C7
Barton Street	D7	Clifton Wood Road	A5	Goodhind Street	F8	Lower Guinea Street	C4	Queen Square	C4-C5	The Grove	C4
Bath Street	F2-F3	Clinton Road	B1	Great George Street	A5-B5-B6	Lower Maudlin Street	C7	Queen Street	D6-E6	The Horsefair	D7
Beauley Road	A3-B3	College Green	B5-C5	Great George Street	E7	Lower Park Row	C6	Queen's Avenue	A7	The Nursery	A1-A2
Belgrave Road	A8	Colston Avenue	C6	Greendale Road	E1	Luckwell Road	A2	Queen's Road	A6-A7	The Pithay	D6
Bell Lane	C6	Colston Parade	D4	Greville Road	A2	Maidstone Street	E1-E2	Queens Parade	A5-B5	Thrissell Street	F7
Bellevue Road	E3-F3	Colston Street	C6	Greville Street	B2	Malago Road	B1-C1-C2	Raleigh Road	A2-A3	Tower Hill	E6
Berkeley Place	A6	Commercial Road	C3-D3	Grosvenor Road	E8	Margate Street	E1	Ravenhill Road	E2-E1-F1	Trenchard Street	C6
Berkeley Square	A6-B6	Constitution Hill	A5	Guinea Street	C4-D4	Marlborough Hill	C7-C8	Raymond Road	D1	Triangle South	A6
Birch Road	A2-A3	Corn Street	C6	Halston Drive	E8	Marlborough Street	C7-D7	Redcatch Road	E1	Triangle West	A6
Bishop Street	E8	Coronation Road	A3-B3-C3-D3	Hamilton Road	A2-A3	Marsh Street	C5	Redcliff Mead Lane	D4-E4	Trinity Road	F7
Bond Street	D7-E7-E6	Cotham Hill	A8-B8	Hampton Road	B8	Mead Street	E3	Redcliffe Backs	D4-D5	Trinity Street	F6-F7
Braggs Lane	E7-F7	Cotham Lawn Road	B8	Hanover Place	A4	Meadow Street	E7	Redcliffe Parade East	D4	Tyndall Avenue	B7
Brandon Steep	B5	Cotham Road	B8-C8	Harbour Way	B4	Melrose Place	C4-D4	Redcliffe Parade West	C4-D4	Tyndall's Park Road	A7-A8-B8
Brandon Street	B5	Cotham Road South	C8	Hartfield Avenue	B8	Merchant Street	D6-D7	Redcliff Street	D4-D5	Tyning Road	E1-E2
Braunton Road	B2	Cotswold Road	C1-C2	Haymarket	D7	Meridian Place	A6	Redcliff Way	D4	Union Road	F5
Brendon Road	C1-D1	Cottage Place	C7	Henry Street	E2-F2	Merrywood Road	B2-B3	Regent Road	C3	Union Street	D6-D7
Bridewell Street	C6-C7	Countership	D5-D6-E6	Herbert Street	C2	Middle Avenue	C5	Richmond Hill	A7	Unity Street	B5-B6
Brighton Street	E8	Cripps Road	A2	Hereford Street	C2	Midland Road	F6	Richmond Street	E3	Unity Street	E6-F6
Brigstocke Road	D8-E8	Cumberland Road	A4-B3-C3-C4	High Street	D6	Milford Street	B2-B3	River Street	E7	University Road	A6-B7
British Road	A1-B1-B2	Dalby Avenue	C2	Highgrove Street	F2	Mill Avenue	C5	Royal Fort Road	B7	Upper Byron Place	A6
Broad Mead	D6-D7	Dale Street	E7	Hill Avenue	D1-E1-E2	Mill Lane	C2	Ruby Street	A1	Upper Maudlin Street	C7
Broad Plain	E6	Dean Lane	B2-B3-C3	Hill Street	B5-B6	Milsom Street	F7-F8	Rupert Street	C6-C7-D7	Upper Perry Hill	B3
Broad Quay	C5-C6	Dean Street	B2	Hill Street	E3	Mitchell Lane	D5	Russ Street	E6	Upton Road	A2-A3
Broad Street	C6	Dean Street	E8	Hillgrove Street	D8	Montague Hill	C8	Saint George's Road	A5-B5	Vicarage Road	A2
Broad Weir	D6-E6	Deanery Road	B5	Holmesdale Road	D1	Montague Place	C8	Saint John's Lane	C1-D1-E1-E2	Victoria Street	D5-E5
Brook Road	C3	Denmark Street	B5-C5	Horfield Road	C7	Montgomery Street	E2	St Augustine's Parade	C5-C6	Vivian Street	D2
Brunswick Square	D7	Diamond Street	B2	Horton Street	F6	Moon Street	D8	St John's Crescent	D1-E1	Wade Street	E7-F7
Brunswick Street	D8	Dighton Street	C7-C8-D8	Hotwell Road	A4-A5	Morley Road	B2-B3	St John's Road	C2-C3	Walker Street	B8-C8
Bruton Place	A6	Dove Lane	E8	Houlton Street	E7	Mount Pleasant Terrace	A2-B2	St John's Street	B2	Wapping Road	C4
Bushy Park	E2-F2	Dove Street	C8-D8	Howard Road	A3-B3	Myrtle Road	B7-B8	St Luke's Road	E2-E3	Waterloo Road	F6
Caledonian Road	A4-B4	Dove Street South	C8-D8	Islington Road	A3-B3	Narrow Plain	E6	St Mathews Road	C8	Waterloo Street	F6
Camden Road	A3	Dunford Road	C1-D1	Jacob Street	E6	Nelson Street	C6-D6	St Mathias Park	E7	Wellington Road	E7
Cannon Street	B2	Dunkerry Road	C1	Jacob's Well Road	A5	New Charlotte Street	C3	St Michael's Hill	B8-B7-C7	Wells Road	F2-F3
Canons Road	C5	Earl Street	C7	Jamaica Street	D8	New Kingsley Road	E5-F6	St Michael's Park	B7	Welsh Back	D4-D5
Canons Way	B4-B5	East Street	B2-C2-C3-D3	Jubilee Street	F6	New Queen Street	D2-D3	St Nicholas Street	C6-D6	Wesley Street	B1-C1
				Kensal Road	D1	New Street	E7	St Paul's Street	B2	West Park	A8
				King Square	C8-D8	Newfoundland Road	E8-F8	St Pauls Road	A7	West Street	A1-B1-B2
				King Square Avenue	D8	Newfoundland Street	E7-E8-F8	St Phillips Road	F6	West Street	F6-F7
				King Street	C5	Newgate	D6	St Stephen's Street	C5-C6	Westbourne Grove	B2
				King William Street	A2	Newport Street	E1	St Thomas Street	D4-D5	Whitehouse Lane	C2-D2
				Kingsdown Parade	C8	Newton Street	F7	Sargent Street	D3	Whitehouse Place	D3
						North Street	A2-B2	Sheene Street	B1-B2	Whitehouse Street	D2-D3
						Nutgrove Avenue	D2-D1-E1	Ship Lane	D3-D4	Whiteladies Road	A7-A8
						Oakfield Road	A8	Silverthorne Lane	F4-F5	Whitson Street	C7
						Old Bread Street	E5	Sion Road	B1-B2	Wilder Street	D8-E8
						Old Market Street	E6	Small Street	C6	William Street	E2-E3
						Osborne Road	B3	Somerset Square	D4	Wilson Street	E8
						Oxford Street	E2-F2-F3	Somerset Street	C8-D8	Windmill Close	D2
						Oxford Street	F5	Somerset Street	D4-E4	Windmill Hill	C1-C2
						Park Avenue	E1	Somerset Terrace	C1-D1-D2	Windsor Terrace	E2
						Park Place	A6-A7	South Road	B1	Wine Street	D6
						Park Road	A3	South Street	B1-A1-A2	Woodland Road	B6-B7-B8-A8
						Park Row	B6	Southville Road	B3-C3	York Road	D3-E3-E4
						Park Street	B6	Southwell Street	B7-C7	York Street	D7-D8

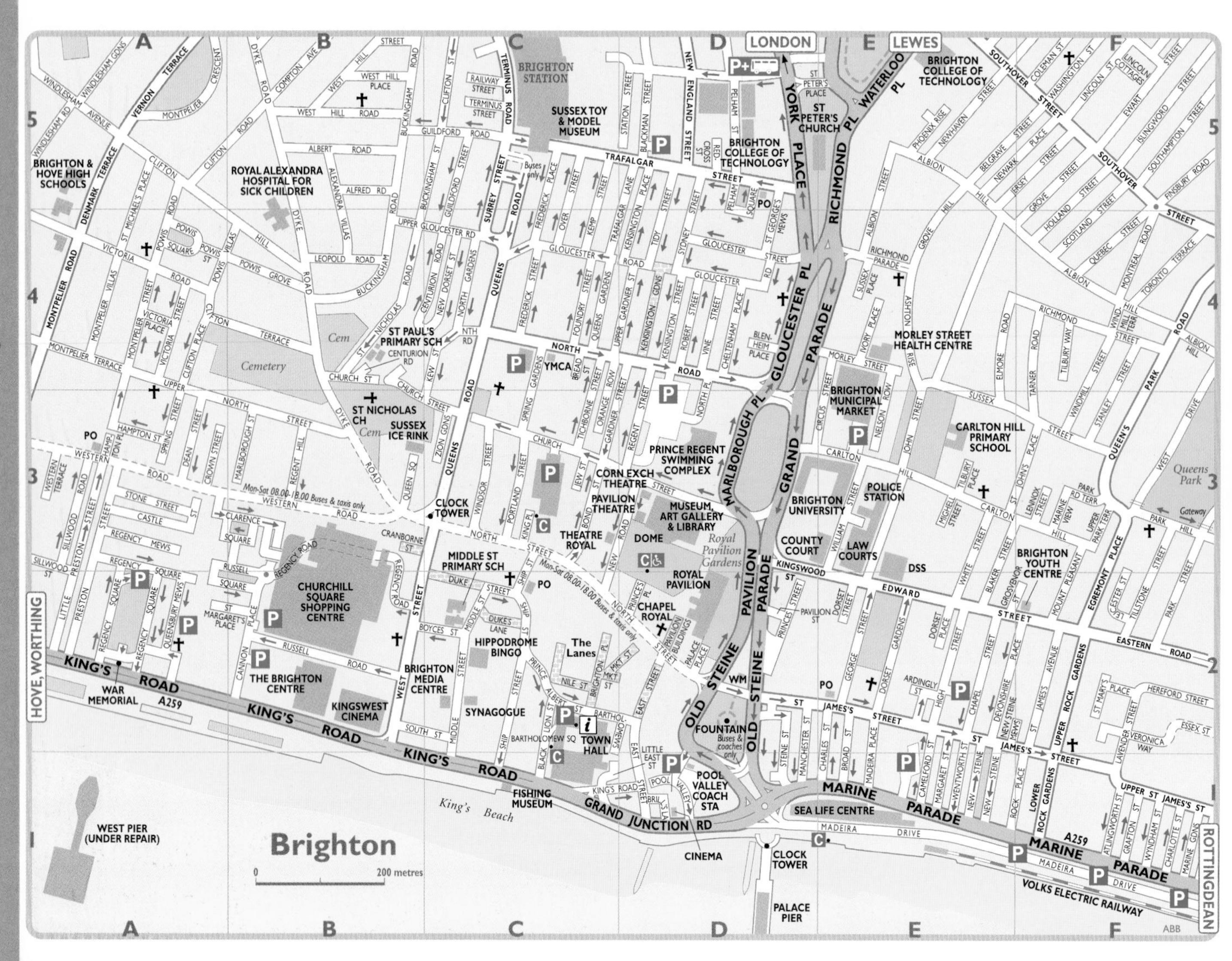

170

Brighton

Brighton is found on atlas page **15**,
grid reference **3104**

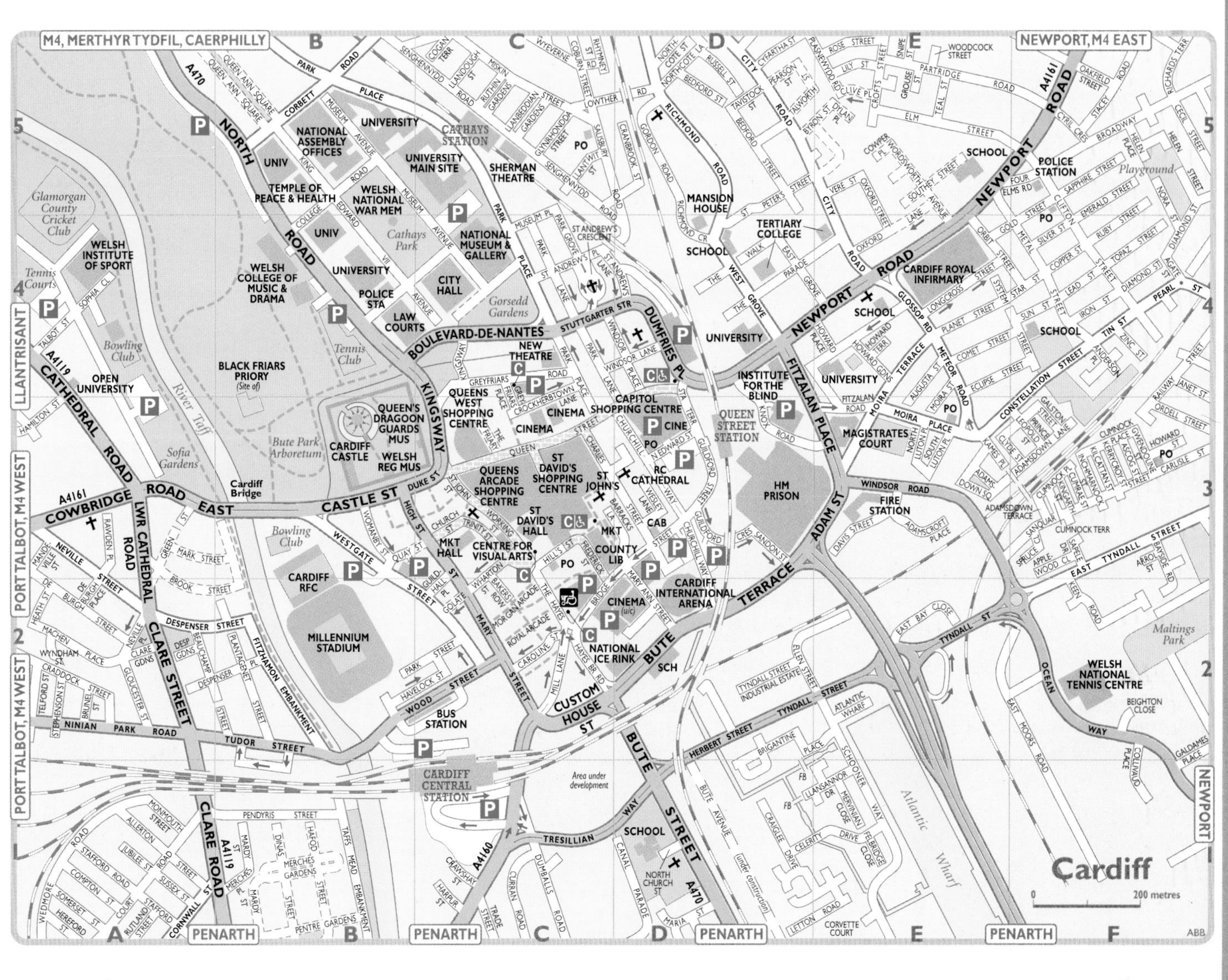

Cardiff

Cardiff is found on atlas page **33**,
grid reference 1876

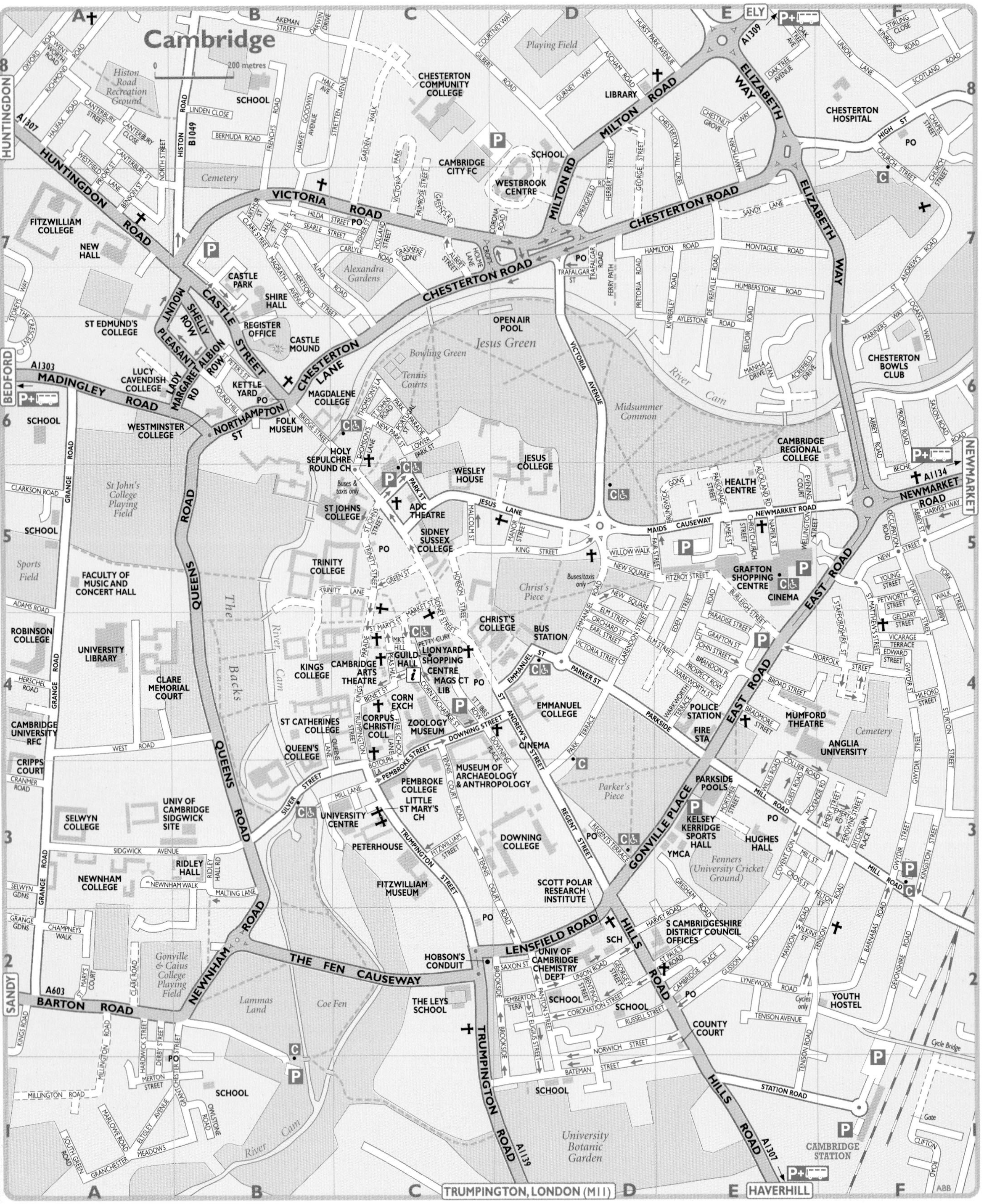

Cambridge

172

ELY
A1309

HUNTINGDON
A1307

HUNTINGDON ROAD

BEDFORD
A1303

MADINGLEY ROAD

SANDY
A603

BARTON ROAD

NEWMARKET
A1134
NEWMARKET ROAD

NEWMARKET ROAD

TRUMPINGTON, LONDON (M11)

HAVERHILL

0 200 metres

Colleges and institutions:

FITZWILLIAM COLLEGE
NEW HALL
ST EDMUND'S COLLEGE
LUCY CAVENDISH COLLEGE
WESTMINSTER COLLEGE
WESTFIELD COLLEGE
ROBINSON COLLEGE
UNIVERSITY LIBRARY
CLARE MEMORIAL COURT
CAMBRIDGE UNIVERSITY RFC
CRIPPS COURT
SELWYN COLLEGE
UNIV OF CAMBRIDGE SIDGWICK SITE
RIDLEY HALL
NEWNHAM COLLEGE
FACULTY OF MUSIC AND CONCERT HALL
KINGS COLLEGE
ST CATHERINES COLLEGE
QUEEN'S COLLEGE
CORPUS CHRISTI COLL
PEMBROKE COLLEGE
LITTLE ST MARY'S CH
PETERHOUSE
FITZWILLIAM MUSEUM
TRINITY COLLEGE
ST JOHNS COLLEGE
ADC THEATRE
SIDNEY SUSSEX COLLEGE
MAGDALENE COLLEGE
FOLK MUSEUM
HOLY SEPULCHRE ROUND CH
CAMBRIDGE ARTS THEATRE
GUILD HALL
CORN EXCH
ZOOLOGY MUSEUM
MUSEUM OF ARCHAEOLOGY & ANTHROPOLOGY
DOWNING COLLEGE
SCOTT POLAR RESEARCH INSTITUTE
CHRIST'S COLLEGE
EMMANUEL COLLEGE
WESLEY HOUSE
JESUS COLLEGE
BUS STATION
GRAFTON SHOPPING CENTRE
CINEMA
POLICE STATION
FIRE STA
MUMFORD THEATRE
ANGLIA UNIVERSITY
PARKSIDE POOLS
KELSEY KERRIDGE SPORTS HALL
YMCA
HUGHES HALL
YOUTH HOSTEL
COUNTY COURT
CAMBRIDGE REGIONAL COLLEGE
HEALTH CENTRE
CHESTERTON BOWLS CLUB
CHESTERTON HOSPITAL
CHESTERTON COMMUNITY COLLEGE
CAMBRIDGE CITY FC
WESTBROOK CENTRE
LION YARD SHOPPING CENTRE
MAGS CT LIB
UNIVERSITY CENTRE
UNIV OF CAMBRIDGE CHEMISTRY DEPT
THE LEYS SCHOOL
HOBSON'S CONDUIT
S CAMBRIDGESHIRE DISTRICT COUNCIL OFFICES
CAMBRIDGE STATION

Roads and places:

VICTORIA ROAD
CHESTERTON ROAD
CHESTERTON LANE
MILTON RD
MILTON ROAD
ELIZABETH WAY
CASTLE STREET
NORTHAMPTON ST
SHELLY ROW
LADY MARGARET RD
ALBION ROW
MOUNT PLEASANT
KETTLE'S YARD
REGISTER OFFICE
SHIRE HALL
CASTLE PARK
CASTLE MOUND
QUEENS ROAD
NEWNHAM ROAD
THE FEN CAUSEWAY
TRUMPINGTON ROAD
A1139
HILLS ROAD
A1307
GONVILLE PLACE
EAST ROAD
PARKER ST
PARKSIDE
EMMANUEL ROAD
MAIDS CAUSEWAY
KING STREET
JESUS LANE
VICTORIA AVENUE
MIDSUMMER COMMON
JESUS GREEN
RIVER CAM
OPEN AIR POOL
BOWLING GREEN
TENNIS COURTS
PARKER'S PIECE
CHRIST'S PIECE
NEW SQUARE
WILLOW WALK
MANOR ST
MALCOLM ST
MANHATTAN DRIVE
LENSFIELD ROAD
UNIVERSITY BOTANIC GARDEN
STATION ROAD
CYCLE BRIDGE
FENNERS (UNIVERSITY CRICKET GROUND)
MILL ROAD
GWYDIR STREET
CEMETERY
COE FEN
LAMMAS LAND
GONVILLE & CAIUS COLLEGE PLAYING FIELD
THE BACKS
ST JOHN'S COLLEGE PLAYING FIELD
SPORTS FIELD
SIDGWICK AVENUE
GRANGE ROAD
WEST ROAD
ADAMS ROAD
HERSCHEL ROAD
CLARKSON ROAD
CRANMER ROAD
SELWYN GDNS
GRANGE GDNS
BARTON ROAD
ALEXANDRA GARDENS
CEMETERY
SCHOOL
PO
LIBRARY
BUS STATION

ABB

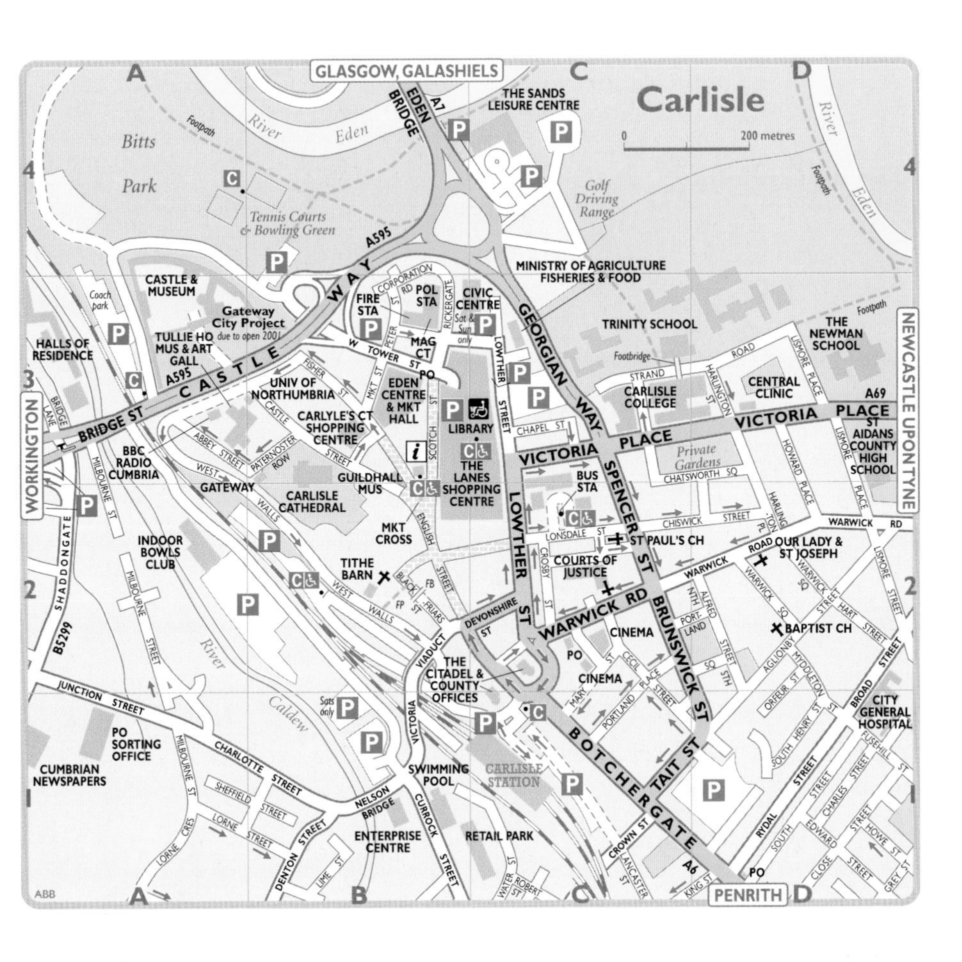

Carlisle

Carlisle is found on atlas page **93**, grid reference **3956**

Abbey Street	A3	Lorne Street	A1-B1
Aglionby Street	D1-D2	Lowther Street	C2-C3
Alfred Street North	D2	Market Street	B3
Alfred Street South	D2	Mary Street	C1-C2
Blackfriars Street	B2	Milbourne Street	A1-A2-A3
Botchergate	C1-D1	Myddleton Street	D1-D2
Bridge Lane	A3	Nelson Bridge	B1
Bridge Street	A3	Orfeur Street	D1-D2
Broad Street	D1-D2	Paternoster Row	B3
Brunswick Street	D1-C2	Peter Street	B3
Castle Street	B2-B3	Portland Place	C1-C2
Castle Way	A3-B3-B4	Portland Square	C2-D2
Cecil Street	C1-C2	Rickergate	B3
Chapel Street	C3	Robert Street	C1
Charles Street	D1	Rydal Street	D1
Charlotte Street	A1-B1	Scotch Street	B2-B3
Chatsworth Square	C3-D3	Shaddongate	A2
Chiswick Street	C2-D2	Sheffield Street	A1-B1
Close Street	D1	South Henry Street	D1
Corporation Road	B3-B4	South Street	D1
Crosby Street	C2	Spencer Street	C2-C3
Crown Street	C1	Strand Road	C3-D3
Currock Street	B1	Tait Street	C1-D1
Denton Street	B1	Victoria Place	C3-D3
Devonshire Street	B2-C2	Victoria Viaduct	B1-B2
Eden Bridge	B4	Warwick Road	C2-D2
Edward Street	D1	Warwick Square	D2
English Street	B2	Water Street	B1-C1
Fisher Street	B3	West Tower Street	B3
Fusehill Street	D1	West Walls	A3-B2
Georgian Way	C3-C4		
Grey Street	D1		
Harlington Place	D2		
Harlington Street	D3		
Hart Street	D2		
Howard Place	D2-D3		
Howe Street	D1		
Junction Street	A1-A2		
King Street	C1-D1		
Lancaster Street	C1		
Lime Street	B1		
Lismore Place	D2-D3		
Lismore Street	D2		
Lonsdale Street	C2		
Lorne Crescent	A1		

173

Cambridge

Cambridge is found on atlas page **53**, grid reference **4558**

Abbey Road	F5-F6	Clare Road	A2	George IV Street	D2	Kingston Street	F3	Oxford Road	A8	Scotland Road	F8
Abbey Street	F5	Clarendon Street	D4-D5	George Street	D7-D8	Kinross Road	F8	Panton Street	D1-D2	Searle Street	B7-C7
Abbey Walk	F4-F5	Clare Street	B7	Gilbert Road	C8-D8	Lady Margaret Road	B6	Paradise Street	E4	Selwyn Gardens	A3
Acrefield Drive	E6	Clarkson Road	A5	Glisson Road	E2-E3	Lensfield Road	C2-D2-D3	Park Parade	C6	Shelly Row	B6-B7
Adams Road	A5	Clifton Road	F1	Gonville Place	D3-E3	Linden Close	B8	Park Street	C5-C6	Sidgwick Avenue	A3-B3
Akeman Street	B8-C8	Collier Road	E3-F3	Grafton Street	E4	Logan's Way	F6-F7	Park Terrace	D3-D4	Sidney Street	C4-C5
Albert Street	C7	Corn Exchange Street	C4	Grange Gardens	A2	Lower Park Street	C6	Parker Street	D4	Silver Street	B3-C3
Albion Row	B6	Corona Road	D7	Grange Road	A2-A4-A6	Lynewode Road	E2	Parkside	D4-E4	South Green Road	A1
Alpha Road	B7-C7-C6	Coronation Street	D2	Granchester Meadows	A1-B1	Madingley Road	A6-B6	Parsonage Street	E5	Springfield Road	D7
Arthur Street	B7	Courtney Way	C8-D8	Granchester Street	B1-B2	Magrath Avenue	B7	Peas Hill	C4	Staffordshire Street	F4-F5
Ascham Road	D8	Covent Garden	E3	Grasmere Gardens	C7	Maids Causeway	D5-E5	Pemberton Terrace	D2	Station Road	E1-F1
Auckland Road	E5	Cranmer Road	A3	Green Street	C5	Malcolm Street	C5	Pembroke Street	C3-C4	Stirling Close	F8
Aylestone Road	D7-E6	Croftholme Lane	C7-D7	Green's Road	C7	Malting Lane	B3	Perowne Street	F3	Storeys Way	A6-A7
Barton Road	A2-B2	Cross Street	E3	Gresham Road	E2-E3	Manhattan Drive	E6	Petty Cury	C4	Stretten Avenue	C8
Bateman Street	C1-D1-E1-E2	Darwin Drive	B8	Guest Road	E3	Manor Street	D5	Petworth Street	F5	Sturton Street	F3-F4-F5
Beche Road	F5-F6	De Freiville Road	E6-E7	Gurney Way	D8	Mariners Way	F6-F7	Portugal Street	C6	Tenison Avenue	E2
Belvoir Road	E6-E7	Derby Street	A1-A2	Gwydir Street	F3-F4	Market Hill	C4	Pound Hill	B6	Tenison Road	E1-E2-F2-F3
Bene't Street	C4	Devonshire Road	F2-F3	Hale Avenue	B8-C8	Market Street	C4-C5	Pretoria Road	D7	Tennis Court Road	C4-C3-D3-D2
Benson Street	A7	Ditchburn Place	F3	Hale Street	B7	Marlowe Road	A1	Primrose Street	C7-C8	The Fen Causeway	B2-C2
Bentinck Street	D2	Downing Place	C4-D4-D3	Halifax Road	A8	Mawson Road	E2-E3	Priory Road	F6	Thomson's Lane	C6
Bermuda Road	B8	Downing Street	C4-D4	Hamilton Road	D7-E7	McKenzie Road	E3-F3	Priory Street	A7-A8	The Crescent	A6-A7
Botolph Lane	C3	Earl Street	D4	Hardwick Street	A1-A2	Merton Street	A1	Prospect Row	E4	Trafalgar Road	D7
Bradmore Street	E4	East Road	E4-E5-F5	Harvest Way	F5	Milford Street	F4	Queens Lane	B3-B4	Trafalgar Street	D7
Brandon Place	E4	Eden Street	E4-E5	Harvey Goodwin Avenue	B8	Mill Lane	B3-C3	Queens Road	B3-B4-B5-B6	Trinity Lane	B5-C5
Bridge Street	B6-C6-C5	Edward Street	F4	Harvey Road	D2-E2-E3	Mill Road	E3-F3	Regent Street	D3	Trinity Street	C5
Broad Street	C2-D2-D1	Elizabeth Way	E8-E7-F7	Hawthorn Way	E7-E8	Mill Street	E3-F3	Regents Terrace	D3	Trumpington Road	C2-C1-D1
Brookside	C2-D2-D1	Elm Street	D5-D4-E4	Herbert Street	D7-D8	Millington Road	A1-A2	Richmond Road	A8	Trumpington Street	C2-C3-C4
Brunswick Gardens	E5	Eltisley Avenue	A1	Herschel Road	A4	Milton Road	D7-D8-E8	Ridley Hall Road	B3	Union Lane	F8
Burleigh Street	E4-E5	Emery Road	F3	Hertford Street	B7-C6	Montague Road	E7-F7	Russell Street	D2-E2	Union Road	D2
Cambridge Place	E2	Emery Street	F3	High Street	E8-F8	Mount Pleasant	B7-A6-B6	St Andrew's Road	F6-F7	Vicarage Terrace	F4
Canterbury Close	A8	Emmanuel Road	D4-D5	Hilda Street	B7-C7	Napier Street	E5	St Andrew's Street	C4-D4-D3	Victoria Avenue	D5-D6-D7
Canterbury Street	A7-A8	Emmanuel Street	D4	Hills Road	D3-D2-E2-E1	New Park Street	C6	St Barnabas Road	F2-F3	Victoria Park	C7-C8
Carlyle Road	B7-C7	Evening Court	E5	Histon Road	B7-B8	New Square	D5	St Eligius Road	D1-D2	Victoria Road	B7-C7-D7
Castle Street	B6-B7	Fair Street	D5-E5	Hobson Street	C4-C5	New Street	F5	St Johns Road	C6	Victoria Street	D4
Champneys Walk	A2	Felton Street	F3	Holland Street	C7	Newmarket Road	E5-F5	St Johns Street	C5	Warkworth Street	E4
Chapel Street	F8	Ferry Path	D7	Humberstone Road	E7-F7	Newnham Road	B2-B3	St Lukes Street	B7	Warkworth Terrace	E4
Chesterton Hall Crescent	E7-E8	Fisher Street	C7	Huntingdon Road	A8-A7-B7	Newnham Walk	A3-B3	St Mary's Court	A2	Wellington Street	E5
Chesterton Lane	B6-C6	Fitzroy Street	E5	Hurst Park Avenue	D8-E8	Norfolk Street	E4-F4	St Mary's Street	C4	Wentworth Road	A8
Chesterton Road	C6-C7-D7-E7	Fitzwilliam Street	C3	James Street	E5	North Street	A7-A8	St Matthew's Street	F4-F5	West Road	A4-B4
Chestnut Grove	E8	Free School Lane	C3-C4	Jesus Lane	C5-D5	Northampton Street	B6	St Paul's Road	E2	Westfield Lane	A7-A8
Christchurch Street	E5	French's Road	B7-B8	John Street	E4	Norwich Street	D1-D2-E2	St Peter's Road	B6	Wilkins Street	E2
Church Street	F7-F8	Garden Walk	C7-C8	Kimberley Road	E6-E7	Oak Tree Avenue	E8	St Tibbs Row	C4	Willis Road	E3
City Road	E4-E5	Geldart Street	F4	King Street	C5-D5	Occupation Road	F5	Sandy Lane	E7	Willow Walk	D5
				Kings Parade	C4	Orchard Street	D4	Saxon Road	F6	York Street	F4-F5
				Kings Road	A2	Owlstone Road	B1	Saxon Street	D2	Young Street	F5

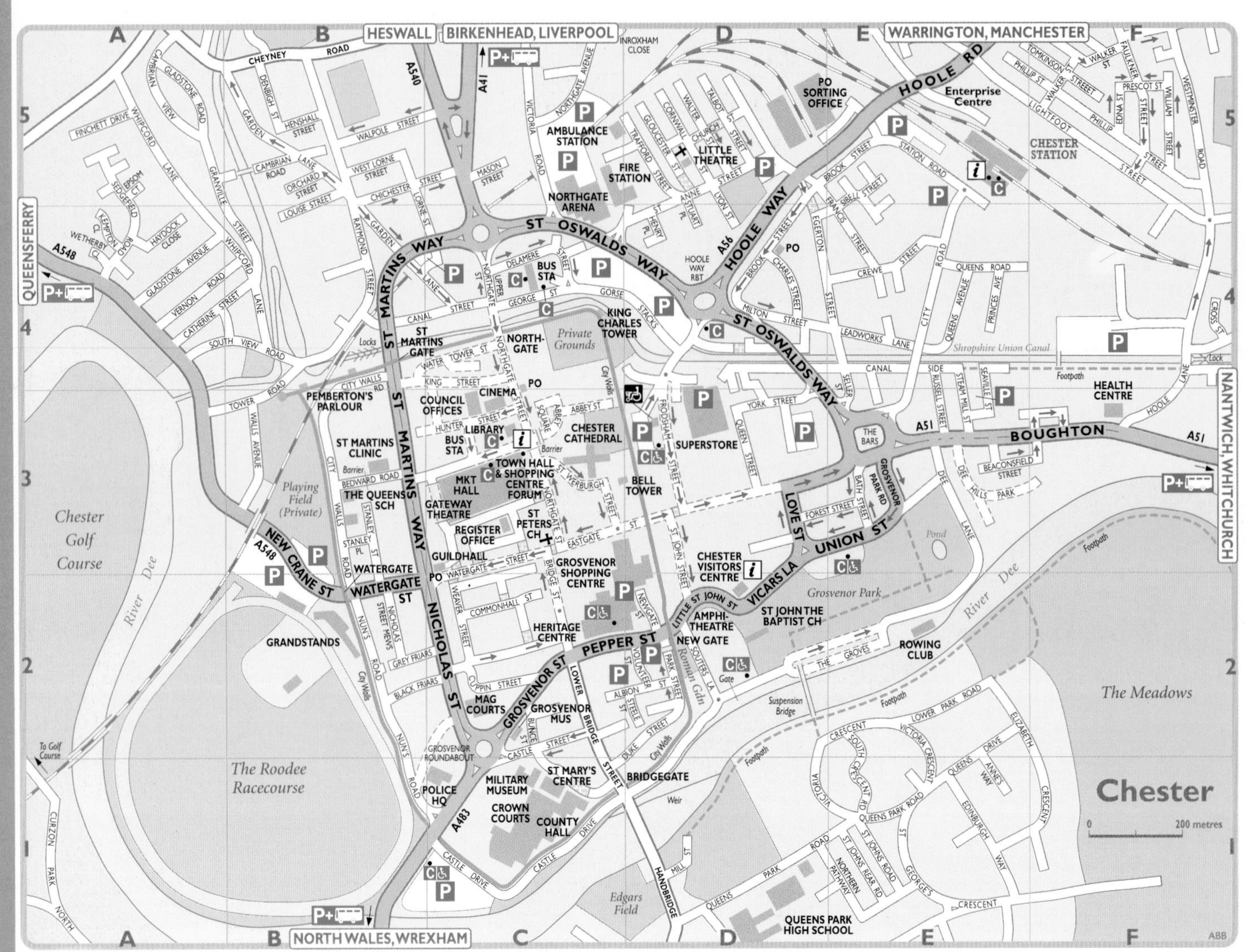

Chester

Chester is found on atlas page **71**,
grid reference **4066**

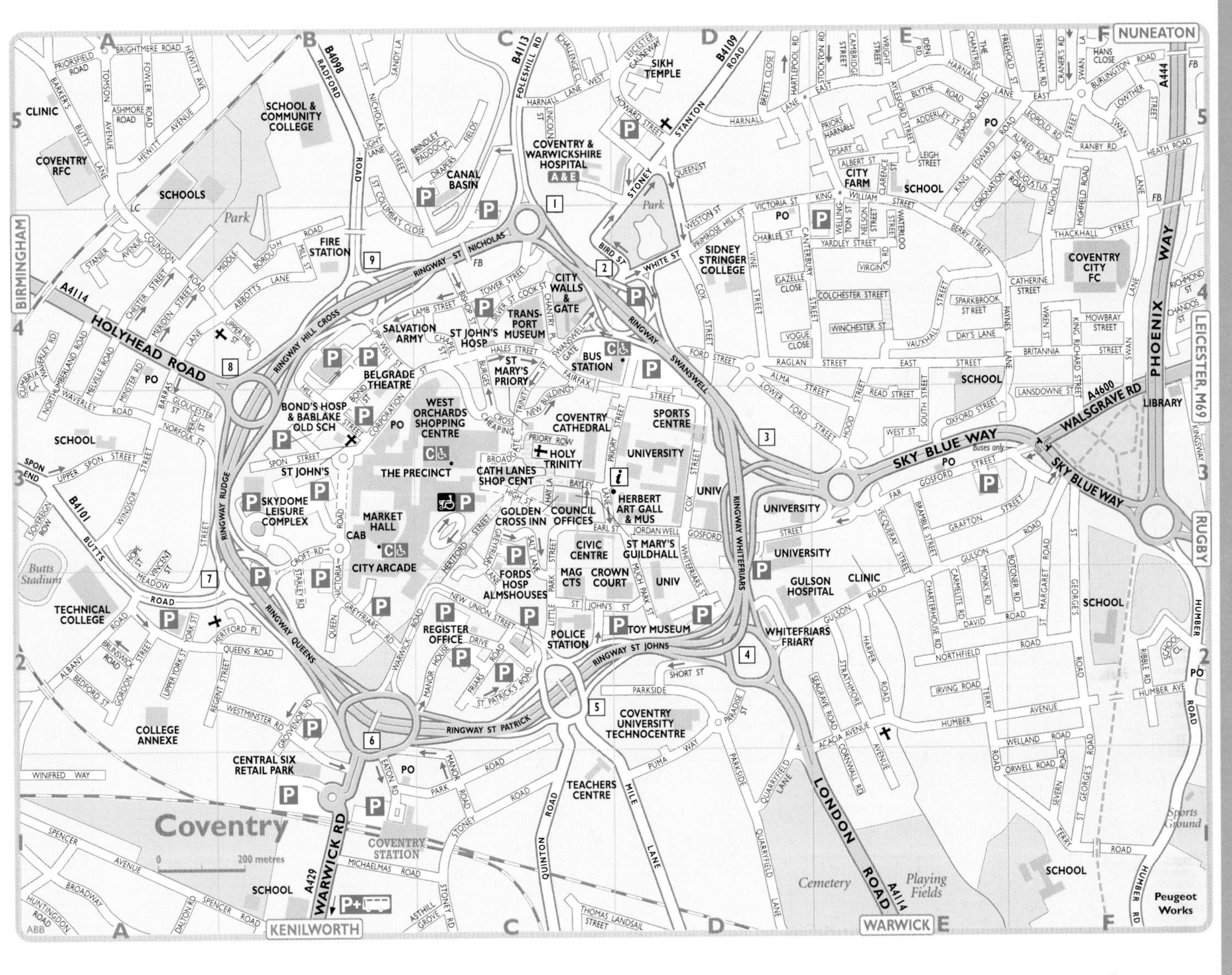

Coventry

Coventry is found on atlas page **61**,
grid reference **3378**

Abbotts Lane	B4	Challenge Close	C5	Gordon Street	A2	Lincoln Street	C5	Queens Road	A2-B2	Stoney Stanton Road	C4-D4-D5
Acacia Avenue	E2	Chandos Street	F4	Gosford Street	D3-E3	Little Park Street	C2-C3	Quinton Road	C1-C2	Strathmore Avenue	E1-E2
Adderley Street	E5	Chantry Place	C4	Grafton Street	E3-F3	London Road	D2-D1-E1	Radford Road	B4-B5	Swan Lane	F4-F5
Albany Road	A2	Chapel Street	C4	Greyfriars Lane	C2-C3	Lower Ford Street	D4-D3-E3	Raglan Street	D4-E4	Swanswell Gate	C4
Albert Street	E5	Charles Street	D4	Greyfriars Road	B2	Lowther Street	F5	Ranby Road	F5	Terry Road	E2-E1-F1
Alfred Road	F5	Charterhouse Road	E2	Grosvenor Road	B1-B2	Manor House Drive	C2	Read Street	E3	Thackhall Street	F4
Alma Street	D4-E3	Chester Street	A4	Gulson Road	D2-E2-E3-F3	Manor Road	B2-C1	Regent Street	A2-B2	The Chantries	E5
Ashmore Road	A5	Clarence Street	E5	Hales Street	C4	Meadow Street	A2-A3	Ribble Road	F2	Thomas Landsail Street	C1-D1
Asthill Grove	B1-C1	Colchester Street	E4	Hans Close	F5	Melville Road	A3-A4	Richmond Street	F4	Tomson Avenue	A5
Augustus Road	F5	Cook Street	C4	Harnall Lane East	D5-E5-F5	Meriden Street	A4	Ringway Hill Cross	B4	Tower Street	C4
Aylesford Street	E5	Cornwall Road	E1-E2	Harnall Lane West	C5	Michaelmas Road	B1-C1	Ringway Queens	B2	Trentham Road	F5
Barker's Butts Lane	A5	Coronation Road	E4-E5-F5	Harper Road	E2	Middleborough Road	A4-B4	Ringway Rudge	B3	Trinity Street	C3-C4
Barras Lane	A3-A4-B4	Corporation Street	B3-B4-C4	Hartlepool Road	D5	Mile Lane	C2-C1-D1	Ringway St Johns	C2-D2	Upper Hill Street	B4
Bayley Lane	C3	Coundon Road	A4	Hay Lane	C3	Mill Street	B4	Ringway St Nicholas	B4-C4	Upper Spon Street	A3
Bedford Street	A2	Cox Street	D3-D4	Heath Road	F5	Minster Road	A3-A4	Ringway St Patrick	C2	Upper Well Street	B4
Berry Street	E4	Craner's Road	F5	Hertford Place	A2-B2	Monks Road	E2-E3	Ringway Swanswell	C4-D4-D3	Upper York Street	A2
Bird Street	C4-D4	Croft Road	B2-B3	Hertford Street	C2-C3	Mowbray Street	F4	Ringway Whitefriars	D2-D3	Vauxhall Street	E4
Bishop Street	C4	Cross Cheaping	C3	Hewitt Avenue	A5	Much Park Street	C3-D3	St Columba's Close	B5-B4-C4	Vecqueray Street	E2-E3
Blythe Road	E5	Cumbria Close	A3-A4	High Street	C3	Nelson Street	E4	St George's Road	F1-F2-F3	Victoria Street	D4-D5
Bond Street	B3-B4	Dalton Road	A1	Highfield Road	F4-F5	New Buildings	C3-C4	St John's Street	C2-D2	Vincent Street	A2-A3
Botoner Road	F2-F3	David Road	E2-F2	Hill Street	B3-B4	New Union Street	C2	St Margaret Road	F2-F3	Vine Street	D4
Bramble Street	E3	Day's Lane	E4	Holyhead Road	A4-B4	Nicholls Street	F4-F5	St Nicholas Street	B5-C5-C4	Virginia Road	E4
Bretts Close	D5	Drapers Fields	C5	Hood Street	E3-E4	Norfolk Street	A3	St Patrick's Road	C2	Vogue Close	D4
Brightmere Road	A5	Dysart Close	E5	Hope Street	A3	Northfield Road	E2-F2	Salt Lane	C2-C3	Walsgrave Road	F4
Brindley Paddocks	C5	Earl Street	C3-D3	Howard Street	D5	Northumberland Road	A3-A4	Sandy Lane	B5	Warwick Road	B1-B2-C2
Britannia Street	F4	East Street	E4	Humber Avenue	E2-F2	Orwell Road	E1-F1	School Close	F2	Waterloo Street	E4
Broadgate	C3	Eaton Road	B1	Humber Road	F1-F2-F3	Oxford Street	E3	Seagrave Road	F2	Waverley Road	A3-A4
Broadway	A1	Fairfax Street	C4-D3	Huntingdon Road	A1	Paradise Street	D2	Severn Road	F1-F2	Welland Road	E2-F2
Brunswick Road	A2	Far Gosford Street	E3	Iden Road	E5	Park Road	B1-C1-C2	Short Street	D2	Wellington Street	E4-E5
Burges	C3-C4	Foleshill Road	C5	Irving Road	E2	Parkside	C2-D2-D1	Silver Street	C4	West Street	E3
Burlington Road	F5	Ford Street	D4	Jesmond Road	E5	Paynes Lane	E4-F4	Sky Blue Way	E3-F3	Westminster Road	B2
Butts Road	A3-A2-B2	Fowler Road	A5	Jordan Well	D3	Percy Street	A3	South Street	E3-E4	Weston Street	D4
Cambridge Street	E5	Freehold Street	E5-F5	King Edward Road	E4-E5-F5	Phoenix Way	F3-F4-F5	Sovereign Row	A3	White Street	D4
Canterbury Street	D4-E4	Friars Road	C2	King Richard Street	F3-F4	Primrose Hill Street	D4	Sparkbrook Street	E4	Whitefriars Street	D2-D3
Carmelite Road	E2	Gazelle Close	D4	King William Street	E4-E5	Priors Harnall	E5	Spencer Avenue	A1	Winchester Street	E4
Catherine Street	F4	Gloucester Street	A3	Kingsway	B4-C4	Priorsfield Road	A5	Spencer Road	A1-B1	Windsor Street	A3
				Lamb Street	B4-C4	Priory Row	C3	Spon End	A3	Winifred Way	A1
				Lansdowne Street	F3	Priory Street	C3-D3	Spon Street	B3	Wren Street	F4
				Leicester Causeway	D5	Puma Way	D1-D2	Stanier Avenue	A4	Wright Street	E5
				Leigh Street	E5	Quarryfield Lane	D1-D2	Starley Road	B2-B3	Yardley Street	E4
				Leopold Road	F5	Queen Street	D5	Stockton Road	E5	York Street	A2
				Light Lane	B5	Queen Victoria Road	B2-B3	Stoney Road	C1		

MATLOCK

CHESTERFIELD

A6 DUFFIELD ROAD

Derwent Park

DERBY ROWING CLUB

PARK GROVE

WHEELDON AVE

STATHAM ST

WHITE STREET

HIGHFIELD ROAD

HIND

CLOSE

ROBIN ROAD

SOUTH DRIVE

RUSKIN ROAD

CHEVIN PLACE

CHEVIN ROAD

KINGSTON STREET

ARTHUR STREET

MILFORD STREET

DERVENTIO CLOSE

CAMP STREET

CHESTER GREEN ROAD

CITY ROAD

ROMAN ROAD

DRAGE ST

MANSFIELD ROAD

CAESAR STREET

CARSIAN ST

A61

P+R

SIR FRANK WHITTLE ROAD

Racecourse Park

NAIRN AVE

BUTE WALK

SHETLAND CLOSE

BERWICK AVENUE

CARDIGAN STREET

SCHOOL

ST MARKS ROAD

DERBYSHIRE COUNTY CRICKET GROUND

GRANDSTAND ROAD

HUNTINGDON GREEN

WESTMORLAND CLOSE

NOTTINGHAM RD

KEDLESTON ROAD

ST ALKMUNDS CHURCH

QUEEN MARY COURT

GARDEN ST

KING ST

SCHOOL

COWLEY ST

LEYLAND ST

WALTER ST

WHITECROSS

GARDENS

PARKER STREET

QUARN WAY

WEST AVENUE

NORTH STREET

NORTH PARADE

BATH STREET

DUKE STREET

HANDYSIDE ST

EDWARD STREET

MARGARET STREET

RIVER STREET

DALEY RD

ST PAULS ROAD

JOHN LOMBE DRIVE

ETRURIA GARDENS

MANSFIELD STREET

ST PANCRAS WAY

ST PAULS RD

MAR BECK COURT

CLARKE STREET

DERWENT BUSINESS CENTRE

LANDAU FORTE COLLEGE

ADLER STREET

EASTON DRIVE

KEYS STREET

ST MARYS ST

STORES ROAD

STORES ROAD

NOTTINGHAM RD

ASHBOURNE

MARKEATON STREET

BRICK ST

MILL STREET

BRIDGE

AGARD STREET

A52 FRIAR GATE

FORD STREET

STAFFORD ST

CURZON STREET

FORMAN STREET

A52

FRIAR

VERNON STREET

YORK STREET

LARGES ST

SOUTH STREET

EATON COURT

MUNDY STREET

WILLIAM ST

VERNON GATE

HORSLEY TERRACE

NUNS STREET

PICKFORD'S HOUSE MUSEUM

FRIARGATE COURT

LODGE LANE

BROOK STREET

ST HELENS STREET

CHAPEL STREET

CATHEDRAL RD

WILLOW ROW

BRIDGE GATE

CAVENDISH

GEORGE ST

BOLD LANE

CHEAPSIDE

THE STRAND

WARDWICK

LIBRARY

ST MARY'S CHURCH

ST MARY'S CHAPEL

Footbridge

ST MARY'S BRIDGE

ST ALKMUND'S WAY

LANCASTER SPORTS CENTRE

CLINIC

QUEENS LEISURE CENTRE

QUEEN STREET

ST MICHAEL'S LANE

FULL STREET

INDUSTRIAL MUSEUM

SILKMILL LANE

CATHEDRAL

POLICE MUSEUM

ST MARY'S GATE

BOLD LANE

OLD BLACKSMITH YARD

SADLER GATE

MARKET PLACE

IRONGATE

CORN MARKET

ASSEMBLY ROOMS

POLICE STATION

MAGISTRATES COURT

DERWENT STREET

EXETER STREET

EXETER PLACE

STUART STREET

P

DARWIN PLACE

Weir

COUNCIL HOUSE

MEADOW ROAD

THE PENTAGON

EASTGATE

A61

A514 NOTTINGHAM

P+R

GREGORYS ROAD

HANSARD GATE

CRANMER ROAD

DUNTON CLOSE

ASHLYN ROAD

Footbridge

Derby

0   200 metres

COUNCIL OFFICES

ST WERBURGH'S ARCADE

MUSEUM & ART GALLERY

OSNABRUK SQUARE

GUILDHALL

ST JAMES STREET

MARKET HALL

VICTORIA ST

ALBERT STREET

MORLEDGE

CROWN & COUNTY COURTS

BUS STATION

THE COCKPITT

STATION APPROACH

B6000

SIDDALS ROAD

COPLAND STREET

LIVERAGE ROAD

PRIDE PARKWAY

B6000

UTTOXETER

A516

UTTOXETER NEW ROAD

TALBOT STREET

KENSINGTON STREET

MANSFIELD STREET

NEWLAND ST

BRAMBLE STREET

COLYEAR ST

BECKETWELL

MACKLIN STREET

GERARD STREET

CROMPTON STREET

WILSON STREET

FORESTER STREET

ROSENGRAVE STREET

ST PETER'S CHURCHYARD

ST PETER'S CHURCH

GREEN LANE

CHEST CLINIC

CINEMA

CROWN WALK

DEVONSHIRE WALK

THEATRE WALK

AUDLEY CENTRE

MARKETS

DERBY PLAYHOUSE THEATRE

EAGLE CENTRE

CASTLE WALK

REGISTER OFFICE

MAIN SHOPPING CENTRE

SALVATION ARMY

OSMASTON RD

BOURNE STREET

TRAFFIC STREET

LONDON ROAD

JOHN STREET

NEW ST

CARRINGTON STREET

TRINITY ST

CANAL STREET

LIVERAGE PL

RAILWAY TERRACE

MIDLAND PLACE

DERBY MIDLAND STATION

FRANCHISE STREET

OLIVE ST

PARLIAMENT STREET

STOCKBROOK

LINTON ST

JACKSON ST

KING ALFRED ST

WERBURGH ST

SCHOOL

COPPERLEAF CLOSE

ABBEY STREET

DRAYCOTT LANE

DREWRY LANE

BAKEWELL STREET

WOLFA STREET

ALMA ST

HARCOURT STREET

WEBSTER STREET

GERARD STREET

WOODS LANE

ABBOTT STREET

ROAD

MACKWORTH COLLEGE

LEOPOLD STREET

CHARNWOOD ST

MOUNT ST

BURTON ROAD

SPA LANE

GREY STREET

SUN STREET

MAY STREET

PITTAR STREET

Recreation Ground

MONK STREET

HARRISON STREET

PERCY ST

LEMAN STREET

BOYER STREET

CROWN MEWS

RIDDINGS STREET

SPRING STREET

SWINBURNE ST

MELBOURNE STREET

HARTINGTON STREET

BRADSHAW WAY

A&E DERBYSHIRE ROYAL INFIRMARY

OSMASTON ROAD

LONDON ROAD

WELLINGTON STREET

LEONARD ST

MIDLAND PO SORTING OFFICE

NELSON STREET

OXFORD ST

BLOOMFIELD ST

SWINNEY ST

MIDLAND ROAD

ROYAL CROWN DERBY

SCHOOL

LONDON ROAD

A6

LOUGHBOROUGH

A5250

BURTON

WHITAKER ROAD

PACKAGE AVE

STONE HILL ROAD

BREEDON HILL ROAD

MOUNT CARMEL ST

DASHWOOD STREET

MOORE STREET

HARRIET STREET

RENALS ST

BELGRAVE STREET

SALISBURY STREET

SCHOOL

BURTON ROAD

MILL HILL LANE

PEAR TREE ST

UPPER BAINBRIDGE ST

LYNDHURST STREET

PROVIDENT ST

CUMMINGS ST

SOCIETY PLACE

CHESTNUT AVE

DEPOT ST

STRUTT ST

ROSE HILL ST

NORMANTON ROAD

LOUDON STREET

ARBORETUM

ARBORETUM STREET

LEESON ST

FERNS CLOSE

GORDON ST

BARLOW STREET

BATEMAN STREET

UTTERLEY LANE

DEXTER STREET

GRAYLING STREET

GRANGE ST

BODEN ST

PO

MOSQUE

MELBOURNE

ABB

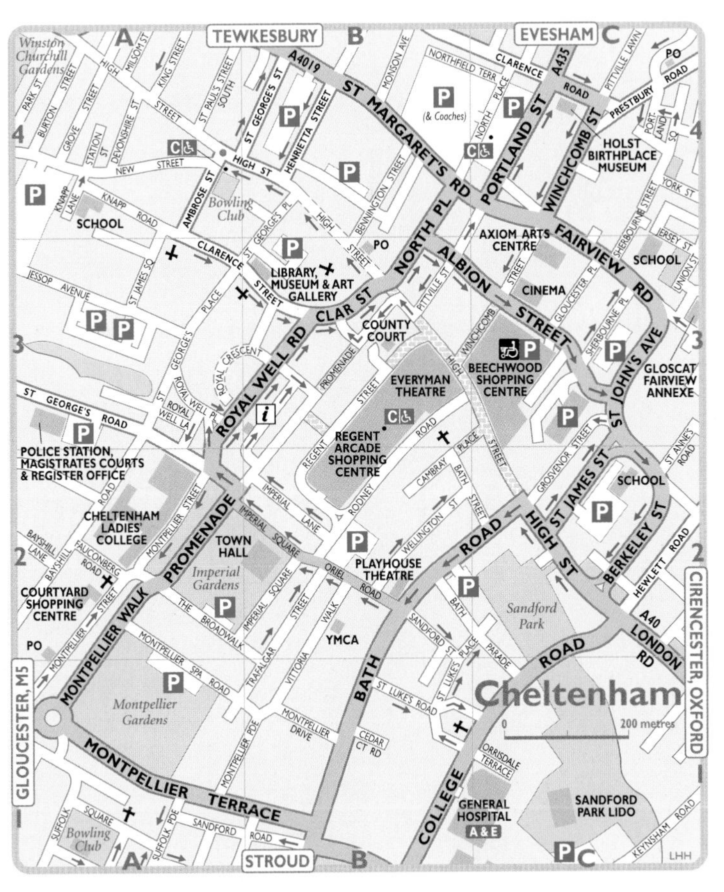

Cheltenham

Cheltenham is found on atlas page **35**,
grid reference **94**2**2**

Albion Street	B3-C3	King Street	A4	Royal Well Place	A3
Ambrose Street	A4	Knapp Lane	A4	Royal Well Road	A3-B3
Bath Parade	B2-C2-C1	Knapp Road	A4	St Anne's Road	C2-C3
Bath Road	B1-B2-C2	London Road	C1-C2	St George's Place	A3-B3-B4
Bath Street	B2-C2	Milsom Street	A4	St George's Road	A3
Bayshill Lane	A2	Monson Avenue	B4	St George's Street	A4-B4
Bayshill Road	A2-A3	Montpellier Drive	B1	St James Square	A3
Bennington Street	B3-B4	Montpellier Parade	A1-B1	St James Street	C2
Berkeley Street	C2	Montpellier Spa Road	A1-A2	St John's Avenue	C3
Burton Street	A4	Montpellier Street	A1-A2	St Luke's Place	B1-B2-C2
Cambray Place	B2-B3-C3	Montpellier Terrace	A1-B1	St Luke's Road	B1
Cedar Court Road	B1	Montpellier Walk	A1-A2	St Margaret's Road	B4-C4
Clarence Road	C4	New Street	A4	St Paul's Street South	A4
Clarence Street	A4-A3-B3	North Place	B3-B4-C4	Sandford Road	A1-B1
College Road	B1-C1-C2	Northfield Terrace	B4-C4	Sandford Street	B2
Devonshire Street	A4	Oriel Road	B2	Sherbourne Place	C3
Fauconberg Road	A2	Orrisdale Terrace	C1	Sherbourne Street	C3-C4
Gloucester Place	C3	Park Street	A4	Station Street	A4
Grosvenor Street	C2-C3	Pittville Lawn	C4	Suffolk Parade	A1
Grove Street	A4	Pittville Street	B3	Suffolk Square	A1
Henrietta Street	B4	Portland Square	C4	The Broadwalk	A2-B2-B1
Hewlett Road	C2	Portland Street	C4	Trafalgar Street	A1-B1-B2
High Street	A4-B4-B3-C2	Prestbury Road	C4	Union Street	C3
Imperial Lane	B2	Promenade	A2-B3	Vittoria Walk	B1-B2
Imperial Square	A2-B2	Regent Street	B2-B3	Wellington Street	B2
Jersey Street	C3-C4	Rodney Road	B2-B3	Winchcomb Street	B3-C3-C4
Jessop Avenue	A3	Royal Crescent	A3-B3	York Street	C4
Keynsham Road	C1	Royal Well Lane	A3		

177

Derby

Derby is found on atlas page **62**,
grid reference **35**3**6**

Abbey Street	B2-B3-B4	Canal Street	E3-E4	Duke Street	C7	Kedleston Road	A8-A7-B7	Nottingham Road	D6-E6-F6	Siddals Road	D4-E4
Adler Court	D8	Cardean Close	D8	Dunkirk Street	B4	Kedleston Street	A6-B7	Nuns Street	A6	Sidney Street	E1
Agard Street	A6-B5	Cardigan Street	F7-F8	Dunton Close	E5	Kensington Street	B4	Old Blacksmith Yard	C5	Silkmill Lane	C6
Albert Street	C5	Carrington Street	D3-E3	East Street	C4-D4-D5	Keys Street	D6	Olive Street	A3	Sir Frank Whittle	
Albion Street	D4	Castle Walk	D4	Eastgate	E6	King Alfred Street	A3-B3-B4	Osmaston Road	D3-D2-E1	Road	E8-E7-E6-F6
Alice Street	D6	Cathedral Road	B6-C6	Eaton Court	A6	King Street	B6-B7	Osnabrük Square	C5	Sitwell Street	C3
Alma Street	B4	Cavendish Street	B5	Edensor Square	A3	Kingston Street	B8	Otter Street	B8-C7	Society Place	C1
Amen Alley	C5	Chapel Street	B6-C6	Edward Street	B7-C7	Larges Street	A5	Oxford Street	E2	South Drive	B8
Arbor Close	B3	Charnwood Street	C2-D3	Elms Street	A7-B7	Leaper Street	A6-A7	Park Grove	A8	South Street	A5
Arboretum Street	D1-D2	Cheapside	B5	Empress Road	A1-B1	Leman Street	A1-A2	Park Street	E3	Sowter Road	C6
Arthur Hind Close	A8	Chequers Road	F5-F6	Etruria Gardens	C7	Leonard Street	D2	Parker Close	B7	Spa Lane	B2-B3
Arthur Street	B6-B7-B8	Chester Green Road	C8-D8	Euston Drive	D7-D8	Leopold Street	C2-C3-D3	Parker Street	A7-B7	Spring Street	A3-B3
Ashlyn Road	E5-F5	Chestnut Avenue	C1	Exchange Street	C5-D4	Leyland Street	A7-A8	Parliament Street	A3	Stafford Street	B4-B5
Avondale Road	C2	Chevin Place	B8	Exeter Place	D5	Lime Avenue	B2-C2	Peet Street	A3-A4	Statham Street	A8
Babington Lane	C3-C4	Chevin Road	B7-B8	Exeter Street	D5-D6	Litchurch Lane	F1	Pelham Street	B3	Station Approach	D4-E4
Back Sitwell Street	C3-D3	City Road	C7-C8	Ford Street	B5-B6	Liversage Place	D3	Percy Street	A2	Stockbrook Street	A2-A3-B3
Bailey Street	B1	Clarke Street	D6-D7	Forester Street	B3-C3	Liversage Road	D3-E3	Phoenix Street	D6	Stone Hill Road	A1-B1
Bakewell Street	A3-A4	Colyear Street	C4	Forman Street	B4	Liversage Street	D4-E3-E4	Pittar Street	B2	Stores Road	E6-E7-E8
Barlow Street	E1-F2	Copeland Street	D4-E4	Fox Street	D6-D7	Lodge Lane	B6	Ponsonby Terrace	A5	Strutt Street	D1
Bateman Street	E1-F1-F2	Copperleaf Close	B3	Franchise Street	A3	London Road	D4-D3-E2-F1	Pride Parkway	E4-F4-F3	Stuart Street	D6
Bath Street	C7	Cornmarket	C5	Friar Gate	A6-A5-B5	Lorne Street	A2	Prime Parkway	D7	Sun Street	B2-B3
Becket Street	B4-B5	Corporation Street	C5	Friargate Court	A5	Loudon Street	C1-D1	Provident Street	C1	Swinburne Street	C2
Becketwell Lane	C4-C5	Cowley Street	A7-A8	Full Street	C5-C6	Lower Eley Street	B2	Quarn Street	A7	Talbot Street	B4
Belgrave Street	C2	Cranmer Road	E5-F5	Garden Street	B7	Lyndhurst Street	C1	Quarn Way	A7	The Cockpitt	D4-D5
Belper Road	B7-B8	Crompton Street	B4-C4	George Street	B5	Lynton Street	A3	Queen Mary Court	A8-B8	The Pentagon	F6
Berwick Avenue	F8	Crown Mews	A2	Gerard Street	B4-B3-B2-C2	Macklin Street	B4-C4	Queen Street	C6	The Strand	C5
Bloomfield Close	E1-E2	Crown Street	A2	Grandstand Road	F7	Madeley Street	D1	Railway Terrace	E4-F3	Theatre Walk	C5
Boden Street	E1	Crown Walk	C4-D4	Grange Street	E1	Mansfield Road	D7-D8	Raven Street	A1-A2	Traffic Street	D3-D4
Bold Lane	B5	Cummings Street	C1	Grayling Street	E1	Mansfield Street	C7-D7	Reginald Street	E1	Trinity Street	E3
Bourne Street	D3	Curzon Street	B4-B5	Great Northern Road	A4	Maplebeck Court	C7	Renals Street	C2	Twyford Street	D1-C2-D2
Boyer Street	A2-B2	Darley Lane	C6-C7	Green Lane	C3-C4	Margaret Street	B7-C7	Riddings Street	A2-B2	Upper Bainbridge Street	B1-C1
Bradshaw Way	D3	Darwin Place	D5-D6	Grey Street	B3	Markeaton Street	A6	River Street	C7	Uttoxeter New Road	A4
Bramble Street	B5	Dashwood Street	C1	Grove Street	C2-D2	Market Place	C5	Robert Street	D6	Vernon Gate	A5
Bramfield Avenue	A1-A2	Dean Street	A1-A2	Handyside Street	C7	May Street	A2-B2	Robin Road	B8	Vernon Street	A5
Breedon Hill Road	B1	Depot Street	C1-D1	Hansard Gate	E5	Meadow Road	E5	Roman Road	D8	Vicarage Avenue	A1-B1
Brick Street	A6	Derventio Close	C8	Harcourt Street	B3-C3	Melbourne Street	C2-D2-D3	Rose Hill Street	C1-D1	Victoria Street	C4-C5
Bridge Street	A5-A6-B6	Derwent Street	C5-D5-D6	Harriet Street	C1-D1	Midland Place	E3	Rosengrave Street	B3-C3	Walter Street	A7
Brook Street	A6-B6	Devonshire Walk	D4	Harrison Street	A2	Midland Road	E2-E3-F3	Ruskin Road	B8	Ward Street	A3
Burton Road	A1-B1-B2-C3	Dexter Street	E1-F1	Hartington Street	C2-D2	Milford Street	B7	St Alkmund's Way	B6-C6-D6	Wardwick	B5-C5
Bute Walk	F8	Drage Street	D8	Henry Street	B7	Mill Hill Lane	B1-C2	St Helens Street	B6	Warner Street	A1-B2
Caesar Street	D8	Drewry Court	A4	Highfield Road	A8-B8	Mill Hill Road	C1	St James Street	C5	Watson Street	A7
Calvert Street	E3	Drewry Lane	A3-A4-B4	Howard Street	B1	Mill Street	A6	St Marks Road	F6-F7	Webster Street	B3
Camp Street	D8	Duffield Road	B7-B8	Hulland Street	E2	Monk Street	B3-B4	St Mary's Bridge	C6	Wellington Street	E2-E3
				Huntingdon Green	F6	Moore Street	C1	St Mary's Gate	B5-C5	Werburgh Street	A3-B3
				Irongate	C5	Morledge	D4-D5	St Mary's Wharf	D7	West Avenue	A7-B7
				Ivy Square	E1	Morleston Street	D2	St Mary's Wharf Road	D7-D8	Western Road	B1-C1
				Jackson Street	A3-A4	Moss Street	A2	St Michael's Lane	C6	Westmorland Close	F6
				John Lombe Drive	C7-D7	Mount Carmel Street	B1	St Pancras Way	D7	Wheeldon Avenue	A8
				John Street	E3-E4	Mount Street	C2	St Pauls Road	C8-D7	Whitaker Road	A1
				Keble Close	E2	Mundy Close	A6	St Peter's Churchyard	C4	White Street	A8
						Mundy Street	A6	St Peter's Street	C4-D4	Whitecross Gardens	A7
						Nairn Avenue	F8	Sacheverel Street	C3	William Street	A7
						Nelson Street	E2-F2	Sadler Gate	C5	Willow Row	B6
						New Street	E3-E4	Salisbury Road	C1-C2	Wilmot Street	C3-D3
						Newland Street	B4	Seale Street	D7	Wilson Street	B3-C4
						Normanton Road	C1-C2	Searl Street	A6	Wolfa Street	A4-B4
						North Parade	C7	Sherwood Street	A2	Woods Lane	A2-B2-B3
						North Street	B7-C7	Shetland Close	F8	York Street	A5

178

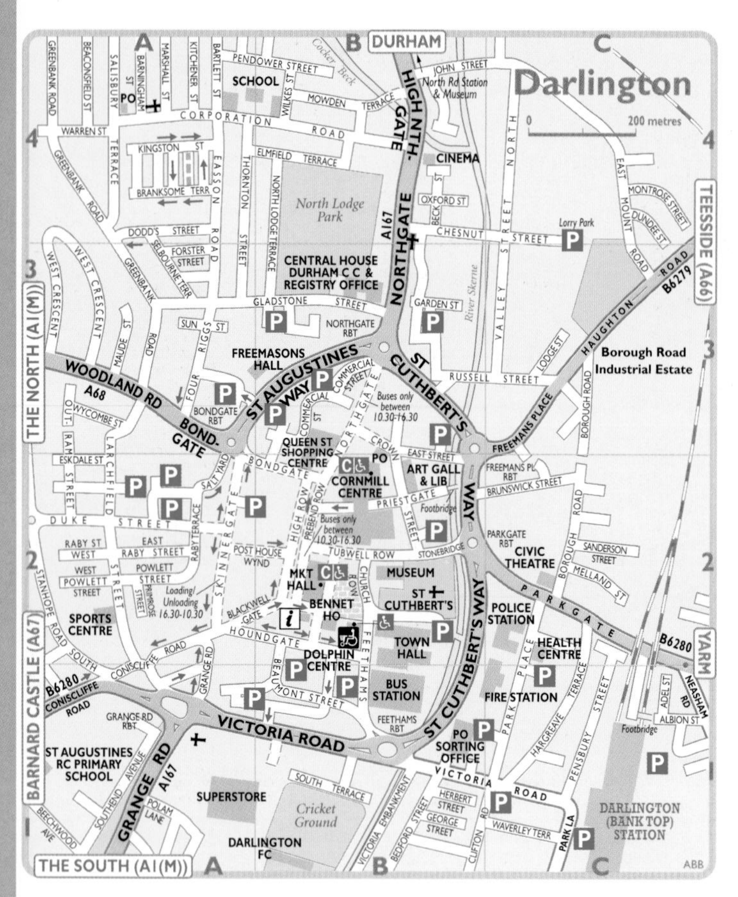

Darlington

Darlington is found on atlas page **89**,
grid reference **2814**

Adelaide Street	C1	John Street	B4-C4	Victoria Road	A1-B1-C1
Albion Street	C1	Kingston Street	A4	Warren Street	A4
Barningham Street	A4	Kitchener Street	A4	Waverley Terrace	C1
Bartlett Street	A4	Larchfield Street	A2-A3	West Crescent	A3-A4
Beaconsfield Street	A4	Lodge Street	C3	West Powlett Street	A2
Beaumont Street	B1-B2	Marshall Street	A4	Wilkes Street	B4
Beck Street	B4	Maude Street	A3	Woodland Road	A3
Bedford Street	B1	Melland Street	C2	Wycombe Street	A3
Beechwood Avenue	A1	Montrose Street	C4		
Blackwell Gate	A2-B2	Mowden Terrace	B4		
Bondgate	A3-A2-B2	Neasham Road	C1		
Borough Road	C2-C3	North Lodge Terrace	B3-B4		
Branksome Terrace	A4	Northgate	B2-B3-B4		
Brunswick Street	B2-C2	Outram Street	A2-A3		
Chestnut Street	B4-C4	Oxford Street	B4		
Church Row	B2	Park Lane	C1		
Clifton Road	B1-C1	Park Place	C1-C2		
Commercial Street	B2-B3	Parkgate	C2		
Coniscliffe Road	A1-A2	Pendower Street	A4-B4		
Corporation Road	A4-B4	Pensbury Street	C1-C2		
Crown Street	B2-B3	Polam lane	A1		
Dodd's Street	A4	Post House Wynd	A2-B2		
Duke Street	A2	Powlett Street	A2		
Dundee Street	C4	Prebend Row	B2		
Easson Road	A3-A4	Priestgate	B2		
East Mount Road	C3-C4	Primrose Street	A2		
East Raby Street	A2	Raby Street West	A2		
East Street	B2-B3	Raby Terrace	A2		
Elmfield Terrace	A4-B4	Russell Street	B3-C3		
Eskdale Street	A2	St Augustines Way	A3-B3		
Feethams	B1-B2	St Cuthbert's Way	B1-B2-B3		
Forster Street	A3	Salisbury Terrace	A4		
Four Riggs	A3	Salt Yard	A2		
Freemans Place	C3	Sanderson Street	C2		
Garden Street	B3	Selbourne Terrace	A3-A4		
George Street	B1	Skinnergate	A2		
Gladstone Street	A3-B3	South Terrace	B1		
Grange Road	A1-A2	Southend Avenue	A1		
Greenbank Road	A3-A4	Stanhope Road South	A1-A2		
Hargreave Terrace	C1-C2	Stonebridge	B2		
Haughton Road	C3-C4	Sun Street	A3		
Herbert Street	B1	Thornton Street	A3-A4		
High Northgate	B4	Tubwell Row	B2		
High Row	B2	Valley Street North	C3-C4		
Houndgate	A2-B2	Victoria Embankment	B1		

Doncaster

Doncaster is found on atlas page **83**,
grid reference **5703**

Apley Road	B2-C2	Prospect Place	B1
Baxter Gate	A3-B3	Queens Road	C4
Beechfield Road	B2-C2	Rainton Road	C1
Broxholme Lane	C4	Ravensworth Road	C1-C2
Carr House Road	A1-B1-C1	Rectory Gardens	C4
Carr Lane	B1	Regent Square	C3
Chequer Avenue	C1	Roberts Road	A1
Chequer Road	B2-C2-C1	Royal Avenue	C4
Childers Street	C1	Rutland Street	C4
Christchurch Road	B4-C4-C3	St James's Bridge	A2
Church View	A4	St James Street	A1-A2-B2-B1
Church Way	A4-B4	St Sepulchre Gate	A3
Clark Avenue	C1	St Sepulchre Gate West	A1-A2
Cleveland Street	A1-A2-B3	St Vincent Road	C4
College Road	B2	Scot Lane	B3
Cooper Street	C1	Silver Street	B3
Coopers Terrace	B4	Somerset Road	C1-C2
Copley Road	B4-C4	South Parade	C3-C2
Cunningham Road	B1-C1	South Street	C1
Dockin Hill Road	B4-C4	Spring Gardens	A3-A2
Duke Street	A3-B3	Stewart Street	A2
East Laith Gate	B3-C3	Stirling Street	A1
Elmfield Road	C2-C1	Thorne Road	C3-C4
Exchange Street	B1	Trafford Way	A3-A2-B2-B1
French Gate	A3	Vaughan Avenue	C4
Glyn Avenue	C4	Waterdale	B2-B3
Grey Friar's Road	A4-B4	West Laith	A2-A3
Grove Place	A2	West Street	A2-A3
Hallgate	B3	Whitburn Road	C2
High Street	A3-B3	Wood Street	B3
Highfield Road	C4		
Jarratt Street	B1		
King's Road	C4		
Lawn Avenue	C3		
Lawn Road	C3		
Low Fisher Gate	B4		
Market Road	B4		
Milton Walk	A2-B2-B1		
Netherhall Road	B4-C4		
North Bridge Road	A4		
North Street	C1		
Oxford Place	A1		
Palmer Street	C1		
Park Road	B3-C3-C4		
Park Terrace	B3-C3		

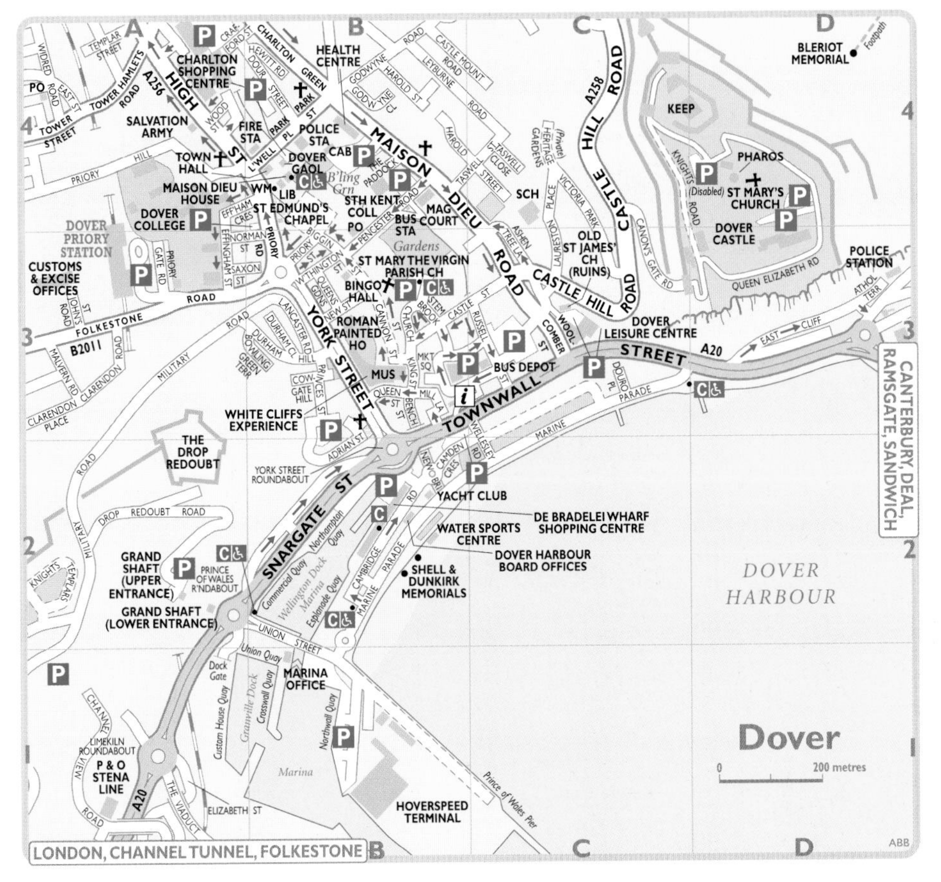

Dover

Dover is found on atlas page **29**, grid reference **3241**

Adrian Street	B2-B3	Maison Dieu Road	B4-C4-C3
Ashen Tree Lane	C3-C4	Malvern Road	A3
Athol Terrace	D3	Marine Parade	B2-C2-C3
Bench Street	B3	Market Square	B3
Biggin Street	B3-B4	Military Road	A2-A3-B3
Bowling Green Terrace	B3	Mill Lane	B3
Bulwark	A1	New Bridge	B2
Cambridge Road	B2	New Street	B3
Camden Crescent	B2-C3	Norman Street	A3-B3-B4
Cannon Street	B3	Park Place	B4
Canon's Gate Road	C3-C4	Park Street	B4
Castle Hill Road	C3-C4	Pencester Road	B3-B4
Castle Mount Road	B4-C4	Princes Street	B3
Castle Street	B3-C3	Priory Gate Road	A3
Channel View Road	A1-A2	Priory Hill	A4
Charlton Green	B4	Priory Road	B3-B4
Church Street	B3	Priory Street	B3
Clarendon Road	A3	Queen Elizabeth Road	D3
Cowgate Hill	B3	Queen Street	B3
Crafford Street	A4-B4	Queens Gardens	B3
De Burgh Street	A4	Russell Street	C3
Dour Street	B4	St John's Road	A3
Douro Place	C3	Saxon Street	A3-B3
Drop Redoubt Road	A2	Snargate Street	B2
Durham Close	B3	Stem Brook	B3
Durham Hill	B3	Taswell Close	C4
East Cliff	D3	Taswell Street	B4-C4
East Street	A4	Templar Street	A4
Effingham Crescent	A4-B4	The Paddock	B4
Effingham Street	A3-A4	The Viaduct	A1
Elizabeth Street	A1	Tower Hamlets Road	A4
Folkestone Road	A3-B3	Tower Street	A4
Godwyne Close	B4	Townwall Street	B3-C3
Godwyne Road	B4	Union Street	B1-B2
Harold Road	B4-C4	Victoria Park	C3-C4
Heritage Gardens	D6	Wellesley Road	C2-C3
Hewitt Road	B4	Widred Road	A4
High Street	A4-B4	Wood Street	A4
King Street	B3	Woolcomber Street	C3
Knights Road	C3-C4	Worthington Street	B3
Knights Templars	A2	York Street	B3
Ladywell	B4		
Lancaster Road	B3		
Laureston Place	C3-C4		
Leyburne Road	B4-C4		

179

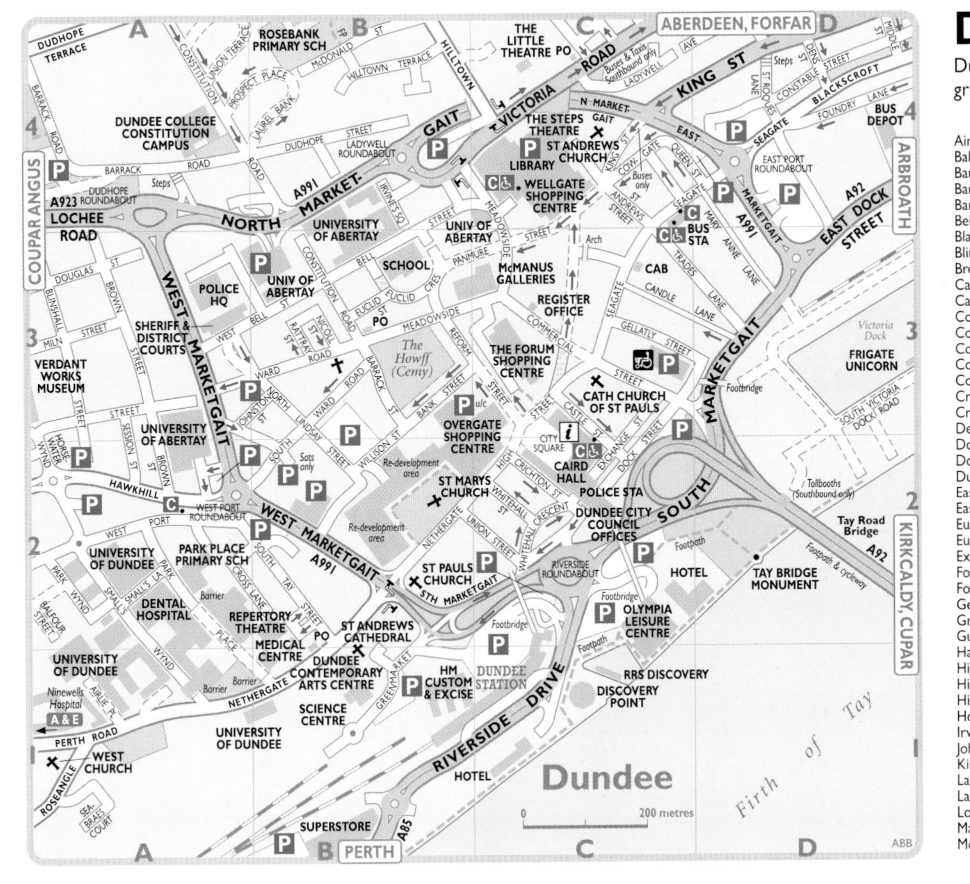

Dundee

Dundee is found on atlas page **126**, grid reference **4030**

Airlie Place	A1	Meadowside	B3-C3-C4
Balfour Place	A1-A2	Middle Street	D4
Bank Street	B2-B3-C3	Miln Street	A3
Barrack Road	A4	Nethergate	A1-B1-B2
Barrack Street	B2-B3	Nicoll Street	B3
Bell Street	B3-C3	North Lindsay Street	B2-B3
Blackscroft	D4	North Marketgait	A3-B3-B4-C4
Blinshall Street	A2-A3	Panmure Street	B3-C3
Brown Street	A2-A3	Panmure Terrace	A4
Candle Lane	C3-D3	Park Place	A2-A1-B1
Castle Street	C2-C3	Park Wynd	B3
Commercial Street	C3	Perth Road	A1
Constable Street	D4	Princes Street	D4
Constitution Road	A4-B4-B3	Prospect Place	A4-B4
Constitution Terrace	A4	Queen Street	C4-D4
Cowgate	C4	Rattray Street	B3
Crichton Street	C2	Reform Street	B3-C3-C2
Cross Lane	A2-B2	Riverside Drive	B1-C1
Dens Street	D4	Roseangle	A1
Dock Street	C2-C3	St Andrews Street	C3-C4
Douglas Street	A3	St Roques Lane	D4
Dudhope Street	B4	Seabraes Court	A1
East Dock Street	D3-D4	Seagate	C3-D4
East Marketgait	C4-D4-D3	Session Street	A2
Euclid Crescent	B3	Small's Lane	A2
Euclid Street	B3	Small's Wynd	A1-A2
Exchange Street	C2-C3	Somerville Place	A4
Forebank Road	C4	South Marketgait	B2-C2-D2-D3
Foundry Lane	D4	South Tay Street	B1-B2
Gellatly Street	C3-D3	South Victoria Dock Road	D2-D3
Greenmarket	B1	South Ward Road	B2-B3
Guthrie Street	A2-A3	Trades Lane	C3-D3
Hawkhill	A2	Union Street	B2-C2
High Street	C2-C3	Union Terrace	A4-B4
Hilltown	B4-C4	Victoria Road	B4-C4-D4
Hilltown Terrace	B4	Ward Road	A3-B3
Horsewater Wynd	A2	West Bell Street	A3-B3
Irvine's Square	B3-B4	West Marketgait	A3-A2-B2
Johnston Street	A2-B3	West Port	A2
King Street	C4-D4	Whitehall Crescent	C2
Ladywell Avenue	C4-D4	Whitehall Street	C2
Laurel Bank	B4	Willison Street	B2
Lochee Road	A3		
Mary Anne Lane	D3-D4		
McDonald Street	B4		

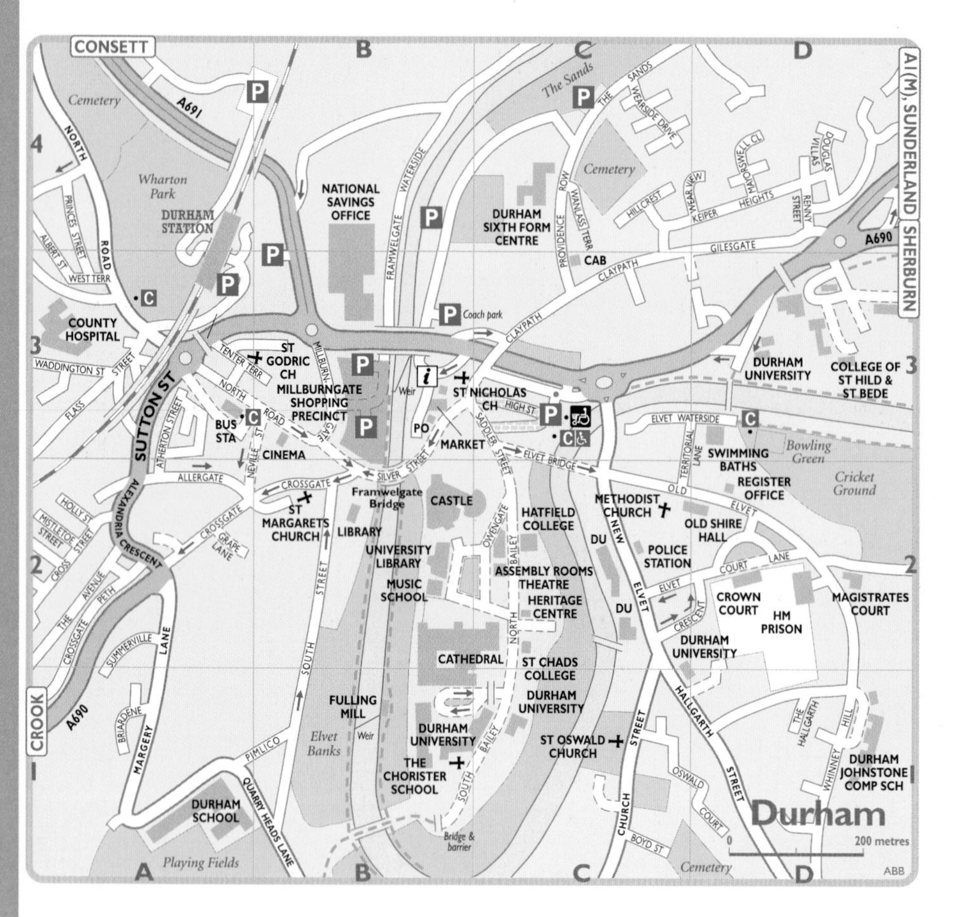

Durham

Durham is found on atlas page **96**, grid reference **2742**

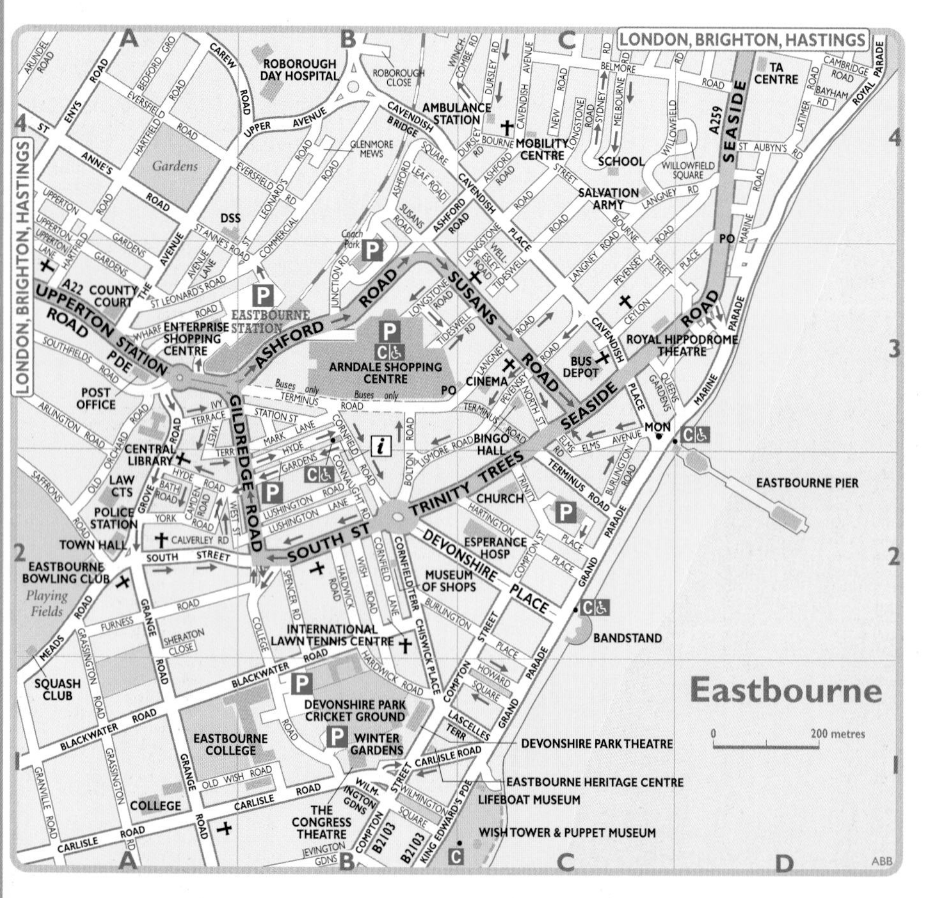

Eastbourne

Eastbourne is found on atlas page **16**, grid reference **6199**

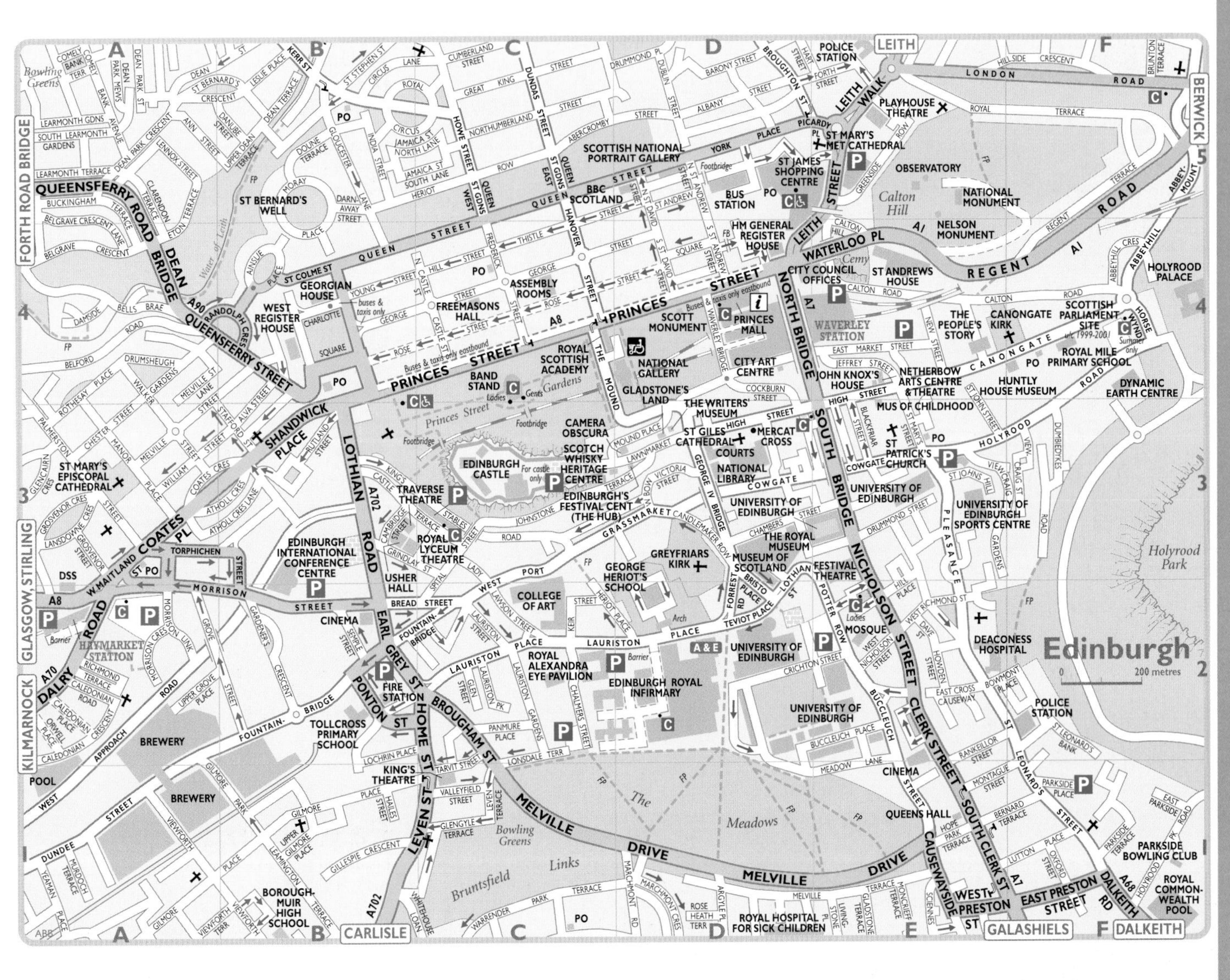

Edinburgh

Edinburgh is found on atlas page 117,
grid reference 2573

182

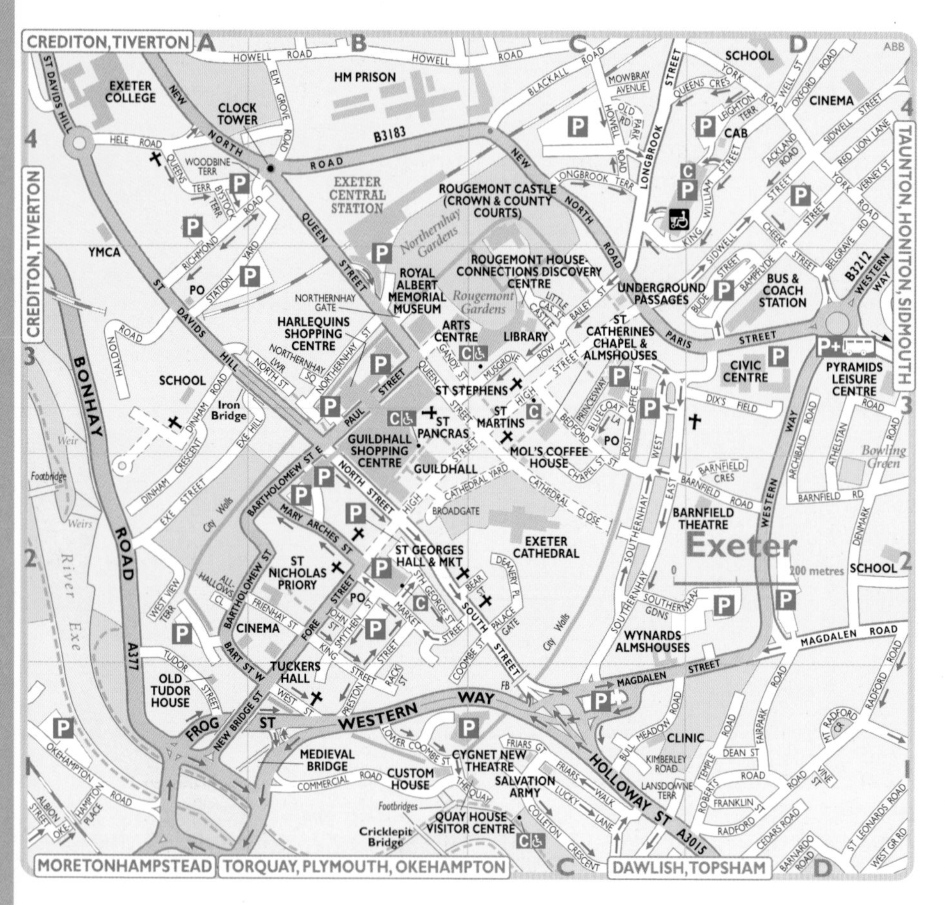

Exeter

Exeter is found on atlas page **9**,
grid reference **9292**

Archibald Road	D2-D3	Lower Coombe Street	B1
Athelstan Road	D2-D3	Lower North Street	B3
Bailey Street	C3	Lucky Lane	C1
Bampfylde Street	D3-D4	Magdalen Road	D2
Barnfield Road	C2-D2	Magdalen Street	C1-D1-D2
Bartholomew Street	A2-B2	Market Street	B2
Bartholomew Street East	B2	Mary Arches Street	B2
Bartholomew Street West	A1-A1-A2	Musgrove Row	B3-C3
Bedford Street	C2-C3	New Bridge Street	A1-B1
Belgrave Road	D3-D4	New North Road	A4-B4-C4-C3
Blackall Road	C4	North Street	B2
Bluecoat Lane	C3	Northernhay Street	B3
Bonhay Road	A1-A2-A3-A4	Okehampton Place	A1
Bull Meadow Road	C1	Okehampton Road	A1
Castle Street	C3	Old Park Road	C4
Cathedral Close	C2-C3	Oxford Road	D4
Cathedral Yard	B2-C2	Palace Gate	C2
Cedars Road	D1	Paris Street	C3-D3
Chapel Street	C2-C3	Paul Street	B3
Cheeke Street	D3-D4	Post Office Lane	C2-C3
Colleton Crescent	C1	Preston Street	B1-B2
Commercial Road	B1	Princesway	C3
Coombe Street	B1-B2-C2	Queen Street	B4-B3-C3
Deanery Place	C2	Queens Crescent	C4-D4
Denmark Road	D2-D3	Queens Terrace	A4
Dinham Crescent	A2-A3	Radford Road	D1-D2
Dinham Road	A3	Richmond Road	A3-A4-B4
Dix's Field	D3	Roberts Road	D1
Elm Grove Road	B4	St Davids Hill	A4-A3-B3
Exe Hill	A3-B3	St Leonards Road	D1
Exe Street	A2	Sidwell Street	C3-D3-D4
Fairpark Road	D1-D2	Smythen Street	B2
Fore Street	B1-B2	South George Street	B2
Friars Walk	C1	South Street	B2-C2-C1
Frienhay Street	B2	Southernhay East	C1-C2-C3
Frog Street	A1-B1	Southernhay Gardens	C2-D2
Haldon Road	A3	Southernhay West	C2-C3
Hele Road	A4	Station Yard	A3-B3-B4
High Street	B2-B3-C3	Temple Road	D1
Holloway Street	C1-D1	Tudor Street	A1-A2
Howell Road	A4-B4-C4	West Street	B1
King Street	B1-B2	West View Terrace	A2
King William Street	C3-C4-D4	Western Way	B1-C1
Longbrook Street	C3-C4	Western Way	D2-D3-D4
Longbrook Terrace	C4	York Road	C4-D4

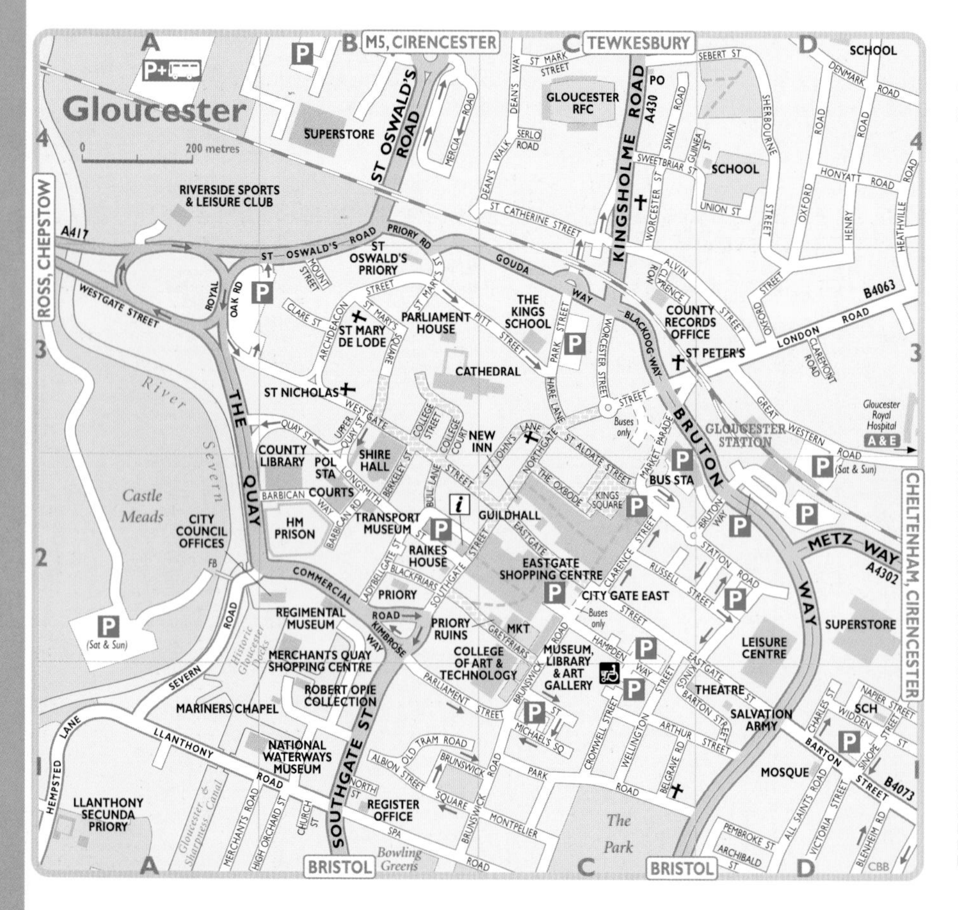

Gloucester

Gloucester is found on atlas page **35**,
grid reference **8318**

Albion Street	B1	Longsmith Street	B2
All Saints Road	D1	Market Parade	C2-C3
Alvin Street	C3-D1	Merchants Road	A1-B1
Archdeacon Street	B3	Mercia Road	B4
Arthur Street	C1-D1	Metz Way	D2
Barbican Road	B2	Montpelier	C1
Barbican Way	B2	Napier Street	D1
Barton Street	D1	Northgate Street	C2-C3
Belgrave Road	C1	Old Tram Road	B1
Berkeley Street	B2-B3	Oxford Road	D3-D4
Blackdog Way	C3	Oxford Street	D3
Blackfriars	B2	Park Road	C1
Brunswick Road	B1-C1-C2	Park Street	C3
Brunswick Square	B1-C1	Parliament Street	B2-B1-C1
Bruton Way	C3-D2-D1	Pembroke Street	D1
Bull Lane	B2	Pitt Street	B3-C3
Charles Street	D1	Priory Road	B4
Clare Street	B3	Quay Street	A3-B3
Clarence Street	C2	Royal Oak Road	A3
College Court	B3	Russell Street	C2-D2
College Street	B3	St Aldate Street	C2-C3
Commercial Road	B2	St Catherine Street	C4
Cromwell Street	C1	St John's Lane	B2-C2-C3
Dean's Walk	C4	St Mary's Square	B3
Dean's Way	C4	St Mary's Street	B3
Denmark Road	D4	St Michael's Square	C1
Eastgate Street	C2-D1	St Oswald's Road	B3-B4
Gouda Way	B3-B4-C3	Sebert Street	C4-D4
Great Western Road	D2-D3	Severn Road	A1-A2
Greyfriars	B2-C2	Sherbourne Street	D3-D4
Guinea Street	C4-D4	Sinope Street	D1
Hampden Way	C1-C2	Southgate Street	B1-B2-C2
Hare Lane	C3	Spa Road	B1-C1
Heathville Road	D3-D4	Station Road	D2
Hempsted Lane	A1	Swan Road	C4
Henry Road	D3-D4	Sweetbriar Street	C4
High Orchard Street	A1-B1	The Oxbode	C2
Honyatt Road	D4	The Quay	A2-A3
Kimbrose Way	B2	Union Street	C4-D4
Kings Barton Street	C1-D1	Upper Quay Street	B2-B3
Kings Square	C2	Victoria Street	D1
Kingsholme Road	C3-C4	Wellington Street	C1-C2
Ladybellgate Street	B2	Westgate Street	A3-B3-B2
Llanthony Road	A1-B1	Widden Street	D1
London Road	D3	Worcester Street	C3, C4

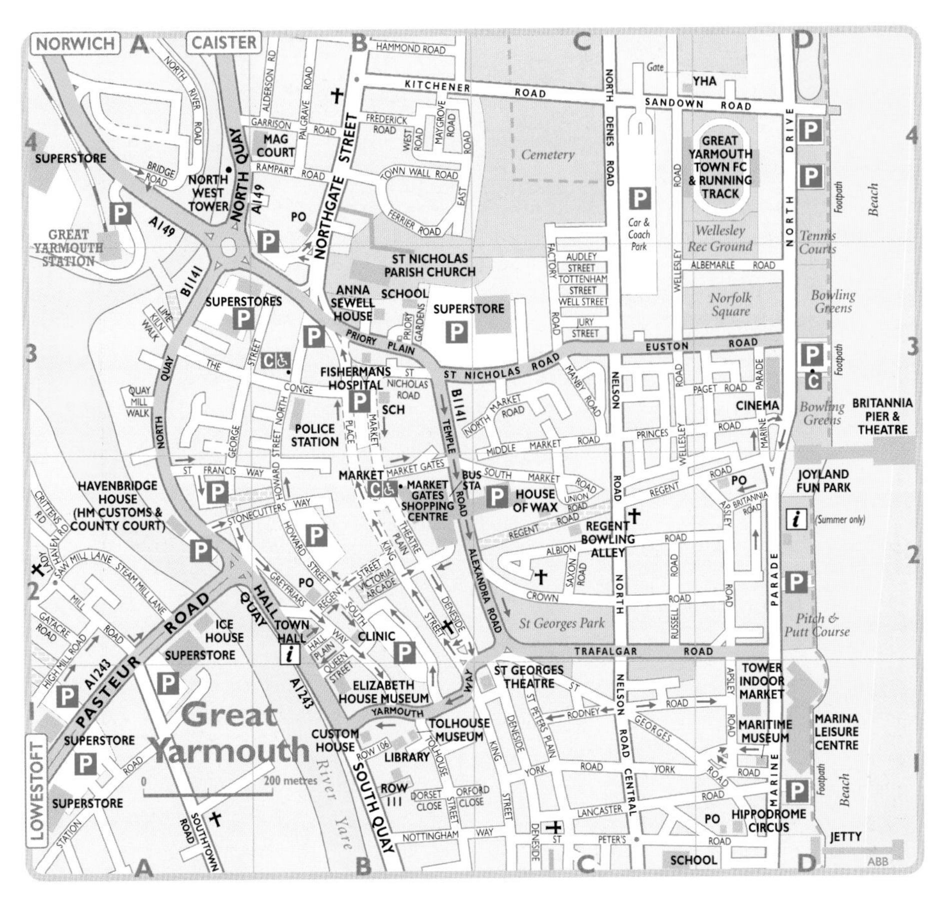

Great Yarmouth

Great Yarmouth is found on atlas page **67**, grid reference **5207**

Albemarle Road	C3-D3	North River Road	A4
Albion Road	C2-D2	Northgate Street	B3-B4
Alderson Road	B4	Nottingham Way	B1-C1
Alexandra Road	C2	Orford Close	B1-C1
Apsley Road	D1-D2	Paget Road	C3-D3
Audley Street	C3	Palgrave Road	B4
Bridge Road	A4	Pasteur Road	A1-A2
Britannia Road	D2	Princes Road	C3-D3
Crown Road	C2-D2	Priory Gardens	B3
Deneside	B2-C1	Priory Plain	B3
Dorset Close	B1	Quay Mill Walk	A3
East Road	B4	Queen Street	B1-B2
Euston Road	C3-D3	Rampart Road	B4
Factory Road	C3-C4	Regent Road	C2-D2
Ferrier Road	B4	Regent Street	B2
Frederick Road	B4	Rodney Road	C1-D1
Garrison Road	A4-B4	Row 106	B1
Gatacre Road	A2	Russell Road	C2
George Street	A2-A3-B3	St Francis Way	A2-B2
Greyfriars Way	A2-B2-B1	St Georges Road	C1-D1
Hall Plain	B2	St Nicholas Road	B3-C3
Hall Quay	B2	St Peter's Road	C1-D1
Hammond Road	B4	St Peters Plain	C1
High Mill Road	A1-A2	Sandown Road	C4-D4
Howard Street North	B2-B3	Saw Mill Lane	A2
Howard Street South	B2	South Market Road	B2-C2
Jury Street	C3	South Quay	B1
King Street	B2-C1	Southtown Road	A1
Kitchener Road	B4-C4	Station Road	A1
Lady Haven Road	A2	Steam Mill Lane	A2
Lancaster Road	C1-D1	Stonecutters Way	A2-B2
Lime Kiln Walk	A3	Temple Road	B3-B2
Manby Road	C3	The Conge	A3-B3
Marine Parade	D1-D2-D3	Theatre Plain	B2
Market Gates	B2	Tolhouse Street	B1
Market Place	B2-B3	Tottenham Street	C3
Maygrove Road	B4	Town Wall Road	B4
Middle Market Road	C2-C3	Trafalgar Road	C2-D2
Mill Road	A2	Union Road	C2
Nelson Road Central	C1	Victoria Arcade	B2
Nelson Road North	C2-C3	Well Street	C3
North Denes Road	C4	Wellesley Road	C2-C3-C4
North Drive	D3-D4	West Road	B4
North Market Road	B3-C3	Yarmouth Way	B1-C1-C2
North Quay	A2-A3-A4	York Road	C1-D1

183

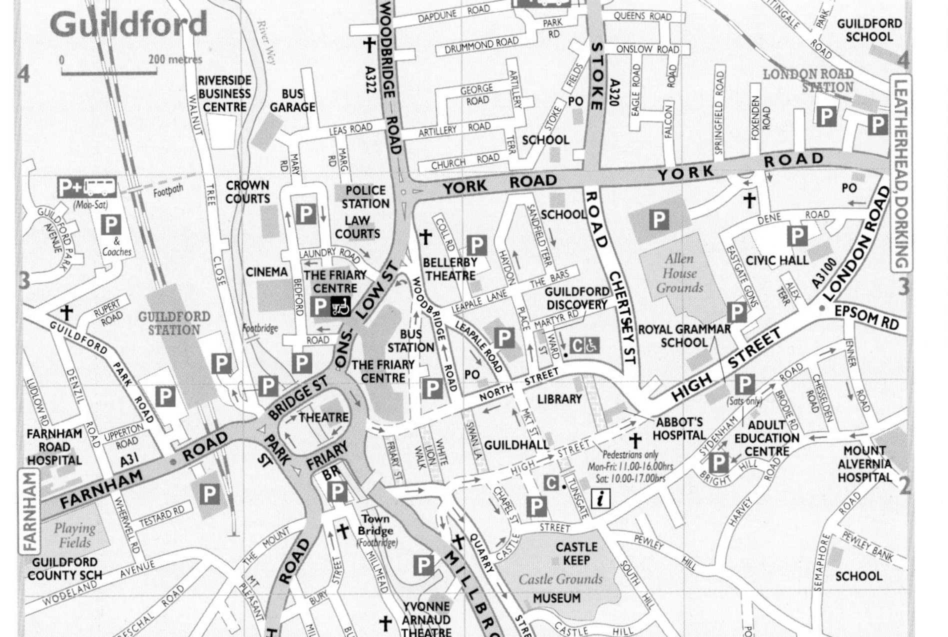

Guildford

Guildford is found on atlas page **25**, grid reference **9949**

Abbot Road	C1	Mareschal Road	A1-A2
Alexandra Terrace	D3	Margaret Road	B3-B4
Artillery Road	B4-C4	Market Street	C2
Artillery Terrace	C4	Martyr Road	C3
Bedford Road	B3	Mary Road	B3-B4
Bridge Street	B2-B3	Millbrook	B2-C2-C1
Bright Hill	D2	Millmead	B1-B2
Brodie Road	D2	Millmead Terrace	B1
Bury Fields	B1	Mount Pleasant	B1-B2
Bury Street	B1-B2	Mountside	A1
Castle Hill	C1	Nightingale Road	D4
Castle Street	C2	North Street	B2-C2-C3
Chapel Street	C2	Onslow Road	C4
Chertsey Street	C3	Onslow Street	B3
Chesselden Road	D2-D3	Park Chase	D4
Church Road	B4-C4	Park Road	C4
College Road	B3-C3	Park Street	B2
Dapdune Road	B4-C4	Pewley Bank	D2
Dene Road	D3	Pewley Hill	C2-D2-D1
Denzil Road	A2-A3	Portsmouth Road	B1-B2
Drummond Road	B4-C4	Poyle Road	D1
Eagle Road	C4	Quarry Street	B2-C2-C1
Eastgate Gardens	D3	Queens Road	C4
Epsom Road	D3	Rupert Road	A3
Falcon Road	C4	Sandfield Terrace	C3
Farnham Road	A2	Semaphore Road	D1-D2
Fort Road	C1-D1	South Hill	C1-C2
Foxenden Road	D4	Springfield Road	D4
Friary Bridge	B2	Stoke Fields	C4
Friary Street	B2	Stoke Road	C3-C4
George Road	B4-C4	Swan Lane	B2-C2
Guildford Park Avenue	A3	Sydenham Road	C2-D2-D3
Guildford Park Road	A2-A3	Testard Road	A2
Harvey Road	D2	The Bars	C3
Haydon Place	C3	The Mount	A1-A2-B2
High Pewley	D1	Tunsgate	C2
High Street	C2-D3	Upperton Road	A2
Jenner Road	D2-D3	Walnut Tree Close	A4-A4-B3
Laundry Road	B3	Ward Street	C3
Lawn Road	B1	Warwicks Road	C1-D1
Leapale Lane	B3-C3	Wherwell Road	A2
Leapale Road	B3-C3	White Lion Walk	B2
Leas Road	B4	Wodeland Avenue	A1-A2
London Road	D3	Woodbridge Road	B2-B3-B4
Ludlow Road	A2-A3	York Road	B3-C3-D3-D4

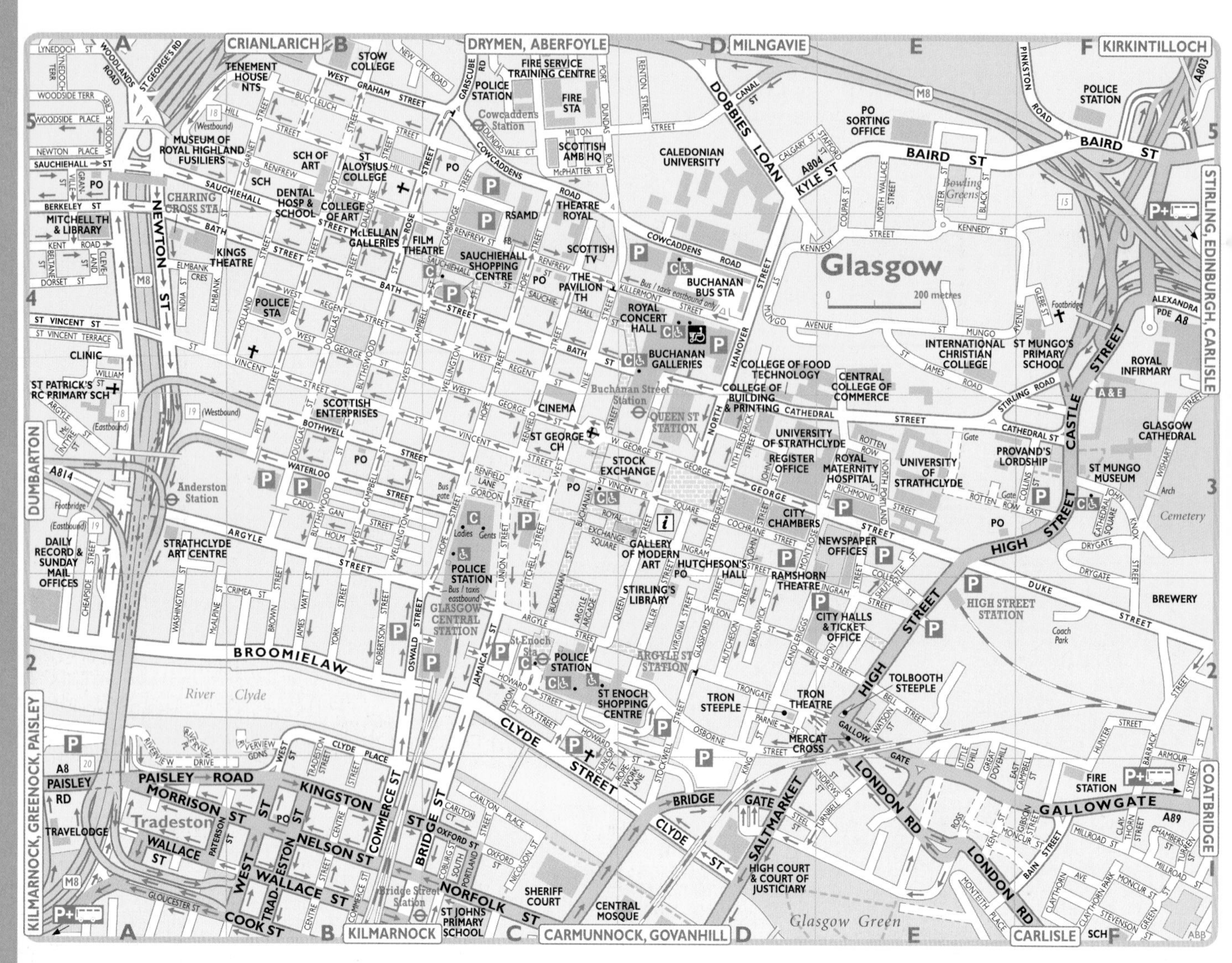

184

Glasgow

Glasgow is found on atlas page **115**,
grid reference **5865**

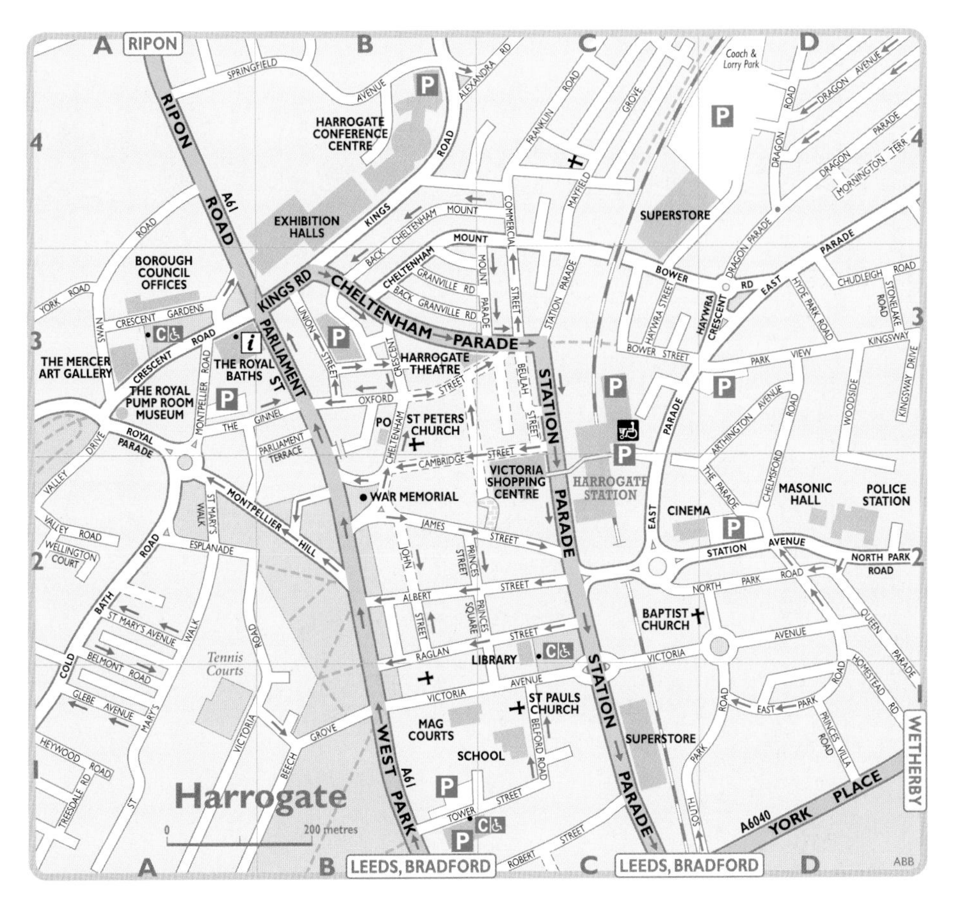

Harrogate

Harrogate is found on atlas page **82**,
grid reference **3054**

Albert Street	B2-C2	North Park Road	C2-D2
Alexandra Road	B4-C4	Oxford Street	B3-C3
Arthington Avenue	D2-D3	Park View	D3
Back Cheltenham Mount	B3-B4-C4	Parliament Street	B3
Back Granville Road	B3	Parliament Terrace	B3
Beech Grove	A1-B1	Princes Square	B2-C2
Belford Road	C1	Princes Street	B2-C2
Belmont Road	A1-A2	Princes Villa Road	D1
Beulah Street	C3	Queen Parade	D1-D2
Bower Road	C4-C3-D3	Raglan Street	B1-B2-C2
Bower Street	C3	Ripon Road	A3-A4
Cambridge Street	B2-C3	Robert Street	C1
Chelmsford Road	D2-D3	Royal Parade	A3
Cheltenham Crescent	B2-B3	St Mary's Avenue	A2
Cheltenham Mount	B3-B4-C4	St Mary's Walk	A1-A2
Cheltenham Parade	B3-C3	South Park Road	C1-D1
Chudleigh Road	D3	Springfield Avenue	A4-B4
Cold Bath Road	A1-A2	Station Avenue	C2-D2
Commercial Street	C3-C4	Station Parade	C1-C2-C3
Crescent Gardens	A3	Stonelake Road	D3
Crescent Road	A3	Swan Road	A3-A4
Dragon Avenue	D4	The Ginnel	A3-B3
Dragon Parade	D3-D4	The Parade	D2
Dragon Road	D4	Tower Street	B1-C1
East Parade	C2-C3-D3-D4	Treesdale Road	A1
East Park Road	D1-D2	Union Street	B3
Esplanade	A2	Valley Drive	A2-A3
Franklin Road	C4	Valley Road	A2
Glebe Avenue	A1	Victoria Avenue	B1-C1-C2-D2
Granville Road	B3	Victoria Road	A1-B1-B2-A2
Haywra Crescent	D3	Wellington Court	A2
Haywra Street	C3	West Park	B1
Heywood Road	A1	Woodside	D2-D3
Homestead Road	D1-D2	York Place	D1
Hyde Park Road	D3	York Road	A3
James Street	B2-C2		
John Street	B2		
Kings Road	B3-B4		
Kingsway	D3		
Kingsway Drive	D3		
Mayfield Grove	C4		
Montpellier Hill	A2-B2		
Montpellier Road	A3		
Mornington Terrace	D4		
Mount Parade	C3		

185

Huddersfield

Huddersfield is found on atlas page **82**,
grid reference **1416**

Albion Street	B1-B2	Market Street	B2
Alfred Street	C1	Merton Street	A1-A2-B2
Back Spring Street	A2	New North Parade	B3
Bath Street	B4	New North Road	A4-A3-B3
Beast Market	C3	New Street	B1-B2-C2
Belmont Street	A4-B4	Northumberland Street	C3
Bow Street	A1-A2	Old Leeds Road	D3-D4
Brook Street	B3-C3	Old Gate	C2-C3
Byram Street	C3	Old South Street	A2
Cambridge Road	B4	Outcote Bank	A1-B1
Castlegate	B1-B2-B3-B4	Page Street	C1
Cecil Street	A2	Park Avenue	A2-A3
Chapel Street	B1-C1	Peel Street	C1-C2
Claremont Street	B4	Pine Street	C3-D3
Cloth Hall Street	B2-C2	Portland Street	A3
Colne Street	D1	Princess Street	B1-C1
Corporation Street	B1-C1-C2	Prospect Street	A1-B1
Cross Church Street	C2	Quay Street	D3
Crossgrove Street	A1	Queen Street	C2
Day Street	D1	Queensgate	C1-C2-D2
Dundas Street	B2	Railway Street	B3
Elmwood Avenue	A4-B4	Ramsden Street	C2
Fenton Square	A1	Rook Street	B4
Firth Street	D1	St Andrews Road	D2-D3-D4
Fitzwilliam Street	A3-B3-B4	St John's Road	B4
Fox Street	B2	St Peter's Street	C3
Garforth Street	D1	Southgate	C3-C2-D2
Gasworks Street	D4	Springrove Street	A1
George Street	B2	Spring Street	A2
Great Northern Street	C4	Springwood Avenue	A2
Greenhead Road	A2	Springwood Street	A2
Half Moon Street	B2	Station Street	B3
Henry Street	B2	Trinity Street	A3-A2-B2
High Street	B2	Westgate	B2-C2
Highfields Road	A4	Upper George Street	A2
Imperial Arcade	B2	Upperhead Row	B2
John William Street	B3-C3	Venn Street	C2-C3
King Street	C2	Victoria Lane	C2
Kings Mill Lane	D1	Wakefield Road	D1-D2
Kirkgate	C2-C3	Water Street	A1-A2
Lord Street	C3	Watergate	D3
Lower Fitzwilliam Street	C4-D4	Waverley Road	A3
Lynton Avenue	A2	William Street	C4
Manchester Road	A1-B1	Wood Street	C3
Market Place	C2	Zetland Street	C2

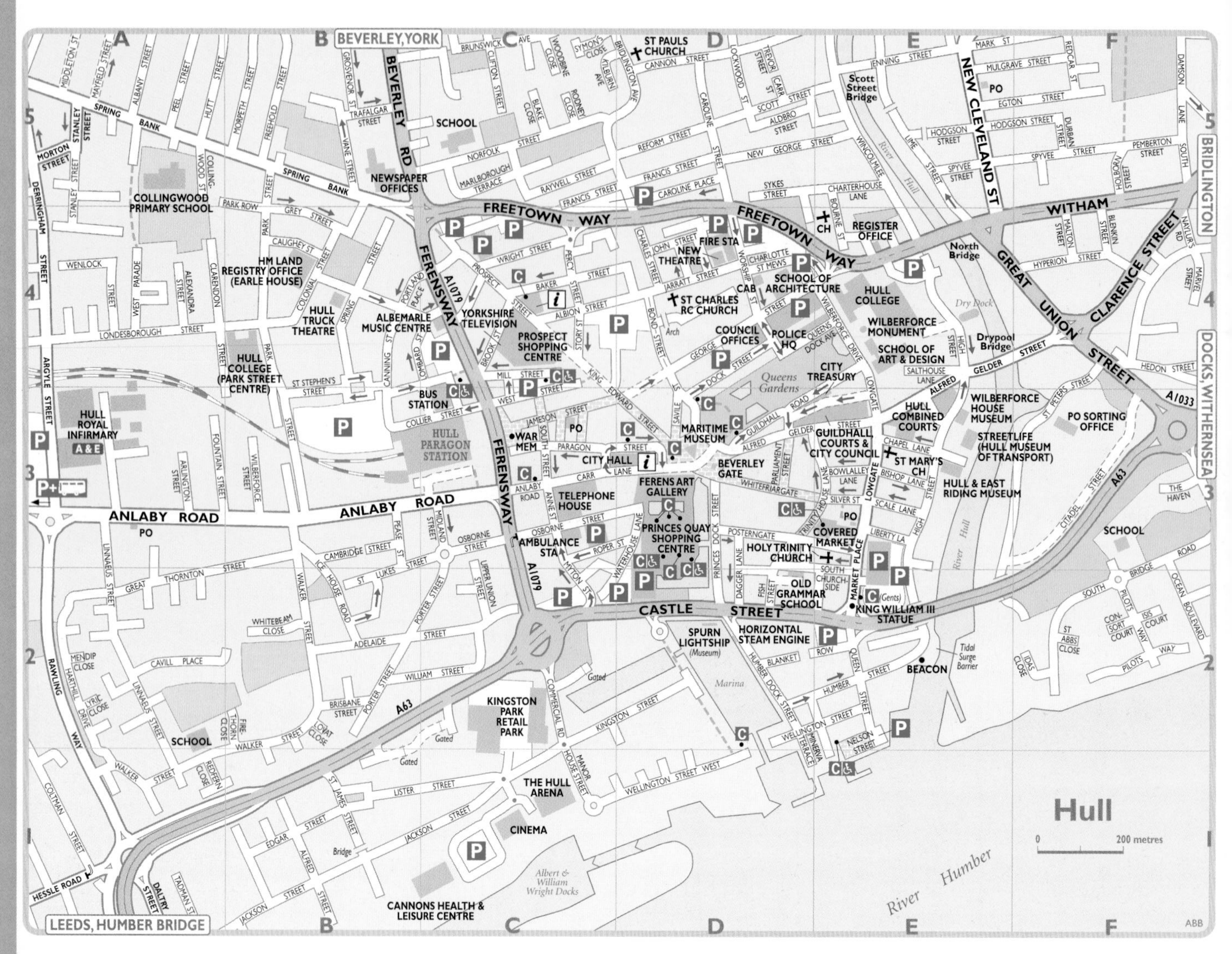

Hull

Hull is found on atlas page **85**,
grid reference **0829**

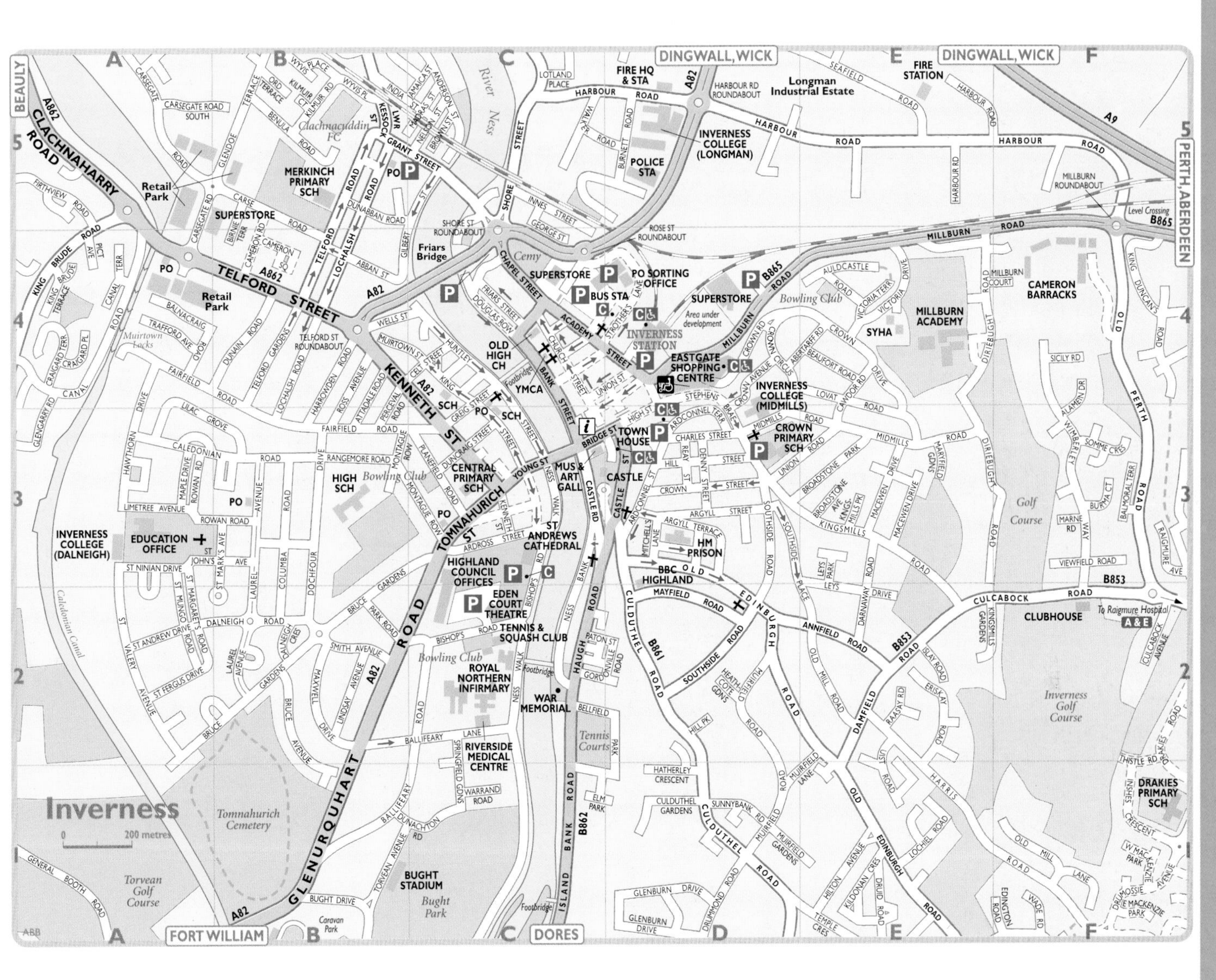

Inverness

Inverness is found on atlas page **140**,
grid reference **6645**

Abban Street	B4	Burma Court	F3	Dalneigh Crescent	B2	Haugh Road	C2-C3	Madras Street	B5-C5	St Margaret's Drive	A2
Abertarff Road	D4-E4	Burnett Road	D5	Dalneigh Road	A2-B2	Hawthorn Drive	A3-A4	Maple Drive	A3	St Mary's Avenue	B2-B3
Academy Street	C4-D4	Caledonian Road	A3-B3	Damfield Road	E1-E2	Heathcote Gardens	D2	Marne Road	F3	St Mungo Road	A2
Ardross Street	C3	Cameron Road	B4	Darnaway Road	E2-E3	High Street	D3	Maryfield Gardens	E5	St Ninian Drive	A3
Alamein Drive	F3-F4	Cameron Square	B4	Denny Street	D3	Hill Park	D2	Maxwell Drive	B2	St Valery Avenue	A2-A3
Anderson Street	C5	Canal Road	A4	Diriebught Road	E2-E3-F3-E4	Hill Street	D3	Mayfield Road	D2	Seafield Road	D5-E5
Annfield Road	D2-E2	Canal Terrace	A4	Dochfour Drive	B2-B3	Hillburn Road	D4-E4-F4	Midmills Road	D3-E3	Shore Street	C4-C5
Ardconnel Street	D3	Carse Road	B4-B5	Douglas Row	C4	Hilton Avenue	E1	Millburn Court	F4	Sicily Road	F4
Ardconnel Terrace	D3	Carsegate Road	A4-A5	Drakies Road	F1-F2	Huntly Street	C3-C4	Millburn Road	D4-E4-F4	Smith Avenue	B2
Argyll Street	D3	Carsegate Road South	A5-B5	Druid Road	E1	India Street	B5-C5	Mitchells Lane	D3	Somme Crescent	F3
Argyll Terrace	D3	Castle Road	C3	Drummond Road	D1	Innes Street	C4-C5	Montague Row	B3-C3	Southside Place	D3-E2
Attadale Road	B3-B4	Castle Street	D3	Drumossie Avenue	F1	Inshes Crescent	F1	Muirfield Gardens	D1-E1	Southside Road	D2-D3
Auldcastle Road	E4	Cawdor Road	E3-E4	Dunabban Road	B4-B5	Island Bank Road	C1-C2	Muirfield Lane	D1-E1	Springfield Gardens	C1-C2
Ballifeary Lane	B2-C2	Celt Street	C4	Dunachton Gardens	B1-C1	Islay Road	E2	Muirfield Road	D1-D2	Stephens Brae	D3
Ballifeary Road	B1-C1-C2	Chapel Street	C4	Dunain Road	B4	Jamaica Street	C5	Muirtown Street	B4-C4	Strother's Lane	D4
Balmoral Terrace	F3	Charles Street	D3	Duncraig Street	C3	Kenneth Street	B4-C3	Nelson Street	C5	Sunnybank Road	D1
Balnacraig Road	A4	Church Street	C3-C4	East Mackenzie Park	F1	Kildonan Crescent	E1	Ness Bank	C2-C3	Telford Gardens	B3-B4
Bank Street	C3-C4	Clachnaharry Road	A5	Edington Road	E1-F1	Kilmuir Court	B5	Ness Walk	C2-C3	Telford Road	B4-B5
Beaufort Road	E4	Columba Road	B2-B3	Elm Park	C1-D1	Kilmuir Road	B5	Old Edinburgh Road	D3-D2-E2-E1	Temple Crescent	E1
Bellfield Park	C2-D2-D1	Craigard Place	A4	Eriskay Road	E1-E2	King Brude Road	A4-A5	Old Mill Lane	F1	Thistle Road	F1
Benula Road	B5	Craigard Terrace	A4	Fairfield Road	A4-B3-C3	King Brude Terrace	A4	Old Mill Road	E2	Tomnahurich Street	C3
Birnie Terrace	B4-B5	Crown Avenue	D3-D4	Firthview Road	A5	King Duncan's Road	F4	Old Perth Road	F2-F3-F4	Torvean Avenue	B1
Bishop's Road	C2-C3	Crown Circus	D4	Friars Street	C4	King Street	C3-C4	Ord Terrace	B5	Trafford Avenue	A4
Bridge Street	C3-D3	Crown Drive	D4-E4	General Booth Road	A1	Kingmills Road	D3-E3-E2	Park Road	B2	Uist Road	E1-E2
Broadstone Avenue	E3	Crown Road	D4	George Street	C4-C5	Kingsmills Gardens	E2-F2	Paton Street	C2-D2	Union Road	D3-E3
Broadstone Park	D3-E3	Crown Street	D3	Gilbert Street	B4-C5	Kingsmills Park	E3	Perceval Road	B3-B4	Union Street	C3-C4-D4
Brown Street	C5	Culcabock Avenue	F2	Glenburn Drive	D1	Laurel Avenue	B2-B3	Pict Avenue	A4	Victoria Drive	E4
Bruce Avenue	B1-B2	Culcabock Road	E2-F2	Glendoe Terrace	B5	Leys Drive	E2	Planefield Road	C3	Victoria Terrace	E4
Bruce Gardens	A1-A2-B2-B3	Culduthel Gardens	D1	Glengarry Road	A3	Leys Park	E2-E3	Raasay Road	E2	Viewfield Road	F3
Bught Drive	B1	Culduthel Road	D1-D2-D3	Glenurquhart Road	B1-B2-C2	Lilac Grove	A3-B3	Raigmore Avenue	F3	Wade Road	F1
				Gordonville Road	C2-D2	Lindsay Avenue	B2	Rangemore Road	B3	Walker Road	C5-D5
				Grant Street	B5-C5	Lochalsh Road	B3-B4-B5	Reay Street	D5	Warrand Road	C1
				Greig Street	C3-C4	Lochiel Road	E1	Ross Avenue	B3-B4	Wells Street	B4-C4
				Harbour Road	C5-D5-E5-F5	Lotland Place	C5	Rowan Road	A3-B3	West Mackenzie Park	F1
				Harris Road	E2-E1-F1	Lovat Road	E3-E4	St Andrew Drive	A2	Wimberley Way	F2-F3-F4
				Harrowden Road	B3-B4	Lower Kessock Street	B5	St Fergus Drive	A2	Wyvis Place	B5
				Hatherley Crescent	D1	Macewen Drive	E3	St John's Avenue	A3-B3		

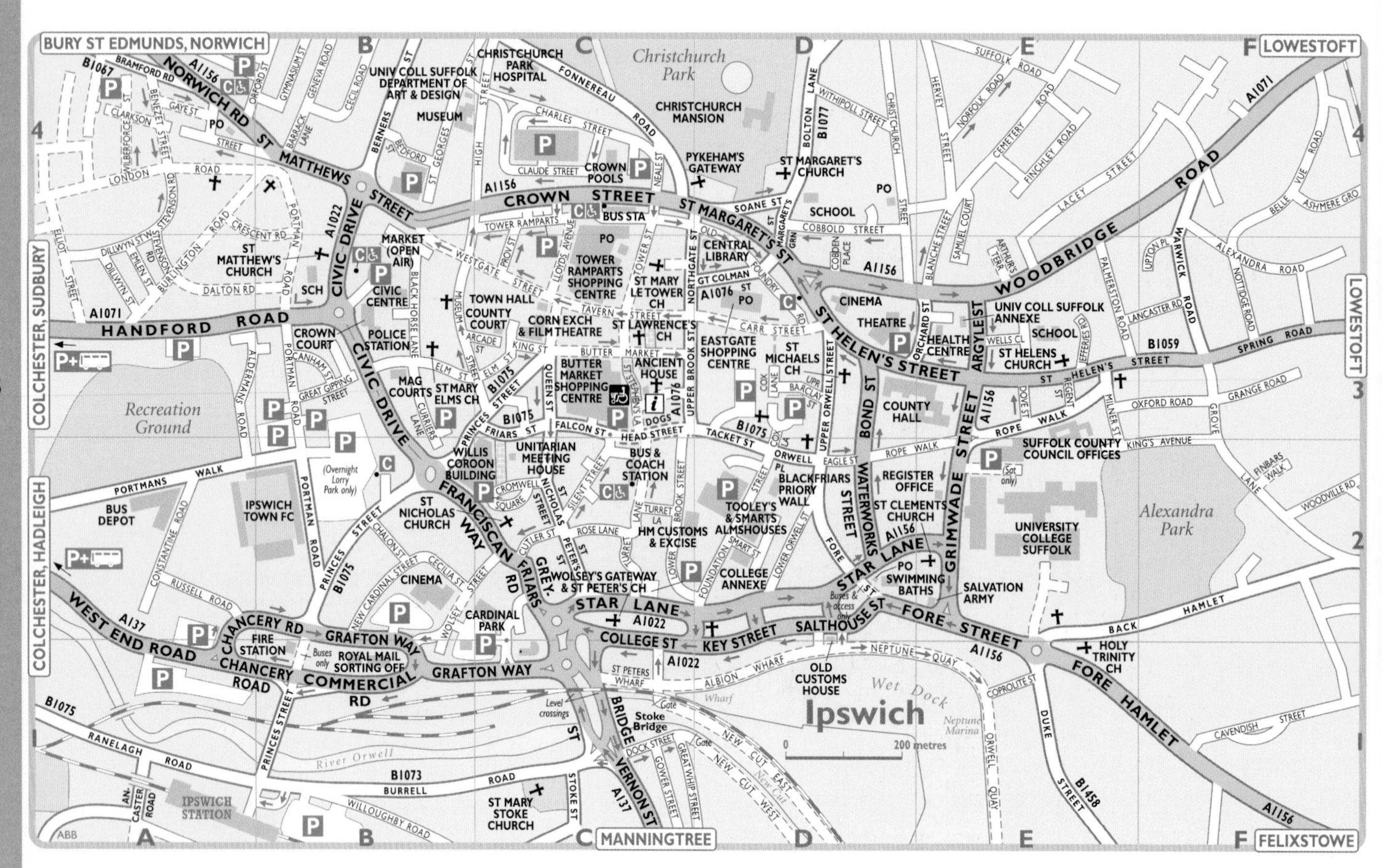

Ipswich

Ipswich is found on atlas page **54**,
grid reference **1644**

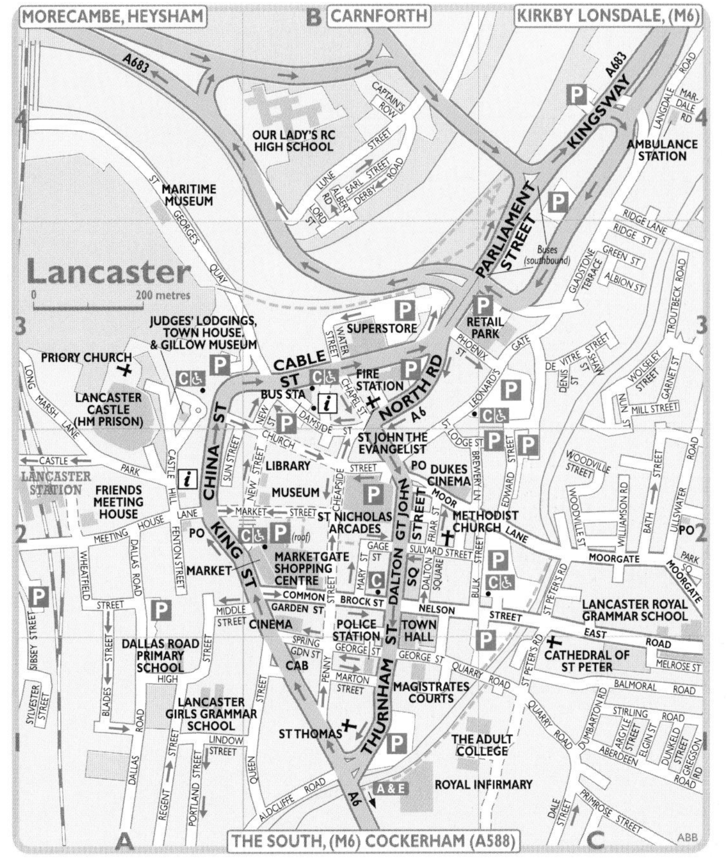

Lancaster

Lancaster is found on atlas page **87**, grid reference **4761**

Aberdeen Road	C1	Langdale Road	C4	Wheatfield Street	A2
Albert Road	B4	Lindow Street	A1-B1	Williamson Road	C2
Albion Street	C3	Lodge Street	B2-B3	Wolseley Street	C3
Aldcliffe Road	B1	Long Marsh Lane	A2-A3	Woodville Street	C2
Argyle Street	C1	Lord Street	B4		
Balmoral Road	C1	Lune Street	B4		
Bath Street	C2	Mardale Road	C4		
Blades Street	A1-A2	Market Street	A2-B2		
Brewery Lane	B2	Marton Street	B1		
Brock Street	B2	Mary Street	B2		
Bulk Street	B2-C2	Meeting House Lane	A2		
Cable Street	B3	Melrose Street	C1		
Captain's Row	B4	Middle Street	A2-B2		
Castle Hill	A2	Mill Street	C3		
Castle Park	A2	Moor Lane	B2-C2		
Chapel Street	B3	Moorgate	C2		
Cheapside	B2	Nelson Street	B2-C2		
China Street	A2-A3	New Street	B2-B3		
Church Street	A3-B2	North Road	B3		
Common Garden Street	B2	Nun Street	C2-C3		
Dale Street	C1	Park Square	C2		
Dallas Road	A1-A2	Parliament Street	C3-C4		
Dalton Square	B2	Penny Street	B1-B2		
Damside Street	B2-B3	Phoenix Street	B3-C3		
De Vitre Street	C3	Portland Street	A1		
Denis Street	C3	Primrose Street	C1		
Derby Road	B4	Quarry Road	B1-C1		
Dumbarton Road	C1	Queen Street	B1		
Dunkeld Street	C1	Regent Street	A1		
Earl Street	B4	Ridge Lane	C3-C4		
East Road	C1-C2	Ridge Street	C3		
Edward Street	C2	St George's Quay	A4-A3-B3		
Elgin Street	C1	St Leonard's Gate	B2-B3-C3		
Fenton Street	A2	St Peter's Road	C1-C2		
Friar Street	B2	Shaw Street	C3		
Gage Street	B2	Sibsey Street	A1-A2		
Garnet Street	C3	Spring Garden Street	B1-B2		
George Street	B1	Stirling Road	C1		
Gladstone Terrace	C3	Sulyard Street	B2		
Great John Street	B2	Sun Street	A2		
Green Street	C3	Sylvester Street	A1		
Gregson Road	C1	Thurnham Street	B1-B2		
High Street	A1-A2	Troutbeck Road	C3		
King Street	A2-B2	Ullswater Road	C2-C3		
Kingsway	C4	Water Street	B3		

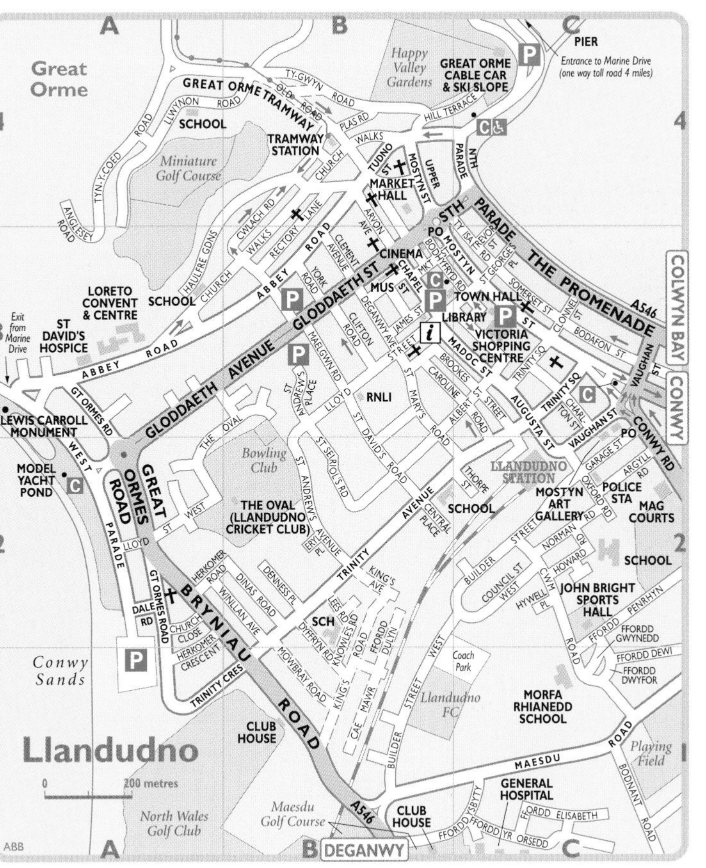

Llandudno

Llandudno is found on atlas page **69**, grid reference **7882**

Abbey Road	A3-C4	Herkomer Road	A2
Albert Street	B2-C3	Hill Terrace	B4-C4
Anglesey Road	A3-A4	Howard Road	C2
Argyll Road	C2	Hywell Place	C2
Arvon Avenue	B3-B4	King's Avenue	B2
Augusta Street	C2-C3	King's Road	B1-B2
Bodafon Street	C3	Knowles Road	B1-B2
Bodnant Road	C1	Lees Road	B2
Brookes Street	B3-C3	Lloyd Street	B3-C3
Bryniau Road	A2-B1	Lloyd Street West	A2
Builder Street	C2	Llwynon Road	A4-B4
Builder Street West	B1-C2	Madoc Street	B3-C3
Cae Mawr	B1	Maelgwn Road	B3
Caroline Road	B3-C3	Maesdu Road	B1-C1
Chapel Street	B3	Mostyn Street	B3-C3
Charlton Street	C3	Mowbray Road	B1
Church Close	A2	Norman Road	C2
Church Walks	A3-B4	North Parade	C4
Clement Avenue	B3	Oxford Road	C2
Clifton Road	B3	Plas Road	B4
Clonnel Street	C3	Rectory Lane	B3-B4
Conwy Road	C2-C3	St Andrew's Avenue	B2-B3
Council Street West	C2	St Andrew's Place	B3
Cwlach Road	B3-B4	St David's Road	B2-B3
Cwm Road	C1-C2	St George's Place	C3
Dale Road	A2	St Mary's Road	B3-C2
Deganwy Avenue	B3	St Seirol's Road	B2-B3
Denness Place	B2	Somerset Street	C3
Dinas Road	B2	South Parade	B4-C3
Dyffryn Road	B1-B2	The Oval	A2-B3
Eryl Place	B2	The Parade	C2
Ffordd Dewi	C1	Thorpe Street	C2
Ffordd Dulyn	B1-B2	Trevor Street	C3
Ffordd Dwyfor	C1	Trinity Avenue	B1-C3
Ffordd Elisabeth	C1	Trinity Crescent	A1-B1
Ffordd Gwynedd	C1	Trinity Square	C3
Ffordd Penrhyn	C1-C2	Tudno Street	B4
Ffordd yr Orsedd	C1	Ty-Gwyn Road	B4
Ffordd Ysbyty	B1-C1	Ty Isa Road	C3-C4
Garage Street	C2-C3	Tyn-y-Coed Road	A4
Gloddaeth Avenue	A2-B3	Upper Mostyn Street	B4
Gloddaeth Street	B3	Vaughan Street	C2-C3
Great Ormes Road	A1-A3	West Parade	A2-A3
Haulfre Gardens	A3	Winllan Avenue	A2-B2
Herkomer Crescent	A1-A2	York Road	B3

189

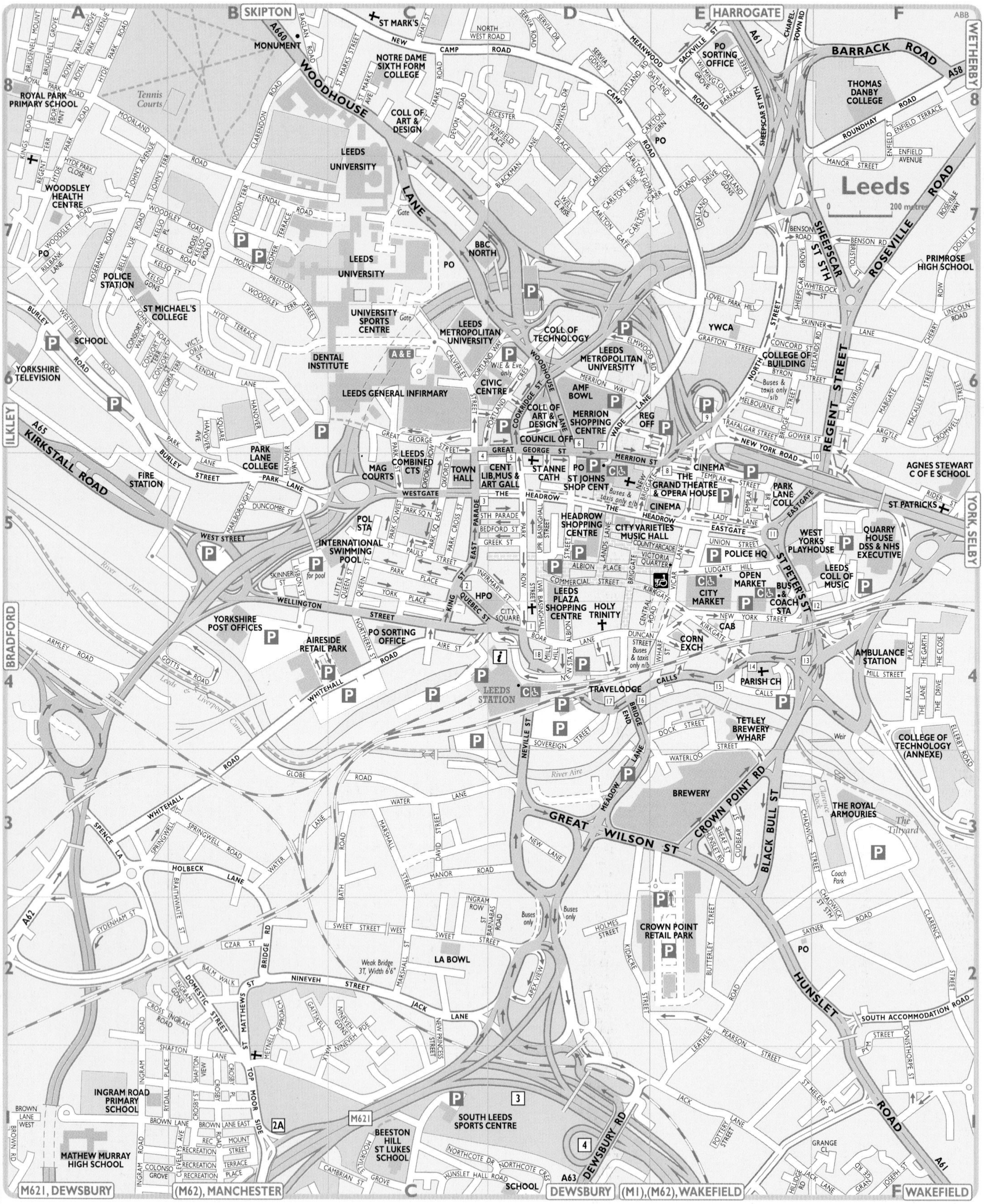

Leeds

A | B SKIPTON | C | D | E HARROGATE | F WETHERBY

ABB

Leeds

0 — 200 metres

BARRACK ROAD A58

THOMAS DANBY COLLEGE

ROYAL PARK PRIMARY SCHOOL

WOODSLEY HEALTH CENTRE

ST MARK'S

NOTRE DAME SIXTH FORM COLLEGE

COLL OF ART & DESIGN

NORTH WEST ROAD

NEW CAMP ROAD

WOODHOUSE LANE

LEEDS UNIVERSITY

LEEDS UNIVERSITY

POLICE STATION

ST MICHAEL'S COLLEGE

YORKSHIRE TELEVISION

UNIVERSITY SPORTS CENTRE

DENTAL INSTITUTE

LEEDS GENERAL INFIRMARY

A & E

LEEDS METROPOLITAN UNIVERSITY

BBC NORTH

COLL OF TECHNOLOGY

LEEDS METROPOLITAN UNIVERSITY

COLLEGE OF BUILDING

YWCA

PRIMROSE HIGH SCHOOL

PO SORTING OFFICE

CIVIC CENTRE

COLL OF ART & DESIGN

COUNCIL OFF

MERRION SHOPPING CENTRE

AMF BOWL

REG OFF

FIRE STATION

PARK LANE COLLEGE

MAG COURTS

LEEDS COMBINED CTS

TOWN HALL

CENT LIB, MUS & ART GALL

ST ANNE CATH

ST JOHNS SHOP CENT

PO

THE GRAND THEATRE & OPERA HOUSE

CINEMA

AGNES STEWART C OF E SCHOOL

ST PATRICKS

PARK LANE COLL

WEST STREET

POL STA

INTERNATIONAL SWIMMING POOL

for pool

HEADROW SHOPPING CENTRE

CITY VARIETIES MUSIC HALL

EASTGATE

WEST YORKS PLAYHOUSE

QUARRY HOUSE DSS & NHS EXECUTIVE

WEST YORKS POLICE HQ

LEEDS COLL OF MUSIC

YORKSHIRE POST OFFICES

HPO

CITY SQUARE

LEEDS PLAZA SHOPPING CENTRE

HOLY TRINITY

OPEN MARKET

CITY MARKET

BUSES & COACH STA

AIRESIDE RETAIL PARK

PO SORTING OFFICE

CORN EXCH

CAB

AMBULANCE STATION

i

LEEDS STATION

TRAVELODGE

PARISH CH

COLLEGE OF TECHNOLOGY (ANNEXE)

TETLEY BREWERY WHARF

THE ROYAL ARMOURIES

The Tiltyard

GREAT WILSON ST

BREWERY

HOLBECK

LA BOWL

CROWN POINT RETAIL PARK

HUNSLET ROAD

INGRAM ROAD PRIMARY SCHOOL

M621

BEESTON HILL ST LUKES SCHOOL

SOUTH LEEDS SPORTS CENTRE

DEWSBURY RD

MATHEW MURRAY HIGH SCHOOL

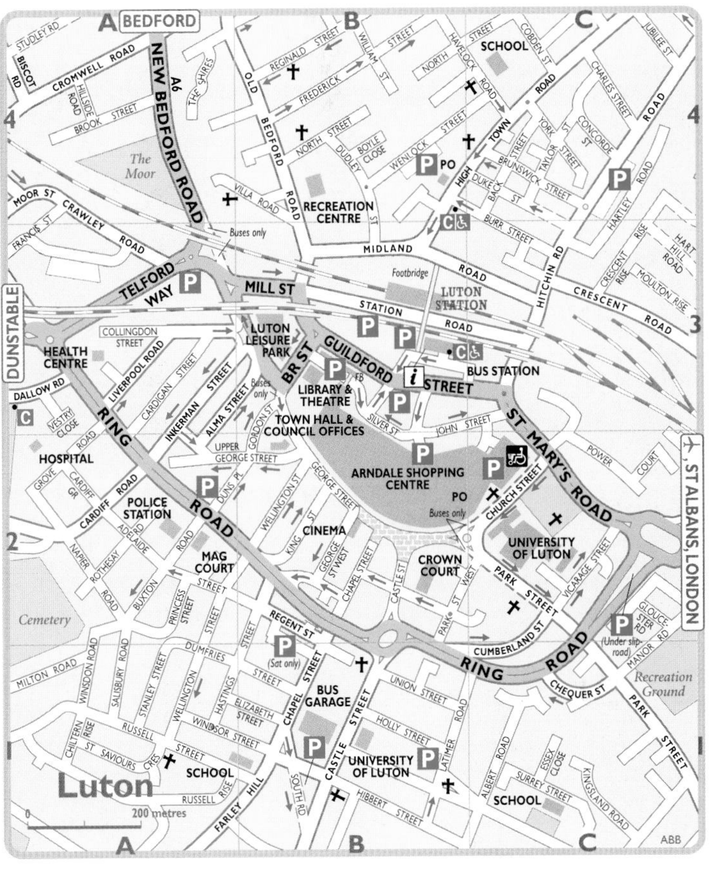

Luton

Luton is found on atlas page **38**, grid reference **0921**

191

Leeds

Leeds is found on atlas page **82**, grid reference **2932**

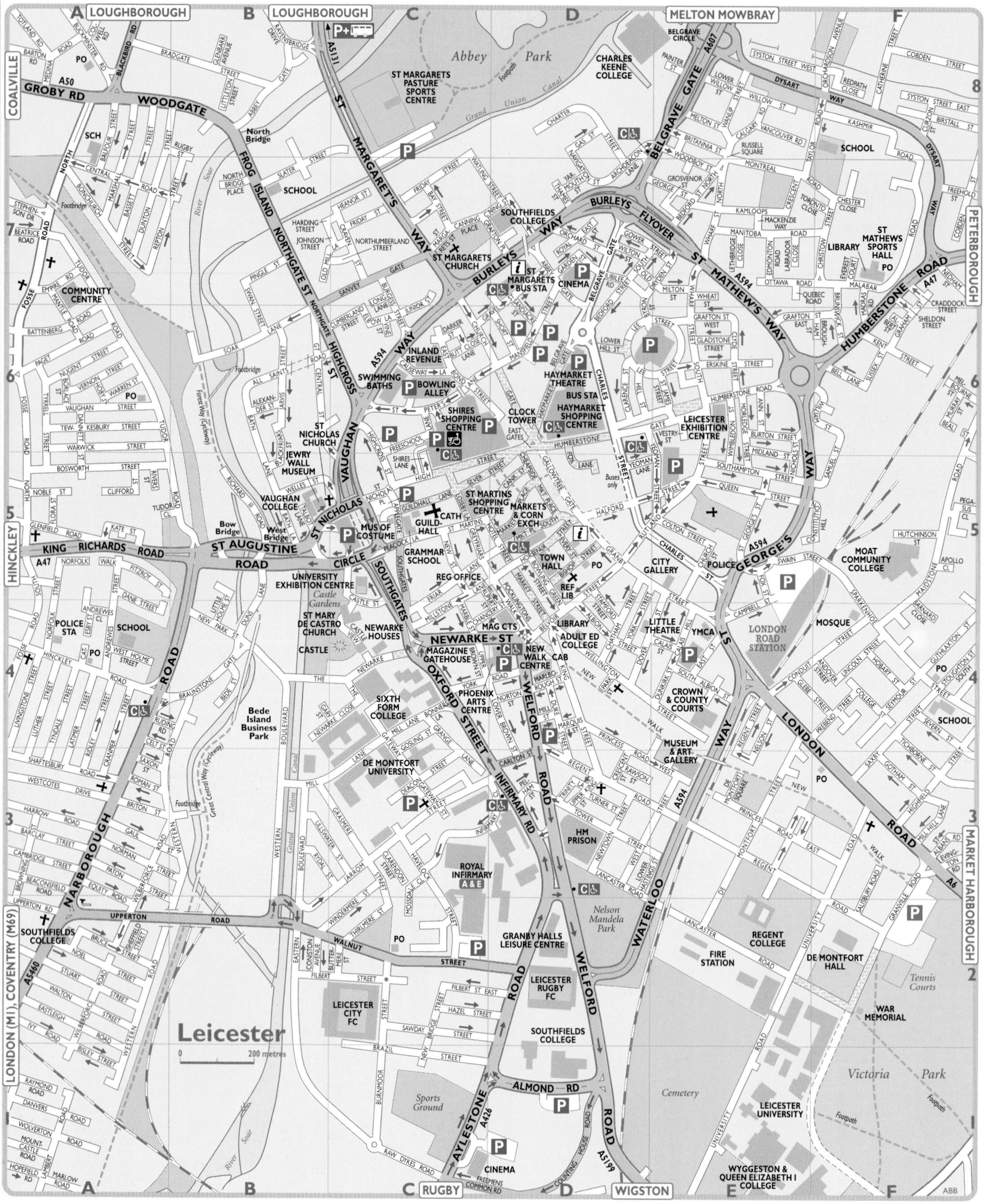

192

Leicester

LOUGHBOROUGH   LOUGHBOROUGH   MELTON MOWBRAY

Abbey Park

COALVILLE
HINCKLEY
London (M1), Coventry (M69)
PETERBOROUGH
MARKET HARBOROUGH
RUGBY   WIGSTON

GROBY RD   A50   WOODGATE
St Margarets Pasture Sports Centre
Charles Keene College
Belgrave Circle
SYSTON STREET WEST
DYSART WAY
SCHOOL
North Bridge
SCHOOL
Grand Union Canal
BURLEYS WAY   BURLEYS FLYOVER   ST MATHEW'S WAY
St Margarets Church
St Margarets Bus Sta
Southfields College
Cinema
Russell Square
LIBRARY
St Mathews Sports Hall
PO
HUMBERSTONE ROAD   A47
Inland Revenue
Swimming Baths
Bowling Alley
Haymarket Theatre
Bus Sta
Haymarket Shopping Centre
Leicester Exhibition Centre
St Nicholas Church
Jewry Wall Museum
Shires Shopping Centre
Clock Tower
Vaughan College
West Bridge
Bow Bridge
Mus of Costume
St Martins Shopping Centre
Markets & Corn Exch
KING RICHARDS ROAD   A47
ST AUGUSTINE ROAD
ST NICHOLAS CIRCLE
Guild Hall   CATH
Grammar School
Reg Office
Town Hall   Ref Lib
City Gallery
POLICE
GEORGE'S WAY   A594
Moat Community College
University Exhibition Centre
Castle Gardens
St Mary de Castro Church
Castle
Newarke Houses
Magazine Gatehouse
NEWARKE ST
New Walk Centre
Library
Adult Ed College
Little Theatre   YMCA
London Road Station
Mosque
POLICE STA   PO   SCHOOL
Bede Island Business Park
Sixth Form College
Phoenix Arts Centre
De Montfort University
OXFORD STREET
INFIRMARY RD
WELFORD ROAD
Crown & County Courts
Museum & Art Gallery
NARBOROUGH ROAD
HM Prison
Royal Infirmary A&E
Nelson Mandela Park
Fire Station
Regent College
De Montfort Hall
Tennis Courts
UPPERTON ROAD
Granby Halls Leisure Centre
WALNUT STREET
WELFORD ROAD
WATERLOO WAY
LONDON ROAD   A6
Leicester City FC
Leicester Rugby FC
Southfields College
War Memorial
Leicester
0   200 metres
Sports Ground
AYLESTONE   A426
ALMOND RD
Cinema
Cemetery
Victoria Park
Leicester University
Wyggeston & Queen Elizabeth I College

A   B   C   D   E   F

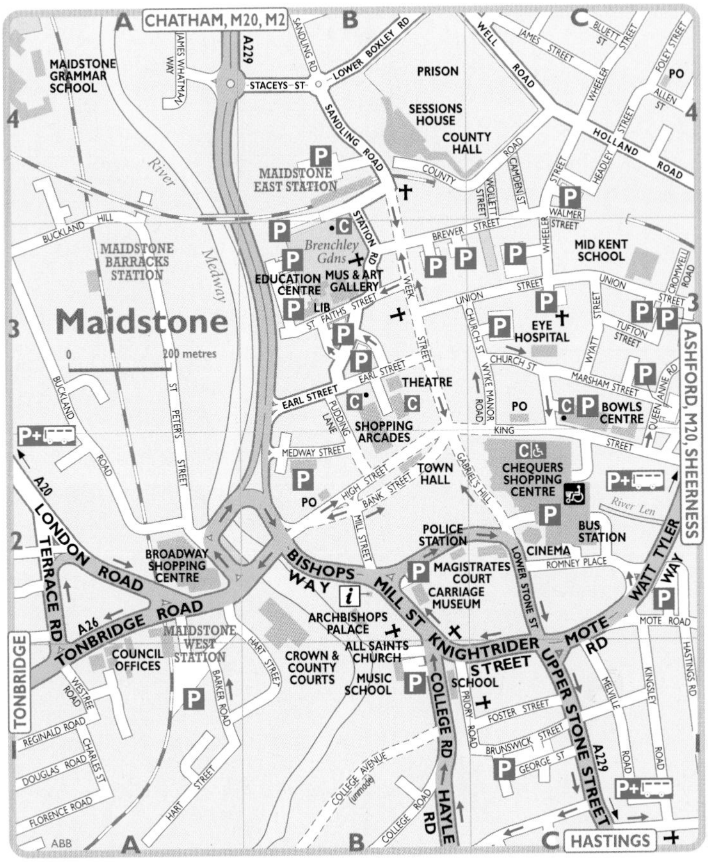
CHATHAM, M20, M2
MAIDSTONE GRAMMAR SCHOOL
PRISON
SESSIONS HOUSE
COUNTY HALL
MAIDSTONE EAST STATION
MAIDSTONE BARRACKS STATION
Maidstone
200 metres
EDUCATION CENTRE
MUS & ART GALLERY
MID KENT SCHOOL
EYE HOSPITAL
THEATRE
SHOPPING ARCADES
BOWLS CENTRE
TOWN HALL
CHEQUERS SHOPPING CENTRE
POLICE STATION
BUS STATION
CINEMA
BROADWAY SHOPPING CENTRE
MAGISTRATES COURT
CARRIAGE MUSEUM
ARCHBISHOPS PALACE
ALL SAINTS CHURCH
MAIDSTONE WEST STATION
COUNCIL OFFICES
CROWN & COUNTY COURTS
MUSIC SCHOOL
SCHOOL
LONDON ROAD
TONBRIDGE ROAD
BISHOPS WAY
MILL ST
KNIGHTRIDER STREET
UPPER STONE STREET
MOTE RD
WATT TYLER WAY
COLLEGE RD
HAYLE RD
ASHFORD, M20, SHEERNESS
TONBRIDGE
HASTINGS

Maidstone

Maidstone is found on atlas page **28**, grid reference **7555**

Allen Street	C4
Bank Street	B2
Barker Road	A1
Bishops Way	B2
Bluett Street	C4
Brewer Street	B3-C3-C4
Brunswick Street	C1
Buckland Hill	A3-A4
Buckland Road	A2-A3
Camden Street	C4
Charles Street	A1
Church Street	C3
College Avenue	B1
College Road	B1
County Road	B4-C4
Cromwell Road	C3
Douglas Road	A1
Earl Street	B3
Florence Road	A1
Foley Street	C4
Foster Street	C1
Gabriel's Hill	B2-C2
George Street	C1
Hart Street	A1-B1-B2-A2
Hastings Road	C1-C2
Hayle Road	B1
Headley Street	C4
High Street	B2
Holland Road	C4
James Street	C4
James Whatman Way	A4
King Street	B3-C2
Kingsley Road	C1-C2
Knightrider Street	B2-B1-C1
London Road	A2
Lower Boxley Road	B4
Lower Stone Street	C2
Marsham Street	C3
Medway Street	B2
Melville Road	C1
Mill Street	B2
Mote Road	C1-C2
Priory Road	B1-C1
Pudding Lane	B2-B3
Queen Anne Road	C2-C3
Reginald Road	A1
Romney Place	C2
St Faiths Street	B3
St Peter's Street	A2-A3
Sandling Road	B4
Staceys Street	B4
Station Road	B3-B4
Terrace Road	A2
Tonbridge Road	A1-A2
Tufton Street	C3
Union Street	B3-C3
Upper Stone Street	C1
Walmer Street	C4
Watt Tyler Way	C2
Week Street	B3
Well Road	C4
Westree Road	A1
Wheeler Street	C3-C4
Wollett Street	C4
Wyatt Street	C3
Wyke Manor Road	C3

Leicester

Leicester is found on atlas page **62**, grid reference **5804**

Abbey Gate	B8
Abbey Gate	D6-D7
Albert Street	F6
Albion Street	D4
Alexander Street	B6
All Saints Road	B6
Almond Road	D1
Andover Street	F4
Andrewes Close	A4
Andrewes Street	A4-A5
Ann Street	E6
Apollo Close	F5
Applegate	C5
Archdeacon Lane	D7-D8
Aylestone Road	C1-D1-D2
Balfour Street	A7-A8
Barclay Street	A3
Barnard Close	F4-F5
Barton Road	A8
Bassett Street	A7-A8
Bath Lane	B5-B6
Battenberg Road	A6
Bay Street	C7
Beaconsfield Road	A3
Beal Street	F6
Beatrice Road	A7
Bede Street	B4
Bedford Street North	E7
Bedford Street South	D6-D7
Belgrave Circle	E8
Belgrave Gate	D6-D7-E8
Bell Lane	F6
Belvoir Street	D4-D5
Birstall Street	F8
Bishop Street	D5
Bisley Street	A1
Blackbird Road	A8
Blackfriars Street	B5-B6
Bonchurch Street	A7
Bonners Lane	C4
Borlace Street	A6
Bosworth Street	A5
Bowling Green Street	D4-D5
Bradgate Street	A8-B8
Braunstone Gate	A4-B4
Brazil Street	C1-C2
Britannia Street	E8
Briton Street	A3
Brougham Street	F6
Browning Street	A3
Bruce Street	A2
Brunswick Street	E6-F6
Buckminster Road	A8
Burgess Street	C6-C7
Burleys Flyover	D7-E7
Burleys Way	C7-D7
Burnmoor Street	C1-C2
Burton Street	E6
Butt Close Lane	C6
Buttermere Street	C2
Byron Street	D6-D7
Calais Hill	E4
Calais Street	E4
Calgary Road	E8
Cambridge Street	A3
Campbell Street	E4-E5
Cank Street	D5
Canning Place	C7
Canning Street	C7-D7
Carlton Street	D3
Castle Street	C4-C5
Castle View	C4
Catesby Street	A4
Catherine Street	F8
Causeway Lane	C6
Celt Street	A4
Central Road	A7-B7
Chancery Street	C4-D4
Charles Street	D6-D5-E5
Charter Street	C7
Chatham Street	D4-D5
Cheapside	D5
Chester Close	F7
Christow Street	F7
Church Gate	C7-C6-D6
Church Street	E5
Clarence Street	D6
Clarendon Street	C3
Clifford Street	A5
Clyde Street	E6
Cobden Street	F7-F8
College Street	F4
Colton Street	E5
Colwell Road	A8
Conduit Street	E4-F4
Coniston Avenue	B2
Constitution Hill	E5-F5
Counting House Road	D1
Craddock Street	F7
Cranmer Street	A3-A4
Craven Street	C7
Crescent Street	D3
Cumberland Street	C6
Curzon Street	F8
Dane Street	A4-A5
Dannett Street	A5-A6
Danvers Road	A1
Darker Street	C6
De Montfort Square	E3
De Montfort Street	E2-E3-E4
Deacon Street	C3
Dover Street	D4-E4-E5
Dryden Street	D7-E7
Duke Street	D3-D4
Dunkirk Street	E4
Duns Lane	B4-B5
Dunton Street	A7-A8-B8
Dysart Way	E8-F8-F7
East Bond Street	C6-D6
East Gates	D6
East Street	E4
Eastern Boulevard	B2-B3
Eastleigh Road	A1-A2
Edmonton Road	E7
Elbow Lane	C6
Empire Road	A7
Equity Road	A2-A3
Erskine Street	E6
Everest Court	F7
Every Street	D5
Evington Road	F3
Filbert Street	B2-C2
Filbert Street East	C2-D2
Fitzroy Street	A5
Flora Street	A5
Fosse Road North	A5-A6-A7-A8
Fosse Road South	A4-A5
Fox Lane	D5-D6
Fox Street	E5
Freehold Street	F7
Freemens Common Road	C1-D1
Freeschool Lane	C6
Friar Lane	C4-C5-D5
Friday Street	C7-C8
Frog Island	B7-B8
Gallowtree Gate	D5-D6
Garden Street	D7
Gary Street	B4
Gas Street	D8
Gateway Street	C3
Gaul Street	A3-B3
George Street	D7-E7
Gladstone Street	E6
Glebe Street	E4-F4
Glenbarr Avenue	B8
Glenfield Road	A5
Gosling Street	C4
Gotham Street	F3
Gower Street	D7-E7
Grafton Place	C7-D7
Grafton Street East	E6-F6
Grafton Street West	E6
Graham Street	F7-F8
Granby Street	D5-E5-E4
Grange Lane	C3-C4
Granville Road	F2-F3
Grasmere Street	B3-C3
Gravel Street	C6-D6-D7
Great Central Street	B6
Greyfriars	C5
Groby Road	A8
Grosvenor Street	E7
Guildhall Lane	C5
Guthlaxton Street	F4
Halford Street	D5-E5
Harding Street	B7-C7
Harrow Road	A3
Havelock Street	C2-C3
Haymarket	D6
Hazel Street	C2-D2
Heanor Street	C7
High Street	C5-D5-D6
Highcross Street	C5-C6
Highfield Street	F3-F4
Hill Street	D6
Hinckley Road	A4
Hobart Street	F4
Hoby Street	A6
Hopefield Road	A1
Horsefair Street	D5
Hotel Street	C5-D5
Humberstone Gate	D6-E6
Humberstone Road	E6-F6-F7
Hutchinson Street	F5
Infirmary Close	C3-D3
Infirmary Road	D3
Ivy Road	A2
Jarrom Street	B2-C3
Jarvis Street	B6
Johnson Street	B7-C7
Jubilee Road	D7
Junior Street	C6-C7
Kamloops Crescent	E7
Kashmir Road	F7-F8
Kate Street	A5
Kent Street	F6
King Richards Road	A5-B5
King Street	D3-D4
Labrador Close	E7
Lambert Road	A1
Lancaster Road	D3-E2
Latimer Street	A3-A4
Lee Street	D6-E6
Lethbridge Close	E7
Lincoln Street	F4
Little Holme Street	B4-B5
Littleton Street	B8
Livingstone Street	A3-A4
London Road	E4-F3
Long Lane	C7
Loseby Lane	C5
Lower Brown Street	D3-D4
Lower Hastings Street	D3-E3
Lower Hill Street	D6
Lower Willow Street	E8
Luther Street	A3-A4
Mackenzie Way	E7
Madras Road	F6-F7
Maidstone Road	F4-F5-F6
Malabar Road	F7
Manitoba Road	E7-F7
Mansfield Street	D6-D7
Mantle Road	A6-A7
Marble Street	C4
Market Place	D5
Market Place South	D5
Market Street	D4-D5
Marlborough Street	D4
Marlow Road	A1
Marquis Street	D4
Marshall Street	A7-A8
Medina Road	A8
Melbourne Street	F6
Melton Street	E8
Midland Street	E5-E6
Mill Hill Lane	F3
Mill Lane	B3-C3-C4
Mill Street	D4
Millstone Lane	C4-C5
Montreal Road	E7-F7
Morledge Street	E5-E6
Mossdale Close	C2-C3
Mountcastle Road	A1
Murray Street	F6
Narborough Road	A2-A3-A4-A5
Navigation Street	D7-D8
Nedham Street	F7
Nelson Street	E3-E4
New Bridge Street	C1-C2
New Park Street	B4
New Street	C5
Newarke Close	B4-C4
Newarke Street	C4-D4
Newtown Street	D3
New Walk	D4-E3-F3
Nichols Street	E5-E6
Noble Street	A5
Noel Street	A2
Norfolk Street	A4-A5
Norfolk Walk	A5
Norman Street	A3-B3
North Bridge Place	B7
Northgate	B6
Northgate Street	B7
Northumberland Street	C7
Norton Street	D4
Nugent Street	A6
Old Mill Lane	B7-C7
Old Milton Street	D7-E7
Orchard Street	D7
Orchardson Avenue	F8
Ottawa Road	E7
Oxford Street	C3-C4
Paget Road	A6
Painter Street	E8
Park Street	D4
Paton Street	A2-A3
Peacock Lane	C5
Pegasus Close	F5
Pelham Street	D3
Pingle Street	B7
Pocklingtons Walk	D4-D5
Prebend Street	F4
Princess Road East	E3-F3
Princess Road West	D4-D3-E3
Quebec Road	E7
Queen Street	E5
Ravensbridge Drive	B8
Raw Dykes Road	C1
Rawson Street	D3
Raymond Road	A1
Redpath Close	F8
Regent Road	D3-E3-F3-F2
Regent Street	E3-E4
Repton Street	A7-B7
Richard III Road	B5
Ridley Street	A3-A4
Rivers Street	A5
Roman Street	A3
Royal East Street	D7
Ruding Road	A4
Rugby Street	B7-B8
Rupert Street	D4-C5
Russell Square	E7-E8
Rutland Street	D5-E5-E6
Rydal Street	B3-C3
St Albans Road	F3
St Augustine Road	B5
St George's Street	E5
St George's Way	E4-E5-E6
St James Street	E6
St Margaret's Way	B8-C8-C7
St Margarets Street	C7
St Martins	C5
St Mathew's Way	E6-E7
St Nicholas Circle	B5-C5
St Nicholas Place	C5
St Peter's Lane	C6
Salisbury Road	F2-F3
Samuel Street	F5-F6
Sandiacre Street	D6-D7
Sanvey Gate	B7-C7
Sawday Street	C2-D2
Saxby Street	F3-F4
Saxon Street	A3
Severn Street	F4
Seymour Street	F4
Shaftesbury Road	A3
Sheffield Street	A2
Sheldon Street	F6-F7
Shires Lane	C5
Short Street	D6
Silver Street	C5-D5
Slater Street	B7-B8-C8
Soar Lane	B6
South Albion Street	E4
Southampton Street	E5
Southgates	C4-C5
Sparkenhoe Street	F4-F5
Stamford Street	D4-D5
Stephenson Drive	A7
Stoughton Street South	F4
Stuart Street	A2
Sussex Street	F6
Swain Street	E5-F5
Swan Street	B6-B7
Syston Street East	F8
Syston Street West	E8-F8
Talbot Lane	B5
Taylor Road	E7-E8-F8
Tewkesbury Street	A6
Thames Street	D7
The Gateway	C3-C4
The Newarke	B4-C4
Thirlmere Street	C2
Tichborne Street	F3-F4
Toronto Close	E7-F7
Totland Road	A8
Tower Street	D3-E3
Trinity Lane	D3
Tudor Close	A5-B5
Tudor Road	A7-A6-A5-B5
Turner Street	D3
Tyndale Street	A3-A4
Tyrrell Street	A5-A6
Ullswater Street	B3-C3
University Road	E1-E2-F2-F3
Upper Brown Street	C4
Upper King Street	D3
Upperton Road	A2-B2
Vancouver Road	E8
Vaughan Street	A6
Vaughan Way	C5-C6-C7
Vernon Street	A6
Vestry Street	E6
Vine Street	C6
Walnut Street	B2-C2-D2
Walton Street	A2
Wanlip Street	E8
Warren Street	A6
Warwick Street	A6
Waterloo Way	D2-E3-E4
Watling Street	C8-C7-D7
Welford Road	D1-D2-D3-D4
Welles Street	B5-C5
Wellington Street	D4-E4
West Holme Street	A4
West Street	D3-E3
Westcotes Drive	A3
Western Boulevard	B2-B3-B4
Western Road	A1-A2-B3-B4
Wharf Street North	E7
Wharf Street South	E6-E7
Wheat Street	E7
Wilberforce Road	A1-A2-A3
William Street	F6
Willow Street	E8
Wilton Street	D7
Wimbledon Street	E5-E6
Windermere Street	B2-C2-C3
Wolverton Road	A1
Woodboy Street	E7-E8
Woodgate	A8-B8
Yarmouth Street	D7
Yeoman Lane	D5
Yeoman Street	D6-E6-E5
York Road	C4-D4
York Street	D4-D5

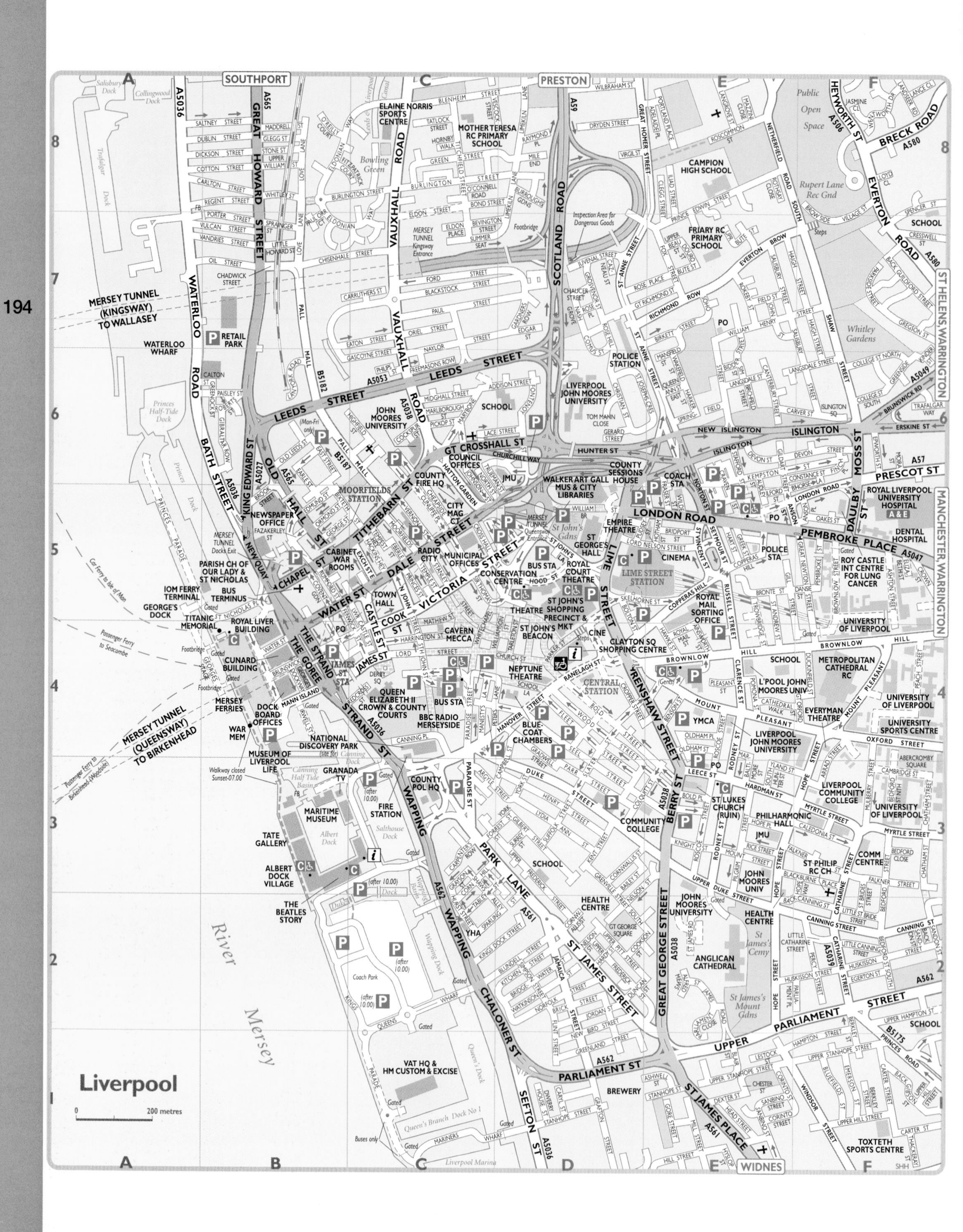
SOUTHPORT
PRESTON
WIDNES
ST HELENS,WARRINGTON
MANCHESTER,WARRINGTON
MERSEY TUNNEL (KINGSWAY) TO WALLASEY
MERSEY TUNNEL (QUEENSWAY) TO BIRKENHEAD
WATERLOO WHARF
RETAIL PARK
ELAINE NORRIS SPORTS CENTRE
MOTHER TERESA RC PRIMARY SCHOOL
CAMPION HIGH SCHOOL
FRIARY RC PRIMARY SCHOOL
Public Open Space
Rupert Lane Rec Gnd
Whitley Gardens
Inspection Area for Dangerous Goods
POLICE STATION
LIVERPOOL JOHN MOORES UNIVERSITY
JOHN MOORES UNIVERSITY
SCHOOL
COUNCIL OFFICES
COUNTY FIRE HQ
MOORFIELDS STATION
CITY MAG CT
WALKER ART GALL MUS & CITY LIBRARIES
COUNTY SESSIONS HOUSE
ROYAL LIVERPOOL UNIVERSITY HOSPITAL A&E
DENTAL HOSPITAL
ROY CASTLE INT CENTRE FOR LUNG CANCER
NEWSPAPER OFFICE
PARISH CH OF OUR LADY & ST NICHOLAS
IOM FERRY TERMINAL
GEORGE'S DOCK
BUS TERMINUS
CABINET WAR ROOMS
RADIO CITY
MUNICIPAL OFFICES
EMPIRE THEATRE
ST GEORGE'S HALL
CINEMA
LIME STREET STATION
POLICE STA
BUS STA
ROYAL COURT THEATRE
CONSERVATION CENTRE
TOWN HALL
ST JOHN'S SHOPPING PRECINCT & MKT
ROYAL MAIL SORTING OFFICE
UNIVERSITY OF LIVERPOOL
TITANIC MEMORIAL
ROYAL LIVER BUILDING
CUNARD BUILDING
CAVERN MECCA
THEATRE
ST JOHN'S BEACON
CLAYTON SQ SHOPPING CENTRE
METROPOLITAN CATHEDRAL RC
MERSEY FERRIES
DOCK BOARD OFFICES
WAR MEM
NEPTUNE THEATRE
CENTRAL STATION
QUEEN ELIZABETH II CROWN & COUNTY COURTS
BUS STA
BBC RADIO MERSEYSIDE
L'POOL JOHN MOORES UNIV
EVERYMAN THEATRE
UNIVERSITY SPORTS CENTRE
YMCA
BLUE-COAT CHAMBERS
NATIONAL DISCOVERY PARK
MUSEUM OF LIVERPOOL LIFE
GRANADA TV
COUNTY POL HQ
FIRE STATION
LIVERPOOL JOHN MOORES UNIVERSITY
LIVERPOOL COMMUNITY COLLEGE
ST LUKES CHURCH (RUIN)
PHILHARMONIC HALL
MARITIME MUSEUM
TATE GALLERY
Albert Dock
ALBERT DOCK VILLAGE
COMMUNITY COLLEGE
JMU
COMM CENTRE
ST PHILIP RC CH
THE BEATLES STORY
SCHOOL
HEALTH CENTRE
JOHN MOORES UNIV
JOHN MOORES UNIVERSITY
HEALTH CENTRE
St James's Cemy
ANGLICAN CATHEDRAL
St James's Mount Gdns
YHA
Coach Park
River Mersey
VAT HQ & HM CUSTOM & EXCISE
BREWERY
SCHOOL
TOXTETH SPORTS CENTRE
Liverpool Marina
LEEDS STREET
SCOTLAND ROAD
GREAT HOWARD STREET
WATERLOO ROAD
BATH STREET
VAUXHALL ROAD
TITHEBARN ST
DALE STREET
VICTORIA STREET
WATER ST
THE STRAND
STRAND ST
WAPPING
CHALONER ST
PARK LANE
ST JAMES STREET
PARLIAMENT ST
UPPER PARLIAMENT STREET
GREAT GEORGE STREET
BERRY ST
RENSHAW STREET
LIME STREET
LONDON ROAD
PEMBROKE PLACE
PRESCOT ST
ISLINGTON
DAULBY ST
MOSS ST
EVERTON ROAD
BRECK ROAD
HEYWORTH ST
ST JAMES PLACE
SEFTON ST
HOPE ST
Liverpool
0 200 metres

Margate

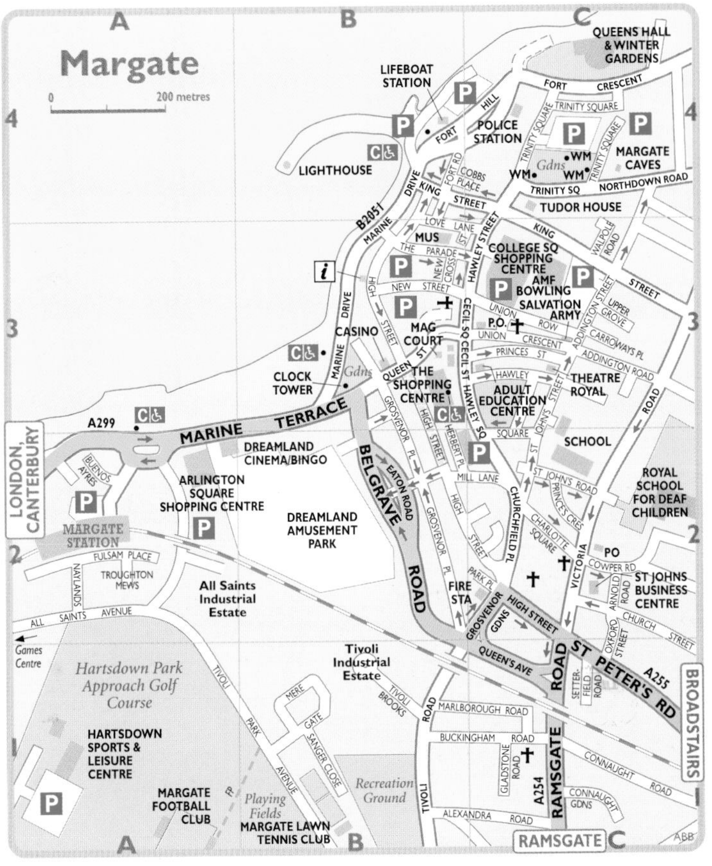

Margate is found on atlas page **29**,
grid reference **3571**

Addington Road	C3	Fort Hill	B4-C4	Northdown Road	C4
Addington Street	C3	Fort Road	B4	Oxford Street	C1-C2
Alexandra Road	B1-C1	Fulsam Place	A2	Park Place	C2
All Saints Avenue	A2	Gladstone Road	C1	Prince's Crescent	C2
Arnold Road	C2	Grosvenor Gardens	C2	Princes Street	C3
Belgrave Road	B2-B3	Grosvenor Place	B2-B3	Queen Street	B3
Buckingham Road	B1-C1	Hawley Square	C2-C3	Queens Avenue	C1
Buenos Ayres	A2	Hawley Street	C3	Ramsgate Road	C1
Carroways Place	C3	Herbert Place	B2	St John's Road	C2
Cecil Square	B3-C3	High Street	B3-B2-C2	St John's Street	C2-C3
Cecil Street	B3-C3	King Street	B4-C4-C3	St Peter's Road	C1
Charlotte Square	C2	Love Lane	B3-C3	Sanger Close	B1
Church Street	C1-C2	Marine Drive	B3-B4	Setterfield Road	C1
Churchfield Place	C2	Marine Terrace	A2-B3	The Parade	B3
Cobbs Place	B4-C4	Marlborough Road	B1-C1	Tivoli Brooks	B1
Connaught Gardens	C1	Mere Gate	B1	Tivoli Park Avenue	A2-A1-B1
Connaught Road	C1	Mill Lane	B2-C2	Tivoli Road	B1
Cowper Road	C2	Naylands	A2	Trinity Square	C4
Eaton Road	B2	New Cross Street	B3	Troughton Mews	A2
Fort Crescent	C4	New Street	B3	Union Crescent	C3
				Union Row	C3
				Upper Grove	C3
				Victoria Road	C2-C3
				Walpole Road	C3

195

Liverpool

Liverpool is found on atlas page **78**,
grid reference **3490**

Abercromby Square	F3-F4	Burlington Street	B8-D8	Dale Street	C5-D5	Great George Square	D2
Addison Street	C6-D6	Burroughs Gardens	D8	Dansie Street	E5-F5	Great George Street	E1-E3
Adelaide Place	E8	Bute Street	E7	Daulby Street	F5	Great Homer Street	D8-E8
Ainsworth Street	E4-E5	Caledonia Street	F3	Derby Square	C4	Great Howard Street	B6-B8
Alfred Mews	E2	Calton Street	B6	Devon Street	E6-F6	Great Newton Street	F4-F5
Anson Place	F5	Cambridge Street	F3	Dexter Street	E1	Great Orford Street	F4
Anson Street	E5	Campbell Street	D3-D4	Dickson Street	A8-A8	Great Richmond Street	D7-E7
Argyle Street	C3-D3	Canning Place	C4	Douro Street	E7	Greek Street	E5
Arrad Street	F3-F4	Canning Street	E2-F2	Dryden Street	D8	Green Street	C8-D8
Ashton Street	F4-F5	Canterbury Street	E6	Dublin Street	A8-B8	Greenland Street	D1
Ashwell Street	E1	Carlton Street	A8-B8	Duckinfield Street	F4	Greenock Street	B6
Audley Street	E5-E6	Carpenter's Row	C3	Duke Street	C4-D3-E3	Greenside	F6
Back Canning Street	E2-F2	Carruthers Street	B7-C7	Duncan Street	D2	Gregson Street	F7
Back Gibson Street	F1	Carter Street	F1	Dwerry House Street	D1	Grenville Street South	D3-E2
Back Guildford Street	F7	Carver Street	E6-F6	Earle Street	B5-B6	Grosvenor Street	D7
Back Sandon Street	F2	Caryl Street	D1	East Street	B6	Hackins Hey	C5
Bailey Street	D3	Castle Street	C4-C5	Eaton Street	B7-C7	Haigh Street	E7-F7-F6
Baltimore Street	E3	Catharine Street	F2-F3	Eberle Street	C5	Hampton Street	E1-F1-F2
Bath Street	A6-B5	Cathedral Walk	E4	Edgar Street	D7	Hanover Street	C3-D4
Bayhorse Lane	E5-F6	Cazneau Street	D7	Edmund Street	B5	Hardman Street	E3
Bedford Close	F3	Chadwick Street	B7	Egerton Street	F2	Hardy Street	D2
Bedford Street	F2-F3	Chaloner Street	C2-D1	Eldon Place	C7	Harker Street	E6
Bedford Street North	F3	Chapel Street	B5	Eldon Street	C7-C8	Harrington Street	C4
Bedford Street South	F2	Chatham Street	F3	Eldonian Way	B8-C8	Hart Street	E5
Benson Street	E4	Chaucer Street	D7	Elizabeth Street	F5	Hatton Garden	C5-C6
Berkley Street	F1-F2	Cheapside	C5-C6	Emerson Street	F1	Hawke Street	E4-E5
Berry Street	E3	Chester Street	E1	Epworth Street	F6	Head Street	E1
Bevington Street	C7-D7	Chisenhale Street	B7-C7	Erskine Street	F6	Henry Street	D3
Bidder Street	E6-E7	Christian Street	D6	Everton Brow	E7	Heyworth Street	F8
Birchfield Street	E6	Church Street	C4-D4	Everton Road	F7-F8	Highfield Street	B6-C6
Birkett Street	E7	Churchill Way	C6-D6	Exchange Street East	C5	Hill Street	E1
Bixteth Street	B5-C5	Clarence Street	E4	Falkner Street	E3-F3	Hood Street	D5
Blackburne Place	E3-F3	Clegg Street	E7-E8	Fazakerley Street	B5	Hope Place	E3
Blackstock Street	C7-D7	Cockspur Street	C6	Fenwick Street	B5-C4	Hope Street	E2-E3-F4
Blair Street	E1	College Street North	F6	Field Street	E7	Hope Way	F3
Blenheim Street	C8-D8	College Street South	F6	Finch Place	F6	Hornby Walk	C8
Bluefields Street	F1	Colquitt Street	D3-E3	Fitzpatrick Court	B8-C8	Hotham Street	E5
Blundell Street	C2-D2	Comus Street	D6-D7	Fleet Street	D3-D4	Hunter Street	D6
Bold Place	E3	Constance Street	E6-F6	Flint Street	D1-D2	Hurst Street	C2-C3
Bold Street	D4-E3	Cook Street	C4-C5	Fontenoy Street	D6	Huskisson Street	E2-F2
Bolton Street	D4-D5	Cookson Street	D2-E2	Ford Street	C7-D7	Hyslop Street	E1
Bond Street	C8-D8	Copperas Hill	D4-E5	Forrest Street	C3-D3	Ilford Street	E5
Breck Road	F8	Corinto Street	E1-F1	Fox Street	D8-E7	Iliad Street	E8
Brick Street	D2	Corn Hill	C3	Fraser Street	E5-E6	Irwell Street	B4
Bridgewater Street	D2	Cornwallis Street	D2-D3	Freemasons Row	C6	Islington	E6-F6
Bridport Street	E5	Cotton Street	A8-B8	Gardners Row	D7	Islington Square	F6
Bronte Street	E5	Covent Garden	B5	Gascoyne Street	B7-C6	Jamaica Street	D1-D2
Brook Street	B5	Craven Street	E5-E6	George Street	B5	James Street	B4-C4
Brow Side	F7-F8	Cresswell Street	F7	George's Dockway	B4	Jasmine Close	F8
Brownlow Hill	E4-F4	Cropper Street	D4-E4	Georges Stage	A4-B4	John Street	E7
Brownlow Street	F4-F5	Cross Hall Street	C5-D5	Gerard Street	D6	Johnson Street	C5-C6
Brunswick Road	F6	Crown Street	F5	Gibraltar Row	B6	Jordan Street	D2
Brunswick Street	B4	Cunliffe Place	C5	Gilbert Street	D2-D3	Juvenal Street	D7
				Gildart Street	E5-E6	Kempston Street	E6-F6
				Gill Street	E5-F4	Kent Street	D3
				Glegg Street	B8	Kinder Street	F6-F7
				Gore Street	E1	King Edward Street	B5-B6
				Gradwell Street	D3-D4	Kings Dock Street	C2-D2
				Grafton Street	D1	Kings Parade	B2-C2-C1
				Grayson Street	C3	Kitchen Street	D2
				Great Crosshall Street	C6-D6	Knight Street	E3
						Lace Street	C6-D6
						Lance Close	F8
						Landseer Road	F8
						Langrove Street	E8
						Langsdale Street	E6-F6
						Lanyork Road	B6
						Leece Street	E3
						Leeds Street	B6-D6
						Lestock Street	E1
						Lime Street	D4-D5
						Limekiln Lane	D7-D8
						Little Canning Street	F2
						Little Catharine Street	F2
						Little Howard Street	B7
						Little St Bride Street	F2
						Lloyd Close	F2
						London Road	D5-E5-F5-F6
						Lord Nelson Street	D5-E5
						Lord Street	C4
						Love Lane	B7-B8
						Lower Castle Street	C4-C5
						Lydia Ann Street	D3
						Maddrell Street	B8
						Manesty's Lane	C4
						Mann Island	B4
						Mansfield Street	E6-E7
						Mariners Wharf	C1-D1

Marlborough Street	C6	St Anne Street	D7-E6
Marybone	C6	St Brides Street	F2-F3
Maryland Street	E4-E3-F3	St James Place	E1
Mathew Street	C4-C5	St James Road	E1-E2
Mazzini Close	E8	St James Street	D2-E2
Midghall Street	C6	St John's Lane	D5
Mile End	D8	St Josephs Crescent	D6-E6
Mill Street	E1	St Nicholas Place	B5
Moira Street	F6	St Vincent Street	E5
Moorfields	C5	Salisbury Street	E7-F6
Moss Street	F6	Saltney Street	A8-B8
Mount Pleasant	E4-F4	Sanbino Street	E1
Mount Street	E3	Sandon Street	F2
Mulberry Street	F3-F4	School Lane	D4
Myrtle Street	F3	Scotland Road	D6-D8
Nash Grove	D7	Seel Street	D4-E3
Naylor Street	C6-D7	Sefton Street	D1
Nelson Street	D2-E3	Seymour Street	E5
Netherfield Road South	E8-F7	Shaw Street	F6-F7
New Bird Street	D1-D2	Shaws Alley	C3-D2
New Islington	E6	Sim Street	E6
New Quay	B5	Simpson Street	D2
Norfolk Street	D2	Sir Thomas Street	C5-D5
North John Street	C4-C5	Skelhorne Street	D5-E5
North Street	C5-C6	Slater Street	D3-D4
Norton Street	E5-E6	Soho Street	E6-E7
O'Connell Road	C8	South Hunter Street	E3
O'Reilly Court	B8	South John Street	C4
Oakes Street	F5	Sparling Street	C2-D2
Oil Street	A7-B7	Spencer Street	F7-F8
Old Hall Street	B5-B6	Sprainger Street	B7
Old Leeds Street	B6	Springfield	E6
Oldham Place	E4	Stafford Street	E5-E6
Oldham Street	E4	Stanhope Street	D1-E1
Oriel Street	C7	Stanley Street	C4-C5
Ormond Street	B5	Stone Street	B8
Oxford Street	F4	Strand Street	B4-C4
Paisley Street	B6	Suffolk Street	D3
Pall Mall	B7-B6-C5	Summer Seat	C7-D7
Paradise Street	C3-C4	Surrey Street	D3
Park Lane	C3-D2	Tabley Street	C2-D3
Parker Street	D4	Tarleton Street	D4-D5
Parkside Street	F7	Tatlock Street	C8
Parliament Close	E1-E2	Tempest Hey	C5
Parliament Place	F2	Temple Street	C5
Parliament Street	D1-E1	Thackeray Street	F1
Parr Street	D3	The Goree	B4-B5
Paul Orr Court	B7	The Strand	B4-B5
Paul Street	C7-D7	Titchfield Street	C7-C8
Peach Street	F4	Tithebarn Street	C5-C6
Pembroke Place	E5-F5	Tom Mann Close	D6
Pembroke Street	F5	Trafalgar Way	F6
Percy Street	F2	Trowbridge Street	E4-E5
Peter's Lane	C4-D4	Trueman Street	C6-D5
Pickop Street	C6	Upper Beau Street	E7
Philips Street	C6	Upper Bute Street	E7
Pilgrim Street	E3	Upper Duke Street	E2-E3
Pleasant Street	E4	Upper Frederick Street	C3-E2
Pomona Street	E4	Upper Hampton Street	F2
Porter Street	A7-B7	Upper Hill Street	F1
Portland Place	E8	Upper Parliament Street	E1-F2
Prescot Street	F6	Upper Pitt Street	D2
Prince Edwin Street	E7-E8	Upper Stanhope Street	E1-F1
Princes Parade	A5-A6	Upper William Street	B8
Princes Road	F1-F2	Vandries Street	A7-B7
Princes Street	C5	Vauxhall Road	C6-C8
Pudsey Street	D5-E5	Vernon Street	C5
Queen Ann Street East	E6	Vescock Street	C8-D8
Queens Wharf	C2	Victoria Street	C5-D5
Ranelagh Street	D4	Village Street	F7-F8
Raymond Place	D8	Virgil Street	D8
Redcross Street	B4-C4	Vulcan Street	A7-B7
Regent Street	A8-B8	Wakefield Street	E6
Renshaw Street	D4-E4	Wapping	C2-C3
Rice Street	E3	Water Street	B4-B5-C5
Richmond Row	D7-E7	Waterloo Road	A6-A8
Roberts Street	B6	Watkinson Street	D2
Rodney Street	E3-E4	Wentworth Drive	F8
Rokeby Street	E7	Whitechapel	C4-D5
Roscoe Street	E3-E4	Whitley Street	B8
Roscommon Street	E8	Wilbraham Street	D8
Rose Hill	D6-D7	Wilde Street	E5
Rose Place	D7-E7	William Brown Street	D5
Rothsay Close	E8	William Henry Street	E7-F7
Royal Mail Street	E4-E5	Williamson Street	C4-D5
Rumford Street	B5	Windsor Street	E1-F1
Russell Street	E4-E5	Wood Street	D3-D4
St Andrew Street	E4-E5	York Street	D3

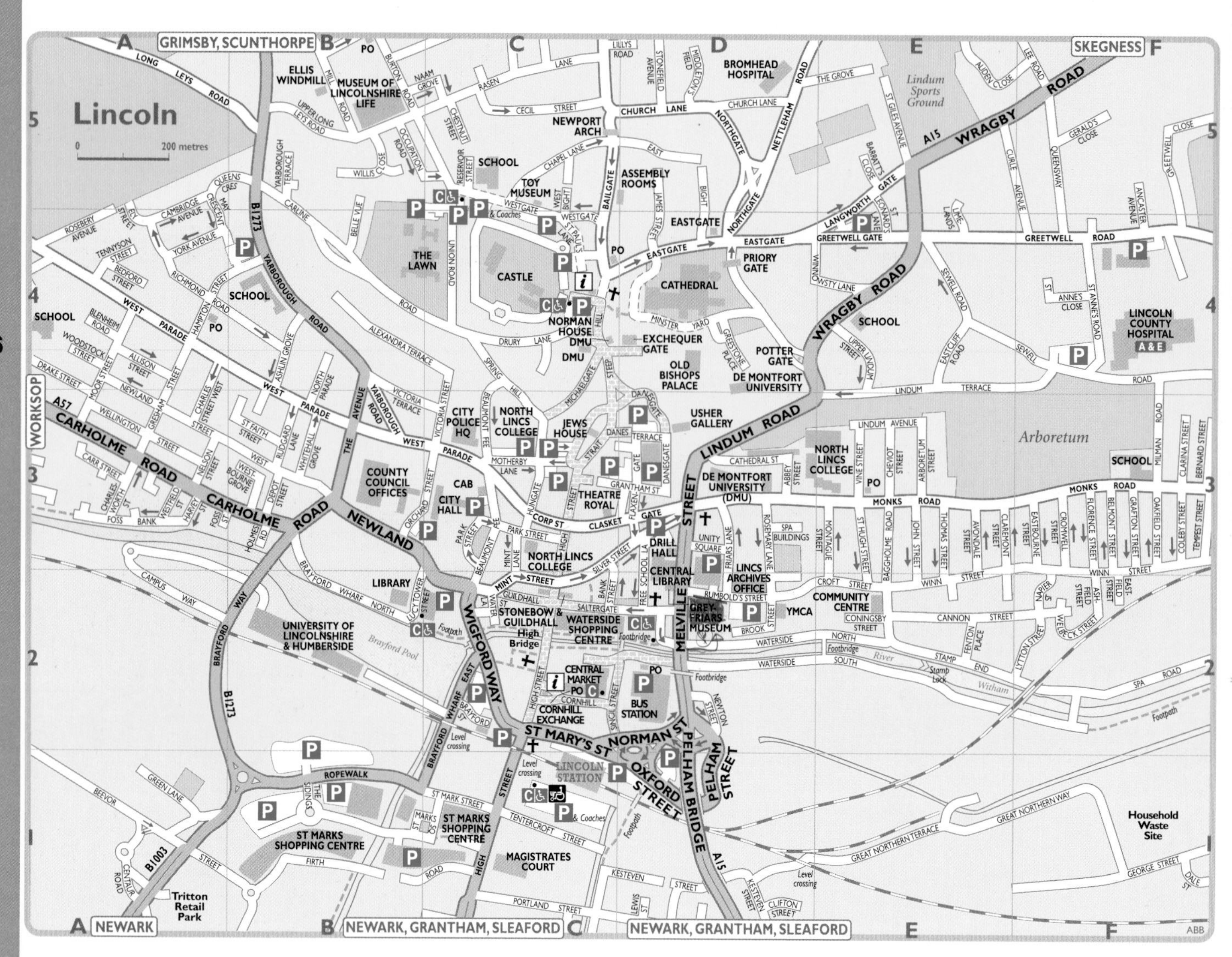

Lincoln

Lincoln is found on atlas page **76**,
grid reference **9771**

196

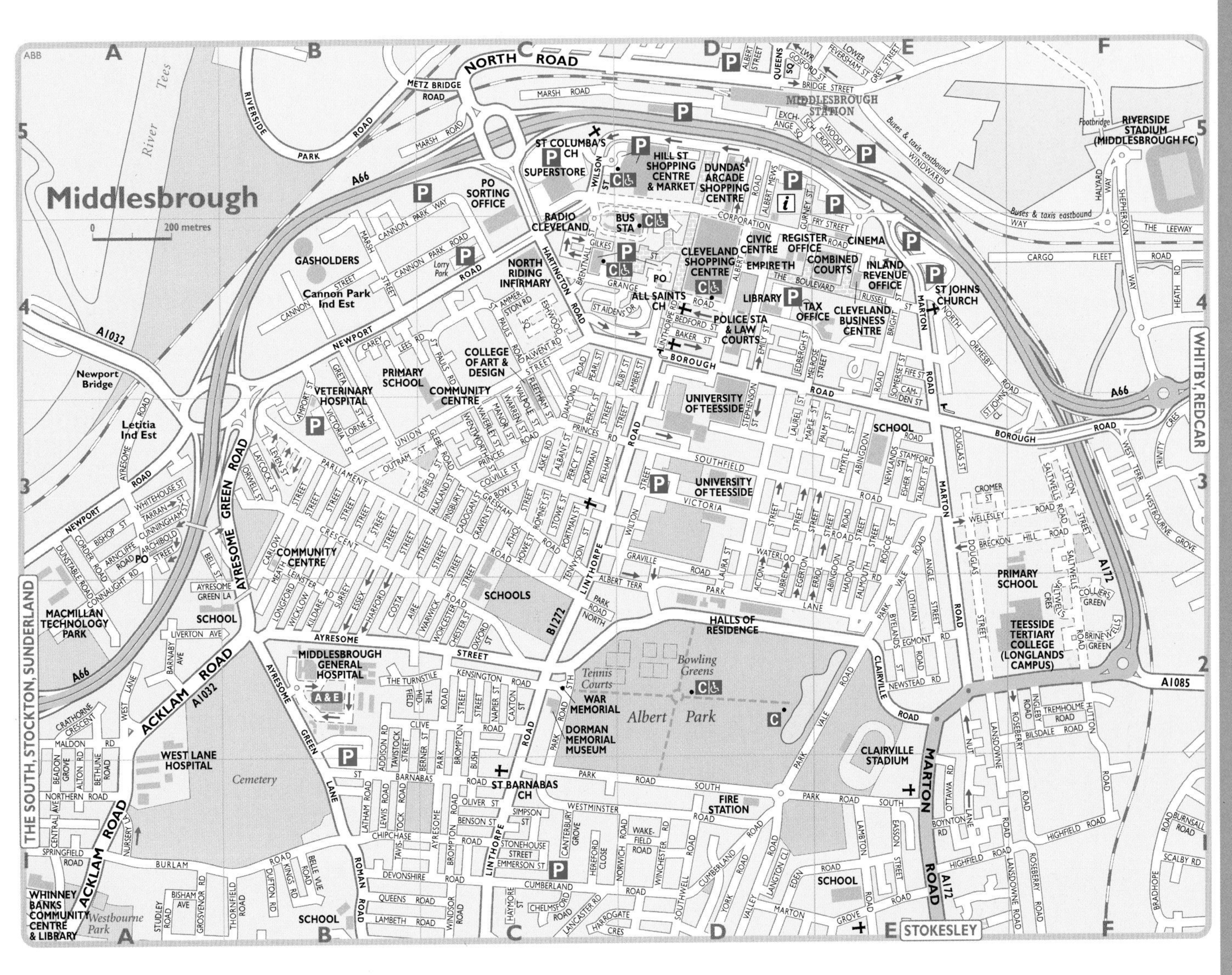

Middlesbrough

Middlesbrough is found on atlas page **97**,
grid reference **4919**

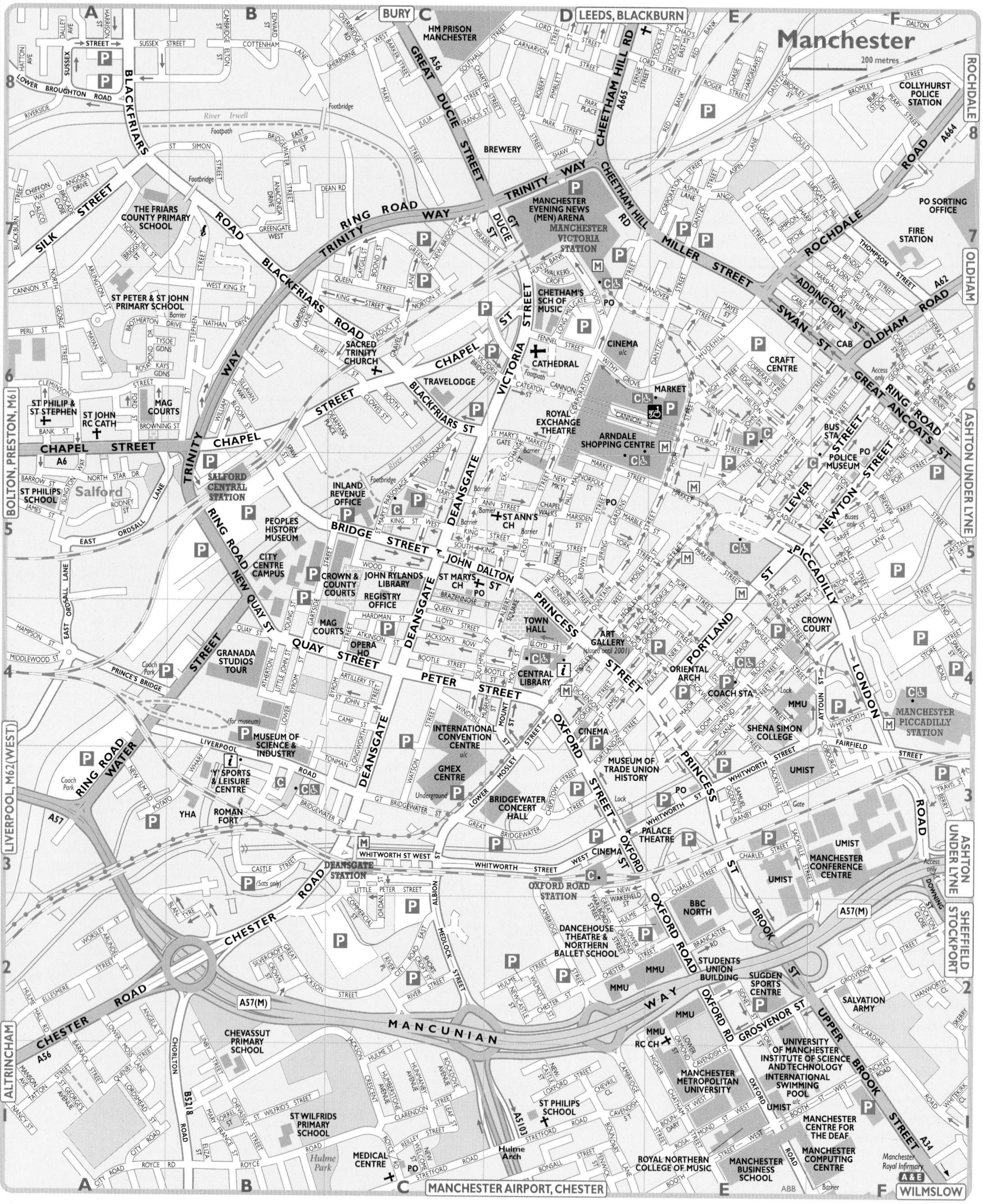

Manchester

198

200 metres

Grid references: A B C D E F / 1 2 3 4 5 6 7 8

BURY

LEEDS, BLACKBURN

ROCHDALE

OLDHAM

ASHTON UNDER LYNE

SHEFFIELD STOCKPORT

WILMSLOW

MANCHESTER AIRPORT, CHESTER

ALTRINCHAM

LIVERPOOL, M62 (WEST)

BOLTON, PRESTON, M61

HM PRISON MANCHESTER

Manchester Evening News (MEN) Arena

MANCHESTER VICTORIA STATION

CHETHAM'S SCH OF MUSIC

CATHEDRAL

ROYAL EXCHANGE THEATRE

ARNDALE SHOPPING CENTRE

MARKET

CRAFT CENTRE

BUS STA

POLICE MUSEUM

THE FRIARS COUNTY PRIMARY SCHOOL

ST PETER & ST JOHN PRIMARY SCHOOL

ST PHILIP & ST STEPHEN

ST JOHN RC CATH

MAG COURTS

SALFORD CENTRAL STATION

PEOPLES HISTORY MUSEUM

CITY CENTRE CAMPUS

CROWN & COUNTY COURTS

JOHN RYLANDS LIBRARY

REGISTRY OFFICE

SACRED TRINITY CHURCH

TRAVELODGE

INLAND REVENUE OFFICE

ST ANN'S CH

ST MARY'S CH

TOWN HALL

ART GALLERY (closed until 2001)

CENTRAL LIBRARY

ORIENTAL ARCH

COACH STA

CROWN COURT

MMU

SHENA SIMON COLLEGE

GRANADA STUDIOS TOUR

OPERA HO

MAG COURTS

MUSEUM OF SCIENCE & INDUSTRY

'Y' SPORTS & LEISURE CENTRE

YHA

ROMAN FORT

INTERNATIONAL CONVENTION CENTRE

GMEX CENTRE

MUSEUM OF TRADE UNION HISTORY

BRIDGEWATER CONCERT HALL

CINEMA

DEANSGATE STATION

OXFORD ROAD STATION

PALACE THEATRE

CINEMA

BBC NORTH

MANCHESTER CONFERENCE CENTRE

UMIST

DANCEHOUSE THEATRE & NORTHERN BALLET SCHOOL

STUDENTS UNION BUILDING

SUGDEN SPORTS CENTRE

SALVATION ARMY

MMU

MANCHESTER METROPOLITAN UNIVERSITY

UNIVERSITY OF MANCHESTER INSTITUTE OF SCIENCE AND TECHNOLOGY

INTERNATIONAL SWIMMING POOL

CHEVASSUT PRIMARY SCHOOL

ST WILFRIDS PRIMARY SCHOOL

ST PHILIPS SCHOOL

MEDICAL CENTRE

Hulme Park

Hulme Arch

ROYAL NORTHERN COLLEGE OF MUSIC

MANCHESTER BUSINESS SCHOOL

MANCHESTER CENTRE FOR THE DEAF

MANCHESTER COMPUTING CENTRE

Manchester Royal Infirmary

A & E

MANCHESTER PICCADILLY STATION

River Irwell

PO SORTING OFFICE

COLLYHURST POLICE STATION

FIRE STATION

CAB

Street names: BLACKFRIARS ROAD, CHAPEL STREET, TRINITY WAY, RING ROAD, DEANSGATE, QUAY STREET, PETER STREET, OXFORD STREET, OXFORD ROAD, PRINCESS STREET, PORTLAND STREET, WHITWORTH STREET, CHESTER ROAD, MANCUNIAN WAY, CHEETHAM HILL RD, MILLER STREET, SWAN ST, GREAT ANCOATS ST, NEWTON ST, PICCADILLY, LONDON ROAD, UPPER BROOK STREET, GROSVENOR ST

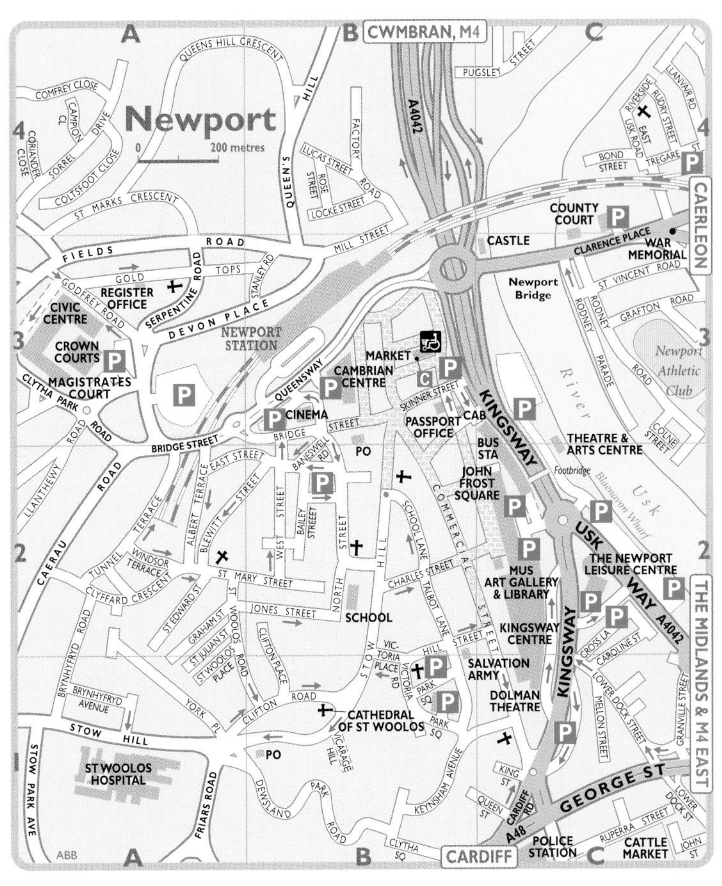

Newport

Newport is found on atlas page **34**,
grid reference 3188

Albert Terrace	A2	Fields Road	A3-B3	Rodney Road	C3
Bailey Street	B2	Friars Road	A1	Rose Street	B4
Baneswell Road	B2-B3	George Street	C1	Rudry Street	C4
Blewitt Street	A2-B2	Godfrey Road	A3	Ruperra Street	C1
Bond Street	C4	Gold Tops	A3-B3	St Edward Street	A2
Bridge Street	A2-A3-B2-B3	Grafton Road	C3	St Julian Street	A1-A2
Brynhyfryd Avenue	A1-A2	Graham Street	A1-A2	St Marks Crescent	A3-A4
Brynhyfryd Road	A1-A2	Granville Street	C1	St Mary Street	A2-B2
Caerau Road	A2	Hill Street	B1-B2-C2	St Vincent Road	C3
Campion Close	A4	John Street	C1	St Woolos Place	A1-A2
Cardiff Road	C1	Jones Street	A2-B2	St Woolos Road	A2-A1-B1
Caroline Street	C1-C2	Keynsham Avenue	B1	School Lane	B2
Charles Street	B2	King Street	C1	Serpentine Road	A3
Clarence Place	C3-C4	Kingsway	C1-C2-C3-B3	Skinner Street	B3
Clifton Place	B2-B1	Llanthewy Road	A2-A3	Sorrel Drive	A4
Clifton Road	A1-B1	Llanvair Road	C4	Stanlet Road	B3
Clyffard Crescent	A2	Locke Street	B4	Stow Hill	A1-B1-B2
Clytha Park Road	A3	Lower Dock Street	C1	Stow Park Avenue	A1
Clytha Square	B1	Lucas Street	B4	Talbot Lane	B2
Colne Street	C3-C2	Mellon Street	C1	Tregare Street	C4
Coltsfoot Close	A4	Mill Street	B3-B4	Tunnel Terrace	A2
Comfrey Close	A4	North Street	B2	Usk Way	C2
Commercial Street	B2-C2-C1	Park Square	B1	Vicarage Hill	B1
Coriander Close	A4	Pugsley Street	B4-C4	Victoria Place	B1
Cross Lane	C1-C2	Queen's Hill	B3-B4	Victoria Road	B1
Devon Place	A3-B3	Queens Hill Crescent	A4-B4	West Street	B2
Dewsland Park Road	A1-B1	Queen Street	C1	Windsor Terrace	A2
East Street	A2-B2	Queensway	A3-B3	York Place	A1-A2
East Usk Road	C4	Riverside	C4		
Factory Road	B4	Rodney Parade	C3		

199

Manchester

Manchester is found on atlas page **79**,
grid reference 8497

Addington Street	E7-F7-F6	Bromley Street	E8-F8	Cornell Street	F6	Middlewood Street	A4	St John Street	C4
Albert Square	D4-D5	Brook Street	E2	Corporation Street	D6-D7-E7-E8	Miller Street	E7	St Mary's Gate	D6
Albion Street	C2-C3	Brotherton Drive	A6-B6	Cottenham Lane	B8	Minshull Street	E4-F4	St Mary's Parsonage	C5
Anaconda Drive	B7	Brown Street	D5	Cotton Street	F6	Mirabel Street	C7-D7	St Mary's Street	C5
Angel Street	E7	Browning Street	A6-B6	Cross Keys Street	F7	Mosley Street	D4-D5-E5	St Simon Street	A8-B8-B7
Angela Street	A2	Burstock Street	B8	Cross Street	D5	Mount Street	D4	St Stephen Street	B6-B7
Angora Drive	A7	Bury Street	B6-C6	Crown Street	B2	Museum Street	C4-D4	St Wilfrid's Street	B1
Arlington Street	A6-A7	Byrom Street	B4-C4	Dale Street	E5-F5	Nancy Street	A1	Sackville Street	F3-E3-E4
Artillery Street	C4	Cable Street	E7-E6-F6	Dalley Avenue	A8	Nathan Drive	B6	Samuel Ogden Street	E3
Arundel Street	A2	Cambridge Street	B8	Dalton Street	F8	New Bridge Street	C7	Sharp Street	E7-F7
Aspin Lane	E7-E8	Cambridge Street	D3-D2-E1	Dantzic Street	E6-E7-E8-F8	New Elm Road	A3	Shaw Street	D8
Atherton Street	B4	Camp Street	C4	Dean Road	B7-C7	New Market	D5	Sherborne Street West	B8-C8
Atkinson Street	C4	Canal Street	E4	Dean Street	F5-F6	New Quay Street	B4-B5	Sherratt Street	F6
Aytoun Street	E5-E4-F4	Cannon Street	A7	Deansgate	C3-C4-C5-C6	New Wakefield Street	D3	Shortcroft Street	C2
Back George Street	D4-E4-F5	Cannon Street	D6-E6	Dearman's Place	C6	New Welcome Street	D2	Shudehill	E6-E7
Back Piccadilly	E5-F5	Carnarvon Street	D8	Dickenson Street	C3-C4	Newcastle Street	D1-D2	Sidney Street	E2
Bank Street	A6	Castle Street	B3	Downing Street	F2-F3	Newton Street	E5-F5-F6	Silk Street	A7
Barker Street	C8	Cateaton Street	D6	Ducie Street	F4-F5	Nicholas Street	D4-E4	Sillavan Way	B6
Barrack Street	A1-A2	Cavendish Street	D1	Dutton Street	D7-D8	Norfolk Street	D5	Silvercroft Street	B2
Barrow Street	A5	Caygill Street	C7	Dyche Street	E7-F7	North George Street	A6-A7	Simpson Street	E7-F7
Bendix Street	F7	Chapel Street	A6-B6-C6-D6	East Ordsall Lane	A4-A5	North Hill Street	A7	Skerry Close	F2
Berry Street	F3	Chapel Walks	D5	East Philip Street	B8	North Star Drive	A5	Sorrel Street	B1
Blackburn Street	A7	Charles Street	E2-E3	Edge Street	E6	Norton Street	C6-C7	South King Street	C5-D5
Blackfriars Road	A8-B7-C6	Charlotte Street	D5-D4-E4	Edward Street	B8	Oak Street	E6	Southall Street	C8-D8
Blackfriars Street	C6	Charter Street	C8-D8	Eliza Street	B1	Oldham Road	F6-F7	Southmill Street	C4-D4
Blantyre Street	B2-C3	Chase Street	E8	Ellesmere Street	A2	Oldham Street	E5-E6-F6	Sparkle Street	F4
Bloom Street	B6	Chatham Street	E4-E5-F5	Elton Street	B8	Overbridge Road	C8	Spaw Street	B5-B6
Bloom Street	E4	Cheetham Hill Road	D7-D8	Exchange Street	D5-D6	Oxford Road	E3-E2-E1	Spear Street	E5-E6-F6
Blossom Street	F6	Chepstow Street	D3	Fairfield Street	F3-F4	Oxford Street	D3-D4	Spring Gardens	D5
Boad Street	F4	Chester Road	A1-A2-B2-C3	Faulkner Street	D4-E4	Pall Mall	D5	Stocks Street	E8
Bonsall Street	D1	Chester Street	D2-E2	Fennel Street	D6	Park Place	D8	Stocks Street East	E8
Boond Street	C7	Chevassut Street	B1	Fenwick Street	C1	Park Street	D8	Store Street	F4
Booth Street	C6	Chevril Close	D1	Fernie Street	D8	Parker Street	E5	Stretford Road	C1-D1
Booth Street	D4-D5	Chiffon Way	A7	Ford Street	A6	Parsonage	C5-C6	Sussex Street	A8-B8
Booth Street West	E1-F1	China Lane	F5	Fountain Street	D4-D5-E5	Paton Street	F5	Swan Street	E7-E6-F6
Bootle Street	C4-C5	Chorlton Road	B1-B2	Francis Street	C8	Peary Street	F8	Tariff Street	F5
Boundary Lane	C1	Chorlton Street	E4	Garden Lane	B6	Peru Street	A6	Tatton Street	A1
Boundary Street West	E1	Church Street	E6	Gartside Street	B4-B5-C5	Peter Street	C4-D4	Thompson Street	F7
Brancaster Road	E2	City Road	A1-B1	George Leigh Street	F6	Piccadilly	E5-F5-F4	Tib Street	E5-E6-F6
Brazenose Street	C5-C4-D4	City Road East	C2	George Street	D4-E4-E5	Pimblett Street	D8	Todd Street	D6-D7
Brewer Street	E2	Clarendon Street	C1	Gould Street	E8-F8-F7	Port Street	F5-F6	Tonman Street	B3-C3
Bridge Street	B5-C5	Cleminson Street	A6-B6	Goulden Street	F6-F7	Portland Street	D3-D4-E4-E5	Trafford Street	F3
Bridgewater Street	B3-C3	Clowes Street	C6	Granby Row	E3	Potato Wharf	A3-B3	Travis Street	F3
Bridgewater Street	B7-B8	Cobourg Street	F3-F4	Gravel Lane	C6-C7	Prince's Bridge	A4	Trinity Way	B5-B6-C7-D7
Briggs Street	A7	Commercial Street	C2	Great Ancoats Street	F5-F6	Princess Street	E3-E4-D4-D5	Turner Street	E6
Brocade Close	A7	Copperas Street	E6	Great Bridgewater Street	C3-D3	Quay Street	B4-C4	Tysoe Gardens	A6-B6
				Great Ducie Street	D7-C7-C8	Queen Street	B7-C7	Upper Brook Street	F1-F2
				Great Jackson Street	B2-C2	Queen Street	C4	Viaduct Street	C6
				Great Marlborough Street	D2-D3	Quenby Street	A1	Victoria Street	D6-D7
				Greengate	C7	Red Bank	E8	Victoria Bridge Street	C6-D6
				Greengate West	B7-C7	Reilley Street	C1	Walkers Croft	D7
				Grosvenor Street	E2-F2	Richmond Street	E4	Water Street	A3-A4-B4
				Hampson Street	A4	River Place	C2	Watson Street	C3-C4
				Hanover Street	D7-E7-E6	River Street	C2	West King Street	B7
Hanworth Close	F2	Middlewood Street	A4			Riverside	A8	West Mosley Street	C4-D5-E5
Hardman Street	C4	Miller Street	E7			Robert Street	D8	Whitekirk Close	F1
Hargreaves Street	E8	Minshull Street	E4-F4			Rochdale Road	E7-F7-F8	Whitworth Street	D3-E3-E4
Harrison Street	A8	Mirabel Street	C7-D7			Rockdove Avenue	C1	Whitworth Street West	C3-D3
Hatton Avenue	A8	Mosley Street	D4-D5-E5			Rodney Street	A5	William Street	B6
Henry Street	F6	Mount Street	D4			Roger Street	E8	Wilmott Street	D2
High Street	E5-E6	Museum Street	C4-D4			Rosamond Drive	A6	Windmill Street	C4-D4
Higher Chatham Street	D2-E1	Nancy Street	A1			Rosamond Street West	E1	Withy Grove	D6
Hilton Street	E6-F6-F5	Nathan Drive	B6			Royce Road	A1-B1-C1	Wood Street	C5
Hope Street	E5	New Bridge Street	C7			St Ann Street	C5-D5	Worsley Street	A2
Houldsworth Street	F5-F6	New Elm Road	A3			St Chad's Street	E8	York Street	D5-E5-E4
Hulme Hall Road	A2	New Market	D5			St George's Avenue	A1	York Street	E1-E2
Hulme Street	C1-C2-D2-E2	New Quay Street	B4-B5			St James Street	D4	Young Street	B4-B5
Humberstone Avenue	C1	New Wakefield Street	D3						
Hunmanby Avenue	C1	New Welcome Street	D2						
Hunts Bank	D7	Newcastle Street	D1-D2						
Inchley Road	F1	Newton Street	E5-F5-F6						
Islington Way	A5-A6	Nicholas Street	D4-E4						
Jackson Crescent	C1-C2	Norfolk Street	D5						
Jackson's Row	C4	North George Street	A6-A7						
James Street	A5	North Hill Street	A7						
John Dalton Street	C5-D5	North Star Drive	A5						
John Street	E6	Norton Street	C6-C7						
Jordan Street	C2-C3	Oak Street	E6						
Julia Street	C8-D8	Oldham Road	F6-F7						
Jutland Street	F4-F5	Oldham Street	E5-E6-F6						
Kays Gardens	A6-B6	Overbridge Road	C8						
Kennedy Street	C5-D4	Oxford Road	E3-E2-E1						
Kincardine Road	F1-F2	Oxford Street	D3-D4						
King Street	B7-C7-C6	Pall Mall	D5						
King Street	C5-D5	Park Place	D8						
King Street West	C5	Park Street	D8						
Laystall Street	F5	Parker Street	E5						
Leaf Street	C1	Parsonage	C5-C6						
Lena Street	F5	Paton Street	F5						
Lever Street	E5-F5-F6	Peary Street	F8						
Linby Street	B1-B2	Peru Street	A6						
Little John Street	B4	Peter Street	C4-D4						
Little Peter Street	C3	Piccadilly	E5-F5-F4						
Liverpool Road	A4-B4-B3-C3	Pimblett Street	D8						
Lloyd Street	C4-C5	Port Street	F5-F6						
Lockton Close	F2	Portland Street	D3-D4-E4-E5						
London Road	F3-F4	Potato Wharf	A3-B3						
Long Millgate	D6-D7	Prince's Bridge	A4						
Longworth Street	C3-C4	Princess Street	E3-E4-D4-D5						
Lord Street	D8-E8	Quay Street	B4-C4						
Lordsmead Street	A1	Queen Street	B7-C7						
Lower Broughton Road	A8	Queen Street	C4						
Lower Byrom Street	B4	Quenby Street	A1						
Lower Mosley Street	C3-D3-D4	Red Bank	E8						
Lower Moss Lane	A1-A2	Reilley Street	C1						
Lower Ormond Street	D2-E2-E1	Richmond Street	E4						
Loxford Street	D1	River Place	C2						
Ludgate Hill	E7-F7	River Street	C2						
Ludgate Street	E7	Riverside	A8						
Major Street	E4	Robert Street	D8						
Mancunian Way	B2-D2-E2-F3	Rochdale Road	E7-F7-F8						
Manson Avenue	A1	Rockdove Avenue	C1						
Marble Street	D5-E5	Rodney Street	A5						
Market Street	D6-D5-E5	Roger Street	E8						
Marsden Street	D5	Rosamond Drive	A6						
Marshall Street	E7-F7-F6	Rosamond Street West	E1						
Mary France Street	B1	Royce Road	A1-B1-C1						
Mary Street	C7-C8	St Ann Street	C5-D5						
Mayan Avenue	A6	St Chad's Street	E8						
Mayes Street	E6-E7	St George's Avenue	A1						
Medlock Street	C2	St James Street	D4						

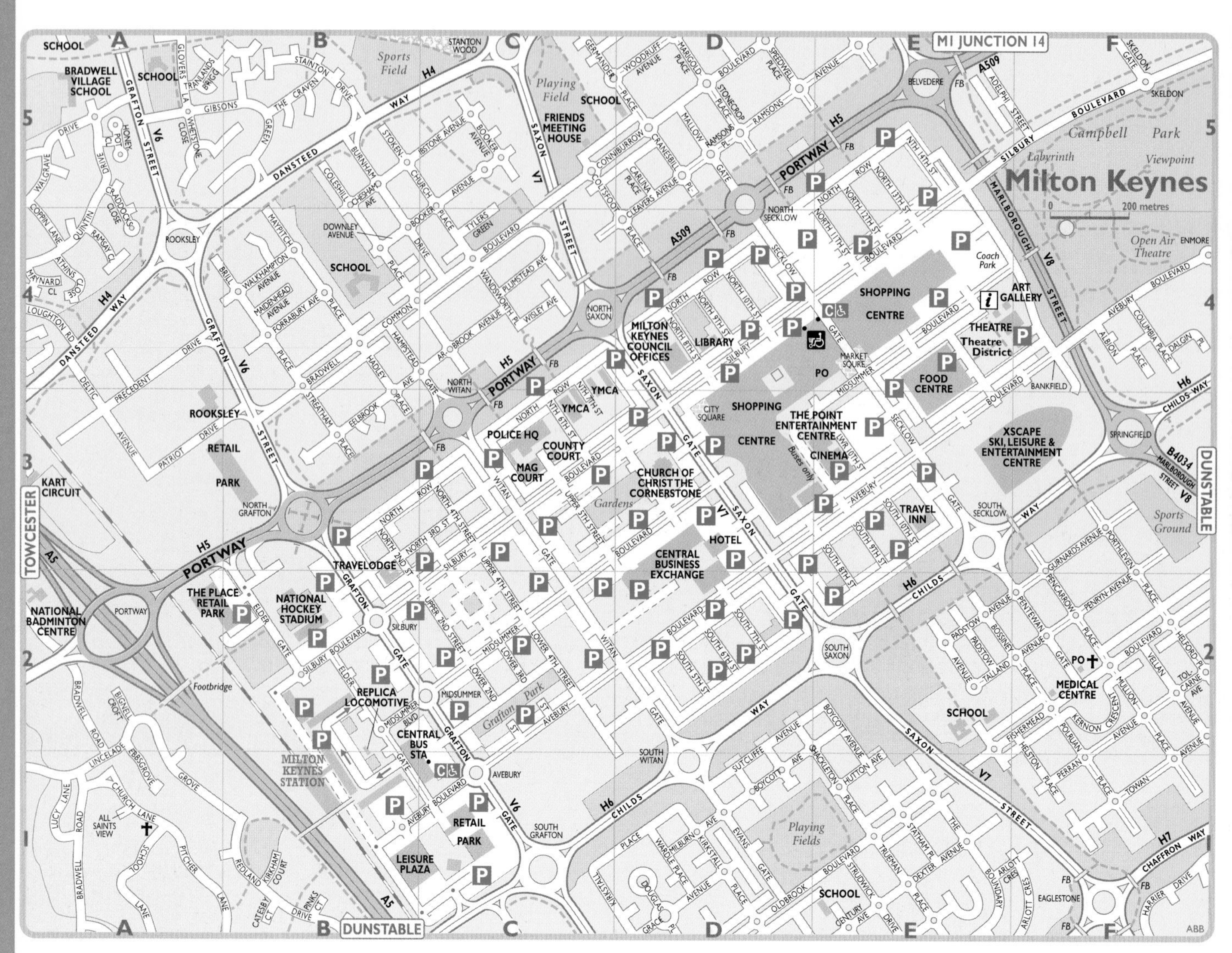

Milton Keynes

Milton Keynes is found on atlas page **38**,
grid reference **8537**

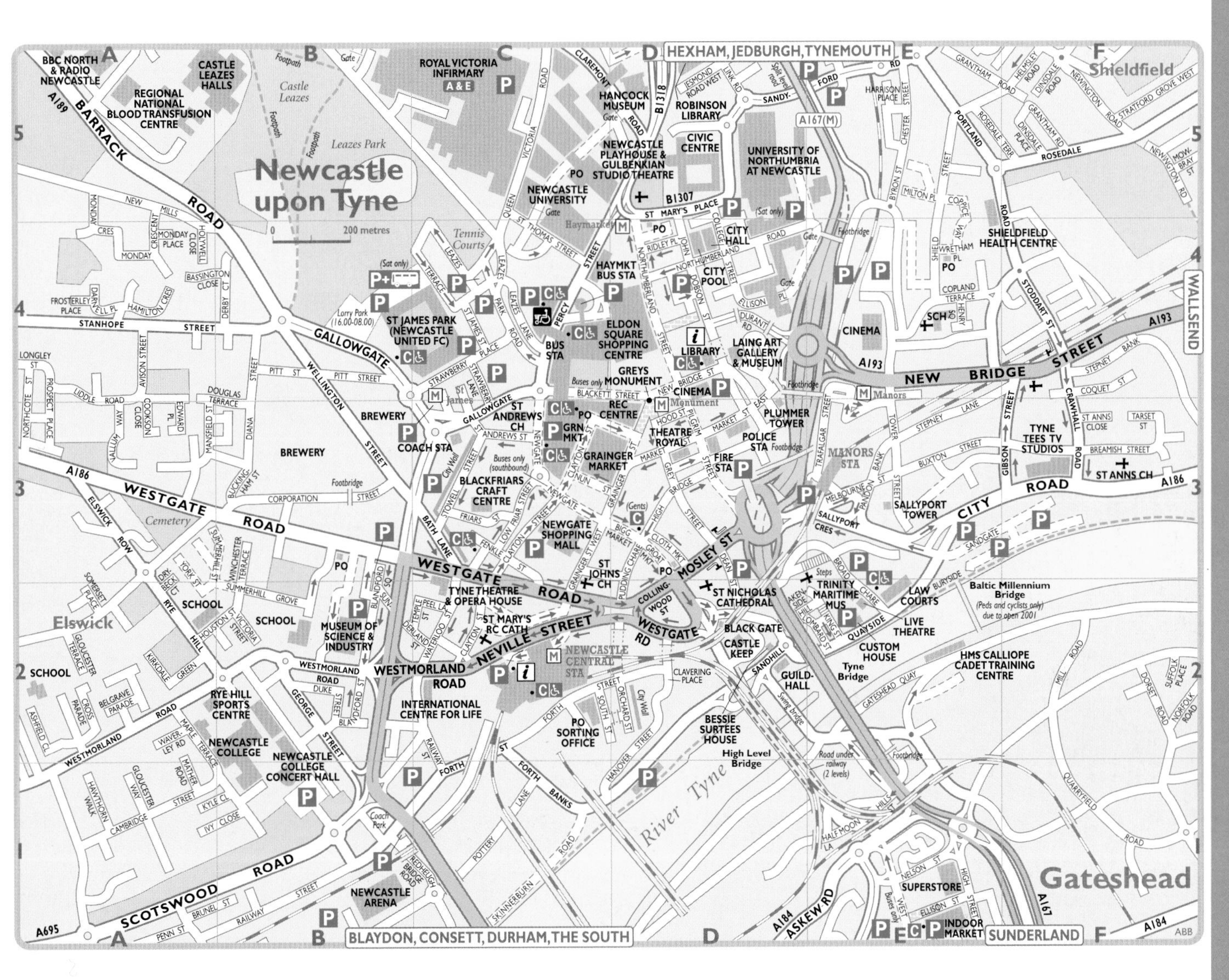

Newcastle upon Tyne

Newcastle upon Tyne is found on atlas page **103**,
grid reference **2464**

Akenside Hill	D2-E2	Corporation Street	B3	Grantham Road	E5-F5	Melbourne Street	E3	Portland Road	E5-F5-F4	Stoddart Street	F4

Akenside Hill	D2-E2	Corporation Street	B3	Grantham Road	E5-F5	Melbourne Street	E3	Portland Road	E5-F5-F4	Stoddart Street	F4
Ashfield Close	A2	Crawhall Road	F3-F4	Grey Street	D3	Mansfield Street	A3	Pottery Lane	C1	Stowell Street	C3
Askew Road	D1-E1	Cross Parade	A2	Groat Market	D3	Maple Terrace	A2-B1	Prospect Place	A3-A4	Stratford Grove West	F5
Avison Street	A4	Darnell Place	A4	Half Moon Lane	E1	Market Street	D3	Pudding Chare	D2-D3	Strawberry Lane	C3-C4
Barrack Road	A5-B4	Dean Street	D2-D3	Hamilton Crescent	A4	Market Street East	D3-D4	Quarryfield Road	F1-F2	Strawberry Place	C4
Bassington Close	A4-B4	Derby Court	B4	Hanover Street	C1-D1-D2	Mather Road	A1-A2	Quayside	E2	Suffolk Place	F2
Bath Lane	C3	Diana Street	B3-B4	Harrison Place	E5	Mill Road	F2	Queen Victoria Road	C4-C5	Summerhill Grove	B2
Belgrave Parade	A2	Dinsdale Place	F5	Hawthorn Walk	A1	Milton Place	E5	Railway Street	A1-B1-C1-C2	Summerhill Street	A3-B3
Bigg Market	C3-D3	Dinsdale Road	F5	Helmsley Road	E5-F5	Monday Crescent	A4-A5	Redheugh Bridge Road	B1-C1	Sunderland Street	B2-C2
Blackett Street	C4-D4	Dorset Road	F2	Henry Square	E4	Monday Place	A4	Ridley Place	D4	Tarset Street	F3
Blandford Square	B2-B3	Douglas Terrace	A4-B3	High Bridge	D3	Mosley Street	D3	Rosedale	F5	Temple Street	B2-C2
Blandford Street	B2	Drybeck Court	A2-A3	High Street	E1	Mowbray Street	F5	Rosedale Terrace	E5-F5	Tower Street	E3
Breamish Street	F3	Duke Street	B2	Hills Street	E1	Nelson Street	E1	Rye Hill	A3-A2-B2	Trafalgar Street	E3-E4
Broad Chare	E2-E3	Durant Road	D4	Holiston Street	A2-B2	New Bridge Street	D4	St Andrews Street	C3	Vallum Way	A3
Brunel Street	A1-B1	Edward Place	A3	Holywell Close	A4	New Bridge Street	E4-F4	St Anns Close	F3	Victoria Street	B2
Buckingham Street	B3	Ellison Place	D4	Hood Street	D3	New Mills	A5-A4	St James Close	C4	Waterloo Street	C2
Buxton Street	E3	Elswick Row	A3	Ivy Close	A1-B1	Newgate	C3	St Mary's Place	D5	Waverley Road	A2
Byron Street	E5	Fenckle Street	C3	Jesmond Road West	D5	Newington Road	F5	St Thomas Street	C4-C5	Wellington Street	B3-B4
Cambridge Street	A1	Forth Banks	C1-C2	John Dobson Street	D4	Norfolk Road	F2	Sallyport Crescent	E3	West Ellison Street	E1
Chester Street	E5	Forth Street	C1-C2-D2	King Street	E2	Northcote Street	A3-A4	Sandgate	E3	Westgate Road	A3-B3-C3-D2
City Road	E3-F3	Friars Street	C3	Kirkdale Green	A2	Northumberland Road	D4-E4	Sandhill	D2	Westmorland Road	A1-A2-B2-C2
Claremont Road	C5-D5	Frosterley Place	A4	Kyle Close	A1-B1	Northumberland Street	D4	Sandyford Road	D5-E5	Winchester Terrace	B2-B3
Clayton Street	C2-C3	Gallowgate	B4-C3-C4	Leazes Lane	C4	Nun Street	C3	Scotswood Road	A1-B1	Wretham Place	E4
Cloth Market	D3	Gateshead Quay	E2	Leazes Park Road	C4	Orchard Street	D2	Shield Street	E4-E5	York Street	A2-A3
College Street	D4-D5	George Street	B1-B2	Leazes Terrace	C4	Pandon Bank	E3	Skinnerburn Road	C1		
Collingwood Street	D2	Gibson Street	F3-F4	Liddle Road	A3-A4	Peel Lane	C2	Somerset Place	A2		
Cookson Close	A3	Gloucester Terrace	A2	Link Road	D5	Penn Street	A1	South Street	C2-D2		
Copland Terrace	E4	Gloucester Way	A1	Lombard Street	D2-E2	Percy Street	C4	Stanhope Street	A4-B4		
Coppice Way	E4-E5	Grainger Street	C3-D3	Longley Street	A4	Pilgrim Street	D3	Stepney Bank	F3-F4		
Coquet Street	F4	Grainger Street West	C2-C3	Low Friar Street	C3	Pitt Street	B4	Stepney Lane	E3-E4		

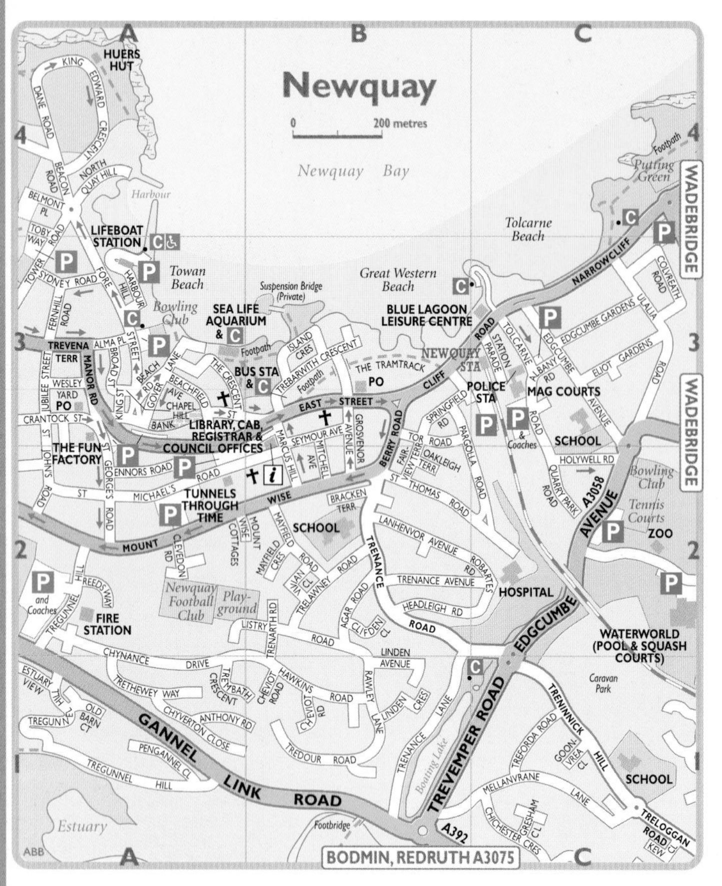

Newquay

Newquay is found on atlas page **4**,
grid reference **8161**

Agar Road	B2	King Street	A3	Trenance Lane	B1-B2
Albany Road	C3	Lanhenvor Avenue	B2	Trenance Road	B2-C2
Alma Place	A3	Linden Avenue	B1-B2	Trenarth Road	B2
Anthony Road	A1-B1	Linden Crescent	B1	Treninnick Hill	C1
Bank Street	A3-B3	Listry Road	A2-B2	Trethewey Way	A1
Beach Road	A3	Manor Road	A3	Trevemper Road	B1-C1
Beachfield Avenue	A3	Marcus Hill	B2-B3	Trevena Terrace	A3
Beacon Road	A4	Mayfield Crescent	B2	Ulalia Road	C3
Belmont Place	A4	Mayfield Road	B2	Vivian Close	B2
Berry Road	B2-B3	Mellanvrane Lane	B1-C1	Wesley Yard	A3
Bracken Terrace	B2	Mitchell Avenue	B2-B3		
Broad Street	A3	Mount Wise	A2-B2		
Chapel Hill	A3	Mount Wise Cottages	A2-B2		
Cheviot Road	B1	Narrowcliff	C3-C4		
Chichester Crescent	C1	North Quay Hill	A4		
Chynance Drive	A1-A2	Oakleigh Terrace	B2		
Chyverton Close	A1	Old Barn Court	A1		
Clevedon Road	A2	Pargolla Road	B3-C2		
Clifden Close	B2	Pengannel Close	A1		
Cliff Road	B3-C3	Quarry Park Road	C2		
Colvreath Road	C3	Rawley Lane	B1		
Crantock Street	A3	Reeds Way	A2		
Dane Road	A4	Robartes Road	C2		
East Street	B3	St George's Road	A2-A3		
Edgcumbe Avenue	C2-C3	St John's Road	A2-A3		
Edgcumbe Gardens	C3	St Michael's Road	A2-B2		
Eliot Gardens	C3	St Thomas Road	B2-C2		
Ennors Road	A2	Seymour Avenue	B3		
Estuary View	A1	Springfield Road	B3		
Fairview Terrace	B2-B3	Station Parade	C3		
Fernhill Road	A2	Sydney Road	A3		
Fore Street	A3-A4	The Crescent	A3		
Gannel Link Road	A2-A1-B1	The Tramtrack	B3		
Goonvrea Close	A1	Toby Way	A4		
Gover Lane	A3	Tolcarne Road	C3		
Gresham Close	C1	Tor Road	B3		
Grosvenor Avenue	B2-B3	Tower Road	A3-A4		
Harbour Hill	A3	Trebarwith Crescent	B3		
Hawkins Road	B1	Tredour Road	B1		
Headleigh Road	B2	Treforda Road	C1		
Holywell Road	C2	Tregunnel Hill	A1-A2		
Island Crescent	B3	Trelawney Road	B2		
Jubilee Street	A3	Treloggan Road	C1		
Kew Close	C1	Trembath Crescent	A1-B1		
King Edward Crescent	A4	Trenance Avenue	B2-C2		

Northampton

Northampton is found on atlas page **49**,
grid reference **7560**

Abington Square	C3	Grafton Street	A4	Upper Bath Street	A3
Abington Street	B2-B3-C3	Great Russell Street	C4	Upper Mounts	B3-B4
Albion Place	B1-B2	Greyfriars	A3-B3-C3	Upper Priory Street	A4
Alcombe Road	C4	Guildhall Road	B1-B2	Victoria Gardens	B1
Alexandra Road	C2-C3	Hazelwood Road	C2	Victoria Promenade	B1-C1
Althorp Street	A3	Herbert Street	A3	Victoria Street	B3-B4
Angel Street	B2	Horsemarket	A2-A3	Wellington Street	B3-C3
Arundel Street	A4	Horseshoe Street	A1-A2	William Street	C3
Ash Street	B4	Hunter Street	C4	York Road	C2-C3
Bailiff Street	B4	King Street	A2		
Barrack Road	A4-B4	Kingswell	A1-A2		
Bath Street	A3	Ladys Lane	A3-B3-C3		
Bedford Road	C1	Lower Harding Street	A4		
Bidders Close	B1	Lower Mounts	C3		
Billing Road	C2	Lower Priory Street	A4		
Bradshaw Street	A2-A3	Margaret Street	B4		
Bridge Street	A1-A2	Market Square	B2		
Broad Street	A3-A4	Mayor Hold	A3		
Campbell Street	A4-B4	Mercer's Row	B2		
Castillian Street	B2	Newland	B3		
Castle Street	A3	Oak Street	B4		
Cattlemarket Road	B1	Overstone Road	C3-C4		
Charles Street	B4-C4	Pike Lane	A2-A3		
Cheyne Walk	C1-C2	Quorn Way	A4		
Church Lane	A3-B3-B4	Regent Street	A4		
Clare Street	C4	Robert Street	B4		
Cloutsham Street	C4	St Andrew's Street	A3-A4		
College Street	A2	St Giles Square	B2		
Commercial Street	A1	St Giles Street	B2-C2		
Connaught Street	B4	St Giles Terrace	C2-C3		
Cranstoun Street	B4-C4	St James Street	A1		
Craven Street	B4-C4	St John's Street	B1		
Crispin Street	A3	St Katherine's Street	A2		
Deal Street	B4	St Mary's Street	A2		
Derngate	C1-C2-B2	St Michael's Road	C3		
Duke Street	B4-C4	St Peter's Way	A1		
Dunster Street	C3-C4	Sheep Street	A3-A4		
Earl Street	B3-C4	Silver Street	A3		
Elm Street	B4	Somerset Street	C4		
Fetter Street	B1-B2	Spencer Parade	C2		
Foundry Street	A1	Spring Gardens	C2		
Gas Street	A1	Swan Street	B1-B2		
George Row	B2	The Drapery	A2-B2		
Georges Street	A4	The Riding	B2-C2		
Gold Street	A2	Tower Street	A3		

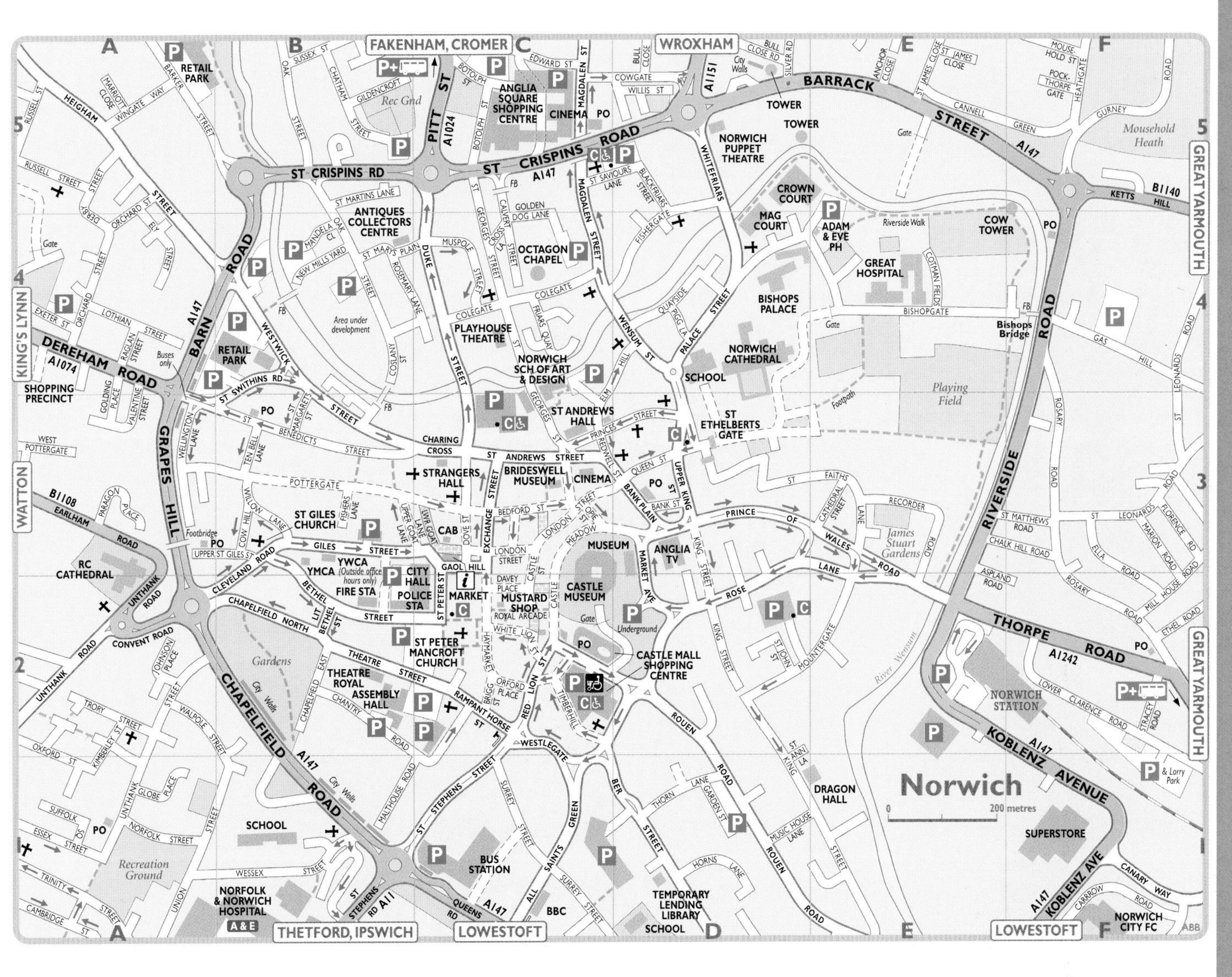

Norwich

Norwich is found on atlas page **67**,
grid reference **2308**

All Saints Green	C1	Chatham Street	B5	Gildencroft	B5	Muspole Street	C4
Anchor Close	E5	Cleveland Road	A2-B2-B3	Giles Street	B3-C3	New Mills Yard	B4
Aspland Road	E3-F2	Colegate	C4	Globe Place	A1	Norfolk Street	A1
Bank Plain	D3	Convent Road	A2	Golden Dog Lane	C4-C5	Oak Street	B4-B5
Bank Street	D3	Coslany Street	B4	Golding Place	A3-A4	Opie Street	C3
Barker Street	A5-B5	Cotman Fields	E4	Grapes Hill	A3	Orchard Street	A4-A5
Barn Road	A4-B4-B5	Cow Hill	B3	Gurney Road	F5	Orford Place	C2
Barrack Street	D5-E5-F5	Cowgate	C5-D5	Haymarket	C2	Oxford Street	A1-A2
Bedford Street	C3	Cross Lane	C4	Heathgate	F5	Palace Street	D4
Ber Street	D2-D1	Davey Place	C2	Heigham Street	A5-A4-B4	Paragon Place	A3
Bethel Street	B3-B2-C2	Derby Street	A4-A5	Hill House Road	F2-F3	Pigg Lane	D4
Bishopgate	E4-F4	Dereham Road	A4	Horns Lane	D1	Pitt Street	C5
Blackfriars Street	D5	Dove Street	C3	Johnson Place	A2	Pockthorpe Gate	F5
Botolph Street	C5	Duke Street	C3-C4-C5	Ketts Hill	F5	Pottergate	A3-B3-C3
Brigg Street	C2	Earlham Road	A3	Kimberley Street	A1-A2	Prince of Wales Road	D3-E3
Bull Close	D5	Edward Street	C5	King Street	D3-D2-D1-E1	Princes Street	C3-D3
Calvert Street	C4-C5	Ella Road	F2-F3	Koblenz Avenue	E2-F2-F1	Quayside	D4
Canary Way	F1	Elm Hill	C3-D4	Little Bethel Street	B2	Queen Street	D3
Cambridge Street	A1	Ely Street	A4-A5	London Street	C3-D3	Raglan Street	A4
Cannell Green	E5-F5	Essex Street	A1	Lothian Street	A4	Rampant Horse Street	C2
Carrow Road	F1	Ethel Road	F2	Lower Clarence Road	F1-F2	Recorder Road	E3
Castle Meadow	C2-C3-D3	Exchange Street	C3	Lower Goat Lane	C3	Red Lion Street	C2
Castle Street	C2-C3	Exeter Street	A4	Magdalen Street	C4-C5	Redwell Street	C3-D3
Cathedral Street	E3	Fishergate	D4-D5	Malthouse Road	B1-C1	Riverside	E1-E2
Chalk Hill Road	E3-F3	Fishers Lane	B3	Mandela Close	B4	Riverside Road	E3-F3-F4-F5
Chantry Road	B2-C2-C1	Florence Road	F3	Marion Road	F3	Rosary Road	F2-F3-F4
Chapelfield East	B2	Friars Quay	C4	Market Avenue	D2-D3	Rose Lane	D2-D3-E3
Chapelfield North	B2	Gaol Hill	C3	Marriott Close	A5	Rosemark Lane	B4-C4
Chapelfield Road	A2-B2-B1	Garden Street	D1	Mountergate	D2-E2	Rouen Road	D2-D1-E1
Charing Cross	C3	Gas Hill	F4	Music House Lane	D1-E1	Royal Arcade	C2

Russell Street	A5	Unthank Street	A1-A2
St Andrews Street	C3	Upper Goat Lane	B3-C3
St Ann Lane	D1-D2	Upper King Street	D3
St Benedicts Street	B3	Upper St Giles Street	A3-B3
St Crispins Road	B5-C5-D5	Valentine Street	A3-A4
St Faiths Lane	D3-E3	Walpole Street	A2-B2
St Georges Street	C3-C4-C5	Wellington Lane	A3
St James Close	E5	Wensum Street	C4-D4
St John Street	D2	Wessex Street	A1-B1
St Leonards Road	F3-F4	West Pottergate	A3
St Margarets Street	B3-B4	Westlegate	C1-C2
St Martins Lane	B5	Westwick Street	B3-B4
St Marys Plain	B4-C4	White Lion Street	C2
St Matthews Road	E3-F3	Whitefriars	D4-D5
St Peter Street	C2-C3	Willis Street	D5
St Saviours Lane	C5-D5	Willow Lane	B3
St Stephens Street	B1-C1-C2	Wingate Way	A5
St Swithins Road	B3-B4		
Stracey Road	F2		
Suffolk Square	A1		
Surrey Street	C1-D1		
Ten Bell Lane	B3		
Theatre Street	B2-C2		
Thorn Lane	D1		
Thorpe Road	E2-F2		
Timberhill	C2		
Trinity Street	A1		
Trory Street	A2		
Union Street	A1-B1		
Unthank Road	A2-A3		

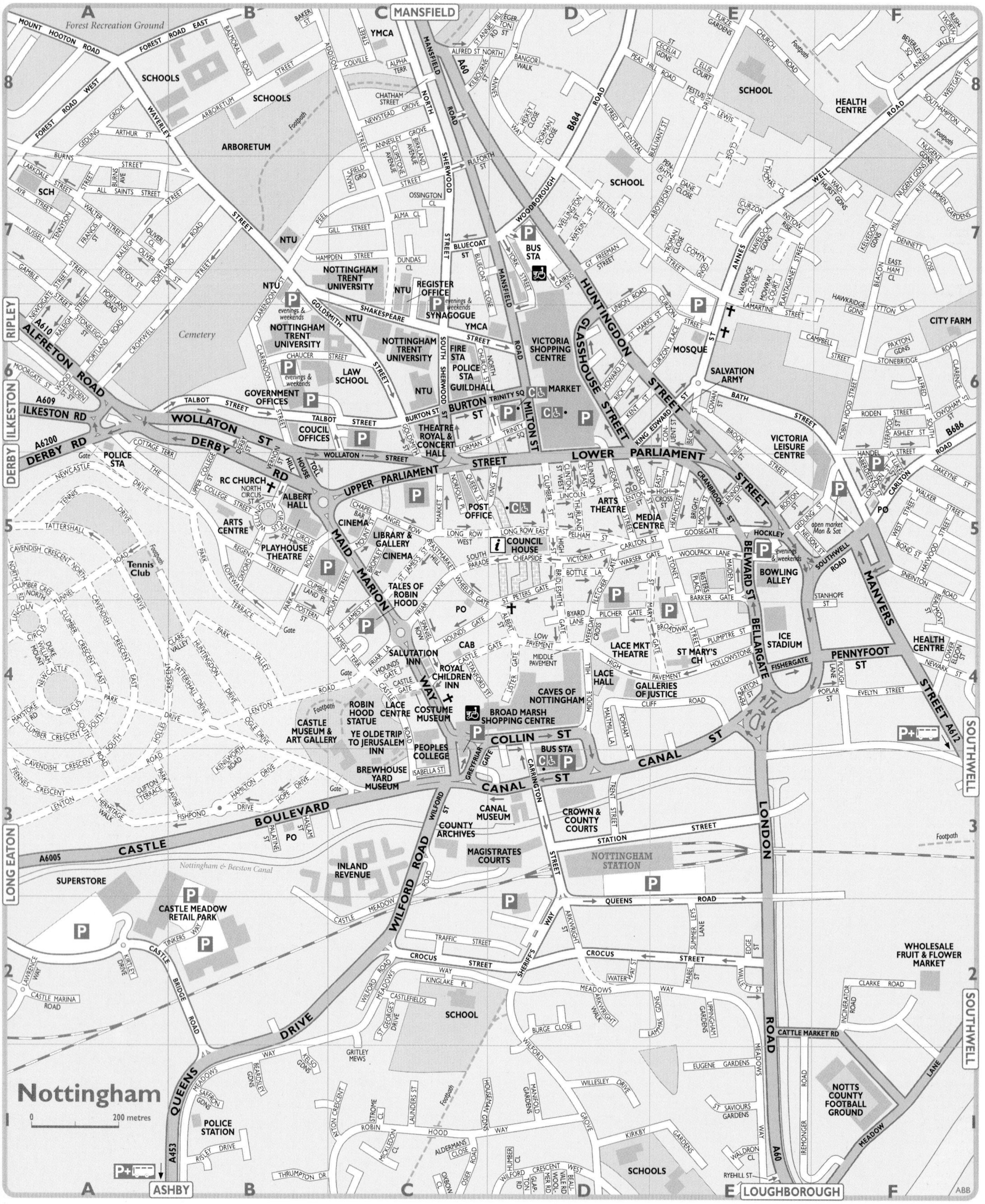

204

Nottingham

MANSFIELD

ASHBY · LOUGHBOROUGH

Forest Recreation Ground

Arboretum

Cemetery

NOTTINGHAM TRET UNIVERSITY (NTU)
NOTTINGHAM TRENT UNIVERSITY
LAW SCHOOL
GOVERNMENT OFFICES
COUCIL OFFICES
Theatre Royal & Concert Hall
REGISTER OFFICE
SYNAGOGUE
YMCA
FIRE STA
POLICE STA
GUILDHALL
VICTORIA SHOPPING CENTRE
Market
BUS STA
SALVATION ARMY
MOSQUE
SCHOOL
HEALTH CENTRE
CITY FARM
VICTORIA LEISURE CENTRE

RC CHURCH
ALBERT HALL
ARTS CENTRE
PLAYHOUSE THEATRE
CINEMA
LIBRARY & GALLERY
CINEMA
TALES OF ROBIN HOOD
POST OFFICE
COUNCIL HOUSE
ARTS THEATRE
MEDIA CENTRE
Hockley
BOWLING ALLEY
ICE STADIUM
HEALTH CENTRE
PENNYFOOT ST

SALUTATION INN
ROYAL CHILDREN INN
CAB
ROBIN HOOD STATUE
LACE CENTRE
COSTUME MUSEUM
CASTLE MUSEUM & ART GALLERY
YE OLDE TRIP TO JERUSALEM INN
PEOPLES COLLEGE
BREWHOUSE YARD MUSEUM
Broad Marsh Shopping Centre
LACE MKT THEATRE
ST MARY'S CH
LACE HALL
CAVES OF NOTTINGHAM
GALLERIES OF JUSTICE
BUS STA

CANAL MUSEUM
COUNTY ARCHIVES
MAGISTRATES COURTS
INLAND REVENUE
CROWN & COUNTY COURTS
NOTTINGHAM STATION
SUPERSTORE
CASTLE MEADOW RETAIL PARK
Tennis Club

WHOLESALE FRUIT & FLOWER MARKET
NOTTS COUNTY FOOTBALL GROUND
SCHOOL
SCHOOLS
POLICE STATION

Nottingham & Beeston Canal
Forest Road East
Mansfield Road
Huntingdon Street
Glasshouse Street
Lower Parliament Street
Upper Parliament Street
Wollaton Street
Derby Road
Maid Marian Way
Canal Street
Collin Street
London Road
Southwell Street
Manvers Street
Alfreton Road
Ilkeston Rd
Castle Boulevard
Queens Drive
Wilford Road
Castle Bridge Road

RIPLEY
DERBY / ILKESTON
LONG EATON
SOUTHWELL

0   200 metres

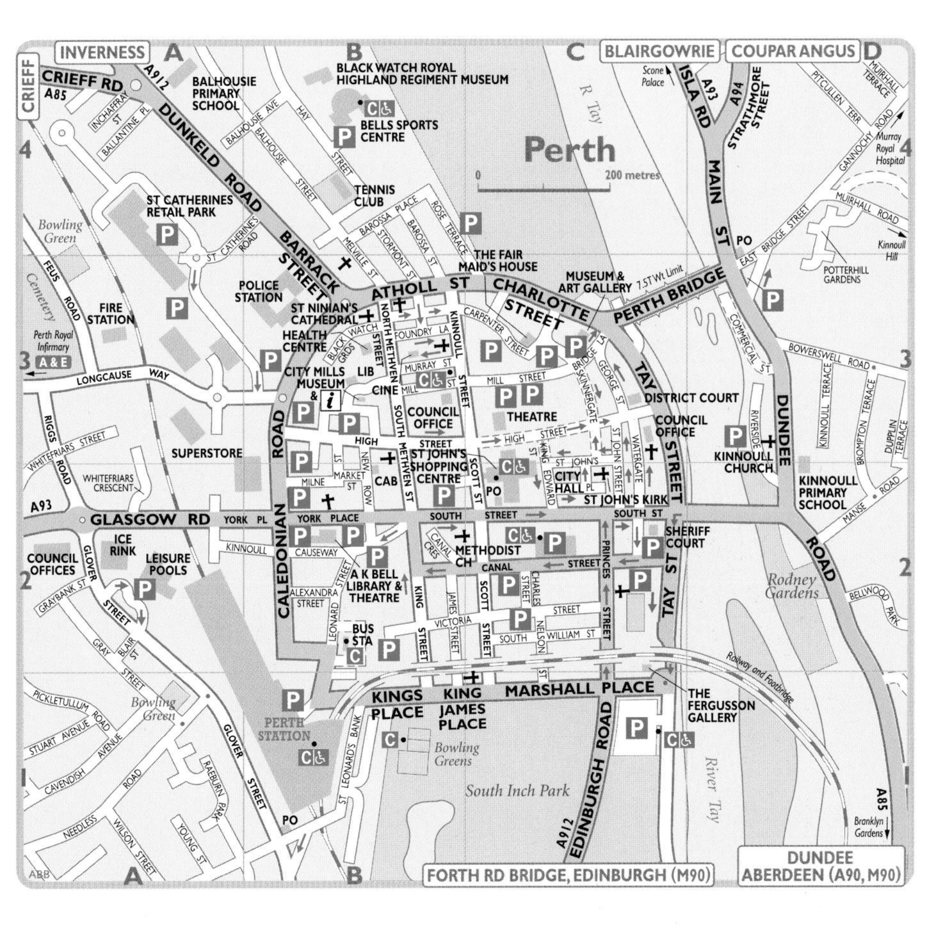

Perth

Perth is found on atlas page **126**,
grid reference **1123**

Alexandra Street	B2	Kinnoull Street	B3-C3
Atholl Street	B3-C3	Kinnoull Terrace	D3
Balhousie Avenue	A4-B4	Leonard Street	B1-B2
Balhousie Street	A4-B4	Longcause Way	A3
Ballantine Place	A4	Main Street	D3-D4
Barossa Place	B4	Manse Road	D2
Barossa Street	B3-B4	Market Street	B2
Barrack Street	B3-B4	Marshall Place	C1
Bellwood Park	D2	Melville Street	B3-B4
Black Watch Gardens	B3	Mill Street	B3-C3
Blair Street	A2	Milne Street	B2-B3
Bowerswell Road	D3	Muirhall Road	D4
Bridge Lane	C3	Muirhall Terrace	D4
Brompton Terrace	D2-D3	Murray Street	B3
Caledonian Road	B2-B3	Needless Road	A1
Canal Crescent	B2	Nelson Street	C2
Canal Street	B2-C2	New Row	B2-B3
Carpenter Street	B3-C3	North Methven Street	B3
Cavendish Avenue	C1	Perth Bridge	C3-D3
Charles Street	C2	Pickletullum Road	A1
Charlotte Street	C3	Pitcullen Terrace	D4
Commercial Street	D3	Potterhill Gardens	D3-D4
Crieff Road	A4	Raeburn Park	A1-B1
Dundee Road	D1-D2-D3	Riggs Road	A2-A3
Dunkeld Road	A4-B4	Riverside	D2-D3
Dupplin Terrace	D2-D3	Rose Terrace	B4-C3
East Bridge Street	D3-D4	St Catherine's Road	A3-A4-B4
Edinburgh Road	C1	St John Street	C2-C3
Feus Road	A3-A4	St John's Place	C2-C3
Foundry Lane	B3	St Leonard's Bank	B1
Gannochy Road	D4	Scott Street	C1-C2-C3
George Street	C3	Skinnergate	C3
Glasgow Road	A2	South Methven Street	B2-B3
Glover Street	A2-A1-B1	South Street	B2-C2
Gray Street	A1-A2	South William Street	C2
Graybank Street	A2	Stormont Street	B3-B4
Hay Street	B4	Strathmore Street	D4
High Street	B3-C3	Stuart Avenue	A1
Inchaffray Street	A4	Tay Street	C2-C3
Isla Road	C4-D4	Victoria Street	B2-C2
James Street	B2	Watergate	C2-C3
King Edward Street	C2-C3	Whitefriars Crescent	A2-A3
King James Place	B1-C1	Whitefriars Street	A2-A3
King Street	B2	Wilson Street	A1
Kings Place	B1	York Place	A2-B2
Kinnoull Causeway	A2-B2	Young Street	A1

205

Nottingham

Nottingham is found on atlas page **62**,
grid reference **5739**

Aberdeen Street	F5	Canal Street	C3-D3-E3-E4	Dundas Close	C7	Kelvedon Gardens	F7	North Sherwood Street	C6-C7-C8	South Road	A3-A4
Abotsford Drive	D7-E7-E8	Carlton Road	F5-F6	East Circus Street	B5	Kent Street	D6-E6	Nugent Gardens	F7-F8	South Sherwood Street	C6
Addison Street	B8-C8-C7	Carlton Street	D5-E5	East Street	E5	Kilbourne Street	C8	Ogle Drive	B4	Southampton Street	F8
Albert Street	D4	Carrington Street	D3-D4	Edge Street	E2	King Edward Street	D6-E6	Old Lenton Street	D5	Southwell Road	F5
Aldermans Close	C1	Castle Boulevard	A3-B3-C3	Ellis Court	E8	King Street	D5	Oliver Street	A7-B7	Spaniel Row	C4
Alfred Street Central	D7-D8	Castle Bridge Road	A2-B2-B1	Eugene Gardens	E1	Kinglake Place	C2	Osier Road	C1	Stanford Street	C4-D4
Alfred Street North	C8-D8	Castle Gate	C4-D4	Evelyn Street	F4	Kirkby Gardens	D1-E1	Ossington Close	C7	Stanhope Street	F4-F5
Alfred Street South	F6	Castle Marina Road	A2	Festus Close	E8	Kirtley Drive	A2	Oxford Street	B5	Station Street	D3-E3
Alfreton Road	A6	Castle Meadow Road	B3-C2-C3	Fiennes Crescent	A3	Lamartine Street	E6-E7	Palatine Street	B3	Stonebridge Road	F6
All Saints Street	A7	Castle Road	C3-C4	Fishergate	E4	Lammas Gardens	D2-E2	Park Drive	A4-B4	Stoneleigh Street	A6
Alma Close	C7	Castlefields	C2	Fishpond Drive	A3-B3	Larkdale Street	A7	Park Ravine	A3-B3	Stoney Street	E4-E5
Alpha Terrace	C8	Cattle Market Road	E2-F2	Fletcher Gate	D4-D5	Launders Street	C1	Park Row	B4-B5-C5	Strome Close	C1
Angel Row	C5	Cavendish Crescent East	A5-A4	Forest Road East	A8-B8	Lawrence Way	A2	Park Terrace	B4-B5	Summer Leys Lane	A3
Annesley Grove	C8	Cavendish Crescent North	A5	Forest Road West	A8	Lennox Street	E5	Park Valley	B4	Talbot Street	A6-B6-C6
Arboretum Street	B8	Cavendish Crescent South	A3-A4	Forman Street	C6-D6	Lenton Road	A3-B4-C4	Paxton Gardens	F6	Tattershall Drive	A5-A4-B4
Arkwright Street	D2	Chapel Bar	C5	Francis Street	A7	Lewis Close	E7-E8	Peas Hill Road	D8-E8	Tennis Drive	A5
Arkwright Walk	D2	Chatham Street	C8	Friar Lane	C4-C5	Limmen Gardens	F7	Peel Street	B7-C7	Tennyson Street	A7
Arthur Street	A8	Chaucer Street	B6-C6	Fulforth Street	C7-D8	Lincoln Circus	A4	Pelham Street	D5	The Ropewalk	A6-A5-B5-B4
Ashley Street	F6	Cheapside	D5	Furze Gardens	A6-A7	Lincoln Street	D5	Pemberton Street	E4	Thomas Close	E7
Ayr Street	A7	Church Road	E8	Gamble Street	A8	Lister Gate	D4	Pennyfoot Street	F4	Thrumpton Drive	B1
Ayton Crescent	C1	Clare Valley	A4-B4	Gedling Grove	A8	Liverpool Street	F6	Penrhyn Close	E7	Thurland Street	D5
Balmoral Road	B8	Clarence Street	F6	Gedling Street	E5-F5	London Road	E1-E2-E3-E4	Pilcher Gate	D4	Tinkers Way	A2-B2
Bangor Walk	D8	Clarendon Street	B6-B7	George Street	D5	Long Row East	D5	Plantaganet Street	E7	Toll House Hill	B5
Barker Gate	E5	Clarke Road	F2	Gill Street	B7-C7	Long Row West	C5	Plough Lane	F4	Traffic Street	C2-D2
Bath Street	E6-F6-F5	Cliff Road	D4-E4	Glasshouse Street	D6	Longden Street	F5	Plumptre Street	E4	Trent Street	D3
Beacon Hill Rise	F7-F8	Clinton Street East	D5	Goldsmith Street	B7-B6-C6-C5	Low Pavement	D4	Popham Street	D3-D4	Trinity Square	D6
Beardsley Gardens	B1	Clinton Street West	D5	Goosegate	E5	Lowdham Street	F6	Poplar Street	F6	Troman Close	F6
Beastmarket Hill	C5	Clipstone Avenue	C7-C8	Great Freeman Street	D7	Lower Parliament Street	D5-D6-E5	Portland Road	A6-A7-B7	Tunnel Road	A4-A5
Beaumont Street	F4-F5	Clumber Crescent East	A4	Greyfriars Gate	C3	Lytton Close	F6-F7	Postern Street	B4	Union Road	D6-D7
Beck Street	E6	Clumber Crescent North	A5	Gritley Mews	C1-C2	Mabel Street	E2	Queen Street	C5	Upper College Street	B5-B6
Bellargate	E4	Clumber Crescent South	A3-A4	Hamilton Drive	B3	Maid Marion Way	B5-C5-C4	Queens Drive	B1-B2-C2	Upper Parliament Street	C5-D5
Belward Street	E5	Clumber Street	D5	Hampden Street	B7-C7	Maiden Lane	E5	Queens Road	D2-E2-E3	Uppingham Gardens	E2
Beverley Square	F8	College Street	B5	Handel Street	F5-F6	Maltmill Lane	D4	Raleigh Street	A6-A7-B7	Vernon Street	B5-B6
Birkland Avenue	C7-C8	Collin Street	C4-D4	Haslam Street	B3	Manifold Gardens	D1	Regent Street	B5	Victoria Street	D5
Bluecoat Close	C7-D7-D6	Colville Street	C8	Havelock Gardens	E7	Mansfield Road	C8-C7-D7-D6	Rick Street	D6	Wadhurst Gardens	F7
Bluecoat Street	C7	Comyn Gardens	E7	Hawkridge Gardens	F6	Manvers Street	F4-F5	Risley Drive	B1	Waldron Close	E1
Bond Street	F5	Conuent Street	E6	Haywood Street	F5	Market Street	C5	Risters Place	E5	Walker Street	F5
Boston Street	E5	Cottage Terrace	A6-B5	Heathcote Street	E5	Maystoke Road	A4	Robin Hood Street	F6	Wallett Street	E2
Bottle Lane	D5	Cowan Street	E6	Hermitage Walk	A3	Meadow Lane	F1-F2	Robin Hood Way	C1-D1	Walter Street	A7
Bridlesmith Gate	D4-D5	Cranbrook Street	E5	Heskey Close	D8	Meadows Way	B1-C2-D2-E1	Roden Street	F6	Warser Gate	D5-E5
Brightmoor Street	E5	Crocus Street	C2-D2-E2	High Cross Street	E5	Mickledon Close	C1	Russell Street	A7	Wasnidge Close	E7
Broad Street	D5-E5	Cromwell Street	A6-B6-B7	High Pavement	D4-E4	Middle Hill	D4	St Annes Hill Road	C8-D8	Waterway Street	D2
Broadway	E4	Cumberland Place	B5-C5	High Street	D5	Middle Pavement	D4	St Annes Valley	F8	Watkin Street	D6
Bromley Place	C5	Curzon Court	E7	Hockley	E5	Milton Street	D6	St Annes Way	D7-D8	Waverley Street	A8-B8-B7
Brook Street	E6-E5-F5	Curzon Place	D6-E6	Holles Crescent	A3-A4-B4	Moorgate Street	A6	St Annes Well Road	E6-E7-F7-F8	Weekday Cross	D4
Bullivant Street	E8	Curzon Street	E6-E7	Hollowstone	E4	Mount Hooton Road	A8	St Cecelia Gardens	E8	Wellington Circus	B5
Burge Close	D2	Dakeyne Street	F5	Hope Drive	B3	Mount Street	B4-C4-C5	St George's Drive	C2	Wellington Street	D7
Burns Street	A8-A7-B7	Dane Close	E7	Hounds Gate	C4-D4	Mowray Court	D6	St James's Street	C4-C5	West Street	F5
Burton Street	C6	Dennett Close	F7	Houseman Gardens	C1-D1	Mount Street	E5-F5	St James's Terrace	C4	Westgate Street	F8
Byard Lane	D4	Derby Road	A5-A6-B6-B5	Howard Street	D6	Nelson Street	E5-F5	St Lukes Street	F5	Wheeler Gate	C4-C5
Cairns Street	D7	Derby Street	B6	Humber Close	D1	Newark Street	F4	St Marks Street	D6-E6	Wilford Crescent West	D1
Campbell Street	E6-F6	Duke William Mount	A4	Huntingdon Drive	B4	Newcastle Circus	A4	St Mary's Gate	D5-D4-E4	Wilford Grove	D1-D2
				Huntingdon Street	C8-D7-E6	Newcastle Drive	A5-B5	St Peters Gate	D4-D5	Wilford Road	C2-C3
				Ilkeston Road	A6	Newdigate Street	A6-A7	St Saviours Gardens	E1	Wilford Street	C3
				Incinerator Road	F2	Newstead Grove	C8	Saffron Gardens	D2	Willesley Drive	D1
				Instow Rise	E7	Nile Street	E5-E6	Shakespeare Street	B7-C7-C6-D6	Wollaton Street	A6-B6-B5-C5
				Iremonger Road	E2-E1-F1	Norfolk Place	C5	Shelton Street	D7-E7	Wood Street	A6
				Ireton Street	A7	Norman Close	D8	Sheriff's Way	D2	Woodborough Road	D7-D8
				Isabella Street	C3	North Church Street	C6-D6	Sneinton Road	F4-F5	Woolpack Lane	E5
				Kelso Gardens	B1	North Circus Street	B5	South Parade	C5-D5	York Street	D6-D7
						North Road	A4-A5				

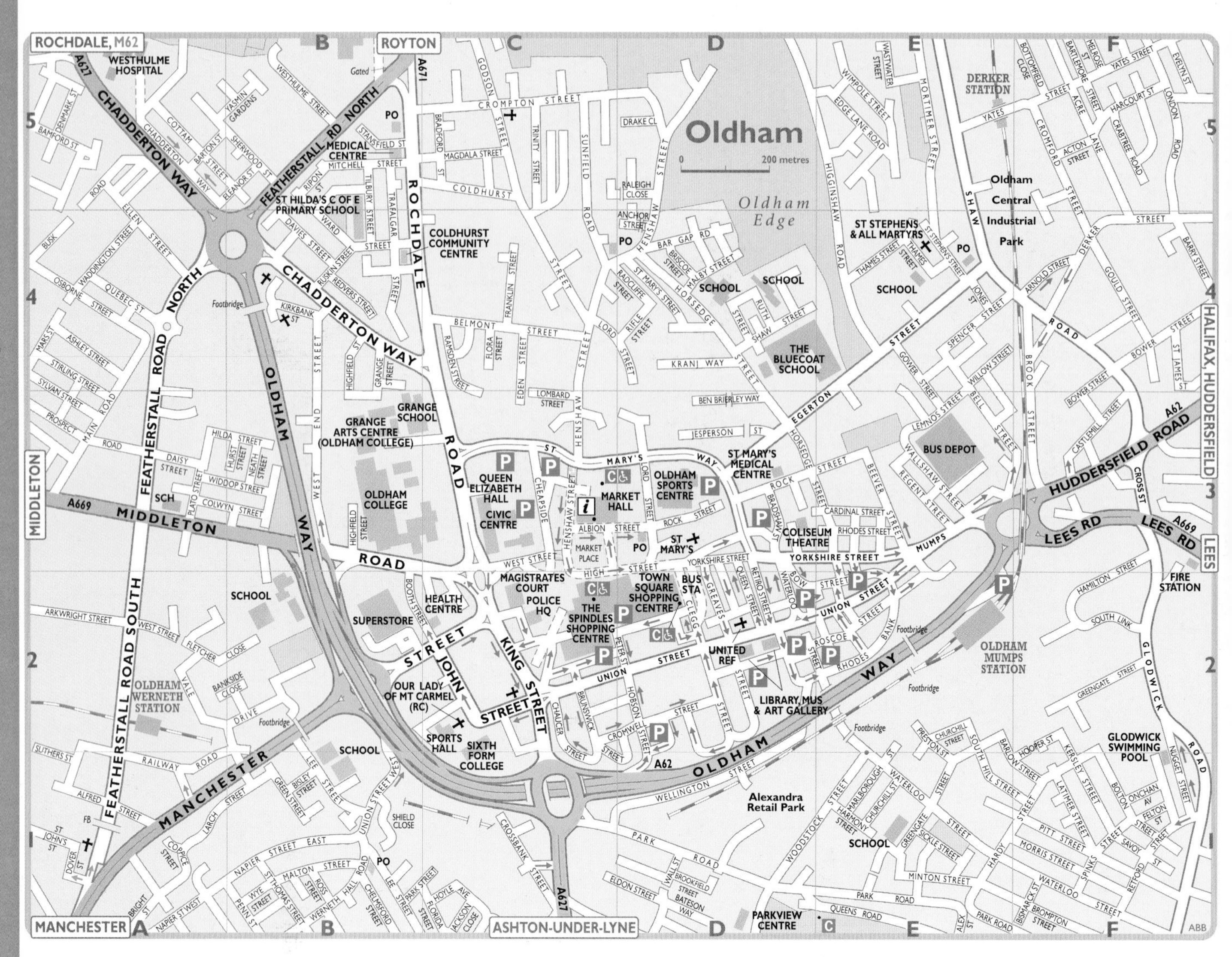

Oldham

Oldham is found on atlas page **79**,
grid reference **9204**

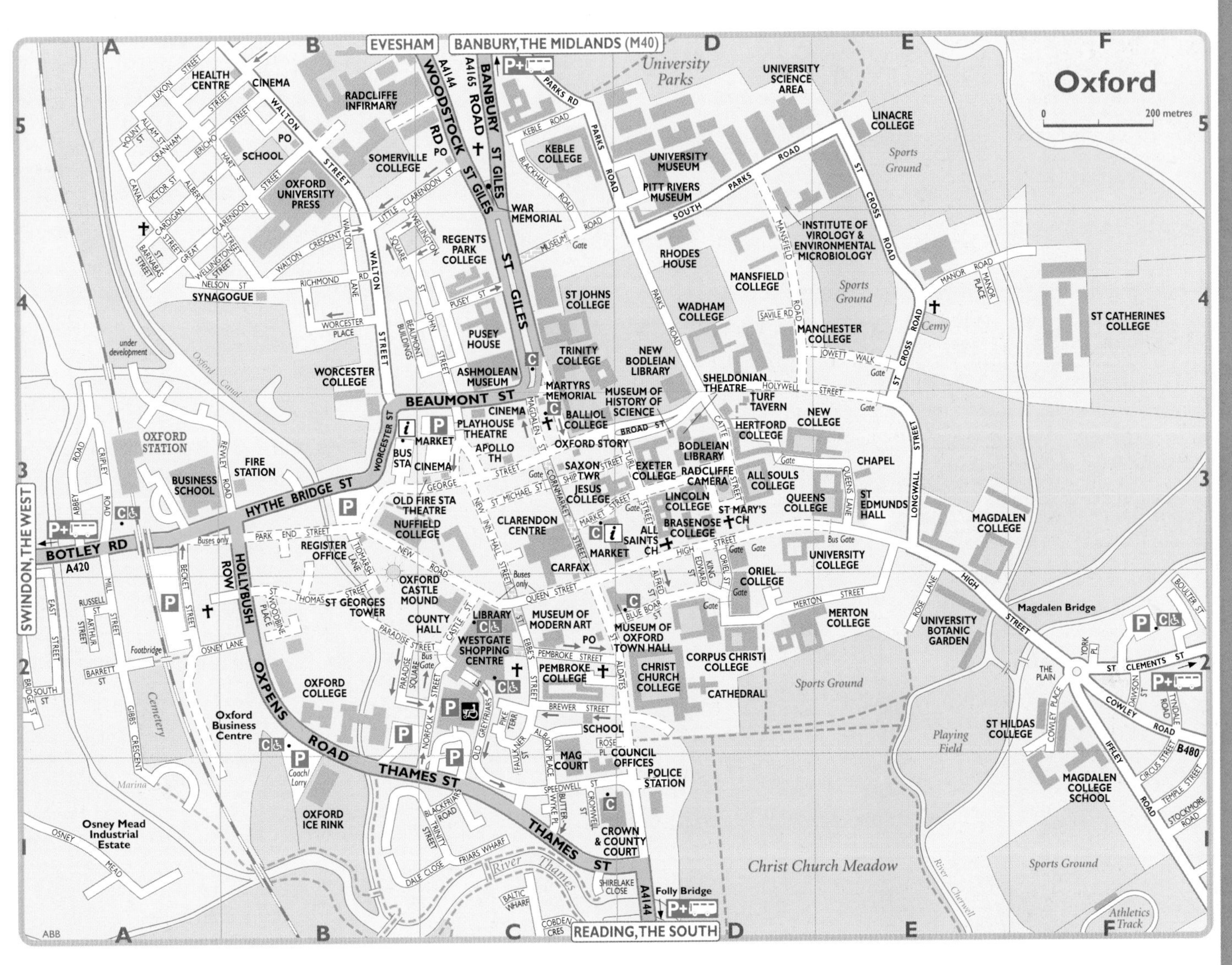

Oxford

Oxford is found on atlas page **37**,
grid reference **5106**

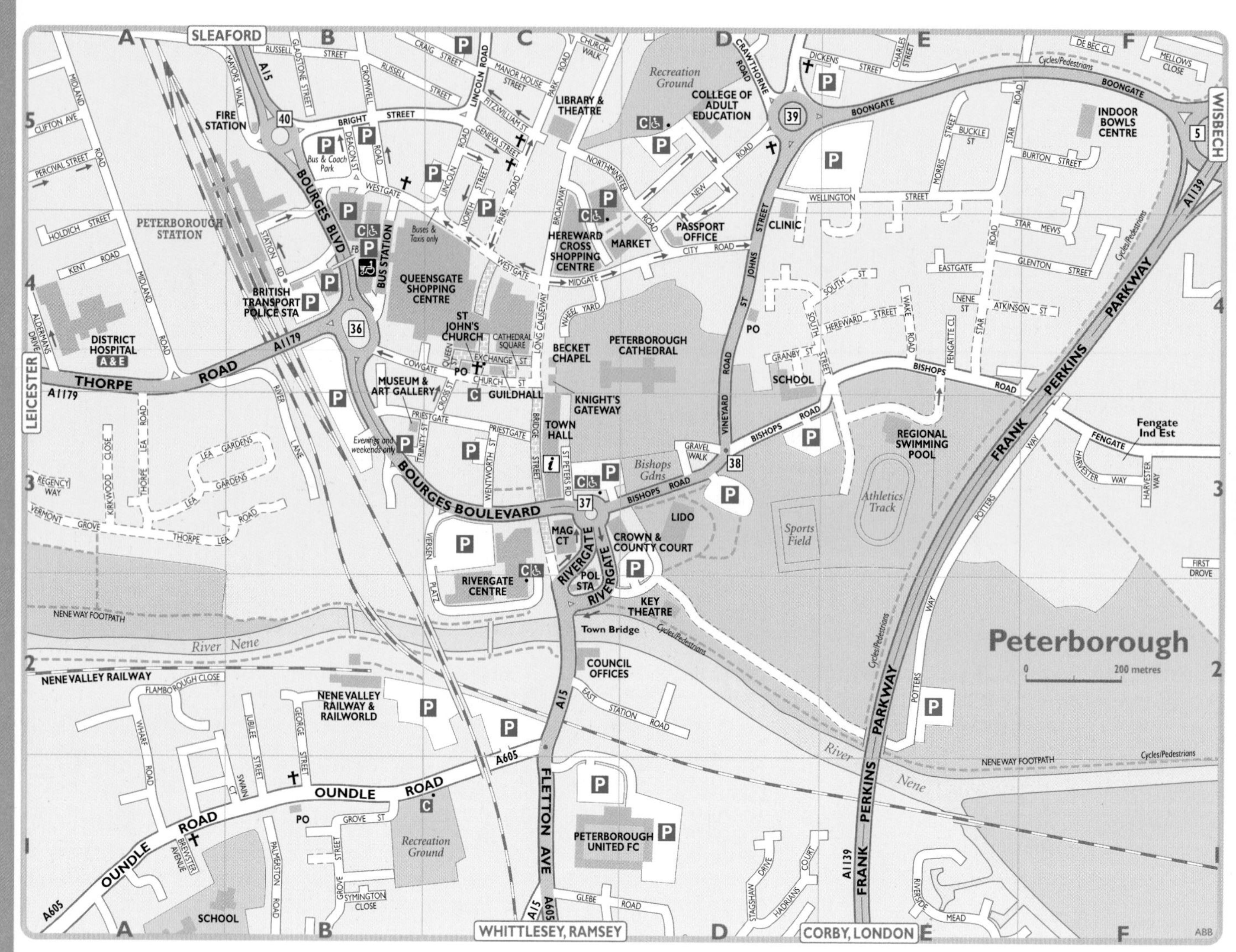

Peterborough

Peterborough is found on atlas page **64**,
grid reference 1998

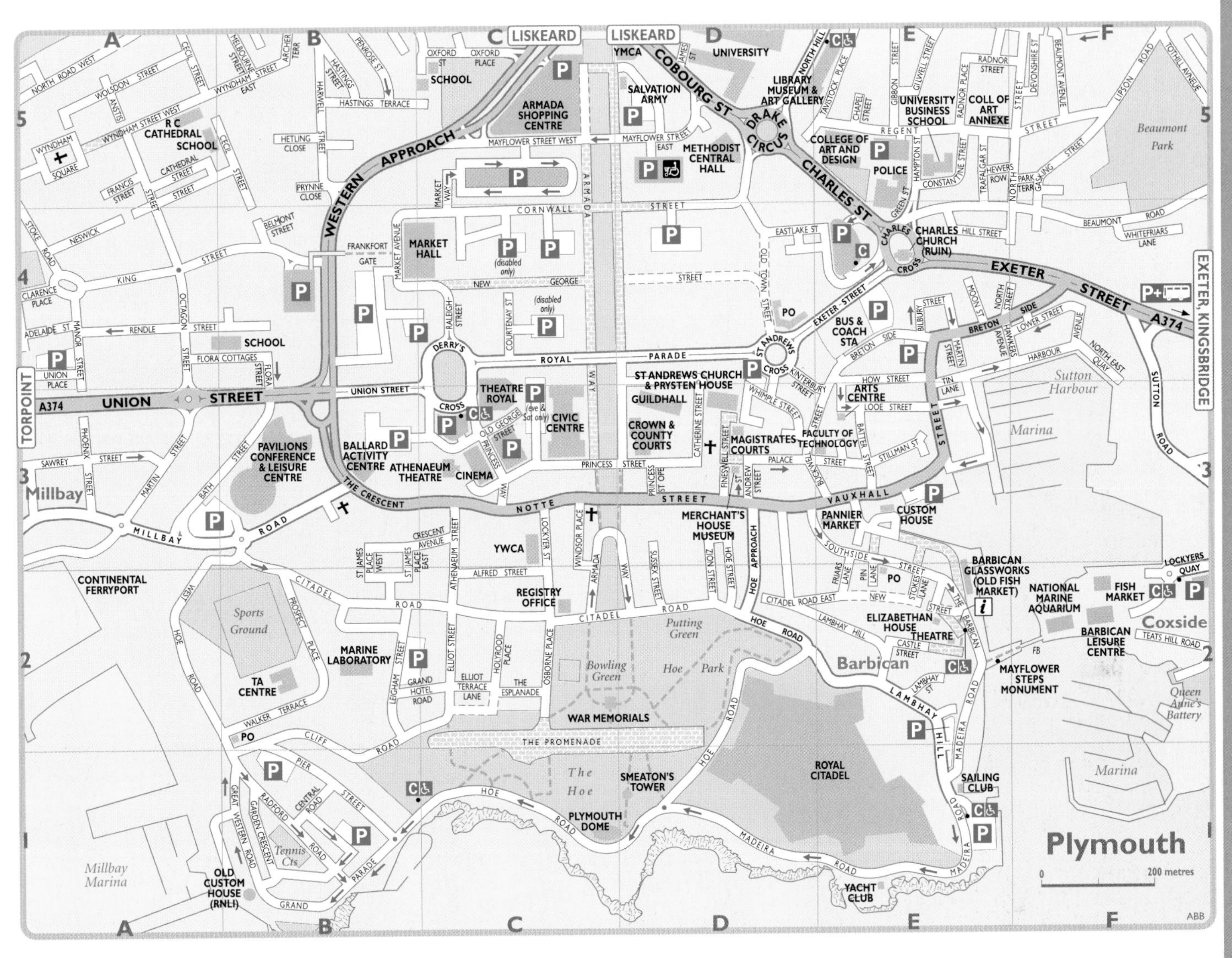

209

Plymouth

Plymouth is found on atlas page **6**,
grid reference **4754**

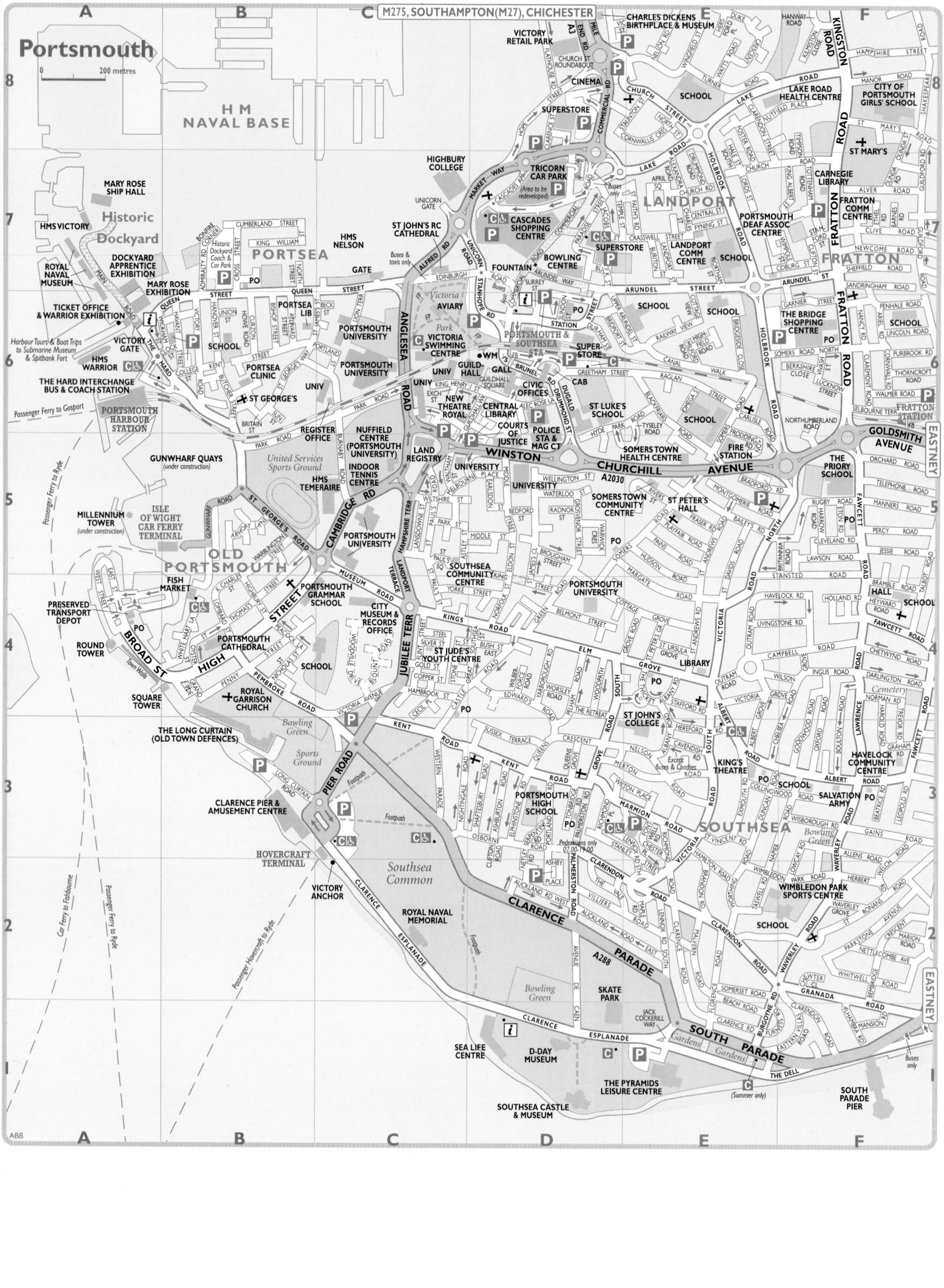

Portsmouth

210

0   200 metres

HM NAVAL BASE

M275, SOUTHAMPTON(M27), CHICHESTER

CHARLES DICKENS BIRTHPLACE & MUSEUM

VICTORY RETAIL PARK

CINEMA

SUPERSTORE

HIGHBURY COLLEGE

TRICORN CAR PARK (Area to be redeveloped)

UNICORN GATE

MARY ROSE SHIP HALL

Historic Dockyard

HMS VICTORY

ROYAL NAVAL MUSEUM

DOCKYARD APPRENTICE EXHIBITION

MARY ROSE EXHIBITION

TICKET OFFICE & WARRIOR EXHIBITION

Harbour Tours & Boat Trips to Submarine Museum & Spitbank Fort

VICTORY GATE

HMS WARRIOR

THE HARD INTERCHANGE BUS & COACH STATION

Passenger Ferry to Gosport

PORTSMOUTH HARBOUR STATION

PORTSEA

Cumberland Street

King William Street

HMS NELSON

GATE

St John's RC Cathedral

Victoria Park

Victoria Aviary

VICTORIA SWIMMING CENTRE

PORTSEA LIB

PORTSMOUTH UNIVERSITY

PORTSMOUTH UNIVERSITY

PORTSEA CLINIC

ST GEORGE'S

UNIV

ANGLESEA ROAD

PARK ROAD

REGISTER OFFICE

NUFFIELD CENTRE (PORTSMOUTH UNIVERSITY)

INDOOR TENNIS CENTRE

HMS TEMERAIRE

United Services Sports Ground

GUNWHARF QUAYS (under construction)

MILLENNIUM TOWER (under construction)

ISLE OF WIGHT CAR FERRY TERMINAL

OLD PORTSMOUTH

FISH MARKET

PRESERVED TRANSPORT DEPOT

ROUND TOWER

BROAD ST

SQUARE TOWER

PORTSMOUTH CATHEDRAL

PORTSMOUTH GRAMMAR SCHOOL

HIGH STREET

ROYAL GARRISON CHURCH

THE LONG CURTAIN (OLD TOWN DEFENCES)

Bowling Green

Sports Ground

CITY MUSEUM & RECORDS OFFICE

JUBILEE TERR

ST JUDE'S YOUTH CENTRE

CLARENCE PIER & AMUSEMENT CENTRE

PIER ROAD

HOVERCRAFT TERMINAL

VICTORY ANCHOR

Southsea Common

ROYAL NAVAL MEMORIAL

Bowling Green

SEA LIFE CENTRE

D-DAY MUSEUM

SOUTHSEA CASTLE & MUSEUM

THE PYRAMIDS LEISURE CENTRE

SKATE PARK

JACK COCKERILL WAY

CLARENCE ESPLANADE

CLARENCE PARADE

SOUTH PARADE

Gardens

THE DELL

SOUTH PARADE PIER

LANDPORT

SUPERSTORE

CASCADES SHOPPING CENTRE

FOUNTAIN

BOWLING CENTRE

LANDPORT COMM CENTRE

SUPERSTORE

PORTSMOUTH & SOUTHSEA STA

GUILD HALL

CIVIC OFFICES

NEW THEATRE ROYAL

CENTRAL LIBRARY

COURTS OF JUSTICE

POLICE STA & MAG CT

WINSTON CHURCHILL AVENUE

LAND REGISTRY

UNIVERSITY

SOMERS TOWN COMMUNITY CENTRE

ST LUKE'S SCHOOL

SOMERSTOWN HEALTH CENTRE

FIRE STATION

ST PETER'S HALL

SOUTHSEA COMMUNITY CENTRE

PORTSMOUTH UNIVERSITY

PORTSMOUTH HIGH SCHOOL

ST JOHN'S COLLEGE

KING'S THEATRE

SOUTHSEA

Bowling Green

WIMBLEDON PARK SPORTS CENTRE

PORTSMOUTH DEAF ASSOC CENTRE

THE BRIDGE SHOPPING CENTRE

FRATTON

FRATTON STATION

GOLDSMITH AVENUE

THE PRIORY SCHOOL

HAVELOCK COMMUNITY CENTRE

SALVATION ARMY

CITY OF PORTSMOUTH GIRLS' SCHOOL

ST MARY'S

CARNEGIE LIBRARY

FRATTON COMM CENTRE

KINGSTON ROAD

EASTNEY

LAKE ROAD HEALTH CENTRE

Car Ferry to Fishbourne

Passenger Ferry to Ryde

Passenger Hovercraft to Ryde

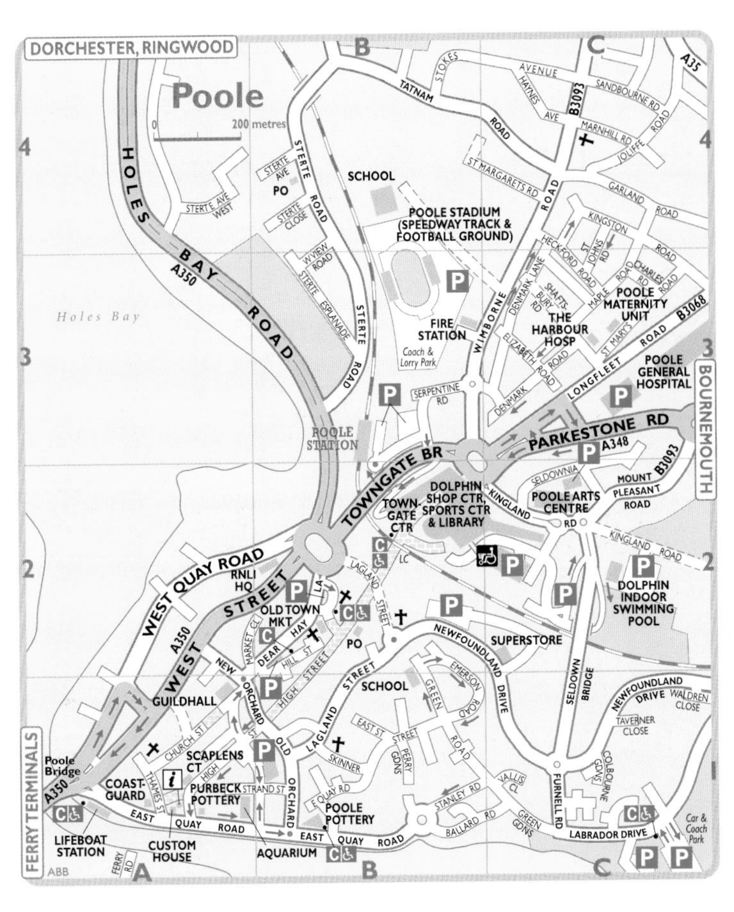

Poole

Poole is found on atlas page 11,
grid reference 0090

Ballard Road	B1-C1	Maple Road	C3-C4	Strand Street	A1-B1
Charles Road	C3	Market Close	A2	Tatnam Road	B4-C4
Church Street	A1	Marnhill Road	C4	Taverner Close	C1
Colbourne Gardens	C1	Mount Pleasant Road	C2	Thames Street	A1
Dear Hay Lane	B2	New Orchard	A2-A1	The Quay	A1-B1
Denmark Lane	C3	Newfoundland Drive	C1	Towngate Bridge	B2-B3
Denmark Road	C3	North Street	B2	Vallis Close	C1
East Quay Road	B1	Old Orchard	B1	Waldren Close	C1
East Street	B1	Parkstone Road	C3	West Quay Road	A1-A2-B2
Elizabeth Road	C3	Perry Gardens	B1	West Street	A1-A2-B2
Emerson Road	B2-B1	St Johns Road	C3-C4	West View Road	B3-B4
Ferry Road	A1	St Margarets Road	B4-C4	Wimborne Road	B3-C3-C4
Garland Road	C4	St Mary's Road	C3		
Green Gardens	C1	Sandbourne Road	C4		
Green Road	B1	Seldown Bridge	C1-C2		
Haynes Avenue	C4	Seldown Lane	C2		
Heckford Road	C3-C4	Serpentine Road	B3		
High Street	A1-B1-B2	Shaftsbury Road	C3		
Hill Street	B2	Skinner Street	B1		
Holes Bay Road	A4-B3-B2	Stanley Road	B1		
Jolliffe Road	C4	Sterte Avenue	B4		
Kingland Road	C2	Sterte Avenue West	A4		
Kingston Road	C3-C4	Sterte Close	B4		
Labrador Drive	C1	Sterte Esplanade	B3		
Lagland Street	B1-B2	Sterte Road	B4-B3		
Longfleet Road	C3	Stokes Avenue	B4-C4		

Portsmouth

Portsmouth is found on atlas page 13,
grid reference 6400

Admiralty Road	B7	Buck Street	D7	Curzon Howe Road	B6	Hanway Road	F8	Nightingale Road	C3-D3	South Parade	E1-F1
Albany Road	E3-E4	Burgoyne Road	E1-E2	Darlington Road	F4	Harold Road	F3-F4	Norfolk Street	D4	Stafford Road	E4
Albert Grove	E3-E4	Burnaby Road	C5-C6	Drummond Road	E7	Harrow Road	F5	Norman Road	F4	Stamford Street	F7
Albert Road	E4-E3-F3	Burton Street	E7	Dugald Drummond Street	D5-D6	Havant Street	B6	North Street	B7	Stanhope Road	D6-D7
Alec Rose Lane	D6	Bush Street East	D4	Duke Crescent	E8	Havelock Road	E4-F4	North Street	E8	Stanley Street	D3-E3-E2
Alexandra Road	E7	Butcher Street	B6	Duncan Road	E3	Herbert Road	F2	Northam Street	E7	Stansted Road	E5-F5
Alfred Road	C7	Cambridge Road	C5	Durham Street	D6	Hereford Road	E3	Northumberland Road	F5-F6	Station Street	D6
Alhambra Road	F1	Campbell Road	E4-F4	Earlsdon Street	D5	Hertford Place	E8	Nutfield Place	E8-F8	Staunton Street	D8-E8
Allens Road	F2-F3	Canal Walk	E6	East Street	A4-A5	Heyward Road	F4	Olinda Road	F7	Steel Street	C4
Alver Road	F7	Carlisle Road	E5-E6	Eastern Villas Road	E1-F1	High Street	B4	Olinda Street	F7-F8	Stone Street	C4
Anglesea Road	C6-C7	Cascades Approach	D7	Edinburgh Road	C7-D7	Highbury Street	B4	Omega Street	E6	Sun Street	B6
April Square	E7	Castle Road	C3-C4-D4	Eldon Street	D5	Highfield Road	E6	Orchard Road	F5	Surrey Street	D6
Ariel Road	F6	Cavendish Road	E3	Elm Grove	D4-E4	Holbrook Road	E8-E7-E6-F5	Osborne Road	C3-D3	Sussex Terrace	D3
Armory Lane	B5	Cecil Place	C4	Elphinstone Road	D3	Holland Road	F4	Outram Road	E4	Talbot Road	F4-F5
Arundel Street	D7-E7-F7	Central Street	E7	Ethel Road	F7	Hope Street	D7-D8	Oxford Road	F3-F4	Taswell Road	E2
Arundel Way	D7	Charles Street	E7	Eton Road	F5	Hudson Road	E4-E5	Oyster Street	B4	Telephone Road	F5
Ashburton Road	D3	Chelsea Road	E3-F3-F4	Exchange Street	C6	Hyde Park Road	D5-D6-E6	Pains Road	E5	Temple Street	D7
Ashby Place	D2	Chester Place	E3	Exmouth Road	E3	Inglis Road	F4	Palmerston Road	D2-D3	The Dell	E1-F1
Astley Street	C5	Chetwynd Road	F4	Fawcett Road	F3-F4-F5	Isambard Brunel Road	D6	Paradise Street	D7	The Hard	A6-B6
Auckland Road East	D2-E2	Chewter Close	F2	Flathouse Road	D8	Jacobs Street	D7	Park Road	B5-B6-C6	The Retreat	D4
Auckland Road West	D2	Church Road	E7-F7	Flint Street	C4	Jessie Road	F5	Park Street	C5	The Thicket	E4
Avenue De Caen	D1-D2	Church Street	D8-E8	Florence Road	E1-E2	Jubilee Terrace	C4	Parkstone Avenue	F2	The Vale	D2-E2
Aylward Street	B6	Claremont Road	F6	Fontwell Road	E3	Kent Road	C3-D3	Peacock Lane	B4	Thorncroft Road	F6
Bailey's Road	E5	Clarence Esplanade	C3-C2-D1-E1	Foster Road	E7-E8	Kent Street	B6	Pelham Road	D3-D4	Timpson Road	F7-F8
Barnes Road	F7	Clarence Parade	D2-E2-E1	Fraser Road	E5	Kilmston Close	F8	Pembroke Road	B4-C4	Tonbridge Road	D3
Beach Road	E1-E2	Clarence Road	E1-E2	Fratton Road	F6-F7-F8	King Albert Street	F7	Penhale Road	F6	Tottenham Road	F7
Beatrice Road	F3	Clarence Street	D8	Froddington Road	E5-E6	King Charles Street	B4	Penny Street	B4	Trevor Road	F3-F4
Beck Street	C6	Clarendon Road	D3-E2-F2-F1	Furness Road	E1-F1	King Henry I Street	C6-D6	Percy Road	F5	Turner Road	E8
Bedford Street	D5	Clarendon Street	E7-E8	Fyning Street	E7	King William Street	B7	Pier Road	C3	Tyseley Road	D6-D5-E5-E6
Belmont Street	D4	Cleveland Road	F5	Gains Road	F3	Kings Road	C4-D4	Playfair Road	E5	Unicorn Gate	C7
Bembridge Crescent	F2	Clifton Road	D3	Garnier Street	F6	Kingston Road	F8	Portland Road	D3	Unicorn Road	C7-D7
Berkshire Close	F6	Clifton Street	F7	Gold Street	C4	Lake Road	E7-E8-F8	Portland Street	C6	Union Street	B6
Bishop Street	B6	Clive Road	F7	Goldsmith Avenue	F5-F6	Landport Street	E7	Purbrook Road	F6	Upper Arundel Street	D6-E6
Blackfriars Road	E5-E6	Clock Street	A6-B6	Goodwood Road	F3-F4	Landport Terrace	C4-C5	Queen Street	A6-B6-B7-C7	Victoria Avenue	C4
Blount Road	C4	Coburg Street	E7-F7	Graham Road	F3	Lansdowne Street	C5	Queens Crescent	D3	Victoria Grove	E4-F4
Bonfire Corner	B7	College Street	B6	Granada Road	F1-F2	Lawrence Road	F3-F4	Queens Grove	D3	Victoria Road North	E4-E5-F5
Boulton Road	F3-F4	Collingwood Road	E3-F3	Grand Parade	B4	Lawson Road	F5	Radnor Street	D5	Victoria Road South	E2-E3-E4
Bradford Road	E5-F5	Commercial Road	D6-D7-D8	Great Southsea Street	C4-D4	Lennox Road South	D3-E3-E2	Raglan Street	E6	Victoria Street	D8-E8
Bramble Road	F4	Copper Street	C4	Green Road	D4-D5	Leopold Street	E6	Railway View	E6	Victory Road	B6
Brandon Road	E2	Cornwall Road	F6	Greetham Street	D6-E6	Lincoln Road	F3	Richmond Place	D3	Villiers Road	D2-E2
Bridgeside Close	E6	Cornwallis Crescent	D8-E8	Grosvenor Street	D5	Lion Terrace	C6	Richmond Road	E2-E3	Vivash Street	F6
Bridport Street	D6	Cottage Grove	D5-D4-E4	Grove Road	D4-E4	Livingstone Road	E4-F4	Rivers Street	E5	Walmer Road	F6
Britain Street	B6	Cottage View	E6	Grove Road South	D3-D4	Lombard Street	B4	Rugby Road	F5	Waltham Street	C5
Britannia Road	E5-F5	Crasswell Street	E7	Guildford Road	F7-F8	Long Curtain Road	B3	St Andrews Road	E4-E5	Warblington Street	B5
Broad Street	A4-B4	Cross Street	B7	Guildhall Square	D6	Lords Street	E7	St Davids Road	E4-E5	Warwick Crescent	D5
Brougham Street	D5	Cumberland Street	B7	Guildhall Walk	C6-D6	Lowcay Road	F2-F3	St Edward's Road	D3-D4	Waterloo Street	D5
				Gunwharf Road	B5	Lucknow Street	F6	St Faith's Road	E7	Watts Road	E8
				Hale Street South	E7-E8	Main Road	A6-A7	St George's Road	B5	Waverley Grove	F2
				Hambrook Street	C4	Malvern Road	E2	St George's Way	B6	Waverley Road	F2-F3
				Hamilton Road	E2-E3	Manners Road	F5	St James's Close	D4-D5	Welch Road	F2-F3
				Hampshire Street	F8	Manor Road	F8	St James's Street	B6-C6	Wellington Street	D5
				Hampshire Terrace	C5	Mansion Road	F1	St Mary's Road	F8	West Street	A4-A5
				Hanover Street	B6	Maple Road	E2	St Nicholas Street	B4	Western Parade	C3
						Margate Road	D5-E5-E4	St Paul's Road	C5	White Hart Lane	B4
						Marion Road	F2	St Paul's Square	C5	Whitwell Road	F2
						Market Way	C7-D7	St Paul's Street	C4-C5	Wickham Street	A6-B6
						Marmion Road	D3-E3	St Peter's Grove	E4	Wilberforce Road	D4
						Melbourne Place	C5-D5	St Ronans Road	F2-F3	Wilson Grove	E4-F4
						Merton Road	D3-E3	St Thomas's Street	B4-B5	Wilton Place	D3-E3
						Middle Street	D5	St Ursula Grove	E4	Wiltshire Street	C5
						Mile End Road	D8	St Vincent Road	E3	Wimbledon Park Road	E2-F2
						Milford Road	E6	Sandringham Road	F7	Wimpole Street	F7
						Montgomerie Road	E5	Selbourne Terrace	F6	Wingfield Street	E8
						Museum Road	C4-C5	Serpentine Road	D3	Winston Churchill	
						Nancy Road	F6	Shaftesbury Road	D3	Avenue	C5-D5-E5
						Napier Road	E2-E3-F3	Shakespeare Road	F8	Wisborough Road	F3
						Nelson Road	D3-E3	Sheffield Road	F7	Woodpath	D4
						Nelson Road	E8	Silver Street	C4	Woodville Drive	C4
						Netley Road	D2-D3	Slindon Street	D6	Worsley Road	D4
						Nettlecombe Avenue	F2	Somers Road	D4-D5-E5-E6	Worthing Road	E2-F2
						Newcome Road	F7	Somers Road North	E6-F6	Yarborough Road	D4
								Somerset Road	E2	Yorke Street	C4-D4

211

212

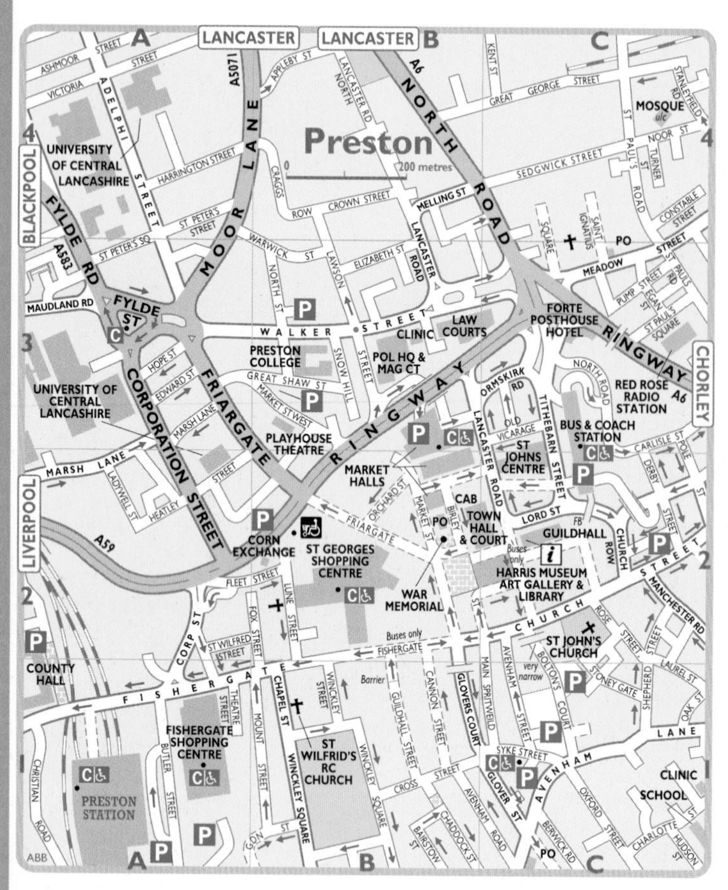

Preston

Preston is found on atlas page **80**,
grid reference **5329**

Adelphi Street	A3-A4	Ladywell Street	A2	Walker Street	A3-B3
Appleby Street	B4	Lancaster Road	B4-B3-C3-C2	Warwick Street	A4-B3
Ashmoor Street	A4	Lancaster Road North	B4	Winckley Square	B1
Avenham Lane	C1	Laurel Street	C1-C2	Winckley Street	B1
Avenham Road	B1-C1	Lawson Street	B3-B4		
Avenham Street	C1-C2	Lord Street	C2		
Bairstow Street	B1	Lune Street	B2		
Berwick Road	C1	Main Spritweild	C1-C2		
Birley Street	B2	Manchester Road	C2		
Bolton's Court	C1-C2	Market Street	B2		
Butler Street	A1	Market Street West	B3		
Cannon Street	B1-B2	Marsh Lane	A2-A3		
Carlisle Street	C3	Maudland Road	A3		
Chaddock Street	B1	Meadow Street	C3-C4		
Chapel Street	B1	Melling Street	B4		
Charlotte Street	C1	Moor Lane	A3-A4		
Christian Road	A1	Mount Street	B1		
Church Row	C2	Noor Street	C4		
Church Street	B2-C2	North Road	B4-C4-C3		
Constable Street	C4	North Street	B3		
Corporation Street	A1-A2-A3	Oak Street	C1		
Craggs Row	B4	Old Vicarage	C3		
Cross Street	B1	Orchard Street	B2		
Crown Street	B4	Ormskirk Road	C3		
Derby Street	C2	Oxford Street	C1		
Edward Street	A3	Pole Street	C2-C3		
Egan Street	C3	Pump Street	C3		
Elizabeth Street	B3	Ringway	B2-B3-C3		
Fishergate	A1-B1-B2	Rose Street	C2		
Fleet Street	A2-B2	Saint Ignatius Square	C3-C4		
Fox Street	B1-B2	St Paul's Road	C3-C4		
Friargate	A3-B2	St Paul's Square	C3		
Fylde Road	A3-A4	St Peter's Square	A3-A4		
Fylde Street	A3	St Peter's Street	A4		
Garden Street	B1	St Wilfred Street	A2		
Glover Street	C1	Sedgwick Street	C4		
Glovers Court	B1-B2	Shepherd Street	C1-C2		
Great George Street	B4-C4	Snow Hill	B3		
Great Shaw Street	A3-B3	Stanleyfield Road	C4		
Guildhall Street	B1-B2	Stoney Gate	C1-C2		
Harrington Street	A4	Syke Street	C1		
Heatley Street	A2	Theatre Street	A1		
Hope Street	A3	Tithebarn Street	C2-C3		
Hudson Street	C1	Turner Street	C4		
Kent Street	C4	Victoria Street	A4		

Ramsgate

Ramsgate is found on atlas page **29**,
grid reference **3865**

Abbot's Hill	B3	Duncan Road	A2	Royal Road	A2-B2-B1
Addington Place	B2	Eagle Hill	A3	Ryton Road	A2
Addington Street	B2	Edith Road	A1	St Luke's Avenue	A4-B4
Albert Road	C4	Effingham Street	B3	St Augustine's Road	A1-B1
Albert Street	B2	Elizabeth Road	C3	St Benedict's Lawn	A1-B1
Albion Place	B3-C3	Ellington Road	A2-A3	St Mildred's Road	A1
Albion Road	C4	Elms Road	B2	School Lane	B3-B4
Alexandra Road	A4	Finsbury Road	A4	Spencer Square	B1-B2
Alma Place	B4	George Street	B3	Spencer Street	B2
Alma Road	A4	Grange Road	A1	Station Approach Road	A3-A4
Alpha Road	A2	Grove Road	A2-A3	Sundew Grove	A4
Anns Road	A4	Harbour Parade	B3-C3	Sussex Street	A4
Archway Road	B2	Harbour Street	B3	The Cloisters	A1-B1
Arklow Square	B4	Hardres Road	B4	Townley Street	B2
Artillery Road	B4	Hardres Street	B3-B4	Truro Road	C4
Augusta Road	B4-C4	Hatfield Road	A3	Turner Street	B3
Avenue Road	B4	Hereson Road	B4	Unity Place	B4
Belgrave Close	A3	Hertford Place	B2	Upper Dumpton Park Road	A4
Bellevue Avenue	B4	Hibernia Street	B3	Vale Place	A2
Bellevue Road	B4-C4	High Street	A3-B3	Vale Road	A1-A2
Belmont Road	A3	Hollicondane Road	A4	Vale Square	A2-B2
Belmont Street	B4	Holly Road	A4	Vereth Road	A1-A2
Beresford Road	A2-B2	King Street	B3-B4	Victoria Parade	C4
Boundary Road	A4-B4	Lawn Villas	B3	Victoria Road	B4-C4
Brights Place	B4	Leopold Street	B2-B3	Waterloo Place	C3-C4
Broad Street	B3	Liverpool Lawn	B2	Wellington Crescent	C3-C4
Brunswick Street	B3	London Road	A1	West Cliff Road	A1-A2
Camden Road	B3	Madeira Walk	B3-C3	Willsons Road	A1-A2
Camden Square	B3	Margate Road	A4	York Street	B3
Cannon Road	A3	Marlborough Road	A2-B2		
Cannonbury Road	A1	Meeting Street	A3-B3		
Carlton Avenue	A2	Monkton	A3		
Cavendish Street	B3	Nelson Crescent	B2		
Chapel Place	A2-A3	North Avenue	A2		
Chatham Place	A3-A4	Paragon Street	B1-B2		
Chatham Street	A3	Percy Road	A4		
Church Hill	B3	Plains of Waterloo	B3-C3		
Church Road	B3-B4	Poplar Road	A3		
Clifton Lawn	B1	Priory Road	B1		
Codrington Road	A2	Queen Street	A2-B2-B3		
Coronation Road	A2	Richmond Road	B2		
Cottage Road	B3-C3	Rodney Street	B2		
Crescent Road	A2	Rose Hill	B2		
D'Este Road	C4	Royal Crescent	B1-B2		
Denmark Road	A4-B4	Royal Esplanade	A1		

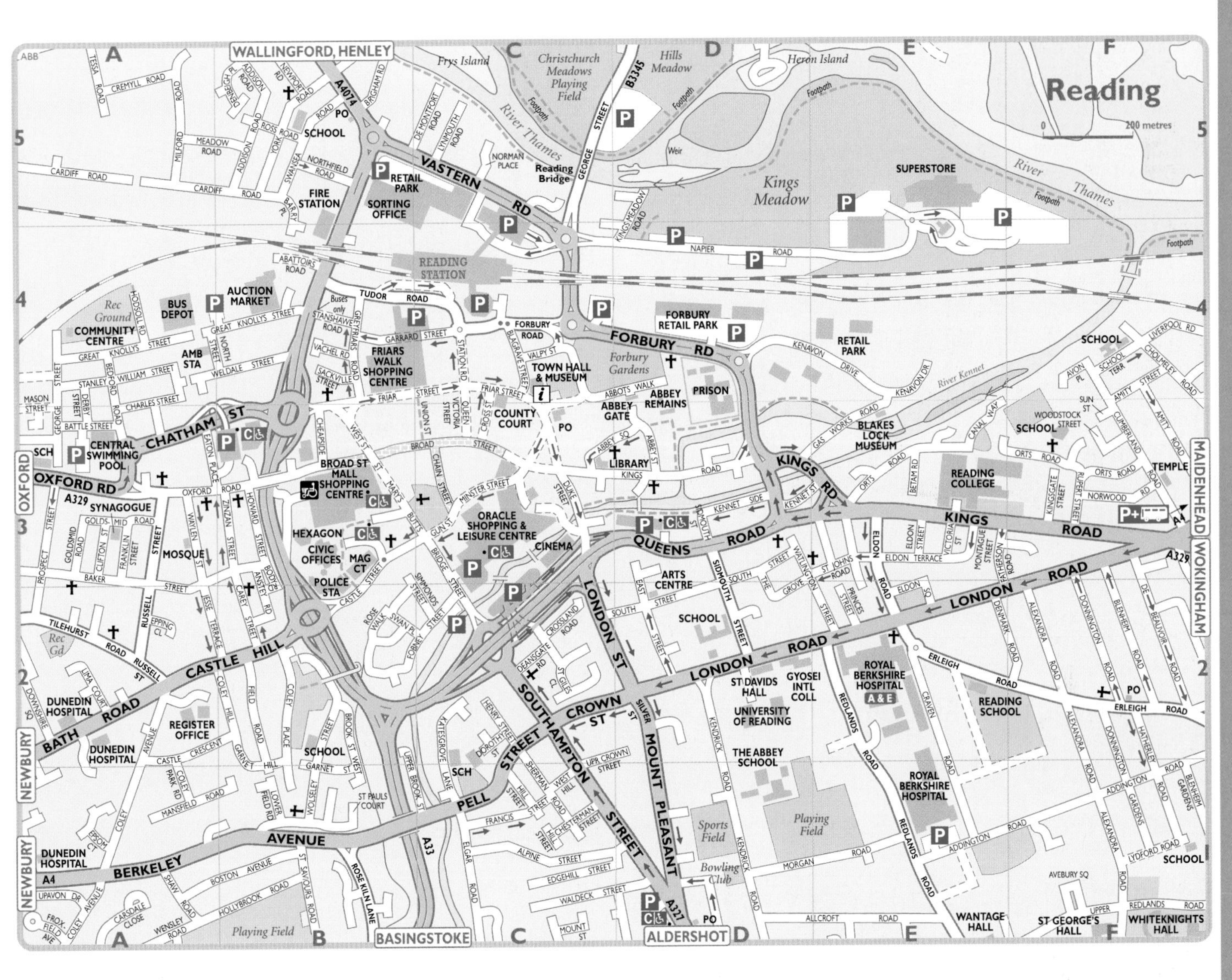

Reading

Reading is found on atlas page **24**,
grid reference **7173**

Abattoirs Road	B4	Castle Crescent	A2-B2	Eldon Road	E2-E3	Kenavon Drive	D4-E4	Queen Victoria Street	C3-C4	Upper Brook Street	B2-C1
Abbey Square	C3-D3	Castle Hill	A2-B2	Eldon Square	E2-E3	Kendrick Road	D1-D2	Queens Road	D3	Upper Crown Street	C1-D2
Abbey Street	D3	Castle Street	B2-B3	Eldon Street	E3	Kennet Side	D3	Redlands Road	E1-E2	Upper Redlands Road	F1
Abbots Walk	C4-D4	Chain Street	C3	Eldon Terrace	E3	Kennet Street	D3-E3	Rose Kiln Lane	B1	Vachel Road	B4
Addington Road	E1-F1-F2	Charles Street	A3-A4	Elgar Road	C1	Kings Meadow Road	D4-D5	Rose Walk	B2	Valpy Street	C4
Addison Road	B5	Chatham Street	A3-B3	Epping Close	A2	Kings Road	C3-D3-E3-F3	Ross Road	B5	Vastern Road	B5-C5-C4
Alexandra Road	F1-F2	Cheapside	B3	Epsom Court	A1	Kingsgate Street	F3	Rupert Street	F3	Victoria Street	E3
Allcroft Road	D1-E1	Chesterman Street	C1	Erleigh Road	E2-F2	Lima Court	A2	Russell Street	A2-A3	Waldeck Street	C1-D1
Alpine Street	C1-D1	Cholmeley Road	F3-F4	Fatherson Road	E2-E3	Liverpool Road	F4	St Giles Close	C2	Watlington Street	D3-E2
Amity Road	F3-F4	Clifton Street	A3	Field Road	B2	London Road	D2-E2-F2-F3	St Johns Road	E3	Waylen Street	A3
Amity Street	F4	Coley Avenue	A1-A2	Forbury Road	C4-D4	London Street	C3-C2-D2	St Mary's Butts	B3-C3	Weldale Street	A4-B4
Anstey Road	B2-B3	Coley Hill	A2-B2	Forney Street	B2-C2	Lower Field Road	B1	St Pauls Court	B1	Wensley Road	A1
Avebury Square	F1	Coley Park Road	A1-A2	Francis Street	C1	Lydford Road	F1	St Saviours Road	B1	West Hill	C1
Avon Place	F4	Coley Place	B1-B2	Franklin Street	A3	Lynmouth Road	C5	Sackville Street	B4	West Street	B3
Baker Street	A2-A3	Cremyll Road	A5	Friar Street	B3-B4-C4	Mansfield Road	A1-B1	School Terrace	F4	Wolseley Street	B1-B2
Barry Place	B4-B5	Cross Street	C3-C4	Froxfield Avenue	A1	Mason Street	A3-A4	Shaw Road	A1	Woodstock Street	F3
Bath Road	A2	Crossland Road	C2	Garnet Hill	B1-B2	Meadow Road	A5-B5	Sherman Road	C1-C2	York Road	B5
Battle Street	A3	Crown Street	C2-D2	Garnet Street	B1-B2	Milford Road	A5	Sidmouth Street	D2-D3	Zinzan Street	B3
Bedford Road	A3-A4	Cumberland Road	F3-F4	Garrard Street	B4-C4	Minster Street	C3	Silver Street	D2		
Berkeley Avenue	A1-B1	De Beauvoir Road	F2-F3	Gas Works Road	D3-E3-E4	Montague Street	E3	Simmonds Street	B3-C2		
Betam Road	E3	De Montfort Road	B5-C5	George Street	A3-A4	Morgan Road	D1-E1	South Street	C2-D2-D3		
Blagrave Street	C4	Deansgate Road	C2	George Street	C4-C5-D5	Mount Pleasant	D1-D2	Southampton Street	C2-C1-D1		
Blenheim Gardens	F1	Denbeigh Place	B5	Goldsmid Road	A3	Mount Street	C1	Stanley William Street	A4		
Blenheim Road	F2-F3	Denmark Road	E2-F2	Great Knollys Street	A4-B4	Napier Road	C4-D4-E4	Stanshawe Road	B4		
Body Road	B2-B3	Derby Street	A3-A4	Greyfriars Road	B4	Newport Road	B5	Station Road	C4		
Boston Avenue	A1-B1	Donnington Gardens	F1-F2	Gun Street	C3	Norman Place	C5	Sun Street	F3		
Bridge Street	C2-C3	Donnington Road	F2-F3	Hatherley Road	F1-F2	North Street	A4-B4	Swan Place	B2-C2		
Brigham Road	B5	Dorothy Street	C2	Henry Street	C2	Northfield Road	B5	Swansea Road	B5		
Broad Street	B3-C3	Downshire Square	A2	Hill Street	C1	Norwood Road	F3	Tessa Road	A5		
Brook Street West	B1-B2	Duke Street	C3	Hodsoll Road	A4	Orts Road	E3-F3	The Grove	D2-D3		
Canal Way	E3	East Street	D2-D3	Hollybrook Road	A1-B1	Oxford Road	A3-B3	Tilehurst Road	A2		
Cardiff Road	A5-B5	Eaton Place	A3-B3	Howard Street	B3	Pell Street	C1-C2	Tudor Road	B4-C4		
Carey Street	B2-B3	Edgehill Street	C1-D1	Jesse Terrace	A2-B2	Princes Street	E2	Union Street	C3-C4		
Carsdale Close	A1			Katesgrove Lane	C1-C2	Prospect Street	A2-A3	Upavon Drive	A1		

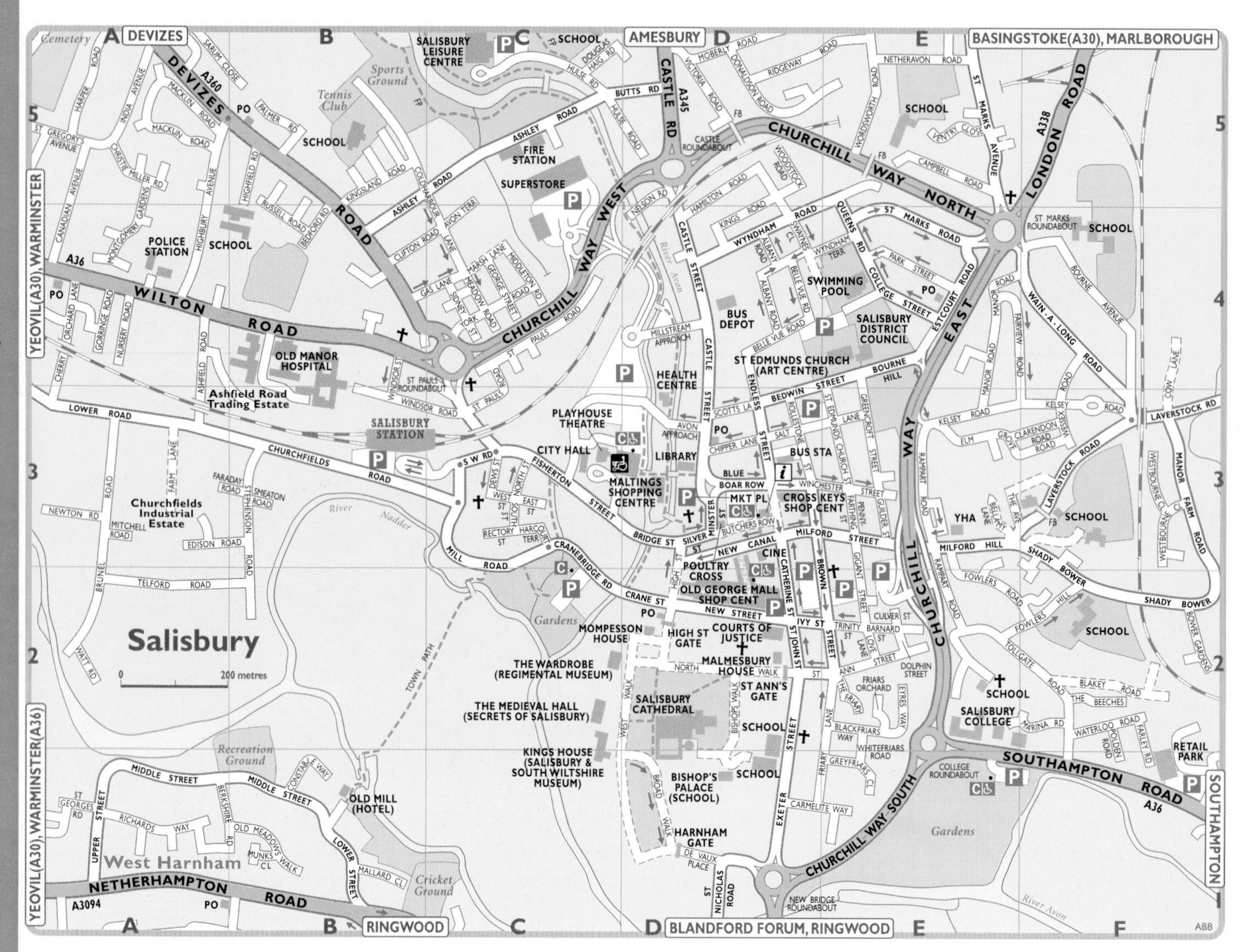

214

Salisbury

Salisbury is found on atlas page **23**,
grid reference **1429**

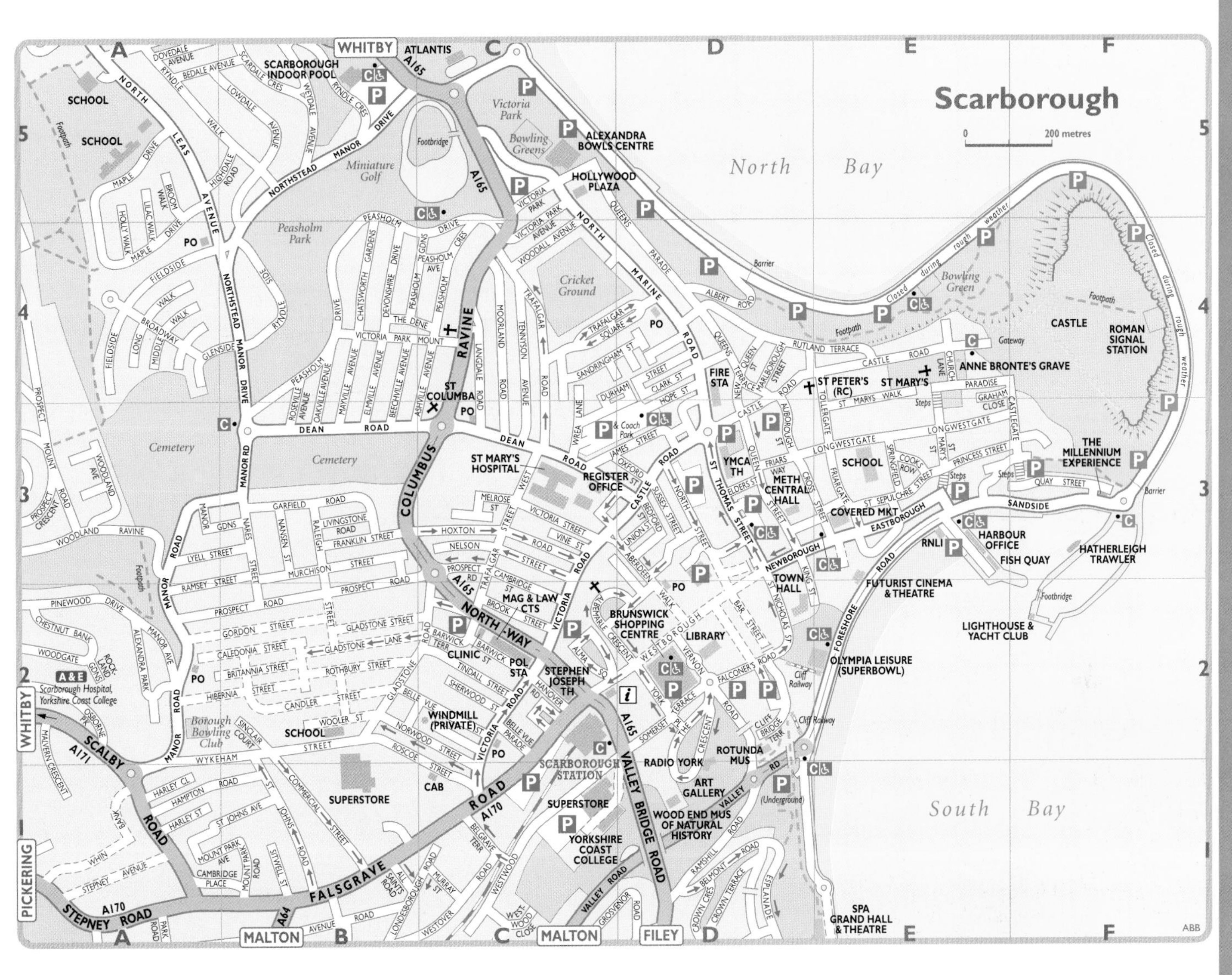

Scarborough

Scarborough is found on atlas page **91**,
grid reference **0488**

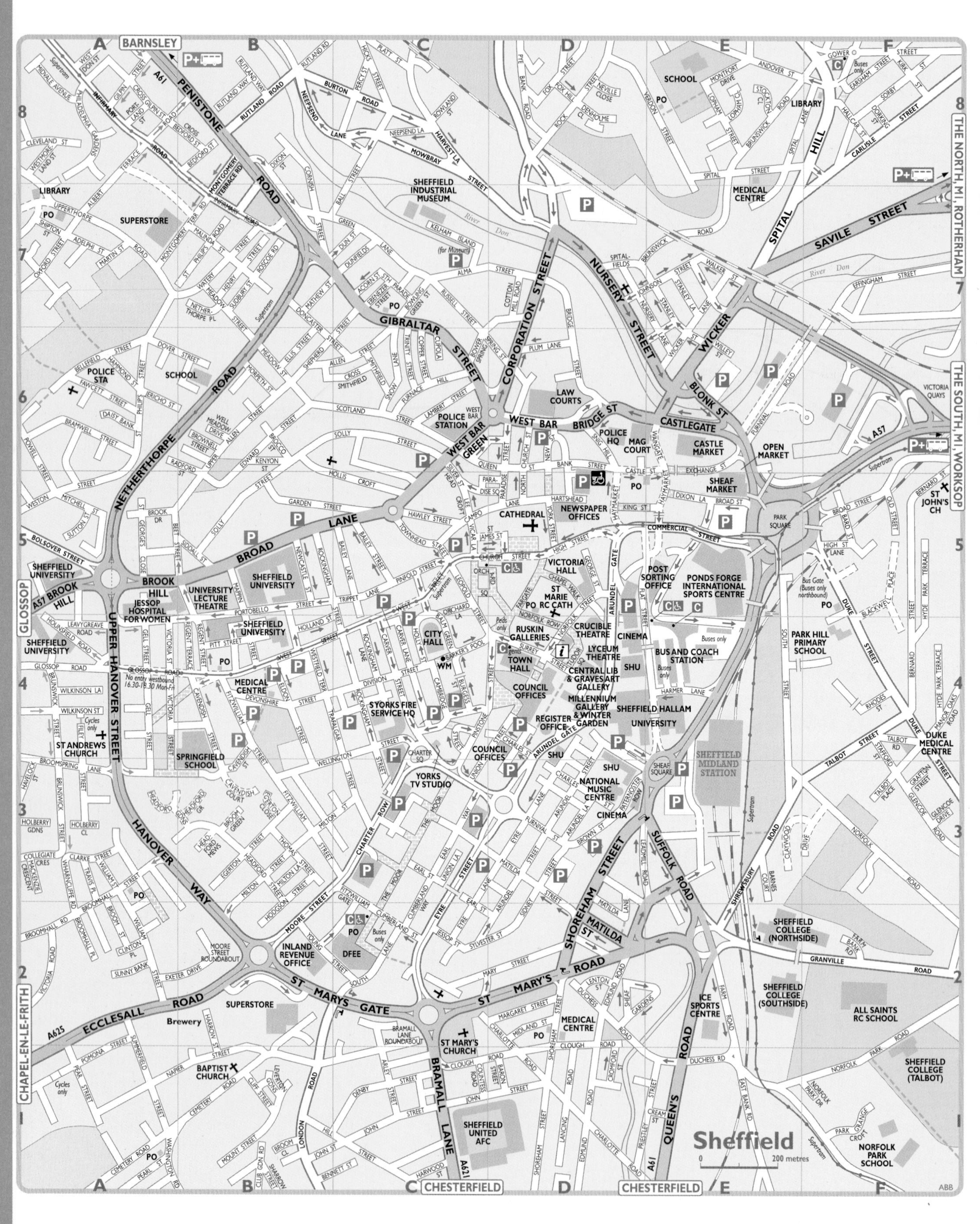
Sheffield
BARNSLEY
CHESTERFIELD
CHESTERFIELD
GLOSSOP
CHAPEL-EN-LE-FRITH
THE NORTH, M1, ROTHERHAM
THE SOUTH, M1, WORKSOP
PENISTONE ROAD
NETHERTHORPE ROAD
GIBRALTAR STREET
CORPORATION STREET
NURSERY STREET
WICKER
SPITAL HILL
SAVILE STREET
BLONK ST
CASTLEGATE
WEST BAR
WEST BAR GREEN
BRIDGE ST
BROAD LANE
BROOK HILL
UPPER HANOVER STREET
HANOVER WAY
ECCLESALL ROAD
ST MARYS GATE
ST MARY'S ROAD
BRAMALL LANE
QUEEN'S ROAD
SUFFOLK ROAD
SHOREHAM STREET
COMMERCIAL STREET
DUKE STREET
SHEFFIELD INDUSTRIAL MUSEUM
LAW COURTS
POLICE STATION
POLICE HQ
MAG COURT
CASTLE MARKET
OPEN MARKET
SHEAF MARKET
CATHEDRAL
NEWSPAPER OFFICES
VICTORIA HALL
ST MARIE RC CATH
POST SORTING OFFICE
PONDS FORGE INTERNATIONAL SPORTS CENTRE
SHEFFIELD UNIVERSITY
UNIVERSITY LECTURE THEATRE
JESSOP HOSPITAL FOR WOMEN
CITY HALL
RUSKIN GALLERIES
TOWN HALL
CRUCIBLE THEATRE
LYCEUM THEATRE
CINEMA
BUS AND COACH STATION
CENTRAL LIB & GRAVES ART GALLERY
COUNCIL OFFICES
MILLENNIUM GALLERY & WINTER GARDEN
SHEFFIELD HALLAM UNIVERSITY
REGISTER OFFICE
S YORKS FIRE SERVICE HQ
MEDICAL CENTRE
SPRINGFIELD SCHOOL
ST ANDREWS CHURCH
YORKS TV STUDIO
NATIONAL MUSIC CENTRE
SHEFFIELD MIDLAND STATION
PARK HILL PRIMARY SCHOOL
DUKE MEDICAL CENTRE
SHEFFIELD COLLEGE (NORTHSIDE)
SHEFFIELD COLLEGE (SOUTHSIDE)
SHEFFIELD COLLEGE (TALBOT)
ALL SAINTS RC SCHOOL
NORFOLK PARK SCHOOL
ICE SPORTS CENTRE
SHEFFIELD UNITED AFC
ST MARY'S CHURCH
BAPTIST CHURCH
INLAND REVENUE OFFICE
DFEE
SUPERSTORE
Brewery
LIBRARY
POLICE STA
SCHOOL
ST JOHN'S CH
PARK SQUARE
SHEAF SQUARE
MOORE STREET ROUNDABOUT
BRAMALL LANE ROUNDABOUT
River Don
Supertram
200 metres
ABB

Shrewsbury

Shrewsbury is found on atlas page **59**, grid reference **4912**

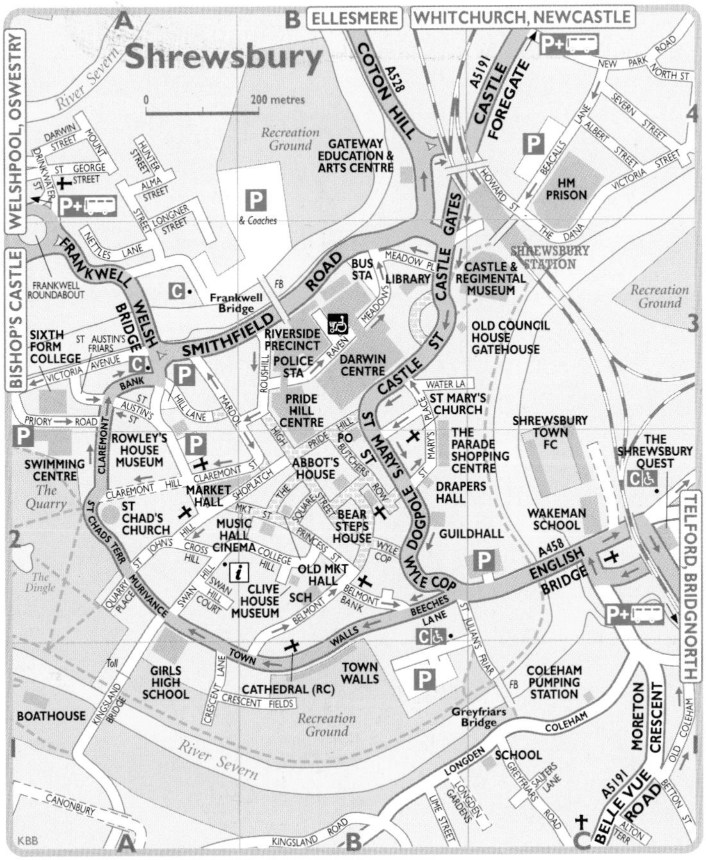

Albert Street C4
Alma Street A4
Beacalls Lane C4
Beeches Lane B2
Belle Vue Road C1
Belmont B1-B2
Belmont Bank B2
Butchers Row B2
Canonbury A1
Castle Foregate C4
Castle Gates B3-B4
Castle Street B3
Claremont Bank A2-A3
Claremont Hill A2
Claremont Street A2-B2
College Hill B2
Coton Hill B4
Crescent Fields A1-B1
Crescent Lane A1
Cross Hill A2
Darwin Street A4
Dogpole B2
Drinkwater Street A4
English Bridge C2
Frankwell A3
Greyfriars Road C1
High Street B2-B3
Hill Lane A3
Howard Street C4
Hunter Street A4
Kingsland Bridge A1
Kingsland Road A1-B1
Lime Street B1
Longden Coleham B1-C1
Longden Gardens B1-C1
Longner Street A3-A4
Mardol A3-B2
Market Street A2-B2
Meadow Place B3
Moreton Crescent C1
Mount Street A3-A4
Murivance A2
Nettles Lane A3
New Park Road C4
Old Coleham C1
Pride Hill B2-B3
Princess Street B2
Priory Road A3
Quarry Place A2
Raven Meadows B3
Roushill B3
St Austin's Friars A3
St Austin's Street A3
St Chads Terrace A2
St George Street A4
St John's Hill A2
St Julian's Friar B2-C2-C1
St Mary's Place B2-B3
St Mary's Street B2-B3
Severn Street C4
Shoplatch A2-B2
Smithfield Road A3-B3
Swan Hill A2
Swan Hill Court A2
The Dana C3-C4
The Square B2
Town Walls A2-A1-B1-B2
Victoria Avenue A3
Victoria Street C4
Water Lane B3-C3
Welsh Bridge A3
Wyle Cop B2

Sheffield

Sheffield is found on atlas page **74**, grid reference **3587**

Acorn Street C7
Adelphi Street A7
Albert Terrace A7-A8
Allen Street B6-C6
Alma Street C7-D7
Andover Street E8
Arley Street C1
Arundel Gate D4-D5
Arundel Lane D3
Arundel Street C2-D2-D3-D4
Bailey Lane C5
Bailey Street C5
Ball Street C7-C8
Balm Green C4-C5
Bank Street D6
Bard Street F5
Barker's Pool C4
Barnes Court E3
Baron Street D1
Bedford Street B8
Beet Street A5-B5
Bellefield Street A6
Bennett Street B1-C1
Bernard Street F4-F5-F6
Blackwell Place F5
Blonk Street E6
Bolsover Street A5
Bower Spring C6
Bowling Green Street C7
Bramall Lane C1-C2
Bramwell Street A6
Bridge Street D6-D7
Broad Lane B5-C5
Broad Street E5
Broad Street F5
Brocco Street B6
Brook Drive A5
Brook Hill A5
Broom Close B1
Broom Green B3
Broom Street A2
Broomhall Place A2
Broomhall Road A2
Broomhall Street A2-A3
Broomspring Lane A3-A4
Brown Street D3
Brownell Street B6
Brunswick Road E7-E8-F8
Brunswick Street A3-A4
Burgess Street C4
Burton Road B8-C8
Cambridge Street C4
Campo Lane C5-D5
Carlisle Street F7-F8
Carver Lane C4
Carver Street C4
Castle Street D6-E6
Castlegate E6
Cavendish Court B3
Cavendish Street B3-B4
Cemetery Road A1-B1
Chapel Walk D5
Charles Street D3-D4
Charlotte Road C2-D2-D1-E1
Charter Row C3
Charter Square C3-C4
Church Street C5-D5
Clarke Street A3
Claywood Drive E3-F3
Cleveland Street A8
Cliff Street B1
Clinton Place A2
Clough Road C1-D1-D2
Club Garden Road B1
Collegiate Crescent A3
Commercial Street D5-E5
Copper Street C6
Cornish Street B7-B8
Corporation Street D6-D7
Cotton Mill Road D7
Countess Road C1
Cream Street E1
Cromford Street D1
Cross Bedford Street A8-B8
Cross Gilpin Street A8
Cross Smithfield B6-C6
Cumberland Street C2
Cumberland Way C2-C3
Cupola C6
Daisy Bank A6
Denby Street C1
Denholme Close D8
Devonshire Street B4
Division Street C4
Dixon Lane E5
Dixon Street B8
Doncaster Street B7-B6-C6
Dorking Street F8
Dover Street A6-B6
Duchess Road D2-D1-E1
Duke Street F3-F4-F5
Dun Street B7-C7
Dunfields C7
Earl Street C3-C2-D2
Earl Way C3
Earsham Street F8
East Bank Road E1
Ebenezer Street C7
Ecclesall Road A1-A2-B2
Edmund Road D1-D2
Edward Street B5-B6
Effingham Street F7
Egerton Close B3
Egerton Street B3
Eldon Street B3-B4
Ellis Street B6
Exchange Street E6
Exeter Drive A2-B2
Eyre Lane C2-C3-D3
Eyre Street C2-C3-D3
Fargate D5
Farm Bank Road F2
Farm Road E1-E2
Fawcett Street A6
Filey Street A3-A4
Fitzwilliam Gate C2-C3
Fitzwilliam Street B4-B3-C3
Fox Hill D8
Fox Street D8
Furnace Hill C6
Furnival Road E6-F6
Furnival Street D3
Garden Street B5-C5
Gell Street A3-A4-A5
George Street D5
Gibraltar Street C6-C7
Gilpin Street A8
Glencoe Drive F3
Glencoe Road F3
Glossop Road A4-B4
Gower Street F8
Grafton Street F3
Granville Road F1-F2
Green Lane B7-C7
Hallcar Street F8
Hammond Street A6
Hanover Way A3-B3-B2
Harmer Lane E4
Harrow Street B2
Hartshead D5
Harvest Lane C8
Harwood Street C1
Havelock Street A3
Hawley Street C5
Haymarket D5
Headford Gardens A3-B3
Headford Grove A3-B3
Headford Mews A3-B3
Headford Street B3
Henry Street B7
Hicks Street C8
High Street D5
High Street Lane F5
Hill Street B1-C1
Hodgson Street B2-B3
Holberry Close A3
Holberry Gardens A3
Holland Street B4
Hollis Croft B6-C5
Holly Street C4-C5
Hounsfield Road A4
Hyde Park Terrace F4-F5
Infirmary Road A8-B8-B7
Jericho Street A6
Jessop Street C2
John Street B1-C1-D1
Johnson Street D7-E7
Kelham Island C7
King Street D5-E5
Kirk Street F8
Lambert Street C6
Lancing Road D1
Leadmill Road D3-E3
Leavygreave Road A4
Lee Croft C5
Lenton Street D2
Leopold Street C4-C5
Leverton Gardens B1
London Road B1-B2
Lopham Close E8
Lopham Street E8
Mackenzie Crescent A3
Malinda Street B7
Manor Oaks Road F4
Mappin Street B4-B5
Margaret Street D2
Martin Street A7
Mary Street C2-D2
Mathew Street B7
Matilda Lane D2-D3
Matilda Street C3-D3-D2
Meadow Street B6-B7
Midland Street D2
Midvale Avenue A8
Milton Lane B3
Milton Street B2-B3-C3
Mitchell Street A5
Montfort Drive E8
Montgomery Terrace Road A7-B8
Moore Street B2-B3-C3
Morpeth Street B6
Mount Street B1
Mowbray Street C8-C7-D7
Napier Street A1-B1
Neepsend Lane B8-C8
Netherthorpe Place B7
Netherthorpe Road A5-A6-B6-B7
Neville Close D8
Newcastle Street B5
Norfolk Park Drive F1
Norfolk Park Road E1-F1-F2
Norfolk Road F2-F3
Norfolk Row D4-D5
Norfolk Street D4-D5
North Church Street D5-D6
Nursery Lane D7-E7-E6
Nursery Street D7-D6-E6
Old Street F5
Orchard Lane C5
Orchard Square C5-D5
Oxford Street A7
Paradise Square C5-D5
Paradise Street D5-D6
Park Grange Croft F1
Park Square E5-F5
Paternoster Row D3
Pear Street A1
Pearl Street A1
Penistone Road A8-B8-B7
Percy Street C8
Philadelphia Gardens A8
Pinfold Street C5
Pinstone Street C3-C4-D4
Pitt Street B4
Platt Street C8
Plum Lane D6
Pomona Street A1-A2
Portland Street A8
Portobello Street B4-B5
Powell Street A5-A6
Priestley Street D1-E1
Pye Bank Road D8
Queen Street C6-D6
Queen's Road E1-E2
Radford Street A6-B6
Regent Street B4
Regent Terrace B4
Rhodes Street F4
Rock Street D8
Rockingham Lane C4
Rockingham Street B5-C5-C4-C3
Roscoe Road B7
Rowland Street C8
Russell Street C7
Rutland Road B8
Rutland Way B8
St George's Close A5
St Mary's Road C2-D2-E2
St Marys Gate B2-C2
St Philip's Road B7
St Philip's Street A6
Savile Street E7-F7
Scotland Street B6-C6
Sharrow Street B1
Sheaf Gardens D2-E2
Shepherd Street B6-C6-C7
Shipton Street A7
Shoreham Street D1-D2-D3
Shrewsbury Road E2-E3
Siddall Street B5
Sidney Street D2-D3
Silver Street Head C5-C6
Smithfield C6
Snig Hill D6
Snow Lane C6
Solly Street B5-B6-C6
Sorby Street F8
South Lane C2
South Parade C7
South Street E3-E4-E5
Spital Hill E7-E8-F8
Spital Lane E8-F8
Spital Street E8
Spitalfields D7
Spring Street D6
Stafford Street F3-F4
Stanley Lane E7
Stanley Street E6-E7
Stockton Close E8
Sudbury Street B7
Suffolk Road E2-E3
Summerfield Street A1-A2
Sunny Bank A2
Surrey Street D4
Sutton Street A5
Sylvester Street C2-D2
Talbot Place F3
Talbot Road F4
Talbot Street F3-F4
Terrace Road A8-B8
The Moor C2-C3
Thomas Street B3
Townhead Street C5
Trafalgar Street B4-C4-C3
Travis Place A3
Trinity Street C6
Trippet Lane C5
Tudor Square D4
Union Lane C3
Union Street C3-D4
Upper Allen Street B5-B6
Upper Hanover Street A3-A4-A5
Upperthorpe Road A7
Verdon Street D8-E8
Vicar Lane C5
Victoria Road A2
Victoria Street A3-A4
Waingate E6
Walker Street E7
Washington Road A1-B1
Watery Street B7
Well Meadow Drive B6
Wellington Street B3-C4
West Bar D6
West Bar Green C6
West Don Street A8
West Street B4-C4-C5
Westfield Terrace B4
Westmoreland Street A8
Weston Street A5-A6
Wharncliffe Road A2-A3
Wicker E6-E7
Wicker Lane E6-E7
Wilkinson Lane A4
Wilkinson Street A4
Willey Street E6
William Street A2-A3
York Street D5
Young Street B2-C2

218

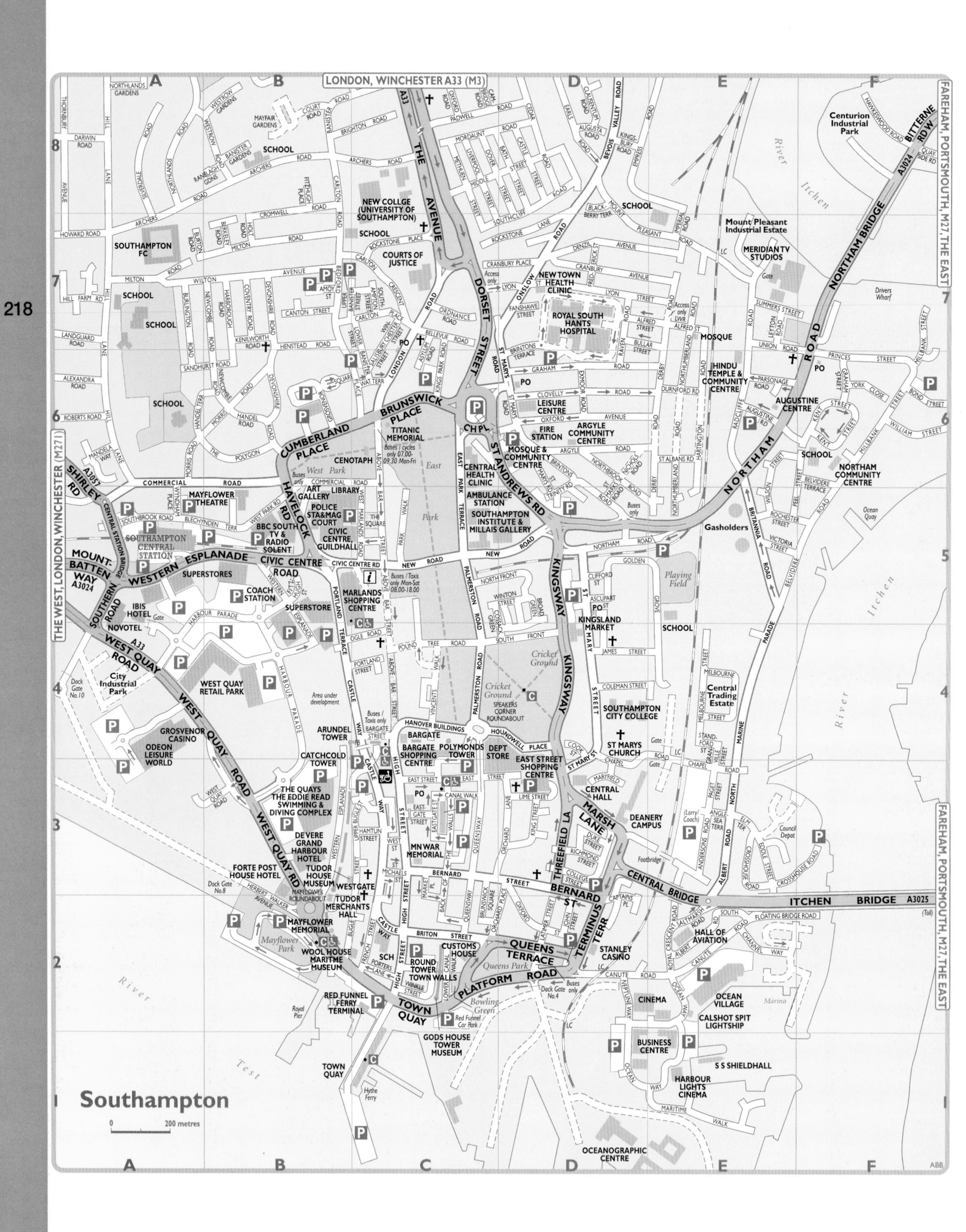

Southampton

0   200 metres

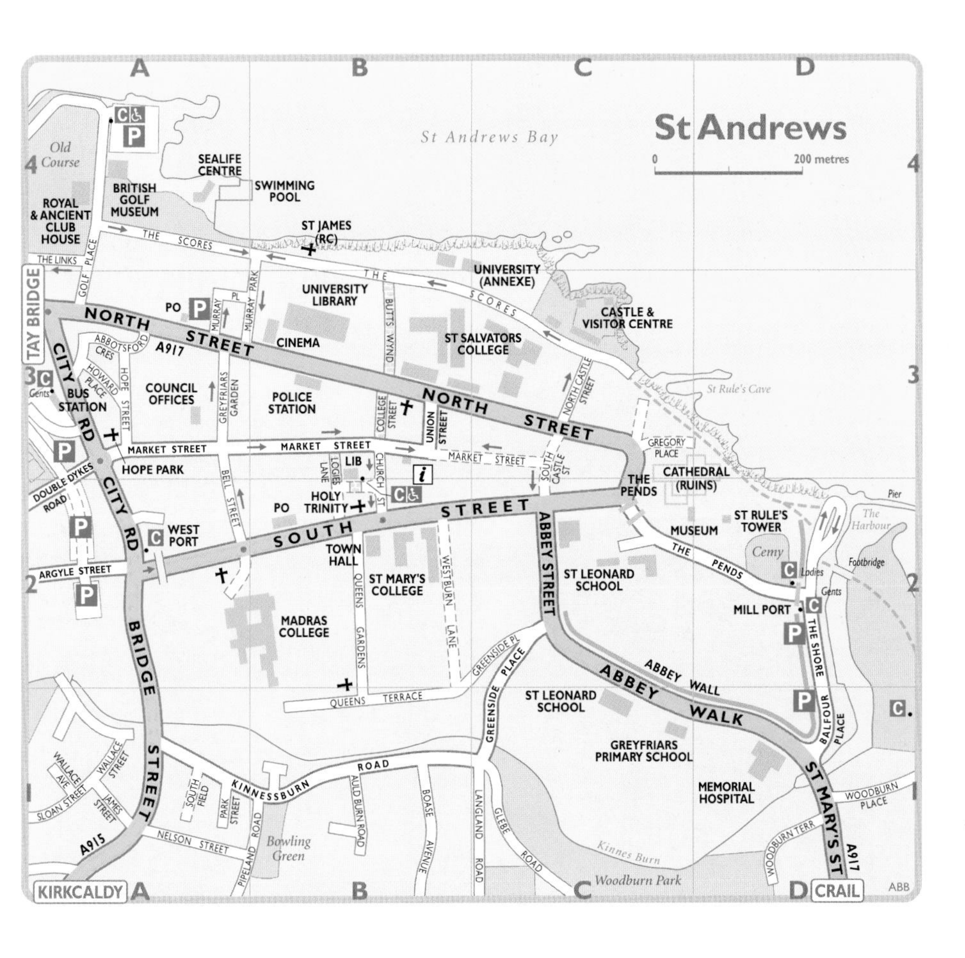

St Andrews

St Andrews is found on atlas page **127**,
grid reference **5I16**

219

Southampton

Southampton is found on atlas page **13**,
grid reference **4II2**

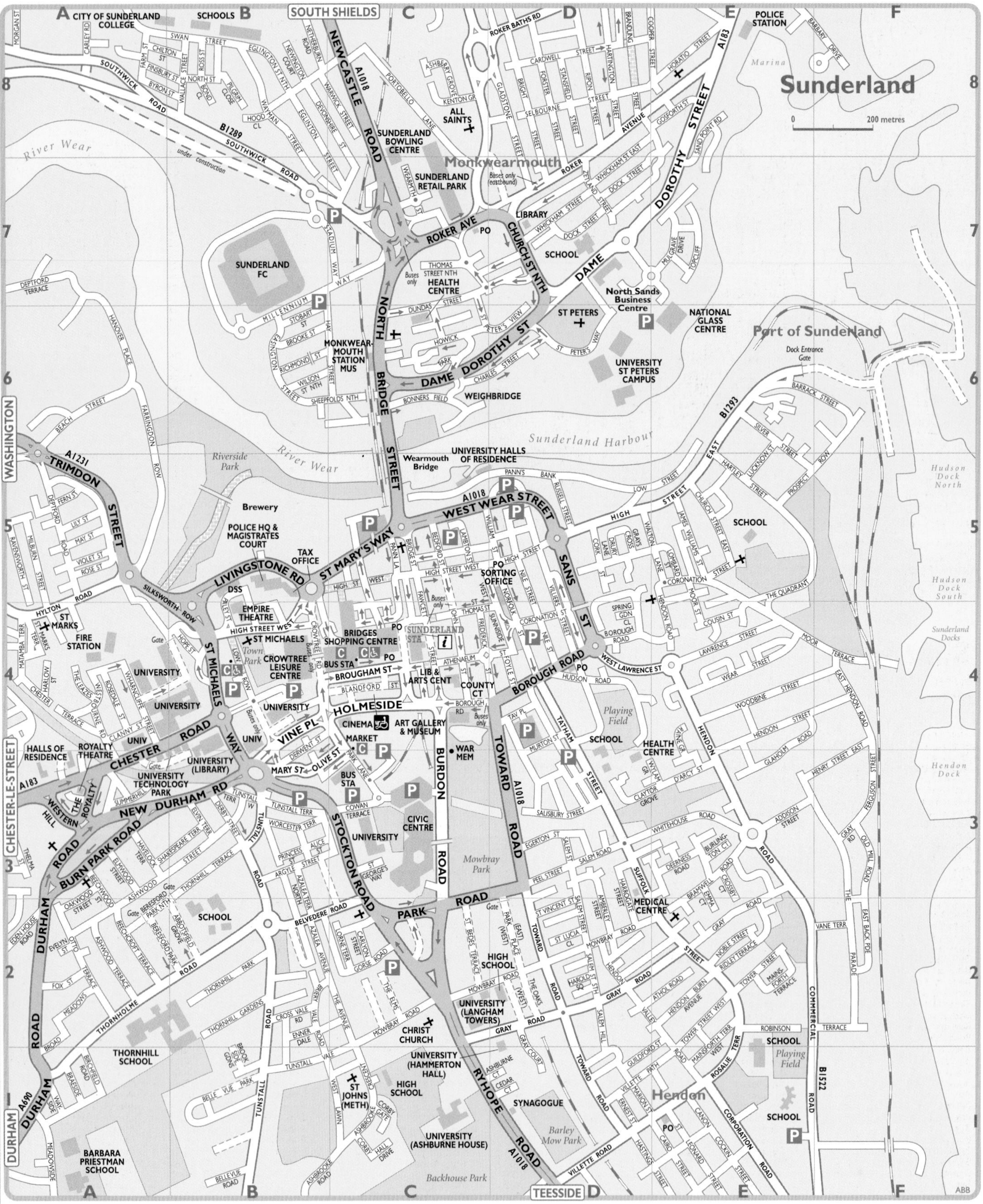

CITY OF SUNDERLAND COLLEGE
SCHOOLS
SOUTH SHIELDS
POLICE STATION

Sunderland

0   200 metres

A B C D E F

SWAN STREET
CHILTON ST
FINSBURY ST
ROSS ST
NORTH ST
EGLINTON ST NTH
NEWBURN
NEWCASTLE ROAD
A1018
PORTOBELLO
ROKER BATHS RD
BRANDLING
COOPER STREET
A183
HORATIO STREET
GOSFORTH ST
Marina
BARBARY DRIVE

SOUTHWICK ROAD
B1289
SOUTHWICK ROAD
under construction
River Wear

BYRON ST
HOOD CL
WAYMAN ST
ASHBERY GROVE
KENTON GR
ALL SAINTS
GLADSTONE STREET
CARDWELL STREET
BRIGHT
FORSTER
STANSFIELD
HPPON
HARTINGTON
COOPER STREET
DOROTHY STREET

SUNDERLAND BOWLING CENTRE
SUNDERLAND RETAIL PARK
Monkwearmouth
Buses only (eastbound)
WHICKHAM ST EAST
DOCK STREET
NORTH BRIDGE STREET
STADIUM WAY
MILLENNIUM WAY

SUNDERLAND FC
ROKER AVE
PO
CHURCH ST NTH
LIBRARY
SCHOOL
DAME DOROTHY STREET
St PETERS
North Sands Business Centre
NATIONAL GLASS CENTRE
Port of Sunderland

STOBART ST
BROOKE ST
RICHMOND
WILSON ST NTH
MONKWEARMOUTH STATION MUS
Buses only
THOMAS STREET NTH
HEALTH CENTRE
DUNDAS STREET
HOWICK
St PETER'S VIEW
PARK
CHARLES STREET
WEIGHBRIDGE
UNIVERSITY St PETERS CAMPUS
Dock Entrance Gate
BARRACK STREET

DEPTFORD TERRACE
HANOVER PLACE
BEACH STREET
FARRINGDON ROW
Riverside Park
River Wear
SHEFFOLDS NTH
BONNERS FIELD
Sunderland Harbour
B1293
SILVER STREET
Hudson Dock North

WASHINGTON
A1231
TRIMDON STREET
Brewery
POLICE HQ & MAGISTRATES COURT
Wearmouth Bridge
Wearmouth Bridge
UNIVERSITY HALLS OF RESIDENCE
PANN'S BANK
RUSSELL STREET
LOW STREET
HIGH STREET EAST
HARTLEY ST
JACKSON ST
PROSPECT ROW
Hudson Dock South

DEPTFORD ROAD
LILY ST
MAY ST
VIOLET ST
ROSE ST
SILKSWORTH ROW
LIVINGSTONE RD
TAX OFFICE
DSS
ST MARY'S WAY
WEST WEAR STREET
A1018
PO SORTING OFFICE
HIGH STREET WEST
WEST
SANS ST
HIGH STREET
CORK STREET
GRAY'S
WALTON LANE
CORONATION
THE QUADRANT
Sunderland Docks

HYLTON ROAD
St MARKS
FIRE STATION
EMPIRE THEATRE
HIGH STREET WEST
St MICHAELS
BRIDGES SHOPPING CENTRE
BUS STA
BROUGHAM ST
BLANDFORD ST
NILE STREET
NORFOLK ST
SPRING GDN CL
BOROUGH ROAD
COUSIN ST
MOOR TERRACE

UNIVERSITY
Town Park
CROWTREE LEISURE CENTRE
UNIVERSITY
HOLMESIDE
SUNDERLAND STA
i
LIB & ARTS CENT
COUNTY CT
BOROUGH RD
Buses only
BOROUGH ROAD
WEST LAWRENCE ST
PO
LAWRENCE STREET
WEAR STREET
EAST HENDON ROAD
WOODBINE STREET
GLAHOLM
Hendon Dock

HALLS OF RESIDENCE
ROYALTY THEATRE
CHESTER ROAD
UNIV
UNIV
VINE PL
MARY ST
OLIVE ST
CINEMA
MARKET
ART GALLERY & MUSEUM
WAR MEM
BURDON ROAD
TOWARD ROAD
A1018
Playing Field
SCHOOL
HEALTH CENTRE

CHESTER-LE-STREET
A183
THE ROYALTY
WESTERN HILL
UNIVERSITY TECHNOLOGY PARK
NEW DURHAM RD
TUNSTALL TERR
UNIVERSITY
CIVIC CENTRE
Mowbray Park
SALISBURY STREET
MEDICAL CENTRE

DURHAM ROAD
A690
BURN PARK ROAD
OAKWOOD STREET
SHAKESPEARE TERR
PRINCESS ST
ALICE ST
ARGYLE ST
AZALEA TERR
STOCKTON ROAD
BELVEDERE ROAD
ST GEORGE'S WAY
PARK ROAD
PARK ROAD
ST VINCENT STREET
St LUCIA
MOWBRAY ROAD
SUFFOLK
HIGH SCHOOL
MEDICAL CENTRE

SCHOOL
THORNHOLME
THORNHILL GARDENS
CROSS VALE
ENNERDALE
MOWBRAY ROAD
HIGH SCHOOL
THE ELMS
UNIVERSITY (LANGHAM TOWERS)
GRAY ROAD
ATHOL ROAD
HENDON BURN AVENUE
TOWER STREET WEST

THORNHILL SCHOOL
TUNSTALL
BELLE VUE RD
St JOHNS (METH)
CHRIST CHURCH
HIGH SCHOOL
UNIVERSITY (HAMMERTON HALL)
SYNAGOGUE
Hendon
PO
SCHOOL
Playing Field

BARBARA PRIESTMAN SCHOOL
BELLEVUE ROAD
ASHBROOKE HALL DRIVE
UNIVERSITY (ASHBURNE HOUSE)
RYHOPE ROAD
A1018
Barley Mow Park
VILLETTE ROAD
CORPORATION ROAD
B1522
SCHOOL
Backhouse Park
TEESSIDE

ABB

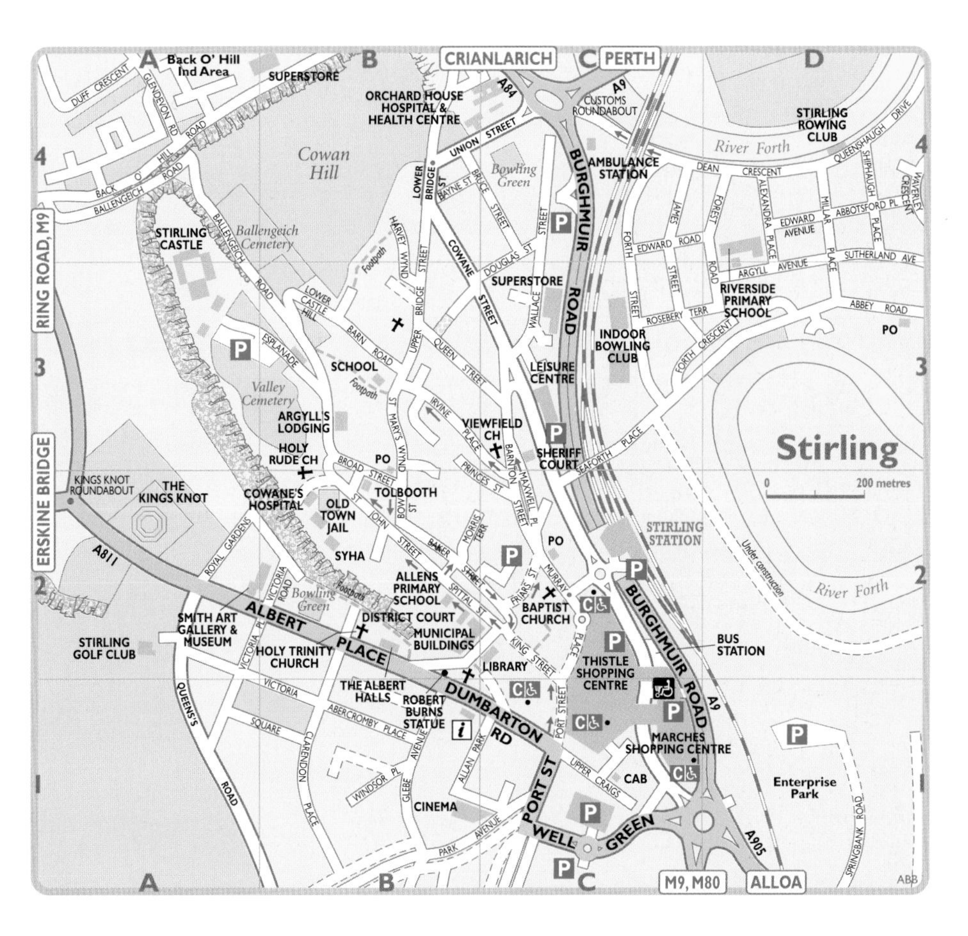

Stirling

Stirling is found on atlas page 116,
grid reference **7993**

Abbey Road	D3	Queen Street	B3-C3
Abbotsford Place	D4	Queenshaugh Drive	D4
Abercromby Place	B1	Queen's Road	A1-A2
Albert Place	A2-B2	Rosebery Terrace	C3-D3
Alexandra Place	D4	Royal Gardens	A2
Allan Park	B1-C1	St John Street	B2
Argyll Avenue	D3-D4	St Mary's Wynd	B2-B3
Back O' Hill Road	A4-B4	Seaforth Place	C2-C3
Baker Street	B2-C2	Shiphaugh Place	D4
Ballengeich Road	A4-A3-B3	Spittal Street	B2-C2
Barn Road	B3	Springbank Road	D1
Barnton Street	C2-C3	Sutherland Avenue	D4
Bayne Street	B4	Union Street	B4-C4
Bow Street	B2	Upper Bridge Street	B3-B4
Broad Street	B2-B3	Upper Craigs	C1
Bruce Street	B4-C4	Victoria Place	A2-B2
Burghmuir Road	C4-C2-D1	Victoria Road	B2
Clarendon Place	B1-B2	Victoria Square	A1-B1
Cowane Street	B4-B3-C3	Wallace Street	C3-C4
Dean Crescent	C4-D4	Waverley Crescent	D4
Douglas Street	B3-C4	Well Green	C1
Duff Crescent	A4	Windsor Place	B1
Dumbarton Road	B1-C1		
Edward Avenue	D4		
Edward Road	C4		
Esplanade	A3-B3		
Forest Road	D3-D4		
Forth Crescent	C3-D3		
Forth Street	C3-C4		
Friars Street	C2		
Glebe Avenue	B1		
Glendevon Road	A4		
Harvey Wynd	B3-B4		
Irvine Place	B3-C3		
James Street	C3-C4		
King Street	C1-C2		
Lower Bridge Street	B4		
Lower Castle Hill	B3		
Maxwell Place	C2-C3		
Millar Place	D3-D4		
Morris Terrace	B2		
Murray Place	C2		
Park Avenue	B1-C1		
Port Street	C1		
Princes Street	B3-B2-C2		

221

Sunderland

Sunderland is found on atlas page **96**,
grid reference **3957**

Abbotsfield Grove	B2	Burn Park Road	A3
Addison Street	E3	Byron Street	A8-B8
Alice Street	B3	Cairo Street	E1
Amberley Street	D2-D3	Canon Cockin Street	E1
Argyle Street	B3-C3	Cardwell Street	D8
Ashberry Grove	C8	Carley Road	A8
Ashbrooke Crescent	C1	Carlyon Street	C2
Ashbrooke Road	B1-C1	Cedar Court	D1
Ashburne Court	C1-C2	Charles Street	C6-D6
Ashwood Street	A2-B3	Chester Road	A3-B4
Ashwood Terrace	A2	Chester Terrace	A4
Athenaeum Street	C4-D4	Chilton Street	A8-B8
Athol Road	D2-E2	Church Street East	E5
Azalea Terrace Avenue	B2	Clanny Street	A4
Azalea Terrace North	B2-B3	Clayton Grove	D3-E3
Barbary Drive	E8-F8	Commercial Road	E1-E2
Beach Street	A6	Cooper Street	E8
Bedford Street	C5	Corby Gate	C1
Beechcroft Terrace	A2	Corby Hall Drive	C1
Beechwood Street	A2-A3	Cork Street	D5
Belle Vue Park	B1	Coronation Street	D4-E5
Belvedere Road	B2-C3	Corporation Road	E1
Beresford Park North	A2-B3	Cousin Street	E4
Beresford Road	A2-B2	Cowan Terrace	C3
Birchfield Road	A1	Crossby Court	E3
Black Road	B7-C7	Cross Vale Road	B2
Blandford Street	C4	Crowtree Road	B4
Bond Close	B8	D'Arcy Street	E3
Bonners Field	C6	Dame Dorothy Street	D6-E8
Borough Road	C4-E4	Deerness Road	E3
Braeside	A1	Deptford Road	A5
Bramwell Road	E2-E3	Deptford Terrace	A7
Brandling Street	D8	Derby Street	B3
Bridge Street	C5	Derwent Street	B3-C3
Briery Vale Road	B1-B2	Devonshire Street	B8-C7
Bright Street	D7-D8	Dock Street	D7-E8
Broad Meadows	A1-A2	Drury Lane	D5
Brooke Street	B6	Dundas Street	C6-C7
Brookside Gardens	B1-B2	Durham Road	A1-A3
Brougham Street	B4-C4	Easington Street	B6
Burdon Road	C2-C4	East Back Poe	F2
Burlington Court	E3	East Barrack Street	D5-F6

East Hendon Road	F4	Horatio Street	E8
Eden House Road	A2	Howick Park	C6
Egerton Street	D3	Hudson Street	D4
Eglinton Street	B8-C7	Hylton Road	A4-A5
Eglinton Street North	B8	James Williams Street	E5
Elmwood Street	A3	John Street	C4-C5
Elvin Terrace	B3	Kenton Grove	C8
Emma Court	E2-E3	Lambton Street	C5
Ennerdale	B2	Lawrence Street	E4
Ernest Street	D1	Lily Street	A5
Evelyn Street	A2	Livingstone Road	B5
Farm Street	A8	Lombard Street	E5
Farringdon Row	A5-A6	Lorne Terrace	C2
Fawcett Street	C4-C5	Low Row	B4
Ferguson Street	F3	Low Street	D5-E6
Fern Street	A5	Lucknow Street	E5-E6
Finsbury Street	A8-B8	Mainsforth Terrace	E2
Forster Street	D7-D8	Mainsforth Terrace West	E1-E2
Fox Street	A2	Marion Street	D1
Foyle Street	D4	Mary Street	B3
Frederick Street	C4-D4	Matamba Terrace	A4
George Street	D5	May Street	A5
Gladstone Street	D7-D8	Meadowside	A1
Glaholm Road	E3-E4	Milburn Street	A5
Gorse Road	C2	Millennium Way	B6-B7-C7
Gosforth Street	E8	Moor Street	E4-E5
Gray Court	D1-D2	Moor Terrace	E4-F4
Gray Road	C2-E3-F3	Mowbray Road	C2-E2
Grays Cross	D5	Mulgrave Drive	E7
Guildford Street	D1-E2	Murton Street	D3-D4
Gunton Street	B8-C7	Netherburn Road	B8
Hanover Place	A6-A7	New Durham Road	A3-B3
Harold Square	D2	Newington Court	D5
Hartington Street	D8	Nile Street	D4-D5
Harlow Street	A4	Noble Street	E2
Harrogate Street	D2-D3	Norfolk Street	D4-D5
Hartley Street	E5-E6	North Bridge Street	C5-C7
Hastings Road	D1-E1	North Street	B8
Havelock Terrace	A3	Old Mill Road	F3
Hay Street	C6-C7	Olive Street	B3-C4
Hendon Burn Avenue	D2-E2	Osman Terrace	D3-E3
Hendon Road	E2-E5	Otto Terrace	A2
Hendon Street	E4-F4	Paley Street	B4-B5
Hendon Valley Road	D2-E1	Pann's Bank	C5-D5
Henry Street East	E3-F4	Pann Lane	C5
High Street	B5-D5	Park Lane	C3-C4
High Street West	B4-B5-C5	Park Place West	D2
Holmside	C4	Park Road	C2-D3
Hood Close	B8	Peel Street	D3
Hope Street	A4-B4	Pilgrim Close	B8

Portobello Lane	C7-C8	The Elms	C2
Princess Street	B3	The Leazes	A4
Prospect Row	E5-F6	The Oaks West	D2
Raine Grove	E4	The Parade	E3-F2
Ravensworth Street	A4-A5	The Quadrant	E5
Richmond Street	B6	The Royalty	A3
Ridley Terrace	E2	Thelma Street	A3
Ripon Street	D8	Thomas Street North	C7
Robinson Terrace	E2-F2	Thornhill Gardens	B2
Roker Avenue	C7-E8	Thornhill Park	B2
Roker Baths Road	D8	Thornhill Terrace	B3
Rosalie Terrace	E1-E2	Thornholme Road	A1-B2
Rose Street	A5	Topcliff	E7
Rosedale Street	A4	Toward Road	D1-D4
Ross Street	B8	Tower Street	E2
Russell Street	D5	Tower Street West	E2
Ryhope Road	C2-D1	Trimdon Street	A5-A6
St Bedes Terrace	C2	Tunstall Road	B1-B3
St George's Way	C3	Tunstall Terrace	B3
St Leonard Street	E1	Tunstall Terrace West	B3
St Lucia Close	D2	Tunstall Vale	B1-C2
St Marks Terrace	A4	Vane Terrace	F2
St Mary's Way	B5-C5	Villette Path	D1-E1
St Michael's Way	B3-B4	Villette Road	D1-E1
St Peter's View	C7-D7	Villiers Street	D4-D5
St Peter's Way	D6-D7	Vine Place	B3-B4
St Thomas Street	C4-D4	Violet Street	A5
St Vincent Street	D2	Wallace Street	B8
Salem Hill	D2	Walton Lane	D5-E5
Salem Road	D3	Warren Street	E6
Salem Street	D2-D3	Warwick Street	B8-C8
Salem Street South	D2	Wayman Street	B8-C7
Salisbury Street	D3	Wayside	A1
Sand Point Road	E7-E8	Wear Street	E4
Sans Street	D4-D5	Wearmouth Street	C2
Selbourne Street	D8	West Lawn	B1-C1
Shakespeare Terrace	A3-B3	West Lawrence Street	D4-E4
Sheepfolds North	B6-C6	West Sunniside	C5-D4
Silksworth Row	A5-B4	West Wear Street	C5-D5
Silver Street	E5-E6	Westbourne Road	A3-A4
Southwick Road	A8-C7	Western Hill	A3
Spring Garden Close	D4	Wharncliffe Road	A4
Stadium Way	B7-C7	Whickham Street	D7-D8
Stansfield Street	D7-D8	Whitehouse Road	D3-E3
Stobart Street	B6-B7	Wilson Street North	B6
Stockton Road	B3-C2	Woodbine Street	E4-F4
Summerhill	A3	Worcester Terrace	B3
Swan Street	A8-B8	Wreath Quay Road	B6-C7
Tavistock Place	D4	Wylam Grove	E3
The Avenue	B2-C2	Zetland Street	D7

222

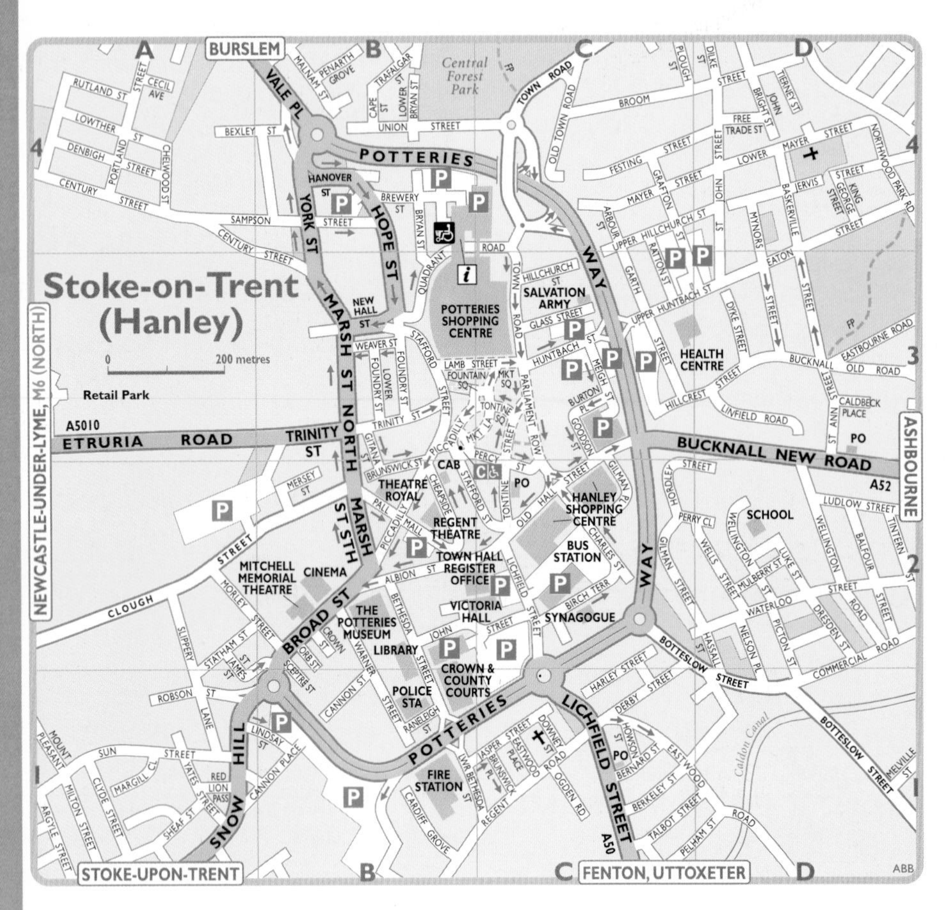

Stoke-on-Trent (Hanley)

Stoke-on-Trent (Hanley) is found on atlas page **72**, grid reference **8847**

Albion Street	B2	Market Lane	B3-C3
Baskerville Street	D3-D4	Market Square	C3
Bethesda Street	B1-B2	Marsh Street North	B2-B3
Birch Terrace	C2	Marsh Street South	B2
Botteslow Street	C2-D1	Mayer Street	C4-D4
Brewery Street	B4	Meigh Street	C3
Broad Street	B2	Mersey Street	B2
Broom Street	C4-D4	Morley Street	A2-B2
Brunswick Street	B2	New Hall Street	B3
Bryan Street	B3-B4	Northwood Park Road	D4
Bucknall New Road	C3-D3-D2	Old Hall Street	C2-C3
Bucknall Old Road	D3	Old Town Road	C4
Burton Place	C3	Pall Mall	B2
Cannon Place	A1-B1	Parliament Row	C3
Cannon Street	B1	Percy Street	C2-C3
Century Street	A4-B3	Piccadilly	B2-B3
Charles Street	C2	Portland Street	A4
Cheapside	B2	Potteries Way	B1-C2-C4-B4
Clough Street	A2-B2	Quadrant Road	B3-B4-C4
Clyde Street	A1	Regent Road	B1-C1
Commercial Road	D1-D2	Sampson Street	A4-B4
Derby Street	C1-C2	Sheaf Street	A1
Dresden Street	D2	Slippery Lane	A1-A2
Eastwood Road	C1-D1	Snow Hill	A1
Eaton Street	D3-D4	St Ann Street	D3
Etruria Road	A3	St John Street	D3-D4
Festing Street	C4-D4	Stafford Street	B3-B2-C2
Foundry Street	B3	Sun Street	A1
Fountain Square	B3-C3	Talbot Street	C1-D1
Garth Street	C3	Tontine Square	C3
Gilman Street	C2-D2	Tontine Street	C2-C3
Glass Street	C3	Town Road	C3-C4
Goodson Street	C3	Trafalgar Street	B4
Harley Street	C1-C2	Trinity Street	B3
Hillcrest Street	C3-D3	Union Street	B4-C4
Hope Street	B3-B4	Upper Hillchurch Street	C3-D4
Huntbach Street	C3	Upper Huntbach Street	C3-D3
Jasper Street	B1-C1	Vale Place	B4
John Street	B2-C2	Warner Street	B1-B2
Lamb Street	B3-C3	Waterloo Street	D2
Lichfield Street	C1-C2	Wellington Road	D2
Lower Bethesda Street	B1-C1	Wells Street	D2
Lower Foundry Street	B3	Yates Street	A1
Lower Mayer Street	D4	York Street	B3-B4
Lowther Street	A4		
Ludlow Street	D2		

Stratford-upon-Avon

Stratford-upon-Avon is found on atlas page **48**, grid reference **2055**

Albany Road	A3	Shreeves Walk	C2-C3
Alcester Road	A3-A4	Southern Lane	B1-B2-C2
Arden Street	A3-A4-B4	Station Road	A4
Avonbank Paddock	B1	Swans Nest Lane	D1-D2
Banbury Road	D1-D2	Tiddington Road	D2
Birmingham Road	B4	Tyler Street	C4
Bridge Foot	C3-D2	Union Street	C3
Bridge Street	C3	Warwick Crescent	D4
Bridge Way	C3-D3	Warwick Way	D4
Broad Street	A2	Waterside	C2
Broad Walk	A2	Wellesbourne Grove	A3
Bull Street	A1-A2	West Street	A1-A2
Chapel Lane	B2-C2	Windsor Street	B4
Chapel Street	B2	Wood Street	B3
Chestnut Walk	A2		
Church Street	A2-B2		
Clopton Bridge	D2		
College Lane	A1		
College Street	A1-B1		
Ely Street	A3-B3-B2		
Evesham Place	A2		
Great William Street	B4-C4		
Greenhill Street	A3-B3		
Grove Road	A2-A3		
Guild Street	B4-C3		
Henley Street	B3-B4		
High Street	B3		
Holtom Street	A1		
John Street	C3-C4		
Lock Close	C4		
Mansell Street	A4-B4		
Meer Street	B3		
Mulberry Street	B4-C4		
Narrow Lane	A1		
New Broad Street	A1		
Old Town	A2-B1		
Paddock Place	A1		
Payton Street	C3-C4		
Rother Road	A2-A3-B3		
St Gregory's Road	C4-D4		
Sanctus Street	A1		
Scholars Lane	A2-B2		
Shakespeare Street	B4		
Sheep Street	B2-C2		
Shipston Road	D1		

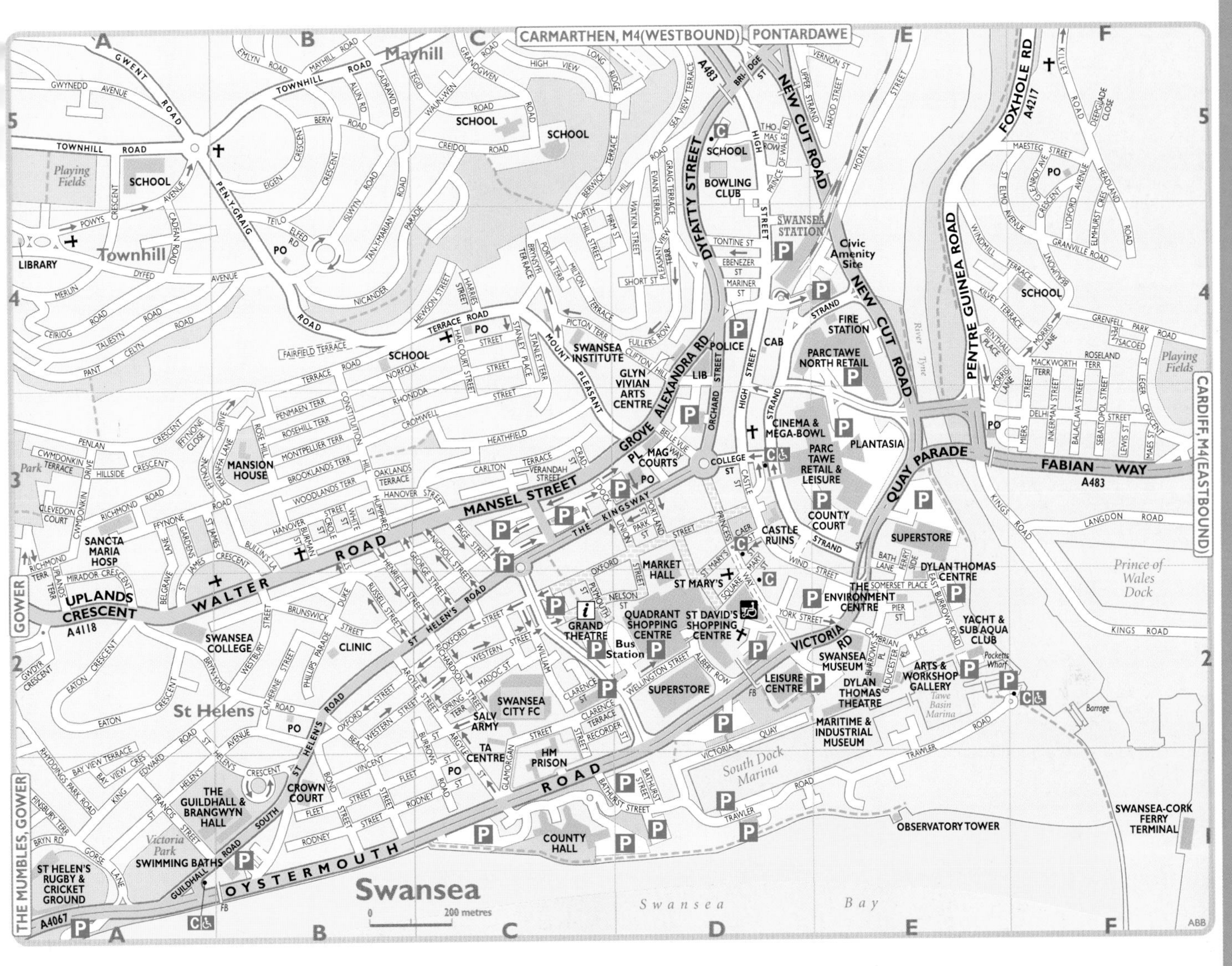

Swansea

Swansea is found on atlas page **32**,
grid reference **6592**

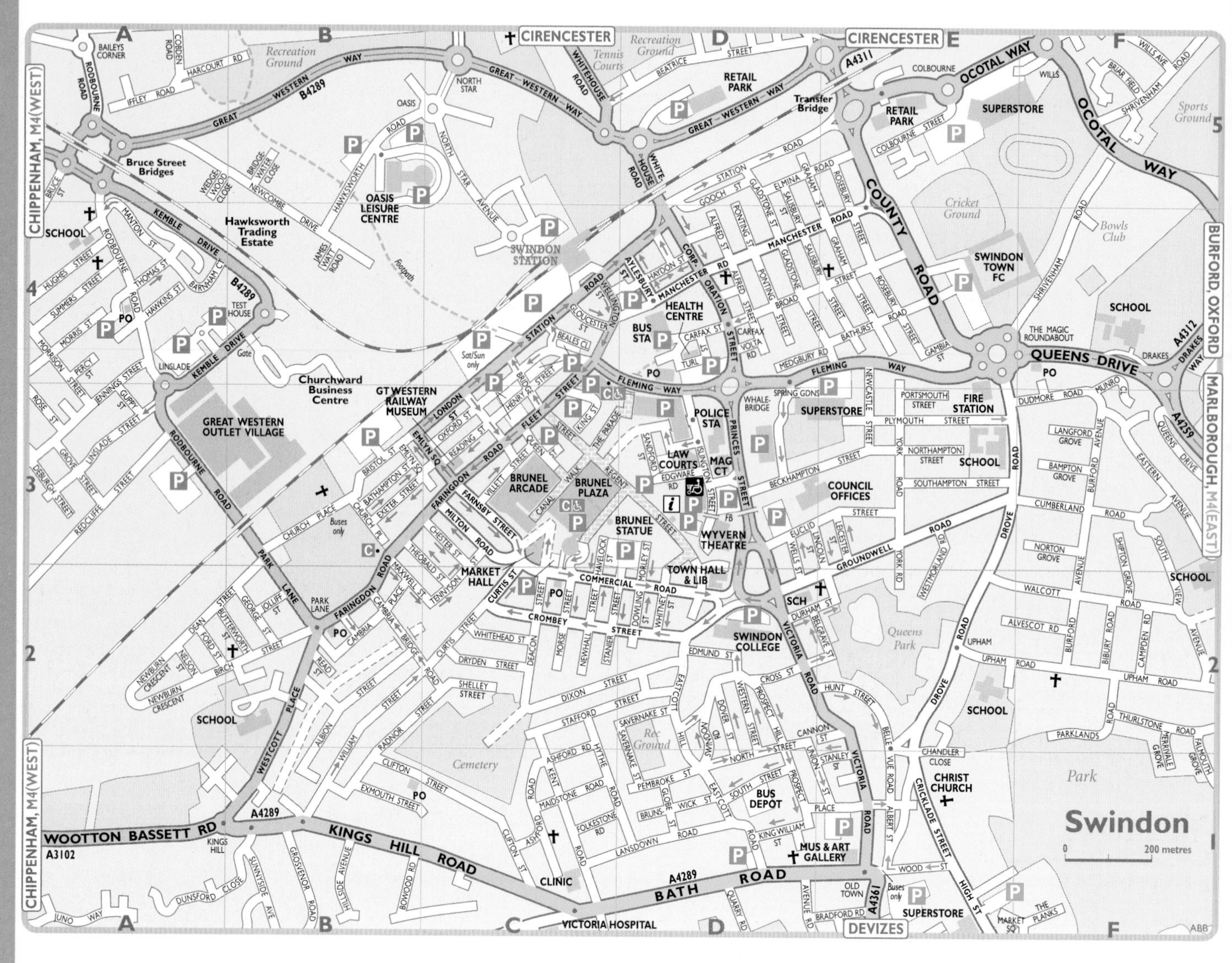

Swindon

Swindon is found on atlas page **36**,
grid reference **1484**

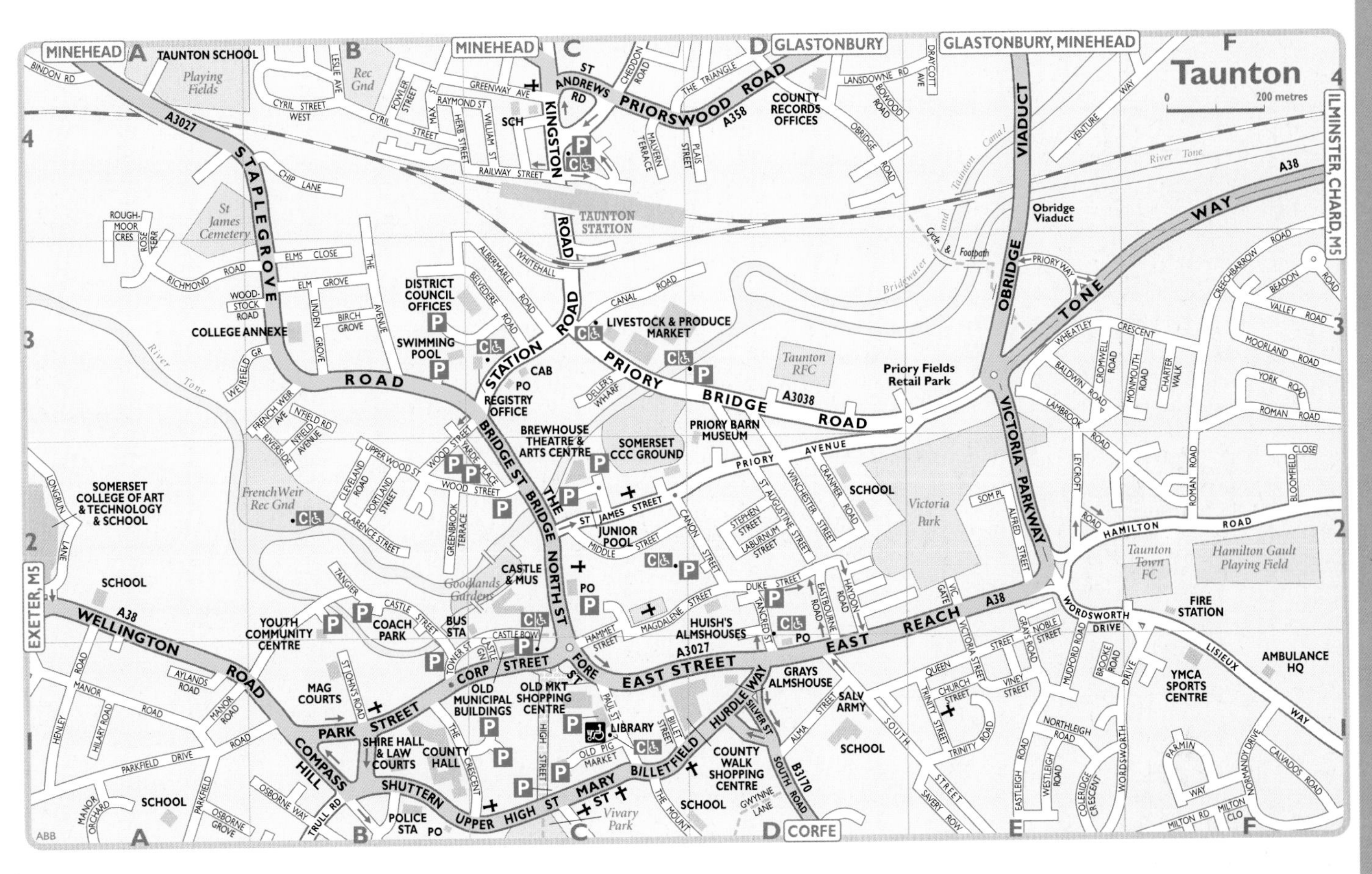

Taunton

Taunton is found on atlas page **20**,
grid reference **2224**

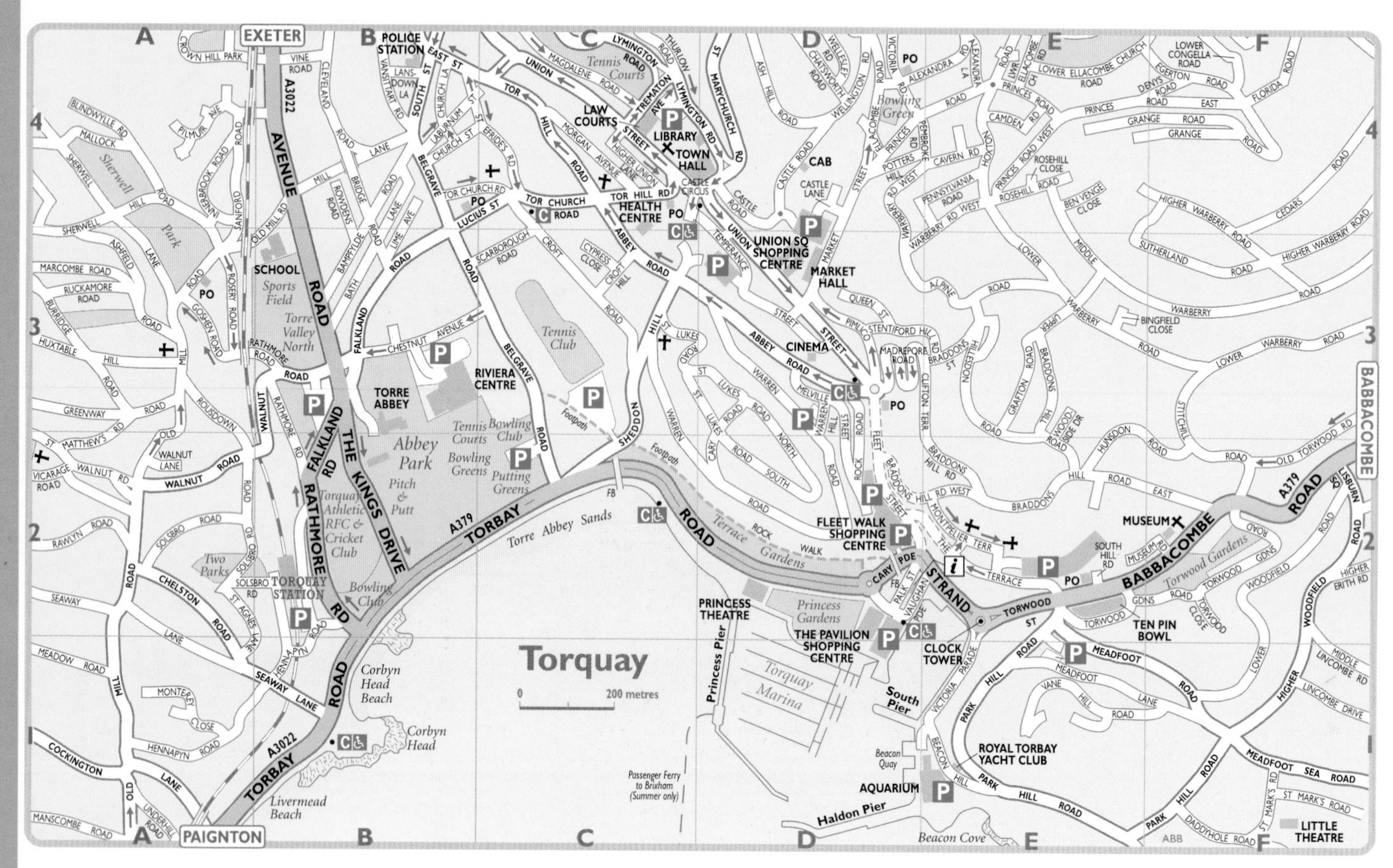

Torquay

Torquay is found on atlas page **7**,
grid reference **9164**

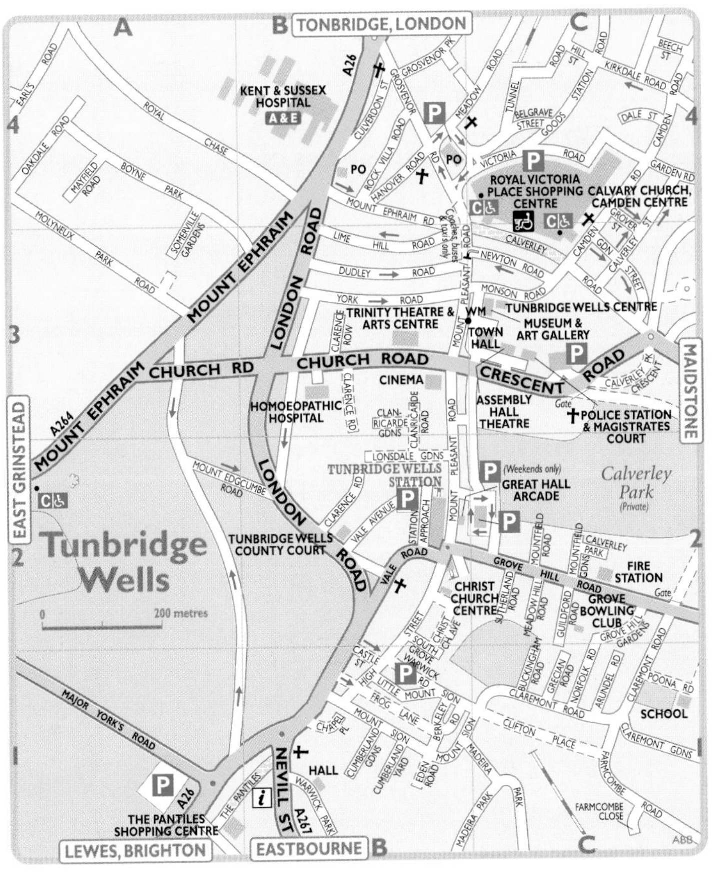

Tunbridge Wells

Tunbridge Wells is found on atlas page 16,
grid reference 5839

Arundel Road	C1	Hill Street	C4
Beech Street	C4	Kirkdale Road	C4
Belgrave Street	C4	Lansdowne Square	C3
Berkeley Road	B1	Lime Hill Road	B3
Boyne Park	A4-B3	Little Mount Sion	B1
Buckingham Road	C1	London Road	B2-B3-B4
Calverley Street	C3-C4	Lonsdale Gardens	B2
Calverley Park	C2	Madeira Park	B1-C1
Calverley Park Crescent	C3	Major York's Road	A1
Calverley Road	C3	Mayfield Road	A4
Camden Road	C3-C4	Meadow Hill Road	C2
Castle Street	B1	Meadow Road	B4-C4
Chapel Place	B1	Molyneux Park Road	A3-A4
Christ Church Avenue	B2	Monson Road	C3
Church Road	A3-B3	Mount Edgcumbe Road	A2-B2
Clanricarde Gardens	B3	Mount Ephraim	A2-A3-B3-B4
Clanricarde Road	B2-B3	Mount Ephraim Road	B4
Claremont Gardens	C1	Mount Pleasant Road	B2-B3-C3-B4
Claremont Road	C1-C2	Mount Sion	B1-C1
Clarence Road	B2-B3	Mountfield Gardens	C2
Clarence Row	B3	Mountfield Road	C2
Clifton Place	C1	Nevill Street	B1
Crescent Road	B3-C3	Newton Road	C3
Culverden Street	B4	Norfolk Road	C1
Cumberland Gardens	B1	Oakdale Road	A4
Cumberland Yard	B1	Poona Road	C1
Dale Street	C4	Rock Villa Road	B4
Dudley Road	B3	Royal Chase	A4-B4
Earl's Road	A4	Somerville Gardens	A3-A4
Eden Road	B1	South Grove	B1-B2
Farmcombe Close	C1	Station Approach	B2
Farmcombe Road	C1	Sutherland Road	C2
Frog Lane	B1	The Pantiles	A1-B1
Garden Road	C4	Tunnel Road	C4
Garden Street	C3	Vale Avenue	B2
Goods Station Road	C4	Vale Road	B2
Grecian Road	C1	Victoria Road	B4-C4
Grosvenor Park	B4	Warwick Park	B1
Grosvenor Road	B4	Warwick Road	B1
Grove Hill Gardens	C2	York Road	B3
Grove Hill Road	B2-C2		
Grover Street	C3-C4		
Guildford Road	C2		
Hanover Road	B4		
High Street	B1-B2		

Warwick

Warwick is found on atlas page 48,
grid reference 2865

Albert Street	A4	St Nicholas Church Street	B2-C3
Archery Fields	C1	Saltisford	A3-A4
Back Lane	A2	Sharpe Close	B4
Banbury Road	B2-C1	Smith Street	B2-C3
Barrack Street	A3	Spring Pool	A4
Bartlett Close	C3	Station Avenue	C4
Bowling Green Street	A2	Station Road	C4
Bridge Brooke Close	B1-C1	Swan Street	A2
Bridge End	B1-C1	The Butts	A3-B2
Brook Street	A2	The Paddocks	C3
Cape Road	A3-A4	Theatre Street	A3
Castle Close	A1	Victoria Street	A3-A4
Castle Hill	B2	Vine Street	B4
Castle Lane	A2-B2	West Street	A1-A2
Castle Street	A2-B2	Woodcote Road	C4
Cattel Road	A4		
Chapel Street	B3		
Cherry Street	C3-C4		
Church Street	A2		
Coten End	C3		
Coventry Road	C3-C4		
Deerpark Drive	A4		
Edward Street	A3-A4		
Gerrard Street	B2-B3		
Guy Street	C3-C4		
Guys Cliffe Terrace	C4		
High Street	A2		
Jury Street	A2-B2		
Lakin Road	C4		
Market Place	A3		
Market Street	A2		
Mill Street	B2		
Myton Road	C1		
New Street	A2-A3		
Northgate Street	A3		
Old Square	A3		
Packmore Street	B4-C4		
Paradise Street	B4-C4		
Park View	B3		
Parkes Street	A3		
Priory Mews	A3		
Priory Road	A3-C3		
Roe Close	B4		
St John's Court	C3		
St Johns	C3		

227

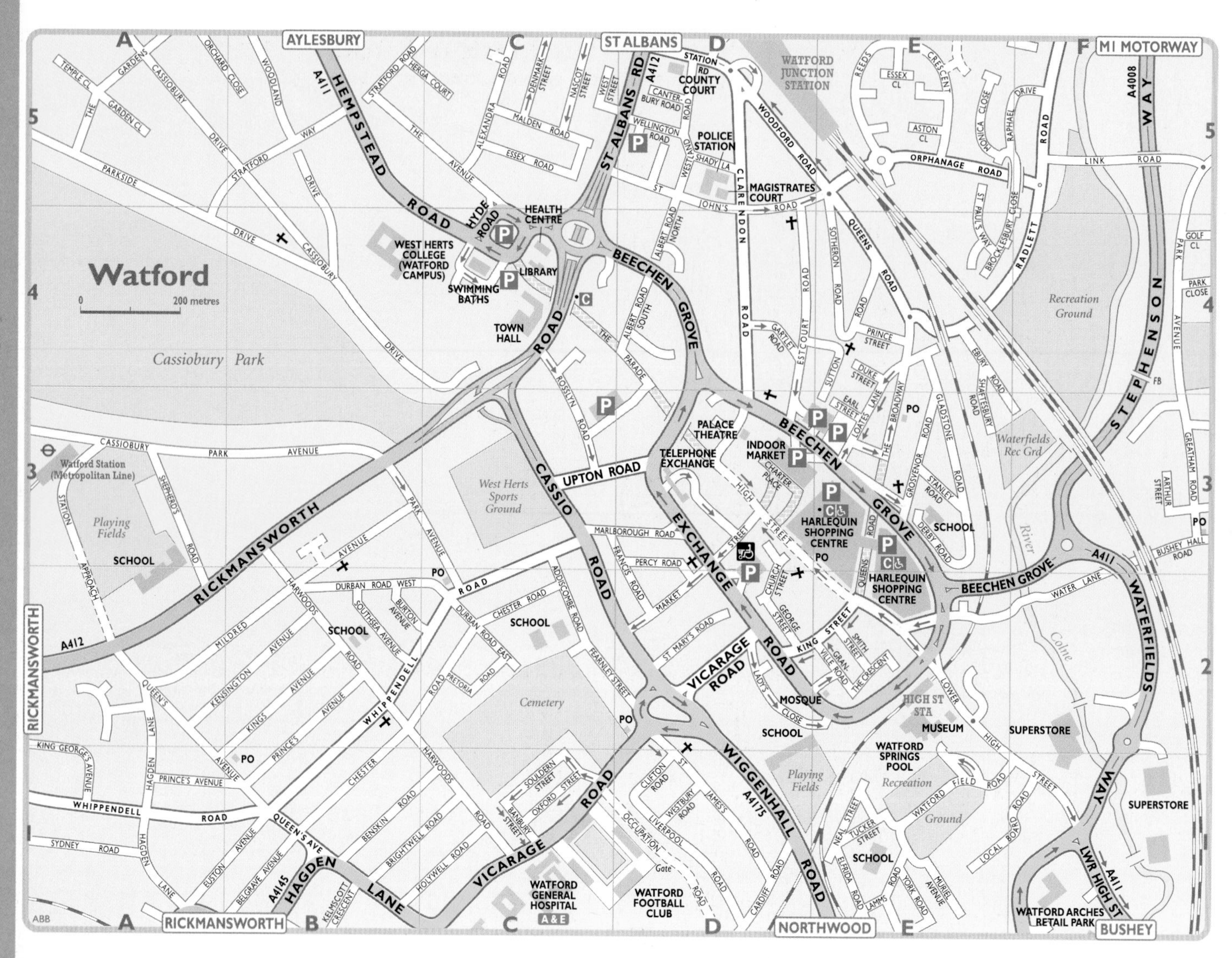

Watford

Watford is found on atlas page **26**,
grid reference 1196

Addiscombe Road	C2-C3	Ebury Road	E4-F3	Lamms Road	E1	Raphael Drive	E5-F5	Tucker Street	E1
Albert Road North	D4-D5	Elfrida Road	E1	Link Road	F5	Reeds Crescent	E5	Upton Road	C3-D3
Albert Road South	D4	Essex Close	E5	Liverpool Road	D1	Rickmansworth Road	A2-B3-C4	Vicarage Road	C1-D1-D2
Alexandra Road	C5	Essex Road	C5	Loates Lane	E3-E4	Rosslyn Road	C3-C4	Water Lane	F2-F3
Arthur Street	F3	Estcourt Road	D3-D4	Local Board Road	E1-F1	Shady Lane	D5	Waterfields Way	F1-F2-F3
Aston Close	E5	Euston Avenue	A1-B1	Lower High Street	E2-F1	Shaftesbury Road	E3-E4	Watford Field Road	E1-F1
Banbury Street	C1	Exchange Road	D3-D2	Malden Road	C5	Shepherd's Road	A2-A3	Wellington Road	D5
Beechen Grove	C4-D3-E2-F3	Fearnley Street	C2-D2	Market Street	D2-D3	Smith Street	E2	West Street	C5
Belgrave Avenue	B1	Francis Road	C3-D3-D2	Marlborough Road	C3-D3	Sotheron Road	E4-E5	Westbury Road	D1
Benskin Road	B1-C1	Garden Close	A5	Mildred Avenue	A2-B2-B3	Souldern Street	C1	Westland Road	D5
Brightwell Road	B1-C1	Gartlet Road	D4	Monica Close	E5	Southsea Avenue	B2	Whippendell Road	A1-B1-B2-C3
Brocklesbury Close	E4-E5-F5	George Street	D2	Muriel Avenue	E1	St Albans Road	C5-D5	Wiggenhall Road	D2-D1-E1
Burton Avenue	B2-C2	Gladstone Road	E3-E4	Nascot Street	C5	St James's Road	D1-D2	Woodford Road	D5-E5
Bushey Hall Road	F3	Golf Close	F4	Neal Street	E1	St John's Road	C5-D5	Woodland Drive	B4-B5
Canterbury Road	D5	Greatham Road	F3	Occupation Road	C1-D1	St Mary's Road	D2	York Road	E1
Cardiff Road	D1	Grosvenor Road	E3	Orchard Close	A5-B5	St Paul's Way	E4-E5		
Cassio Road	C3-C2-D2	Hagden Lane	A2-A1-B1	Orphanage Road	E5-F5	Stanley Road	E3		
Cassiobury Drive	A5-B5-B4-C4	Harwoods Road	B3-B2-C1	Oxford Street	C1	Station Approach	A2-A3		
Cassiobury Park Avenue	A3-B3	Hempstead Road	B5-C4	Park Avenue	B3-C3-C2	Station Road	D5		
Charter Place	D3	Herga Court	B5-C5	Park Avenue	F4-F5	Stephenson Way	F3-F4-F5		
Chester Road	B1-B2-C2	High Street	D3	Park Close	F4	Stratford Road	B5		
Church Street	D2-D3	Holywell Road	B1-C1	Parkside Drive	A5-A4-B4	Stratford Way	A4-A5-B5		
Clarendon Road	D3-D4-D5	Hyde Road	C4	Percy Road	D2-D3	Sutton Road	E3-E4		
Clifton Road	D1	Kelmscott Crescent	B1	Pretoria Road	C2	Sydney Road	A1		
Denmark Street	C5	Kensington Avenue	A2-B2	Prince Street	E4	Temple Close	A5		
Derby Road	E3	King George's Avenue	A1-A2	Prince's Avenue	A1-B1-B2	The Avenue	B5-C5		
Duke Street	E4	King Street	D2-E2	Queen's Avenue	A2-A1-B1	The Broadway	E3-E4		
Durban Road East	C2	Kings Avenue	A1-B1-B2	Queens Road	E2-E3	The Crescent	E2		
Durban Road West	B2-C2	Lady's Close	D2-E2	Queens Road	E4-E5	The Gardens	A5		
Earl Street	E3			Radlett Road	E4-F4-F5	The Parade	C4-D4		

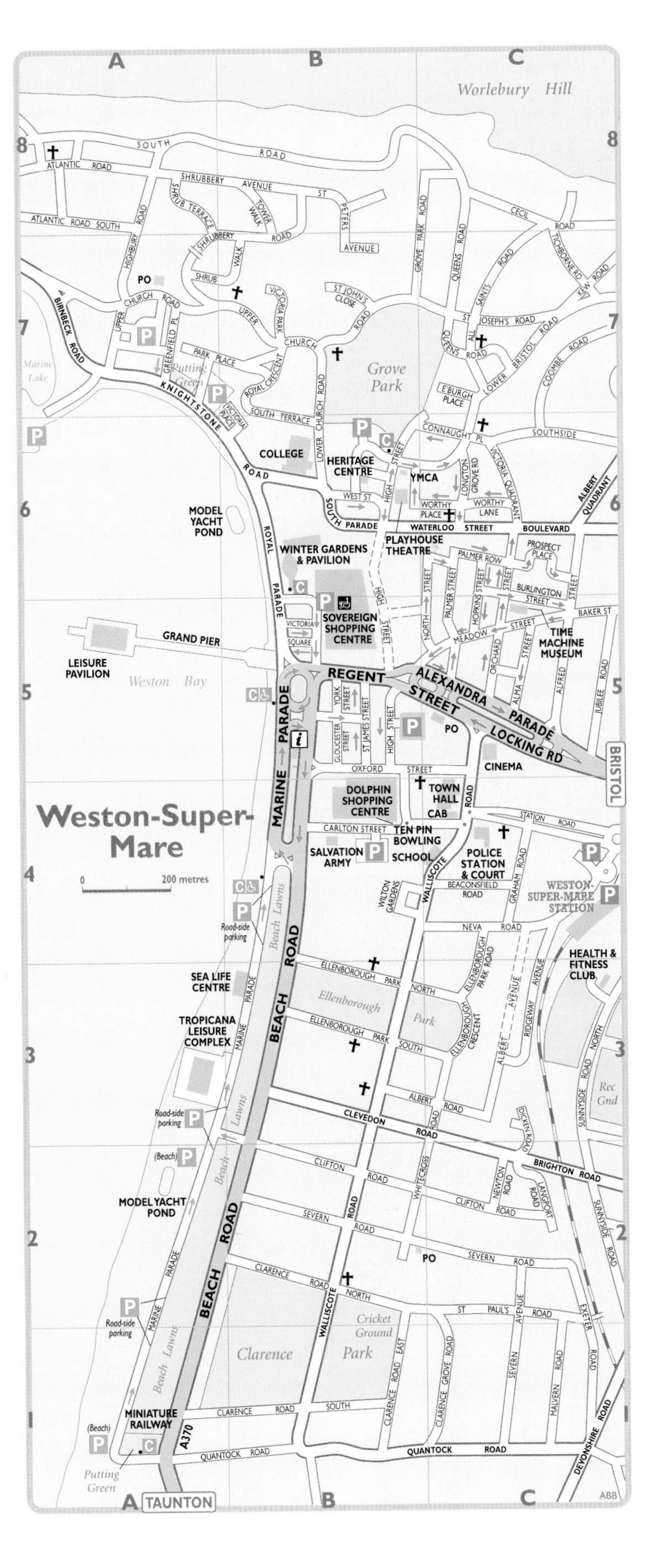

Weston-Super-Mare

Weston-Super-Mare is found on atlas page **21**, grid reference **3260**

229

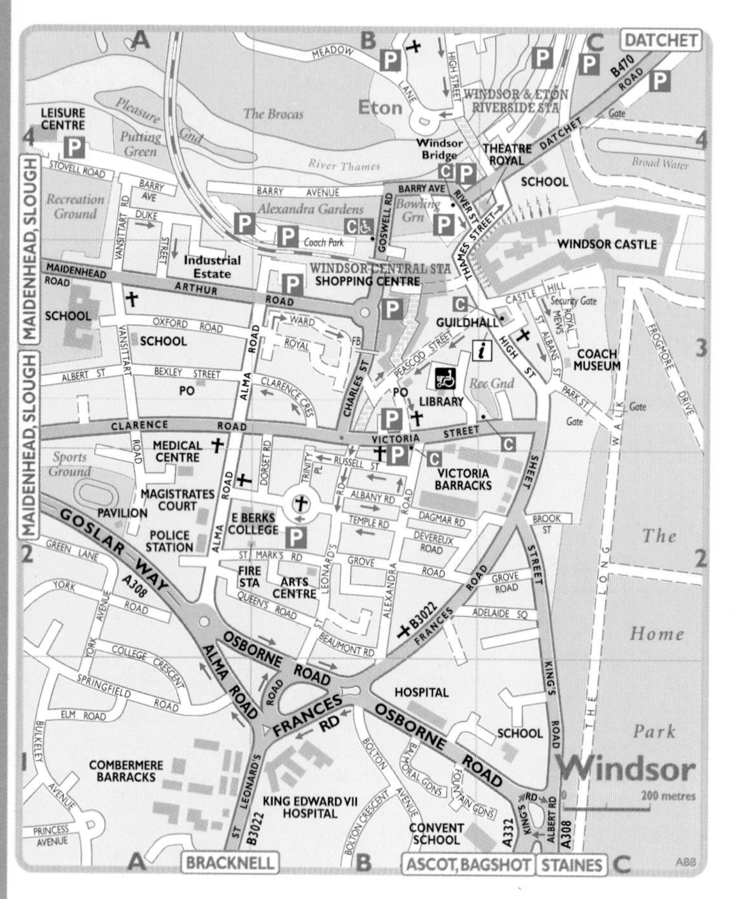

Windsor

Windsor is found on atlas page **26**, grid reference **9576**

Adelaide Square	B2-C2	Royal Mews	C3
Albany Road	B2	Russell Street	B2
Albert Road	C1	St Albans Street	C3
Albert Street	A3	St Leonard's Road	A1-B1-B2-B3
Alexandra Road	B1-B2-B3	St Mark's Road	A2-B2
Alma Road	B1-B2-B3	Sheet Street	C2-C3
Arthur Road	A3-B3	Springfield Road	A1-A2
Balmoral Gardens	B1	Stovell Road	A4
Barry Avenue	A4-B4	Temple Road	B2
Beaumont Road	B2	Thames Street	B3-C4
Bexley Street	A3	The Long Walk	C1-C2-C3
Bolton Avenue	B1	Trinity Place	B2-B3
Bolton Crescent	B1	Vansittart Road	A2-A3-A4
Brook Street	C2	Victoria Street	B3-C3
Bulkeley Avenue	A1	Ward Royal	B3
Castle Hill	C3	York Avenue	A1-A2
Charles Street	B3	York Road	A2
Clarence Crescent	B3		
Clarence Road	A3-B3		
College Crescent	A1-A2		
Dagmar Road	B2		
Datchet Road	C4		
Devereux Road	B2		
Dorset Road	B2-B3		
Duke Street	A3-A4		
Elm Road	A1		
Fountain Gardens	B1-C1		
Frances Road	B1-B2-C2		
Frogmore Drive	C3		
Goslar Way	A2		
Goswell Road	B3-B4		
Green Lane	A2		
Grove Road	B2-C2		
High Street (Eton)	B4		
High Street (Windsor)	C3		
King's Road	C1-C2		
Maidenhead Road	A3		
Meadow Lane	A4-B4		
Osborne Road	A2-B2-B1-C1		
Oxford Road	A3		
Park Street	C3		
Peascod Street	B3		
Princess Avenue	A1		
Queen's Road	A2-B2		
River Street	B4		

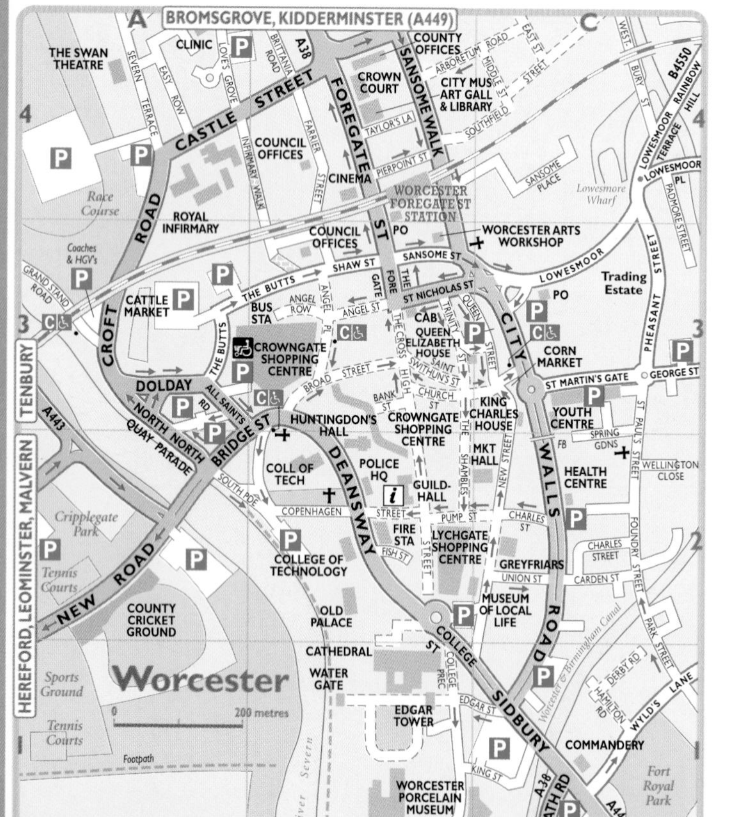

Worcester

Worcester is found on atlas page **47**, grid reference **8554**

All Saints Road	A3	Pheasant Street	C3-C4
Angel Place	B3	Pierpoint Street	B4
Angel Row	B3	Pump Street	B2-C2
Angel Street	B3	Queen Street	B3-C3
Arboretum Road	B4-C4	St Martin's Gate	C3
Bank Street	B3	St Nicholas Street	B3
Bath Road	C1	St Paul's Street	C2-C3
Bridge Street	A2-B3	St Swithun's Street	B3
Brittania Road	B4	Sansome Place	B4-C4
Broad Street	B3	Sansome Street	B3
Castle Street	A4-B4	Sansome Walk	B4
Charles Street	C2	Severn Street	B1
Church Street	B3	Severn Terrace	A4
City Walls Road	C1-C2-C3	Shaw Street	B3
College Precinct	B1	Sidbury	C1
College Street	B1-B2	South Parade	A2-B2
Copenhagen Street	B2	Southfield Street	B4-C4
Croft Road	A3-A4	Spring Gardens	C2-C3
Deansway	B2-B3	Taylor's Lane	B4
Derby Road	C1	The Butts	A3-B3
Dolday	A3	The Cross	B3
East Street	C4	The Shambles	B2-B3
Easy Row	A4	Trinity Street	B3
Edgar Street	B1-C1	Union Street	C2
Farrier Street	B3-B4	Westbury Street	C4
Foregate	B3	Wyld's Lane	C1
Foregate Street	B3-B4		
Foundry Street	C2		
Garden Street	C2		
George Street	C3		
Grand Stand Road	A3		
Hamilton Road	C1		
High Street	B2-B3		
Infirmary Walk	A4-B4-B3		
King Street	B1-C1		
Love's Grove	A4		
Lowesmoor	C3-C4		
Lowesmoor Place	C4		
Lowesmoor Terrace	C4		
Middle Street	C4		
New Road	A2		
New Street	C2-C3		
North Quay	A2-A3		
Padmore Street	C3-C4		
Park Street	C1-C2		

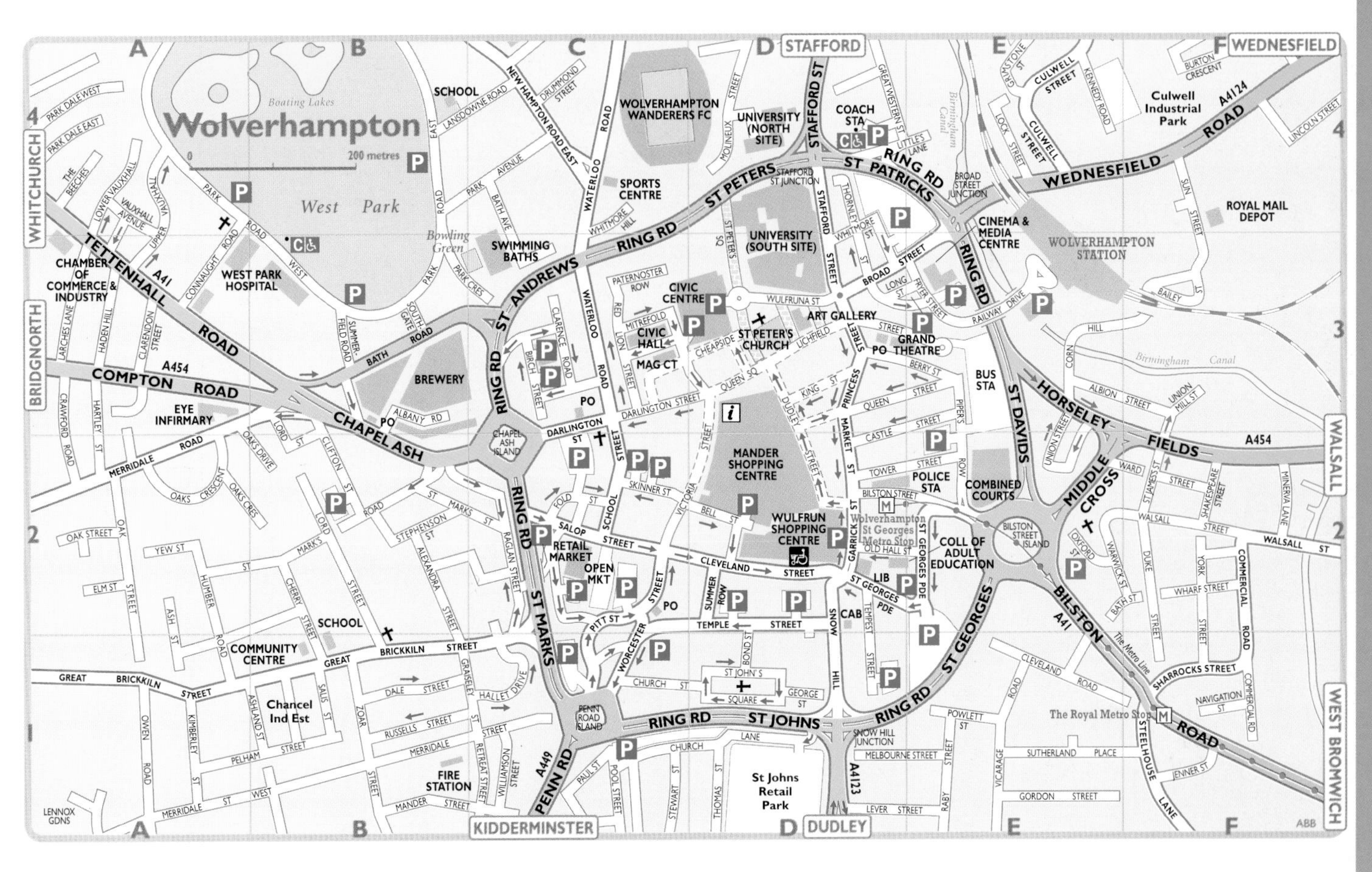

Wolverhampton

Wolverhampton is found on atlas page **60**,
grid reference **9198**

Albany Road	B3	Elm Street	A2	Minerva Lane	F2	Ring Road St Peters	C3-C4-D4	Warwick Street	E2-F2
Albion Street	E3-F3	Fold Street	C2	Mitrefold	C3	Russell Street	B1	Waterloo Road	C3-C4
Alexandra Street	B1-B2	Fryer Street	E3	Molineux Street	D4	St Georges Parade	D2-E2	Wednesfield Road	E4-F4
Ash Street	A1-A2	Garrick Street	D2	Navigation Street	F1	St James's Street	F2	Wharf Street	F2
Ashland Street	B1	George Street	D1	New Hampton Road East	C4	St John's Square	D1	Whitmore Hill	C4
Bailey Street	F3	Gordon Street	E1	Oak Street	A1-A2	St Mark's Road	A2-B2	Whitmore Street	D3-D4
Bath Avenue	C3-C4	Gramstone Street	E4	Oaks Crescent	A2-B2	St Marks Street	B2-C2	Williamson Street	C1
Bath Road	B3-C3	Greasely Street	B1-C1	Oaks Drive	A3-A2-B2	St Peter's Square	D3-D4	Worcester Street	C1-C2
Bath Street	E2-F2	Great Brick Kiln Street	A1-B1-C1	Old Hall Street	D2-E2	Salisbury Street	B1	Wulfruna Street	D3
Bell Street	D2	Great Western Street	D4	Owen Road	A1	Salop Street	C2	Yew Street	A2
Berry Street	D3-E3	Haden Hill	A3	Oxford Street	E2	School Street	C2-C3	York Street	F1-F2
Bilston Road	E2-E1-F1	Hallet Drive	C1	Park Avenue	B4-C4	Sharrocks Street	F1	Zoar Street	B1
Bilston Street	D2-E2	Hartley Street	A2-A3	Park Crescent	B3-C3	Shakespeare Street	F2		
Birch Street	C3	Herbert Street	D4	Park Dale East	A4	Skinner Street	C2		
Bond Street	D1	Horseley Fields	E3-E2-F2	Park Dale West	A4	Snow Hill	D1-D2		
Broad Street	D3-E3	Humber Road	A1-A2	Park Road East	B3-B4	Southgate	B3		
Burton Crescent	F4	Jenner Street	F1	Park Road West	B3-B4-A4	Stafford Street	D3-D4		
Castle Street	D2-D3-C3	Kennedy Road	E4	Paternoster Row	C3	Steelhouse Lane	F1		
Chapel Ash	B3-B2	Kimberley Street	A1	Paul Street	C1	Stephenson Street	B2		
Cheapside	D3	King Street	D3	Pelham Street	A1-B1	Stewart Street	C1		
Cherry Street	B1-B2	Laburnum Street	A1-B2	Penn Road	C1	Summer Row	D2		
Church Lane	C1-D1	Lansdowne Road	B4-C4	Piper's Row	E2-E3	Summerfield Road	B3		
Church Street	C1-D1	Larches Lane	A3	Pitt Street	C2	Sun Street	F3-F4		
Clarence Road	C3	Lennox Gardens	A1	Pool Street	C1	Sutherland Place	E1-F1		
Clarendon Street	A3	Lever Street	D1-E1	Powlett Street	E1	Tempest Street	D1-D2		
Cleveland Road	E1-F1	Lichfield Street	D3-E3	Princess Street	D3	Temple Street	D1-D2-C1-C2		
Cleveland Street	C2-D2	Lincoln Street	F4	Queen Street	D3-E3	Tettenhall Road	A4-A3-B3		
Clifton Street	B2-B3	Little's Lane	D4-E4	Queen Square	D3	The Beeches	A4		
Commercial Road	F1-F2	Lock Street	E4	Raby Street	E1	Thomas Street	D1		
Compton Road	A3-B3	Long Street	D3-E3	Raglan Street	C2	Thornley Street	D3-D4		
Connaught Road	A3-A4	Lord Street	B1-B2-B3	Railway Drive	E3	Tower Street	D2-E2		
Corn Hill	E3-F3	Lower Vauxhall	A4	Red Lion Street	C3	Union Mill Street	F3		
Crawford Road	A2-A3	Mander Street	B1-C1	Retreat Street	C1	Union Street	E2-E3		
Culwell Street	E4	Market Street	D2-D3	Ring Road St Andrews	C3	Upper Vauxhall Avenue	A3-A4		
Dale Street	B1	Melbourne Street	D1-E1	Ring Road St Davids	E2-E3	Vauxhall Avenue	A4		
Darlington Square	C2-C3-D3	Merridale Road	A2-A3-B3	Ring Road St Georges	D1-E1-E2	Vicarage Road	E1		
Drummond Street	C4	Merridale Street	B1-C1	Ring Road St Johns	C1-D1	Victoria Street	C2-D2-D3		
Dudley Street	D2-D3	Merridale Street West	A1-B1	Ring Road St Marks	C1-C2	Walsall Street	E2-F2		
Duke Street	F1-F2	Middle Cross	E2	Ring Road St Patricks	D4-E4	Ward Street	E2-F2		

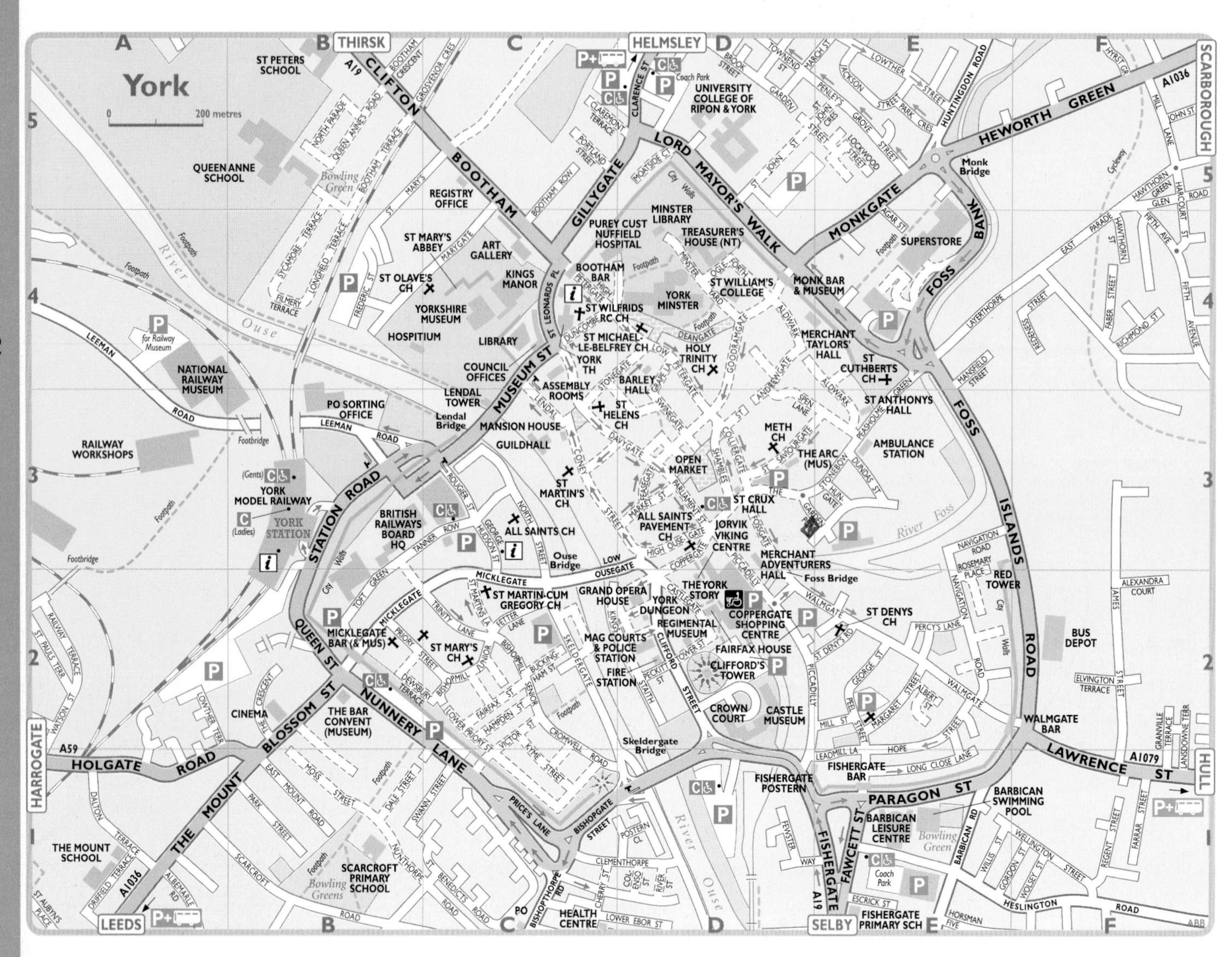

York

York is found on atlas page **83**,
grid reference **6051**

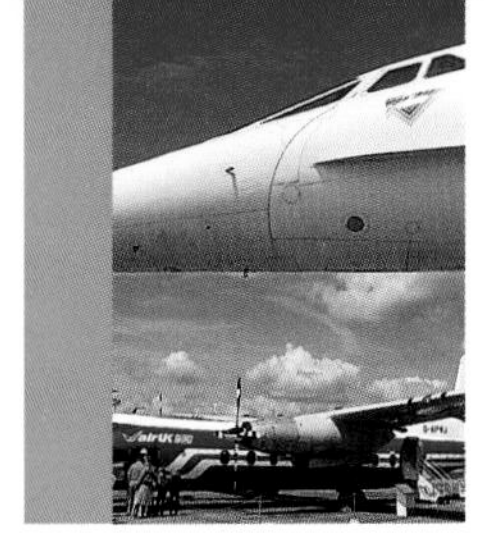

ports and airports

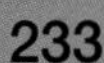

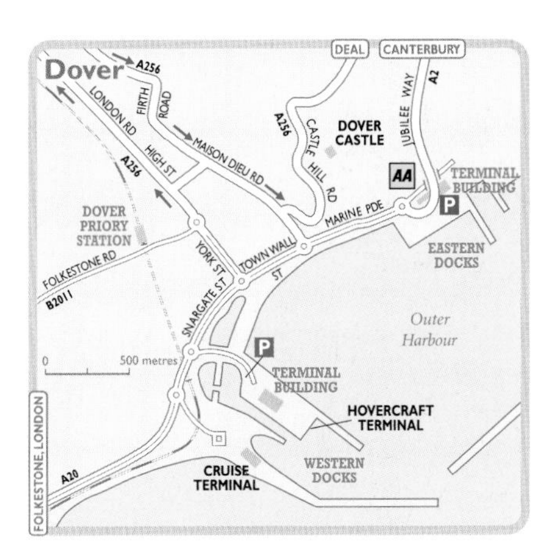

Pay-on-return parking is available at the Dover Eastern Docks and pay-and-display at the Hovercraft Terminal.
For further information tel: 01304 241427
Other long-stay parking facilities are available with a collection and delivery service.
For details tel: 01304 201227

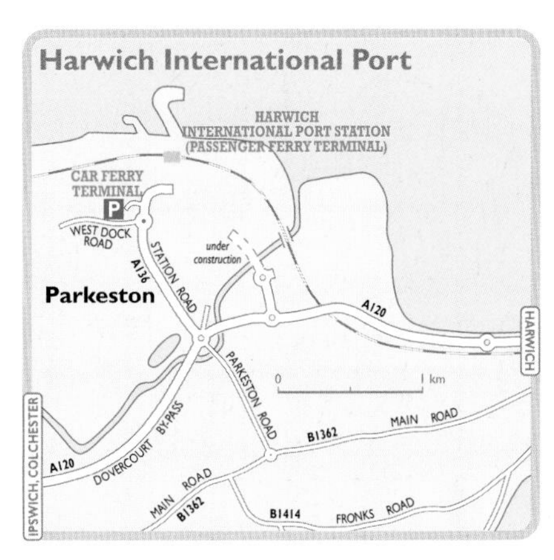

Open-air parking is available at the terminal.
For charge details tel: 01255 242000
Further parking is available 5 miles from Harwich International Port with a collection and delivery service.
For charge details tel: 01255 870217

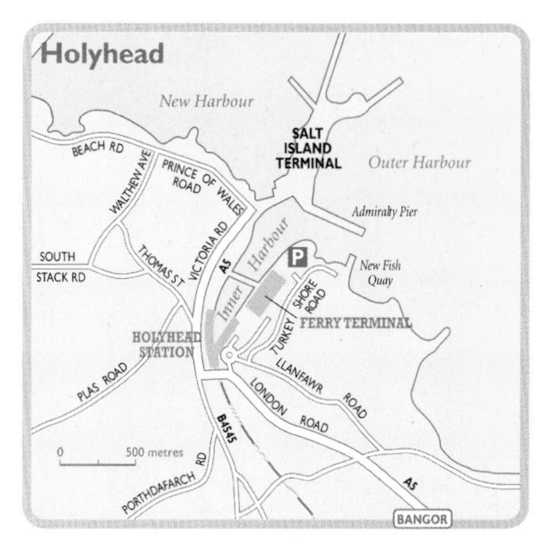

Open-air pay-and-display parking is available close to the Ferry Terminal.
For charge details tel: 01407 762304 or 606732

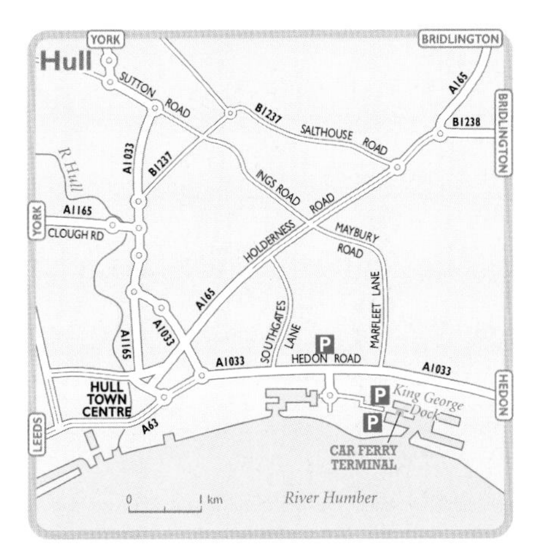

Free open-air parking is available at King George Dock (left at owners' risk).
Tel: 01482 795141
Undercover parking is also available.
For charge details tel: 01482 781021

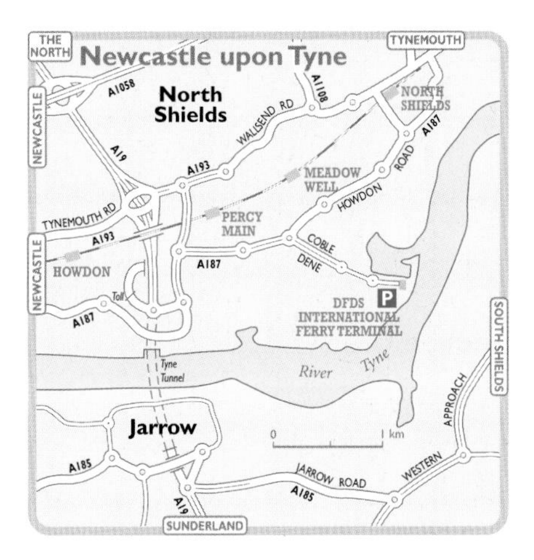

Open-air secure parking is available at the DFDS International Ferry Terminal, Royal Quays.
For charge details tel: 0191 296 0202

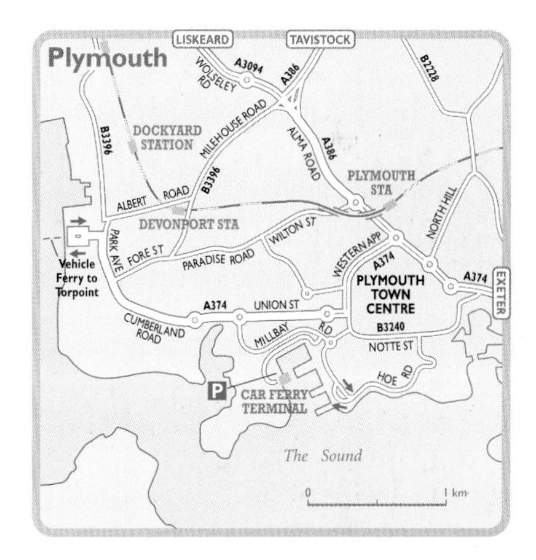

Free open-air parking is available outside the terminal building.
Tel: 0990 360360

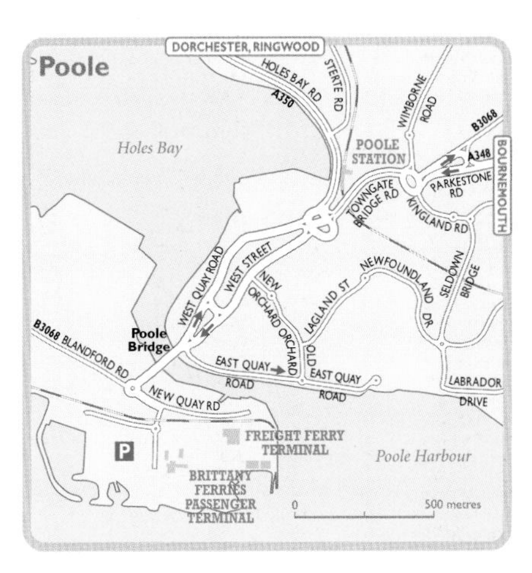

Open-air parking for 600 vehicles is available adjacent to the Ferry Terminal.
For charge details tel: 01202 440220

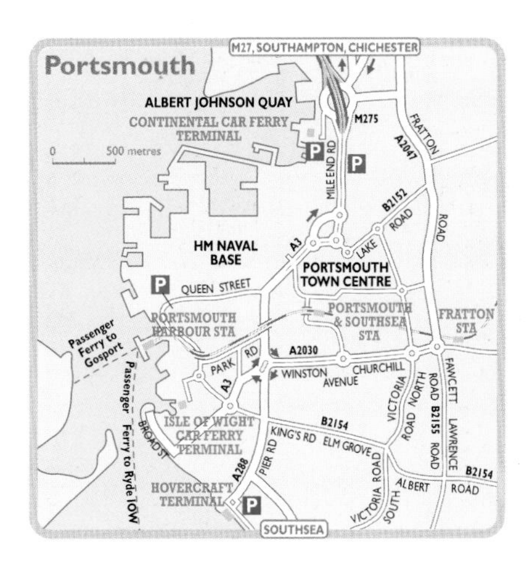

Secure parking facilities are available at the Continental Car Ferry Terminal and long-stay parking off Mile End Rd.
For charge details tel: 023 9275 1261
Pay-and-display parking is available opposite the Hovercraft Terminal.
Multi-storey parking is available close to the Isle of Wight Passenger Ferry Terminal.
For charge details tel: 023 9282 3153

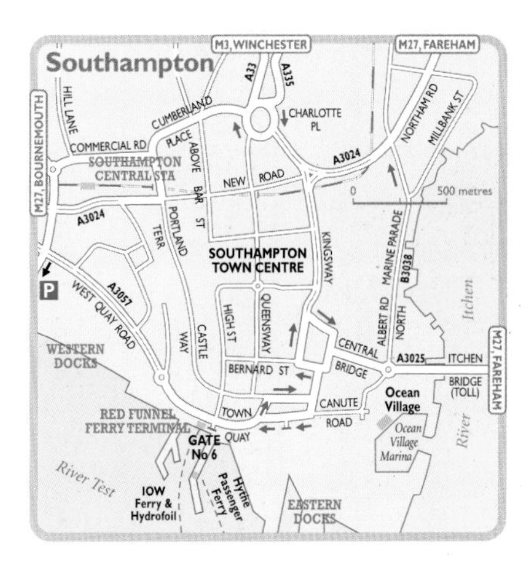

Covered or fenced compound parking for 2,000 vehicles is available within the Western Docks with a collection and delivery service.
For charge details tel: 023 8022 8001/2/3

major airports

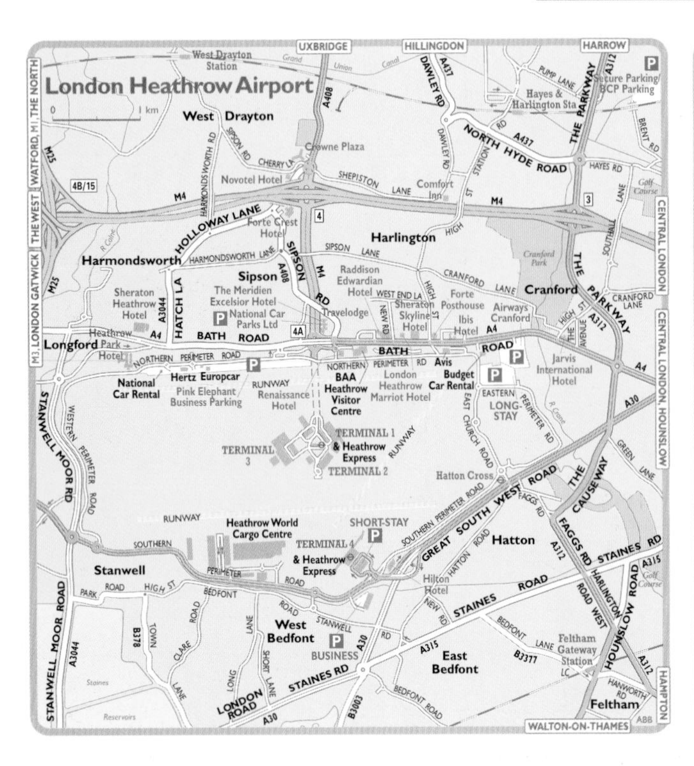

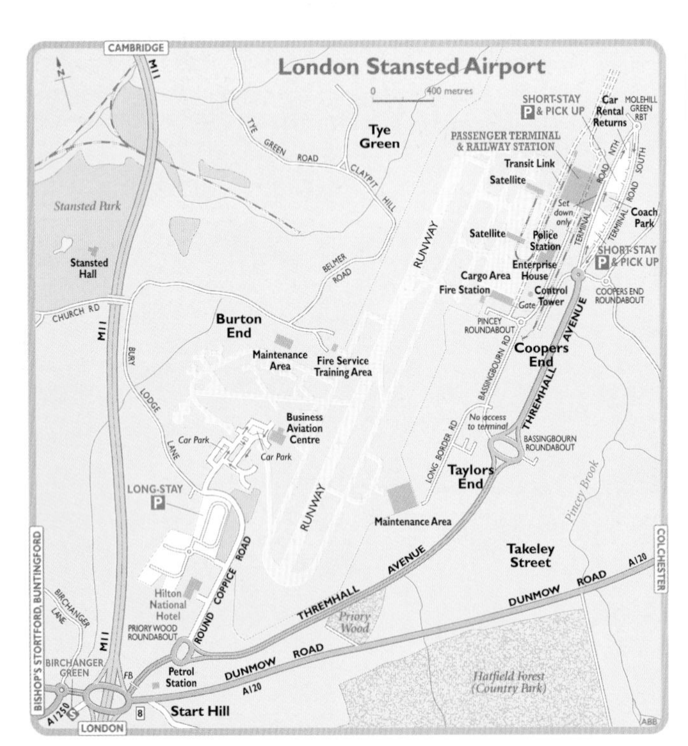

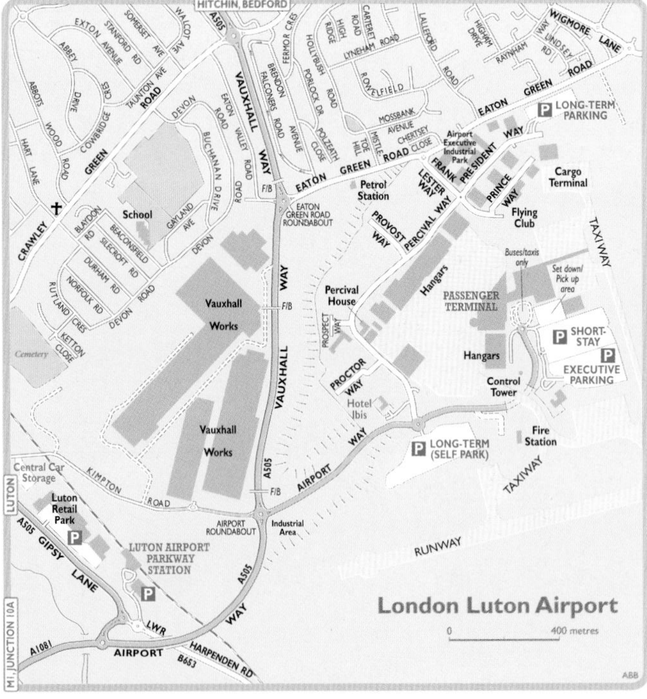

London Heathrow Airport – 16 miles west of London

Telephone: 020 8759 4321 or visit www.baa.co.uk
Parking: short-stay, long-stay and business parking is available.
For charge details tel: 0345 405000
Public Transport: coach, bus, rail and London Underground.
There are several 4-star and 3-star hotels within easy reach of the airport.
Car hire facilities are available.

London Gatwick Airport – 35 miles south of London

Telephone: 01293 535353 or visit www.baa.co.uk
Parking: short and long-stay parking is available at both the North and South terminals.
For charge details tel: 0345 405000
Public Transport: coach, bus and rail.
There are several 4-star and 3-star hotels within easy reach of the airport.
Car hire facilities are available.

London Stansted Airport – 36 miles north-east of London

Telephone: 01279 680500 or visit www.baa.co.uk
Parking: short and long-stay open-air parking is available.
For charge details tel: 01279 681192
Public Transport: coach, bus and direct rail link to London on the 'Stansted Skytrain'.
There is one 3-star hotel within easy reach of the airport.
Car hire facilities are available.

London Luton Airport – 33 miles north of London

Telephone: 01582 405100 or visit www.london-luton.com
Parking: short and long-stay open-air parking is available.
For charge details tel: 01582 395249
Public Transport: coach, bus and rail.
There is one 2-star hotel at the airport and two 3-star hotels within easy reach of the airport.
Car hire facilities are available.

major airports

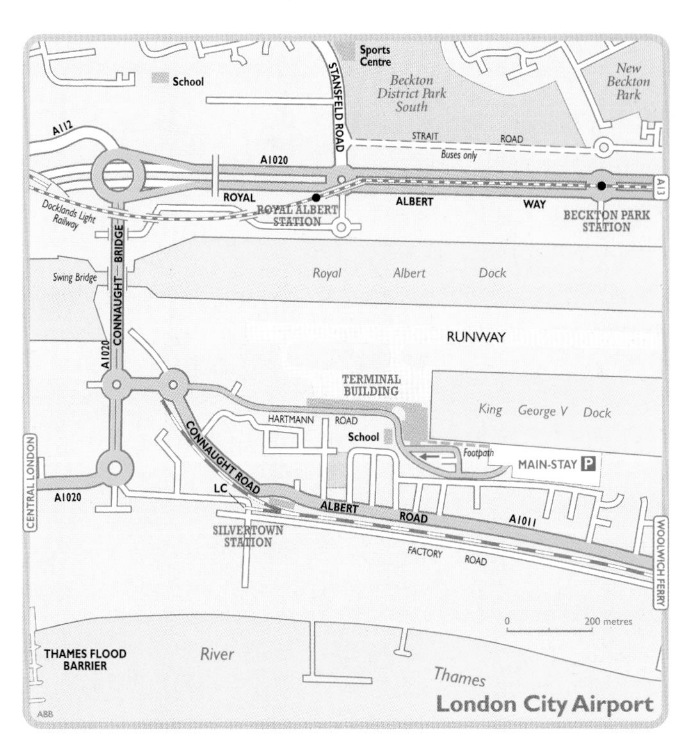

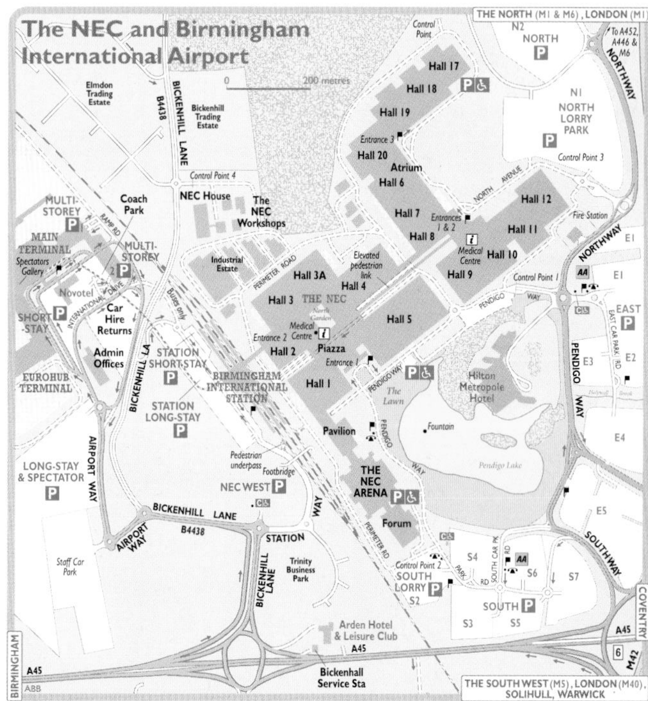

London City Airport – 7 miles east of London

Telephone: 020 7646 0088 or visit www.londoncityairport.com
Parking: open-air parking is available.
For charge details tel: 020 7646 0088
Public Transport: shuttle-bus service into London (Liverpool Street). Easy access to the rail network and the London Underground.
There are 5-star, 4-star and 3-star hotels within easy reach of the airport.
Car hire facilities are available.

Birmingham International Airport – 8 miles east of Birmingham

Telephone: 0121 767 5511 (Main Terminal), 0121 767 7502 (Eurohub Terminal) or visit www.bhx.co.uk
Parking: short and long-stay parking is available. For charge details tel: 0121 767 7861
Public Transport: shuttle-bus service to Birmingham International railway station and the NEC.
There is one 3-star hotel adjacent to the airport and several 4 and 3-star hotels within easy reach of the airport. Car hire facilities are available.

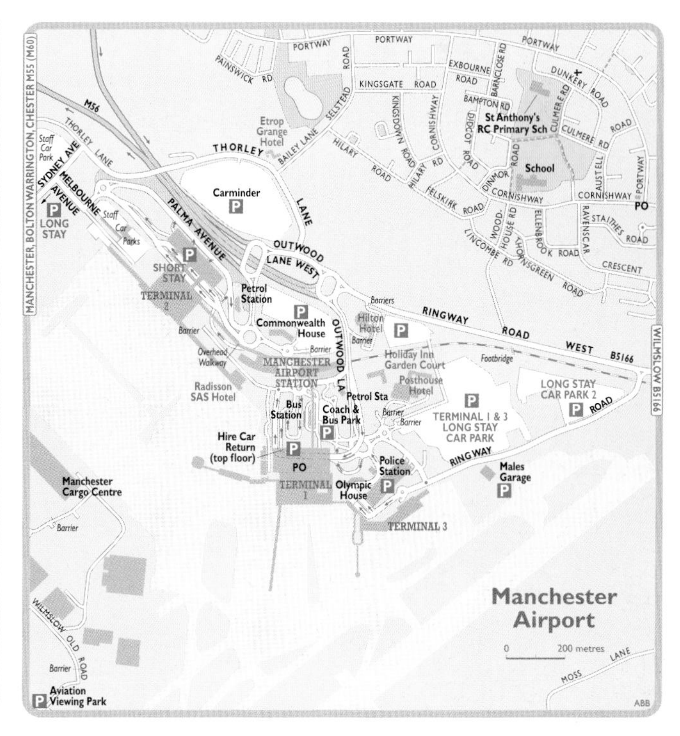

East Midlands Airport – 15 miles south-west of Nottingham, next to the M1 at junctions 23A and 24

Telephone: 01332 852852 or visit www.eastmidsairport.co.uk
Parking: short and long-stay parking is available.
For charge details tel: 0800 128128
Public Transport: bus and coach services to major towns and cities in the East Midlands.
There is one 4-star hotel and several 3-star hotels within easy reach of the airport.
Car hire facilities are available.

Manchester Airport – 10 miles south of Manchester

Telephone: 0161 489 3000 or visit www.manairport.co.uk
Parking: short and long-stay parking is available. For charge details tel: 0161 489 3723
Public Transport: bus, coach and rail. Manchester airport railway station connects with the rail network.
There is one 4-star hotel and several 3-star hotels within easy reach of the airport.
Car hire facilities are available.

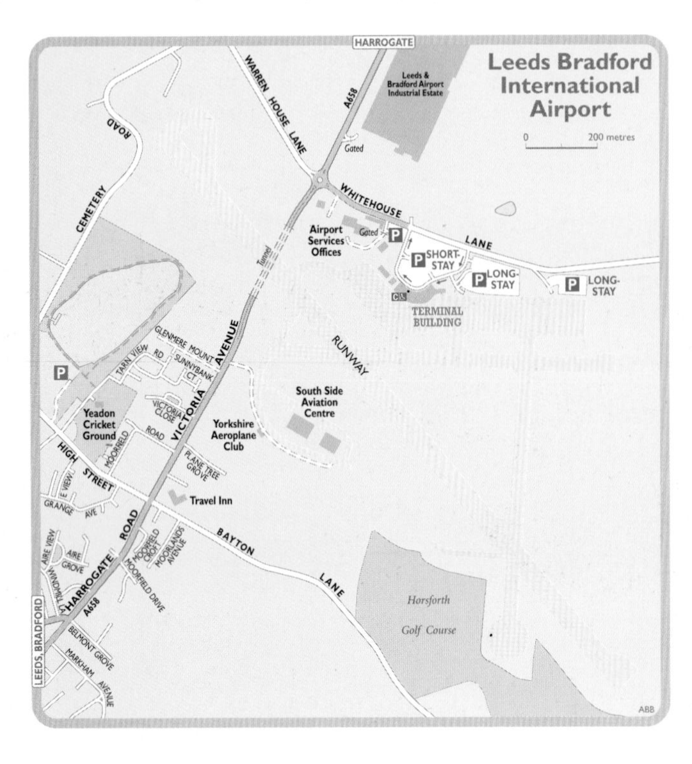

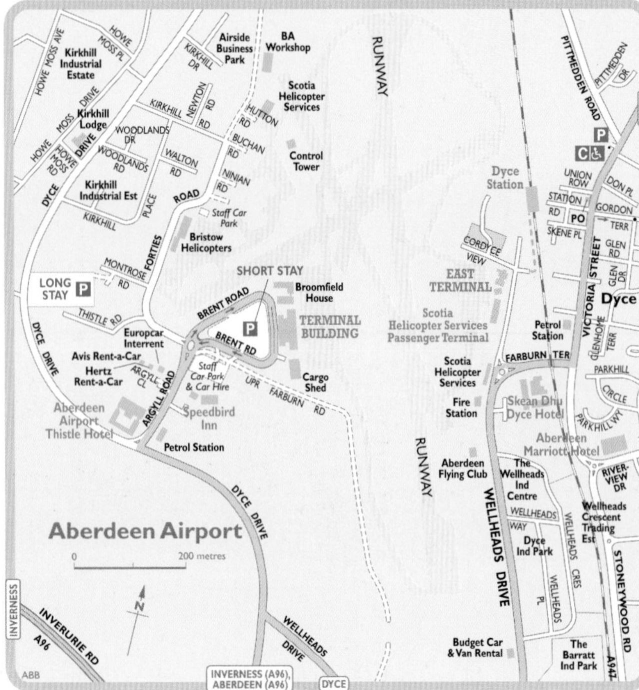

236

Leeds Bradford International Airport – 7 miles north-east of Bradford and 9 miles north-west of Leeds

Telephone: 0113 250 9696 or visit www.lbia.co.uk
Parking: short and long-stay parking is available.
Public Transport: bus from Leeds and Bradford.
There are several 4-star and 3-star hotels within easy reach of the airport.
Car hire facilities are available.

Aberdeen Airport – 7 miles north-west of Aberdeen

Telephone: 01224 722331 or visit www.baa.co.uk
Parking: open-air parking is available.
For charge details tel: 01224 722331 ext 5142
Public Transport: regular bus to central Aberdeen.
There are several 4-star and 3-star hotels within easy reach of the airport.
Car hire facilities are available.

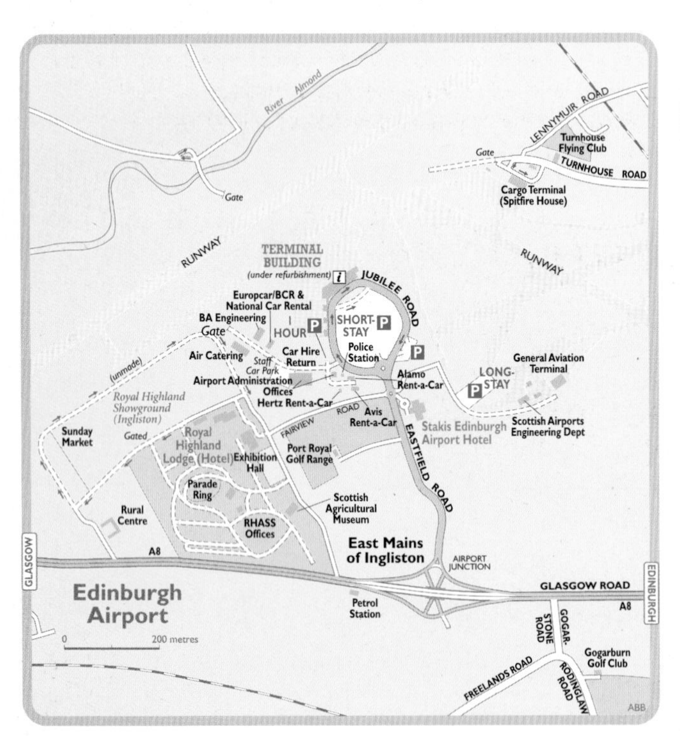

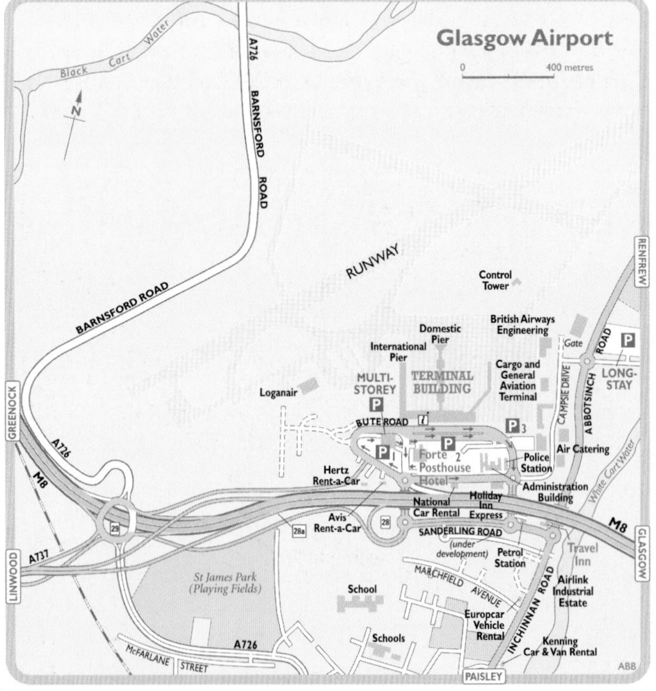

Edinburgh Airport – 7 miles west of Edinburgh

Telephone: 0131 333 1000 or visit www.baa.co.uk
Parking: open-air parking is available.
For charge details tel: 0131 344 3197
Public Transport: regular bus services operate between central Edinburgh and Glasgow.
There is one 4-star hotel and several 3-star hotels within easy reach of the airport.
Car hire facilities are available.

Glasgow Airport – 8 miles west of Glasgow

Telephone: 0141 887 1111 or visit www.baa.co.uk
Parking: short and long-stay parking is available, mostly open-air.
For charge details tel: 0141 889 2751
Public Transport: regular coach services operate between central Glasgow and Edinburgh.
There are several 3-star hotels within easy reach of the airport.
Car hire facilities are available.

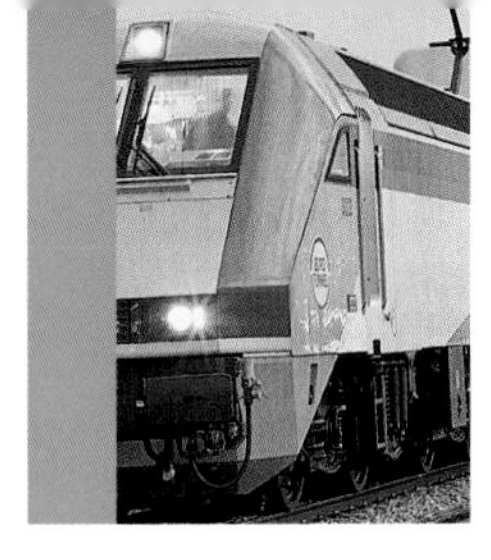

the Channel Tunnel

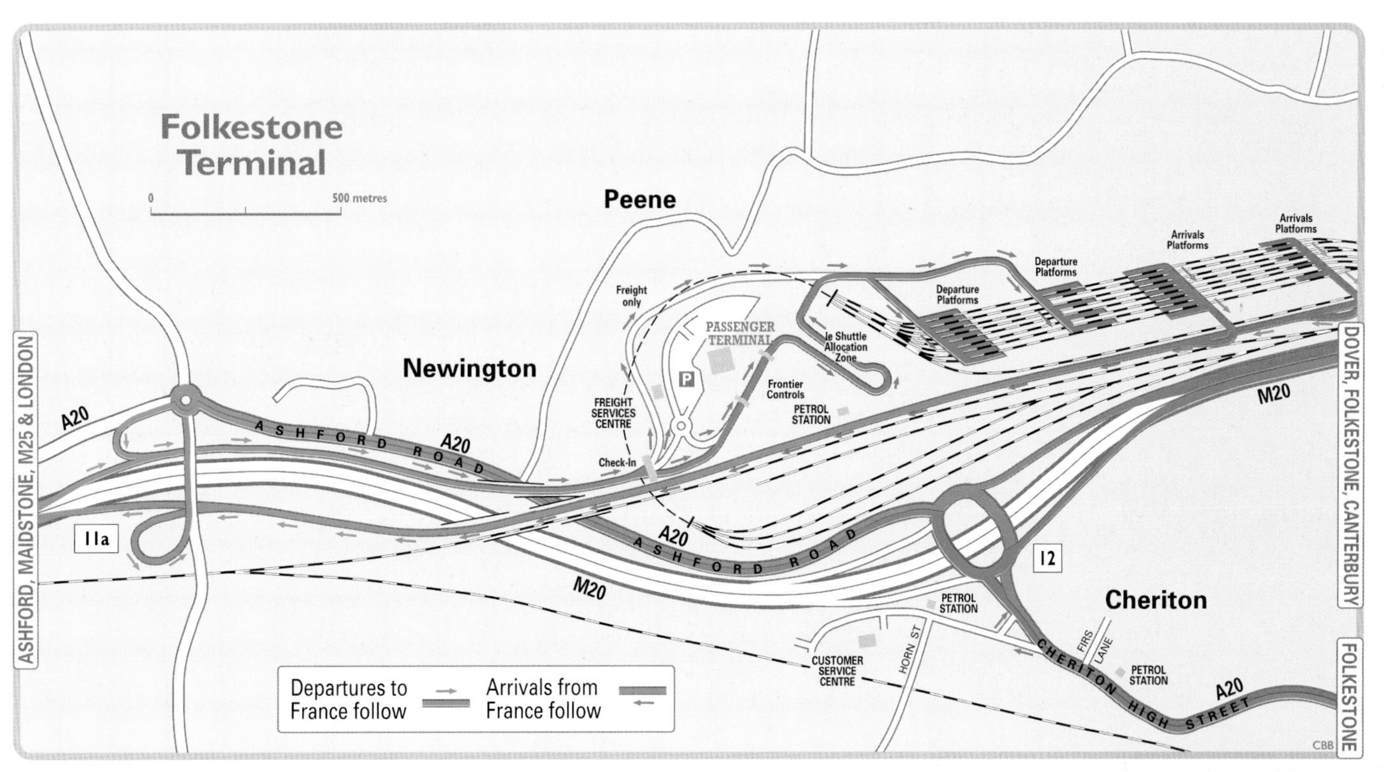

Services to Europe

The Eurotunnel Shuttle service for cars, cars towing caravans and trailers, motorcycles, coaches and HGV vehicles runs between terminals at Folkestone and Calais/Coquelles.
It takes just over one hour to travel from the M20 motorway in Kent, via the Channel Tunnel, to the A16 autoroute in France. The service runs 24 hours a day, every day of the year. Call the Eurotunnel Call Centre (tel: 0990 353535) or visit www.eurotunnel.com for the latest ticket and travel information.

There are up to four departures per hour at peak times, with the journey in the tunnel from platform to platform taking just 35 minutes (45 minutes at night). Travellers pass through British and French frontier controls on departure, saving time on the other side of the Channel. Each terminal has bureaux de change, restaurants and a variety of shops. In Calais/Coquelles, the Cité de l'Europe contains numerous shops and restaurants, hotels and a hypermarket.

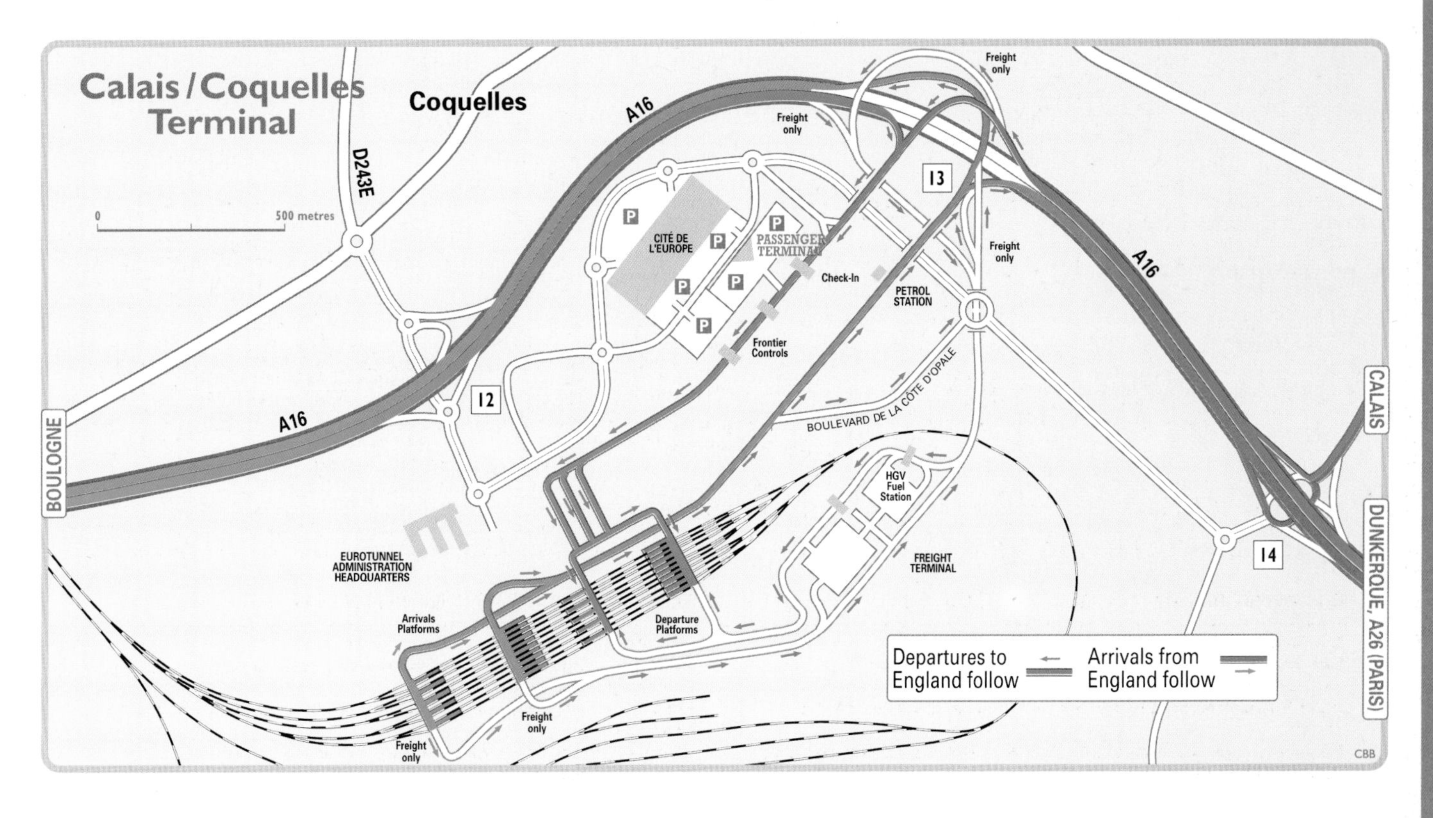

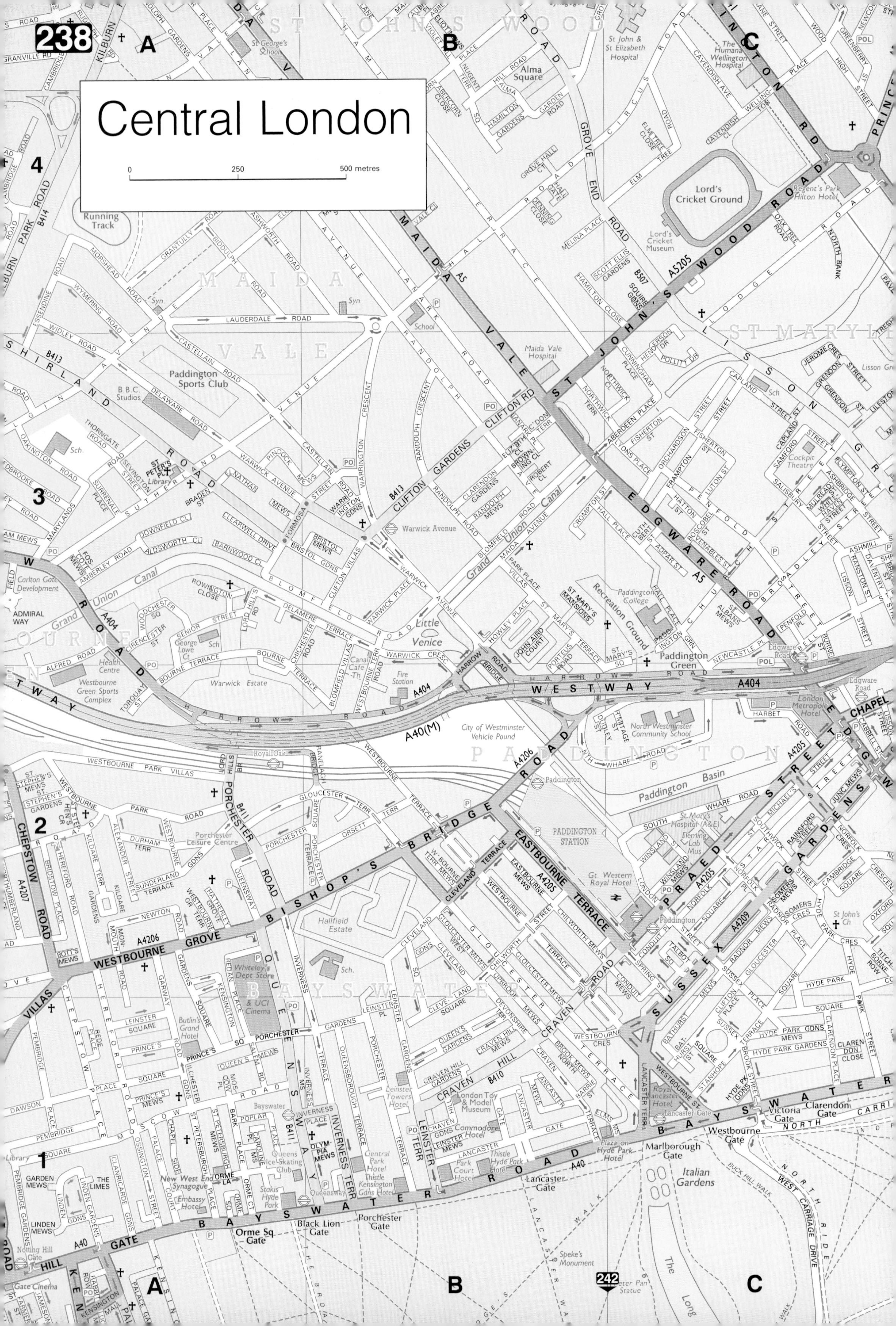
Central London
0
250
500 metres
A
B
C
A
B
C
1
2
3
4
242
ST JOHN'S WOOD
MAIDA VALE
ST MARYLEBONE
PADDINGTON
BAYSWATER
St George's School
St John & St Elizabeth Hospital
The Humana Wellington Hospital
Alma Square
Lord's Cricket Ground
Lord's Cricket Museum
Regent's Park Hilton Hotel
Running Track
Paddington Sports Club
B.B.C. Studios
Maida Vale Hospital
School
Syn
Syn.
Sch.
St Peter's Library
Warwick Avenue
Little Venice
Grand Union Canal
Canal Cafe Th
Fire Station
Carlton Gate Development
Admiral Way
George Lowe Ct
Health Centre
Westbourne Green Sports Complex
Warwick Estate
Paddington College
Recreation Ground
Paddington Green
Edgware Road
London Metropole Hotel
Cockpit Theatre
City of Westminster Vehicle Pound
North Westminster Community School
Royal Oak
Paddington Basin
Paddington Station
St Mary's Hospital (A&E)
Fleming Lab Mus
Gt. Western Royal Hotel
Paddington
Porchester Leisure Centre
Hallfield Estate
Whiteley's Dept Store & UCI Cinema
Butlin's Grand Hotel
St John's Ch
Leinster Towers Hotel
London Toy & Model Museum
Commodore Hotel
Royal Lancaster Hotel
Lancaster Gate
Victoria Gate
Clarendon Gate
Westbourne Gate
Marlborough Gate
Italian Gardens
Plaza on Hyde Park Hotel
Thistle Hyde Park Hotel
Park Court Hotel
Central Park Hotel
Thistle Kensington Gdns Hotel
Queens Ice Skating Club
Queensway
Bayswater
Stakis Hyde Park
Embassy Hotel
New West End Synagogue
Black Lion Gate
Porchester Gate
Orme Sq Gate
Notting Hill Gate
Gate Cinema
Speke's Monument
Peter Pan Statue
Library
A5
A5205
A404
A40(M)
A4206
A4205
A4209
A4207
A40
B413
B414
B411
B410
B507
MAIDA VALE
EDGWARE ROAD
ST JOHN'S WOOD ROAD
LISSON GROVE
WELLINGTON RD
GROVE END ROAD
CIRCUS ROAD
HAMILTON TERRACE
ABERCORN PLACE
CLIFTON GARDENS
CLIFTON RD
WARWICK AVENUE
RANDOLPH AVENUE
SHIRLAND ROAD
ELGIN AVENUE
LAUDERDALE ROAD
CASTELLAIN ROAD
DELAWARE ROAD
SUTHERLAND AVENUE
HARROW ROAD
WESTWAY
BISHOP'S BRIDGE ROAD
WESTBOURNE GROVE
PORCHESTER ROAD
QUEENSWAY
EASTBOURNE TERRACE
PRAED STREET
SUSSEX GARDENS
CRAVEN ROAD
CRAVEN HILL
BAYSWATER ROAD
NOTTING HILL GATE
CHEPSTOW ROAD
CHEPSTOW VILLAS
INVERNESS TERRACE
LEINSTER TERR
LANCASTER TERR
NORTH CARRIAGE DRIVE
WEST CARRIAGE DRIVE
NORTH RIDE
BUCK HILL WALK
LANCASTER WALK
KENSINGTON PALACE GARDENS
HYDE PARK GARDENS
HYDE PARK SQUARE
EDGWARE ROAD
CHAPEL

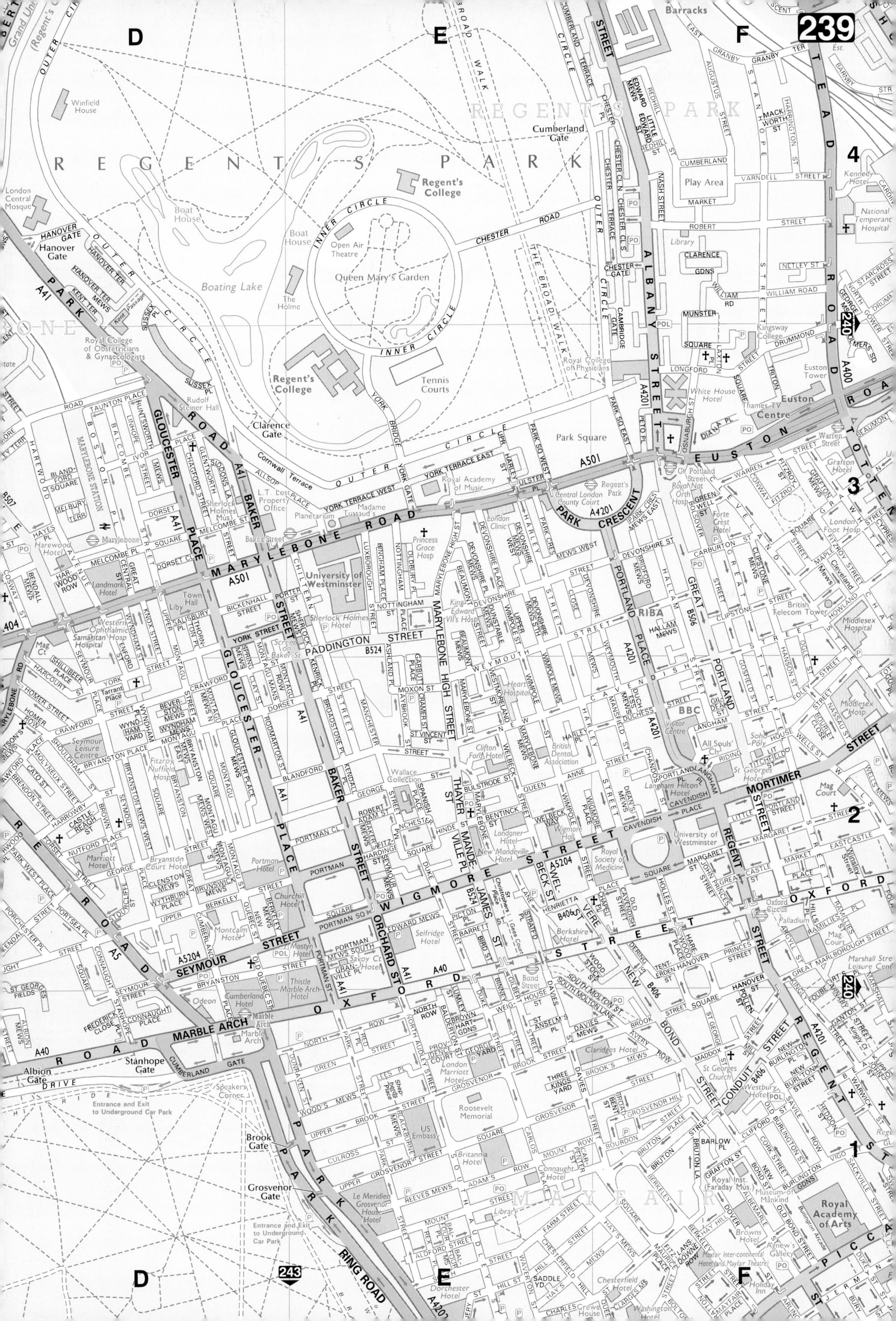
D
E
F
4
3
2
1
REGENT'S PARK
Winfield House
London Central Mosque
Hanover Gate
Boat House
Boating Lake
The Holme
Open Air Theatre
Queen Mary's Garden
INNER CIRCLE
OUTER CIRCLE
Regent's College
Tennis Courts
Clarence Gate
Cumberland Gate
CHESTER ROAD
THE BROAD WALK
Royal College of Obstetricians & Gynaecologists
Royal College of Physicians
Cornwall Terrace
YORK TERRACE EAST
YORK TERRACE WEST
Madame Tussaud's
Planetarium
L.T. Lost Property Office
Park Square
PARK CRESCENT
EUSTON ROAD
A501
Euston Centre
Euston Tower
Thames TV
White House Hotel
Kingsway College
Barracks
Play Area
Library
National Temperance Hospital
Kennedy Hotel
ALBANY STREET
HAMPSTEAD ROAD
A400
TOTTENHAM COURT ROAD
MARYLEBONE STATION
Marylebone
Baker Street
Sherlock Holmes Mus.
Harewood Hotel
Landmark Hotel
Town Hall
Western Ophthalmic Hosp
Samaritan Hosp
MARYLEBONE ROAD
University of Westminster
Princess Grace Hosp
London Clinic
King Edward VII's Hosp
Sherlock Holmes Hotel
Heart Hospital
RIBA
BBC
All Souls'
Langham Hilton Hotel
British Telecom Tower
Middlesex Hospital
London Foot Hosp
Cleveland Mews
GLOUCESTER PLACE
BAKER STREET
PORTLAND PLACE
GREAT PORTLAND STREET
MARYLEBONE HIGH STREET
PADDINGTON STREET
WIGMORE STREET
MORTIMER STREET
CAVENDISH SQUARE
OXFORD STREET
Oxford Circus
REGENT STREET
Wallace Collection
Clifton Ford Hotel
Londoner Hotel
New Mandeville Hotel
Wigmore Hall
Royal Society of Medicine
British Dental Association
University of Westminster
St Georges Hotel
Palladium
Marshall St Leisure Cent
Portman Hotel
Churchill Hotel
Montcalm Hotel
Selfridge Hotel
Mostyn Hotel
Thistle Marble Arch Hotel
Cumberland Hotel
Odeon
Berkshire Hotel
Bond Street
SEYMOUR STREET
MARBLE ARCH
Marble Arch
EDGWARE ROAD
A5
BAYSWATER ROAD
A40
Albion Gate
Stanhope Gate
Speakers Corner
Entrance and Exit to Underground Car Park
Brook Gate
Grosvenor Gate
PARK LANE
Claridges Hotel
London Marriott Hotel
Roosevelt Memorial
US Embassy
Britannia Hotel
Connaught Hotel
Le Meridien Grosvenor House Hotel
Dorchester Hotel
St Georges Church
Westbury Hotel
Royal Inst. (Faraday Mus.)
Museum of Mankind
Browns Hotel
Mayfair Inter-continental Hotel and Mayfair Theatre
Royal Academy of Arts
Burlington Arcade
Holiday Inn
Chesterfield Hotel
Washington Hotel
MAYFAIR
BOND STREET
CONDUIT STREET
PICCADILLY
RING ROAD
A4202
243
240

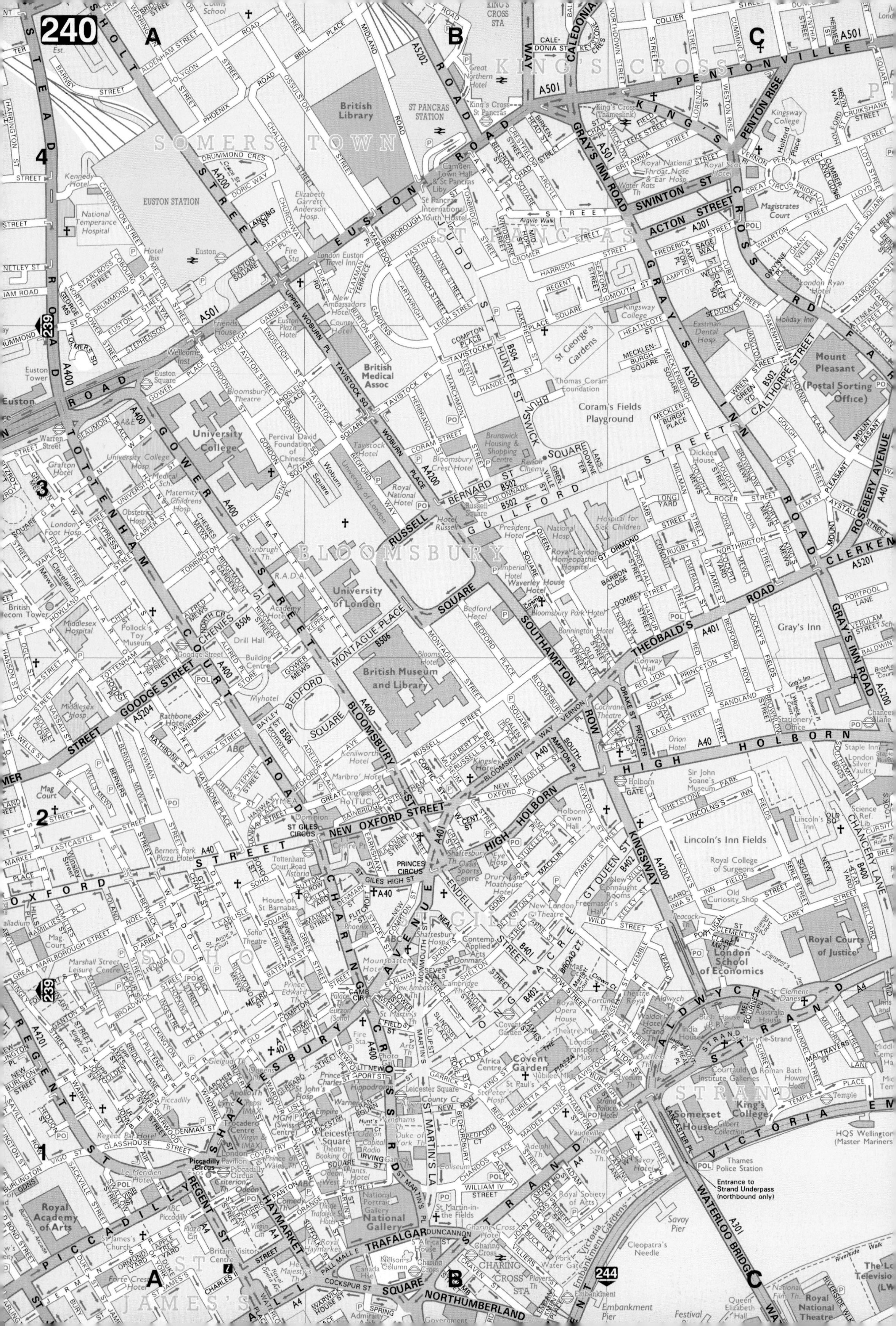
A
B
C
4
3
2
1
239
244
KING'S CROSS
SOMERS TOWN
ST PANCRAS
BLOOMSBURY
ST GILES
SOHO
STRAND
ST JAMES'S
British Library
ST PANCRAS STATION
KING'S CROSS STA
Great Northern Hotel
King's Cross St Pancras
King's Cross (Thameslink)
EUSTON STATION
Euston
Euston Square
Euston Tower
Kennedy Hotel
National Temperance Hospital
Hotel Ibis
Friends House
Wellcome Inst
Camden Town Hall & St Pancras Liby
St Pancras International Youth Hostel
Elizabeth Garrett Anderson Hosp.
London Euston Travel Inn
New Ambassadors Hotel
Euston Plaza Hotel
County Hotel
British Medical Assoc
Fire Sta
St George's Gardens
Thomas Coram Foundation
Coram's Fields Playground
Kingsway College
Eastman Dental Hosp.
Royal National Throat Nose & Ear Hosp
Royal Scot Hotel
Water Rats Th
Magistrates Court
London Ryan Hotel
Holiday Inn
Mount Pleasant (Postal Sorting Office)
Brunswick Housing & Shopping Centre
Renoir Cinema
Bloomsbury Crest Hotel
Royal National Hotel
Tavistock Hotel
University College
University College Hosp.
Bloomsbury Theatre
Percival David Foundation of Chinese Art
University of London
Woburn Square
Dickens House
Hospital for Sick Children
President Hotel
National Hosp.
Royal London Homeopathic Hospital
Imperial Hotel
Waverley House Hotel
Bloomsbury Park Hotel
Bonnington Hotel
Hotel Russell
Russell Square
Gray's Inn
Conway Hall
Cochrane Theatre
Orion Hotel
Stationery Office
Staple Inn
London Silver Vaults
Warren Street
Grafton Hotel
London Foot Hosp
British Telecom Tower
Middlesex Hospital
Pollock's Toy Museum
Goodge Street
Drill Hall
Building Centre
R.A.D.A.
Vanbrugh Th.
Academy Hotel
Myhotel
Rathbone Hotel
Middlesex Hosp.
British Museum and Library
Bedford Hotel
Kenilworth Hotel
Marlbro' Hotel
Kingsley Hotel
Congress Ho (TUC)
YMCA
Dominion
ST GILES CIRCUS
Centre Pt
Tottenham Court Road
Astoria
Berners Park Plaza Hotel
Mag Court
Marshall Street Leisure Centre
House of St Barnabas
Soho Theatre
PRINCES CIRCUS
Shaftesbury Eye Hosp
Oasis Sports Centre
Drury Lane Moathouse Hotel
Holborn Town Hall
Holborn
Sir John Soane's Museum
Lincoln's Inn Fields
Lincoln's Inn
Royal College of Surgeons
Old Curiosity Shop
New Connaught Rooms
Freemason's Hall
New London Theatre
London School of Economics
Royal Courts of Justice
Science Ref. Lib
Shaftesbury Th.
Contemp Applied Arts
Mountbatten Hotel
SEVEN DIALS
Cambridge Th.
Prince Edward Th
CAMB CIR
Palace Th
Curzon (Soho)
Fire Sta.
St Martin's Th
Covent Garden
London Transport Mus
Theatre Mus
Royal Opera House
Fortune Th
Theatre Royal
Aldwych Th
Waldorf Hotel
Strand Th
Bush House (B.B.C.)
India House
Australia House
St Clement Danes
St Mary-le-Strand
Courtauld Institute Galleries
Roman Bath
Somerset House
King's College
Lyceum Th
Duchess Th
Strand Palace Hotel
Savoy Hotel
Savoy Th.
Vaudeville Th
Adelphi Th
Jubilee Mkt
St Paul's
St Peter's Hosp
Hippodrome
Leicester Square
Empire
Warner
Wyndhams Th
Duke of York Th
Albery Th
Coliseum
Garrick Th
Prince Charles Th
St John's Hosp
Trocadero Centre
Apollo Th
Queen's Th
Gielgud Th
Lyric Th
Piccadilly Th
Regent Pal Hotel
Piccadilly Circus
London Pavilion
Criterion Th
Comedy Th
Le Meridien Hotel
Royal Academy of Arts
St James's Church
Britain Visitor Centre
Forte Crest Hotel
Her Majesty's Th
Haymarket
National Portrait Gallery
National Gallery
St Martin-in-the-Fields
Nelson's Column
Canada House
South Africa House
Charing Cross Hotel
CHARING CROSS STA
Royal Society of Arts
York Water Gate
Embankment
Embankment Pier
Cleopatra's Needle
Savoy Pier
Thames Police Station
Entrance to Strand Underpass (northbound only)
HQS Wellington (Master Mariners)
Temple
Queen Elizabeth Hall
National Film Th.
Royal National Theatre
Victoria Embankment Gardens
PICCADILLY
REGENT ST
HAYMARKET
TRAFALGAR SQUARE
NORTHUMBERLAND AVE
STRAND
ALDWYCH
KINGSWAY
HIGH HOLBORN
NEW OXFORD STREET
OXFORD STREET
SHAFTESBURY AVENUE
CHARING CROSS RD
TOTTENHAM COURT ROAD
GOWER STREET
EUSTON ROAD
GRAY'S INN ROAD
KING'S CROSS RD
PENTONVILLE ROAD
THEOBALD'S ROAD
SOUTHAMPTON ROW
RUSSELL SQUARE
BLOOMSBURY STREET
WATERLOO BRIDGE
VICTORIA EMBANKMENT
ROSEBERY AVENUE
CLERKENWELL ROAD
GOODGE STREET
A501
A400
A40
A4200
A5200
A201
A401
A5201
A4
A301
B502
B504
B506
B402
B401
A5204

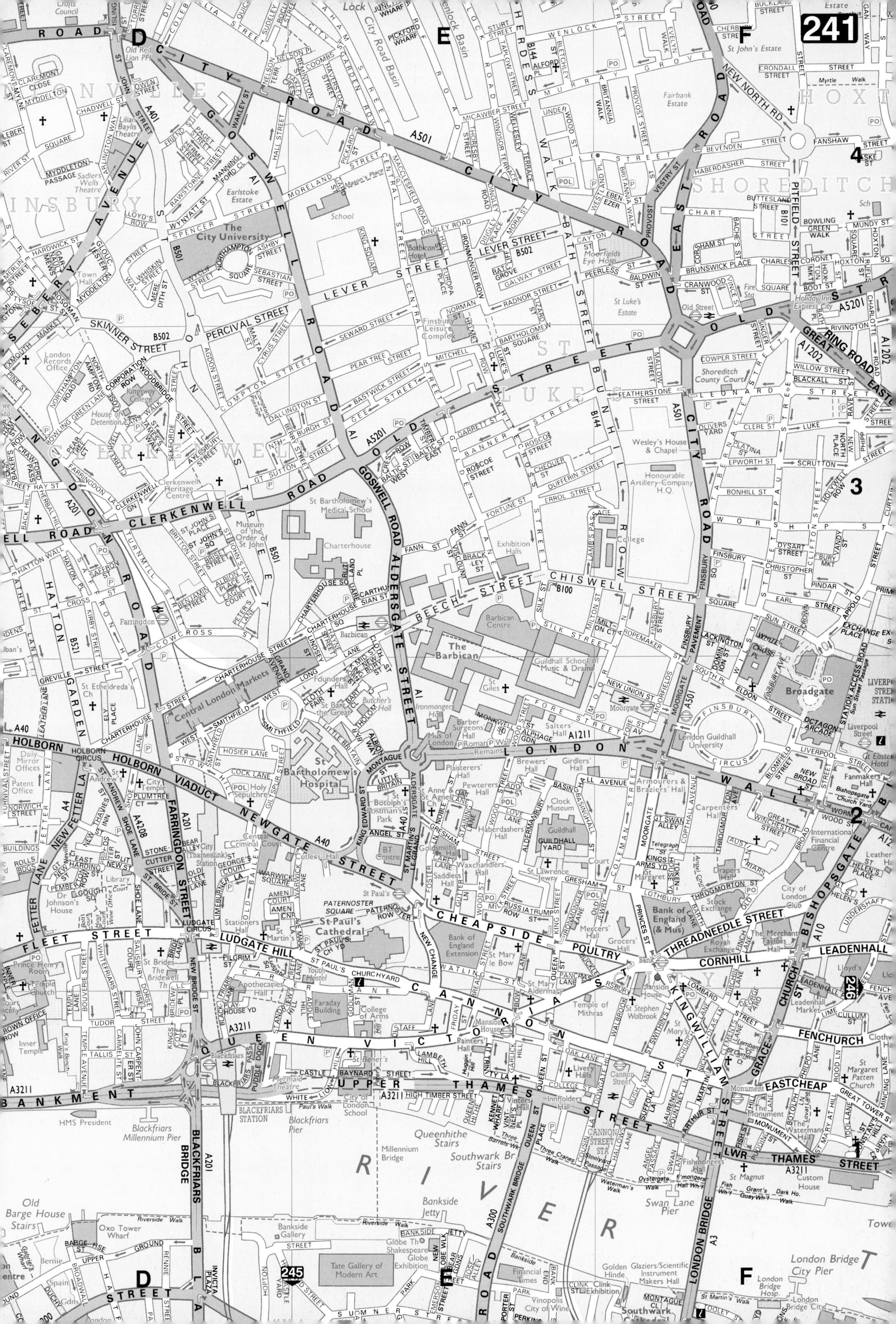
D
E
F
4
3
2
1
D
E
F
CITY ROAD
GOSWELL ROAD
A501
A1
CLERKENWELL
INSBURY
SHOREDITCH
HOXTON
ST LUKE'S
CLERKENWELL
CITY
RIVER
OLD STREET
CLERKENWELL ROAD
ROSEBERY AVENUE
FARRINGDON ROAD
ALDERSGATE STREET
BEECH STREET
CHISWELL STREET
LONDON WALL
HOLBORN
HOLBORN VIADUCT
NEWGATE STREET
FLEET STREET
LUDGATE HILL
CHEAPSIDE
POULTRY
CORNHILL
LEADENHALL
THREADNEEDLE STREET
QUEEN VICTORIA STREET
CANNON STREET
KING WILLIAM STREET
UPPER THAMES STREET
LWR THAMES STREET
EASTCHEAP
FENCHURCH
BISHOPSGATE
GRACECHURCH
LONDON BRIDGE
SOUTHWARK BRIDGE
BLACKFRIARS BRIDGE
EMBANKMENT
FARRINGDON STREET
NEW NORTH RD
EAST ROAD
GREAT EASTERN STREET
CITY ROAD
FINSBURY PAVEMENT
MOORGATE
BUNHILL ROW
WHITECROSS STREET
GOLDEN LANE
PERCIVAL STREET
SKINNER STREET
LEVER STREET
WENLOCK
MURRAY GROVE
The City University
Barbican Centre
The Barbican
Central London Markets
St Bartholomew's Hospital
St Paul's Cathedral
Charterhouse
Bank of England (& Mus)
Mansion House
Guildhall
Broadgate
Honourable Artillery Company H.Q.
Wesley's House & Chapel
Faraday Building
College of Arms
Tate Gallery of Modern Art
Globe Theatre Shakespeare Globe Exhibition
Millennium Bridge
Blackfriars Millennium Pier
HMS President
Old Barge House Stairs
Oxo Tower Wharf
Bankside Gallery
Bankside Jetty
Queenhithe Stairs
Southwark Br Stairs
Swan Lane Pier
London Bridge City Pier
Custom House
Monument
Stock Exchange
Royal Exchange
Lloyd's
Liverpool Street
Moorgate
Barbican
Farringdon
Old Street
St Paul's
Blackfriars
Cannon Street
Bank
Museum of London
London Guildhall University
Finsbury Leisure Complex
Moorfields Eye Hosp
St Luke's Estate
Fairbank Estate
St John's Estate
Earlstoke Estate
City Road Basin
Wenlock Basin
Sadlers Wells Theatre
Lilian Baylis Theatre
London Records Office
Kingsway College
House of Detention
Clerkenwell Heritage Centre
Museum of the Order of St John
St Bartholomew's Medical School
Shoreditch County Court
Holiday Inn Express City
Exhibition Halls
Guildhall School of Music & Drama
Ironmongers Hall
Barber Surgeons Hall
St Giles
Founders Hall
Butcher's Hall
St Bart the Great
Holy Sepulchre
Central Criminal Court
City Thameslink Station
Stationers Hall
Apothecaries Hall
Youth Hostel
Mermaid Theatre
City of London School
Blackfriars Station
Blackfriars Pier
St Brides
The Bridewell Th
Prince Henry's Room
Temple Church
Inner Temple
Dr Johnson's House
Daily Mirror Offices
Patent Office
St Etheldreda's Ch
Cutlers' Hall
Goldsmiths Hall
Saddlers Hall
Waxchandlers' Hall
Haberdashers Hall
Pewterers Hall
Plaisterers' Hall
Brewers' Hall
Girdlers' Hall
Armourers & Braziers' Hall
Carpenters' Hall
Drapers Hall
Mercers' Hall
Grocers' Hall
Temple of Mithras
St Stephen Walbrook
St Mary Aldermary
St Mary le Bow
Bank of England Extension
Painters' Hall
Vintners Hall
Innholders Hall
Fishmongers Hall
St Magnus
The Watermans Hall
St Margaret Pattens Church
Leadenhall Market
The Merchant Taylors Hall
City of London Club
International Financial Centre
Fanmakers Hall
Great Eastern Hotel
Cannon Street Sta
Financial Times
Vinopolis City of Wine
Clink Exhibition
Golden Hinde
Glaziers/Scientific Instrument Makers Hall
London Bridge Hosp.
A40
A201
A1211
A3211
A5201
A1202
A10
A3
A300
A4
A4208
B502
B501
B144
B100
B101
B521
245
246
200

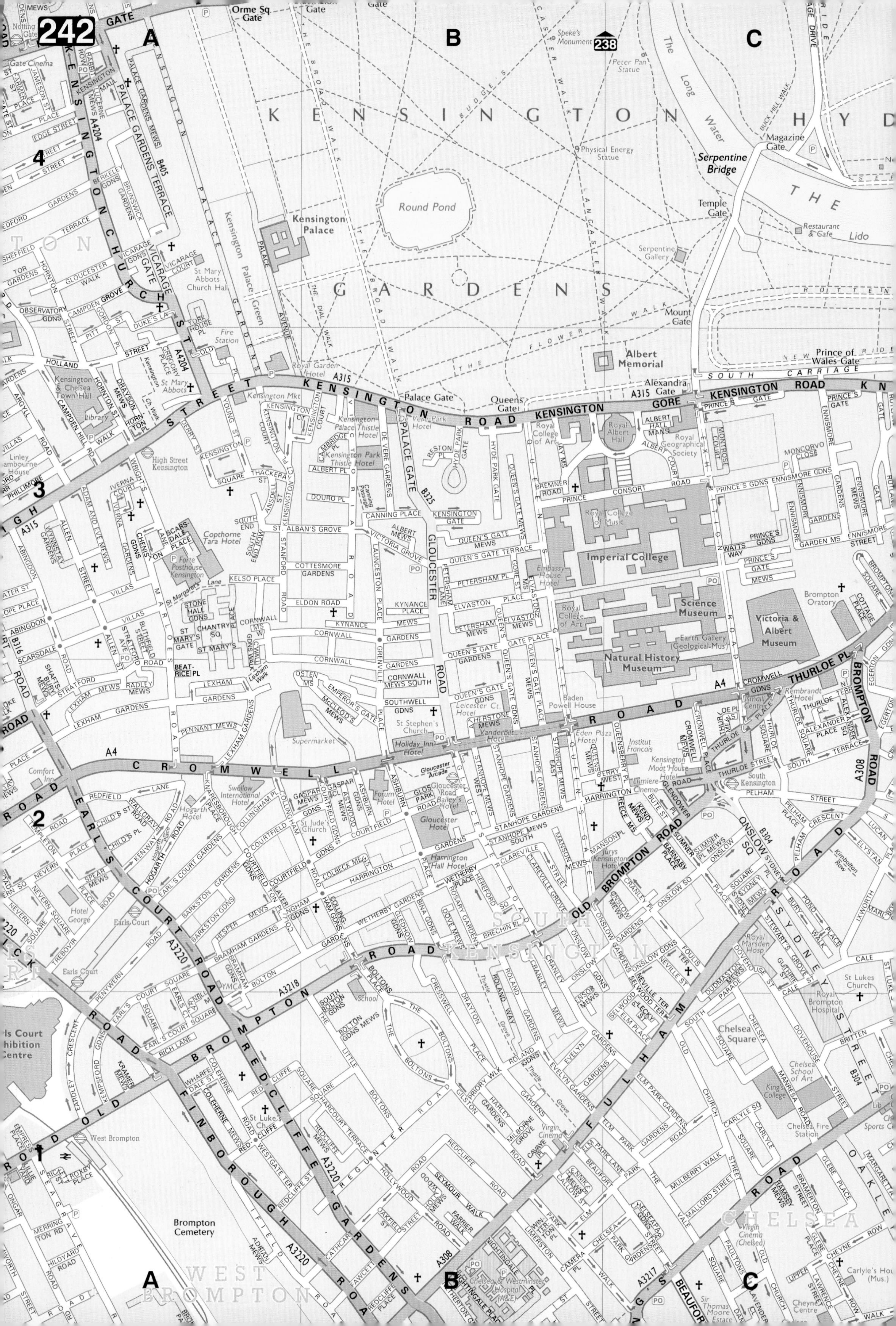
242
A
B
C
238
4
3
2
1
KENSINGTON GARDENS
HYDE PARK
Round Pond
Kensington Palace
Orme Sq Gate
Speke's Monument
Peter Pan Statue
The Long Water
Physical Energy Statue
Magazine Gate
Serpentine Bridge
Temple Gate
THE Lido
Restaurant & Cafe
Serpentine Gallery
Mount Gate
Albert Memorial
Prince of Wales Gate
SOUTH CARRIAGE
Alexandra Gate
Queens Gate
Palace Gate
KENSINGTON ROAD
KENSINGTON GORE
Royal Albert Hall
Royal College of Art
Royal Geographical Society
Royal College of Music
Imperial College
Science Museum
Victoria & Albert Museum
Natural History Museum
Earth Gallery (Geological Mus)
Brompton Oratory
Embassy House Hotel
Baden Powell House
Institut Francais
Kensington Moat House Hotel
South Kensington
CROMWELL ROAD
A4
THURLOE PL
BROMPTON ROAD
A308
Rembrandt Hotel
St Stephen's Church
Holiday Inn Hotel
Vanderbilt Hotel
Eden Plaza Hotel
Gloucester Arcade
Gloucester Road
Forum Hotel
Gloucester Hotel
Harrington Hall Hotel
Jurys Kensington Hotel
Bailey's Hotel
Supermarket
Swallow International Hotel
Hogarth Hotel
Comfort Inn
Earls Court
Hotel George
EARL'S COURT ROAD
A3220
Earls Court Exhibition Centre
West Brompton
Brompton Cemetery
WEST BROMPTON
OLD BROMPTON ROAD
A3218
St Luke's Ch
The Boltons
School
SOUTH KENSINGTON
FULHAM ROAD
SYDNEY STREET
Royal Marsden Hosp
Royal Brompton Hospital
St Lukes Church
Chelsea Square
Chelsea School of Art
King's College
Chelsea Fire Station
Virgin Cinema
Virgin Cinema (Chelsea)
Chelsea & Westminster Hospital (A&E)
CHELSEA
KING'S ROAD
A3217
Carlyle's House (Mus.)
Cheyne Centre
Sir Thomas Moore Estate
FINBOROUGH ROAD
REDCLIFFE GARDENS
HOLLAND STREET
KENSINGTON HIGH STREET
A315
High Street Kensington
Kensington & Chelsea Town Hall
Library
St Mary Abbots Church Hall
Fire Station
Royal Garden Hotel
Kensington Mkt
Kensington Palace Thistle Hotel
De Vere Park Hotel
Kensington Park Thistle Hotel
Copthorne Tara Hotel
Forte Posthouse Kensington
KENSINGTON CHURCH STREET
A4204
PALACE GARDENS TERRACE
VICARAGE GATE
KENSINGTON PALACE GARDENS
Kensington Palace Green
GLOUCESTER ROAD
PALACE GATE
B325
QUEEN'S GATE
HYDE PARK GATE
Linley Sambourne House
Notting Hill Gate
Gate Cinema

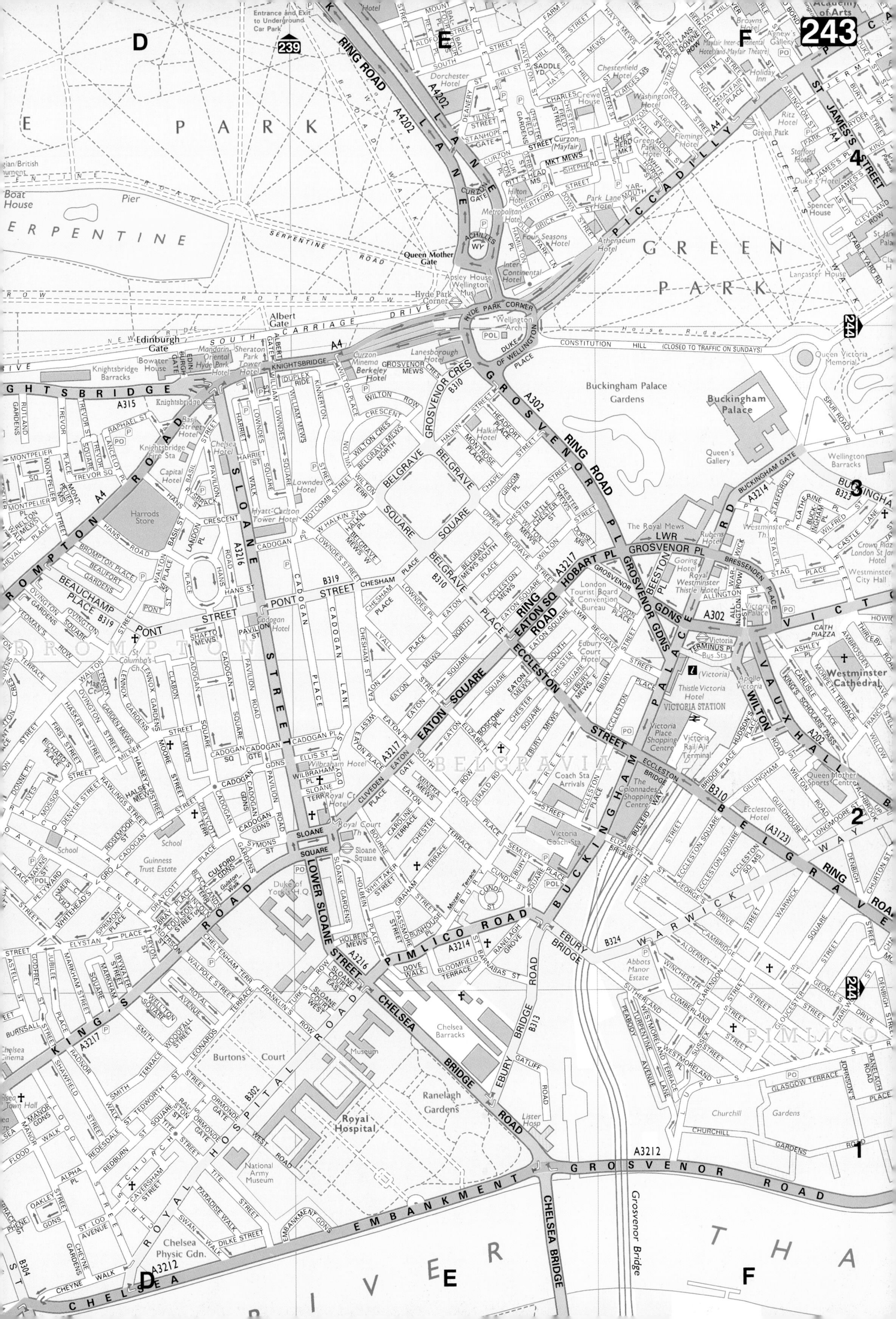

243
D
E
F
239
244
Entrance and Exit to Underground Car Park
PARK
SERPENTINE
Boat House
Pier
SERPENTINE ROAD
ROTTEN ROW
SOUTH CARRIAGE DRIVE
Albert Gate
Edinburgh Gate
Hyde Park Corner
Queen Mother Gate
Apsley House (Wellington Mus)
Wellington Arch
RING ROAD
PARK LANE
A4202
CURZON GATE
ACHILLES WY
Dorchester Hotel
Hilton Hotel
Metropolitan Hotel
Four Seasons Hotel
Inter Continental Hotel
Athenaeum Hotel
Park Lane Hotel
Chesterfield Hotel
Washington Hotel
Green Park Hotel
Flemings Hotel
Holiday Inn
Ritz Hotel
Stafford Hotel
Duke's Hotel
Spencer House
Lancaster House
Brown's Hotel
Mayfair Inter-Continental Hotel and Mayfair Theatre
Royal Academy of Arts
Agnew's Gallery
Crewe House
Curzon (Mayfair)
SHEPHERD MKT
MKT MEWS
PICCADILLY
A4
Green Park
GREEN PARK
ST JAMES'S STREET
CONSTITUTION HILL (CLOSED TO TRAFFIC ON SUNDAYS)
Horse Ride
Queen Victoria Memorial
Buckingham Palace Gardens
Buckingham Palace
Queen's Gallery
Wellington Barracks
BUCKINGHAM GATE
The Royal Mews
Rubens Hotel
Goring Hotel
Royal Westminster Thistle Hotel
Westminster Cathedral
Westminster City Hall
Crowne Plaza London St James Hotel
CATH PIAZZA
VICTORIA STREET
Victoria Palace
Victoria
TERMINUS PL
Bus Sta
Apollo Victoria
Thistle Victoria Hotel
VICTORIA STATION
Victoria Place Shopping Centre
Victoria Rail/Air Terminal
The Colonnades Shopping Centre
Coach Sta Arrivals
Victoria Coach Sta
London Tourist Board and Convention Bureau
Edbury Court Hotel
Eccleston Hotel
Queen Mother Sports Centre
VAUXHALL BRIDGE ROAD
A202
BELGRAVE ROAD
(A3123)
B310
WARWICK WAY
PIMLICO
Abbots Manor Estate
Churchill Gardens
GROSVENOR ROAD
A3212
Grosvenor Bridge
GROSVENOR PL
A302
GROSVENOR CRES
DUKE OF WELLINGTON PLACE
Lanesborough Hotel
Curzon Minema
Berkeley Hotel
Halkin Hotel
BELGRAVE SQUARE
EATON SQUARE
A3217
ECCLESTON STREET
BUCKINGHAM PALACE ROAD
BELGRAVIA
KNIGHTSBRIDGE
A315
Knightsbridge Barracks
Bowater House
Mandarin Oriental Hyde Park Hotel
Sheraton Park Tower Hotel
Knightsbridge
Basil Street Hotel
Knightsbridge Fire Sta
Capital Hotel
Harrods Store
Chelsea Hotel
Lowndes Hotel
Hyatt-Carlton Tower Hotel
BROMPTON ROAD
SLOANE STREET
A3216
Cadogan Hotel
PONT STREET
B319
BROMPTON
St Columba's Ch
Wilbraham Hotel
Royal Ct Hotel
Royal Court Th
SLOANE SQUARE
Sloane Square
LOWER SLOANE STREET
Duke of York's H.Q
Guinness Trust Estate
School
KING'S ROAD
PIMLICO ROAD
A3214
CHELSEA BRIDGE ROAD
Chelsea Barracks
Museum
Burtons Court
Ranelagh Gardens
Royal Hospital
National Army Museum
Lister Hosp
ROYAL HOSPITAL ROAD
B302
EBURY BRIDGE
B324
Chelsea Cinema
Chelsea Town Hall
Chelsea Physic Gdn.
CHELSEA EMBANKMENT
CHELSEA BRIDGE
RIVER
THAMES
1
2
3
4

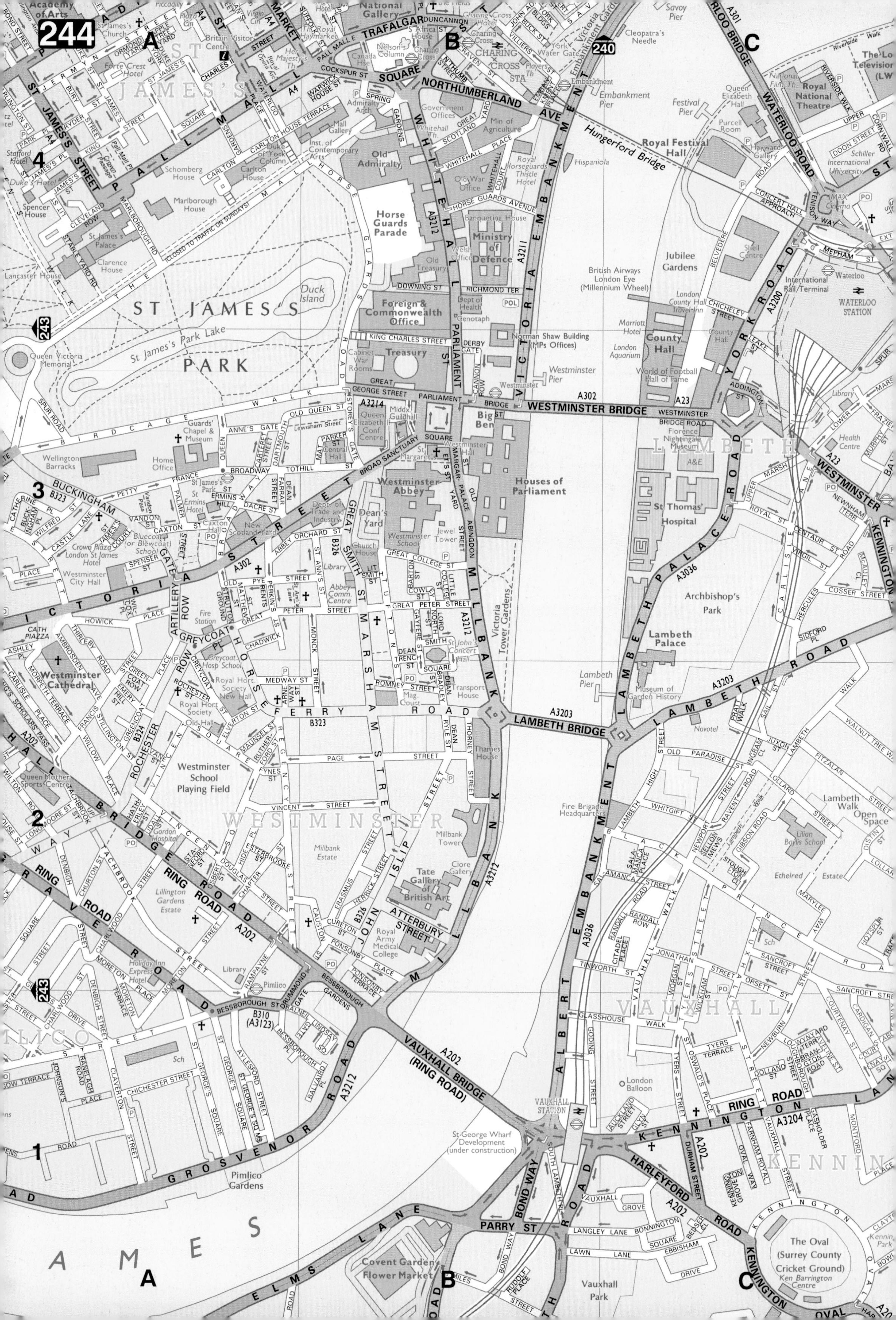

A
B
C
240
243
4
3
2
1
ST JAMES'S
PALL MALL
TRAFALGAR SQUARE
National Gallery
Nelson's Column
Charing Cross
CHARING CROSS STA
NORTHUMBERLAND AVE
Embankment
Embankment Pier
Cleopatra's Needle
Savoy Pier
WATERLOO BRIDGE
Royal National Theatre
National Film Th.
Queen Elizabeth Hall
Festival Pier
Purcell Room
Royal Festival Hall
Hungerford Bridge
Hayward Gallery
Schiller International University
WATERLOO ROAD
IMAX Cinema
Waterloo
International Rail Terminal
WATERLOO STATION
Shell Centre
MEPHAM ST
Jubilee Gardens
British Airways London Eye (Millennium Wheel)
London County Hall Travel Inn
County Hall
Marriott Hotel
London Aquarium
World of Football Hall of Fame
YORK ROAD
A3200
A301
Admiralty Arch
Government Offices
Min of Agriculture
Old Admiralty
Horse Guards Parade
Royal Horseguards Thistle Hotel
Old War Office
Banqueting House
Ministry of Defence
WHITEHALL
A3212
A3211
VICTORIA EMBANKMENT
Old Treasury
DOWNING ST
RICHMOND TER
Foreign & Commonwealth Office
KING CHARLES STREET
Treasury
Cabinet War Rooms
Norman Shaw Building (MPs Offices)
Westminster Pier
Westminster
PARLIAMENT ST
WESTMINSTER BRIDGE
A302
A23
Big Ben
Houses of Parliament
Florence Nightingale Museum
St Thomas' Hospital
LAMBETH
Schomberg House
Marlborough House
St James's Palace
Clarence House
Lancaster House
Spencer House
Duke of York Column
Carlton House
Inst. of Contemporary Arts
Mall Galleries
ST JAMES'S PARK
Duck Island
St James's Park Lake
Queen Victoria Memorial
BIRDCAGE WALK
Guards' Chapel & Museum
Wellington Barracks
Home Office
BUCKINGHAM GATE
Crown Plaza London St James Hotel
Westminster City Hall
New Scotland Yard
Queen Elizabeth II Conf. Centre
Middx. Guildhall
Central Hall
Westminster Abbey
Dean's Yard
Westminster School
Jewel Tower
Dept. of Trade and Industry
BROADWAY
VICTORIA STREET
Westminster Cathedral
GREYCOAT PL
HORSEFERRY ROAD
Royal Hort. Society New Hall
Royal Hort. Society Old Hall
Fire Station
Transport House
Thames House
MILLBANK
A3203
LAMBETH BRIDGE
Lambeth Pier
Lambeth Palace
Museum of Garden History
Archbishop's Park
LAMBETH ROAD
LAMBETH PALACE ROAD
A3036
Victoria Tower Gardens
Westminster School Playing Field
WESTMINSTER
Millbank Tower
Millbank Estate
Tate Gallery of British Art
Clore Gallery
Royal Army Medical College
Lillington Gardens Estate
Holiday Inn Express Hotel
Pimlico
VAUXHALL BRIDGE ROAD
A202
VAUXHALL BRIDGE (RING ROAD)
GROSVENOR ROAD
A3212
B310 (A3123)
Pimlico Gardens
St George Wharf Development (under construction)
VAUXHALL STATION
London Balloon
ALBERT EMBANKMENT
Fire Brigade Headquarters
Novotel
Lambeth Walk Open Space
Lilian Baylis School
Ethelred Estate
VAUXHALL
KENNINGTON
KENNINGTON LANE
RING ROAD
A3204
HARLEYFORD ROAD
The Oval (Surrey County Cricket Ground)
Ken Barrington Centre
Covent Garden Flower Market
Vauxhall Park
NINE ELMS LANE
PARRY ST
BOND WAY
SOUTH LAMBETH ROAD
THAMES

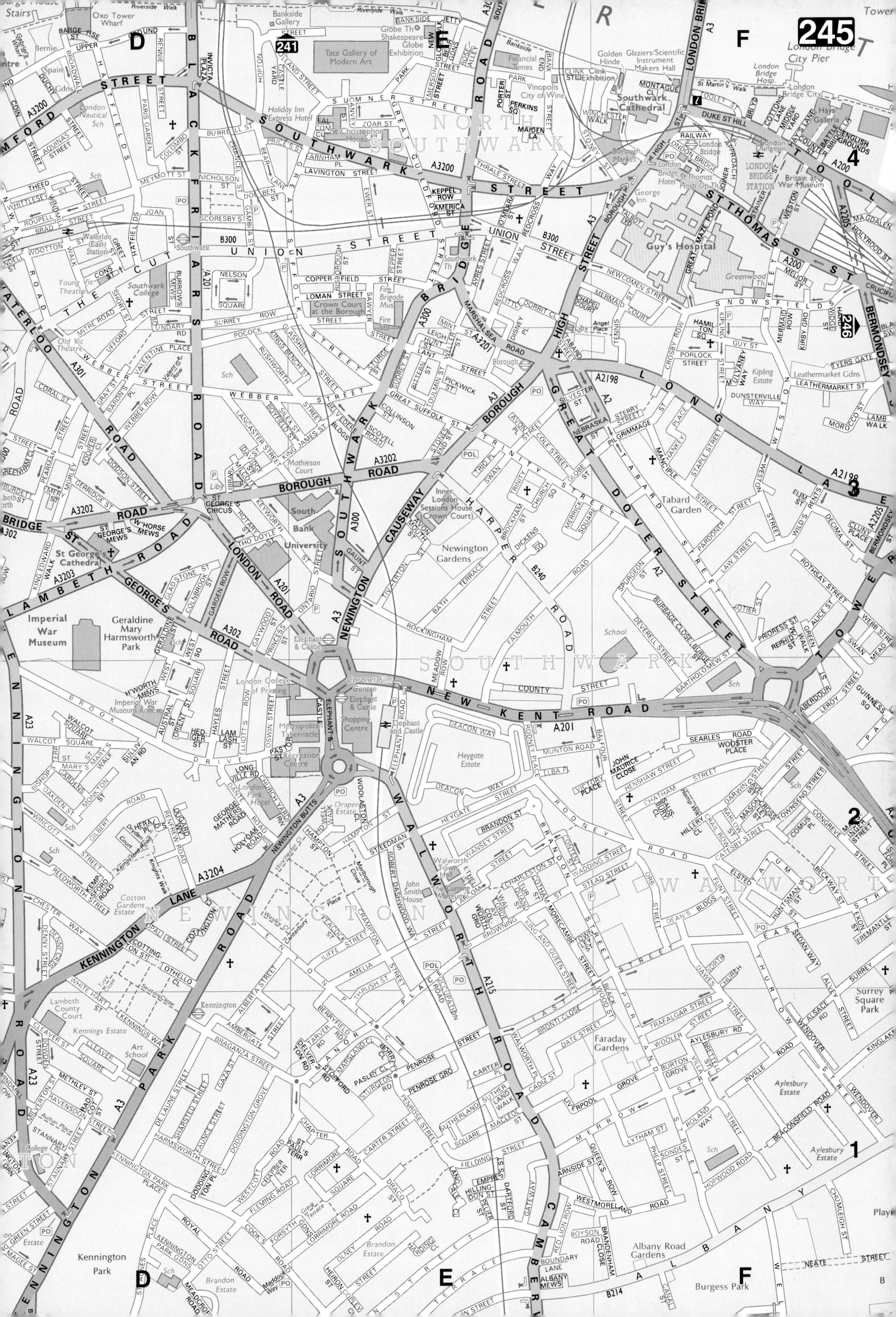
D
E
F
4
3
2
1
241
246
Oxo Tower Wharf
Bankside Gallery
Tate Gallery of Modern Art
Globe Th Shakespeare Globe Exhibition
Financial Times
Golden Hinde
Glaziers/Scientific Instrument Makers Hall
Clink Exhibition
Vinopolis City of Wine
Southwark Cathedral
London Bridge City Pier
London Bridge Hosp.
London Dungeon
Hays Galleria
Britain at War Museum
LONDON BRIDGE STATION
Guy's Hospital
Greenwood Th
Holiday Inn Express Hotel
NORTH SOUTHWARK
Borough Market
George Inn
Southwark
Waterloo (East) Station
Young Vic Theatre
Southwark College
Old Vic Theatre
Crown Court at the Borough
Fire Brigade Mus
Kipling Estate
Leathermarket Gdns
Mathieson Court
South Bank University
Inner London Sessions House (Crown Court)
Newington Gardens
Tabard Garden
St George's Cathedral
Imperial War Museum
Geraldine Mary Harmsworth Park
Imperial War Museum Annexe
London College of Printing
Elephant & Castle
Elephant & Castle Shopping Centre
Metropolitan Tabernacle
Recreation Centre
Coronet Film Centre
Heygate Estate
SOUTHWARK
London Park Hotel
Draper Estate
Walworth Town Hall
The Cuming Museum
John Smith House
WALWORTH
Cotton Gardens Estate
NEWINGTON
Kennington
Lambeth County Court
Kennings Estate
Art School
Faraday Gardens
Surrey Square Park
Aylesbury Estate
Albany Road Gardens
Burgess Park
Kennington Park
Brandon Estate
SOUTHWARK STREET
BLACKFRIARS ROAD
SOUTHWARK BRIDGE ROAD
UNION STREET
BOROUGH HIGH STREET
ST THOMAS STREET
TOOLEY STREET
LONG LANE
BOROUGH ROAD
LONDON ROAD
NEWINGTON CAUSEWAY
ST GEORGE'S ROAD
LAMBETH ROAD
GREAT DOVER STREET
TOWER BRIDGE ROAD
NEW KENT ROAD
WALWORTH ROAD
KENNINGTON PARK ROAD
KENNINGTON LANE
KENNINGTON ROAD
NEWINGTON BUTTS
CAMBERWELL ROAD
ALBANY ROAD
BERMONDSEY STREET
A3200
A3
A300
A3201
A3202
A201
A2
A2198
A200
A2205
A302
A3203
A3204
A23
A215
B300
B240
B214

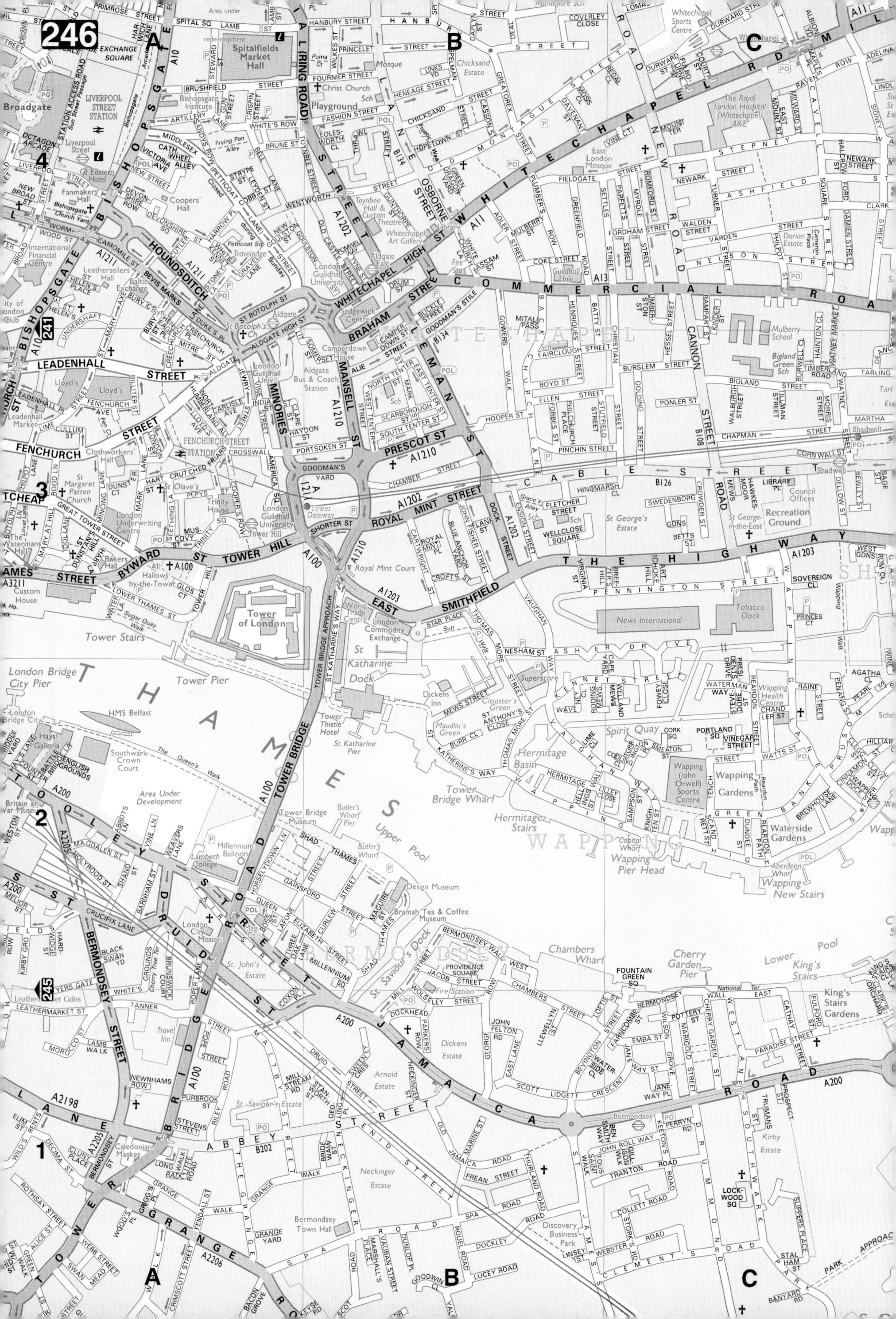
A
B
C
4
3
2
1
241
245
Spitalfields Market Hall
Liverpool Street Station
Broadgate
Bishopsgate
Houndsditch
Leadenhall Street
Fenchurch Street
Aldgate
Minories
Mansell St
Leman St
Prescot St
Royal Mint Street
Whitechapel High St
Whitechapel Rd
Commercial Road
Cable Street
The Highway
East Smithfield
Pennington Street
News International
Tobacco Dock
Wapping
Wapping High St
Wapping Lane
Tower of London
Tower Hill
Byward St
Tower Bridge
Tower Bridge Approach
Tower Bridge Road
St Katharine Dock
Royal Mint Court
Tower Pier
Tower Stairs
HMS Belfast
London Bridge City Pier
Thames
Tooley Street
Hays Galleria
Southwark Crown Court
Area Under Development
Design Museum
Butler's Wharf
Upper Pool
Bermondsey
Bermondsey Wall West
Bermondsey Street
Jamaica Road
Druid St
Abbey Street
Spa Road
Grange Road
Tower Bridge Road
Long Lane
Neckinger Estate
Bermondsey Town Hall
Dickens Estate
Cherry Garden Pier
King's Stairs Gardens
Southwark Park Rd
Clements Road
Hermitage Basin
Wapping Gardens
Wapping Pier Head
Wapping New Stairs
Waterside Gardens
Shadwell
Cannon Street Road
Whitechapel
Royal London Hospital (Whitechapel) A&E
East London Mosque
Mulberry School
Toynbee Hall & Curtain Theatre
Whitechapel Art Gallery
Aldgate East
Tower Gateway
Tower Hill
Fenchurch Street Station
Lloyd's
Custom House
Lower Thames St
Recreation Ground
St George's Estate
Millennium Balloon
Lambeth College
Bramah Tea & Coffee Museum
Tower Bridge Museum
Discovery Business Park

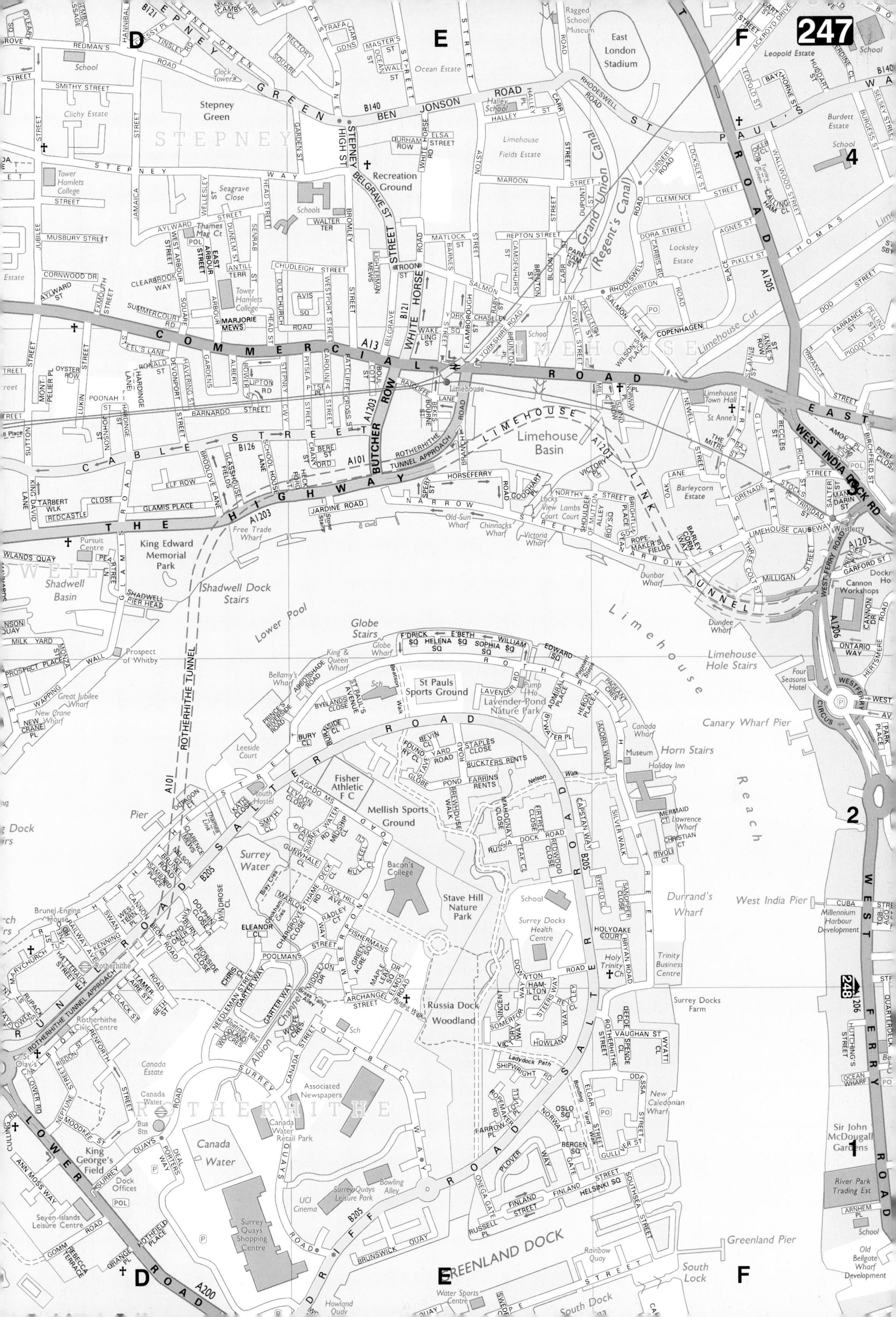
D
E
F
4
3
2
1
Stepney Green
STEPNEY
Ocean Estate
East London Stadium
Ragged School Museum
Leopold Estate
Burdett Estate
Limehouse Fields Estate
Recreation Ground
Tower Hamlets College
Seagrave Close
Clichy Estate
Grand Union Canal
(Regent's Canal)
Locksley Estate
LIMEHOUSE
Limehouse Cut
Limehouse Town Hall
COMMERCIAL ROAD
EAST INDIA DOCK RD
WEST INDIA DOCK RD
BEN JONSON ROAD
STEPNEY WAY
CABLE STREET
THE HIGHWAY
BUTCHER ROW
ROTHERHITHE TUNNEL APPROACH
LIMEHOUSE LINK
LIMEHOUSE LINK TUNNEL
NARROW STREET
Limehouse Basin
Barleycorn Estate
King Edward Memorial Park
Shadwell Basin
Shadwell Dock Stairs
Free Trade Wharf
Lower Pool
Globe Stairs
Prospect of Whitby
Limehouse Reach
Limehouse Hole Stairs
Canary Wharf Pier
Four Seasons Hotel
Cannon Workshops
WESTFERRY CIRCUS
St Pauls Sports Ground
Lavender Pond Nature Park
Fisher Athletic F C
Mellish Sports Ground
Surrey Water
Bacon's College
Stave Hill Nature Park
Surrey Docks Health Centre
Russia Dock Woodland
Horn Stairs
Holiday Inn
Durrand's Wharf
West India Pier
Millennium Harbour Development
Trinity Business Centre
Holy Trinity Ch
Surrey Docks Farm
New Caledonian Wharf
ROTHERHITHE
ROTHERHITHE TUNNEL
SALTER ROAD
REDRIFF ROAD
LOWER ROAD
Canada Estate
Canada Water
Associated Newspapers
Canada Water Retail Park
Surrey Quays Leisure Park
Surrey Quays Shopping Centre
UCI Cinema
Bowling Alley
King George's Field
Seven Islands Leisure Centre
Brunel Engine House
Rotherhithe Civic Centre
GREENLAND DOCK
Greenland Pier
South Lock
South Dock
Water Sports Centre
Howland Quay
Rainbow Quay
WEST FERRY ROAD
Sir John McDougall Gardens
River Park Trading Est
Old Bellgate Wharf Development
A13
A1203
A1205
A101
A200
A1206
B140
B121
B126
B205
248

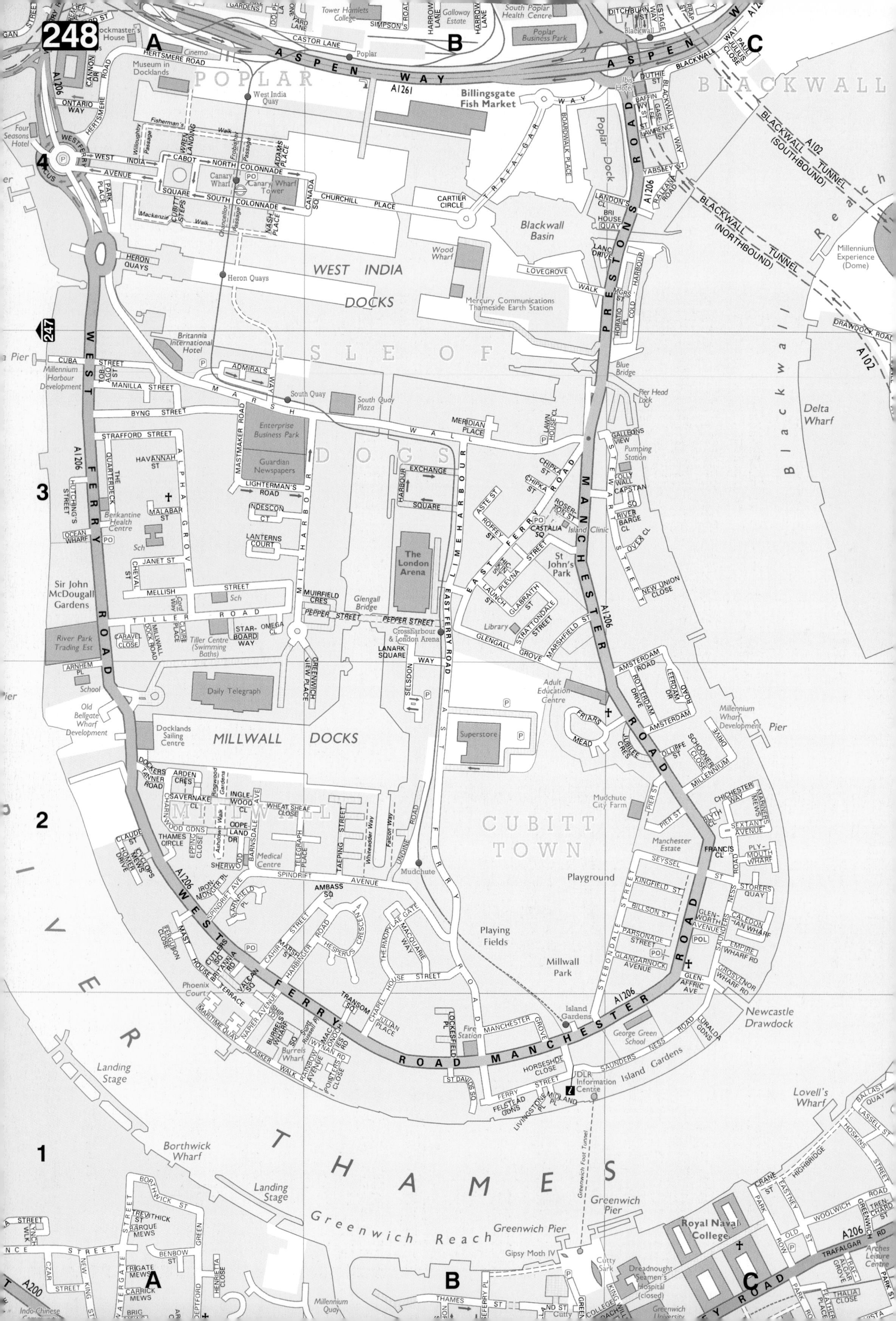

248
247
A
B
C
4
3
2
1
POPLAR
BLACKWALL
ASPEN WAY
A1261
A1206
A102
Billingsgate Fish Market
Museum in Docklands
HERTSMERE ROAD
Cinema
CASTOR LANE
Poplar
Tower Hamlets College
SIMPSON'S RD
Galloway Estate
South Poplar Health Centre
Poplar Business Park
Blackwall
West India Quay
Canary Wharf
Canary Wharf Tower
NORTH COLONNADE
SOUTH COLONNADE
CABOT
SQUARE
WEST INDIA AVENUE
CHURCHILL PLACE
CARTIER CIRCLE
TRAFALGAR WAY
Poplar Dock
Blackwall Basin
BLACKWALL TUNNEL (SOUTHBOUND)
BLACKWALL TUNNEL (NORTHBOUND)
Millennium Experience (Dome)
Heron Quays
HERON QUAYS
WEST INDIA DOCKS
Wood Wharf
Mercury Communications Thameside Earth Station
PRESTONS ROAD
LOVEGROVE WALK
Blue Bridge
Pier Head Lock
DRAWDOCK ROAD
Delta Wharf
Blackwall Reach
ISLE OF DOGS
Britannia International Hotel
Millennium Harbour Development
CUBA STREET
MANILLA STREET
BYNG STREET
South Quay
South Quay Plaza
MARSH WALL
MERIDIAN PLACE
Enterprise Business Park
Guardian Newspapers
MASTMAKER ROAD
LIGHTERMAN'S ROAD
HARBOUR EXCHANGE SQUARE
LIMEHARBOUR
MILLHARBOUR
STRAFFORD STREET
ALPHA GROVE
WEST FERRY ROAD
Berkantine Health Centre
Sir John McDougall Gardens
The London Arena
MANCHESTER ROAD
EAST FERRY ROAD
St John's Park
Island Clinic
Library
GLENGALL GROVE
Glengall Bridge
PEPPER STREET
Crossharbour & London Arena
TILLER ROAD
Tiller Centre (Swimming Baths)
River Park Trading Est
School
Daily Telegraph
Old Bellgate Wharf Development
Docklands Sailing Centre
MILLWALL DOCKS
Superstore
Adult Education Centre
Millennium Wharf Development
Pier
MILLWALL
CUBITT TOWN
Mudchute City Farm
Mudchute
Manchester Estate
Playground
Playing Fields
Millwall Park
SPINDRIFT AVENUE
Medical Centre
Phoenix Court
Landing Stage
Island Gardens
George Green School
Newcastle Drawdock
Fire Station
DLR Information Centre
Greenwich Foot Tunnel
RIVER THAMES
Greenwich Reach
Borthwick Wharf
Greenwich Pier
Gipsy Moth IV
Cutty Sark
Royal Naval College
Dreadnought Seamen's Hospital (closed)
Greenwich University
Lovell's Wharf
Millennium Quay
TRAFALGAR RD
A206
A200
Arches Leisure Centre

Central London street index

In the index the street names are listed in alphabetical order and written in full, but may be abbreviated on the map. Postal codes are listed where information is available. Each entry is followed by its map page number in bold type, and an arbitrary letter and grid reference number. For example, for Exhibition Road SW7 **242** C3, turn to page 242. The letter 'C' refers to the grid square located at the bottom of the page; the figure '3' refers to the grid square located at the left-hand side of the page. Exhibition Road is found within the intersecting square. SW7 is the postcode. A proportion of street names and their references are also followed by the name of another street in italics. These entries do not appear on the map due to insufficient space but can be located adjacent to the name of the road in italics.

249

250

C

D

Harpur Street — Marylebone Mews

252

Harpur Street WC1 240 C3
Harriet Street SW1 243 D3
Harriet Walk SW1 243 D3
Harrington Gardens SW7 242 B2
Harrington Road SW7 242 C2
Harrington Street NW1 239 F4
Harrison Street WC1 240 B4
Harrow Place E1 246 A4
Harrow Road W2, W9, W10 & NW10 238 B2
Harrow Road Bridge W2 238 B2
Harrowby Street W1 239 D2
Hart Street EC3 246 A3
Harwich Lane EC2 246 A4
Harwood Row NW1 239 D3
Hasker Street SW3 243 D2
Hastings Street WC1 240 B4
Hatfields SE1 245 D4
Hatherley Grove W2 238 A2
Hatherley Street SW1 244 A2
Hatteraick Street SE16 247 D2
Hatton Garden EC1 241 D3
Hatton Place EC1 241 D3
Hatton Place EC1 241 D3
Hatton Street NW8 238 C3
Hatton Wall EC1 241 D3
Haunch of Venison Yard W1 238 C1
Brook Street
Havannah Street E14 248 A3
Havering Street E1 247 D3
Haverstock Street N1 241 E4
Hawkesmoor Mews E1 246 C3
Hay Hill W1 239 F1
Hay's Lane SE1 245 F4
Hay's Mews W1 239 F1
Hayes Place NW1 239 D3
Hayles Street SE11 245 D2
Haymarket SW1 240 A1
Hayne Street EC1 241 E3
Hayward's Place EC1 241 D3
Headfort Place SW1 243 E3
Heathcote Street WC1 240 C3
Heckford Street E1 247 E3
Heddon Street W1 239 F1
Hedger Street SE11 245 D2
Heiron Street SE17 245 E1
Helena Square SE16 247 E3
Hellings Street E1 246 B2
Helmet Row EC1 241 E3
Helsinki Square SE16 247 E2
Hemp Walk SE17 245 F2
Henderson Drive NW8 238 C3
Heneage Lane EC3 246 A4
Heneage Place EC3 246 A4
Heneage Street E1 246 B4
Henniker Mews SW3 242 B1
Henrietta Close SE8 248 A1
Henrietta Place W1 239 E2
Henrietta Street WC2 240 B1
Henriques Street E1 246 C4
Henshaw Street SE17 245 F2
Herald's Place SE11 245 D2
Herbal Hill EC1 241 D3
Herbrand Street WC1 240 B3
Hercules Road SE1 244 C3
Hereford Road W2 238 A2
Hereford Square SW7 242 B2
Hermes Street N1 240 C4
Hermit Street EC1 241 D4
Hermitage Street W2 238 C2
Hermitage Wall E1 246 B2
Heron Place SE16 247 E2
Heron Quays E14 248 A4
Herrick Street SW1 244 B2
Hertford Street W1 243 E4
Hertsmere Road E14 248 A4
Hesper Mews SW5 242 A2
Hesperus Crescent E14 248 B2
Hessel Street E1 246 C3
Heygate Street SE17 245 E2
Hickin Street E14 248 B3
Hide Place SW1 244 A2
High Holborn WC1 240 B2
High Timber Street EC4 241 E1
Highbridge SE10 248 C1
Hildyard Road SW6 242 A1
Hill Road W9 238 B4
Hill Street W1 239 F2
Hillery Close SE17 245 F2
Hilliard's Court E1 246 C2
Hillingdon Street SE5 & SE17 245 E1
Pelier Street
Hind Court EC4 241 D2
Hinde Street W1 239 E2
Hindmarsh Close E1 246 B3
Hobart Place SW1 243 F3
Hogarth Court EC3 241 F1
Fenchurch Street
Hogarth Place SW5 242 A2
Hogarth Road SW5 242 A2
Holbein Mews SW1 243 E2
Holbein Place SW1 243 E2
Holborn EC1 241 D2
Holborn Circus EC1 241 D2
Holborn Viaduct EC1 241 D2
Holford Place WC1 240 C4
Holford Street WC1 240 C4
Holland Street SE1 245 D4
Holland Street W8 242 A3
Hollen Street W1 240 A2
Wardour Street
Holles Street W1 239 F2
Holley Mews SW10 242 B1
Drayton Gardens
Hollywood Mews SW10 242 B1
Hollywood Road SW10 242 B1
Holyoak Road SE11 245 D2
Holyoake Court SE16 247 F2
Holyrood Street SE1 246 A2
Holywell Row EC2 241 F3
Homer Drive E14 248 A2
Homer Row W1 239 D2
Homer Street W1 239 D2
Honduras Street EC1 241 E3
Old Street
Hooper Street E1 246 B3
Hop Gardens WC2 240 B1
St Martin's Lane
Hope Wharf SE16 247 D2
Hopetown Street E1 246 B4
Hopkins Street W1 240 A1
Hopton Street SE1 245 D4
Hopwood Road SE17 245 F1
Horatio Place E14 248 C4
Horley Crescent SE16 247 D2
Marlow Way
Hornton Place W8 242 A3
Hornton Street W8 242 A3
Horse Guards Avenue SW1 244 B4
Horse Guards Road SW1 244 B4
Horse Ride SW1 243 F3
Horseferry Road E14 247 E3
Horseferry Road SW1 244 A3
Horselydown Lane SE1 246 A2
Horseshoe Close E14 248 B2
Hosier Lane EC1 241 D2
Hoskins Street SE10 248 C1
Hothfield Place SE16 247 D1
Hotspur Street SE11 244 C2
Houghton Street WC2 240 C1
Aldwych
Houndsditch EC3 246 A4
Howard Place SW1 240 A2
Carlisle Street
Howell Walk SE1 245 E2
Howick Place SW1 244 A3
Howland Street W1 240 A3
Howland Way SE16 247 E1
Howley Place W2 238 B3
Hoxton Market N1 241 F4
Hoxton Square N1 241 F4
Huddart Street E3 247 F4
Hudson's Place SW1 243 F2
Huggin Hill EC4 241 E1
Hugh Street SW1 243 F2
Hull Close SE16 247 E2
Hull Street EC1 241 E4
Hunt's Court WC2 240 B1
Hunter Close SE1 245 F3
Prioress Street
Hunter Street WC1 240 B3
Huntley Street WC1 240 A3
Huntsman Street SE17 245 F2
Huntsworth Mews NW1 239 D3
Hutching's Street E14 248 A3
Hutton Street EC4 241 D1
Hyde Park Corner W1 243 E4
Hyde Park Crescent W2 238 C2
Hyde Park Gardens W2 238 C1
Hyde Park Gardens Mews W2 238 C1
Hyde Park Gate SW7 242 B3
Hyde Park Square W2 238 C2
Hyde Park Street W2 238 C2

I

Idol Lane EC3 246 A3
Ifield Road SW10 242 A1
Ilchester Gardens W2 238 A1
Iliffe Street SE17 245 E2
Indescon Court E14 248 A3
India Place WC2 240 C1
Montreal Place
India Street EC3 246 A3
Ingestre Place W1 240 A1
Inglebert Street EC1 241 D4
Inglewood Close E14 248 A2
Ingram Close SE11 244 C2
Inigo Place WC2 240 B1
Bedford Street
Inner Temple Lane EC4 241 D2
Inverness Gardens W8 242 A4
Palace Garden Terrace
Inverness Mews W2 238 B1
Inverness Place W2 238 B1
Inverness Terrace W2 238 B1
Invicta Plaza SE1 245 D4
Inville Road SE17 245 F1
Ireland Yard EC4 241 D1
St Andrew's Hill
Ironmonger Lane EC2 241 E2
Ironmonger Place E14 248 A2
Ironmonger Row EC1 241 E4
Ironside Close SE16 247 D2
Irving Street WC2 240 B1
Isambard Place SE16 247 D2
Island Row E14 247 F3
Iverna Court W8 242 A3
Iverna Gardens W8 242 A3
Ives Street SW3 243 D2
Ivor Place NW1 239 D3
Ixworth Place SW3 242 C2

J

Jacob Street SE1 246 B2
Jamaica Road SE1 & SE16 246 B1
Jamaica Street E1 247 D4
James Street W1 239 E2
James Street WC2 240 B1
Long Acre
Jameson Street W8 242 A4
Janet Street E14 248 A3
Janeway Place SE16 246 C1
Janeway Street SE16 246 C1
Jardine Road E1 247 E3
Jay Mews SW7 242 B3
Jermyn Street SW1 244 A4
Jerome Crescent NW8 238 C3
Jewry Street EC3 246 A3
Joan Street SE1 245 D4
Jockey's Fields WC1 240 C3
John Adams Street WC2 244 B4
John Aird Court W2 238 B3
John Carpenter Street EC4 241 D1
John Felton Road SE16 246 B1
John Fisher Street E1 246 B3
John Islip Street SW1 244 B2
John Maurice Close SE17 245 F2
John Princes Street W1 239 F2
John Roll Way SE16 246 C1
John Street WC1 240 C3
John's Mews WC1 240 C3
Johnson Street E1 247 D3
Johnson's Place SW1 244 A1
Joiner Street SE1 245 F4
Jonathan Street SE11 244 C2
Jones Street W1 239 A3
Bourdon Street
Jubilee Crescent E14 248 C2
Jubilee Place SW3 243 D2
Jubilee Street E1 247 D4
Judd Street WC1 240 B4
Julian Place E14 248 B1
Junction Mews W2 238 C2
Juxon Street SE11 244 C2

K

Katherine Close SE16 247 D2
Kean Street WC2 240 C2
Keel Close SE16 247 E2
Keeley Street WC2 240 C2
Keeton's Road SE16 246 C1
Kelso Place W8 242 A3
Kemble Street WC2 240 C2
Kempsford Gardens SW5 242 A1
Kempsford Road SE11 245 D2
Kempton Court E1 246 C4
Durward Street
Kendal Street W2 239 C2
Kendall Place W1 239 D2
Kendrick Mews SW7 242 C2
Kendrick Place SW7 242 C2
Reece Mews
Kennet Street E1 246 B2
Kennet Wharf Lane EC4 241 E1
Kenning Street SE16 247 D2
Kennings Way SE11 245 B2
Kennington Green SE11 245 D1
Kennington Grove SE11 244 C1
Kennington Lane SE11 244 C1
Kennington Oval SE11 244 C1
Kennington Park Gardens SE11 245 D1
Kennington Park Place SE11 245 D1
Kennington Park Road SE11 245 D1
Kennington Road SE1 & SE11 244 C3
Kenrick Place W1 239 E2
Kensington Church Street W8 242 A4
Kensington Church Walk W8 242 A3
Kensington Court W8 242 A3
Kensington Court Place W8 242 A3
Kensington Gardens Square W2 238 A2
Kensington Gate W8 242 B3
Kensington Gore SW7 242 B3
Kensington High Street W8 & W14 242 A3
Kensington Mall W8 242 A4
Kensington Palace Gardens W8 242 A4
Kensington Road W8 & SW7 242 B3
Kensington Square W8 242 A3
Kent Passage NW1 239 D4
Kent Terrace NW1 239 D4
Kenton Street WC1 239 B3
Kenway Road SW5 241 A2
Keppel Row SE1 245 E4
Keppel Street WC1 240 B3
Keyse Road SE1 246 B1
Keystone Crescent N1 240 B4
Keyworth Street SE1 245 D3
Kilburn Park Road NW6 238 A4
Kildare Gardens W2 238 A2
Kildare Terrace W2 238 A2
Kimbolton Row SW3 242 C2
Fulham Road
Kinburn Street SE16 247 D2
Kinder Street E1 246 C3
King and Queen Street SE17 245 E2
King Charles Street SW1 244 B3
King David Lane E1 247 D3
King Edward III Mews SE16 246 C1
Paradise Street
King Edward Street EC1 241 E2
King Edward Walk SE1 245 D3
King James Street SE1 245 E3
King Square EC1 241 E4
King Street EC2 241 E2
King Street SW1 244 A4
King Street WC2 240 B1
King William Street EC4 241 F1
King's Bench Walk EC4 241 D1
King's Cross Road WC1 240 C4
King's Mews WC1 240 C3
King's Road SW3, SW6 & SW10 243 D1
King's Scholars' Passage SW1 243 F2
King's Stairs Close SE16 246 C2
Kingfield Street E14 248 C2
Kinghorn Street EC1 241 E3
Kinglake Street SE17 245 F2
Kingly Court W1 240 A1
Kingly Street W1 239 F1
Kings Arms Yard EC2 241 F2
Kings Bench Street SE1 245 D3
Kingscote Street EC4 241 D1
Kingsway WC2 240 C2
Kinnerton Street SW1 243 E3
Kipling Street SE1 245 F4
Kirby Grove SE1 245 F3
Kirby Street EC1 241 D3
Knaresborough Place SW5 242 A2
Knight's Walk SE11 245 D2
Knighten Street E1 246 C2
Knightrider Street EC4 241 E1
Godliman Street
Knightsbridge SW1 & SW7 243 D3
Knightsbridge Green SW1 243 D3
Brompton Road
Knox Street W1 239 D3
Kramer Mews SW5 242 A1
Kynance Mews SW7 242 B3

L

Lackington Street EC2 241 F3
Lafone Street SE1 246 A2
Lagado Mews SE16 247 E2
Lamb Street E1 246 A4
Lamb Walk SE1 245 F3
Lamb's Conduit Street WC1 240 C3
Lamb's Passage EC1 241 F3
Lambeth Bridge SW1 & SE11 244 B2
Lambeth High Street SE1 244 C2
Lambeth Hill EC4 241 E1
Lambeth Palace Road SE1 244 C2
Lambeth Road SE1 244 C2
Lambeth Walk SE11 244 C2
Lamlash Street SE11 245 D2
Lanark Place W9 238 B3
Lanark Road W9 238 A4
Lanark Square E14 248 B3
Lancaster Drive E14 248 B4
Lancaster Gate W2 238 B1
Lancaster Mews W2 238 B1
Lancaster Place WC2 240 C1
Lancaster Street SE1 245 D3
Lancaster Terrace W2 238 C1
Lancaster Walk W2 238 B1
Lancelot Place SW7 243 D3
Lancing Street NW1 240 A4
Landon Place SW1 243 D3
Landon's Close E14 248 B4
Langdale Close SE17 245 E1
Langham Place W1 239 F2
Langham Street W1 239 F2
Langley Lane SW8 244 B1
Langley Street WC2 240 B1
Langton Close WC1 240 C3
Lansdowne Row W1 239 F1
Lansdowne Terrace WC1 240 B3
Lant Street SE1 245 E3
Lanterns Court E14 248 A3
Larcom Street SE17 245 E2
Lassell Street SE10 248 C1
Lauderdale Road W9 238 A4
Launcelot Street SE1 244 C3
Lower Marsh
Launceston Place W8 242 B3
Launch Street E14 248 B3
Laurence Pountney Lane EC4 241 F1
Lavender Close SW3 242 C1
Lavender Road SE16 247 E2
Laverton Place SW5 242 A2
Lavington Street SE1 245 E4
Law Street SE1 245 F3
Lawn House Close E14 248 B3
Lawn Lane SW8 244 B1
Lawrence Lane EC2 241 E2
Trump Street
Lawrence Street SW3 242 C1
Laxton Place NW1 239 F3
Laystall Street EC1 240 C3
Layton's Buildings SE1 245 E4
Borough High Street
Leadenhall Place EC3 241 F1
Leadenhall Street EC3 241 F2
Leake Street SE1 244 C3
Leather Lane EC1 241 D3
Leathermarket Court SE1 245 F3
Leathermarket Street
Leathermarket Street SE1 245 F3
Lecky Street SW7 242 C1
Leerdam Drive E14 248 C2
Lees Place W1 239 E1
Leicester Court WC2 240 B1
Cranbourn Street
Leicester Place WC2 240 A1
Lisle Street
Leicester Square WC2 240 B1
Leicester Street WC2 240 B1
Leigh Hunt Street SE1 245 E3
Leigh Street WC1 240 B4
Leinster Gardens W2 238 B1
Leinster Mews W2 238 B1
Leinster Place W2 238 B1
Leinster Square W2 238 A1
Leinster Terrace W2 238 B1
Leman Street E1 246 B3
Lennox Gardens SW1 243 D2
Lennox Gardens Mews SW1 243 D2
Leonard Street EC2 241 F3
Leopold Street E3 247 F4
Leroy Street SE1 245 F2
Lever Street EC1 241 E4
Leverett Street SW3 243 D2
Mossop Street
Lewisham Street SW1 244 B3
Lexham Gardens W8 242 A2
Lexham Mews W8 242 A2
Lexham Walk W8 242 A2
Lexington Street W1 240 A1
Leyden Street E1 246 A4
Leydon Close SE16 247 E2
Library Place E1 246 C3
Library Street SE1 245 D3
Lighterman Mews E1 247 E4
Lightermans Road E14 248 A3
Lilestone Street NW8 238 C3
Lilley Close E1 246 B2
Lillie Yard SW6 242 A1
Lime Close E1 246 B2
Lime Street EC3 241 F1
Lime Street Passage EC3 241 F1
Lime Street
Limeburner Lane EC4 241 D2
Limeharbour E14 248 B3
Limehouse Causeway E14 247 F3
Limehouse Link Tunnel E14 247 E3
Limerston Street SW10 242 B1
Lincoln Street SW3 243 D2
Lincoln's Inn Fields WC2 240 C2
Linden Gardens W2 238 A1
Linden Mews W2 238 A1
Lindley Street E1 246 C4
Lindsay Square SW1 244 B2
Lindsey Street EC1 241 E3
Linhope Street NW1 238 D3
Links Yard E1 246 B4
Linsey Street SE16 246 B1
Lipton Road E1 247 D3
Lisle Street W1 240 A1
Lisson Grove NW1 & NW8 238 C3
Lisson Street NW1 238 C3
Litchfield Street WC2 240 B1
Little Argyll Street W1 244 A2
Regent Street
Little Britain EC1 241 E2
Little Chester Street SW1 243 E3
Little College Street SW1 244 B3
Little Dorrit Close SE1 245 E4
Little Edward Street NW1 239 F4
Little George Street SW1 244 B3
Great George Street
Little London Court SE1 246 B1
Mill Street
Little Marlborough Street W1 239 F1
Kingly Street
Little New Street EC4 241 D2
New Street Square
Little Newport Street WC2 240 B1
Little Portland Street W1 239 F2
Little Russell Street WC1 240 B2
Little Sanctuary SW1 244 B3
Broad Sanctuary
Little Smith Street SW1 244 B3
Little Somerset Street E1 244 A3
Little St James's Street SW1 244 A4
Little Titchfield Street W1 239 F2
Little Trinity Lane EC4 241 E1
Liverpool Grove SE17 245 E1
Liverpool Street EC2 241 F2
Livingstone Place E14 248 B1
Livonia Street W2 240 A2
Lizard Street EC1 241 E4
Llewellyn Street SE16 246 B1
Lloyd Baker Street WC1 240 C4
Lloyd Square WC1 240 C4
Lloyd Street WC1 240 C4
Lloyd's Avenue EC3 246 A3
Lloyd's Row EC1 241 D4
Lockesfield Place E14 248 B1
Locksley Street E14 247 F4
Lockwood Square SE16 246 C1
Lodge Road NW8 238 C4
Loftie Street SE16 246 B1
Lolesworth Close E1 246 B4
Lollard Street SE11 244 C2
Loman Street SE1 245 E4
Lomas Street E1 246 C4
Lombard Court EC4 241 F1
Lombard Lane EC4 241 A2
Temple Lane
London Bridge EC4 & SE1 241 F1
London Bridge Street SE1 245 F4
London Road SE1 245 D3
London Street EC3 246 A3
London Street W2 238 C2
London Wall EC2 241 E2
Long Acre WC2 240 B1
Long Lane EC1 241 E2
Long Lane SE1 245 F3
Long Walk SE1 246 A1
Long Yard WC1 240 C3
Longford Street NW1 239 F3
Longmoore Street SW1 243 F2
Longville Road SE11 245 D2
Lord Hill's Bridge W2 238 A2
Lord Hill's Road W2 238 A3
Lord North Street SW1 244 B3
Lordship Place SW3 242 C1
Lawrence Street
Lorenzo Street WC1 240 C4
Lorrimore Road SE17 245 E1
Lorrimore Square SE17 245 E1
Lothbury EC2 241 F2
Loughborough Street SE11 244 C1
Lovat Lane EC3 241 F1
Love Lane EC2 241 E2
Lovegrove Walk E14 248 B4
Lovell Place SE16 247 E1
Lovers' Walk W1 243 E4
Lowell Street E14 247 E4
Lower Belgrave Street SW1 243 E3
Lower Grosvenor Place SW1 243 F3
Lower James Street W1 240 A1
Lower John Street W1 240 A1
Lower Marsh SE1 244 C3
Lower Road SE8 & SE16 247 D1
Lower Robert Street WC2 240 B1
Savoy Place
Lower Sloane Street SW1 243 E1
Lower Thames Street EC3 241 F1
Lowndes Place SW1 243 E3
Lowndes Square SW1 243 D3
Lowndes Street SW1 243 E3
Lowood Street E1 246 C3
Bewley Street
Loxham Street WC1 240 B3
Cromer Street
Lucan Place SW3 242 C2
Lucerne Mews W8 242 A4
Lucey Road SE16 246 B1
Ludgate Broadway EC4 241 D2
Pilgrim Street
Ludgate Circus EC4 241 D2
Ludgate Square EC4 241 D2
Luke Street EC2 241 F3
Lukin Street E1 247 D3
Lumley Street W1 239 E1
Brown Hart Garden
Lupus Street SW1 243 F1
Luralda Gardens E14 248 C1
Luton Street NW8 238 C3
Luxborough Street W1 239 E3
Lyall Street SW1 243 E3
Lygon Place SW1 243 F3
Lynch Walk SE8 248 A1
Lyons Place NW8 238 C3
Lytham Street SE17 245 F1

M

Mabledon Place WC1 240 B4
Macclesfield Road EC1 241 E4
Mackenzie Walk E14 248 A4
Macklin Street WC2 240 B2
Mackworth Street NW1 239 F4
Macleod Street SE17 245 E1
Maconochies Road E14 248 B1
Macquarie Way E14 248 B2
Maddock Way SE17 245 D1
Maddox Street W1 239 F1
Magdalen Street SE1 246 A2
Magee Street SE11 245 D1
Magellan Place E14 248 A1
Maritime Quay
Maguire Street SE1 246 B2
Mahognay Close SE16 247 E2
Maida Avenue W2 238 B3
Maida Vale W9 238 B4
Maiden Lane WC2 240 B1
Maiden Lane SE1 245 E4
Makins Street SW3 246 D2
Malabar Street E14 248 A3
Malet Street WC1 240 A3
Mallord Street SW3 242 C1
Mallory Street NW8 238 C3
Mallow Street EC1 241 F3
Malta Street EC1 241 D3
Maltby Street SE1 246 A1
Maltravers Street WC2 240 C1
Managers Street E14 248 C4
Manchester Grove E14 248 B2
Manchester Road E14 248 B3
Manchester Square W1 239 E2
Manchester Street W1 239 E2
Manciple Street SE1 245 F3
Mandarin Street E14 247 F3
Mandeville Place W1 239 E2
Manette Street W1 240 B2
Manilla Street E14 248 A3
Manningford Close EC1 241 D4
Manningtree Street E1 246 B4
Commercial Road
Manor Place SE17 245 E1
Manresa Road SW3 242 C1
Mansell Street E1 246 B3
Mansfield Mews W1 239 F2
Mansfield Street
Mansfield Street W1 239 F2
Mansion House Place EC4 241 A1
St Swithun's Lane
Manson Mews SW7 242 B2
Manson Place SW7 242 C2
Maple Leaf Square SE16 247 E2
Maple Street W1 239 F3
Maples Place E1 246 C4
Marble Arch W1 239 D1
Marchmont Street WC1 240 B3
Margaret Court W1 239 F2
Margaret Street
Margaret Street W1 239 F2
Margaretta Terrace SW3 242 C1
Margery Street WC1 240 C4
Marigold Street SE16 246 C1
Mariners Mews E14 248 C2
Maritime Quay E14 248 A1
Marjorie Mews E1 247 D4
Mark Lane EC3 246 A3
Market Court W1 239 E1
Oxford Street
Market Mews W1 243 E4
Market Place W1 239 F2
Markham Place SW3 243 D2
Elystan Place
Markham Square SW3 243 D2
Markham Street SW3 243 D2
Marlborough Close SE17 245 E2
Marlborough Road SW1 244 A4
Marlborough Street SW3 242 C2
Marloes Road W8 242 A3
Marlow Way SE16 247 E2
Marne Street W10 246 B1
Maroon Street E14 247 E4
Marsh Street E14 248 A2
Marsh Wall E14 248 A3
Marshall Street W1 240 A1
Marshall's Place SE16 246 B1
Marshalsea Road SE1 245 E4
Marsham Street SW1 244 B3
Marshfield Street E14 248 B3
Marsland Close SE17 245 E1
Martha Street E1 246 C3
Martin Lane EC4 241 F1
Martin's Street WC2 240 B1
Martlett Court WC2 240 B2
Marylands Road W9 238 A3
Marylebone High Street W1 239 E3
Marylebone Lane W1 239 E2
Marylebone Mews W1 239 E2

253

Queen Square Swallow Street

Queen Square WC1 240 B3
Queen Street EC4 241 E1
Queen Street W1 241 F4
Queen Street Place EC1 241 E1
Queen Victoria Street EC4 241 D1
Queen's Gardens SW1 243 F3
Queen's Gardens W2 238 B1
Queen's Gate SW7 242 B3
Queen's Gate Gardens SW7 242 B2
Queen's Gate Mews SW7 242 B3
Queen's Gate Place SW7 242 B3
Queen's Gate Place Mews SW7 242 B2
Queen's Gate Terrace SW7 242 B3
Queen's Mews W2 238 A1
Queen's Row SE17 245 E1
Queen's Walk SW1 243 F4
Queenhithe EC4 241 E1
Queensberry Mews West SW7 242 B2
Queensberry Place SW7 239 F4
Harrington Street
Queensborough Terrace W2 238 B1
Queensway W2 238 A2
Quick Street N1 241 D4

R

Rabbit Row W8 242 A4
Raby Street E14 247 E4
Radcliffe Road SE1 246 A1
Radcot Street SE11 245 D1
Radley Court SE16 247 E2
Radley Mews W8 242 A2
Radnor Mews W2 238 C2
Radnor Place W2 238 C2
Radnor Street EC1 241 D3
Radnor Walk SW3 243 D1
Railway Approach SE1 245 F4
Railway Avenue SE16 247 D2
Rainbow Avenue E14 248 B1
Raine Street E1 246 C2
Rainsford Street W2 238 C2
Raleana Road E14 248 C4
Ralston Street SW3 243 D1
Ramillies Place W1 239 F2
Ramillies Street W1 240 A2
Rampart Street E1 246 C4
Rampayne Street SW1 244 A2
Ramsey Mews SW3 242 C1
Randall Road SE11 244 C2
Randall Row SE11 244 C2
Randolph Avenue W9 238 A4
Randolph Crescent W9 238 B3
Randolph Mews W9 238 B3
Randolph Road W9 238 B2
Ranelagh Bridge W2 238 B2
Ranelagh Grove SW1 243 E2
Ranelagh Road SW1 244 A1
Ranston Street NW1 238 C3
Raphael Street SW7 243 D3
Ratcliff Grove EC1 241 E4
Ratcliffe Cross Street E1 247 E3
Ratcliffe Lane E14 247 E3
Rathbone Place W1 240 A2
Raven Row E1 246 C4
Ravensdon Street SE11 245 D1
Ravent Road SE11 244 C2
Ravey Street EC2 241 F3
Rawlings Street SW3 243 D2
Rawstorne Place EC1 241 D4
Rawstorne Street
Rawstorne Street EC1 241 D4
Ray Street EC1 241 D3
Reardon Path E1 246 C2
Reardon Street E1 246 C2
Rebecca Terrace SE16 247 D1
Rectory Square E1 247 E4
Red Lion Row SE17 245 E1
Red Lion Square WC1 240 C2
Red Lion Street WC1 240 C2
Redan Place W2 238 A2
Redburn Street SW3 243 D1
Redcastle Close E1 247 D3
Redcliffe Gardens SW10 & SW5 242 A1
Redcliffe Mews SW10 242 B1
Redcliffe Place SW10 242 B1
Redcliffe Road SW10 242 B1
Redcliffe Square SW10 242 A1
Redcliffe Street SW10 242 A1
Redcross Way SE1 245 E4
Rede Place W2 238 A1
Redesdale Street SW3 243 D1
Redfield Lane SW5 242 A2
Redhill Street NW1 239 F4
Redman's Road E1 247 D4
Redmead Lane E1 246 B2
Wapping High Street
Redriff Road SE16 247 E1
Redwood Close SE16 247 E2
Reece Mews SW7 242 C2
Reedworth Street SE11 245 D2
Reeves Mews W1 239 E1
Regal Close E1 246 C4
Regan Way N1 241 F4
Regency Street SW1 244 A2
Regent Square WC1 240 B4
Regent Street W1 & SW1 239 F2
Regnart Buildings NW1 240 A4
Euston Street
Relton Mews SW7 243 D3
Remington Street N1 241 E4
Remnant Street WC2 240 C2
Kingsway
Renforth Street SE16 247 D1
Renfrew Road SE11 245 D2
Rennie Street SE1 241 E1
Rephidim Street SE1 245 F3
Repton Street E14 247 E4
Reston Place SW7 242 B3
Reveley Close SE16 247 E1
Rex Place W1 239 E1
Rhodeswell Road E14 247 F4
Rich Lane SW5 242 A1
Rich Street E14 247 F3
Richard's Place SW3 243 D2
Richbell Place WC1 240 C3
Emerald Street
Richmond Buildings W1 240 A2
Dean Street
Richmond Mews W1 240 A2
Richmond Terrace SW1 244 B4
Rickett Street SW6 242 A1
Ridgmount Gardens WC1 240 A3
Ridgmount Street WC1 240 A3
Riding House Street W1 239 F2
Riley Road SE1 246 A1
Ringwood Gardens E14 248 A2
Risborough Street SE1 245 E4
Risdon Street SE16 247 D1
River Barge Close E14 248 C3
River Street EC1 241 D4
Riverside Walk SE1 244 C4
Rivington Street EC2 241 F3
Robert Adam Street W1 239 E2
Robert Close W9 238 B3
Robert Dashwood Way SE17 245 E2
Robert Street NW1 239 F4
Robert Street WC2 240 B1
Roberts Place EC1 241 D3
Bowling Green Lane
Robinson Street SW3 243 D1
Flood Street
Rochester Row SW1 244 A2
Rochester Street SW1 244 A2
Rockingham Street SE1 245 E3
Rocliffe Street N1 241 E4
Roding Mews E1 246 B2
Rodmarton Street W1 239 D2
Rodney Place SE17 245 E2
Rodney Road SE17 245 E2
Roffey Street E14 248 B3
Roger Street WC1 240 C3
Roland Gardens SW7 242 B1
Roland Way SE17 245 F1
Roland Way SW7 242 B1
Rolls Buildings EC4 241 D2
Rolls Passage EC4 240 C2
Romford Street E1 246 C4
Romilly Street W1 240 A1
Romney Mews W1 239 E3
Chiltern Street
Romney Street SW1 244 B2
Ronald Street E1 247 D3
Rood Lane EC3 241 F1
Rope Street SE16 247 E1
Ropemaker Road SE16 247 E1
Ropemaker Street EC2 241 F3
Ropemaker's Fields E14 247 F3
Roper Lane SE1 246 A1
Rosary Gardens SW7 242 B2
Roscoe Street EC1 241 E3
Rose & Crown Yard SW1 244 A4
King Street
Rose Alley SE1 245 E4
Rose Street WC2 240 B1
Rosebery Avenue EC1 243 D3
Rosemoor Street SW3 243 D2
Roserton Street E14 248 B3
Rosoman Place EC1 241 D4
Rosoman Street
Rosoman Street EC1 241 D4
Rossmore Road NW1 239 D3
Rotary Street SE1 245 D3
Rotherhithe Street SE16 247 D2
Rotherhithe Tunnel Approach
E14 247 E3
Rotherhithe Tunnel Approach
SE16 247 F1
Rothsay Street SE1 245 F3
Rotten Row SW7 & SW1 242 C4
Rotterdam Drive E14 248 C2
Rouel Road SE16 246 B1
Roupell Street SE1 245 D4
Rowington Close W2 238 A3
Roxby Place SW6 242 A1
Roy Square E14 247 F3
Royal Avenue SW3 243 D1
Royal Exchange Buildings EC3 241 F2
Cornhill
Royal Hospital Road SW3 243 D1
Royal Mint Place E1 246 B3
Royal Mint Street E1 246 B3
Royal Opera Arcade SW1 244 A4
Royal Road SE17 245 D1
Royal Street SE1 244 C3
Rudolf Place SW8 244 B1
Rudolph Road NW6 238 A4
Rufus Street N1 241 F4
Rugby Street WC1 240 C3
Rugg Street E14 247 F3
Rum Close E1 246 C3
Rupack Street SE16 247 D1
Rupert Street W1 240 A1
Rushworth Street SE1 245 D3
Russell Court SW1 244 A4
Cleveland Row
Russell Place SE16 247 E1
Russell Square WC1 240 B3
Russell Street WC2 240 C1
Russia Dock Road SE16 247 E2
Russia Row EC2 241 E2
Russia Walk SE16 247 E1
Rutherford Street SW1 244 A2
Rutland Gardens SW7 243 D3
Rutland Gate SW7 242 C3
Rutland Gate Mews SW7 242 C3
Rutland Gate
Rutland Mews East SW7 242 C3
Ennismore Street
Rutland Mews South SW7 242 C3
Ennismore Street
Rutland Place EC1 241 E3
Rutland Street SW7 242 C3
Rysbrack Street SW3 243 D3

S

Sackville Street W1 240 A1
Saddle Yard W1 243 E4
Saffron Hill EC1 241 D3
Saffron Street EC1 241 D3
Sage Street E1 246 C3
Sage Way WC1 240 C4
Sail Street SE11 244 C2
St Agnes Place SE11 245 D1
St Alban's Grove W8 242 A3
St Alban's Street SW1 240 A1
St Albans Mews W2 238 C3
St Alphage Garden EC2 241 E2
St Andrew Street EC4 241 D2
St Andrew's Hill EC4 241 D1
St Ann's Lane SW1 244 A3
St Ann's Row E14 247 F3
St Ann's Street SW1 244 B3
St Anne Street E14 247 F3
St Anne's Court W1 240 A2
St Anselm's Place W1 239 E1
St Anthony's Close E1 246 B2
St Barnabas Street SW1 243 E2
St Botolph Street EC3 246 A4
St Bride Street EC4 241 D2
St Catherines Mews SW3 243 D2
Milner Street
St Chad's Place WC1 240 B4
St Chad's Street WC1 240 B4
St Christopher's Place W1 239 E2
St Clare Street EC3 246 A3
St Clement's Lane WC2 240 C2
St Clements Court EC4 241 F1
St Cross Street EC1 241 D3
St David's Square E14 248 B1
St Dunstan's Court EC4 241 D2
Fleet Street
St Dunstan's Lane EC3 241 F1
St Mary at Hill
St Dunstans Alley EC3 246 A3
St Dunstans Hill
St Dunstans Hill EC3 246 A3
St Ermins Hill SW1 244 A3
St George Street W1 239 F1
St George's Circus SE1 245 D3
St George's Court EC4 241 D2
St George's Drive SW1 243 F2
St George's Mews SE1 245 D3
St George's Road SE1 245 D3
St George's Square SW1 244 A1
St George's Square E14 247 E3
St George's Square Mews SW1 244 A1
St Georges Fields W2 239 D1
St Giles High Street WC2 240 B2
St Helen's Place EC3 241 F2
St Helena Street WC1 240 C4
St James's Court SW1 244 A3
St James's Market SW1 240 A1
Haymarket
St James's Place SW1 243 F4
St James's Road SE1 & SE16 246 B1
St James's Row EC1 241 D3
St James's Walk
St James's Square SW1 244 A4
St James's Street SW1 244 A4
St James's Walk EC1 241 D3
St John Street EC1 241 D4
St John's Lane EC1 241 D3
St John's Place EC1 241 D3
St John's Square EC1 241 D3
St John's Villas W8 242 A3
St Mary's Place
St John's Wood High Street
NW8 238 C4
St John's Wood Road NW8 238 C4
St Katherine's Row EC3 241 F1
Fenchurch Street
St Katherine's Way E1 246 B1
St Lawrence Street E14 248 C4
St Leonard's Terrace SW3 243 D1
St Loo Avenue SW3 243 D1
St Luke's Close EC1 241 E3
St Luke's Street SW3 242 C1
St Margaret's Lane W8 242 A3
St Margaret's Street SW1 244 B3
St Mark Street E1 246 B3
St Martin's Court WC2 240 B1
St Martin's Lane
St Martin's Lane WC2 240 B1
St Martin's Place WC2 240 B1
St Martin's Street WC2 240 B1
St Martin's-le-Grand EC1 241 E2
St Mary at Hill EC3 241 F1
St Mary Axe EC3 246 A3
St Mary's Gardens SE11 245 D2
St Mary's Gate W8 242 A3
St Mary's Mansions W2 238 B3
St Mary's Place W8 242 A3
St Mary's Square W2 238 C3
St Mary's Terrace W2 238 B3
St Mary's Walk SE11 245 D2
St Marychurch Street SE16 247 D1
St Matthew Street SW1 244 A3
St Michael's Street W2 238 C2
St Olav's Square SE16 247 D1
Lower Road
St Oswald's Place SE11 244 C1
St Paul's Avenue SE16 247 E2
St Paul's Churchyard EC4 241 E2
St Paul's Terrace SE17 245 E1
St Paul's Way E3 247 F4
St Peter's Place W9 238 A3
St Petersburgh Mews W2 238 A1
St Petersburgh Place W2 238 A1
St Stephen's Crescent W2 238 A2
St Stephen's Gardens W2 238 A2
St Stephen's Mews W2 238 A2
St Swithin's Lane EC4 241 F1
St Thomas Street SE1 245 F4
St Vincent Street W1 239 E2
Salamanca Place SE1 244 C2
Salamanca Street SE1 & SE11 244 C2
Salem Road W2 238 A1
Salisbury Close SE17 245 F2
Salisbury Court EC4 241 D2
Salisbury Place W1 239 D3
Salisbury Square EC4 241 D2
Salisbury Court
Salisbury Street NW8 238 C3
Salmon Lane E14 247 E4
Salter Road SE16 247 E1
Salter Street E14 247 F3
Samford Street NW8 238 C3
Sampson Street E1 246 C2
Sancroft Street SE11 244 C2
Sanctuary Street SE1 245 E4
Marshalsea Road
Sandell Street SE1 245 D4
Sandland Street WC1 240 C2
Sandpiper Close SE16 247 F2
Sandwich Street WC1 240 B4
Sandys Row E1 246 A4
Sans Walk EC1 243 D3
Sardinia Street WC2 240 C2
Saunders Court E14 247 F3
Limehouse Causeway
Saunders Ness Road E14 248 C2
Savage Gardens EC3 246 A3
Pepys Street
Savernake Close E14 248 A2
Savile Row W1 239 F1
Savoy Buildings WC2 240 C1
Savoy Hill WC2 240 C1
Savoy Way
Savoy Place WC2 240 B1
Savoy Row WC2 240 C1
Savoy Street
Savoy Steps WC2 240 C1
Savoy Way
Savoy Street WC2 240 C1
Savoy Way WC2 240 C1
Sawyer Street SE1 245 E4
Scala Street W1 240 A2
Scandrett Street E1 246 C2
Scarborough Street E1 246 B3
Scarsdale Place W8 242 A3
Scarsdale Villas W8 242 A3
School House Lane E1 247 D3
Schooner Close SE16 247 D2
Schooner Close E14 248 C2
Scoresby Street SE1 245 D4
Scotswood Street EC1 243 D3
Sans Walk
Scott Ellis Gardens NW8 238 B4
Scott Lidgett Crescent SE16 246 B1
Scott Russell Place E14 248 B1
Scovell Road SE1 245 E3
Scrutton Street EC2 241 F3
Seagrave Road SW6 242 A1
Searles Road SE1 245 F2
Seaton Close SE11 245 D1
Sebastian Street EC1 241 D4
Secker Street SE1 244 C4
Sedan Way SE17 245 F2
Sedding Street SW1 243 E2
Sloane Square
Seddon Street WC1 240 C4
Sedley Place W1 239 F2
Woodstock Street
Seething Lane EC3 246 A3
Sekforde Street EC1 241 D3
Sellon Mews SE11 244 C2
Selsdon Way E14 248 B2
Selsey Street E14 247 F4
Selwood Terrace SW7 242 C2
Selwood Place SW7 242 C1
Semley Place SW1 243 E2
Senior Street W2 238 A3
Senrab Street E1 247 D4
Serle Street WC2 240 C2
Serpentine Road W2 242 C1
Seth Street SE16 247 D1
Settles Street E1 246 C4
Seven Dials WC2 240 B2
Seville Street SW1 243 D3
Knightsbridge
Sevington Street W9 238 A3
Seward Street EC1 241 E3
Sextant Avenue E14 248 C2
Seymour Mews W1 239 E2
Seymour Place W1 239 D2
Seymour Street W2 239 D1
Seymour Walk SW10 242 B1
Seyssel Street E14 248 C2
Shad Thames SE1 246 A2
Shadwell Pier Head E1 247 D3
Shadwell Place E1 246 C3
Shaftesbury Avenue W1 & WC2 240 A1
Shaftesbury Mews W8 242 A2
Shafto Mews SW1 243 D3
Shand Street SE1 246 A2
Sharsted Street SE17 245 D1
Shawfield Street SW3 243 D1
Sheffield Street WC2 240 C2
Portugal Street
Sheffield Terrace W8 242 A4
Shelmerdine Close E3 247 F4
Shelton Street WC2 240 B2
Shepherd Market W1 243 F4
Shepherd Street W1 243 E4
Shepherd's Place W1 239 E1
Shepherdess Place N1 241 E4
Shepherdess Walk
Shepherdess Walk N1 241 E4
Sheraton Street W1 240 A2
Wardour Street
Sherlock Mews W1 239 E3
Sherwood Gardens E14 248 A2
Sherwood Street W1 240 A1
Shillibeer Place W1 239 D2
Ship Yard E14 248 A1
Shipwright Road SE16 247 E1
Shirland Road W9 238 A3
Shoe Lane EC4 241 D2
Short Street SE1 245 D4
Short's Gardens WC2 240 B2
Shorter Street E1 246 B3
Shoulder of Mutton Alley E14 247 F2
Shouldham Street W1 239 D2
Shroton Street NW1 238 C3
Sicilian Avenue WC1 240 B2
Vernon Place
Siddons Lane NW1 239 D3
Sidford Place SE1 244 C2
Sidmouth Street WC1 240 C4
Sidney Square E1 247 D4
Sidney Street E1 246 C4
Silex Street SE1 245 D3
Silk Street EC2 241 E3
Silver Walk SE16 247 F2
Silvester Street SE1 245 E3
Simpson's Road E14 248 B4
Singer Street EC2 241 F3
Sise Lane EC4 241 E2
Pancras Lane
Skinner Street EC1 241 D3
Skinners Lane EC4 241 F4
Queen Street
Sleaford Street SW8 240 B4
Slingsby Place WC2 240 B1
Slippers Place SE16 246 C1
Sloane Avenue SW3 243 D2
Sloane Court East SW3 243 E2
Sloane Court West SW3 243 E1
Sloane Gardens SW1 243 E2
Sloane Square SW1 243 E2
Sloane Street SW1 243 D3
Sloane Terrace SW1 243 E2
Sly Street E1 246 C3
Cannon Street Road
Smart's Place WC2 240 B2
Smeaton Street E1 246 C2
Smith Close SE16 247 D2
Smith Square SW1 244 B3
Smith Street SW3 243 D1
Smith Terrace SW3 243 D1
Smithfield Street EC1 241 D2
Smithy Street E1 247 D4
Snow Hill EC1 241 D2
Snowsfields SE1 245 F4
Soho Square W1 240 A2
Soho Street W1 240 A2
Somerford Way SE16 247 E1
Somers Crescent W2 238 C2
Somers Mews W2 238 C2
Sondes Street SE17 245 F1
Sophia Square SE16 247 E3
South Audley Street W1 239 E1
South Bolton Gardens SW5 242 B1
South Carriage Drive
SW1 & SW7 242 C3
South Collonnade E14 248 A4
South Crescent WC1 240 A2
Store Street
South Eaton Place SW1 243 E2
South End W8 242 A3
South End Row W8 242 A3
South Lambeth Place SW8 244 B1
South Molton Lane W1 239 E1
South Molton Street W1 239 E2
South Parade SW3 242 C1
South Place EC2 241 F2
South Street W1 243 E4
South Tenter Street E1 246 B3
South Terrace SW7 242 C2
South Wharf Road W2 238 C2
Southall Place SE1 245 F3
Long Lane
Southampton Buildings WC2 240 C2
Southampton Place WC1 240 B2
Southampton Row WC1 240 B3
Southampton Street WC2 240 B1
Southsea Street SE16 247 F1
Southwark Bridge EC4 & SE1 241 E1
Southwark Bridge Road SE1 245 E3
Southwark Park Road SE16 246 C1
Southwark Street SE1 245 D4
Southwell Gardens SW7 242 B2
Southwick Street W2 238 C2
Hyde Park Crescent
Sovereign Close E1 246 C3
Spa Road SE16 246 B1
Spanish Place W1 239 E2
Spear Mews SW5 242 A2
Spelman Street E1 246 B4
Spence Close SE16 247 F1
Spencer Street EC1 241 D4
Spenser Street SW1 244 A3
Spert Street E14 247 E3
Spindrift Avenue E14 248 A2
Spital Square E1 246 A4
Spital Street E1 246 B4
Sprimont Place SW3 243 D2
Spring Gardens SW1 244 B4
Spring Mews W1 239 D3
Spring Street W2 238 C2
Spur Road SW1 243 F3
Spur Road SE1 244 C3
Lower Marsh
Spurgeon Street SE1 245 F3
Squire Gardens NW8 238 C4
Stable Yard Road SW1 244 A4
Stables Way SE11 244 C1
Stacey Street WC2 240 B2
Staff Street EC1 241 F4
Vince Street
Stafford Place SW1 243 F3
Stag Place SW1 243 F3
Stainer Street SE1 245 F4
Staining Lane EC2 241 E2
Stalbridge Street NW1 238 C3
Stalham Street SE16 246 C1
Stamford Street SE1 244 C4
Stanford Road W8 242 A3
Stanford Street SW1 244 A2
Stanhope Gardens SW7 242 B2
Stanhope Gate W1 243 E4
Hertford Street
Stanhope Mews East SW7 242 B2
Stanhope Mews South SW7 242 B2
Stanhope Mews West SW7 242 B2
Stanhope Place W2 242 B2
Stanhope Street NW1 239 F4
Stanhope Terrace W2 238 C1
Stannary Place SE11 245 D1
Stannary Street SE11 245 D1
Stanworth Street SE1 246 B1
Staple Inn Buildings WC1 240 C2
Staple Street SE1 245 F3
Staples Close SE16 247 E2
Star Place E1 246 B3
Star Street W2 238 C2
Star Yard WC2 240 C2
Starboard Way E14 248 A3
Starcross Street NW1 240 A3
Station Acces Road EC2 241 F2
Stave Yard Road SE16 247 E2
Stead Street SE17 245 E2
Stebondale Street E14 248 C2
Stedham Place WC1 240 B2
New Oxford Street
Steedman Street SE17 245 E2
Steel's Lane E1 247 D3
Steelyard Passage EC4 241 E1
Steers Way SE16 247 E1
Stephen Mews W1 240 A2
Gresse Street
Stephen Street W1 240 A2
Stephen's Row EC4 241 F1
Walbrook
Stephenson Way NW1 240 A3
Stepney Causeway E1 247 D3
Stepney Green E1 247 D4
Stepney High Street E1 247 E4
Stepney Way E1 246 C4
Sterling Street SW7 243 D3
Montpelier Place
Sterry Street SE1 245 F3
Stevedore Street E1 246 C2
Stevens Street SE1 246 A1
Steward Street E1 246 A4
Stewart Street E14 248 C3
Stewart's Grove SW3 242 C2
Stillington Street SW1 244 A2
Stockholm Way E1 246 B2
Vaughan Way
Stocks Place E14 247 F3
Stone Buildings WC2 240 C2
Chancery Lane
Stone Hall Gardens W8 242 A3
Stone Hall Place W8 242 A3
Stone Hall Gardens
Stone Stairs E1 247 E3
Stonecutter Street EC4 241 D2
Stones End Street SE1 245 E3
Stoney Lane E1 246 A4
Stoney Street SE1 245 F4
Stopford Road SE17 245 E1
Store Street WC1 240 A2
Storers Quay E14 248 C2
Storey's Gate SW1 244 B3
Stork's Road SE16 246 C1
Stoughton Close SE11 244 C2
Stourcliffe Street W1 239 D2
Strafford Street E14 248 A3
Strand WC2 240 B1
Stratford Avenue W8 242 A3
Stratford Place W1 239 E2
Stratford Road W8 242 A2
Strathearn Place W2 238 C2
Hyde Park Square
Strathmore Gardens W8 242 A4
Palace Gardens Terrace
Stratton Street W1 243 F4
Strattondale Street E14 248 B3
Streatham Street WC1 240 B2
Dyott Street
Strutton Ground SW1 244 A3
Strype Street E1 246 A4
Stukeley Street WC2 240 B2
Sturge Street SE1 245 E3
Sturgeon Road SE17 245 E1
Sturt Street N1 241 E4
Stutfield Street E1 246 B3
Sudeley Street N1 241 D4
Sudrey Street SE1 245 E3
Suffolk Lane EC4 241 F1
Suffolk Place SW1 240 B1
Suffolk Street
Suffolk Street SW1 240 B1
Sugar Quay Walk EC3 246 A3
Sullivan Road SE1 245 D2
Summercourt Road E1 247 D4
Summers Street EC1 241 D3
Back Hill
Sumner Place SW7 242 C2
Sumner Place Mews SW7 242 C2
Sumner Street SE1 245 E4
Sun Street EC2 241 F3
Sun Street Passage EC2 241 F2
Sun Walk E1 246 B3
Sunderland Terrace W2 238 A2
Sunningdale Gardens W8 242 A2
Stratford Road
Surrenale Place W9 238 A3
Surrey Quays Road SE16 247 D1
Surrey Row SE1 245 D4
Surrey Square SE17 245 F2
Surrey Street WC2 240 C1
Surrey Water Road SE16 247 E2
Sussex Gardens W2 238 C1
Sussex Place NW1 239 D4
Sussex Place W2 238 C2
Sussex Square W2 238 C1
Sussex Street SW1 243 F1
Sutherland Avenue W9 238 A3
Sutherland Row SW1 243 F1
Sutherland Street
Sutherland Square SE17 245 E1
Sutherland Street SW1 243 F1
Sutherland Walk SE17 245 E1
Sutton Row W1 240 B2
Swallow Street W1 240 A1

255

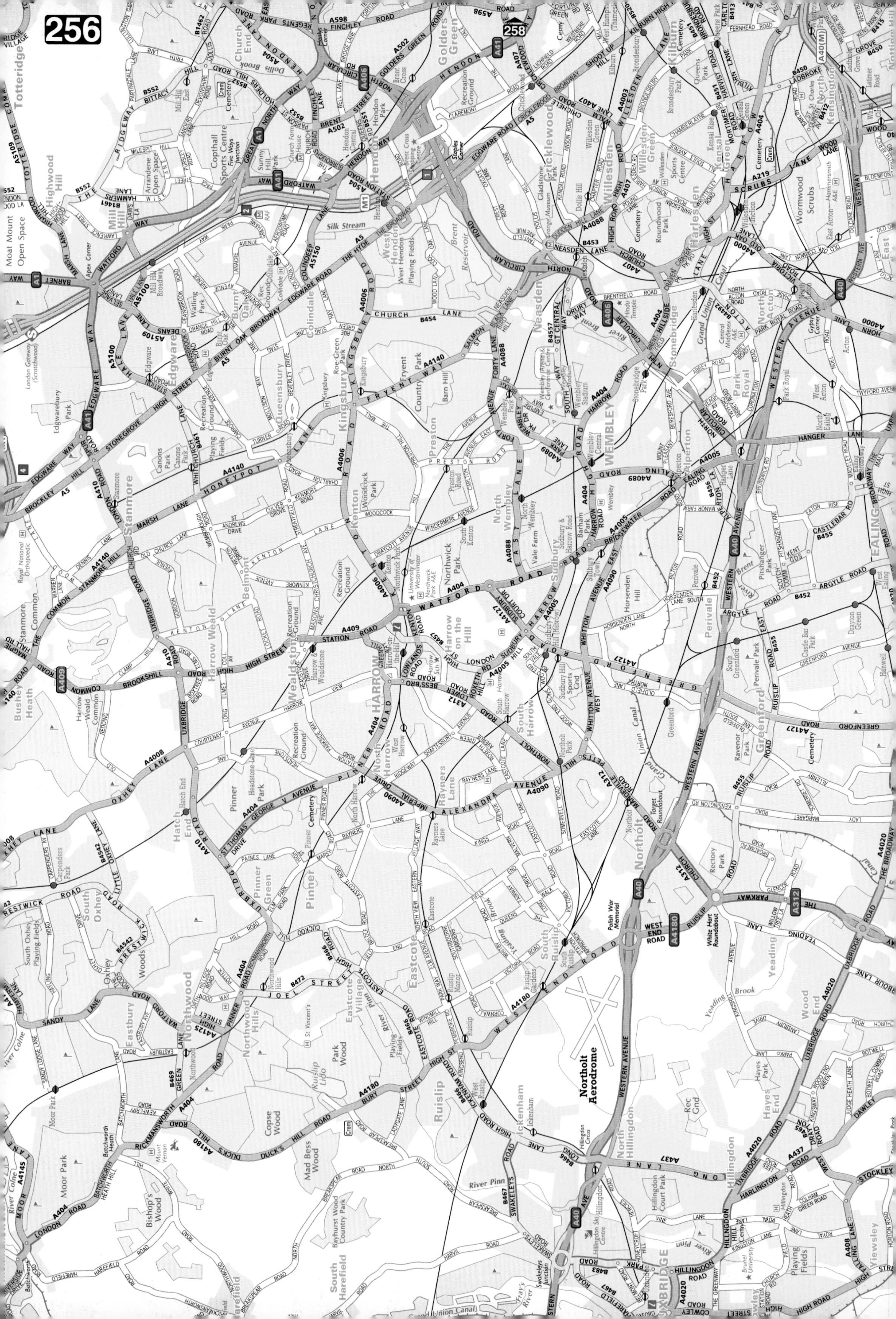
258
Totteridge
Church End
Golders Green
Kilburn
Highwood Hill
Mill Hill
Hendon
Cricklewood
Willesden
Willesden Green
Kensal Green
Harlesden
Wormwood Scrubs
Moat Mount Open Space
Copthall Sports Centre
Burnt Oak
Colindale
Edgware
West Hendon
Brent Reservoir
Neasden
Stonebridge
North Acton
Park Royal
Queensbury
Kingsbury
Fryent Country Park
Barn Hill
Wembley
Preston
Alperton
Stanmore
Canons Park
Kenton
Belmont
North Wembley
Sudbury
Northwick Park
Harrow on the Hill
Wealdstone
Harrow Weald
Harrow
Horsenden Hill
Perivale
Ealing
Bushey Heath
Stanmore Common
South Harrow
Greenford
North Harrow
Rayners Lane
Headstone Lane
Hatch End
Pinner
Pinner Green
Northolt
Eastcote
Eastcote Village
Carpenders Park
South Oxhey
Oxhey Woods
Northwood
Northwood Hills
Eastbury
Ruislip Manor
South Ruislip
Ruislip
Yeading
Park Wood
Ruislip Lido
Copse Wood
Northolt Aerodrome
Hayes End
Ickenham
Moor Park
Mad Bess Wood
North Hillingdon
Hillingdon
Bishop's Wood
Bayhurst Wood Country Park
South Harefield
Uxbridge
Harefield
Viewsley
Grand Union Canal
River Pinn

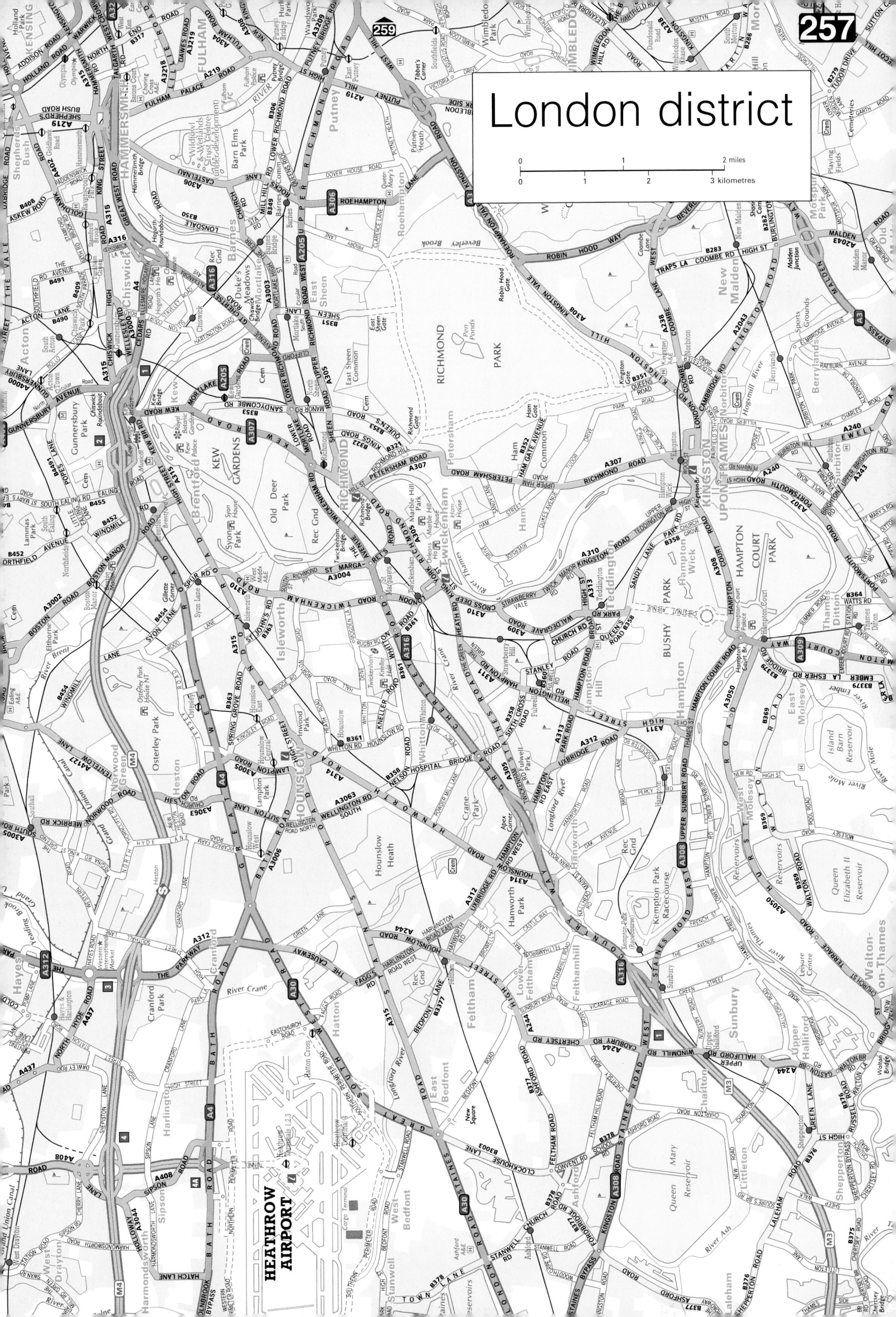
London district
0 1 2 miles
0 1 2 3 kilometres
259
RICHMOND PARK
Pen Ponds
Robin Hood Gate
Beverley Brook
HAMMERSMITH
FULHAM
Putney
Barnes
Mortlake
Chiswick
Kew
KEW GARDENS
Brentford
RICHMOND
Petersham
Ham
Twickenham
Teddington
KINGSTON UPON THAMES
New Malden
Norbiton
Surbiton
Berrylands
Isleworth
Osterley Park
HOUNSLOW
Hounslow Heath
Whitton
Heston
Norwood Green
Cranford
Hayes
Harlington
Sipson
Harmondsworth
West Drayton
HEATHROW AIRPORT
Hatton
Feltham
Lower Feltham
Hanworth
Hampton
Hampton Hill
BUSHY PARK
HAMPTON COURT PARK
East Molesey
West Molesey
Thames Ditton
Queen Elizabeth II Reservoir
Island Barn Reservoir
Kempton Park Racecourse
Sunbury
Upper Halliford
Charlton
Littleton
Shepperton
Queen Mary Reservoir
Ashford
Stanwell
East Bedfont
West Bedfont
Walton-on-Thames
River Thames
River Crane
River Mole
Acton
Shepherds Bush
Gunnersbury Park
Old Deer Park
Syon Park
Wimbledon Park
Motspur Park

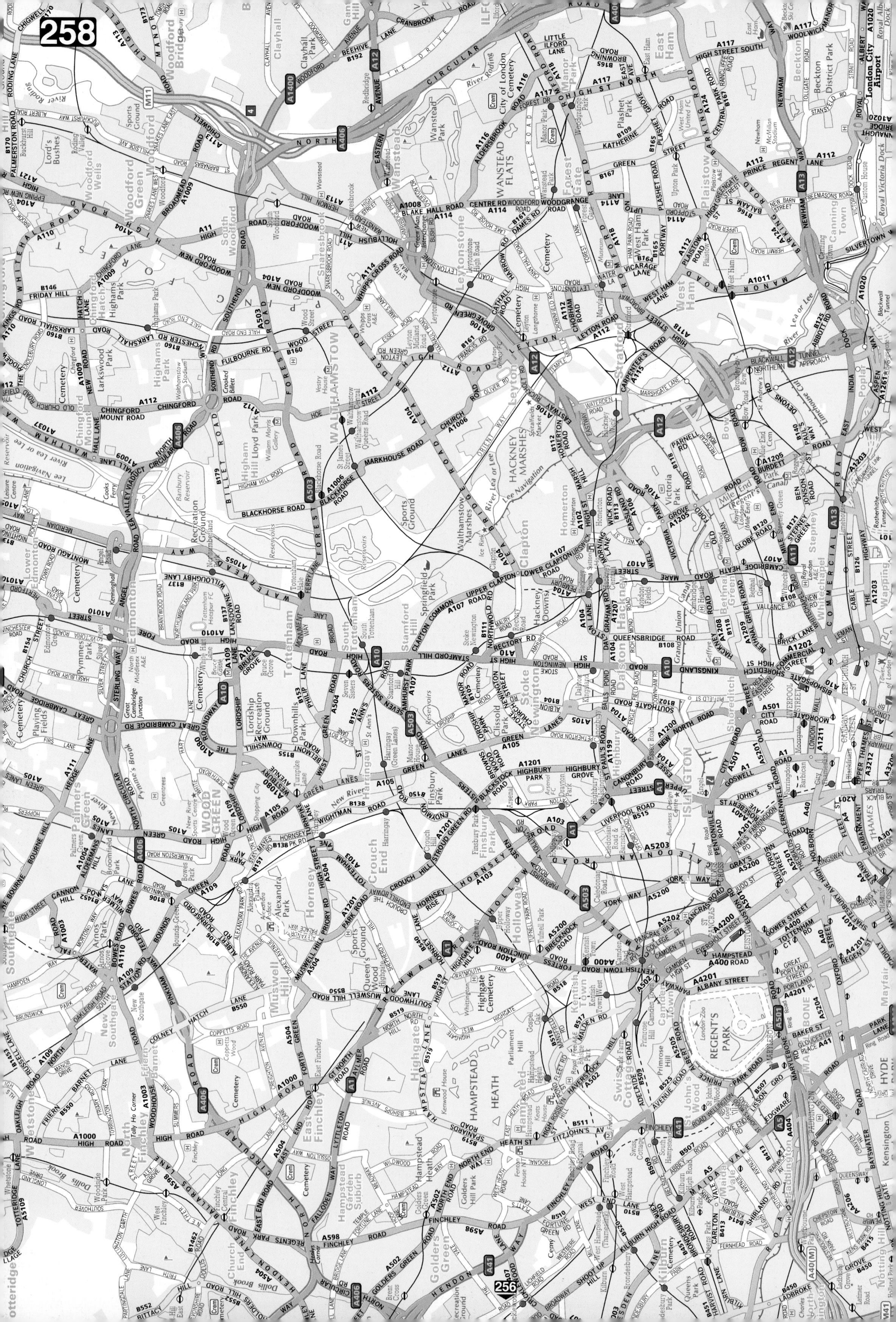

Woodford Bridge
Clayhall
Barkingside
Wanstead
Wanstead Park
Wanstead Flats
Manor Park
East Ham
Beckton
Beckton District Park
London City Airport
Royal Victoria Dock
Buckhurst Hill
Woodford Green
Woodford Wells
South Woodford
Snaresbrook
Leytonstone
Forest Gate
Plaistow
West Ham
Canning Town
Chingford Hatch
Highams Park
Walthamstow
Leyton
Stratford
Hackney Marshes
Bow
Poplar
Mile End
Stepney
Whitechapel
Wapping
Chingford Mount
Higham Hill
Lloyd Park
Upper Edmonton
Edmonton
Lower Edmonton
Tottenham
South Tottenham
Stamford Hill
Clapton
Hackney
Homerton
Bethnal Green
Shoreditch
Dalston
Stoke Newington
Hackney Downs
Springfield Park
Walthamstow Marshes
Sports Ground
Reservoirs
Palmers Green
Wood Green
Harringay
Hornsey
Finsbury Park
Highbury
Islington
Canonbury
Crouch End
Alexandra Park
Muswell Hill
Holloway
Upper Holloway
Highgate
Highgate Cemetery
Kentish Town
Camden Town
Regent's Park
Marylebone
Mayfair
Hyde Park
Bowes Park
Arnos Park
Southgate
New Southgate
Friern Barnet
North Finchley
East Finchley
Finchley
Church End
Whetstone
Totteridge
Hampstead
Hampstead Heath
Hampstead Garden Suburb
Golders Green
Swiss Cottage
St John's Wood
Maida Vale
Kilburn
Paddington
Notting Hill
Kensington
Bayswater
Thames
256

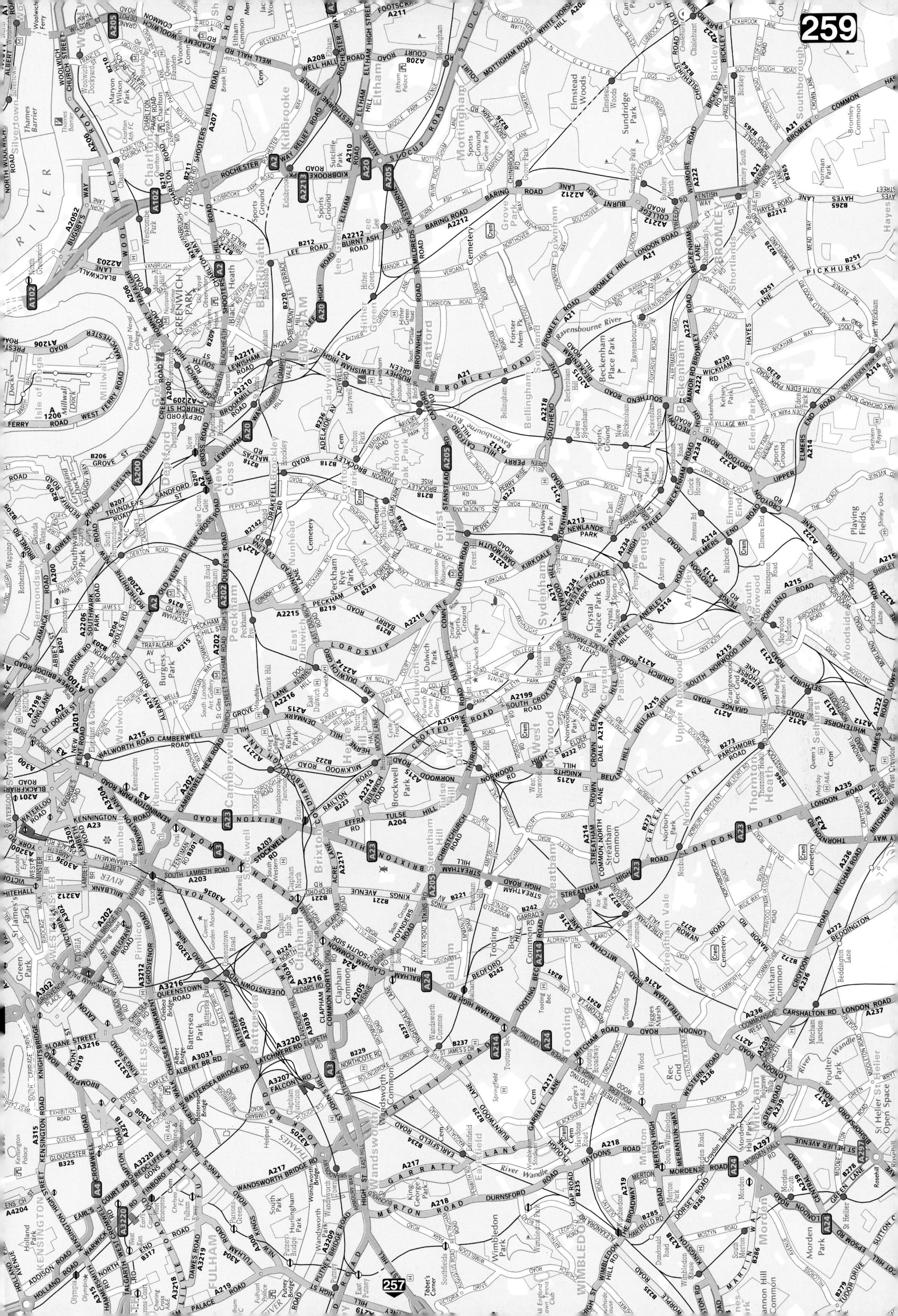

Woolwich
Silvertown
Thames Barrier
Charlton
Kidbrooke
Eltham
Mottingham
Elmstead Woods
Sundridge Park
Chislehurst
Bickley
Southborough
Bromley Common
Blackheath
Greenwich
Greenwich Park
Lee Green
Lee
Grove Park
Downham
Bromley
Shortlands
Isle of Dogs
Millwall Dock
Deptford
Lewisham
Hither Green
Catford
Southend
Beckenham
Beckenham Place Park
Hayes
West Wickham
Eden Park
New Cross
Brockley
Ladywell
Crofton Park
Honor Oak Park
Forest Hill
Bellingham
Ravensbourne River
Rotherhithe
Bermondsey
Southwark Park
Peckham
Nunhead
Peckham Rye Park
Sydenham
Penge
Anerley
Elmers End
Kent House
Crystal Palace Park
Crystal Palace
Upper Norwood
South Norwood
Woodside
Shirley
Playing Fields
Camberwell
Burgess Park
Walworth
Kennington
East Dulwich
Dulwich
Dulwich Park
West Dulwich
Herne Hill
Brockwell Park
Tulse Hill
West Norwood
Gipsy Hill
Thornton Heath
Selhurst
Norwood Junction
Brixton
Stockwell
Lambeth
Vauxhall
Westminster
Waterloo
Southwark
Elephant & Castle
Streatham Hill
Streatham
Streatham Common
Streatham Vale
Norbury
Norbury Park
Pimlico
Victoria
Green Park
St James's Park
Clapham
Clapham Common
Balham
Tooting
Tooting Bec
Mitcham
Mitcham Common
Battersea
Battersea Park
Chelsea
Wandsworth
Wandsworth Common
Earlsfield
Tooting Graveney
Colliers Wood
Merton
Morden
Morden Park
St Helier
Poulter Park
Beddington Lane
Fulham
Kensington
Holland Park
Putney
Southfields
Wimbledon
Wimbledon Park
South Wimbledon
River Wandle
Morden Hall Park

257

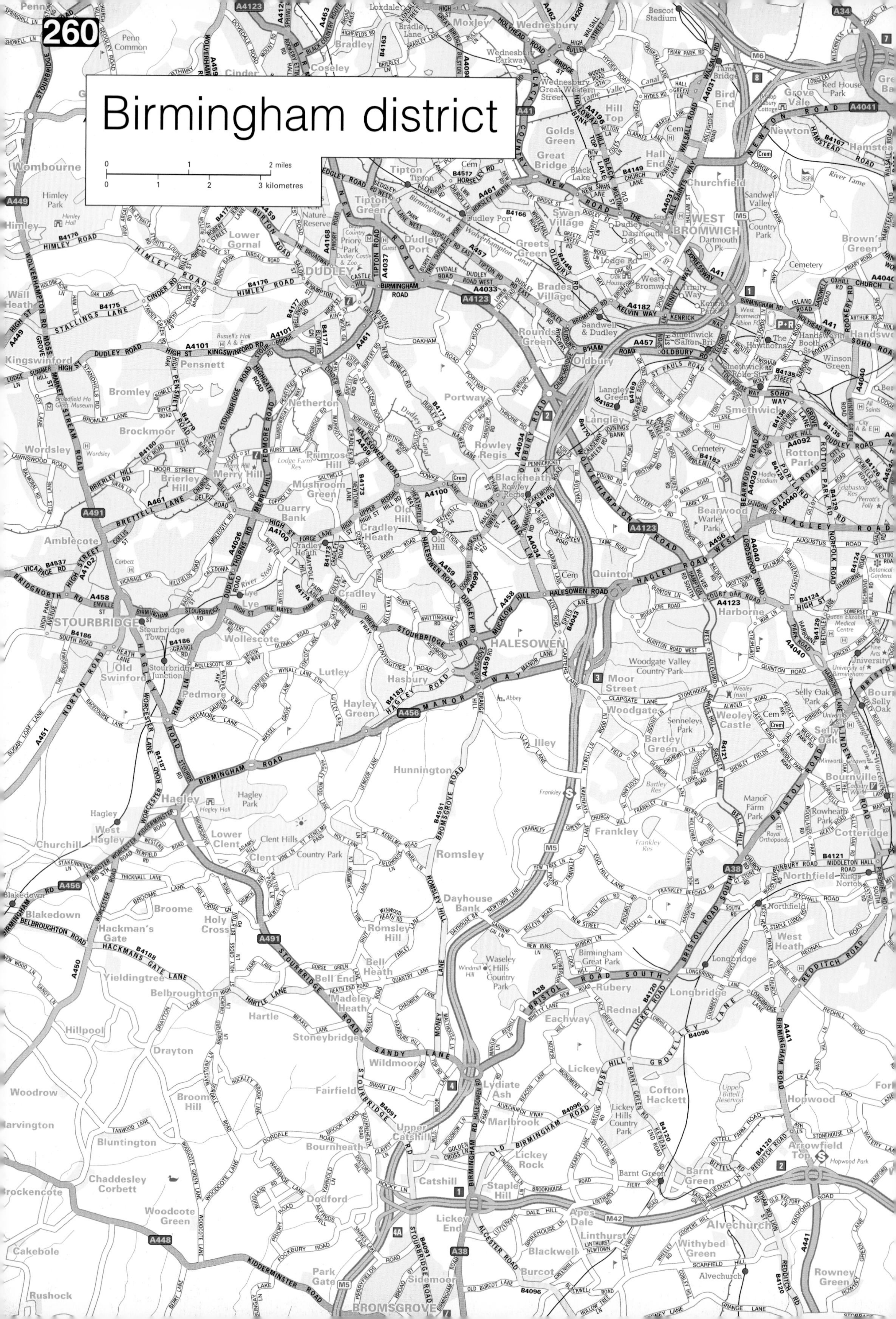

Birmingham district
0 1 2 miles
0 1 2 3 kilometres
Penn Common
Coseley
Moxley
Wednesbury
Bescot Stadium
Wombourne
Himley Park
Himley
Lower Gornal
DUDLEY
Tipton
Tipton Green
Dudley Port
Great Bridge
Golds Green
Hill Top
Hall End
Churchfield
WEST BROMWICH
Sandwell Valley Country Park
Newton
Hamstead
Grove Vale
Red House Park
Wall Heath
Kingswinford
Pensnett
Bromley
Brockmoor
Wordsley
Brierley Hill
Merry Hill
Netherton
Primrose Hill
Mushroom Green
Quarry Bank
Oldbury
Langley Green
Langley
Smethwick
Rowley Regis
Blackheath
Portway
Rounds Green
Brades Village
Amblecote
STOURBRIDGE
Stourbridge Town
Lye
Cradley
Cradley Heath
Old Hill
Wollescote
Old Swinford
Pedmore
Lutley
Hasbury
Hayley Green
HALESOWEN
Quinton
Harborne
Bearwood
Warley Park
Moor Street
Woodgate
Bartley Green
Weoley Castle
Selly Oak
Bournville
Illey
Hunnington
Frankley
Romsley
Hagley
West Hagley
Churchill
Blakedown
Broome
Clent
Lower Clent
Clent Hills Country Park
Hackman's Gate
Holy Cross
Yieldingtree
Belbroughton
Bell Heath
Bell End
Madeley Heath
Hartle
Hillpool
Drayton
Stoneybridge
Wildmoor
Dayhouse Bank
Romsley Hill
Waseley Hills Country Park
Rubery
Rednal
Longbridge
Northfield
West Heath
Cotteridge
Eachway
Lickey
Cofton Hackett
Hopwood
Lydiate Ash
Fairfield
Marlbrook
Lickey Hills Country Park
Barnt Green
Upper Catshill
Catshill
Lickey Rock
Staple Hill
Lickey End
Apes Dale
Linthurst
Blackwell
Burcot
Alvechurch
Withybed Green
Arrowfield Top
Rowney Green
Woodrow
Broom Hill
Bluntington
Chaddesley Corbett
Woodcote Green
Cakebole
Rushock
Bournheath
Dodford
Park Gate
Sidemoor
BROMSGROVE

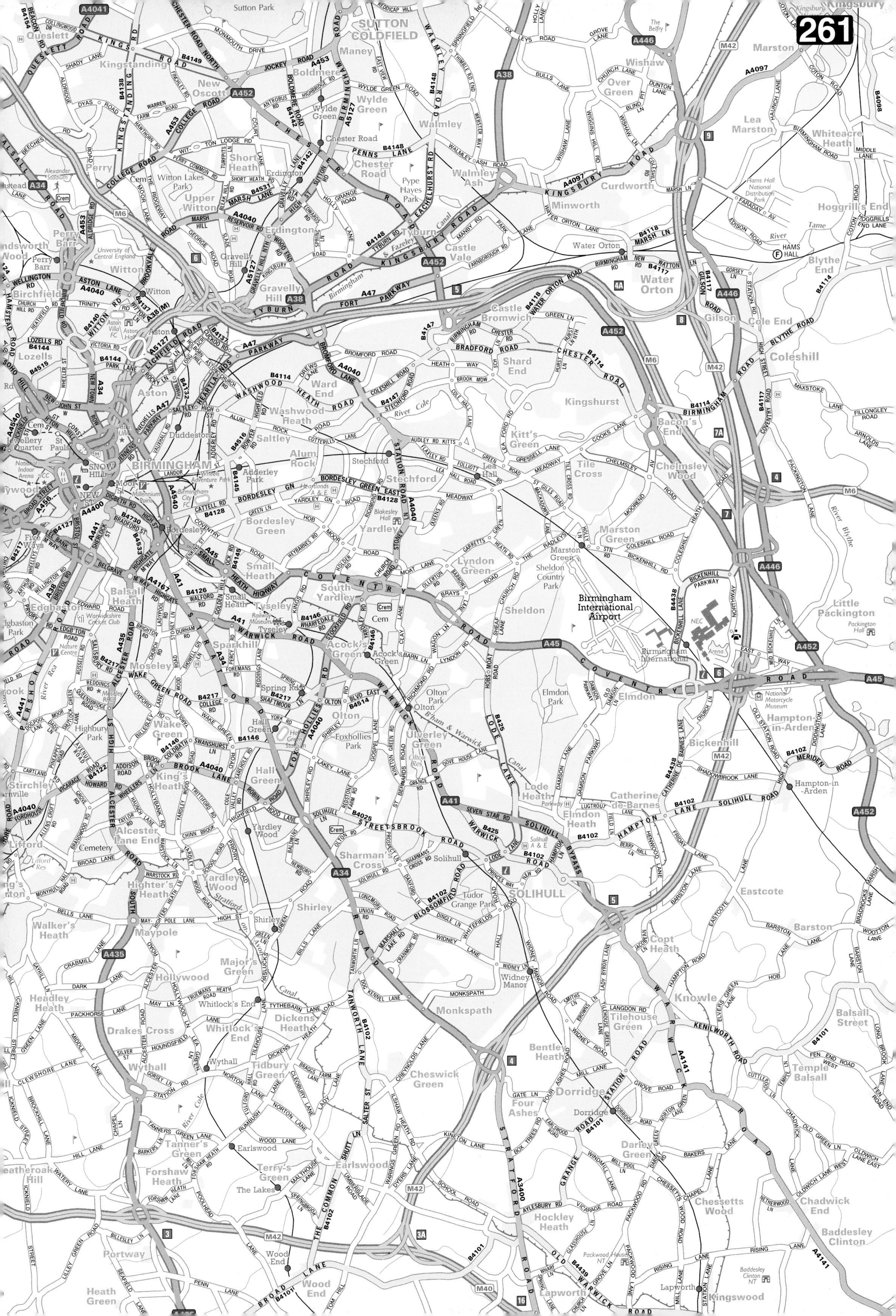
Sutton Park
SUTTON COLDFIELD
Kingsbury
Marston
Wishaw
Over Green
The Belfry
Queslett
Kingstanding
New Oscott
Boldmere
Maney
Wylde Green
Walmley
Chester Road
Lea Marston
Whiteacre Heath
Perry
Short Heath
Erdington
Pype Hayes Park
Walmley Ash
Curdworth
Minworth
Hams Hall National Distribution Park
Hoggrill's End
Witton Lakes Park
Upper Witton
Alexander Stadium
Perry Barr
University of Central England
Witton
Gravelly Hill
Tyburn
Castle Vale
Water Orton
Hams Hall
River Tame
Blythe End
Handsworth Wood
Birchfield
Gravelly Hill
Aston Villa FC
Aston
Castle Bromwich
Shard End
Gilson
Cole End
Coleshill
Lozells
Ward End
Washwood Heath
Kingshurst
Bacon's End
Saltley
Alum Rock
Stechford
Kitt's Green
Tile Cross
Chelmsley Wood
Duddeston
Jewellery Quarter
St Pauls
Snow Hill
BIRMINGHAM
Adderley Park
Lea Hall
National Indoor Arena
ICC
Moor St
New St
Millennium Point
Birmingham City FC
Bordesley Green
Heartlands A & E
Blakesley Hall
Yardley
Marston Green
Five Ways
Bordesley
Small Heath
Lyndon Green
Marston Green
Sheldon Country Park
Edgbaston
Balsall Heath
South Yardley
Tyseley
Sheldon
Birmingham International Airport
Little Packington
Packington Hall
Warwickshire Cricket Club
Railway Museum
Sparkhill
Acock's Green
NEC
Birmingham International
Arena
Moseley
Elmdon Park
Elmdon
National Motorcycle Museum
Hampton-in-Arden
Olton Park
Olton
Spring Rd
Hall Green
Highbury Park
Wake Green
Foxhollies Park
Ulverley Green
Bickenhill
Olton Res
Hall Green
King's Heath
Stirchley
Lode Heath
Catherine-de-Barnes
Hampton-in-Arden
Elmdon Heath
Yardley Wood
Alcester Lane End
Cemetery
Lifford
Sharman's Cross
Solihull
SOLIHULL
Highter's Heath
Yardley Wood
Tudor Grange Park
Shirley
Eastcote
Barston
Walker's Heath
Maypole
Shirley Green
Copt Heath
Major's Green
Hollywood
Widney Manor
Knowle
Headley Heath
Whitlock's End
Dickens Heath
Monkspath
Tilehouse Green
Balsall Street
Drakes Cross
Whitlock's End
Bentley Heath
Temple Balsall
Wythall
Tidbury Green
Cheswick Green
Four Ashes
Dorridge
Tanner's Green
Earlswood
Darley Green
Heatheroak Hill
Forshaw Heath
Terry's Green
Earlswood
The Lakes
Chessetts Wood
Chadwick End
Hockley Heath
Baddesley Clinton
Portway
Wood End
Packwood House NT
Baddesley Clinton NT
Lapworth
Kingswood
Wood End
Heath Green
M6
M42
M40
A38
A45
A452
A446
A4097
A34
A41
A435
A3400
A4141
Coventry Road
Warwick Road
Stratford Road
Kingsbury Road
Chester Road
Birmingham Road
Solihull Bypass

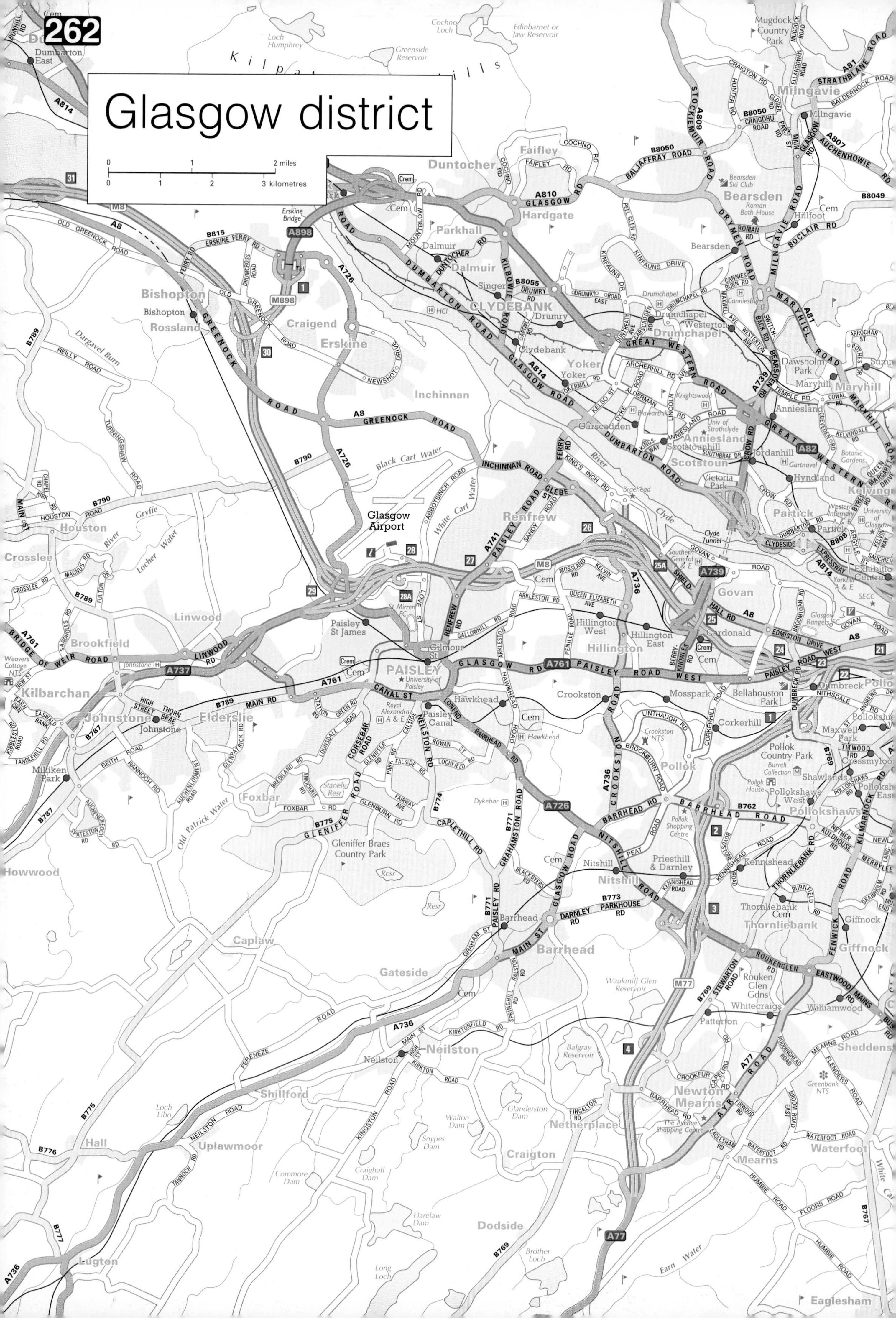
Glasgow district
0
1
2 miles
0
1
2
3 kilometres
Kilpatrick Hills
Loch Humphrey
Cochno Loch
Greenside Reservoir
Edinbarnet or Jaw Reservoir
Mugdock Country Park
Dumbarton East
A814
M8
A8
OLD GREENOCK ROAD
B815
ERSKINE FERRY RD
Erskine Bridge
A898
M898
A726
Duntocher
Faifley
Hardgate
A810
GLASGOW RD
Parkhall
Dalmuir
Singer
CLYDEBANK
Drumry
Clydebank
B8055
DUMBARTON ROAD
KILBOWIE RD
Bishopton
Rossland
GREENOCK ROAD
Craigend
Erskine
NEWSHOT DRIVE
Inchinnan
GREENOCK ROAD
B789
REILLY ROAD
Dargavel Burn
TURNINGSHAW ROAD
B790
Black Cart Water
INCHINNAN ROAD
ABBOTSINCH ROAD
White Cart Water
Glasgow Airport
Renfrew
A741
PAISLEY ROAD
Houston
HOUSTON ROAD
River Gryffe
Locher Water
Crosslee
MAGNUS RD
FULTON DR
Linwood
Brookfield
BRIDGE OF WEIR ROAD
A761
A737
LINWOOD RD
Weavers Cottage NTS
Kilbarchan
Johnstone
Elderslie
B787
B789
MAIN RD
Milliken Park
Foxbar
FOXBAR RD
B775
GLENIFFER RD
Gleniffer Braes Country Park
Old Patrick Water
Howwood
Paisley St James
St Mirren FC
Gilmour St
PAISLEY
University of Paisley
CANAL ST
Royal Alexandra A & E
Paisley Canal
Hawkhead
NEILSTON RD
CORSEBAR ROAD
B774
CAPLETHILL RD
Stanely Resr
Resr
B771
GRAHAMSTON ROAD
A726
BARRHEAD RD
GLASGOW RD
A761
PAISLEY ROAD WEST
Crookston
Crookston NTS
Mosspark
Bellahouston Park
Corkerhill
Pollok
Pollok Shopping Centre
Pollok Country Park
Burrell Collection
Pollok House
A736
CROOKSTON ROAD
ARKLESTON RD
GALLOWHILL RD
M8
MOSSLAND RD
KELVIN AVE
QUEEN ELIZABETH AVE
Hillington West
Hillington East
Hillington
Cardonald
Govan
A739
SHIELD HALL RD
Clyde Tunnel
Southern General A & E
Yoker
Garscadden
Scotstoun
Scotstounhill
Victoria Park
Knightswood
Anniesland
Univ of Strathclyde
Jordanhill
Gartnavel
Hyndland
Partick
Kelvingrove
Botanic Gardens
Western Infirmary A & E
University of Glasgow
CLYDESIDE EXPRESSWAY
A814
SECC
Yorkhill A & E
Exhibition Centre
Glasgow Rangers FC
EDMISTON DRIVE
Dumbreck
Maxwell Park
Pollokshields
Shawlands
Pollokshaws West
Pollokshaws
Cressmyloof
B762
BARRHEAD ROAD
B769
Kennishead
Thornliebank
THORNLIEBANK RD
Giffnock
FENWICK ROAD
Priesthill & Darnley
Nitshill
NITSHILL ROAD
B773
PARKHOUSE RD
DARNLEY RD
Barrhead
MAIN ST
Gateside
Caplaw
Waukmill Glen Reservoir
M77
ROUKENGLEN RD
Rouken Glen Gdns
Whitecraigs
Williamwood
EASTWOOD MAINS RD
Patterton
STEWARTON ROAD
A77
AYR ROAD
Newton Mearns
The Avenue Shopping Centre
Mearns
Waterfoot
Sheddens
Greenbank NTS
Eaglesham
Earn Water
Brother Loch
Long Loch
Netherplace
Craigton
Dodside
Balgray Reservoir
Glanderston Dam
Walton Dam
Snypes Dam
Craighall Dam
Harelaw Dam
Commore Dam
Neilston
KIRKTONFIELD RD
A736
Shillford
Loch Libo
Uplawmoor
NEILSTON ROAD
Hall
B775
B776
B777
Lugton
Drumchapel
Westerton
GREAT WESTERN ROAD
A82
Bearsden
Bearsden Ski Club
Roman Bath House
DRYMEN ROAD
Milngavie
STRATHBLANE ROAD
A81
MILNGAVIE ROAD
Hillfoot
BOCLAIR RD
B8049
Canniesburn
Dawsholm Park
Maryhill
Temple
Annieslea
MARYHILL ROAD
STOCKIEMUIR ROAD
A809
BALJAFFRAY ROAD
B8050
A807
AUCHENHOWIE ROAD
Cem
Crem
HCl

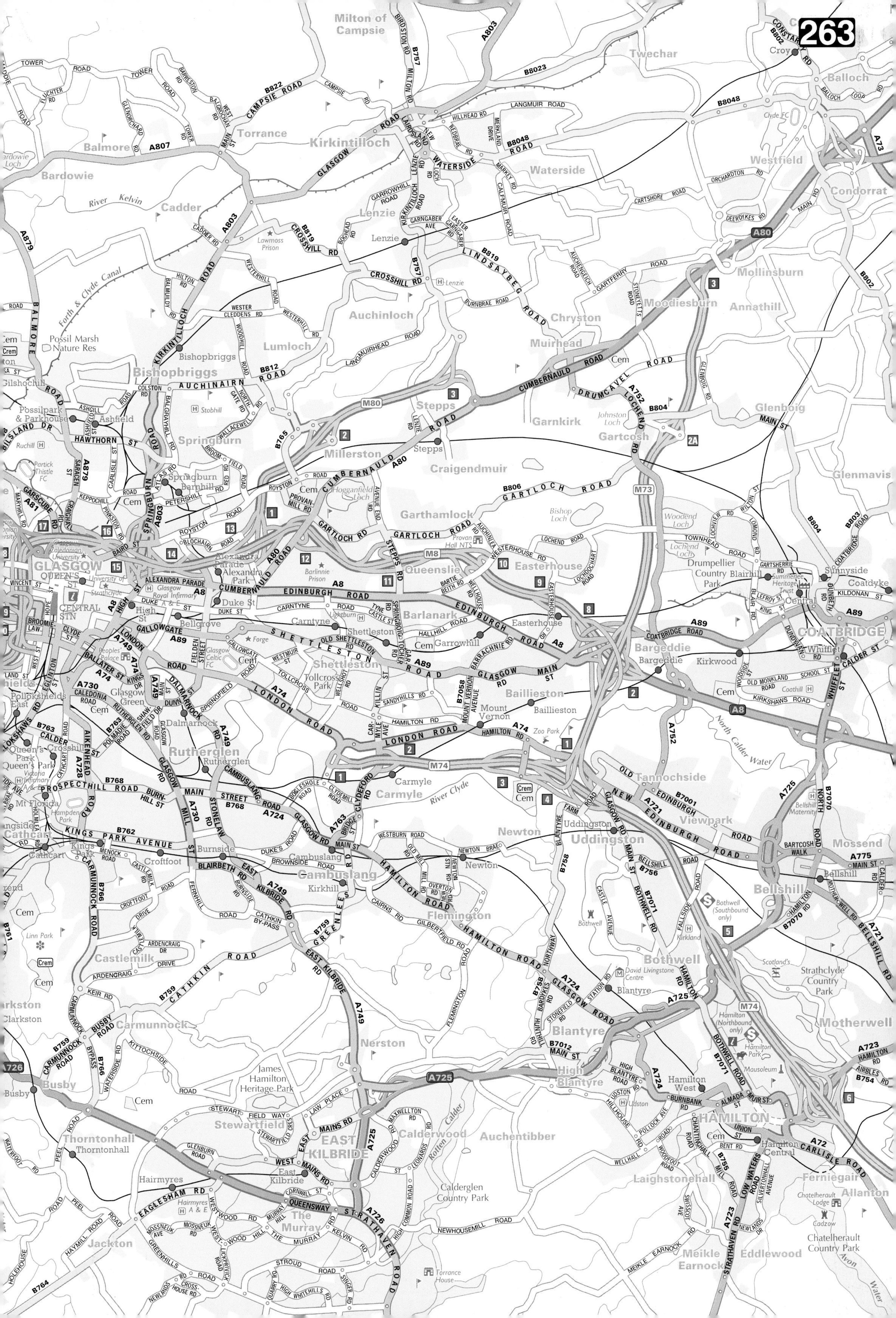

Milton of Campsie
Twechar
Croy
Balloch
Clyde FC
Westfield
Condorrat
Mollinsburn
Annathill
Torrance
Kirkintilloch
Balmore
Bardowie
Bardowie Loch
River Kelvin
Cadder
Lenzie
Lawmoss Prison
Waterside
Forth & Clyde Canal
Possil Marsh Nature Res
Auchinloch
Lumloch
Bishopbriggs
Chryston
Muirhead
Moodiesburn
Glenboig
Stepps
Garnkirk
Johnston Loch
Gartcosh
Millerston
Craigendmuir
Glenmavis
Possilpark & Parkhouse
Ashfield
Stobhill
Springburn
Ruchill
Partick Thistle FC
Barnhill
Hogganfield Loch
Garthamlock
Bishop Loch
Woodend Loch
Lochend Loch
Drumpellier Country Park
Blairhill
Summerlee Heritage Trust
Central
Sunnyside
Coatdyke
Glasgow Caledonian University
GLASGOW
QUEEN'S ST
University of Strathclyde
CENTRAL STN
Alexandra Parade
Alexandra Park
Barlinnie Prison
Provan Hall NTS
Queenslie
Easterhouse
Glasgow Royal Infirmary
Duke St
High St
Bellgrove
Barlanark
Carntyne
Shettleston
Garrowhill
Bargeddie
Kirkwood
COATBRIDGE
Whifflet
Coathill
Peoples Palace
Glasgow Green
Glasgow Celtic FC
Shettleston
Tollcross Park
Baillieston
Mount Vernon
Zoo Park
North Calder Water
Pollokshields
Pollokshields East
Dalmarnock
Rutherglen
Queen's Park
Crosshill
Victoria Infirmary
Mt Florida
Hampden Park
Cathcart
Kings Park
Croftfoot
Carmyle
River Clyde
Tannochside
Viewpark
Uddingston
Newton
Bellshill
Bellshill Maternity
Mossend
Burnside
Cambuslang
Gambuslang
Kirkhill
Flemington
Bothwell
Bothwell (Southbound only)
Kirkland
Linn Park
Castlemilk
Carmunnock
Clarkston
Busby
David Livingstone Centre
Blantyre
Scotland's
Strathclyde Country Park
Motherwell
Hamilton (Northbound only)
Hamilton Park
Mausoleum
Nerston
James Hamilton Heritage Park
High Blantyre
Udston
Hamilton West
HAMILTON
Hamilton Central
Stewartfield
EAST KILBRIDE
Calderwood
Auchentibber
Thorntonhall
Hairmyres
Hairmyres A & E
East Kilbride
Calderglen Country Park
The Murray
Laighstonehall
Ferniegair
Allanton
Chatelherault Lodge
Cadzow
Chatelherault Country Park
Jackton
Meikle Earnock
Eddlewood
Torrance House
Avon Water
M8
M73
M74
M80
A80
A8
A89
A74
A725
A726
A749
A752
A763
A803
A879
A807
A730
A728
A724
A721
A723
A775
A72
A73
B757
B822
B8023
B8048
B819
B812
B806
B804
B802
B803
B7001
B7058
B7070
B7071
B756
B758
B759
B762
B763
B766
B768
B7012
B754
B755
B761
B764
CAMPSIE ROAD
GLASGOW ROAD
CUMBERNAULD ROAD
GARTLOCH ROAD
EDINBURGH ROAD
LONDON ROAD
HAMILTON ROAD
KINGS PARK AVENUE
PROSPECTHILL ROAD
MAIN STREET
EAST KILBRIDE ROAD
GLASGOW ROAD
CATHKIN ROAD
QUEENSWAY
STRATHAVEN ROAD
EAGLESHAM RD
CARLISLE ROAD
BOTHWELL ROAD
LOW WATERS RD

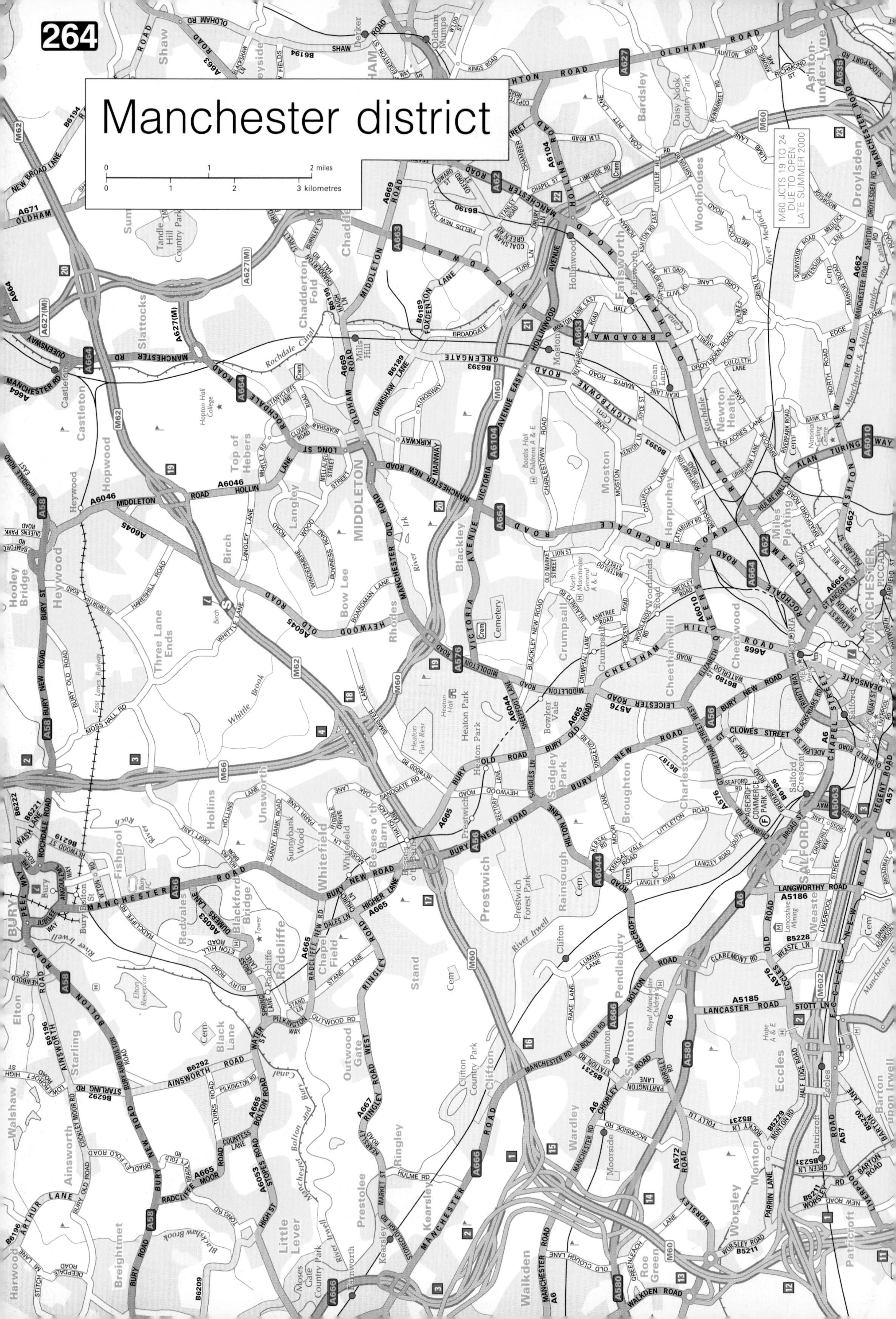

Manchester district
0 1 2 miles
0 1 2 3 kilometres
M60 JCTS 19 TO 24 DUE TO OPEN LATE SUMMER 2000
Shaw
Ashton-under-Lyne
Bardsley
Daisy Nook Country Park
Droylsden
Woodhouses
Failsworth
Hollinwood
Chadderton
Chadderton Fold
Slattocks
Tandle Hill Country Park
Castleton
Hopwood
Heywood
Hooley Bridge
Top of Hebers
Middleton
Mills Hill
Moston
Dean Lane
Newton Heath
Miles Platting
Harpurhey
Blackley
Langley
Birch
Three Lane Ends
Bow Lee
Rhodes
Crumpsall
Cheetham Hill
Cheetwood
Woodlands Road
Manchester
Piccadilly
Victoria
Salford
Salford Crescent
Heaton Park
Heaton Park Resr
Bowker Vale
Sedgley Park
Broughton
Charlestown
Prestwich
Prestwich Forest Park
Rainsough
Clifton
Pendlebury
Swinton
Eccles
Weaste
Patricroft
Barton upon Irwell
Monton
Worsley
Wardley
Moorside
Walkden
Roe Green
Kearsley
Ringley
Prestolee
Stand
Outwood Gate
Clifton Country Park
Unsworth
Hollins
Whitefield
Besses o' th' Barn
Sunnybank Wood
Fishpool
Bury
Redvales
Blackford Bridge
Radcliffe
Chapel Field
Black Lane
Starling
Elton
Walshaw
Ainsworth
Breightmet
Little Lever
Moses Gate Country Park
Farnworth
Harwood
Elton Reservoir
River Irwell
River Irk
River Medlock
Rochdale Canal
Whittle Brook
Hopton Hall College
Booths Hall Childrens A & E
North Manchester General A & E
Royal Manchester Children's
Hope A & E
National Cycling Centre
Lancashire Mining

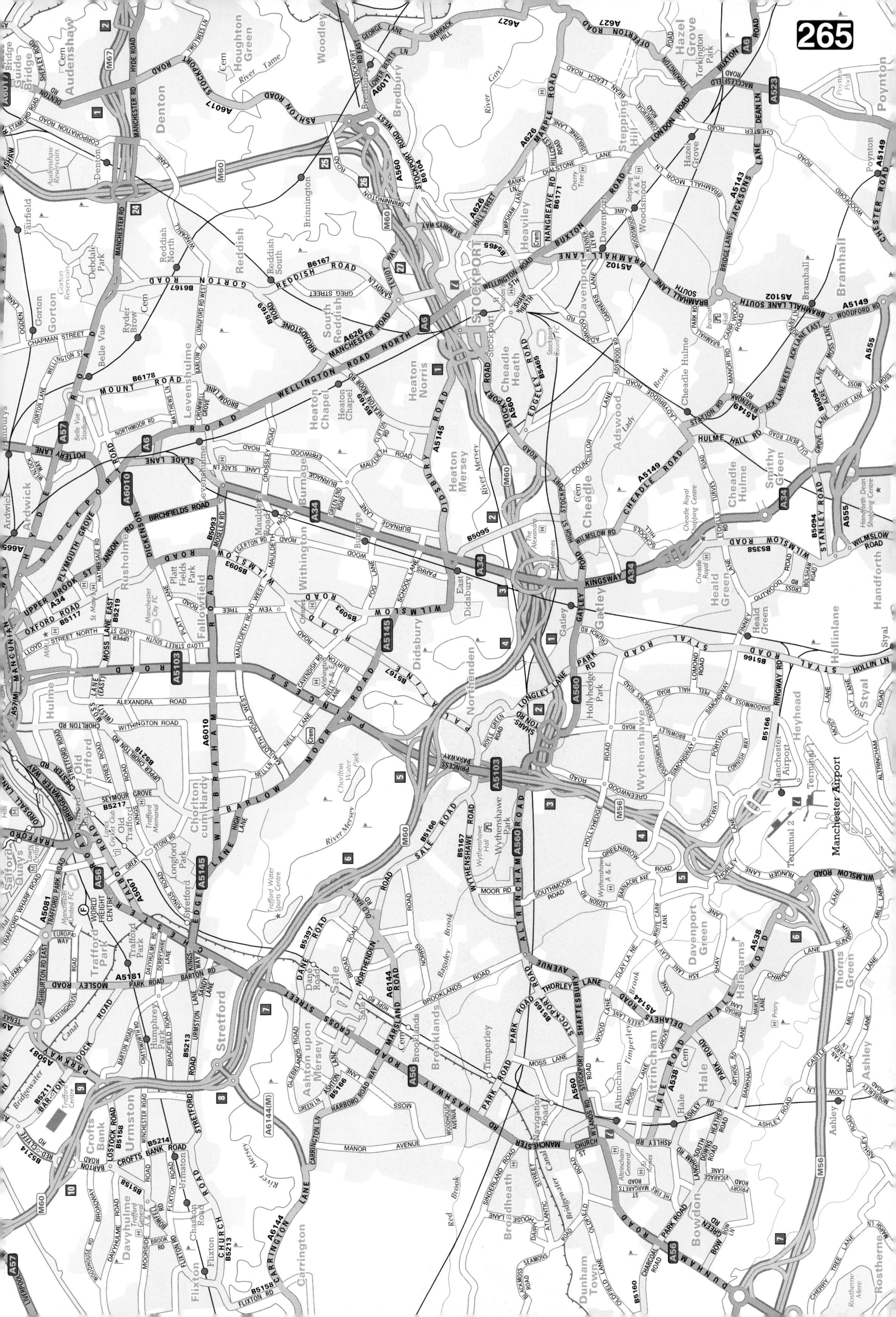
Audenshaw
Guide Bridge
Denton
Houghton Green
Woodley
Bredbury
Hazel Grove
Torkington Park
Poynton
Stepping Hill
Heaviley
Woodsmoor
Davenport
Reddish
Reddish North
Reddish South
South Reddish
Brinnington
Gorton
Belle Vue
Debdale Park
Ryder Brow
Levenshulme
Heaton Chapel
Heaton Norris
Stockport
Cheadle Heath
Cheadle Hulme
Bramhall
Adswood
Heaton Mersey
Burnage
Cheadle
Smithy Green
Ardwick
Rusholme
Fallowfield
Platt Fields Park
Withington
Didsbury
East Didsbury
Gatley
Heald Green
Handforth
Hollinlane
Styal
Heyhead
Manchester Airport
Mauldeth Road
Mancunian Way
Hulme
Old Trafford
Chorlton cum Hardy
Northenden
Wythenshawe
Wythenshawe Park
Hollyhedge Park
Salford Quays
Trafford Park
Longford Park
Stretford
Sale
Dane Road
Brooklands
Ashton upon Mersey
Timperley
Altrincham
Hale
Halebarns
Davenport Green
Thorns Green
Ashley
Humphrey Park
Urmston
Davyhulme
Crofts Bank
Flixton
Chassen Road
Carrington
Broadheath
Navigation Road
Dunham Town
Bowdon
Rostherne
River Tame
River Goyt
River Mersey
Baguley Brook
Chorlton Water Park
Trafford Water Sports Centre
Bridgewater Canal
Stockport County FC
Belle Vue Stadium
Manchester City FC
Manchester United FC
Lancs Cricket Club
Trafford Centre
Cheadle Royal Shopping Centre
Handforth Dean Shopping Centre
Terminal 1
Terminal 2
M60
M67
M56
A57(M)
A6
A34
A560
A5103
A5145
A6010
A56
A538
A523
A555
A5149
A6144
A6144(M)
A6017
A627
A626
A5102
A5143
WILMSLOW ROAD
KINGSWAY
PRINCESS PARKWAY
WASHWAY ROAD
CROSS STREET
CHESTER ROAD
BARLOW MOOR ROAD
PALATINE ROAD
WELLINGTON ROAD NORTH
STOCKPORT ROAD
HYDE ROAD
ASHTON ROAD
BUXTON ROAD
LONDON ROAD
MARPLE ROAD
OFFERTON ROAD
BRAMHALL LANE SOUTH
STYAL ROAD
DUNHAM ROAD
MANCHESTER ROAD
CARRINGTON LANE
MOSLEY ROAD
ALTRINCHAM ROAD
SHAFTESBURY AVENUE
HALE ROAD
PARK ROAD

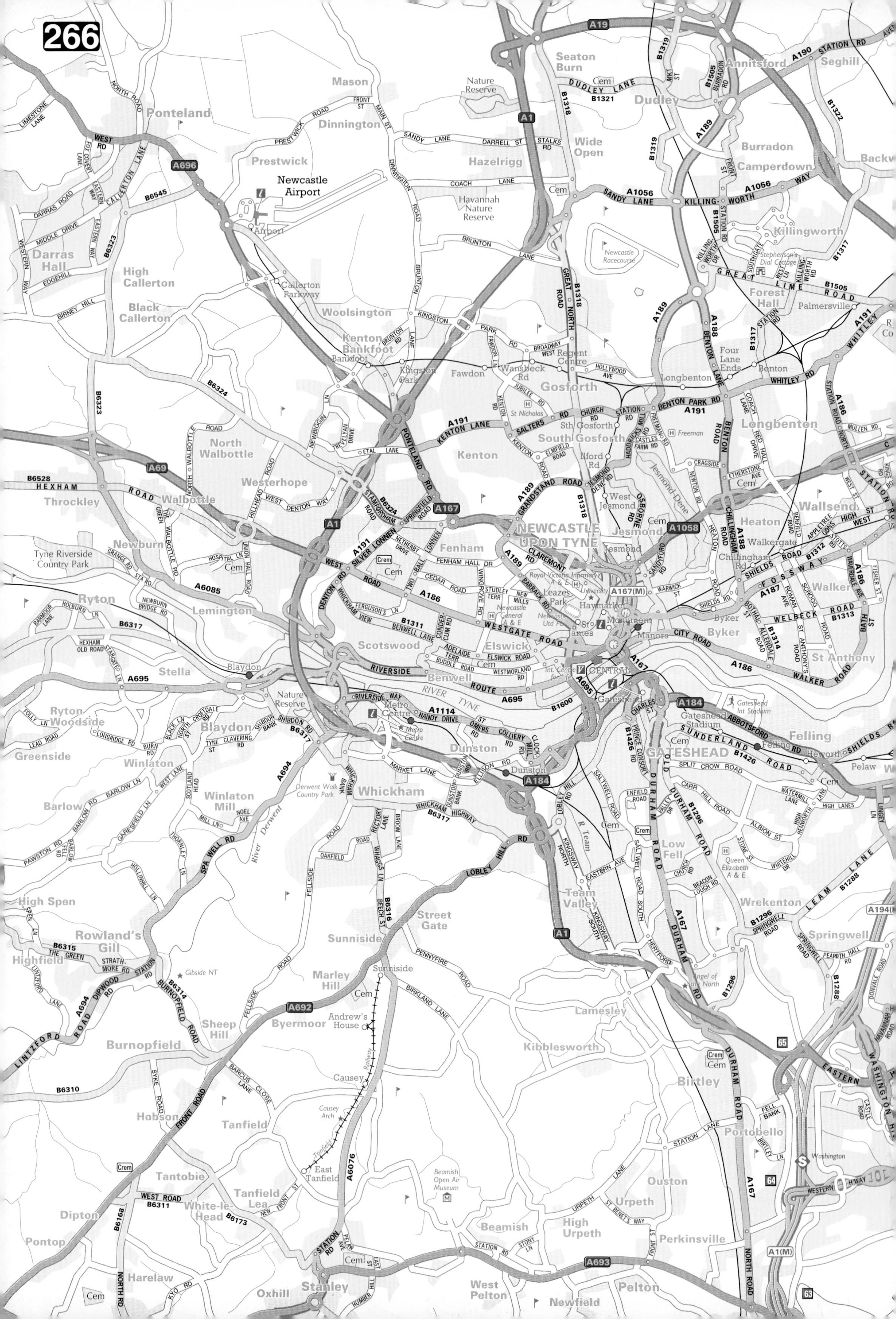
A19
Seaton Burn
Cem
Dudley Lane
B1321
Dudley
Annitsford
A190
Station Rd
Seghill
B1322
Mason
Nature Reserve
Ponteland
Dinnington
North Road
Front St
Main St
Prestwick Road
Limestone Lane
West Rd
Sandy Lane
Darrell St
Stalks Rd
Wide Open
B1318
B1319
A1
A189
Burradon
Camperdown
Backworth
Prestwick
Hazelrigg
A696
Newcastle Airport
Coach Lane
Cem
A1056
Sandy Lane
Killingworth Way
A1056
B6545
Havannah Nature Reserve
Killingworth
Darras Road
Middle Drive
Western Way
Eastern Way
Darras Hall
B6323
Edgehill
High Callerton
Brunton Lane
Newcastle Racecourse
Stephenson's Dial Cottage
Great Lime Road
B1505
B1317
Forest Hall
Palmersville
Callerton Parkway
Black Callerton
Birney Hill
Woolsington
Great North Road
Kingston Park Rd
Broadway
West
Regent Centre
Four Lane Ends
Benton
Whitley Rd
A191
Kenton Bankfoot
Bankfoot
Kingston Park
Fawdon
Wansbeck Rd
Hollywood Ave
Longbenton
Gosforth
B6324
Jubilee Rd
Salters Rd
Church Rd
Station Rd
Benton Park Rd
A191
A186
Kenton Lane
Sth Gosforth
South Gosforth
Freeman
Longbenton
North Walbottle
Road
Kenton
Etal Lane
Elmfield Road
Ilford Rd
Cragside
Etherstone Ave
Cem
A69
Hexham Road
B6528
Throckley
Walbottle
Westerhope
West Denton Way
Grandstand Road
West Jesmond
Osborne Rd
Jesmond Dene
Wallsend
Heaton
A167
A1
Stamfordham Road
B6324
Springfield Road
Newcastle upon Tyne
Cem
Jesmond
A1058
Newburn
Tyne Riverside Country Park
Silver Lonnen
Fenham
Claremont Rd
Walkergate
Chillingham Rd
Shields Road
Fossway
B1312
Cem
West Road
Crem
Cem
Fenham Hall Dr
Royal Victoria Infirmary A & E
University
A167(M)
Warwick St
Walker
A6085
Cedar Road
Leazes Park
Haymarket
A187
Welbeck Road
Ryton
Lemington
Newburn Bridge Rd
Denton Rd
Whickham View
Ferguson's Ln
Benwell Lane
B1311
A186
Westgate Road
Condercum Rd
Newcastle General A & E
Newcastle Utd FC
St James
Monument
Manors
Byker
City Road
B6317
Hexham Old Road
Scotswood
Elswick
Adelaide Terr
Elswick Road
Buddle Road
Cem
Westmorland Road
Int. Centre for Life
Central
A186
Walker Road
St Anthony
Blaydon
Stella
A695
Riverside
Benwell
Route
A695
B1600
Gateshead
Charles St
A184
Gateshead Int Stadium
Nature Reserve
Riverside Way
River Tyne
Metro Centre
A1114
Handy Drive
Colliery Rd
Clock Mill Rd
Gateshead Stadium
Abbotsford
Felling
Ryton Woodside
Blaydon
Shibdon Bank
B6317
Sunderland Road
Felling
Heworth
Shields Rd
Greenside
Winlaton
Dunston
Dunston
Prince Consort Rd
B1426
Gateshead
Split Crow Road
Pelaw
A694
Market Lane
A184
Cem
Barlow
Barlow Ln
Winlaton Mill
Derwent Walk Country Park
Whickham
Whickham Highway
B6317
Lobley Hill
Saltwell Road
Enfield Road
Old Durham Road
Carr Hill Road
B1296
Watermill Lane
High Lanes
Albion St
Spa Well Rd
River Derwent
Fellside
Oakfield
Whaggs Ln
Lobley Hill Rd
R Team
Kingsway North
Cem
Crem
Low Fell
Durham Road
Queen Elizabeth A & E
Eastern Ave
Saltwell Road South
Beacon Lough Rd
Leam Lane
B1288
High Spen
B6316 Beech St
Team Valley
Kingsway South
Wrekenton
A194(M)
Rowland's Gill
Street Gate
A1
Springwell Road
B1296
Springwell
Highfield
B6315
Sunniside
Gibside NT
Pennyfire Road
Hertford
A167 Durham Road
Angel of the North
B1296
B6314
Burnopfield Road
Marley Hill
Sunniside
Cem
Birkland Lane
Lamesley
A694
Dipwood Rd
Lintzford Road
A692
Andrew's House
Byermoor
Sheep Hill
Burnopfield
Kibblesworth
Crem
Cem
Eastern
Washington
Railway
Causey
Barcus Close Lane
Birtley
B6310
Syke Road
Front Road
Hobson
Causey Arch
Tanfield
Tanfield Railway
Station Lane
Portobello
Durham Road
Fell Bank
Birtley Ln
Washington
Crem
Tantobie
East Tanfield
A6076
Beamish Open Air Museum
Ouston
Urpeth Lane
Western Highway
West Road
B6311
Tanfield Lea
Front St
White-le-Head
B6173
Urpeth
St Benet's Way
A167
Dipton
High Urpeth
Perkinsville
B6168
Beamish
Pontop
Station Rd
Stony Ln
A1(M)
North Road
Cem
A693
Harelaw
Cem
Kyo Rd
Oxhill
Stanley
Humber Hill
West Pelton
Pelton
Newfield
Front St

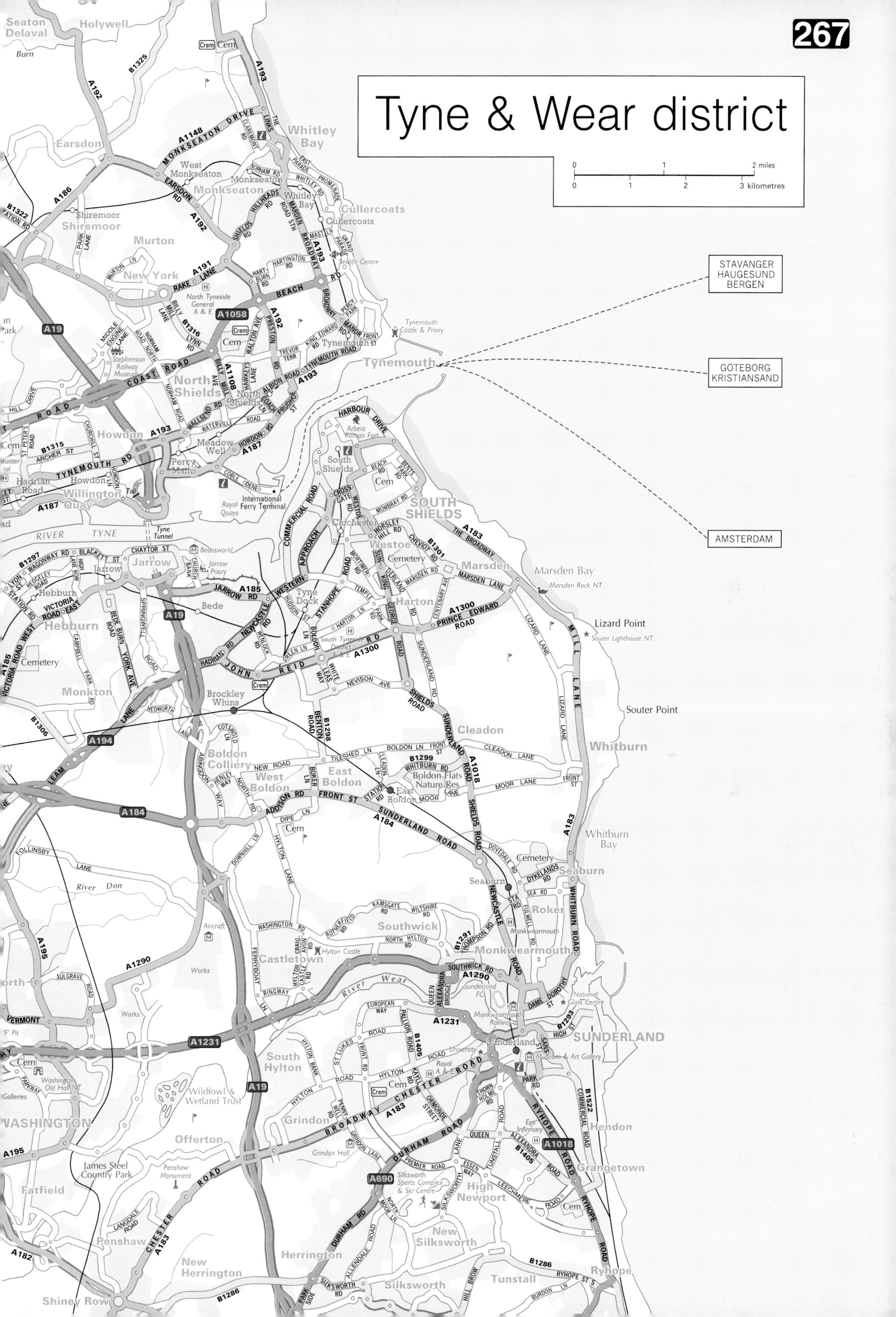

Tyne & Wear district

index to place names

England

5	*Beds*	**Bedfordshire**
6	*Berks*	**Berkshire**
10	*Bristl*	**Bristol**
11	*Bucks*	**Buckinghamshire**
13	*Cambs*	**Cambridgeshire**
17	*Ches*	**Cheshire**
22	*Cnwll*	**Cornwall**
23	*Cumb*	**Cumbria**
25	*Derbys*	**Derbyshire**
26	*Devon*	**Devon**
27	*Dorset*	**Dorset**
30	*Dur*	**Durham**
35	*E R Yk*	**East Riding of Yorkshire**
36	*E Susx*	**East Sussex**
37	*Essex*	**Essex**
41	*Gloucs*	**Gloucestershire**
42	*Gt Lon*	**Greater London**
43	*Gt Man*	**Greater Manchester**
46	*Hants*	**Hampshire**
47	*Herefs*	**Herefordshire**
48	*Herts*	**Hertfordshire**
53	*IOW*	**Isle of Wight**
54	*IOS*	**Isles of Scilly**
56	*Kent*	**Kent**
57	*Lancs*	**Lancashire**
58	*Leics*	**Leicestershire**
59	*Lincs*	**Lincolnshire**
60	*Mersyd*	**Merseyside**
67	*Norfk*	**Norfolk**
70	*N York*	**North Yorkshire**
71	*Nhants*	**Northamptonshire**
72	*Nthumb*	**Northumberland**
73	*Notts*	**Nottinghamshire**
75	*Oxon*	**Oxfordshire**
81	*Rutlnd*	**Rutland**
83	*Shrops*	**Shropshire**
84	*Somset*	**Somerset**
87	*S York*	**South Yorkshire**
88	*Staffs*	**Staffordshire**
90	*Suffk*	**Suffolk**
91	*Surrey*	**Surrey**
94	*T & W*	**Tyne & Wear**
96	*Warwks*	**Warwickshire**
100	*W Mids*	**West Midlands**
101	*W Susx*	**West Sussex**
102	*W York*	**West Yorkshire**
103	*Wilts*	**Wiltshire**
104	*Worcs*	**Worcestershire**

Wales

7	*Blae G*	**Blaenau Gwent**
9	*Brdgnd*	**Bridgend**
12	*Caerph*	**Caerphilly**
14	*Cardif*	**Cardiff**
15	*Carmth*	**Carmarthenshire**
16	*Cerdgn*	**Ceredigion**
21	*Conwy*	**Conwy**
24	*Denbgs*	**Denbighshire**
40	*Flints*	**Flintshire**
45	*Gwynd*	**Gwynedd**
51	*IOA*	**Isle of Anglesey**
61	*Myr Td*	**Merthyr Tydfil**
63	*Mons*	**Monmouthshire**
65	*Neath*	**Neath Port Talbot**
66	*Newpt*	**Newport**
76	*Pembks*	**Pembrokeshire**
78	*Powys*	**Powys**
80	*Rhondd*	**Rhondda Cynon Taff**
92	*Swans*	**Swansea**
93	*Torfn*	**Torfaen**
95	*V Glam*	**Vale of Glamorgan**
105	*Wrexhm*	**Wrexham**

Scotland

1	*Aber C*	**Aberdeen City**
2	*Abers*	**Aberdeenshire**
3	*Angus*	**Angus**
4	*Ag & B*	**Argyll & Bute**
8	*Border*	**Borders (Scottish)**
18	*C Edin*	**City of Edinburgh**
19	*C Glas*	**City of Glasgow**
20	*Clacks*	**Clackmannanshire**
28	*D & G*	**Dumfries & Galloway**
29	*Dund C*	**Dundee City**
31	*E Ayrs*	**East Ayrshire**
32	*E Duns*	**East Dunbartonshire**
33	*E Loth*	**East Lothian**
34	*E Rens*	**East Renfrewshire**
38	*Falk*	**Falkirk**
39	*Fife*	**Fife**
49	*Highld*	**Highland**
50	*Inver*	**Inverclyde**
62	*Mdloth*	**Midlothian**
64	*Moray*	**Moray**
68	*N Ayrs*	**North Ayrshire**
69	*N Lans*	**North Lanarkshire**
74	*Ork*	**Orkney Islands**
77	*P & K*	**Perth & Kinross**
79	*Rens*	**Renfrewshire**
82	*Shet*	**Shetland Islands**
85	*S Ayrs*	**South Ayrshire**
86	*S Lans*	**South Lanarkshire**
89	*Stirlg*	**Stirling**
97	*W Isls*	**Western Isles**
98	*W Duns*	**West Dunbartonshire**
99	*W Loth*	**West Lothian**

The Channel Islands & Isle of Man

44	*Guern*	**Guernsey**
55	*Jersey*	**Jersey**
52	*IOM*	**Isle of Man**

Each place name entry in this index is identified with its County, County Borough or Council Area name. These are shown in *italics*, and can be identified using the key map below. A list of the abbreviated forms used is shown on the left.

To locate a place name in the atlas turn to the map page indicated in bold type in the index and use the 4-figure grid reference.

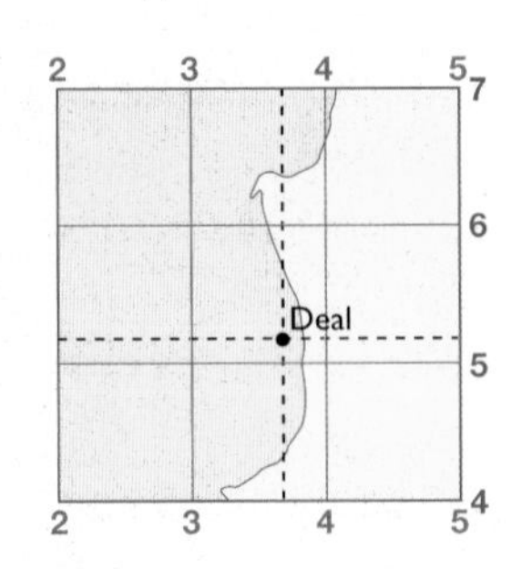

Example:

Deal *Kent* **29** 3752

Turn to page **29**

Find **3** along the bottom or top of the page

Move a further **7** tenths of the square to the right (easting)

Find **5** up the side of the page

Move a further **2** tenths up (northing)

Deal will be found where the easting and northing intersect

The National Grid two-letter prefixes are also shown on the map pages to denote the 100km square, e.g. Deal TR3752

100 places of interest are indexed in red.

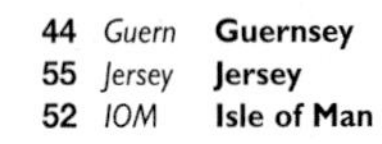

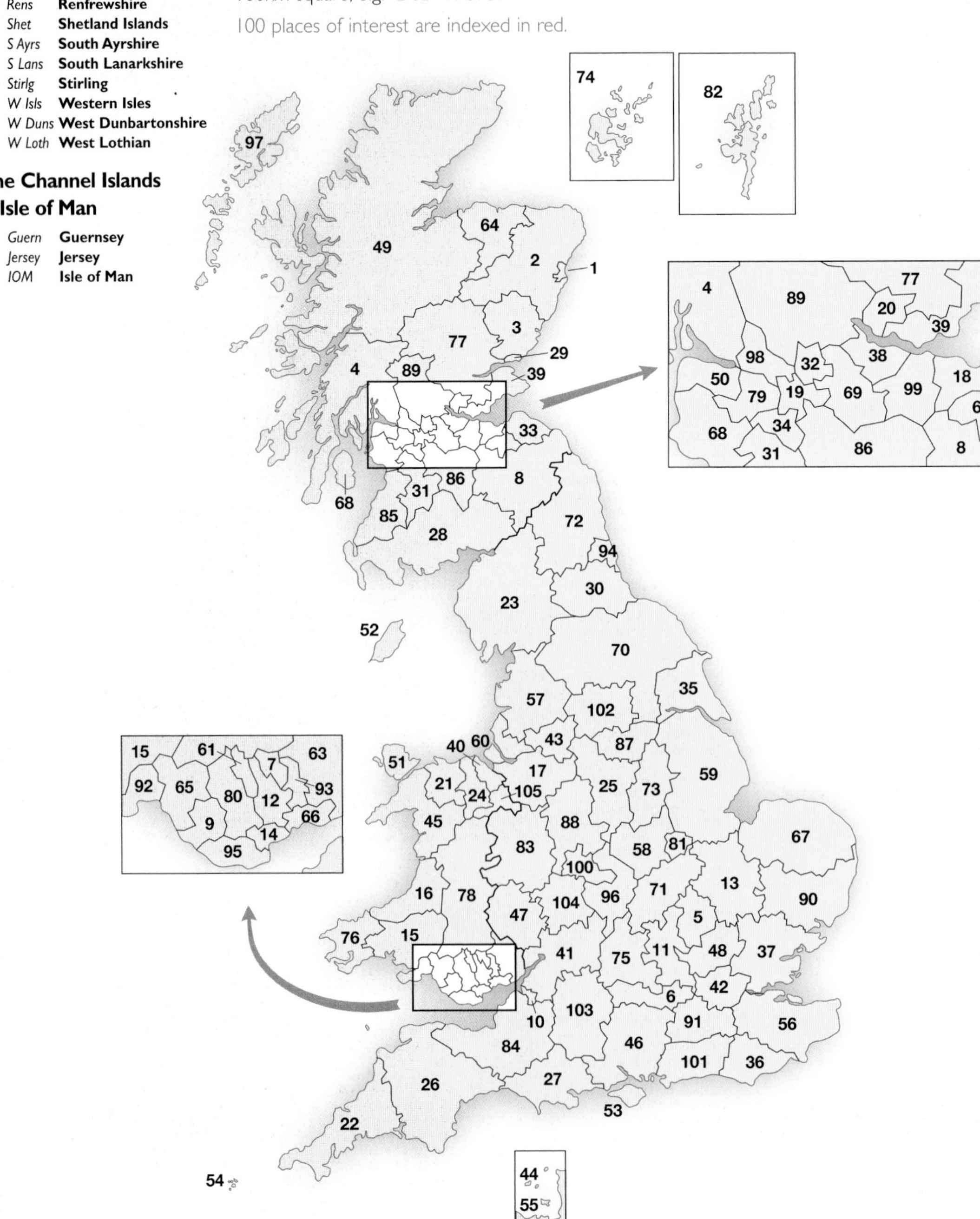

A'Chill Anlaby

A

A'Chill Highld 128 2705
Ab Kettleby Leics 63 7223
Ab Lench Worcs 47 0151
Abbas Combe Somset 22 7022
Abberley Worcs 47 7467
Abberley Common Worcs 47 7467
Abberton Essex 41 0019
Abberton Worcs 47 9953
Abberwick Nthumb 111 1313
Abbess Roding Essex 40 5711
Abbey Devon 9 1410
Abbey Dore Herefs 46 3830
Abbey Green Staffs 72 9757
Abbey Hill Somset 10 2718
Abbey St Bathans Border 119 7661
Abbey Town Cumb 93 1750
Abbey Village Lancs 81 6422
Abbey Wood Gt Lon 27 4779
Abbeycwmhir Powys 45 0571
Abbeydale S York 74 3281
Abbeystead Lancs 81 5654
Abbot's Chair Derbys 74 0290
Abbot's Salford Warwks 48 0650
Abbotrule Border 110 6113
Abbots Bickington Devon 18 3813
Abbots Bromley Staffs 73 0724
Abbots Deuglie P & K 126 1111
Abbots Langley Herts 26 0901
Abbots Leigh Somset 34 5474
Abbots Morton Worcs 48 0255
Abbots Ripton Cambs 52 2377
Abbots Worthy Hants 24 4932
Abbotsbury Dorset 10 5785
Abbotsham Devon 18 4226
Abbotskerswell Devon 7 8568
Abbotsleigh Devon 7 8048
Abbotsley Cambs 52 2256
Abbotstone Hants 24 5634
Abbotswood Hants 23 3623
Abbott Street Dorset 11 9800
Abbotts Ann Hants 23 3243
Abcott Shrops 46 3978
Abdon Shrops 59 5786
Abenhall Gloucs 35 6717
Aber Clydach Powys 33 1021
Aber-arad Carmth 31 3140
Aber-banc Cerdgn 31 3541
Aber-giar Carmth 44 5040
Aber-Magwr Cerdgn 43 6673
Aber-meurig Cerdgn 44 5656
Aber-nant Rhondd 33 0103
Aberaeron Cerdgn 42 4562
Aberaman Rhondd 33 0100
Aberangell Gwynd 57 8410
Aberarder Highld 140 6225
Aberargie P & K 126 1615
Aberarth Cerdgn 42 4763
Aberavon Neath 32 7489
Aberbargoed Caerph 33 1500
Aberbeeg Blae G 33 2002
Abercairny P & K 125 9222
Abercanaid Myr Td 33 0503
Abercarn Caerph 33 2194
Abercastle Pembks 30 8533
Abercegir Powys 57 8001
Aberchalder Lodge Highld 131 3403
Aberchirder Abers 142 6252
Abercoed Cerdgn 44 6757
Abercraf Powys 33 8212
Abercregan Neath 33 8496
Abercwmboi Rhondd 33 0299
Abercych Pembks 31 2441
Abercynon Rhondd 33 0794
Aberdalgie P & K 125 0720
Aberdare Rhondd 33 0002
Aberdaron Gwynd 56 1726
Aberdeen Aber C 135 9306
Aberdeen Airport 135 8712
Aberdesach Gwynd 68 4251
Aberdour Fife 117 1985
Aberdulais Neath 32 7799
Aberdyfi Gwynd 43 6196
Aberedw Powys 45 0847
Abereiddy Pembks 30 7931
Abererch Gwynd 56 3936
Aberfan Myr Td 33 0700
Aberfeldy P & K 125 8549
Aberffraw IOA 68 3569
Aberffrwd Cerdgn 43 6878
Aberford W York 83 4337
Aberfoyle Stirlg 115 5200
Abergarw Brdgnd 33 9184
Abergarwed Neath 33 8102
Abergavenny Mons 34 2914
Abergele Conwy 70 9477
Abergorlech Carmth 44 5833
Abergwesyn Powys 45 8552
Abergwili Carmth 31 4320
Abergwydol Powys 57 7903
Abergwynfi Neath 33 8995
Abergwyngregyn Gwynd 69 6572
Abergynolwyn Gwynd 57 6806
Aberhafesp Powys 58 0792
Aberhosan Powys 43 8197
Aberkenfig Brdgnd 33 8984
Aberlady E Loth 118 4679
Aberlemno Angus 127 5255
Aberllefenni Powys 57 7609
Aberllynfi Powys 45 1737
Aberlour Moray 141 2642
Abermorddu Flints 71 3056
Abermule Powys 58 1694
Abernant Carmth 31 3323
Abernethy P & K 126 1816
Abernyte P & K 126 2531
Aberporth Cerdgn 42 2651
Abersoch Gwynd 56 3127
Abersychan Torfn 34 2603
Aberthin V Glam 33 0074
Abertillery Blae G 33 2104
Abertridwr Caerph 33 1289
Abertridwr Powys 58 0319
Abertysswg Caerph 33 1305
Aberuthven P & K 125 9615
Aberyscir Powys 45 9929
Aberystwyth Cerdgn 43 5881
Abingdon Oxon 37 4997
Abinger Surrey 14 1145
Abinger Hammer Surrey 14 0947
Abington Nhants 50 7861
Abington S Lans 108 9323
Abington Pigotts Cambs 39 3044
Ablington Gloucs 36 1007
Ablington Wilts 23 1546
Abney Derbys 74 1980
Above Church Staffs 73 0150
Aboyne Abers 134 5298
Abram Gt Man 78 6001
Abriachan Highld 139 5535
Abridge Essex 27 4696
Abson Gloucs 35 7074
Abthorpe Nhants 49 6446
Aby Lincs 77 4078
Acaster Malbis N York 83 5845
Acaster Selby N York 83 5741
Accott Devon 19 6432
Accrington Lancs 81 7628
Acha Ag & B 120 1854
Acha Mor W Isls 152 3029
Achahoish Ag & B 113 7877
Achalader P & K 126 1245
Achaleven Ag & B 122 9233
Achanalt Highld 139 2661
Achandunie Highld 146 6472
Achany Highld 146 5602
Acharacle Highld 121 6767
Acharn Highld 122 7050
Acharn P & K 124 7543
Achavanich Highld 151 1842
Achduart Highld 145 0403
Achfary Highld 148 2939
Achiltibuie Highld 144 0208
Achinhoan Ag & B 105 7516
Achintee Highld 138 9441
Achintraid Highld 138 8438
Achmelvich Highld 148 0524
Achmore Highld 138 8533
Achmore W Isls 152 3029
Achnacarnin Highld 148 0432
Achnacarry Highld 131 1787
Achnacloich Highld 129 5908
Achnaconeran Highld 139 4118
Achnacroish Ag & B 122 8541
Achnadrish Lodge Ag & B 121 4652
Achnafauld P & K 125 8736
Achnagarron Highld 146 6870
Achnaha Highld 128 4668
Achnahaird Highld 144 0013
Achnairn Highld 146 5512
Achnalea Highld 130 8561
Achnamara Ag & B 113 7887
Achnasheen Highld 138 1658
Achnashellach Station Highld 138 0048
Achnastank Moray 141 2733
Achosnich Highld 121 4467
Achranich Highld 122 7047
Achreamie Highld 150 0166
Achriabhach Highld 131 1468
Achriesgill Highld 148 2554
Achtoty Highld 149 6762
Achurch Nhants 51 0283
Achvaich Highld 146 7194
Ackergill Highld 151 3553
Acklam N York 97 4817
Acklam N York 90 7861
Ackleton Shrops 60 7698
Acklington Nthumb 103 2301
Ackton W York 83 4121
Ackworth Moor Top W York 83 4316
Acle Norfk 67 4010
Acock's Green W Mids 61 1283
Acol Kent 29 3067
Acomb N York 83 5651
Acomb Nthumb 102 9366
Acombe Somset 9 1914
Aconbury Herefs 46 5133
Acre Lancs 81 7924
Acrefair Wrexhm 70 2743
Acresford Derbys 61 2913
Acton Ches 71 6352
Acton Dorset 11 9978
Acton Gt Lon 26 2080
Acton Staffs 72 8241
Acton Suffk 54 8945
Acton Worcs 47 8467
Acton Beauchamp Herefs 47 6850
Acton Bridge Ches 71 5975
Acton Burnell Shrops 59 5302
Acton Green Herefs 47 6950
Acton Park Wrexhm 71 3451
Acton Pigott Shrops 59 5402
Acton Round Shrops 59 6395
Acton Scott Shrops 59 4589
Acton Trussell Staffs 72 9318
Acton Turville Gloucs 35 8080
Adbaston Staffs 72 7627
Adber Dorset 21 5920
Adbolton Notts 62 5938
Adderbury Oxon 49 4735
Adderley Shrops 72 6640
Adderstone Nthumb 111 1330
Addiewell W Loth 117 9962
Addingham W York 82 0749
Addington Bucks 49 7428
Addington Gt Lon 27 3664
Addington Kent 28 6559
Addiscombe Gt Lon 27 3366
Addlestone Surrey 26 0564
Addlestonemoor Surrey 26 0565
Addlethorpe Lincs 77 5468
Adeney Shrops 72 6918
Adeyfield Herts 38 0708
Adfa Powys 58 0601
Adforton Herefs 46 4071
Adisham Kent 29 2253
Adlestrop Gloucs 48 2426
Adlingfleet E R Yk 84 8421
Adlington Ches 79 9180
Adlington Lancs 81 6013
Admaston Shrops 59 6313
Admaston Staffs 73 0423
Admington Warwks 48 2045
Adsborough Somset 20 2729
Adscombe Somset 20 1837
Adstock Bucks 49 7329
Adstone Nhants 49 5951
Adswood Gt Man 79 8888
Adversane W Susx 14 0723
Advie Highld 141 1234
Adwalton W York 82 2328
Adwell Oxon 37 6999
Adwick Le Street S York 83 5308
Adwick upon Dearne S York 83 4701
Ae D & G 100 9889
Ae Bridgend D & G 100 0186
Affetside Gt Man 81 7513
Affleck Abers 142 5540
Affpuddle Dorset 11 8093
Affric Lodge Highld 138 1822
Afon-wen Flints 70 1371
Afton Devon 7 8462
Afton IOW 12 3486
Agglethorpe N York 89 0885
Aigburth Mersyd 78 3886
Aike E R Yk 84 0446
Aiketgate Cumb 94 4846
Aikhead Cumb 93 2349
Aikton Cumb 93 2753
Ailby Lincs 77 4376
Ailey Herefs 46 3348
Ailsworth Cambs 64 1198
Ainderby Quernhow N York 89 3480
Ainderby Steeple N York 89 3392
Aingers Green Essex 41 1120
Ainsdale Mersyd 80 3112
Ainsdale-on-Sea Mersyd 80 2912
Ainstable Cumb 94 5246
Ainsworth Gt Man 79 7610
Ainthorpe N York 90 7007
Aintree Mersyd 78 3898
Ainville W Loth 117 1063
Aird Ag & B 113 7600
Aird D & G 98 0960
Aird W Isls 152 5635
Aird a Mhulaidh W Isls 152 1810
Aird Asaig W Isls 152 1202
Aird Dhubh Highld 137 7040
Aird of Kinloch Ag & B 121 5228
Aird of Sleat Highld 129 5900
Aird Uig W Isls 152 0533
Airdeny Ag & B 122 9929
Airdrie N Lans 116 7565
Airdriehill N Lans 116 7867
Airds Bay Ag & B 122 9932
Airds of Kells D & G 99 6770
Airidh a bhruaich W Isls 152 2417
Airieland D & G 99 7556
Airlie Angus 126 3150
Airmyn E R Yk 84 7224
Airntully P & K 125 0935
Airor Highld 129 7205
Airth Falk 116 9087
Airton N York 88 9059
Aisby Lincs 76 8692
Aisby Lincs 64 0138
Aisgill Cumb 88 7797
Aish Devon 7 6960
Aish Devon 7 8458
Aisholt Somset 20 1935
Aiskew N York 89 2788
Aislaby Dur 89 4012
Aislaby N York 90 8608
Aislaby N York 90 7785
Aisthorpe Lincs 76 9480
Aith Shet 153 3455
Akeld Nthumb 111 9529
Akeley Bucks 49 7037
Akenham Suffk 54 1449
Albaston Devon 6 4270
Alberbury Shrops 59 3614
Albourne W Susx 15 2516
Albourne Green W Susx 15 2616
Albrighton Shrops 59 4918
Albrighton Shrops 60 8004
Alburgh Norfk 55 2687
Albury Herts 39 4324
Albury Oxon 37 6505
Albury Surrey 14 0447
Albury End Herts 39 4223
Albury Heath Surrey 14 0646
Alby Hill Norfk 67 1934
Alcaig Highld 139 5657
Alcaston Shrops 59 4587
Alcester Warwks 48 0857
Alcester Lane End W Mids 61 0780
Alciston E Susx 16 5005
Alcombe Wilts 35 8169
Alconbury Cambs 52 1875
Alconbury Weston Cambs 52 1777
Aldborough N York 89 4066
Aldborough Norfk 66 1834
Aldbourne Wilts 36 2676
Aldbrough E R Yk 85 2438
Aldbrough St John N York 89 2011
Aldbury Herts 38 9612
Aldcliffe Lancs 87 4660
Aldclune P & K 132 8964
Aldeburgh Suffk 55 4656
Aldeby Norfk 67 4493
Aldenham Herts 26 1498
Alder Moor Staffs 73 2226
Alderbury Wilts 23 1827
Aldercar Derbys 62 4447
Alderford Norfk 66 1218
Alderholt Dorset 12 1212
Alderley Gloucs 35 7690
Alderley Edge Ches 79 8478
Aldermans Green W Mids 61 3683
Aldermaston Berks 24 5965
Alderminster Warwks 48 2348
Aldershot Hants 25 8650
Alderton Gloucs 47 0033
Alderton Nhants 49 7446
Alderton Shrops 59 4924
Alderton Suffk 55 3441
Alderton Wilts 35 8482
Alderwasley Derbys 73 3053
Aldfield N York 89 2669
Aldford Ches 71 4159
Aldgate Rutlnd 63 9804
Aldham Essex 40 9126
Aldham Suffk 54 0545
Aldingbourne W Susx 14 9205
Aldingham Cumb 86 2870
Aldington Kent 29 0736
Aldington Worcs 48 0644
Aldington Corner Kent 29 0636
Aldivalloch Moray 141 3526
Aldochlay Ag & B 115 3591
Aldon Shrops 46 4379
Aldoth Cumb 92 1448
Aldreth Cambs 53 4473
Aldridge W Mids 61 0500
Aldringham Suffk 55 4461
Aldro N York 90 8162
Aldsworth Gloucs 36 1509
Aldsworth W Susx 14 7608
Aldunie Moray 141 3626
Aldwark Derbys 74 2257
Aldwark N York 89 4663
Aldwick W Susx 14 9198
Aldwincle Nhants 51 0081
Aldworth Berks 37 5579
Alexandria W Duns 115 3979
Aley Somset 20 1838
Alfardisworthy Devon 18 2911
Alfington Devon 9 1197
Alfold Surrey 14 0333
Alfold Bars W Susx 14 0333
Alfold Crossways Surrey 14 0335
Alford Abers 142 5715
Alford Lincs 77 4575
Alford Somset 21 6032
Alfreton Derbys 74 4155
Alfrick Worcs 47 7453
Alfrick Pound Worcs 47 7452
Alfriston E Susx 16 5103
Algarkirk Lincs 64 2935
Alhampton Somset 21 6234
Alkborough Lincs 84 8821
Alkerton Gloucs 35 7705
Alkerton Oxon 48 3743
Alkham Kent 29 2542
Alkington Shrops 71 5339
Alkmonton Derbys 73 1838
All Cannings Wilts 23 0661
All Saints South Elmham Suffk 55 3482
All Stretton Shrops 59 4595
Allaleigh Devon 7 8053
Allanaquoich Abers 133 1291
Allanbank N Lans 116 8458
Allanton Border 119 8654
Allanton N Lans 116 8457
Allanton S Lans 116 7454
Allaston Gloucs 35 6304
Allbrook Hants 13 4521
Allen End Warwks 61 1696
Allen's Green Herts 39 4516
Allendale Nthumb 95 8355
Allenheads Nthumb 95 8645
Allensford Dur 95 0750
Allensmore Herefs 46 4635
Allenton Derbys 62 3732
Aller Devon 19 7625
Aller Somset 21 4029
Allerby Cumb 92 0839
Allercombe Devon 9 0494
Allerford Somset 20 9046
Allerston N York 90 8782
Allerthorpe E R Yk 84 7847
Allerton Mersyd 78 3987
Allerton W York 82 1234
Allerton Bywater W York 83 4227
Allerton Mauleverer N York 89 4157
Allesley W Mids 61 3080
Allestree Derbys 62 3439
Allet Common Cnwll 3 7948
Allexton Leics 51 8100
Allgreave Ches 72 9767
Allhallows Kent 28 8377
Allhallows-on-Sea Kent 40 8478
Alligin Shuas Highld 137 8357
Allimore Green Staffs 72 8519
Allington Dorset 10 4693
Allington Kent 28 7557
Allington Lincs 63 8540
Allington Wilts 35 8975
Allington Wilts 23 0663
Allington Wilts 23 2039
Allithwaite Cumb 87 3876
Alloa Clacks 116 8892
Allonby Cumb 92 0842
Allostock Ches 79 7471
Alloway S Ayrs 106 3318
Allowenshay Somset 10 3913
Allscott Shrops 59 6113
Allscott Shrops 60 7396
Alltami Flints 70 2665
Alltchaorunn Highld 123 1951
Alltmawr Powys 45 0746
Alltwalis Carmth 31 4431
Alltwen Neath 32 7303
Alltyblaca Cerdgn 44 5245
Allweston Dorset 11 6614
Allwood Green Suffk 54 0472
Almeley Herefs 46 3351
Almeley Wooton Herefs 46 3352
Almer Dorset 11 9199
Almholme S York 83 5808
Almington Staffs 72 7034
Almodington W Susx 14 8297
Almondbank P & K 125 0625
Almondbury W York 82 1614
Almondsbury Gloucs 34 6084
Alne N York 90 4965
Alnesbourn Priory Suffk 55 1940
Alness Highld 146 6569
Alnham Nthumb 111 9810
Alnmouth Nthumb 111 2410
Alnwick Nthumb 111 1813
Alperton Gt Lon 26 1883
Alphamstone Essex 54 8735
Alpheton Suffk 54 8750
Alphington Devon 9 9190
Alpington Norfk 67 2901
Alport Derbys 74 2264
Alpraham Ches 71 5859
Alresford Essex 41 0621
Alrewas Staffs 61 1614
Alsager Ches 72 7955
Alsagers Bank Staffs 72 7948
Alsop en le Dale Derbys 73 1554
Alston Cumb 94 7146
Alston Devon 10 3002
Alston Sutton Somset 21 4151
Alstone Gloucs 47 9832
Alstone Somset 21 3146
Alstone Green Staffs 72 8518
Alstonefield Staffs 73 1355
Alswear Devon 19 7222
Alt Gt Man 79 9403
Altandhu Highld 144 9812
Altarnun Cnwll 5 2281
Altass Highld 146 5000
Altcreich Ag & B 122 6938
Altgaltraig Ag & B 114 0473
Altham Lancs 81 7732
Althorne Essex 40 9198
Althorpe Lincs 84 8309
Altnabreac Station Highld 150 0045
Altnacraig Ag & B 122 8429
Altnaharra Highld 149 5635
Altofts W York 83 3823
Alton Derbys 74 3664
Alton Hants 24 7139
Alton Staffs 73 0741
Alton Wilts 23 1546
Alton Barnes Wilts 23 1062
Alton Pancras Dorset 11 7002
Alton Priors Wilts 23 1162
Alton Towers 73 0743
Altrincham Gt Man 79 7687
Altskeith Hotel Stirlg 124 4602
Alva Clacks 116 8897
Alvah Abers 142 6760
Alvanley Ches 71 4974
Alvaston Derbys 62 3833
Alvechurch Worcs 60 0272
Alvecote Warwks 61 2404
Alvediston Wilts 22 9723
Alveley Shrops 60 7584
Alverdiscott Devon 19 5225
Alverstoke Hants 13 6098
Alverstone IOW 13 5785
Alverthorpe W York 82 3121
Alverton Notts 63 7942
Alves Moray 141 1362
Alvescot Oxon 36 2704
Alveston Gloucs 35 6388
Alveston Warwks 48 2356
Alvingham Lincs 77 3691
Alvington Gloucs 34 6000
Alwalton Cambs 64 1396
Alwinton Nthumb 110 9106
Alwoodley W York 82 2840
Alwoodley Gates W York 82 3140
Alyth P & K 126 2448
Amber Hill Lincs 76 2346
Amber Row Derbys 74 3856
Ambergate Derbys 74 3451
Amberley Gloucs 35 8501
Amberley W Susx 14 0213
Amberstone E Susx 16 5911
Amble Nthumb 103 2604
Amblecote W Mids 60 8985
Ambler Thorn W York 82 0929
Ambleside Cumb 87 3704
Ambleston Pembks 30 0025
Ambrosden Oxon 37 6019
Amcotts Lincs 84 8514
America Cambs 53 4378
Amersham Bucks 26 9597
Amersham on the Hill Bucks 26 9798
Amerton Staffs 73 9927
Amesbury Wilts 23 1541
Amhuinnsuidhe W Isls 152 0408
Amington Staffs 61 2304
Amisfield Town D & G 100 0082
Amlwch IOA 68 4492
Ammanford Carmth 32 6212
Amotherby N York 90 7473
Ampfield Hants 13 4023
Ampleforth N York 90 5878
Ampney Crucis Gloucs 36 0601
Ampney St Mary Gloucs 36 0802
Ampney St Peter Gloucs 36 0801
Amport Hants 23 3044
Ampthill Beds 38 0337
Ampton Suffk 54 8671
Amroth Pembks 31 1608
Amulree P & K 125 8936
Amwell Herts 39 1613
An T-ob W Isls 152 0286
Anaheilt Highld 130 8162
Ancaster Lincs 63 9843
Anchor Shrops 58 1785
Ancroft Nthumb 111 9945
Ancrum Border 110 6224
Ancton W Susx 14 9800
Anderby Lincs 77 5275
Andersea Somset 21 3333
Andersfield Somset 20 2434
Anderson Dorset 11 8797
Anderton Ches 79 6475
Anderton Cnwll 6 4351
Andover Hants 23 3645
Andoversford Gloucs 35 0219
Andreas IOM 158 4199
Anelog Gwynd 56 1527
Anerley Gt Lon 27 3369
Anfield Mersyd 78 3692
Angarrack Cnwll 2 5838
Angarrick Cnwll 3 7937
Angelbank Shrops 46 5776
Angersleigh Somset 20 1918
Angerton Cumb 93 2257
Angle Pembks 30 8603
Angmering W Susx 14 0604
Angram N York 88 8899
Angram N York 83 5248
Angrouse Cnwll 2 6619
Anick Nthumb 102 9465
Ankerville Highld 147 8174
Ankle Hill Leics 63 7518
Anlaby E R Yk 84 0328

Avon Dassett

Batford

271

Avon Dassett Warwks 49 4150
Avonbridge Falk 116 9172
Avonmouth Bristl 34 5178
Avonwick Devon 7 7158
Awbridge Hants 12 3224
Awkley Gloucs 34 5985
Awliscombe Devon 9 1301
Awre Gloucs 35 7008
Awsworth Notts 62 4844
Axborough Worcs 60 8579
Axbridge Somset 21 4354
Axford Hants 24 6043
Axford Wilts 36 2370
Axminster Devon 10 2998
Axmouth Devon 10 2591
Axton Flints 70 1080
Aycliffe Dur 96 2822
Aydon Nthumb 103 0065
Aylburton Gloucs 34 6101
Ayle Cumb 94 7149
Aylesbeare Devon 9 0392
Aylesbury Bucks 38 8213
Aylesby Lincs 85 2007
Aylesford Kent 28 7359
Aylesham Kent 29 2452
Aylestone Leics 50 5700
Aylestone Park Leics 50 5800
Aylmerton Norfk 66 1839
Aylsham Norfk 67 1926
Aylton Gloucs 47 6537
Aylworth Gloucs 36 1021
Aymestrey Herefs 46 4265
Aynho Nhants 49 5133
Ayot Green Herts 39 2214
Ayot St Lawrence Herts 39 1916
Ayot St Peter Herts 39 2115
Ayr S Ayrs 106 3321
Aysgarth N York 88 0088
Ayshford Devon 9 0415
Ayside Cumb 87 3983
Ayston Rutlnd 51 8600
Aythorpe Roding Essex 40 5815
Ayton Border 119 9260
Azerley N York 89 2574

B

Babbacombe Devon 7 9265
Babbington Notts 62 4943
Babbinswood Shrops 59 3329
Babbs Green Herts 39 3916
Babcary Somset 21 5628
Babel Carmth 44 8235
Babel Green Suffk 53 7348
Babell Flints 70 1573
Babeny Devon 7 6775
Babington Somset 22 7051
Bablock Hythe Oxon 36 4304
Babraham Cambs 53 5150
Babworth Notts 75 6880
Bachau IOA 68 4383
Bache Shrops 59 4681
Bacheldre Powys 58 2492
Bachelor's Bump E Susx 17 8412
Back o' th' Brook Staffs 73 0751
Back of Keppoch Highld 129 6587
Back Street Suffk 53 7458
Backaland Ork 153 5630
Backbarrow Cumb 87 3584
Backe Carmth 31 2615
Backfolds Abers 143 0252
Backford Ches 71 3971
Backford Cross Ches 71 3873
Backies Highld 147 8302
Backlass Highld 151 2053
Backwell Somset 21 4968
Backworth T & W 103 3072
Bacon's End W Mids 61 1888
Baconsthorpe Norfk 66 1236
Bacton Herefs 46 3732
Bacton Norfk 67 3433
Bacton Suffk 54 0567
Bacton Green Suffk 54 0365
Bacup Lancs 81 8622
Badachro Highld 137 7873
Badbury Wilts 36 1980
Badby Nhants 49 5658
Badcall Highld 148 1541
Badcall Highld 148 2455
Badcaul Highld 144 0291
Baddeley Edge Staffs 72 9150
Baddeley Green Staffs 72 9151
Baddesley Clinton Warwks 61 2072
Baddesley Ensor Warwks 61 2798
Baddidarrach Highld 145 0822
Baddinsgill Border 117 1254
Badenscoth Abers 142 6938
Badenyon Abers 141 3319
Badgall Cnwll 5 2486
Badgeney Cambs 65 4397
Badger Shrops 60 7699
Badger's Cross Cnwll 2 4833
Badgers Mount Kent 27 4962
Badgeworth Gloucs 35 9019
Badgworth Somset 21 3952
Badharlick Cnwll 5 2686
Badicaul Highld 137 7529
Badingham Suffk 55 3068
Badlesmere Kent 28 0153
Badlieu Border 108 0518
Badlipster Highld 151 2448
Badluachrach Highld 144 9994
Badninish Highld 147 7594
Badrallach Highld 145 0691
Badsey Worcs 48 0743
Badshot Lea Surrey 25 8648
Badsworth W York 83 4614
Badwell Ash Suffk 54 9868
Badwell Green Suffk 54 0169
Bag Enderby Lincs 77 3571
Bagber Dorset 11 7513
Bagby N York 89 4680
Bagendon Gloucs 35 0106
Bagginswood Shrops 60 6881
Baggrow Cumb 93 1741
Bagh a Chaisteil W Isls 152 6698
Bagh a Tuath W Isls 152 7003
Bagham Kent 29 0753
Bagillt Flints 70 2175
Baginton Warwks 61 3474
Baglan Neath 32 7492
Bagley Shrops 59 4027
Bagley Somset 21 4645
Bagley W York 82 2235
Bagmore Hants 24 6544
Bagnall Staffs 72 9250
Bagnor Berks 24 4569
Bagot Shrops 46 5873
Bagshot Surrey 25 9063
Bagshot Wilts 23 3165
Bagstone Gloucs 35 6987
Bagthorpe Notts 75 4651
Bagworth Leics 62 4408
Bagwy Llydiart Herefs 46 4426
Baildon W York 82 1539
Baildon Green W York 82 1439
Baile a Mhanaich W Isls 152 7755
Baile Ailein W Isls 152 2920
Baile Mor Ag & B 120 2824
Bailey Green Hants 13 6627
Baileyhead Cumb 101 5179
Bailiff Bridge W York 82 1425
Baillieston C Glas 116 6764
Bailrigg Lancs 87 4858
Bainbridge N York 88 9390
Bainshole Abers 142 6035
Bainton Cambs 64 0906
Bainton E R Yk 84 9652
Bainton Oxon 49 5827
Baintown Fife 126 3503
Bairnkine Border 110 6515
Baker Street Essex 40 6381
Baker's End Herts 39 3917
Bakewell Derbys 74 2168
Bala Gwynd 58 9235
Balallan W Isls 152 2920
Balbeg Highld 139 4431
Balbeggie P & K 126 1629
Balblair Highld 139 5145
Balblair Highld 140 7066
Balby S York 75 5600
Balcary D & G 92 8149
Balchraggan Highld 139 5343
Balchreick Highld 148 1960
Balcombe W Susx 15 3130
Balcombe Lane W Susx 15 3132
Balcomie Links Fife 127 6209
Baldersby N York 89 3578
Baldersby St James N York 89 3676
Balderstone Gt Man 79 9010
Balderstone Lancs 81 6332
Balderton Notts 75 8151
Baldhu Cnwll 3 7743
Baldinnie Fife 127 4211
Baldinnies P & K 125 0216
Baldock Herts 39 2434
Baldovie Dund C 127 4533
Baldrine IOM 158 4281
Baldslow E Susx 17 8013
Baldwin IOM 158 3581
Baldwin's Gate Staffs 72 7939
Baldwin's Hill Surrey 15 3839
Baldwinholme Cumb 93 3351
Bale Norfk 66 0136
Baledgarno P & K 126 2730
Balemartine Ag & B 120 9841
Balerno C Edin 117 1666
Balfarg Fife 126 2803
Balfield Angus 134 5468
Balfour Ork 153 4716
Balfron Stirlg 115 5489
Balgaveny Abers 142 6540
Balgavies Angus 127 5451
Balgonar Fife 117 0293
Balgowan D & G 98 1142
Balgowan Highld 132 6494
Balgown Highld 136 3868
Balgracie D & G 98 9860
Balgray Angus 126 4038
Balgray S Lans 108 8824
Balham Gt Lon 27 2873
Balhary P & K 126 2646
Balholmie P & K 126 1436
Baligill Highld 150 8565
Balintore Angus 133 2859
Balintore Highld 147 8675
Balintraid Highld 146 7370
Balivanich W Isls 152 7755
Balk N York 89 4780
Balkeerie Angus 126 3244
Balkholme E R Yk 84 7828
Ball Green Staffs 72 8952
Ball Haye Green Staffs 72 9856
Ball Hill Hants 24 4163
Ball's Green Gloucs 35 8699
Ballabeg IOM 158 2570
Ballachulish Highld 130 0858
Ballafesson IOM 158 2070
Ballakilpheric IOM 158 2271
Ballamodha IOM 158 2773
Ballanlay Ag & B 114 0462
Ballantrae S Ayrs 98 0882
Ballards Gore Essex 40 9092
Ballards Green Warwks 61 2791
Ballasalla IOM 158 2870
Ballater Abers 134 3695
Ballaugh IOM 158 3493
Ballchraggan Highld 147 7675
Ballencrieff E Loth 118 4878
Ballevullin Ag & B 120 9546
Ballidon Derbys 73 2054
Balliekine N Ayrs 105 8739
Balliemore Ag & B 114 1099
Balligmorrie S Ayrs 106 2290
Ballimore Ag & B 114 9283
Ballimore Stirlg 124 5317
Ballindalloch Moray 141 1636
Ballindean P & K 126 2529
Ballingdon Essex 54 8640
Ballinger Common Bucks 38 9103
Ballingham Herefs 46 5731
Ballingry Fife 117 1797
Ballinluig P & K 125 9752
Ballinshoe Angus 126 4153
Ballintuim P & K 126 1055
Balloch Highld 140 7247
Balloch N Lans 116 7374
Balloch P & K 125 8419
Balloch S Ayrs 106 3295
Balloch W Duns 115 3982
Ballogie Abers 134 5795
Balls Cross W Susx 14 9826
Balls Green E Susx 16 4936
Ballygown Ag & B 121 4343
Ballygrant Ag & B 112 3966
Ballyhaugh Ag & B 120 1758
Ballymenoch Ag & B 115 3086
Ballymichael N Ayrs 105 9231
Balmacara Highld 137 8028
Balmaclellan D & G 99 6579
Balmae D & G 99 6844
Balmaha Stirlg 115 4290
Balmalcolm Fife 126 3208
Balmangan D & G 99 6445
Balmedie Abers 143 9618
Balmer Heath Shrops 59 4434
Balmerino Fife 126 3524
Balmerlawn Hants 12 3003
Balmoral Castle Grounds 133 2594
Balmore E Duns 115 5973
Balmuchy Highld 147 8678
Balmuir Angus 127 5648
Balmule Fife 117 2088
Balmullo Fife 127 4220
Balnacoil Lodge Highld 147 8011
Balnacra Highld 138 9846
Balnacroft Abers 133 2894
Balnafoich Highld 140 6835
Balnaguard P & K 125 9451
Balnahard Ag & B 121 4534
Balnahard Ag & B 112 4199
Balnain Highld 139 4430
Balnakeil Highld 149 3968
Balnapaling Highld 147 7969
Balne N York 83 5918
Balquharn P & K 125 0235
Balquhidder Stirlg 124 5320
Balsall Common W Mids 61 2376
Balsall Heath W Mids 61 0784
Balsall Street W Mids 61 2276
Balscote Oxon 48 3942
Balsham Cambs 53 5850
Baltasound Shet 153 6208
Baltasound Airport 153 6207
Balterley Staffs 72 7650
Balterley Green Staffs 72 7650
Balterley Heath Staffs 72 7450
Baltersan D & G 99 4261
Baltonsborough Somset 21 5434
Balvarran P & K 133 0761
Balvicar Ag & B 122 7616
Balvraid Highld 129 8416
Balvraid Highld 140 8231
Balwest Cnwll 2 5930
Bamber Bridge Lancs 81 5625
Bamber's Green Essex 40 5722
Bamburgh Nthumb 111 1734
Bamburgh Castle 111 1835
Bamff P & K 126 2251
Bamford Derbys 74 2083
Bamford Gt Man 81 8612
Bampton Cumb 94 5118
Bampton Devon 20 9522
Bampton Oxon 36 3103
Bampton Grange Cumb 94 5218
Banavie Highld 130 1177
Banbury Oxon 49 4540
Banc-y-ffordd Carmth 31 4037
Bancffosfelen Carmth 32 4811
Banchory Abers 135 6995
Banchory-Devenick Abers 135 9002
Bancycapel Carmth 31 4214
Bancyfelin Carmth 31 3218
Bandirran P & K 126 2030
Bandrake Head Cumb 86 3187
Banff Abers 142 6863
Bangor Gwynd 69 5772
Bangor's Green Lancs 78 3709
Bangor-is-y-coed Wrexhm 71 3845
Bangors Cnwll 18 2099
Bangrove Suffk 54 9372
Banham Norfk 54 0687
Bank Hants 12 2807
Bank Ground Cumb 86 3196
Bank Newton N York 81 9053
Bank Street Worcs 47 6362
Bank Top Lancs 78 5207
Bank Top W York 82 1024
Bankend D & G 100 0268
Bankfoot P & K 125 0635
Bankglen E Ayrs 107 5912
Bankhead Aber C 135 9009
Bankhead S Lans 116 9844
Banknock Falk 116 7779
Banks Cumb 101 5664
Banks Lancs 80 3920
Banks Green Worcs 47 9967
Bankshill D & G 101 1982
Banningham Norfk 67 2129
Bannister Green Essex 40 6920
Bannockburn Stirlg 116 8190
Banstead Surrey 27 2559
Bantham Devon 7 6643
Banton N Lans 116 7480
Banwell Somset 21 3959
Bapchild Kent 28 9263
Bapton Wilts 22 9938
Bar Hill Cambs 52 3863
Barabhas W Isls 152 3649
Barassie S Ayrs 106 3232
Barbaraville Highld 146 7472
Barber Booth Derbys 74 1184
Barber Green Cumb 87 3982
Barbieston S Ayrs 107 4317
Barbon Cumb 87 6282
Barbridge Ches 71 6156
Barbrook Devon 19 7147
Barby Nhants 50 5470
Barcaldine Ag & B 122 9641
Barcheston Warwks 48 2639
Barclose Cumb 101 4462
Barcombe E Susx 15 4114
Barcombe Cross E Susx 15 4115
Barcroft W York 82 0437
Barden N York 89 1493
Barden Park Kent 16 5746
Bardfield End Green Essex 40 6231
Bardfield Saling Essex 40 6826
Bardney Lincs 76 1269
Bardon Leics 62 4412
Bardon Mill Nthumb 102 7764
Bardowie E Duns 115 5873
Bardown E Susx 16 6629
Bardrainney Inver 115 3373
Bardsea Cumb 86 3074
Bardsey W York 83 3643
Bardsley Gt Man 79 9201
Bardwell Suffk 54 9473
Bare Lancs 87 4564
Bareppa Cnwll 3 7729
Barewood Herefs 46 3856
Barfad D & G 98 3266
Barford Norfk 66 1107
Barford Warwks 48 2760
Barford St John Oxon 49 4433
Barford St Martin Wilts 23 0531
Barford St Michael Oxon 49 4332
Barfrestone Kent 29 2650
Bargate Derbys 62 3546
Bargeddie N Lans 116 6964
Bargoed Caerph 33 1599
Bargrennan D & G 98 3577
Barham Cambs 52 1375
Barham Kent 29 2050
Barham Suffk 54 1451
Barholm Lincs 64 0810
Barkby Leics 63 6309
Barkby Thorpe Leics 63 6309
Barkers Green Shrops 59 5228
Barkestone-le-Vale Leics 63 7734
Barkham Berks 25 7766
Barking Gt Lon 27 4484
Barking Suffk 54 0753
Barking Tye Suffk 54 0652
Barkingside Gt Lon 27 4489
Barkisland W York 82 0519
Barkla Shop Cnwll 3 7350
Barkston Lincs 63 9341
Barkston Ash N York 83 4936
Barkway Herts 39 3835
Barlanark C Glas 116 6664
Barlaston Staffs 72 8938
Barlavington W Susx 14 9716
Barlborough Derbys 75 4777
Barlby N York 83 6333
Barlestone Leics 62 4205
Barley Herts 39 4038
Barley Lancs 81 8240
Barley Hole S York 74 3697
Barleycroft End Herts 39 4327
Barleythorpe Rutlnd 63 8409
Barling Essex 40 9389
Barlings Lincs 76 0774
Barlochan D & G 92 8157
Barlow Derbys 74 3474
Barlow N York 83 6428
Barlow T & W 96 1561
Barmby Moor E R Yk 84 7748
Barmby on the Marsh E R Yk 83 6928
Barmer Norfk 66 8133
Barming Heath Kent 28 7255
Barmollack Ag & B 105 8043
Barmouth Gwynd 57 6116
Barmpton Dur 96 3118
Barmston E R Yk 91 1659
Barnaby Green Suffk 55 4780
Barnacarry Ag & B 114 0094
Barnack Cambs 64 0705
Barnacle Warwks 61 3884
Barnard Castle Dur 95 0516
Barnard Gate Oxon 36 4010
Barnardiston Suffk 53 7148
Barnbarroch D & G 92 8456
Barnburgh S York 83 4803
Barnby Suffk 55 4789
Barnby Dun S York 83 6109
Barnby in the Willows Notts 76 8552
Barnby Moor Notts 75 6684
Barncorkrie D & G 98 0935
Barnes Gt Lon 26 2276
Barnes Street Kent 16 6447
Barnet Gt Lon 26 2496
Barnet Gate Gt Lon 26 2195
Barnetby le Wold Lincs 84 0509
Barney Norfk 66 9932
Barnham Suffk 54 8779
Barnham W Susx 14 9503
Barnham Broom Norfk 66 0807
Barnhead Angus 135 6657
Barnhill Ches 71 4854
Barnhill Dund C 127 4731
Barnhill Moray 141 1457
Barnhills D & G 98 9871
Barningham Dur 89 0810
Barningham Suffk 54 9676
Barnoldby le Beck Lincs 85 2303
Barnoldswick Lancs 81 8746
Barns Green W Susx 14 1226
Barnsdale Bar N York 83 5014
Barnsley Gloucs 36 0704
Barnsley S York 83 3406
Barnsley Shrops 60 7592
Barnsole Kent 29 2756
Barnstaple Devon 19 5633
Barnston Essex 40 6419
Barnston Mersyd 78 2783
Barnstone Notts 63 7335
Barnt Green Worcs 60 0173
Barnton C Edin 117 1874
Barnton Ches 71 6375
Barnwell All Saints Nhants 51 0484
Barnwell St Andrew Nhants 51 0584
Barnwood Gloucs 35 8518
Baron's Cross Herefs 46 4758
Barons Wood Devon 8 7003
Baronwood Cumb 94 5143
Barr S Ayrs 106 2794
Barra Airport 152 7005
Barrachan D & G 99 3649
Barrapoll Ag & B 120 9442
Barras Cumb 88 8312
Barrasford Nthumb 102 9173
Barrets Green Ches 71 5859
Barrhead E Rens 115 4958
Barrhill S Ayrs 98 2382
Barrington Cambs 52 3849
Barrington Somset 10 3818
Barripper Cnwll 2 6338
Barrmill N Ayrs 115 3651
Barrnacarry Bay Ag & B 122 8122
Barrock Highld 151 2570
Barrow Gloucs 47 8824
Barrow Lancs 81 7338
Barrow Rutlnd 63 8815
Barrow Shrops 59 6500
Barrow Somset 22 7231
Barrow Suffk 53 7663
Barrow Bridge Gt Man 81 6811
Barrow Burn Nthumb 110 8610
Barrow Gurney Somset 21 5268
Barrow Haven Lincs 84 0622
Barrow Hill Derbys 74 4275
Barrow Island Cumb 86 1968
Barrow Nook Lancs 78 4402
Barrow Street Wilts 22 8330
Barrow upon Soar Leics 62 5717
Barrow upon Trent Derbys 62 3528
Barrow Vale Somset 21 6460
Barrow's Green Ches 78 5287
Barrow's Green Ches 72 6857
Barrow-in-Furness Cumb 86 2068
Barrow-upon-Humber Lincs 84 0620
Barroway Drove Norfk 65 5703
Barrowby Lincs 63 8736
Barrowden Rutlnd 51 9400
Barrowford Lancs 81 8539
Barry Angus 127 5334
Barry V Glam 20 1268
Barry Island V Glam 20 1166
Barsby Leics 63 6911
Barsham Suffk 55 3989
Barston W Mids 61 2078
Bartestree Herefs 46 5640
Barthol Chapel Abers 143 8133
Bartholomew Green Essex 40 7221
Barthomley Ches 72 7652
Bartley Hants 12 3012
Bartley Green W Mids 60 0081
Bartlow Cambs 53 5845
Barton Cambs 52 4055
Barton Ches 71 4454
Barton Cumb 94 4826
Barton Devon 7 9167
Barton Gloucs 48 0925
Barton Herefs 46 2957
Barton Lancs 78 3509
Barton Lancs 80 5137
Barton N York 89 2208
Barton Oxon 37 5507
Barton Warwks 48 1051
Barton Bendish Norfk 65 7105
Barton End Gloucs 35 8498
Barton Green Staffs 73 1717
Barton Hartshorn Bucks 49 6430
Barton Hill N York 90 7064
Barton in Fabis Notts 62 5132
Barton in the Beans Leics 62 3906
Barton Mills Suffk 53 7173
Barton Seagrave Nhants 51 8877
Barton St David Somset 21 5432
Barton Stacey Hants 24 4341
Barton Town Devon 19 6840
Barton Turf Norfk 67 3522
Barton upon Irwell Gt Man 79 7697
Barton Waterside Lincs 84 0222
Barton-le-Clay Beds 38 0830
Barton-le-Street N York 90 7274
Barton-le-Willows N York 90 7163
Barton-on-Sea Hants 12 2393
Barton-on-the-Heath Warwks 48 2532
Barton-under-Needwood Staffs 73 1818
Barton-upon-Humber Lincs 84 0221
Barugh S York 82 3108
Barugh Green S York 82 3107
Barvas W Isls 152 3649
Barway Cambs 53 5575
Barwell Leics 50 4496
Barwick Devon 8 5907
Barwick Herts 39 3819
Barwick Somset 10 5513
Barwick in Elmet W York 83 4037
Baschurch Shrops 59 4221
Bascote Warwks 48 4063
Bascote Heath Warwks 48 3962
Base Green Suffk 54 0163
Basford Green Staffs 72 9851
Bashall Eaves Lancs 81 6943
Bashall Town Lancs 81 7142
Bashley Hants 12 2496
Basildon Berks 37 6078
Basildon Essex 40 7189
Basingstoke Hants 24 6352
Baslow Derbys 74 2572
Bason Bridge Somset 21 3446
Bassaleg Newpt 34 2786
Bassendean Border 110 6245
Bassenthwaite Cumb 93 2332
Bassett Hants 13 4216
Bassingbourn Cambs 39 3343
Bassingfield Notts 62 6137
Bassingham Lincs 76 9060
Bassingthorpe Lincs 63 9628
Bassus Green Herts 39 3025
Basted Kent 27 6055
Baston Lincs 64 1113
Bastwick Norfk 67 4217
Batch Somset 21 3255
Batchworth Herts 26 0694
Batchworth Heath Herts 26 0792
Batcombe Dorset 10 6103
Batcombe Somset 22 6938
Bate Heath Ches 79 6879
Batford Herts 38 1415

Birchington

Bosoughan

273

Birchington *Kent* 29 3069
Birchley Heath *Warwks* 61 2894
Birchmoor Green *Beds* 38 9534
Birchover *Derbys* 74 2362
Birchwood *Ches* 79 6591
Birchyfield *Herefs* 47 6453
Bircotes *Notts* 75 6391
Bird End *W Mids* 60 0194
Bird Street *Suffk* 54 0052
Birdbrook *Essex* 53 7041
Birdforth *N York* 90 4875
Birdham *W Susx* 14 8200
Birdingbury *Warwks* 50 4368
Birdlip *Gloucs* 35 9214
Birdoswald *Cumb* 102 6166
Birds Edge *W York* 82 2007
Birds Green *Essex* 40 5808
Birdsall *N York* 90 8165
Birdsgreen *Shrops* 60 7785
Birdsmoorgate *Dorset* 10 3900
Birdwell *S York* 83 3401
Birdwood *Gloucs* 35 7418
Birgham *Border* 110 7939
Birichin *Highld* 147 7592
Birkacre *Lancs* 81 5714
Birkby *N York* 89 3202
Birkdale *Mersyd* 80 3214
Birkenbog *Abers* 142 5365
Birkenhead *Mersyd* 78 3288
Birkenhills *Abers* 142 7445
Birkenshaw *W York* 82 2028
Birkhall *Abers* 134 3493
Birkhill *Angus* 126 3534
Birkhill *D & G* 109 2015
Birkholme *Lincs* 63 9623
Birkin *N York* 83 5326
Birks *W York* 82 2626
Birkshaw *Nthumb* 102 7765
Birley *Herefs* 46 4553
Birley Carr *S York* 74 3392
Birling *Kent* 28 6860
Birling *Nthumb* 111 2406
Birling Gap *E Susx* 16 5596
Birlingham *Worcs* 47 9343
Birmingham *W Mids* 61 0786
Birmingham Airport 61 1883
Birmingham Museum & Art Gallery 61 0786
Birnam *P & K* 125 0341
Birness *Abers* 143 9933
Birse *Abers* 134 5697
Birsemore *Abers* 134 5297
Birstall *Leics* 62 5909
Birstall *W York* 82 2225
Birstwith *N York* 89 2359
Birthorpe *Lincs* 64 1033
Birtley *Herefs* 46 3669
Birtley *Nthumb* 102 8778
Birtley *T & W* 96 2756
Birts Street *Worcs* 47 7836
Bisbrooke *Rutlnd* 51 8899
Biscathorpe *Lincs* 76 2284
Biscovey *Cnwll* 3 0552
Bish Mill *Devon* 19 7425
Bisham *Berks* 26 8485
Bishampton *Worcs* 47 9951
Bishop Auckland *Dur* 96 2028
Bishop Burton *E R Yk* 84 9839
Bishop Middleham *Dur* 96 3231
Bishop Monkton *N York* 89 3266
Bishop Norton *Lincs* 76 9892
Bishop Sutton *Somset* 21 5859
Bishop Thornton *N York* 89 2563
Bishop Wilton *E R Yk* 84 7955
Bishop's Castle *Shrops* 59 3288
Bishop's Caundle *Dorset* 11 6913
Bishop's Cleeve *Gloucs* 47 9627
Bishop's Frome *Herefs* 47 6648
Bishop's Green *Essex* 40 6217
Bishop's Green *Hants* 24 5063
Bishop's Itchington *Warwks* 48 3857
Bishop's Norton *Gloucs* 47 8424
Bishop's Nympton *Devon* 19 7523
Bishop's Offley *Staffs* 72 7729
Bishop's Stortford *Herts* 39 4821
Bishop's Sutton *Hants* 24 6032
Bishop's Tachbrook *Warwks* 48 3161
Bishop's Tawton *Devon* 19 5729
Bishop's Waltham *Hants* 13 5517
Bishop's Wood *Staffs* 60 8309
Bishopbridge *Lincs* 76 0391
Bishopbriggs *E Duns* 116 6070
Bishopmill *Moray* 141 2163
Bishops Cannings *Wilts* 23 0364
Bishops Gate *Surrey* 25 9871
Bishops Hull *Somset* 20 2024
Bishops Lydeard *Somset* 20 1729
Bishopsbourne *Kent* 29 1852
Bishopsteignton *Devon* 7 9073
Bishopstoke *Hants* 13 4619
Bishopston *Swans* 32 5789
Bishopstone *Bucks* 38 8010
Bishopstone *E Susx* 16 4701
Bishopstone *Herefs* 46 4143
Bishopstone *Kent* 29 2068
Bishopstone *Wilts* 23 0625
Bishopstone *Wilts* 36 2483
Bishopstrow *Wilts* 22 8943
Bishopswood *Somset* 10 2612
Bishopsworth *Bristl* 21 5768
Bishopthorpe *N York* 83 5947
Bishopton *Dur* 96 3621
Bishopton *Rens* 115 4371
Bishopton *Warwks* 48 1956
Bishton *Newpt* 34 3887
Bishton *Staffs* 73 0220
Bisley *Gloucs* 35 9005
Bisley *Surrey* 25 9559
Bisley Camp *Surrey* 25 9357
Bispham *Lancs* 80 3140
Bispham Green *Lancs* 80 4813
Bissoe *Cnwll* 3 7741
Bisterne *Hants* 12 1401
Bitchet Green *Kent* 27 5654
Bitchfield *Lincs* 63 9828
Bittadon *Devon* 19 5441
Bittaford *Devon* 7 6656
Bittering *Norfk* 66 9417
Bitterley *Shrops* 46 5677
Bitterne *Hants* 13 4513
Bitteswell *Leics* 50 5385
Bitton *Gloucs* 35 6869
Bix *Oxon* 37 7284
Blaby *Leics* 50 5697
Black Bourton *Oxon* 36 2804
Black Callerton *T & W* 103 1769
Black Car *Norfk* 66 0995
Black Corner *W Susx* 15 2939
Black Corries *Highld* 123 2956
Black Crofts *Ag & B* 122 9234
Black Cross *Cnwll* 4 9060
Black Dog *Devon* 19 8009
Black Heddon *Nthumb* 103 0775
Black Lane *Gt Man* 79 7708
Black Lane Ends *Lancs* 81 9243
Black Moor *W York* 82 2939
Black Notley *Essex* 40 7620
Black Pill *Swans* 32 6190
Black Street *Suffk* 55 5186
Black Tar *Pembks* 30 9909
Black Torrington *Devon* 18 4605
Blackadder *Border* 119 8452
Blackawton *Devon* 7 8051
Blackbank *Warwks* 61 3586
Blackbeck *Cumb* 86 0207
Blackborough *Devon* 9 0909
Blackborough End *Norfk* 65 6615
Blackboys *E Susx* 16 5220
Blackbrook *Derbys* 62 3347
Blackbrook *Staffs* 72 7638
Blackbrook *Surrey* 15 1846
Blackburn *Abers* 135 8212
Blackburn *Lancs* 81 6827
Blackburn *S York* 74 3992
Blackburn *W Loth* 117 9865
Blackcraig *E Ayrs* 107 6308
Blackden Heath *Ches* 79 7871
Blackdog *Abers* 135 9513
Blackdown *Devon* 5 5079
Blackdown *Dorset* 10 3903
Blackdyke *Cumb* 92 1452
Blackenall Heath *W Mids* 60 0002
Blacker *S York* 83 3309
Blacker Hill *S York* 83 3602
Blackfen *Gt Lon* 27 4674
Blackfield *Hants* 13 4402
Blackford *Cumb* 101 3961
Blackford *P & K* 125 8908
Blackford *Somset* 21 4147
Blackford *Somset* 21 6526
Blackford Bridge *Gt Man* 79 8007
Blackfordby *Leics* 62 3217
Blackgang *IOW* 13 4876
Blackhall *C Edin* 117 1975
Blackhall *Dur* 97 4638
Blackhall Colliery *Dur* 97 4539
Blackhaugh *Border* 109 4238
Blackheath *Essex* 40 0021
Blackheath *Gt Lon* 27 3876
Blackheath *Suffk* 55 4274
Blackheath *Surrey* 14 0346
Blackheath *W Mids* 60 9786
Blackhill *Abers* 143 0039
Blackhill *Abers* 143 0755
Blackhill *Abers* 143 0843
Blackhill *Dur* 95 0851
Blackhill of Clackriach *Abers* 143 9246
Blackhorse *Devon* 9 9893
Blackhorse Hill *E Susx* 17 7714
Blackjack *Lincs* 64 2639
Blackland *Somset* 19 8336
Blackland *Wilts* 22 0168
Blacklaw *D & G* 108 0408
Blackley *Gt Man* 79 8502
Blacklunans *P & K* 133 1460
Blackmarstone *Herefs* 46 5038
Blackmill *Brdgnd* 33 9386
Blackmoor *Hants* 14 7733
Blackmoor *Somset* 21 4661
Blackmoorfoot *W York* 82 0913
Blackmore *Essex* 40 6001
Blackmore End *Essex* 40 7430
Blackmore End *Herts* 39 1716
Blackness *Falk* 117 0579
Blacknest *Berks* 25 9568
Blacknest *Hants* 25 7941
Blacko *Lancs* 81 8541
Blackpool *Devon* 7 8547
Blackpool *Devon* 7 8174
Blackpool *Lancs* 80 3036
Blackpool Airport 80 3131
Blackpool Gate *Cumb* 101 5377
Blackridge *W Loth* 116 8967
Blackrock *Cnwll* 2 6534
Blackrock *Mons* 33 2112
Blackrock *Mons* 34 5188
Blackrod *Gt Man* 78 6110
Blacksboat *Moray* 141 1838
Blackshaw *D & G* 100 0465
Blackshaw Head *W York* 82 9527
Blacksmith's Green *Suffk* 54 1465
Blacksnape *Lancs* 81 7121
Blackstone *W Susx* 15 2316
Blackthorn *Oxon* 37 6219
Blackthorpe *Suffk* 54 9063
Blacktoft *E R Yk* 84 8324
Blacktop *Aber C* 135 8604
Blackwall *Derbys* 73 2549
Blackwater *Cnwll* 3 7346
Blackwater *Hants* 25 8459
Blackwater *IOW* 13 5086
Blackwater *Somset* 10 2615
Blackwaterfoot *N Ayrs* 105 9028
Blackwell *Cumb* 93 4053
Blackwell *Derbys* 74 1272
Blackwell *Derbys* 75 4458
Blackwell *Dur* 89 2713
Blackwell *Warwks* 48 2443
Blackwell *Worcs* 60 9972
Blackwellsend Green *Gloucs* 47 7825
Blackwood *Caerph* 33 1797
Blackwood *D & G* 100 9087
Blackwood *S Lans* 116 7844
Blackwood Hill *Staffs* 72 9255
Blacon *Ches* 71 3868
Bladbean *Kent* 29 1847
Bladnoch *D & G* 99 4254
Bladon *Oxon* 37 4514
Bladon *Somset* 21 4220
Blaen Dyryn *Powys* 45 9336
Blaen-y-Coed *Carmth* 31 3427
Blaen-y-cwm *Blae G* 33 1311
Blaen-y-cwm *Rhondd* 33 9298
Blaenannerch *Cerdgn* 42 2448
Blaenau Ffestiniog *Gwynd* 57 7045
Blaenavon *Torfn* 34 2508
Blaenffos *Pembks* 31 1937
Blaengarw *Brdgnd* 33 9092
Blaengeuffardd *Cerdgn* 43 6480
Blaengwrach *Neath* 33 8605
Blaengwynfi *Neath* 33 8996
Blaenllechau *Rhondd* 33 0097
Blaenpennal *Cerdgn* 43 6264
Blaenplwyf *Cerdgn* 43 5775
Blaenporth *Cerdgn* 42 2648
Blaenrhondda *Rhondd* 33 9299
Blaenwaun *Carmth* 31 2327
Blaenycwm *Cerdgn* 43 8275
Blagdon *Devon* 7 8561
Blagdon *Somset* 20 2118
Blagdon *Somset* 21 5059
Blagdon Hill *Somset* 9 2117
Blagill *Cumb* 94 7347
Blaguegate *Lancs* 78 4506
Blaich *Highld* 130 0376
Blain *Highld* 129 6769
Blaina *Blae G* 33 2008
Blair Atholl *P & K* 132 8665
Blair Drummond *Stirlg* 116 7399
Blair's Ferry *Ag & B* 114 9869
Blairgowrie *P & K* 126 1745
Blairingone *P & K* 117 9896
Blairlogie *Stirlg* 116 8396
Blairmore *Ag & B* 114 1983
Blairmore *Highld* 148 1959
Blairnamarrow *Moray* 141 2015
Blaisdon *Gloucs* 35 7017
Blake End *Essex* 40 7023
Blakebrook *Worcs* 60 8276
Blakedown *Worcs* 60 8878
Blakeley Lane *Staffs* 72 9746
Blakemere *Ches* 71 5571
Blakemere *Herefs* 46 3641
Blakemore *Devon* 7 7660
Blakeney *Gloucs* 35 6707
Blakeney *Norfk* 66 0243
Blakenhall *Ches* 72 7247
Blakenhall *W Mids* 60 9197
Blakeshall *Worcs* 60 8381
Blakesley *Nhants* 49 6250
Blanchland *Nthumb* 95 9650
Bland Hill *N York* 82 2053
Blandford Camp *Dorset* 11 9107
Blandford Forum *Dorset* 11 8806
Blandford St Mary *Dorset* 11 8805
Blanefield *Stirlg* 115 5479
Blankney *Lincs* 76 0660
Blantyre *S Lans* 116 6957
Blar a' Chaorainn *Highld* 130 1066
Blargie *Highld* 132 6094
Blarmachfoldach *Highld* 130 0969
Blashford *Hants* 12 1506
Blaston *Leics* 51 8095
Blatherwycke *Nhants* 51 9795
Blawith *Cumb* 86 2888
Blawquhairn *D & G* 99 6282
Blaxhall *Suffk* 55 3656
Blaxton *S York* 75 6700
Blaydon *T & W* 103 1863
Bleadney *Somset* 21 4845
Bleadon *Somset* 21 3456
Bleak Street *Somset* 22 7631
Blean *Kent* 29 1260
Bleasby *Lincs* 76 1384
Bleasby *Notts* 75 7149
Bleasdale *Lancs* 81 5745
Bleatarn *Cumb* 94 7313
Bleathwood *Herefs* 46 5570
Blebocraigs *Fife* 127 4214
Bleddfa *Powys* 45 2068
Bledington *Gloucs* 36 2422
Bledlow *Bucks* 37 7702
Bledlow Ridge *Bucks* 37 7997
Bleet *Wilts* 22 8958
Blegbie *E Loth* 118 4861
Blencarn *Cumb* 94 6331
Blencogo *Cumb* 93 1947
Blendworth *Hants* 13 7113
Blennerhasset *Cumb* 93 1741
Bletchingdon *Oxon* 37 5018
Bletchingley *Surrey* 27 3250
Bletchley *Bucks* 38 8633
Bletchley *Shrops* 59 6233
Bletherston *Pembks* 31 0721
Bletsoe *Beds* 51 0258
Blewbury *Oxon* 37 5385
Blickling *Norfk* 66 1728
Blidworth *Notts* 75 5956
Blidworth Bottoms *Notts* 75 5954
Blindburn *Nthumb* 110 8210
Blindcrake *Cumb* 92 1434
Blindley Heath *Surrey* 15 3645
Blisland *Cnwll* 4 1073
Bliss Gate *Worcs* 60 7472
Blissford *Hants* 12 1713
Blisworth *Nhants* 49 7253
Blithbury *Staffs* 73 0819
Blitterlees *Cumb* 92 1052
Blo Norton *Norfk* 54 0179
Blockley *Gloucs* 48 1634
Blofield *Norfk* 67 3309
Bloomfield *Border* 110 5824
Blore *Staffs* 72 7234
Blore *Staffs* 73 1349
Blounts Green *Staffs* 73 0732
Blowick *Mersyd* 80 3516
Bloxham *Oxon* 49 4336
Bloxholm *Lincs* 76 0653
Bloxwich *W Mids* 60 9902
Bloxworth *Dorset* 11 8894
Blubberhouses *N York* 82 1655
Blue Anchor *Cnwll* 4 9157
Blue Anchor *Somset* 20 0243
Blue Bell Hill *Kent* 28 7462
Blue John Cavern 74 1384
Blundellsands *Mersyd* 78 3099
Blundeston *Suffk* 67 5297
Blunham *Beds* 52 1551
Blunsdon St Andrew *Wilts* 36 1389
Bluntington *Worcs* 60 9074
Bluntisham *Cambs* 52 3674
Blunts *Cnwll* 5 3463
Blunts Green *Warwks* 48 1468
Blurton *Staffs* 72 8941
Blyborough *Lincs* 76 9394
Blyford *Suffk* 55 4276
Blymhill *Staffs* 60 8112
Blymhill Lawn *Staffs* 60 8211
Blyth *Notts* 75 6287
Blyth *Nthumb* 103 3181
Blyth Bridge *Border* 117 1345
Blythburgh *Suffk* 55 4475
Blythe *Border* 110 5849
Blythe Bridge *Staffs* 72 9541
Blythe End *Warwks* 61 2190
Blythe Marsh *Staffs* 72 9640
Blyton *Lincs* 76 8594
Bo'ness *Falk* 117 0081
Boar's Head *Gt Man* 78 5708
Boarhills *Fife* 127 5613
Boarhunt *Hants* 13 6008
Boarley *Kent* 28 7659
Boars Hill *Oxon* 37 4902
Boarsgreave *Lancs* 81 8420
Boarshead *E Susx* 16 5332
Boarstall *Bucks* 37 6214
Boasley Cross *Devon* 5 5093
Boat of Garten *Highld* 140 9319
Boath *Highld* 146 5774
Bobbing *Kent* 28 8865
Bobbington *Staffs* 60 8090
Bobbingworth *Essex* 39 5305
Bocaddon *Cnwll* 4 1858
Bochym *Cnwll* 2 6920
Bocking *Essex* 40 7623
Bocking Churchstreet *Essex* 40 7525
Bockleton *Worcs* 46 5961
Boconnoc *Cnwll* 4 1460
Boddam *Abers* 143 1342
Boddam *Shet* 153 3915
Boddington *Gloucs* 47 8925
Bodedern *IOA* 68 3380
Bodelwyddan *Denbgs* 70 0075
Bodenham *Herefs* 46 5350
Bodenham *Wilts* 23 1626
Bodenham Moor *Herefs* 46 5450
Bodewryd *IOA* 68 4090
Bodfari *Denbgs* 70 0970
Bodffordd *IOA* 68 4277
Bodfuan *Gwynd* 56 3237
Bodham *Norfk* 66 1240
Bodiam *E Susx* 17 7825
Bodiam Castle 17 7825
Bodicote *Oxon* 49 4538
Bodieve *Cnwll* 4 9973
Bodinnick *Cnwll* 3 1352
Bodle Street Green *E Susx* 16 6514
Bodmin *Cnwll* 4 0667
Bodnant Garden 69 8072
Bodney *Norfk* 66 8298
Bodorgan *IOA* 68 3867
Bodrean *Cnwll* 3 8448
Bodsham Green *Kent* 29 1045
Bodwen *Cnwll* 4 0360
Bodymoor Heath *Warwks* 61 1996
Bogallan *Highld* 140 6350
Bogbrae *Abers* 143 0335
Boghall *Mdloth* 117 2465
Boghall *W Loth* 117 9867
Boghead *S Lans* 107 7742
Boghead Farm *Moray* 141 3559
Bogmoor *Moray* 141 3563
Bogmuir *Abers* 135 6471
Bogniebrae *Abers* 142 5945
Bognor Regis *W Susx* 14 9399
Bogroy *Highld* 140 9022
Bogue *D & G* 99 6481
Bohetherick *Devon* 5 4167
Bohortha *Cnwll* 3 8532
Bohuntine *Highld* 131 2983
Bojewyan *Cnwll* 2 3934
Bokiddick *Cnwll* 4 0562
Bolam *Dur* 96 1922
Bolam *Nthumb* 103 1082
Bolberry *Devon* 7 6939
Bold Heath *Mersyd* 78 5389
Boldmere *W Mids* 61 1194
Boldon Colliery *T & W* 96 3462
Boldre *Hants* 12 3198
Boldron *Dur* 95 0314
Bole *Notts* 75 7987
Bole Hill *Derbys* 74 3374
Bolehill *Derbys* 73 2955
Bolenowe *Cnwll* 2 6738
Bolham *Devon* 9 9515
Bolham Water *Devon* 9 1612
Bolingey *Cnwll* 3 7653
Bollington *Ches* 79 9377
Bollington Cross *Ches* 79 9277
Bollow *Gloucs* 35 7413
Bolney *W Susx* 15 2622
Bolnhurst *Beds* 51 0859
Bolshan *Angus* 127 6252
Bolsover *Derbys* 75 4770
Bolster Moor *W York* 82 0815
Bolsterstone *S York* 74 2696
Boltby *N York* 90 4886
Boltenstone *Abers* 134 4110
Bolter End *Bucks* 37 7992
Bolton *Cumb* 94 6323
Bolton *E Loth* 118 5070
Bolton *E R Yk* 84 7752
Bolton *Gt Man* 79 7108
Bolton *Nthumb* 111 1013
Bolton Abbey *N York* 82 0754
Bolton Bridge *N York* 82 0653
Bolton by Bowland *Lancs* 81 7849
Bolton Hall *N York* 88 0789
Bolton le Sands *Lancs* 87 4867
Bolton Low Houses *Cumb* 93 2344
Bolton New Houses *Cumb* 93 2444
Bolton Percy *N York* 83 5341
Bolton Town End *Lancs* 87 4867
Bolton Upon Dearne *S York* 83 4502
Bolton-on-Swale *N York* 89 2599
Boltonfellend *Cumb* 101 4768
Boltongate *Cumb* 93 2340
Bolventor *Cnwll* 4 1876
Bomarsund *Nthumb* 103 2684
Bomere Heath *Shrops* 59 4719
Bonar Bridge *Highld* 146 6191
Bonawe *Ag & B* 122 0033
Bonby *Lincs* 84 0015
Boncath *Pembks* 31 2038
Bonchester Bridge *Border* 110 5812
Bonchurch *IOW* 13 5778
Bond's Green *Herefs* 46 3554
Bondleigh *Devon* 8 6505
Bonds *Lancs* 80 4944
Bone *Cnwll* 2 4632
Bonehill *Devon* 8 7277
Bonehill *Staffs* 61 1902
Boney Hay *Staffs* 61 0410
Bonhill *W Duns* 115 3979
Boningale *Shrops* 60 8202
Bonjedward *Border* 110 6522
Bonkle *N Lans* 116 8457
Bonnington *Angus* 127 5739
Bonnington *Kent* 17 0535
Bonnybank *Fife* 126 3503
Bonnybridge *Falk* 116 8279
Bonnykelly *Abers* 143 8653
Bonnyrigg *Mdloth* 117 3065
Bonnyton *Angus* 126 3338
Bonsall *Derbys* 74 2758
Bonshaw Tower *D & G* 101 2472
Bont *Mons* 57 3819
Bont-Dolgadfan *Powys* 57 8800
Bontddu *Gwynd* 57 6718
Bonthorpe *Lincs* 77 4872
Bontnewydd *Cerdgn* 43 6165
Bontnewydd *Gwynd* 68 4859
Bontuchel *Denbgs* 70 0857
Bonvilston *V Glam* 33 0673
Bonwm *Denbgs* 70 1042
Bonymaen *Swans* 32 6795
Boode *Devon* 19 5037
Boohay *Devon* 7 8952
Booker *Bucks* 37 8391
Booley *Shrops* 59 5625
Boon *Border* 110 5745
Boon Hill *Staffs* 72 8150
Boorley Green *Hants* 13 5014
Boosbeck *N York* 97 6617
Boose's Green *Essex* 40 8431
Boot *Cnwll* 5 2697
Boot *Cumb* 86 1700
Boot Street *Suffk* 55 2248
Booth *E R Yk* 84 7326
Booth *W York* 82 0427
Booth Green *Ches* 79 9280
Booth Town *W York* 82 0926
Boothby Graffoe *Lincs* 76 9859
Boothby Pagnell *Lincs* 63 9730
Boothstown *Gt Man* 79 7200
Boothville *Nhants* 50 7864
Bootle *Cumb* 86 1088
Bootle *Mersyd* 78 3495
Boots Green *Ches* 79 7572
Booze *N York* 88 0102
Boraston *Shrops* 46 6169
Bordeaux *Guern* 158 0000
Borden *Kent* 28 8862
Borden *W Susx* 14 8324
Border *Cumb* 92 1654
Bordley *N York* 88 9465
Bordon *Hants* 14 8035
Bordon Camp *Hants* 14 7936
Boreham *Essex* 40 7609
Boreham *Wilts* 22 8944
Boreham Street *E Susx* 16 6611
Borehamwood *Herts* 26 1996
Boreland *D & G* 100 1691
Boreraig *Highld* 136 1853
Boreston *Devon* 7 7653
Boreton *Ches* 59 5106
Borgh *W Isls* 152 4055
Borgh *W Isls* 152 6501
Borgie *Highld* 149 6759
Borgue *D & G* 99 6248
Borgue *Highld* 151 1326
Borley *Essex* 54 8443
Borley Green *Essex* 54 8442
Borley Green *Suffk* 54 9960
Borneskitaig *Highld* 136 3770
Borness *D & G* 99 6145
Borough Green *Kent* 27 6157
Boroughbridge *N York* 89 3966
Borras Head *Wrexhm* 71 3653
Borrowash *Derbys* 62 4234
Borrowby *N York* 97 7715
Borrowby *N York* 89 4289
Borrowdale *Cumb* 93 2514
Borrowstoun *Falk* 117 9980
Borstal *Kent* 28 7366
Borth *Cerdgn* 43 6090
Borth-y-Gest *Gwynd* 57 5637
Borthwickbrae *Border* 109 4113
Borthwickshiels *Border* 109 4315
Borve *Highld* 136 4448
Borve *W Isls* 152 4055
Borve *W Isls* 152 6501
Borve *W Isls* 152 0394
Borwick *Lancs* 87 5272
Borwick Lodge *Cumb* 87 3499
Borwick Rails *Cumb* 86 1879
Bosavern *Cnwll* 2 3730
Bosbury *Herefs* 47 6943
Boscarne *Cnwll* 4 0367
Boscastle *Cnwll* 4 0990
Boscombe *Dorset* 12 1191
Boscombe *Wilts* 23 2038
Boscoppa *Cnwll* 3 0353
Bosham *W Susx* 14 8003
Bosham Hoe *W Susx* 14 8102
Bosherston *Pembks* 30 9694
Boskednan *Cnwll* 2 4434
Boskenna *Cnwll* 2 4223
Bosley *Ches* 72 9165
Bosoughan *Cnwll* 4 8760

Bossall
Brimscombe
274

Bossall N York 90 7160
Bossiney Cnwll 4 0688
Bossingham Kent 29 1548
Bossington Somset 19 8947
Bostock Green Ches 79 6769
Boston Lincs 64 3343
Boston Spa W York 83 4245
Boswarthan Cnwll 2 4433
Boswinger Cnwll 3 9841
Botallack Cnwll 2 3732
Botanic Gardens 115 5666
Botany Bay Gt Lon 27 2999
Botcheston Leics 62 4804
Botesdale Suffk 54 0475
Bothal Nthumb 103 2386
Bothampstead Berks 37 5076
Bothamsall Notts 75 6773
Bothel Cumb 93 1838
Bothenhampton Dorset 10 4791
Bothwell S Lans 116 7058
Botley Bucks 26 9802
Botley Hants 13 5113
Botley Oxon 37 4806
Botolph Claydon Bucks 49 7324
Botolph's Bridge Kent 17 1233
Botolphs W Susx 15 1909
Bottesford Leics 63 8038
Bottesford Lincs 84 8906
Bottisham Cambs 53 5460
Bottom o' th' Moor Gt Man 81 6511
Bottom of Hutton Lancs 80 4827
Bottomcraig Fife 126 3724
Bottoms Cnwll 2 3824
Bottoms W York 81 9321
Botts Green Warwks 61 2492
Botusfleming Cnwll 5 4061
Botwnnog Gwynd 56 2631
Bough Beech Kent 16 4847
Boughrood Powys 45 1239
Boughspring Gloucs 34 5597
Boughton Cambs 52 1965
Boughton Nhants 50 7565
Boughton Norfk 65 7002
Boughton Notts 75 6768
Boughton Aluph Kent 28 0246
Boughton End Beds 38 9838
Boughton Green Kent 28 7650
Boughton Malherbe Kent 28 8849
Boughton Monchelsea Kent 28 7650
Boughton Street Kent 28 0559
Boulby N York 97 7618
Boulder Clough W York 82 0323
Bouldnor IOW 12 3789
Bouldon Shrops 59 5485
Boulge Suffk 55 2552
Boulmer Nthumb 111 2614
Boulston Pembks 30 9712
Boultham Lincs 76 9669
Bourn Cambs 52 3256
Bourne Lincs 64 0920
Bourne End Beds 38 9644
Bourne End Beds 51 0160
Bourne End Bucks 26 8987
Bourne End Herts 38 0206
Bournebridge Essex 27 5094
Bournebrook W Mids 61 0483
Bournemouth Dorset 12 0890
Bournemouth Airport 12 1198
Bournes Green Essex 40 9186
Bournes Green Gloucs 35 9104
Bournheath Worcs 60 9574
Bournstream Gloucs 35 7494
Bournville W Mids 61 0481
Bourton Dorset 22 7630
Bourton Oxon 36 2386
Bourton Shrops 59 5996
Bourton Somset 21 3864
Bourton Wilts 23 0464
Bourton on Dunsmore Warwks 50 4370
Bourton-on-the-Hill Gloucs 48 1732
Bourton-on-the-Water Gloucs 36 1620
Bousd Ag & B 120 2563
Boustead Hill Cumb 93 2959
Bouth Cumb 86 3285
Bouthwaite N York 89 1271
Bouts Worcs 48 0359
Bovain Stirlg 124 5430
Boveney Berks 26 9377
Boveridge Dorset 12 0514
Bovey Tracey Devon 8 8178
Bovingdon Herts 38 0103
Bovingdon Green Bucks 37 8386
Bovinger Essex 39 5205
Bovington Dorset 11 8288
Bovington Camp Dorset 11 8389
Bovington Tank Museum 11 8388
Bow Cumb 93 3356
Bow Devon 8 7201
Bow Devon 7 8156
Bow Gt Lon 27 3683
Bow Ork 153 3693
Bow Brickhill Bucks 38 9034
Bow Lee Gt Man 79 8406
Bow of Fife Fife 126 3212
Bow Street Cerdgn 43 6285
Bow Street Norfk 66 0198
Bowbank Dur 95 9423
Bowbridge Gloucs 35 8505
Bowburn Dur 96 3037
Bowcombe IOW 13 4786
Bowd Devon 9 1090
Bowden Border 109 5530
Bowden Devon 7 8449
Bowden Hill Wilts 22 9367
Bowdon Gt Man 79 7686
Bower Highld 151 2362
Bower Ashton Bristl 34 5671
Bower Hinton Somset 10 4517
Bower House Tye Suffk 54 9840
Bower's Row W York 83 4028
Bowerchalke Wilts 23 0223
Bowerhill Wilts 22 9162
Bowermadden Highld 151 2464
Bowers Staffs 72 8135
Bowers Gifford Essex 40 7588
Bowershall Fife 117 0991
Bowes Dur 95 9913
Bowgreave Lancs 80 4943
Bowhouse D & G 100 0165
Bowithick Cnwll 4 1882
Bowker's Green Lancs 78 4004
Bowland Border 109 4540
Bowland Bridge Cumb 87 4189
Bowley Herefs 46 5452
Bowley Town Herefs 46 5352
Bowlhead Green Surrey 25 9138
Bowling W Duns 115 4373
Bowling W York 82 1731
Bowling Bank Wrexhm 71 3948
Bowling Green Worcs 47 8251
Bowmanstead Cumb 86 3096
Bowmore Ag & B 112 3159
Bowness-on-Solway Cumb 101 2262
Bowness-on-Windermere Cumb 87 4097
Bowriefauld Angus 127 5147
Bowscale Cumb 93 3531
Bowsden Nthumb 111 9941
Bowston Cumb 87 4996
Bowthorpe Norfk 66 1709
Box Gloucs 35 8600
Box Wilts 22 8268
Box End Beds 38 0049
Box Hill Surrey 26 1951
Box's Shop Cnwll 18 2101
Boxbush Gloucs 35 6720
Boxbush Gloucs 35 7413
Boxford Berks 24 4271
Boxford Suffk 54 9640
Boxgrove W Susx 14 9007
Boxley Kent 28 7758
Boxmoor Herts 38 0406
Boxted Essex 41 9933
Boxted Suffk 54 8251
Boxted Cross Essex 41 0032
Boxted Heath Essex 41 0031
Boxwell Gloucs 35 8192
Boxworth Cambs 52 3464
Boxworth End Cambs 52 3667
Boyden End Suffk 53 7355
Boyden Gate Kent 29 2265
Boylestone Derbys 73 1835
Boyndie Abers 142 6463
Boyndlie Abers 143 9162
Boynton E R Yk 91 1367
Boys Hill Dorset 11 6710
Boysack Angus 127 6249
Boythorpe Derbys 74 3869
Boyton Cnwll 5 3292
Boyton Suffk 55 3747
Boyton Wilts 22 9539
Boyton Cross Essex 40 6409
Boyton End Suffk 53 7244
Bozeat Nhants 51 9058
Braaid IOM 158 3276
Brabling Green Suffk 55 2964
Brabourne Kent 29 1041
Brabourne Lees Kent 29 0840
Brabstermire Highld 151 3169
Bracadale Highld 136 3538
Braceborough Lincs 64 0713
Bracebridge Heath Lincs 76 9867
Bracebridge Low Fields Lincs 76 9666
Braceby Lincs 64 0135
Bracewell Lancs 81 8648
Brackenfield Derbys 74 3759
Brackenhirst N Lans 116 7468
Brackenthwaite Cumb 93 2946
Brackenthwaite N York 82 2851
Bracklesham W Susx 14 8096
Brackletter Highld 131 1882
Brackley Nhants 49 5837
Brackley Hatch Nhants 49 6441
Bracknell Berks 25 8769
Braco P & K 125 8309
Bracobrae Moray 142 5053
Bracon Ash Norfk 66 1899
Bracora Highld 129 7192
Bracorina Highld 129 7292
Bradaford Devon 5 3994
Bradbourne Derbys 73 2052
Bradbury Dur 96 3128
Bradden Nhants 49 6448
Braddock Cnwll 4 1662
Bradeley Staffs 72 8851
Bradenham Bucks 37 8297
Bradenstoke Wilts 35 0079
Bradfield Berks 24 6072
Bradfield Devon 9 0509
Bradfield Essex 41 1430
Bradfield Norfk 67 2733
Bradfield S York 74 2692
Bradfield Combust Suffk 54 8957
Bradfield Green Ches 72 6859
Bradfield Heath Essex 41 1430
Bradfield St Clare Suffk 54 9057
Bradfield St George Suffk 54 9059
Bradford Cnwll 4 1175
Bradford Devon 18 4207
Bradford Nthumb 111 1532
Bradford Nthumb 103 0679
Bradford W York 82 1632
Bradford Abbas Dorset 10 5813
Bradford Leigh Wilts 22 8362
Bradford Peverell Dorset 11 6593
Bradford-on-Avon Wilts 22 8261
Bradford-on-Tone Somset 20 1722
Bradford Devon 19 5534
Brading IOW 13 6087
Bradley Ches 71 5377
Bradley Derbys 73 2246
Bradley Hants 24 6341
Bradley Lincs 85 2406
Bradley N York 88 0380
Bradley Staffs 72 8717
Bradley W Mids 60 9595
Bradley W York 82 1720
Bradley Worcs 47 9860
Bradley Wrexhm 71 3253
Bradley Green Ches 71 5045
Bradley Green Somset 20 2538
Bradley Green Warwks 61 2800
Bradley Green Worcs 47 9862
Bradley in the Moors Staffs 73 0541
Bradley Stoke Gloucs 34 6181
Bradmore Notts 62 5830
Bradney Somset 21 3338
Bradninch Devon 19 6133
Bradninch Devon 9 9904
Bradnop Staffs 73 0155
Bradnor Green Herefs 46 2957
Bradpole Dorset 10 4894
Bradshaw Gt Man 81 7312
Bradshaw W York 82 0514
Bradshaw W York 82 0729
Bradstone Devon 5 3880
Bradwall Green Ches 72 7563
Bradwell Bucks 38 8340
Bradwell Derbys 74 1781
Bradwell Devon 19 5042
Bradwell Essex 40 8122
Bradwell Norfk 67 5003
Bradwell Waterside Essex 41 9907
Bradwell-on-Sea Essex 41 0006
Bradworthy Devon 18 3214
Brae Highld 140 6662
Brae Shet 153 3568
Brae Roy Lodge Highld 131 3391
Braeface Falk 116 7880
Braehead Angus 127 6952
Braehead D & G 99 4152
Braehead S Lans 117 9550
Braemar Abers 133 1591
Braemore Highld 150 0829
Braemore Highld 145 2079
Braes of Coul Angus 133 2857
Braes of Enzie Moray 142 3957
Braeside Inver 114 2374
Braeswick Ork 153 6137
Braevallich Ag & B 122 9507
Brafferton Dur 96 2921
Brafferton N York 89 4370
Brafield-on-the-Green Nhants 51 8258
Bragar W Isls 152 2947
Bragbury End Herts 39 2621
Braidwood S Lans 116 8448
Brailsford Derbys 73 2541
Brailsford Green Derbys 73 2541
Brain's Green Gloucs 35 6609
Braintree Essex 40 7523
Braiseworth Suffk 54 1371
Braishfield Hants 23 3725
Braithwaite Cumb 93 2323
Braithwaite W York 82 0341
Braithwell S York 75 5394
Braken Hill W York 83 4216
Bramber W Susx 15 1810
Brambridge Hants 13 4721
Bramcote Notts 62 5037
Bramcote Warwks 61 4088
Bramdean Hants 24 6128
Bramerton Norfk 67 2904
Bramfield Herts 39 2915
Bramfield Suffk 55 3973
Bramford Suffk 54 1246
Bramhall Gt Man 79 8984
Bramham W York 83 4242
Bramhope W York 82 2543
Bramley Derbys 74 4079
Bramley Hants 24 6559
Bramley S York 75 4892
Bramley Surrey 25 0044
Bramley W York 82 2435
Bramley Corner Hants 24 6359
Bramley Green Hants 24 6658
Bramley Head N York 89 1258
Bramling Kent 29 2256
Brampford Speke Devon 9 9298
Brampton Cambs 52 2170
Brampton Cumb 101 5361
Brampton Cumb 94 6723
Brampton Lincs 76 8479
Brampton Norfk 67 2223
Brampton S York 83 4101
Brampton Suffk 55 4381
Brampton Abbotts Herefs 46 6026
Brampton Ash Nhants 50 7987
Brampton Bryan Herefs 46 3772
Brampton-en-le-Morthen S York 75 4887
Bramshall Staffs 73 0532
Bramshaw Hants 12 2615
Bramshill Hants 24 7461
Bramshott Hants 14 8432
Bramwell Somset 21 4329
Bran End Essex 40 6525
Branault Highld 128 5269
Brancaster Norfk 65 7743
Brancaster Staithe Norfk 66 7944
Brancepeth Dur 96 2237
Branchill Moray 141 0852
Brand End Lincs 64 3745
Brand Green Gloucs 47 7328
Branderburgh Moray 141 2371
Brandesburton E R Yk 85 1147
Brandeston Suffk 55 2460
Brandis Corner Devon 18 4104
Brandiston Norfk 66 1421
Brandon Dur 96 2340
Brandon Lincs 76 9048
Brandon Nthumb 111 0417
Brandon Suffk 53 7886
Brandon Warwks 50 4176
Brandon Bank Norfk 53 6289
Brandon Creek Norfk 65 6091
Brandon Parva Norfk 66 0708
Brandsby N York 90 5872
Brandy Wharf Lincs 76 0196
Brane Cnwll 2 4028
Branksome Dorset 12 0492
Branksome Park Dorset 12 0590
Bransbury Hants 24 4242
Bransby Lincs 76 8978
Branscombe Devon 9 1988
Bransford Worcs 47 7952
Bransgore Hants 12 1897
Bransholme E R Yk 85 1033
Bransley Shrops 47 6575
Branson's Cross Worcs 61 0970
Branston Leics 63 8129
Branston Lincs 76 0166
Branston Staffs 73 2221
Branston Booths Lincs 76 0668
Branstone IOW 13 5583
Brant Broughton Lincs 76 9154
Brantham Suffk 54 1034
Branthwaite Cumb 92 0525
Branthwaite Cumb 93 2937
Brantingham E R Yk 84 9429
Branton Nthumb 111 0416
Branton S York 83 6401
Branton Green N York 89 4362
Branxton Nthumb 110 8937
Brassey Green Ches 71 5260
Brassington Derbys 73 2254
Brasted Kent 27 4755
Brasted Chart Kent 27 4653
Brathens Abers 135 6798
Bratoft Lincs 77 4764
Brattleby Lincs 76 9481
Bratton Shrops 59 6413
Bratton Somset 20 9446
Bratton Wilts 22 9152
Bratton Clovelly Devon 5 4691
Bratton Fleming Devon 19 6437
Bratton Seymour Somset 22 6729
Braughing Herts 39 3925
Braughing Friars Herts 39 4124
Braunston Nhants 50 5466
Braunston Rutlnd 63 8306
Braunstone Leics 62 5502
Braunton Devon 18 4836
Brawby N York 90 7378
Brawdy Pembks 30 8524
Brawl Highld 150 8166
Braworth N York 90 5007
Bray Berks 26 9079
Bray Shop Cnwll 5 3374
Bray's Hill E Susx 16 6714
Braybrooke Nhants 50 7684
Braydon Wilts 36 0488
Braydon Brook Wilts 35 9891
Braydon Side Wilts 35 0185
Brayford Devon 19 6834
Braystones Cumb 86 0106
Braythorn N York 82 2449
Brayton N York 83 6030
Braywick Berks 26 8979
Braywoodside Berks 26 8775
Brazacott Cnwll 5 2691
Breach Kent 28 8465
Breach Kent 29 1947
Breachwood Green Herts 39 1522
Breaden Heath Shrops 59 4436
Breadsall Derbys 62 3639
Breadstone Gloucs 35 7000
Breadward Herefs 46 2854
Breage Cnwll 2 6128
Breakachy Highld 139 4644
Brealangwell Lodge Highld 146 5192
Bream Gloucs 34 6005
Breamore Hants 12 1517
Brean Somset 20 2956
Breanais W Isls 152 9925
Brearley W York 82 0225
Brearton N York 89 3261
Breascleit W Isls 152 2135
Breasclete W Isls 152 2135
Breaston Derbys 62 4533
Brechfa Carmth 44 5230
Brechin Angus 134 6060
Breckles Norfk 66 9594
Breckonside D & G 100 8489
Brecon Powys 45 0428
Bredbury Gt Man 79 9291
Brede E Susx 17 8218
Bredenbury Herefs 46 6056
Bredfield Suffk 55 2653
Bredgar Kent 28 8860
Bredhurst Kent 28 7962
Bredon Worcs 47 9236
Bredon's Hardwick Worcs 47 9135
Bredon's Norton Worcs 47 9339
Bredwardine Herefs 46 3344
Breedon on the Hill Leics 62 4022
Breich W Loth 117 9560
Breightmet Gt Man 79 7409
Breighton E R Yk 84 7033
Breinton Herefs 46 4739
Bremhill Wilts 35 9773
Bremridge Devon 19 6929
Brenchley Kent 28 6741
Brendon Devon 18 3607
Brendon Devon 19 7748
Brendon Hill Somset 20 0234
Brenfield Ag & B 113 8482
Brenish W Isls 152 9925
Brenkley T & W 103 2175
Brent Eleigh Suffk 54 9448
Brent Knoll Somset 21 3350
Brent Mill Devon 7 6959
Brent Pelham Herts 39 4330
Brentford Gt Lon 26 1777
Brentingby Leics 63 7818
Brentwood Essex 27 5993
Brenzett Kent 17 0027
Brenzett Green Kent 17 0128
Brereton Staffs 73 0516
Brereton Green Ches 72 7764
Brereton Heath Ches 72 8065
Brereton Hill Staffs 73 0515
Bressingham Norfk 54 0780
Bressingham Common Norfk 54 0981
Bretby Derbys 73 2922
Bretford Warwks 50 4377
Bretforton Worcs 48 0943
Bretherdale Head Cumb 87 5705
Bretherton Lancs 80 4720
Brettabister Shet 153 4857
Brettenham Norfk 54 9383
Brettenham Suffk 54 9654
Bretton Derbys 74 2078
Bretton Flints 71 3563
Brewer Street Surrey 27 3251
Brewers End Essex 39 5521
Brewood Staffs 60 8808
Briantspuddle Dorset 11 8193
Brick End Essex 40 5725
Brick Houses S York 74 3081
Brickendon Herts 39 3208
Bricket Wood Herts 26 1202
Brickkiln Green Essex 40 7331
Bricklehampton Worcs 47 9742
Bride IOM 158 4401
Bridekirk Cumb 92 1133
Bridell Pembks 31 1742
Bridestowe Devon 5 5189
Brideswell Abers 142 5738
Bridford Devon 8 8186
Bridge Cnwll 2 6744
Bridge Kent 29 1854
Bridge End Beds 38 0050
Bridge End Cumb 93 3748
Bridge End Cumb 86 1884
Bridge End Devon 7 6946
Bridge End Dur 95 0236
Bridge End Essex 40 6731
Bridge End Lincs 64 1436
Bridge End Nthumb 102 8965
Bridge End Surrey 26 0756
Bridge Green Essex 39 4636
Bridge Hewick N York 89 3370
Bridge of Alford Abers 142 5617
Bridge of Allan Stirlg 116 7997
Bridge of Avon Moray 141 1835
Bridge of Avon Moray 141 1520
Bridge of Balgie P & K 124 5746
Bridge of Brewlands Angus 133 1961
Bridge of Brown Highld 141 1120
Bridge of Cally P & K 126 1351
Bridge of Canny Abers 135 6597
Bridge of Craigisla Angus 126 2553
Bridge of Dee D & G 99 7359
Bridge of Don Aber C 135 9409
Bridge of Dulsie Highld 140 9341
Bridge of Dye Abers 135 6586
Bridge of Earn P & K 126 1318
Bridge of Ericht P & K 131 5258
Bridge of Feugh Abers 135 7094
Bridge of Forss Highld 150 0368
Bridge of Gairn Abers 134 3597
Bridge of Gaur P & K 124 5056
Bridge of Marnoch Abers 142 5950
Bridge of Orchy Ag & B 123 2939
Bridge of Tilt P & K 132 8765
Bridge of Tynet Moray 141 3861
Bridge of Walls Shet 153 2752
Bridge of Weir Rens 115 3965
Bridge Reeve Devon 19 6613
Bridge Sollers Herefs 46 4142
Bridge Street Suffk 54 8749
Bridge Trafford Ches 71 4571
Bridge Yate Gloucs 35 6872
Bridgefoot Cumb 92 0529
Bridgehampton Somset 21 5624
Bridgehill Dur 95 0951
Bridgehouse Gate N York 89 1565
Bridgemary Hants 13 5803
Bridgemere Ches 72 7145
Bridgend Abers 142 5135
Bridgend Ag & B 112 3362
Bridgend Angus 134 5368
Bridgend Brdgnd 33 9079
Bridgend Cerdgn 42 1745
Bridgend Cumb 93 4014
Bridgend D & G 108 0708
Bridgend Devon 6 5548
Bridgend Fife 126 3911
Bridgend Moray 141 3731
Bridgend P & K 126 1224
Bridgend W Loth 117 0475
Bridgend of Lintrathen Angus 126 2854
Bridgerule Devon 18 2702
Bridges Shrops 59 3996
Bridgetown Devon 5 3389
Bridgetown Somset 20 9233
Bridgham Norfk 54 9685
Bridgnorth Shrops 60 7193
Bridgtown Staffs 60 9808
Bridgwater Somset 20 2937
Bridlington E R Yk 91 1866
Bridport Dorset 10 4692
Bridstow Herefs 46 5824
Brierfield Lancs 81 8436
Brierley Gloucs 35 6215
Brierley Herefs 46 4955
Brierley W York 83 4010
Brierley Hill W Mids 60 9186
Brierton Dur 97 4730
Briery Cumb 93 2824
Brig o'Turk Stirlg 124 5306
Brigg Lincs 84 0007
Briggate Norfk 67 3127
Briggswath N York 90 8608
Brigham Cumb 92 0830
Brigham Cumb 93 2823
Brigham E R Yk 85 0753
Brighouse W York 82 1422
Brighstone IOW 13 4282
Brightgate Derbys 74 2659
Brighthampton Oxon 36 3803
Brightholmlee Derbys 74 2895
Brightley Devon 8 6097
Brightling E Susx 16 6820
Brightlingsea Essex 41 0817
Brighton Cnwll 3 9054
Brighton E Susx 15 3104
Brighton le Sands Mersyd 78 3098
Brightons Falk 116 9277
Brightor Cnwll 5 3561
Brightwalton Berks 36 4279
Brightwalton Green Berks 36 4278
Brightwalton Holt Berks 36 4377
Brightwell Suffk 55 2543
Brightwell Baldwin Oxon 37 6595
Brightwell Upperton Oxon 37 6594
Brightwell-cum-Sotwell Oxon 37 5790
Brignall Dur 95 0712
Brigsley Lincs 85 2501
Brigsteer Cumb 87 4889
Brigstock Nhants 51 9485
Brill Bucks 37 6513
Brill Cnwll 3 7229
Brilley Herefs 46 2648
Brimfield Herefs 46 5267
Brimfield Cross Herefs 46 5368
Brimington Derbys 74 4073
Brimley Devon 8 8077
Brimpsfield Gloucs 35 9312
Brimpton Berks 24 5564
Brimscombe Gloucs 35 8702

Brimstage
Burn Naze
275

Brimstage Mersyd 78 3082
Brincliffe S York 74 3284
Brind E R Yk 84 7430
Brindham Somset 21 5139
Brindister Shet 153 2857
Brindle Lancs 81 5924
Brineton Staffs 60 8013
Bringhurst Leics 51 8492
Brington Cambs 51 0875
Briningham Norfk 66 0434
Brinkely Notts 75 7153
Brinkhill Lincs 77 3773
Brinkley Cambs 53 6354
Brinklow Warwks 50 4379
Brinkworth Wilts 35 0184
Brinscall Lancs 81 6221
Brinscombe Somset 21 4251
Brinsea Somset 21 4461
Brinsley Notts 75 4548
Brinsop Herefs 46 4444
Brinsworth S York 74 4289
Brinton Norfk 66 0335
Brinyan Ork 153 4327
Brisco Cumb 93 4252
Brisley Norfk 66 9421
Brislington Bristl 35 6270
Brissenden Green Kent 28 9439
Bristol Bristl 34 5972
Bristol Airport 21 5065
Bristol Zoo 34 5773
Briston Norfk 66 0632
Brisworthy Devon 6 5665
Britannia Lancs 81 8821
Britford Wilts 23 1627
Brithdir Caerph 33 1401
Brithdir Gwynd 57 7618
British Torfn 34 2503
British Legion Village Kent 28 7257
Briton Ferry Neath 32 7394
Britwell Salome Oxon 37 6792
Brixham Devon 7 9255
Brixton Devon 6 5552
Brixton Gt Lon 27 3175
Brixton Deverill Wilts 22 8638
Brixworth Nhants 50 7470
Brize Norton Oxon 36 2907
Brize Norton Airport 36 2905
Broad Alley Worcs 47 8867
Broad Blunsdon Wilts 36 1491
Broad Campden Gloucs 48 1537
Broad Carr W York 82 0919
Broad Chalke Wilts 23 0325
Broad Clough Lancs 81 8623
Broad Ford Kent 28 7139
Broad Green Essex 40 8823
Broad Green Suffk 53 7859
Broad Green Worcs 47 7756
Broad Green Worcs 60 9970
Broad Haven Pembks 30 8613
Broad Hill Cambs 53 5976
Broad Hinton Wilts 36 1075
Broad Laying Hants 24 4362
Broad Marston Worcs 48 1446
Broad Meadow Staffs 72 8348
Broad Oak Cumb 86 1194
Broad Oak E Susx 17 8219
Broad Oak E Susx 16 6022
Broad Oak Hants 24 7551
Broad Oak Herefs 34 4821
Broad Oak Kent 29 1761
Broad Oak Mersyd 78 5395
Broad Road Suffk 55 2676
Broad Street E Susx 17 8616
Broad Street Essex 39 5516
Broad Street Kent 28 7672
Broad Street Kent 28 8356
Broad Street Wilts 23 1059
Broad Street Green Essex 40 8509
Broad Town Wilts 36 0977
Broad's Green Essex 40 6912
Broadbottom Gt Man 79 9993
Broadbridge W Susx 14 8105
Broadbridge Heath W Susx 15 1431
Broadclyst Devon 9 9897
Broadfield Inver 115 3373
Broadfield Pembks 31 1303
Broadford Highld 129 6423
Broadford Bridge W Susx 14 0921
Broadgairhill Border 109 2010
Broadgate Lincs 64 3610
Broadgrass Green Suffk 54 9663
Broadhaugh Border 119 8655
Broadheath Gt Man 79 7689
Broadheath Worcs 47 6665
Broadhembury Devon 9 1004
Broadhempston Devon 7 8066
Broadholme Notts 76 8874
Broadland Row E Susx 17 8319
Broadlay Carmth 31 3709
Broadley Essex 39 4207
Broadley Gt Man 81 8816
Broadley Moray 142 3961
Broadley Common Essex 39 4207
Broadmayne Dorset 11 7286
Broadmere Hants 24 6247
Broadmoor Gloucs 35 6415
Broadmoor Pembks 31 0906
Broadnymett Devon 8 7001
Broadoak Dorset 10 4396
Broadoak Gloucs 35 6912
Broadoak Wrexhm 71 3658
Broadstairs Kent 29 3967
Broadstone Dorset 11 0095
Broadstone Mons 34 5102
Broadstone Shrops 59 5489
Broadwas Worcs 47 7555
Broadwater Herts 39 2422
Broadwater W Susx 15 1404
Broadwaters Worcs 60 8477
Broadway Carmth 31 2910
Broadway Carmth 31 3808
Broadway Pembks 30 8713
Broadway Somset 10 3215
Broadway Suffk 55 3979
Broadway Worcs 48 0937
Broadwell Gloucs 34 5811
Broadwell Gloucs 48 2027
Broadwell Oxon 36 2504
Broadwell Warwks 50 4565
Broadwey Dorset 11 6683
Broadwindsor Dorset 10 4302
Broadwood Kelly Devon 8 6106
Broadwoodwidger Devon 5 4189
Brobury Herefs 46 3444
Brochel Highld 137 5846
Brock Lancs 80 5140
Brock's Green Hants 24 5061
Brockamin Worcs 47 7753
Brockbridge Hants 13 6118
Brockdish Norfk 55 2179
Brockencote Worcs 60 8873
Brockenhurst Hants 12 3002
Brocketsbrae S Lans 108 8239
Brockford Green Suffk 54 1265
Brockford Street Suffk 54 1167
Brockhall Nhants 49 6362
Brockham Surrey 15 1949
Brockhampton Gloucs 47 9326
Brockhampton Gloucs 36 0322
Brockhampton Hants 13 7106
Brockhampton Herefs 46 5931
Brockhampton Green Dorset 11 7106
Brockholes W York 82 1510
Brockhurst Derbys 74 3364
Brockhurst Warwks 50 4683
Brocklebank Cumb 93 3042
Brocklesby Lincs 85 1311
Brockley Somset 21 4666
Brockley Suffk 54 8371
Brockley Green Suffk 53 7247
Brockley Green Suffk 54 8254
Brockleymoor Cumb 94 4937
Brockmoor W Mids 60 9088
Brockscombe Devon 5 4695
Brockton Shrops 59 3104
Brockton Shrops 60 7103
Brockton Shrops 59 3285
Brockton Shrops 59 5794
Brockton Staffs 72 8131
Brockweir Gloucs 34 5401
Brockwood Park Hants 13 6226
Brockworth Gloucs 35 8916
Brocton Cnwll 4 0168
Brocton Staffs 72 9619
Brodick N Ayrs 105 0135
Brodie Moray 140 9757
Brodsworth S York 83 5007
Brogaig Highld 136 4767
Brogborough Beds 38 9638
Broken Cross Ches 79 6873
Broken Cross Ches 79 8973
Brokenborough Wilts 35 9189
Brokerswood Wilts 22 8352
Bromborough Mersyd 78 3582
Brome Suffk 54 1376
Brome Street Suffk 54 1576
Bromeswell Suffk 55 3050
Bromfield Cumb 93 1746
Bromfield Shrops 46 4876
Bromham Beds 38 0051
Bromham Wilts 22 9665
Bromley Gt Lon 27 4069
Bromley S York 74 3298
Bromley Shrops 60 7395
Bromley W Mids 60 9088
Bromley Common Gt Lon 27 4266
Bromley Cross Essex 41 0627
Bromlow Shrops 59 3201
Brompton Kent 28 7668
Brompton N York 89 3796
Brompton N York 91 9482
Brompton Shrops 59 5408
Brompton Ralph Somset 20 0832
Brompton Regis Somset 20 9531
Brompton-on-Swale N York 89 2199
Bromsash Herefs 47 6524
Bromsberrow Gloucs 47 7433
Bromsberrow Heath Gloucs 47 7333
Bromsgrove Worcs 60 9670
Bromstead Heath Staffs 72 7917
Bromyard Herefs 47 6554
Bromyard Downs Herefs 47 6655
Bronaber Gwynd 57 7131
Bronant Cerdgn 43 6467
Broncroft Shrops 59 5486
Brongest Cerdgn 42 3245
Bronington Wrexhm 71 4839
Bronllys Powys 45 1434
Bronwydd Carmth 31 4123
Bronydd Powys 45 2245
Bronygarth Shrops 58 2637
Brook Carmth 31 2609
Brook Hants 12 2714
Brook Hants 23 3429
Brook IOW 13 3983
Brook Kent 29 0644
Brook Surrey 14 9237
Brook Surrey 14 0546
Brook End Beds 51 0763
Brook End Beds 52 1547
Brook End Bucks 38 9244
Brook End Cambs 51 0773
Brook Hill Hants 12 2714
Brook House Denbgs 70 0765
Brook Street Essex 27 5793
Brook Street Kent 17 9333
Brook Street Suffk 54 8248
Brook Street W Susx 15 3026
Brooke Norfk 67 2899
Brooke Rutlnd 63 8405
Brookfield Rens 115 4164
Brookhampton Oxon 37 6098
Brookhampton Somset 21 6327
Brookhouse Lancs 87 5464
Brookhouse S York 75 5188
Brookhouse Green Ches 72 8161
Brookhouses Derbys 74 0388
Brookland Kent 17 9926
Brooklands Gt Man 79 7890
Brookmans Park Herts 39 2404
Brooks Powys 58 1499
Brooks End Kent 29 2967
Brooks Green W Susx 14 1224
Brooksby Leics 63 6715
Brookthorpe Gloucs 35 8312
Brookville Norfk 65 7396
Brookwood Surrey 25 9557
Broom Beds 39 1742
Broom Dur 96 2441
Broom S York 75 4491
Broom Warwks 48 0853
Broom Green Norfk 66 9823
Broom Hill Dorset 12 0302
Broom Hill Notts 62 5447
Broom Hill S York 83 4102
Broom Hill Worcs 60 9175
Broom Street Kent 28 0462
Broom's Green Gloucs 47 7132
Broome Norfk 67 3591
Broome Shrops 59 4080
Broome Worcs 60 9078
Broome Park Nthumb 111 1012
Broomedge Ches 79 7085
Broomer's Corner W Susx 14 1220
Broomershill W Susx 14 0619
Broomfield Essex 40 7010
Broomfield Kent 28 8452
Broomfield Kent 29 1966
Broomfield Somset 20 2232
Broomfields Shrops 59 4217
Broomfleet E R Yk 84 8727
Broomhall Surrey 25 9566
Broomhaugh Nthumb 103 0261
Broomhill Nthumb 103 2401
Broomhill Green Ches 71 6247
Broomley Nthumb 103 0360
Broomsthorpe Norfk 66 8428
Brora Highld 147 9103
Broseley Shrops 60 6701
Brotherhouse Bar Lincs 64 2614
Brotherlee Dur 95 9237
Brothertoft Lincs 77 2746
Brotherton N York 83 4825
Brotton N York 97 6819
Broubster Highld 150 0359
Brough Cumb 95 7914
Brough Derbys 74 1882
Brough E R Yk 84 9326
Brough Highld 151 2273
Brough Notts 76 8458
Brough Shet 153 5665
Brough Lodge Shet 153 5892
Brough Sowerby Cumb 95 7912
Broughall Shrops 71 5741
Broughton Border 108 1136
Broughton Bucks 38 8413
Broughton Bucks 38 8939
Broughton Cambs 52 2878
Broughton Flints 71 3363
Broughton Gt Man 79 8201
Broughton Hants 23 3033
Broughton Lancs 80 5234
Broughton Lincs 84 9608
Broughton N York 82 9451
Broughton N York 90 7673
Broughton Nhants 51 8375
Broughton Oxon 49 4138
Broughton Staffs 72 7634
Broughton V Glam 33 9270
Broughton Astley Leics 50 5292
Broughton Beck Cumb 86 2882
Broughton Gifford Wilts 22 8763
Broughton Green Worcs 47 9561
Broughton Hackett Worcs 47 9254
Broughton Mains D & G 99 4545
Broughton Mills Cumb 86 2290
Broughton Moor Cumb 92 0533
Broughton Poggs Oxon 36 2303
Broughton Tower Cumb 86 2187
Broughton-in-Furness Cumb 86 2187
Broughty Ferry Dund C 127 4630
Brow End Cumb 86 2674
Brow-of-the-Hill Norfk 65 6819
Brown Candover Hants 24 5739
Brown Edge Lancs 80 3614
Brown Edge Staffs 72 9053
Brown Heath Ches 71 4564
Brown Lees Staffs 72 8756
Brown Street Suffk 54 0663
Brown's Green W Mids 61 0591
Brownber Cumb 87 7005
Brownheath Shrops 59 4629
Brownhill Abers 143 8640
Brownhills Fife 127 5215
Brownhills W Mids 61 0405
Brownieside Nthumb 111 1623
Browninghill Green Hants 24 5859
Brownlow Heath Ches 72 8360
Brownrigg Cumb 92 0420
Brownrigg Cumb 92 1652
Browns Hill Gloucs 35 8802
Brownsham Devon 18 2826
Brownsover Warwks 50 5177
Brownston Devon 7 6952
Browston Green Norfk 67 4901
Broxa N York 91 9491
Broxbourne Herts 39 3606
Broxburn E Loth 119 6977
Broxburn W Loth 117 0872
Broxfield Nthumb 111 2016
Broxted Essex 40 5727
Broxton Ches 71 4754
Broxwood Herefs 46 3654
Broyle Side E Susx 16 4513
Bruan Highld 151 3139
Bruar P & K 132 8265
Brucefield Highld 147 9386
Bruchag Ag & B 114 1157
Bruera Ches 71 4360
Bruern Abbey Oxon 36 2620
Bruichladdich Ag & B 112 2661
Bruisyard Suffk 55 3266
Bruisyard Street Suffk 55 3365
Brumby Lincs 84 8909
Brund Staffs 74 1061
Brundall Norfk 67 3308
Brundish Suffk 55 2769
Brundish Street Suffk 55 2671
Brunnion Cnwll 2 5036
Brunslow Shrops 59 3684
Bruntcliffe W York 82 2526
Brunthwaite W York 82 0546
Bruntingthorpe Leics 50 6089
Brunton Fife 126 3220
Brunton Nthumb 111 2024
Brunton Wilts 23 2456
Brushford Somset 20 9225
Brushford Barton Devon 8 6707
Bruton Somset 22 6835
Bryan's Green Worcs 47 8868
Bryanston Dorset 11 8607
Bryant's Bottom Bucks 26 8599
Brydekirk D & G 101 1870
Brymbo Wrexhm 71 2953
Brympton Somset 10 5115
Bryn Ches 71 6072
Bryn Gt Man 78 5600
Bryn Neath 33 8192
Bryn Shrops 59 2985
Bryn Du IOA 68 3472
Bryn Gates Lancs 78 5901
Bryn Golau Rhondd 33 0088
Bryn Saith Marchog Denbgs 70 0750
Bryn-bwbach Gwynd 57 6236
Bryn-coch Neath 32 7499
Bryn-Eden Gwynd 57 7129
Bryn-Henllan Pembks 30 0139
Bryn-mawr Gwynd 56 2433
Bryn-newydd Denbgs 70 1842
Bryn-penarth Powys 58 1004
Bryn-y-bal Flints 70 2564
Bryn-y-Maen Conwy 69 8376
Bryn-yr-Eos Wrexhm 71 2840
Brynaman Carmth 32 7114
Brynberian Pembks 31 1035
Brynbryddan Neath 32 7792
Bryncae Rhondd 33 9982
Bryncethin Brdgnd 33 9183
Bryncir Gwynd 56 4844
Bryncroes Gwynd 56 2231
Bryncrug Gwynd 57 6103
Bryneglwys Denbgs 70 1447
Brynfields Wrexhm 71 3044
Brynford Flints 70 1774
Bryngwran IOA 68 3577
Bryngwyn Mons 34 3909
Bryngwyn Powys 45 1849
Brynhoffnant Cerdgn 42 3351
Bryning Lancs 80 4029
Brynithel Blae G 33 2101
Brynmawr Blae G 33 1911
Brynmenyn Brdgnd 33 9084
Brynmill Swans 32 6392
Brynna Rhondd 33 9883
Brynrefail Gwynd 69 5562
Brynrefail IOA 68 4886
Brynsadler Rhondd 33 0280
Brynsiencyn IOA 68 4867
Brynteg IOA 68 4982
Bualintur Highld 128 4020
Buarth-draw Flints 70 1779
Bubbenhall Warwks 61 3672
Bubwith E R Yk 84 7136
Buchanan Smithy Stirlg 115 4689
Buchanhaven Abers 143 1247
Buchanty P & K 125 9328
Buchany Stirlg 124 7102
Buchlyvie Stirlg 115 5793
Buck's Cross Devon 18 3522
Buck's Mills Devon 18 3523
Buckabank Cumb 93 3749
Buckden Cambs 52 1967
Buckden N York 88 9477
Buckenham Norfk 67 3505
Buckerell Devon 9 1200
Buckfast Devon 7 7467
Buckfastleigh Devon 7 7366
Buckhaven Fife 118 3598
Buckholt Mons 34 5016
Buckhorn Weston Dorset 22 7524
Buckhurst Hill Essex 27 4194
Buckie Moray 142 4265
Buckingham Bucks 49 6933
Buckland Bucks 38 8812
Buckland Devon 7 6743
Buckland Gloucs 48 0835
Buckland Hants 12 3196
Buckland Herts 39 3533
Buckland Kent 29 3042
Buckland Oxon 36 3498
Buckland Surrey 26 2150
Buckland Brewer Devon 18 4220
Buckland Common Bucks 38 9207
Buckland Dinham Somset 22 7551
Buckland Filleigh Devon 18 4609
Buckland in the Moor Devon 7 7273
Buckland Monachorum Devon 6 4968
Buckland Newton Dorset 11 6805
Buckland Ripers Dorset 11 6582
Buckland St Mary Somset 10 2613
Buckland-Tout-Saints Devon 7 7645
Bucklebury Berks 24 5570
Bucklers Hard Hants 13 4000
Bucklesham Suffk 55 2441
Buckley Flints 70 2763
Buckley Green Warwks 48 1567
Buckley Mountain Flints 70 2765
Bucklow Hill Ches 79 7383
Buckminster Leics 63 8722
Bucknall Lincs 76 1668
Bucknall Staffs 72 9047
Bucknell Oxon 49 5625
Bucknell Shrops 46 3574
Buckpool Moray 142 4165
Bucks Green W Susx 14 0833
Bucks Hill Herts 26 0500
Bucks Horn Oak Hants 25 8041
Bucksburn Aber C 135 8909
Buckshead Cnwll 3 8346
Buckton E R Yk 91 1872
Buckton Herefs 46 3873
Buckton Nthumb 111 0838
Buckworth Cambs 52 1476
Budby Notts 75 6169
Budd's Titson Cnwll 18 2401
Buddileigh Staffs 72 7449
Buddon Angus 127 5232
Bude Cnwll 18 2105
Budge's Shop Cnwll 5 3259
Budlake Devon 9 9800
Budle Nthumb 111 1535
Budleigh Salterton Devon 9 0682
Budlett's Common E Susx 16 4723
Budock Water Cnwll 3 7831
Buerton Ches 72 6843
Bugbrooke Nhants 49 6757
Bugford Devon 7 8350
Buglawton Ches 72 8763
Bugle Cnwll 4 0158
Bugley Dorset 22 7824
Bugthorpe E R Yk 90 7757
Buildwas Shrops 59 6204
Builth Road Powys 45 0353
Builth Wells Powys 45 0350
Bulbourne Herts 38 9313
Bulbridge Wilts 23 0830
Bulby Lincs 64 0526
Buldoo Highld 150 0067
Bulford Wilts 23 1643
Bulford Barracks Wilts 23 1843
Bulkeley Ches 71 5354
Bulkington Warwks 61 3986
Bulkington Wilts 22 9458
Bulkworthy Devon 18 3914
Bull Bay IOA 68 4294
Bull's Green Herts 39 2717
Bull's Green Norfk 67 4194
Bullamore N York 89 3994
Bullbridge Derbys 74 3552
Bullbrook Berks 25 8869
Bullen's Green Herts 39 2105
Bulley Gloucs 35 7619
Bullgill Cumb 92 0938
Bullinghope Herefs 46 5136
Bullington Hants 24 4541
Bullington Lincs 76 0877
Bullington End Bucks 38 8145
Bullockstone Kent 29 1665
Bulmer Essex 54 8440
Bulmer N York 90 6967
Bulmer Tye Essex 54 8438
Bulphan Essex 40 6385
Bulstone Devon 9 1789
Bulstrode Herts 26 0302
Bulstrode Park Bucks 26 9888
Bulverhythe E Susx 17 7708
Bulwark Abers 143 9345
Bulwell Notts 62 5343
Bulwick Nhants 51 9694
Bumble's Green Essex 39 4005
Bunacaimb Highld 129 6588
Bunarkaig Highld 131 1887
Bunbury Ches 71 5657
Bunbury Heath Ches 71 5558
Bunchrew Highld 140 6246
Buncton W Susx 15 1413
Bundalloch Highld 138 8927
Bunessan Ag & B 121 3821
Bungay Suffk 55 3389
Bunker's Hill Lincs 77 2653
Bunnahabhain Ag & B 112 4173
Bunny Notts 62 5829
Buntait Highld 139 4030
Buntingford Herts 39 3629
Bunwell Norfk 66 1292
Bunwell Street Norfk 66 1193
Bupton Derbys 73 2237
Burbage Derbys 74 0472
Burbage Leics 50 4492
Burbage Wilts 23 2261
Burcher Herefs 46 3360
Burchett's Green Berks 26 8481
Burchett's Green E Susx 16 6631
Burcombe Wilts 23 0730
Burcot Oxon 37 5695
Burcot Worcs 60 9871
Burcote Shrops 60 7495
Burcott Bucks 38 8415
Burcott Bucks 38 8823
Burdale N York 90 8762
Bures Essex 54 9034
Burford Oxon 36 2512
Burford Shrops 46 5868
Burg Ag & B 121 3845
Burgates Hants 14 7728
Burge End Herts 38 1432
Burgess Hill W Susx 15 3218
Burgh Suffk 55 2351
Burgh by Sands Cumb 93 3259
Burgh Castle Norfk 67 4805
Burgh Heath Surrey 26 2457
Burgh Hill E Susx 17 7226
Burgh le Marsh Lincs 77 5065
Burgh next Aylsham Norfk 67 2125
Burgh on Bain Lincs 76 2186
Burgh St Margaret Norfk 67 4413
Burgh St Peter Norfk 67 4693
Burghclere Hants 24 4761
Burghead Moray 141 1168
Burghfield Berks 24 6668
Burghfield Common Berks 24 6566
Burghill Herefs 46 4844
Burghwallis S York 83 5311
Burham Kent 28 7262
Buriton Hants 13 7419
Burland Ches 71 6153
Burlawn Cnwll 4 9970
Burleigh Berks 25 9169
Burleigh Gloucs 35 8601
Burlescombe Devon 9 0716
Burleston Dorset 11 7794
Burlestone Devon 7 8248
Burley Hants 12 2102
Burley Rutlnd 63 8810
Burley Shrops 59 4881
Burley Gate Herefs 46 5947
Burley in Wharfedale W York 82 1646
Burley Lawn Hants 12 2103
Burley Street Hants 12 2004
Burley Wood Head W York 82 1544
Burleydam Ches 71 6042
Burlingham Green Norfk 67 3610
Burlingjobb Powys 46 2558
Burlington Shrops 60 7711
Burlton Shrops 59 4526
Burmarsh Kent 17 1032
Burmington Warwks 48 2637
Burn N York 83 5928
Burn Cross S York 74 3496
Burn Naze Lancs 80 3443

Carlisle Airport 101 4860
Carloggas *Cnwll* 4 8765
Carlops *Border* 117 1656
Carloway *W Isls* 152 2043
Carlton *Beds* 51 9555
Carlton *Cambs* 53 6452
Carlton *Dur* 96 3921
Carlton *Leics* 62 3904
Carlton *N York* 88 0684
Carlton *N York* 90 6086
Carlton *N York* 83 6423
Carlton *Notts* 62 6041
Carlton *S York* 83 3610
Carlton *Suffk* 55 3764
Carlton *W York* 83 3327
Carlton Colville *Suffk* 55 5189
Carlton Curlieu *Leics* 50 6997
Carlton Green *Cambs* 53 6451
Carlton Husthwaite *N York* 90 4976
Carlton in Lindrick *Notts* 75 5883
Carlton Miniott *N York* 89 3981
Carlton Scroop *Lincs* 63 9445
Carlton-in-Cleveland *N York* 90 5004
Carlton-le-Moorland *Lincs* 76 9058
Carlton-on-Trent *Notts* 75 7963
Carluddon *Cnwll* 3 0255
Carluke *S Lans* 116 8450
Carlyon Bay *Cnwll* 3 0552
Carmacoup *S Lans* 107 7927
Carmarthen *Carmth* 31 4120
Carmel *Carmth* 32 5816
Carmel *Flints* 70 1676
Carmel *Gwynd* 68 4954
Carmichael *S Lans* 108 9238
Carminowe *Cnwll* 2 6623
Carmunnock *C Glas* 115 5957
Carmyle *C Glas* 116 6462
Carmyllie *Angus* 127 5442
Carn Brea *Cnwll* 2 6841
Carn-gorm *Highld* 138 9520
Carnaby *E R Yk* 91 1465
Carnbee *Fife* 127 5206
Carnbo *P & K* 125 0503
Carnbrogie *Abers* 143 8527
Carndu *Highld* 138 8827
Carnduff *S Lans* 116 6646
Carne *Cnwll* 3 7724
Carne *Cnwll* 3 9138
Carne *Cnwll* 4 9558
Carnell *E Ayrs* 107 4731
Carnewas *Cnwll* 4 8569
Carnforth *Lancs* 87 4970
Carnhedryn *Pembks* 30 8027
Carnhell Green *Cnwll* 2 6137
Carnie *Abers* 135 8005
Carnkie *Cnwll* 2 7134
Carnkiet *Cnwll* 3 7852
Carno *Powys* 58 9696
Carnoch *Highld* 130 8696
Carnock *Fife* 117 0489
Carnon Downs *Cnwll* 3 7940
Carnousie *Abers* 142 6650
Carnoustie *Angus* 127 5534
Carnwath *S Lans* 117 9846
Carnyorth *Cnwll* 2 3733
Carol Green *W Mids* 61 2577
Carpalla *Cnwll* 3 9654
Carperby *N York* 88 0089
Carr *Gt Man* 81 7816
Carr *S York* 75 5090
Carr Gate *W York* 82 3123
Carr Shield *Nthumb* 95 8047
Carr Vale *Derbys* 75 4669
Carradale *Ag & B* 105 8138
Carrbridge *Highld* 140 9022
Carrbrook *Gt Man* 79 9800
Carrefour *Jersey* 158 0000
Carreglefn *IOA* 68 3889
Carrhouse *Lincs* 84 7706
Carrick *Ag & B* 114 9086
Carrick Castle *Ag & B* 114 1994
Carriden *Falk* 117 0181
Carrington *Gt Man* 79 7492
Carrington *Lincs* 77 3155
Carrington *Mdloth* 117 3160
Carrismerry *Cnwll* 4 0158
Carrog *Conwy* 69 7647
Carrog *Denbgs* 70 1043
Carron *Falk* 116 8882
Carron *Moray* 141 2241
Carron Bridge *Stirlg* 116 7483
Carronbridge *D & G* 100 8698
Carronshore *Falk* 116 8983
Carrow Hill *Mons* 34 4390
Carruth House *Inver* 115 3566
Carrutherstown *D & G* 100 1071
Carrville *Dur* 96 3043
Carrycoats Hall *Nthumb* 102 9279
Carsaig *Ag & B* 121 5421
Carse Gray *Angus* 127 4553
Carseriggan *D & G* 98 3167
Carsethorn *D & G* 92 9959
Carshalton *Gt Lon* 27 2764
Carsington *Derbys* 73 2553
Carskey *Ag & B* 104 6508
Carsluith *D & G* 99 4854
Carsphairn *D & G* 107 5693
Carstairs *S Lans* 116 9345
Carstairs Junction *S Lans* 117 9545
Carswell Marsh *Oxon* 36 3299
Carter's Clay *Hants* 23 3024
Carters Green *Essex* 39 5110
Carterton *Oxon* 36 2806
Carterway Heads *Dur* 95 0451
Carthew *Cnwll* 3 0056
Carthorpe *N York* 89 3083
Cartington *Nthumb* 103 0204
Cartland *S Lans* 116 8646
Cartledge *Derbys* 74 3276
Cartmel *Cumb* 87 3878
Cartmel Fell *Cumb* 87 4188
Carway *Carmth* 32 4606
Carwinley *Cumb* 101 4072
Cashe's Green *Gloucs* 35 8205
Cashmoor *Dorset* 11 9713
Cassington *Oxon* 37 4511
Cassop Colliery *Dur* 96 3438
Castallack *Cnwll* 2 4525
Castell *Conwy* 69 7669
Castell-y-bwch *Torfn* 34 2792
Casterton *Lancs* 87 6279
Castle *Cnwll* 4 0958
Castle Acre *Norfk* 66 8115
Castle Ashby *Nhants* 51 8659
Castle Bolton *N York* 88 0391
Castle Bromwich *W Mids* 61 1489
Castle Bytham *Lincs* 63 9818
Castle Caereinion *Powys* 58 1605
Castle Camps *Cambs* 53 6242
Castle Carrock *Cumb* 94 5455
Castle Cary *Somset* 21 6432
Castle Combe *Wilts* 35 8477
Castle Donington *Leics* 62 4427
Castle Douglas *D & G* 99 7662
Castle Eaton *Wilts* 36 1496
Castle Eden *Dur* 96 4238
Castle End *Cambs* 64 1208
Castle Frome *Herefs* 47 6645
Castle Gate *Cnwll* 2 4934
Castle Green *Cumb* 87 5392
Castle Green *Surrey* 25 9761
Castle Gresley *Derbys* 73 2717
Castle Hedingham *Essex* 53 7835
Castle Hill *Kent* 28 6942
Castle Hill *Suffk* 54 1446
Castle Kennedy *D & G* 98 1159
Castle Lachlan *Ag & B* 114 0195
Castle Morris *Pembks* 30 9031
Castle O'er *D & G* 101 2492
Castle Pulverbatch *Shrops* 59 4202
Castle Rising *Norfk* 65 6624
Castle Street *W York* 82 9524
Castle Stuart *Highld* 140 7449
Castlebay *W Isls* 152 6698
Castlebythe *Pembks* 30 0229
Castlecary *Falk* 116 7878
Castleford *W York* 83 4225
Castlehill *Border* 109 2135
Castlehill *Highld* 151 1968
Castlehill *W Duns* 115 3875
Castlemartin *Pembks* 30 9198
Castlemilk *C Glas* 115 5958
Castlemorton *Worcs* 47 7937
Castlerigg 93 2823
Castleside *Dur* 95 0748
Castlethorpe *Bucks* 38 8044
Castlethorpe *Lincs* 84 9807
Castleton *Border* 101 5189
Castleton *Derbys* 74 1582
Castleton *Gt Man* 79 8810
Castleton *N York* 90 6807
Castleton *Newpt* 34 2583
Castletown *Dorset* 11 6874
Castletown *Highld* 151 1967
Castletown *IOM* 158 2667
Castletown *T & W* 96 3658
Castley *N York* 82 2646
Caston *Norfk* 66 9597
Castor *Cambs* 64 1298
Caswell Bay *Swans* 32 5987
Cat and Fiddle *Ches* 79 0072
Cat's Ash *Newpt* 34 3790
Catacol *N Ayrs* 105 9149
Catbrook *Mons* 34 5102
Catch *Flints* 70 2070
Catchall *Cnwll* 2 4228
Catchem's Corner *W Mids* 61 2576
Catchgate *Dur* 96 1652
Catcliffe *S York* 74 4288
Catcomb *Wilts* 35 0076
Catcott *Somset* 21 3939
Catcott Burtle *Somset* 21 4043
Catel *Guern* 158 0000
Caterham *Surrey* 27 3455
Catfield *Norfk* 67 3821
Catfield Common *Norfk* 67 4021
Catfirth *Shet* 153 4354
Catford *Gt Lon* 27 3773
Catforth *Lancs* 80 4735
Cathcart *C Glas* 115 5860
Cathedine *Powys* 45 1425
Catherine Slack *W York* 82 0928
Catherine-de-Barnes *W Mids* 61 1780
Catherington *Hants* 13 6914
Catherston Leweston *Dorset* 10 3694
Catherton *Shrops* 47 6578
Catisfield *Hants* 13 5506
Catley *Herefs* 47 6844
Catley Lane Head *Gt Man* 81 8715
Catlodge *Highld* 132 6392
Catlow *Lancs* 81 8836
Catlowdy *Cumb* 101 4576
Catmere End *Essex* 39 4939
Catmore *Berks* 37 4580
Caton *Devon* 7 7872
Caton *Lancs* 87 5364
Caton Green *Lancs* 87 5565
Cator Court *Devon* 8 6877
Catrine *E Ayrs* 107 5225
Catsfield *E Susx* 17 7213
Catsfield Stream *E Susx* 17 7113
Catsgore *Somset* 21 5025
Catsham *Somset* 21 5533
Catshill *Worcs* 60 9573
Catstree *Shrops* 60 7496
Cattadale *Ag & B* 105 6710
Cattal *N York* 83 4454
Cattawade *Suffk* 41 1033
Catterall *Lancs* 80 4942
Catteralslane *Shrops* 71 5640
Catterick *N York* 89 2397
Catterick Bridge *N York* 89 2299
Catterick Garrison *N York* 89 1897
Catterlen *Cumb* 94 4833
Catterline *Abers* 135 8678
Catterton *N York* 83 5145
Catteshall *Surrey* 25 9844
Catthorpe *Leics* 50 5578
Cattishall *Suffk* 54 8865
Cattistock *Dorset* 10 5999
Catton *Cumb* 95 8257
Catton *N York* 89 3678
Catton *Norfk* 67 2312
Catwick *E R Yk* 85 1345
Catworth *Cambs* 51 0873
Caudle Green *Gloucs* 35 9410
Caulcott *Beds* 38 0042
Caulcott *Oxon* 49 5024
Cauldcots *Angus* 127 6547
Cauldhame *Stirlg* 116 6493
Cauldmill *Border* 109 5315
Cauldon *Staffs* 73 0749
Cauldon Lowe *Staffs* 73 0747
Cauldwell *Derbys* 73 2517
Caulkerbush *D & G* 92 9257
Caulside *D & G* 101 4480
Caundle Marsh *Dorset* 11 6713
Caunsall *Worcs* 60 8581
Caunton *Notts* 75 7460
Causeway *Hants* 13 7422
Causeway End *Cumb* 87 4885
Causeway End *D & G* 99 4260
Causeway End *Essex* 40 6819
Causewayend *S Lans* 108 0336
Causewayhead *Cumb* 92 1253
Causewayhead *Stirlg* 116 8095
Causey Park *Nthumb* 103 1794
Causey Park Bridge *Nthumb* 103 1894
Causeyend *Abers* 143 9419
Cavendish *Suffk* 54 8046
Cavenham *Suffk* 53 7670
Caversfield *Oxon* 49 5825
Caversham *Berks* 24 7274
Caverswall *Staffs* 72 9542
Caverton Mill *Border* 110 7425
Cavil *E R Yk* 84 7730
Cawdor *Highld* 140 8450
Cawkwell *Lincs* 77 2879
Cawood *N York* 83 5737
Cawsand *Cnwll* 6 4350
Cawston *Norfk* 66 1323
Cawston *Warwks* 50 4773
Cawthorn *N York* 90 7788
Cawthorne *S York* 82 2808
Cawton *N York* 90 6476
Caxton *Cambs* 52 3058
Caxton End *Cambs* 52 3157
Caxton Gibbet *Cambs* 52 2960
Caynham *Shrops* 46 5573
Caythorpe *Lincs* 76 9348
Caythorpe *Notts* 63 6845
Cayton *N York* 91 0583
Ceann a Bhaigh *W Isls* 152 7468
Ceannacroc Lodge *Highld* 131 2211
Cearsiadar *W Isls* 152 3320
Ceciliford *Mons* 34 5003
Cefn *Newpt* 34 2788
Cefn Berain *Conwy* 70 9969
Cefn Byrle *Powys* 33 8311
Cefn Canel *Powys* 58 2331
Cefn Coch *Powys* 58 1026
Cefn Cribwr *Brdgnd* 33 8582
Cefn Cross *Brdgnd* 33 8682
Cefn Mably *Caerph* 34 2283
Cefn-brith *Conwy* 70 9350
Cefn-bryn-brain *Carmth* 32 7413
Cefn-coed-y-cymmer *Myr Td* 33 0308
Cefn-ddwysarn *Gwynd* 70 9638
Cefn-Einion *Shrops* 58 2886
Cefn-mawr *Wrexhm* 70 2842
Cefn-y-bedd *Wrexhm* 71 3156
Cefn-y-pant *Carmth* 31 1925
Cefneithin *Carmth* 32 5513
Cefngorwydd *Powys* 45 9045
Cefnpennar *Rhondd* 33 0300
Ceint *IOA* 68 4875
Cellan *Cerdgn* 44 6149
Cellardyke *Fife* 127 5704
Cellarhead *Staffs* 72 9547
Celleron *Cumb* 94 4925
Celynen *Caerph* 33 2195
Cemaes *IOA* 68 3793
Cemmaes *Powys* 57 8406
Cemmaes Road *Powys* 57 8104
Cenarth *Cerdgn* 31 2641
Cerbyd *Pembks* 30 8227
Ceres *Fife* 126 4011
Cerne Abbas *Dorset* 11 6601
Cerney Wick *Gloucs* 36 0796
Cerrigceinwen *IOA* 68 4274
Cerrigydrudion *Conwy* 70 9548
Cess *Norfk* 67 4417
Ceunant *Gwynd* 69 5361
Chaceley *Gloucs* 47 8530
Chacewater *Cnwll* 3 7544
Chackmore *Bucks* 49 6835
Chacombe *Nhants* 49 4944
Chadbury *Worcs* 47 0146
Chadderton *Gt Man* 79 9005
Chadderton Fold *Gt Man* 79 9006
Chaddesden *Derbys* 62 3836
Chaddesley Corbett *Worcs* 60 8973
Chaddlehanger *Devon* 5 4678
Chaddleworth *Berks* 36 4178
Chadlington *Oxon* 36 3321
Chadshunt *Warwks* 48 3453
Chadwell *Leics* 63 7824
Chadwell *Shrops* 60 7814
Chadwell End *Beds* 51 0865
Chadwell Heath *Gt Lon* 27 4888
Chadwell St Mary *Essex* 40 6478
Chadwick *Worcs* 47 8369
Chadwick End *W Mids* 61 2073
Chadwick Green *Mersyd* 78 5299
Chaffcombe *Somset* 10 3510
Chafford Hundred *Essex* 40 6079
Chagford *Devon* 8 7087
Chailey *E Susx* 15 3919
Chainbridge *Cambs* 27 4200
Chainhurst *Kent* 28 7248
Chalbury *Dorset* 12 0206
Chalbury Common *Dorset* 12 0206
Chaldon *Surrey* 27 3155
Chaldon Herring or
East Chaldon *Dorset* 11 7983
Chale *IOW* 13 4877
Chale Green *IOW* 13 4879
Chalfont Common *Bucks* 26 0092
Chalfont St Giles *Bucks* 26 9893
Chalfont St Peter *Bucks* 26 0090
Chalford *Gloucs* 35 8903
Chalford *Oxon* 37 7200
Chalford *Wilts* 22 8650
Chalgrave *Beds* 38 0127
Chalgrove *Oxon* 37 6396
Chalk *Kent* 28 6773
Chalk End *Essex* 40 6310
Chalkhouse Green *Berks* 37 7178
Chalkway *Somset* 10 3707
Chalkwell *Kent* 28 8963
Challaborough *Devon* 7 6544
Challacombe *Devon* 19 6940
Challoch *D & G* 99 3867
Challock *Kent* 28 0050
Chalmington *Dorset* 10 5900
Chalton *Beds* 38 0326
Chalton *Beds* 52 1450
Chalton *Hants* 13 7315
Chalvey *Berks* 26 9679
Chalvington *E Susx* 16 5109
Chambers Green *Kent* 28 9243
Chandler's Cross *Herts* 26 0698
Chandler's Ford *Hants* 13 4319
Chandlers Cross *Worcs* 47 7738
Channel's End *Beds* 51 1056
Chantry *Somset* 22 7146
Chantry *Suffk* 54 1443
Chapel *Cumb* 93 2231
Chapel *Fife* 117 2593
Chapel Allerton *Somset* 21 4050
Chapel Allerton *W York* 82 3037
Chapel Amble *Cnwll* 4 9975
Chapel Brampton *Nhants* 50 7266
Chapel Chorlton *Staffs* 72 8137
Chapel Cross *E Susx* 16 6120
Chapel End *Beds* 38 0542
Chapel End *Beds* 51 1058
Chapel End *Cambs* 52 1282
Chapel End *Warwks* 61 3393
Chapel Field *Gt Man* 79 7906
Chapel Green *Warwks* 61 2785
Chapel Green *Warwks* 49 4660
Chapel Haddlesey *N York* 83 5826
Chapel Hill *Abers* 143 0635
Chapel Hill *Lincs* 76 2054
Chapel Hill *Mons* 34 5399
Chapel Hill *N York* 83 3446
Chapel Lawn *Shrops* 46 3176
Chapel le Dale *N York* 88 7377
Chapel Leigh *Somset* 20 1229
Chapel Milton *Derbys* 74 0581
Chapel of Garioch *Abers* 142 7124
Chapel Rossan *D & G* 98 1044
Chapel Row *Berks* 24 5769
Chapel Row *E Susx* 16 6312
Chapel Row *Essex* 40 7900
Chapel St Leonards *Lincs* 77 5672
Chapel Stile *Cumb* 86 3205
Chapel Town *Cnwll* 3 8855
Chapel-en-le-Frith *Derbys* 74 0580
Chapelbridge *Cambs* 64 2993
Chapelend Way *Essex* 53 7039
Chapelgate *Lincs* 65 4124
Chapelhall *N Lans* 116 7862
Chapelhope *Border* 109 2318
Chapelknowe *D & G* 101 3173
Chapels *Cumb* 86 2383
Chapelton *Angus* 127 6247
Chapelton *Devon* 19 5726
Chapelton *S Lans* 116 6848
Chapeltown *Lancs* 81 7315
Chapeltown *Moray* 141 2320
Chapeltown *S York* 74 3596
Chapmans Well *Devon* 5 3593
Chapmanslade *Wilts* 22 8247
Chapmore End *Herts* 39 3216
Chappel *Essex* 40 8928
Charaton *Cnwll* 5 3069
Chard *Somset* 10 3208
Chard Junction *Somset* 10 3404
Chardleigh Green *Somset* 10 3110
Chardstock *Devon* 10 3004
Charfield *Gloucs* 35 7292
Chargrove *Gloucs* 35 9219
Charing *Kent* 28 9549
Charing Heath *Kent* 28 9249
Charing Hill *Kent* 28 9550
Charingworth *Gloucs* 48 1939
Charlbury *Oxon* 36 3519
Charlcombe *Somset* 22 7467
Charlcutt *Wilts* 35 9875
Charlecote *Warwks* 48 2656
Charles *Devon* 19 6832
Charles Tye *Suffk* 54 0252
Charleshill *Surrey* 25 8944
Charleston *Angus* 126 3845
Charlestown *Aber C* 135 9300
Charlestown *Cnwll* 3 0351
Charlestown *Derbys* 74 0392
Charlestown *Dorset* 11 6579
Charlestown *Fife* 117 0683
Charlestown *Gt Man* 79 8100
Charlestown *Highld* 144 8174
Charlestown *Highld* 140 6448
Charlestown *W York* 82 9726
Charlestown *W York* 82 1638
Charlesworth *Derbys* 79 0092
Charlinch *Somset* 20 2338
Charlottetown *Fife* 126 2910
Charlton *Gt Lon* 27 4178
Charlton *Hants* 23 3547
Charlton *Herts* 39 1728
Charlton *Nhants* 49 5335
Charlton *Nthumb* 102 8184
Charlton *Oxon* 36 4088
Charlton *Shrops* 59 5911
Charlton *Somset* 20 2926
Charlton *Somset* 21 6343
Charlton *Somset* 22 6852
Charlton *Surrey* 26 0869
Charlton *W Susx* 14 8812
Charlton *Wilts* 22 9022
Charlton *Wilts* 35 9588
Charlton *Wilts* 23 1156
Charlton *Worcs* 60 8371
Charlton *Worcs* 47 0045
Charlton Abbots *Gloucs* 48 0324
Charlton Adam *Somset* 21 5328
Charlton Hill *Shrops* 59 5807
Charlton Horethorne *Somset* 22 6623
Charlton Kings *Gloucs* 35 9621
Charlton Mackrell *Somset* 21 5328
Charlton Marshall *Dorset* 11 9004
Charlton Musgrove *Somset* 22 7229
Charlton on the Hill *Dorset* 11 8903
Charlton-all-Saints *Wilts* 23 1723
Charlton-on-Otmoor *Oxon* 37 5616
Charlwood *Hants* 24 6731
Charlwood *Surrey* 15 2441
Charminster *Dorset* 11 6792
Charmouth *Dorset* 10 3693
Charndon *Bucks* 49 6724
Charney Bassett *Oxon* 36 3894
Charnock Green *Lancs* 81 5516
Charnock Richard *Lancs* 81 5515
Charsfield *Suffk* 55 2556
Chart Corner *Kent* 28 7950
Chart Hill *Kent* 28 7949
Chart Sutton *Kent* 28 8049
Charter Alley *Hants* 24 5958
Charterhall *Border* 110 7647
Charterhouse *Somset* 21 4955
Chartershall *Stirlg* 116 7990
Charterville Allotments *Oxon* 36 3110
Chartham *Kent* 29 1054
Chartham Hatch *Kent* 29 1056
Chartridge *Bucks* 38 9303
Chartway Street *Kent* 28 8350
Charwelton *Nhants* 49 5356
Chase Terrace *Staffs* 61 0309
Chasetown *Staffs* 61 0408
Chastleton *Oxon* 48 2429
Chasty *Devon* 18 3402
Chatburn *Lancs* 81 7644
Chatcull *Staffs* 72 7934
Chatham *Caerph* 33 2188
Chatham *Kent* 28 7567
Chatham Green *Essex* 40 7115
Chathill *Nthumb* 111 1827
Chatley *Worcs* 47 8561
Chatsworth House 74 2570
Chattenden *Kent* 28 7572
Chatter End *Essex* 39 4725
Chatteris *Cambs* 52 3985
Chatterton *Lancs* 81 7918
Chattisham *Suffk* 54 0942
Chatto *Border* 110 7717
Chatton *Nthumb* 111 0528
Chaul End *Beds* 38 0521
Chawleigh *Devon* 19 7112
Chawley *Oxon* 37 4604
Chawston *Beds* 52 1556
Chawton *Hants* 24 7037
Chaxhill *Gloucs* 35 7414
Chazey Heath *Oxon* 37 6977
Cheadle *Gt Man* 79 8688
Cheadle *Staffs* 73 0043
Cheadle Heath *Gt Man* 79 8789
Cheadle Hulme *Gt Man* 79 8786
Cheam *Gt Lon* 26 2463
Cheapside *Berks* 25 9469
Chearsley *Bucks* 37 7110
Chebsey *Staffs* 72 8528
Checkendon *Oxon* 37 6683
Checkley *Ches* 72 7346
Checkley *Staffs* 73 0237
Checkley Green *Ches* 72 7245
Chedburgh *Suffk* 53 7957
Cheddar *Somset* 21 4553
Cheddington *Bucks* 38 9217
Cheddleton *Staffs* 72 9752
Cheddleton Heath *Staffs* 72 9853
Cheddon Fitzpaine *Somset* 20 2427
Chedglow *Wilts* 35 9493
Chedgrave *Norfk* 67 3699
Chedington *Dorset* 10 4805
Chediston *Suffk* 55 3577
Chediston Green *Suffk* 55 3578
Chedworth *Gloucs* 36 0512
Chedzoy *Somset* 21 3437
Cheesden *Gt Man* 81 8216
Cheeseman's Green *Kent* 28 0338
Cheetham Hill *Gt Man* 79 8401
Cheetwood *Gt Man* 79 8399
Cheldon *Devon* 19 7313
Chelford *Ches* 79 8174
Chellaston *Derbys* 62 3730
Chellington *Beds* 51 9555
Chelmarsh *Shrops* 60 7288
Chelmick *Shrops* 59 4791
Chelmondiston *Suffk* 55 2037
Chelmorton *Derbys* 74 1169
Chelmsford *Essex* 40 7007
Chelmsley Wood *W Mids* 61 1887
Chelsea *Gt Lon* 27 2778
Chelsfield *Gt Lon* 27 4864
Chelsham *Surrey* 27 3758
Chelston *Somset* 20 1521
Chelsworth *Suffk* 54 9748
Cheltenham *Gloucs* 35 9422
Chelveston *Nhants* 51 9969
Chelvey *Somset* 21 4668
Chelwood *Somset* 21 6361
Chelwood Common *E Susx* 15 4128
Chelwood Gate *E Susx* 15 4130
Chelworth *Wilts* 35 9694
Chelworth Lower Green *Wilts* 36 0892
Chelworth Upper Green *Wilts* 36 0893
Cheney Longville *Shrops* 59 4284
Chenies *Bucks* 26 0198
Chepstow *Mons* 34 5393
Chequerbent *Gt Man* 79 6706
Chequers Corner *Norfk* 65 4908
Cherhill *Wilts* 36 0370
Cherington *Gloucs* 35 9098
Cherington *Warwks* 48 2936
Cheriton *Devon* 19 7346
Cheriton *Hants* 24 5828
Cheriton *Kent* 29 2037
Cheriton *Swans* 32 4593
Cheriton Bishop *Devon* 8 7793
Cheriton Fitzpaine *Devon* 9 8606
Cheriton or
Stackpole Elidor *Pembks* 30 9897
Cherrington *Shrops* 72 6619
Cherry Burton *E R Yk* 84 9841
Cherry Hinton *Cambs* 53 4856
Cherry Orchard *Worcs* 47 8553
Cherry Willingham *Lincs* 76 0272
Chertsey *Surrey* 26 0466

278

Coalville Leics 62 4214
Coanwood Nthumb 94 6859
Coat Somset 21 4520
Coatbridge N Lans 116 7365
Coatdyke N Lans 116 7465
Coate Wilts 23 0462
Coate Wilts 36 1882
Coates Cambs 64 3097
Coates Gloucs 35 9701
Coates Lincs 75 8181
Coates Lincs 76 9083
Coates W Susx 14 9917
Coatham N York 97 5925
Coatham Mundeville Dur 96 2820
Cobbaton Devon 19 6126
Coberley Gloucs 35 9616
Cobhall Common Herefs 46 4535
Cobham Kent 28 6768
Cobham Surrey 26 1060
Coblers Green Essex 40 6819
Cobley Dorset 12 0220
Cobnash Herefs 46 4560
Cobo Guern 158 0000
Cobridge Staffs 72 8747
Coburby Abers 143 9164
Cock & End Suffk 53 7253
Cock Alley Derbys 74 4170
Cock Bank Wrexhm 71 3545
Cock Bevington Warwks 48 0552
Cock Bridge Abers 133 2509
Cock Clarks Essex 40 8102
Cock Green Essex 40 6919
Cock Marling E Susx 17 8718
Cock Street Kent 28 7850
Cockayne N York 90 6198
Cockayne Hatley Beds 52 2649
Cockburnspath Border 119 7770
Cockenzie and
Port Seton E Loth 118 4075
Cocker Bar Lancs 80 5022
Cocker Brook Lancs 81 7425
Cockerham Lancs 80 4651
Cockermouth Cumb 92 1230
Cockernhoe Green Herts 38 1223
Cockersdale W York 82 2329
Cockett Swans 32 6394
Cockfield Dur 96 1224
Cockfield Suffk 54 9054
Cockfosters Gt Lon 27 2796
Cocking W Susx 14 8717
Cocking Causeway W Susx 14 8819
Cockington Devon 7 8963
Cocklake Somset 21 4449
Cockle Park Nthumb 103 2091
Cockley Beck Cumb 86 2501
Cockley Cley Norfk 66 7904
Cockpole Green Berks 37 7981
Cocks Cnwll 3 7652
Cockshutford Shrops 59 5885
Cockshutt Shrops 59 4328
Cockthorpe Norfk 66 9842
Cockwells Cnwll 2 5234
Cockwood Devon 9 9780
Cockwood Somset 20 2242
Cockyard Derbys 74 0479
Cockyard Herefs 46 4133
Coddenham Suffk 54 1354
Coddington Ches 71 4555
Coddington Herefs 47 7142
Coddington Notts 76 8354
Codford St Mary Wilts 22 9739
Codford St Peter Wilts 22 9639
Codicote Herts 39 2118
Codmore Hill W Susx 14 0520
Codnor Derbys 74 4149
Codrington Gloucs 35 7278
Codsall Staffs 60 8603
Codsall Wood Staffs 60 8404
Coed Morgan Mons 34 3511
Coed Talon Flints 70 2659
Coed Ystumgwern Gwynd 57 5824
Coed-y-Bryn Cerdgn 42 3545
Coed-y-caerau Newpt 34 3891
Coed-y-paen Mons 34 3398
Coed-yr-ynys Powys 33 1520
Coedana IOA 68 4382
Coedely Rhondd 33 0285
Coedkernew Newpt 34 2783
Coedpoeth Wrexhm 70 2851
Coedway Powys 59 3315
Coelbren Powys 33 8511
Coffinswell Devon 7 8968
Coffle End Beds 51 0159
Cofton Devon 9 9680
Cofton Hackett Worcs 60 0075
Cogan V Glam 33 1771
Cogenhoe Nhants 51 8260
Cogges Oxon 36 3609
Coggeshall Essex 40 8522
Coggin's Mill E Susx 16 5927
Coignafearn Highld 140 7018
Coilacriech Abers 134 3296
Coilantogle Stirlg 124 5907
Coillore Highld 136 3537
Coiltry Highld 131 3506
Coity Brdgnd 33 9281
Col W Isls 152 4739
Colaboll Highld 146 5610
Colan Cnwll 4 8661
Colaton Raleigh Devon 9 0787
Colbost Highld 136 2148
Colburn N York 89 1999
Colbury Hants 12 3410
Colby Cumb 94 6620
Colby IOM 158 2370
Colby Norfk 67 2231
Colchester Essex 41 9925
Cold Ash Berks 24 5169
Cold Ashby Nhants 50 6576
Cold Ashton Gloucs 35 7572
Cold Aston Gloucs 36 1219
Cold Blow Pembks 31 1212
Cold Brayfield Bucks 38 9252
Cold Cotes N York 88 7171
Cold Green Herefs 47 6842
Cold Hanworth Lincs 76 0383
Cold Harbour Herts 38 1415
Cold Harbour Oxon 37 6379
Cold Harbour Wilts 22 8645
Cold Hatton Shrops 59 6221
Cold Hatton Heath Shrops 59 6321
Cold Hesledon Dur 96 4146
Cold Hiendley W York 83 3714
Cold Higham Nhants 49 6653
Cold Kirby N York 90 5384
Cold Newton Leics 63 7106
Cold Northcott Cnwll 5 2086
Cold Norton Essex 40 8500
Cold Overton Leics 63 8010
Cold Weston Shrops 59 5583
Coldbackie Highld 149 6160
Coldbeck Cumb 88 7204
Coldean E Susx 15 3308
Coldeast Devon 7 8174
Colden W York 82 9628
Colden Common Hants 13 4822
Coldfair Green Suffk 55 4360
Coldham Cambs 65 4303
Coldharbour Cnwll 3 7548
Coldharbour Devon 9 0612
Coldharbour Gloucs 34 5503
Coldharbour Surrey 15 1443
Coldingham Border 119 9065
Coldmeece Staffs 72 8532
Coldred Kent 29 2747
Coldridge Devon 8 6907
Coldstream Border 110 8439
Coldwaltham W Susx 14 0216
Coldwell Herefs 46 4235
Coldwells Abers 143 9538
Cole Somset 22 6733
Cole End Warwks 61 2089
Cole Green Herts 39 2811
Cole Green Herts 39 4330
Cole Henley Hants 24 4651
Cole's Cross Devon 7 7746
Colebatch Shrops 59 3287
Colebrook Devon 9 0006
Colebrook Devon 6 5457
Colebrooke Devon 8 7699
Coleby Lincs 84 8919
Coleby Lincs 76 9760
Coleford Devon 8 7701
Coleford Gloucs 34 5710
Coleford Somset 22 6848
Coleford Water Somset 20 1133
Colegate End Norfk 55 1987
Colehill Dorset 12 0201
Coleman Green Herts 39 1812
Coleman's Hatch E Susx 16 4433
Colemere Shrops 59 4332
Colemore Hants 24 7030
Colemore Green Shrops 60 7197
Colenden P & K 126 1029
Coleorton Leics 62 4017
Colerne Wilts 35 8271
Coles Cross Dorset 10 3902
Coles Green Suffk 54 1041
Colesbourne Gloucs 35 0013
Colesden Beds 52 1255
Coleshill Bucks 26 9495
Coleshill Oxon 36 2393
Coleshill Warwks 61 2089
Colestocks Devon 9 0900
Coley Somset 21 5855
Colgate W Susx 15 2332
Colinsburgh Fife 127 4703
Colinton C Edin 117 2168
Colintraive Ag & B 114 0374
Colkirk Norfk 66 9126
Collace P & K 126 2032
Collafirth Shet 153 3482
Collaton Devon 7 7139
Collaton Devon 7 7952
Collaton St Mary Devon 7 8660
College Green Somset 21 5736
College of Roseisle Moray 141 1466
College Town Berks 25 8560
Collessie Fife 126 2813
Colleton Mills Devon 19 6615
Collier Row Gt Lon 27 5091
Collier Street Kent 28 7145
Collier's End Herts 39 3720
Collier's Green Kent 17 7822
Colliers Green Kent 28 7538
Colliery Row T & W 96 3249
Collieston Abers 143 0328
Collin D & G 100 0276
Collingbourne Ducis Wilts 23 2453
Collingbourne Kingston Wilts 23 2355
Collingham Notts 76 8262
Collingham W York 83 3945
Collington Herefs 47 6460
Collingtree Nhants 49 7555
Collins Green Ches 78 5594
Collins Green Worcs 47 7457
Colliston Angus 127 6045
Colliton Devon 9 0804
Collyweston Nhants 63 9902
Colmonell S Ayrs 98 1485
Colmworth Beds 51 1058
Coln Rogers Gloucs 36 0809
Coln St Aldwyns Gloucs 36 1405
Coln St Dennis Gloucs 36 0810
Colnbrook Berks 26 0277
Colne Cambs 52 3775
Colne Lancs 81 8939
Colne Bridge W York 82 1720
Colne Edge Lancs 81 8841
Colne Engaine Essex 40 8430
Colney Norfk 66 1807
Colney Heath Herts 39 2005
Colney Street Herts 26 1502
Colpy Abers 142 6432
Colquhar Border 109 3341
Colquite Cnwll 4 0570
Colscott Devon 18 3614
Colsterdale N York 89 1381
Colsterworth Lincs 63 9324
Colston Bassett Notts 63 7033
Colt Hill Hants 24 7551
Colt's Hill Kent 16 6443
Coltfield Moray 141 1163
Coltishall Norfk 67 2719
Colton Cumb 86 3185
Colton N York 83 5444
Colton Norfk 66 1009
Colton Staffs 73 0420
Colton W York 83 3732
Columbjohn Devon 9 9699
Colva Powys 45 1952
Colvend D & G 92 8654
Colwall Herefs 47 7542
Colwell Nthumb 102 9575
Colwich Staffs 73 0121
Colwick Notts 62 6140
Colwinston V Glam 33 9375
Colworth W Susx 14 9103
Colwyn Bay Conwy 69 8578
Colyford Devon 10 2592
Colyton Devon 9 2494
Combe Berks 23 3760
Combe Devon 7 7238
Combe Devon 7 8448
Combe Herefs 46 3463
Combe Oxon 36 4116
Combe Almer Dorset 11 9597
Combe Common Surrey 14 9436
Combe Down Somset 22 7662
Combe Fishacre Devon 7 8465
Combe Florey Somset 20 1531
Combe Hay Somset 22 7359
Combe Martin Devon 19 5846
Combe Raleigh Devon 9 1502
Combe St Nicholas Somset 10 3011
Combeinteignhead Devon 7 9071
Comberbach Ches 79 6477
Comberford Staffs 61 1907
Comberton Cambs 52 3856
Comberton Herefs 46 4968
Combpyne Devon 10 2892
Combridge Staffs 73 0937
Combrook Warwks 48 3051
Combs Derbys 74 0478
Combs Suffk 54 0456
Combs Ford Suffk 54 0457
Combwich Somset 20 2542
Comers Abers 135 6707
Comhampton Worcs 47 8367
Commercial Pembks 31 1416
Commercial End Cambs 53 5563
Commins Coch Powys 57 8402
Common Edge Lancs 80 3232
Common End Cumb 92 0022
Common Moor Cnwll 5 2469
Common Platt Wilts 36 1186
Common Side Derbys 74 3375
Commondale N York 90 6610
Commonside Ches 71 5473
Commonside Derbys 73 2441
Commonwood Shrops 59 4828
Commonwood Wrexhm 71 3753
Compass Somset 20 2934
Compstall Gt Man 79 9690
Compstonend D & G 99 6652
Compton Berks 37 5280
Compton Devon 7 8664
Compton Hants 23 3529
Compton Hants 13 4625
Compton Staffs 60 8284
Compton Surrey 25 9546
Compton W Susx 14 7714
Compton Wilts 23 1351
Compton Abbas Dorset 22 8618
Compton Abdale Gloucs 36 0516
Compton Bassett Wilts 36 0372
Compton Beauchamp Oxon 36 2786
Compton Bishop Somset 21 3955
Compton Chamberlayne Wilts 23 0229
Compton Dando Somset 21 6464
Compton Dundon Somset 21 4932
Compton Durville Somset 10 4117
Compton Greenfield Gloucs 34 5681
Compton Martin Somset 21 5457
Compton Pauncefoot Somset 21 6426
Compton Valence Dorset 10 5993
Compton Verney Warwks 48 3152
Comrie Fife 117 0289
Comrie P & K 124 7722
Conaglen House Highld 130 0268
Conchra Highld 138 8827
Concraigie P & K 125 0944
Conder Green Lancs 80 4556
Conderton Worcs 47 9637
Condicote Gloucs 48 1528
Condorrat N Lans 116 7373
Condover Shrops 59 4905
Coney Hill Gloucs 35 8517
Coney Weston Suffk 54 9578
Coneyhurst Common W Susx 14 1023
Coneysthorpe N York 90 7171
Coneythorpe W York 89 3958
Conford Hants 14 8233
Congdon's Shop Cnwll 5 2878
Congerstone Leics 62 3605
Congham Norfk 65 7123
Conghurst Kent 17 7628
Congl-y-wal Gwynd 57 7044
Congleton Ches 72 8562
Congresbury Somset 21 4363
Congreve Staffs 60 9013
Conheath D & G 100 9969
Conicavel Moray 140 9853
Coningsby Lincs 76 2257
Conington Cambs 52 1885
Conington Cambs 52 3266
Conisbrough S York 75 5098
Conisholme Lincs 77 4095
Coniston Cumb 86 3097
Coniston E R Yk 85 1535
Coniston Cold N York 81 9054
Conistone N York 88 9867
Connah's Quay Flints 71 2969
Connel Ag & B 122 9134
Connel Park E Ayrs 107 6012
Connor Downs Cnwll 2 5939
Conon Bridge Highld 139 5455
Cononley N York 82 9846
Consall Staffs 72 9848
Consett Dur 95 1051
Constable Burton N York 89 1690
Constable Lee Lancs 81 8123
Constantine Cnwll 3 7329
Constantine Bay Cnwll 4 8774
Contin Highld 139 4556
Conwy Conwy 69 7877
Conyer Kent 28 9664
Conyer's Green Suffk 54 8867
Cooden E Susx 17 7107
Cook's Green Essex 41 1818
Cookbury Devon 18 4006
Cookbury Wick Devon 18 3905
Cookham Berks 26 8985
Cookham Dean Berks 26 8685
Cookham Rise Berks 26 8885
Cookhill Warwks 48 0558
Cookley Suffk 55 3475
Cookley Worcs 60 8480
Cookley Green Oxon 37 6990
Cookney Abers 135 8693
Cooks Green Suffk 54 9753
Cooksbridge E Susx 15 4013
Cooksey Green Worcs 47 9069
Cookshill Staffs 72 9443
Cooksland Cnwll 4 0867
Cooksmill Green Essex 40 6306
Cookson Green Ches 71 5774
Cookson's Green Dur 96 2933
Coolham W Susx 14 1122
Cooling Kent 28 7575
Cooling Street Kent 28 7474
Coombe Cnwll 2 6242
Coombe Cnwll 3 8340
Coombe Devon 8 8384
Coombe Devon 7 9373
Coombe Devon 9 1091
Coombe Gloucs 35 7694
Coombe Hants 13 6620
Coombe Wilts 23 1450
Coombe Bissett Wilts 23 1026
Coombe Cellars Devon 7 9072
Coombe Cross Hants 13 6620
Coombe End Somset 20 0329
Coombe Hill Gloucs 47 8826
Coombe Keynes Dorset 11 8484
Coombe Pafford Devon 7 9166
Coombe Street Somset 22 7631
Coombes W Susx 15 1808
Coombes-Moor Herefs 46 3663
Coombeswood W Mids 60 9785
Cooper Street Kent 29 3060
Cooper Turning Gt Man 79 6308
Cooper's Corner Kent 16 4849
Cooperhill Moray 141 9953
Coopers Green E Susx 16 4723
Coopers Green Herts 39 1909
Coopersale Common Essex 27 4702
Coopersale Street Essex 27 4701
Cootham W Susx 14 0714
Cop Street Kent 27 2959
Copdock Suffk 54 1242
Copford Green Essex 40 9222
Copgrove N York 89 3463
Copister Shet 153 4879
Cople Beds 38 1048
Copley Dur 95 0825
Copley Gt Man 79 9798
Copley W York 82 0822
Coplow Dale Derbys 74 1679
Copmanthorpe N York 83 5646
Copmere End Staffs 72 8029
Copp Lancs 80 4239
Coppathorne Cnwll 18 2000
Coppenhall Staffs 72 9019
Coppenhall Moss Ches 72 7058
Copperhouse Cnwll 2 5637
Coppicegate Shrops 60 7379
Coppingford Cambs 52 1679
Coppins Corner Kent 28 9448
Copplestone Devon 8 7702
Coppull Lancs 81 5614
Coppull Moor Lancs 81 5512
Copsale W Susx 15 1724
Copster Green Lancs 81 6733
Copston Magna Warwks 50 4588
Copt Heath W Mids 61 1777
Copt Hewick N York 89 3471
Copt Oak Leics 62 4812
Copthall Green Essex 27 4201
Copthorne Cnwll 5 2692
Copthorne W Susx 15 3139
Copy's Green Norfk 66 9439
Copythorne Hants 12 3014
Coram Street Suffk 54 0042
Corbets Tey Gt Lon 27 5685
Corbiere Jersey 158 0000
Corbridge Nthumb 103 9964
Corby Nhants 51 8988
Corby Glen Lincs 63 0024
Corby Hill Cumb 94 4857
Cordon N Ayrs 105 0230
Cordwell Derbys 74 3176
Coreley Shrops 46 6173
Cores End Bucks 26 9087
Corfe Somset 20 2319
Corfe Castle Dorset 11 9681
Corfe Mullen Dorset 11 9896
Corfton Shrops 59 4985
Corgarff Abers 133 2708
Corhampton Hants 13 6120
Corks Pond Kent 28 6540
Corley Warwks 61 3085
Corley Ash Warwks 61 2986
Corley Moor Warwks 61 2884
Cormuir Angus 134 3066
Cornard Tye Suffk 54 9041
Corndon Devon 8 6985
Corner Row Lancs 80 4134
Corney Cumb 86 1191
Cornforth Dur 96 3134
Cornhill Abers 142 5858
Cornhill-on-Tweed Nthumb 110 8639
Cornholme W York 81 9126
Cornish Hall End Essex 53 6836
Cornoigmore Ag & B 120 9846
Cornriggs Dur 95 8441
Cornsay Dur 96 1443
Cornsay Colliery Dur 96 1643
Corntown Highld 139 5556
Corntown V Glam 33 9177
Cornwell Oxon 48 2727
Cornwood Devon 6 6059
Cornworthy Devon 7 8255
Corpach Highld 130 0976
Corpusty Norfk 66 1129
Corrachree Abers 134 4604
Corran Cnwll 3 9946
Corran Highld 130 8409
Corran Highld 130 0263
Corrany IOM 158 4589
Corrie D & G 101 2086
Corrie N Ayrs 105 0242
Corriecravie N Ayrs 105 9223
Corriegills N Ayrs 105 0335
Corriegour Lodge Hotel Highld 131 2692
Corriemoille Highld 139 3663
Corrimony Highld 139 3730
Corringham Essex 40 7083
Corringham Lincs 76 8691
Corris Gwynd 57 7508
Corris Uchaf Gwynd 57 7408
Corrow Ag & B 114 1800
Corry Highld 137 6424
Cors-y-Gedol Gwynd 57 6022
Corscombe Devon 8 6296
Corscombe Dorset 10 5105
Corse Gloucs 47 7826
Corse Lawn Gloucs 47 8330
Corsham Wilts 35 8770
Corsindae Abers 135 6808
Corsley Wilts 22 8246
Corsley Heath Wilts 22 8245
Corsock D & G 99 7576
Corston Somset 22 6965
Corston Wilts 35 9283
Corstorphine C Edin 117 1972
Cortachy Angus 134 3959
Corton Suffk 67 5497
Corton Wilts 22 9340
Corton Denham Somset 21 6322
Coruanan Lodge Highld 130 0668
Corwen Denbgs 70 0743
Coryates Dorset 10 6285
Coryton Devon 5 4583
Coryton Essex 40 7382
Cosby Leics 50 5495
Coseley W Mids 60 9494
Cosford Shrops 60 8005
Cosgrove Nhants 38 7942
Cosham Hants 13 6505
Cosheston Pembks 30 0003
Coshieville P & K 124 7749
Cossall Notts 62 4842
Cossall Marsh Notts 62 4842
Cossington Leics 62 6013
Cossington Somset 21 3540
Costessey Norfk 66 1711
Costock Notts 62 5726
Coston Leics 63 8422
Coston Norfk 66 0506
Cote Oxon 36 3502
Cote Somset 21 3444
Cotebrook Ches 71 5765
Cotehill Cumb 93 4650
Cotes Cumb 87 4886
Cotes Leics 62 5520
Cotes Staffs 72 8434
Cotes Heath Staffs 72 8334
Cotesbach Leics 50 5382
Cotgrave Notts 63 6435
Cothal Abers 143 8715
Cotham Notts 63 7947
Cothelstone Somset 20 1831
Cotherstone Dur 95 0119
Cothill Oxon 37 4699
Cotleigh Devon 9 2002
Cotmanhay Derbys 62 4543
Coton Cambs 52 4058
Coton Nhants 50 6771
Coton Shrops 59 5334
Coton Staffs 72 8120
Coton Staffs 72 9731
Coton Staffs 61 1804
Coton Clanford Staffs 72 8723
Coton Hayes Staffs 72 9832
Coton Hill Shrops 59 4813
Coton in the Clay Staffs 73 1628
Coton in the Elms Derbys 73 2415
Coton Park Derbys 73 2617
Cott Devon 7 7861
Cottage End Hants 24 4143
Cottam E R Yk 91 9964
Cottam Lancs 80 5032
Cottam Notts 75 8179
Cottenham Cambs 53 4467
Cotterdale N York 88 8393
Cottered Herts 39 3129
Cotteridge W Mids 61 0480
Cotterstock Nhants 51 0490
Cottesbrooke Nhants 50 7173
Cottesmore Rutlnd 63 9013
Cottingham E R Yk 84 0432
Cottingham Nhants 51 8490
Cottingley W York 82 1137
Cottisford Oxon 49 5831
Cotton Suffk 54 0666
Cotton End Beds 38 0845
Cotton Tree Lancs 81 9039
Cottown Abers 142 5026
Cottown Abers 142 7615
Cottown of Gight Abers 143 8140
Cottrell V Glam 33 0774
Cotts Devon 6 4365
Cotwall Shrops 59 6017
Cotwalton Staffs 72 9234
Couch's Mill Cnwll 4 1459
Coughton Herefs 34 5921
Coughton Warwks 48 0860
Coulaghailtro Ag & B 113 7165
Coulags Highld 138 9645
Coulderton Cumb 86 9808
Coull Abers 134 5102
Coulport Ag & B 114 2187
Coulsdon Gt Lon 27 2959
Coulston Wilts 22 9554
Coulter S Lans 108 0234
Coultershaw Bridge W Susx 14 9719
Coultings Somset 20 2241
Coulton N York 90 6373
Coultra Fife 126 3523

280

Culkein Dittisham
281

Culkein *Highld* 148 0333
Culkein Drumbeg *Highld* 148 1133
Culkerton *Gloucs* 35 9395
Cullen *Moray* 142 5167
Cullercoats *T & W* 103 3570
Cullerlie *Abers* 135 7603
Cullicudden *Highld* 140 6463
Cullingworth *W York* 82 0636
Cullipool House *Ag & B* 122 7413
Cullivoe *Shet* 153 5402
Culloden *Highld* 140 7246
Cullompton *Devon* 9 0207
Culm Davy *Devon* 9 1215
Culmington *Shrops* 59 4982
Culmstock *Devon* 9 1013
Culnacraig *Highld* 145 0603
Culnaightrie *D & G* 92 7750
Culnaknock *Highld* 137 5162
Culpho *Suffk* 55 2149
Culrain *Highld* 146 5794
Culross *Fife* 117 9886
Culroy *S Ayrs* 106 3114
Culsalmond *Abers* 142 6532
Culscadden *D & G* 99 4748
Culshabbin *D & G* 98 3051
Culswick *Shet* 153 2745
Cultercullen *Abers* 143 9223
Cults *Aber C* 135 8903
Culverstone Green *Kent* 27 6362
Culverthorpe *Lincs* 64 0240
Culworth *Nhants* 49 5446
Culzean Castle 106 2310
Cumbernauld *N Lans* 116 7674
Cumbernauld Village *N Lans* 116 7676
Cumberworth *Lincs* 77 5073
Cumdivock *Cumb* 93 3448
Cuminestown *Abers* 143 8050
Cumledge *Border* 119 7956
Cummersdale *Cumb* 93 3953
Cummertrees *D & G* 100 1366
Cummingston *Moray* 141 1368
Cumnock *E Ayrs* 107 5620
Cumnor *Oxon* 37 4504
Cumrew *Cumb* 94 5550
Cumrue *D & G* 100 0686
Cumwhinton *Cumb* 93 4552
Cumwhitton *Cumb* 94 5052
Cundall *N York* 89 4272
Cunninghamhead *N Ayrs* 106 3741
Cupar *Fife* 126 3714
Cupar Muir *Fife* 126 3613
Cupernham *Hants* 23 3622
Curbar *Derbys* 74 2574
Curbridge *Hants* 13 5211
Curbridge *Oxon* 36 3308
Curdridge *Hants* 13 5213
Curdworth *Warwks* 61 1792
Curland *Somset* 10 2717
Curridge *Berks* 24 4972
Currie *C Edin* 117 1867
Curry Mallet *Somset* 21 3221
Curry Rivel *Somset* 21 3925
Curteis Corner *Kent* 28 8539
Curtisden Green *Kent* 28 7440
Curtisknowle *Devon* 7 7353
Cury *Cnwll* 2 6721
Cushnie *Abers* 134 5211
Cushuish *Somset* 20 1930
Cusop *Herefs* 46 2441
Cutcloy *D & G* 99 4534
Cutcombe *Somset* 20 9339
Cutgate *Gt Man* 81 8614
Cuthill *Highld* 147 7587
Cutiau *Gwynd* 57 6317
Cutler's Green *Essex* 40 5930
Cutmadoc *Cnwll* 4 0963
Cutmere *Cnwll* 5 3260
Cutnall Green *Worcs* 47 8868
Cutsdean *Gloucs* 48 0830
Cutsyke *W York* 83 4224
Cutthorpe *Derbys* 74 3473
Cuttivett *Cnwll* 5 3662
Cuxham *Oxon* 37 6695
Cuxton *Kent* 28 7066
Cuxwold *Lincs* 85 1701
Cwm *Blae G* 33 1805
Cwm *Denbgs* 70 0677
Cwm Capel *Carmth* 32 4502
Cwm Crawnon *Powys* 33 1419
Cwm Dulais *Swans* 32 6103
Cwm Irfon *Powys* 45 8549
Cwm Morgan *Carmth* 31 2934
Cwm Penmachno *Conwy* 69 7547
Cwm-bach *Carmth* 32 4801
Cwm-celyn *Blae G* 33 2008
Cwm-Cewydd *Gwynd* 57 8713
Cwm-cou *Cerdgn* 31 2942
Cwm-Ifor *Carmth* 44 6625
Cwm-Llinau *Powys* 57 8408
Cwm-y-glo *Carmth* 32 5513
Cwm-y-glo *Gwynd* 69 5562
Cwmafan *Neath* 32 7791
Cwmaman *Rhondd* 33 0099
Cwmann *Carmth* 44 5847
Cwmavon *Torfn* 34 2706
Cwmbach *Carmth* 31 2526
Cwmbach *Powys* 45 1639
Cwmbach *Rhondd* 33 0201
Cwmbach Llechrhyd *Powys* 45 0254
Cwmbelan *Powys* 58 9481
Cwmbran *Torfn* 34 2994
Cwmbrwyno *Cerdgn* 43 7180
Cwmcarn *Caerph* 34 2293
Cwmcarvan *Mons* 34 4707
Cwmdare *Rhondd* 33 9803
Cwmdu *Carmth* 44 6330
Cwmdu *Powys* 45 1823
Cwmdu *Swans* 32 6494
Cwmduad *Carmth* 31 3731
Cwmdwr *Carmth* 44 7132
Cwmergyr *Cerdgn* 43 7982
Cwmfelin *Brdgnd* 33 8589
Cwmfelin *Myr Td* 33 0901
Cwmfelin Boeth *Carmth* 31 1919
Cwmfelin Mynach *Carmth* 31 2224
Cwmfelinfach *Caerph* 33 1891
Cwmffrwd *Carmth* 31 4217
Cwmgiedd *Powys* 32 7911
Cwmgorse *Carmth* 32 7010
Cwmgwili *Carmth* 32 5710
Cwmgwrach *Neath* 33 8604
Cwmhiraeth *Carmth* 31 3437
Cwmisfael *Carmth* 32 4915
Cwmllynfell *Neath* 32 7412
Cwmmawr *Carmth* 32 5312
Cwmparc *Rhondd* 33 9495
Cwmpengraig *Carmth* 31 3536
Cwmpennar *Rhondd* 33 0300
Cwmrhos *Powys* 45 1824
Cwmrhydyceirw *Swans* 32 6699
Cwmsychbant *Cerdgn* 44 4746
Cwmtillery *Blae G* 33 2105
Cwmyoy *Mons* 46 2923
Cwmystwyth *Cerdgn* 43 7874
Cwrt *Gwynd* 32 6800
Cwrt-newydd *Cerdgn* 44 4947
Cwrt-y-gollen *Powys* 34 2317
Cyfronydd *Powys* 58 1408
Cylibebyll *Neath* 32 7404
Cymer *Neath* 33 8695
Cymmer *Rhondd* 33 0290
Cynghordy *Carmth* 44 8040
Cynheidre *Carmth* 32 4907
Cynonville *Neath* 33 8395
Cynwyd *Denbgs* 70 0541
Cynwyl Elfed *Carmth* 31 3727

D

Daccombe *Devon* 7 9068
Dacre *Cumb* 93 4526
Dacre *N York* 89 1960
Dacre Banks *N York* 89 1962
Daddry Shield *Dur* 95 8937
Dadford *Bucks* 49 6638
Dadlington *Leics* 61 4097
Dafen *Carmth* 32 5201
Daffy Green *Norfk* 66 9609
Dagenham *Gt Lon* 27 5084
Daglingworth *Gloucs* 35 9905
Dagnall *Bucks* 38 9916
Dagworth *Suffk* 54 0361
Dailly *S Ayrs* 106 2701
Dainton *Devon* 7 8566
Dairsie *Fife* 126 4117
Daisy Hill *Gt Man* 79 6504
Daisy Hill *W York* 82 2728
Dalabrog *W Isls* 152 7521
Dalavich *Ag & B* 122 9612
Dalbeattie *D & G* 100 8361
Dalbury *Derbys* 73 2634
Dalby *IOM* 158 2178
Dalby *Lincs* 77 4169
Dalby *N York* 90 6371
Dalcapon *P & K* 125 9754
Dalchalm *Highld* 147 9105
Dalchreichart *Highld* 131 2812
Dalchruin *P & K* 124 7116
Dalcrue *P & K* 125 0427
Dalderby *Lincs* 77 2565
Dalditch *Devon* 9 0483
Dale *Cumb* 94 5443
Dale *Derbys* 62 4338
Dale *Pembks* 30 8005
Dale Bottom *Cumb* 93 2921
Dale End *Derbys* 74 2161
Dale End *N York* 82 9645
Dale Hill *E Susx* 16 7030
Dalehouse *N York* 97 7717
Dalgarven *N Ayrs* 115 2846
Dalgety Bay *Fife* 117 1683
Dalgig *E Ayrs* 107 5512
Dalginross *P & K* 124 7721
Dalguise *P & K* 125 9847
Dalhalvaig *Highld* 150 8954
Dalham *Suffk* 53 7261
Daliburgh *W Isls* 152 7521
Dalkeith *Mdloth* 118 3367
Dallas *Moray* 141 1252
Dallinghoo *Suffk* 55 2655
Dallington *E Susx* 16 6519
Dallington *Nhants* 49 7362
Dallow *N York* 89 1971
Dalmally *Ag & B* 123 1627
Dalmary *Stirlg* 115 5195
Dalmellington *E Ayrs* 107 4705
Dalmeny *C Edin* 117 1477
Dalmigavie *Highld* 140 7319
Dalmigavie Lodge *Highld* 140 7523
Dalmore *Highld* 140 6668
Dalmuir *W Duns* 115 4871
Dalnabreck *Highld* 129 7069
Dalnacardoch *P & K* 132 7270
Dalnahaitnach *Highld* 140 8519
Dalnaspidal *P & K* 132 6473
Dalnawillan Lodge *Highld* 150 0340
Daloist *P & K* 124 7857
Dalqueich *P & K* 125 0804
Dalquhairn *S Ayrs* 106 3296
Dalreavoch Lodge *Highld* 147 7508
Dalry *N Ayrs* 115 2949
Dalrymple *E Ayrs* 106 3514
Dalserf *S Lans* 116 7950
Dalsmeran *Ag & B* 104 6413
Dalston *Cumb* 93 3650
Dalston *Gt Lon* 27 3384
Dalswinton *D & G* 100 9385
Dalton *Cumb* 87 5476
Dalton *D & G* 100 1173
Dalton *Lancs* 78 4908
Dalton *N York* 89 1108
Dalton *N York* 89 4376
Dalton *Nthumb* 103 1172
Dalton *S York* 75 4594
Dalton Magna *S York* 75 4692
Dalton Parva *S York* 75 4593
Dalton Piercy *Dur* 97 4631
Dalton-in-Furness *Cumb* 86 2274
Dalton-le-Dale *Dur* 96 4048
Dalton-on-Tees *N York* 89 2907
Dalveen *D & G* 108 8806
Dalveich *Stirlg* 124 6124
Dalwhinnie *Highld* 132 6384
Dalwood *Devon* 9 2400
Dam Green *Norfk* 54 0485
Damask Green *Herts* 39 2529
Damerham *Hants* 12 1016
Damgate *Norfk* 67 4009
Dan-y-Parc *Powys* 34 2217
Danaway *Kent* 28 8663
Danbury *Essex* 40 7805
Danby *N York* 90 7008
Danby Bottom *N York* 90 6904
Danby Wiske *N York* 89 3398
Dandaleith *Moray* 141 2846
Danderhall *Mdloth* 117 3069
Dane End *Herts* 39 3321
Dane Hills *Leics* 62 5604
Dane Street *Kent* 28 0552
Danebridge *Ches* 72 9665
Danegate *E Susx* 16 5633
Danehill *E Susx* 15 4027
Danemoor Green *Norfk* 66 0505
Danesford *Shrops* 60 7391
Danesmoor *Derbys* 74 4063
Daniel's Water *Kent* 28 9541
Danshillock *Abers* 142 7157
Danskine *E Loth* 118 5667
Danthorpe *E R Yk* 85 2532
Danzey Green *Warwks* 48 1269
Dapple Heath *Staffs* 73 0425
Darby Green *Hants* 25 8360
Darcy Lever *Gt Man* 79 7308
Daren-felen *Mons* 34 2212
Darenth *Kent* 27 5671
Daresbury *Ches* 78 5882
Darfield *S York* 83 4104
Darfoulds *Notts* 75 5578
Dargate *Kent* 29 0861
Darite *Cnwll* 5 2569
Darland *Kent* 28 7865
Darland *Wrexhm* 71 3757
Darlaston *Staffs* 72 8835
Darlaston *W Mids* 60 9796
Darlaston Green *W Mids* 60 9797
Darley *N York* 89 2059
Darley Abbey *Derbys* 62 3538
Darley Bridge *Derbys* 74 2661
Darley Dale *Derbys* 74 2663
Darley Green *Warwks* 61 1874
Darley Head *N York* 89 1959
Darleyhall *Herts* 38 1422
Darlingscott *Warwks* 48 2342
Darlington *Dur* 89 2814
Darliston *Shrops* 59 5733
Darlton *Notts* 75 7773
Darnford *Staffs* 61 1308
Darnick *Border* 109 5334
Darowen *Powys* 57 8201
Darra *Abers* 142 7447
Darracott *Cnwll* 18 2811
Darracott *Devon* 18 2317
Darracott *Devon* 18 4739
Darras Hall *Nthumb* 103 1570
Darrington *W York* 83 4820
Darsham *Suffk* 55 4169
Darshill *Somset* 21 6144
Dartford *Kent* 27 5474
Dartington *Devon* 7 7862
Dartmeet *Devon* 7 6773
Dartmouth *Devon* 7 8751
Darton *S York* 82 3110
Darvel *E Ayrs* 107 5637
Darwell Hole *E Susx* 16 6919
Darwen *Lancs* 81 6922
Datchet *Berks* 26 9877
Datchworth *Herts* 39 2619
Datchworth Green *Herts* 39 2718
Daubhill *Gt Man* 79 7007
Dauntsey *Wilts* 35 9782
Dauntsey Green *Wilts* 35 9981
Dava *Highld* 141 0038
Davenham *Ches* 79 6571
Davenport *Gt Man* 79 9088
Davenport Green *Ches* 79 8379
Davenport Green *Gt Man* 79 8086
Daventry *Nhants* 49 5762
David Street *Kent* 27 6464
Davidson's Mains *C Edin* 117 2175
Davidstow *Cnwll* 4 1587
Davington *D & G* 109 2302
Davington Hill *Kent* 28 0161
Daviot *Abers* 142 7428
Daviot *Highld* 140 7239
Daviot House *Highld* 140 7240
Davis's Town *E Susx* 16 5217
Davoch of Grange *Moray* 142 4751
Davyhulme *Gt Man* 79 7595
Daw End *W Mids* 61 0300
Daw's House *Cnwll* 5 3182
Dawesgreen *Surrey* 15 2147
Dawley *Shrops* 60 6808
Dawlish *Devon* 9 9576
Dawlish Warren *Devon* 9 9778
Dawn *Conwy* 69 8672
Daws Green *Somset* 20 1921
Daws Heath *Essex* 40 8188
Dawsmere *Lincs* 65 4430
Day Green *Ches* 72 7757
Daybrook *Notts* 62 5744
Dayhills *Staffs* 72 9532
Dayhouse Bank *Worcs* 60 9678
Daylesford *Gloucs* 48 2425
Ddol *Flints* 70 1471
Ddol-Cownwy *Powys* 58 0117
Deal *Kent* 29 3752
Dean *Cumb* 92 0725
Dean *Devon* 19 6245
Dean *Devon* 19 7048
Dean *Devon* 7 7364
Dean *Dorset* 11 9715
Dean *Hants* 24 4431
Dean *Hants* 13 5619
Dean *Lancs* 81 8525
Dean *Oxon* 36 3422
Dean *Somset* 22 6743
Dean Bottom *Kent* 27 5868
Dean Court *Oxon* 37 4705
Dean End *Dorset* 11 9717
Dean Head *S York* 74 2600
Dean Prior *Devon* 7 7363
Dean Row *Ches* 79 8781
Dean Street *Kent* 28 7453
Deanburnhaugh *Border* 109 3911
Deancombe *Devon* 7 7264
Deane *Gt Man* 79 6907
Deane *Hants* 24 5450
Deanhead *W York* 82 0415
Deanland *Dorset* 22 9918
Deanlane End *W Susx* 13 7412
Deanraw *Nthumb* 102 8162
Deans *W Loth* 117 0369
Deanscales *Cumb* 92 0926
Deanshanger *Nhants* 49 7639
Deanshaugh *Moray* 141 3550
Deanston *Stirlg* 124 7101
Dearham *Cumb* 92 0736
Dearnley *Gt Man* 81 9215
Debach *Suffk* 55 2454
Debden *Essex* 53 5533
Debden *Essex* 27 4496
Debden Green *Essex* 40 5831
Debenham *Suffk* 54 1763
Deblin's Green *Worcs* 47 8148
Dechmont *W Loth* 117 0370
Dechmont Road *W Loth* 117 0269
Deddington *Oxon* 49 4631
Dedham *Essex* 41 0533
Dedham Heath *Essex* 41 0531
Dedworth *Berks* 26 9476
Deene *Nhants* 51 9492
Deenethorpe *Nhants* 51 9591
Deepcar *S York* 74 2897
Deepcut *Surrey* 25 9057
Deepdale *Cumb* 88 7184
Deepdale *N York* 88 8979
Deeping Gate *Lincs* 64 1509
Deeping St James *Lincs* 64 1609
Deeping St Nicholas *Lincs* 64 2115
Deerhurst *Gloucs* 47 8730
Deerhurst Walton *Gloucs* 47 8828
Deerton Street *Kent* 28 9762
Defford *Worcs* 47 9143
Defynnog *Powys* 45 9227
Deganwy *Conwy* 69 7779
Degnish *Ag & B* 122 7812
Deighton *N York* 89 3801
Deighton *N York* 83 6244
Deighton *W York* 82 1519
Deiniolen *Gwynd* 69 5763
Delabole *Cnwll* 4 0683
Delamere *Ches* 71 5668
Delfrigs *Abers* 143 9620
Dell Quay *W Susx* 14 8302
Delley *Devon* 19 5424
Delliefure *Highld* 141 0730
Delly End *Oxon* 36 3513
Delmonden Green *Kent* 17 7330
Delnashaugh Inn *Moray* 141 1835
Delny *Highld* 146 7372
Delph *Gt Man* 82 9807
Delves *Dur* 95 1149
Delvine *P & K* 126 1240
Dembleby *Lincs* 64 0437
Demelza *Cnwll* 4 9763
Den of Lindores *Fife* 126 2616
Denaby *S York* 75 4899
Denaby Main *S York* 75 4999
Denbies *Surrey* 26 1450
Denbigh *Denbgs* 70 0566
Denbrae *Fife* 126 3818
Denbury *Devon* 7 8268
Denby *Derbys* 62 3946
Denby Bottles *Derbys* 62 3846
Denby Dale *W York* 82 2208
Denchworth *Oxon* 36 3891
Dendron *Cumb* 86 2470
Denel End *Beds* 38 0335
Denfield *P & K* 125 9517
Denford *Nhants* 51 9976
Dengie *Essex* 41 9802
Denham *Bucks* 26 0487
Denham *Suffk* 53 7561
Denham *Suffk* 55 1974
Denham End *Suffk* 53 7663
Denham Green *Bucks* 26 0488
Denham Green *Suffk* 55 1974
Denhead *Abers* 143 9952
Denhead *Fife* 127 4613
Denhead of Gray *Dund C* 126 3531
Denholm *Border* 110 5718
Denholme *W York* 82 0734
Denholme Clough *W York* 82 0732
Denio *Gwynd* 56 3635
Denmead *Hants* 13 6512
Denmore *Aber C* 135 9411
Denne Park *W Susx* 15 1628
Dennington *Suffk* 55 2867
Denny *Falk* 116 8082
Dennyloanhead *Falk* 116 8080
Denshaw *Gt Man* 82 9710
Denside *Abers* 135 8095
Densole *Kent* 29 2141
Denston *Suffk* 53 7652
Denstone *Staffs* 73 0940
Denstroude *Kent* 29 1061
Dent *Cumb* 87 7086
Denton *Cambs* 52 1587
Denton *Dur* 96 2118
Denton *E Susx* 16 4502
Denton *Gt Man* 79 9295
Denton *Kent* 28 6673
Denton *Kent* 29 2147
Denton *Lincs* 63 8632
Denton *N York* 82 1448
Denton *Nhants* 51 8358
Denton *Norfk* 55 2788
Denton *Oxon* 37 5902
Denver *Norfk* 65 6001
Denwick *Nthumb* 111 2014
Deopham *Norfk* 66 0400
Deopham Green *Norfk* 66 0499
Depden *Suffk* 53 7857
Depden Green *Suffk* 53 7756
Deptford *Gt Lon* 27 3777
Deptford *Wilts* 22 0138
Derby *Derbys* 62 3536
Derby *Devon* 19 5633
Derbyhaven *IOM* 158 2867
Derculich *P & K* 125 8852
Dereham *Norfk* 66 9913
Deri *Caerph* 33 1201
Derril *Devon* 18 3003
Derringstone *Kent* 29 2049
Derrington *Staffs* 72 8922
Derriton *Devon* 18 3303
Derry Hill *Wilts* 35 9670
Derrythorpe *Lincs* 84 8208
Dersingham *Norfk* 65 6830
Dervaig *Ag & B* 121 4352
Derwen *Denbgs* 70 0750
Derwen Fawr *Carmth* 44 5722
Derwenlas *Powys* 57 7298
Derwydd *Carmth* 32 6117
Desborough *Nhants* 51 8083
Desford *Leics* 62 4703
Deskford *Moray* 142 5061
Detchant *Nthumb* 111 0836
Detling *Kent* 28 7958
Deuxhill *Shrops* 60 6987
Devauden *Mons* 34 4898
Devil's Bridge *Cerdgn* 43 7376
Deviock *Cnwll* 5 3155
Devitts Green *Warwks* 61 2790
Devizes *Wilts* 22 0061
Devonport *Devon* 6 4554
Devonside *Clacks* 116 9196
Devoran *Cnwll* 3 7939
Dewarton *Mdloth* 118 3763
Dewlish *Dorset* 11 7798
Dewsbury *W York* 82 2421
Dewsbury Moor *W York* 82 2321
Deytheur *Powys* 58 2317
Dial *Somset* 21 5366
Dial Green *W Susx* 14 9227
Dial Post *W Susx* 15 1519
Dibberford *Dorset* 10 4504
Dibden *Hants* 13 4008
Dibden Purlieu *Hants* 13 4106
Dickens Heath *W Mids* 61 1176
Dickleburgh *Norfk* 54 1682
Didbrook *Gloucs* 48 0531
Didcot *Oxon* 37 5290
Didcot Railway Centre 37 5290
Diddington *Cambs* 52 1965
Diddlebury *Shrops* 59 5085
Didley *Herefs* 46 4532
Didling *W Susx* 14 8318
Didmarton *Gloucs* 35 8287
Didsbury *Gt Man* 79 8491
Didworthy *Devon* 7 6862
Digby *Lincs* 76 0854
Digg *Highld* 136 4668
Diggle *Gt Man* 82 0007
Digmoor *Lancs* 78 4905
Digswell *Herts* 39 2415
Digswell Water *Herts* 39 2514
Dihewyd *Cerdgn* 44 4855
Dilham *Norfk* 67 3325
Dilhorne *Staffs* 72 9743
Dillington *Cambs* 52 1365
Dilston *Nthumb* 102 9763
Dilton *Wilts* 22 8548
Dilton Marsh *Wilts* 22 8449
Dilwyn *Herefs* 46 4154
Dimple *Derbys* 74 2960
Dimple *Gt Man* 81 7015
Dinas *Carmth* 31 2730
Dinas *Cnwll* 4 9274
Dinas *Gwynd* 56 2735
Dinas *Pembks* 30 0138
Dinas *Rhondd* 33 0091
Dinas Dinlle *Gwynd* 68 4356
Dinas Powys *V Glam* 33 1571
Dinas-Mawddwy *Gwynd* 57 8515
Dinder *Somset* 21 5744
Dinedor *Herefs* 46 5336
Dingestow *Mons* 34 4510
Dingle *Mersyd* 78 3687
Dingleden *Kent* 17 8131
Dingley *Nhants* 50 7787
Dingwall *Highld* 139 5458
Dinham *Mons* 34 4792
Dinmael *Conwy* 70 0044
Dinnet *Abers* 134 4598
Dinnington *S York* 75 5285
Dinnington *Somset* 10 4012
Dinnington *T & W* 103 2073
Dinorwic *Gwynd* 69 5961
Dinton *Bucks* 37 7610
Dinton *Wilts* 22 0131
Dinwoodie *D & G* 100 1190
Dinworthy *Devon* 18 3015
Dipford *Somset* 20 2021
Dipley *Hants* 24 7457
Dippen *Ag & B* 105 7937
Dippen *N Ayrs* 105 0422
Dippenhall *Surrey* 25 8146
Dippermill *Devon* 18 4406
Dippertown *Devon* 5 4284
Dipple *Moray* 141 3258
Dipple *S Ayrs* 106 2002
Diptford *Devon* 7 7256
Dipton *Dur* 96 1554
Diptonmill *Nthumb* 102 9361
Dirleton *E Loth* 118 5184
Dirt Pot *Nthumb* 95 8545
Discoed *Powys* 46 2764
Diseworth *Leics* 62 4524
Dishforth *N York* 89 3873
Disley *Ches* 79 9784
Diss *Norfk* 54 1180
Disserth *Powys* 45 0358
Distington *Cumb* 92 0023
Ditchampton *Wilts* 23 0831
Ditchburn *Nthumb* 111 1320
Ditcheat *Somset* 21 6236
Ditchingham *Norfk* 67 3391
Ditchley *Oxon* 36 3820
Ditchling *E Susx* 15 3215
Ditherington *Shrops* 59 5014
Ditteridge *Wilts* 35 8169
Dittisham *Devon* 7 8655

Ditton Earls Common

282

Ditton Ches 78 4986
Ditton Kent 28 7158
Ditton Green Cambs 53 6558
Ditton Priors Shrops 59 6089
Dixton Gloucs 47 9830
Dixton Mons 34 5113
Dizzard Cnwll 4 1698
Dobcross Gt Man 82 9906
Dobroyd Castle W York 81 9323
Dobwalls Cnwll 5 2165
Doccombe Devon 8 7786
Dochgarroch Highld 140 6140
Dockenfield Surrey 25 8240
Docker Lancs 87 5774
Docking Norfk 65 7636
Docklow Herefs 46 5657
Dockray Cumb 93 2649
Dockray Cumb 93 3921
Dod's Leigh Staffs 73 0134
Dodbrooke Devon 7 7444
Dodd's Green Ches 71 6043
Doddinghurst Essex 27 5999
Doddington Cambs 52 4090
Doddington Kent 28 9357
Doddington Lincs 76 8970
Doddington Nthumb 111 9932
Doddington Shrops 46 6176
Doddiscombsleigh Devon 8 8586
Doddshill Norfk 65 6930
Doddy Cross Cnwll 5 3062
Dodford Nhants 49 6160
Dodford Worcs 60 9373
Dodington Gloucs 35 7580
Dodington Somset 20 1740
Dodleston Ches 71 3661
Dodscott Devon 19 5419
Dodside E Rens 115 5053
Dodworth S York 82 3105
Dodworth Bottom S York 83 3204
Dodworth Green S York 82 3004
Doe Bank W Mids 61 1197
Doe Lea Derbys 75 4666
Dog Village Devon 9 9896
Dogdyke Lincs 76 2055
Dogley Lane W York 82 1813
Dogmersfield Hants 25 7852
Dogridge Wilts 36 0887
Dogsthorpe Cambs 64 1901
Dol-for Powys 57 8106
Dol-gran Carmth 31 4334
Dolanog Powys 58 0612
Dolau Powys 45 1467
Dolaucothi Carmth 44 6640
Dolbenmaen Gwynd 56 5043
Doley Shrops 72 7429
Dolfach Powys 58 9101
Dolfor Powys 58 1087
Dolgarrog Conwy 69 7767
Dolgellau Gwynd 57 7217
Dolgoch Gwynd 57 6504
Doll Highld 147 8803
Dollar Clacks 117 9698
Dollarfield Clacks 117 9697
Dolley Green Powys 46 2865
Dollwen Cerdgn 43 6881
Dolphin Flints 70 1973
Dolphinholme Lancs 80 5253
Dolphinton S Lans 117 1046
Dolton Devon 19 5712
Dolwen Conwy 69 8874
Dolwyddelan Conwy 69 7352
Dolybont Cerdgn 43 6288
Dolyhir Powys 46 2457
Domgay Powys 58 2818
Donaldson's Lodge Nthumb 110 8741
Doncaster S York 83 5703
Doncaster Carr S York 83 5801
Donhead St Andrew Wilts 22 9124
Donhead St Mary Wilts 22 9024
Donibristle Fife 117 1688
Doniford Somset 20 0842
Donington Lincs 64 2035
Donington on Bain Lincs 76 2382
Donington Southing Lincs 64 2034
Donisthorpe Leics 61 3113
Donkey Street Kent 17 1032
Donkey Town Surrey 25 9360
Donnington Berks 24 4668
Donnington Gloucs 48 1928
Donnington Herefs 47 7034
Donnington Shrops 59 5708
Donnington Shrops 60 7114
Donnington W Susx 14 8501
Donnington Wood Shrops 60 7012
Donyatt Somset 10 3314
Doomsday Green W Susx 15 1929
Doonfoot S Ayrs 106 3219
Doonholm S Ayrs 106 3317
Dorback Lodge Highld 141 0716
Dorchester Dorset 11 6990
Dorchester Oxon 37 5794
Dordon Warwks 61 2500
Dore S York 74 3181
Dores Highld 140 5934
Dorking Surrey 15 1649
Dorking Tye Suffk 54 9236
Dormans Land Surrey 15 4041
Dormans Park Surrey 15 3940
Dormington Herefs 46 5840
Dormston Worcs 47 9857
Dorn Gloucs 48 2034
Dorney Bucks 26 9378
Dornie Highld 138 8826
Dornoch Highld 147 7989
Dornock D & G 101 2366
Dorrery Highld 150 0754
Dorridge W Mids 61 1775
Dorrington Lincs 76 0852
Dorrington Shrops 59 4702
Dorrington Shrops 72 7340
Dorsington Warwks 48 1349
Dorstone Herefs 46 3141
Dorton Bucks 37 6814
Dosthill Staffs 61 2199
Dottery Dorset 10 4595
Doublebois Cnwll 5 1964
Doughton Gloucs 35 8791
Douglas IOM 158 3775
Douglas S Lans 108 8330
Douglas and Angus Dund C 127 4233
Douglas Castle S Lans 108 8431
Douglas Pier Ag & B 114 1999
Douglas Water S Lans 108 8736
Douglas West S Lans 108 8231
Douglastown Angus 126 4147
Doulting Somset 21 6443
Dounby Ork 153 2920
Doune Highld 146 4400
Doune Stirlg 116 7201
Dounepark S Ayrs 106 1897
Dounie Highld 146 5690
Dousland Devon 6 5369
Dovaston Shrops 59 3521
Dove Green Notts 75 4652
Dove Holes Derbys 74 0777
Dovenby Cumb 92 0933
Dover Gt Man 78 6000
Dover Kent 29 3241
Dover Castle 29 3241
Dovercourt Essex 41 2431
Doverdale Worcs 47 8666
Doveridge Derbys 73 1133
Doversgreen Surrey 15 2548
Dowally P & K 125 0048
Dowbridge Lancs 80 4331
Dowdeswell Gloucs 35 0019
Dowlais Myr Td 33 0607
Dowland Devon 19 5610
Dowlish Ford Somset 10 3513
Dowlish Wake Somset 10 3712
Down Ampney Gloucs 36 0996
Down Hatherley Gloucs 35 8622
Down St Mary Devon 8 7404
Down Thomas Devon 6 5050
Downacarey Devon 5 3790
Downderry Cnwll 5 3154
Downe Gt Lon 27 4361
Downend Berks 37 4775
Downend Gloucs 35 6577
Downend Gloucs 35 8398
Downend IOW 13 5387
Downfield Dund C 126 3932
Downgate Cnwll 5 2871
Downgate Cnwll 5 3672
Downham Essex 40 7296
Downham Gt Lon 27 3871
Downham Lancs 81 7844
Downham Nthumb 110 8633
Downham Market Norfk 65 6103
Downhead Somset 21 5625
Downhead Somset 22 6945
Downhill Cnwll 4 8669
Downhill P & K 125 0930
Downholland Cross Lancs 78 3606
Downholme N York 89 1197
Downies Abers 135 9294
Downing Flints 70 1578
Downley Bucks 26 8495
Downside Somset 21 6244
Downside Somset 21 6450
Downside Surrey 26 1057
Downton Hants 12 2693
Downton Wilts 12 1821
Downton on the Rock Herefs 46 4273
Dowsby Lincs 64 1129
Dowsdale Lincs 64 2810
Dowsland Green Essex 40 8724
Doxey Staffs 72 8923
Doxford Nthumb 111 1823
Doynton Gloucs 35 7274
Draethen Caerph 34 2287
Draffan S Lans 116 7945
Dragonby Lincs 84 9014
Dragons Green W Susx 15 1423
Drakeholes Notts 75 7090
Drakelow Worcs 60 8180
Drakemyre N Ayrs 115 2950
Drakes Broughton Worcs 47 9248
Drakes Cross Worcs 61 0876
Drakewalls Cnwll 6 4270
Draughton N York 82 0352
Draughton Nhants 50 7676
Drax N York 83 6726
Drax Hales N York 83 6725
Draycot Foliat Wilts 36 1777
Draycote Warwks 50 4470
Draycott Derbys 62 4433
Draycott Gloucs 48 1835
Draycott Shrops 60 8093
Draycott Somset 21 4751
Draycott Somset 21 5521
Draycott Worcs 47 8548
Draycott in the Clay Staffs 73 1528
Draycott in the Moors Staffs 72 9840
Drayford Devon 19 7813
Draynes Cnwll 5 2169
Drayton Hants 13 6705
Drayton Leics 51 8392
Drayton Lincs 64 2439
Drayton Norfk 66 1813
Drayton Oxon 49 4241
Drayton Oxon 37 4894
Drayton Somset 21 4024
Drayton Worcs 60 9075
Drayton Bassett Staffs 61 1900
Drayton Beauchamp Bucks 38 9011
Drayton Manor Park 61 1901
Drayton Parslow Bucks 38 8328
Drayton St Leonard Oxon 37 5996
Drebley N York 88 0559
Dreemskerry IOM 158 4791
Dreen Hill Pembks 30 9214
Drefach Carmth 31 3538
Drefach Carmth 32 5213
Drefach Cerdgn 44 4945
Drefelin Carmth 31 3637
Dreghorn N Ayrs 106 3538
Drellingore Kent 29 2441
Drem E Loth 118 5079
Dresden Staffs 72 9142
Drewsteignton Devon 8 7391
Driby Lincs 77 3874
Driffield E R Yk 91 0257
Driffield Gloucs 36 0799
Driffield Cross Roads Gloucs 36 0698
Drift Cnwll 2 4328
Drigg Cumb 86 0699
Drighlington W York 82 2228
Drimnin Highld 121 5554
Drimpton Dorset 10 4104
Drimsallie Highld 130 9578
Dringhoe E R Yk 85 1454
Dringhouses N York 83 5849
Drinkstone Suffk 54 9561
Drinkstone Green Suffk 54 9660
Drinsey Nook Notts 76 8773
Drive End Dorset 10 5808
Driver's End Herts 39 2220
Drointon Staffs 73 0226
Droitwich Worcs 47 8963
Dron P & K 126 1416
Dronfield Derbys 74 3578
Dronfield Woodhouse Derbys 74 3378
Drongan E Ayrs 107 4418
Dronley Angus 126 3435
Droop Dorset 11 7508
Dropping Well S York 74 3994
Droxford Hants 13 6018
Droylsden Gt Man 79 9097
Druid Denbgs 70 0443
Druids Heath W Mids 61 0502
Druidston Pembks 30 8616
Druimachoish Highld 123 1246
Druimarbin Highld 130 0770
Druimdrishaig Ag & B 113 7370
Druimindarroch Highld 129 6884
Drum Ag & B 114 9276
Drum P & K 117 0400
Drumalbin S Lans 108 9038
Drumbeg Highld 148 1232
Drumblade Abers 142 5840
Drumbreddon D & G 98 0843
Drumbuie Highld 137 7730
Drumburgh Cumb 93 2659
Drumburn D & G 92 8854
Drumchapel C Glas 115 5270
Drumchastle P & K 132 6858
Drumclog S Lans 107 6438
Drumeldrie Fife 127 4403
Drumelzier Border 108 1334
Drumfearn Highld 129 6716
Drumfrennie Abers 135 7298
Drumguish Highld 132 7900
Drumhead Abers 134 6092
Drumin Moray 141 1830
Drumjohn D & G 107 5297
Drumlamford S Ayrs 98 2876
Drumlasie Abers 135 6405
Drumleaning Cumb 93 2751
Drumlemble Ag & B 104 6619
Drumlithie Abers 135 7880
Drummoddie D & G 99 3845
Drummore D & G 98 1336
Drummuir Moray 141 3843
Drumnadrochit Highld 139 5030
Drumnagorrach Moray 142 5252
Drumpark D & G 100 8779
Drumrunie Lodge Highld 145 1604
Drumshang S Ayrs 106 2514
Drumuie Highld 136 4546
Drumuillie Highld 140 9420
Drumvaich Stirlg 124 6704
Drunzie P & K 126 1308
Druridge Nthumb 103 2796
Drury Flints 71 2964
Dry Doddington Lincs 63 8546
Dry Drayton Cambs 52 3861
Dry Sandford Oxon 37 4600
Dry Street Essex 40 6986
Drybeck Cumb 94 6615
Drybridge Moray 142 4362
Drybridge N Ayrs 106 3536
Drybrook Gloucs 35 6417
Dryburgh Border 110 5932
Drym Cnwll 2 6133
Drymen Stirlg 115 4788
Drymuir Abers 143 9046
Drynoch Highld 136 4031
Dryslwyn Carmth 32 5520
Dryton Shrops 59 5806
Dubford Abers 143 7963
Dublin Suffk 54 1669
Duchally Highld 145 3817
Duck End Beds 38 0544
Duck End Cambs 52 2464
Duck End Essex 40 6526
Duck End Essex 53 6833
Duck's Cross Beds 52 1156
Duckend Green Essex 40 7223
Duckington Ches 71 4851
Ducklington Oxon 36 3507
Duddingston C Edin 117 2872
Duddington Nhants 51 9800
Duddlestone Somset 20 2321
Duddleswell E Susx 16 4628
Duddlewick Shrops 59 6583
Duddo Nthumb 110 9342
Duddon Ches 71 5164
Duddon Bridge Cumb 86 1988
Dudleston Shrops 71 3438
Dudleston Heath Shrops 59 3736
Dudley T & W 103 2573
Dudley W Mids 60 9490
Dudley Hill W York 82 1830
Dudley Port W Mids 60 9691
Dudnill Shrops 47 6474
Dudsbury Dorset 12 0798
Dudswell Herts 38 9609
Duffield Derbys 62 3443
Duffryn Neath 33 8495
Dufftown Moray 141 3240
Duffus Moray 141 1668
Dufton Cumb 94 6825
Duggleby N York 90 8767
Duirinish Highld 137 7831
Duisdalemore Highld 129 7013
Duisky Highld 130 0076
Duke Street Suffk 54 0742
Dukestown Blae G 33 1410
Dukinfield Gt Man 79 9397
Dulas IOA 68 4789
Dulcote Somset 21 5644
Dulford Devon 9 0706
Dull P & K 125 8049
Dullatur N Lans 116 7476
Dullingham Cambs 53 6357
Dullingham Ley Cambs 53 6456
Dulnain Bridge Highld 141 9925
Duloe Beds 52 1560
Duloe Cnwll 5 2358
Dulverton Somset 20 9127
Dulwich Gt Lon 27 3373
Dumbarton W Duns 115 3975
Dumbleton Gloucs 47 0135
Dumfries D & G 100 9776
Dumgoyne Stirlg 115 5283
Dummer Hants 24 5846
Dumpton Kent 29 3966
Dun Angus 135 6659
Dunalastair P & K 132 7158
Dunan Ag & B 114 1571
Dunan Highld 137 5828
Dunan P & K 124 4757
Dunaverty Ag & B 105 6807
Dunball Somset 21 3141
Dunbar E Loth 118 6778
Dunbeath Highld 151 1629
Dunbeg Ag & B 122 8833
Dunblane Stirlg 116 7801
Dunbog Fife 126 2817
Dunbridge Hants 23 3226
Duncanston Highld 139 5856
Duncanstone Abers 142 5726
Dunchideock Devon 9 8787
Dunchurch Warwks 50 4871
Duncote Nhants 49 6750
Duncow D & G 100 9683
Duncrievie P & K 126 1309
Duncton W Susx 14 9617
Dundee Dund C 126 4030
Dundee Airport 126 3728
Dundon Somset 21 4832
Dundonald S Ayrs 106 3634
Dundonnell Highld 145 0987
Dundraw Cumb 93 2149
Dundreggan Highld 131 3214
Dundrennan D & G 99 7447
Dundry Somset 21 5666
Dunecht Abers 135 7509
Dunfermline Fife 117 0987
Dunfield Gloucs 36 1497
Dunford Bridge S York 82 1502
Dungate Kent 28 9159
Dungavel S Lans 107 6537
Dunge Wilts 22 8954
Dungworth S York 74 2789
Dunham Notts 75 8074
Dunham Town Gt Man 79 7387
Dunham Woodhouses Gt Man 79 7287
Dunham-on-the-Hill Ches 71 4772
Dunhampstead Worcs 47 9160
Dunhampton Worcs 47 8466
Dunholme Lincs 76 0279
Dunino Fife 127 5311
Dunipace Falk 116 8083
Dunk's Green Kent 27 6152
Dunkeld P & K 125 0242
Dunkerton Somset 22 7159
Dunkeswell Devon 9 1407
Dunkeswick W York 82 3047
Dunkirk Ches 71 3872
Dunkirk Gloucs 35 7885
Dunkirk Kent 29 0759
Dunkirk Staffs 72 8152
Dunkirk Wilts 22 9962
Dunlappie Angus 134 5867
Dunley Hants 24 4553
Dunley Worcs 47 7869
Dunlop E Ayrs 115 4049
Dunmaglass Highld 140 5922
Dunmere Cnwll 4 0467
Dunmore Falk 116 8989
Dunn Street Kent 28 7961
Dunnet Highld 151 2171
Dunnichen Angus 127 5048
Dunning P & K 125 0114
Dunnington E R Yk 85 1551
Dunnington N York 83 6652
Dunnington Warwks 48 0654
Dunnockshaw Lancs 81 8127
Dunoon Ag & B 114 1776
Dunphail Moray 141 0048
Dunragit D & G 98 1557
Duns Border 119 7853
Duns Tew Oxon 49 4528
Dunsa Derbys 74 2470
Dunsby Lincs 64 1026
Dunscar Gt Man 81 7113
Dunscore D & G 100 8684
Dunscroft S York 83 6409
Dunsdale N York 97 6019
Dunsden Green Oxon 37 7377
Dunsdon Devon 18 3008
Dunsfold Surrey 14 0035
Dunsford Devon 8 8189
Dunshalt Fife 126 2410
Dunshillock Abers 143 9848
Dunsill Notts 75 4661
Dunsley N York 90 8511
Dunsley Staffs 60 8583
Dunsmore Bucks 38 8605
Dunsop Bridge Lancs 81 6649
Dunstable Beds 38 0122
Dunstall Staffs 73 1820
Dunstall Common Worcs 47 8843
Dunstall Green Suffk 53 7460
Dunstan Nthumb 111 2419
Dunstan Steads Nthumb 111 2422
Dunster Somset 20 9943
Dunston Lincs 76 0662
Dunston Norfk 67 2202
Dunston Staffs 72 9217
Dunston T & W 96 2362
Dunston Heath Staffs 72 9017
Dunstone Devon 6 5951
Dunstone Devon 7 7175
Dunsville S York 83 6407
Dunswell E R Yk 85 0735
Dunsyre S Lans 117 0748
Dunterton Devon 5 3779
Dunthrop Oxon 48 3528
Duntisbourne Abbots Gloucs 35 9607
Duntisbourne Rouse Gloucs 35 9805
Duntish Dorset 11 6906
Duntocher W Duns 115 4872
Dunton Beds 39 2344
Dunton Bucks 38 8224
Dunton Norfk 66 8830
Dunton Bassett Leics 50 5490
Dunton Green Kent 27 5157
Dunton Wayletts Essex 40 6590
Duntulm Highld 136 4174
Dunure S Ayrs 106 2515
Dunvant Swans 32 5993
Dunvegan Highld 136 2547
Dunwich Suffk 55 4770
Dunwood Staffs 72 9455
Durdar Cumb 93 4051
Durgan Cnwll 3 7727
Durham Dur 96 2742
Durham Cathedral 96 2742
Durisdeer D & G 108 8903
Durisdeermill D & G 108 8804
Durkar W York 82 3116
Durleigh Somset 20 2736
Durley Hants 13 5116
Durley Wilts 23 2364
Durley Street Hants 13 5217
Durlock Kent 29 2757
Durlock Kent 29 3164
Durlow Common Gloucs 47 6339
Durmgley Angus 127 4250
Durn Gt Man 82 9416
Durness Highld 149 4068
Duror Highld 122 9955
Durran Ag & B 122 9607
Durrington W Susx 14 1105
Durrington Wilts 23 1544
Durris Abers 135 7796
Dursley Gloucs 35 7598
Dursley Cross Gloucs 35 6920
Durston Somset 20 2928
Durweston Dorset 11 8508
Duston Nhants 49 7261
Duthil Highld 140 9324
Dutlas Powys 45 2177
Duton Hill Essex 40 6027
Dutson Cnwll 5 3485
Dutton Ches 71 5779
Duxford Cambs 53 4846
Duxford Oxon 36 3600
Duxford Aircraft Museum 53 4645
Dwygyfylchi Conwy 69 7376
Dwyran IOA 68 4465
Dyce Aber C 135 8812
Dyer's End Essex 53 7238
Dyfatty Carmth 32 4500
Dyffrydan Gwynd 57 6914
Dyffryn Brdgnd 33 8593
Dyffryn Myr Td 33 0603
Dyffryn V Glam 33 0971
Dyffryn Ardudwy Gwynd 57 5823
Dyffryn Castell Cerdgn 43 7782
Dyffryn Cellwen Neath 33 8510
Dyke Lincs 64 1022
Dyke Moray 140 9858
Dykehead Angus 126 2453
Dykehead Angus 134 3859
Dykehead N Lans 116 8759
Dykehead Stirlg 115 5997
Dykelands Abers 135 7068
Dykends Angus 133 2557
Dykeside Abers 142 7243
Dylife Powys 43 8694
Dymchurch Kent 17 1029
Dymock Gloucs 47 7031
Dyrham Gloucs 35 7475
Dysart Fife 117 3093
Dyserth Denbgs 70 0578

E

Eachway Worcs 60 9876
Eachwick Nthumb 103 1171
Eagland Hill Lancs 80 4345
Eagle Lincs 76 8766
Eagle Barnsdale Lincs 76 8865
Eagle Moor Lincs 76 8868
Eaglescliffe Dur 96 4215
Eaglesfield Cumb 92 0928
Eaglesfield D & G 101 2374
Eaglesham E Rens 115 5751
Eagley Gt Man 81 7112
Eairy IOM 158 2977
Eakley Lanes Bucks 38 8250
Eakring Notts 75 6762
Ealand Lincs 84 7811
Ealing Gt Lon 26 1780
Eals Nthumb 94 6756
Eamont Bridge Cumb 94 5228
Earby Lancs 81 9046
Earcroft Lancs 81 6823
Eardington Shrops 60 7290
Eardisland Herefs 46 4158
Eardisley Herefs 46 3149
Eardiston Shrops 59 3725
Eardiston Worcs 47 6968
Earith Cambs 52 3875
Earl Shilton Leics 50 4697
Earl Soham Suffk 55 2363
Earl Sterndale Derbys 74 0966
Earl Stonham Suffk 54 1059
Earl's Croome Worcs 47 8642
Earl's Down E Susx 16 6419
Earl's Green Suffk 54 0366
Earle Nthumb 111 9826
Earlestown Mersyd 78 5795
Earley Berks 24 7472
Earlham Norfk 67 1908
Earlish Highld 136 3861
Earls Barton Nhants 51 8563
Earls Colne Essex 40 8528
Earls Common Worcs 47 9559

Earlsditton Elmbridge

283

Earlsditton Shrops 47 6275
Earlsdon W Mids 61 3278
Earlsferry Fife 118 4800
Earlsfield Gt Lon 27 2573
Earlsford Abers 143 8334
Earlsheaton W York 82 2621
Earlston Border 110 5738
Earlston E Ayrs 106 4035
Earlswood Surrey 15 2749
Earlswood Warwks 61 1174
Earlswood Common Mons 34 4594
Earnley W Susx 14 8196
Earnshaw Bridge Lancs 80 5222
Earsdon Nthumb 103 1993
Earsdon T & W 103 3272
Earsham Norfk 55 3288
Earswick N York 90 6157
Eartham W Susx 14 9309
Earthcott Gloucs 35 6585
Easby N York 90 5708
Easdale Ag & B 122 7417
Easebourne W Susx 14 9023
Easenhall Warwks 50 4679
Eashing Surrey 25 9443
Easington Bucks 37 6810
Easington Dur 96 4143
Easington E R Yk 85 3919
Easington N York 97 7417
Easington Nthumb 111 1234
Easington Oxon 37 6697
Easington Colliery Dur 96 4344
Easington Lane T & W 96 3646
Easingwold N York 90 5269
Easole Street Kent 29 2652
Eassie and Nevay Angus 126 3344
East Aberthaw V Glam 20 0366
East Allington Devon 7 7748
East Anstey Devon 19 8626
East Anton Hants 23 3747
East Appleton N York 89 2395
East Ashey IOW 13 5888
East Ashling W Susx 14 8107
East Aston Hants 24 4445
East Ayton N York 91 9985
East Balsdon Cnwll 5 2898
East Bank Blae G 33 2105
East Barkwith Lincs 76 1681
East Barming Kent 28 7254
East Barnby N York 90 8212
East Barnet Gt Lon 27 2795
East Barns E Loth 119 7176
East Barsham Norfk 66 9133
East Beckham Norfk 66 1639
East Bedfont Gt Lon 26 0873
East Bergholt Suffk 54 0734
East Bierley W York 82 1929
East Bilney Norfk 66 9519
East Blatchington E Susx 16 4800
East Bloxworth Dorset 11 8894
East Boldon T & W 96 3661
East Boldre Hants 12 3700
East Bolton Nthumb 111 1216
East Bower Somset 21 3237
East Bradenham Norfk 66 9308
East Brent Somset 21 3451
East Bridgford Notts 63 6943
East Briscoe Dur 95 9719
East Buckland Devon 19 6831
East Budleigh Devon 9 0684
East Burnham Bucks 26 9584
East Burton Dorset 11 8287
East Butsfield Dur 95 1145
East Butterwick Lincs 84 8306
East Calder W Loth 117 0867
East Carleton Norfk 66 1701
East Carlton Nhants 51 8389
East Carlton W York 82 2143
East Challow Oxon 36 3888
East Charleton Devon 7 7642
East Chelborough Dorset 10 5505
East Chevington Nthumb 103 2699
East Chiltington E Susx 15 3715
East Chinnock Somset 10 4913
East Chisenbury Wilts 23 1452
East Cholderton Hants 23 2945
East Clandon Surrey 26 0651
East Claydon Bucks 49 7325
East Clevedon Somset 34 4171
East Coker Somset 10 5412
East Combe Somset 20 1631
East Compton Somset 21 6141
East Cornworthy Devon 7 8455
East Cote Cumb 92 1255
East Cottingwith E R Yk 84 7042
East Cowes IOW 13 5095
East Cowick E R Yk 83 6620
East Cowton N York 89 3003
East Cramlington Nthumb 103 2776
East Cranmore Somset 22 6743
East Creech Dorset 11 9382
East Curthwaite Cumb 93 3348
East Dean E Susx 16 5598
East Dean Gloucs 35 6520
East Dean Hants 23 2726
East Dean W Susx 14 9012
East Down Devon 19 6041
East Drayton Notts 75 7775
East Dulwich Gt Lon 27 3375
East Dundry Somset 21 5766
East Ella E R Yk 84 0529
East End Beds 38 9642
East End Beds 51 1055
East End Bucks 38 9344
East End E R Yk 85 1931
East End E R Yk 85 2927
East End Essex 39 4210
East End Hants 24 4161
East End Hants 12 3696
East End Herts 39 4527
East End Kent 17 8335
East End Kent 28 9673
East End Oxon 36 3915
East End Somset 34 4770
East End Somset 22 6746
East Everleigh Wilts 23 2053
East Farleigh Kent 28 7353
East Farndon Nhants 50 7184
East Ferry Lincs 75 8199
East Firsby Lincs 76 0085
East Ford Suffk 54 1035
East Fortune E Loth 118 5479
East Garforth W York 83 4133
East Garston Berks 36 3576
East Ginge Oxon 37 4486
East Goscote Leics 63 6413
East Grafton Wilts 23 2560
East Green Suffk 55 4065
East Grimstead Wilts 23 2227
East Grinstead W Susx 15 3938
East Guldeford E Susx 17 9321
East Haddon Nhants 50 6668
East Hagbourne Oxon 37 5288
East Halton Lincs 85 1319
East Ham Gt Lon 27 4283
East Hanney Oxon 36 4193
East Hanningfield Essex 40 7701
East Hardwick W York 83 4618
East Harling Norfk 54 9986
East Harlsey N York 89 4299
East Harnham Wilts 23 1428
East Harptree Somset 21 5655
East Hartburn Dur 96 4217
East Hartford Nthumb 103 2679
East Harting W Susx 14 7919
East Hatch Wilts 22 9228
East Hatley Cambs 52 2850
East Hauxwell N York 89 1693
East Haven Angus 127 5836
East Heckington Lincs 64 1944
East Hedleyhope Dur 96 1540
East Helmsdale Highld 147 0315
East Hendred Oxon 37 4588
East Heslerton N York 91 9276
East Hewish Somset 21 4064
East Hoathly E Susx 16 5216
East Holme Dorset 11 8986
East Horrington Somset 21 5846
East Horsley Surrey 26 0952
East Horton Nthumb 111 0330
East Howe Dorset 12 0795
East Huntington N York 83 6155
East Huntspill Somset 21 3445
East Hyde Beds 38 1217
East Ilkerton Devon 19 7147
East Ilsley Berks 37 4980
East Keal Lincs 77 3863
East Kennett Wilts 23 1167
East Keswick W York 83 3644
East Kilbride S Lans 116 6354
East Kimber Devon 5 4998
East Kirkby Lincs 77 3362
East Knighton Dorset 11 8185
East Knowstone Devon 19 8423
East Knoyle Wilts 22 8830
East Kyloe Nthumb 111 0639
East Lambrook Somset 10 4318
East Langdon Kent 29 3346
East Langton Leics 50 7292
East Laroch Highld 130 0858
East Lavant W Susx 14 8608
East Lavington W Susx 14 9416
East Layton N York 89 1609
East Leake Notts 62 5526
East Learmouth Nthumb 110 8637
East Leigh Devon 8 6905
East Leigh Devon 7 6852
East Leigh Devon 7 7657
East Lexham Norfk 66 8517
East Linton E Loth 118 5977
East Liss Hants 14 7827
East Lockinge Oxon 36 4287
East Lound Lincs 75 7899
East Lulworth Dorset 11 8682
East Lutton N York 91 9469
East Lydeard Somset 20 1829
East Lydford Somset 21 5731
East Malling Kent 28 7056
East Malling Heath Kent 28 6955
East Marden W Susx 14 8014
East Markham Notts 75 7373
East Martin Hants 12 0719
East Marton N York 81 9050
East Meon Hants 13 6822
East Mere Devon 9 9916
East Mersea Essex 41 0414
East Midlands Airport 62 4626
East Molesey Surrey 26 1467
East Morden Dorset 11 9194
East Morton D & G 108 8800
East Morton W York 82 0942
East Ness N York 90 6978
East Newton E R Yk 85 2638
East Norton Leics 50 7800
East Ogwell Devon 7 8370
East Orchard Dorset 11 8317
East Ord Nthumb 119 9751
East Panson Devon 5 3692
East Parley Dorset 12 1097
East Peckham Kent 28 6648
East Pennar Pembks 30 9602
East Pennard Somset 21 5937
East Perry Cambs 52 1566
East Portlemouth Devon 7 7538
East Prawle Devon 7 7836
East Preston W Susx 14 0602
East Pulham Dorset 11 7209
East Putford Devon 18 3616
East Quantoxhead Somset 20 1343
East Rainham Kent 28 8267
East Rainton T & W 96 3347
East Ravendale Lincs 76 2399
East Raynham Norfk 66 8825
East Rigton W York 83 3743
East Rolstone Somset 21 3962
East Rounton N York 89 4203
East Rudham Norfk 66 8228
East Runton Norfk 67 1942
East Ruston Norfk 67 3427
East Saltoun E Loth 118 4767
East Scrafton N York 89 0884
East Sheen Gt Lon 26 2075
East Shefford Berks 36 3874
East Sleekburn Nthumb 103 2883
East Somerton Norfk 67 4719
East Stockwith Lincs 75 7894
East Stoke Dorset 11 8686
East Stoke Notts 75 7549
East Stour Dorset 22 8022
East Stourmouth Kent 29 2662
East Stowford Devon 19 6326
East Stratton Hants 24 5440
East Studdal Kent 29 3149
East Sutton Kent 28 8349
East Taphouse Cnwll 4 1863
East Thirston Nthumb 89 1900
East Tilbury Essex 28 6877
East Tisted Hants 24 7032
East Torrington Lincs 76 1483
East Tuddenham Norfk 66 0711
East Tytherley Hants 23 2929
East Tytherton Wilts 35 9674
East Village Devon 8 8405
East Wall Shrops 59 5293
East Walton Norfk 65 7416
East Water Somset 21 5350
East Week Devon 8 6692
East Wellow Hants 12 3020
East Wemyss Fife 118 3497
East Whitburn W Loth 117 9665
East Wickham Gt Lon 27 4677
East Williamston Pembks 31 0904
East Winch Norfk 65 6916
East Winterslow Wilts 23 2434
East Wittering W Susx 14 7997
East Witton N York 89 1486
East Woodburn Nthumb 102 9086
East Woodhay Hants 24 4061
East Woodlands Somset 22 7944
East Worldham Hants 24 7538
East Wretham Norfk 54 9190
East Youlstone Devon 18 2715
East-the-Water Devon 18 4526
Eastbourne Dur 89 3013
Eastbourne E Susx 16 6199
Eastbridge Suffk 55 4566
Eastbrook V Glam 33 1671
Eastburn W York 82 0144
Eastbury Berks 36 3477
Eastbury Herts 26 1092
Eastby N York 82 0154
Eastchurch Kent 28 9871
Eastcombe Gloucs 35 8904
Eastcote Gt Lon 26 1088
Eastcote Nhants 49 6853
Eastcote W Mids 61 1979
Eastcott Cnwll 18 2515
Eastcott Wilts 23 0255
Eastcourt Wilts 35 9792
Eastcourt Wilts 23 2361
Eastdown Devon 7 8249
Eastend Essex 40 9492
Eastend S Lans 108 9537
Easter Balmoral Abers 133 2694
Easter Compton Gloucs 34 5782
Easter Dalziel Highld 140 7550
Easter Howgate Mdloth 117 2463
Easter Kinkell Highld 139 5755
Easter Moniack Highld 139 5543
Easter Ord Abers 135 8304
Easter Pitkierie Fife 127 5606
Easter Skeld Shet 153 3144
Easter Softlaw Border 110 7532
Eastergate W Susx 14 9405
Easterhouse C Glas 116 6865
Eastern Green W Mids 61 2879
Easterton Wilts 23 0254
Eastertown Somset 21 3454
Eastfield N Lans 116 8964
Eastfield N York 91 0484
Eastgate Dur 95 9538
Eastgate Lincs 64 1019
Eastgate Norfk 66 1423
Eastham Mersyd 78 3680
Eastham Ferry Mersyd 78 3681
Easthampstead Berks 25 8667
Easthampton Herefs 46 4063
Eastheath Berks 25 7967
Easthope Shrops 59 5695
Easthorpe Essex 40 9121
Easthorpe Notts 75 7053
Eastington Devon 19 7408
Eastington Gloucs 36 1213
Eastington Gloucs 35 7705
Eastlands D & G 100 8172
Eastleach Martin Gloucs 36 2004
Eastleach Turville Gloucs 36 1905
Eastleigh Devon 18 4827
Eastleigh Hants 13 4519
Eastling Kent 28 9656
Eastmoor Norfk 65 7303
Eastney Hants 13 6698
Eastnor Herefs 47 7237
Eastoft Lincs 84 8016
Easton Berks 24 4172
Easton Cambs 52 1371
Easton Cumb 93 2759
Easton Devon 8 7289
Easton Dorset 11 6971
Easton Hants 24 5132
Easton IOW 12 3486
Easton Lincs 63 9326
Easton Norfk 66 1310
Easton Somset 21 5147
Easton Suffk 55 2858
Easton Wilts 35 8970
Easton Grey Wilts 35 8887
Easton Maudit Nhants 51 8858
Easton on the Hill Nhants 64 0104
Easton Royal Wilts 23 2060
Easton-in-Gordano Somset 34 5175
Eastpeek Devon 5 3494
Eastrea Cambs 64 2997
Eastriggs D & G 101 2466
Eastrington E R Yk 84 7929
Eastrop Wilts 36 2092
Eastry Kent 29 3054
Eastshaw W Susx 14 8724
Eastville Bristl 35 6174
Eastville Lincs 77 4056
Eastwell Leics 63 7728
Eastwick Herts 39 4311
Eastwood Essex 40 8688
Eastwood Notts 62 4646
Eastwood W York 82 9726
Eastwood End Cambs 65 4292
Eathorpe Warwks 48 3969
Eaton Ches 71 5763
Eaton Ches 72 8765
Eaton Leics 63 7928
Eaton Norfk 67 2006
Eaton Notts 75 7077
Eaton Oxon 37 4403
Eaton Shrops 59 3789
Eaton Shrops 59 5089
Eaton Bishop Herefs 46 4439
Eaton Bray Beds 38 9720
Eaton Constantine Shrops 59 5906
Eaton Ford Beds 52 1759
Eaton Green Beds 38 9621
Eaton Hastings Oxon 36 2598
Eaton Mascott Shrops 59 5305
Eaton Socon Cambs 52 1759
Eaton upon Tern Shrops 72 6523
Eaves Brow Ches 79 6393
Eaves Green W Mids 61 2682
Ebberston N York 91 8982
Ebbesborne Wake Wilts 22 9924
Ebbw Vale Blae G 33 1609
Ebchester Dur 95 1055
Ebdon Somset 21 3664
Ebford Devon 9 9887
Ebley Gloucs 35 8205
Ebnal Ches 71 4948
Ebnall Herefs 46 4758
Ebrington Gloucs 48 1840
Ebsworthy Town Devon 5 5090
Ecchinswell Hants 24 4959
Ecclaw Border 119 7568
Ecclefechan D & G 101 1974
Eccles Border 110 7641
Eccles Gt Man 79 7798
Eccles Kent 28 7360
Eccles Green Herefs 46 3748
Eccles on Sea Norfk 67 4128
Eccles Road Norfk 54 0189
Ecclesall S York 74 3284
Ecclesfield S York 74 3593
Eccleshall Staffs 72 8329
Eccleshill W York 82 1736
Ecclesmachan W Loth 117 0573
Eccleston Ches 71 4162
Eccleston Lancs 80 5217
Eccleston Mersyd 78 4895
Eccleston Green Lancs 80 5216
Echt Abers 135 7405
Eckford Border 110 7026
Eckington Derbys 75 4379
Eckington Worcs 47 9241
Ecton Nhants 51 8263
Ecton Staffs 74 0958
Edale Derbys 74 1285
Eday Airport 153 5634
Edburton W Susx 15 2311
Edderside Cumb 92 1045
Edderton Highld 146 7084
Eddington Kent 29 1867
Eddleston Border 117 2447
Eddlewood S Lans 116 7153
Eden Mount Cumb 87 4077
Eden Park Gt Lon 27 3667
Edenbridge Kent 16 4446
Edenfield Lancs 81 8019
Edenhall Cumb 94 5632
Edenham Lincs 64 0621
Edensor Derbys 74 2469
Edentaggart Ag & B 115 3293
Edenthorpe S York 83 6206
Edern Gwynd 56 2739
Edgarley Somset 21 5238
Edgbaston W Mids 61 0684
Edgcombe Cnwll 2 7133
Edgcott Bucks 37 6722
Edgcott Somset 19 8438
Edge Gloucs 35 8409
Edge Shrops 59 3908
Edge End Gloucs 34 5913
Edge Green Ches 71 4851
Edgebolton Shrops 59 5721
Edgefield Norfk 66 0934
Edgefield Green Norfk 66 0934
Edgefold Gt Man 79 7005
Edgehill Warwks 48 3747
Edgerley Shrops 59 3518
Edgerton W York 82 1317
Edgeside Lancs 81 8322
Edgeworth Gloucs 35 9406
Edgeworthy Devon 19 8413
Edgiock Worcs 48 0461
Edgmond Shrops 72 7119
Edgmond Marsh Shrops 72 7120
Edgton Shrops 59 3885
Edgware Gt Lon 26 1991
Edgworth Lancs 81 7416
Edial Staffs 61 0808
Edinbane Highld 136 3450
Edinburgh C Edin 117 2573
Edinburgh Airport 117 1473
Edinburgh Castle 117 2573
Edinburgh Zoo 117 2173
Edingale Staffs 61 2111
Edingham D & G 100 8363
Edingley Notts 75 6655
Edingthorpe Norfk 67 3132
Edingthorpe Green Norfk 67 3031
Edington Border 119 8955
Edington Nthumb 103 1582
Edington Somset 21 3839
Edington Wilts 22 9253
Edington Burtle Somset 21 3943
Edingworth Somset 21 3653
Edith Weston Rutlnd 63 9205
Edithmead Somset 21 3249
Edlesborough Bucks 38 9719
Edlingham Nthumb 111 1109
Edlington Lincs 76 2371
Edmond Castle Cumb 94 4958
Edmondsham Dorset 12 0611
Edmondsley Dur 96 2349
Edmondthorpe Leics 63 8517
Edmonton Cnwll 4 9672
Edmonton Gt Lon 27 3492
Edmundbyers Dur 95 0150
Ednam Border 110 7337
Ednaston Derbys 73 2341
Edradynate P & K 125 8751
Edrom Border 119 8255
Edstaston Shrops 59 5132
Edstone Warwks 48 1861
Edvin Loach Herefs 47 6658
Edwalton Notts 62 5935
Edwardstone Suffk 54 9442
Edwardsville Myr Td 33 0896
Edwinsford Carmth 44 6334
Edwinstowe Notts 75 6266
Edworth Beds 39 2241
Edwyn Ralph Herefs 47 6457
Edzell Angus 134 6068
Efail Isaf Rhondd 33 0884
Efail-fach Neath 32 7895
Efail-Rhyd Powys 58 1626
Efailnewydd Gwynd 56 3535
Efailwen Carmth 31 1325
Efenechtyd Denbgs 70 1155
Effgill D & G 101 3092
Effingham Surrey 26 1153
Efflinch Staffs 73 1816
Efford Devon 9 8901
Egbury Hants 24 4352
Egdean W Susx 14 9920
Egerton Gt Man 81 7014
Egerton Kent 28 9147
Eggbuckland Devon 6 5057
Eggesford Devon 19 6811
Eggington Beds 38 9525
Egginton Derbys 73 2628
Egglescliffe Dur 89 4113
Eggleston Dur 95 9923
Egham Surrey 25 0071
Egham Wick Surrey 25 9870
Eginswell Devon 7 8866
Egleton Rutlnd 63 8707
Eglingham Nthumb 111 1019
Egloshayle Cnwll 4 0072
Egloskerry Cnwll 5 2786
Eglwys Cross Wrexhm 71 4740
Eglwys-Brewis V Glam 20 0068
Eglwysbach Conwy 69 8070
Eglwysfach Cerdgn 43 6996
Eglwyswrw Pembks 31 1438
Egmanton Notts 75 7368
Egremont Cumb 86 0110
Egremont Mersyd 78 3192
Egton N York 90 8006
Egton Bridge N York 90 8004
Eight and Forty E R Yk 84 8529
Eight Ash Green Essex 40 9425
Eilanreach Highld 129 8018
Elan Village Powys 45 9364
Elberton Gloucs 34 6088
Elbridge W Susx 14 9101
Elburton Devon 6 5353
Elcombe Wilts 36 1280
Elcot Berks 36 3969
Elder Street Essex 53 5734
Eldernell Cambs 64 3298
Eldersfield Worcs 47 7931
Elderslie Rens 115 4463
Eldmire N York 89 4274
Eldon Dur 96 2328
Eldwick W York 82 1240
Elfhill Abers 135 8085
Elford Nthumb 111 1831
Elford Staffs 61 1810
Elgin Moray 141 2162
Elgol Highld 128 5213
Elham Kent 29 1744
Elie Fife 118 4900
Elilaw Nthumb 111 9708
Elim IOA 68 3584
Eling Hants 12 3612
Elkesley Notts 75 6975
Elkstone Gloucs 35 9612
Ella Abers 142 6459
Ellacombe Devon 7 9164
Ellanbeich Ag & B 122 7417
Elland W York 82 1120
Elland Lower Edge W York 82 1221
Ellary Ag & B 113 7376
Ellastone Staffs 73 1143
Ellel Lancs 80 4856
Ellemford Border 119 7260
Ellen's Green Surrey 14 0935
Ellenborough Cumb 92 0435
Ellenbrook Gt Man 79 7201
Ellenhall Staffs 72 8426
Ellerbeck N York 89 4396
Ellerby N York 90 7914
Ellerdine Heath Shrops 59 6122
Ellerhayes Devon 9 9702
Elleric Ag & B 123 0448
Ellerker E R Yk 84 9229
Ellers N York 82 0043
Ellerton E R Yk 84 7039
Ellerton N York 89 2598
Ellerton Shrops 72 7125
Ellesborough Bucks 38 8306
Ellesmere Shrops 59 3934
Ellesmere Port Ches 71 4076
Ellicombe Somset 20 9844
Ellingham Hants 12 1408
Ellingham Norfk 67 3592
Ellingham Nthumb 111 1725
Ellingstring N York 89 1783
Ellington Cambs 52 1671
Ellington Nthumb 103 2791
Ellington Thorpe Cambs 52 1670
Elliots Green Somset 22 7945
Ellisfield Hants 24 6446
Ellishader Highld 137 5065
Ellistown Leics 62 4310
Ellon Abers 143 9530
Ellonby Cumb 93 4235
Ellough Suffk 55 4486
Elloughton E R Yk 84 9428
Ellwood Gloucs 34 5908
Elm Cambs 65 4707
Elm Green Essex 40 7705
Elm Grove Norfk 67 4803
Elm Park Gt Lon 27 5385
Elmbridge Worcs 47 9068

284

Fetcham Fulstone

Fetcham Surrey 26 1455
Fetterangus Abers 143 9850
Fettercairn Abers 135 6573
Fewcott Oxon 49 5428
Fewston N York 82 1954
Ffair Rhos Cerdgn 43 7368
Ffairfach Carmth 32 6321
Ffald-y-Brenin Carmth 44 6344
Ffawyddog Powys 33 2018
Ffestiniog Gwynd 57 7042
Ffestiniog Railway 57 6541
Ffordd-las Denbgs 70 1264
Fforest Carmth 32 5704
Fforest Mons 34 2820
Fforest Fach Swans 32 6295
Fforest Goch Neath 32 7401
Ffostrasol Cerdgn 42 3747
Ffrith Flints 70 2855
Ffynnon-Oer Cerdgn 44 5353
Ffynnonddewi Cerdgn 42 3852
Ffynnongroyw Flints 70 1382
Fiag Lodge Highld 149 4528
Fickleshole Surrey 27 3860
Fiddington Gloucs 47 9231
Fiddington Somset 20 2140
Fiddleford Dorset 11 8013
Fiddlers Green Cnwll 3 8155
Fiddlers Hamlet Essex 27 4701
Field Staffs 73 0233
Field Broughton Cumb 87 3881
Field Dalling Norfk 66 0038
Field Head Leics 62 4909
Fieldhead Cumb 93 4539
Fife Keith Moray 142 4250
Fifehead Magdalen Dorset 22 7821
Fifehead Neville Dorset 11 7610
Fifehead St Quintin Dorset 11 7710
Fifield Berks 26 9076
Fifield Oxon 36 2418
Fifield Wilts 23 1450
Figheldean Wilts 23 1547
Filands Wilts 35 9388
Filby Norfk 67 4613
Filey N York 91 1180
Filgrave Bucks 38 8648
Filkins Oxon 36 2304
Filleigh Devon 19 6627
Filleigh Devon 19 7410
Fillingham Lincs 76 9485
Fillongley Warwks 61 2887
Filmore Hill Hants 13 6627
Filton Gloucs 34 6079
Fimber E R Yk 91 8960
Finavon Angus 127 4956
Fincham Norfk 65 6806
Finchampstead Berks 25 7963
Fincharn Ag & B 122 9003
Finchdean Hants 13 7312
Finchingfield Essex 40 6832
Finchley Gt Lon 27 2690
Findern Derbys 73 3030
Findhorn Moray 141 0364
Findhorn Bridge Highld 140 8027
Findo Gask P & K 125 0019
Findochty Moray 142 4667
Findon Abers 135 9397
Findon W Susx 14 1208
Findon Mains Highld 140 6060
Findrack House Abers 134 6004
Finedon Nhants 51 9172
Fineshade Nhants 51 9798
Fingal Street Suffk 55 2169
Fingask P & K 126 1619
Fingest Bucks 37 7791
Finghall N York 89 1889
Fingland Cumb 93 2557
Fingland D & G 107 7517
Finglesham Kent 29 3353
Fingringhoe Essex 41 0220
Finkle Green Essex 53 7040
Finkle Street S York 74 3099
Finlarig Stirlg 124 5733
Finmere Oxon 49 6332
Finnart P & K 124 5157
Finningham Suffk 54 0669
Finningley S York 75 6799
Finsbay W Isls 152 0786
Finstall Worcs 60 9770
Finsthwaite Cumb 87 3687
Finstock Oxon 36 3616
Finstown Ork 153 3513
Fintry Abers 142 7554
Fintry Stirlg 116 6186
Finzean Abers 134 5993
Fionnphort Ag & B 120 3023
Fionnsbhagh W Isls 152 0786
Fir Tree Dur 96 1434
Firbank Cumb 87 6293
Firbeck S York 75 5688
Firby N York 89 2686
Firby N York 90 7466
Firgrove Gt Man 81 9113
Firsby Lincs 77 4562
Firsdown Dorset 23 2133
Fishbourne IOW 13 5592
Fishbourne W Susx 14 8304
Fishbourne Roman Palace 14 8305
Fishburn Dur 96 3632
Fishcross Clacks 116 8995
Fisher W Susx 14 8700
Fisher's Pond Hants 13 4820
Fisher's Row Lancs 80 4148
Fisherford Abers 142 6735
Fisherrow E Loth 118 3472
Fisherstreet W Susx 14 9431
Fisherton Highld 140 7451
Fisherton S Ayrs 106 2717
Fisherton de la Mere Wilts 22 0038
Fisherwick Staffs 61 1708
Fishery Estate Berks 26 8980
Fishguard Pembks 30 9537
Fishlake S York 83 6513
Fishleigh Devon 8 5405
Fishmere End Lincs 64 2837
Fishnish Pier Ag & B 121 6542
Fishpond Bottom Dorset 10 3698
Fishponds Bristl 35 6375
Fishpool Gt Man 79 8009
Fishtoft Lincs 64 3642
Fishtoft Drove Lincs 77 3148
Fishwick Lancs 81 5629
Fiskavaig Highld 136 3334
Fiskerton Lincs 76 0471
Fiskerton Notts 75 7351
Fitling E R Yk 85 2534
Fittleton Wilts 23 1449
Fittleworth W Susx 14 0019
Fitton End Cambs 65 4313
Fitz Shrops 59 4417
Fitzhead Somset 20 1228
Fitzroy Somset 20 1927
Fitzwilliam W York 83 4115
Five Ash Down E Susx 16 4723
Five Ashes E Susx 16 5525
Five Bells Somset 20 0642
Five Bridges Herefs 47 6446
Five Lanes Mons 34 4490
Five Oak Green Kent 16 6445
Five Oaks Jersey 158 0000
Five Oaks W Susx 14 0928
Five Roads Carmth 32 4805
Five Wents Kent 28 8050
Fivecrosses Ches 71 5276
Fivehead Somset 21 3522
Fivelanes Cnwll 5 2280
Flack's Green Essex 40 7614
Flackwell Heath Bucks 26 8989
Fladbury Worcs 47 9946
Fladdabister Shet 153 4332
Flagg Derbys 74 1368
Flamborough E R Yk 91 2270
Flamingo Land Theme Park 90 7880
Flamstead Herts 38 0714
Flansham W Susx 14 9601
Flanshaw W York 82 3020
Flappit Spring W York 82 0536
Flasby N York 82 9456
Flash Staffs 74 0266
Flashader Highld 136 3453
Flaunden Herts 26 0100
Flawborough Notts 63 7842
Flawith N York 90 4865
Flax Bourton Somset 21 5069
Flaxby N York 89 3957
Flaxley Gloucs 35 6815
Flaxmere Ches 71 5572
Flaxpool Somset 20 1435
Flaxton N York 90 6762
Fleckney Leics 50 6493
Flecknoe Warwks 49 5163
Fledborough Notts 75 8072
Fleet Dorset 10 6380
Fleet Hants 13 7201
Fleet Hants 25 8053
Fleet Lincs 64 3823
Fleet Hargate Lincs 65 3925
Fleetend Hants 13 5006
Fleetwood Lancs 80 3348
Flemingston V Glam 20 0169
Flemington S Lans 116 6559
Flempton Suffk 54 8169
Fletcher Green Kent 16 5349
Fletchersbridge Cnwll 4 1065
Fletchertown Cumb 93 2042
Fletching E Susx 16 4223
Fleur-de-lis Caerph 33 1696
Flexbury Cnwll 18 2107
Flexford Surrey 25 9350
Flimby Cumb 92 0233
Flimwell E Susx 17 7131
Flint Flints 70 2472
Flint Mountain Flints 70 2470
Flint's Green W Mids 61 2680
Flintham Notts 63 7445
Flinton E R Yk 85 2136
Flishinghurst Kent 28 7537
Flitcham Norfk 65 7326
Flitton Beds 38 0535
Flitwick Beds 38 0334
Flixborough Lincs 84 8714
Flixborough Stather Lincs 84 8614
Flixton Gt Man 79 7494
Flixton N York 91 0479
Flixton Suffk 55 3186
Flockton W York 82 2314
Flockton Green W York 82 2515
Flodden Nthumb 110 9235
Flodigarry Highld 136 4671
Flookburgh Cumb 87 3675
Flordon Norfk 66 1897
Flore Nhants 49 6460
Flotterton Nthumb 103 9902
Flowers Green E Susx 16 6311
Flowton Suffk 54 0846
Flushdyke W York 82 2820
Flushing Cnwll 3 8034
Fluxton Devon 9 0893
Flyford Flavell Worcs 47 9755
Fobbing Essex 40 7183
Fochabers Moray 141 3458
Fochriw Caerph 33 1005
Fockerby Lincs 84 8519
Foddington Somset 21 5729
Foel Powys 58 9911
Foel y Dyffryn Brdgnd 33 8594
Foelgastell Carmth 32 5414
Foggathorpe E R Yk 84 7537
Fogo Border 110 7649
Fogwatt Moray 141 2356
Foindle Highld 148 1948
Folda Angus 133 1963
Fole Staffs 73 0437
Foleshill W Mids 61 3582
Foliejon Park Berks 25 8974
Folke Dorset 11 6613
Folkestone Kent 29 2336
Folkingham Lincs 64 0733
Folkington E Susx 16 5603
Folksworth Cambs 52 1489
Folkton N York 91 0579
Folla Rule Abers 142 7332
Follifoot N York 83 3452
Folly Gate Devon 8 5798
Folly Hill Surrey 25 8348
Fonmon V Glam 20 0467
Font-y-gary V Glam 20 0566
Fonthill Bishop Wilts 22 9333
Fonthill Gifford Wilts 22 9231
Fontmell Magna Dorset 11 8616
Fontmell Parva Dorset 11 8214
Fontwell W Susx 14 9407
Foolow Derbys 74 1976
Foots Cray Gt Lon 27 4770
Forbestown Abers 134 3513
Forcett N York 89 1712
Ford Ag & B 122 8603
Ford Bucks 37 7709
Ford Derbys 74 4080
Ford Devon 18 4124
Ford Devon 6 6150
Ford Devon 7 7940
Ford Gloucs 48 0829
Ford Nthumb 110 9437
Ford Shrops 59 4113
Ford Somset 20 0928
Ford Somset 21 5953
Ford Staffs 73 0653
Ford W Susx 14 9903
Ford Wilts 35 8475
Ford Wilts 23 1632
Ford End Essex 40 6716
Ford Green Lancs 80 4746
Ford Heath Shrops 59 4011
Ford Street Somset 20 1518
Ford's Green Suffk 54 0666
Forda Devon 8 5390
Fordcombe Kent 16 5240
Fordell Fife 117 1588
Forden Powys 58 2201
Forder Devon 8 6789
Forder Green Devon 7 7967
Fordham Cambs 53 6370
Fordham Essex 40 9228
Fordham Norfk 65 6199
Fordham Heath Essex 40 9426
Fordingbridge Hants 12 1414
Fordon E R Yk 91 0475
Fordoun Abers 135 7475
Fordstreet Essex 40 9226
Fordton Devon 8 8399
Fordwells Oxon 36 3013
Fordwich Kent 29 1859
Fordyce Abers 142 5563
Forebridge Staffs 72 9322
Foremark Derbys 62 3326
Forest Guern 158 0000
Forest N York 89 2700
Forest Becks Lancs 81 7851
Forest Chapel Ches 79 9772
Forest Gate Gt Lon 27 4085
Forest Green Surrey 14 1241
Forest Hall Cumb 87 5401
Forest Hall T & W 103 2769
Forest Head Cumb 94 5857
Forest Hill Gt Lon 27 3672
Forest Hill Oxon 37 5807
Forest Lane Head N York 83 3356
Forest Lodge Ag & B 123 2742
Forest Mill Clacks 117 9694
Forest Row E Susx 16 4234
Forest Side IOW 13 4889
Forest Town Notts 75 5662
Forest-in-Teesdale Dur 95 8630
Forestburn Gate Nthumb 103 0696
Forestside W Susx 14 7612
Forfar Angus 127 4550
Forgandenny P & K 125 0818
Forge Powys 57 7699
Forge Hammer Torfn 34 2895
Forge Side Torfn 34 2408
Forgie Moray 141 3854
Forgieside Moray 142 4053
Forgue Abers 142 6145
Forhill Worcs 61 0575
Formby Mersyd 78 3006
Forncett End Norfk 66 1493
Forncett St Mary Norfk 66 1694
Forncett St Peter Norfk 66 1693
Fornham All Saints Suffk 54 8367
Fornham St Martin Suffk 54 8567
Fornside Cumb 93 3220
Forres Moray 141 0358
Forsbrook Staffs 72 9641
Forse Highld 151 2234
Forse House Highld 151 2135
Forshaw Heath Warwks 61 0873
Forsinard Highld 150 8942
Forston Dorset 11 6695
Fort Augustus Highld 131 3709
Fort Hommet Guern 158 0000
Fort le Marchant Guern 158 0000
Fort William Highld 130 1074
Forteviot P & K 125 0517
Forth S Lans 116 9453
Forthampton Gloucs 47 8532
Fortingall P & K 124 7347
Fortnighty Highld 140 9350
Forton Hants 24 4143
Forton Lancs 80 4851
Forton Shrops 59 4316
Forton Somset 10 3307
Forton Staffs 72 7521
Fortrie Abers 142 6645
Fortrose Highld 140 7256
Fortuneswell Dorset 11 6873
Forty Green Bucks 26 9291
Forty Hill Gt Lon 27 3398
Forward Green Suffk 54 1059
Fosbury Wilts 23 3157
Foscot Oxon 36 2421
Foscote Nhants 49 6546
Fosdyke Lincs 64 3133
Fosdyke Bridge Lincs 64 3232
Foss P & K 132 7858
Foss-y-ffin Cerdgn 42 4460
Fossebridge Gloucs 36 0711
Foster Street Essex 39 4809
Fosterhouses S York 83 6514
Foston Derbys 73 1931
Foston Leics 50 6094
Foston Lincs 63 8542
Foston N York 90 6965
Foston on the Wolds E R Yk 85 1055
Fotherby Lincs 77 3191
Fothergill Cumb 92 0234
Fotheringhay Nhants 51 0593
Foul End Warwks 61 2494
Foul Mile E Susx 16 6215
Foulbridge Cumb 93 4248
Foulby W York 83 3917
Foulden Border 119 9355
Foulden Norfk 65 7699
Foulridge Lancs 81 8942
Foulsham Norfk 66 0324
Fountainhall Border 118 4249
Four Ashes Staffs 60 9108
Four Ashes Staffs 60 8087
Four Ashes Suffk 54 0070
Four Ashes W Mids 61 1575
Four Cabots Guern 158 0000
Four Crosses Powys 58 2618
Four Crosses Staffs 60 9509
Four Elms Kent 16 4648
Four Foot Somset 21 5833
Four Forks Somset 20 2336
Four Gates Gt Man 79 6407
Four Gotes Cambs 65 4516
Four Lane End S York 82 2702
Four Lane Ends Ches 71 5561
Four Lanes Cnwll 2 6838
Four Marks Hants 24 6735
Four Mile Bridge IOA 68 2778
Four Oaks E Susx 17 8524
Four Oaks Gloucs 47 6928
Four Oaks W Mids 61 1098
Four Oaks W Mids 61 2480
Four Points Berks 37 5579
Four Roads Carmth 32 4409
Four Shire Stone Warwks 48 2232
Four Throws Kent 17 7729
Four Wents Kent 27 6251
Fourlanes End Ches 72 8059
Fourpenny Highld 147 8094
Fourstones Nthumb 102 8867
Fovant Wilts 22 0028
Foveran Abers 143 9723
Fowey Cnwll 3 1251
Fowley Common Ches 79 6795
Fowlhall Kent 28 6946
Fowlis Angus 126 3233
Fowlis Wester P & K 125 9224
Fowlmere Cambs 53 4245
Fownhope Herefs 46 5834
Fox Corner Surrey 25 9654
Fox Hatch Essex 27 5798
Fox Street Essex 41 0227
Foxbar Rens 115 4561
Foxcombe Devon 5 4887
Foxcote Gloucs 35 0118
Foxcote Somset 22 7155
Foxdale IOM 158 2778
Foxearth Essex 54 8344
Foxendown Kent 27 6466
Foxfield Cumb 86 2185
Foxham Wilts 35 9777
Foxhills Hants 12 3411
Foxhole Cnwll 3 9654
Foxhole Swans 32 6694
Foxholes N York 91 0173
Foxhunt Green E Susx 16 5417
Foxley Nhants 49 6451
Foxley Norfk 66 0422
Foxley Wilts 35 8986
Foxley Green Wilts 35 8985
Foxlydiate Worcs 47 0167
Foxt Staffs 73 0348
Foxton Cambs 52 4148
Foxton Dur 96 3624
Foxton Leics 50 7089
Foxton N York 89 4296
Foxup N York 88 8676
Foxwist Green Ches 71 6268
Foxwood Shrops 47 6276
Foy Herefs 46 5928
Foyers Highld 139 4921
Foynesfield Highld 140 8953
Fraddam Cnwll 2 5834
Fraddon Cnwll 4 9158
Fradley Staffs 61 1513
Fradswell Staffs 73 9931
Fraisthorpe E R Yk 91 1561
Framfield E Susx 16 4920
Framingham Earl Norfk 67 2702
Framingham Pigot Norfk 67 2703
Framlingham Suffk 55 2863
Frampton Dorset 10 6295
Frampton Lincs 64 3239
Frampton Cotterell Gloucs 35 6682
Frampton Mansell Gloucs 35 9202
Frampton on Severn Gloucs 35 7407
Frampton West End Lincs 64 3041
Framsden Suffk 55 1959
Framwellgate Moor Dur 96 2644
Frances Green Lancs 81 6236
Franche Worcs 60 8278
Frandley Ches 71 6379
Frankaborough Devon 5 3991
Frankby Mersyd 78 2486
Frankfort Norfk 67 3024
Franklands Gate Herefs 46 5346
Frankley Worcs 60 9980
Franksbridge Powys 45 1156
Frankton Warwks 50 4270
Frant E Susx 16 5835
Fraserburgh Abers 143 9966
Frating Essex 41 0722
Frating Green Essex 41 0823
Fratton Hants 13 6500
Freathy Cnwll 5 3952
Freckenham Suffk 53 6672
Freckleton Lancs 80 4329
Freebirch Derbys 74 3072
Freeby Leics 63 8020
Freefolk Hants 24 4848
Freehay Staffs 73 0241
Freeland Oxon 36 4112
Freethorpe Norfk 67 4005
Freethorpe Common Norfk 67 4004
Freiston Lincs 64 3743
Fremington Devon 19 5132
Fremington N York 88 0499
French Street Kent 27 4552
Frenchay Gloucs 35 6377
Frenchbeer Devon 8 6785
Frenich P & K 132 8258
Frensham Surrey 25 8441
Freshfield Mersyd 78 2907
Freshford Somset 22 7860
Freshwater IOW 12 3487
Freshwater Bay IOW 12 3485
Freshwater East Pembks 30 0198
Fressingfield Suffk 55 2677
Freston Suffk 54 1638
Freswick Highld 151 3667
Fretherne Gloucs 35 7210
Frettenham Norfk 67 2417
Freuchie Fife 126 2806
Freystrop Pembks 30 9511
Friar Waddon Dorset 11 6486
Friar's Gate E Susx 16 4933
Friars' Hill N York 90 7485
Friday Bridge Cambs 65 4604
Friday Street E Susx 16 6203
Friday Street Suffk 55 2459
Friday Street Suffk 55 3351
Friday Street Suffk 55 3760
Friday Street Surrey 14 1245
Fridaythorpe E R Yk 90 8759
Friden Derbys 74 1660
Friendly W York 82 0524
Friern Barnet Gt Lon 27 2892
Friesland Bay Ag & B 120 1954
Friesthorpe Lincs 76 0683
Frieston Lincs 63 9347
Frieth Bucks 37 7990
Friezeland Notts 75 4750
Frilford Oxon 37 4497
Frilsham Berks 24 5473
Frimley Surrey 25 8757
Frimley Green Surrey 25 8856
Frindsbury Kent 28 7469
Fring Norfk 65 7334
Fringford Oxon 49 6029
Frinsted Kent 28 8957
Frinton-on-Sea Essex 41 2320
Friockheim Angus 127 5949
Friog Gwynd 57 6112
Frisby on the Wreake Leics 63 6917
Friskney Lincs 77 4655
Friskney Eaudike Lincs 77 4755
Friston E Susx 16 5598
Friston Suffk 55 4160
Fritchley Derbys 74 3552
Frith Bank Lincs 77 3147
Frith Common Worcs 47 6969
Fritham Hants 12 2314
Frithelstock Devon 18 4619
Frithelstock Stone Devon 18 4518
Frithend Hants 25 8039
Frithsden Herts 38 0109
Frithville Lincs 77 3150
Frittenden Kent 28 8140
Frittiscombe Devon 7 8043
Fritton Norfk 67 4600
Fritton Norfk 67 2293
Fritwell Oxon 49 5229
Frizinghall W York 82 1435
Frizington Cumb 92 0316
Frocester Gloucs 35 7803
Frodesley Shrops 59 5101
Frodsham Ches 71 5177
Frog End Cambs 52 3946
Frog End Cambs 53 5358
Frog Pool Worcs 47 8065
Frogden Border 110 7628
Froggatt Derbys 74 2476
Froghall Staffs 73 0247
Frogham Hants 12 1612
Frogham Kent 29 2550
Frogmore Devon 7 7742
Frognall Lincs 64 1610
Frogpool Cnwll 3 7540
Frogwell Cnwll 5 3468
Frolesworth Leics 50 5090
Frome Somset 22 7747
Frome St Quintin Dorset 10 5902
Frome Whitfield Dorset 11 6991
Fromes Hill Herefs 47 6846
Fron Denbgs 70 0666
Fron Gwynd 56 3539
Fron Gwynd 68 5054
Fron Powys 58 2203
Fron Powys 58 1797
Fron Isaf Wrexhm 70 2740
Fron-goch Gwynd 70 9039
Froncysyllte Denbgs 70 2640
Frostenden Suffk 55 4781
Frosterley Dur 95 0237
Froxfield Beds 38 9733
Froxfield Wilts 23 2968
Froxfield Green Hants 13 7025
Fryern Hill Hants 13 4320
Fryerning Essex 40 6300
Fryton N York 90 6874
Fuinary Highld 121 6246
Fulbeck Lincs 76 9450
Fulbourn Cambs 53 5256
Fulbrook Oxon 36 2513
Fulflood Hants 24 4730
Fulford N York 83 6149
Fulford Somset 20 2029
Fulford Staffs 72 9537
Fulham Gt Lon 27 2576
Fulking W Susx 15 2411
Full Sutton E R Yk 84 7455
Fullaford Devon 19 6838
Fullarton N Ayrs 106 3238
Fuller Street Essex 40 7416
Fuller Street Kent 27 5656
Fuller's End Essex 39 5325
Fuller's Moor Ches 71 4954
Fullerton Hants 23 3739
Fulletby Lincs 77 2973
Fullready Warwks 48 2846
Fullwood E Ayrs 115 4450
Fulmer Bucks 26 9985
Fulmodeston Norfk 66 9930
Fulnetby Lincs 76 0979
Fulney Lincs 64 2623
Fulstone W York 82 1709

285

H

Harton Shrops 59 4888
Harton T & W 103 3765
Hartpury Gloucs 47 7924
Hartshead W York 82 1822
Hartshead Moor Side W York 82 1625
Hartshill Staffs 72 8546
Hartshill Warwks 61 3194
Hartshorne Derbys 62 3221
Hartside Nthumb 111 9716
Hartsop Cumb 93 4013
Hartswell Somset 20 0827
Hartwell Nhants 38 7850
Hartwith N York 89 2161
Hartwood N Lans 116 8459
Hartwoodmyres Border 109 4324
Harvel Kent 28 6563
Harvington Worcs 60 8775
Harvington Worcs 48 0549
Harwell Notts 75 6891
Harwell Oxon 37 4989
Harwich Essex 41 2531
Harwood Dur 95 8233
Harwood Gt Man 79 7410
Harwood Nthumb 103 0189
Harwood Dale N York 91 9695
Harwood Lee Gt Man 81 7411
Harworth Notts 75 6191
Hasbury W Mids 60 9582
Hascombe Surrey 25 0039
Haselbech Nhants 50 7177
Haselbury Plucknett Somset 10 4710
Haseley Warwks 48 2367
Haseley Green Warwks 48 2369
Haseley Knob Warwks 61 2371
Haselor Warwks 48 1257
Hasfield Gloucs 47 8227
Hasguard Pembks 30 8509
Haskayne Lancs 78 3508
Hasketon Suffk 55 2450
Hasland Derbys 74 3969
Hasland Green Derbys 74 3968
Haslemere Surrey 14 9032
Haslingden Lancs 81 7823
Haslingden Grane Lancs 81 7522
Haslingfield Cambs 52 4052
Haslington Ches 72 7355
Hassall Ches 72 7657
Hassall Green Ches 72 7858
Hassell Street Kent 29 0946
Hassingham Norfk 67 3605
Hassness Cumb 93 1816
Hassocks W Susx 15 3015
Hassop Derbys 74 2272
Haste Hill Surrey 14 9032
Haster Highld 151 3251
Hasthorpe Lincs 77 4869
Hastingleigh Kent 29 0945
Hastings E Susx 17 8209
Hastings Somset 10 3116
Hastingwood Essex 39 4807
Hastoe Herts 38 9209
Haswell Dur 96 3743
Haswell Plough Dur 96 3742
Hatch Beds 52 1547
Hatch Beauchamp Somset 20 3020
Hatch End Beds 51 0760
Hatch End Gt Lon 26 1390
Hatchet Gate Hants 12 3701
Hatching Green Herts 38 1312
Hatchmere Ches 71 5571
Hatcliffe Lincs 76 2100
Hatfield Herefs 46 5959
Hatfield Herts 39 2308
Hatfield S York 83 6609
Hatfield Worcs 47 8750
Hatfield Broad Oak Essex 39 5416
Hatfield Heath Essex 39 5215
Hatfield Peverel Essex 40 7911
Hatfield Woodhouse S York 83 6708
Hatford Oxon 36 3395
Hatherden Hants 23 3450
Hatherleigh Devon 8 5404
Hathern Leics 62 5022
Hatherop Gloucs 36 1505
Hathersage Derbys 74 2381
Hathersage Booths Derbys 74 2480
Hatherton Ches 72 6847
Hatherton Staffs 60 9510
Hatley St George Cambs 52 2751
Hatt Cnwll 5 4062
Hattersley Gt Man 79 9894
Hattingley Hants 24 6437
Hatton Abers 143 0537
Hatton Angus 127 4642
Hatton Ches 78 5982
Hatton Derbys 73 2130
Hatton Gt Lon 26 0975
Hatton Lincs 76 1776
Hatton Shrops 59 4790
Hatton Warwks 48 2367
Hatton Heath Ches 71 4561
Hatton of Fintray Abers 143 8316
Haugh E Ayrs 107 4925
Haugh Lincs 77 4175
Haugh W York 81 9311
Haugh Head Nthumb 111 0026
Haugh of Glass Moray 142 4238
Haugh of Urr D & G 100 8066
Haugham Lincs 77 3381
Haughhead Inn E Duns 116 6079
Haughley Suffk 54 0262
Haughley Green Suffk 54 0264
Haughton Notts 75 6872
Haughton Powys 59 3018
Haughton Shrops 59 3726
Haughton Shrops 59 5516
Haughton Shrops 60 7408
Haughton Shrops 60 6896
Haughton Staffs 72 8620
Haughton Green Gt Man 79 9393
Haughton le Skerne Dur 96 3116
Haughton Moss Ches 71 5756
Haultwick Herts 39 3323
Haunton Staffs 61 2310
Hautes Croix Jersey 158 0000
Hauxley Nthumb 103 2703
Hauxton Cambs 53 4452
Havannah Ches 72 8664
Havant Hants 13 7106
Haven Herefs 46 4054
Haven Bank Lincs 76 2352
Haven Side E R Yk 85 1827
Havenstreet IOW 13 5690
Havercroft W York 83 3913
Haverfordwest Pembks 30 9515
Haverhill Suffk 53 6745
Haverigg Cumb 86 1578
Havering-atte-Bower Essex 27 5193
Haversham Bucks 38 8242
Haverthwaite Cumb 87 3483
Haverton Hill Dur 97 4822
Havyat Somset 21 4761
Havyatt Somset 21 5338
Hawarden Flints 71 3165
Hawbridge Worcs 47 9049
Hawbush Green Essex 40 7820
Hawcoat Cumb 86 2071
Hawe's Green Norfk 67 2399
Hawen Cerdgn 42 3446
Hawes N York 88 8789
Hawford Worcs 47 8460
Hawick Border 109 5014
Hawk Green Gt Man 79 9687
Hawkchurch Devon 10 3400
Hawkedon Suffk 53 7953
Hawkenbury Kent 28 8045
Hawkeridge Wilts 22 8653
Hawkerland Devon 9 0588
Hawkes End W Mids 61 2982
Hawkesbury Gloucs 35 7686
Hawkesbury Warwks 61 3784
Hawkesbury Upton Gloucs 35 7786
Hawkhill Nthumb 111 2212
Hawkhurst Kent 17 7530
Hawkhurst Common E Susx 16 5217
Hawkinge Kent 29 2139
Hawkley Hants 24 7429
Hawkridge Somset 19 8630
Hawksdale Cumb 93 3648
Hawkshaw Gt Man 81 7615
Hawkshead Cumb 87 3598
Hawkshead Hill Cumb 86 3398
Hawksland S Lans 108 8439
Hawkspur Green Essex 40 6532
Hawkstone Shrops 59 5830
Hawkswick N York 88 9570
Hawksworth Notts 63 7543
Hawksworth W York 82 1641
Hawkwell Essex 40 8591
Hawkwell Nthumb 103 0771
Hawley Hants 25 8657
Hawley Kent 27 5471
Hawling Gloucs 36 0622
Hawnby N York 90 5489
Haworth W York 82 0337
Hawstead Suffk 54 8559
Hawstead Green Suffk 54 8658
Hawthorn Dur 96 4145
Hawthorn Hants 24 6733
Hawthorn Rhondd 33 0987
Hawthorn Hill Berks 25 8773
Hawthorn Hill Lincs 76 2155
Hawthorpe Lincs 64 0427
Hawton Notts 75 7851
Haxby N York 90 6058
Haxby Gates N York 83 6056
Haxey Lincs 75 7799
Haxey Turbary Lincs 84 7501
Haxted Surrey 16 4245
Haxton Wilts 23 1449
Hay Cnwll 3 8651
Hay Cnwll 3 9243
Hay Cnwll 3 9552
Hay Cnwll 4 9770
Hay Green Norfk 65 5418
Hay Street Herts 39 3926
Hay-on-Wye Powys 45 2342
Haydock Mersyd 78 5697
Haydon Dorset 11 6715
Haydon Somset 20 2523
Haydon Somset 22 6853
Haydon Bridge Nthumb 102 8464
Haydon Wick Wilts 36 1387
Haye Cnwll 5 3570
Hayes Gt Lon 26 0980
Hayes Gt Lon 27 4066
Hayes End Gt Lon 26 0882
Hayfield Ag & B 123 0723
Hayfield Derbys 74 0386
Haygate Shrops 59 6410
Hayhillock Angus 127 5242
Hayle Cnwll 2 5537
Hayley Green W Mids 60 9582
Haymoor Green Ches 72 6850
Hayne Devon 9 9515
Hayne Devon 8 7685
Haynes (Church End) Beds 38 0740
Haynes (Northwood End) Beds 38 0941
Haynes (Silver End) Beds 38 1042
Haynes (West End) Beds 38 0640
Hayscastle Pembks 30 8925
Hayscastle Cross Pembks 30 9125
Haysden Kent 16 5745
Hayton Cumb 92 1041
Hayton Cumb 94 5157
Hayton E R Yk 84 8245
Hayton Notts 75 7284
Hayton's Bent Shrops 59 5280
Haytor Vale Devon 8 7777
Haytown Devon 18 3814
Haywards Heath W Susx 15 3324
Haywood Herefs 46 4834
Haywood S York 83 5812
Haywood Oaks Notts 75 6055
Hazards Green E Susx 16 6812
Hazel Grove Gt Man 79 9287
Hazel Street Kent 28 6939
Hazel Stub Suffk 53 6544
Hazelbank S Lans 116 8345
Hazelbury Bryan Dorset 11 7408
Hazeleigh Essex 40 8203
Hazeley Hants 24 7458
Hazelford Notts 75 7249
Hazelhurst Gt Man 79 9600
Hazelslade Staffs 60 0212
Hazelton Walls Fife 126 3322
Hazelwood Derbys 62 3245
Hazlemere Bucks 26 8895
Hazlerigg T & W 103 2372
Hazles Staffs 73 0047
Hazleton Gloucs 36 0718
Heacham Norfk 65 6737
Headbourne Worthy Hants 24 4832
Headbrook Herefs 46 2854
Headcorn Kent 28 8344
Headingley W York 82 2836
Headington Oxon 37 5407
Headlam Dur 96 1818
Headland Dur 97 5234
Headless Cross Worcs 48 0365
Headlesscross N Lans 116 9158
Headley Hants 24 5162
Headley Hants 14 8236
Headley Surrey 26 2054
Headley Down Hants 14 8336
Headley Heath Worcs 61 0676
Headon Notts 75 7476
Heads S Lans 116 7247
Heads Nook Cumb 94 5054
Heage Derbys 74 3750
Healaugh N York 88 0199
Healaugh N York 83 5047
Heald Green Gt Man 79 8485
Heale Devon 19 6446
Heale Somset 20 2420
Heale Somset 21 3825
Healey Lancs 81 8816
Healey N York 89 1780
Healey Nthumb 95 0158
Healey W York 82 2719
Healeyfield Dur 95 0648
Healing Lincs 85 2110
Heamoor Cnwll 2 4631
Heanor Derbys 62 4346
Heanton Punchardon Devon 19 5035
Heapey Lancs 81 5920
Heapham Lincs 76 8788
Hearn Hants 14 8337
Hearts Delight Kent 28 8862
Heasley Mill Devon 19 7332
Heast Highld 129 6417
Heath Derbys 75 4567
Heath W York 83 3520
Heath and Reach Beds 38 9228
Heath Common W Susx 14 0915
Heath End Bucks 26 8898
Heath End Hants 24 4161
Heath End Leics 62 3621
Heath End Surrey 25 8549
Heath End Warwks 48 2360
Heath Green Worcs 61 0771
Heath Hall D & G 100 9979
Heath Hayes & Wimblebury Staffs 60 0110
Heath Hill Shrops 60 7613
Heath House Somset 21 4146
Heath Town W Mids 60 9399
Heathbrook Shrops 59 6228
Heathcote Derbys 74 1460
Heathcote Shrops 72 6528
Heathencote Nhants 49 7147
Heather Leics 62 3910
Heathfield Devon 8 8376
Heathfield E Susx 16 5821
Heathfield N York 89 1367
Heathfield Somset 20 1626
Heathrow Airport 26 0775
Heathstock Devon 9 2402
Heathton Shrops 60 8192
Heatley Gt Man 79 7088
Heatley Staffs 73 0626
Heaton Gt Man 79 6909
Heaton Lancs 87 4460
Heaton Staffs 72 9562
Heaton T & W 103 2666
Heaton W York 82 1335
Heaton Chapel Gt Man 79 8891
Heaton Mersey Gt Man 79 8690
Heaton Norris Gt Man 79 8890
Heaton's Bridge Lancs 80 4011
Heaverham Kent 27 5758
Heaviley Gt Man 79 9088
Heavitree Devon 9 9492
Hebburn T & W 103 3164
Hebden N York 88 0263
Hebden Bridge W York 82 9927
Hebden Green Ches 71 6365
Hebing End Herts 39 3122
Hebron Carmth 31 1827
Hebron IOA 68 4584
Hebron Nthumb 103 1989
Heckfield Hants 24 7260
Heckfield Green Suffk 54 1875
Heckfordbridge Essex 40 9421
Heckington Lincs 64 1444
Heckmondwike W York 82 1824
Heddington Wilts 22 9966
Heddon-on-the-Wall Nthumb 103 1366
Hedenham Norfk 67 3193
Hedge End Hants 13 4912
Hedgerley Bucks 26 9687
Hedgerley Green Bucks 26 9787
Hedging Somset 20 3029
Hedley on the Hill Nthumb 95 0759
Hednesford Staffs 60 9912
Hedon E R Yk 85 1928
Hedsor Bucks 26 9086
Hegdon Hill Herefs 46 5853
Heglibister Shet 153 3851
Heighington Dur 96 2422
Heighington Lincs 76 0269
Heightington Worcs 60 7671
Heiton Border 110 7130
Hele Cnwll 5 2198
Hele Devon 19 5347
Hele Devon 9 9902
Hele Devon 7 7470
Hele Somset 20 1824
Hele Lane Devon 19 7910
Helebridge Cnwll 18 2103
Helensburgh Ag & B 115 2982
Helenton S Ayrs 106 3830
Helford Cnwll 3 7526
Helford Passage Cnwll 3 7626
Helhoughton Norfk 66 8626
Helions Bumpstead Essex 53 6541
Hell Corner Berks 23 3864
Hellaby S York 75 5092
Helland Cnwll 4 0771
Hellandbridge Cnwll 4 0671
Hellescott Cnwll 5 2888
Hellesdon Norfk 67 2010
Hellesveor Cnwll 2 5040
Hellidon Nhants 49 5158
Hellifield N York 81 8556
Hellingly E Susx 16 5812
Hellington Norfk 67 3103
Helm Nthumb 103 1896
Helmdon Nhants 49 5943
Helme W York 82 0912
Helmingham Suffk 54 1857
Helmington Row Dur 96 1835
Helmsdale Highld 147 0315
Helmshore Lancs 81 7821
Helmsley N York 90 6183
Helperby N York 89 4469
Helperthorpe N York 91 9570
Helpringham Lincs 64 1440
Helpston Cambs 64 1205
Helsby Ches 71 4975
Helsey Lincs 77 5172
Helston Cnwll 2 6527
Helstone Cnwll 4 0881
Helton Cumb 94 5021
Helwith N York 88 0702
Helwith Bridge N York 88 8069
Hemblington Norfk 67 3411
Hemel Hempstead Herts 38 0507
Hemerdon Devon 6 5657
Hemingbrough N York 83 6730
Hemingby Lincs 76 2374
Hemingfield S York 83 3801
Hemingford Abbots Cambs 52 2871
Hemingford Grey Cambs 52 2970
Hemingstone Suffk 54 1454
Hemington Nhants 51 0985
Hemington Somset 22 7253
Hemley Suffk 55 2842
Hemlington N York 90 5014
Hempholme E R Yk 85 0850
Hempnall Norfk 67 2494
Hempnall Green Norfk 67 2493
Hempriggs Moray 141 1063
Hempstead Essex 53 6338
Hempstead Kent 28 7964
Hempstead Norfk 66 1037
Hempstead Norfk 67 4028
Hempsted Gloucs 35 8116
Hempton Norfk 66 9129
Hempton Oxon 49 4431
Hemsby Norfk 67 4917
Hemswell Lincs 76 9290
Hemswell Cliff Lincs 76 9489
Hemsworth W York 83 4213
Hemyock Devon 9 1313
Henbury Bristl 34 5678
Henbury Ches 79 8773
Hendersyde Park Border 110 7435
Hendham Devon 7 7450
Hendomen Powys 58 2197
Hendon Gt Lon 26 2389
Hendon T & W 96 4055
Hendra Cnwll 3 7237
Hendra Cnwll 4 0275
Hendre Brdgnd 33 9381
Hendre Flints 70 1867
Hendre Mons 34 4614
Hendy Carmth 32 5803
Heneglwys IOA 68 4276
Henfield W Susx 15 2115
Henford Devon 5 3794
Henghurst Kent 28 9536
Hengoed Caerph 33 1594
Hengoed Powys 45 2253
Hengoed Shrops 58 2833
Hengrave Suffk 54 8268
Henham Essex 39 5428
Henhurst Kent 28 6669
Heniarth Powys 58 1208
Henlade Somset 20 2623
Henley Dorset 11 6904
Henley Gloucs 35 9016
Henley Shrops 59 4588
Henley Shrops 46 5476
Henley Somset 21 4232
Henley Suffk 54 1551
Henley W Susx 14 8925
Henley Green W Mids 61 3681
Henley Park Surrey 25 9352
Henley Street Kent 28 6667
Henley's Down E Susx 17 7312
Henley-in-Arden Warwks 48 1566
Henley-on-Thames Oxon 37 7682
Henllan Cerdgn 31 3540
Henllan Denbgs 70 0268
Henllan Amgoed Carmth 31 1819
Henllys Torfn 34 2691
Henlow Beds 39 1738
Hennock Devon 8 8381
Henny Street Essex 54 8738
Henry's Moat (Castell Hendre) Pembks 30 0427
Henryd Conwy 69 7774
Hensall N York 83 5923
Henshaw Nthumb 102 7664
Hensingham Cumb 92 9816
Henstead Suffk 55 4885
Hensting Hants 13 4922
Henstridge Somset 22 7219
Henstridge Ash Somset 22 7220
Henstridge Marsh Somset 22 7320
Henton Oxon 37 7602
Henton Somset 21 4945
Henwick Worcs 47 8355
Henwood Cnwll 5 2673
Henwood Oxon 37 4602
Heol Senni Powys 45 9223
Heol-las Swans 32 6998
Heol-y-Cyw Brdgnd 33 9484
Hepburn Nthumb 111 0624
Hepple Nthumb 103 9901
Hepscott Nthumb 103 2284
Heptonstall W York 82 9828
Hepworth Suffk 54 9874
Hepworth W York 82 1606
Herbrandston Pembks 30 8707
Hereford Herefs 46 5139
Hereson Kent 29 3865
Heribusta Highld 136 3970
Heriot Border 118 3953
Hermiston C Edin 117 1870
Hermit Hill S York 74 3200
Hermitage Berks 24 5072
Hermitage Border 101 5095
Hermitage Dorset 11 6506
Hermitage Hants 13 7505
Hermon IOA 68 3968
Hermon Pembks 31 2031
Herne Kent 29 1865
Herne Bay Kent 29 1768
Herne Common Kent 29 1765
Herne Hill Gt Lon 27 3274
Herne Pound Kent 28 6654
Herner Devon 19 5826
Hernhill Kent 29 0660
Herodsfoot Cnwll 5 2160
Heronden Kent 29 2954
Herongate Essex 40 6291
Heronsford S Ayrs 98 1283
Heronsgate Herts 26 0294
Herriard Hants 24 6646
Herring's Green Beds 38 0844
Herringfleet Suffk 67 4797
Herringswell Suffk 53 7270
Herringthorpe S York 75 4492
Herrington T & W 96 3453
Hersden Kent 29 2062
Hersham Cnwll 18 2507
Hersham Surrey 26 1164
Herstmonceux E Susx 16 6312
Herston Dorset 11 0178
Herston Ork 153 4191
Hertford Herts 39 3212
Hertford Heath Herts 39 3510
Hertingfordbury Herts 39 3012
Hesket Newmarket Cumb 93 3438
Hesketh Bank Lancs 80 4423
Hesketh Lane Lancs 81 6141
Heskin Green Lancs 80 5315
Hesleden Dur 96 4438
Hesleden N York 88 8874
Hesley S York 75 6194
Hesleyside Nthumb 102 8183
Heslington N York 83 6250
Hessay N York 83 5253
Hessenford Cnwll 5 3057
Hessett Suffk 54 9361
Hessle E R Yk 84 0326
Hessle W York 83 4317
Hest Bank Lancs 87 4666
Hestley Green Suffk 54 1567
Heston Gt Lon 26 1277
Hestwall Ork 153 2618
Heswall Mersyd 78 2681
Hethe Oxon 49 5929
Hethersett Norfk 66 1404
Hethersgill Cumb 101 4767
Hetherside Cumb 101 4366
Hetherson Green Ches 71 5250
Hethpool Nthumb 110 8928
Hett Dur 96 2836
Hetton N York 88 9658
Hetton Steads Nthumb 111 0335
Hetton-le-Hole T & W 96 3547
Heugh Nthumb 103 0873
Heugh Head Border 119 8762
Heughhead Abers 134 3811
Heveningham Suffk 55 3372
Hever Kent 16 4745
Heversham Cumb 87 4983
Hevingham Norfk 67 1921
Hewas Water Cnwll 3 9649
Hewelsfield Gloucs 34 5602
Hewenden W York 82 0736
Hewish Somset 21 4064
Hewish Somset 10 4208
Hewood Dorset 10 3502
Hexham Nthumb 102 9364
Hextable Kent 27 5170
Hexthorpe S York 83 5602
Hexton Herts 38 1030
Hexworthy Cnwll 5 3581
Hexworthy Devon 7 6572
Hey Lancs 81 8843
Hey Houses Lancs 80 3429
Heybridge Essex 40 8508
Heybridge Essex 40 6398
Heybridge Basin Essex 40 8707
Heybrook Bay Devon 6 4949
Heydon Cambs 39 4339
Heydon Norfk 66 1127
Heydour Lincs 63 0039
Heyhead Gt Man 79 8285
Heylipoll Ag & B 120 9743
Heylor Shet 153 2980
Heyrod Gt Man 79 9799
Heysham Lancs 87 4160
Heyshaw N York 89 1761
Heyshott W Susx 14 8917
Heyside Gt Man 79 9307
Heytesbury Wilts 22 9242
Heythrop Oxon 48 3527
Heywood Gt Man 79 8510
Heywood Wilts 22 8753
Hibaldstow Lincs 84 9702
Hickleton S York 83 4805
Hickling Norfk 67 4124
Hickling Notts 63 6928
Hickling Green Norfk 67 4123
Hickling Heath Norfk 67 4022
Hickmans Green Kent 29 0658
Hicks Forstal Kent 29 1863
Hickstead W Susx 15 2620
Hidcote Bartrim Gloucs 48 1742
Hidcote Boyce Gloucs 48 1742
High Ackworth W York 83 4417
High Angerton Nthumb 103 0985
High Ardwell D & G 98 0745
High Auldgirth D & G 100 9187
High Bankhill Cumb 94 5542

290

Place	Ref
Hood Hill *S York*	74 3697
Hooe *Devon*	6 5052
Hooe *E Susx*	16 6910
Hoohill *Lancs*	80 3237
Hook *Cambs*	65 4293
Hook *Devon*	10 3005
Hook *E R Yk*	84 7625
Hook *Hants*	13 5105
Hook *Hants*	24 7254
Hook *Kent*	27 6170
Hook *Pembks*	30 9711
Hook *Surrey*	26 1864
Hook *Wilts*	36 0784
Hook Bank *Worcs*	47 8140
Hook End *Essex*	40 5900
Hook Green *Kent*	16 6535
Hook Norton *Oxon*	48 3533
Hook Street *Gloucs*	35 6799
Hook Street *Wilts*	36 0884
Hookagate *Shrops*	59 4609
Hooke *Dorset*	10 5300
Hookgate *Staffs*	72 7435
Hookway *Devon*	8 8598
Hookwood *Surrey*	15 2643
Hooley *Surrey*	27 2856
Hooley Bridge *Gt Man*	81 8511
Hooton *Ches*	71 3678
Hooton Levitt *S York*	75 5291
Hooton Pagnell *S York*	83 4807
Hooton Roberts *S York*	75 4897
Hop Pole *Lincs*	64 1813
Hopcrofts Holt *Oxon*	49 4625
Hope *Derbys*	74 1783
Hope *Devon*	7 6740
Hope *Flints*	71 3058
Hope *Powys*	58 2507
Hope *Shrops*	59 3401
Hope *Shrops*	46 5974
Hope *Staffs*	73 1254
Hope Bowdler *Shrops*	59 4792
Hope End Green *Essex*	40 5720
Hope Mansell *Herefs*	35 6219
Hope under Dinmore *Herefs*	46 5052
Hopehouse *Border*	109 2916
Hopeman *Moray*	147 1469
Hopesay *Shrops*	59 3983
Hopetown *W York*	83 3923
Hopgrove *N York*	83 6354
Hopperton *N York*	83 4256
Hopsford *Warwks*	50 4284
Hopstone *Shrops*	60 7894
Hopton *Derbys*	73 2653
Hopton *Shrops*	59 3820
Hopton *Staffs*	72 9425
Hopton *Suffk*	54 9979
Hopton Cangeford *Shrops*	59 5480
Hopton Castle *Shrops*	46 3678
Hopton on Sea *Norfk*	67 5299
Hopton Wafers *Shrops*	47 6376
Hoptonheath *Shrops*	46 3877
Hopwas *Staffs*	61 1804
Hopwood *Gt Man*	79 8609
Hopwood *Worcs*	61 0375
Horam *E Susx*	16 5717
Horbling *Lincs*	64 1135
Horbury *W York*	82 2918
Horcott *Gloucs*	36 1500
Horden *Dur*	96 4440
Horderley *Shrops*	59 4086
Hordle *Hants*	12 2795
Hordley *Shrops*	59 3831
Horeb *Carmth*	32 4905
Horeb *Cerdgn*	31 3942
Horfield *Bristl*	34 5976
Horham *Suffk*	55 2072
Horkesley Green *Essex*	41 9831
Horkesley Heath *Essex*	41 9829
Horkstow *Lincs*	84 9817
Horley *Oxon*	49 4144
Horley *Surrey*	15 2842
Horn Hill *Bucks*	26 0192
Horn Street *Kent*	29 1836
Hornblotton Green *Somset*	21 5833
Hornby *Lancs*	87 5868
Hornby *N York*	89 3605
Hornby *N York*	89 2293
Horncastle *Lincs*	77 2669
Hornchurch *Gt Lon*	27 5387
Horncliffe *Nthumb*	110 9249
Horndean *Border*	110 9049
Horndean *Hants*	13 7013
Horndon *Devon*	5 5280
Horndon on the Hill *Essex*	40 6683
Horne *Surrey*	15 3344
Horne Row *Essex*	40 7704
Horner *Somset*	20 9045
Horners Green *Suffk*	54 9641
Horney Common *E Susx*	16 4525
Horning *Norfk*	67 3417
Horninghold *Leics*	51 8097
Horninglow *Staffs*	73 2425
Horningsea *Cambs*	53 4962
Horningsham *Wilts*	22 8141
Horningtoft *Norfk*	66 9323
Horningtops *Cnwll*	5 2760
Horns Cross *Devon*	18 3823
Horns Cross *E Susx*	17 8222
Hornsbury *Somset*	10 3310
Hornsby *Cumb*	94 5150
Hornsbygate *Cumb*	94 5250
Hornsea *E R Yk*	85 1947
Hornsey *Gt Lon*	27 3089
Hornton *Oxon*	48 3945
Horpit *Wilts*	36 2183
Horra *Shet*	153 4693
Horrabridge *Devon*	6 5169
Horridge *Devon*	7 7674
Horringer *Suffk*	54 8261
Horringford *IOW*	13 5485
Horrocks Fold *Gt Man*	81 7012
Horrocksford *Lancs*	81 7543
Horsacott *Devon*	19 5231
Horsebridge *Devon*	5 4075
Horsebridge *E Susx*	16 5811
Horsebridge *Hants*	23 3430
Horsebridge *Shrops*	59 3606
Horsebridge *Staffs*	72 9553
Horsebrook *Staffs*	60 8810

Place	Ref
Horsecastle *Somset*	21 4265
Horsedown *Cnwll*	2 6134
Horsegate *Lincs*	64 1510
Horsehay *Shrops*	60 6707
Horseheath *Cambs*	53 6147
Horsehouse *N York*	88 0480
Horsell *Surrey*	25 9959
Horseman's Green *Wrexhm*	71 4441
Horsenden *Bucks*	37 7902
Horsey *Norfk*	67 4622
Horsey *Somset*	21 3239
Horsey Corner *Norfk*	67 4523
Horsford *Norfk*	67 1916
Horsforth *W York*	82 2338
Horsham *W Susx*	15 1731
Horsham *Worcs*	47 7358
Horsham St Faith *Norfk*	67 2115
Horsington *Lincs*	76 1968
Horsington *Somset*	22 7023
Horsley *Derbys*	62 3744
Horsley *Gloucs*	35 8497
Horsley *Nthumb*	102 8496
Horsley *Nthumb*	103 0965
Horsley Cross *Essex*	41 1229
Horsley Woodhouse *Derbys*	62 3944
Horsley's Green *Bucks*	37 7894
Horsleygate *Derbys*	74 3076
Horsleyhill *Border*	109 5319
Horsmonden *Kent*	28 7040
Horspath *Oxon*	37 5705
Horstead *Norfk*	67 2619
Horsted Keynes *W Susx*	15 3828
Horton *Berks*	26 0175
Horton *Bucks*	38 9219
Horton *Dorset*	12 0307
Horton *Gloucs*	35 7584
Horton *Lancs*	81 8550
Horton *Nhants*	51 8154
Horton *Shrops*	59 4929
Horton *Shrops*	60 6814
Horton *Somset*	10 3214
Horton *Staffs*	72 9457
Horton *Surrey*	26 1962
Horton *Swans*	32 4785
Horton *Wilts*	23 0463
Horton Cross *Somset*	10 3315
Horton Green *Ches*	71 4549
Horton Heath *Hants*	13 4916
Horton in Ribblesdale *N York*	88 8017
Horton Kirby *Kent*	27 5668
Horton-cum-Studley *Oxon*	37 5912
Horwich *Gt Man*	81 6311
Horwich End *Derbys*	79 0080
Horwood *Devon*	19 5027
Hoscar *Lancs*	80 4611
Hoscote *Border*	109 3911
Hose *Leics*	63 7329
Hosey Hill *Kent*	27 4553
Hosh *P & K*	125 8523
Hoswick *Shet*	153 4123
Hotham *E R Yk*	84 8934
Hothfield *Kent*	28 9644
Hoton *Leics*	62 5722
Hott *Nthumb*	102 7785
Hough *Ches*	72 7151
Hough *Ches*	79 8578
Hough End *W York*	82 2433
Hough Green *Ches*	78 4886
Hough-on-the-Hill *Lincs*	63 9246
Hougham *Lincs*	63 8844
Houghton *Cambs*	52 2872
Houghton *Cumb*	93 4159
Houghton *Hants*	23 3432
Houghton *Nthumb*	103 1266
Houghton *Pembks*	30 9807
Houghton *W Susx*	14 0111
Houghton Conquest *Beds*	38 0441
Houghton Gate *T & W*	96 3051
Houghton Green *Ches*	79 6291
Houghton Green *E Susx*	17 9222
Houghton le Side *Dur*	96 2221
Houghton le Spring *T & W*	96 3449
Houghton on the Hill *Leics*	63 6703
Houghton Regis *Beds*	38 0123
Houghton St Giles *Norfk*	66 9235
Hound Green *Hants*	24 7359
Houndslow *Border*	110 6347
Houndsmoor *Somset*	20 1225
Houndwood *Border*	119 8463
Hounslow *Gt Lon*	26 1375
Hounslow Green *Essex*	40 6518
Househill *Highld*	140 8855
Houses Hill *W York*	82 1916
Housesteads Roman Fort	102 7868
Housieside *Abers*	143 8926
Houston *Rens*	115 4066
Houstry *Highld*	151 1534
Houton *Ork*	153 3104
Hove *E Susx*	15 2804
Hove Edge *W York*	82 1324
Hoveringham *Notts*	63 6946
Hoveton *Norfk*	67 3018
Hovingham *N York*	90 6675
How Caple *Herefs*	46 6030
How End *Beds*	38 0340
How Mill *Cumb*	94 5056
Howbrook *S York*	74 3298
Howden *E R Yk*	84 7428
Howden-le-Wear *Dur*	96 1633
Howe *Highld*	151 3061
Howe *IOM*	158 1968
Howe *N York*	89 3580
Howe *Norfk*	67 2799
Howe Bridge *Gt Man*	79 6602
Howe Green *Essex*	40 7403
Howe of Teuchar *Abers*	143 7946
Howe Street *Essex*	40 6914
Howe Street *Essex*	53 6934
Howegreen *Essex*	40 8301
Howell *Lincs*	76 1346
Howes *D & G*	101 1866
Howey *Powys*	45 0558
Howgate *Mdloth*	117 2457
Howgill *N York*	81 8246
Howick *Nthumb*	111 2517
Howle *Dur*	95 0926
Howle *Shrops*	72 6923

Place	Ref
Howle Hill *Herefs*	34 6020
Howlett End *Essex*	53 5834
Howley *Somset*	10 2609
Howmore *W Isls*	152 7536
Hownam *Border*	110 7719
Howrigg *Cumb*	93 3347
Howsham *Lincs*	84 0404
Howsham *N York*	90 7362
Howt Green *Kent*	28 8965
Howtel *Nthumb*	110 8934
Howton *Devon*	8 7487
Howton *Herefs*	46 4129
Howtown *Cumb*	93 4419
Howwood *Rens*	115 3960
Hoxne *Suffk*	54 1777
Hoylake *Mersyd*	78 2189
Hoyland Common *S York*	74 3600
Hoyland Nether *S York*	74 3700
Hoyland Swaine *S York*	82 2604
Hoyle *W Susx*	14 9018
Hoyle Mill *S York*	83 3506
Hubberholme *N York*	88 9278
Hubberston *Pembks*	30 8906
Hubbert's Bridge *Lincs*	64 2643
Huby *N York*	82 2747
Huby *N York*	90 5665
Huccaby *Devon*	7 6673
Hucclecote *Gloucs*	35 8717
Hucking *Kent*	28 8458
Hucknall *Notts*	75 5349
Huddersfield *W York*	82 1416
Huddington *Worcs*	47 9457
Hudswell *N York*	89 1400
Huggate *E R Yk*	84 8855
Hugglescote *Leics*	62 4212
Hugh Town *IOS*	2 9010
Hughenden Valley *Bucks*	26 8697
Hughley *Shrops*	59 5698
Huish *Devon*	19 5311
Huish *Wilts*	23 1463
Huish Champflower *Somset*	20 0529
Huish Episcopi *Somset*	21 4326
Hulberry *Kent*	27 5265
Hulcote *Beds*	38 9438
Hulcott *Bucks*	38 8516
Hulham *Devon*	9 0183
Hull *E R Yk*	85 0829
Hulland *Derbys*	73 2446
Hulland Ward *Derbys*	73 2546
Hullavington *Wilts*	35 8981
Hullbridge *Essex*	40 8095
Hulme *Ches*	78 6091
Hulme *Gt Man*	79 8396
Hulme *Staffs*	72 9345
Hulme End *Staffs*	74 1059
Hulme Walfield *Ches*	72 8465
Hulse Heath *Ches*	72 7283
Hulton Lane Ends *Gt Man*	79 6905
Hulver Street *Norfk*	66 9311
Hulver Street *Suffk*	55 4686
Hulverstone *IOW*	13 3984
Humber *Devon*	7 8975
Humber *Herefs*	46 5356
Humberside Airport	85 0910
Humberston *Lincs*	85 3105
Humberstone *Leics*	63 6305
Humberton *N York*	89 4168
Humbie *E Loth*	118 4662
Humbleton *E R Yk*	85 2234
Humbleton *Nthumb*	111 9728
Humby *Lincs*	63 0032
Hume *Border*	110 7041
Humshaugh *Nthumb*	102 9171
Huna *Highld*	151 3573
Huncoat *Lancs*	81 7730
Huncote *Leics*	50 5197
Hundalee *Border*	110 6418
Hundall *Derbys*	74 3876
Hunderthwaite *Dur*	95 9821
Hundle Houses *Lincs*	77 2453
Hundleby *Lincs*	77 3966
Hundleton *Pembks*	30 9600
Hundon *Suffk*	53 7348
Hundred Acres *Hants*	13 5911
Hundred End *Lancs*	80 4122
Hundred House *Powys*	45 1154
Hungarton *Leics*	63 6907
Hungate End *Bucks*	38 7946
Hunger Hill *Lancs*	80 5411
Hungerford *Berks*	23 3368
Hungerford *Hants*	12 1612
Hungerford *Somset*	20 0440
Hungerford Newtown *Berks*	36 3571
Hungerstone *Herefs*	46 4435
Hungerton *Lincs*	63 8729
Hungryhatton *Shrops*	72 6626
Hunmanby *N York*	91 0977
Hunningham *Warwks*	48 3767
Hunnington *Worcs*	60 9681
Hunny Hill *IOW*	13 4990
Hunsdon *Herts*	39 4114
Hunsingore *N York*	83 4253
Hunslet *W York*	82 3130
Hunsonby *Cumb*	94 5835
Hunstanton *Norfk*	65 6740
Hunstanworth *Dur*	95 9448
Hunsterson *Ches*	72 6946
Hunston *Suffk*	54 9768
Hunston *W Susx*	14 8601
Hunston Green *Suffk*	54 9866
Hunstrete *Somset*	21 6462
Hunsworth *W York*	82 1827
Hunt End *Worcs*	48 0364
Hunt's Corner *Norfk*	54 0588
Hunt's Cross *Mersyd*	78 4385
Hunter's Inn *Devon*	19 6548
Hunter's Quay *Ag & B*	114 1879
Huntham *Somset*	21 3426
Hunthill Lodge *Angus*	134 4771
Huntingdon *Cambs*	52 2471
Huntingfield *Suffk*	55 3374
Huntingford *Dorset*	22 8030
Huntington *Ches*	71 4264
Huntington *E Loth*	118 4874
Huntington *Herefs*	46 2553
Huntington *Herefs*	46 4841
Huntington *N York*	83 6156
Huntington *Staffs*	60 9712

Place	Ref
Huntley *Gloucs*	35 7219
Huntly *Abers*	142 5339
Hunton *Hants*	24 4840
Hunton *Kent*	28 7149
Hunton *N York*	89 1892
Hunton Bridge *Herts*	26 0800
Hunts Green *Bucks*	38 8903
Hunts Green *Warwks*	61 1897
Huntscott *Somset*	20 9144
Huntsham *Devon*	20 0020
Huntshaw *Devon*	19 5023
Huntshaw Cross *Devon*	19 5222
Huntspill *Somset*	21 3145
Huntstile *Somset*	20 2633
Huntworth *Somset*	21 3134
Hunwick *Dur*	96 1832
Hunworth *Norfk*	66 0635
Hurcott *Somset*	10 3916
Hurdcott *Wilts*	23 1733
Hurdsfield *Ches*	79 9274
Hurley *Berks*	37 8283
Hurley *Warwks*	61 2495
Hurley Bottom *Berks*	37 8283
Hurley Common *Warwks*	61 2496
Hurlford *E Ayrs*	107 4536
Hurlston Green *Lancs*	80 3911
Hurn *Dorset*	12 1296
Hurn's End *Lincs*	77 4249
Hursley *Hants*	13 4225
Hurst *Berks*	25 7973
Hurst *Dorset*	11 7990
Hurst *N York*	88 0402
Hurst *Somset*	10 4518
Hurst Green *E Susx*	17 7327
Hurst Green *Essex*	41 0916
Hurst Green *Lancs*	81 6838
Hurst Green *Surrey*	27 3951
Hurst Hill *W Mids*	60 9393
Hurst Wickham *W Susx*	15 2816
Hurstbourne Priors *Hants*	24 4346
Hurstbourne Tarrant *Hants*	23 3853
Hurstley *Herefs*	46 3548
Hurstpierpoint *W Susx*	15 2716
Hurstway Common *Herefs*	46 2949
Hurstwood *Lancs*	81 8831
Hurtiso *Ork*	153 5001
Hurtmore *Surrey*	25 9445
Hurworth Burn *Dur*	96 4033
Hurworth Place *Dur*	89 2909
Hurworth-on-Tees *Dur*	89 3009
Hury *Dur*	95 9519
Husbands Bosworth *Leics*	50 6484
Husborne Crawley *Beds*	38 9635
Husthwaite *N York*	90 5175
Hut Green *N York*	83 5623
Hutcherleigh *Devon*	7 7850
Huthwaite *N York*	90 4801
Huthwaite *Notts*	75 4659
Huttoft *Lincs*	77 5176
Hutton *Border*	119 9053
Hutton *Cumb*	93 4326
Hutton *E R Yk*	84 0253
Hutton *Essex*	40 6395
Hutton *Lancs*	80 4926
Hutton *Somset*	21 3558
Hutton Bonville *N York*	89 3300
Hutton Buscel *N York*	91 9784
Hutton Conyers *N York*	89 3273
Hutton Cranswick *E R Yk*	84 0252
Hutton End *Cumb*	93 4538
Hutton Hall *N York*	90 6014
Hutton Hang *N York*	89 1788
Hutton Henry *Dur*	96 4236
Hutton Lowcross *N York*	90 5914
Hutton Magna *Dur*	89 1212
Hutton Mulgrave *N York*	90 8309
Hutton Roof *Cumb*	93 3734
Hutton Roof *Cumb*	87 5677
Hutton Rudby *N York*	89 4606
Hutton Sessay *N York*	89 4776
Hutton Wandesley *N York*	83 5050
Hutton-le-Hole *N York*	90 7090
Huxham *Devon*	9 9497
Huxham Green *Somset*	21 5936
Huxley *Ches*	71 5061
Huyton *Mersyd*	78 4490
Hycemoor *Cumb*	86 0989
Hyde *Gloucs*	35 8801
Hyde *Gt Man*	79 9494
Hyde *Hants*	12 1612
Hyde End *Berks*	24 7266
Hyde Heath *Bucks*	26 9300
Hyde Lea *Staffs*	72 9120
Hyde Park Corner *Somset*	20 2832
Hydestile *Surrey*	25 9640
Hykeham Moor *Lincs*	76 9366
Hyndford Bridge *S Lans*	108 9141
Hynish *Ag & B*	120 9839
Hyssington *Powys*	59 3194
Hystfield *Gloucs*	35 6695
Hythe *Hants*	13 4207
Hythe *Kent*	29 1634
Hythe *Somset*	21 4452
Hythe End *Berks*	26 0172
Hyton *Cumb*	86 0987

Place	Ref
Ibberton *Dorset*	11 7807
Ible *Derbys*	74 2457
Ibsley *Hants*	12 1509
Ibstock *Leics*	62 4009
Ibstone *Bucks*	37 7593
Ibthorpe *Hants*	23 3753
Iburndale *N York*	90 8707
Ibworth *Hants*	24 5654
Icelton *Somset*	21 3765
Ickburgh *Norfk*	66 8195
Ickenham *Gt Lon*	26 0786
Ickford *Bucks*	37 6407
Ickham *Kent*	29 2258

Place	Ref
Ickleford *Herts*	39 1831
Icklesham *E Susx*	17 8716
Ickleton *Cambs*	39 4943
Icklingham *Suffk*	53 7772
Ickornshaw *N York*	82 9642
Ickwell Green *Beds*	52 1545
Ickworth	54 8262
Icomb *Gloucs*	36 2122
Idbury *Oxon*	36 2319
Iddesleigh *Devon*	19 5508
Ide *Devon*	9 8990
Ide Hill *Kent*	27 4851
Ideford *Devon*	9 8977
Iden *E Susx*	17 9123
Iden Green *Kent*	28 7437
Iden Green *Kent*	17 8031
Idle *W York*	82 1737
Idless *Cnwll*	3 8147
Idlicote *Warwks*	48 2844
Idmiston *Wilts*	23 1937
Idridgehay *Derbys*	73 2849
Idrigill *Highld*	136 3863
Idstone *Oxon*	36 2584
Iffley *Oxon*	37 5203
Ifield *W Susx*	15 2537
Ifold *W Susx*	14 0231
Iford *Dorset*	12 1393
Iford *E Susx*	15 4007
Ifton Mons	34 4688
Ifton Heath *Shrops*	59 3237
Ightfield *Shrops*	71 5938
Ightham *Kent*	27 5956
Iken *Suffk*	55 4155
Ilam *Staffs*	73 1350
Ilchester *Somset*	21 5222
Ilderton *Nthumb*	111 0121
Ilford *Gt Lon*	27 4486
Ilford *Somset*	10 3617
Ilfracombe *Devon*	19 5247
Ilkeston *Derbys*	62 4641
Ilketshall St Andrew *Suffk*	55 3887
Ilketshall St Margaret *Suffk*	55 3485
Ilkley *W York*	82 1147
Illand *Cnwll*	5 2878
Illey *W Mids*	60 9881
Illidge Green *Ches*	72 7963
Illingworth *W York*	82 0728
Illogan *Cnwll*	2 6743
Illston on the Hill *Leics*	50 7099
Ilmer *Bucks*	37 7605
Ilmington *Warwks*	48 2143
Ilminster *Somset*	10 3614
Ilsington *Devon*	7 7875
Ilsington *Dorset*	11 7592
Ilston *Swans*	32 5590
Ilton *N York*	89 1978
Ilton *Somset*	10 3517
Imachar *N Ayrs*	105 8640
Immingham *Lincs*	85 1814
Immingham Dock *Lincs*	85 1916
Impington *Cambs*	53 4463
Ince *Ches*	71 4576
Ince Blundell *Mersyd*	78 3203
Ince-in-Makerfield *Gt Man*	78 5904
Inchbae Lodge Hotel *Highld*	146 4069
Inchbare *Angus*	134 6065
Inchberry *Moray*	141 3055
Inchinnan *Rens*	115 4769
Inchlaggan *Highld*	131 1701
Inchmichael *P & K*	126 2425
Inchnacardoch Hotel *Highld*	131 3810
Inchnadamph *Highld*	145 2521
Inchture *P & K*	126 2728
Inchvuilt *Highld*	139 2438
Inchyra *P & K*	126 1820
Indian Queens *Cnwll*	4 9159
Ingate Place *Suffk*	55 4288
Ingatestone *Essex*	40 6499
Ingbirchworth *S York*	82 2205
Ingerthorpe *N York*	89 2866
Ingestre *Staffs*	72 9724
Ingham *Lincs*	76 9483
Ingham *Norfk*	67 3926
Ingham *Suffk*	54 8570
Ingham Corner *Norfk*	67 3927
Ingleborough *Norfk*	65 4715
Ingleby *Derbys*	62 3426
Ingleby Arncliffe *N York*	89 4400
Ingleby Barwick *N York*	89 4414
Ingleby Cross *N York*	89 4500
Ingleby Greenhow *N York*	90 5706
Ingleigh Green *Devon*	8 6007
Inglesbatch *Somset*	22 7061
Inglesham *Wilts*	36 2098
Ingleston *D & G*	100 9865
Ingleton *Dur*	96 1720
Ingleton *N York*	87 6972
Inglewhite *Lancs*	80 5439
Ingmire Hall *Cumb*	87 6391
Ingoe *Nthumb*	103 0374
Ingoldisthorpe *Norfk*	65 6832
Ingoldmells *Lincs*	77 5668
Ingoldsby *Lincs*	64 0129
Ingram *Nthumb*	111 0115
Ingrave *Essex*	40 6291
Ingrow *W York*	82 0539
Ings *Cumb*	87 4498
Ingst *Gloucs*	34 5887
Ingthorpe *Lincs*	63 9908
Ingworth *Norfk*	47 1929
Inkberrow *Worcs*	47 0157
Inkerman *Dur*	95 1139
Inkhorn *Abers*	143 9239
Inkpen *Berks*	23 3664
Inkstack *Highld*	151 2570
Inmarsh *Wilts*	22 9460
Innellan *Ag & B*	114 1570
Innerleithen *Border*	109 3336
Innerleven *Fife*	118 3700
Innermessan *D & G*	98 0862
Innerwick *E Loth*	119 7273
Innesmill *Moray*	141 2863
Insch *Abers*	142 6228
Insh *Highld*	132 8101
Inskip *Lancs*	80 4637
Inskip Moss Side *Lancs*	80 4636
Instow *Devon*	18 4730
Insworke *Cnwll*	6 4252

Intake Kinerarach

Intake *S York* 74 3884
Inver *Abers* 133 2293
Inver *Highld* 147 8682
Inver *P & K* 125 0142
Inver-boyndie *Abers* 142 6664
Inverailort *Highld* 129 7681
Inveralligin *Highld* 138 8457
Inverallochy *Abers* 143 0365
Inveran *Highld* 146 5797
Inveraray *Ag & B* 123 0908
Inverarish *Highld* 137 5535
Inverarity *Angus* 127 4544
Inverarnan *Stirlg* 123 3118
Inverasdale *Highld* 144 8284
Inveravon *Falk* 117 9579
Inverawe *Ag & B* 122 0231
Inverbeg *Ag & B* 115 3497
Inverbervie *Abers* 135 8272
Inverbroom *Highld* 145 1883
Invercreran House Hotel *Ag & B* 122 0146
Inverdruie *Highld* 132 8911
Inveresk *E Loth* 118 3471
Inveresragan *Ag & B* 122 9835
Inverewe Garden 144 8682
Inverey *Abers* 133 0889
Inverfarigaig *Highld* 139 5123
Inverfolla *Ag & B* 122 9544
Invergarry *Highld* 131 3001
Invergeldie *P & K* 124 7327
Invergloy *Highld* 131 2288
Invergordon *Highld* 140 7068
Invergowrie *P & K* 126 3430
Inverguseran *Highld* 129 7407
Inverhadden *P & K* 124 6757
Inverherive Hotel *Stirlg* 123 3626
Inverie *Highld* 129 7600
Inverinan *Ag & B* 122 9917
Inverinate *Highld* 138 9221
Inverkeilor *Angus* 127 6649
Inverkeithing *Fife* 117 1383
Inverkeithny *Abers* 142 6247
Inverkip *Inver* 114 2072
Inverkirkaig *Highld* 145 0719
Inverlael *Highld* 145 1885
Inverlair *Highld* 131 3479
Inverliever Lodge *Ag & B* 122 8905
Inverlochy *Ag & B* 123 1927
Invermark *Angus* 134 4480
Invermarkie *Abers* 142 4239
Invermoriston *Highld* 139 4216
Inverness *Highld* 140 6645
Inverness Dalcross Airport 140 7752
Invernoaden *Ag & B* 114 1297
Inveroran Hotel *Ag & B* 123 2741
Inverquharity *Angus* 134 4057
Inverquhomery *Abers* 143 0146
Inverroy *Highld* 131 2581
Inversanda *Highld* 130 9459
Invershiel *Highld* 138 9319
Invershin *Highld* 146 5796
Invershore *Highld* 151 2435
Inversnaid Hotel *Stirlg* 123 3308
Inverugie *Abers* 143 0948
Inveruglas *Ag & B* 123 3109
Inveruglass *Highld* 132 8000
Inverurie *Abers* 142 7721
Inwardleigh *Devon* 8 5699
Inworth *Essex* 40 8717
Iochdar *W Isls* 152 7646
Iping *W Susx* 14 8522
Ipplepen *Devon* 7 8366
Ipsden *Oxon* 37 6285
Ipstones *Staffs* 73 0149
Ipswich *Suffk* 54 1644
Irby *Mersyd* 78 2584
Irby in the Marsh *Lincs* 77 4663
Irby upon Humber *Lincs* 85 1904
Irchester *Nhants* 51 9265
Ireby *Cumb* 93 2338
Ireby *Lancs* 87 6575
Ireland *Beds* 38 1341
Ireleth *Cumb* 86 2277
Ireshopeburn *Dur* 95 8638
Ireton Wood *Derbys* 73 2847
Irlam *Gt Man* 79 7294
Irnham *Lincs* 64 0226
Iron Acton *Glouc*s 35 6783
Iron Bridge *Cambs* 65 4898
Iron Bridge Museum 60 6603
Iron Cross *Warwks* 48 0552
Ironbridge *Shrops* 60 6703
Ironmacannie *D & G* 99 6675
Irons Bottom *Surrey* 15 2446
Ironville *Derbys* 75 4351
Irstead *Norfk* 67 3620
Irthington *Cumb* 101 4961
Irthlingborough *Nhants* 51 9470
Irton *N York* 91 0184
Irvine *N Ayrs* 106 3238
Isauld *Highld* 150 9865
Isbister *Shet* 153 3790
Isfield *E Susx* 16 4417
Isham *Nhants* 51 8873
Isington *Hants* 25 7842
Islandpool *Worcs* 60 8780
Islay Airport 112 3251
Isle Abbotts *Somset* 21 3520
Isle Brewers *Somset* 21 3621
Isle of Dogs *Gt Lon* 27 3779
Isle of Man Ronaldsway Airport 158 2868
Isle of Whithorn *D & G* 99 4736
Isleham *Cambs* 53 6474
Isleornsay *Highld* 129 7012
Isles of Scilly St Mary's Airport 2 9210
Islesteps *D & G* 100 9672
Islet Village *Guern* 158 0000
Isleworth *Gt Lon* 26 1575
Isley Walton *Leics* 62 4224
Islibhig *W Isls* 152 0029
Islington *Gt Lon* 27 3184
Islip *Nhants* 51 9879
Islip *Oxon* 37 5214
Islivig *W Isls* 152 0029
Isombridge *Shrops* 59 6113
Istead Rise *Kent* 27 6370
Itchen Abbas *Hants* 24 5333
Itchen Stoke *Hants* 24 5532
Itchingfield *W Susx* 15 1328
Itchington *Gloucs* 35 6587
Itteringham *Norfk* 66 1430
Itton *Devon* 8 6899
Itton *Mons* 34 4995
Ivegill *Cumb* 93 4143
Ivelet *N York* 88 9398
Iver *Bucks* 26 0381
Iver Heath *Bucks* 26 0283
Iveston *Dur* 96 1350
Ivinghoe *Bucks* 38 9416
Ivinghoe Aston *Bucks* 38 9517
Ivington *Herefs* 46 4756
Ivington Green *Herefs* 46 4656
Ivy Cross *Dorset* 22 8623
Ivy Hatch *Kent* 27 5854
Ivy Todd *Norfk* 66 8909
Ivybridge *Devon* 6 6356
Ivychurch *Kent* 17 0327
Iwade *Kent* 28 9067
Iwerne Courtney or Shroton *Dorset* 11 8512
Iwerne Minster *Dorset* 11 8614
Ixworth *Suffk* 54 9370
Ixworth Thorpe *Suffk* 54 9173

J

Jack Green *Lancs* 81 5925
Jack Hill *N York* 82 1951
Jack's Bush *Hants* 23 2636
Jack-in-the-Green *Devon* 9 0195
Jacksdale *Notts* 75 4451
Jackson Bridge *W York* 82 1607
Jackton *S Lans* 115 5952
Jacobs Well *Surrey* 25 0053
Jacobstow *Cnwll* 5 1995
Jacobstowe *Devon* 8 5801
Jameston *Pembks* 30 0598
Jamestown *Highld* 139 4756
Jamestown *W Duns* 115 3981
Janets-town *Highld* 151 3551
Janetstown *Highld* 151 1932
Jardine Hall *D & G* 100 1088
Jarrow *T & W* 103 3364
Jarvis Brook *E Susx* 16 5329
Jasper's Green *Essex* 40 7226
Jawcraig *Falk* 116 8475
Jaywick *Essex* 41 1513
Jealott's Hill *Berks* 25 8673
Jeater Houses *N York* 89 4394
Jedburgh *Border* 110 6420
Jeffreyston *Pembks* 31 0906
Jemimaville *Highld* 140 7165
Jerbourg *Guern* 158 0000
Jersey Airport 158 0000
Jerusalem *Lincs* 76 9170
Jesmond *T & W* 103 2566
Jevington *E Susx* 16 5601
Jingle Street *Mons* 34 4710
Jockey End *Herts* 38 0413
Jodrell Bank *Ches* 79 7970
John o' Groats *Highld* 151 3872
John's Cross *E Susx* 17 7421
Johnby *Cumb* 93 4332
Johnshaven *Abers* 135 7967
Johnson's Street *Norfk* 67 3717
Johnston *Pembks* 30 9310
Johnstone *D & G* 109 2400
Johnstone *Rens* 115 4263
Johnstonebridge *D & G* 100 1092
Johnstown *Carmth* 31 3919
Johnstown *Wrexhm* 71 3046
Joppa *C Edin* 118 3173
Joppa *Cerdgn* 43 5666
Joppa *S Ayrs* 106 4119
Jordans *Bucks* 26 9791
Jordanston *Pembks* 30 9132
Jordanthorpe *S York* 74 3580
Joyden's Wood *Kent* 27 5072
Jubilee Corner *Kent* 28 8447
Jump *S York* 83 3801
Jumper's Town *E Susx* 16 4632
Juniper *Nthumb* 95 9358
Juniper Green *C Edin* 117 1968
Jurby *IOM* 158 3698
Jurston *Devon* 8 6984

K

Kaber *Cumb* 88 7911
Kaimend *S Lans* 117 9945
Kames *Ag & B* 114 9771
Kames *E Ayrs* 107 6926
Kea *Cnwll* 3 8142
Keadby *Lincs* 84 8311
Keal Cotes *Lincs* 77 3660
Kearby Town End *N York* 83 3447
Kearsley *Gt Man* 79 7504
Kearsley *Nthumb* 103 0275
Kearsney *Kent* 29 2844
Kearstwick *Cumb* 87 6079
Kearton *N York* 88 9998
Keasden *N York* 88 7266
Keason *Cnwll* 5 3168
Keaton *Devon* 7 6454
Keckwick *Ches* 78 5783
Keddington *Lincs* 77 3488
Keddington Corner *Lincs* 77 3589
Kedington *Suffk* 53 7046
Kedleston *Derbys* 73 3040
Keelby *Lincs* 85 1610
Keele *Staffs* 72 8045
Keele University *Staffs* 72 8144
Keeley Green *Beds* 38 0046
Keelham *W York* 82 0732
Keeston *Pembks* 30 9019
Keevil *Wilts* 22 9258
Kegworth *Leics* 62 4826
Kehelland *Cnwll* 2 6241
Keig *Abers* 142 6119
Keighley *W York* 82 0541
Keilarsbrae *Clacks* 116 8994
Keillour *P & K* 125 9725
Keiloch *Abers* 133 1891
Keils *Ag & B* 113 5268
Keinton Mandeville *Somset* 21 5430
Keir Mill *D & G* 100 8593
Keirsleywell Row *Nthumb* 94 7751
Keisby *Lincs* 64 0328
Keisley *Cumb* 94 7124
Keiss *Highld* 151 3461
Keith *Moray* 142 4250
Keithick *P & K* 126 2038
Keithock *Angus* 134 6063
Keithtown *Highld* 139 5256
Kelbrook *Lancs* 81 9044
Kelburn *N Ayrs* 114 2156
Kelby *Lincs* 63 0041
Keld *Cumb* 94 5514
Keld *N York* 88 8900
Keld Head *N York* 90 7884
Keldholme *N York* 90 7086
Kelfield *Lincs* 84 8201
Kelfield *N York* 83 5938
Kelham *Notts* 75 7755
Kelhead *D & G* 100 1469
Kellacott *Devon* 5 4088
Kellamergh *Lancs* 80 4029
Kellas *Angus* 127 4535
Kellas *Moray* 141 1654
Kellaton *Devon* 7 8039
Kelleth *Cumb* 87 6605
Kelling *Norfk* 66 0942
Kellington *N York* 83 5524
Kelloe *Dur* 96 3436
Kelloholm *D & G* 107 7411
Kells *Cumb* 92 9616
Kelly *Devon* 5 3981
Kelly Bray *Cnwll* 5 3671
Kelmarsh *Nhants* 50 7379
Kelmscot *Oxon* 36 2499
Kelsale *Suffk* 55 3865
Kelsall *Ches* 71 5268
Kelshall *Herts* 39 3336
Kelsick *Cumb* 93 1950
Kelso *Border* 110 7234
Kelstedge *Derbys* 74 3363
Kelstern *Lincs* 77 2489
Kelsterton *Flints* 70 2770
Kelston *Somset* 22 7067
Keltneyburn *P & K* 124 7749
Kelton *D & G* 100 9970
Kelty *Fife* 117 1494
Kelvedon *Essex* 40 8619
Kelvedon Hatch *Essex* 27 5698
Kelynack *Cnwll* 2 3729
Kemacott *Devon* 19 6647
Kemback *Fife* 126 4115
Kemberton *Shrops* 60 7204
Kemble *Gloucs* 35 9897
Kemble Wick *Gloucs* 35 9895
Kemerton *Worcs* 47 9536
Kemeys Commander *Mons* 34 3404
Kemnay *Abers* 142 7316
Kemp Town *E Susx* 15 3303
Kempe's Corner *Kent* 28 0346
Kempley *Gloucs* 47 6629
Kempley Green *Gloucs* 47 6728
Kemps Green *Warwks* 61 1470
Kempsey *Worcs* 47 8549
Kempsford *Gloucs* 36 1696
Kempshott *Hants* 24 6050
Kempston *Beds* 38 0347
Kempston Hardwick *Beds* 38 0344
Kempton *Shrops* 59 3682
Kemsing *Kent* 27 5558
Kemsley *Kent* 28 9166
Kemsley Street *Kent* 28 8062
Kenardington *Kent* 17 9732
Kenchester *Herefs* 46 4342
Kencot *Oxon* 36 2504
Kendal *Cumb* 87 5192
Kenderchurch *Herefs* 46 4028
Kendleshire *Gloucs* 35 6679
Kenfig *Brdgnd* 32 8081
Kenfig Hill *Brdgnd* 33 8382
Kenidjack *Cnwll* 2 3632
Kenilworth *Warwks* 61 2871
Kenley *Gt Lon* 27 3260
Kenley *Shrops* 59 5500
Kenmore *Highld* 137 7557
Kenmore *P & K* 124 7745
Kenn *Devon* 9 9285
Kenn *Somset* 21 4268
Kennacraig *Ag & B* 113 8262
Kennards House *Cnwll* 5 2883
Kenneggy *Cnwll* 2 5628
Kennerleigh *Devon* 8 8107
Kennessee Green *Mersyd* 78 3801
Kennet *Clacks* 116 9291
Kennethmont *Abers* 142 5428
Kennett *Cambs* 53 7068
Kennford *Devon* 9 9186
Kenninghall *Norfk* 54 0386
Kennington *Kent* 28 0245
Kennington *Oxon* 37 5201
Kennoway *Fife* 126 3502
Kenny *Somset* 10 3117
Kennyhill *Suffk* 53 6679
Kennythorpe *N York* 90 7865
Kenovay *Ag & B* 120 9946
Kensaleyre *Highld* 136 4151
Kensham Green *Kent* 17 8229
Kensington *Gt Lon* 27 2579
Kensworth *Beds* 38 0319
Kensworth Common *Beds* 38 0317
Kent End *Wilts* 36 0594
Kent Green *Ches* 72 8458
Kent Street *E Susx* 17 7816
Kent Street *Kent* 28 6654
Kent's Green *Gloucs* 47 7423
Kent's Oak *Hants* 23 3224
Kentallen *Highld* 122 0057
Kentchurch *Herefs* 46 4125
Kentford *Suffk* 53 7066
Kentisbeare *Devon* 9 0608
Kentisbury *Devon* 19 6243
Kentisbury Ford *Devon* 19 6242
Kentish Town *Gt Lon* 27 2884
Kentmere *Cumb* 87 4504
Kenton *Devon* 9 9583
Kenton *Gt Lon* 26 1788
Kenton *Suffk* 55 1965
Kenton *T & W* 103 2267
Kenton Bankfoot *Nthumb* 103 2069
Kentra *Highld* 129 6569
Kents Bank *Cumb* 87 3975
Kenwick *Shrops* 59 4230
Kenwyn *Cnwll* 3 8145
Kenyon *Ches* 79 6395
Keoldale *Highld* 149 3866
Keppoch *Highld* 138 8924
Kepwick *N York* 89 4690
Keresley *W Mids* 61 3282
Keresley Green *Warwks* 61 3283
Kergilliak *Cnwll* 3 7833
Kernborough *Devon* 7 7941
Kerne Bridge *Herefs* 34 5818
Kerridge *Ches* 79 9376
Kerridge-end *Ches* 79 9475
Kerris *Cnwll* 2 4427
Kerry *Powys* 58 1490
Kerrycroy *Ag & B* 114 1061
Kersall *Notts* 75 7162
Kersbrook *Devon* 9 0683
Kerscott *Devon* 19 6329
Kersey *Suffk* 54 0044
Kersey Tye *Suffk* 54 9843
Kersey Upland *Suffk* 54 9942
Kershader *W Isls* 152 3320
Kershopefoot *Cumb* 101 4782
Kersoe *Worcs* 47 9940
Kerswell *Devon* 9 0806
Kerswell Green *Worcs* 47 8646
Kerthen Wood *Cnwll* 2 5833
Kesgrave *Suffk* 55 2245
Kessingland *Suffk* 55 5286
Kessingland Beach *Suffk* 55 5385
Kestle *Cnwll* 3 9845
Kestle Mill *Cnwll* 4 8459
Keston *Gt Lon* 27 4164
Keswick *Cumb* 93 2623
Keswick *Norfk* 67 2004
Ketsby *Lincs* 77 3676
Kettering *Nhants* 51 8678
Ketteringham *Norfk* 66 1603
Kettins *Angus* 126 2338
Kettle Green *Herts* 39 4118
Kettlebaston *Suffk* 54 9650
Kettlebridge *Fife* 126 3007
Kettlebrook *Staffs* 61 2103
Kettleburgh *Suffk* 55 2660
Kettleholm *D & G* 100 1476
Kettleness *N York* 97 8315
Kettleshulme *Ches* 79 9879
Kettlesing *N York* 82 2256
Kettlesing Bottom *N York* 89 2357
Kettlestone *Norfk* 66 9631
Kettlethorpe *Lincs* 76 8475
Kettletoft *Ork* 153 6538
Kettlewell *N York* 88 9672
Ketton *Rutlnd* 63 9704
Kew *Gt Lon* 26 1876
Kew Gardens 27 1877
Kewstoke *Somset* 21 3363
Kexbrough *S York* 82 3009
Kexby *Lincs* 76 8785
Kexby *N York* 84 7050
Key Green *Ches* 72 8963
Key Green *N York* 90 8004
Key Street *Kent* 28 8764
Key's Toft *Lincs* 77 4858
Keyham *Leics* 63 6706
Keyhaven *Hants* 12 3091
Keyingham *E R Yk* 85 2425
Keymer *W Susx* 15 3115
Keynsham *Somset* 21 6568
Keysoe *Beds* 51 0762
Keysoe Row *Beds* 51 0861
Keyston *Cambs* 51 0475
Keyworth *Notts* 62 6130
Kibbear *Somset* 20 2222
Kibblesworth *T & W* 96 2456
Kibworth Beauchamp *Leics* 50 6893
Kibworth Harcourt *Leics* 50 6894
Kidbrooke *Gt Lon* 27 4176
Kidburngill *Cumb* 92 0621
Kidd's Moor *Norfk* 66 1103
Kiddemore Green *Staffs* 60 8509
Kidderminster *Worcs* 60 8376
Kiddington *Oxon* 49 4123
Kidlington *Oxon* 37 4913
Kidmore End *Oxon* 37 6979
Kidsdale *D & G* 99 4336
Kidsgrove *Staffs* 72 8454
Kidstones *N York* 88 9581
Kidwelly *Carmth* 31 4006
Kiel Crofts *Ag & B* 122 9039
Kielder *Nthumb* 102 6293
Kiells *Ag & B* 112 4168
Kilbarchan *Rens* 115 4063
Kilbeg *Highld* 129 6506
Kilberry *Ag & B* 113 7164
Kilbirnie *N Ayrs* 115 3154
Kilbride *Ag & B* 122 8525
Kilbride *Ag & B* 113 7279
Kilbride *Ag & B* 114 0367
Kilbuiack *Moray* 141 0960
Kilburn *Derbys* 62 3845
Kilburn *Gt Lon* 26 2483
Kilburn *N York* 90 5179
Kilby *Leics* 50 6295
Kilchamaig *Ag & B* 113 8060
Kilchattan *Ag & B* 112 3795
Kilchattan *Ag & B* 114 1054
Kilcheran *Ag & B* 122 8239
Kilchoan *Highld* 121 4863
Kilchoman *Ag & B* 112 2163
Kilchrenan *Ag & B* 122 0322
Kilconquhar *Fife* 127 4802
Kilcot *Gloucs* 47 6925
Kilcoy *Highld* 139 5751
Kilcreggan *Ag & B* 114 2480
Kildale *N York* 90 6009
Kildalloig *Ag & B* 105 7518
Kildary *Highld* 147 7674
Kildavaig *Ag & B* 114 9866
Kildavanan *Ag & B* 114 0266
Kildonan *Highld* 147 9120
Kildonan *N Ayrs* 105 0321
Kildonan Lodge *Highld* 147 9022
Kildonnan *Highld* 128 4885
Kildrochet House *D & G* 98 0856
Kildrummy *Abers* 142 4617
Kildwick *N York* 82 0046
Kilfinan *Ag & B* 114 9378
Kilfinnan *Highld* 131 2795
Kilford *Denbgs* 70 0766
Kilgetty *Pembks* 31 1207
Kilgrammie *S Ayrs* 106 2502
Kilgwrrwg Common *Mons* 34 4797
Kilham *E R Yk* 91 0664
Kilham *Nthumb* 110 8832
Kilkenneth *Ag & B* 120 9444
Kilkenzie *Ag & B* 105 6724
Kilkhampton *Cnwll* 18 2511
Killamarsh *Derbys* 75 4581
Killay *Swans* 32 6092
Killearn *Stirlg* 115 5286
Killerby *Dur* 96 1919
Killerton *Devon* 9 9700
Killichonan *P & K* 132 5458
Killiechronan *Ag & B* 121 5441
Killiecrankie *P & K* 132 9162
Killilan *Highld* 138 9430
Killin *Stirlg* 124 5733
Killinghall *N York* 89 2858
Killington *Cumb* 87 6188
Killington *Devon* 19 6646
Killingworth *T & W* 103 2770
Killiow *Cnwll* 3 8042
Killivose *Cnwll* 3 8049
Killochyett *Border* 118 4545
Kilmacolm *Inver* 115 3567
Kilmahog *Stirlg* 124 6108
Kilmahumaig *Ag & B* 113 7893
Kilmaluag *Highld* 136 4374
Kilmany *Fife* 126 3821
Kilmarnock *E Ayrs* 107 4237
Kilmartin *Ag & B* 113 8398
Kilmaurs *E Ayrs* 106 4141
Kilmelford *Ag & B* 122 8512
Kilmersdon *Somset* 22 6952
Kilmeston *Hants* 13 5825
Kilmichael *Ag & B* 105 6922
Kilmichael Glassary *Ag & B* 113 8593
Kilmichael of Inverlussa *Ag & B* 113 7786
Kilmington *Devon* 10 2797
Kilmington *Wilts* 22 7736
Kilmington Common *Wilts* 22 7735
Kilmington Street *Wilts* 22 7835
Kilmorack *Highld* 139 4944
Kilmore *Ag & B* 122 8825
Kilmore *Highld* 129 6507
Kilmory *Ag & B* 113 7074
Kilmory *Highld* 128 5270
Kilmory *N Ayrs* 105 9621
Kilmuir *Highld* 136 2547
Kilmuir *Highld* 136 3770
Kilmuir *Highld* 140 6749
Kilmuir *Highld* 147 7573
Kilmun *Ag & B* 114 1781
Kiln Green *Berks* 37 8178
Kiln Pit Hill *Nthumb* 95 0355
Kilnave *Ag & B* 112 2871
Kilncadzow *S Lans* 116 8848
Kilndown *Kent* 16 7035
Kilnhill *Cumb* 93 2132
Kilnhouses *Ches* 71 6366
Kilnhurst *S York* 75 4597
Kilninver *Ag & B* 122 8221
Kilnsea *E R Yk* 85 4115
Kilnsey *N York* 88 9767
Kilnwick *E R Yk* 84 9949
Kilnwick Percy *E R Yk* 84 8249
Kiloran *Ag & B* 112 3996
Kilpatrick *N Ayrs* 105 9026
Kilpeck *Herefs* 46 4430
Kilpin *E R Yk* 84 7726
Kilpin Pike *E R Yk* 84 7626
Kilrenny *Fife* 127 5704
Kilsby *Nhants* 50 5671
Kilspindie *P & K* 126 2125
Kilstay *D & G* 98 1238
Kilsyth *N Lans* 116 7178
Kiltarlity *Highld* 139 5041
Kilton *N York* 97 7018
Kilton Thorpe *N York* 97 6917
Kilvaxter *Highld* 136 3869
Kilve *Somset* 20 1442
Kilvington *Notts* 63 8042
Kilwinning *N Ayrs* 106 3043
Kimberley *Norfk* 66 0603
Kimberley *Notts* 62 4944
Kimberworth *S York* 74 4093
Kimble Wick *Bucks* 38 8007
Kimblesworth *Dur* 96 2547
Kimbolton *Cambs* 51 1067
Kimbolton *Herefs* 46 5261
Kimcote *Leics* 50 5886
Kimmeridge *Dorset* 11 9179
Kimmerston *Nthumb* 111 9535
Kimpton *Hants* 23 2746
Kimpton *Herts* 39 1718
Kimworthy *Devon* 18 3112
Kinbrace *Highld* 150 8631
Kinbuck *Stirlg* 125 7905
Kincaple *Fife* 127 4618
Kincardine *Fife* 116 9387
Kincardine *Highld* 146 6089
Kincardine O'Neil *Abers* 134 5999
Kinclaven *P & K* 126 1538
Kincorth *Aber C* 135 9403
Kincorth House *Moray* 141 0161
Kincraig *Highld* 132 8305
Kincraigie *P & K* 125 9849
Kindallachan *P & K* 125 9949
Kinerarach *Ag & B* 113 6553

Kineton Lamorran

Kineton *Gloucs* 48 0926
Kineton *Warwks* 48 3350
Kinfauns *P & K* 126 1622
Kinfold *S Ayrs* 106 3634
King Arthur's Labyrinth 57 7407
King Sterndale *Derbys* 74 0972
King's Acre *Herefs* 46 4841
King's Bromley *Staffs* 73 1216
King's Cliffe *Nhants* 51 0097
King's Coughton *Warwks* 48 0859
King's Heath *W Mids* 61 0781
King's Hill *Warwks* 61 3274
King's Lynn *Norfk* 65 6120
King's Mills *Guern* 158 0000
King's Moss *Lancs* 78 5000
King's Newton *Derbys* 62 3825
King's Norton *Leics* 50 6800
King's Norton *W Mids* 61 0579
King's Nympton *Devon* 19 6819
King's Pyon *Herefs* 46 4450
King's Somborne *Hants* 23 3531
King's Stag *Dorset* 11 7210
King's Stanley *Gloucs* 35 8103
King's Sutton *Oxon* 49 4936
King's Walden *Herts* 39 1623
Kingarth *Ag & B* 114 0956
Kingcausie *Abers* 135 8699
Kingcoed *Mons* 34 4305
Kingerby *Lincs* 76 0592
Kingford *Devon* 18 2806
Kingham *Oxon* 48 2624
Kingholm Quay *D & G* 100 9773
Kinghorn *Fife* 117 2686
Kinglassie *Fife* 117 2298
Kingoldrum *Angus* 126 3355
Kingoodie *P & K* 126 3329
Kings Bridge *Swans* 32 5997
Kings Caple *Herefs* 46 5528
Kings Green *Gloucs* 47 7734
Kings Hill *Kent* 28 6755
Kings Hill *W Mids* 60 9896
Kings House Hotel *Highld* 123 2654
Kings Langley *Herts* 26 0702
Kings Meaburn *Cumb* 94 6221
Kings Muir *Border* 109 2539
Kings Newnham *Warwks* 50 4577
Kings Ripton *Cambs* 52 2676
Kings Weston *Bristl* 34 5477
Kings Worthy *Hants* 24 4932
Kingsand *Cnwll* 6 4350
Kingsash *Bucks* 38 8805
Kingsbarns *Fife* 127 5912
Kingsbridge *Devon* 7 7344
Kingsbridge *Somset* 20 9837
Kingsburgh *Highld* 136 3955
Kingsbury *Gt Lon* 26 1988
Kingsbury *Warwks* 61 2196
Kingsbury Episcopi *Somset* 21 4321
Kingsclere *Hants* 24 5258
Kingscote *Gloucs* 35 8196
Kingscott *Devon* 19 5318
Kingscross *N Ayrs* 105 0428
Kingsdon *Somset* 21 5126
Kingsdown *Kent* 29 3748
Kingsdown *Wilts* 22 8167
Kingsdown *Wilts* 36 1688
Kingseat *Fife* 117 1290
Kingsey *Bucks* 37 7406
Kingsfold *W Susx* 15 1636
Kingsford *Aber C* 135 8506
Kingsford *E Ayrs* 115 4447
Kingsford *Worcs* 60 8181
Kingsgate *Kent* 29 3970
Kingshall Street *Suffk* 54 9161
Kingsheanton *Devon* 19 5537
Kingshouse Hotel *Stirlg* 124 5620
Kingshurst *W Mids* 61 1688
Kingside Hill *Cumb* 92 1551
Kingskerswell *Devon* 7 8767
Kingskettle *Fife* 126 3008
Kingsland *Dorset* 10 4597
Kingsland *Herefs* 46 4461
Kingsland *IOA* 68 2581
Kingsley *Ches* 71 5574
Kingsley *Hants* 25 7838
Kingsley *Staffs* 73 0146
Kingsley Green *W Susx* 14 8930
Kingsley Park *Nhants* 49 7762
Kingslow *Shrops* 60 7998
Kingsmead *Hants* 13 5813
Kingsmuir *Angus* 127 4849
Kingsmuir *Fife* 127 5308
Kingsnorth *Kent* 28 0039
Kingstanding *W Mids* 61 0794
Kingsteignton *Devon* 7 8773
Kingsthorne *Herefs* 46 4931
Kingsthorpe *Nhants* 49 7563
Kingston *Cambs* 52 3455
Kingston *Cnwll* 5 3675
Kingston *Devon* 6 6347
Kingston *Devon* 9 0687
Kingston *Dorset* 11 7509
Kingston *Dorset* 11 9579
Kingston *E Loth* 118 5482
Kingston *Hants* 12 1401
Kingston *IOW* 13 4781
Kingston *Kent* 29 1950
Kingston *W Susx* 14 0802
Kingston Bagpuize *Oxon* 36 4098
Kingston Blount *Oxon* 37 7399
Kingston Deverill *Wilts* 22 8437
Kingston Lisle *Oxon* 36 3287
Kingston near Lewes *E Susx* 15 3908
Kingston on Soar *Notts* 62 5027
Kingston on Spey *Moray* 141 3365
Kingston Russell *Dorset* 10 5791
Kingston Seymour *Somset* 21 4066
Kingston St Mary *Somset* 20 2229
Kingston Stert *Oxon* 37 7200
Kingston upon Thames *Gt Lon* 26 1869
Kingstone *Herefs* 46 4235
Kingstone *Somset* 10 3713
Kingstone *Staffs* 73 0629
Kingstone Winslow *Oxon* 36 2685
Kingstown *Cumb* 93 3959
Kingswear *Devon* 7 8851
Kingswells *Aber C* 135 8606
Kingswinford *W Mids* 60 8888
Kingswood *Bucks* 37 6919
Kingswood *Gloucs* 35 6473
Kingswood *Gloucs* 35 7491
Kingswood *Kent* 28 8350
Kingswood *Powys* 58 2302
Kingswood *Somset* 20 1037
Kingswood *Surrey* 26 2455
Kingswood *Warwks* 61 1871
Kingswood Brook *Warwks* 61 1970
Kingswood Common *Herefs* 46 2954
Kingswood Common *Staffs* 60 8302
Kingthorpe *Lincs* 76 1275
Kington *Gloucs* 35 6290
Kington *Herefs* 46 2956
Kington *Worcs* 47 9956
Kington Langley *Wilts* 35 9276
Kington Magna *Dorset* 22 7622
Kington St Michael *Wilts* 35 9077
Kingussie *Highld* 132 7500
Kingweston *Somset* 21 5230
Kinharrachie *Abers* 143 9231
Kinharvie *D & G* 100 9266
Kinkell Bridge *P & K* 125 9316
Kinknockie *Abers* 143 0041
Kinleith *C Edin* 117 1866
Kinlet *Shrops* 60 7180
Kinloch *Highld* 149 3434
Kinloch *Highld* 149 5552
Kinloch *Highld* 128 4099
Kinloch *P & K* 126 1444
Kinloch *P & K* 126 2644
Kinloch Hourn *Highld* 130 9506
Kinloch Rannoch *P & K* 132 6658
Kinlochard *Stirlg* 124 4502
Kinlochbervie *Highld* 148 2256
Kinlocheil *Highld* 130 9779
Kinlochewe *Highld* 138 0261
Kinlochlaggan *Highld* 131 5289
Kinlochleven *Highld* 131 1861
Kinlochmoidart *Highld* 129 7072
Kinlochnanuagh *Highld* 129 7384
Kinloss *Moray* 141 0661
Kinmel Bay *Conwy* 70 9880
Kinmuck *Abers* 143 8119
Kinmundy *Abers* 143 8817
Kinnabus *Ag & B* 104 2942
Kinnadie *Abers* 143 9743
Kinnaird *P & K* 133 9559
Kinnaird Castle *Angus* 134 6357
Kinneddar *Moray* 141 2269
Kinneff *Abers* 135 8477
Kinnelhead *D & G* 108 0201
Kinnell *Angus* 127 6150
Kinnerley *Shrops* 59 3320
Kinnersley *Herefs* 46 3449
Kinnersley *Worcs* 47 8743
Kinnerton *Powys* 46 2463
Kinnerton *Shrops* 59 3796
Kinnerton Green *Flints* 71 3361
Kinnesswood *P & K* 126 1702
Kinninvie *Dur* 95 0521
Kinnordy *Angus* 126 3655
Kinoulton *Notts* 63 6730
Kinross *P & K* 126 1102
Kinrossie *P & K* 126 1832
Kinsbourne Green *Herts* 38 1016
Kinsey Heath *Ches* 72 6642
Kinsham *Herefs* 46 3665
Kinsham *Worcs* 47 9335
Kinsley *W York* 83 4114
Kinson *Dorset* 12 0796
Kintbury *Berks* 23 3866
Kintessack *Moray* 141 0060
Kintillo *P & K* 126 1317
Kinton *Herefs* 46 4174
Kinton *Shrops* 59 3719
Kintore *Abers* 143 7916
Kintour *Ag & B* 112 4551
Kintra *Ag & B* 120 3125
Kintraw *Ag & B* 122 8204
Kinveachy *Highld* 140 9018
Kinver *Staffs* 60 8483
Kiplin *N York* 89 2897
Kippax *W York* 83 4130
Kippen *Stirlg* 116 6494
Kippford or Scaur *D & G* 92 8354
Kipping's Cross *Kent* 16 6440
Kirbister *Ork* 153 3607
Kirburd *Border* 117 1244
Kirby Bedon *Norfk* 67 2705
Kirby Bellars *Leics* 63 7117
Kirby Cane *Norfk* 67 3794
Kirby Corner *W Mids* 61 2976
Kirby Cross *Essex* 41 2120
Kirby Fields *Leics* 62 5203
Kirby Grindalythe *N York* 91 9067
Kirby Hill *N York* 89 1406
Kirby Hill *N York* 89 3968
Kirby Knowle *N York* 89 4687
Kirby le Soken *Essex* 41 2121
Kirby Misperton *N York* 90 7779
Kirby Muxloe *Leics* 62 5104
Kirby Row *Norfk* 67 3792
Kirby Sigston *N York* 89 4194
Kirby Underdale *E R Yk* 90 8058
Kirby Wiske *N York* 89 3784
Kirconnel *D & G* 100 9868
Kirdford *W Susx* 14 0126
Kirk *Highld* 151 2859
Kirk Bramwith *S York* 83 6211
Kirk Deighton *N York* 83 3950
Kirk Ella *E R Yk* 84 0129
Kirk Hallam *Derbys* 62 4540
Kirk Hammerton *N York* 83 4655
Kirk Ireton *Derbys* 73 2650
Kirk Langley *Derbys* 73 2838
Kirk Merrington *Dur* 96 2631
Kirk Michael *IOM* 158 3190
Kirk of Shotts *N Lans* 116 8462
Kirk Sandall *S York* 83 6108
Kirk Smeaton *N York* 83 5216
Kirk Yetholm *Border* 110 8228
Kirkabister *Shet* 153 4938
Kirkandrews *D & G* 99 6048
Kirkandrews upon Eden *Cumb* 93 3558
Kirkbampton *Cumb* 93 3056
Kirkbean *D & G* 92 9759
Kirkbride *Cumb* 93 2256
Kirkbridge *N York* 89 2590
Kirkbuddo *Angus* 127 5043
Kirkburn *Border* 109 2938
Kirkburn *E R Yk* 84 9855
Kirkburton *W York* 82 1912
Kirkby *Lincs* 76 0592
Kirkby *Mersyd* 78 4099
Kirkby *N York* 90 5305
Kirkby Fleetham *N York* 89 2894
Kirkby Green *Lincs* 76 0857
Kirkby Hall *N York* 89 2795
Kirkby in Ashfield *Notts* 75 4856
Kirkby la Thorpe *Lincs* 76 0946
Kirkby Lonsdale *Cumb* 87 6178
Kirkby Malham *N York* 88 8960
Kirkby Mallory *Leics* 50 4500
Kirkby Malzeard *N York* 89 2374
Kirkby Mills *N York* 90 7085
Kirkby on Bain *Lincs* 77 2462
Kirkby Overblow *N York* 83 3249
Kirkby Stephen *Cumb* 88 7708
Kirkby Thore *Cumb* 94 6325
Kirkby Underwood *Lincs* 64 0727
Kirkby Wharf *N York* 83 5041
Kirkby Woodhouse *Notts* 75 4954
Kirkby-in-Furness *Cumb* 86 2282
Kirkbymoorside *N York* 90 6986
Kirkcaldy *Fife* 117 2892
Kirkcambeck *Cumb* 101 5368
Kirkchrist *D & G* 99 6751
Kirkcolm *D & G* 98 0268
Kirkconnel *D & G* 107 7311
Kirkconnell *D & G* 99 6760
Kirkcowan *D & G* 98 3260
Kirkcudbright *D & G* 99 6850
Kirkdale *Mersyd* 78 3493
Kirkfieldbank *S Lans* 108 8643
Kirkgunzeon *D & G* 100 8666
Kirkham *Lancs* 80 4232
Kirkham *N York* 90 7365
Kirkhamgate *W York* 82 2922
Kirkharle *Nthumb* 103 0182
Kirkhaugh *Nthumb* 94 6949
Kirkheaton *Nthumb* 103 0177
Kirkheaton *W York* 82 1818
Kirkhill *Highld* 139 5545
Kirkhope *S Lans* 108 9606
Kirkhouse *Cumb* 94 5759
Kirkhouse Green *S York* 83 6213
Kirkibost *Highld* 129 5518
Kirkinch *P & K* 126 3044
Kirkinner *D & G* 99 4251
Kirkintilloch *E Duns* 116 6573
Kirkland *Cumb* 92 0718
Kirkland *Cumb* 94 6432
Kirkland *D & G* 107 7213
Kirkland *D & G* 100 8190
Kirkland *D & G* 100 0389
Kirkland Guards *Cumb* 93 1840
Kirkleatham *N York* 97 5921
Kirklevington *N York* 89 4309
Kirkley *Suffk* 67 5391
Kirklington *N York* 89 3181
Kirklington *Notts* 75 6757
Kirklinton *Cumb* 101 4367
Kirkliston *C Edin* 117 1274
Kirkmabreck *D & G* 99 4856
Kirkmaiden *D & G* 98 1236
Kirkmichael *P & K* 133 0759
Kirkmichael *S Ayrs* 106 3408
Kirkmuirhill *S Lans* 107 7842
Kirknewton *Nthumb* 110 9130
Kirknewton *W Loth* 117 1166
Kirkney *Abers* 142 5132
Kirkoswald *Cumb* 94 5541
Kirkoswald *S Ayrs* 106 2407
Kirkpatrick *D & G* 100 9090
Kirkpatrick *IOM* 158 2482
Kirkpatrick Durham *D & G* 100 7870
Kirkpatrick-Fleming *D & G* 101 2770
Kirksanton *Cumb* 86 1380
Kirkstall *W York* 82 2635
Kirkstead *Lincs* 76 1762
Kirkstile *Abers* 142 5235
Kirkstile *D & G* 101 3690
Kirkstone Pass Inn *Cumb* 87 4007
Kirkstyle *Highld* 151 3472
Kirkthorpe *W York* 83 3621
Kirkton *Abers* 142 6425
Kirkton *Abers* 143 8243
Kirkton *D & G* 100 9781
Kirkton *Fife* 126 3625
Kirkton *Highld* 137 8227
Kirkton *Highld* 138 9141
Kirkton *P & K* 125 9618
Kirkton Manor *Border* 109 2238
Kirkton of Airlie *Angus* 126 3151
Kirkton of Auchterhouse *Angus* 126 3438
Kirkton of Barevan *Highld* 140 8347
Kirkton of Collace *P & K* 126 1931
Kirkton of Glenbuchat *Abers* 141 3715
Kirkton of Logie Buchan *Abers* 143 9829
Kirkton of Menmuir *Angus* 134 5364
Kirkton of Monikie *Angus* 127 5138
Kirkton of Rayne *Abers* 142 6930
Kirkton of Skene *Abers* 135 8007
Kirkton of Strathmartine *Angus* 126 3735
Kirkton of Tealing *Angus* 126 4038
Kirktown *Abers* 143 9965
Kirktown *Abers* 143 0852
Kirktown of Bourtie *Abers* 143 8025
Kirktown of Fetteresso *Abers* 135 8486
Kirktown of Mortlach *Moray* 141 3138
Kirktown of Slains *Abers* 143 0329
Kirkwall *Ork* 153 4411
Kirkwall Airport 153 4808
Kirkwhelpington *Nthumb* 103 9984
Kirmincham *Ches* 79 8068
Kirmington *Lincs* 85 1011
Kirmond le Mire *Lincs* 76 1892
Kirn *Ag & B* 114 1878
Kirriemuir *Angus* 126 3853
Kirstead Green *Norfk* 67 2997
Kirtlebridge *D & G* 101 2372
Kirtling *Cambs* 53 6857
Kirtling Green *Suffk* 53 6855
Kirtlington *Oxon* 37 4919
Kirtomy *Highld* 150 7463
Kirton *Abers* 134 6113
Kirton *Lincs* 64 3038
Kirton *Notts* 75 6969
Kirton *Suffk* 55 2740
Kirton End *Lincs* 64 2940
Kirton Holme *Lincs* 64 2642
Kirton in Lindsey *Lincs* 76 9398
Kirtonhill *W Duns* 115 3875
Kirwaugh *D & G* 99 4054
Kishorn *Highld* 138 8440
Kislingbury *Nhants* 49 6959
Kite Green *Warwks* 48 1666
Kitebrook *Warwks* 48 2431
Kites Hardwick *Warwks* 50 4768
Kitleigh *Cnwll* 18 2499
Kitt Green *Gt Man* 78 5405
Kittisford *Somset* 20 0822
Kittle *Swans* 32 5789
Kitts Green *W Mids* 61 1587
Kittybrewster *Aber C* 135 9207
Kitwood *Hants* 24 6633
Kivernoll *Herefs* 46 4632
Kiveton Park *S York* 75 4982
Knaith *Lincs* 75 8284
Knaith Park *Lincs* 76 8485
Knap Corner *Dorset* 22 8023
Knaphill *Surrey* 25 9658
Knaplock *Somset* 19 8633
Knapp *Somset* 20 3025
Knapp Hill *Hants* 13 4023
Knapthorpe *Notts* 75 7458
Knapton *N York* 83 5652
Knapton *N York* 90 8876
Knapton *Norfk* 67 3034
Knapton Green *Herefs* 46 4452
Knapwell *Cambs* 52 3362
Knaresborough *N York* 89 3557
Knarsdale *Nthumb* 94 6754
Knaven *Abers* 143 8943
Knayton *N York* 89 4387
Knebworth *Herts* 39 2520
Knedlington *E R Yk* 84 7327
Kneesall *Notts* 75 7064
Kneesworth *Cambs* 39 3444
Kneeton *Notts* 63 7146
Knelston *Swans* 32 4688
Knenhall *Staffs* 72 9237
Knettishall *Suffk* 54 9780
Knightacott *Devon* 19 6539
Knightcote *Warwks* 48 4054
Knightley *Staffs* 72 8125
Knightley Dale *Staffs* 72 8123
Knighton *Devon* 6 5349
Knighton *Dorset* 10 6111
Knighton *Dorset* 12 0497
Knighton *Leics* 62 6001
Knighton *Powys* 46 2872
Knighton *Somset* 20 1944
Knighton *Staffs* 72 7240
Knighton *Staffs* 72 7527
Knighton *Wilts* 36 2971
Knighton on Teme *Worcs* 47 6369
Knightsbridge *Gloucs* 47 8926
Knightsmill *Cnwll* 4 0780
Knightwick *Worcs* 47 7356
Knill *Herefs* 46 2960
Knipton *Leics* 63 8231
Knitsley *Dur* 95 1048
Kniveton *Derbys* 73 2050
Knock *Cumb* 94 6727
Knock *Highld* 129 6709
Knock *Moray* 142 5452
Knock *W Isls* 152 4931
Knock Castle *N Ayrs* 114 1963
Knockally *Highld* 151 1429
Knockan *Highld* 145 2110
Knockando *Moray* 141 1941
Knockbain *Highld* 139 5543
Knockbain *Highld* 140 6256
Knockdee *Highld* 151 1760
Knockdown *Wilts* 35 8388
Knockeen *S Ayrs* 106 3195
Knockenkelly *N Ayrs* 105 0427
Knockentiber *E Ayrs* 106 4039
Knockhall *Kent* 27 5974
Knockholt *Kent* 27 4658
Knockholt Pound *Kent* 27 4859
Knockin *Shrops* 59 3322
Knockinlaw *E Ayrs* 107 4239
Knockmill *Kent* 27 5761
Knocknain *D & G* 98 9764
Knocksheen *D & G* 99 5882
Knockvennie Smithy *D & G* 99 7571
Knodishall *Suffk* 55 4262
Knole *Somset* 21 4825
Knole Park *Gloucs* 34 5983
Knolls Green *Ches* 79 8079
Knolton *Wrexhm* 71 3739
Knook *Wilts* 22 9341
Knossington *Leics* 63 8008
Knott End-on-Sea *Lancs* 80 3548
Knotting *Beds* 51 0063
Knotting Green *Beds* 51 0062
Knottingley *W York* 83 5023
Knotty Green *Bucks* 26 9392
Knowbury *Shrops* 46 5775
Knowe *D & G* 98 3171
Knowehead *D & G* 107 6090
Knoweside *S Ayrs* 106 2512
Knowl Green *Essex* 53 7841
Knowl Hill *Berks* 37 8279
Knowle *Bristl* 34 6070
Knowle *Devon* 18 4938
Knowle *Devon* 8 7801
Knowle *Devon* 9 0007
Knowle *Devon* 9 0582
Knowle *Shrops* 46 5973
Knowle *Somset* 20 9643
Knowle *W Mids* 61 1876
Knowle Cross *Devon* 9 0397
Knowle Green *Lancs* 81 6338
Knowle Hill *Surrey* 25 9966
Knowle St Giles *Somset* 10 3411
Knowlefield *Cumb* 93 4057
Knowlton *Dorset* 12 0209
Knowlton *Kent* 29 2853
Knowsley *Mersyd* 78 4395
Knowsley Safari Park 78 4694
Knowstone *Devon* 19 8323
Knox *N York* 89 2957
Knox Bridge *Kent* 28 7840
Knucklas *Powys* 46 2574
Knuston *Nhants* 51 9266
Knutsford *Ches* 79 7578
Knutton *Staffs* 72 8347
Knypersley *Staffs* 72 8856
Krumlin *W York* 82 0518
Kuggar *Cnwll* 3 7216
Kyle of Lochalsh *Highld* 137 7627
Kyleakin *Highld* 137 7526
Kylerhea *Highld* 129 7820
Kyles Scalpay *W Isls* 152 2198
Kylesku *Highld* 148 2233
Kylesmorar *Highld* 129 8093
Kylestrome *Highld* 148 2234
Kyloe *Nthumb* 111 0540
Kynaston *Herefs* 47 6435
Kynaston *Shrops* 59 3520
Kynnersley *Shrops* 72 6716
Kyre Green *Worcs* 46 6162
Kyre Park *Worcs* 47 6263
Kyrewood *Worcs* 46 5967
Kyrle *Somset* 20 0522

L

293

L'Ancresse *Guern* 158 0000
L'Eree *Guern* 158 0000
L'Etacq *Jersey* 158 0000
La Bellieuse *Guern* 158 0000
La Fontenelle *Guern* 158 0000
La Fosse *Guern* 158 0000
La Greve *Guern* 158 0000
La Greve de Lecq *Jersey* 158 0000
La Hougue Bie *Jersey* 158 0000
La Houguette *Guern* 158 0000
La Passee *Guern* 158 0000
La Pulente *Jersey* 158 0000
La Rocque *Jersey* 158 0000
La Rousaillerie *Guern* 158 0000
La Villette *Guern* 158 0000
Lacadal *W Isls* 152 4234
Lacasaigh *W Isls* 152 3321
Laceby *Lincs* 85 2106
Lacey Green *Bucks* 37 8200
Lach Dennis *Ches* 79 7071
Lackenby *N York* 97 5619
Lackford *Suffk* 53 7970
Lackford Green *Suffk* 53 7970
Lacock *Wilts* 22 9168
Ladbroke *Warwks* 49 4158
Ladderedge *Staffs* 72 9654
Laddingford *Kent* 28 6948
Lade Bank *Lincs* 77 3954
Ladock *Cnwll* 3 8950
Lady Hall *Cumb* 86 1986
Lady Village *Ork* 153 6841
Lady's Green *Suffk* 53 7559
Ladybank *Fife* 126 3009
Ladycross *Cnwll* 5 3188
Ladygill *S Lans* 108 9428
Ladykirk *Border* 110 8847
Ladyridge *Herefs* 46 5931
Ladywood *W Mids* 61 0586
Ladywood *Worcs* 47 8661
Lag *D & G* 100 8786
Laga *Highld* 121 6361
Lagavulin *Ag & B* 104 4045
Lagg *N Ayrs* 105 9521
Laggan *Highld* 131 2997
Laggan *Highld* 132 6194
Laid *Highld* 149 4159
Laide *Highld* 144 9091
Laig *Highld* 128 4687
Laigh Clunch *E Ayrs* 115 4647
Laigh Fenwick *E Ayrs* 107 4542
Laigh Glenmuir *E Ayrs* 107 6120
Laighstonehall *S Lans* 116 7054
Laindon *Essex* 40 6889
Lairg *Highld* 146 5806
Laisterdyke *W York* 82 1932
Laithes *Cumb* 93 4633
Lake *Devon* 19 5531
Lake *Devon* 5 5289
Lake *Dorset* 11 9990
Lake *IOW* 13 5883
Lake *Wilts* 23 1339
Lakenheath *Suffk* 53 7182
Laker's Green *Surrey* 14 0335
Lakesend *Norfk* 65 5196
Lakeside *Cumb* 87 3787
Laleham *Surrey* 26 0568
Laleston *Brdgnd* 33 8779
Lamancha *Border* 117 2052
Lamanva *Cnwll* 3 7631
Lamarsh *Essex* 54 8835
Lamas *Norfk* 67 2423
Lamb Roe *Lancs* 81 7337
Lambden *Border* 110 7443
Lamberhurst *Kent* 28 6736
Lamberhurst Down *Kent* 16 6735
Lamberton *Border* 119 9658
Lambeth *Gt Lon* 27 3178
Lambfair Green *Suffk* 53 7153
Lambley *Notts* 63 6345
Lambley *Nthumb* 94 6658
Lambourn *Berks* 36 3278
Lambourne End *Essex* 27 4794
Lambs Green *W Susx* 15 2136
Lambston *Pembks* 30 9016
Lamellion *Cnwll* 5 2463
Lamerton *Devon* 5 4577
Lamesley *T & W* 96 2557
Lamington *S Lans* 108 9731
Lamlash *N Ayrs* 105 0231
Lamonby *Cumb* 93 4036
Lamorick *Cnwll* 4 0364
Lamorna *Cnwll* 2 4424
Lamorran *Cnwll* 3 8741

Lampen Lingwood

294

Lampen Cnwll 4 1867
Lampeter Cerdgn 44 5747
Lampeter Velfrey Pembks 31 1514
Lamphey Pembks 30 0100
Lamplugh Cumb 92 0820
Lamport Nhants 50 7574
Lamyatt Somset 21 6536
Lana Devon 18 3007
Lana Devon 5 3496
Lanark S Lans 108 8843
Lanarth Cnwll 3 7621
Lancaster Lancs 87 4761
Lancaut Gloucs 34 5396
Lanchester Dur 96 1647
Lancing W Susx 15 1804
Land's End Cnwll 2 3425
Land's End Airport 2 3728
Land-hallow Highld 151 1833
Landbeach Cambs 53 4765
Landcross Devon 18 4523
Landerberry Abers 135 7404
Landford Wilts 12 2519
Landimore Swans 32 4692
Landkey Devon 19 6031
Landkey Town Devon 19 5931
Landore Swans 32 6695
Landrake Cnwll 5 3760
Landscove Devon 7 7766
Landshipping Pembks 30 0211
Landue Cnwll 5 3579
Landulph Cnwll 6 4361
Landwade Suffk 53 6268
Landywood Staffs 60 9805
Lane Cnwll 4 8260
Lane Bottom Lancs 81 8735
Lane End Bucks 37 8091
Lane End Ches 79 6890
Lane End Cnwll 4 0369
Lane End Hants 13 5525
Lane End Kent 27 5671
Lane End Lancs 81 8747
Lane End Wilts 22 8145
Lane End Waberthwaite Cumb 86 1093
Lane Ends Derbys 73 2334
Lane Ends Dur 96 1833
Lane Ends Lancs 81 7930
Lane Ends N York 82 9743
Lane Green Staffs 60 8703
Lane Head Dur 89 1211
Lane Head Gt Man 79 6296
Lane Head W Mids 35 9700
Lane Heads Lancs 80 4339
Lane Side Lancs 81 7922
Laneast Cnwll 5 2283
Laneham Notts 75 8076
Lanehead Dur 95 8441
Lanehead Nthumb 102 7985
Laneshaw Bridge Lancs 81 9240
Langaford Devon 18 4199
Langaller Somset 20 2626
Langar Notts 63 7234
Langbank Rens 115 3873
Langbar N York 82 0951
Langbaurgh N York 90 5511
Langcliffe N York 88 8264
Langdale End N York 91 9391
Langdon Cnwll 5 3089
Langdon Beck Dur 95 8531
Langdown Hants 13 4206
Langdyke Fife 126 3304
Langenhoe Essex 41 0018
Langford Beds 39 1841
Langford Devon 9 0203
Langford Essex 40 8309
Langford Notts 75 8258
Langford Oxon 36 2402
Langford Somset 21 4560
Langford Budville Somset 20 1122
Langford End Beds 52 1753
Langham Dorset 22 7725
Langham Essex 41 0333
Langham Norfk 66 0141
Langham Rutlnd 63 8411
Langham Suffk 54 9769
Langham Moor Essex 41 0131
Langham Wick Essex 41 0231
Langho Lancs 81 7034
Langholm D & G 101 3684
Langland Swans 32 6087
Langlee Border 109 5035
Langley Berks 26 0178
Langley Ches 79 9471
Langley Derbys 62 4445
Langley Gloucs 47 0028
Langley Gt Man 79 8506
Langley Hants 13 4401
Langley Herts 39 2122
Langley Kent 28 8052
Langley Nthumb 102 8261
Langley Oxon 36 2915
Langley Somset 20 0828
Langley W Susx 14 8029
Langley Warwks 48 1962
Langley Burrell Wilts 35 9375
Langley Castle Nthumb 102 8362
Langley Common Derbys 73 2937
Langley Green Derbys 73 2738
Langley Green Essex 40 8722
Langley Green Warwks 48 1962
Langley Lower Green Essex 39 4334
Langley Marsh Somset 20 0729
Langley Mill Derbys 62 4446
Langley Moor Dur 96 2540
Langley Park Dur 96 2145
Langley Street Norfk 67 3601
Langley Upper Green Essex 39 4434
Langleybury Herts 26 0700
Langney E Susx 16 6302
Langold Notts 75 5886
Langore Cnwll 5 2986
Langport Somset 21 4226
Langrick Lincs 77 2648
Langridge Somset 35 7469
Langridge Ford Devon 19 5722
Langrigg Cumb 92 1645
Langrish Hants 13 7023
Langsett S York 74 2100
Langside P & K 125 7913
Langstone Hants 13 7204
Langstone Newpt 34 3789
Langthorne N York 89 2491
Langthorpe N York 89 3867
Langthwaite N York 88 0001
Langtoft E R Yk 91 0066
Langtoft Lincs 64 1212
Langton Dur 96 1619
Langton Lincs 76 2368
Langton Lincs 77 3970
Langton N York 90 7966
Langton by Wragby Lincs 76 1476
Langton Green Kent 16 5439
Langton Green Suffk 54 1474
Langton Herring Dorset 10 6182
Langton Matravers Dorset 11 0078
Langtree Devon 18 4515
Langtree Week Devon 18 4715
Langwathby Cumb 94 5733
Langwell House Highld 147 1122
Langworth Lincs 76 0676
Langworthy Devon 5 4894
Lanhydrock House & Gardens 4 0863
Lanivet Cnwll 4 0464
Lanjeth Cnwll 3 9752
Lank Cnwll 4 0875
Lanlivery Cnwll 4 0759
Lanner Cnwll 2 7139
Lanoy Cnwll 5 2977
Lanreath Cnwll 4 1857
Lansallos Cnwll 4 1751
Lanteglos Cnwll 4 0882
Lanteglos Highway Cnwll 3 1453
Lanton Border 110 6221
Lanton Nthumb 110 9231
Lapford Somset 19 7308
Laphroaig Ag & B 104 3845
Lapley Staffs 60 8712
Lapworth Warwks 61 1671
Larachbeg Highld 122 6948
Larbert Falk 116 8582
Larbreck Lancs 80 4040
Largie Abers 142 6131
Largiemore Ag & B 114 9486
Largoward Fife 127 4607
Largs N Ayrs 114 2059
Largybeg N Ayrs 105 0423
Largymore N Ayrs 105 0424
Larkbeare Devon 9 0797
Larkfield Inver 114 2475
Larkfield Kent 28 7058
Larkhall S Lans 116 7651
Larkhill Wilts 23 1244
Larling Norfk 54 9889
Lartington Dur 95 0117
Lasborough Gloucs 35 8294
Lasham Hants 24 6742
Lashbrook Devon 18 4305
Lashenden Kent 28 8440
Lask Edge Staffs 72 9156
Lassodie Fife 117 1292
Lasswade Mdloth 117 3065
Lastingham N York 90 7290
Latcham Somset 21 4447
Latchford Herts 39 3920
Latchford Oxon 37 6501
Latchingdon Essex 40 8800
Latchley Cnwll 5 4173
Latebrook Staffs 72 8453
Lately Common Gt Man 79 6797
Lathbury Bucks 38 8744
Latheron Highld 151 2033
Latheronwheel Highld 151 1832
Lathones Fife 127 4708
Latimer Bucks 26 0099
Latteridge Gloucs 35 6684
Lattiford Somset 22 6926
Latton Wilts 36 0995
Lauder Border 118 5347
Laugharne Carmth 31 3010
Laughterton Lincs 76 8375
Laughton E Susx 16 4913
Laughton Leics 50 6688
Laughton Lincs 76 8497
Laughton Lincs 64 0731
Laughton-en-le-Morthen S York 75 5187
Launcells Cnwll 18 2405
Launcells Cross Cnwll 18 2605
Launceston Cnwll 5 3384
Launton Oxon 37 6022
Laurencekirk Abers 135 7171
Laurieston D & G 99 6864
Laurieston Falk 116 9179
Lavendon Bucks 51 9153
Lavenham Suffk 54 9149
Lavernock V Glam 20 1868
Laversdale Cumb 101 4762
Laverstock Wilts 23 1630
Laverstoke Hants 24 4948
Laverton Gloucs 48 0735
Laverton N York 89 2273
Laverton Somset 22 7753
Lavister Wrexhm 71 3758
Law S Lans 116 8252
Law Hill S Lans 116 8251
Lawers P & K 124 6739
Lawford Essex 41 0831
Lawford Somset 20 1336
Lawgrove P & K 125 0926
Lawhitton Cnwll 5 3582
Lawkland N York 88 7766
Lawkland Green N York 88 7765
Lawley Shrops 60 6608
Lawnhead Staffs 72 8325
Lawrence End Herts 38 1419
Lawrenny Pembks 30 0106
Lawshall Suffk 54 8654
Lawshall Green Suffk 54 8853
Lawton Herefs 46 4459
Laxay W Isls 152 3321
Laxdale W Isls 152 4234
Laxey IOM 158 4384
Laxfield Suffk 55 2972
Laxford Bridge Highld 148 2346
Laxo Shet 153 4463
Laxton E R Yk 84 7925
Laxton Nhants 51 9596
Laxton Notts 75 7267
Laycock W York 82 0341
Layer Breton Essex 40 9417
Layer Marney Essex 40 9217
Layer-de-la-Haye Essex 41 9620
Layham Suffk 54 0240
Layland's Green Berks 23 3866
Laymore Dorset 10 3804
Layter's Green Bucks 26 9890
Laytham E R Yk 84 7439
Laythes Cumb 93 2455
Lazenby N York 97 5719
Lazonby Cumb 94 5439
Le Bigard Guern 158 0000
Le Bourg Guern 158 0000
Le Bourg Jersey 158 0000
Le Gron Guern 158 0000
Le Haguais Jersey 158 0000
Le Hocq Jersey 158 0000
Le Villocq Guern 158 0000
Lea Derbys 74 3257
Lea Herefs 35 6521
Lea Lincs 75 8286
Lea Shrops 59 4108
Lea Shrops 59 3589
Lea Wilts 35 9586
Lea Bridge Derbys 74 3156
Lea Heath Staffs 73 0225
Lea Marston Warwks 61 2093
Lea Town Lancs 80 4730
Lea Yeat Cumb 88 7686
Leachkin Highld 140 6344
Leadburn Mdloth 117 2355
Leaden Roding Essex 40 5913
Leadenham Lincs 76 9452
Leadgate Dur 96 1251
Leadgate Nthumb 95 1159
Leadhills S Lans 108 8815
Leadingcross Green Kent 28 8951
Leadmill Derbys 74 2380
Leafield Oxon 36 3115
Leagrave Beds 38 0523
Leahead Ches 72 6864
Leake N York 89 4390
Leake Common Side Lincs 77 3952
Lealholm N York 90 7607
Lealholm Side N York 90 7607
Lealt Highld 137 5060
Leam Derbys 74 2379
Leamington Hastings Warwks 50 4467
Leamington Spa Warwks 48 3265
Leamonsley Staffs 61 1009
Leamside Dur 96 3146
Leap Cross E Susx 16 5810
Leasgill Cumb 87 4983
Leasingham Lincs 76 0548
Leasingthorne Dur 96 2530
Leatherhead Surrey 26 1656
Leathley N York 82 2347
Leaton Shrops 59 4618
Leaton Shrops 59 6111
Leaveland Kent 28 0053
Leavenheath Suffk 54 9537
Leavening N York 90 7863
Leaves Green Gt Lon 27 4161
Lebberston N York 91 0782
Lechlade Gloucs 36 2199
Lecht Gruinart Ag & B 112 2768
Leck Lancs 87 6476
Leckbuie P & K 124 7040
Leckford Hants 23 3737
Leckhampstead Berks 36 4375
Leckhampstead Bucks 49 7237
Leckhampstead Thicket Berks 36 4276
Leckhampton Gloucs 35 9419
Leckmelm Highld 145 1689
Leckwith V Glam 33 1574
Leconfield E R Yk 84 0143
Ledaig Ag & B 122 9037
Ledburn Bucks 38 9021
Ledbury Herefs 47 7137
Leddington Gloucs 47 6834
Ledgemoor Herefs 46 4150
Ledicot Herefs 46 4162
Ledmore Junction Highld 145 2412
Ledsham Ches 71 3574
Ledsham W York 83 4529
Ledston W York 83 4328
Ledston Luck W York 83 4330
Ledstone Devon 7 7446
Ledwell Oxon 49 4128
Lee Devon 18 4846
Lee Gt Lon 27 3875
Lee Hants 12 3617
Lee Shrops 59 4032
Lee Brockhurst Shrops 59 5427
Lee Chapel Essex 40 6987
Lee Clump Bucks 38 9004
Lee Common Bucks 38 9103
Lee Green Ches 72 6661
Lee Mill Devon 6 5955
Lee Moor Devon 6 5762
Lee Street Surrey 15 2743
Lee-on-the-Solent Hants 13 5600
Leebotwood Shrops 59 4798
Leece Cumb 86 2469
Leedon Beds 38 9325
Leeds Kent 28 8253
Leeds W York 82 2932
Leeds Bradford Airport 82 2241
Leeds Castle 28 8353
Leedstown Cnwll 2 6034
Leek Staffs 72 9856
Leek Wootton Warwks 48 2868
Leeming N York 89 2989
Leeming W York 82 0434
Leeming Bar N York 89 2889
Lees Derbys 73 2637
Lees Gt Man 79 9504
Lees W York 82 0437
Lees Green Derbys 73 2637
Lees Hill Cumb 101 5568
Leesthorpe Leics 63 7813
Leeswood Flints 70 2660
Leetown P & K 126 2121
Leftwich Ches 79 6672
Legbourne Lincs 77 3784
Legburthwaite Cumb 93 3219
Legerwood Border 110 5843
Legoland 26 9474
Legsby Lincs 76 1385
Leicester Leics 62 5804
Leicester Forest East Leics 62 5202
Leigh Devon 19 7212
Leigh Dorset 10 6108
Leigh Gloucs 47 8626
Leigh Gt Man 79 6599
Leigh Kent 16 5446
Leigh Shrops 59 3303
Leigh Surrey 15 2246
Leigh Wilts 36 0692
Leigh Worcs 47 7853
Leigh Beck Essex 40 8183
Leigh Delamere Wilts 35 8879
Leigh Green Kent 17 9033
Leigh Knoweglass S Lans 116 6350
Leigh Park Dorset 12 0299
Leigh Sinton Worcs 47 7750
Leigh upon Mendip Somset 22 6947
Leigh Woods Somset 34 5672
Leigh-on-Sea Essex 40 8286
Leighland Chapel Somset 20 0336
Leighterton Gloucs 35 8290
Leighton N York 89 1679
Leighton Powys 58 2306
Leighton Shrops 59 6105
Leighton Somset 22 7043
Leighton Bromswold Cambs 52 1175
Leighton Buzzard Beds 38 9225
Leinthall Earls Herefs 46 4467
Leinthall Starkes Herefs 46 4369
Leintwardine Herefs 46 4074
Leire Leics 50 5290
Leiston Suffk 55 4462
Leitfie P & K 126 2545
Leith C Edin 117 2776
Leitholm Border 110 7944
Lelant Cnwll 2 5437
Lelley E R Yk 85 2032
Lem Hill Worcs 60 7275
Lemmington Hall Nthumb 111 1211
Lempitlaw Border 110 7832
Lemreway W Isls 152 3711
Lemsford Herts 39 2212
Lenchwick Worcs 48 0347
Lendalfoot S Ayrs 106 1390
Lendrick Stirlg 124 5506
Lendrum Terrace Abers 143 1141
Lenham Kent 28 8952
Lenham Heath Kent 28 9149
Lenie Highld 139 5126
Lennel Border 110 8540
Lennox Plunton D & G 99 6051
Lennoxtown E Duns 116 6277
Lent Bucks 26 9381
Lenton Lincs 64 0230
Lenton Notts 62 5539
Lenwade Norfk 66 0918
Lenzie E Duns 116 6572
Leochel-Cushnie Abers 134 5210
Leominster Herefs 46 4959
Leonard Stanley Gloucs 35 8003
Leoville Jersey 158 0000
Lepe Hants 13 4498
Lephin Highld 136 1749
Leppington N York 90 7661
Lepton W York 82 2015
Lerryn Cnwll 4 1457
Lerwick Shet 153 4741
Les Arquets Guern 158 0000
Les Hubits Guern 158 0000
Les Lohiers Guern 158 0000
Les Murchez Guern 158 0000
Les Nicolles Guern 158 0000
Les Quartiers Guern 158 0000
Les Quennevais Jersey 158 0000
Les Sages Guern 158 0000
Les Villets Guern 158 0000
Lesbury Nthumb 111 2311
Leslie Abers 142 5924
Leslie Fife 126 2501
Lesmahagow S Lans 108 8139
Lesnewth Cnwll 4 1390
Lessingham Norfk 67 3928
Lessonhall Cumb 93 2250
Lestowder Cnwll 3 7924
Leswalt D & G 98 0163
Letchmore Heath Herts 26 1597
Letchworth Herts 39 2232
Letcombe Bassett Oxon 36 3784
Letcombe Regis Oxon 36 3886
Letham Angus 127 5348
Letham Border 110 6708
Letham Falk 116 8986
Letham Fife 126 3014
Letham Grange Angus 127 6345
Lethendy P & K 126 1341
Lethenty Abers 142 5820
Lethenty Abers 143 8140
Letheringham Suffk 55 2757
Letheringsett Norfk 66 0638
Lett's Green Kent 27 4559
Lettaford Devon 8 7084
Letterewe Highld 144 9571
Letterfearn Highld 138 8823
Letterfinlay Lodge Hotel Highld 131 2491
Lettermorar Highld 129 7389
Letters Highld 145 1687
Lettershaw S Lans 108 8920
Letterston Pembks 30 9429
Lettoch Highld 141 0219
Lettoch Highld 141 1032
Letton Herefs 46 3346
Letton Herefs 46 3770
Letty Green Herts 39 2810
Letwell S York 75 5686
Leuchars Fife 127 4521
Leumrabhagh W Isls 152 3711
Leurbost W Isls 152 3725
Levalsa Meor Cnwll 3 0049
Levedale Staffs 72 8916
Level's Green Essex 39 4724
Leven E R Yk 85 1045
Leven Fife 118 3800
Levens Cumb 87 4886
Levens Green Herts 39 3522
Levenshulme Gt Man 79 8794
Levenwick Shet 153 4021
Leverburgh W Isls 152 0286
Leverington Cambs 65 4411
Leverstock Green Herts 38 0806
Leverton Lincs 77 4047
Levington Suffk 55 2339
Levisham N York 90 8390
Lew Oxon 36 3206
Lewannick Cnwll 5 2780
Lewdown Devon 5 4586
Lewes E Susx 15 4110
Leweston Dorset 10 6312
Leweston Pembks 30 9322
Lewis Wych Herefs 46 3357
Lewisham Gt Lon 27 3774
Lewiston Highld 139 5129
Lewknor Oxon 37 7197
Leworthy Devon 18 3201
Leworthy Devon 19 6738
Lewson Street Kent 28 9661
Lewth Lancs 80 4836
Lewtrenchard Devon 5 4586
Lexden Essex 41 9625
Lexworthy Somset 20 2535
Ley Cnwll 4 1766
Ley Hill Bucks 26 9902
Leybourne Kent 28 6858
Leyburn N York 89 1190
Leycett Staffs 72 7946
Leygreen Herts 39 1624
Leyland Lancs 80 5422
Leyland Green Mersyd 78 5500
Leylodge Abers 135 7613
Leys Abers 143 0052
Leys Angus 126 2537
Leys of Cossans Angus 126 3849
Leysdown-on-Sea Kent 28 0370
Leysmill Angus 127 6047
Leysters Herefs 46 5664
Leyton Gt Lon 27 3786
Leytonstone Gt Lon 27 3987
Lezant Cnwll 5 3479
Lezayre IOM 158 4294
Lezerea Cnwll 2 6833
Lhanbryde Moray 141 2761
Libanus Powys 45 9925
Libberton S Lans 108 9943
Liberton C Edin 117 2769
Lichfield Staffs 61 1109
Lickey Worcs 60 9975
Lickey End Worcs 60 9772
Lickey Rock Worcs 60 9774
Lickfold W Susx 14 9226
Liddaton Green Devon 5 4582
Liddesdale Highld 130 7759
Liddington Wilts 36 2081
Lidgate Derbys 74 3077
Lidgate Suffk 53 7258
Lidget S York 75 6500
Lidgett Notts 75 6365
Lidham Hill E Susx 17 8316
Lidlington Beds 38 9939
Lidsing Kent 28 7862
Liff Angus 126 3332
Lifford W Mids 61 0580
Lifton Devon 5 3885
Liftondown Devon 5 3685
Lighthazles W York 82 0220
Lighthorne Warwks 48 3355
Lighthorne Heath Warwks 48 3555
Lightwater Surrey 25 9362
Lightwood Staffs 72 9241
Lightwood Green Ches 71 6342
Lightwood Green Wrexhm 71 3840
Lilbourne Nhants 50 5676
Lilburn Tower Nthumb 111 0224
Lilleshall Shrops 72 7315
Lilley Berks 37 4479
Lilley Herts 38 1126
Lilliesleaf Border 109 5325
Lillingstone Dayrell Bucks 49 7039
Lillingstone Lovell Bucks 49 7140
Lillington Dorset 10 6212
Lilliput Dorset 12 0489
Lilstock Somset 20 1645
Lilyhurst Shrops 60 7413
Limbrick Lancs 81 6016
Limbury Beds 38 0724
Lime Street Worcs 47 8130
Limebrook Herefs 46 3766
Limefield Gt Man 81 8012
Limekilnburn S Lans 116 7050
Limekilns Fife 117 0883
Limerigg Falk 116 8571
Limerstone IOW 13 4482
Limestone Brae Nthumb 95 7949
Limington Somset 21 5422
Limmerhaugh E Ayrs 107 6127
Limpenhoe Norfk 67 3903
Limpley Stoke Wilts 22 7860
Limpsfield Surrey 27 4053
Limpsfield Chart Surrey 27 4251
Linby Notts 75 5351
Linchmere W Susx 14 8630
Lincluden D & G 100 9677
Lincoln Lincs 76 9771
Lincomb Worcs 47 8268
Lincombe Devon 7 7440
Lindal in Furness Cumb 86 2475
Lindale Cumb 87 4180
Lindfield W Susx 15 3425
Lindford Hants 14 8036
Lindley W York 82 1217
Lindley Green N York 82 2248
Lindow End Ches 79 8178
Lindridge Worcs 47 6769
Lindsell Essex 40 6427
Lindsey Suffk 54 9745
Lindsey Tye Suffk 54 9845
Liney Somset 21 3535
Linford Essex 40 6779
Linford Hants 12 1806
Lingbob W York 82 0935
Lingdale N York 97 6716
Lingen Herefs 46 3667
Lingfield Surrey 15 3843
Lingley Green Ches 78 5588
Lingwood Norfk 67 3508

Lower Gledfield Marley

Lower Gledfield *Highld* 146 5890
Lower Godney *Somset* 21 4742
Lower Gornal *W Mids* 60 9191
Lower Gravenhurst *Beds* 38 1035
Lower Green *Gt Man* 79 7098
Lower Green *Herts* 39 1832
Lower Green *Herts* 39 4233
Lower Green *Kent* 16 5640
Lower Green *Kent* 16 6341
Lower Green *Nhants* 51 8159
Lower Green *Norfk* 66 9837
Lower Green *Staffs* 60 9007
Lower Green *Suffk* 53 7465
Lower Hacheston *Suffk* 55 3156
Lower Halliford *Surrey* 26 0866
Lower Halstock Leigh *Dorset* 10 5207
Lower Halstow *Kent* 28 8567
Lower Hamworthy *Dorset* 11 9990
Lower Hardres *Kent* 29 1553
Lower Harpton *Herefs* 46 2760
Lower Hartlip *Kent* 28 8464
Lower Hartshay *Derbys* 74 3851
Lower Hartwell *Bucks* 38 7912
Lower Hatton *Staffs* 72 8236
Lower Hawthwaite *Cumb* 86 2189
Lower Hergest *Herefs* 46 2755
Lower Heyford *Oxon* 49 4824
Lower Heysham *Lancs* 87 4160
Lower Higham *Kent* 28 7172
Lower Holbrook *Suffk* 54 1834
Lower Hordley *Shrops* 59 3929
Lower Horncroft *W Susx* 14 0017
Lower Howsell *Worcs* 47 7848
Lower Irlam *Gt Man* 79 7193
Lower Kilburn *Derbys* 62 3744
Lower Kilcott *Gloucs* 35 7889
Lower Killeyan *Ag & B* 104 2742
Lower Kingcombe *Dorset* 10 5599
Lower Kingswood *Surrey* 26 2453
Lower Kinnerton *Ches* 71 3462
Lower Langford *Somset* 21 4560
Lower Largo *Fife* 126 4102
Lower Leigh *Staffs* 73 0135
Lower Lemington *Gloucs* 48 2134
Lower Llanfadog *Powys* 45 9567
Lower Lovacott *Devon* 19 5227
Lower Loxhore *Devon* 19 6137
Lower Lydbrook *Gloucs* 34 5916
Lower Lye *Herefs* 46 4066
Lower Machen *Newpt* 34 2288
Lower Maes-coed *Herefs* 46 3430
Lower Mannington *Dorset* 12 0604
Lower Marston *Somset* 22 7644
Lower Meend *Gloucs* 34 5504
Lower Merridge *Somset* 20 2034
Lower Middleton Cheney *Nhants* 49 5041
Lower Milton *Somset* 21 5347
Lower Moor *W Mids* 47 9747
Lower Morton *Gloucs* 35 6491
Lower Nazeing *Essex* 39 3906
Lower Norton *Warwks* 48 2363
Lower Nyland *Dorset* 22 7521
Lower Penarth *V Glam* 20 1869
Lower Penn *Staffs* 60 8796
Lower Pennington *Hants* 12 3193
Lower Penwortham *Lancs* 80 5327
Lower Peover *Ches* 79 7474
Lower Place *Gt Man* 81 9011
Lower Pollicott *Bucks* 37 7013
Lower Pond Street *Essex* 39 4537
Lower Quinton *Warwks* 48 1847
Lower Rainham *Kent* 28 8167
Lower Raydon *Suffk* 54 0338
Lower Roadwater *Somset* 20 0339
Lower Salter *Lancs* 87 6063
Lower Seagry *Wilts* 35 9580
Lower Sheering *Essex* 39 4914
Lower Shelton *Beds* 38 9942
Lower Shiplake *Oxon* 37 7679
Lower Shuckburgh *Warwks* 49 4862
Lower Slaughter *Gloucs* 36 1622
Lower Soothill *W York* 82 2523
Lower Soudley *Gloucs* 35 6609
Lower Standen *Kent* 29 2340
Lower Stanton St Quintin *Wilts* 35 9180
Lower Stoke *Kent* 28 8375
Lower Stone *Gloucs* 35 6794
Lower Stonnall *Staffs* 61 0803
Lower Stow Bedon *Norfk* 66 9694
Lower Street *Dorset* 11 8399
Lower Street *E Susx* 16 7012
Lower Street *Norfk* 67 2635
Lower Street *Suffk* 53 7852
Lower Street *Suffk* 54 1052
Lower Stretton *Ches* 79 6281
Lower Stroud *Dorset* 10 4598
Lower Sundon *Beds* 38 0526
Lower Swanwick *Hants* 13 4909
Lower Swell *Gloucs* 48 1725
Lower Tadmarton *Oxon* 48 4036
Lower Tale *Devon* 9 0601
Lower Tean *Staffs* 73 0138
Lower Thurlton *Norfk* 67 4299
Lower Town *Cnwll* 2 6528
Lower Town *Devon* 7 7172
Lower Town *Herefs* 47 6342
Lower Town *Pembks* 30 9637
Lower Trebullett *Cnwll* 5 3277
Lower Tregantle *Cnwll* 5 3953
Lower Treluswell *Cnwll* 3 7735
Lower Tysoe *Warwks* 48 3445
Lower Ufford *Suffk* 55 2952
Lower Upcott *Devon* 9 8880
Lower Upham *Hants* 13 5219
Lower Upnor *Kent* 28 7571
Lower Vexford *Somset* 20 1135
Lower Walton *Ches* 78 6086
Lower Waterston *Dorset* 11 7395
Lower Weare *Somset* 21 4053
Lower Weedon *Nhants* 49 6259
Lower Welson *Herefs* 46 2950
Lower Westmancote *Worcs* 47 9337
Lower Whatcombe *Dorset* 11 8401
Lower Whatley *Somset* 22 7447
Lower Whitley *Ches* 71 6179
Lower Wick *Gloucs* 35 7096
Lower Wick *Worcs* 47 8352
Lower Wield *Hants* 24 6340
Lower Wigginton *Herts* 38 9409
Lower Willingdon *E Susx* 16 5803
Lower Withington *Ches* 79 8169
Lower Woodend *Bucks* 37 8187
Lower Wraxhall *Dorset* 10 5700
Lower Wyche *Worcs* 47 7743
Lower Wyke *W York* 82 1525
Lowerhouse *Lancs* 81 8032
Lowesby *Leics* 63 7207
Lowestoft *Suffk* 67 5493
Loweswater *Cumb* 92 1421
Lowfield Heath *W Susx* 15 2739
Lowgill *Cumb* 87 6297
Lowgill *Lancs* 87 6564
Lowick *Cumb* 86 2885
Lowick *Nhants* 51 9881
Lowick *Nthumb* 111 0139
Lowick Bridge *Cumb* 86 2986
Lowick Green *Cumb* 86 2985
Lowlands *Dur* 96 1325
Lowlands *Torfn* 34 2996
Lowsonford *Warwks* 48 1868
Lowther *Cumb* 94 5323
Lowther Castle *Cumb* 94 5223
Lowthorpe *E R Yk* 91 0860
Lowton *Devon* 8 6604
Lowton *Gt Man* 78 6197
Lowton *Somset* 20 1918
Lowton Common *Gt Man* 79 6397
Lowton St Mary's *Gt Man* 79 6397
Loxbeare *Devon* 9 9116
Loxhill *Surrey* 25 0038
Loxhore *Devon* 19 6138
Loxhore Cott *Devon* 19 6138
Loxley *Warwks* 48 2553
Loxley Green *Staffs* 73 0630
Loxter *Herefs* 47 7140
Loxton *Somset* 21 3755
Loxwood *W Susx* 14 0331
Loyal Lodge *Highld* 149 6146
Lubenham *Leics* 50 7087
Lucas Green *Surrey* 25 9460
Lucasgate *Lincs* 77 4147
Luccombe *Somset* 20 9243
Luccombe Village *IOW* 13 5879
Lucker *Nthumb* 111 1530
Luckett *Cnwll* 5 3873
Lucking Street *Essex* 54 8134
Luckington *Wilts* 35 8383
Lucknam *Wilts* 35 8272
Luckwell Bridge *Somset* 20 9038
Lucott *Somset* 19 8645
Lucton *Herefs* 46 4364
Lucy Cross *N York* 89 2112
Ludag *W Isls* 152 7714
Ludborough *Lincs* 77 2995
Ludbrook *Devon* 7 6654
Ludchurch *Pembks* 31 1411
Luddenden *W York* 82 0426
Luddenden Foot *W York* 82 0325
Luddenham Court *Kent* 28 9963
Luddesdown *Kent* 28 6666
Luddington *Lincs* 84 8316
Luddington *Warwks* 48 1652
Luddington in the Brook *Nhants* 51 1083
Ludford *Lincs* 76 1989
Ludford *Shrops* 46 5174
Ludgershall *Bucks* 37 6517
Ludgershall *Wilts* 23 2650
Ludgvan *Cnwll* 2 5033
Ludham *Norfk* 67 3818
Ludlow *Shrops* 46 5175
Ludney *Somset* 10 3812
Ludwell *Wilts* 22 9122
Ludworth *Dur* 96 3641
Luffenhall *Herts* 39 2928
Luffincott *Devon* 5 3394
Luffness *E Loth* 118 4780
Lugar *E Ayrs* 107 5921
Lugg Green *Herefs* 46 4462
Luggate Burn *E Loth* 118 5974
Luggiebank *N Lans* 116 7672
Lugsdale *Ches* 78 5285
Lugton *E Ayrs* 115 4152
Lugwardine *Herefs* 46 5540
Luib *Highld* 137 5627
Lulham *Herefs* 46 4141
Lullington *Derbys* 61 2412
Lullington *E Susx* 16 5202
Lullington *Somset* 22 7851
Lulsgate Bottom *Somset* 21 5165
Lulsley *Worcs* 47 7455
Lulworth Camp *Dorset* 11 8381
Lumb *Lancs* 81 8324
Lumb *W York* 82 0221
Lumbutts *W York* 82 9523
Lumby *N York* 83 4830
Lumloch *E Duns* 116 6370
Lumphanan *Abers* 134 5804
Lumphinnans *Fife* 117 1792
Lumsden *Abers* 142 4722
Lunan *Angus* 127 6851
Lunanhead *Angus* 127 4752
Luncarty *P & K* 125 0929
Lund *E R Yk* 84 9647
Lund *N York* 83 6532
Lundie *Angus* 126 2836
Lundie *Stirlg* 124 7304
Lundin Links *Fife* 126 4002
Lundin Mill *Fife* 126 4102
Lundy Green *Norfk* 67 2392
Lunna *Shet* 153 4869
Lunsford *Kent* 28 6959
Lunsford's Cross *E Susx* 17 7210
Lunt *Mersyd* 78 3402
Luntley *Herefs* 46 3955
Luppitt *Devon* 9 1606
Lupridge *Devon* 7 7153
Lupset *W York* 82 3119
Lupton *Cumb* 87 5581
Lurgashall *W Susx* 14 9326
Lurley *Devon* 9 9215
Lusby *Lincs* 77 3467
Luscombe *Devon* 7 7957
Luson *Devon* 6 6050
Luss *Ag & B* 115 3692
Lusta *Highld* 136 2656
Lustleigh *Devon* 8 7881
Luston *Herefs* 46 4863
Luthermuir *Abers* 135 6568
Luthrie *Fife* 126 3319
Lutley *Worcs* 60 9382
Luton *Beds* 38 0921
Luton *Devon* 9 0802
Luton *Devon* 9 9076
Luton *Kent* 28 7766
Luton Airport 38 1220
Lutterworth *Leics* 50 5484
Lutton *Devon* 6 5959
Lutton *Devon* 7 6961
Lutton *Lincs* 65 4325
Lutton *Nhants* 52 1187
Luxborough *Somset* 20 9738
Luxulyan *Cnwll* 4 0558
Luzley *Gt Man* 79 9600
Lybster *Highld* 151 2435
Lydbury North *Shrops* 59 3486
Lydcott *Devon* 19 6936
Lydd *Kent* 17 0420
Lydd Airport 17 0621
Lydden *Kent* 29 2645
Lydden *Kent* 29 3567
Lyddington *Rutlnd* 51 8797
Lyde Green *Hants* 24 7057
Lydeard St Lawrence *Somset* 20 1332
Lydeway *Wilts* 23 0557
Lydford *Devon* 5 5185
Lydford on Fosse *Somset* 21 5630
Lydgate *Gt Man* 82 9516
Lydgate *W York* 81 9225
Lydham *Shrops* 59 3391
Lydiard Green *Wilts* 36 0885
Lydiard Millicent *Wilts* 36 0986
Lydiard Tregoze *Wilts* 36 1085
Lydiate *Mersyd* 78 3604
Lydiate Ash *Worcs* 60 9775
Lydlinch *Dorset* 11 7413
Lydney *Gloucs* 35 6303
Lydstep *Pembks* 31 0898
Lye *W Mids* 60 9284
Lye Cross *Somset* 21 4962
Lye Green *Bucks* 38 9703
Lye Green *E Susx* 16 5134
Lye Green *Warwks* 48 1965
Lye Head *Worcs* 60 7573
Lye's Green *Wilts* 22 8146
Lyford *Oxon* 36 3994
Lymbridge Green *Kent* 29 1244
Lyme Regis *Dorset* 10 3492
Lyminge *Kent* 29 1641
Lymington *Hants* 12 3295
Lyminster *W Susx* 14 0204
Lymm *Ches* 79 6887
Lympne *Kent* 17 1135
Lympsham *Somset* 21 3354
Lympstone *Devon* 9 9984
Lynbridge *Devon* 19 7248
Lynch *Somset* 20 9047
Lynch Green *Norfk* 66 1505
Lynchat *Highld* 132 7801
Lyndhurst *Hants* 12 3008
Lyndon *Rutlnd* 63 9004
Lyndon Green *W Mids* 61 1485
Lyne *Border* 109 2041
Lyne *Surrey* 26 0166
Lyne Down *Herefs* 47 6431
Lyne of Skene *Abers* 135 7610
Lyneal *Shrops* 59 4433
Lyneham *Devon* 8 8579
Lyneham *Oxon* 36 2720
Lyneham *Wilts* 35 0278
Lyneham Airport 35 0178
Lyneholmford *Cumb* 101 5172
Lynemouth *Nthumb* 103 2991
Lyness *Ork* 153 3094
Lyng *Norfk* 66 0617
Lyng *Somset* 21 3329
Lynhales *Herefs* 46 3255
Lynmouth *Devon* 19 7249
Lynn *Shrops* 72 7815
Lynn *Staffs* 61 0704
Lynn of Shenval *Moray* 141 2129
Lynsted *Kent* 28 9460
Lynstone *Cnwll* 18 2005
Lynton *Devon* 19 7249
Lyon's Gate *Dorset* 11 6505
Lyonshall *Herefs* 46 3355
Lytchett Matravers *Dorset* 11 9495
Lytchett Minster *Dorset* 11 9693
Lyth *Highld* 151 2762
Lytham *Lancs* 80 3627
Lytham St Anne's *Lancs* 80 3427
Lythbank *Shrops* 59 4607
Lythe *N York* 90 8413
Lythmore *Highld* 150 0566

M

Mabe Burnthouse *Cnwll* 3 7634
Mabie *D & G* 100 9570
Mablethorpe *Lincs* 77 5085
Macclesfield *Ches* 79 9173
Macduff *Abers* 142 7064
Macharioch *Ag & B* 105 7309
Machen *Caerph* 33 2189
Machrie *N Ayrs* 105 8934
Machrihanish *Ag & B* 104 6320
Machrins *Ag & B* 112 3693
Machynlleth *Powys* 57 7400
Machynys *Carmth* 32 5198
Mackworth *Derbys* 62 3137
Macmerry *E Loth* 118 4372
Maddaford *Devon* 8 5494
Madderty *P & K* 125 9522
Maddington *Wilts* 23 0744
Maddiston *Falk* 116 9476
Madehurst *W Susx* 14 9810
Madeley *Shrops* 60 6904
Madeley *Staffs* 72 7744
Madeley Heath *Staffs* 72 7845
Madford *Devon* 9 1411
Madingley *Cambs* 52 3960
Madley *Herefs* 46 4238
Madresfield *Worcs* 47 8047
Madron *Cnwll* 2 4531
Maen-y-groes *Cerdgn* 42 3858
Maenaddwyn *IOA* 68 4684
Maenan *Conwy* 69 7965
Maenclochog *Pembks* 31 0827
Maendy *V Glam* 33 0076
Maenporth *Cnwll* 3 7829
Maentwrog *Gwynd* 57 6640
Maer *Cnwll* 18 2008
Maer *Staffs* 72 7938
Maerdy *Carmth* 44 6527
Maerdy *Rhondd* 33 9798
Maes-glas *Newpt* 34 2985
Maesbrook *Shrops* 59 3021
Maesbury *Shrops* 59 3026
Maesbury Marsh *Shrops* 59 3125
Maesgwynne *Carmth* 31 2024
Maeshafn *Denbgs* 70 2061
Maesllyn *Cerdgn* 42 3644
Maesmynis *Powys* 45 0146
Maesmynis *Powys* 45 0350
Maesteg *Brdgnd* 33 8590
Maesybont *Carmth* 32 5616
Maesycwmmer *Caerph* 33 1594
Magdalen Laver *Essex* 39 5108
Maggieknockater *Moray* 141 3145
Maggots End *Essex* 39 4827
Magham Down *E Susx* 16 6011
Maghull *Mersyd* 78 3703
Magor *Mons* 34 4286
Maiden Bradley *Wilts* 22 8038
Maiden Head *Somset* 21 5666
Maiden Law *Dur* 96 1749
Maiden Newton *Dorset* 10 5997
Maiden Wells *Pembks* 30 9799
Maidenbower *W Susx* 15 2935
Maidencombe *Devon* 7 9268
Maidenhayne *Devon* 10 2795
Maidenhead *Berks* 26 8980
Maidens *S Ayrs* 106 2107
Maidens Green *Berks* 25 8972
Maidenwell *Lincs* 77 3179
Maidford *Nhants* 49 6052
Maids Moreton *Bucks* 49 7035
Maidstone *Kent* 28 7555
Maidwell *Nhants* 50 7476
Maindee *Newpt* 34 3288
Mains of Balhall *Angus* 134 5163
Mains of Balnakettle *Abers* 134 6274
Mains of Dalvey *Highld* 141 1132
Mains of Haulkerton *Abers* 135 7172
Mainsforth *Dur* 96 3131
Mainsriddle *D & G* 92 9456
Mainstone *Shrops* 58 2787
Maisemore *Gloucs* 35 8121
Major's Green *Worcs* 61 1077
Makeney *Derbys* 62 3544
Malborough *Devon* 7 7139
Malcoff *Derbys* 74 0782
Malden *Surrey* 26 2166
Malden Rushett *Gt Lon* 26 1761
Maldon *Essex* 40 8506
Malham *N York* 88 9063
Mallaig *Highld* 129 6796
Mallaigvaig *Highld* 129 6897
Malleny Mills *C Edin* 117 1665
Mallows Green *Essex* 39 4726
Malltraeth *IOA* 68 4068
Mallwyd *Gwynd* 57 8612
Malmesbury *Wilts* 35 9387
Malmsmead *Somset* 19 7947
Malpas *Ches* 71 4847
Malpas *Cnwll* 3 8442
Malpas *Newpt* 34 3090
Malswick *Gloucs* 47 7324
Maltby *Lincs* 77 3183
Maltby *N York* 89 4613
Maltby *S York* 75 5392
Maltby le Marsh *Lincs* 77 4681
Malting Green *Essex* 41 9720
Maltman's Hill *Kent* 28 9043
Malton *N York* 90 7871
Malvern Link *Worcs* 47 7947
Malvern Wells *Worcs* 47 7742
Malzie *D & G* 99 3754
Mamble *Worcs* 60 6871
Mamhilad *Mons* 34 3003
Manaccan *Cnwll* 3 7624
Manafon *Powys* 58 1102
Manais *W Isls* 152 1089
Manaton *Devon* 8 7581
Manby *Lincs* 77 3986
Mancetter *Warwks* 61 3296
Manchester *Gt Man* 79 8497
Manchester Airport 79 8184
Mancot *Flints* 71 3167
Mandally *Highld* 131 2900
Manderston House 119 8154
Manea *Cambs* 53 4789
Maney *W Mids* 61 1195
Manfield *N York* 89 2113
Mangerton *Dorset* 10 4995
Mangotsfield *Gloucs* 35 6676
Mangrove Green *Herts* 38 1224
Manhay *Cnwll* 2 6930
Manish *W Isls* 152 1089
Mankinholes *W York* 82 9523
Manley *Ches* 71 5071
Manmoel *Caerph* 33 1803
Mannel *Ag & B* 120 9840
Manning's Heath *W Susx* 15 2028
Manningford Bohune *Wilts* 23 1357
Manningford Bruce *Wilts* 23 1358
Manningham *W York* 82 1435
Mannington *Dorset* 12 0605
Manningtree *Essex* 41 1031
Mannofield *Aber C* 135 9104
Manor Park *Gt Lon* 27 4285
Manorbier *Pembks* 30 0697
Manorbier Newton *Pembks* 30 0400
Manordeilo *Carmth* 44 6726
Manorhill *Border* 110 6632
Manorowen *Pembks* 30 9336
Mansell Gamage *Herefs* 46 3944
Mansell Lacy *Herefs* 46 4245
Mansergh *Cumb* 87 6082
Mansfield *E Ayrs* 107 6214
Mansfield *Notts* 75 5361
Mansfield Woodhouse *Notts* 75 5363
Mansriggs *Cumb* 86 2980
Manston *Dorset* 11 8115
Manston *Kent* 29 3466
Manston *W York* 83 3634
Manston Airport 29 3365
Manswood *Dorset* 11 9708
Manthorpe *Lincs* 63 9137
Manthorpe *Lincs* 64 0715
Manton *Lincs* 84 9302
Manton *Notts* 75 6078
Manton *Rutlnd* 63 8704
Manton *Wilts* 23 1768
Manuden *Essex* 39 4926
Manwood Green *Essex* 39 5412
Maperton *Somset* 22 6726
Maple Cross *Herts* 26 0393
Maplebeck *Notts* 75 7060
Mapledurham *Oxon* 37 6776
Mapledurwell *Hants* 24 6851
Maplehurst *W Susx* 15 1824
Maplescombe *Kent* 27 5664
Mapleton *Derbys* 73 1647
Mapleton *Kent* 16 4649
Mapperley *Derbys* 62 4342
Mapperley Park *Notts* 62 5842
Mapperton *Dorset* 10 5099
Mappleborough Green *Warwks* 48 0866
Mappleton *E R Yk* 85 2243
Mapplewell *S York* 83 3210
Mappowder *Dorset* 11 7306
Marazanvose *Cnwll* 3 7950
Marazion *Cnwll* 2 5130
Marbury *Ches* 71 5645
March *Cambs* 65 4196
March *S Lans* 108 9914
Marcham *Oxon* 37 4596
Marchamley *Shrops* 59 5929
Marchamley Wood *Shrops* 59 5831
Marchington *Staffs* 73 1330
Marchington Woodlands *Staffs* 73 1128
Marchros *Gwynd* 56 3125
Marchwiel *Wrexhm* 71 3547
Marchwood *Hants* 12 3810
Marcross *V Glam* 20 9269
Marden *Herefs* 46 5146
Marden *Kent* 28 7444
Marden *Wilts* 23 0857
Marden Ash *Essex* 27 5502
Marden Beech *Kent* 28 7442
Marden Thorn *Kent* 28 7642
Mardens Hill *E Susx* 16 5032
Mardlebury *Herts* 39 2618
Mardy *Mons* 34 3015
Marefield *Leics* 63 7407
Mareham le Fen *Lincs* 77 2761
Mareham on the Hill *Lincs* 77 2867
Marehay *Derbys* 62 3947
Marehill *W Susx* 14 0618
Maresfield *E Susx* 16 4624
Marfleet *E R Yk* 85 1429
Marford *Wrexhm* 71 3556
Margam *Neath* 32 7887
Margaret Marsh *Dorset* 22 8218
Margaret Roding *Essex* 40 5912
Margaretting *Essex* 40 6701
Margaretting Tye *Essex* 40 6800
Margate *Kent* 29 3571
Margnaheglish *N Ayrs* 105 0332
Margrie *D & G* 99 5950
Margrove Park *N York* 97 6515
Marham *Norfk* 65 7009
Marhamchurch *Cnwll* 18 2203
Marholm *Cambs* 64 1401
Marian-glas *IOA* 68 5084
Mariansleigh *Devon* 19 7422
Marine Town *Kent* 28 9274
Marionburgh *Abers* 135 7006
Marishader *Highld* 136 4963
Maristow *Devon* 6 4764
Maritime Centre 142 4265
Marjoriebanks *D & G* 100 0883
Mark *Somset* 21 3847
Mark Causeway *Somset* 21 3547
Mark Cross *E Susx* 16 5010
Mark Cross *E Susx* 16 5831
Mark's Corner *IOW* 13 4692
Markbeech *Kent* 16 4742
Markby *Lincs* 77 4878
Markeaton *Derbys* 62 3237
Market Bosworth *Leics* 62 4002
Market Deeping *Lincs* 64 1310
Market Drayton *Shrops* 72 6734
Market Harborough *Leics* 50 7387
Market Lavington *Wilts* 22 0154
Market Overton *Rutlnd* 63 8816
Market Rasen *Lincs* 76 1089
Market Stainton *Lincs* 76 2279
Market Weighton *E R Yk* 84 8741
Market Weston *Suffk* 54 9877
Markfield *Leics* 62 4809
Markham *Caerph* 33 1601
Markham Moor *Notts* 75 7173
Markinch *Fife* 126 2901
Markington *N York* 89 2865
Markle *E Loth* 118 5777
Marks Tey *Essex* 40 9023
Marksbury *Somset* 22 6662
Markwell *Cnwll* 5 3758
Markyate *Herts* 38 0616
Marl Bank *Worcs* 47 7840
Marlborough *Wilts* 23 1868
Marlbrook *Herefs* 46 5154
Marlbrook *Worcs* 60 9774
Marlcliff *Warwks* 48 0950
Marldon *Devon* 7 8663
Marle Green *E Susx* 16 5816
Marlesford *Suffk* 55 3258
Marley *Kent* 29 1850
Marley *Kent* 29 3353

298

N

300

Newton on Trent *Lincs* **76** 8373
Newton Poppleford *Devon* **9** 0889
Newton Purcell *Oxon* **49** 6230
Newton Regis *Warwks* **61** 2707
Newton Reigny *Cumb* **93** 4731
Newton Row *Highld* **151** 3449
Newton Solney *Derbys* **73** 2825
Newton St Cyres *Devon* **9** 8898
Newton St Faith *Norfk* **67** 2217
Newton St Loe *Somset* **22** 7064
Newton St Petrock *Devon* **18** 4112
Newton Stacey *Hants* **24** 4140
Newton Stewart *D & G* **99** 4065
Newton Toney *Wilts* **23** 2140
Newton Tracey *Devon* **19** 5226
Newton under
Roseberry *N York* **90** 5713
Newton Underwood *Nthumb* **103** 1486
Newton upon Derwent *E R Yk* **84** 7149
Newton Valence *Hants* **24** 7232
Newton Wamphray *D & G* **100** 1195
Newton with Scales *Lancs* **80** 4530
Newton-by-the-Sea *Nthumb* **111** 2325
Newton-le-Willows *Mersyd* **78** 5995
Newton-le-Willows *N York* **89** 2189
Newton-on-Rawcliffe *N York* **90** 8090
Newton-on-the-Moor *Nthumb* **111** 1705
Newtongarry Croft *Abers* **142** 5735
Newtongrange *Mdloth* **118** 3364
Newtonhill *Abers* **135** 9193
Newtonloan *Mdloth* **118** 3362
Newtonmill *Angus* **134** 6064
Newtonmore *Highld* **132** 7098
Newtown *Blae G* **33** 1709
Newtown *Ches* **71** 6247
Newtown *Ches* **72** 9060
Newtown *Ches* **71** 5278
Newtown *Cnwll* **2** 5729
Newtown *Cnwll* **3** 7423
Newtown *Cnwll* **3** 1052
Newtown *Cnwll* **5** 2978
Newtown *Cumb* **92** 1048
Newtown *Cumb* **101** 5062
Newtown *Cumb* **94** 5224
Newtown *Cumb* **101** 3862
Newtown *D & G* **107** 7710
Newtown *Derbys* **79** 9984
Newtown *Devon* **9** 0699
Newtown *Devon* **19** 7625
Newtown *Dorset* **10** 4802
Newtown *Dorset* **12** 0393
Newtown *Gloucs* **35** 6702
Newtown *Gt Man* **78** 5604
Newtown *Hants* **12** 2710
Newtown *Hants* **24** 4763
Newtown *Hants* **13** 6013
Newtown *Herefs* **46** 4757
Newtown *Herefs* **46** 5333
Newtown *Herefs* **46** 6145
Newtown *Herefs* **47** 7037
Newtown *Highld* **131** 3504
Newtown *IOW* **13** 4290
Newtown *Lancs* **80** 5118
Newtown *Nthumb* **111** 9631
Newtown *Nthumb* **103** 0300
Newtown *Nthumb* **103** 0425
Newtown *Powys* **58** 1091
Newtown *Rhondd* **33** 0598
Newtown *Shrops* **59** 4222
Newtown *Shrops* **59** 4731
Newtown *Somset* **10** 2712
Newtown *Staffs* **60** 9904
Newtown *Wilts* **22** 9129
Newtown *Wilts* **23** 2963
Newtown *Worcs* **47** 8755
Newtown *Worcs* **60** 9478
Newtown Linford *Leics* **62** 5209
Newtown of Beltrees *Rens* **115** 3758
Newtown St Boswells *Border* **110** 5732
Newtown Unthank *Leics* **62** 4904
Newtyle *Angus* **126** 2941
Newyears Green *Gt Lon* **26** 0788
Newyork *Ag & B* **122** 9611
Nextend *Herefs* **46** 3357
Neyland *Pembks* **30** 9605
Niarbyl *IOM* **158** 2177
Nibley *Gloucs* **35** 6606
Nibley *Gloucs* **35** 6982
Nibley Green *Gloucs* **35** 7396
Nicholashayne *Devon* **9** 1016
Nicholaston *Swans* **32** 5288
Nickies Hill *Cumb* **101** 5667
Nidd *N York* **89** 3060
Nigg *Aber C* **135** 9402
Nigg *Highld* **147** 8071
Nightcott *Somset* **19** 8925
Nimlet *Somset* **35** 7470
Nine Elms *Wilts* **36** 1085
Nine Wells *Pembks* **30** 7924
Ninebanks *Nthumb* **94** 7853
Nineveh *Worcs* **47** 6265
Ninfield *E Susx* **16** 7012
Ningwood *IOW* **13** 3989
Nisbet *Border* **110** 6725
Nisbet Hill *Border* **119** 7950
Niton *IOW* **13** 5076
Nitshill *C Glas* **115** 5260
No Man's Heath *Ches* **71** 5148
No Man's Heath *Warwks* **61** 2808
No Man's Land *Cnwll* **4** 9470
No Man's Land *Cnwll* **5** 2756
Noah's Ark *Kent* **27** 5557
Noak Bridge *Essex* **40** 6990
Noak Hill *Essex* **27** 5494
Nobold *Shrops* **59** 4710
Nobottle *Nhants* **49** 6763
Nocton *Lincs* **76** 0564
Nogdam End *Norfk* **67** 3900
Noke *Oxon* **37** 5413
Nolton *Pembks* **30** 8618
Nolton Haven *Pembks* **30** 8618
Nomansland *Devon* **19** 8313
Nomansland *Wilts* **12** 2517
Noneley *Shrops* **59** 4828
Nonington *Kent* **29** 2552
Nook *Cumb* **101** 4679
Nook *Cumb* **87** 5481

Norbiton *Gt Lon* **26** 1969
Norbreck *Lancs* **80** 3140
Norbridge *Herefs* **47** 7144
Norbury *Ches* **71** 5547
Norbury *Derbys* **73** 1241
Norbury *Gt Lon* **27** 3069
Norbury *Shrops* **59** 3692
Norbury *Staffs* **72** 7823
Norbury Common *Ches* **71** 5548
Norbury Junction *Staffs* **72** 7923
Norchard *Worcs* **47** 8568
Norcott Brook *Ches* **78** 6080
Norcross *Lancs* **80** 3341
Nordelph *Norfk* **65** 5501
Norden *Gt Man* **81** 8614
Nordley *Shrops* **60** 6996
Norham *Nthumb* **110** 9047
Norland Town *W York* **82** 0622
Norley *Ches* **71** 5772
Norleywood *Hants* **12** 3597
Norlington *E Susx* **16** 4413
Norman Cross *Cambs* **52** 1690
Norman's Bay *E Susx* **16** 6805
Norman's Green *Devon* **9** 0503
Normanby *Lincs* **84** 8816
Normanby *Lincs* **76** 9988
Normanby *N York* **97** 5418
Normanby *N York* **90** 7381
Normanby le Wold *Lincs* **76** 1295
Normandy *Surrey* **25** 9351
Normanton *Derbys* **62** 3433
Normanton *Leics* **63** 8140
Normanton *Lincs* **63** 9446
Normanton *Notts* **75** 7054
Normanton *Rutlnd* **63** 9305
Normanton *W York* **83** 3822
Normanton *Wilts* **23** 1340
Normanton le Heath *Leics* **62** 3712
Normanton on Soar *Notts* **62** 5122
Normanton on the Wolds *Notts* **62** 6232
Normanton on Trent *Notts* **75** 7868
Normoss *Lancs* **80** 3437
Norney *Surrey* **25** 9444
Norrington Common *Wilts* **22** 8864
Norris Green *Cnwll* **5** 4169
Norristhorpe *W York* **82** 2123
North Anston *S York* **75** 5184
North Aston *Oxon* **49** 4828
North Baddesley *Hants* **13** 3920
North Ballachulish *Highld* **130** 0560
North Barrow *Somset* **21** 6129
North Barsham *Norfk* **66** 9135
North Benfleet *Essex* **40** 7588
North Bersted *W Susx* **14** 9201
North Berwick *E Loth* **118** 5485
North Bitchburn *Dur* **96** 1732
North Blyth *Nthumb* **103** 3082
North Boarhunt *Hants* **13** 6010
North Bockhampton *Hants* **12** 1797
North Bovey *Devon* **8** 7484
North Bradley *Wilts* **22** 8555
North Brentor *Devon* **5** 4881
North Brewham *Somset* **22** 7236
North Bridge *Surrey* **14** 9636
North Brook End *Cambs* **39** 2944
North Buckland *Devon* **18** 4840
North Burlingham *Norfk* **67** 3609
North Cadbury *Somset* **21** 6327
North Carlton *Lincs* **76** 9477
North Carlton *Notts* **75** 5984
North Cave *E R Yk* **84** 8932
North Cerney *Gloucs* **35** 0107
North Chailey *E Susx* **15** 3921
North Charford *Hants* **12** 1919
North Charlton *Nthumb* **111** 1622
North Cheam *Gt Lon* **26** 2365
North Cheriton *Somset* **22** 6925
North Chideock *Dorset* **10** 4294
North Cliffe *E R Yk* **84** 8736
North Clifton *Notts* **75** 8272
North Close *Dur* **96** 2532
North Cockerington *Lincs* **77** 3790
North Connel *Ag & B* **122** 9034
North Cornelly *Brdgnd* **33** 8181
North Corner *Cnwll* **3** 7818
North Corry *Highld* **122** 8353
North Cotes *Lincs* **77** 3400
North Country *Cnwll* **2** 6943
North Cove *Suffk* **55** 4689
North Cowton *N York* **89** 2803
North Crawley *Bucks* **38** 9244
North Cray *Gt Lon* **27** 4872
North Creake *Norfk* **66** 8538
North Curry *Somset* **21** 3125
North Dalton *E R Yk* **84** 9351
North Deighton *N York* **83** 3951
North Duffield *N York* **83** 6837
North Duntulm *Highld* **136** 4274
North Elham *Kent* **29** 1844
North Elkington *Lincs* **77** 2890
North Elmham *Norfk* **66** 9820
North Elmsall *W York* **83** 4712
North End *Cumb* **93** 3259
North End *Dorset* **22** 8427
North End *E R Yk* **85** 1941
North End *E R Yk* **85** 2831
North End *Essex* **40** 6618
North End *Hants* **12** 1016
North End *Hants* **24** 5828
North End *Hants* **13** 6502
North End *Leics* **62** 5715
North End *Lincs* **85** 1022
North End *Lincs* **85** 3101
North End *Lincs* **76** 0499
North End *Lincs* **64** 2341
North End *Lincs* **77** 4289
North End *Mersyd* **78** 3004
North End *Nhants* **51** 9668
North End *Norfk* **66** 9992
North End *Nthumb* **103** 1301
North End *Somset* **21** 4266
North End *W Susx* **14** 9703
North End *W Susx* **14** 1109
North Erradale *Highld* **144** 7480
North Evington *Leics* **62** 6204
North Fambridge *Essex* **40** 8597
North Ferriby *E R Yk* **84** 9826
North Frodingham *E R Yk* **85** 1053

North Gorley *Hants* **12** 1611
North Green *Norfk* **55** 2288
North Green *Suffk* **55** 3162
North Green *Suffk* **55** 3966
North Grimston *N York* **90** 8467
North Halling *Kent* **28** 7065
North Hayling *Hants* **13** 7303
North Hazelrigg *Nthumb* **111** 0533
North Heasley *Devon* **19** 7333
North Heath *W Susx* **14** 0621
North Hele *Somset* **20** 0323
North Hill *Cnwll* **5** 2776
North Hillingdon *Gt Lon* **26** 0784
North Hinksey *Oxon* **37** 4905
North Holmwood *Surrey* **15** 1647
North Huish *Devon* **7** 7156
North Hykeham *Lincs* **76** 9465
North Kelsey *Lincs* **84** 0401
North Kessock *Highld* **140** 6548
North Killingholme *Lincs* **85** 1417
North Kilvington *N York* **89** 4285
North Kilworth *Leics* **50** 6183
North Kingston *Hants* **12** 1603
North Kyme *Lincs* **76** 1552
North Landing *E R Yk* **91** 2471
North Lee *Bucks* **38** 8308
North Lees *N York* **89** 2973
North Leigh *Kent* **29** 1347
North Leigh *Oxon* **36** 3813
North Leverton
with Habblesthorpe *Notts* **75** 7882
North Littleton *Worcs* **48** 0847
North Lopham *Norfk* **54** 0382
North Luffenham *Rutlnd* **63** 9303
North Marden *W Susx* **14** 8016
North Marston *Bucks* **37** 7722
North Middleton *Mdloth* **118** 3559
North Middleton *Nthumb* **111** 9924
North Milmain *D & G* **98** 0852
North Molton *Devon* **19** 7329
North Moreton *Oxon* **37** 5689
North Mundham *W Susx* **14** 8702
North Muskham *Notts* **75** 7958
North Newbald *E R Yk* **84** 9136
North Newington *Oxon* **49** 4240
North Newnton *Wilts* **23** 1257
North Newton *Somset* **20** 3031
North Nibley *Gloucs* **35** 7495
North Oakley *Hants* **24** 5354
North Ockendon *Gt Lon* **27** 5985
North Ormesby *N York* **97** 5119
North Ormsby *Lincs* **77** 2893
North Otterington *N York* **89** 3689
North Owersby *Lincs* **76** 0594
North Perrott *Somset* **10** 4709
North Petherton *Somset* **20** 2833
North Petherwin *Cnwll* **5** 2789
North Pickenham *Norfk* **66** 8606
North Piddle *Worcs* **47** 9654
North Pool *Devon* **7** 7741
North Poorton *Dorset* **10** 5298
North Poulner *Hants* **12** 1606
North Quarme *Somset* **20** 9236
North Queensferry *C Edin* **117** 1380
North Radworthy *Devon* **19** 7534
North Rauceby *Lincs* **76** 0246
North Reston *Lincs* **77** 3883
North Rigton *N York* **82** 2749
North Ripley *Hants* **12** 1699
North Rode *Ches* **72** 8866
North Ronaldsay Airport **153** 7554
North Row *Cumb* **93** 2232
North Runcton *Norfk* **65** 6416
North Scale *Cumb* **86** 1869
North Scarle *Lincs* **76** 8466
North Seaton *Nthumb* **103** 2986
North Seaton Colliery *Nthumb* **103** 2986
North Shian *Ag & B* **122** 9143
North Shields *T & W* **103** 3568
North Shoebury *Essex* **40** 9286
North Shore *Lancs* **80** 3037
North Side *Cambs* **64** 2799
North Side *Cumb* **92** 9929
North Skelton *N York* **97** 6718
North Somercotes *Lincs* **77** 4296
North Stainley *N York* **89** 2876
North Stainmore *Cumb* **95** 8314
North Stifford *Essex* **40** 6080
North Stoke *Oxon* **37** 6186
North Stoke *Somset* **35** 7069
North Stoke *W Susx* **14** 0110
North Street *Berks* **24** 6371
North Street *Cambs* **53** 5868
North Street *Hants* **12** 1518
North Street *Hants* **24** 6433
North Street *Kent* **28** 8174
North Street *Kent* **28** 0157
North Sunderland *Nthumb* **111** 2131
North Tamerton *Cnwll* **5** 3197
North Tawton *Devon* **8** 6601
North Third *Stirlg* **116** 7589
North Thoresby *Lincs* **77** 2998
North Tidworth *Wilts* **23** 2349
North Town *Berks* **26** 8882
North Town *Devon* **19** 5109
North Town *Somset* **21** 5642
North Tuddenham *Norfk* **66** 0314
North Walbottle *T & W* **103** 1767
North Walsham *Norfk* **67** 2830
North Waltham *Hants* **24** 5646
North Warnborough *Hants* **24** 7351
North Weald Bassett *Essex* **39** 4904
North Wheatley *Notts* **75** 7585
North Whilborough *Devon* **7** 8766
North Wick *Somset* **21** 5865
North Widcombe *Somset* **21** 5758
North Willingham *Lincs* **76** 1688
North Wingfield *Derbys* **74** 4065
North Witham *Lincs* **63** 9221
North Wootton *Dorset* **11** 6514
North Wootton *Norfk* **65** 6424
North Wootton *Somset* **21** 5641
North Wraxall *Wilts* **35** 8175
North Wroughton *Wilts* **36** 1481
Northacre *Norfk* **66** 9598
Northall *Bucks* **38** 9520
Northall Green *Norfk* **66** 9914
Northallerton *N York* **89** 3694

Northam *Devon* **18** 4529
Northam *Hants* **13** 4312
Northampton *Nhants* **49** 7560
Northampton *Worcs* **47** 8365
Northaw *Herts* **27** 2702
Northay *Somset* **10** 2811
Northborough *Cambs* **64** 1507
Northbourne *Kent* **29** 3352
Northbridge Street *E Susx* **17** 7324
Northbrook *Hants* **24** 5139
Northbrook *Oxon* **37** 4922
Northchapel *W Susx* **14** 9529
Northchurch *Herts* **38** 9708
Northcott *Devon* **9** 0912
Northcott *Devon* **9** 1209
Northcott *Devon* **5** 3392
Northcourt *Oxon* **37** 4998
Northdown *Kent* **29** 3770
Northedge *Derbys* **74** 3665
Northend *Bucks* **37** 7392
Northend *Warwks* **48** 3952
Northend Woods *Bucks* **26** 9089
Northenden *Gt Man* **79** 8289
Northfield *Aber C* **135** 9008
Northfield *E R Yk* **84** 0326
Northfield *W Mids* **60** 0279
Northfields *Lincs* **64** 0208
Northfleet *Kent* **27** 6374
Northiam *E Susx* **17** 8324
Northill *Beds* **52** 1446
Northington *Gloucs* **35** 7008
Northington *Hants* **24** 5637
Northlands *Lincs* **77** 3453
Northleach *Gloucs* **36** 1114
Northleigh *Devon* **19** 6034
Northleigh *Devon* **19** 1995
Northlew *Devon* **19** 5099
Northload Bridge *Somset* **21** 4939
Northmoor *Oxon* **36** 4202
Northmoor *Somset* **20** 9028
Northmuir *Angus* **126** 3854
Northney *Hants* **13** 7303
Northolt *Gt Lon* **26** 1384
Northop *Flints* **70** 2468
Northop Hall *Flints* **70** 2667
Northorpe *Lincs* **76** 8997
Northorpe *Lincs* **64** 0917
Northorpe *Lincs* **64** 2036
Northorpe *W York* **82** 2221
Northover *Somset* **21** 4838
Northover *Somset* **21** 5223
Northowram *W York* **82** 1126
Northport *Dorset* **11** 9288
Northrepps *Norfk* **67** 2439
Northton *W Isls* **152** 9989
Northway *Somset* **20** 1329
Northway *Swans* **32** 5889
Northwich *Ches* **79** 6673
Northwick *Gloucs* **34** 5686
Northwick *Somset* **21** 3548
Northwick *Worcs* **47** 8458
Northwold *Norfk* **65** 7597
Northwood *Derbys* **74** 2664
Northwood *Gt Lon* **26** 0990
Northwood *IOW* **13** 4992
Northwood *Shrops* **59** 4633
Northwood *Staffs* **72** 8949
Northwood Green *Gloucs* **35** 7216
Norton *Ches* **78** 5581
Norton *Cnwll* **4** 0869
Norton *Dur* **96** 4421
Norton *E Susx* **16** 4701
Norton *Gloucs* **47** 8524
Norton *Herts* **39** 2334
Norton *IOW* **12** 3488
Norton *Mons* **34** 4420
Norton *N York* **90** 7971
Norton *Nhants* **49** 5963
Norton *Notts* **75** 5771
Norton *Powys* **46** 3067
Norton *S York* **83** 5415
Norton *S York* **74** 3681
Norton *Shrops* **59** 5609
Norton *Shrops* **60** 7200
Norton *Shrops* **59** 4681
Norton *Shrops* **59** 6382
Norton *Somset* **21** 3463
Norton *Suffk* **54** 9565
Norton *Swans* **32** 6188
Norton *W Susx* **14** 9206
Norton *Wilts* **35** 8884
Norton *Worcs* **47** 8751
Norton *Worcs* **48** 0447
Norton Bavant *Wilts* **22** 9043
Norton Bridge *Staffs* **72** 8630
Norton Canes *Staffs* **60** 0107
Norton Canon *Herefs* **46** 3847
Norton Corner *Norfk* **66** 0928
Norton Disney *Lincs* **76** 8859
Norton Ferris *Wilts* **22** 7936
Norton Fitzwarren *Somset* **20** 1925
Norton Green *IOW* **12** 3488
Norton Green *Staffs* **60** 0107
Norton Hawkfield *Somset* **21** 5964
Norton Heath *Essex* **40** 6004
Norton in Hales *Shrops* **72** 7038
Norton in the Moors *Staffs* **72** 8951
Norton Lindsey *Warwks* **48** 2263
Norton Little Green *Suffk* **54** 9766
Norton Malreward *Somset* **21** 6064
Norton Mandeville *Essex* **40** 5804
Norton St Philip *Somset* **22** 7755
Norton sub Hamdon *Somset* **10** 4615
Norton Subcourse *Norfk* **67** 4198
Norton Wood *Herefs* **46** 3648
Norton-Juxta-Twycross *Leics* **61** 3207
Norton-le-Clay *N York* **89** 4071
Norwell *Notts* **75** 7761
Norwell Woodhouse *Notts* **75** 7362
Norwich *Norfk* **67** 2308
Norwich Airport **67** 2113
Norwich Cathedral **67** 2308
Norwich *Shet* **153** 6414
Norwood Clacks **116** 8793
Norwood *Kent* **17** 0530
Norwood *S York* **75** 4681
Norwood End *Essex* **40** 5608
Norwood Green *Gt Lon* **26** 1378

Norwood Green *W York* **82** 1326
Norwood Hill *Surrey* **15** 2343
Norwoodside *Cambs* **65** 4197
Noseley *Leics* **50** 7398
Noss Mayo *Devon* **6** 5547
Nosterfield *N York* **89** 2780
Nosterfield End *Cambs* **53** 6344
Nostie *Highld* **138** 8527
Notgrove *Gloucs* **36** 1020
Nottage *Brdgnd* **33** 8177
Notter *Cnwll* **5** 3960
Nottingham *Notts* **62** 5739
Nottington *Dorset* **11** 6682
Notton *W York* **83** 3413
Notton *Wilts* **35** 9169
Nottswood Hill *Gloucs* **35** 7018
Nounsley *Essex* **40** 7910
Noutard's Green *Worcs* **47** 8066
Nowton *Suffk* **54** 8660
Nox *Shrops* **59** 4110
Nuffield *Oxon* **37** 6687
Nun Monkton *N York* **90** 5057
Nunburnholme *E R Yk* **84** 8447
Nuncargate *Notts* **75** 5054
Nunclose *Cumb* **94** 4945
Nuneaton *Warwks* **61** 3691
Nuneham Courtenay *Oxon* **37** 5599
Nunhead *Gt Lon* **27** 3475
Nunkeeling *E R Yk* **85** 1449
Nunney *Somset* **22** 7345
Nunney Catch *Somset* **22** 7344
Nunnington *Herefs* **46** 5543
Nunnington *N York* **90** 6679
Nunnykirk *Nthumb* **103** 0793
Nunsthorpe *Lincs* **85** 2607
Nunthorpe *N York* **83** 6050
Nunthorpe *N York* **97** 5314
Nunthorpe Village *N York* **90** 5413
Nunton *Wilts* **23** 1526
Nunwick *N York* **89** 3274
Nunwick *Nthumb* **102** 8774
Nup End *Bucks* **38** 8619
Nupdown *Gloucs* **35** 6395
Nupend *Gloucs* **35** 7806
Nuptow *Berks* **25** 8873
Nursling *Hants* **12** 3716
Nursted *Hants* **13** 7521
Nursteed *Wilts* **23** 0260
Nurton *Staffs* **60** 8399
Nutbourne *W Susx* **14** 7705
Nutbourne *W Susx* **14** 0718
Nutfield *Surrey* **27** 3050
Nuthall *Notts* **62** 5243
Nuthampstead *Herts* **39** 4034
Nuthurst *W Susx* **15** 1925
Nutley *E Susx* **16** 4427
Nutley *Hants* **24** 6044
Nuttal Lane *Gt Man* **81** 7915
Nutwell *S York* **83** 6304
Nybster *Highld* **151** 3663
Nyetimber *W Susx* **14** 8998
Nyewood *W Susx* **14** 8021
Nymet Rowland *Devon* **19** 7108
Nymet Tracey *Devon* **8** 7200
Nympsfield *Gloucs* **35** 8000
Nynehead *Somset* **20** 1422
Nythe *Somset* **21** 4234
Nyton *W Susx* **14** 9305

O

Oad Street *Kent* **28** 8762
Oadby *Leics* **50** 6200
Oak Cross *Devon* **8** 5399
Oak Tree *Dur* **89** 3613
Oakall Green *Worcs* **47** 8161
Oakamoor *Staffs* **73** 0444
Oakbank *W Loth* **117** 0766
Oakdale *Caerph* **33** 1898
Oake *Somset* **20** 1525
Oaken *Staffs* **60** 8602
Oakenclough *Lancs* **80** 5447
Oakengates *Shrops* **60** 7010
Oakenholt *Flints* **70** 2571
Oakenshaw *Dur* **96** 1937
Oakenshaw *W York* **82** 1727
Oaker Side *Derbys* **74** 2760
Oakerthorpe *Derbys* **74** 3854
Oakford *Cerdgn* **42** 4558
Oakford *Devon* **20** 9121
Oakfordbridge *Devon* **20** 9122
Oakgrove *Ches* **79** 9169
Oakham *Rutlnd* **63** 8608
Oakhanger *Ches* **72** 7754
Oakhanger *Hants* **14** 7635
Oakhill *Somset* **21** 6347
Oakhurst *Kent* **27** 5550
Oakington *Cambs* **52** 4164
Oaklands *Powys* **45** 0450
Oakle Street *Gloucs* **35** 7517
Oakley *Beds* **51** 0153
Oakley *Bucks* **37** 6412
Oakley *Dorset* **11** 0198
Oakley *Fife* **117** 0289
Oakley *Hants* **24** 5650
Oakley *Oxon* **37** 7500
Oakley *Suffk* **54** 1677
Oakley Green *Berks* **26** 9276
Oakley Park *Powys* **58** 9886
Oakridge *Gloucs* **35** 9103
Oaks *Dur* **96** 1525
Oaks *Lancs* **81** 6733
Oaks Green *Derbys* **73** 1533
Oaks Green *Derbys* **59** 4204
Oaksey *Wilts* **35** 9993
Oakshaw *Cumb* **101** 5176
Oakshott *Hants* **13** 7427
Oakthorpe *Leics* **61** 3212
Oakwood *Derbys* **62** 3738
Oakwood *Nthumb* **102** 9465
Oakwoodhill *Surrey* **15** 1337

Oakworth

Parson Drove

302

Oakworth W York 82 0338
Oare Kent 28 0063
Oare Somset 19 7947
Oare Wilts 23 1563
Oasby Lincs 63 0039
Oath Somset 21 3827
Oathlaw Angus 127 4756
Oatlands Park Surrey 26 0865
Oban Ag & B 122 8629
Obley Shrops 46 3377
Obney P & K 125 0237
Oborne Dorset 11 6518
Obthorpe Lincs 64 0914
Occold Suffk 54 1570
Occumster Highld 151 2635
Ochiltree E Ayrs 107 5021
Ockbrook Derbys 62 4235
Ocker Hill W Mids 60 9793
Ockeridge Worcs 47 7762
Ockham Surrey 26 0756
Ockle Highld 129 5570
Ockley Surrey 15 1440
Ocle Pychard Herefs 46 5945
Octon E R Yk 91 0369
Odcombe Somset 10 5015
Odd Down Somset 22 7462
Oddingley Worcs 47 9159
Oddington Gloucs 48 2225
Oddington Oxon 37 5515
Odell Beds 51 9657
Odham Devon 18 4703
Odiham Hants 24 7451
Odsal W York 82 1529
Odsey Herts 39 2938
Odstock Wilts 23 1426
Odstone Leics 62 3907
Offchurch Warwks 48 3565
Offenham Worcs 48 0546
Offerton T & W 96 3455
Offham E Susx 15 4012
Offham Kent 28 6557
Offham W Susx 14 0208
Offleymarsh Shrops 72 7829
Offord Cluny Cambs 52 2267
Offord Darcy Cambs 52 2266
Offton Suffk 54 0649
Offwell Devon 9 1999
Ogbourne Maizey Wilts 36 1871
Ogbourne St Andrew Wilts 36 1872
Ogbourne St George Wilts 36 2074
Ogden W York 82 0730
Ogle Nthumb 103 1378
Oglet Mersyd 78 4481
Ogmore V Glam 33 8876
Ogmore Vale Brdgnd 33 9390
Ogmore-by-Sea V Glam 33 8675
Ogwen Bank Gwynd 69 6265
Okeford Fitzpaine Dorset 11 8010
Okehampton Devon 8 5995
Olchard Devon 9 8777
Old Nhants 50 7872
Old Aberdeen Aber C 135 9407
Old Alresford Hants 24 5834
Old Auchenbrack D & G 107 7597
Old Basford Notts 62 5543
Old Basing Hants 24 6652
Old Bewick Nthumb 111 0621
Old Bolingbroke Lincs 77 3565
Old Bracknell Berks 25 8668
Old Bramhope W York 82 2343
Old Brampton Derbys 74 3371
Old Bridge of Urr D & G 100 7767
Old Buckenham Norfk 66 0691
Old Burghclere Hants 24 4657
Old Byland N York 90 5585
Old Cassop Dur 96 3339
Old Castle Brdgnd 33 9079
Old Churchstoke Powys 58 2894
Old Clee Lincs 85 2808
Old Cleeve Somset 20 0441
Old Clipstone Notts 75 6064
Old Colwyn Conwy 69 8678
Old Dailly S Ayrs 106 2299
Old Dalby Leics 63 6723
Old Dam Derbys 74 1179
Old Deer Abers 143 9747
Old Ditch Somset 21 5049
Old Edlington S York 75 5397
Old Eldon Dur 96 2427
Old Ellerby E R Yk 85 1637
Old Felixstowe Suffk 55 3135
Old Fletton Cambs 64 1997
Old Forge Herefs 34 5518
Old Furnace Herefs 46 4923
Old Glossop Derbys 74 0494
Old Goole E R Yk 84 7422
Old Grimsby IOS 2 8915
Old Hall Green Herts 39 3722
Old Hall Street Norfk 67 3033
Old Harlow Essex 39 4711
Old Heath Essex 41 0122
Old Hunstanton Norfk 65 6842
Old Hurst Cambs 52 3077
Old Hutton Cumb 87 5688
Old Kea Cnwll 3 8441
Old Kilpatrick W Duns 115 4672
Old Knebworth Herts 39 2320
Old Lakenham Norfk 67 2205
Old Langho Lancs 81 7035
Old Laxey IOM 158 4683
Old Leake Lincs 77 4050
Old Malton N York 90 7972
Old Micklefield W York 83 4433
Old Milton Hants 12 2394
Old Milverton Warwks 48 2967
Old Newton Suffk 54 0562
Old Quarrington Dur 96 3237
Old Radford Notts 62 5540
Old Radnor Powys 46 2558
Old Rayne Abers 142 6728
Old Romney Kent 17 0325
Old Shoreham W Susx 15 2006
Old Soar Kent 27 6254
Old Sodbury Gloucs 35 7581
Old Somerby Lincs 63 9633
Old Stratford Nhants 49 7741
Old Swinford W Mids 60 9083
Old Tebay Cumb 87 6105
Old Thirsk N York 89 4382
Old Town Cumb 93 4743
Old Town Cumb 87 5982
Old Town E Susx 16 5999
Old Town IOS 2 9110
Old Town Nthumb 102 8891
Old Town W York 82 0028
Old Trafford Gt Man 79 8196
Old Tupton Derbys 74 3865
Old Warden Beds 38 1343
Old Weston Cambs 51 0977
Old Wick Highld 151 3649
Old Windsor Berks 25 9874
Old Wives Lees Kent 29 0754
Old Woking Surrey 26 0157
Old Wolverton Bucks 38 8041
Old Woods Shrops 59 4520
Oldany Highld 148 0932
Oldberrow Warwks 48 1265
Oldburry Kent 27 5956
Oldbury Shrops 60 7192
Oldbury W Mids 60 9888
Oldbury Warwks 61 3194
Oldbury Naite Gloucs 35 6293
Oldbury on the Hill Gloucs 35 8188
Oldbury-on-Severn Gloucs 34 6092
Oldcastle Mons 46 3224
Oldcastle Heath Ches 71 4745
Oldcotes Notts 75 5888
Oldfield W York 82 0037
Oldfield Worcs 47 8464
Oldford Somset 22 7850
Oldhall Green Suffk 54 8956
Oldham Gt Man 79 9204
Oldhamstocks E Loth 119 7470
Oldland Gloucs 35 6771
Oldmeldrum Abers 143 8127
Oldmill Cnwll 5 3673
Oldmixon Somset 21 3358
Oldridge Devon 8 8296
Oldshoremore Highld 148 2058
Oldstead N York 90 5379
Oldwall Cumb 101 4761
Oldwalls Swans 32 4891
Oldways End Somset 19 8724
Olive Green Staffs 73 1118
Oliver Border 108 0924
Oliver's Battery Hants 13 4527
Ollaberry Shet 153 3680
Ollach Highld 137 5137
Ollerton Ches 79 7776
Ollerton Notts 75 6567
Ollerton Shrops 72 6425
Olmarch Cerdgn 44 6255
Olmstead Green Cambs 53 6341
Olney Bucks 38 8951
Olrig House Highld 151 1866
Olton W Mids 61 1382
Olveston Gloucs 34 6086
Ombersley Worcs 47 8463
Ompton Notts 75 6865
Once Brewed Nthumb 102 7466
Onchan IOM 158 3978
Onecote Staffs 73 0455
Onehouse Suffk 54 0159
Onen Mons 34 4314
Ongar Street Herefs 46 3967
Onibury Shrops 46 4579
Onich Highld 130 0261
Onllwyn Neath 33 8410
Onneley Staffs 72 7542
Onslow Village Surrey 25 9849
Onston Ches 71 5873
Openwoodgate Derbys 62 3647
Opinan Highld 137 7472
Orbliston Moray 141 3057
Orbost Highld 136 2543
Orby Lincs 77 4967
Orchard Portman Somset 20 2421
Orcheston Wilts 23 0545
Orcop Herefs 46 4726
Orcop Hill Herefs 46 4727
Ord Abers 142 6258
Ordhead Abers 135 6610
Ordie Abers 134 4501
Ordiequish Moray 141 3357
Ordley Nthumb 95 9459
Ordsall Notts 75 7079
Ore E Susx 17 8311
Oreleton Common Herefs 46 4768
Oreton Shrops 59 6580
Orford Ches 78 6190
Orford Suffk 55 4250
Organford Dorset 11 9392
Orgreave Staffs 73 1415
Orlestone Kent 17 0034
Orleton Herefs 46 4967
Orleton Worcs 47 7067
Orlingbury Nhants 51 8572
Ormathwaite Cumb 93 2625
Ormesby N York 97 5317
Ormesby St Margaret Norfk 67 4914
Ormesby St Michael Norfk 67 4714
Ormiscaig Highld 144 8590
Ormiston E Loth 118 4169
Ormsaigmore Highld 121 4763
Ormsary Ag & B 113 7472
Ormskirk Lancs 78 4108
Ornsby Hill Dur 96 1648
Oronsay Ag & B 112 3588
Orphir Ork 153 3404
Orpington Gt Lon 27 4666
Orrell Gt Man 78 5303
Orrell Mersyd 78 3496
Orrell Post Gt Man 78 5305
Orrisdale IOM 158 3292
Orroland D & G 92 7746
Orsett Essex 40 6482
Orslow Staffs 72 8015
Orston Notts 63 7740
Orthwaite Cumb 93 2534
Ortner Lancs 80 5354
Orton Cumb 87 6208
Orton Nhants 51 8079
Orton Staffs 60 8795
Orton Longueville Cambs 64 1796
Orton Rigg Cumb 93 3352
Orton Waterville Cambs 64 1595
Orton-on-the-Hill Leics 61 3003
Orwell Cambs 52 3650
Osbaldeston Lancs 81 6431
Osbaldeston Green Lancs 81 6432
Osbaldwick N York 83 6251
Osbaston Leics 62 4204
Osbaston Shrops 59 3222
Osborne IOW 13 5194
Osborne House 13 5195
Osbournby Lincs 64 0638
Oscroft Ches 71 5067
Ose Highld 136 3140
Osgathorpe Leics 62 4319
Osgodby Lincs 76 0792
Osgodby N York 83 6433
Osgodby N York 91 0584
Oskaig Highld 137 5438
Oskamull Ag & B 121 4540
Osmaston Derbys 73 1943
Osmington Dorset 11 7283
Osmington Mills Dorset 11 7381
Osmondthorpe W York 83 3333
Osmotherley N York 89 4596
Osney Oxon 37 4906
Ospringe Kent 28 0060
Ossett W York 82 2720
Ossington Notts 75 7564
Ostend Essex 40 9397
Osterley Gt Lon 26 1577
Oswaldkirk N York 90 6278
Oswaldtwistle Lancs 81 7327
Oswestry Shrops 59 2929
Otford Kent 27 5359
Otham Kent 28 7953
Otham Hole Kent 28 8052
Othery Somset 21 3831
Otley Suffk 55 2055
Otley W York 82 2045
Otley Green Suffk 55 2156
Otter Ferry Ag & B 114 9384
Otterbourne Hants 13 4522
Otterburn N York 88 8857
Otterburn Nthumb 102 8893
Otterham Cnwll 4 1690
Otterham Quay Kent 28 8366
Otterhampton Somset 20 2443
Otternish W Isls 152 9079
Ottershaw Surrey 26 0263
Otterswick Shet 153 5285
Otterton Devon 9 0684
Otterwood Hants 13 4102
Ottery Devon 6 4475
Ottery St Mary Devon 9 1095
Ottinge Kent 29 1642
Ottringham E R Yk 85 2624
Oughterby Cumb 93 2955
Oughtershaw N York 88 8780
Oughterside Cumb 92 1140
Oughtibridge S York 74 3093
Oughtrington Ches 79 6987
Oulston N York 90 5474
Oulton Cumb 93 2450
Oulton Norfk 66 1328
Oulton Staffs 72 7822
Oulton Staffs 72 9035
Oulton Suffk 67 5294
Oulton W York 83 3628
Oulton Broad Suffk 67 5192
Oulton Street Norfk 66 1527
Oundle Nhants 51 0388
Ounsdale Staffs 60 8693
Ousby Cumb 94 6134
Ousden Suffk 53 7459
Ousefleet E R Yk 84 8323
Ouston Dur 96 2554
Out Elmstead Kent 29 2050
Out Newton E R Yk 85 3821
Out Rawcliffe Lancs 80 4041
Outchester Nthumb 111 1433
Outgate Cumb 87 3599
Outhgill Cumb 88 7801
Outhill Warwks 48 1066
Outlands Staffs 72 7630
Outlane W York 82 0817
Outwell Norfk 65 5103
Outwick Hants 12 1417
Outwood Surrey 15 3145
Outwood W York 83 3323
Outwood Gate Gt Man 79 7805
Outwoods Leics 62 4018
Outwoods Staffs 72 7817
Outwoods Warwks 61 2484
Ouzlewell Green W York 83 3326
Ovenden W York 82 0827
Over Cambs 52 3770
Over Ches 71 6365
Over Gloucs 35 8119
Over Gloucs 34 5882
Over Burrows Derbys 73 2639
Over Compton Dorset 10 5816
Over End Cambs 51 0893
Over Green Warwks 61 1694
Over Haddon Derbys 74 2066
Over Kellet Lancs 87 5169
Over Kiddington Oxon 36 4021
Over Monnow Mons 34 5012
Over Norton Oxon 48 3128
Over Peover Ches 79 7873
Over Silton N York 89 4493
Over Stowey Somset 20 1838
Over Stratton Somset 10 4315
Over Tabley Ches 79 7279
Over Wallop Hants 23 2838
Over Whitacre Warwks 61 2590
Over Woodhouse Derbys 75 4671
Over Worton Oxon 49 4329
Overbury Worcs 47 9537
Overcombe Dorset 11 6982
Overgreen Derbys 74 3273
Overleigh Somset 21 4835
Overley Staffs 73 1515
Overpool Ches 71 3877
Overscaig Hotel Highld 149 4123
Overseal Derbys 73 2915
Oversland Kent 28 0557
Oversley Green Warwks 48 0957
Overstone Nhants 50 7966
Overstrand Norfk 67 2440
Overstreet Wilts 23 0637
Overthorpe Nhants 49 4840
Overton Aber C 143 8714
Overton Ches 71 5277
Overton Hants 24 5149
Overton Lancs 87 4358
Overton N York 83 5555
Overton Shrops 46 5072
Overton Swans 32 4685
Overton W York 82 2516
Overton Wrexhm 71 3741
Overton Bridge Wrexhm 71 3542
Overton Green Ches 72 8060
Overtown Lancs 87 6275
Overtown N Lans 116 8053
Overtown W York 83 3516
Overtown Wilts 36 1579
Overy Oxon 37 5893
Oving Bucks 37 7821
Oving W Susx 14 9004
Ovingdean E Susx 15 3503
Ovingham Nthumb 103 0863
Ovington Dur 89 1314
Ovington Essex 53 7642
Ovington Hants 24 5631
Ovington Norfk 66 9202
Ovington Nthumb 103 0663
Ower Hants 12 3216
Ower Hants 13 4702
Owermoigne Dorset 11 7685
Owl's Green Suffk 55 2869
Owlbury Shrops 59 3191
Owlerton S York 74 3389
Owlpen Gloucs 35 7998
Owlsmoor Berks 25 8462
Owlswick Bucks 37 7806
Owmby Lincs 85 0704
Owmby Lincs 76 0087
Owslebury Hants 13 5123
Owston Leics 63 7707
Owston S York 83 5511
Owston Ferry Lincs 75 8000
Owstwick E R Yk 85 2732
Owthorne E R Yk 85 3328
Owthorpe Notts 63 6733
Oxborough Norfk 65 7401
Oxbridge Dorset 10 4797
Oxcombe Lincs 77 3177
Oxcroft Derbys 75 4873
Oxen End Essex 40 6629
Oxen Park Cumb 86 3187
Oxenholme Cumb 87 5389
Oxenhope W York 82 0334
Oxenpill Somset 21 4441
Oxenton Gloucs 47 9531
Oxenwood Wilts 23 3058
Oxford Oxon 37 5106
Oxhey Herts 26 1295
Oxhill Dur 96 1852
Oxhill Warwks 48 3146
Oxley W Mids 60 9001
Oxley Green Essex 40 9014
Oxley's Green E Susx 16 6921
Oxlode Cambs 53 4886
Oxnam Border 110 6918
Oxnead Norfk 67 2224
Oxshott Surrey 26 1460
Oxshott Heath Surrey 26 1361
Oxspring S York 82 2601
Oxted Surrey 27 3852
Oxton Border 118 4953
Oxton N York 83 5042
Oxton Notts 75 6351
Oxwich Swans 32 4986
Oxwich Green Swans 32 4985
Oxwick Norfk 66 9125
Oykel Bridge Hotel Highld 145 3801
Oyne Abers 142 6725
Oystermouth Swans 32 6187
Ozleworth Gloucs 35 7993

P

Pabail W Isls 152 5231
Packers Hill Dorset 11 7110
Packington Leics 62 3614
Packmoor Staffs 72 8654
Packmores Warwks 48 2866
Padanaram Angus 127 4251
Padbury Bucks 49 7230
Paddington Ches 79 6389
Paddington Gt Lon 27 2681
Paddlesworth Kent 28 6862
Paddlesworth Kent 29 1939
Paddock Wood Kent 28 6744
Paddolgreen Shrops 59 5032
Padeswood Flints 70 2762
Padfield Derbys 74 0296
Padgate Ches 79 6389
Padhams Green Essex 40 6497
Padiham Lancs 81 7933
Padside N York 89 1659
Padstow Cnwll 4 9175
Padworth Berks 24 6166
Page Bank Dur 96 2335
Pagham W Susx 14 8897
Paglesham Essex 40 9293
Paignton Devon 7 8860
Pailton Warwks 50 4781
Paine's Cross E Susx 16 6223
Painleyhill Staffs 73 0333
Painscastle Powys 45 1646
Painshawfield Nthumb 103 0560
Painsthorpe E R Yk 90 8158
Painswick Gloucs 35 8609
Painter's Forstal Kent 28 9958
Paisley Rens 115 4864
Pakefield Suffk 55 5390
Pakenham Suffk 54 9267
Pale Gwynd 58 9836
Pale Green Essex 53 6542
Palestine Hants 23 2640
Paley Street Berks 26 8776
Palfrey W Mids 60 0196
Palgrave Suffk 54 1178
Pallington Dorset 11 7891
Palmers Green Gt Lon 27 3192
Palmersbridge Cnwll 5 1977
Palmerston E Ayrs 107 5019
Palmerstown V Glam 20 1369
Palnackie D & G 92 8157
Palnure D & G 99 4563
Palterton Derbys 75 4768
Pamber End Hants 24 6158
Pamber Green Hants 24 6159
Pamber Heath Hants 24 6162
Pamington Gloucs 47 9433
Pamphill Dorset 11 9900
Pampisford Cambs 53 4948
Panborough Somset 21 4745
Panbride Angus 127 5635
Pancrasweek Devon 18 2905
Pancross V Glam 20 0469
Pandy Caerph 33 1587
Pandy Gwynd 57 6202
Pandy Gwynd 57 8729
Pandy Mons 34 3322
Pandy Powys 58 9004
Pandy Wrexhm 58 1935
Pandy Tudur Conwy 69 8564
Pandy'r Capel Denbgs 70 0850
Panfield Essex 40 7325
Pangbourne Berks 37 6376
Pangdean W Susx 15 2911
Panks Bridge Herefs 47 6248
Pannal N York 82 3051
Pannal Ash N York 82 2953
Pannanich Wells Hotel Abers 134 4097
Pant Shrops 58 2722
Pant Glas Gwynd 68 4747
Pant Mawr Powys 43 8482
Pant-ffrwyth Brdgnd 33 9483
Pant-Gwyn Carmth 44 5925
Pant-lasau Swans 32 6600
Pant-pastynog Denbgs 70 0461
Pant-y-dwr Powys 45 9874
Pant-y-ffridd Powys 58 1502
Pant-y-gog Brdgnd 33 9090
Pant-y-mwyn Flints 70 1964
Pantasaph Flints 70 1675
Panteg Pembks 30 9234
Pantersbridge Cnwll 4 1667
Pantglas Powys 43 7797
Panton Lincs 76 1778
Pantperthog Gwynd 57 7404
Pantyffynnon Carmth 32 6210
Pantygasseg Torfn 34 2599
Pantymenyn Carmth 31 1426
Panxworth Norfk 67 3513
Papa Westray Airport 153 4851
Papcastle Cumb 92 1031
Papigoe Highld 151 3851
Papple E Loth 118 5972
Papplewick Notts 75 5451
Papworth Everard Cambs 52 2862
Papworth St Agnes Cambs 52 2664
Par Cnwll 3 0753
Paramour Street Kent 29 2961
Parbold Lancs 80 4911
Parbrook Somset 21 5736
Parbrook W Susx 14 0825
Parc Gwynd 57 8834
Parc Seymour Newpt 34 4091
Parcllyn Cerdgn 42 2451
Pardshaw Cumb 92 0924
Parham Suffk 55 3060
Park Abers 135 7898
Park D & G 100 9091
Park Nthumb 102 6861
Park Bottom Cnwll 2 6642
Park Bridge Gt Man 79 9402
Park Corner Berks 26 8582
Park Corner E Susx 16 5336
Park Corner Oxon 37 6988
Park End Beds 38 9952
Park End Nthumb 102 8675
Park End Staffs 72 7851
Park Gate Hants 13 5108
Park Gate W York 82 1841
Park Gate Worcs 60 9371
Park Green Essex 39 4628
Park Green Suffk 54 1364
Park Head Cumb 94 5841
Park Head Derbys 74 3654
Park Hill Gloucs 34 5799
Park Royal Gt Lon 26 1982
Park Street Herts 39 1404
Park Street W Susx 14 1131
Parkend Gloucs 34 6108
Parkers Green Kent 16 6148
Parkeston Essex 41 2332
Parkeston Quay Essex 41 2332
Parkfield Cnwll 5 3167
Parkgate Ches 70 2878
Parkgate Cumb 93 2146
Parkgate D & G 100 0288
Parkgate E Susx 17 7214
Parkgate Essex 40 6829
Parkgate Kent 27 5064
Parkgate Kent 17 8534
Parkgate Surrey 15 2043
Parkhall W Duns 115 4871
Parkham Devon 18 3921
Parkham Ash Devon 18 3620
Parkhill Notts 75 6952
Parkhill House Abers 143 8914
Parkhouse Mons 34 5003
Parkmill Swans 32 5489
Parkside Dur 96 4248
Parkside N Lans 116 8058
Parkside Wrexhm 71 3855
Parkstone Dorset 12 0391
Parley Green Dorset 12 1097
Parlington W York 83 4235
Parmoor Bucks 37 7989
Parndon Essex 39 4308
Parracombe Devon 19 6745
Parrog Pembks 30 0539
Parson Drove Cambs 64 3708

Pyrford Riseden

Pyrford Surrey 26 0358
Pyrton Oxon 37 6896
Pytchley Nhants 51 8574
Pyworthy Devon 18 3102

Q

Quabbs Shrops 58 2180
Quadring Lincs 64 2233
Quadring Eaudike Lincs 64 2433
Quainton Bucks 37 7420
Quaker's Yard Myr Td 33 0995
Quaking Houses Dur 96 1850
Quarley Hants 23 2743
Quarndon Derbys 62 3340
Quarr Hill IOW 13 5792
Quarrier's Village Inver 115 3666
Quarrington Lincs 64 0544
Quarrington Hill Dur 96 3337
Quarry Bank W Mids 60 9386
Quarrybank Ches 71 5465
Quarrywood Moray 141 1763
Quarter N Ayrs 114 1961
Quarter S Lans 116 7251
Quatford Shrops 60 7391
Quatt Shrops 60 7588
Quebec Dur 96 1743
Quedgeley Gloucs 35 8014
Queen Adelaide Cambs 53 5681
Queen Camel Somset 21 5924
Queen Charlton Somset 21 6367
Queen Dart Devon 19 8316
Queen Oak Dorset 22 7831
Queen Street Kent 28 6845
Queen Street Wilts 35 0287
Queen's Bower IOW 13 5684
Queen's Head Shrops 59 3327
Queen's Park Beds 38 0349
Queen's Park Nhants 49 7562
Queenborough Kent 28 9172
Queenhill Worcs 47 8537
Queensbury W York 82 1030
Queensferry Flints 71 3168
Queenslie C Glas 116 6565
Queenzieburn N Lans 116 6977
Quendon Essex 39 5130
Queniborough Leics 63 6412
Quenington Gloucs 36 1404
Quernmore Lancs 87 5160
Quernmore Park Hall Lancs 87 5162
Queslett W Mids 61 0695
Quethiock Cnwll 5 3164
Quick's Green Berks 37 5876
Quidenham Norfk 54 0287
Quidhampton Hants 24 5150
Quidhampton Wilts 23 1030
Quina Brook Shrops 59 5232
Quinbury End Nhants 49 6250
Quinton Nhants 49 7754
Quinton W Mids 60 9984
Quinton Green Nhants 50 7853
Quintrell Downs Cnwll 4 8460
Quither Devon 5 4481
Quixhall Staffs 73 1041
Quixwood Border 119 7863
Quoditch Devon 5 4097
Quorn Leics 62 5616
Quothquan S Lans 108 9939
Quoyburray Ork 153 5005
Quoyloo Ork 153 2420

R

Rabbit's Cross Kent 28 7847
Rableyheath Herts 39 2319
Raby Cumb 93 1951
Raby Mersyd 71 3179
Rachan Mill Border 108 1134
Rachub Gwynd 69 6267
Rackenford Devon 19 8518
Rackham W Susx 14 0413
Rackheath Norfk 67 2814
Racks D & G 100 0274
Rackwick Ork 153 2099
Radbourne Derbys 73 2836
Radcliffe Gt Man 79 7806
Radcliffe Nthumb 103 2602
Radcliffe on Trent Notts 63 6439
Radclive Bucks 49 6734
Radcot Oxon 36 2899
Raddington Somset 20 0225
Radernie Fife 127 4609
Radford Semele Warwks 48 3464
Radlet Somset 20 2038
Radlett Herts 26 1600
Radley Devon 19 7323
Radley Oxon 37 5398
Radley Green Essex 40 6205
Radmore Green Ches 71 5955
Radnage Bucks 37 7897
Radstock Somset 22 6854
Radstone Nhants 49 5840
Radway Warwks 48 3648
Radway Green Ches 72 7754
Radwell Beds 51 0057
Radwell Herts 39 2335
Radwinter Essex 53 6037
Radwinter End Essex 53 6139
Radyr Cardif 33 1280
RAF College (Cranwell) Lincs 76 0049
Rafford Moray 141 0556
Ragdale Leics 63 6619
Ragdon Shrops 59 4591
Raginnis Cnwll 2 4625
Raglan Mons 34 4107
Ragnall Notts 75 8073
Raigbeg Highld 140 8128
Rainbow Hill Worcs 47 8555
Rainford Mersyd 78 4700
Rainham Gt Lon 27 5282
Rainham Kent 28 8165
Rainhill Mersyd 78 4991
Rainhill Stoops Mersyd 78 5090
Rainow Ches 79 9475
Rainsough Gt Man 79 8002
Rainton N York 89 3675
Rainworth Notts 75 5858
Raisbeck Cumb 87 6407
Raise Cumb 94 7046
Raisthorpe N York 90 8561
Rait P & K 126 2226
Raithby Lincs 77 3084
Raithby Lincs 77 3766
Raithwaite N York 90 8611
Rake W Susx 14 8027
Rakewood Gt Man 82 9414
Ralia Highld 132 7097
Ram Carmth 44 5846
Ram Hill Gloucs 35 6779
Ram Lane Kent 28 9646
Ramasaig Highld 136 1644
Rame Cnwll 3 7233
Rame Cnwll 6 4249
Rampisham Dorset 10 5602
Rampside Cumb 86 2366
Rampton Cambs 53 4267
Rampton Notts 75 8078
Ramsbottom Gt Man 81 7916
Ramsbury Wilts 36 2771
Ramscraigs Highld 151 1427
Ramsdean Hants 13 7022
Ramsdell Hants 24 5857
Ramsden Oxon 36 3515
Ramsden Worcs 47 9246
Ramsden Bellhouse Essex 40 7194
Ramsden Heath Essex 40 7095
Ramsey Cambs 52 2885
Ramsey Essex 41 2130
Ramsey IOM 158 4594
Ramsey Forty Foot Cambs 52 3087
Ramsey Heights Cambs 52 2484
Ramsey Island Essex 40 9405
Ramsey Mereside Cambs 52 2889
Ramsey St Mary's Cambs 52 2587
Ramsgate Kent 29 3865
Ramsgill N York 89 1170
Ramshaw Dur 95 9547
Ramsholt Suffk 55 3141
Ramshope Nthumb 102 7304
Ramshorn Staffs 73 0845
Ramsley Devon 8 6593
Ramsnest Common Surrey 14 9432
Ranby Lincs 76 2278
Ranby Notts 75 6580
Rand Lincs 76 1078
Randwick Gloucs 35 8306
Ranfurly Rens 115 3865
Rangemore Staffs 73 1822
Rangeworthy Gloucs 35 6986
Rank's Green Essex 40 7418
Rankinston E Ayrs 107 4513
Ranksborough Rutlnd 63 8311
Rann Lancs 81 7124
Rannoch Station P & K 124 4257
Ranscombe Somset 20 9443
Ranskill Notts 75 6587
Ranton Staffs 72 8524
Ranton Green Staffs 72 8423
Ranworth Norfk 67 3514
Raploch Stirlg 116 7894
Rapness Ork 153 5141
Rapps Somset 10 3316
Rascarrel D & G 92 7948
Rashfield Ag & B 114 1483
Rashwood Worcs 47 9165
Raskelf N York 90 4971
Rassau Blae G 33 1511
Rastrick W York 82 1421
Ratagan Highld 138 9119
Ratby Leics 62 5105
Ratcliffe Culey Leics 61 3299
Ratcliffe on Soar Notts 62 4928
Ratcliffe on the Wreake Leics 63 6314
Ratfyn Wilts 23 1642
Rathen Abers 143 9960
Rathillet Fife 126 3620
Rathmell N York 88 8059
Ratho C Edin 117 1370
Rathven Moray 142 4465
Ratlake Hants 13 4123
Ratley Warwks 48 3847
Ratling Kent 29 2453
Ratlinghope Shrops 59 4096
Rattan Row Norfk 65 5114
Rattar Highld 151 2673
Ratten Row Cumb 93 3240
Ratten Row Cumb 93 3949
Ratten Row Lancs 80 4241
Rattery Devon 7 7461
Rattlesden Suffk 54 9758
Ratton Village E Susx 16 5901
Rattray P & K 126 1845
Raughton Cumb 93 3947
Raughton Head Cumb 93 3745
Raunds Nhants 51 9972
Raven Meols Mersyd 78 2805
Ravenfield S York 75 4895
Ravenglass Cumb 86 0896
Ravenhills Green Worcs 47 7454
Raveningham Norfk 67 3996
Ravenscar N York 91 9801
Ravenscliffe Staffs 72 8452
Ravensdale IOM 158 3592
Ravensden Beds 51 0754
Ravenshead Notts 75 5654
Ravensmoor Ches 71 6150
Ravensthorpe Nhants 50 6670
Ravensthorpe W York 82 2220
Ravenstone Bucks 38 8451
Ravenstone Leics 62 4013
Ravenstonedale Cumb 88 7203
Ravenstruther S Lans 116 9245
Ravensworth N York 89 1308
Raw N York 91 9305
Rawcliffe E R Yk 83 6822
Rawcliffe N York 83 5854
Rawcliffe Bridge E R Yk 83 6921
Rawdon W York 82 2139
Rawling Street Kent 28 9059
Rawmarsh S York 75 4396
Rawnsley Staffs 60 0212
Rawreth Essex 40 7893
Rawridge Devon 9 2006
Rawtenstall Lancs 81 8123
Raydon Suffk 54 0438
Raylees Nthumb 102 9291
Rayleigh Essex 40 8090
Raymond's Hill Devon 10 3296
Rayne Essex 40 7222
Raynes Park Gt Lon 26 2368
Rea Gloucs 35 8016
Reach Cambs 53 5666
Read Lancs 81 7634
Reading Berks 24 7173
Reading Street Kent 17 9230
Reading Street Kent 29 3869
Reagill Cumb 94 6017
Rearquhar Highld 146 7492
Rearsby Leics 63 6514
Reaseheath Shrops 72 6454
Reay Highld 150 9664
Reculver Kent 29 2269
Red Ball Somset 9 0917
Red Bull Ches 72 8254
Red Cross Cambs 53 4754
Red Cross Cnwll 18 2605
Red Dial Cumb 93 2546
Red Hill Dorset 12 0995
Red Hill Warwks 48 1356
Red Lodge Suffk 53 6970
Red Lumb Gt Man 81 8415
Red Rock Gt Man 78 5809
Red Roses Carmth 31 2011
Red Row T & W 103 2599
Red Street Staffs 72 8251
Red Wharf Bay IOA 68 5281
Redberth Pembks 31 0804
Redbourn Herts 38 1012
Redbourne Lincs 76 9799
Redbrook Gloucs 34 5309
Redbrook Wrexhm 71 5041
Redbrook Street Kent 28 9336
Redburn Highld 140 9447
Redburn Nthumb 102 7764
Redcar N York 97 6024
Redcastle D & G 100 8165
Redcastle Highld 139 5849
Redding Falk 116 9278
Reddingmuirhead Falk 116 9177
Reddish Gt Man 79 8993
Redditch Worcs 48 0467
Rede Suffk 54 8055
Redenhall Norfk 55 2684
Redenham Hants 23 3049
Redesmouth Nthumb 102 8682
Redford Abers 135 7570
Redford Angus 127 5644
Redford W Susx 14 8626
Redfordgreen Border 109 3616
Redgate Rhondd 33 0188
Redgorton P & K 125 0828
Redgrave Suffk 54 0477
Redhill Abers 135 7704
Redhill Herts 39 3033
Redhill Somset 21 4962
Redhill Surrey 27 2750
Redisham Suffk 55 4084
Redland Bristl 34 5775
Redland Ork 153 3724
Redlingfield Suffk 54 1870
Redlingfield Green Suffk 54 1871
Redlynch Somset 22 7033
Redlynch Wilts 12 2021
Redmain Cumb 92 1333
Redmarley Worcs 47 7666
Redmarley D'Abitot Gloucs 47 7531
Redmarshall Dur 96 3821
Redmile Leics 63 7935
Redmire N York 88 0491
Redmyre Abers 135 7575
Rednal Shrops 59 3628
Rednal W Mids 60 0076
Redpath Border 110 5835
Redpoint Highld 137 7368
Redruth Cnwll 2 6942
Redstocks Wilts 22 9362
Redstone P & K 126 1834
Redstone Cross Pembks 31 1015
Redvales Gt Man 79 8008
Redwick Gloucs 34 5486
Redwick Newpt 34 4184
Redworth Dur 96 2423
Reed Herts 39 3636
Reedham Norfk 67 4201
Reedness E R Yk 84 7923
Reeds Beck Lincs 76 2065
Reeds Holme Lancs 81 8024
Reepham Lincs 76 0473
Reepham Norfk 66 1022
Reeth N York 88 0399
Reeves Green W Mids 61 2677
Regaby IOM 158 4397
Reiff Highld 144 9614
Reigate Surrey 27 2550
Reighton N York 91 1375
Reisque Abers 143 8819
Reiss Highld 151 3354
Rejerrah Cnwll 3 7956
Releath Cnwll 2 6532
Relubbus Cnwll 2 5631
Relugas Moray 141 9948
Remenham Berks 37 7684
Remenham Hill Berks 37 7882
Rempstone Notts 62 5724
Rendcomb Gloucs 35 0209
Rendham Suffk 55 3464
Rendlesham Suffk 55 3453
Renfrew Rens 115 5067
Renhold Beds 38 0952
Renishaw Derbys 75 4577
Rennington Nthumb 111 2118
Renton W Duns 115 3877
Renwick Cumb 94 5943
Repps Norfk 67 4217
Repton Derbys 73 3026
Resaurie Highld 140 7045
Rescassa Cnwll 3 9842
Rescorla Cnwll 3 9848
Resipole Highld 121 7264
Reskadinnick Cnwll 2 6341
Resolis Highld 140 6765
Resolven Neath 33 8302
Rest and be thankful Ag & B 123 2307
Reston Border 119 8862
Restronguet Cnwll 3 8136
Reswallie Angus 127 5051
Reterth Cnwll 4 9463
Retew Cnwll 4 9257
Retford Notts 75 7081
Retire Cnwll 4 0064
Rettendon Essex 40 7698
Retyn Cnwll 4 8858
Revesby Lincs 77 2961
Rew Devon 7 7570
Rew Devon 7 7138
Rew Street IOW 13 4794
Rewe Devon 9 9499
Rexon Devon 5 4188
Reydon Suffk 55 4977
Reymerston Norfk 66 0206
Reynalton Pembks 31 0908
Reynoldston Swans 32 4889
Rezare Cnwll 5 3677
Rhadyr Mons 34 3602
Rhandirmwyn Carmth 44 7843
Rhayader Powys 45 9768
Rheindown Highld 139 5147
Rhes-y-cae Flints 70 1871
Rhewl Denbgs 70 1060
Rhewl Denbgs 70 1744
Rhewl Mostyn Flints 70 1580
Rhewl-fawr Flints 70 1381
Rhicarn Highld 148 0825
Rhiconich Highld 148 2552
Rhicullen Highld 146 6971
Rhigos Rhondd 33 9205
Rhireavach Highld 144 0295
Rhives Highld 147 8200
Rhiwbina Cardif 33 1682
Rhiwbryfdir Gwynd 57 6946
Rhiwderyn Newpt 34 2687
Rhiwen Gwynd 69 5763
Rhiwinder Rhondd 33 0287
Rhiwlas Gwynd 69 5765
Rhiwlas Gwynd 58 9237
Rhiwlas Powys 58 1932
Rhiwsaeson Cardif 33 0682
Rhode Somset 20 2734
Rhoden Green Kent 28 6845
Rhodes Gt Man 79 8505
Rhodes Minnis Kent 29 1542
Rhodesia Notts 75 5679
Rhodiad-y-brenin Pembks 30 7627
Rhonehouse D & G 99 7459
Rhoose V Glam 20 0666
Rhos Carmth 31 3835
Rhos Denbgs 70 1261
Rhos Neath 32 7302
Rhos Powys 45 1731
Rhos Haminiog Cerdgn 43 5464
Rhos Lligwy IOA 68 4886
Rhos y-brithdir Powys 58 1323
Rhos-fawr Gwynd 56 3838
Rhos-on-Sea Conwy 69 8480
Rhos-y-garth Cerdgn 43 6373
Rhos-y-gwaliau Gwynd 58 9434
Rhos-y-llan Gwynd 56 2337
Rhos-y-meirch Powys 46 2769
Rhosbeirio IOA 68 3991
Rhoscefnhir IOA 68 5276
Rhoscolyn IOA 68 2675
Rhoscrowther Pembks 30 9002
Rhosesmor Flints 70 2168
Rhosgadfan Gwynd 68 5057
Rhosgoch IOA 68 4089
Rhosgoch Powys 45 1847
Rhoshill Pembks 31 1940
Rhoshirwaun Gwynd 56 2029
Rhoslan Gwynd 56 4840
Rhoslefain Gwynd 57 5705
Rhosllanerchrugog Wrexhm 71 2946
Rhosmaen Carmth 44 6423
Rhosmeirch IOA 68 4677
Rhosneigr IOA 68 3173
Rhosnesni Wrexhm 71 3550
Rhosrobin Wrexhm 71 3252
Rhossili Swans 31 4187
Rhostryfan Gwynd 68 4957
Rhostyllen Wrexhm 71 3148
Rhosybol IOA 68 4288
Rhosygadfa Shrops 59 3234
Rhosymedre Wrexhm 71 2842
Rhu Ag & B 115 2684
Rhuallt Denbgs 70 0775
Rhubodach Ag & B 114 0273
Rhuddall Heath Ches 71 5562
Rhuddlan Cerdgn 44 4943
Rhuddlan Denbgs 70 0278
Rhulen Powys 45 1349
Rhunahaorine Ag & B 105 7048
Rhyd Gwynd 57 6341
Rhyd-Ddu Gwynd 69 5652
Rhyd-lydan Conwy 69 8950
Rhyd-uchaf Gwynd 58 9037
Rhyd-y pennau Cerdgn 43 6385
Rhyd-y-clafdy Gwynd 56 3234
Rhyd-y-foel Conwy 70 9176
Rhyd-y-groes Gwynd 69 5867
Rhyd-y-meirch Mons 34 3107
Rhyd-y-sarn Gwynd 57 6842
Rhyd-yr-onnen Gwynd 57 6102
Rhydargaeau Carmth 31 4326
Rhydcymerau Carmth 44 5738
Rhydd Worcs 47 8345
Rhydding Neath 32 7499
Rhydgaled Conwy 70 9964
Rhydlanfair Conwy 69 8252
Rhydlewis Cerdgn 42 3447
Rhydlios Gwynd 56 1929
Rhydowen Cerdgn 42 4445
Rhydrosser Cerdgn 43 5667
Rhydspence Herefs 46 2447
Rhydtalog Flints 70 2354
Rhydycroesau Shrops 58 2430
Rhydyfelin Cerdgn 43 5979
Rhydyfelin Rhondd 33 0988
Rhydyfro Neath 32 7105
Rhydymain Gwynd 57 8022
Rhydymwyn Flints 70 2066
Rhyl Denbgs 70 0081
Rhymney Caerph 33 1107
Rhynd P & K 126 1520
Rhynie Abers 142 4927
Rhynie Highld 147 8479
Ribbesford Worcs 60 7874
Ribbleton Lancs 81 5631
Ribby Lancs 80 4031
Ribchester Lancs 81 6535
Riber Derbys 74 3059
Riby Lincs 85 1807
Riccall N York 83 6237
Riccarton Border 101 5494
Riccarton E Ayrs 107 4236
Rich's Holford Somset 20 1434
Richards Castle Herefs 46 4969
Richings Park Bucks 26 0278
Richmond Gt Lon 26 1774
Richmond N York 89 1701
Richmond S York 74 4085
Richmond Fort Guern 158 0000
Rickerscote Staffs 72 9220
Rickford Somset 21 4859
Rickham Devon 7 7537
Rickinghall Suffk 54 0475
Rickling Essex 39 4931
Rickling Green Essex 39 5129
Rickmansworth Herts 26 0694
Riddell Border 109 5124
Riddings Cumb 101 4075
Riddings Derbys 74 4252
Riddlecombe Devon 19 6113
Riddlesden W York 82 0742
Ridge Dorset 11 9386
Ridge Herts 26 2100
Ridge Somset 21 5556
Ridge Wilts 22 9531
Ridge Green Surrey 15 3048
Ridge Lane Warwks 61 2994
Ridge Row Kent 29 2042
Ridgebourne Powys 45 0560
Ridgehill Somset 21 5462
Ridgeway Derbys 74 3551
Ridgeway Derbys 74 4081
Ridgeway Worcs 48 0461
Ridgeway Cross Herefs 47 7147
Ridgewell Essex 53 7340
Ridgewood E Susx 16 4719
Ridgmont Beds 38 9736
Riding Mill Nthumb 103 0161
Ridley Kent 27 6164
Ridley Nthumb 102 7963
Ridley Green Ches 71 5554
Ridlington Norfk 67 3430
Ridlington Rutlnd 63 8402
Ridlington Street Norfk 67 3430
Ridsdale Nthumb 102 9084
Rievaulx N York 90 5785
Rievaulx Abbey 90 5784
Rigg D & G 101 2966
Riggend N Lans 116 7670
Righoul Highld 140 8851
Rigmadon Park Cumb 87 6184
Rigsby Lincs 77 4375
Rigside S Lans 108 8735
Riley Green Lancs 81 6225
Rileyhill Staffs 61 1114
Rilla Mill Cnwll 5 2973
Rillaton Cnwll 5 2973
Rillington N York 90 8574
Rimington Lancs 81 8045
Rimpton Somset 21 6121
Rimswell E R Yk 85 3128
Rinaston Pembks 30 9825
Rindleford Shrops 60 7395
Ring o'Bells Lancs 78 4510
Ring's End Cambs 65 3902
Ringford D & G 99 6957
Ringinglow Derbys 74 2883
Ringland Norfk 66 1313
Ringles Cross E Susx 16 4722
Ringlestone Kent 28 8755
Ringley Gt Man 79 7605
Ringmer E Susx 16 4412
Ringmore Devon 7 6546
Ringmore Devon 7 9272
Ringorm Moray 141 2644
Ringsfield Suffk 55 4088
Ringsfield Corner Suffk 55 4087
Ringshall Bucks 38 9814
Ringshall Suffk 54 0452
Ringshall Stocks Suffk 54 0551
Ringstead Nhants 51 9875
Ringstead Norfk 65 7040
Ringwood Hants 12 1505
Ringwould Kent 29 3548
Rinsey Cnwll 2 5927
Rinsey Croft Cnwll 2 6028
Ripe E Susx 16 5110
Ripley Derbys 74 3950
Ripley Hants 12 1698
Ripley N York 89 2860
Ripley Surrey 26 0556
Riplingham E R Yk 84 9631
Riplington Hants 13 6623
Ripon N York 89 3171
Rippingale Lincs 64 0927
Ripple Kent 29 3550
Ripple Worcs 47 8737
Ripponden W York 82 0319
Risabus Ag & B 104 3143
Risbury Herefs 46 5455
Risby Lincs 84 9114
Risby Suffk 54 8066
Risca Caerph 34 2391
Rise E R Yk 85 1542
Riseden E Susx 16 6130

306

S

Seworgan Slindon

308

Seworgan Cnwll 2 7030
Sewstern Leics 63 8821
Sexhow N York 89 4706
Sezincote Gloucs 48 1731
Sgiogarstaigh W Isls 152 5461
Shabbington Bucks 37 6606
Shackerstone Leics 62 3706
Shacklecross Derbys 62 4234
Shackleford Surrey 25 9345
Shade W York 81 9323
Shader W Isls 152 3854
Shadforth Dur 96 3440
Shadingfield Suffk 55 4384
Shadoxhurst Kent 28 9737
Shadwell Norfk 54 9383
Shadwell W York 83 3439
Shaftenhoe End Herts 39 4037
Shaftesbury Dorset 22 8623
Shaftholme S York 83 5708
Shafton S York 83 3911
Shafton Two Gates S York 83 3910
Shakespeare's Birthplace 48 1955
Shalbourne Wilts 23 3163
Shalcombe IOW 13 3985
Shalden Hants 24 6941
Shalden Green Hants 24 7043
Shaldon Devon 7 9372
Shalfleet IOW 13 4189
Shalford Essex 40 7229
Shalford Surrey 25 0047
Shalford Green Essex 40 7127
Shallowford Staffs 72 8729
Shalmsford Street Kent 29 0954
Shalstone Bucks 49 6436
Shamley Green Surrey 14 0343
Shandford Angus 134 4962
Shandon Ag & B 114 2586
Shandwick Highld 147 8575
Shangton Leics 50 7196
Shankhouse Nthumb 103 2778
Shanklin IOW 13 5881
Shap Cumb 94 5615
Shapwick Dorset 11 9301
Shapwick Somset 21 4138
Shard End W Mids 61 1588
Shardlow Derbys 62 4330
Shareshill Staffs 60 9406
Sharlston W York 83 3918
Sharlston Common W York 83 3919
Sharman's Cross W Mids 61 1279
Sharnal Street Kent 28 7974
Sharnbrook Beds 51 9959
Sharneyford Lancs 81 8824
Sharnford Leics 50 4891
Sharnhill Green Dorset 11 7105
Sharoe Green Lancs 80 5333
Sharow N York 89 3371
Sharp Green Norfk 67 3820
Sharpenhoe Beds 38 0630
Sharperton Nthumb 102 9503
Sharpness Gloucs 35 6702
Sharpthorne W Susx 15 3732
Sharptor Cnwll 5 2573
Sharpway Gate Worcs 47 9565
Sharrington Norfk 66 0337
Shatterford Worcs 60 7981
Shatterling Kent 29 2658
Shaugh Prior Devon 6 5463
Shave Cross Dorset 10 4198
Shavington Ches 72 6951
Shaw Berks 24 4768
Shaw Gt Man 79 9308
Shaw W York 82 0235
Shaw Wilts 22 8965
Shaw Wilts 36 1185
Shaw Common Gloucs 47 6826
Shaw Green Herts 39 3032
Shaw Green Lancs 80 5218
Shaw Green N York 82 2652
Shaw Hill Lancs 81 5720
Shaw Mills N York 89 2562
Shawbost W Isls 152 2646
Shawbury Shrops 59 5521
Shawclough Gt Man 81 8914
Shawdon Hill Nthumb 111 0813
Shawell Leics 50 5480
Shawford Hants 13 4625
Shawforth Lancs 81 8920
Shawhead D & G 100 8675
Shawsburn S Lans 116 7750
Shear Cross Wilts 22 8642
Shearington D & G 100 0266
Shearsby Leics 50 6290
Shearston Somset 20 2830
Shebbear Devon 18 4409
Shebdon Staffs 72 7625
Shebster Highld 150 0164
Sheddens E Rens 115 5757
Shedfield Hants 13 5613
Sheen Derbys 74 1161
Sheep Hill Dur 96 1757
Sheep-ridge W York 82 1519
Sheepbridge Derbys 74 3674
Sheepscar W York 82 3134
Sheepscombe Gloucs 35 8910
Sheepstor Devon 6 5667
Sheepwash Devon 18 4806
Sheepwash Nthumb 103 2585
Sheepway Somset 34 4976
Sheepy Magna Leics 61 3201
Sheepy Parva Leics 62 3301
Sheering Essex 39 5014
Sheerness Kent 28 9174
Sheerwater Surrey 26 0461
Sheet Hants 13 7524
Sheffield Cnwll 2 4526
Sheffield S York 74 3587
Sheffield Bottom Berks 24 6469
Sheffield City Airport 74 4088
Sheffield Green E Susx 15 4125
Shefford Beds 38 1439
Sheigra Highld 148 1860
Sheinton Shrops 59 6003
Shelderton Shrops 46 4077
Sheldon Derbys 74 1768
Sheldon Devon 9 1208
Sheldon W Mids 61 1584
Sheldwich Kent 28 0156
Sheldwich Lees Kent 28 0156
Shelf W York 82 1228
Shelfanger Norfk 54 1083
Shelfield W Mids 61 0302
Shelfield Warwks 48 1263
Shelfield Green Warwks 48 1261
Shelford Notts 63 6642
Shelford Warwks 50 4288
Shellacres Border 110 8943
Shelley Essex 39 5505
Shelley Suffk 54 0238
Shelley W York 82 2011
Shelley Far Bank W York 82 2010
Shellingford Oxon 36 3193
Shellow Bowells Essex 40 6007
Shelsley Beauchamp Worcs 47 7363
Shelsley Walsh Worcs 47 7263
Shelton Beds 51 0368
Shelton Norfk 67 2291
Shelton Notts 63 7844
Shelton Shrops 59 4613
Shelton Green Norfk 55 2390
Shelton Lock Derbys 62 3730
Shelton Under Harley Staffs 72 8139
Shelve Shrops 59 3399
Shelwick Herefs 46 5242
Shenfield Essex 40 6095
Shenington Oxon 48 3742
Shenley Herts 26 1800
Shenley Brook End Bucks 38 8335
Shenley Church End Bucks 38 8336
Shenleybury Herts 26 1801
Shenmore Herefs 46 3937
Shennanton D & G 98 3363
Shenstone Staffs 61 1004
Shenstone Worcs 60 8673
Shenstone Woodend Staffs 61 1101
Shenton Leics 61 3800
Shepeau Stow Lincs 64 3012
Shephall Herts 39 2623
Shepherd's Bush Gt Lon 26 2380
Shepherd's Green Oxon 37 7183
Shepherds Cnwll 3 8154
Shepherds Patch Gloucs 35 7304
Shepherdswell Kent 29 2647
Shepley W York 82 1909
Shepperdine Gloucs 35 6295
Shepperton Surrey 26 0766
Shepperton Green Surrey 26 0767
Shepreth Cambs 52 3947
Shepshed Leics 62 4819
Shepton Beauchamp Somset 10 4017
Shepton Mallet Somset 21 6143
Shepton Montague Somset 22 6831
Shepway Kent 28 7753
Sheraton Dur 96 4435
Sherborne Dorset 10 6316
Sherborne Gloucs 36 1614
Sherborne Somset 21 5855
Sherborne Causeway Dorset 22 8323
Sherborne St John Hants 24 6255
Sherbourne Warwks 48 2661
Sherburn Dur 96 3142
Sherburn N York 91 9576
Sherburn Hill Dur 96 3342
Sherburn in Elmet N York 83 4933
Shere Surrey 14 0747
Shereford Norfk 66 8829
Sherfield English Hants 23 2922
Sherfield on Loddon Hants 24 6858
Sherfin Lancs 81 7925
Sherford Devon 7 7844
Sherford Dorset 11 9193
Sheriff Hutton N York 90 6566
Sheriffhales Shrops 60 7512
Sheringham Norfk 66 1543
Sherington Bucks 38 8846
Shermanbury W Susx 15 2019
Shernborne Norfk 65 7132
Sherrington Wilts 22 9639
Sherston Wilts 35 8586
Sherwood Notts 62 5643
Shettleston C Glas 116 6464
Shevington Gt Man 78 5408
Shevington Moor Gt Man 78 5410
Shevington Vale Gt Man 78 5309
Sheviock Cnwll 5 3755
Shibden Head W York 82 0928
Shide IOW 13 5088
Shidlaw Nthumb 110 8037
Shiel Bridge Highld 138 9318
Shieldaig Highld 137 8154
Shieldhill D & G 100 0385
Shieldhill Falk 116 8976
Shieldhill House Hotel S Lans 108 0040
Shields N Lans 116 7755
Shielfoot Highld 129 6670
Shielhill Angus 134 4257
Shielhill Inver 114 2472
Shifford Oxon 36 3701
Shifnal Shrops 60 7407
Shilbottle Nthumb 111 1908
Shildon Dur 96 2226
Shillford E Rens 115 4556
Shillingford Devon 20 9824
Shillingford Oxon 37 5992
Shillingford Abbot Devon 9 9088
Shillingford St George Devon 9 9087
Shillingstone Dorset 11 8211
Shillington Beds 38 1234
Shillmoor Nthumb 110 8807
Shilton Oxon 36 2608
Shilton Warwks 61 4084
Shilvinghampton Dorset 10 6284
Shimpling Norfk 54 1583
Shimpling Suffk 54 8651
Shimpling Street Suffk 54 8753
Shincliffe Dur 96 2940
Shiney Row T & W 96 3252
Shinfield Berks 24 7368
Shingay Cambs 52 3046
Shingle Street Suffk 55 3642
Shinnersbridge Devon 7 7862
Shinness Highld 146 5215
Shipbourne Kent 27 5952
Shipbrookhill Ches 79 6771
Shipdham Norfk 66 9507
Shipham Somset 21 4457
Shiphay Devon 7 8965
Shiplake Oxon 37 7678
Shiplake Row Oxon 37 7478
Shiplate Somset 21 3556
Shipley Derbys 62 4444
Shipley Shrops 60 8095
Shipley W Susx 15 1421
Shipley W York 82 1537
Shipley Bridge Surrey 15 3040
Shipley Hatch Kent 28 0038
Shipmeadow Suffk 55 3790
Shippea Hill Station Cambs 53 6484
Shippon Oxon 37 4898
Shipston on Stour Warwks 48 2540
Shipton Bucks 49 7727
Shipton Gloucs 36 0318
Shipton N York 90 5558
Shipton Shrops 59 5692
Shipton Bellinger Hants 23 2345
Shipton Gorge Dorset 10 4991
Shipton Green W Susx 14 8099
Shipton Moyne Gloucs 35 8989
Shipton-on-Cherwell Oxon 37 4716
Shipton-under-Wychwood Oxon 36 2817
Shiptonthorpe E R Yk 84 8543
Shirburn Oxon 37 6995
Shirdley Hill Lancs 80 3612
Shire Cumb 94 6135
Shire Oak W Mids 61 0504
Shirebrook Derbys 75 5267
Shiregreen S York 74 3691
Shirehampton Bristl 34 5376
Shiremoor T & W 103 3171
Shirenewton Mons 34 4793
Shireoaks Notts 75 5580
Shirkoak Kent 17 9435
Shirl Heath Herefs 46 4359
Shirland Derbys 74 4058
Shirlett Shrops 59 6497
Shirley Derbys 73 2141
Shirley Gt Lon 27 3565
Shirley Hants 13 4014
Shirley W Mids 61 1278
Shirrell Heath Hants 13 5714
Shirvan Ag & B 113 8784
Shirwell Devon 19 6037
Shirwell Cross Devon 19 5936
Shiskine N Ayrs 105 9129
Shittlehope Dur 95 0039
Shobdon Herefs 46 4062
Shobley Hants 12 1806
Shobrooke Devon 9 8601
Shoby Leics 63 6820
Shocklach Ches 71 4349
Shocklach Green Ches 71 4349
Shoeburyness Essex 40 9385
Sholden Kent 29 3552
Sholing Hants 13 4511
Shoose Cumb 92 0127
Shoot Hill Shrops 59 4112
Shop Cnwll 18 2214
Shop Cnwll 4 8773
Shop Street Suffk 55 2268
Shopwyke W Susx 14 8805
Shore Gt Man 81 9216
Shoreditch Gt Lon 27 3382
Shoreditch Somset 20 2422
Shoreham Kent 27 5161
Shoreham Airport 15 2005
Shoreham-by-Sea W Susx 15 2105
Shoreswood Nthumb 110 9446
Shorley Hants 13 5726
Shorncote Gloucs 35 0296
Shorne Kent 28 6971
Shorne Ridgeway Kent 28 6970
Short Heath W Mids 60 9700
Short Heath W Mids 61 0992
Shorta Cross Cnwll 5 2857
Shortbridge E Susx 16 4521
Shortfield Common Surrey 25 8442
Shortgate E Susx 16 4915
Shortheath Hants 14 7636
Shortlanesend Cnwll 3 8047
Shortstown Beds 38 0747
Shorwell IOW 13 4583
Shoscombe Somset 22 7156
Shotesham Norfk 67 2499
Shotgate Essex 40 7592
Shotley Suffk 55 2335
Shotley Bridge Dur 95 0953
Shotley Gate Suffk 41 2433
Shotley Street Suffk 55 2335
Shotleyfield Nthumb 95 0553
Shottenden Kent 28 0454
Shottermill Surrey 14 8832
Shottery Warwks 48 1854
Shotteswell Warwks 49 4245
Shottisham Suffk 55 3244
Shottle Derbys 74 3149
Shottlegate Derbys 62 3147
Shotton Dur 96 3625
Shotton Dur 96 4139
Shotton Flints 71 3168
Shotton Nthumb 110 8430
Shotton Nthumb 103 2277
Shotton Colliery Dur 96 3941
Shotts N Lans 116 8759
Shotwick Ches 71 3371
Shougle Moray 141 2155
Shouldham Norfk 65 6709
Shouldham Thorpe Norfk 65 6607
Shoulton Worcs 47 8159
Shover's Green E Susx 16 6530
Shraleybrook Staffs 72 7849
Shrawardine Shrops 59 3915
Shrawley Worcs 47 8065
Shreding Green Bucks 26 0280
Shrewley Warwks 48 2167
Shrewsbury Shrops 59 4912
Shrewton Wilts 23 0743
Shripney W Susx 14 9302
Shrivenham Oxon 36 2389
Shropham Norfk 66 9893
Shrub End Essex 41 9723
Shucknall Herefs 46 5842
Shudy Camps Cambs 53 6244
Shurdington Gloucs 35 9218
Shurlock Row Berks 25 8374
Shurnock Worcs 48 0360
Shurrery Highld 150 0458
Shurrery Lodge Highld 150 0456
Shurton Somset 20 2044
Shustoke Warwks 61 2290
Shut Heath Staffs 72 8621
Shute Devon 9 8900
Shute Devon 10 2597
Shutford Oxon 48 3840
Shuthonger Gloucs 47 8935
Shutlanger Nhants 49 7249
Shutt Green Staffs 60 8709
Shutterton Devon 9 9679
Shuttington Warwks 61 2505
Shuttlewood Derbys 75 4673
Shuttlewood Common Derbys 75 4773
Shuttleworth Lancs 81 8017
Siabost W Isls 152 2646
Siadar W Isls 152 3854
Sibbertoft Nhants 50 6882
Sibdon Carwood Shrops 59 4183
Sibford Ferris Oxon 48 3537
Sibford Gower Oxon 48 3537
Sible Hedingham Essex 53 7734
Sibley's Green Essex 40 6128
Siblyback Cnwll 5 2372
Sibsey Lincs 77 3550
Sibsey Fenside Lincs 77 3452
Sibson Cambs 51 0997
Sibson Leics 61 3500
Sibster Highld 151 3253
Sibthorpe Notts 75 7273
Sibthorpe Notts 63 7645
Sibton Suffk 55 3669
Sicklesmere Suffk 54 8760
Sicklinghall N York 83 3648
Sid Cop S York 83 3809
Sidbrook Somset 20 2527
Sidbury Devon 9 1391
Sidbury Shrops 60 6885
Sidcot Somset 21 4257
Sidcup Gt Lon 27 4672
Siddick Cumb 92 0031
Siddington Ches 79 8470
Siddington Gloucs 36 0399
Sidemoor Worcs 60 9571
Sidestrand Norfk 67 2539
Sidford Devon 9 1390
Sidlesham W Susx 14 8599
Sidlesham Common W Susx 14 8599
Sidley E Susx 17 7408
Sidmouth Devon 9 1287
Siefton Shrops 59 4883
Sigford Devon 7 7773
Sigglesthorne E R Yk 85 1545
Sigingstone V Glam 33 9771
Signet Oxon 36 2410
Silchester Hants 24 6261
Sileby Leics 62 6015
Silecroft Cumb 86 1381
Silfield Norfk 66 1299
Silian Cerdgn 44 5751
Silk Willoughby Lincs 64 0542
Silkstead Hants 13 4424
Silkstone S York 82 2805
Silkstone Common S York 82 2904
Silksworth T & W 96 3752
Silloth Cumb 92 1153
Silpho N York 91 9692
Silsden W York 82 0446
Silsoe Beds 38 0835
Silton Dorset 22 7829
Silver End Essex 40 8119
Silver Street Kent 28 8760
Silver Street Somset 21 5432
Silverburn Mdloth 117 2060
Silverdale Lancs 87 4674
Silverdale Staffs 72 8146
Silverdale Green Lancs 87 4674
Silverford Abers 142 7763
Silvergate Norfk 66 1727
Silverlace Green Suffk 55 3160
Silverley's Green Suffk 55 2976
Silverstone Nhants 49 6743
Silverton Devon 9 9502
Silverwell Cnwll 3 7448
Silvington Shrops 47 6279
Simmondley Derbys 74 0293
Simonburn Nthumb 102 8773
Simons Burrow Devon 9 1416
Simonsbath Somset 19 7739
Simonstone Lancs 81 7734
Simonstone N York 88 8791
Simprim Border 110 8445
Simpson Bucks 38 8836
Simpson Cross Pembks 30 8919
Sinclair's Hill Border 119 8150
Sinclairston E Ayrs 107 4716
Sinderby N York 89 3482
Sinderhope Nthumb 95 8451
Sinderland Green Gt Man 79 7389
Sindlesham Berks 25 7769
Single Street Gt Lon 27 4359
Singleborough Bucks 49 7631
Singleton Lancs 80 3838
Singleton W Susx 14 8713
Singlewell Kent 28 6570
Sinkhurst Green Kent 28 8142
Sinnarhard Abers 134 4713
Sinnington N York 90 7485
Sinton Worcs 47 8160
Sinton Green Worcs 47 8160
Sipson Gt Lon 26 0777
Sirhowy Blae G 33 1410
Sissinghurst Kent 28 7937
Siston Gloucs 35 6875
Sitcott Devon 5 3691
Sithney Cnwll 2 6328
Sithney Common Cnwll 2 6428
Sithney Green Cnwll 2 6429
Sittingbourne Kent 28 9063
Six Ashes Staffs 60 7988
Six Bells Blae G 34 2202
Six Mile Bottom Cambs 53 5756
Six Rues Jersey 158 0000
Sixhills Lincs 76 1787
Sixmile Cottages Kent 29 1344
Sixpenny Handley Dorset 11 9917
Sizergh Castle 87 4987
Sizewell Suffk 55 4762
Skaill Ork 153 5806
Skares E Ayrs 107 5317
Skateraw Abers 135 9193
Skateraw E Loth 119 7375
Skeabost Highld 136 4148
Skeeby N York 89 1902
Skeffington Leics 63 7402
Skeffling E R Yk 85 3719
Skegby Notts 75 4961
Skegby Notts 75 7869
Skegness Lincs 77 5663
Skelbo Highld 147 7895
Skelbo Street Highld 147 7994
Skelbrooke S York 83 5012
Skeldyke Lincs 64 3337
Skellingthorpe Lincs 76 9272
Skellorm Green Ches 79 9281
Skellow S York 83 5310
Skelmanthorpe W York 82 2310
Skelmersdale Lancs 78 4606
Skelmorlie N Ayrs 114 1967
Skelpick Highld 150 7256
Skelston D & G 100 8285
Skelton Cumb 93 4335
Skelton E R Yk 84 7625
Skelton N York 89 0900
Skelton N York 97 6618
Skelton N York 89 3668
Skelton N York 83 5756
Skelwith Bridge Cumb 87 3403
Skendleby Lincs 77 4369
Skene House Abers 135 7610
Skenfrith Mons 34 4520
Skerne E R Yk 84 0455
Skerray Highld 149 6563
Skerricha Highld 148 2350
Skerton Lancs 87 4763
Sketchley Leics 50 4292
Sketty Swans 32 6292
Skewen Neath 32 7296
Skewsby N York 90 6270
Skeyton Norfk 67 2425
Skeyton Corner Norfk 67 2527
Skiall Highld 150 0267
Skidbrooke Lincs 77 4393
Skidbrooke North End Lincs 77 4395
Skidby E R Yk 84 0133
Skigersta W Isls 152 5461
Skilgate Somset 20 9827
Skillington Lincs 63 8925
Skinburness Cumb 92 1256
Skinflats Falk 116 9082
Skinidin Highld 136 2247
Skinners Green Berks 24 4465
Skinningrove N York 97 7119
Skipness Ag & B 114 9057
Skipper's Bridge Cumb 101 3783
Skiprigg Cumb 93 3945
Skipsea E R Yk 85 1654
Skipsea Brough E R Yk 85 1454
Skipton N York 82 9851
Skipton-on-Swale N York 89 3679
Skipwith N York 83 6638
Skirlaugh E R Yk 85 1439
Skirling Border 108 0739
Skirmett Bucks 37 7790
Skirpenbeck E R Yk 84 7456
Skirwith Cumb 94 6132
Skirwith N York 87 7073
Skirza Highld 151 3868
Skitby Cumb 101 4465
Skittle Green Bucks 37 7703
Skulamus Highld 129 6622
Skyborry Green Shrops 46 2674
Skye Green Essex 40 8722
Skye of Curr Highld 141 9924
Skyreholme N York 88 0660
Slack Derbys 74 3362
Slack W York 82 9728
Slack Head Cumb 87 4978
Slackcote Gt Man 82 9709
Slackholme End Lincs 77 5370
Slacks of Cairnbanno Abers 143 8445
Slad Gloucs 35 8707
Slade Devon 19 5046
Slade Devon 9 1108
Slade Somset 19 8327
Slade End Oxon 37 5990
Slade Green Kent 27 5276
Slade Heath Staffs 60 9106
Slade Hooton S York 75 5288
Slades Green Worcs 47 8134
Sladesbridge Cnwll 4 0171
Slaggyford Nthumb 94 6752
Slaid Hill W York 83 3240
Slaidburn Lancs 81 7152
Slaithwaite W York 82 0813
Slaley Derbys 74 2757
Slaley Nthumb 95 9657
Slamannan Falk 116 8572
Slapton Bucks 38 9320
Slapton Devon 7 8245
Slapton Nhants 49 6446
Slattocks Gt Man 79 8808
Slaugham W Susx 15 2528
Slaughterford Wilts 35 8473
Slawston Leics 50 7894
Sleaford Hants 25 8038
Sleaford Lincs 64 0645
Sleagill Cumb 94 5919
Sleap Shrops 59 4826
Sleapford Shrops 59 6315
Sleasdairidh Highld 146 6496
Sledge Green Worcs 47 8134
Sledmere E R Yk 91 9364
Sleight Dorset 11 9898
Sleightholme Dur 88 9510
Sleights N York 90 8607
Slepe Dorset 11 9293
Slickly Highld 151 2966
Sliddery N Ayrs 105 9323
Sligachan Highld 136 4829
Sligrachan Ag & B 114 1791
Slimbridge Gloucs 35 7303
Slindon Staffs 72 8232
Slindon W Susx 14 9608

Slinfold W Susx 14 1131
Sling Gwynd 69 6066
Slingsby N York 90 6974
Slip End Beds 38 0718
Slip End Herts 39 2837
Slipton Nhants 51 9579
Slitting Mill Staffs 73 0217
Slockavullin Ag & B 113 8297
Slogarie D & G 99 6568
Sloley Norfk 67 2924
Sloncombe Devon 8 7386
Sloothby Lincs 77 4970
Slough Berks 26 9879
Slough Green Somset 20 2719
Slough Green W Susx 15 2826
Slumbay Highld 138 8938
Slyfield Green Surrey 25 9952
Slyne Lancs 87 4765
Smailholm Border 110 6436
Small Dole W Susx 15 2112
Small Heath W Mids 61 1085
Small Hythe Kent 17 8930
Small Wood Hey Lancs 80 3948
Smallbridge Gt Man 81 9115
Smallbrook Devon 9 8698
Smallbrook Gloucs 34 5900
Smallburgh Norfk 67 3324
Smalldale Derbys 74 0977
Smalldale Derbys 74 1781
Smalley Derbys 62 4044
Smalley Common Derbys 62 4042
Smalley Green Derbys 62 4043
Smallfield Surrey 15 3143
Smallridge Devon 10 3001
Smallthorne Staffs 72 8850
Smallways N York 89 1111
Smallwood Ches 72 8060
Smallworth Norfk 54 0080
Smannell Hants 23 3749
Smardale Cumb 88 7308
Smarden Kent 28 8742
Smarden Bell Kent 28 8742
Smart's Hill Kent 16 5242
Smeafield Nthumb 111 0937
Smearisary Highld 129 6476
Smeatharpe Devon 9 1910
Smeeth Kent 29 0739
Smeeton Westerby Leics 50 6892
Smelthouses N York 89 1964
Smerral Highld 151 1733
Smestow Staffs 60 8591
Smethwick W Mids 60 0287
Smethwick Green Ches 72 8063
Smisby Derbys 62 3418
Smith End Green Worcs 47 7752
Smith Green Lancs 80 4955
Smith's End Herts 39 4037
Smith's Green Essex 40 5721
Smith's Green Essex 53 6640
Smitheclose IOW 13 5391
Smithfield Cumb 101 4465
Smithies S York 83 3508
Smithincott Devon 9 0611
Smithstown Highld 144 7977
Smithton Highld 140 7145
Smithy Bridge Gt Man 81 9215
Smithy Green Ches 79 7474
Smithy Green Gt Man 79 8785
Smithy Houses Derbys 62 3846
Smockington Leics 50 4589
Smoo Highld 149 4167
Smythe's Green Essex 40 9218
Snade D & G 100 8485
Snailbeach Shrops 59 3702
Snailwell Cambs 53 6467
Snainton N York 91 9282
Snaith E R Yk 83 6422
Snake Pass Inn Derbys 74 1190
Snape N York 89 2684
Snape Suffk 55 3959
Snape Green Mersyd 80 3813
Snape Street Suffk 55 3958
Snaresbrook Gt Lon 27 4089
Snarestone Leics 62 3409
Snarford Lincs 76 0482
Snargate Kent 17 9928
Snave Kent 17 0129
Sneachill Worcs 47 9053
Snead Powys 59 3192
Sneath Common Norfk 54 1689
Sneaton N York 91 8907
Sneatonthorpe N York 91 9006
Snelland Lincs 76 0780
Snelson Ches 79 8074
Snelston Derbys 73 1543
Snetterton Norfk 66 9991
Snettisham Norfk 65 6834
Snibston Leics 62 4114
Snig's End Gloucs 47 7828
Snitter Nthumb 103 0203
Snitterby Lincs 76 9894
Snitterfield Warwks 48 2159
Snitterton Derbys 74 2760
Snittlegarth Cumb 93 2138
Snitton Shrops 46 5575
Snoadhill Kent 28 9442
Snodhill Herefs 46 3240
Snodland Kent 28 7061
Snoll Hatch Kent 28 6648
Snow End Herts 39 4032
Snow Street Norfk 54 0981
Snowden Hill S York 74 2600
Snowshill Gloucs 48 0933
Soake Hants 13 6611
Soar Cardif 33 0983
Soar Devon 7 7037
Soar Powys 45 9731
Soberton Hants 13 6116
Soberton Heath Hants 13 6014
Sockbridge Cumb 94 4926
Sockburn Dur 89 3406
Sodom Denbgs 70 0971
Sodylt Bank Shrops 71 3439
Soham Cambs 53 5973
Soham Cotes Cambs 53 5775
Solas W Isls 152 8074
Solbury Pembks 30 8912
Soldon Devon 18 3210
Soldon Cross Devon 18 3210
Soldridge Hants 24 6535
Sole Street Kent 28 6567
Sole Street Kent 29 0949
Solihull W Mids 61 1679
Sollers Dilwyn Herefs 46 4255
Sollers Hope Herefs 46 6132
Sollom Lancs 80 4518
Solva Pembks 30 8024
Solwaybank D & G 101 3077
Somerby Leics 63 7710
Somerby Lincs 84 0606
Somercotes Derbys 74 4253
Somerford Dorset 12 1793
Somerford Keynes Gloucs 35 0195
Somerley W Susx 14 8198
Somerleyton Suffk 67 4897
Somersal Herbert Derbys 73 1335
Somersby Lincs 77 3472
Somersham Cambs 52 3678
Somersham Suffk 54 0848
Somerton Oxon 49 4928
Somerton Somset 21 4928
Somerton Suffk 54 8153
Somerwood Shrops 59 5614
Sompting W Susx 15 1505
Sonning Berks 37 7575
Sonning Common Oxon 37 7180
Sonning Eye Oxon 37 7476
Sontley Wrexhm 71 3347
Sopley Hants 12 1596
Sopworth Wilts 35 8286
Sorbie D & G 99 4346
Sordale Highld 151 1462
Sorisdale Ag & B 120 2763
Sorn E Ayrs 107 5526
Sortat Highld 151 2863
Sosgill Cumb 92 1024
Sotby Lincs 76 2078
Sots Hole Lincs 76 1264
Sotterly Suffk 55 4484
Soughton Flints 70 2466
Soulbury Bucks 38 8826
Soulby Cumb 93 4625
Soulby Cumb 88 7411
Souldern Oxon 49 5231
Souldrop Beds 51 9861
Sound Muir Moray 141 3652
Soundwell Gloucs 35 6575
Sourton Devon 8 5390
Soutergate Cumb 86 2281
South Acre Norfk 66 8114
South Alkham Kent 29 2441
South Allington Devon 7 7938
South Alloa Falk 116 8791
South Ambersham W Susx 14 9120
South Anston S York 75 5183
South Ascot Berks 25 9268
South Ashford Kent 28 0041
South Baddesley Hants 12 3596
South Bank N York 97 5320
South Bank N York 83 5950
South Barrow Somset 21 6028
South Beddington Gt Lon 27 2863
South Beer Cnwll 5 3091
South Benfleet Essex 40 7787
South Bersted W Susx 14 9300
South Bockhampton Dorset 12 1795
South Bowood Dorset 10 4498
South Bramwith S York 83 6211
South Brent Devon 7 6960
South Brewham Somset 22 7236
South Broomhill Nthumb 103 2499
South Burlingham Norfk 67 3807
South Cadbury Somset 21 6325
South Carlton Lincs 76 9476
South Carlton Notts 75 5883
South Cave E R Yk 84 9230
South Cerney Gloucs 36 0497
South Chailey E Susx 15 3918
South Chard Somset 10 3205
South Charlton Nthumb 111 1620
South Cheriton Somset 22 6924
South Church Dur 96 2128
South Cleatlam Dur 96 1218
South Cliffe E R Yk 84 8735
South Clifton Notts 75 8270
South Cockerington Lincs 77 3888
South Cornelly Brdgnd 33 8280
South Cove Suffk 55 4981
South Creake Norfk 66 8536
South Crosland W York 82 1112
South Croxton Leics 63 6810
South Dalton E R Yk 84 9645
South Darenth Kent 27 5669
South Duffield N York 83 6833
South Elkington Lincs 77 2988
South Elmsall W York 83 4711
South End E R Yk 85 3918
South End Hants 12 1015
South End Herefs 47 7444
South End Lincs 85 1120
South End Norfk 54 9990
South Erradale Highld 137 7471
South Fambridge Essex 40 8694
South Fawley Berks 36 3880
South Ferriby Lincs 84 9820
South Field E R Yk 84 0225
South Godstone Surrey 15 3648
South Gorley Hants 12 1610
South Gosforth T & W 103 2467
South Green Essex 41 0319
South Green Essex 40 6893
South Green Kent 28 8560
South Green Norfk 66 0510
South Green Suffk 54 1775
South Gyle C Edin 117 1871
South Hanningfield Essex 40 7497
South Harting W Susx 14 7819
South Hayling Hants 13 7299
South Hazelrigg Nthumb 111 0532
South Heath Bucks 26 9101
South Heighton E Susx 16 4402
South Hetton Dur 96 3845
South Hiendley W York 83 3912
South Hill Cnwll 5 3272
South Hill Somset 21 4726
South Hinksey Oxon 37 5104
South Hole Devon 18 2220
South Holmwood Surrey 15 1744
South Hornchurch Gt Lon 27 5183
South Huish Devon 7 6941
South Hykeham Lincs 76 9364
South Hylton T & W 96 3556
South Kelsey Lincs 76 0498
South Kessock Highld 140 6547
South Killingholme Lincs 85 1416
South Kilvington N York 89 4284
South Kilworth Nhants 50 6081
South Kirkby W York 83 4410
South Knighton Devon 7 8172
South Kyme Lincs 76 1749
South Lawn Oxon 36 2814
South Leigh Oxon 36 3909
South Leverton Notts 75 7881
South Littleton Worcs 48 0746
South Lopham Norfk 54 0481
South Luffenham Rutlnd 63 9301
South Malling E Susx 16 4210
South Marston Wilts 36 1987
South Merstham Surrey 27 2952
South Middleton Nthumb 111 9923
South Milford N York 83 4931
South Milton Devon 7 7042
South Mimms Herts 26 2201
South Molton Devon 19 7125
South Moor Dur 96 1951
South Moreton Oxon 37 5688
South Mundham W Susx 14 8700
South Muskham Notts 75 7957
South Newbald E R Yk 84 9035
South Newington Oxon 48 4033
South Newton Wilts 23 0834
South Normanton Derbys 75 4456
South Norwood Gt Lon 27 3368
South Nutfield Surrey 15 3049
South Ockendon Essex 27 5983
South Ormsby Lincs 77 3675
South Ossett W York 82 2819
South Otterington N York 89 3787
South Owersby Lincs 76 0693
South Park Surrey 15 2448
South Perrott Dorset 10 4706
South Petherton Somset 10 4316
South Petherwin Cnwll 5 3181
South Pickenham Norfk 66 8504
South Pill Cnwll 6 4259
South Pool Devon 7 7740
South Poorton Dorset 10 5297
South Quarme Somset 20 9236
South Queensferry C Edin 117 1378
South Radworthy Devon 19 7432
South Rauceby Lincs 64 0245
South Raynham Norfk 66 8723
South Reddish Gt Man 79 8891
South Reston Lincs 77 4083
South Runcton Norfk 65 6308
South Scarle Notts 76 8463
South Shian Ag & B 122 9042
South Shields T & W 103 3666
South Shore Lancs 80 3033
South Somercotes Lincs 77 4193
South Stainley N York 89 3063
South Stifford Essex 27 5978
South Stoke Lincs 63 9127
South Stoke Oxon 37 5983
South Stoke Somset 22 7461
South Stoke W Susx 14 0209
South Stour Kent 28 0338
South Street Kent 27 6363
South Street Kent 28 0557
South Street Kent 29 1265
South Tarbrax S Lans 117 0353
South Tawton Devon 8 6594
South Thoresby Lincs 77 4076
South Thorpe Dur 95 1013
South Tidworth Wilts 23 2347
South Town Hants 24 6536
South Walsham Norfk 67 3613
South Warnborough Hants 24 7247
South Weald Essex 27 5694
South Weston Oxon 37 7098
South Wheatley Cnwll 5 2492
South Widcombe Somset 21 5856
South Wigston Leics 50 5897
South Willesborough Kent 28 0240
South Willingham Lincs 76 1983
South Wingate Dur 96 4134
South Wingfield Derbys 74 3755
South Witham Lincs 63 9219
South Wonston Hants 24 4636
South Woodham Ferrers Essex 40 8097
South Wootton Norfk 65 6422
South Wraxall Wilts 22 8364
South Zeal Devon 8 6593
Southall Gt Lon 26 1279
Southam Gloucs 47 9725
Southam Warwks 49 4161
Southampton Hants 13 4112
Southampton Airport 13 4516
Southborough Gt Lon 27 4267
Southborough Kent 16 5842
Southbourne Dorset 12 1491
Southbourne W Susx 14 7705
Southbrook Dorset 11 8494
Southburgh Norfk 66 0005
Southburn E R Yk 84 9854
Southchurch Essex 40 9086
Southcott Cnwll 5 1995
Southcott Devon 18 4416
Southcott Devon 8 5495
Southcott Devon 8 7580
Southcott Wilts 23 1659
Southcourt Bucks 38 8112
Southease E Susx 16 4205
Southend Ag & B 105 6908
Southend Wilts 36 1973
Southend Airport 40 8789
Southend-on-Sea Essex 40 8885
Southernby Cumb 93 3639
Southernden Kent 28 8645
Southerndown V Glam 33 8873
Southerness D & G 92 9754
Southerton Devon 9 0790
Southery Norfk 65 6194
Southfield Falk 116 8472
Southfleet Kent 27 6171
Southford IOW 13 5179
Southgate Gt Lon 27 2994
Southgate Norfk 65 6833
Southgate Norfk 66 8635
Southgate Norfk 66 1324
Southgate Swans 32 5587
Southill Beds 39 1542
Southington Hants 24 5049
Southleigh Devon 9 2093
Southminster Essex 40 9599
Southmoor Oxon 36 3998
Southmuir Angus 126 3852
Southoe Cambs 52 1864
Southolt Suffk 55 1968
Southorpe Cambs 64 0803
Southover Dorset 10 6294
Southover E Susx 16 6525
Southowram W York 82 1123
Southport Mersyd 80 3317
Southrepps Norfk 67 2536
Southrey Lincs 76 1366
Southrop Gloucs 36 1903
Southrope Hants 24 6644
Southsea Hants 13 6599
Southsea Wrexhm 71 3051
Southside Dur 95 1026
Southtown Norfk 67 5106
Southtown Somset 10 3216
Southwaite Cumb 93 4445
Southwark Gt Lon 27 3279
Southwater W Susx 15 1526
Southwater Street W Susx 15 1427
Southway Somset 21 5242
Southwell Dorset 11 6870
Southwell Notts 75 6953
Southwick Hants 13 6208
Southwick Nhants 51 0292
Southwick Somset 21 3646
Southwick T & W 96 3758
Southwick W Susx 15 2405
Southwick Wilts 22 8355
Southwold Suffk 55 5076
Southwood Norfk 67 3905
Southwood Somset 21 5533
Sowe Common W Mids 61 3782
Sower Carr Lancs 80 3743
Sowerby N York 89 4380
Sowerby W York 82 0423
Sowerby Bridge W York 82 0523
Sowerby Row Cumb 93 3940
Sowerhill Somset 19 8924
Sowhill Torfn 34 2700
Sowley Green Suffk 53 7050
Sowood W York 82 0818
Sowton Devon 6 5065
Sowton Devon 9 9792
Soyland Town W York 82 0320
Spa Common Norfk 67 2930
Spain's End Essex 53 6637
Spalding Lincs 64 2422
Spaldington E R Yk 84 7633
Spaldwick Cambs 52 1372
Spalford Notts 76 8369
Spanby Lincs 64 0938
Spanish Green Hants 24 6958
Sparham Norfk 66 0719
Sparhamill Norfk 66 0818
Spark Bridge Cumb 86 3084
Sparket Cumb 93 4325
Sparkford Somset 21 6025
Sparkhill W Mids 61 1083
Sparkwell Devon 6 5857
Sparrow Green Norfk 66 9414
Sparrowpit Derbys 74 0880
Sparrows Green E Susx 16 6332
Sparsholt Hants 24 4331
Sparsholt Oxon 36 3487
Spartylea Cumb 95 8548
Spath Staffs 73 0835
Spaunton N York 90 7289
Spaxton Somset 20 2237
Spean Bridge Highld 131 2281
Spear Hill W Susx 15 1317
Spearywell Hants 23 3127
Speen Berks 24 4567
Speen Bucks 26 8499
Speeton N York 91 1574
Speke Mersyd 78 4383
Speldhurst Kent 16 5541
Spellbrook Herts 39 4817
Spelmonden Kent 28 7037
Spelsbury Oxon 36 3421
Spen W York 82 1925
Spen Green Ches 72 8160
Spencers Wood Berks 24 7166
Spennithorne N York 89 1388
Spennymoor Dur 96 2533
Spernall Warwks 48 0862
Spestos Devon 8 7298
Spetchley Worcs 47 8953
Spetisbury Dorset 11 9102
Spexhall Suffk 55 3780
Spey Bay Moray 141 3565
Speybridge Highld 141 0326
Speyview Moray 141 2541
Spilsby Lincs 77 4066
Spindlestone Nthumb 111 1533
Spinkhill Derbys 75 4578
Spinningdale Highld 146 6789
Spirthill Wilts 35 9976
Spital Berks 26 9675
Spital Mersyd 78 3482
Spital Hill S York 75 6193
Spital in the Street Lincs 76 9690
Spithurst E Susx 16 4217
Spittal E Loth 118 4677
Spittal E R Yk 84 7652
Spittal Highld 151 1654
Spittal Nthumb 119 0051
Spittal Pembks 30 9723
Spittal of Glenmuick Abers 134 3085
Spittal of Glenshee P & K 133 1070
Spittal-on-Rule Border 110 5819
Spittalfield P & K 126 1040
Spixworth Norfk 67 2415
Splatt Cnwll 4 9476
Splatt Cnwll 5 2288
Splatt Devon 8 6005
Splayne's Green E Susx 16 4224
Splottlands Cardif 33 2077
Spodegreen Ches 79 7385
Spofforth N York 83 3651
Spon Green Flints 70 2863
Spondon Derbys 62 4036
Spooner Row Norfk 66 0997
Sporle Norfk 66 8411
Spott E Loth 118 6775
Spottiswoode Border 110 6049
Spratton Nhants 50 7169
Spreakley Surrey 25 8341
Spreyton Devon 8 6996
Spriddlestone Devon 6 5351
Spridlington Lincs 76 0084
Spring Gardens Dur 96 1726
Spring Vale S York 82 2502
Springburn C Glas 116 6068
Springfield D & G 101 3268
Springfield Essex 40 7208
Springfield Fife 126 3411
Springhill Staffs 60 9704
Springhill Staffs 61 0705
Springholm D & G 100 8070
Springside N Ayrs 106 3738
Springthorpe Lincs 76 8789
Springwell T & W 96 2858
Sproatley E R Yk 85 1934
Sproston Green Ches 72 7366
Sprotbrough S York 83 5301
Sproughton Suffk 54 1244
Sprouston Border 110 7535
Sprowston Norfk 67 2512
Sproxton Leics 63 8524
Sproxton N York 90 6181
Sprytown Devon 5 4185
Spunhill Shrops 59 4133
Spurstow Ches 71 5556
Spyway Dorset 10 5293
Square & Compass Pembks 30 8431
Stableford Shrops 60 7598
Stableford Staffs 72 8138
Stacey Bank Derbys 74 2890
Stackhouse N York 88 8165
Stackpole Pembks 30 9896
Stacksford Norfk 54 0590
Stacksteads Lancs 81 8521
Staddiscombe Devon 6 5151
Staddlethorpe E R Yk 84 8328
Staden Derbys 74 0771
Stadhampton Oxon 37 6098
Stadhlaigearraidh W Isls 152 7638
Staffield Cumb 94 5442
Staffin Highld 136 4967
Stafford Staffs 72 9223
Stagsden Beds 38 9848
Stainborough S York 83 3203
Stainburn Cumb 92 0129
Stainburn N York 82 2548
Stainby Lincs 63 9022
Staincross S York 83 3210
Staindrop Dur 96 1220
Staines Surrey 26 0371
Stainfield Lincs 64 0824
Stainfield Lincs 76 1172
Stainforth N York 88 8267
Stainforth S York 83 6411
Staining Lancs 80 3436
Stainland W York 82 0719
Stainsacre N York 91 9108
Stainsby Derbys 75 4565
Stainton Cumb 93 3857
Stainton Cumb 94 4828
Stainton Cumb 87 5285
Stainton Dur 95 0718
Stainton N York 97 4714
Stainton N York 89 1096
Stainton S York 75 5593
Stainton by Langworth Lincs 76 0677
Stainton le Vale Lincs 76 1794
Stainton with Adgarley Cumb 86 2472
Staintondale N York 91 9998
Stair Cumb 93 2321
Stair E Ayrs 107 4423
Stair Haven D & G 98 2153
Stairfoot S York 83 3705
Staithes N York 97 7818
Stake Pool Lancs 80 4147
Stakeford Nthumb 103 2685
Stakes Hants 13 6808
Stalbridge Dorset 11 7317
Stalbridge Weston Dorset 11 7116
Stalham Norfk 67 3725
Stalham Green Norfk 67 3824
Stalisfield Green Kent 28 9552
Stallen Dorset 10 6016
Stalling Busk N York 88 9186
Stallingborough Lincs 85 1911
Stallington Staffs 72 9439
Stalmine Lancs 80 3745
Stalmine Moss Side Lancs 80 3845
Stalybridge Gt Man 79 9698
Stambourne Essex 53 7238
Stambourne Green Essex 53 6938
Stamford Lincs 64 0307
Stamford Nthumb 111 2219
Stamford Bridge Ches 71 4667
Stamford Bridge E R Yk 84 7155
Stamford Hill Gt Lon 27 3387
Stamfordham Nthumb 103 0771
Stanah Lancs 80 3542
Stanborough Herts 39 2211
Stanbridge Beds 38 9624
Stanbridge Dorset 11 0004
Stanbury W York 82 0137
Stand Gt Man 79 7905
Stand N Lans 116 7668
Standburn Falk 116 9274
Standeford Staffs 60 9107
Standen Kent 28 8540
Standen Street Kent 17 8030
Standerwick Somset 22 8150
Standford Hants 14 8134
Standingstone Cumb 92 0533
Standish Gloucs 35 7908
Standish Gt Man 78 5610
Standish Lower Ground Gt Man 78 5507

Standlake Strefford

310

Standlake *Oxon* **36** 3903
Standon *Hants* **13** 4226
Standon *Herts* **39** 3922
Standon *Staffs* **72** 8135
Standon Green End *Herts* **39** 3620
Standwell Green *Suffk* **54** 1369
Stane *N Lans* **116** 8859
Stanfield *Norfk* **66** 9320
Stanford *Beds* **39** 1640
Stanford *Kent* **29** 1238
Stanford *Shrops* **59** 3313
Stanford Bishop *Herefs* **47** 6851
Stanford Bridge *Shrops* **72** 7024
Stanford Bridge *Worcs* **47** 7265
Stanford Dingley *Berks* **24** 5771
Stanford in the Vale *Oxon* **36** 3493
Stanford le Hope *Essex* **40** 6882
Stanford on Avon *Nhants* **50** 5978
Stanford on Soar *Notts* **62** 5421
Stanford on Teme *Worcs* **47** 7065
Stanford Rivers *Essex* **27** 5301
Stanfree *Derbys* **75** 4773
Stanghow *N York* **97** 6715
Stanground *Cambs* **64** 2097
Stanhill *Lancs* **81** 7227
Stanhoe *Norfk* **66** 8036
Stanhope *Border* **108** 1229
Stanhope *Dur* **95** 9939
Stanhope Bretby *Derbys* **73** 2921
Stanion *Nhants* **51** 9186
Stanklin *Worcs* **60** 8574
Stanley *Derbys* **62** 4140
Stanley *Dur* **96** 1953
Stanley *Notts* **75** 4662
Stanley *P & K* **126** 1033
Stanley *Shrops* **60** 7483
Stanley *Staffs* **72** 9352
Stanley *W York* **83** 3422
Stanley Common *Derbys* **62** 4042
Stanley Crook *Dur* **96** 1637
Stanley Ferry *W York* **83** 3522
Stanley Gate *Lancs* **78** 4405
Stanley Moor *Staffs* **72** 9251
Stanley Pontlarge *Gloucs* **47** 0030
Stanmer *E Susx* **15** 3309
Stanmore *Berks* **37** 4778
Stanmore *Gt Lon* **26** 1692
Stanmore *Hants* **24** 4628
Stannersburn *Nthumb* **102** 7286
Stanningfield *Suffk* **54** 8756
Stanningley *W York* **82** 2234
Stannington *Nthumb* **103** 2179
Stannington *S York* **74** 2987
Stannington Station *Nthumb* **103** 2181
Stansbatch *Herefs* **46** 3461
Stansfield *Suffk* **53** 7852
Stanshope *Staffs* **73** 1253
Stanstead *Suffk* **54** 8449
Stanstead Abbotts *Herts* **39** 3811
Stanstead Street *Suffk* **54** 8448
Stansted *Kent* **27** 6062
Stansted Airport **39** 5322
Stansted Mountfitchet *Essex* **39** 5125
Stanton *Derbys* **73** 2718
Stanton *Devon* **7** 7050
Stanton *Gloucs* **48** 0634
Stanton *Mons* **34** 3021
Stanton *Nthumb* **103** 1390
Stanton *Staffs* **73** 1245
Stanton *Suffk* **54** 9673
Stanton Butts *Cambs* **52** 2372
Stanton by Bridge *Derbys* **62** 3726
Stanton by Dale *Derbys* **62** 4637
Stanton Drew *Somset* **21** 5963
Stanton Fitzwarren *Wilts* **36** 1790
Stanton Harcourt *Oxon* **36** 4105
Stanton Hill *Notts* **75** 4760
Stanton in Peak *Derbys* **74** 2364
Stanton Lacy *Shrops* **46** 4978
Stanton Lees *Derbys* **74** 2562
Stanton Long *Shrops* **59** 5791
Stanton on the Wolds *Notts* **63** 6330
Stanton Prior *Somset* **22** 6762
Stanton St Bernard *Wilts* **23** 0961
Stanton St John *Oxon* **37** 5709
Stanton St Quintin *Wilts* **35** 9079
Stanton Street *Suffk* **54** 9566
Stanton under Bardon *Leics* **62** 4610
Stanton upon Hine Heath *Shrops* **59** 5624
Stanton Wick *Somset* **21** 6162
Stantway *Gloucs* **35** 7313
Stanwardine in the Field *Shrops* **59** 4124
Stanwardine in the Wood *Shrops* **59** 4227
Stanway *Essex* **40** 9424
Stanway *Gloucs* **48** 0632
Stanway Green *Essex* **40** 9523
Stanway Green *Suffk* **55** 2470
Stanwell *Surrey* **26** 0574
Stanwell Moor *Surrey* **26** 0474
Stanwick *Nhants* **51** 9771
Stanwix *Cumb* **93** 4057
Staoinebrig *W Isls* **152** 7532
Stape *N York* **90** 7994
Stapehill *Dorset* **12** 0500
Stapeley *Ches* **72** 6749
Stapenhill *Staffs* **73** 2521
Staple *Kent* **29** 2756
Staple *Somset* **20** 1141
Staple Cross *Devon* **20** 0320
Staple Cross *E Susx* **17** 7822
Staple Fitzpaine *Somset* **10** 2618
Staple Hill *Worcs* **60** 9773
Staplefield *W Susx* **15** 2728
Stapleford *Cambs* **53** 4751
Stapleford *Herts* **39** 3117
Stapleford *Leics* **63** 8018
Stapleford *Lincs* **76** 8857
Stapleford *Notts* **62** 4837
Stapleford *Wilts* **23** 0737
Stapleford Abbotts *Essex* **27** 5194
Stapleford Tawney *Essex* **27** 5099
Staplegrove *Somset* **20** 2126
Staplehay *Somset* **20** 2121
Staplehurst *Kent* **28** 7843
Staplers *IOW* **13** 5189
Staplestreet *Kent* **29** 0660
Staplet *Cumb* **101** 5071
Stapleton *Herefs* **46** 3265
Stapleton *Leics* **50** 4398
Stapleton *N York* **89** 2612
Stapleton *Shrops* **59** 4704
Stapleton *Somset* **21** 4621
Stapley *Somset* **9** 1913
Staploe *Beds* **52** 1560
Staplow *Herefs* **47** 6941
Star *Fife* **126** 3103
Star *Pembks* **31** 2434
Star *Somset* **21** 4358
Starbeck *N York* **83** 3255
Starbotton *N York* **88** 9574
Starcross *Devon* **9** 9781
Stareton *Warwks* **61** 3371
Starkholmes *Derbys* **74** 3058
Starling *Gt Man* **79** 7710
Starlings Green *Essex* **39** 4631
Starr's Green *E Susx* **17** 7615
Starston *Norfk* **55** 2384
Start *Devon* **7** 8044
Startforth *Dur* **95** 0415
Startley *Wilts* **35** 9482
Statenborough *Kent* **29** 3155
Statham *Ches* **79** 6787
Stathe *Somset* **21** 3728
Stathern *Leics* **63** 7731
Station Town *Dur* **96** 4036
Staughton Green *Cambs* **52** 1365
Staughton Highway *Cambs* **52** 1364
Staunton *Gloucs* **34** 5512
Staunton *Gloucs* **47** 7829
Staunton Green *Herefs* **46** 3661
Staunton in the Vale *Notts* **63** 8043
Staunton on Arrow *Herefs* **46** 3660
Staunton on Wye *Herefs* **46** 3644
Staveley *Cumb* **87** 3786
Staveley *Cumb* **87** 4698
Staveley *Derbys* **75** 4374
Staveley *N York* **89** 3662
Staverton *Devon* **7** 7964
Staverton *Gloucs* **47** 8923
Staverton *Nhants* **49** 5361
Staverton *Wilts* **22** 8560
Staverton Bridge *Gloucs* **35** 8722
Stawell *Somset* **21** 3738
Stawley *Somset* **20** 0622
Staxigoe *Highld* **151** 3852
Staxton *N York* **91** 0179
Staylittle *Cerdgn* **43** 6489
Staylittle *Powys* **43** 8891
Staynall *Lancs* **80** 3643
Staythorpe *Notts* **75** 7554
Stead *W York* **82** 1446
Stean *N York* **89** 0973
Steane *Nhants* **49** 5538
Stearsby *N York* **90** 6171
Steart *Somset* **20** 2745
Stebbing *Essex* **40** 6624
Stebbing Green *Essex* **40** 6823
Stebbing Park *Essex* **40** 6524
Stechford *W Mids* **61** 1287
Stede Quarter *Kent* **28** 8738
Stedham *W Susx* **14** 8622
Steel *Nthumb* **95** 9458
Steel Cross *E Susx* **16** 5331
Steel Green *Cumb* **86** 1679
Steel Heath *Shrops* **59** 5436
Steele Road *Border* **101** 5293
Steelend *Fife* **117** 0392
Steen's Bridge *Herefs* **46** 5357
Steep *Hants* **13** 7425
Steep Lane *W York* **82** 0223
Steephill *IOW* **13** 5477
Steeple *Dorset* **11** 9080
Steeple *Essex* **40** 9303
Steeple Ashton *Wilts* **22** 9056
Steeple Aston *Oxon* **49** 4725
Steeple Barton *Oxon* **49** 4424
Steeple Bumpstead *Essex* **53** 6841
Steeple Claydon *Bucks* **49** 7026
Steeple Gidding *Cambs* **52** 1381
Steeple Langford *Wilts* **23** 0337
Steeple Morden *Cambs* **39** 2842
Steeton *W York* **82** 0344
Stein *Highld* **136** 2656
Stella *T & W* **103** 1763
Stelling Minnis *Kent* **29** 1447
Stembridge *Somset* **21** 4220
Stenalees *Cnwll* **3** 0156
Stenhouse *D & G* **100** 8093
Stenhousemuir *Falk* **116** 8783
Stenigot *Lincs* **77** 2480
Stenscholl *Highld* **136** 4767
Stenton *E Loth* **118** 6274
Steornabhagh *W Isls* **152** 4232
Stepaside *Pembks* **31** 1407
Stepney *Gt Lon* **27** 3681
Stepping Hill *Gt Man* **79** 9187
Steppingley *Beds* **38** 0035
Stepps *N Lans* **116** 6568
Sternfield *Suffk* **55** 3861
Sterridge *Devon* **19** 5545
Stert *Wilts* **23** 0259
Stetchworth *Cambs* **53** 6459
Steven's Crouch *E Susx* **17** 7115
Stevenage *Herts* **39** 2325
Stevenston *N Ayrs* **106** 2742
Steventon *Hants* **24** 5447
Steventon *Oxon* **37** 4691
Steventon End *Essex* **53** 5942
Stevington *Beds* **51** 9853
Stewartby *Beds* **38** 0142
Stewartfield *S Lans* **116** 6255
Stewarton *E Ayrs* **115** 4245
Stewkley *Bucks* **38** 8526
Stewley *Somset* **10** 3118
Stewton *Lincs* **77** 3587
Steyne Cross *IOW* **13** 6487
Steyning *W Susx* **15** 1711
Steynton *Pembks* **30** 9107
Stibb *Cnwll* **18** 2210
Stibb Cross *Devon* **18** 4314
Stibb Green *Wilts* **23** 2262
Stibbard *Norfk* **66** 9828
Stibbington *Cambs* **51** 0898
Stichill *Border* **110** 7138
Sticker *Cnwll* **3** 9750
Stickford *Lincs* **77** 3560
Sticklepath *Devon* **8** 6494
Sticklepath *Somset* **20** 0436
Stickling Green *Essex* **39** 4732
Stickney *Lincs* **77** 3457
Stiff Street *Kent* **28** 8761
Stiffkey *Norfk* **66** 9742
Stifford's Bridge *Herefs* **47** 7347
Stile Bridge *Kent* **28** 7547
Stileway *Somset* **21** 4641
Stilligarry *W Isls* **152** 7638
Stillingfleet *N York* **83** 5940
Stillington *Dur* **96** 3723
Stillington *N York* **90** 5867
Stilton *Cambs* **52** 1689
Stinchcombe *Gloucs* **35** 7298
Stinsford *Dorset* **11** 7091
Stiperstones *Shrops* **59** 3600
Stirchley *Shrops* **60** 6907
Stirchley *W Mids* **61** 0581
Stirling *Abers* **143** 1242
Stirling *Stirlg* **116** 7993
Stirtloe *Cambs* **52** 1966
Stirton *N York* **82** 9752
Stisted *Essex* **40** 8024
Stitchcombe *Wilts* **36** 2369
Stithians *Cnwll* **3** 7336
Stivichall *W Mids* **61** 3376
Stixwould *Lincs* **76** 1765
Stoak *Ches* **71** 4273
Stobo *Border* **109** 1837
Stoborough *Dorset* **11** 9286
Stoborough Green *Dorset* **11** 9285
Stobs Castle *Border* **109** 5008
Stobswood *Nthumb* **103** 2195
Stock *Essex* **40** 6998
Stock *Somset* **21** 4561
Stock Green *Worcs* **47** 9859
Stock Wood *Worcs* **47** 0058
Stockbridge *Hants* **23** 3535
Stockbriggs *S Lans* **107** 7936
Stockbury *Kent* **28** 8461
Stockcross *Berks* **24** 4368
Stockdale *Cnwll* **3** 7837
Stockdalewath *Cumb* **93** 3845
Stocker's Hill *Kent* **28** 9650
Stockerston *Leics* **51** 8397
Stocking *Herefs* **47** 6230
Stocking Green *Bucks* **38** 8047
Stocking Pelham *Herts* **39** 4529
Stockingford *Warwks* **61** 3391
Stockland *Devon* **9** 2404
Stockland Bristol *Somset* **20** 2443
Stockland Green *Kent* **16** 5642
Stockleigh English *Devon* **8** 8506
Stockleigh Pomeroy *Devon* **9** 8703
Stockley *Wilts* **22** 9967
Stockley Hill *Herefs* **46** 3738
Stocklinch *Somset* **10** 3817
Stockmoor *Herefs* **46** 3954
Stockport *Gt Man* **79** 8990
Stocksbridge *S York* **74** 2698
Stocksfield *Nthumb* **103** 0561
Stockstreet *Essex* **40** 8222
Stockton *Herefs* **46** 5261
Stockton *Norfk* **67** 3894
Stockton *Shrops* **58** 2601
Stockton *Shrops* **72** 7716
Stockton *Shrops* **60** 7299
Stockton *Warwks* **49** 4363
Stockton *Wilts* **22** 9838
Stockton Brook *Staffs* **72** 9151
Stockton Heath *Ches* **78** 6185
Stockton on Teme *Worcs* **47** 7167
Stockton on the Forest *N York* **83** 6556
Stockton-on-Tees *Dur* **96** 4419
Stockwell *Gloucs* **35** 9414
Stockwell End *W Mids* **60** 8900
Stockwell Heath *Staffs* **73** 0521
Stockwood *Bristl* **21** 6368
Stockwood *Dorset* **10** 5906
Stodday *Lancs* **87** 4658
Stodmarsh *Kent* **29** 2260
Stody *Norfk* **66** 0535
Stoer *Highld* **148** 0328
Stoford *Somset* **10** 5613
Stoford *Wilts* **23** 0835
Stogumber *Somset* **20** 0937
Stogursey *Somset* **20** 2042
Stoke *Devon* **18** 2324
Stoke *Hants* **24** 4051
Stoke *Hants* **13** 7202
Stoke *Kent* **28** 8274
Stoke *W Mids* **61** 3778
Stoke Abbott *Dorset* **10** 4500
Stoke Albany *Nhants* **51** 8088
Stoke Ash *Suffk* **54** 1170
Stoke Bardolph *Notts* **63** 6441
Stoke Bliss *Worcs* **47** 6563
Stoke Bruerne *Nhants* **49** 7449
Stoke by Clare *Suffk* **53** 7443
Stoke Canon *Devon* **9** 9398
Stoke Charity *Hants* **24** 4839
Stoke Climsland *Cnwll* **5** 3674
Stoke Cross *Herefs* **47** 6250
Stoke D'Abernon *Surrey* **26** 1258
Stoke Doyle *Nhants* **51** 0286
Stoke Dry *Rutlnd* **51** 8596
Stoke Edith *Herefs* **46** 6040
Stoke End *Warwks* **61** 1797
Stoke Farthing *Wilts* **23** 0525
Stoke Ferry *Norfk* **65** 7000
Stoke Fleming *Devon* **7** 8648
Stoke Gabriel *Devon* **7** 8557
Stoke Gifford *Gloucs* **35** 6279
Stoke Golding *Leics* **61** 3997
Stoke Goldington *Bucks* **38** 8348
Stoke Green *Bucks* **26** 9882
Stoke Hammond *Bucks* **38** 8829
Stoke Heath *Shrops* **72** 6529
Stoke Heath *W Mids* **61** 3681
Stoke Heath *Worcs* **47** 9468
Stoke Holy Cross *Norfk* **67** 2301
Stoke Lacy *Herefs* **47** 6249
Stoke Lyne *Oxon* **49** 5628
Stoke Mandeville *Bucks* **38** 8310
Stoke Newington *Gt Lon* **27** 3386
Stoke Orchard *Gloucs* **47** 9128
Stoke Poges *Bucks* **26** 9783
Stoke Pound *Worcs* **47** 9667
Stoke Prior *Herefs* **46** 5256
Stoke Prior *Worcs* **47** 9467
Stoke Rivers *Devon* **19** 6335
Stoke Rochford *Lincs* **63** 9127
Stoke Row *Oxon* **37** 6884
Stoke St Gregory *Somset* **21** 3427
Stoke St Mary *Somset* **20** 2622
Stoke St Michael *Somset* **22** 6646
Stoke St Milborough *Shrops* **59** 5682
Stoke sub Hamdon *Somset* **10** 4717
Stoke Talmage *Oxon* **37** 6799
Stoke Trister *Somset* **22** 7428
Stoke upon Tern *Shrops* **59** 6328
Stoke Wake *Dorset* **11** 7606
Stoke Wharf *Worcs* **47** 9567
Stoke-by-Nayland *Suffk* **54** 9836
Stoke-on-Trent *Staffs* **72** 8847
Stoke-upon-Trent *Staffs* **72** 8745
Stokeford *Dorset* **11** 8687
Stokeham *Notts* **75** 7876
Stokeinteignhead *Devon* **7** 9170
Stokenchurch *Bucks* **37** 7696
Stokenham *Devon* **7** 8042
Stokesay *Shrops* **59** 4381
Stokesay Castle **59** 4381
Stokesby *Norfk* **67** 4310
Stokesley *N York* **90** 5208
Stolford *Somset* **20** 2345
Ston Easton *Somset* **21** 6253
Stondon Massey *Essex* **27** 5800
Stone *Bucks* **37** 7812
Stone *Gloucs* **35** 6895
Stone *Kent* **27** 5774
Stone *Kent* **17** 9427
Stone *S York* **75** 5589
Stone *Somset* **21** 5834
Stone *Staffs* **72** 9034
Stone *Worcs* **60** 8675
Stone Allerton *Somset* **21** 3951
Stone Bridge Corner *Cambs* **64** 2700
Stone Chair *W York* **82** 1227
Stone Cross *E Susx* **16** 5128
Stone Cross *E Susx* **16** 6104
Stone Cross *E Susx* **16** 6431
Stone Cross *Kent* **16** 5239
Stone Cross *Kent* **28** 0236
Stone Cross *Kent* **29** 3257
Stone Hill *S York* **83** 6809
Stone House *Cumb* **88** 7685
Stone Street *Kent* **27** 5754
Stone Street *Suffk* **54** 9639
Stone Street *Suffk* **54** 0143
Stone Street *Suffk* **55** 3882
Stone-edge-Batch *Somset* **34** 4671
Stonea *Cambs* **65** 4593
Stonebridge *Norfk* **54** 9290
Stonebridge *Somset* **21** 3859
Stonebridge *W Mids* **61** 2182
Stonebroom *Derbys* **74** 4059
Stonecross Green *Suffk* **54** 8257
Stonecrouch *Kent* **16** 7033
Stoneferry *E R Yk* **85** 1031
Stonefield Castle Hotel *Ag & B* **113** 8671
Stonegate *E Susx* **16** 6628
Stonegate *N York* **90** 7708
Stonegrave *N York* **90** 6577
Stonehall *Worcs* **47** 8848
Stonehaugh *Nthumb* **102** 7976
Stonehaven *Abers* **135** 8786
Stonehenge **23** 1142
Stonehill Green *Gt Lon* **27** 5070
Stonehouse *Ches* **71** 5070
Stonehouse *D & G* **100** 8268
Stonehouse *Devon* **6** 4654
Stonehouse *Gloucs* **35** 8005
Stonehouse *Nthumb* **94** 6958
Stonehouse *S Lans* **116** 7546
Stoneleigh *Warwks* **61** 3372
Stoneley Green *Ches* **71** 6151
Stonely *Cambs* **52** 1167
Stoner Hill *Hants* **13** 7225
Stones Green *Essex* **41** 1626
Stonesby *Leics* **63** 8224
Stonesfield *Oxon* **36** 3917
Stonestreet Green *Kent* **29** 0637
Stonethwaite *Cumb* **93** 2613
Stonewells *Moray* **141** 2865
Stonewood *Kent* **27** 5972
Stoney Cross *Hants* **12** 2611
Stoney Middleton *Derbys* **74** 2375
Stoney Stanton *Leics* **50** 4994
Stoney Stoke *Somset* **22** 7032
Stoney Stratton *Somset* **21** 6539
Stoney Stretton *Shrops* **59** 3809
Stoneybridge *W Isls* **152** 7532
Stoneybridge *Worcs* **60** 9476
Stoneyburn *W Loth* **117** 9862
Stoneygate *Leics* **62** 6002
Stoneyhills *Essex* **40** 9597
Stoneykirk *D & G* **98** 0853
Stoneywood *Aber C* **135** 8811
Stoneywood *Falk* **116** 7982
Stonham Aspal *Suffk* **54** 1359
Stonnall *Staffs* **61** 0603
Stonor *Oxon* **37** 7388
Stonton Wyville *Leics* **50** 7395
Stony Cross *Herefs* **46** 5466
Stony Cross *Herefs* **47** 7247
Stony Houghton *Derbys* **75** 4966
Stony Stratford *Bucks* **38** 7840
Stonyford *Hants* **12** 3215
Stonywell *Staffs* **61** 0712
Stoodleigh *Devon* **19** 6532
Stoodleigh *Devon* **20** 9218
Stopham *W Susx* **14** 0219
Stopsley *Beds* **38** 1023
Stoptide *Cnwll* **4** 9475
Storeton *Mersyd* **78** 3084
Storeyard Green *Herefs* **47** 7144
Stormy Corner *Lancs* **78** 4707
Stornoway *W Isls* **152** 4232
Stornoway Airport **152** 4632
Storridge *Herefs* **47** 7548
Storrington *W Susx* **14** 0814
Storth *Cumb* **87** 4779
Storwood *E R Yk* **84** 7144
Stotfield *Moray* **141** 2270
Stotfold *Beds* **39** 2136
Stottesdon *Shrops* **60** 6782
Stoughton *Leics* **63** 6402
Stoughton *Surrey* **25** 9851
Stoughton *W Susx* **14** 8011
Stoul *Highld* **129** 7594
Stoulton *Worcs* **47** 9049
Stour Provost *Dorset* **22** 7921
Stour Row *Dorset* **22** 8221
Stourbridge *W Mids* **60** 8983
Stourpaine *Dorset* **11** 8609
Stourport-on-Severn *Worcs* **60** 8171
Stourton *Staffs* **60** 8684
Stourton *W York* **83** 3230
Stourton *Warwks* **48** 2936
Stourton *Wilts* **22** 7734
Stourton Caundle *Dorset* **11** 7115
Stout *Somset* **21** 4331
Stove *Shet* **153** 4224
Stoven *Suffk* **55** 4481
Stow *Border* **118** 4544
Stow *Lincs* **76** 8882
Stow Bardolph *Norfk* **65** 6206
Stow Bedon *Norfk* **66** 9596
Stow Longa *Cambs* **51** 1070
Stow Maries *Essex* **40** 8399
Stow-cum-Quy *Cambs* **53** 5260
Stow-on-the-Wold *Gloucs* **48** 1925
Stowbridge *Norfk* **65** 6007
Stowe *Gloucs* **34** 5606
Stowe *Shrops* **46** 3173
Stowe by Chartley *Staffs* **73** 0026
Stowehill *Nhants* **49** 6458
Stowell *Somset* **22** 6822
Stowey *Somset* **21** 5959
Stowford *Devon* **5** 4398
Stowford *Devon* **19** 6541
Stowford *Devon* **5** 4387
Stowford *Devon* **9** 1189
Stowlangtoft *Suffk* **54** 9568
Stowmarket *Suffk* **54** 0458
Stowting *Kent* **29** 1242
Stowting Common *Kent* **29** 1243
Stowupland *Suffk* **54** 0760
Straanruie *Moray* **141** 9916
Strachan *Abers* **135** 6792
Strachur *Ag & B* **114** 0901
Stracthro Hospital *Angus* **134** 6265
Stradbroke *Suffk* **55** 2373
Stradbrook *Wilts* **22** 9152
Stradishall *Suffk* **53** 7552
Stradsett *Norfk* **65** 6605
Stragglethorpe *Lincs* **76** 9152
Stragglethorpe *Notts* **63** 6537
Straight Soley *Wilts* **36** 3172
Straiton *Mdloth* **117** 2766
Straiton *S Ayrs* **106** 3804
Straloch *Abers* **143** 8620
Straloch *P & K* **133** 0463
Stramshall *Staffs* **73** 0735
Strang *IOM* **158** 3578
Strangford *Herefs* **46** 5827
Stranraer *D & G* **98** 0560
Strata Florida *Cerdgn* **43** 7465
Stratfield Mortimer *Berks* **24** 6664
Stratfield Saye *Hants* **24** 6861
Stratfield Turgis *Hants* **24** 6959
Stratford *Beds* **52** 1748
Stratford *Gt Lon* **27** 3884
Stratford St Andrew *Suffk* **55** 3560
Stratford St Mary *Suffk* **54** 0434
Stratford sub Castle *Wilts* **23** 1332
Stratford Tony *Wilts* **23** 0926
Stratford-upon-Avon *Warwks* **48** 2055
Strath *Highld* **144** 7978
Strathan *Highld* **145** 0821
Strathan *Highld* **149** 5764
Strathaven *S Lans* **116** 7044
Strathblane *Stirlg* **115** 5679
Strathcanaird *Highld* **145** 1501
Strathcarron Station *Highld* **138** 9442
Strathcoil *Ag & B* **122** 6830
Strathdon *Abers* **134** 3512
Strathkinness *Fife* **127** 4516
Strathloanhead *W Loth* **116** 9272
Strathmashie House *Highld* **132** 5891
Strathmiglo *Fife* **126** 2109
Strathpeffer *Highld* **139** 4858
Strathtay *P & K* **125** 9153
Strathwhillan *N Ayrs* **105** 0235
Strathy *Highld* **150** 8464
Strathy Inn *Highld* **150** 8365
Strathyre *Stirlg* **124** 5617
Stratton *Cnwll* **18** 2306
Stratton *Dorset* **11** 6593
Stratton *Gloucs* **35** 0103
Stratton Audley *Oxon* **49** 6025
Stratton St Margaret *Wilts* **36** 1786
Stratton St Michael *Norfk* **67** 2093
Stratton Strawless *Norfk* **67** 2220
Stratton-on-the-Fosse *Somset* **22** 6650
Stravithie *Fife* **127** 5313
Stream *Somset* **20** 0639
Streat *E Susx* **15** 3515
Streatham *Gt Lon* **27** 3071
Streatley *Beds* **38** 0728
Streatley *Berks* **37** 5980
Street *Devon* **9** 1888
Street *Lancs* **80** 5252
Street *N York* **90** 7304
Street *Somset* **21** 4836
Street Ashton *Warwks* **50** 4582
Street Dinas *Shrops* **71** 3338
Street End *E Susx* **16** 6023
Street End *Kent* **29** 1453
Street End *W Susx* **14** 8599
Street Gate *T & W* **96** 2159
Street Houses *N York* **97** 7419
Street Houses *N York* **83** 5245
Street Lane *Derbys* **74** 3848
Street on the Fosse *Somset* **21** 6239
Streethay *Staffs* **61** 1410
Streetlam *N York* **89** 3098
Streetly *W Mids* **61** 0898
Streetly End *Cambs* **53** 6148
Strefford *Shrops* **59** 4485

Strelitz Tendring Green

Strelitz P & K 126 1836
Strelley Notts 62 5141
Strensall N York 90 6360
Strensham Worcs 47 9140
Stretcholt Somset 20 2943
Strete Devon 7 8446
Stretford Gt Man 79 7994
Stretford Herefs 46 4455
Stretford Herefs 46 5257
Strethall Essex 39 4839
Stretham Cambs 53 5174
Strettington W Susx 14 8907
Stretton Ches 71 4452
Stretton Ches 79 6282
Stretton Derbys 74 3961
Stretton Rutlnd 63 9415
Stretton Staffs 60 8811
Stretton Staffs 73 2526
Stretton en le Field Leics 61 3011
Stretton Grandison Herefs 47 6344
Stretton Heath Shrops 59 3610
Stretton on Fosse Warwks 48 2238
Stretton Sugwas Herefs 46 4642
Stretton under Fosse Warwks 50 4581
Stretton Westwood Shrops 59 5998
Stretton-on-Dunsmore Warwks 61 4072
Strichen Abers 143 9455
Strines Gt Man 79 9786
Stringston Somset 20 1742
Strixton Nhants 51 9061
Stroat Gloucs 34 5797
Stromeferry Highld 138 8634
Stromness Ork 153 2508
Stronachlachar Stirlg 123 4010
Stronafian Ag & B 114 0281
Stronchrubie Highld 145 2419
Strone Ag & B 114 1980
Strone Highld 131 1481
Stronenaba Highld 131 2084
Stronmilchan Ag & B 123 1528
Stronsay Airport 153 6329
Strontian Highld 130 8161
Strood Kent 28 7268
Strood Kent 17 8532
Strood Green Surrey 15 2048
Strood Green W Susx 14 0224
Stroud Gloucs 35 8505
Stroud Hants 13 7223
Stroud Green Essex 40 8590
Stroud Green Gloucs 35 8007
Stroude Surrey 25 0068
Stroxton Lincs 63 9030
Struan Highld 136 3438
Struan P & K 132 8065
Strubby Lincs 77 4582
Strumpshaw Norfk 67 3407
Strutherhill S Lans 116 7649
Struthers Fife 126 3709
Struy Highld 139 4040
Stryd-y-Facsen IOA 68 3383
Stryt-issa Wrexhm 70 2845
Stuartfield Abers 143 9745
Stubbers Green W Mids 61 0401
Stubbington Hants 13 5503
Stubbins N York 81 7918
Stubbs Green Norfk 67 2598
Stubhampton Dorset 11 9113
Stubley Derbys 74 3378
Stubshaw Cross Gt Man 78 5899
Stubton Lincs 76 8748
Stuchbury Nhants 49 5643
Stuckeridge Devon 20 9221
Stuckton Hants 12 1613
Stud Green Berks 26 8877
Studfold N York 88 8169
Studham Beds 38 0215
Studholme Cumb 93 2556
Studland Dorset 12 0382
Studley Warwks 48 0764
Studley Wilts 35 9671
Studley Common Warwks 48 0664
Studley Roger N York 89 2970
Studley Royal N York 89 2770
Stump Cross Cambs 39 5044
Stuntney Cambs 53 5578
Stunts Green E Susx 16 6213
Sturbridge Staffs 72 8330
Sturgate Lincs 76 8888
Sturmer Essex 53 6943
Sturminster Common Dorset 11 7812
Sturminster Marshall Dorset 11 9500
Sturminster Newton Dorset 11 7814
Sturry Kent 29 1760
Sturton Lincs 84 9604
Sturton by Stow Lincs 76 8980
Sturton le Steeple Notts 75 7883
Stuston Suffk 54 1377
Stutton N York 83 4841
Stutton Suffk 54 1534
Styal Ches 79 8383
Stydd Lancs 81 6536
Stynie Moray 141 3360
Styrrup Notts 75 6090
Succoth Ag & B 123 2905
Suckley Worcs 47 7251
Suckley Green Worcs 47 7253
Sudborough Nhants 51 9682
Sudbourne Suffk 55 4153
Sudbrook Lincs 63 9744
Sudbrook Mons 34 5087
Sudbrooke Lincs 76 0376
Sudbury Derbys 73 1631
Sudbury Gt Lon 26 1685
Sudbury Suffk 54 8741
Sudden Gt Man 81 8812
Suddie Highld 140 6554
Suddington Worcs 47 8463
Sudgrove Gloucs 35 9308
Suffield N York 91 9890
Suffield Norfk 67 2232
Sugdon Shrops 59 6015
Sugnall Staffs 72 7931
Sugwas Pool Herefs 46 4541
Suisnish Highld 129 5816
Sulby IOM 158 3894
Sulgrave Nhants 49 5544
Sulgrave Manor 49 5645
Sulham Berks 24 6474
Sulhamstead Berks 24 6368
Sulhamstead Abbots Berks 24 6467
Sulhamstead Bannister Berks 24 6368
Sullington W Susx 14 0913
Sullom Shet 153 3573
Sullom Voe Shet 153 4075
Sully V Glam 20 1568
Sumburgh Airport 153 3810
Summer Heath Bucks 37 7490
Summer Hill Wrexhm 71 3153
Summerbridge N York 89 2062
Summercourt Cnwll 3 8856
Summerfield Norfk 65 7538
Summerfield Worcs 60 8473
Summerhouse Dur 96 2019
Summerlands Cumb 87 5386
Summerley Derbys 74 3778
Summersdale W Susx 14 8606
Summerseat Gt Man 81 7914
Summertown Oxon 37 5009
Summit Gt Man 79 9109
Summit N York 82 9418
Sunbiggin N York 87 6608
Sunbury Surrey 26 1168
Sundaywell D & G 100 8284
Sunderland Ag & B 112 2464
Sunderland Cumb 93 1735
Sunderland Lancs 80 4255
Sunderland T & W 96 3957
Sunderland Bridge Dur 96 2637
Sundhope Border 109 3325
Sundon Park Beds 38 0525
Sundridge Kent 27 4855
Sunk Island E R Yk 85 2619
Sunningdale Berks 25 9567
Sunninghill Surrey 25 9367
Sunningwell Oxon 37 4900
Sunniside Dur 96 1438
Sunniside T & W 96 2059
Sunny Bank Lancs 81 7720
Sunny Brow Dur 96 1934
Sunnyhill Derbys 62 3432
Sunnyhurst Lancs 81 6722
Sunnylaw Stirlg 116 7998
Sunnymead Oxon 37 5009
Sunton Wilts 23 2454
Surbiton Gt Lon 26 1867
Surfleet Lincs 64 2528
Surfleet Seas End Lincs 64 2628
Surlingham Norfk 67 3106
Surrex Essex 40 8722
Sustead Norfk 66 1837
Susworth Lincs 84 8302
Sutcombe Devon 18 3411
Sutcombemill Devon 18 3411
Suton Norfk 66 0999
Sutterby Lincs 77 3872
Sutterton Lincs 64 2835
Sutton Beds 52 2247
Sutton Cambs 51 0998
Sutton Cambs 53 4479
Sutton Devon 8 7202
Sutton Devon 7 7042
Sutton E Susx 16 4999
Sutton Gt Lon 27 2564
Sutton Kent 29 3349
Sutton Mersyd 78 5393
Sutton N York 83 4925
Sutton Norfk 67 3823
Sutton Notts 75 6784
Sutton Notts 63 7637
Sutton Oxon 36 4106
Sutton Pembks 30 9115
Sutton S York 83 5512
Sutton Shrops 59 3527
Sutton Shrops 59 5010
Sutton Shrops 72 6631
Sutton Shrops 60 7386
Sutton Staffs 72 7622
Sutton Suffk 55 3046
Sutton W Susx 14 9715
Sutton at Hone Kent 27 5569
Sutton Bassett Nhants 50 7790
Sutton Benger Wilts 35 9478
Sutton Bingham Somset 10 5410
Sutton Bonington Notts 62 5024
Sutton Bridge Lincs 65 4721
Sutton Cheney Leics 50 4100
Sutton Coldfield W Mids 61 1295
Sutton Courtenay Oxon 37 5094
Sutton Crosses Lincs 65 4321
Sutton Fields Notts 62 4926
Sutton Grange N York 89 2873
Sutton Green Oxon 36 4107
Sutton Green Surrey 25 0054
Sutton Green Wrexhm 71 4048
Sutton Howgrave N York 89 3179
Sutton in Ashfield Notts 75 4958
Sutton in the Elms Leics 50 5193
Sutton Lane Ends Ches 79 9270
Sutton Maddock Shrops 60 7201
Sutton Mallet Somset 21 3736
Sutton Mandeville Wilts 22 9828
Sutton Manor Mersyd 78 5190
Sutton Marsh Herefs 46 5544
Sutton Montis Somset 21 6224
Sutton on Sea Lincs 77 5281
Sutton on the Hill Derbys 73 2333
Sutton on Trent Notts 75 7965
Sutton Poyntz Dorset 11 7083
Sutton Scotney Hants 24 4639
Sutton St Edmund Lincs 64 3613
Sutton St James Lincs 65 3918
Sutton St Nicholas Herefs 46 5245
Sutton Street Kent 28 8055
Sutton upon Derwent E R Yk 84 7047
Sutton Valence Kent 28 8149
Sutton Veny Wilts 22 9041
Sutton Waldron Dorset 11 8615
Sutton Weaver Ches 71 5479
Sutton Wick Oxon 37 4894
Sutton Wick Somset 21 5759
Sutton-in-Craven N York 82 0043
Sutton-on-Hull E R Yk 85 1232
Sutton-on-the-Forest N York 90 5864
Sutton-under-Brailes Warwks 48 3037
Sutton-under-Whitestonecliffe N York 90 4882
Swaby Lincs 77 3877
Swadlincote Derbys 73 2919
Swaffham Norfk 66 8108
Swaffham Bulbeck Cambs 53 5562
Swaffham Prior Cambs 53 5764
Swafield Norfk 67 2832
Swainby N York 89 4701
Swainshill Herefs 46 4641
Swainsthorpe Norfk 67 2101
Swainswick Somset 22 7668
Swalcliffe Oxon 48 3737
Swalecliffe Kent 29 1367
Swallow Lincs 85 1703
Swallow Beck Lincs 76 9467
Swallow Nest S York 75 4585
Swallowcliffe Wilts 22 9627
Swallowfield Berks 24 7264
Swallows Cross Essex 40 6198
Swampton Hants 24 4150
Swan Green Ches 79 7373
Swan Street Essex 40 8927
Swan Village W Mids 60 9892
Swanage Dorset 12 0378
Swanbourne Bucks 38 8026
Swanbridge V Glam 20 1667
Swancote Shrops 60 7494
Swanland E R Yk 84 9928
Swanley Kent 27 5168
Swanley Village Kent 27 5369
Swanmore Hants 13 5716
Swannington Leics 62 4116
Swannington Norfk 66 1319
Swanpool Garden Suburb Lincs 76 9569
Swanscombe Kent 27 6074
Swansea Swans 32 6592
Swansea Airport 32 5691
Swanton Abbot Norfk 67 2625
Swanton Morley Norfk 66 0117
Swanton Novers Norfk 66 0231
Swanton Street Kent 28 8759
Swanwick Derbys 74 4053
Swanwick Hants 13 5109
Swarby Lincs 64 0440
Swardeston Norfk 67 2002
Swarkestone Derbys 62 3728
Swarland Nthumb 103 1602
Swarland Estate Nthumb 103 1603
Swarraton Hants 24 5636
Swartha W York 82 0546
Swarthmoor Cumb 86 2777
Swaton Lincs 64 1337
Swavesey Cambs 52 3668
Sway Hants 12 2798
Swayfield Lincs 63 9922
Swaythling Hants 13 4416
Sweet Green Worcs 47 6462
Sweetham Devon 9 8899
Sweethaws E Susx 16 5028
Sweetlands Corner Kent 28 7845
Sweets Cnwll 4 1595
Sweetshouse Cnwll 4 0861
Swefling Suffk 55 3463
Swepstone Leics 62 3610
Swerford Oxon 48 3731
Swettenham Ches 72 8067
Swffryd Blae G 33 2198
Swift's Green Kent 28 8744
Swilland Suffk 54 1852
Swillbrook Lancs 80 4834
Swillington W York 83 3830
Swimbridge Devon 19 6230
Swimbridge Newland Devon 19 6030
Swinbrook Oxon 36 2812
Swincliffe N York 89 2458
Swincliffe W York 82 2027
Swincombe Devon 19 6941
Swinden N York 81 8554
Swinderby Lincs 76 8663
Swindon Gloucs 47 9325
Swindon Nthumb 102 9799
Swindon Staffs 60 8690
Swindon Wilts 36 1484
Swine E R Yk 85 1335
Swinefleet E R Yk 84 7621
Swineford Gloucs 35 6969
Swineshead Beds 51 0565
Swineshead Lincs 64 2340
Swineshead Bridge Lincs 64 2242
Swiney Highld 151 2335
Swinford Leics 50 5679
Swinford Oxon 37 4408
Swingfield Minnis Kent 29 2142
Swingfield Street Kent 29 2343
Swingleton Green Suffk 54 9647
Swinhoe Nthumb 111 2128
Swinhope Lincs 76 2196
Swinithwaite N York 88 0489
Swinmore Common Herefs 47 6741
Swinscoe Staffs 73 1247
Swinside Cumb 93 2421
Swinstead Lincs 64 0122
Swinthorpe Lincs 76 0680
Swinton Border 110 8347
Swinton Gt Man 79 7701
Swinton N York 89 2179
Swinton N York 90 7573
Swinton S York 75 4599
Swithland Leics 62 5512
Swordale Highld 139 5765
Swordland Highld 129 7891
Swordly Highld 150 7463
Sworton Heath Ches 79 6884
Swyddffynnon Cerdgn 43 6966
Swynnerton Staffs 72 8535
Swyre Dorset 10 5288
Sycharth Powys 58 2025
Sychnant Powys 45 9777
Sychtyn Powys 58 9907
Sydallt Flints 71 3055
Syde Gloucs 35 9511
Sydenham Gt Lon 27 3671
Sydenham Oxon 37 7301
Sydenham Damerel Devon 5 4176
Sydenhurst Surrey 14 9534
Syderstone Norfk 66 8332
Sydling St Nicholas Dorset 10 6399
Sydmonton Hants 24 4857
Sydnal Lane Shrops 60 8005
Syerston Notts 63 7447
Sygun Copper Mine 69 6048
Syke Gt Man 81 8915
Sykehouse S York 83 6316
Syleham Suffk 55 2078
Sylen Carmth 32 5106
Symbister Shet 153 5462
Symington S Ayrs 106 3831
Symington S Lans 108 9935
Symonds Yat Herefs 34 5515
Symondsbury Dorset 10 4493
Sympson Green W York 82 1838
Synderford Dorset 10 3803
Synod Inn Cerdgn 42 4054
Syre Highld 149 6943
Syreford Gloucs 35 0220
Syresham Nhants 49 6241
Syston Leics 62 6211
Syston Lincs 63 9240
Sytchampton Worcs 47 8466
Sywell Nhants 51 8267

T

Tabley Hill Ches 79 7379
Tackley Oxon 37 4719
Tacolneston Norfk 66 1495
Tadcaster N York 83 4843
Taddington Derbys 74 1471
Taddington Gloucs 48 0831
Taddiport Devon 18 4818
Tadley Hants 24 6061
Tadlow Cambs 52 2847
Tadmarton Oxon 48 3937
Tadwick Somset 35 7470
Tadworth Surrey 26 2257
Tafarn-y-bwlch Pembks 31 0834
Tafarn-y-Gelyn Denbgs 70 1961
Tafarnaubach Blae G 33 1210
Taff's Well Cardif 33 1283
Tafolwern Powys 57 8902
Tai'r Bull Powys 45 9925
Taibach Neath 32 7788
Tain Highld 151 2266
Tain Highld 147 7781
Tairbeart W Isls 152 1500
Takeley Essex 40 5621
Takeley Street Essex 39 5421
Tal-y-bont Conwy 69 7668
Tal-y-bont Gwynd 57 5921
Tal-y-bont Gwynd 69 6070
Tal-y-Cafn Conwy 69 7871
Tal-y-coed Mons 34 4115
Tal-y-garn Rhondd 33 0379
Tal-y-llyn Gwynd 57 7109
Tal-y-Waun Torfn 34 2604
Talachddu Powys 45 0833
Talacre Flints 70 1183
Talaton Devon 9 0699
Talbenny Pembks 30 8411
Talbot Green Rhondd 33 0382
Talbot Village Dorset 12 0793
Taleford Devon 9 0997
Talerddig Powys 58 9300
Talgarreg Cerdgn 42 4251
Talgarth Powys 45 1533
Taliesin Cerdgn 43 6591
Talisker Highld 136 3230
Talke Staffs 72 8253
Talke Pits Staffs 72 8353
Talkin Cumb 94 5557
Talla Linnfoots Border 108 1320
Talladale Highld 144 9170
Tallaminnock S Ayrs 106 4098
Tallarn Green Wrexhm 71 4444
Tallentire Cumb 92 1035
Talley Carmth 44 6332
Tallington Lincs 64 0908
Tallwrn Wrexhm 71 2947
Talmine Highld 149 5863
Talog Carmth 31 3325
Talsarn Cerdgn 44 5456
Talsarnau Gwynd 57 6135
Talskiddy Cnwll 4 9165
Talwrn IOA 68 4877
Talwrn Wrexhm 71 3847
Talybont Cerdgn 43 6589
Talybont-on-Usk Powys 33 1122
Talysarn Gwynd 68 4952
Talywern Powys 57 8200
Tamer Lane End Gt Man 79 6401
Tamerton Foliot Devon 6 4761
Tamworth Staffs 61 2003
Tamworth Green Lincs 64 3842
Tan Hill N York 88 8906
Tan Office Green Suffk 53 7858
Tan-y-Bwlch Gwynd 57 6540
Tan-y-fron Conwy 70 9564
Tan-y-fron Wrexhm 71 2952
Tan-y-Grisiau Gwynd 57 6945
Tan-y-groes Cerdgn 42 2849
Tancred N York 89 4558
Tancredston Pembks 30 8826
Tandridge Surrey 27 3750
Tanfield Dur 96 1855
Tanfield Lea Dur 96 1854
Tangiers Pembks 30 9518
Tangley Hants 23 3252
Tangmere W Susx 14 9006
Tangusdale W Isls 152 6500
Tankerness Ork 153 5109
Tankersley S York 74 3499
Tankerton Kent 29 1166
Tannach Highld 151 3247
Tannachie Abers 135 7884
Tannadice Angus 134 4758
Tanner's Green Worcs 61 0874
Tannington Suffk 55 2467
Tannochside N Lans 116 7061
Tansley Derbys 74 3259
Tansor Nhants 51 0590
Tantobie Dur 96 1754
Tanton N York 90 5210
Tanwood Worcs 60 9074
Tanworth in Arden Warwks 61 1170
Taobh Tuath W Isls 152 9989
Taplow Bucks 26 9182
Tarbert Ag & B 113 6551
Tarbert Ag & B 113 8668
Tarbert W Isls 152 1500
Tarbet Ag & B 123 3104
Tarbet Highld 148 1649
Tarbet Highld 129 7992
Tarbock Green Mersyd 78 4687
Tarbolton S Ayrs 107 4327
Tarbrax S Lans 117 0255
Tardebigge Worcs 47 9969
Tarfside Angus 134 4879
Tarland Abers 134 4804
Tarleton Lancs 80 4520
Tarlscough Lancs 80 4314
Tarlton Gloucs 35 9599
Tarnock Somset 21 3752
Tarns Cumb 92 1248
Tarnside Cumb 87 4390
Tarporley Ches 71 5562
Tarr Somset 19 8632
Tarr Somset 20 1030
Tarrant Crawford Dorset 11 9203
Tarrant Gunville Dorset 11 9213
Tarrant Hinton Dorset 11 9311
Tarrant Keyneston Dorset 11 9204
Tarrant Launceston Dorset 11 9409
Tarrant Monkton Dorset 11 9408
Tarrant Rawston Dorset 11 9306
Tarrant Rushton Dorset 11 9305
Tarring Neville E Susx 16 4403
Tarrington Herefs 46 6140
Tarskavaig Highld 129 5810
Tarves Abers 143 8631
Tarvie P & K 133 0164
Tarvin Ches 71 4966
Tarvin Sands Ches 71 4967
Tasburgh Norfk 67 1996
Tasley Shrops 60 6894
Taston Oxon 36 3521
Tatenhill Staffs 73 2021
Tathall End Bucks 38 8246
Tatham Lancs 87 6069
Tathwell Lincs 77 3182
Tatsfield Surrey 27 4156
Tattenhall Ches 71 4858
Tatterford Norfk 66 8628
Tattersett Norfk 66 8429
Tattershall Lincs 76 2157
Tattershall Bridge Lincs 76 1956
Tattershall Thorpe Lincs 76 2159
Tattingstone Suffk 54 1337
Tattingstone White Horse Suffk 54 1338
Tatworth Somset 10 3205
Tauchers Moray 141 3749
Taunton Somset 20 2224
Taverham Norfk 66 1613
Taverners Green Essex 40 5618
Tavernspite Pembks 31 1812
Tavistock Devon 6 4874
Taw Green Devon 8 6597
Tawstock Devon 19 5529
Taxal Derbys 79 0079
Taychreggan Hotel Ag & B 123 0421
Tayinloan Ag & B 105 6946
Taynton Gloucs 35 7222
Taynton Oxon 36 2313
Taynuilt Ag & B 122 0031
Tayport Fife 127 4628
Tayvallich Ag & B 113 7487
Tealby Lincs 76 1590
Team Valley T & W 103 2459
Teangue Highld 129 6609
Teanord Highld 140 5964
Tebay Cumb 87 6104
Tebworth Beds 38 9926
Tedburn St Mary Devon 8 8194
Teddington Gloucs 47 9633
Teddington Gt Lon 26 1670
Tedstone Delamere Herefs 47 6958
Tedstone Wafer Herefs 47 6759
Teesport N York 97 5423
Teesside Airport 89 3713
Teesside Park N York 97 4618
Teeton Nhants 50 6970
Teffont Evias Wilts 22 9931
Teffont Magna Wilts 22 9932
Tegryn Pembks 31 2233
Teigh Rutlnd 63 8615
Teigncombe Devon 8 6787
Teigngrace Devon 7 8574
Teignmouth Devon 7 9473
Teindside Border 109 4408
Telford Shrops 60 6908
Tellisford Somset 22 8055
Telscombe E Susx 15 4003
Telscombe Cliffs E Susx 15 4001
Tempar P & K 124 6857
Templand D & G 100 0886
Temple Cnwll 4 1473
Temple Mdloth 117 3158
Temple Balsall W Mids 61 2076
Temple Bar Cerdgn 44 5354
Temple Cloud Somset 21 6257
Temple End Suffk 53 6650
Temple Ewell Kent 29 2844
Temple Grafton Warwks 48 1255
Temple Guiting Gloucs 48 0928
Temple Hirst N York 83 6024
Temple Normanton Derbys 74 4167
Temple of Fiddes Abers 135 8080
Temple Pier Highld 139 5330
Temple Sowerby Cumb 94 6127
Templecombe Somset 22 7022
Templeton Devon 19 8813
Templeton Pembks 31 1111
Templetown Dur 95 1050
Tempsford Beds 52 1653
Ten Mile Bank Norfk 65 5996
Tenbury Wells Worcs 46 5968
Tenby Pembks 31 1300
Tendring Essex 41 1424
Tendring Green Essex 41 1325

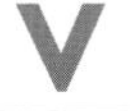

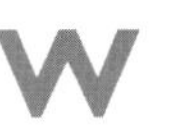

315

Wood Street Zouch
318

Wood Street Surrey 25 9550
Wood Top Lancs 81 5643
Wood Walton Cambs 52 2180
Wood's Corner E Susx 16 6619
Wood's Green E Susx 16 6333
Woodale N York 88 0279
Woodall S York 75 4880
Woodbastwick Norfk 67 3315
Woodbeck Notts 75 7777
Woodborough Notts 63 6347
Woodborough Wilts 23 1159
Woodbridge Devon 9 1895
Woodbridge Dorset 22 8518
Woodbridge Suffk 55 2649
Woodbury Devon 9 0087
Woodbury Salterton Devon 9 0189
Woodchester Gloucs 35 8302
Woodchurch Kent 17 9434
Woodchurch Mersyd 78 2786
Woodcombe Somset 20 9546
Woodcote Gt Lon 27 2962
Woodcote Oxon 37 6482
Woodcote Shrops 72 7615
Woodcote Green Worcs 60 9172
Woodcott Hants 24 4354
Woodcroft Gloucs 34 5495
Woodcutts Dorset 11 9717
Wooditton Cambs 53 6559
Woodeaton Oxon 37 5312
Wooden Pembks 31 1105
Woodend Highld 130 7861
Woodend Nhants 49 6149
Woodend Staffs 73 1726
Woodend W Loth 116 9269
Woodend W Susx 14 8108
Woodend Green Essex 39 5528
Woodfalls Wilts 12 1920
Woodford Devon 7 7950
Woodford Gloucs 35 6995
Woodford Gt Lon 27 4191
Woodford Gt Man 79 8882
Woodford Nhants 51 9676
Woodford Bridge Gt Lon 27 4291
Woodford Halse Nhants 49 5452
Woodford Wells Gt Lon 27 4093
Woodgate Devon 9 1015
Woodgate Norfk 66 8915
Woodgate Norfk 66 0215
Woodgate W Mids 60 9982
Woodgate W Susx 14 9304
Woodgate Worcs 47 9666
Woodgreen Hants 12 1717
Woodgreen Oxon 36 3610
Woodhall Lincs 76 2267
Woodhall N York 88 9790
Woodhall Hill W York 82 2035
Woodhall Spa Lincs 76 1963
Woodham Bucks 37 7018
Woodham Dur 96 2826
Woodham Surrey 26 0462
Woodham Ferrers Essex 40 7999
Woodham Mortimer Essex 40 8104
Woodham Walter Essex 40 8007
Woodhead Abers 142 7838
Woodhill Somset 21 3527
Woodhorn Nthumb 103 2988
Woodhorn Demesne Nthumb 103 3088
Woodhouse Leics 62 5314
Woodhouse S York 74 4284
Woodhouse W York 82 2935
Woodhouse W York 83 3821
Woodhouse Eaves Leics 62 5214
Woodhouse Green Staffs 72 9162
Woodhouse Mill S York 75 4385
Woodhouselee Mdloth 117 2364
Woodhouselees D & G 101 3975
Woodhouses Cumb 93 3252
Woodhouses Gt Man 79 9100
Woodhouses Staffs 61 0709
Woodhouses Staffs 73 1518
Woodhuish Devon 7 9152
Woodhurst Cambs 52 3176
Woodingdean E Susx 15 3505
Woodkirk W York 82 2725
Woodland Abers 143 8723
Woodland Devon 7 7968
Woodland Devon 6 6256
Woodland Dur 95 0726
Woodland Kent 29 1441
Woodland S Ayrs 106 1795
Woodland Head Devon 8 7796
Woodland Street Somset 21 5337
Woodland View S York 74 3188
Woodlands Abers 135 7895
Woodlands Dorset 12 0509
Woodlands Hants 12 3211
Woodlands Kent 27 5660
Woodlands N York 83 3254
Woodlands S York 83 5308
Woodlands Somset 20 1640
Woodlands Park Berks 26 8678
Woodlands St Mary Berks 36 3375
Woodleigh Devon 7 7349
Woodlesford W York 83 3629
Woodley Berks 25 7773
Woodley Gt Man 79 9392
Woodmancote Gloucs 47 9727
Woodmancote Gloucs 35 0008
Woodmancote Gloucs 35 7597
Woodmancote W Susx 14 7707
Woodmancote W Susx 15 2314
Woodmancote Worcs 47 9142
Woodmancott Hants 24 5642
Woodmansey E R Yk 84 0538
Woodmansgreen W Susx 14 8627
Woodmansterne Surrey 27 2759
Woodmanton Devon 9 0186
Woodmarsh Wilts 22 8555
Woodmill Staffs 73 1320
Woodminton Wilts 22 0022
Woodnesborough Kent 29 3157
Woodnewton Nhants 51 0394
Woodnook Notts 75 4752
Woodplumpton Lancs 80 4934
Woodrising Norfk 66 9803
Woodrow Worcs 60 8975
Woodseaves Shrops 72 6831
Woodseaves Staffs 72 7925
Woodsend Wilts 36 2176
Woodsetts S York 75 5483
Woodsford Dorset 11 7590
Woodside Berks 25 9371
Woodside Cumb 92 0434
Woodside Essex 39 4704
Woodside Fife 127 4207
Woodside Gt Lon 27 3467
Woodside Hants 12 3294
Woodside Herts 39 2406
Woodside P & K 126 2037
Woodside Green Kent 28 9053
Woodstock Oxon 37 4416
Woodstock Pembks 30 0325
Woodston Cambs 64 1897
Woodthorpe Derbys 75 4574
Woodthorpe Leics 62 5417
Woodthorpe Lincs 77 4380
Woodton Norfk 67 2994
Woodtown Devon 18 4123
Woodvale Mersyd 78 3010
Woodville Derbys 62 3118
Woodwall Green Staffs 72 7831
Woody Bay Devon 19 6748
Woodyates Dorset 12 0219
Woofferton Shrops 46 5268
Wookey Somset 21 5145
Wookey Hole Somset 21 5347
Wool Dorset 11 8486
Woolacombe Devon 18 4643
Woolage Green Kent 29 2349
Woolage Village Kent 29 2350
Woolaston Gloucs 34 5899
Woolaston Common Gloucs 34 5801
Woolavington Somset 21 3441
Woolbeding W Susx 14 8722
Woolbrook Devon 9 1289
Woolcotts Somset 20 9631
Wooldale W York 82 1508
Wooler Nthumb 111 9927
Woolfardisworthy Devon 18 3321
Woolfardisworthy Devon 19 8208
Woolfold Gt Man 81 7811
Woolfords S Lans 117 0056
Woolhampton Berks 24 5766
Woolhanger Devon 19 6945
Woolhope Herefs 46 6135
Woolland Dorset 11 7707
Woollard Somset 21 6364
Woollensbrook Herts 39 3609
Woolley Cambs 52 1574
Woolley Cnwll 18 2516
Woolley Derbys 74 3760
Woolley Somset 22 7468
Woolley W York 83 3212
Woolley Bridge Derbys 79 0194
Woolley Green Berks 26 8480
Woolmer Green Herts 39 2518
Woolmere Green Worcs 47 9663
Woolmerston Somset 20 2833
Woolminstone Somset 10 4108
Woolpack Kent 28 8537
Woolpit Suffk 54 9762
Woolpit Green Suffk 54 9761
Woolscott Warwks 50 5068
Woolsgrove Devon 8 7902
Woolsington T & W 103 1870
Woolstaston Shrops 59 4598
Woolsthorpe Lincs 63 8333
Woolsthorpe-by-
Colsterworth Lincs 63 9224
Woolston Ches 79 6489
Woolston Devon 7 7141
Woolston Devon 7 7150
Woolston Hants 13 4310
Woolston Shrops 59 3224
Woolston Shrops 59 4287
Woolston Somset 20 0939
Woolston Somset 21 6527
Woolston Green Devon 7 7766
Woolstone Bucks 38 8738
Woolstone Gloucs 47 9630
Woolstone Oxon 36 2987
Woolton Mersyd 78 4286
Woolton Hill Hants 24 4361
Woolverstone Suffk 54 1738
Woolverton Somset 22 7953
Woolwich Gt Lon 27 4478
Woonton Herefs 46 3552
Woonton Herefs 46 5562
Wooperton Nthumb 111 0420
Woore Shrops 72 7342
Wootten Green Suffk 55 2372
Wootton Beds 38 0044
Wootton Hants 12 2498
Wootton Herefs 46 3252
Wootton IOW 13 5392
Wootton Kent 29 2246
Wootton Lincs 85 0815
Wootton Nhants 49 7656
Wootton Oxon 37 4419
Wootton Oxon 37 4701
Wootton Shrops 59 3327
Wootton Staffs 72 8227
Wootton Staffs 73 1044
Wootton Bassett Wilts 36 0682
Wootton Bridge IOW 13 5492
Wootton Broadmead Beds 38 0243
Wootton Common IOW 13 5391
Wootton Courtenay Somset 20 9343
Wootton Fitzpaine Dorset 10 3695
Wootton Rivers Wilts 23 1962
Wootton St Lawrence Hants 24 5953
Wootton Wawen Warwks 48 1563
Worcester Worcs 47 8554
Worcester Park Gt Lon 26 2165
Wordsley W Mids 60 8987
Worfield Shrops 60 7595
Worgret Dorset 11 9087
Workhouse End Beds 38 1052
Workington Cumb 92 0028
Worksop Notts 75 5879
Worlaby Lincs 84 0113
Worlaby Lincs 77 3476
World's End Berks 37 4877
Worlds End Bucks 38 8509
Worlds End Hants 13 6311
Worlds End W Susx 15 3220
Worle Somset 21 3562
Worleston Ches 72 6556
Worlingham Suffk 55 4489
Worlington Devon 19 7713
Worlington Suffk 53 6973
Worlingworth Suffk 55 2368
Wormald Green N York 89 3065
Wormbridge Herefs 46 4230
Wormegay Norfk 65 6611
Wormelow Tump Herefs 46 4930
Wormhill Derbys 74 1274
Wormhill Herefs 46 4239
Wormingford Essex 40 9332
Worminghall Bucks 37 6308
Wormington Gloucs 48 0336
Worminster Somset 21 5743
Wormit Fife 126 4026
Wormleighton Warwks 49 4553
Wormley Herts 39 3605
Wormley Surrey 25 9438
Wormley Hill S York 83 6616
Wormleybury Herts 39 3506
Wormshill Kent 28 8857
Wormsley Herefs 46 4247
Worplesdon Surrey 25 9753
Worrall S York 74 3092
Worrall Hill Gloucs 34 6014
Worsbrough S York 83 3602
Worsbrough Bridge S York 83 3503
Worsbrough Dale S York 83 3604
Worsley Gt Man 79 7500
Worsley Mesnes Gt Man 78 5703
Worstead Norfk 67 3025
Worsthorne Lancs 81 8732
Worston Devon 6 5953
Worston Lancs 81 7742
Worth Kent 29 3355
Worth Somset 21 5144
Worth W Susx 15 3036
Worth Abbey Surrey 15 3134
Worth Matravers Dorset 11 9777
Wortham Suffk 54 0877
Worthen Shrops 59 3204
Worthenbury Wrexhm 71 4146
Worthing Norfk 66 9919
Worthing W Susx 15 1403
Worthington Leics 62 4020
Worthybrook Mons 34 4711
Worting Hants 24 5952
Wortley S York 74 3099
Wortley W York 82 2732
Worton N York 88 9589
Worton Wilts 22 9757
Wortwell Norfk 55 2784
Wotherton Shrops 58 2800
Wothorpe Cambs 64 0205
Wotter Devon 6 5661
Wotton Surrey 14 1247
Wotton Underwood Bucks 37 6815
Wotton-under-Edge Gloucs 35 7593
Woughton on the Green Bucks 38 8737
Wouldham Kent 28 7164
Woundale Shrops 60 7793
Wrabness Essex 41 1731
Wrafton Devon 18 4935
Wragby Lincs 76 1378
Wragby W York 83 4116
Wramplingham Norfk 66 1106
Wrangaton Devon 7 6758
Wrangbrook W York 83 4913
Wrangle Lincs 77 4250
Wrangle Common Lincs 77 4253
Wrangle Lowgate Lincs 77 4451
Wrangway Somset 20 1218
Wrantage Somset 20 3022
Wrawby Lincs 84 0108
Wraxall Somset 34 4971
Wraxall Somset 21 6036
Wray Lancs 87 6067
Wray Castle Cumb 87 3700
Wraysbury Berks 25 0074
Wrayton Lancs 87 6172
Wrea Green Lancs 80 3931
Wreaks End Cumb 86 2286
Wreay Cumb 93 4348
Wreay Cumb 93 4423
Wrecclesham Surrey 25 8244
Wrekenton T & W 96 2759
Wrelton N York 90 7686
Wrenbury Ches 71 5947
Wrench Green N York 91 9689
Wreningham Norfk 66 1698
Wrentham Suffk 55 4982
Wrenthorpe W York 82 3122
Wrentnall Shrops 59 4203
Wressle E R Yk 84 7131
Wressle Lincs 84 9709
Wrestlingworth Beds 52 2547
Wretton Norfk 65 6900
Wrexham Wrexhm 71 3350
Wribbenhall Worcs 60 7975
Wrickton Shrops 59 6486
Wright's Green Essex 39 5017
Wrightington Bar Lancs 80 5313
Wrinehill Staffs 72 7547
Wrington Somset 21 4762
Wringworthy Cnwll 5 2658
Writhlington Somset 22 6954
Writtle Essex 40 6706
Wrockwardine Shrops 59 6212
Wroot Lincs 84 7103
Wrose W York 82 1636
Wrotham Kent 27 6158
Wrotham Heath Kent 27 6357
Wrottesley Staffs 60 8200
Wroughton Wilts 36 1480
Wroxall IOW 13 5579
Wroxall Warwks 61 2271
Wroxeter Shrops 59 5608
Wroxham Norfk 67 3017
Wroxton Oxon 49 4141
Wyaston Derbys 73 1842
Wyatt's Green Essex 40 5999
Wyberton East Lincs 64 3240
Wyberton West Lincs 64 3142
Wyboston Beds 52 1656
Wybunbury Ches 72 6949
Wych Dorset 10 4791
Wych Cross E Susx 15 4131
Wychbold Worcs 47 9266
Wychnor Staffs 73 1715
Wyck Hants 24 7539
Wyck Rissington Gloucs 36 1821
Wycliffe Dur 95 1114
Wycoller Lancs 81 9339
Wycomb Leics 63 7724
Wycombe Marsh Bucks 26 8892
Wyddial Herts 39 3731
Wye Kent 28 0546
Wyesham Mons 34 5211
Wyfordby Leics 63 7918
Wyke Devon 9 8799
Wyke Devon 10 2996
Wyke Dorset 22 7926
Wyke Shrops 59 6402
Wyke Surrey 25 9251
Wyke W York 82 1526
Wyke Champflower Somset 22 6634
Wyke Regis Dorset 11 6677
Wykeham N York 90 8175
Wykeham N York 91 9683
Wyken Shrops 60 7695
Wyken W Mids 61 3780
Wykey Shrops 59 3824
Wykin Leics 61 4095
Wylam Nthumb 103 1164
Wylde Green W Mids 61 1294
Wylye Wilts 22 0037
Wymeswold Leics 62 6023
Wymington Beds 51 9564
Wymondham Leics 63 8418
Wymondham Norfk 66 1001
Wyndham Brdgnd 33 9392
Wynford Eagle Dorset 10 5896
Wynyard Park Dur 96 4326
Wyre Piddle Worcs 47 9647
Wysall Notts 62 6027
Wyson Herefs 46 5267
Wythall Worcs 61 0774
Wytham Oxon 37 4708
Wythburn Cumb 93 3214
Wythenshawe Gt Man 79 8386
Wythop Mill Cumb 93 1729
Wyton Cambs 52 2772
Wyton E R Yk 85 1733
Wyverstone Suffk 54 0468
Wyverstone Street Suffk 54 0367
Wyville Lincs 63 8729

Y

Y Felinheli Gwynd 68 5267
Y Ferwig Cerdgn 42 1849
Y Ffor Gwynd 56 3939
Y Gyffylliog Denbgs 70 0557
Y Maerdy Conwy 70 0144
Y Nant Wrexhm 71 2850
Y Rhiw Gwynd 56 2227
Yaddlethorpe Lincs 84 8806
Yafford IOW 13 4481
Yafforth N York 89 3494
Yalberton Devon 7 8658
Yalding Kent 28 6950
Yanwath Cumb 94 5127
Yanworth Gloucs 36 0713
Yapham E R Yk 84 7851
Yapton W Susx 14 9703
Yarborough Somset 21 3857
Yarbridge IOW 13 6086
Yarburgh Lincs 77 3592
Yarcombe Devon 9 2408
Yard Devon 19 7721
Yardley W Mids 61 1386
Yardley Gobion Nhants 49 7644
Yardley Hastings Nhants 51 8657
Yardley Wood W Mids 61 1079
Yardro Powys 45 2258
Yarford Somset 20 2029
Yarkhill Herefs 46 6042
Yarley Somset 21 5044
Yarlington Somset 21 6529
Yarlsber N York 87 7072
Yarm N York 89 4112
Yarmouth IOW 12 3589
Yarnacott Devon 19 6230
Yarnbrook Wilts 22 8654
Yarner Devon 9 7778
Yarnfield Staffs 72 8632
Yarnscombe Devon 19 5623
Yarnton Oxon 37 4711
Yarpole Herefs 46 4764
Yarrow Border 109 3528
Yarrow Somset 21 3746
Yarrow Feus Border 109 3325
Yarrowford Border 109 4030
Yarsop Herefs 46 4047
Yarwell Nhants 51 0697
Yate Gloucs 35 7081
Yateley Hants 25 8161
Yatesbury Wilts 36 0671
Yattendon Berks 24 5574
Yatton Herefs 46 4366
Yatton Herefs 47 6330
Yatton Somset 21 4365
Yatton Keynell Wilts 35 8676
Yaverland IOW 13 6185
Yawl Devon 10 3194
Yawthorpe Lincs 76 8992
Yaxham Norfk 66 0010
Yaxley Cambs 64 1891
Yaxley Suffk 54 1273
Yazor Herefs 46 4046
Yeading Gt Lon 26 1182
Yeadon W York 82 2041
Yealand Conyers Lancs 87 5074
Yealand Redmayne Lancs 87 5075
Yealand Storrs Lancs 87 4975
Yealmbridge Devon 6 5852
Yealmpton Devon 6 5851
Yearby N York 97 5921
Yearngill Cumb 92 1443
Yearsley N York 90 5874
Yeaton Shrops 59 4319
Yeaveley Derbys 73 1840
Yeavering Nthumb 110 9330
Yedingham N York 91 8979
Yelford Oxon 36 3604
Yelland Devon 18 4931
Yelling Cambs 52 2662
Yelvertoft Nhants 50 5975
Yelverton Devon 6 5267
Yelverton Norfk 67 2902
Yenston Somset 22 7121
Yeo Mill Somset 19 8426
Yeo Vale Devon 18 4223
Yeoford Devon 8 7899
Yeolmbridge Cnwll 5 3187
Yeovil Somset 10 5515
Yeovil Marsh Somset 10 5418
Yeovilton Somset 21 5423
Yeovilton Fleet
Air Arm Museum 21 5523
Yerbeston Pembks 30 0609
Yesnaby Ork 153 2215
Yetlington Nthumb 111 0209
Yetminster Dorset 10 5910
Yetson Devon 7 8056
Yettington Devon 9 0585
Yetts o' Muckhart Clacks 117 0001
Yew Green Warwks 48 2367
Yews Green W York 82 0931
Yielden Beds 51 0167
Yieldingtree Worcs 60 8977
Yieldshields S Lans 116 8750
Yiewsley Gt Lon 26 0680
Ynysboeth Rhondd 33 0695
Ynysddu Caerph 33 1792
Ynysforgan Swans 32 6799
Ynyshir Rhondd 33 0292
Ynyslas Cerdgn 43 6193
Ynysmaerdy Rhondd 33 0383
Ynysmeudwy Neath 32 7305
Ynystawe Swans 32 6800
Ynyswen Powys 33 8313
Ynyswen Rhondd 33 9597
Ynysybwl Rhondd 33 0594
Ynysymaengwyn Gwynd 57 5902
Yockenthwaite N York 88 9078
Yockleton Shrops 59 3910
Yokefleet E R Yk 84 8124
Yoker C Glas 115 5069
York Lancs 81 7133
York N York 83 6051
York Minster 83 6052
York Town Surrey 25 8660
Yorkletts Kent 29 0963
Yorkley Gloucs 35 6307
Yorton Heath Shrops 59 5022
Youlgreave Derbys 74 2064
Youlthorpe E R Yk 84 7655
Youlton N York 90 4963
Young's End Essex 40 7319
Youngsbury Herts 39 3618
Yoxall Staffs 73 1418
Yoxford Suffk 55 3969
Yoxford Little Street Suffk 55 3869
Ysbyty Cynfyn Cerdgn 43 7578
Ysbyty Ifan Conwy 69 8448
Ysbyty Ystwyth Cerdgn 43 7371
Ysceifiog Flints 70 1571
Ysgubor-y-Coed Cerdgn 43 6895
Ystalyfera Powys 32 7608
Ystrad Rhondd 33 9895
Ystrad Aeron Cerdgn 44 5256
Ystrad Ffin Carmth 44 7846
Ystrad Meurig Cerdgn 43 7067
Ystrad Mynach Caerph 33 1494
Ystradfellte Powys 33 9313
Ystradgynlais Powys 32 7910
Ystradowen V Glam 33 0077
Ystumtuen Cerdgn 43 7378
Ythanbank Abers 143 9033
Ythanwells Abers 142 6338
Ythsie Abers 143 8830

Z

Zeal Monachorum Devon 8 7204
Zeals Wilts 22 7831
Zelah Cnwll 3 8151
Zennor Cnwll 2 4538
Zoar Cnwll 3 7619
Zouch Notts 62 5023

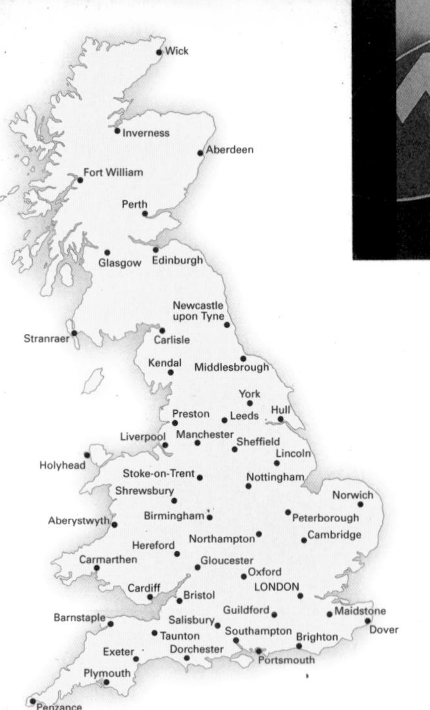

distances and journey times

The distances between towns on the mileage chart are given to the nearest mile, and are measured along the normal AA-recommended routes. It should be noted that AA-recommended routes do not necessarily follow the shortest distance between places but are based on the quickest travelling time, making maximum use of motorways and dual carriageways.

These times are average off-peak journey times based on normal AA-recommended routes. The times given do not take into account rest breaks, fuel stops or any unforeseen traffic delays, and therefore should be used as a guide only.

Example: Glasgow to Norwich, a journey of 379 miles taking approximately 7 hours 31 minutes.

journey times

	Aberystwyth	Barnstaple	Birmingham	Brighton	Bristol	Cambridge	Cardiff	Carlisle	Carmarthen	Dorchester	Dover	Edinburgh	Exeter	Fort William	Glasgow	Gloucester	Guildford	Hereford	Holyhead	Hull	Inverness	Kendal	Leeds	Lincoln	Liverpool	Maidstone	Manchester	Middlesbrough	Newcastle	Northampton	Norwich	Nottingham	Oxford	Penzance	Perth	Peterborough	Plymouth	Portsmouth	Preston	Salisbury	Sheffield	Shrewsbury	Southampton	Stoke-on-Trent	Stranraer	Taunton	Wick	York	LONDON
Aberdeen	904	1050	747	1050	911	907	935	424	1012	1045	1110	234	1024	355	258	834	1004	849	845	733	237	515	652	752	633	1028	630	543	508	837	1008	753	905	1244	150	836	1112	1037	556	1007	724	748	1021	700	502	948	510	643	952
Aberystwyth		437	249	540	301	430	229	445	115	432	613	646	411	902	625	248	443	158	239	438	956	359	344	430	244	532	305	459	529	339	553	338	352	630	718	420	458	454	318	410	351	154	439	249	713	334	1229	414	454
Barnstaple			324	423	200	501	235	631	334	206	515	833	115	1048	812	228	339	303	642	548	1142	545	529	508	456	434	449	630	700	406	624	422	317	232	905	453	147	324	504	232	501	405	307	401	900	109	1415	545	403
Birmingham				311	146	153	210	328	309	320	336	530	259	745	509	109	225	123	339	233	839	242	214	157	153	255	146	315	346	101	316	107	126	518	602	143	347	258	201	242	145	102	242	058	557	223	1112	230	216
Brighton					302	215	338	631	438	233	156	833	353	1048	812	303	104	349	642	455	1143	546	436	355	457	116	449	537	607	222	321	329	201	613	905	250	442	110	504	152	408	406	128	401	900	321	1415	452	126
Bristol						316	100	452	159	144	339	654	134	910	633	049	206	124	503	409	1004	407	350	329	318	258	310	451	522	221	439	243	132	353	726	314	222	217	325	128	322	227	202	222	721	058	1236	406	218
Cambridge							350	449	449	340	213	638	435	907	630	249	153	303	520	250	1001	424	241	150	335	132	320	337	407	110	135	145	159	654	723	046	523	246	343	248	222	244	238	239	718	359	1234	252	128
Cardiff								516	116	230	415	717	209	933	656	118	241	117	459	432	1027	430	413	352	341	334	334	515	545	256	511	307	208	428	749	337	256	253	349	208	346	236	237	245	744	133	1300	430	254
Carlisle									552	626	652	206	605	422	145	415	544	429	425	316	516	056	235	334	213	610	210	200	125	417	551	335	445	824	238	419	652	617	136	548	307	328	602	240	233	528	749	225	532
Carmarthen										329	514	754	308	1010	733	218	341	204	353	532	1104	507	452	452	358	433	414	607	637	356	610	406	307	528	827	437	356	352	426	308	445	248	337	345	822	232	1337	522	354
Dorchester											347	828	123	1044	807	223	207	258	637	543	1138	541	524	454	452	306	444	625	656	314	503	417	222	343	900	357	212	135	459	102	456	401	118	356	855	104	1410	540	242
Dover												841	447	1110	833	340	146	426	704	453	1204	607	444	353	518	047	511	540	610	241	319	348	238	707	926	249	535	240	526	256	425	427	246	422	921	413	1437	455	147
Edinburgh													807	310	100	617	747	632	628	505	332	258	424	523	416	800	413	315	240	620	740	524	648	1027	051	608	855	820	339	750	456	531	805	443	303	731	605	414	735
Exeter														1022	746	202	311	237	616	522	1117	520	503	442	431	406	423	604	635	341	558	356	251	226	839	427	059	254	438	204	435	340	238	335	834	043	1349	519	338
Fort William															242	832	1002	847	843	734	139	513	652	752	631	1028	628	612	537	834	1008	753	903	1241	234	837	1110	1035	553	1005	724	745	1019	658	443	946	413	643	949
Glasgow																555	724	609	606	456	350	236	415	515	353	751	351	340	305	557	731	516	626	1004	112	559	833	757	316	728	447	508	742	421	207	709	622	406	712
Gloucester																	208	050	426	332	927	330	313	252	241	259	233	414	445	154	410	206	110	421	649	237	250	219	248	147	245	150	204	145	644	126	1159	329	217
Guildford																		254	556	409	1057	500	350	315	411	105	403	451	521	136	309	243	115	531	819	210	359	059	418	120	322	320	106	315	814	237	1329	406	048
Hereford																			355	346	941	344	327	306	252	345	248	429	459	210	425	221	156	456	703	251	325	305	303	233	300	119	250	159	658	201	1214	344	303
Holyhead																				419	937	340	325	431	225	622	247	440	510	428	643	356	457	835	700	503	704	628	259	559	332	244	613	252	655	540	1210	355	543
Hull																					828	251	108	106	218	412	149	200	234	239	335	141	325	742	550	220	610	457	211	445	115	313	442	228	545	446	1100	058	350
Inverness																						607	746	846	725	1122	722	641	606	929	1103	847	957	1336	243	931	1204	1129	648	1059	818	840	1113	752	554	1040	237	737	1044
Kendal																							156	309	128	525	125	149	204	331	526	259	400	738	329	354	607	532	050	502	224	242	516	155	324	443	840	210	446
Leeds																								126	124	403	056	122	153	220	342	122	306	723	509	211	551	438	117	427	045	227	423	140	504	427	1019	038	335
Lincoln																									237	312	205	222	252	149	229	056	236	701	608	117	530	407	229	356	108	244	353	200	603	406	1119	137	250
Liverpool																										436	046	239	310	242	453	210	311	649	447	317	518	443	046	413	144	137	427	106	442	354	957	154	357
Maidstone																											430	458	529	200	238	307	157	626	845	207	454	159	445	214	344	346	205	341	840	332	1355	413	106
Manchester																												210	241	235	421	143	304	642	443	250	511	435	044	406	106	146	420	059	439	347	954	125	350
Middlesbrough																													047	320	438	222	407	823	400	306	652	539	226	527	154	341	523	254	429	528	914	109	435
Newcastle																														352	509	254	438	855	325	337	723	610	244	558	225	413	555	325	354	559	839	144	507
Northampton																															232	113	056	600	652	059	428	228	251	216	152	153	212	148	647	304	1202	236	121
Norwich																																252	322	817	823	153	646	405	443	411	322	407	401	356	818	522	1333	351	245
Nottingham																																	200	616	609	115	444	331	218	320	054	151	316	107	604	321	1120	138	228
Oxford																																		511	720	154	339	136	319	124	238	221	120	216	715	215	1230	322	115
Penzance																																			1058	646	145	514	657	424	654	559	458	554	1053	302	1608	738	557
Perth																																				652	926	851	410	822	539	602	836	514	316	802	516	458	806
Peterborough																																					516	303	314	305	152	233	255	214	648	352	1203	221	146
Plymouth																																						343	526	252	523	427	326	423	922	131	1437	607	425
Portsmouth																																							451	054	410	352	030	348	847	222	1402	454	142
Preston																																								421	144	201	435	113	405	401	920	147	405
Salisbury																																									359	322	037	317	816	130	1332	443	151
Sheffield																																										225	355	125	535	359	1050	109	307
Shrewsbury																																											334	102	557	301	1113	257	304
Southampton																																												332	831	205	1347	439	141
Stoke-on-Trent																																													510	259	1025	210	302
Stranraer																																														757	826	454	801
Taunton																																															1313	443	301
Wick																																																1010	1316
York																																																	351

distances

	Aberdeen	Aberystwyth	Barnstaple	Birmingham	Brighton	Bristol	Cambridge	Cardiff	Carlisle	Carmarthen	Dorchester	Dover	Edinburgh	Exeter	Fort William	Glasgow	Gloucester	Guildford	Hereford	Holyhead	Hull	Inverness	Kendal	Leeds	Lincoln	Liverpool	Maidstone	Manchester	Middlesbrough	Newcastle	Northampton	Norwich	Nottingham	Oxford	Penzance	Perth	Peterborough	Plymouth	Portsmouth	Preston	Salisbury	Sheffield	Shrewsbury	Southampton	Stoke-on-Trent	Stranraer	Taunton	Wick	York
Aberystwyth	468
Barnstaple	603	214
Birmingham	431	124	180
Brighton	605	288	208	171
Bristol	513	128	99	90	169
Cambridge	462	215	267	97	120	170
Cardiff	531	110	127	109	201	44	203
Carlisle	231	236	372	199	375	282	257	300
Carmarthen	513	48	190	171	264	106	266	67	282
Dorchester	595	206	94	172	119	62	179	119	363	182
Dover	587	325	273	207	82	206	124	238	400	301	200
Edinburgh	125	335	470	298	473	380	333	398	98	381	462	458
Exeter	587	198	55	164	175	84	251	111	355	174	55	245	455
Fort William	156	446	581	409	584	491	466	509	209	491	573	590	133	565
Glasgow	147	333	468	296	472	379	353	397	96	379	461	478	49	453	102
Gloucester	479	111	125	56	155	35	150	61	247	124	117	192	347	109	456	343
Guildford	563	224	175	128	44	106	91	138	332	201	97	97	432	147	541	428	99
Hereford	481	78	144	58	189	54	153	57	250	88	136	225	350	128	459	346	33	132
Holyhead	459	101	339	167	343	250	259	201	227	149	332	369	327	324	436	323	215	300	155
Hull	375	228	321	140	260	231	139	249	170	312	313	264	247	305	379	266	196	239	199	219
Inverness	106	494	630	457	633	540	514	558	257	540	622	639	158	614	66	174	505	591	508	485	428
Kendal	279	190	325	153	329	236	245	254	47	236	318	355	147	310	256	143	201	286	204	181	164	305
Leeds	331	174	302	121	263	212	146	230	126	220	294	271	202	286	335	222	177	220	180	165	60	383	71
Lincoln	387	199	276	89	216	186	95	204	182	267	245	220	258	260	391	278	151	173	154	204	47	439	176	72
Liverpool	357	110	274	102	277	184	193	202	126	163	266	304	225	258	335	222	150	235	121	101	128	383	79	74	140
Maidstone	548	286	234	168	50	167	85	199	361	262	161	41	419	206	570	458	153	58	186	329	225	619	315	233	181	263
Manchester	355	134	261	89	264	171	160	189	123	180	253	291	223	245	332	219	137	222	140	125	97	381	77	44	85	35	251
Middlesbrough	276	245	357	177	318	268	198	286	95	291	350	322	147	342	280	191	233	276	236	236	89	308	84	63	123	145	283	115
Newcastle	234	276	388	208	349	299	229	317	60	322	381	353	106	373	239	154	264	307	267	267	142	266	102	94	154	176	314	146	38
Northampton	479	173	210	55	132	114	54	159	248	222	158	155	348	194	457	344	76	90	110	216	152	505	201	133	92	150	116	137	188	219
Norwich	488	277	329	159	171	233	63	264	282	327	241	175	359	313	491	379	212	162	214	320	151	540	276	173	104	241	135	186	223	254	116
Nottingham	393	162	234	54	195	144	86	163	188	226	226	218	265	218	397	284	110	153	113	178	92	446	164	74	38	112	179	71	129	160	66	119
Oxford	503	159	170	68	109	73	81	105	271	168	115	146	371	154	480	367	48	67	81	239	189	529	225	171	130	173	106	161	226	257	43	144	103
Penzance	697	308	108	274	287	194	361	221	465	284	167	357	565	110	674	562	219	259	238	433	414	723	419	396	369	367	317	355	451	482	304	423	328	264
Perth	87	382	518	345	521	428	402	446	145	428	510	527	42	502	102	62	393	478	396	373	315	114	193	268	327	271	487	266	192	151	395	428	334	418	611
Peterborough	433	204	262	86	158	173	38	191	227	254	205	162	304	247	436	324	138	116	141	223	110	485	221	118	51	157	123	131	168	199	43	77	57	86	356	349
Plymouth	628	239	67	205	218	125	292	152	396	215	97	288	496	44	605	492	150	190	169	364	345	654	350	326	300	298	248	286	382	413	235	354	259	195	77	542	288
Portsmouth	588	243	162	154	53	125	132	157	357	220	73	140	457	129	566	453	118	46	151	325	275	615	310	256	214	259	101	246	312	343	128	204	189	85	240	503	157	171
Preston	321	147	282	110	285	192	201	211	89	193	274	312	189	266	298	186	158	243	161	138	122	347	43	68	134	36	272	32	103	139	159	234	121	183	376	235	180	307	268
Salisbury	544	183	118	121	90	53	139	96	313	159	39	159	412	90	522	409	72	62	105	281	260	570	266	241	200	215	120	202	296	327	113	201	174	70	202	458	164	133	43	223
Sheffield	365	167	272	76	233	182	122	201	159	264	264	247	236	256	368	255	148	191	151	158	66	417	125	36	47	79	207	39	100	131	103	147	44	141	366	281	93	297	227	83	211
Shrewsbury	416	75	221	49	225	132	141	109	185	109	214	251	284	206	394	281	97	182	52	104	163	442	138	122	125	65	212	74	193	224	99	203	87	122	315	330	129	246	208	95	164	90
Southampton	570	225	142	135	66	106	131	138	339	201	53	152	439	109	548	435	100	49	133	307	257	596	292	238	197	241	112	228	293	324	110	193	171	67	220	484	157	151	20	249	23	208	188
Stoke-on-Trent	387	115	221	48	224	131	138	149	155	212	213	248	255	205	364	251	97	182	99	123	129	413	109	93	92	57	209	45	163	194	96	173	54	121	315	301	99	246	207	66	163	53	38	189
Stranraer	232	342	478	305	481	388	363	406	106	388	470	487	133	462	188	86	354	439	356	333	276	258	153	228	288	231	448	226	201	163	355	388	294	378	572	146	333	503	464	195	420	265	291	446	262
Taunton	554	165	50	132	160	51	218	79	323	142	45	224	423	34	532	419	77	126	96	291	272	581	276	253	227	225	184	212	308	339	162	280	186	121	144	469	215	75	114	234	70	223	172	94	172	429
Wick	208	596	732	559	735	642	617	660	360	642	724	741	260	716	167	276	608	693	610	587	530	105	407	482	542	485	702	480	410	369	609	642	548	632	826	216	587	757	718	449	674	519	545	700	516	361	683
York	322	202	315	134	276	225	155	243	117	248	307	280	193	299	326	213	191	233	193	193	38	374	91	24	80	103	240	72	50	89	146	180	86	184	409	238	126	340	269	97	254	58	151	251	121	223	266	477
LONDON	544	238	216	120	59	120	60	152	313	215	128	79	413	200	522	409	102	30	136	281	187	571	266	198	143	215	39	202	253	284	68	115	131	56	310	458	86	241	74	223	88	168	162	80	162	419	167	673	211